THE NAGEL EDITION

חומש קורן לב לדעת
THE KOREN LEV LADAAT ḤUMASH

ספר שמות
SHEMOT/EXODUS

KOREN

THE NAGEL EDITION

חומש קורן לב לדעת
THE KOREN LEV LADAAT ḤUMASH

SHEMOT / EXODUS

TORAH TRANSLATION BY
Rabbi Lord Jonathan Sacks שליט״א

COMMENTARIES BY
Rabbi Shlomo Einhorn, Executive Editor
and Rabbi Dr. Zvi Grumet, Senior Editor

MANAGING EDITOR
Rabbi Yedidya Naveh

•

KOREN PUBLISHERS JERUSALEM

The Koren Lev Ladaat Ḥumash
Volume 2: Shemot
First Edition, 2020

Koren Publishers Jerusalem Ltd.
POB 4044, Jerusalem 9104001, ISRAEL
POB 8531, New Milford, CT, 06776, USA

www.korenpub.com

Torah Translation © 2019, Jonathan Sacks, from the Magerman Edition of the Koren Tanakh
Koren Tanakh Font ©1962, 2020 Koren Publishers Jerusalem Ltd.
Commentary © Koren Publishers Jerusalem Ltd.

Images used with the generous permission of Rabbi Menachem Makover,
originally printed in *Otzar Hamishkan*, published by Dani Sefarim.

Considerable research and expense have gone into the creation of this publication.
Unauthorized copying may be considered *geneivat da'at* and breach of copyright law.
No part of this publication (content or design, including use of the Koren fonts)
may be reproduced, stored in a retrieval system or transmitted in any form or by any
means electronic, mechanical, photocopying or otherwise, without the prior written
permission of the publisher, except in the case of brief quotations
embedded in critical articles or reviews.

The creation of this work was made possible with the generous support of the Jewish Book Trust Inc.

Printed in PRC

ISBN 978-965-7766-27-9

YAHEX01

THE NAGEL EDITION
OF THE KOREN YOUNG ADULT ḤUMASH LEV LADAAT
IS DEDICATED TO THE MEMORY OF

Jack M. Nagel z"l
ר׳ יעקב אלימלך ז״ל

A beloved husband, devoted father, adoring grandfather and great grandfather.
A true Visionary, who survived the Shoah, and whose philosophy was
to deal compassionately and kindly with all people.
His love for Torah and being a mensch guided him throughout his life.
He believed Education was the key to Jewish survival, and he made it his life's mission
to enrich the Los Angeles community with all aspects of Jewish scholarship and culture.
He established and remained committed to many yeshivot and Centers of Jewish
Learning throughout the United States and in his cherished homeland, Israel.

He had great faith, great heart, and great courage and was blessed
together with his Eshet Chayil, our Mother Gitta,
to leave a legacy of Tzedaka, Chesed and Emunah.

מרבה תורה מרבה חיים. מרבה צדקה מרבה שלום.
"The more Torah, the more life. The more charity, the more peace." (Avot 2:8)

Dedicated with love by his children:

Dr. Ronnie and Cheryl Nagel	Los Angeles, California, USA
Esther and Dr. Paul Lerer	Englewood, New Jersey, USA
David and Marnie Nagel	Los Angeles, California, USA
Careena and Drew Parker	Englewood, New Jersey, USA
And his devoted wife, Dr. Gitta Nagel	Los Angeles, California, USA

CONTENTS

מבוא ix Preface

הקדמה x Introduction

ספר שמות: לב לדעת **SEFER SHEMOT: LEV LADAAT**

שמות 1 Shemot
וארא 41 Va'era
בא 79 Bo
בשלח 111 Beshalaḥ
יתרו 151 Yitro
משפטים 181 Mishpatim
תרומה 211 Teruma
תצוה 239 Tetzaveh
כי תשא 269 Ki Tisa
ויקהל 311 Vayak-hel
פקודי 331 Pekudei

ספר שמות עם רש"י 349 **SEFER SHEMOT WITH RASHI**

נספח – פרשני התורה 515 Appendix – The Classic Commentators

PUBLISHER'S PREFACE

"דור לדור ישבח מעשיך" (תהלים קמה, ד)

"One generation will praise Your works to the next…" (Psalms 145:4)

It is with gratitude and a certain ambition that we introduce this volume of **THE NAGEL EDITION OF THE KOREN LEV LADAAT ḤUMASH**, a Ḥumash designed to encourage connection, reflection and learning of our foundation stone, the Torah.

The connection between Jewish young adults and the Torah is critical. Our children must learn the text of the Ḥumash and the classical commentators who have illuminated difficult passages. But it is just as important – and all-too-often neglected – that the student or young adult engage emotionally and experientially with the text. How does the Torah give them a prism to view the world around them? The need for this deeper, spiritual interaction gives rise to the name of this edition: **Lev Ladaat: The Understanding Heart**. For our ambition is that every Jew engage with the Torah and incorporate its values into his or her daily life, not just as an academic exercise.

It is with this ambition that Koren Publishers Jerusalem has created this edition, designed for high school students and young adults in synagogue *minyanim*. Since 1962, the Koren Tanakh has been recognized for its textual accuracy and innovative graphic design. We have remained committed to these qualities, and we have recently had the privilege of enriching the Ḥumash text with the eloquent English translation of one of the most articulate and original Jewish thinkers of our time, Rabbi Lord Jonathan Sacks, שליט״א.

It is with gratitude that we acknowledge Rabbi Sacks for this exceptional translation of the Torah. And our thanks are no less due to Rabbi Shlomo Einhorn, from whose fertile imagination and broad educational experience the concept for this Young Adult Ḥumash sprang. Likewise to Rabbi Dr. Zvi Grumet, whose intimate knowledge of the Ḥumash and its commentaries has enriched these pages inestimably. And to Rabbi Yedidya Naveh, our Managing Editor, who brought it all together into a handsome and useful edition.

None of this would have been possible without the support and detailed involvement of the Nagel Family of California and New Jersey, who understood both the ambitions and methods of this edition. **THE NAGEL EDITION OF THE KOREN LEV LADAAT ḤUMASH** is dedicated to the memory of Jack Nagel, z"l, who was an exceptional community leader. He and his beloved wife Gitta have enabled so much of Jewish life in the Los Angeles community, especially in the area of Jewish education: *yeshivot*, high schools and so much more. Surviving the Holocaust and making a new life for himself and family, Jack's was an exemplary Jewish life, combining *Torah im derekh eretz*. Koren is honored to be associated with his memory.

On behalf of all our *rabbanim*, scholars and designers, we thank the Nagel Family. And to the many thousands of readers, in this and future generations: We are forever in your debt.

We hope the use of this Ḥumash will bring Jews closer and closer to the Torah and all the good it represents.

Matthew Miller, Publisher
Jerusalem, Autumn 5781 (2020)

EDITOR'S INTRODUCTION

What if there were no more bookstores left on Earth? What if we woke up to discover that the written word had been almost eliminated? This is the frightening possibility we confront when we visit "The Last Bookstore" in downtown Los Angeles. The Last Bookstore takes the guise of a survival shelter where all of Earth's great books are sold, in case there may one day be no other places to find books. I once had the opportunity to spend some time there, and I found my way to a Bible, which included a commentary for teenagers. It roused my curiosity – why is there no edition of the Ḥumash directed toward young adults? Ought we be simply waiting for young Jewish people to come to the Torah, instead of bringing the Torah to them?

Some might say that teens aren't interested in the Ḥumash. They are mistaken. For 22 years I have been teaching young adults, and I have always found them to be as hungry for knowledge and connection as any other group. Whenever I look past a student's distracted veneer and genuinely engage them with some profound thought, it opens a reservoir of dialogue that I could not have found elsewhere.

With social media and technology becoming a constant part of our lives, our need for real and deep connection has only grown stronger. The Torah, we know, is an עץ חיים למחזיקים בה – a tree of life for all who hold on to it.

Putting together a project like this Ḥumash is complex. It's very easy to slip into anachronistic concepts aimed at grabbing attention. But we owe more to ourselves; we are hungry for substantive and truly thought-provoking conversations.

To you, our young adults, we now offer this Ḥumash. Will you use it? Will you allow it to guide you? When you are having a hard day and the walls seem to close in on you, will you pick this Torah up and let it lift you up? Will you let God into your life? We find Him in these words.

Why do we study Torah?

- *The Torah is a blueprint of the universe*, starting at the beginning – Bereshit. The Midrash teaches that God "looked into the Torah and created a world." Do we want to understand the world? "We should look at where it came from."

- *How to practice Judaism.* Torah teaches us how to live as Jews. It teaches us how to practice our Judaism. The Gemara teaches: "תלמוד גדול, שהתלמוד מביא לידי מעשה" – learning is great in that it moves us to action. I love the word *halakha*, which denotes Jewish Law. It means to walk. We can't walk in the ways of Judaism unless we know the *halakha*.

- *The values of Judaism.* The Torah guides us not only in how to practice Judaism's laws but, at times more importantly, how to live its values. The emphasis that our people places on charity, education, visiting the sick – it's all derived from the sensibilities of the Torah.

- *To help us do battle.* The sages interpret the wars described in the Torah as symbolic of our struggle against the *yetzer hara*, our evil inclination. Our shadow side is cunning. We have only one weapon against it, says the Gemara in Kiddushin: Torah study.

- *It is our oxygen, our life force.* The Gemara in Berakhot teaches us that just as a fish cannot live without water, so too we cannot exist without Torah. There isn't an example of a Jewish community that has thrived and flourished over multiple generations without a love and appreciation for producing Torah.

- *Crisis management.* Think about what enabled Yosef to survive trauma after trauma in Egypt? What made him so resilient? What did Yosef have that allowed him to survive? Rashi tells us that before he was thrown into the pit, Yosef would spend his time with Yaakov, studying the Torah taught by Shem and Ever. Shem and Ever were survivors. They had endured the flood and the generation of the dispersion. Deep down, Yaakov knew that Yosef would need this Torah.

- *To develop a relationship with God.* Part of our mission in this world is to cleave to the Almighty. Through a relationship with God one learns what it means to be a proper human being. We enter into a relationship with our Father in Heaven by learning His word.

◂ *It's the*

- *It's the Great Equalizer.* Rav Boruch Ber, the great rosh yeshiva, is quoted to have once said that Torah is the great equalizer. A child starting sixth grade could learn Bava Metzia, as though it's the most basic and simple piece of the Gemara. But at the same time, it's one of the hardest parts of the Talmud, challenging even the most advanced scholars. Torah is accessible to everyone at all levels.

- *It's your story.* Project years ahead and imagine bringing your spouse back to the house of your parents. While you're cleaning up the house, you find your old yearbook. You can't wait to share it with the person that you love. Why are you so excited? Because you are going to share the story of your life. That's why we open up the Torah. Our entire legacy is there; where we came from, what we went through, where our customs come from, and where our identity has come from.

- *And finally: It's your way out.* Imagine you are lost in a maze. You cannot find the way out. Suddenly, you're told by the maze keeper, who stands above the maze, that there is one way out. It's the simplest way of all – the way that you came in. Retrace your steps, and that's how you'll find a way out. The Jews have survived the Shoah and have rebuilt a remarkable edifice called the State of Israel. We have done amazing things in America and around the world. We have built *yeshivot* filled to the brim with students. But we also find ourselves at a crossroads, facing multiple challenges. God's guidance for us is: Retrace your steps. Figure out where you became lost, because that will tell us how to get through the maze of life. That's why we need the Torah.

With all these ideas in mind, we have designed this Ḥumash in such a way as to maximize the student's opportunity for reflection, connection, and learning. In addition to Rabbi Lord Jonathan Sacks's beautiful new translation of the Torah, we have included several different commentaries to add meaning to your journey:

WISDOM OF THE HEART: This commentary is designed to make you think critically about the stories, laws, and poetry in the Torah and how they relate to your life. It often includes a question about your own experiences and opinions.

THE CLASSIC COMMENTATORS: This section begins with a guiding issue or question and brings two or three classic commentaries from Jewish history who have offered answers. Compare the answers given by the different commentaries. With whom do you agree? These are followed by *Questions for Thought,* which push you to read the commentaries more closely and find hidden ideas below the surface.

TEXTUAL SKILLS: These questions encourage you to read the text of the Torah more closely. The exact ways words and phrases appear carry tremendous meaning, and by paying attention to details we can make ourselves better readers.

QUICK BITES: This section provides a brief thought about the Torah that we can take with us out of the classroom and share with family and friends. It can be a jumping-off point for a deeper conversation.

EXPLORING HASHKAFA: This essay at the end of most *parashot* deals with a "big idea" that challenges us as Jews in the modern world. It is not meant to give us easy answers, but to help us learn to think in creative ways about complex questions.

I write these words with profound gratitude to God. It is my hope that this project brings about a deeper love and understanding of God among the Jewish people.

It is an honor to work on this project together with Koren Publishers. Their professionalism, responsibility to tradition, and keen sense of style have made this a truly wonderful experience. Thank you to Matthew and all the talented and hardworking editorial staff at Koren.

Thank you to my wonderful school and community, Yeshivat Yavneh, where many of these teachings were first developed and shared with teenagers.

Thank you to my wife, Shira. We were standing on the shore of the Mediterranean Sea when you held a rough draft of this Ḥumash in your hand. You looked at me and said: "This project must happen."

Thank you to my parents and family who continue to encourage, praise, and support my work.

Thank you to the Nagel family. The connection between our families goes back over sixty years, and our bond of Torah began with a family *ḥavura* on Wilshire Boulevard.

◂ Together

Together with Jack, of blessed memory, we completed Sanhedrin and then began Bava Batra. It has been an exceptional privilege, and I have the *zekhut* of continuing this tradition with the family. This work was made possible by the incredible family vision gifted to the Nagels by Jack and Gitta. To Dr. Ronnie, Esther, David, and Careena, my blessing is that the merit of this project may stand for your whole family's long life and health. May we continue to follow your trailblazing path, as together we celebrate this very historic moment – *The Koren Lev Ladaat Ḥumash.*

Rabbi Shlomo Einhorn
Executive Editor

פרשת שמות
PARASHAT SHEMOT

The world of Genesis is no longer; the legendary, pioneering forefathers and foremothers are memories we learned about through stories we were told. We have grown so fast and so large that we are no longer just a family but the beginning of a nation, the descendants of Israel. And yet, with all of our success and comfort, there is a nagging feeling that something may not be right. Our neighbors look at us as differently. We feel that we don't really belong in the mainstream of society. And we struggle with our identity – are we who we are because of our ancient traditions, or because we are not like those around us?

PARASHAT SHEMOT

Yaakov and his twelve sons, all listed by name, went down to Egypt with their families – seventy in all. But in Egypt their clan became so big that "the land was filled with them."

1 1 And these are the names of the sons of Yisrael who came to Egypt with Yaakov, each with
2 his household: Reuven, Shimon, Levi and Yehuda; Yissakhar, Zevulun and Binyamin;
3
4 Dan and Naftali; Gad and Asher. The descendants of Yaakov were seventy in all, and
5
6 Yosef was already in Egypt. Then Yosef died, and all his brothers, and all that generation.
7 But the Israelites were fruitful and burgeoned; they multiplied and became exceptionally strong, until the land was filled with them.

TEXTUAL SKILLS

1. Notice that the term בני ישראל appears twice in this passage, and once at the beginning of the next passage. Does it mean the children of the man named *Yisrael* or the Israelite people?

2. Do you recognize the words פרו וישרצו וירבו ויעצמו במאד מאד ותמלא הארץ אותם from the book of Genesis? How do you know?

WISDOM OF THE HEART

Names in Tanakh are meaningful – they say something about the people described.

The man named Yaakov earned for himself an additional name, Yisrael. Those two names have very different connotations. The name Yaakov comes initially from the word עקב, "heel," as Yaakov was holding Esav's heel at birth, but also has echoes of trickery or deception. It was the wily, streetwise Yaakov who took Esav's blessing and who worked hard to outwit Lavan. By contrast, the name Yisrael contains the word ישר – "straight," "honest" – and is used to describe the man who "takes the high road."

Interestingly, in these opening verses the Torah uses both the names Yaakov and Yisrael in referencing the family that went down to Egypt. As descendants of Yaakov, they may need to be streetwise in dealing with the Egyptians on their way out of the bitter exile; as descendants of Yisrael, they will learn that to fulfill their ultimate destiny they will need to rise above that.

The Talmud cites a teaching from Reish Lakish: "God does not wound Israel unless He first creates for them the remedy" (Megilla 13b). The Stichiner Rebbe comments that before beginning the slavery in Egypt, God brought them their remedy – their names, their identity, their purpose. Yaakov *and* Yisrael.

How does your name affect or express your identity?

פרשת שמות

א וְאֵ֗לֶּה שְׁמוֹת֙ בְּנֵ֣י יִשְׂרָאֵ֔ל הַבָּאִ֖ים מִצְרָ֑יְמָה אֵ֣ת יַעֲקֹ֔ב אִ֥ישׁ
ב וּבֵית֖וֹ בָּֽאוּ: רְאוּבֵ֣ן שִׁמְע֔וֹן לֵוִ֖י וִיהוּדָֽה: יִשָּׂשכָ֥ר זְבוּלֻ֖ן וּבִנְיָמִֽן:
ג דָּ֥ן וְנַפְתָּלִ֖י גָּ֥ד וְאָשֵֽׁר: וַֽיְהִ֗י כָּל־נֶ֛פֶשׁ יֹצְאֵ֥י יֶֽרֶךְ־יַעֲקֹ֖ב שִׁבְעִ֣ים
ה נָ֑פֶשׁ וְיוֹסֵ֖ף הָיָ֥ה בְמִצְרָֽיִם: וַיָּ֤מָת יוֹסֵף֙ וְכָל־אֶחָ֔יו וְכֹ֖ל הַדּ֥וֹר
ו הַהֽוּא: וּבְנֵ֣י יִשְׂרָאֵ֗ל פָּר֧וּ וַיִּשְׁרְצ֛וּ וַיִּרְבּ֥וּ וַיַּֽעַצְמ֖וּ בִּמְאֹ֣ד מְאֹ֑ד
ז וַתִּמָּלֵ֥א הָאָ֖רֶץ אֹתָֽם:

CLASSIC COMMENTATORS

The passage opens with a brief listing of Yaakov and his clan of seventy as they descend to Egypt. The commentaries want to know why this is necessary, since there is a longer version of this listing (beginning and ending almost identically!) in Genesis 46:7–27.

RASHI — רש"י

Even though He counted them when they were alive, He counted them again after they had died to indicate how much He loves them.

אף על פי שמנאן בחייהן בשמותן, חזר ומנאן במיתתן, להודיע חיבתן, שנמשלו לכוכבים שמוציאן ומכניסן במספר ובשמות, שנאמר (ישעיה מ) "המוציא במספר צבאם לכולם בשם יקרא".

RASHBAM — רשב"ם

Because the Torah wanted to highlight that "*Benei Yisrael* were fruitful and burgeoned…" (1:7), it repeated that when they first came down to Egypt there were only seventy.

מפני שרוצה לפרש ולומר "ובני ישראל פרו וישרצו" וגו' הוצרך לכפול ולומר בבואם למצרים לא היו אלא שבעים ואחר מות דור ההוא פרו וישרצו.

RAMBAN — רמב"ן

Since the Torah wanted to begin the story of the exile from the time they actually went down to Egypt [not from the time the enslavement started], it repeated what it had said earlier.

כי הכתוב ירצה למנות ענין הגלות מעת רדתם למצרים, כי אז גלו בראש גולים, כאשר פירשתי, ולפיכך יחזור אל תחילת הענין שהוא מפסוק "וכל זרעו הביא אתו מצרימה" (בראשית מו ז).

QUESTIONS FOR THOUGHT

- Which of the above commentaries sees the entire passage as a unit?
- Which of the above suggests that we need to view Jewish history in a broad context of what comes before and after?
- Which of the above would serve as a message of consolation when the Jewish people are suffering and feeling abandoned by God?

8 Then a new king arose over Egypt, who had not known Yosef. And he said to his people,
9
10 "You see that the Israelite people are many and more powerful than we. Come, let us deal wisely with them in case they increase, and if war breaks out they may join our enemies and fight against us and escape from the land." So they placed slave masters over the
11 Israelites to oppress them with forced labor; they built supply cities for Pharaoh: Pitom
12 and Ramesses. But the more they were oppressed, the more they increased and spread;
13 and the Egyptians came to dread the Israelites. The Egyptians imposed backbreaking
14 labor on the Israelites, embittering their lives with harsh work in mortar and brick and

TEXTUAL SKILLS

1. This passage describes a project to build a city using חומר and לבנים, and includes the words הנה, הבה, פן. Now look at the story of the tower of Babel (Gen. 11:1–9) and see the similarities!
2. Notice which nation in these verses is consistently described in the plural and which in the singular. Based on that, how should you understand the phrase למען ענותו בסבלותם?
3. In preparing the Egyptians to isolate *Benei Yisrael*, Pharaoh claims that *Benei Yisrael* have become many and more powerful ממנו. The word ממנו, translated "than we" here (as in "more powerful than we") can also mean "from us." This would mean that Pharaoh is accusing *Benei Yisrael* of leeching from the Egyptians in order to grow. Do you know anywhere else where one of Avraham's descendants is accused of become mighty at the expense of his host?

WISDOM OF THE HEART

Abolitionist, reformer, and runaway slave Frederick Douglass once said: "The life of the nation is secure only while the nation is honest, truthful, and virtuous." It is difficult to describe Pharaoh and his plan to enslave Israel as honest or virtuous. He slowly turned the people against Israel – first by painting Israel as a foreign implant, then by stoking fear that the outsiders are dangerous, that they will take over. The lies, fearmongering, and alienation fed on each other, until all of Israel was drafted into a national service which ultimately morphed into full servitude.

According to the Global Slavery Index, in 2017 there were an estimated forty million people enslaved worldwide. Are you aware of societies, even perhaps our own, that contain elements of Pharaoh's plan to alienate and put down others because they are different or because their numbers are growing?

The experience of Israel's slavery in Egypt is described in Tanakh (Deut. 4:20) as a כור הברזל, "smelting furnace" used for iron, suggesting that the exile there purified and strengthened the nation just as iron is purified and strengthened in a furnace. That trial by fire didn't destroy us, but helped to prepare us for our future challenges.

There is another aspect to this imagery. According to the *Hovot HaLevavot*, the positive side of pain is that it humbles us. It shatters our arrogant thinking that we are all powerful.

Ego is a very powerful force. The need to feel significant, stand out, and be relevant can sometimes derail our best intentions. While a healthy sense of self is necessary, allowing one's ego to take the driver's seat can lead to devastating consequences. The *kur habarzel* of Egypt helped Israel to purify itself of its arrogance and appreciate the role of a Supreme Being.

How have painful or challenging experiences impacted you?

שמות | פרק א

ח וַיָּקָם מֶלֶךְ־חָדָשׁ עַל־מִצְרָיִם אֲשֶׁר לֹא־יָדַע אֶת־יוֹסֵף: וַיֹּאמֶר
ט אֶל־עַמּוֹ הִנֵּה עַם בְּנֵי יִשְׂרָאֵל רַב וְעָצוּם מִמֶּנּוּ: הָבָה נִתְחַכְּמָה
י לוֹ פֶּן־יִרְבֶּה וְהָיָה כִּי־תִקְרֶאנָה מִלְחָמָה וְנוֹסַף גַּם־הוּא עַל־
יא שֹׂנְאֵינוּ וְנִלְחַם־בָּנוּ וְעָלָה מִן־הָאָרֶץ: וַיָּשִׂימוּ עָלָיו שָׂרֵי מִסִּים
לְמַעַן עַנֹּתוֹ בְּסִבְלֹתָם וַיִּבֶן עָרֵי מִסְכְּנוֹת לְפַרְעֹה אֶת־פִּתֹם
יב וְאֶת־רַעַמְסֵס: וְכַאֲשֶׁר יְעַנּוּ אֹתוֹ כֵּן יִרְבֶּה וְכֵן יִפְרֹץ וַיָּקֻצוּ מִפְּנֵי
יג בְּנֵי יִשְׂרָאֵל: וַיַּעֲבִדוּ מִצְרַיִם אֶת־בְּנֵי יִשְׂרָאֵל בְּפָרֶךְ: וַיְמָרְרוּ
אֶת־חַיֵּיהֶם בַּעֲבֹדָה קָשָׁה בְּחֹמֶר וּבִלְבֵנִים וּבְכָל־עֲבֹדָה בַּשָּׂדֶה

CLASSIC COMMENTATORS

The Torah tells us that "a new king arose over Egypt, who had not known Yosef." Even though many years have passed since Yosef was influential, given his immense legacy in Egypt, the commentaries want to know how it is possible that Pharaoh would not know Yosef.

RABBI OVADYA SFORNO
The royal Egyptian annals had undoubtedly recorded Yosef's achievements…However, the new king did not imagine that Yosef was one of the Hebrews, nor that Israel deserved to be treated favorably because of him.

ר' עובדיה ספורנו
ויקם מלך חדש על מצרים אשר לא ידע את יוסף – אף על פי שהיה זכרונו ממנו בדברי הימים למלכים בלי ספק ... לא עלתה על לב המלך החדש אפשרות היותו מזה העם, ושיהיה עם זה ראוי לשאת פנים לעמו בעבורו.

RABBI SAMSON RAPHAEL HIRSCH
We have before us the earliest case of anti-Semitism in Jewish history.

ר' שמשון רפאל הירש
ויקם מלך חדש על מצרים וגו' – לפנינו כאן הדוגמא הקדומה ביותר של רשעות נגד היהודים.

RABBI DAVID TZVI HOFFMAN
The verse is telling us that the king adopted new policies.

רב דוד צבי הופמן
מלך – חדש – מלך שנהג על-פי קווי-מדיניות חדשים.

QUESTIONS FOR THOUGHT

- Which of the commentaries understands that Pharaoh's forgetting of Yosef was part of a natural political process of changing economic policy?
- Which of the commentaries understands Pharaoh's decrees as a classic story of anti-Semitism?
- According to which of the commentaries is the forgetting of Yosef an innocent mistake?
- Do you see this Pharaoh instituting policies which are similar to, or dramatically different from, Yosef's policies in Genesis 47?

SHEMOT | CHAPTER 1

When the Egyptian king fails to control the growth of Benei Yisrael, he instructs the midwives to secretly kill the male newborns. In the privacy of the birthing rooms, the midwives undermine the king's secret plan, but when that fails, he issues a public instruction to throw all male babies into the Nile.

15 all field labors; all the work they forced upon them was intended to break them. Then the king of Egypt said to the midwives of the Hebrews (one named Shifra, the other Puah),
16 "When you help a Hebrew woman give birth, look on the birthstool. If it is a boy, kill
17 him, and if it is a girl, let her live." But the midwives feared God, and did not do as the
18 king of Egypt ordered them. They let the babies live. Then the king of Egypt summoned the midwives and demanded, "Why have you done this; why have you let the children
19 live?" But "Hebrew women," the midwives replied, "are not like Egyptians. They are full of
20 vigor, and have already given birth by the time the midwife arrives." God was good to the
21 midwives; and the people multiplied and grew very strong. And because the midwives
22 feared God, He granted them households. Then Pharaoh commanded his entire people, saying, "Throw every boy that is born into the Nile, and let all the girls live."

QUESTIONS FOR THOUGHT

- According to which of the commentaries would it have been easiest for Pharaoh to have kept this decree a secret?
- According to which interpretation was Pharaoh more likely to succeed with his plot?
- Which explanation do you think fits the story best?

TEXTUAL SKILLS

1. Which three-letter Hebrew root appears eleven times in this passage? What do you think the Torah is trying to emphasize?
2. In the Torah, the phrase ירא א-להים is not used frequently, and is often used to mean "being moral." In this passage it is used twice(!) to describe the midwives. Do you think it makes more sense here to understand it as "God-fearing" or as "moral?"

WISDOM OF THE HEART

The Torah states that the midwives didn't kill the babies because they feared God. Really? Do you need the fear of God to resist killing newborns?

Rabbi Mordechai Gifter once explained that we sometimes make all sorts of calculations to justify our actions. Here's one the midwives could have used: "If I kill just a few babies, I can keep Pharaoh's wrath at bay and save the rest of Israel." This utilitarian approach, one that calculates which action will have the most benefit, demands that we ignore the immorality of the act itself. Yet some things are simply wrong, no matter the calculations. When a command in the Torah tells us that something is categorically wrong, it is wrong.

It is this fear of God – this recognition that there are some things that we just don't do, regardless of the cost-benefit analysis – that the Torah ascribes to the midwives.

Are there things you've done, which you rationalized with all sorts of justifications and calculations, that you later regretted? If you knew that you would eventually regret it, would you do it again?

טו אֶת־כָּל־עֲבֹדָתָ֔ם אֲשֶׁר־עָבְד֥וּ בָהֶ֖ם בְּפָֽרֶךְ׃ וַיֹּ֙אמֶר֙ מֶ֣לֶךְ מִצְרַ֔יִם לַֽמְיַלְּדֹ֖ת הָֽעִבְרִיֹּ֑ת אֲשֶׁ֨ר שֵׁ֤ם הָֽאַחַת֙ שִׁפְרָ֔ה וְשֵׁ֥ם הַשֵּׁנִ֖ית פּוּעָֽה׃

טז וַיֹּ֗אמֶר בְּיַלֶּדְכֶן֙ אֶת־הָֽעִבְרִיּ֔וֹת וּרְאִיתֶ֖ן עַל־הָאָבְנָ֑יִם אִם־בֵּ֥ן הוּא֙ וַהֲמִתֶּ֣ן אֹת֔וֹ וְאִם־בַּ֥ת הִ֖וא וָחָֽיָה׃

יז וַתִּירֶ֤אןָ הַֽמְיַלְּדֹת֙ אֶת־הָ֣אֱלֹהִ֔ים וְלֹ֣א עָשׂ֔וּ כַּֽאֲשֶׁ֛ר דִּבֶּ֥ר אֲלֵיהֶ֖ן מֶ֣לֶךְ מִצְרָ֑יִם וַתְּחַיֶּ֖יןָ אֶת־הַיְלָדִֽים׃

שני יח וַיִּקְרָ֤א מֶֽלֶךְ־מִצְרַ֙יִם֙ לַֽמְיַלְּדֹ֔ת וַיֹּ֣אמֶר לָהֶ֔ן מַדּ֥וּעַ עֲשִׂיתֶ֖ן הַדָּבָ֣ר הַזֶּ֑ה וַתְּחַיֶּ֖יןָ אֶת־הַיְלָדִֽים׃

יט וַתֹּאמַ֤רְןָ הַֽמְיַלְּדֹת֙ אֶל־פַּרְעֹ֔ה כִּ֣י לֹ֧א כַנָּשִׁ֛ים הַמִּצְרִיֹּ֖ת הָֽעִבְרִיֹּ֑ת כִּֽי־חָי֣וֹת הֵ֔נָּה בְּטֶ֨רֶם תָּב֧וֹא אֲלֵהֶ֛ן הַֽמְיַלֶּ֖דֶת וְיָלָֽדוּ׃

כ וַיֵּ֥יטֶב אֱלֹהִ֖ים לַֽמְיַלְּדֹ֑ת וַיִּ֧רֶב הָעָ֛ם וַיַּֽעַצְמ֖וּ מְאֹֽד׃

כא וַיְהִ֕י כִּֽי־יָֽרְא֥וּ הַֽמְיַלְּדֹ֖ת אֶת־הָֽאֱלֹהִ֑ים וַיַּ֥עַשׂ לָהֶ֖ם בָּתִּֽים׃

כב וַיְצַ֣ו פַּרְעֹ֔ה לְכָל־עַמּ֖וֹ לֵאמֹ֑ר כָּל־הַבֵּ֣ן הַיִּלּ֗וֹד הַיְאֹ֙רָה֙ תַּשְׁלִיכֻ֔הוּ וְכָל־הַבַּ֖ת תְּחַיּֽוּן׃

CLASSIC COMMENTATORS

As the oppression intensifies, Pharaoh instructs the midwives to kill the males as they are born. The midwives are called the מילדות העבריות, which could be read as "the Hebrew midwives" or as the "midwives for the Hebrews."

RASHI

Shifra – This is another name for Yokheved. She is referred to as Shifra because she would beautify [*meshaperet*] the children she birthed.

Puah – This is another name for Miriam. She is referred to as Puah because she would call [*poah*] and coo to the child as women will do to soothe babies.

רש"י

שפרה – יוכבד, על שם שמשפרת את הוולד.
פועה – מרים, שפועה ומדברת והוגה לוולד, כדרך הנשים לפייס תינוק הבוכה.

ABARBANEL

These midwives were clearly not Hebrews, for Pharaoh would hardly have trusted Hebrew women to kill their own people. Rather, they were Egyptian women who worked for the Hebrews, as is it stated: "When you help a Hebrew woman give birth" (1:16).

אברבנאל

ולא היו עבריות, כי איך יבטח ליבו בנשים העבריות שימיתו ולדיהן, אבל היו נשים מצריות מילדות את העבריות, ר"ל עוזרות אותן ללדת, כמו שאמר "בילדכן את העבריות".

IBN EZRA

For there must have been more than five hundred midwives, and these two [Shifra and Puah] were in charge of all them.

אבן עזרא

אין ספק כי הרבה מחמש מאות מילדות היו, אלה שתיהן היו שרות עליהן.

SHEMOT | CHAPTER 2   SHEMOT | 8

With the decree to kill male babies in the background, the scene shifts to one child, nameless, saved by a series of acts of kindness by anonymous women – his mother, his sister, and Pharaoh's daughter. Like the midwives in the previous passage, these anonymous women successfully defy the seemingly all-powerful king.

2 1 A man of the house of Levi went and married a daughter of Levi. And she became preg-
2 nant and gave birth to a son. She saw what a fine child he was, and for three months she
3 kept him hidden. And when she could no longer hide him, she took a papyrus basket
and coated it with tar and pitch. She laid the child in it and placed it among the reeds by
4 the bank of the Nile, and his sister stood by at a distance to see what would happen to
5 him. Pharaoh's daughter came down to bathe in the Nile, while her attendants walked
by the riverbank. She saw the basket among the reeds and sent her maid to fetch it.
6 When she opened it she saw him there, the child; the boy was crying, and she was
7 moved to pity for him: "This must be one of the Hebrew boys." Then his sister asked
Pharaoh's daughter, "Shall I go and fetch one of the Hebrew women to nurse the child
8 for you?" "Go," said Pharaoh's daughter. So the girl went away and called the child's
9 mother. "Take this child," Pharaoh's daughter told her; "nurse him for me, and I will

---

QUESTIONS FOR THOUGHT

- Which of the commentaries thinks that there was something miraculously different about Moshe?
- Why do you think that some commentaries go out of their way to show that Moshe was a "miracle baby" while others insist on demonstrating that, while there was something different about him, it was not extraordinary?

TEXTUAL SKILLS

1. The phrase כי טוב, used to describe Moshe, is used in only one other place in the Torah. Where? What do you think the connection between those two places is?

2. Notice that the names of all the people in this scene are missing. Why do you think the Torah does this?

WISDOM OF THE HEART

Here is an incredible irony. Pharaoh's decree to throw the babies into the water leads to the story of Moshe in the reeds. That leads to his being saved by Pharaoh's daughter, which ends with Moshe being raised in the palace, where he learns diplomacy and leadership from Pharaoh's court! Pharaoh believed that he was undermining Israel. Little did he know that he was strengthening it.

In many of the Eastern martial arts, you use your opponent's energy and inertia to your own advantage. Can you think of ways of taking charge of the energies that drive you to act improperly and using those very energies positively?

ב ב וַיֵּלֶךְ אִישׁ מִבֵּית לֵוִי וַיִּקַּח אֶת־בַּת־לֵוִי: וַתַּהַר הָאִשָּׁה וַתֵּלֶד
ג בֵּן וַתֵּרֶא אֹתוֹ כִּי־טוֹב הוּא וַתִּצְפְּנֵהוּ שְׁלֹשָׁה יְרָחִים: וְלֹא־
יָכְלָה עוֹד הַצְּפִינוֹ וַתִּקַּח־לוֹ תֵּבַת גֹּמֶא וַתַּחְמְרָה בַחֵמָר
וּבַזָּפֶת וַתָּשֶׂם בָּהּ אֶת־הַיֶּלֶד וַתָּשֶׂם בַּסּוּף עַל־שְׂפַת הַיְאֹר:
ה וַתֵּתַצַּב אֲחֹתוֹ מֵרָחֹק לְדֵעָה מַה־יֵּעָשֶׂה לוֹ: וַתֵּרֶד בַּת־פַּרְעֹה
לִרְחֹץ עַל־הַיְאֹר וְנַעֲרֹתֶיהָ הֹלְכֹת עַל־יַד הַיְאֹר וַתֵּרֶא אֶת־
הַתֵּבָה בְּתוֹךְ הַסּוּף וַתִּשְׁלַח אֶת־אֲמָתָהּ וַתִּקָּחֶהָ: וַתִּפְתַּח
וַתִּרְאֵהוּ אֶת־הַיֶּלֶד וְהִנֵּה־נַעַר בֹּכֶה וַתַּחְמֹל עָלָיו וַתֹּאמֶר
מִיַּלְדֵי הָעִבְרִים זֶה: וַתֹּאמֶר אֲחֹתוֹ אֶל־בַּת־פַּרְעֹה הַאֵלֵךְ
וְקָרָאתִי לָךְ אִשָּׁה מֵינֶקֶת מִן הָעִבְרִיֹּת וְתֵינִק לָךְ אֶת־הַיָּלֶד:
ח וַתֹּאמֶר־לָהּ בַּת־פַּרְעֹה לֵכִי וַתֵּלֶךְ הָעַלְמָה וַתִּקְרָא אֶת־אֵם
הַיָּלֶד: וַתֹּאמֶר לָהּ בַּת־פַּרְעֹה הֵילִיכִי אֶת־הַיֶּלֶד הַזֶּה וְהֵינִקִהוּ
לִי וַאֲנִי אֶתֵּן אֶת־שְׂכָרֵךְ וַתִּקַּח הָאִשָּׁה הַיֶּלֶד וַתְּנִיקֵהוּ:

CLASSIC COMMENTATORS

All mothers think that their babies are beautiful and would do anything to protect their newborns, yet the Torah says about Moshe specifically that his mother saw that he was **טוב** and therefore hid him. What was different about Moshe?

RASHI

רש״י

כשנולד, נתמלא כל הבית כולו אורה.

When [Moshe] was born, the entire house was filled with light.

RASHBAM

רשב״ם

משה נולד לסוף ששה חדשים, ולפיכך יכלה להצפינו שלשה חדשים, שהמצריים היו מבקרים למעוברות לסוף תשעה חדשים. לכן נסתכלה בו בשעת לידה אם הוא נפל ולא תטרח בהטמנתו, וראתהו כי טוב ויפה הוא, וראתהו כי טוב ויפה הוא – כי גמרו סימניו שערו וציפורניו ... וידעה שהוא בר קיימא.

Moshe was born after a six-month pregnancy (this is why she was able to hide him for three months, for the Egyptians would only visit the pregnant women after nine months). She examined him as soon as he was born to make sure he had survived. If he had been a stillborn, she would not have had to go through the trouble of hiding him. But she saw that he was a fine, healthy child, with fully developed hair and nails…and she knew that he was viable.

10 pay you your wage." So the woman took the child and nursed him. The child grew, and she brought him to Pharaoh's daughter and he became her son. She named him Moshe,
11 "because," she said, "I drew him out of the water." One day, when Moshe had grown up, he went out to his people and saw their forced labor. And he noticed an Egyptian
12 striking a Hebrew: one of his brothers. Looking this way and that and seeing no one, he
13 struck down the Egyptian and hid his body in the sand. The next day he went out and saw two Hebrews fighting. He asked the guilty one, "Why are you striking your own
14 neighbor?" The man said, "Who made you a ruler and judge over us? Do you intend to kill me as you killed the Egyptian?" Then Moshe was afraid; "Surely," he thought,
15 "the thing has become known." Word reached Pharaoh and he sought to kill Moshe. But Moshe fled his presence and went to live in the land of Midian. There he sat down

---

- What two possibilities do the commentaries suggest as to how Moshe knew that he was from *Benei Yisrael*? According to which of those explanations would Moshe have been more likely to feel a deep connection with them?
- Being raised in the palace, Moshe could probably have chosen to identify as an Egyptian and lived his life as an Egyptian prince. Why would he choose to give that up? Would you?
- Was it an accident or part of the divine plan that the future redeemer was not raised amongst his own people? What does Ibn Ezra say about this? What can you add to his points?

TEXTUAL SKILLS

1. Notice that ויגדל משה is written twice in two consecutive verses.
2. Notice that in the first passage of this chapter, the word ילד appears eight times. Which word, which replaces ילד, appears five times in this passage?

WISDOM OF THE HEART

Immediately after the Torah records that Moshe grew up, it says that he saw the suffering of his kinsmen.

Rabbi Yitzḥak Eliyahu Landau comments that Moshe's greatness was directly linked to his sensitivity to the suffering of others. Rabbi Yitzḥak of Volozhin similarly comments that the essence of being a human is being humane – caring and empathetic to others.

How does helping others enhance your own character?

QUICK BITE

The Torah states that before striking the Egyptian, Moshe looked "this way and that." A wise man once commented that the Torah is describing Moshe's internal struggle at that moment. Moshe was at a critical decision point: he needed to choose between two ways. One way would have him continue his life as an Egyptian prince; the other way would have him abandon the power and prestige and embrace the heritage of his people. But in this place of conflict: וירא כי אין איש – "he saw that he was no man." If we cannot take a stand as to who we really are, we lose our own identity, as a people and as individuals.

וַיִּגְדַּל הַיֶּלֶד וַתְּבִאֵהוּ לְבַת־פַּרְעֹה וַיְהִי־לָהּ לְבֵן וַתִּקְרָא שְׁמוֹ יֹ
מֹשֶׁה וַתֹּאמֶר כִּי מִן־הַמַּיִם מְשִׁיתִהוּ: וַיְהִי ׀ בַּיָּמִים הָהֵם יא *שלישי*
וַיִּגְדַּל מֹשֶׁה וַיֵּצֵא אֶל־אֶחָיו וַיַּרְא בְּסִבְלֹתָם וַיַּרְא אִישׁ מִצְרִי
מַכֶּה אִישׁ־עִבְרִי מֵאֶחָיו: וַיִּפֶן כֹּה וָכֹה וַיַּרְא כִּי אֵין אִישׁ וַיַּךְ יב
אֶת־הַמִּצְרִי וַיִּטְמְנֵהוּ בַּחוֹל: וַיֵּצֵא בַּיּוֹם הַשֵּׁנִי וְהִנֵּה שְׁנֵי־אֲנָשִׁים יג
עִבְרִים נִצִּים וַיֹּאמֶר לָרָשָׁע לָמָּה תַכֶּה רֵעֶךָ: וַיֹּאמֶר מִי שָׂמְךָ יד
לְאִישׁ שַׂר וְשֹׁפֵט עָלֵינוּ הַלְהָרְגֵנִי אַתָּה אֹמֵר כַּאֲשֶׁר הָרַגְתָּ אֶת־
הַמִּצְרִי וַיִּירָא מֹשֶׁה וַיֹּאמַר אָכֵן נוֹדַע הַדָּבָר: וַיִּשְׁמַע פַּרְעֹה טו
אֶת־הַדָּבָר הַזֶּה וַיְבַקֵּשׁ לַהֲרֹג אֶת־מֹשֶׁה וַיִּבְרַח מֹשֶׁה מִפְּנֵי

CLASSIC COMMENTATORS

Moshe was raised by Pharaoh's daughter from a very early age, yet he identifies himself in this incident with *Benei Yisrael*. Where did that identity come from?

ABARBANEL

Moshe had always been attached to Yokheved, who had begun to raise him, and to her children. Once he grew up, he learned from them his true identity, that he was a Hebrew child, even though Pharaoh's daughter had raised him as a son. He therefore began to go out to his Hebrew kinsmen.

IBN EZRA

Perhaps God arranged that Moshe should grow up in the royal household so that he would be erudite and cultured, rather than vulgar and slavish. This noble character was expressed when he killed the Egyptian for performing an injustice and when he gallantly saved the daughters of the Midianite from the oppression of the shepherds, who had been stealing their water.

RABBI SAMSON RAPHAEL HIRSCH

Pharaoh's daughter did not name the foundling "Mashui," meaning "one drawn up from the water," but "Moshe" – "he who redeems from the water." Perhaps by choosing the latter, the princess had already begun her efforts to shape the character of her adopted son. Furthermore, his Hebrew name would always remind him of his origin.

אברבנאל

לפי שמשה תמיד דבקה נפשו ביוכבד אשר גדלתו ובבניה ואחרי שנתגדל ידע מהם אמתת ענינו ושהוא מילדי העברים עם היות שבת פרעה גדלתו כבן ולכן היה יוצא אל אחיו העברים.

אבן עזרא

אולי סבב השם זה שיגדל משה בבית המלכות להיות נפשו העליונה בדרך מלכות והרגילות, ולא תהיה נפשו שפלה רגילה להיות בבית עבדים. הלא תראה, כי הרג המצרי בעבור שהוא עושה חמס. והושיע בנות מדין מהרועים, בעבור שהיו עושים חמס להשקות צאנם המים שדלו.

ר' שמשון רפאל הירש

לא קראה לו בשם "משוי" – "מי שנמשה מתוך המים", אלא "משה" – "הגואל מן המים". אפשר שיש בכך רמז לכיוון החינוך שנתנה בת המלך לבנה המאומץ. בנוסף על כך, שמו העברי יעשה אותו תמיד מודע למוצאו.

QUESTIONS FOR THOUGHT

Moshe flees Pharaoh and goes to Midian, where he again saves helpless people from their tormentors. This time his efforts are rewarded: he is invited to stay with Yitro, whose daughters he rescued. He marries Tzipora, one of the daughters, and has a son whom he names Gershom.

16 beside a well. The priest of Midian had seven daughters; they came to draw water and
17 filled the troughs to water their father's flock. Then the shepherds arrived and started to drive the young women away. But Moshe stood up to defend them, and then watered
18 their flock. When the sisters returned to Reuel their father, he asked them, "How is it
19 that you have come back so quickly today?" They said, "An Egyptian rescued us from the
20 shepherds. He even drew water for us and watered the flock." "Where is he?" he asked his daughters. "Why did you leave him there? Invite him in to have something to eat."
21 Moshe accepted an invitation to stay with the man, and he gave Moshe his daughter
22 Tzipora in marriage. She gave birth to a son, and Moshe named him Gershom, saying, "I have been a stranger in an alien land."

TEXTUAL SKILLS

1. Notice that in the beginning of this chapter Moshe is saved through the kindness of women; in the end of the chapter it is he who shows kindness to and saves women he has never met before.

2. Who did Yitro's daughters think Moshe was?

WISDOM OF THE HEART

Women are an essential part of this redemption saga. Notice the stars of this story:

1. The midwives, who disobey Pharaoh's command to kill the baby Hebrew boys.
2. Moshe's mother, who defies the royal edict and hides baby Moshe.
3. Moshe's sister, who doesn't let her baby brother out of her sight.
4. Pharaoh's daughter, who defies her father and rescues the Hebrew baby.

After Moshe is saved by all these women, it is his turn, as he saves Yitro's daughters – one of whom will become his wife and will ultimately save him too!

What are ways we can be players, rather than bystanders, in the history of the Jewish people?

QUICK BITE

After killing the Egyptian, Moshe runs away and remains in Midian for many years, perhaps in search of spiritual elevation, like his father-in-law, Yitro. But God will not let him escape his destiny. He summons Moshe from his spiritual quest in order to save *Benei Yisrael*. In case Moshe had any second thoughts about abandoning his spiritual mission for an earthly one, Tzipora – in circumcising their son, binding him to his people, and thereby saving Moshe's life – reminds Moshe that he cannot cut himself off from his people, even in pursuit of a path to higher spirituality.

טז פַּרְעֹה וַיֵּשֶׁב בְּאֶרֶץ־מִדְיָן וַיֵּשֶׁב עַל־הַבְּאֵר: וּלְכֹהֵן מִדְיָן שֶׁבַע
בָּנוֹת וַתָּבֹאנָה וַתִּדְלֶנָה וַתְּמַלֶּאנָה אֶת־הָרְהָטִים לְהַשְׁקוֹת
יז צֹאן אֲבִיהֶן: וַיָּבֹאוּ הָרֹעִים וַיְגָרְשׁוּם וַיָּקָם מֹשֶׁה וַיּוֹשִׁעָן וַיַּשְׁקְ
יח אֶת־צֹאנָם: וַתָּבֹאנָה אֶל־רְעוּאֵל אֲבִיהֶן וַיֹּאמֶר מַדּוּעַ מִהַרְתֶּן
יט בֹּא הַיּוֹם: וַתֹּאמַרְןָ אִישׁ מִצְרִי הִצִּילָנוּ מִיַּד הָרֹעִים וְגַם־דָּלֹה
דָלָה לָנוּ וַיַּשְׁקְ אֶת־הַצֹּאן: וַיֹּאמֶר אֶל־בְּנֹתָיו וְאַיּוֹ לָמָּה זֶּה
כא עֲזַבְתֶּן אֶת־הָאִישׁ קִרְאֶן לוֹ וְיֹאכַל לָחֶם: וַיּוֹאֶל מֹשֶׁה לָשֶׁבֶת
כב אֶת־הָאִישׁ וַיִּתֵּן אֶת־צִפֹּרָה בִתּוֹ לְמֹשֶׁה: וַתֵּלֶד בֵּן וַיִּקְרָא אֶת־
שְׁמוֹ גֵּרְשֹׁם כִּי אָמַר גֵּר הָיִיתִי בְּאֶרֶץ נָכְרִיָּה:

CLASSIC COMMENTATORS

The Torah uses an unusual word, ויואל, to describe Moshe's decision to stay with Yitro. The commentaries debate the meaning of this word, which affects our understanding of Moshe's decision.

RALBAG
רלב״ג

ויואל משה – הוא מענין החפץ והרצון.

The term ויואל suggests that Moshe willingly and happily stayed in Yitro's home.

MALBIM
מלבי״ם

ויואל – כבר בארתי (הושע ה) שפעל יאל מורה שנתרצה אחר שמאן תחלה בדבר, מבואר שמשה לא נתרצה תיכף, וכן אחר שנתרצה לא נתרצה מצד שהוא כהן מדין רק לשבת את האיש מצד מעלתו וחכמתו, כי כהונתו לע״ז היה נגד רצון משה.

I have explained (Hos. 5) that the verb י-א-ל denotes a person's agreement to something after having first refused it. It is clear then that Moshe did not immediately agree, and even after he consented, he did so not out of regard for Yitro's priesthood, but for his virtue and wisdom. For the fact that Yitro was a priest in the worship of idols was distasteful to Moshe.

QUESTIONS FOR THOUGHT

- Why would Moshe want to stay with Yitro? Why would he not want to stay? Which of these do you think makes more sense in this scene?
- There is a similar story to this one in the book of Genesis – about someone who runs away from his homeland, comes to a well, acts heroically to ensure that there is water for a local woman's sheep, and ends up marrying her. Which story is that? What might we learn from that story about whether or not Moshe wanted to stay with Yitro?

Shemot | Chapter 2

Pharaoh dies, and the suffering of Benei Yisrael causes them to cry out. God hears their cries and decides that the time has come to fulfill the covenant he made with Avraham, Yitzḥak, and Yaakov.

23 Years passed, and the king of Egypt died. The Israelites sighed in their enslavement and
24 cried out, and from their servitude their plea for help rose up to God. And God heard their groaning, and remembered His covenant with Avraham, with Yitzḥak, and with
25 Yaakov. God saw the Israelites, and God knew.

QUESTIONS FOR THOUGHT

- Ralbag suggests that the slavery intensified after Pharaoh's death, even though the Torah mentions nothing about it. What forced Ralbag to suggest an interpretation that seems to have no grounding in the Torah?
- One of the commentaries suggests that there is no connection at all between the death of Pharaoh and the cries of *Benei Yisrael*. If so, then why does the Torah even mention the death of Pharaoh?
- Which commentary says that the suffering did not change at all with the death of Pharaoh? If there was no change, then why did they start to cry out now? Can you imagine a similar thing happening today with, say, an important figure in your school or community replacing one who is retiring?

TEXTUAL SKILLS

1. Notice how verbs are used in these three verses to describe the relationship between God and the cries of the people. Can you figure out how those verbs are different?

2. Look carefully at the description of *Benei Yisrael* crying. Are they crying to God or not?

WISDOM OF THE HEART

It is a popular notion that God waits for us to cry out before he helps us. The Rebbe of Izhbitz suggests that sometimes we are so used to being crushed that we don't even have the capacity to dream of a better life. Rather than letting us suffer endlessly, sometimes God will allow us to be squeezed just a little more, forcing us to recognize that we cannot bear it anymore. It is then that we cry out, allowing God to do what He long waited to do: redeem us from our suffering. The first light of dawn comes after the darkest part of the night.

Are there things about yourself that are not as you would like them to be but you just accept them as is?

QUICK BITE

Moshe sees the plight of his brothers. That "seeing" is far more than vision – it is the capacity to understand what others do not, the ability to empathize with those in pain. At the end of ברכת המזון there is a quote from Psalms, which contains King David's declaration: "I have been young, and now I am old, yet I have not seen the righteous forsaken" (Ps. 37:25). Is that real? Did he never live amongst real people, where even the righteous suffer? Rabbi Leo Jung suggests that this means that, like Moshe, King David never saw a righteous person suffering and left him to suffer.

How good are we at truly seeing other people – their pain, their struggles?

כג וַיְהִי בַיָּמִים הָרַבִּים הָהֵם וַיָּמָת מֶלֶךְ מִצְרַיִם וַיֵּאָנְחוּ בְנֵי־יִשְׂרָאֵל מִן־הָעֲבֹדָה וַיִּזְעָקוּ וַתַּעַל שַׁוְעָתָם אֶל־הָאֱלֹהִים מִן־הָעֲבֹדָה:
כד וַיִּשְׁמַע אֱלֹהִים אֶת־נַאֲקָתָם וַיִּזְכֹּר אֱלֹהִים אֶת־בְּרִיתוֹ אֶת־
כה אַבְרָהָם אֶת־יִצְחָק וְאֶת־יַעֲקֹב: וַיַּרְא אֱלֹהִים אֶת־בְּנֵי יִשְׂרָאֵל

CLASSIC COMMENTATORS

The Torah seems to connect the death of Pharaoh with the cries of *Benei Yisrael*, but one would think that there would have actually been some relief after the death of their chief oppressor. Therefore, the commentaries try to explain the link between the death of Pharaoh and their cries.

RALBAG

רלב״ג

The Torah is describing here the events that occurred during the lengthy time between Moshe's departure from Egypt and the birth of his son Gershom. While he was away from his people, the king who had threatened him died and was succeeded by a new monarch. The latter greatly intensified the labor requirements of *Benei Yisrael*. That in turn led the nation to sigh in their enslavement and to cry out to the Lord. But He heard their agony and was aware of their suffering.

אמר שבזה העת הרב שהיה מעת צאת משה ממצרים עד הזמן שנולד בו גרשום, מת מלך מצרים, וקם תחתיו מלך אחר והוא הכביד העבודה מאד, ולזה נאנחו בני ישראל מן העבודה, ויצעקו אל ה' יתע׳׳ל, ועלתה צעקתם אליו מן העבודה.

RABBI YOSEF BEKHOR SHOR

ר' יוסף בכור שור

So long as the previous king was alive, there was anticipation that when he would die, the decrees would be annulled. So when he died and the decrees continued, they said: "Now we see that there is no end to this business; we will never be freed from this labor," and they sighed.

כל זמן שהיה אותו מלך חי, היו מצפים שמא כשימות זה יתבטלו גזירות. וכיון שמת ולא נתבטלו גזירותיו, אמרו: עתה אין לדבר סוף, לא נצא עוד מעמל זה, ויאנחו.

RABBI YOSEF KARA

ר' יוסף קרא

As long as Pharaoh lived, the Holy One, blessed be He, refrained from ordering Moshe to go to Egypt to confront the king. Had God not waited, Moshe would have justifiably responded: How can I show my face before Pharaoh? The man seeks my death! For the verse states, "Word reached Pharaoh and he sought to kill Moshe" (2:15). This is why God assured Moshe that he could safely return to Egypt, telling him that "all those who sought your life have died" (4:19).

שכל זמן שהיה פרעה קיים, אם יאמר הקדוש ברוך הוא למשה לכה ואשלחך אל פרעה, משה ישיבנו איך אלך אל פרעה והוא מבקש להרגני, כדכתיב ויבקש להרוג את משה. וזהו שאמר לו כי מתו כל האנשים המבקשים את נפשך.

SHEMOT | CHAPTER 3

While chapter 1 speaks about the suffering of all of Benei Yisrael, chapter 2 shifts the focus specifically to Moshe. In this chapter Moshe is brought into the story of Benei Yisrael, and it begins with his first encounter with God, at the burning bush.

3 1 One day Moshe was tending the flock of his father-in-law Yitro, priest of Midian. He led the flock to the far side of the wilderness and came to Ḥorev, the mountain of God. 2 Then an angel of the LORD appeared to him in flames of fire from the midst of a bush 3 – and he saw – the bush was ablaze with fire but was not consumed. Moshe said, "I 4 must turn aside to see this wonder. Why does the bush not burn up?" The LORD saw that he had turned aside to look, and God called to him from within the bush: "Moshe, 5 Moshe." He answered, "Here I am." Then God said, "Do not come close. Remove the

---

TEXTUAL SKILLS

1. The word סנה appears only six times in all of Tanakh – five times here and once in Deuteronomy, referring back to this scene. Why would the Torah choose a word whose meaning we can only guess to describe the medium for this encounter?
2. The word מדבר, usually translated as "desert" or "wilderness," actually means "the place where sheep are led to graze," since it is far away from where crops are cultivated.
3. There are only two places in Tanakh where someone is told to take off his shoes in the context of an encounter with a divine being. Where is the other one?

WISDOM OF THE HEART

Moshe's encounter at the bush sets in motion an irreversible process in which a fugitive from Egypt who became a Midianite shepherd becomes Moshe Rabbeinu. The scene in which the first encounter happens, including the imagery of the bush that burns but doesn't burn up, is filled with meaning. Let's look at three messages relevant for leadership.

1. Leadership demands passion (burning) and resilience (doesn't burn up). Great leaders need the stamina to recover and learn from setbacks, and that can be fueled by a passion to accomplish the mission.
2. Moshe's first reaction to the mission with which he is tasked is to question himself. "Who am I?" he asks. Stephen Covey, in *The 7 Habits of Highly Effective People*, says that one of the essential components of leadership is seeking not to change others but rather to begin with addressing who you are internally. Like Moshe.
3. The prize is sometimes within the flames – getting dirty and bruised and singed. Garth Brooks, the legendary country singer, expressed it this way: "Life is not tried, it is merely survived, if you're standing outside the fire." Our most significant moments of growth and accomplishment take work, commitment, pain, and perseverance. You can't rescue the kingdom without slaying the dragon; and certainly, one can't create a flame of eternity without giving something up.

Have you ever had a "burning bush" moment? Are there things that you feel passionately about, that you would be prepared to sacrifice for?

שמות | פרק ג

א וּמֹשֶׁ֗ה הָיָ֥ה רֹעֶ֛ה אֶת־צֹ֛אן יִתְר֥וֹ חֹתְנ֖וֹ וַיֵּ֣דַע אֱלֹהִֽים: ב רביעי
כֹּהֵ֣ן מִדְיָ֑ן וַיִּנְהַ֤ג אֶת־הַצֹּאן֙ אַחַ֣ר הַמִּדְבָּ֔ר וַיָּבֹ֛א אֶל־הַ֥ר הָאֱלֹהִ֖ים
חֹרֵֽבָה: וַיֵּ֠רָ֠א מַלְאַ֨ךְ יְהֹוָ֥ה אֵלָ֛יו בְּלַבַּת־אֵ֖שׁ מִתּ֣וֹךְ הַסְּנֶ֑ה וַיַּ֗רְא
ג וְהִנֵּ֤ה הַסְּנֶה֙ בֹּעֵ֣ר בָּאֵ֔שׁ וְהַסְּנֶ֖ה אֵינֶ֥נּוּ אֻכָּֽל: וַיֹּ֣אמֶר מֹשֶׁ֔ה אָסֻֽרָה־
נָּ֣א וְאֶרְאֶ֔ה אֶת־הַמַּרְאֶ֥ה הַגָּדֹ֖ל הַזֶּ֑ה מַדּ֖וּעַ לֹא־יִבְעַ֥ר הַסְּנֶֽה:
ד וַיַּ֥רְא יְהֹוָ֖ה כִּ֣י סָ֣ר לִרְא֑וֹת וַיִּקְרָא֩ אֵלָ֨יו אֱלֹהִ֜ים מִתּ֣וֹךְ הַסְּנֶ֗ה
ה וַיֹּ֛אמֶר מֹשֶׁ֥ה מֹשֶׁ֖ה וַיֹּ֥אמֶר הִנֵּֽנִי: וַיֹּ֕אמֶר אַל־תִּקְרַ֣ב הֲלֹ֑ם שַׁל־
נְעָלֶ֨יךָ֙ מֵעַ֣ל רַגְלֶ֔יךָ כִּ֣י הַמָּק֗וֹם אֲשֶׁ֤ר אַתָּה֙ עוֹמֵ֣ד עָלָ֔יו אַדְמַת־

CLASSIC COMMENTATORS

The Torah describes that Moshe had guided Yitro's sheep to "the far side of the wilderness" (אחר המדבר). This unusual phrase does not appear anywhere else in Tanakh, so the commentaries assume that it is coming to teach something special about this.

RASHI — רש״י

This was so that the sheep would not graze in others' fields, to distance himself from theft.

להתרחק מן הגזל, שלא ירעו בשדות אחרים.

RABBI YOSEF BEKHOR SHOR — ר' יוסף בכור שור

Moshe led Yitro's flock past the wilderness, for the wilderness contains no pasture land for sheep to graze on.

העביר להם המדבר, שבמדבר לא היה מרעה, כי בארץ מדבר אין עולין עשבים.

HAAMEK DAVAR — העמק דבר

By telling us that Moshe "led the flock to the far side of the wilderness," the text reveals that Moshe was drawn to the solitary landscapes of the desert. It was there that he would be able to meditate, and to ruminate about God and other lofty matters.

המשמעות שהיה משתדל להנהיג במקום שהוא יותר מדבר, ונמשך אחר מקום מדבר, כדי שיוכל להתבודד ולחקור אחר אלקות וכדומה.

QUESTIONS FOR THOUGHT

- Which quality of Moshe does each of the commentaries suggest that the Torah is trying to highlight?
- Which of those qualities do you think is most essential for the person who is going to take on God's mission and bring *Benei Yisrael* out of Egypt?

> God introduces Himself to Moshe and describes the suffering of Benei Yisrael. He states His intention to save them from their oppression and bring them to the land of the Canaanites. Finally, He tells Moshe that He intends for Moshe to go to Pharaoh and take Benei Yisrael out of Egypt.

6 shoes from your feet, for the place where you stand is holy ground. I," He said, "am the God of your father, the God of Avraham, the God of Yitzḥak, and the God of Yaakov."
7 Then Moshe hid his face, for he was afraid to look at God. The LORD continued, "I have seen My people's suffering in Egypt; I have heard them cry out amid their oppressors;
8 I know their anguish. So I have come to rescue them from the hand of the Egyptians and bring them up from that land to one that is good, spacious, a land flowing with milk and honey, the place of the Canaanites, Hittites, Amorites, Perizzites, Hivites and
9 Jebusites. Now the cry of the Israelites has reached Me; I have seen the oppression the
10 Egyptians subject them to. So go: I am sending you to Pharaoh to bring My people, the

TEXTUAL SKILLS

1. There are two halves to verse 10. How are they connected?
2. At the end of the previous chapter, when we hear that God has decided to intervene, we are told that God hears the groans of *Benei Yisrael*. When God speaks with Moshe here, He says that he sees their suffering. In this context, is there a difference between God seeing and God hearing?

WISDOM OF THE HEART

In *The 7 Habits of Highly Effective People*, Stephen Covey writes that that second habit of successful individuals is that they begin with the end in mind – סוף מעשה במחשבה תחילה. To know what to do, you need to know where you want to end up. When that becomes clear, then all the things we need to do in order to get there become meaningful stepping stones toward that goal.

How do we figure out what our big goals in life are?

QUICK BITE

It was the last few weeks of high school, and Shlomo's mother told him that a great rabbi was staying at their neighbor's house. The Kaliver Rebbe was in town, known for his piercing insight and his spiritual vision. Shlomo walked over and waited for him in the backyard. The rabbi appeared, majestic in his gold and white Sabbath clothes, a calmness on his worn face. He shook Shlomo's hand and looked deep into his eyes. They stood there, frozen, for what felt like a long time. And then he spoke:

"When Moshe approached the burning bush God told him to take off his נעל, "shoe," for the place upon which he was standing was holy. But there is a deeper, richer understanding of this: consider that the word נעל can also mean "lock." This gives completely different meaning to the command. 'Remove the shackles from your feet, for if you realize that anywhere you stand is holy ground – you are free.'"

At that moment Shlomo felt a surge of exhilaration. *You are never trapped*, he thought. *There is always another way.*

ו קֹ֣דֶשׁ הֽוּא׃ וַיֹּ֗אמֶר אָֽנֹכִי֙ אֱלֹהֵ֣י אָבִ֔יךָ אֱלֹהֵ֧י אַבְרָהָ֛ם אֱלֹהֵ֥י יִצְחָ֖ק וֵֽאלֹהֵ֣י יַעֲקֹ֑ב וַיַּסְתֵּ֤ר מֹשֶׁה֙ פָּנָ֔יו כִּ֣י יָרֵ֔א מֵהַבִּ֖יט אֶל־הָאֱלֹהִֽים׃

ז וַיֹּ֣אמֶר יְהֹוָ֔ה רָאֹ֥ה רָאִ֛יתִי אֶת־עֳנִ֥י עַמִּ֖י אֲשֶׁ֣ר בְּמִצְרָ֑יִם וְאֶת־

ח צַעֲקָתָ֤ם שָׁמַ֙עְתִּי֙ מִפְּנֵ֣י נֹֽגְשָׂ֔יו כִּ֥י יָדַ֖עְתִּי אֶת־מַכְאֹבָֽיו׃ וָאֵרֵ֞ד לְהַצִּיל֣וֹ ׀ מִיַּ֣ד מִצְרַ֗יִם וּֽלְהַעֲלֹתוֹ֮ מִן־הָאָ֣רֶץ הַהִוא֒ אֶל־אֶ֤רֶץ טוֹבָה֙ וּרְחָבָ֔ה אֶל־אֶ֛רֶץ זָבַ֥ת חָלָ֖ב וּדְבָ֑שׁ אֶל־מְק֤וֹם הַֽכְּנַעֲנִי֙

ט וְהַ֣חִתִּ֔י וְהָֽאֱמֹרִי֙ וְהַפְּרִזִּ֔י וְהַחִוִּ֖י וְהַיְבוּסִֽי׃ וְעַתָּ֕ה הִנֵּ֛ה צַעֲקַ֥ת בְּנֵי־יִשְׂרָאֵ֖ל בָּ֣אָה אֵלָ֑י וְגַם־רָאִ֙יתִי֙ אֶת־הַלַּ֔חַץ אֲשֶׁ֥ר מִצְרַ֖יִם

י לֹחֲצִ֥ים אֹתָֽם׃ וְעַתָּ֣ה לְכָ֔ה וְאֶֽשְׁלָחֲךָ֖ אֶל־פַּרְעֹ֑ה וְהוֹצֵ֛א אֶת־עַמִּ֥י

CLASSIC COMMENTATORS

Language describing God's physical attributes or movement makes many of the commentaries uncomfortable. This is called *anthropomorphism*, the use of human attributes to describe something that is not human. The language here that God "descended" to save *Benei Yisrael* is an example of that.

RAMBAN

רמב״ן

שנתגליתי על ההר הזה באש.

I have revealed Myself on this mountain through fire.

RABBI SAMSON RAPHAEL HIRSCH

ר׳ שמשון רפאל הירש

ה׳ יורד ומתערב בעניני העולם, כדי למנוע את הגדלת המרחק שבין השמים והארץ. בכך הוא מקרב את העולם צעד אחד קדימה לייעודו - ליום בו שכינתו תוכל לשוב ולשכון בתחתונים.

The Lord does make a practice of descending to earth in order to intervene in the running of His world. In this way, He prevents the gap between heaven and earth from widening. This in turn has the effect of drawing the world closer to its destiny, to an era when the Divine Presence can once again return and dwell in the lower realms of His creation.

QUESTIONS FOR THOUGHT

- The word וארד, translated here as "I have come," literally means "I have descended." According to Ramban, when God says that He descended to save *Benei Yisrael*, when did that actually happen?
- According to Rabbi Hirsch, what does "God descending" actually mean?
- According to which of the two commentaries can we sometimes still reasonably expect God to descend even today?

Shemot | Chapter 3

Moshe, who fled Egypt decades earlier and who has settled into the comfortable life of a Midianite shepherd, has multiple hesitations about accepting God's mission. He questions his own worthiness as well as his ability to handle questions from Benei Yisrael.

11 Israelites, out of Egypt." But "Who am I," said Moshe to God, "to go to Pharaoh, to bring
12 the Israelites out of Egypt?" God replied, "I will be with you. Proof that I have sent you will come when, having brought the people out of Egypt, you come to serve God upon
13 this mountain." Moshe said to God, "When I go to the Israelites and tell them, 'Your fathers' God has sent me to you,' they will ask me, 'What is His name?' What shall I
14 say?" God replied to Moshe, "I will be what I will be." He said, "This is what you shall tell
15 the Israelites: I will be sent me to you." Then God said to Moshe, "You shall say this to the Israelites: The LORD God of your fathers, the God of Avraham, the God of Yitzḥak,

QUESTIONS FOR THOUGHT

- According to which of the commentaries are the two doubts that Moshe expressed connected to each other?
- Each of the commentaries has a very different understanding of Moshe's view of *Benei Yisrael*. According to one, Moshe was afraid that he was unworthy of leading them; according to a second, he thought that *Benei Yisrael* were unworthy of leaving Egypt; and a third opinion says that *Benei Yisrael* need a good leader who can transform them and Moshe believes that he lacks those qualities. Can you match the commentaries with their opinions?
- Do you think that Moshe is really concerned about these things, or is he just looking for excuses not to go?

TEXTUAL SKILLS

1. In the Torah, when one person is speaking, the next ויאמר usually indicates that the other party is responding. In unusual circumstances, ויאמר appears two or more times in a row – all referring the same person speaking – and there is always a good reason for breaking up the speech that way. Look at verses 14–15 – how many times can you find ויאמר in a row that all refer to God speaking? Can you figure out why?

2. In verse 12, it is not clear how the various parts of the verse fit together. Can you figure out the problem?

WISDOM OF THE HEART

When Pharaoh's daughter discovers the baby in the basket, the Torah states that "she saw that the baby was crying." Rabbi Menaḥem Mendel of Vorke, from whom we have only eight teachings, asks: why doesn't the Torah say that she heard that the baby was crying? The Rebbe of Vorke responds that the baby wasn't actually crying out loud; rather, it was crying in its heart.

The Biale Rebbe suggests that God's message of אהיה אשר אהיה is meant to convey the idea that in exile, God sees the prayers of Israel, even when those prayers are in their hearts because they cannot find the words with which to express themselves.

How do you think a person can develop the capacity to see someone else's pain even before it is expressed?

שמות | פרק ג

יא בְנֵי־יִשְׂרָאֵל מִמִּצְרָיִם: וַיֹּאמֶר מֹשֶׁה אֶל־הָאֱלֹהִים מִי אָנֹכִי כִּי
יב אֵלֵךְ אֶל־פַּרְעֹה וְכִי אוֹצִיא אֶת־בְּנֵי יִשְׂרָאֵל מִמִּצְרָיִם: וַיֹּאמֶר
כִּי־אֶהְיֶה עִמָּךְ וְזֶה־לְּךָ הָאוֹת כִּי אָנֹכִי שְׁלַחְתִּיךָ בְּהוֹצִיאֲךָ אֶת־
יג הָעָם מִמִּצְרַיִם תַּעַבְדוּן אֶת־הָאֱלֹהִים עַל הָהָר הַזֶּה: וַיֹּאמֶר
מֹשֶׁה אֶל־הָאֱלֹהִים הִנֵּה אָנֹכִי בָא אֶל־בְּנֵי יִשְׂרָאֵל וְאָמַרְתִּי
לָהֶם אֱלֹהֵי אֲבוֹתֵיכֶם שְׁלָחַנִי אֲלֵיכֶם וְאָמְרוּ־לִי מַה־שְּׁמוֹ מָה
יד אֹמַר אֲלֵהֶם: וַיֹּאמֶר אֱלֹהִים אֶל־מֹשֶׁה אֶהְיֶה אֲשֶׁר אֶהְיֶה
טו וַיֹּאמֶר כֹּה תֹאמַר לִבְנֵי יִשְׂרָאֵל אֶהְיֶה שְׁלָחַנִי אֲלֵיכֶם: וַיֹּאמֶר
עוֹד אֱלֹהִים אֶל־מֹשֶׁה כֹּה־תֹאמַר אֶל־בְּנֵי יִשְׂרָאֵל יְהוָה אֱלֹהֵי

CLASSIC COMMENTATORS

Moshe expresses doubts about the mission, related to both himself and *Benei Yisrael*, but the exact content of those doubts is a subject of great debate.

רש״י

מי אנכי – מה אני חשוב לדבר עם המלכים.
וכי אוציא את בני ישראל – ואף אם חשוב אני, מה זכו
ישראל שיעשה להם נס.

RASHI

"Who am I" – what is my importance that I might speak with kings?
"To bring the Israelites out" – And even if I am important, what did the Israelites do to merit a miracle being performed for them?

כלי יקר

וכי אוציא את בני ישראל כי אומה גבוהה ורמה כזאת
בני אברהם יצחק ויעקב עם גדול ורם איך ילכו אחרי
שפל ובזוי כמוני?

KELI YAKAR

Moshe believed himself unworthy of leading the great and exalted nation of *Benei Yisrael* – the descendants of Avraham, Yitzḥak, and Yaakov. For why would a noble and distinguished people like the Israelites agree to follow such a lowly and despised individual like him?

ר׳ שמשון רפאל הירש

משה ... ידע היטב שאין בו מאומה מהחומר, אשר
מלהיבי ההמונים, מנהיגים, מפקדי צבאות, גיבורים
ושליטים, נוצרים ממנו. היה זה אך טבע שאדם כזה
יהסס מלקבל על עצמו שליחות כזאת ... האם אין צד
שהשליחות כולה תבוא לידי כשלון, מכיון שהוא עלול
להיות חסר אונים בפני פרעה ... ובמקרה כזה, האם
לא ימיט אך ורק אסון כפול ומכופל על ראש אחיו?
וכי לא היה רשאי להיות מסופק, אם יש לאישיותו
את הכח המרשים והכובש את לב האחרים, הנדרש
בכדי להפוך אומה של עבדים לעם ה׳?

RABBI SAMSON RAPHAEL HIRSCH

Moshe...recognized in himself an absence of those characteristics possessed by agitators of multitudes, leaders of armies, heroes, and rulers. It was only natural that such a person would hesitate to accept such a mission upon himself... Because Moshe was bereft of any inherent leadership abilities, he believed that the job God was foisting on him was doomed to failure... And if that were to happen, would not Moshe's bumbling bring even greater suffering upon the heads of his brethren? Surely Moshe could be excused for doubting whether he possessed the skill to capture the imagination of the masses, a quality necessary for transforming the people from a nation of quivering slaves into the proud servants of the Lord.

SHEMOT | CHAPTER 3

16 and the God of Yaakov, has sent me to you. This is My name forever, and this is how I will be remembered through the ages. Go, gather the elders of Israel and tell them: The Lord God of your fathers appeared to me – the God of Avraham, Yitzḥak, and Yaakov
17 – saying: I have taken note of you and what is being inflicted upon you in Egypt. And I promise to bring you out of the misery of Egypt to the land of the Canaanites and Hittites, the Amorites and Perizzites, the Hivites and Jebusites, to a land flowing with
18 milk and honey. They will listen to you. Then you and the elders of Israel shall go to the king of Egypt and tell him, 'The Lord God of the Hebrews has revealed Himself to us. Send us forth now for a three-day journey into the wilderness to sacrifice to the
19 Lord our God.' But I know that even by a mighty hand the king of Egypt would not
20 send you forth. So I will stretch out My hand and strike Egypt with all the wonders I
21 will do there. After that, he will send you forth. And I will grant this people favor in the
22 eyes of the Egyptians, so that when you leave, you will not leave empty-handed. Every woman shall ask her neighbor, ask any woman lodging with her, for objects of silver and

---

RABBI OVADYA SFORNO

Although you will receive all of these objects from the Egyptians as loans, and you will be obligated to return them, you will later acquire all of it rightfully. This will happen when Egypt chases after you to fight you and to take your plunder. Since they will die in that battle when God fights on Israel's behalf, it will be justifiable, measure for measure, for the pursued to collect the plunder of their pursuers. Such is the custom in any war.

ר׳ עובדיה ספורנו

אף על פי שתקבלו הכל מהם דרך השאלה, ותהיו חייבים להחזיר, הנה תקנו אחר כך את הכל בדין, בדרפם אחריכם להלחם בכם ולשלול את שללכם. כי אמנם כאשר מתו באותה המלחמה, כי ה׳ נלחם, היה בדין מדה כנגד מדה כל שלל הרודפים לנרדפים, כמנהג בכל מלחמה.

RABBI DAVID TZVI HOFFMAN

Because the plan for Israel's escape involved telling the Egyptians that the people were only leaving for a three-day furlough to sacrifice to God, the nation would necessarily have to leave a good deal of their possessions behind. To compensate the Israelites for that impending loss [for they were never to return to reclaim their property], the Lord promised the nation that they would not quit Egypt empty handed. In exchange for their homes and the articles they would be unable to take with them, the nation would be given "objects of silver and gold." These are the items that they would ask from the Egyptians before the exodus.

ר׳ דוד צבי הופמן

לפי שהאמתלה ללכת דרך שלושת ימים לזבוח וכו׳ תגרור אחריה שבני ישראל ייאלצו להשאיר את רכושם בארץ מצרים, מבטיח ה׳ כי למרות זאת לא יצאו משם ריקם, אלא שבעד הרכוש שישאירו במצרים יפוצו על ידי אותם כלי כסף וכלי זהב שישאלו – ידרשו מן המצרים.

QUESTIONS FOR THOUGHT

- Which of the commentaries suggests that initially they were supposed to borrow the gold and silver? Why does he think that that is not ethically problematic?
- Which of the commentaries understands that the plan was for them to request parting gifts from the Egyptians?
- According to Rabbi David Tzvi Hoffman, it was a justified deception. What made it justified?
- Which of the above explanations do you find the least ethically uncomfortable? The most?

אֲבֹתֵיכֶם אֱלֹהֵי אַבְרָהָם אֱלֹהֵי יִצְחָק וֵאלֹהֵי יַעֲקֹב שְׁלָחַנִי
אֲלֵיכֶם זֶה־שְּׁמִי לְעֹלָם וְזֶה זִכְרִי לְדֹר דֹּר: לֵךְ וְאָסַפְתָּ אֶת־ טז
זִקְנֵי יִשְׂרָאֵל וְאָמַרְתָּ אֲלֵהֶם יְהֹוָה אֱלֹהֵי אֲבֹתֵיכֶם נִרְאָה אֵלַי
אֱלֹהֵי אַבְרָהָם יִצְחָק וְיַעֲקֹב לֵאמֹר פָּקֹד פָּקַדְתִּי אֶתְכֶם וְאֶת־
הֶעָשׂוּי לָכֶם בְּמִצְרָיִם: וָאֹמַר אַעֲלֶה אֶתְכֶם מֵעֳנִי מִצְרַיִם אֶל־ יז
אֶרֶץ הַכְּנַעֲנִי וְהַחִתִּי וְהָאֱמֹרִי וְהַפְּרִזִּי וְהַחִוִּי וְהַיְבוּסִי אֶל־אֶרֶץ
זָבַת חָלָב וּדְבָשׁ: וְשָׁמְעוּ לְקֹלֶךָ וּבָאתָ אַתָּה וְזִקְנֵי יִשְׂרָאֵל יח
אֶל־מֶלֶךְ מִצְרַיִם וַאֲמַרְתֶּם אֵלָיו יְהֹוָה אֱלֹהֵי הָעִבְרִיִּים נִקְרָה
עָלֵינוּ וְעַתָּה נֵלְכָה־נָּא דֶּרֶךְ שְׁלֹשֶׁת יָמִים בַּמִּדְבָּר וְנִזְבְּחָה
לַיהֹוָה אֱלֹהֵינוּ: וַאֲנִי יָדַעְתִּי כִּי לֹא־יִתֵּן אֶתְכֶם מֶלֶךְ מִצְרַיִם יט
לַהֲלֹךְ וְלֹא בְּיָד חֲזָקָה: וְשָׁלַחְתִּי אֶת־יָדִי וְהִכֵּיתִי אֶת־מִצְרַיִם כ
בְּכֹל נִפְלְאֹתַי אֲשֶׁר אֶעֱשֶׂה בְּקִרְבּוֹ וְאַחֲרֵי־כֵן יְשַׁלַּח אֶתְכֶם:
וְנָתַתִּי אֶת־חֵן הָעָם־הַזֶּה בְּעֵינֵי מִצְרָיִם וְהָיָה כִּי תֵלֵכוּן לֹא כא
תֵלְכוּ רֵיקָם: וְשָׁאֲלָה אִשָּׁה מִשְּׁכֶנְתָּהּ וּמִגָּרַת בֵּיתָהּ כְּלֵי־כֶסֶף כב

חמישי

TEXTUAL SKILLS

1. The Torah speaks about requesting items from Egyptian neighbors or people who live in the same house. What does this suggest about the slavery in Egypt?

2. There is another place where God instructs *Benei Yisrael* to ask the Egyptians for their things, in Exodus 11:2. What are the differences between that verse and this one?

CLASSIC COMMENTATORS

God tells Moshe to instruct *Benei Yisrael* to request items of gold and silver, and even clothes, from their Egyptian neighbors before they leave on their three-day journey. This raises serious ethical questions about deceiving the Egyptians (since they were not planning to return those items). The commentaries grapple with this question.

RASHBAM   רשב״ם

As a genuine and unconditional gift, for "I will grant this people favor [in the eyes of the Egyptians]" (3:21).

במתנה גמורה וחלוטה, שהריא ונתתי את חן העם (שמות ג, כ״א).

gold, and clothing, and you shall put these on your sons and daughters, and despoil the Egyptians." But Moshe replied, "They will not believe me. They will not listen to me. They will say, 'The LORD has not appeared to you.'" "What is that in your hand?" asked the LORD. "A staff," he replied. "Throw it to the ground." He threw it, and it turned into a snake; and Moshe fled back from it. The LORD told Moshe, "Reach out your hand and take hold of its tail." He reached out his hand and grasped it, and in his hand it turned back into a staff. "This is so that they will believe that the LORD God of their fathers, the God of Avraham, Yitzḥak, and Yaakov, appeared to you." The LORD spoke to him again: "Put your hand inside your cloak." He put his hand inside his cloak; when he took it out it was as white as snow. "Put it back inside your cloak," He said. Moshe put his hand back inside his cloak and when he took it out the skin color had returned. "If they do not believe you and are not persuaded by the first sign, they will believe the evidence of the second sign. And if they do not believe either of these signs, and will not listen to you, then take some water from the Nile and spill it on the ground. The water you

---

RABBEINU BAḤYA

With the two signs of the changing of the staff and the affliction of the **צרעת**, the Holy One, blessed be He, taught Moshe that He has the ability to kill the living and to revive the dead. For the staff in Moshe's hand started as a piece of dry and lifeless wood which was then changed into a living snake.

רבינו בחיי

ויש לפרש כי בשני אותות האלה כלומר אות המטה ואות הצרעת רמז לו הקב״ה שבידו להחיות את המת ולהמית את החי, כי המטה היה עץ יבש כמו מת ונעשה נחש חי.

QUESTIONS FOR THOUGHT

- Interestingly, all of the commentaries suggest that the sign of the snake was designed to send a message to Moshe in addition to trying to convince *Benei Yisrael*. According to one it is a message of encouragement, according to another it was a hint that the mission would be difficult, and according to a third it was a rebuke to Moshe. Which of the commentaries says which?
- Do you think that it was appropriate for Moshe to be questioning his effectiveness on this mission?

TEXTUAL SKILLS

1. Notice which of the signs God gives Moshe are reversible and which is not.

2. Is the third sign the same as the plague of blood? How do you know?

שמות | פרק ד

וּכְלֵי זָהָב וּשְׂמָלֹת וְשַׂמְתֶּם עַל־בְּנֵיכֶם וְעַל־בְּנְֹתֵיכֶם וְנִצַּלְתֶּם
אֶת־מִצְרָיִם: וַיַּעַן מֹשֶׁה וַיֹּאמֶר וְהֵן לֹא־יַאֲמִינוּ לִי וְלֹא יִשְׁמְעוּ
בְּקֹלִי כִּי יֹאמְרוּ לֹא־נִרְאָה אֵלֶיךָ יְהֹוָה: וַיֹּאמֶר אֵלָיו יְהֹוָה מזה מַה־זֶּה
בְיָדֶךָ וַיֹּאמֶר מַטֶּה: וַיֹּאמֶר הַשְׁלִיכֵהוּ אַרְצָה וַיַּשְׁלִכֵהוּ אַרְצָה
וַיְהִי לְנָחָשׁ וַיָּנָס מֹשֶׁה מִפָּנָיו: וַיֹּאמֶר יְהֹוָה אֶל־מֹשֶׁה שְׁלַח
יָדְךָ וֶאֱחֹז בִּזְנָבוֹ וַיִּשְׁלַח יָדוֹ וַיַּחֲזֶק־בּוֹ וַיְהִי לְמַטֶּה בְּכַפּוֹ: לְמַעַן
יַאֲמִינוּ כִּי־נִרְאָה אֵלֶיךָ יְהֹוָה אֱלֹהֵי אֲבֹתָם אֱלֹהֵי אַבְרָהָם
אֱלֹהֵי יִצְחָק וֵאלֹהֵי יַעֲקֹב: וַיֹּאמֶר יְהֹוָה לוֹ עוֹד הָבֵא־נָא יָדְךָ
בְּחֵיקֶךָ וַיָּבֵא יָדוֹ בְּחֵיקוֹ וַיּוֹצִאָהּ וְהִנֵּה יָדוֹ מְצֹרַעַת כַּשָּׁלֶג:
וַיֹּאמֶר הָשֵׁב יָדְךָ אֶל־חֵיקֶךָ וַיָּשֶׁב יָדוֹ אֶל־חֵיקוֹ וַיּוֹצִאָהּ מֵחֵיקוֹ
וְהִנֵּה־שָׁבָה כִּבְשָׂרוֹ: וְהָיָה אִם־לֹא יַאֲמִינוּ לָךְ וְלֹא יִשְׁמְעוּ
לְקֹל הָאֹת הָרִאשׁוֹן וְהֶאֱמִינוּ לְקֹל הָאֹת הָאַחֲרוֹן: וְהָיָה
אִם־לֹא יַאֲמִינוּ גַּם לִשְׁנֵי הָאֹתוֹת הָאֵלֶּה וְלֹא יִשְׁמְעוּן לְקֹלֶךָ
וְלָקַחְתָּ מִמֵּימֵי הַיְאֹר וְשָׁפַכְתָּ הַיַּבָּשָׁה וְהָיוּ הַמַּיִם אֲשֶׁר

א
ב
ג
ד
ה
ו
ז
ח
ט

CLASSIC COMMENTATORS

The commentaries are curious about the signs that God gave Moshe – why these? Do they symbolize some kind of idea?

RASHI

God thereby hinted to Moshe that by speaking ill of the children of Israel, he had adopted the tactics of the snake [who spoke slanderously of God; see Genesis 3].

רש״י

רמז לו שסיפר לשון הרע על ישראל, ותפש אומנותו של נחש.

IBN EZRA

The commentator Yefet writes that the sign of the staff was an allusion to Pharaoh's various stages of transformation. For although the king was initially soft [tame] like a staff, and subsequently turned [nasty] like a snake, he would eventually be forced to revert to his initial compliant state. Pharaoh would end up being like one who had never existed.

אבן עזרא

אמר יפת: זה המופת רמז כי פרעה היה בתחלה דבר רך כמו מטה, ונהפך לנחש ... ובסוף ישוב כבראשונה, והיה כלא היה.

10 take from the Nile will become blood on the ground." Then Moshe said to the Lord, "Please, my Lord, I am not a man of words; I was not yesterday, nor the day before, and
11 still I am not since You spoke to Your servant. I am slow of speech and tongue." "Who gives man speech?" said the Lord to him. "Who makes people dumb or deaf? Who
12 gives them sight or blindness? Is it not I, the Lord? Now go. I will help you speak and
13 I will teach you what to say." But, "Please, my Lord," he said, "send someone else." Then
14 the Lord's anger blazed against Moshe. "Have you not a brother, Aharon the Levite? He, I know, is able to speak. Even now he is setting out to meet you, and when he sees
15 you his heart will rejoice. You shall speak to him and place words in his mouth. I will
16 help you both to speak, and I will teach you what to do. He will speak on your behalf
17 to the people – he will be your voice; and you will be his access to God. Take this staff in your hand. With it, you shall perform the signs."

RAMBAN

רמב״ן

ועל דרך הפשט יאמר: כי אני כבד פה גם מתמול גם משלשום, כי מנעורי הייתי כבד פה, אף כי עתה כי אני זקן. וגם מאז דברך היום אל עבדך, כי לא הסירות כבדות פי בצוותך אותי ללכת אל פרעה לדבר בשמך, ואם כן, איך אלך לפניו. והנה משה, מרוב חפצו שלא ילך, לא התפלל לפניו יתברך שיסיר כבדות פיו, אבל טען אחרי שלא הסירות כבדות פי מעת שדברת לי ללכת, אל תצוני שאלך, כי לא יתכן לאדון הכל לשלוח שליח ערל שפתים למלך עמים.

The straightforward meaning of the verse is that Moshe complained that he had been slow of speech and tongue from his early childhood, a problem that had only become more acute with his old age. Furthermore, Moshe pointed out, God had not alleviated his difficulty speaking since He first appeared to him and commanded that Moshe go to Egypt to speak in His name. How then could Moshe possibly appear before the king?

Out of a deep desire to avoid the mission, Moshe did not pray to God to heal his speech impediment at this point. Instead he contended: Since You have not corrected my speech problem since You first told me to go, do not command me to proceed. It is inconceivable that the Master of all things should employ an emissary with deficient speech to appeal to a great king.

HAAMEK DAVAR

העמק דבר

הענין הזה נדרש להיות איש דברים עם ישראל להסביר להם כל נס על מה הוא בא ומראה, וכן הסבר דבר ה' במאמרים הקודמים, ואני איני ראוי לכך.

One must be a man of words to explain to Israel the reason for and significance of each miracle. And I will need to explain the word of God in my preceding statements. But I am not fit for any of that.

QUESTIONS FOR THOUGHT

- One of the commentaries reads the text as is, that Moshe had a speech defect, while another is horrified by the notion that the greatest prophet would have such a flaw. Can you figure out which of the above align with those positions?
- Would you pay more attention to what someone says because of their speaking ability or because of the content of what they say?
- According to the Haamek Davar, there was no physical defect, but Moshe was simply not an eloquent speaker. Is eloquence a gift from God or something that we can develop?

י תִּקַּח מִן־הַיְאֹר וְהָיוּ לְדָם בַּיַּבָּשֶׁת: וַיֹּאמֶר מֹשֶׁה אֶל־יהוה בִּי אֲדֹנָי לֹא אִישׁ דְּבָרִים אָנֹכִי גַּם מִתְּמוֹל גַּם מִשִּׁלְשֹׁם גַּם

יא מֵאָז דַּבֶּרְךָ אֶל־עַבְדֶּךָ כִּי כְבַד־פֶּה וּכְבַד לָשׁוֹן אָנֹכִי: וַיֹּאמֶר יהוה אֵלָיו מִי שָׂם פֶּה לָאָדָם אוֹ מִי־יָשׂוּם אִלֵּם אוֹ חֵרֵשׁ

יב אוֹ פִקֵּחַ אוֹ עִוֵּר הֲלֹא אָנֹכִי יהוה: וְעַתָּה לֵךְ וְאָנֹכִי אֶהְיֶה

יג עִם־פִּיךָ וְהוֹרֵיתִיךָ אֲשֶׁר תְּדַבֵּר: וַיֹּאמֶר בִּי אֲדֹנָי שְׁלַח־נָא

יד בְּיַד־תִּשְׁלָח: וַיִּחַר־אַף יהוה בְּמֹשֶׁה וַיֹּאמֶר הֲלֹא אַהֲרֹן אָחִיךָ הַלֵּוִי יָדַעְתִּי כִּי־דַבֵּר יְדַבֵּר הוּא וְגַם הִנֵּה־הוּא יֹצֵא לִקְרָאתֶךָ

טו וְרָאֲךָ וְשָׂמַח בְּלִבּוֹ: וְדִבַּרְתָּ אֵלָיו וְשַׂמְתָּ אֶת־הַדְּבָרִים בְּפִיו וְאָנֹכִי אֶהְיֶה עִם־פִּיךָ וְעִם־פִּיהוּ וְהוֹרֵיתִי אֶתְכֶם אֵת אֲשֶׁר

טז תַּעֲשׂוּן: וְדִבֶּר־הוּא לְךָ אֶל־הָעָם וְהָיָה הוּא יִהְיֶה־לְּךָ לְפֶה

יז וְאַתָּה תִּהְיֶה־לּוֹ לֵאלֹהִים: וְאֶת־הַמַּטֶּה הַזֶּה תִּקַּח בְּיָדֶךָ אֲשֶׁר תַּעֲשֶׂה־בּוֹ אֶת־הָאֹתֹת:

CLASSIC COMMENTATORS

What kind of speech defect did Moshe think would interfere with his ability to fulfill God's mission?

RASHBAM — רשב״ם

This means only that Moshe was not proficient in the nuances of the Egyptian language, for in his youth he had run away from Egypt, and now he was eighty years old.... It cannot be that a prophet who would speak to God face to face and received the Torah had a speech impediment.

איני בקי בלשון מצרים בחיתוך לשון, כי בקטנותי ברחתי משם ועתה אני בן שמונים ... וכי איפשר נביא אשר ידעו השם פנים אל פנים וקיבל תורה מידו לידו היה מגמגם בלשונו.

18 Moshe left and returned to Yeter his father-in-law. He said to him, "Let me go back to
19 my brothers in Egypt, to see if they are still alive." Yitro said to him, "Go in peace." While Moshe was still in Midian, the Lord said to him, "Go, return to Egypt. All those who
20 sought your life have died." So Moshe took his wife and sons and put them on a donkey,
21 and he set out to return to Egypt, taking in his hand the staff of God. The Lord said to Moshe, "When you return to Egypt, see that you perform for Pharaoh all the wonders I have placed in your power. But still I will strengthen his heart and he will not send the
22 people forth. Tell Pharaoh: This is what the Lord says, 'Israel is My son, My firstborn. I
23 have told you: Send forth My son, so that he may serve Me. If you refuse to let him go, I
24 will kill your son, your firstborn.'" At a lodging place on the way, the Lord confronted
25 Moshe and was about to kill him. But Tzipora took a flint knife and cut off her son's foreskin, throwing it down at his feet, and said, "You are a bridegroom of blood to me."
26 So He let him go. Then "A bridegroom of blood," she said, "because of circumcision."

RASHBAM

רשב"ם

The attack came because Moshe was lazy about going, [encumbering himself by] taking his wife and sons along.

כי היה מתעצל בהליכתו ומוליך אשתו ובניו.

RABBI DAVID TZVI HOFFMAN

ר' דוד צבי הופמן

Tzipora immediately understood that circumcising her son's foreskin would serve to rescue her husband from mortal danger. We must conclude that although Moshe had previously explained to Tzipora the obligation he bore to circumcise his sons, his wife had objected to the ritual. Yitro too had prevented Moshe from performing the procedure. And in the face of his family's disapproval, Moshe lacked the fortitude to insist on fulfilling the Lord's commandment.

אנו רואים שציפורה חשה תיכף ומיד, כי כריתת ערלת בנה תושיע את בעלה, ומכאן שכבר אמר לה משה קודם לכן, שחובה זו מוטלת עליו, אלא שהיא התנגדה, יחד עם אביה, לדבר זה, ומשה לא היה חזק דיו כדי לעשות את מצוות ה' בלי להתחשב בהתנגדות זו.

QUESTIONS FOR THOUGHT

- According to one of the above commentaries, Moshe rationalized why the timing for the circumcision was wrong; according to another, Moshe lacked the fortitude to push past the opposition of his wife and father-in-law. The third opinion doesn't address the circumcision, but offers a different explanation as to why God wanted to kill Moshe. What is that explanation?
- Why would circumcision be so important prior to this specific mission?

TEXTUAL SKILLS

1. Which of Moshe's sons needed to be circumcised in this story?
2. When God says to Moshe, "I will kill your son, your firstborn" (v. 23), is that part of the message that Moshe is supposed to deliver to Pharaoh or a message that God is telling Moshe about himself?
3. The story with the circumcision happens at a מלון. That word appears only two other times in all of the Torah, in Genesis 42:27 and Genesis 43:21 (both are referring to the same event). What is the connection between the appearance of this word here and in the story in Genesis?

יח וַיֵּ֨לֶךְ מֹשֶׁ֜ה וַיָּ֣שָׁב ׀ אֶל־יֶ֣תֶר חֹֽתְנ֗וֹ וַיֹּ֤אמֶר לוֹ֙ אֵ֣לְכָה נָּ֔א וְאָשׁ֨וּבָה֙ ששי ג
אֶל־אַחַ֣י אֲשֶׁר־בְּמִצְרַ֔יִם וְאֶרְאֶ֖ה הַעוֹדָ֣ם חַיִּ֑ים וַיֹּ֧אמֶר יִתְר֛וֹ
לְמֹשֶׁ֖ה לֵ֥ךְ לְשָׁלֽוֹם׃
יט וַיֹּ֨אמֶר יְהֹוָ֤ה אֶל־מֹשֶׁה֙ בְּמִדְיָ֔ן לֵ֖ךְ שֻׁ֣ב
מִצְרָ֑יִם כִּי־מֵ֨תוּ֙ כָּל־הָ֣אֲנָשִׁ֔ים הַֽמְבַקְשִׁ֖ים אֶת־נַפְשֶֽׁךָ׃
כ וַיִּקַּ֨ח מֹשֶׁ֜ה אֶת־אִשְׁתּ֣וֹ וְאֶת־בָּנָ֗יו וַיַּרְכִּבֵם֙ עַֽל־הַחֲמֹ֔ר וַיָּ֖שָׁב אַ֣רְצָה
מִצְרָ֑יִם וַיִּקַּ֥ח מֹשֶׁ֛ה אֶת־מַטֵּ֥ה הָאֱלֹהִ֖ים בְּיָדֽוֹ׃
כא וַיֹּ֣אמֶר יְהֹוָה֮
אֶל־מֹשֶׁה֒ בְּלֶכְתְּךָ֙ לָשׁ֣וּב מִצְרַ֔יְמָה רְאֵ֗ה כָּל־הַמֹּֽפְתִים֙ אֲשֶׁר־
שַׂ֣מְתִּי בְיָדֶ֔ךָ וַעֲשִׂיתָ֖ם לִפְנֵ֣י פַרְעֹ֑ה וַאֲנִי֙ אֲחַזֵּ֣ק אֶת־לִבּ֔וֹ וְלֹ֥א
יְשַׁלַּ֖ח אֶת־הָעָֽם׃
כב וְאָמַרְתָּ֖ אֶל־פַּרְעֹ֑ה כֹּ֚ה אָמַ֣ר יְהֹוָ֔ה בְּנִ֥י בְכֹרִ֖י
יִשְׂרָאֵֽל׃
כג וָאֹמַ֣ר אֵלֶ֗יךָ שַׁלַּ֤ח אֶת־בְּנִי֙ וְיַֽעַבְדֵ֔נִי וַתְּמָאֵ֖ן לְשַׁלְּח֑וֹ
הִנֵּה֙ אָנֹכִ֣י הֹרֵ֔ג אֶת־בִּנְךָ֖ בְּכֹרֶֽךָ׃
כד וַיְהִ֥י בַדֶּ֖רֶךְ בַּמָּל֑וֹן וַיִּפְגְּשֵׁ֣הוּ
יְהֹוָ֔ה וַיְבַקֵּ֖שׁ הֲמִיתֽוֹ׃
כה וַתִּקַּ֨ח צִפֹּרָ֜ה צֹ֗ר וַתִּכְרֹת֙ אֶת־עָרְלַ֣ת בְּנָ֔הּ
וַתַּגַּ֖ע לְרַגְלָ֑יו וַתֹּ֕אמֶר כִּ֧י חֲתַן־דָּמִ֛ים אַתָּ֖ה לִֽי׃
כו וַיִּ֖רֶף מִמֶּ֑נּוּ אָ֚ז
אָֽמְרָ֔ה חֲתַ֥ן דָּמִ֖ים לַמּוּלֹֽת׃

CLASSIC COMMENTATORS

The story of Moshe's mysterious encounter with God is puzzling in many ways. One of the questions that bothered the commentaries was why Moshe hadn't circumcised his son.

IBN EZRA

There was a tradition not to circumcise a baby if he was sick or if he was traveling on the eighth day, since it would not be possible to tarry during a journey. Since Moshe could not delay the fulfillment of God's mission, he thought it best not to circumcise his son and risk endangering the baby on the journey. Subsequently God sent an angel to remind Moshe, encouraging him to change his mind, circumcise his son, and proceed on the journey by himself. The baby would then remain with his mother until he recovered.

אבן עזרא

היתה קבלה בידם שלא יומל הבן בשמיני אם הוא חולה, או הוא בדרך שאין יכולת במוליכו להתעכב. ובעבור כי משה לא יוכל להתעכב בשליחות השם, ראה בעצתו שלא יומל, כי יסתכן הנער אם יוליכו. הנה שלח השם מלאכו להזכיר משה שינוח עצמו, ויומל הנער, וילך לו לבדו, והנער יהיה עם אמו עד שיתרפא.

SHEMOT | CHAPTER 4

On his way to Egypt Moshe is met by Aharon, with whom he shares God's messages. Together they go to the elders of Israel. Aharon tells them the message he heard from Moshe and performs the signs that God had given to Moshe. The elders believe that God has heard their cries and remembered them, and they bow in gratitude.

27 The Lord said to Aharon, "Go and meet Moshe in the wilderness." And he went and
28 met him at God's mountain, and kissed him. And Moshe told Aharon all that the Lord had said about his mission, and all the miraculous signs He had commanded him to
29 perform. So Moshe and Aharon went and gathered all the elders of Israel. Aharon told
30 them everything the Lord had said to Moshe, and he performed the signs before the
31 people. And the people believed. When they heard that the Lord was watching over the Israelites, and that He had seen their misery, they bowed their heads and prostrated

QUESTIONS FOR THOUGHT

- According to which two commentaries does Moshe include unflattering things about himself? Why would that be important to include?
- Only one of the commentaries mentions specifically that he told Aharon about his role. Why would that be important? Why do the other commentaries not think that it is important to mention?
- According to one of the commentaries, Moshe told Aharon every detail of the mission. What was the effect of sharing all that? Do you think that leaders should always share everything with their partners, or is it sometimes wiser to keep some things hidden?

TEXTUAL SKILLS

1. Was Moshe supposed to perform the signs right away or only after *Benei Yisrael* expressed hesitation about believing him?
2. There are two other brother-reunions in the Torah – Yaakov and Esav, and Yosef and his brothers. In what way is the reunion between Moshe and Aharon different from those others?
3. Notice that in the previous passage and here Moshe has an encounter, which the Torah describes using the word ויפגשהו. (Note: these are the only two times in all of Tanakh that this word appears!) Do these two encounters have anything in common?

QUICK BITE

One might wonder: why did God never remove Moshe's speech impediment? Perhaps it was to let us know that true leadership is not about charisma or personality but about substance and character. If we reflect further, perhaps the message is that the perfection of the messenger is unimportant. God wants each and every one of us, with all our imperfections, to do the best we can with what we have.

There is an extraordinary story about Itzhak Perlman, a wheelchair-bound world-class violinist. At the beginning of one performance a string on his violin broke, yet he did not miss a beat and continued to play the entire piece with only three strings. Afterward he said, "You just have to play with what you have."

שמות | פרק ד

כז וַיֹּ֤אמֶר יְהֹוָה֙ אֶֽל־אַהֲרֹ֔ן לֵ֛ךְ לִקְרַ֥את מֹשֶׁ֖ה הַמִּדְבָּ֑רָה וַיֵּ֗לֶךְ
כח וַֽיִּפְגְּשֵׁ֛הוּ בְּהַ֥ר הָאֱלֹהִ֖ים וַיִּשַּׁק־לֽוֹ: וַיַּגֵּ֤ד מֹשֶׁה֙ לְאַהֲרֹ֔ן אֵ֥ת כׇּל־
כט דִּבְרֵ֥י יְהֹוָ֖ה אֲשֶׁ֣ר שְׁלָח֑וֹ וְאֵ֥ת כׇּל־הָאֹתֹ֖ת אֲשֶׁ֥ר צִוָּֽהוּ: וַיֵּ֥לֶךְ מֹשֶׁ֖ה
ל וְאַהֲרֹ֑ן וַיַּ֣אַסְפ֔וּ אֶת־כׇּל־זִקְנֵ֖י בְּנֵ֥י יִשְׂרָאֵֽל: וַיְדַבֵּ֣ר אַהֲרֹ֗ן אֵ֚ת כׇּל־
הַדְּבָרִ֔ים אֲשֶׁר־דִּבֶּ֥ר יְהֹוָ֖ה אֶל־מֹשֶׁ֑ה וַיַּ֥עַשׂ הָאֹתֹ֖ת לְעֵינֵ֥י הָעָֽם:
לא וַֽיַּאֲמֵ֖ן הָעָ֑ם וַֽיִּשְׁמְע֡וּ כִּֽי־פָקַ֨ד יְהֹוָ֜ה אֶת־בְּנֵ֣י יִשְׂרָאֵ֗ל וְכִ֤י רָאָה֙

CLASSIC COMMENTATORS

The Torah says that Moshe told Aharon "all" that God had said to him, and repeats "all" later in the verse. The commentaries want to know what the Torah is trying to highlight

ר' יוסף אבן כספי

ספר לו שלש הנבואות שהגיעו למשה בשלשה זמנים זה אחר זה, כי ראוי שידע אהרן עתה בתחלת העניינים כל סודות משה שגילה לו השם, וגם הוא, רצוני אהרן נתחבר למשה בכל המוסכם, וייטב בעיניו מאד, לכן וילך משה ואהרן.

RABBI YOSEF IBN KASPI

Moshe relayed to Aharon the three prophecies that he had received on three different occasions. For it was necessary that Aharon be made aware of all the secrets that God had revealed to Moshe, so that he could become a full and committed partner in the enterprise his brother was embarking on. This alliance is reflected in the verse which states, "After this, Moshe and Aharon came to Pharaoh" (5:1).

רמב״ן

שהגיד לו כל הדברים שהיו בינו ובין הקדוש ברוך הוא, וכל אשר היה מסרב בשליחות, וכי על כרחו נשתלח, וזה טעם כל.

RAMBAN

Moshe related to Aharon the entire conversation that passed between him and God. He told him that he had initially refused the mission, and that he was being sent against his will. This is what the word "all" connotes.

חזקוני

הגיד לו כל אשר קרהו ושהביא אשתו במלון ראשון.

HIZKUNI

Moshe reported to Aharon everything that had happened to him, and that he had brought his wife with him to the lodging place.

מלבי״ם

הגיד לו כל מה שדבר עמו והודיע כי אהרן ניתן לו לפה להציע הדברים ולעשות האותות לפני בני ישראל.

MALBIM

He told him all that God had spoken about with him. He also informed Aharon that he was to be his spokesman, to explicate the words of God and to perform the signs before the Israelites.

SHEMOT | CHAPTER 5   SHEMOT | 32

After their successful meeting with the elders of Israel, Moshe and Aharon present God's message to Pharaoh. Pharaoh's initial reaction is not positive, and when they press their point, Pharaoh instructs the Egyptian taskmasters to increase the workload by making the people forage for their own straw while demanding the same output of bricks.

5 1 themselves. After this, Moshe and Aharon came to Pharaoh; they said, "Thus says the Lord, God of Israel: Send My people forth so that they may hold a festival for Me in
2 the wilderness." But Pharaoh said, "Who is this Lord that I should obey Him and send
3 Israel forth? I do not know the Lord, and I will not send Israel forth." "The God of the Hebrews has revealed Himself to us," they said. "Let us take a three-day journey into the wilderness and sacrifice to the Lord our God, or He may strike us with the plague
4 or with the sword." The king of Egypt said to them, "Why, Moshe and Aharon, would
5 you take the people from their work? Get back to your labor! Look," said Pharaoh, "how numerous the people of the land have become; and yet you would have them
6 rest from their labors." That day, Pharaoh gave orders to the people's taskmasters and
7 foremen: "Do not give the people straw for bricks as before. Let them go and gather
8 their own straw. But require them to make the same quota of bricks as before. Do not reduce it. They are lazy. That is why they are crying out, 'Send us forth to sacrifice to
9 our God.' Make the work harder for the people; and make sure they do it instead of

---

QUESTIONS FOR THOUGHT

- According to one of the commentaries, this phrase is Pharaoh's response to something that Moshe and Aharon said earlier. According to the other, it is connected to the continuation of Pharaoh's new decree. Can you figure out which is which?
- Can you think of other situations in which context can completely change the meaning of what someone is saying?

TEXTUAL SKILLS

1. In verse 4, Pharaoh is speaking to Moshe and Aharon. In verse 5 he is still speaking, yet the Torah opens the verse with an extra ויאמר, suggesting that this was the beginning of a new speech (rather than a continuation of the previous one). What do you think happened, or was supposed to happen, between Pharaoh's first speech and his second?

2. The word סבל, meaning "heavy burden," appears only six times in the Torah – and all of them are in the story of the exodus! In fact, it appears twice in these verses alone. One interesting point is that sometimes it is used to describe the burden of the Egyptians, and sometimes the burden of Israel!

WISDOM OF THE HEART

According to Ramban, Pharaoh's initial plan to enslave the Hebrews was sophisticated, since an unprovoked attack on a people invited to the kingdom would have been unacceptable. Initially, they were to be isolated – treated as not "real" Egyptians and a potential threat. Then they were slowly drawn into a form of national service, perhaps to demonstrate their loyalty, which morphed into compulsory work on a project of major importance. From there it was a short step to slavery, and ultimately to oppression. The work element was an essential step, so that when Moshe and Aharon ask for a reprieve from the work Pharaoh seizes on that as an attempt to reverse the process he had carefully constructed.

שמות | פרק ה

שביעי

א אֶת־עֵינָיִם וַיִּקְּדוּ וַיִּשְׁתַּחֲוֽוּ: וְאַחַ֗ר בָּ֚אוּ מֹשֶׁ֣ה וְאַהֲרֹ֔ן וַיֹּאמְר֖וּ אֶל־פַּרְעֹ֑ה כֹּֽה־אָמַ֤ר יְהֹוָה֙ אֱלֹהֵ֣י יִשְׂרָאֵ֔ל שַׁלַּח֙ אֶת־עַמִּ֔י וְיָחֹ֥גּוּ

ב לִ֖י בַּמִּדְבָּֽר: וַיֹּ֣אמֶר פַּרְעֹ֔ה מִ֣י יְהֹוָ֔ה אֲשֶׁ֥ר אֶשְׁמַ֣ע בְּקֹל֔וֹ לְשַׁלַּ֖ח אֶת־יִשְׂרָאֵ֑ל לֹ֤א יָדַ֙עְתִּי֙ אֶת־יְהֹוָ֔ה וְגַ֥ם אֶת־יִשְׂרָאֵ֖ל לֹ֥א אֲשַׁלֵּֽחַ:

ג וַיֹּ֣אמְר֔וּ אֱלֹהֵ֥י הָעִבְרִ֖ים נִקְרָ֣א עָלֵ֑ינוּ נֵ֣לֲכָה נָּ֡א דֶּרֶךְ֩ שְׁלֹ֨שֶׁת יָמִ֜ים בַּמִּדְבָּ֗ר וְנִזְבְּחָה֙ לַֽיהֹוָ֣ה אֱלֹהֵ֔ינוּ פֶּ֨ן־יִפְגָּעֵ֔נוּ בַּדֶּ֖בֶר א֥וֹ

ד בֶחָֽרֶב: וַיֹּ֤אמֶר אֲלֵהֶם֙ מֶ֣לֶךְ מִצְרַ֔יִם לָ֚מָּה מֹשֶׁ֣ה וְאַהֲרֹ֔ן תַּפְרִ֥יעוּ אֶת־הָעָ֖ם מִמַּֽעֲשָׂ֑יו לְכ֖וּ לְסִבְלֹתֵיכֶֽם: וַיֹּ֣אמֶר פַּרְעֹ֔ה הֵן־רַבִּ֥ים

ה עַתָּ֖ה עַ֣ם הָאָ֑רֶץ וְהִשְׁבַּתֶּ֥ם אֹתָ֖ם מִסִּבְלֹתָֽם: וַיְצַ֥ו פַּרְעֹ֖ה בַּיּ֣וֹם

ו הַה֑וּא אֶת־הַנֹּגְשִׂ֣ים בָּעָ֔ם וְאֶת־שֹֽׁטְרָ֖יו לֵאמֹֽר: לֹ֣א תֹֽאסִפ֞וּן לָתֵ֨ת תֶּ֧בֶן לָעָ֛ם לִלְבֹּ֥ן הַלְּבֵנִ֖ים כִּתְמ֣וֹל שִׁלְשֹׁ֑ם הֵ֚ם יֵֽלְכ֔וּ וְקֹֽשְׁשׁ֥וּ

ז לָהֶ֖ם תֶּֽבֶן: וְאֶת־מַתְכֹּ֨נֶת הַלְּבֵנִ֜ים אֲשֶׁ֣ר הֵם֩ עֹשִׂ֨ים תְּמ֤וֹל שִׁלְשֹׁם֙

ח תָּשִׂ֣ימוּ עֲלֵיהֶ֔ם לֹ֥א תִגְרְע֖וּ מִמֶּ֑נּוּ כִּֽי־נִרְפִּ֣ים הֵ֔ם עַל־כֵּ֗ן הֵ֤ם צֹֽעֲקִים֙

ט לֵאמֹ֔ר נֵֽלְכָ֖ה נִזְבְּחָ֥ה לֵֽאלֹהֵֽינוּ: תִּכְבַּ֧ד הָעֲבֹדָ֛ה עַל־הָֽאֲנָשִׁ֖ים

CLASSIC COMMENTATORS

Following Moshe and Aharon's second presentation to Pharaoh, he begins his reply by saying, "How numerous the people of the land have become" (5:5). What is Pharaoh trying to explain with this phrase?

RASHI — רש״י

The labor they perform is so extensive, that if you cause them to cease working it will constitute immeasurable loss [to the state].

שהעבודה מוטלת עליהם, ואתם משביתים אותם מסבלותם, הפסד גדול הוא זה.

IBN EZRA — אבן עזרא

The laborers had become so numerous that [Pharaoh] was indifferent if the plague or the sword struck down some of them.

לא נחוש אם יבוא דבר או חרב עליכם, כי רבים הם אלה הסבלים.

The Egyptian taskmasters deliver the new decree, and the people scramble to gather straw for the bricks. As the task is nearly impossible to complete, the Israelite foremen responsible for the work production are beaten by their taskmasters for not filling their daily quotas. When the Israelite foremen complain to Pharaoh, he explains that it was all a result of their request to worship God.

10 listening to lies." So the taskmasters and foremen went out and told the people, "This
11 is what Pharaoh says: I will no longer give you straw. You must go and get your own
12 straw wherever you can find it. Your production must not fall short of what it was." So
13 the people spread out all over Egypt to collect stubble for straw. The taskmasters kept
14 pressuring them, saying, "Complete your daily work quota just as when there was straw."
And the Israelite foremen whom Pharaoh's slave drivers had appointed were flogged.
"Why have you not fulfilled your quota of bricks," they were asked, "either yesterday or
15 today as you did before?" The Israelite foremen came and protested to Pharaoh, "Why
16 are you treating your servants like this? Your servants are given no straw, yet they tell
17 us, 'Make bricks!' We are being flogged for your people's failing." But he said, "Lazy,
18 that is what you are – lazy! That is why you keep saying, 'Send us forth to sacrifice to the

---

QUESTIONS FOR THOUGHT

- According to Bekhor Shor, what did Pharaoh claim was motivating the request to leave for worship? Do you think that Pharaoh really believed this, or was this just an excuse to punish them for making the request?
- According to Abarbanel, what was the purpose of increasing their workload? Do you think that making the work crushingly hard is effective in the long term at keeping a population under control, or will that just increase their desire to rebel?

TEXTUAL SKILLS

1. There are two different words to describe the supervisors of the work – one describes the Israelite foremen who were appointed to manage the work, while the other describes the Egyptian taskmasters who were responsible for the Israelite foremen. Can you identify the terms used in the Torah to describe each?

2. Notice that the verb לקושש, used to mean "to gather straw," is a play on the word קש, meaning "straw." Can you find another verb-noun pair in this passage (and the same one in the previous passage!) where the verb describes the action used to produce the noun?

QUICK BITE

The Israelite foremen were selected by the Egyptians to maintain control over the rest of Israel and ensure that they met their labor quotas. Three millennia later, in the Nazi labor camps, Jews were also forced into becoming *kapos*. The purpose of this system was two-fold: (1) Cost efficiency. Having slaves control the other slaves saves money; and (2) To turn victim against victim. This was one of the sickest twists of the Holocaust. Elie Wiesel, in his memoir *Night*, writes about a kapo named Idek: "I happened to cross his path. He threw himself on me like a wild beast, beating me in the chest, on my head, throwing me to the ground and picking me up again, crushing me with ever more violent blows, until I was covered in blood." In times of hardship, loyalty and kindness to one another can be the greatest challenge.

שמות | פרק ה

י וַיֵּעָשׂוּ־בָהּ וְאַל־יִשְׁעוּ בְּדִבְרֵי־שָׁקֶר: וַיֵּצְאוּ נֹגְשֵׂי הָעָם וְשֹׁטְרָיו וַיֹּאמְרוּ אֶל־הָעָם לֵאמֹר כֹּה אָמַר פַּרְעֹה אֵינֶנִּי נֹתֵן לָכֶם תֶּבֶן:
יא אַתֶּם לְכוּ קְחוּ לָכֶם תֶּבֶן מֵאֲשֶׁר תִּמְצָאוּ כִּי אֵין נִגְרָע מֵעֲבֹדַתְכֶם
יב דָּבָר: וַיָּפֶץ הָעָם בְּכָל־אֶרֶץ מִצְרָיִם לְקֹשֵׁשׁ קַשׁ לַתֶּבֶן: וְהַנֹּגְשִׂים
יג אָצִים לֵאמֹר כַּלּוּ מַעֲשֵׂיכֶם דְּבַר־יוֹם בְּיוֹמוֹ כַּאֲשֶׁר בִּהְיוֹת
יד הַתֶּבֶן: וַיֻּכּוּ שֹׁטְרֵי בְּנֵי יִשְׂרָאֵל אֲשֶׁר־שָׂמוּ עֲלֵהֶם נֹגְשֵׂי פַרְעֹה לֵאמֹר מַדּוּעַ לֹא כִלִּיתֶם חָקְכֶם לִלְבֹּן כִּתְמוֹל שִׁלְשֹׁם גַּם־תְּמוֹל
טו גַּם־הַיּוֹם: וַיָּבֹאוּ שֹׁטְרֵי בְּנֵי יִשְׂרָאֵל וַיִּצְעֲקוּ אֶל־פַּרְעֹה לֵאמֹר
טז לָמָּה תַעֲשֶׂה כֹה לַעֲבָדֶיךָ: תֶּבֶן אֵין נִתָּן לַעֲבָדֶיךָ וּלְבֵנִים אֹמְרִים
יז לָנוּ עֲשׂוּ וְהִנֵּה עֲבָדֶיךָ מֻכִּים וְחָטָאת עַמֶּךָ: וַיֹּאמֶר נִרְפִּים אַתֶּם
יח נִרְפִּים עַל־כֵּן אַתֶּם אֹמְרִים נֵלְכָה נִזְבְּחָה לַיהוה: וְעַתָּה לְכוּ

CLASSIC COMMENTATORS

In response to Moshe and Aharon's request, Pharaoh accuses *Benei Yisrael* of being lax in their work. He repeats this accusation to explain the new work rules to the Israelite foremen who complain to him. The commentaries want to understand the connection between the accusation and the reality of the request and complaint.

RABBI YOSEF BEKHOR SHOR   ר' יוסף בכור שור

According to Pharaoh, because the workload imposed on the Israelites was not so severe that the people lacked free time, they spent those hours devising strategies to get out of the labor completely.

רפה עליהם המלאכה, וחושבים איך יבטלוה לגמרי.

ABARBANEL   אברבנאל

Pharaoh argued that because the Israelite population had swelled, the quota of bricks they had to produce was easily met by the number of slaves in his employ. This meant that Israel had periods of idleness…and that, in turn, led them to picture themselves engaging in religious activities – a luxury not available to workers who are constantly kept busy. Because they were not thoroughly engaged, the Israelites demanded "Let us take a journey…and sacrifice to the Lord" (5:3).

אין מתכונת הלבנים ומספרם קשה עליכם כי נרפים ופנויים אתם במלאכתכם יען אתם עתה רבים יותר ממה שהייתם בתחלה... על כן אתם צועקים נלכה נזבחה לא-לוהינו כי מי שהוא פנוי מהעבודה מחשב בדברים העיוניים והאלוהיים אשר כאלה.

19 LORD.' Now go. Get to work. Straw will not be given you, and you must complete your count of bricks." When the Israelite foremen saw that they were not to reduce each day's
20 quota, they knew that harm was coming to them. Leaving Pharaoh, they met Moshe
21 and Aharon, who stood awaiting them. They said to them, "May the LORD look on you and judge, because you have made us repellent in the eyes of Pharaoh and his officials;
22 you have put a sword in their hands to kill us." Then Moshe returned to the LORD and
23 said, "Why, Lord, have You brought harm to this people? Is this why You sent me? Ever since I came to Pharaoh to speak in Your name, he has dealt worse with this people; and
6 1 You have done nothing to deliver Your people." But the LORD said to Moshe, "Now you are about to see what I will do to Pharaoh. By a mighty hand he will send them forth, and by a mighty hand he will drive them from his land."

ר' שמשון רפאל הירש

זה הרגע שאליו ציפיתי. תחילה, יש לאפשר לחוסר־האונים ולייאוש להתגלות במלואם; שיהיה ברור שבאמצעים הרגילים שביד האדם לא ניתן להשיג דבר, ושאין כל תועלת בפניות לפרעה ... ויהיה ברור וניכר שמשה אינו אלא כלי ביד ה', ומעשיו אינם אלא מעשי ה'.

RABBI SAMSON RAPHAEL HIRSCH

This is the moment I have been waiting for. First it had to be made clear to Israel that they were themselves utterly powerless. It would be proved that the efforts of man can achieve nothing, as all appeals to Pharaoh were futile.... All would recognize that Moshe was a mere instrument of God, and that his actions were in fact the actions of God.

QUESTIONS FOR THOUGHT

- Which of the commentaries understands that the events just before this conversation with God were necessary in order to bring about the redemption?
- Two of the commentaries disagree as to whether the events just before this conversation were part of a natural process or exactly the opposite, a supernatural process. Can you identify the two commentaries?
- Do you think that redemption is a natural or supernatural process?

TEXTUAL SKILLS

1. The word ב-א-ש appears only seven times in the Torah, and it means to have a bad smell. Twice it is used as a metaphor, meaning something like "to make someone look bad." Once is in this passage; the other time it is used in Yaakov's rebuke to Shimon and Levi (Gen. 34:30).

WISDOM OF THE HEART

After *Benei Yisrael* leave Egypt they are given a commandment to redeem a firstborn donkey with a sheep to commemorate the event. That's a strange way to commemorate this!

Rabbi Yosef Dov Fishof suggests that the answer lies in the distinction between a donkey and a sheep. Historically, the donkey was a hardworking beast of burden while the sheep was a domesticated animal tenderly cared for by the shepherd. When *Benei Yisrael* were in Egypt they were treated by the Egyptians as donkeys, but God redeemed them to be his loyal flock, and He provided a faithful shepherd, Moshe, to guide them. This transition is commemorated in the commandment to redeem a firstborn donkey with a sheep.

Do you surround yourself with people who elevate you, who help to influence and transform you positively?

שמות | פרק ה

יט עֲבֹדוּ וְתֶ֫בֶן לֹא־יִנָּתֵ֥ן לָכֶ֖ם וְתֹ֣כֶן לְבֵנִ֑ים תִּתֵּֽנוּ: וַיִּרְא֞וּ שֹׁטְרֵ֤י בְנֵֽי־יִשְׂרָאֵל֙ אֹתָ֖ם בְּרָ֣ע לֵאמֹ֑ר לֹא־תִגְרְע֥וּ מִלִּבְנֵיכֶ֖ם דְּבַר־י֥וֹם בְּיוֹמֽוֹ:
כ וַֽיִּפְגְּעוּ֙ אֶת־מֹשֶׁ֣ה וְאֶֽת־אַהֲרֹ֔ן נִצָּבִ֖ים לִקְרָאתָ֑ם בְּצֵאתָ֖ם
כא מֵאֵ֣ת פַּרְעֹֽה: וַיֹּאמְר֣וּ אֲלֵהֶ֔ם יֵ֧רֶא יְהוָ֛ה עֲלֵיכֶ֖ם וְיִשְׁפֹּ֑ט אֲשֶׁ֧ר הִבְאַשְׁתֶּ֣ם אֶת־רֵיחֵ֗נוּ בְּעֵינֵ֤י פַרְעֹה֙ וּבְעֵינֵ֣י עֲבָדָ֔יו לָֽתֶת־חֶ֥רֶב
כב בְּיָדָ֖ם לְהָרְגֵֽנוּ: וַיָּ֧שָׁב מֹשֶׁ֛ה אֶל־יְהוָ֖ה וַיֹּאמַ֑ר אֲדֹנָ֗י לָמָ֤ה הֲרֵעֹ֙תָה֙ [מפטיר]
כג לָעָ֣ם הַזֶּ֔ה לָ֥מָּה זֶּ֖ה שְׁלַחְתָּֽנִי: וּמֵאָ֞ז בָּ֤אתִי אֶל־פַּרְעֹה֙ לְדַבֵּ֣ר
ו א בִּשְׁמֶ֔ךָ הֵרַ֖ע לָעָ֣ם הַזֶּ֑ה וְהַצֵּ֥ל לֹא־הִצַּ֖לְתָּ אֶת־עַמֶּֽךָ: וַיֹּ֤אמֶר יְהוָה֙ אֶל־מֹשֶׁ֔ה עַתָּ֣ה תִרְאֶ֔ה אֲשֶׁ֥ר אֶֽעֱשֶׂ֖ה לְפַרְעֹ֑ה כִּ֣י בְיָ֤ד חֲזָקָה֙ יְשַׁלְּחֵ֔ם וּבְיָ֣ד חֲזָקָ֔ה יְגָרְשֵׁ֖ם מֵאַרְצֽוֹ:

CLASSIC COMMENTATORS

In God's response to Moshe He says, "Now you are about to see…" The commentaries want to know the significance of the word "now," and why Moshe would believe God now more than he did before.

KELI YAKAR
כלי יקר

God answered Moshe: "Now you are about to see." It is known that it is always darkest before the dawn breaks….So too on winter days, the cold is most intense just prior to sunrise but is defeated by the sun. This is a natural phenomenon….So it was with regard to Pharaoh, who was treating the Israelites worse now than in the past. This was a clear sign that his end was nigh and that the hour of redemption was coming to defeat all of Pharaoh's efforts.

השיב לו הקב"ה עתה תראה וגו', כי מהידוע שכך היא המדה שבכל יום סמוך לעלות השחר החושך מחשיך ביותר מן חשכת הלילה ואח"כ אור השחר בוקע ועולה, ... וכן בימות החורף סמוך לעלית השמש הקור הולך וגובר ולסוף הוא מנוצח מן השמש, וזה דבר טבעי ... כמו כן מה שהרע פרעה לישראל עכשיו יותר ממה שעשה לשעבר זה מופת חותך שקרב קיצו, ושזמן הגאולה קרובה לבטל כל פעולותיו של פרעה.

MALBIM
מלבים

What God meant by this is that the redemption required preparation before the time for Israel's salvation came. The groundwork had to be laid in order to punish Pharaoh and his people for their wickedness… Pharaoh had not yet perpetrated quite enough villainy…Then Pharaoh's wickedness was consummated: not only did he not obey God's command, but he added to Israel's suffering in order to antagonize the Almighty.

ר"ל שלגאולה זו צריך הכנה שיגיע עת לתשועת ישראל וגם צריך הכנה שיגיע עת שישעיר פרעה ועמו על רשעתם, והיה חסר עדיין איזה ... חטא לפרעה ... ונשלם רשעת פרעה שלא די שלא שמע בקול ה' עוד הוסיף לענותם למען הכעיסו.

MORE QUICK BITES

- **1:1** Rashi comments that even though *Benei Yisrael* are counted in Genesis as they descend to Egypt, they are counted again in the beginning of Exodus as a demonstration of God's love for them – as in the verse: "He who brings out their host by number, He calls them all by name" (Is. 40:26). In explaining the comparison of *Benei Yisrael* to the stars, Rabbi Aharon Leib Steinman suggests that just as counting the stars serves no purpose other than to appreciate the wonder of God's creation, so is God's counting of *Benei Yisrael* an expression of His adoration for them.

- **1:5** As *Benei Yisrael* are counted in the beginning of Exodus, all seventy are referred to as a single נפש, or life force. This is contrasted to the counting of Esav's descendants, who are referred to in the plural (Gen. 36:6). Rabbi Samson Raphael Hirsch explains that *Benei Yisrael* were bonded by a unity of purpose, and so they existed as a single living entity.

- **1:15** Rashi teaches that the names of the midwives related to their actions. Shifra, from the Aramaic word for "good," and Puah, for the cooing sounds she would make for the newborns. Rabbi Chaim Friedlander asks: why were they not given names celebrating their heroism in saving those infants? He responds that saving a baby's life is the most natural thing for a person, but the Torah is celebrating the fact that they went beyond saving babies and cared for them as if they were their own.

- **2:1** In the story about Moshe's birth, his parents are left anonymous. To explain this, Rabbi Dessler suggests that the Torah was making it clear at the outset that Moshe was simply a man born of a man, a human – not a deity. The Torah does not turn its heroes into gods.

- **2:6** The word used by the Torah to describe Pharaoh's daughter's reaction to Moshe is חמלה. Malbim comments that unlike other similar words, this particular word means to recognize the inherent goodness in someone or something and care for it lest it be destroyed. Rabbi Reuven P. Bulka applies this interpretation to the wonderful prayer of מודה אני, recited by Jews upon awakening in the morning, in which we give gratitude to God for exercising His חמלה in restoring our souls. God recognizes the inherent precious value in each and every one of us, and so He restores our souls every morning.

EXPLORING HASHKAFA
Exodus and Archaeology

Many people are troubled by the apparent lack of archaeological evidence for the exodus from Egypt. After all, wouldn't you expect that there would be all sorts of findings supporting such a momentous event?

It turns out that such an expectation is not wholly reasonable. First, we need to keep in mind that just because proof hasn't been found yet doesn't mean that it's not there. Like the Mishna (Eduyot 2:2) says, the fact that we haven't seen something cannot be proof of its non-existence. For example, many secular historians doubted the existence of King David until the 1990s, when archaeologists unearthed an Aramean inscription at Tel Dan making reference to the House of David (בית דוד). Second, the Torah describes almost everything about the exodus in completely miraculous terms – the signs Moshe makes, the plagues, the splitting of the sea, the clouds which protect and guide *Benei Yisrael*, and even the food they eat in the desert. As Moshe says: "Your garments did not grow old upon you, nor did your feet swell, these forty years" (Deut. 8:4). Given the description of this supernatural existence, we should not expect that they would leave the normal traces of life for archaeologists to find.

As far as written records go, it's important to be aware that in the ancient world there was no concept of recording history as a truthful account of events. For the most part, histories were commissioned by emperors and kings to glorify themselves and leave a legacy of their successes – they will not write accounts of their own defeat. It would have been ridiculous for a royal Egyptian scribe to have written the story of the defeat of his empire! As an aside, that is one of the ways that the Torah is distinct: it does record our failures, because the purpose of the Torah is to provide moral and religious guidance for future generations, and that includes learning from mistakes and failures.

And finally, while there may be no direct archaeological proof of the exodus, there is much historical and archaeological evidence for the context of the exodus given in the Torah. For example, the Torah uses names of people and places in Egypt in ways that match the archaeological record, supporting the idea that *Benei Yisrael* were really there. Archaeology also tells us that around the time of the exodus (in the late thirteenth century BCE, under the reign of Pharaoh Ramesses II and shortly afterward) Egyptian control of Canaan and Sinai weakened, and groups of Semitic nomads began traveling through these areas, including the Sinai desert and the eastern side of the Jordan River, where the Torah says *Benei Yisrael* wandered. During this period, small farming communities began to be established in the hills of Canaan with features that indicate they were likely Israelite (for example, a lack of pig bones). Also at this time, the Egyptian pharaoh Merneptah writes of battles he has with a group called "Israel." There is a huge amount of evidence – both in archaeology and in the writings of other empires that existed – broadly supporting the context in which the events of the Tanakh, including the exodus, happened.

The bottom line is: For those who believe in the truth of the Torah there is no need to feel threatened by the arguments based on archaeology. Archaeological and historical research can actually enrich our understanding of the Torah by giving us more context as to how events occurred.

פרשת וארא
PARASHAT VA'ERA

"The secret to success is to be ready when your opportunity comes."
Benjamin Disraeli

Was God's plan backfiring? What seemed to Moshe like a sure bet took a turn for the worse. But maybe that isn't so surprising. We feel like we're on a roll, like nothing can stop us, and then something goes wrong – something we didn't expect. We stumble, lose momentum, and feel like we failed. The truly determined won't let that obstacle stand in their way – they find a reservoir of strength they never realized they had. And that's the moment when God reveals to you that together, you can do it.

PARASHAT VA'ERA

After Moshe's initial frustration with God's apparent failure to save the people as he expected, God reiterates His commitment to redeem the people, but now – for the first time – He makes explicit reference to the covenant with Avraham, Yitzhak, and Yaakov as a significant part of the redemption. Moshe tells the people about God's promise, but this time they cannot accept his message. Nevertheless, God perseveres by sending Moshe to Pharaoh.

6 2 Then God spoke to Moshe. "I am the Lord," He said to him. "As El Shaddai I appeared
3 to Avraham, Yitzhak, and Yaakov – but by My name the Lord I did not make Myself
4 known to them. And I made a covenant with them to give them the land of Canaan, the
5 land where they lived as strangers. And now, I have heard the groaning of the Israelites
6 whom the Egyptians are holding as slaves, and I remember My covenant. Therefore, say to the Israelites: I am the Lord, and I will free you from the forced labor of the Egyptians, I will rescue you from slavery. I will liberate you with an outstretched arm
7 and with great acts of judgment. I will take you as My people and I will be your God. Then you will know that I am the Lord your God, freeing you from Egyptian forced

---

QUESTIONS FOR THOUGHT

- Which of the commentaries emphasizes God's power? How will that power manifest itself?
- Which of the commentaries sees God's comment as part of His response to Moshe's complaint at the end of *Parashat Shemot*?
- According to one of the commentaries, God is introducing an entirely new concept of a god – one who feels a closeness and a commitment to people.
- Which of the above approaches do you think would provide the best reassurance to Moshe and the people?

TEXTUAL SKILLS

1. Find the two-word phrase which both opens and closes this passage (and appears twice more in the middle!).
2. This passage follows a structure sometimes called a chiastic structure. In its simplest form, it looks like A-B-A, in which there is an opening theme or phrase which appears again in the close, and a second theme in the middle. Chiastic structures can get more complicated, like A-B-B-A or A-B-C-D-E-D-C-B-A. The structure here has four levels. In the middle, you'll find the term סבלות מצרים twice. Surrounding those two references you'll find references to the ארץ. Try to find the other two layers of the chiastic structure.

פרשת וארא

וַיְדַבֵּ֥ר אֱלֹהִ֖ים אֶל־מֹשֶׁ֑ה וַיֹּ֥אמֶר אֵלָ֖יו אֲנִ֥י יְהוָֽה: וָאֵרָ֗א אֶל־אַבְרָהָ֛ם אֶל־יִצְחָ֥ק וְאֶֽל־יַעֲקֹ֖ב בְּאֵ֣ל שַׁדָּ֑י וּשְׁמִ֣י יְהוָ֔ה לֹ֥א נוֹדַ֖עְתִּי לָהֶֽם: וְגַ֨ם הֲקִמֹ֤תִי אֶת־בְּרִיתִי֙ אִתָּ֔ם לָתֵ֥ת לָהֶ֖ם אֶת־אֶ֣רֶץ כְּנָ֑עַן אֵ֛ת אֶ֥רֶץ מְגֻרֵיהֶ֖ם אֲשֶׁר־גָּ֥רוּ בָֽהּ: וְגַ֣ם ׀ אֲנִ֣י שָׁמַ֗עְתִּי אֶֽת־נַאֲקַת֙ בְּנֵ֣י יִשְׂרָאֵ֔ל אֲשֶׁ֥ר מִצְרַ֖יִם מַעֲבִדִ֣ים אֹתָ֑ם וָאֶזְכֹּ֖ר אֶת־בְּרִיתִֽי: לָכֵ֞ן אֱמֹ֥ר לִבְנֵֽי־יִשְׂרָאֵל֮ אֲנִ֣י יְהוָה֒ וְהוֹצֵאתִ֣י אֶתְכֶ֗ם מִתַּ֨חַת֙ סִבְלֹ֣ת מִצְרַ֔יִם וְהִצַּלְתִּ֥י אֶתְכֶ֖ם מֵעֲבֹדָתָ֑ם וְגָאַלְתִּ֤י אֶתְכֶם֙ בִּזְר֣וֹעַ נְטוּיָ֔ה וּבִשְׁפָטִ֖ים גְּדֹלִֽים: וְלָקַחְתִּ֨י אֶתְכֶ֥ם לִי֙ לְעָ֔ם וְהָיִ֥יתִי לָכֶ֖ם לֵֽאלֹהִ֑ים וִֽידַעְתֶּ֗ם כִּ֣י אֲנִ֤י יְהוָה֙ אֱלֹ֣הֵיכֶ֔ם הַמּוֹצִ֣יא אֶתְכֶ֔ם

CLASSIC COMMENTATORS

There seems to be an emphasis in God's words on the importance of which name He uses. The first verse begins by telling us that אלהים tells Moshe that His name is יהוה. What is the significance of this switch?

RASHI

My name is יהוה – I can be trusted to keep My word. For I made a promise to them that I have not yet fulfilled.

רש״י

שמי ה', נאמן לאמת הדברים, שהרי הבטחתים ולא קיימתים.

RAMBAN

He did not make Himself known to them under the name יהוה, which He employed in the creation of the world. That is to say, God did not create any miraculous phenomena for the patriarchs by altering nature.

רמב״ן

לא נודעתי להם לברוא להם חדשות בשנוי התולדות.

RABBI DAVID TZVI HOFFMAN

The name יהוה connotes that God is humanity's Father in heaven who loves them... He has chosen Israel to be His select nation with whom He wishes to forge a particularly close relationship. In other words – He will be their God. God did not share this sort of close connection with the patriarchs.

ר' דוד צבי הופמן

ה' הוא אביהם האוהב של האנשים...הבוחר בישראל להיות עמו וחפץ לקיים עמם יחסים קרובים במיוחד – להיות לו לאלהים. יחסים כאלה לא היו בין ה' ובין האבות.

8 labor. And I will bring you to the land that I promised to give to Avraham, Yitzḥak,
9 and Yaakov; to you I will give it as a possession. I am the Lord." Moshe told this to the Israelites, but in the brokenness of their spirit and the brutal labor they did not listen to him.
10
11 Then the Lord said to Moshe, "Go, tell Pharaoh King of Egypt to send the Israelites forth from his land."
12 But Moshe said to the Lord, "The Israelites, You see, have not listened to me. How then will Pharaoh listen? And I am a man of uncircumcised
13 lips." The Lord spoke to Moshe and Aharon; and He charged them with regard to the Israelites and to Pharaoh King of Egypt, to bring the Israelites out of the land of Egypt.

WISDOM OF THE HEART

The famous "four expressions of redemption" are preceded by God instructing Moshe to announce to *Benei Yisrael* that "I am God." One of the commentaries explains this announcement as being the catalyst for a cascade of events: The knowledge of God will itself bring about a cessation of slavery (והוצאתי), which will allow the people to leave Egypt (והצלתי). The ultimate redemption (וגאלתי) will come with the drowning of the Egyptians, and a new understanding of "I am Lord" will become evident with the revelation at Sinai (ולקחתי).

These expressions can be understood as universal mantras of freedom. What words do you use to pick yourself up?

The nature of Moshe's speech impediment is unclear. Some midrashim suggest that he was unable to pronounce the letter ר, while others believe that it was the letter פ. Interestingly, both of those letters are prominent in the final message Yosef left his family, פקוד יפקוד, that God will remember and bring them to their destiny (Gen. 50:24). Those words served as a "code" to authenticate Moshe as God's messenger (Ex. 3:16), so these midrashim may be implying that Moshe was concerned that he would be unable to convey it properly. Ultimately, he did convey the message, transcending his limitations.

One aspect of greatness is transcending what you believe are your limitations. Much of what we think we can't do we really can, but we are not willing to make that extra effort to push ourselves beyond our limitations. Greatness is found within those who face their weaknesses and drive themselves to overcome them.

ח מִתַּחַת סִבְלוֹת מִצְרָיִם: וְהֵבֵאתִי אֶתְכֶם אֶל־הָאָרֶץ אֲשֶׁר נָשָׂאתִי אֶת־יָדִי לָתֵת אֹתָהּ לְאַבְרָהָם לְיִצְחָק וּלְיַעֲקֹב וְנָתַתִּי

ט אֹתָהּ לָכֶם מוֹרָשָׁה אֲנִי יְהֹוָה: וַיְדַבֵּר מֹשֶׁה כֵּן אֶל־בְּנֵי יִשְׂרָאֵל וְלֹא שָׁמְעוּ אֶל־מֹשֶׁה מִקֹּצֶר רוּחַ וּמֵעֲבֹדָה קָשָׁה:

י וַיְדַבֵּר יְהֹוָה אֶל־מֹשֶׁה לֵּאמֹר: בֹּא דַבֵּר אֶל־פַּרְעֹה מֶלֶךְ

יא מִצְרָיִם וִישַׁלַּח אֶת־בְּנֵי־יִשְׂרָאֵל מֵאַרְצוֹ: וַיְדַבֵּר מֹשֶׁה לִפְנֵי

יב יְהֹוָה לֵאמֹר הֵן בְּנֵי־יִשְׂרָאֵל לֹא־שָׁמְעוּ אֵלַי וְאֵיךְ יִשְׁמָעֵנִי פַרְעֹה וַאֲנִי עֲרַל שְׂפָתָיִם:

יג וַיְדַבֵּר יְהֹוָה אֶל־מֹשֶׁה וְאֶל־אַהֲרֹן וַיְצַוֵּם אֶל־בְּנֵי יִשְׂרָאֵל וְאֶל־פַּרְעֹה מֶלֶךְ מִצְרָיִם לְהוֹצִיא אֶת־בְּנֵי־יִשְׂרָאֵל מֵאֶרֶץ

QUICK BITES

Moshe tells God, "*Benei Yisrael* didn't listen to me; surely Pharaoh won't listen" – yet God seems to ignore this very reasonable argument. Sometimes, we look at the path ahead of us and are convinced that there is no way to move forward. The obstacles are simply too great to overcome. That's what Moshe was thinking. But God knew that all Moshe needed to do was to believe that he could, to push just a little harder. Success sometimes hangs on making that extra push when we think that it is hopeless – that we have nothing left to give.

Verses 6–7 contain the four expressions of redemption: "I will free you," "I will rescue you," "I will liberate you," and "I will take you as my people." The four cups that we drink at the Seder represent these four expressions. But for those familiar with the progression of the Seder, there is an issue with the cadence: The space between the first, second, and third cups are roughly equal. But the move from the third cup to the fourth cup is almost instantaneous. How come? The first three cups parallel the first three expressions of redemption. Those verbs: "free," "rescue," and "liberate," all express the removal of a circumstance we don't want to be in. This is what we call *sur mera*, the removal of bad, undesired elements of our lives. But it's not enough to stop there. A vacuum, where our live are empty of meaning, can be even more spiritually dangerous than what was there beforehand. So we must jump immediately to fill that void with a positive value – *aseh tov* – here expressed by the words "I will take you as my people."

Shemot | Chapter 6

14 These were the heads of their ancestral houses. The sons of Reuven, Yisrael's firstborn, were Ḥanokh, Palu, Ḥetzron and Karmi; these were the families of Reuven. Shimon's
15 sons were Yemuel, Yamin, Ohad, Yakhin, Tzoḥar, and Sha'ul, son of a Canaanite woman;
16 these are the families of Shimon. These are the names of Levi's sons by their lineage:
17 Gershon, Kehat, and Merari. Levi lived 137 years. The sons of Gershon were Livni and
18 Shimi, by their families. The sons of Kehat were Amram, Yitzhar, Ḥevron, and Uzziel.
19 Kehat lived 133 years. The sons of Merari were Maḥli and Mushi. These are the families of
20 the Levites by their lineage. Amram married Yokheved, his father's sister, who bore him
21 Aharon and Moshe. Amram lived 137 years. The sons of Yitzhar were Koraḥ, Nefeg, and
22 Zikhri. The sons of Uzziel were Mishael, Eltzafan, and Sitri. Aharon married Elisheva,
23 daughter of Amminadav and sister of Naḥshon, and she bore him Nadav and Avihu,
24 Elazar and Itamar. The sons of Koraḥ were Assir, Elkana, and Aviasaf; these are the
25 families of the Korahites. Elazar, Aharon's son, married one of the daughters of Putiel, and she bore him Pinḥas. These were the heads of the Levite clans by their families.
26 These were the Aharon and Moshe to whom the Lord said, "Bring the Israelites out of
27 Egypt by their battalions." It was they who spoke up to Pharaoh King of Egypt to bring
28 the Israelites out of Egypt – this same Moshe and Aharon. So it came to pass on the

---

RASHI
Because on his deathbed the patriarch Yaakov chastised these three tribes [Reuven, Shimon, and Levi, in Genesis 49:4–7], the text returns to them now and records only their lineages to stress their importance

רש"י
לפי שקינטרם יעקב אביהם לשלשה שבטים הללו בשעת מותו, חזר הכתוב לייחסם כאן לבדם, לומר שחשובין הם.

RABBI DAVID TZVI HOFFMAN
The only reason that this tabulation begins with Reuven and Shimon is to remind readers that Levi was not Yaakov's firstborn son, but merely his third child.

ר׳ דוד צפי הופמן
וגם תחילתו של לוח זה לא נמסרה כאן אלא ללמדנו-להזכירנו שלוי היה רק בנו השלישי של יעקב, ואינו אפוא שבט הבכור.

MALBIM
The Torah here followed the custom of all historians, to first mention some less important details before arriving at the main issue, which it will discuss at length and in detail.

מלבי"ם
ונהג בזה כדרך הכתובים בכל ספורי התולדות להזכיר תחלה את הטפל בקצרה עד שבא אל העקר שבו יאריך בכל פרטיו.

QUESTIONS FOR THOUGHT

- Malbim and R. David Tzvi Hoffman express opinions which are exactly the opposite of one another. Try to figure out in what way they are exactly opposite!
- In what way is Rashi's commentary very different from the other two?
- Which of these commentaries do you think makes the most sense in the context of where the Torah chose to include it?

שמות | פרק ו

מִצְרָיִם׃ אֵלֶּה רָאשֵׁי בֵית־אֲבֹתָם בְּנֵי רְאוּבֵן בְּכֹר יד
יִשְׂרָאֵל חֲנוֹךְ וּפַלּוּא חֶצְרוֹן וְכַרְמִי אֵלֶּה מִשְׁפְּחֹת רְאוּבֵן׃ וּבְנֵי טו
שִׁמְעוֹן יְמוּאֵל וְיָמִין וְאֹהַד וְיָכִין וְצֹחַר וְשָׁאוּל בֶּן־הַכְּנַעֲנִית
אֵלֶּה מִשְׁפְּחֹת שִׁמְעוֹן׃ וְאֵלֶּה שְׁמוֹת בְּנֵי־לֵוִי לְתֹלְדֹתָם גֵּרְשׁוֹן טז
וּקְהָת וּמְרָרִי וּשְׁנֵי חַיֵּי לֵוִי שֶׁבַע וּשְׁלֹשִׁים וּמְאַת שָׁנָה׃ בְּנֵי
גֵרְשׁוֹן לִבְנִי וְשִׁמְעִי לְמִשְׁפְּחֹתָם׃ וּבְנֵי קְהָת עַמְרָם וְיִצְהָר יז יח
וְחֶבְרוֹן וְעֻזִּיאֵל וּשְׁנֵי חַיֵּי קְהָת שָׁלֹשׁ וּשְׁלֹשִׁים וּמְאַת שָׁנָה׃
וּבְנֵי מְרָרִי מַחְלִי וּמוּשִׁי אֵלֶּה מִשְׁפְּחֹת הַלֵּוִי לְתֹלְדֹתָם׃ וַיִּקַּח יט
עַמְרָם אֶת־יוֹכֶבֶד דֹּדָתוֹ לוֹ לְאִשָּׁה וַתֵּלֶד לוֹ אֶת־אַהֲרֹן וְאֶת־
מֹשֶׁה וּשְׁנֵי חַיֵּי עַמְרָם שֶׁבַע וּשְׁלֹשִׁים וּמְאַת שָׁנָה׃ וּבְנֵי יִצְהָר כא
קֹרַח וָנֶפֶג וְזִכְרִי׃ וּבְנֵי עֻזִּיאֵל מִישָׁאֵל וְאֶלְצָפָן וְסִתְרִי׃ וַיִּקַּח כב כג
אַהֲרֹן אֶת־אֱלִישֶׁבַע בַּת־עַמִּינָדָב אֲחוֹת נַחְשׁוֹן לוֹ לְאִשָּׁה
וַתֵּלֶד לוֹ אֶת־נָדָב וְאֶת־אֲבִיהוּא אֶת־אֶלְעָזָר וְאֶת־אִיתָמָר׃
וּבְנֵי קֹרַח אַסִּיר וְאֶלְקָנָה וַאֲבִיאָסָף אֵלֶּה מִשְׁפְּחֹת הַקָּרְחִי׃ כד
וְאֶלְעָזָר בֶּן־אַהֲרֹן לָקַח־לוֹ מִבְּנוֹת פּוּטִיאֵל לוֹ לְאִשָּׁה וַתֵּלֶד לוֹ כה
אֶת־פִּינְחָס אֵלֶּה רָאשֵׁי אֲבוֹת הַלְוִיִּם לְמִשְׁפְּחֹתָם׃ הוּא אַהֲרֹן כו
וּמֹשֶׁה אֲשֶׁר אָמַר יְהוָה לָהֶם הוֹצִיאוּ אֶת־בְּנֵי יִשְׂרָאֵל מֵאֶרֶץ
מִצְרַיִם עַל־צִבְאֹתָם׃ הֵם הַמְדַבְּרִים אֶל־פַּרְעֹה מֶלֶךְ־מִצְרַיִם כז
לְהוֹצִיא אֶת־בְּנֵי־יִשְׂרָאֵל מִמִּצְרָיִם הוּא מֹשֶׁה וְאַהֲרֹן׃ וַיְהִי כח

CLASSIC COMMENTATORS

Before describing the extended family of Levi leading to Moshe and Aharon, the Torah provides a brief description of Levi's older brothers, Reuven and Shimon. Since the rest of this story does not involve either of those two elder brothers, the commentaries are curious as to why they are included.

SHEMOT | CHAPTER 6   VA'ERA | 48

29 day the Lord spoke to Moshe in Egypt. The Lord said to Moshe, "I am the Lord. Tell
30 Pharaoh King of Egypt all that I am telling you." But Moshe replied to the Lord, "You know that I have uncircumcised lips. How then will Pharaoh listen to me?
7 1 Then the Lord said to Moshe, "I am making you now like a god to Pharaoh, and your
2 brother Aharon will be your prophet. All that I command you, you are to speak, and your brother Aharon to convey to Pharaoh, that he send the Israelites forth from his
3 land. But I will harden Pharaoh's heart and multiply My signs and wonders in the land
4 of Egypt. Still Pharaoh will not listen to you. Then I will set My hand against Egypt and, with great acts of judgment, bring My battalions, My people the Israelites, forth
5 out of the land of Egypt. When I stretch out My hand against Egypt and bring the
6 Israelites out from among them, the Egyptians will know that I am the Lord." Moshe
7 and Aharon did so; they did exactly as the Lord commanded them. Moshe was eighty

---

RABBI SAMSON RAPHAEL HIRSCH

ר׳ שמשון רפאל הירש

הכרת ה׳ אשר תושג באמצעות אותות ומופתים אלה, תאחד את ישראל כ"צבא" מסביב לה׳ ותלכדם כ"עם ה׳."

After the signs and wonders that Moshe performs convince the people to acknowledge the Lord, the Israelites will unite as God's army and rally around Him to form "the nation of the Lord."

QUESTIONS FOR THOUGHT

- In what way is Rabbi Avraham ben HaRambam similar to Ibn Ezra?
- What does Rabbi Avraham ben HaRambam add that Ibn Ezra doesn't say?
- Rabbi Samson Raphael Hirsch is the only one of the above who tries to explain why *Benei Yisrael* are called צבא ה׳ here. It has to do with carefully reading the context in which it is used. Try to figure out his explanation and how it fits the words of these verses.

TEXTUAL SKILLS

1. This is only the second time in the Torah that word נביא is used; the first one is in Genesis 20. They mean two different things. Try to figure out what נביא means here.

2. The plagues are only hinted to in this passage. According to what it says in this passage, what purpose are they designed to serve?

WISDOM OF THE HEART

It is naturally hard for Pharaoh and Egypt to accept the idea that they will no longer be masters of *Benei Yisrael*, but it seems like *Benei Yisrael* themselves also need a long time to accept the reality of their new future, even after the amazing wonders God performs in Egypt. Rav Avraham Blass explains that it was easier for them to believe in the power of God than it was for them to believe in their own capabilities to function as free people. Indeed, prisoners and slaves who are used to having their lives managed by someone else are often afraid of living independently.

How much of what we believe to be our limitations are actually self-imposed?

שמות | פרק ו ואראל | 49

כט בְּי֗וֹם דִּבֶּ֧ר יְהֹוָ֛ה אֶל־מֹשֶׁ֖ה בְּאֶ֥רֶץ מִצְרָֽיִם: וַיְדַבֵּ֧ר *שלישי*
יְהֹוָ֛ה אֶל־מֹשֶׁ֖ה לֵּאמֹ֑ר אֲנִ֣י יְהֹוָ֑ה דַּבֵּ֗ר אֶל־פַּרְעֹה֙ מֶ֣לֶךְ מִצְרַ֔יִם
ל אֵ֛ת כָּל־אֲשֶׁ֥ר אֲנִ֖י דֹּבֵ֣ר אֵלֶֽיךָ: וַיֹּ֥אמֶר מֹשֶׁ֖ה לִפְנֵ֣י יְהֹוָ֑ה הֵ֤ן אֲנִי֙
עֲרַ֣ל שְׂפָתַ֔יִם וְאֵ֕יךְ יִשְׁמַ֥ע אֵלַ֖י פַּרְעֹֽה:

ז א וַיֹּ֤אמֶר יְהֹוָה֙ אֶל־מֹשֶׁ֔ה רְאֵ֛ה נְתַתִּ֥יךָ אֱלֹהִ֖ים לְפַרְעֹ֑ה וְאַהֲרֹ֥ן
ב אָחִ֖יךָ יִהְיֶ֥ה נְבִיאֶֽךָ: אַתָּ֣ה תְדַבֵּ֔ר אֵ֖ת כָּל־אֲשֶׁ֣ר אֲצַוֶּ֑ךָּ וְאַהֲרֹ֤ן
ג אָחִ֨יךָ֙ יְדַבֵּ֣ר אֶל־פַּרְעֹ֔ה וְשִׁלַּ֥ח אֶת־בְּנֵֽי־יִשְׂרָאֵ֖ל מֵאַרְצֽוֹ: וַאֲנִ֥י
אַקְשֶׁ֖ה אֶת־לֵ֣ב פַּרְעֹ֑ה וְהִרְבֵּיתִ֧י אֶת־אֹתֹתַ֛י וְאֶת־מוֹפְתַ֖י בְּאֶ֥רֶץ
ד מִצְרָֽיִם: וְלֹֽא־יִשְׁמַ֤ע אֲלֵכֶם֙ פַּרְעֹ֔ה וְנָתַתִּ֥י אֶת־יָדִ֖י בְּמִצְרָ֑יִם
וְהוֹצֵאתִ֨י אֶת־צִבְאֹתַ֜י אֶת־עַמִּ֤י בְנֵֽי־יִשְׂרָאֵל֙ מֵאֶ֣רֶץ מִצְרַ֔יִם
ה בִּשְׁפָטִ֖ים גְּדֹלִֽים: וְיָדְע֤וּ מִצְרַ֨יִם֙ כִּֽי־אֲנִ֣י יְהֹוָ֔ה בִּנְטֹתִ֥י אֶת־יָדִ֖י
ו עַל־מִצְרָ֑יִם וְהוֹצֵאתִ֥י אֶת־בְּנֵֽי־יִשְׂרָאֵ֖ל מִתּוֹכָֽם: וַיַּ֥עַשׂ מֹשֶׁ֖ה
וְאַהֲרֹ֑ן כַּאֲשֶׁ֨ר צִוָּ֧ה יְהֹוָ֛ה אֹתָ֖ם כֵּ֥ן עָשֽׂוּ: וּמֹשֶׁה֙ בֶּן־שְׁמֹנִ֣ים שָׁנָ֔ה
ז וְאַהֲרֹ֔ן בֶּן־שָׁלֹ֥שׁ וּשְׁמֹנִ֖ים שָׁנָ֑ה בְּדַבְּרָ֖ם אֶל־פַּרְעֹֽה:

CLASSIC COMMENTATORS

In 7:4, for the first time ever, *Benei Yisrael* are called the **צבא** of God – literally, "God's army." The commentaries want to know what this new term is trying to convey.

IBN EZRA

אבן עזרא

Just like the angels fill the ranks of the Lord's army in the heavens, similarly do the Israelites serve as God's soldiers on earth.

כמו שהמלאכים הם צבאות ה' בשמים, כך הם ישראל בארץ.

RABBI AVRAHAM BEN HARAMBAM

ר' אברהם בן הרמב"ם

Now just as God has selected His favorites among the celestial beings, i.e., the angels, whom He honors and considers His possessions, so too did He choose an elect group from among His earthly creatures to call His own. This group is referred to as God's "battalions," connoting Israel's treasured and respected status.

וכמו שהוא יתעלה עשה לו סגולה מן העליונים שכיבד אותם והם המלאכים שהוא מיחס אותם אליו כן עשה לו סגולה מן הנמצאים בארץ ויחס אותם אליו וקרא אותם צבאתי.

God sends Moshe and Aharon to Pharaoh and tells them that if Pharaoh asks for a sign, then Aharon should throw down his staff, which will become a crocodile. Pharaoh is unimpressed, as his own sorcerers do the same with their staffs, and even after Aharon's staff swallows theirs, Pharaoh maintains his steely will.

8 years old, and Aharon eighty-three, when they spoke to Pharaoh. Then the LORD said
9 to Moshe, and to Aharon, "When Pharaoh says to you, 'Perform a miracle,' tell Aharon:
10 Take your staff and throw it down before Pharaoh and it will become a snake." So Moshe and Aharon went to Pharaoh and did just as the LORD had commanded. Aharon threw
11 down his staff before Pharaoh and his officials, and it became a snake. Pharaoh then summoned his sages and sorcerers, and the Egyptian magicians did the same thing by
12 their sorcery. Each threw down his staff, and they became snakes – but Aharon's staff
13 swallowed up theirs. Pharaoh, nonetheless, was obstinate, and he would not listen to

QUESTIONS FOR THOUGHT

- While Ibn Ezra takes a clear stand that there is no such thing as magic, Ramban firmly believes that magic is real. Where does Ralbag stand?
- According to Rambam, there are no supernatural forces in the world operating independent of God. Ramban disagrees. According to each, why do you think that the Torah later forbids magic?
- With whom do you agree, Ibn Ezra and Rambam, or Ramban?

TEXTUAL SKILLS

1. Notice that here the Torah talks about the staff turning into a תנין, while at the burning bush Moshe's staff turns into a נחש. Look at other places these words appear in Tanakh. Do they mean the same thing?

2. God here anticipates that Pharaoh will ask for a מופת, while at the burning bush He provides Moshe with an אות to demonstrate to *Benei Yisrael*. Are these words synonymous?

WISDOM OF THE HEART

According to a midrash, Pharaoh became exceedingly frightened when Aharon's staff swallows those of the sorcerers because his staff did not grow any fatter after swallowing them. (Does that remind you of an earlier dream of Pharaoh?) *Ketav Sofer* explains that Pharaoh understood the symbolism – Israel would swallow up all the nations to the extent that there would be no trace of them.

Aharon's staff became a symbol of the power of Israel. What staffs do you have? What untapped strengths can you tap into?

ט וַיֹּ֣אמֶר יְהוָ֗ה אֶל־מֹשֶׁה֙ וְאֶֽל־אַהֲרֹ֣ן לֵאמֹ֔ר: כִּי֩ יְדַבֵּ֨ר אֲלֵכֶ֤ם ה *רביעי*
פַּרְעֹה֙ לֵאמֹ֔ר תְּנ֥וּ לָכֶ֖ם מוֹפֵ֑ת וְאָמַרְתָּ֣ אֶֽל־אַהֲרֹ֗ן קַ֧ח אֶֽת־מַטְּךָ֛
י וְהַשְׁלֵ֥ךְ לִפְנֵֽי־פַרְעֹ֖ה יְהִ֥י לְתַנִּֽין: וַיָּבֹ֨א מֹשֶׁ֤ה וְאַהֲרֹן֙ אֶל־פַּרְעֹ֔ה
וַיַּ֣עֲשׂוּ כֵ֔ן כַּאֲשֶׁ֖ר צִוָּ֣ה יְהוָ֑ה וַיַּשְׁלֵ֨ךְ אַהֲרֹ֜ן אֶת־מַטֵּ֗הוּ לִפְנֵ֥י פַרְעֹ֛ה
יא וְלִפְנֵ֥י עֲבָדָ֖יו וַיְהִ֥י לְתַנִּֽין: וַיִּקְרָא֙ גַּם־פַּרְעֹ֔ה לַֽחֲכָמִ֖ים וְלַֽמְכַשְּׁפִ֑ים
יב וַיַּֽעֲשׂ֨וּ גַם־הֵ֜ם חַרְטֻמֵּ֥י מִצְרַ֛יִם בְּלַהֲטֵיהֶ֖ם כֵּֽן: וַיַּשְׁלִ֨יכוּ֙ אִ֣ישׁ
יג מַטֵּ֔הוּ וַיִּהְי֖וּ לְתַנִּינִ֑ם וַיִּבְלַ֥ע מַטֵּֽה־אַהֲרֹ֖ן אֶת־מַטֹּתָֽם: וַיֶּחֱזַק֙ לֵ֣ב

CLASSIC COMMENTATORS

Is there really such a thing as magic, or is it all just deception?

IBN EZRA

To distinguish Moshe's authentic display of transforming a staff into a living snake from the trickery of the magicians, the text mentions their use of "sorcery." The trick performed by Pharaoh's servants is a mere illusion whose effects will immediately vanish.

אבן עזרא

הנה הכתוב הפריש בין מעשה משה למעשה החרטומים, שאמר שהם לא עשו כי אם בדרך להט ... דבר שייראה לעין רגע אחד ולא יעמוד.

RAMBAN

According to our Rabbis, the Egyptian sorcerers managed their witchcraft by enlisting the help of angels of destruction…Specifically the magicians were assisted by "the flaming ones" – angels of fire.

רמב״ן

אמרו רבותינו שהם מעשה כשפים ועל ידי מלאכי חבלה הם נעשים ... והענין: כי הם נעשים על ידי לוהטים, מלאכי אש.

RALBAG

The verse refers to Pharaoh's servants as "wise men" for they possessed the wisdom to produce witchcraft and execute unnatural activities. In fact, what these performers were doing was merely sleight of hand that tricked observers into thinking they were witnessing true magic. The sorcerers did this by manipulating ordinary objects in ways that resembled witchcraft. Alternatively, it is possible that these men really had mastered techniques of bending the laws of nature. If that is what the Torah is describing here, the art of witchcraft the Egyptians possessed has been lost to history.

רלב״ג

ועניין החכמה ההיא היתה להמציא פעולת הכישוף, ויעשו בה פעולות זרות, אין מדרך הטבע שיגיעו ממנו. וזה, אם בשיאחזו העינים, ויבאו לחשוב שיעשו מה שאינם עושים; אם בשימציאו תחבולות טבעיות יתחדשו בהם עניינים זרים ידמו למפעולות הכשפים; או בשיעשו אלו הפעולות הזרות על דרך הכישוף – אם היה שיהיה אפשר חידושם על דרך הכישוף. והנה לא נודע לנו עד היום מהות זה הכישוף ועניינו.

After Pharaoh refuses to accept Moshe's message, God tells Moshe to meet Pharaoh by the riverside and warn him that if he does not let Benei Yisrael go to worship, then Moshe will hit the water with his staff and turn it into blood.

14 them, just as the Lord had predicted. Then the Lord said to Moshe, "Pharaoh's heart is
15 unyielding. He refuses to send the people forth. So go to Pharaoh in the morning as he goes out to the water. Place yourself by the bank of the Nile where you will encounter
16 him, taking in your hand the staff that turned into a snake. Say to him: The Lord, God of the Hebrews, has sent me to tell you: Send My people forth, so that they may serve
17 Me in the wilderness. So far, you have not listened. This is what the Lord says: This will make it known to you that I am the Lord. With the staff in my hand I will strike
18 the water in the Nile and it will become blood. The fish in the Nile will die; the Nile will

QUESTIONS FOR THOUGHT
- According to which of the commentaries is the choice of the riverside as a meeting place tailored specifically for Pharaoh?
- According to the different commentaries, is the riverside a place where Pharaoh demonstrates strength or where he goes to hide his weakness?
- Do you think that the riverside warning was meant to humiliate Pharaoh or to provide a private opportunity for him to hear Moshe's request with no onlookers?

TEXTUAL SKILLS

1. In the verse immediately preceding this passage the Torah describes Pharaoh's heart as being חזק (literally, "strong"), while in the opening of this passage God describes his heart as being כבד (literally, "heavy"). Do those two words mean the same thing?

2. The word ונלאו comes from the root ל-א-ה, and means "to become exhausted from repeatedly trying and not succeeding." It is used only twice in the Torah (the other is Gen. 19:11). Why do you think that word was chosen to describe to Pharaoh the impact of the first of the plagues?

WISDOM OF THE HEART

The Nile was the source of pride and strength for all Egyptians – it was the very center of their lives. What would it have been like for any ordinary Egyptian to wake up one random morning and discover that the Nile had turned into blood?

Are there things on which you are too dependent?

שמות | פרק ז | וארא

יד פַּרְעֹה וְלֹא שָׁמַע אֲלֵהֶם כַּאֲשֶׁר דִּבֶּר יְהוָֹה: וַיֹּאמֶר
טו יְהוָֹה אֶל־מֹשֶׁה כָּבֵד לֵב פַּרְעֹה מֵאֵן לְשַׁלַּח הָעָם: לֵךְ אֶל־פַּרְעֹה
בַּבֹּקֶר הִנֵּה יֹצֵא הַמַּיְמָה וְנִצַּבְתָּ לִקְרָאתוֹ עַל־שְׂפַת הַיְאֹר
טז וְהַמַּטֶּה אֲשֶׁר־נֶהְפַּךְ לְנָחָשׁ תִּקַּח בְּיָדֶךָ: וְאָמַרְתָּ אֵלָיו יְהוָֹה
אֱלֹהֵי הָעִבְרִים שְׁלָחַנִי אֵלֶיךָ לֵאמֹר שַׁלַּח אֶת־עַמִּי וְיַעַבְדֻנִי
בַּמִּדְבָּר וְהִנֵּה לֹא־שָׁמַעְתָּ עַד־כֹּה: כֹּה אָמַר יְהוָֹה בְּזֹאת תֵּדַע
יז כִּי אֲנִי יְהוָֹה הִנֵּה אָנֹכִי מַכֶּה ׀ בַּמַּטֶּה אֲשֶׁר־בְּיָדִי עַל־הַמַּיִם
יח אֲשֶׁר בַּיְאֹר וְנֶהֶפְכוּ לְדָם: וְהַדָּגָה אֲשֶׁר־בַּיְאֹר תָּמוּת וּבָאַשׁ

CLASSIC COMMENTATORS

The specificity of the riverside as the meeting place intrigued many of the commentaries.

RASHI

[He went] to relieve himself. Pharaoh professed to be a god who was above such bodily functions. He would rise early and steal down to the Nile to tend to his needs.

רש״י

הנה הכתוב הפריש בין מעשה משה למעשה החרטומים, שאמר שהם לא עשו כי אם בדרך להט ... דבר שייראה לעין רגע אחד ולא יעמוד.

IBN EZRA

It is likely that this was the time that the level of the Nile's waters was expected to rise, and Pharaoh went down to the river bank to inspect its progress. God therefore commanded Moshe to execute his sign on the river while Pharaoh watched.

אבן עזרא

יתכן שהיה זה קרוב מעת עלות היאור המעלות הידועות, והמלך יוצא לראותו. וצוה השם לעשות זה המופת ביאור לעיני פרעה בצאתו שמה.

RABBI YOSEF KARA

Pharaoh went down to the Nile, as is the custom of many people who live by the water, to bathe in the river first thing in the morning and refresh himself.

ר׳ יוסף קרא

כדרך בני אדם המשכימים בבקר על שפת נהרות ורוחצין ממימי הנהר להאיר עיניהם.

RABBI DAVID TZVI HOFFMAN

It seems that Pharaoh made his way down to the river in order to worship the Nile. It was therefore appropriate that Moshe intercept him en route and prove to the king the inefficacy and inabilities of his god. At the same time Moshe would demonstrate the omnipotence of the Lord.

ר׳ דוד צבי הופמן

מסתבר להבין שהלך לסגוד לו ליאור, ודווקא בדרכו זו צריך היה להראות לו את אפסותם של אליליו ואת כל־יכולתו של ה׳.

Following the warning to Pharaoh, God instructs Moshe to tell Aharon to use his staff to strike the water. They do as they are told, and all the water in the Nile and its tributaries turns to blood. But when Pharaoh's sorcerers copy Aharon's actions, Pharaoh grows determined to ignore the message brought by Moshe and Aharon. For seven days there is no water from the Nile, the fish die, and the Egyptians dig wells to tap into the ground water to drink.

19 stink and the Egyptians will be unable to drink its water." Then the LORD said to Moshe, "Tell Aharon: Take your staff and stretch out your hand over the waters of Egypt, their rivers, canals, ponds and reservoirs, and they will turn into blood. There will be blood
20 throughout Egypt, even inside vessels of wood and of stone." Moshe and Aharon did just as the LORD commanded. Aharon raised his staff, in full view of Pharaoh and his officials, and struck the water of the Nile, and all the Nile's water turned into blood.
21 The Nile fish died, and the river stank so that the Egyptians could not drink its water.
22 Throughout the land of Egypt, blood appeared. But the Egyptian magicians did the same thing by their sorcery. So Pharaoh's heart remained adamant, and he would not
23 listen to them, just as the LORD had predicted. Pharaoh turned and went back into his
24 palace and did not take even this to heart. The Egyptians all dug along the Nile to get
25 drinking water, unable to drink of the waters of the Nile. And seven days went by after the LORD's striking of the Nile.

QUESTIONS FOR THOUGHT
- On what basis does Ibn Ezra suggest that even *Benei Yisrael* were affected?
- On what basis does Baal Haturim disagree?
- Which do you think should have greater influence on our understanding of Torah – a careful reading of the text or our intuition?
- Look at 8:18. Does that verse seem to support Ibn Ezra or Baal Haturim?

TEXTUAL SKILLS

1. Compare verse 19 and verse 20 in this chapter. What did Moshe do?
2. The Egyptian sorcerers do something wondrous in this passage, but they also performed something wondrous in the previous passage. Find the word which describes the tool used by the sorcerers, and notice the difference between the tools used in the different plagues. Do you think that they are the same tool described slightly differently or different ones?

WISDOM OF THE HEART

There are many ways to organize the plagues in an attempt to understand them. One way to view the first plagues is to understand them as an attack on the Nile, the source of the Egyptian economy and power, and an Egyptian deity. Moshe confronts Pharaoh on the banks of the river, the blood renders the Nile powerless, and the frogs emerging from the Nile spread destruction and stench from the Nile rather than cleansing, life-giving waters.

When do our strengths turn into weaknesses?

יט הַיְאֹר וְנִלְאוּ מִצְרַיִם לִשְׁתּוֹת מַיִם מִן־הַיְאֹר: וַיֹּאמֶר
יְהוָֹה אֶל־מֹשֶׁה אֱמֹר אֶל־אַהֲרֹן קַח מַטְּךָ וּנְטֵה־יָדְךָ עַל־מֵימֵי
מִצְרַיִם עַל־נַהֲרֹתָם ׀ עַל־יְאֹרֵיהֶם וְעַל־אַגְמֵיהֶם וְעַל כָּל־
מִקְוֵה מֵימֵיהֶם וְיִהְיוּ־דָם וְהָיָה דָם בְּכָל־אֶרֶץ מִצְרַיִם וּבָעֵצִים
וּבָאֲבָנִים: וַיַּעֲשׂוּ־כֵן מֹשֶׁה וְאַהֲרֹן כַּאֲשֶׁר ׀ צִוָּה יְהוָֹה וַיָּרֶם בַּמַּטֶּה כ
וַיַּךְ אֶת־הַמַּיִם אֲשֶׁר בַּיְאֹר לְעֵינֵי פַרְעֹה וּלְעֵינֵי עֲבָדָיו וַיֵּהָפְכוּ
כָּל־הַמַּיִם אֲשֶׁר־בַּיְאֹר לְדָם: וְהַדָּגָה אֲשֶׁר־בַּיְאֹר מֵתָה וַיִּבְאַשׁ כא
הַיְאֹר וְלֹא־יָכְלוּ מִצְרַיִם לִשְׁתּוֹת מַיִם מִן־הַיְאֹר וַיְהִי הַדָּם
בְּכָל־אֶרֶץ מִצְרָיִם: וַיַּעֲשׂוּ־כֵן חַרְטֻמֵּי מִצְרַיִם בְּלָטֵיהֶם וַיֶּחֱזַק כב
לֵב־פַּרְעֹה וְלֹא־שָׁמַע אֲלֵהֶם כַּאֲשֶׁר דִּבֶּר יְהוָֹה: וַיִּפֶן פַּרְעֹה וַיָּבֹא כג
אֶל־בֵּיתוֹ וְלֹא־שָׁת לִבּוֹ גַּם־לָזֹאת: וַיַּחְפְּרוּ כָל־מִצְרַיִם סְבִיבֹת כד
הַיְאֹר מַיִם לִשְׁתּוֹת כִּי לֹא יָכְלוּ לִשְׁתֹּת מִמֵּימֵי הַיְאֹר: וַיִּמָּלֵא כה
שִׁבְעַת יָמִים אַחֲרֵי הַכּוֹת־יְהוָֹה אֶת־הַיְאֹר:

CLASSIC COMMENTATORS

Did the plague of blood affect *Benei Yisrael*? The answer is not clear.

IBN EZRA

Many commentators argue that the water remained red in the possession of the Egyptians but turned clear when handed to an Israelite. If that were true, however, such a patent miracle would have been stated explicitly in the Torah. In my opinion, the three plagues of blood, frogs, and lice struck the Hebrews as severely as they did the Egyptians. For it is my policy to follow the Torah text [and not aggadic reports].

RABBI YAAKOV BAAL HATURIM

According to Rabbi Avraham Ibn Ezra, the water which had become blood for the Egyptians reverted to its natural state when held by an Israelite... But while the commentator's pursuit of the text's straightforward meaning compels him to argue that Israel too was stricken during this plague, I find such an approach objectionable – why would God cause Israel such suffering? Rather, the Lord is fully capable of punishing one who deserves it while shielding his innocent neighbor from harm.

אבן עזרא

רבים אומרים, כי המים היו ביד המצרי אדומים כדם ונתלבנו ביד הישראלי, אם כן למה לא נכתב אות זה בתורה? ולפי דעתי, כי מכת הדם והצפרדעים והכנים היתה כוללת המצרים והעברים, כי אחר הכתוב נרדף.

ר׳ יעקב בעל הטורים

כתב ר׳ אברהם "רבים אומרים כי המים היו ביד המצרי ... ". ורודפו אחר הפשט הביאו לזה הדעת, כי חלילה להכות את ישראל ולהכות אשר ירצה.

Shemot | Chapter 7

26 Then the Lord said to Moshe, "Go to Pharaoh and say to him: This is what the Lord
27 says: Send My people forth, so that they may serve Me. And if you should refuse to
28 send them forth – I will scourge your land with frogs from end to end. The Nile will
teem with frogs. They will come up into your palace, into your bedroom and up onto
your bed, into the houses of your officials and of all your people, into your ovens and
29 your kneading pans. The frogs shall climb up onto you and your people and all your
8 1 officials." The Lord said to Moshe, "Speak to Aharon: Stretch out your hand that holds
your staff, over the rivers, the canals and the pools, and cause frogs to climb up and out
2 onto the land of Egypt." So Aharon stretched out his hand over the waters of Egypt, and
3 frogs climbed up and covered the Egyptian land. But the magicians used their sorcery
4 and did the same, making frogs climb up over the land of Egypt. Then Pharaoh called
for Moshe and Aharon and said, "Pray to the Lord to take the frogs away from me and

---

RABBI DAVID TZVI HOFFMAN
ר' דוד צבי הופמן

Pharaoh was prepared to make concessions because he was personally suffering from the plague's effects.

כיון שהוא עצמו הוטרד מן המכה, הוא נכון לוויתורים

QUESTIONS FOR THOUGHT

- Two of the commentaries think that this plague was fundamentally different from the others. One commentary disagrees and says that this is a test. Which commentary is that, and what is the test?
- According to R. David Tzvi Hoffman, what was different about the plague itself that may have convinced Pharaoh?
- What can you find in v. 28 that supports R. Hoffman's explanation?

TEXTUAL SKILLS

1. The word **משארת**, meaning a basket used to knead dough, appears only four times in Tanakh; one is here, a second one is in the story of leaving Egypt (12:34). Based on the root of the word, venture an educated guess why that kneading basket is called a **משארת**?

2. In the first plague, the Torah describes in detail the multiple collections of water that will turn into blood (7:19). In the second plague, the Torah is very brief about those sources of water but describes in great detail where the frogs will get to. Suggest a reason for the difference.

WISDOM OF THE HEART

Rashi cites a midrashic opinion that the plague of frogs started with a single frog which multiplied when hit. You would think that after the first one or two times, the Egyptians would have realized that they should stop hitting the frog. Commenting on this, the Steipler Gaon notes that this demonstrates the insanity of anger – it drives us to irrational, self-destructive behavior.

Making decisions from a place of anger will usually worsen your problems.

כו וַיֹּאמֶר יהוה אֶל־מֹשֶׁה בֹּא אֶל־פַּרְעֹה וְאָמַרְתָּ אֵלָיו כֹּה אָמַר
כז יהוה שַׁלַּח אֶת־עַמִּי וְיַעַבְדֻנִי: וְאִם־מָאֵן אַתָּה לְשַׁלֵּחַ הִנֵּה
כח אָנֹכִי נֹגֵף אֶת־כָּל־גְּבוּלְךָ בַּצְפַרְדְּעִים: וְשָׁרַץ הַיְאֹר צְפַרְדְּעִים
וְעָלוּ וּבָאוּ בְּבֵיתֶךָ וּבַחֲדַר מִשְׁכָּבְךָ וְעַל־מִטָּתֶךָ וּבְבֵית עֲבָדֶיךָ
כט וּבְעַמֶּךָ וּבְתַנּוּרֶיךָ וּבְמִשְׁאֲרוֹתֶיךָ: וּבְכָה וּבְעַמְּךָ וּבְכָל־עֲבָדֶיךָ
ח א יַעֲלוּ הַצְפַרְדְּעִים: וַיֹּאמֶר יהוה אֶל־מֹשֶׁה אֱמֹר אֶל־אַהֲרֹן נְטֵה
אֶת־יָדְךָ בְּמַטֶּךָ עַל־הַנְּהָרֹת עַל־הַיְאֹרִים וְעַל־הָאֲגַמִּים וְהַעַל
ב אֶת־הַצְפַרְדְּעִים עַל־אֶרֶץ מִצְרָיִם: וַיֵּט אַהֲרֹן אֶת־יָדוֹ עַל מֵימֵי
מִצְרָיִם וַתַּעַל הַצְפַרְדֵּעַ וַתְּכַס אֶת־אֶרֶץ מִצְרָיִם: וַיַּעֲשׂוּ־כֵן
ג הַחַרְטֻמִּים בְּלָטֵיהֶם וַיַּעֲלוּ אֶת־הַצְפַרְדְּעִים עַל־אֶרֶץ מִצְרָיִם:
ד וַיִּקְרָא פַרְעֹה לְמֹשֶׁה וּלְאַהֲרֹן וַיֹּאמֶר הַעְתִּירוּ אֶל־יהוה וְיָסֵר
הַצְפַרְדְּעִים מִמֶּנִּי וּמֵעַמִּי וַאֲשַׁלְּחָה אֶת־הָעָם וְיִזְבְּחוּ לַיהוה:

CLASSIC COMMENTATORS

When Pharaoh's sorcerers turn their staffs into crocodiles, Pharaoh strengthens his will to refuse Moshe's request. Later, when his sorcerers turn water into blood, that again strengthens Pharaoh's will to resist Moshe's request. This time, however, even though the sorcerers replicate Aharon's plague, Pharaoh calls Moshe and Aharon to ask them to remove the frogs. Why does he seem to give in now when his sorcerers demonstrate again that they can do what Aharon did?

IBN EZRA
אבן עזרא

And so he summoned Moshe, having understood that although his servants might be able to add a few frogs to the ordeal, they certainly would fail at ridding his kingdom of the pests. For only a person who has introduced a phenomenon is capable of removing it.

על כן קרא למשה, כי ראה כי החרטומים הוסיפו על המכה, ולא יכלו לחסר אותה, כי אין יכולת באדם לחסרה, כי אם מי שהביאה.

RALBAG
רלב״ג

Pharaoh's motive for asking Moshe and Aharon to call off the frogs was to test whether in fact it was they who had lured the amphibians to the land in the first place. For the king thought that perhaps the arrival of the frogs was a completely natural event that the Hebrew leaders took credit for, having somehow been able to anticipate the invasion.

לא עשה זה כי אם לנסות אם זה הפועל בא על ידי משה ואהרן, או הוא מקרה קרה להם וידעו משה ואהרן זה המקרה באחד מהדרכים אשר ידע האדם בהם העתידות.

> Moshe not only agrees to pray to remove the frogs but invites Pharaoh to decide the timing of that removal. Pharaoh asks for the frogs to be removed on the following day. Moshe prays to God, and the frogs die – leaving the Egyptians with a huge mess of dead frogs to clean up. Once the threat of the frogs is over, Pharaoh's heart grows heavy and he returns to his refusal to listen to Moshe and Aharon.

5 from my people, and I will send your people forth to sacrifice to the Lord." Moshe said to Pharaoh, "Gloat over me: you name the time when I should pray that the frogs be removed, for you and your officials, and your people, from you and your homes, 6 remaining only in the Nile." "Tomorrow," he replied. Moshe said, "It will be as you say. 7 Then you will know that there is none like the Lord our God. The frogs will depart from you and from your homes, your officials, all your people. They will only remain in 8 the Nile." Moshe and Aharon departed Pharaoh's presence, and Moshe cried out to the 9 Lord about the frogs He had brought upon Pharaoh. The Lord did as Moshe said, and 10 the frogs in the houses, courtyards and fields died; they gathered them up into heaping 11 piles, and the stench filled the whole land. But when Pharaoh saw that respite had come,

---

QUESTIONS FOR THOUGHT

- According Ibn Ezra, what did Pharaoh believe about Moshe's ability to bring the frogs?
- Does Bekhor Shor agree or disagree with Ibn Ezra?
- According to Ramban, did Pharaoh think that he was giving Moshe a long time or a short time to remove the plague?
- Which of the above approaches do you think is closest to capturing Pharaoh's thoughts?

TEXTUAL SKILLS

1. Notice the root ב-א-ש in verse 10 to describe what happened to the land. Where have you seen that word recently, and what was it describing?
2. The root צ-ב-ר, meaning "accumulate," appears in only two contexts in the Torah. One is here; the other is in Genesis ch. 41. Look there to see what they are accumulating. What do you think the connection between these two is?

WISDOM OF THE HEART

The Baal Shem Tov is cited as commenting on Psalms 69:19 that before we pray for ultimate redemption we must pray for our personal redemption, the redemption of our soul. You can't fix the world before you fix yourself. The Slonimer Rebbe writes in his *Darkhei Noam* that *galut* is not just the place where you live, but it is also how you live. The story of Egypt is not just about how Israel was redeemed from *galut* many years ago, but serves as a metaphor for our personal journeys.

What kind of personal redemption would you like to work for in your own life?

שמות | פרק ח

ה וַיֹּ֨אמֶר מֹשֶׁ֤ה לְפַרְעֹה֙ הִתְפָּאֵ֣ר עָלַ֔י לְמָתַ֣י ׀ אַעְתִּ֣יר לְךָ֗ וְלַעֲבָדֶ֨יךָ֙ וּלְעַמְּךָ֔ לְהַכְרִית֙ הַֽצֲפַרְדְּעִ֔ים מִמְּךָ֖ וּמִבָּתֶּ֑יךָ רַ֥ק בַּיְאֹ֖ר תִּשָּׁאַֽרְנָה׃
ו וַיֹּ֖אמֶר לְמָחָ֑ר וַיֹּ֨אמֶר֙ כִּדְבָ֣רְךָ֔ לְמַ֣עַן תֵּדַ֔ע כִּי־אֵ֖ין כַּיהֹוָ֥ה אֱלֹהֵֽינוּ׃
ז וְסָר֣וּ הַֽצֲפַרְדְּעִ֗ים מִמְּךָ֙ וּמִבָּ֣תֶּ֔יךָ וּמֵעֲבָדֶ֖יךָ וּמֵעַמֶּ֑ךָ רַ֥ק בַּיְאֹ֖ר תִּשָּׁאַֽרְנָה׃ *חמישי*
ח וַיֵּצֵ֥א מֹשֶׁ֛ה וְאַהֲרֹ֖ן מֵעִ֣ם פַּרְעֹ֑ה וַיִּצְעַ֤ק מֹשֶׁה֙ אֶל־יְהֹוָ֔ה עַל־דְּבַ֥ר הַֽצֲפַרְדְּעִ֖ים אֲשֶׁר־שָׂ֥ם לְפַרְעֹֽה׃
ט וַיַּ֥עַשׂ יְהֹוָ֖ה כִּדְבַ֣ר מֹשֶׁ֑ה וַיָּמֻ֨תוּ֙ הַֽצֲפַרְדְּעִ֔ים מִן־הַבָּתִּ֥ים מִן־הַחֲצֵרֹ֖ת וּמִן־הַשָּׂדֹֽת׃
י וַיִּצְבְּר֥וּ אֹתָ֖ם חֳמָרִ֣ם חֳמָרִ֑ם וַתִּבְאַ֖שׁ הָאָֽרֶץ׃
יא וַיַּ֣רְא פַּרְעֹ֗ה כִּ֤י הָֽיְתָה֙ הָֽרְוָחָ֔ה וְהַכְבֵּד֙ אֶת־לִבּ֔וֹ וְלֹ֥א שָׁמַ֖ע אֲלֵהֶ֑ם

CLASSIC COMMENTATORS

Moshe's invitation to Pharaoh to determine the timing of the removal of the frogs is often understood as a form of mocking flattery, as if to say, "You, Pharaoh, are of course in charge." The great irony is the close of Moshe's statement: "Then you will know that there is none like the Lord our God." In that context, Pharaoh's request that the frogs be gone the next day seems odd. If they are so uncomfortable that Pharaoh needed to summon Moshe to remove them, why not ask for them to be removed immediately?

אבן עזרא

אמר רב שמואל בן חפני: אין מנהג האדם לבקש רק שתסור המכה ממנו מיד. ופרעה חשב כי מערכת כוכבי שמים הביאה הצפרדעים על מצרים, ומשה היה יודע זה. וידע פרעה כי עתה הגיע עת סור הצפרדעים, על כן נסהו והאריך ואמר "למחר".

IBN EZRA

Rav Shmuel ben Ḥofni asks: Is it not reasonable for a person suffering from a plague to ask that his torment end as soon as possible? Indeed, Pharaoh believed that it was the heavenly constellations that had inflicted the frog infestation upon his people, a belief that Moshe was well aware of. But because the king also thought that the alignment of the stars meant that the frogs were about to immediately disappear, he tested Moshe to see if the Hebrew could keep the animals in place until the following day.

ר' יוסף בכור שור

אמר "אני אתן לך זמן עד למחר, ואפילו הכי לא תוכל עשות".

RABBI YOSEF BEKHOR SHOR

Pharaoh's challenge to Moshe was as follows: Even if I give you until tomorrow I do not believe that you are capable of removing the frogs.

רמב"ן

כי בעבור שאמר למתי אעתיר לך, חשב פרעה כי ביקש זמן, ועל כן נתן לו זמן קצר, ויאמר למחר.

RAMBAN

When Moshe challenged Pharaoh: "You name the time when I should pray [that the frogs be removed]" (8:5), the king thought that Moshe was playing for time. In response, he suggested the shortest possible time for Moshe to get the job done, saying: "Tomorrow."

> *Pharaoh refused to accept the sign of the staff turning into a crocodile, was unmoved by the plague of the blood, and made himself stubborn even after summoning Moshe to remove the plague of the frogs. It could be argued that Pharaoh was unconvinced since in each case his sorcerers were able to replicate the miracle using their magic. The third plague, however, was different. Not only was there no warning, but the sorcerers were unable to generate lice from the earth. Despite their proclamation that this was clearly the "finger of God," Pharaoh continues to ignore Moshe's and Aharon's demand.*

12 he hardened his heart and would not listen, just as the Lord had predicted. Then the Lord said to Moshe, "Tell Aharon: Extend your staff and strike the dust of the earth;
13 all over Egypt it will be transformed into lice." They did so. Aharon extended the hand that held his staff and struck the dust of the earth, and suddenly there were lice on the
14 people, on the animals. The dust of the earth was turned to lice all across Egypt. The magicians tried to produce lice with their sorcery, but they could not. Meanwhile the
15 lice still infested people and animals alike. "This," the magicians told Pharaoh, "is the finger of God." But Pharaoh's heart was toughened, and – as the Lord had predicted – he

---

- Which of the commentaries understands that the "finger of God" comment was not about God at all, but that it is an expression meaning that it is completely out of the control of humans (similar to how insurance companies today call hurricanes "an act of God")?
- Do you think that the sorcerers were actually convinced that God was doing the miracles and that Moshe and Aharon were God's messengers? Would you be convinced by a supernatural event seemingly directed by a human?

TEXTUAL SKILLS

1. The lice are described here in the singular, even though it is clear that there were many. Which other plague is described in the singular even though there were many?

2. Notice that this time Aharon uses his staff to strike the earth. What has he struck up until now?

QUICK BITE

Immediately following the plague of lice, the Torah jumps right into the next plague. R. Shalom Schwadron asks: Why do we never hear that the lice went away? Why was there was no resolution to that plague as there was with all the others? He answers that in all other cases Pharaoh asked for relief. One of the fundamental aspects of prayer and God's providence is that one needs to be able to ask for the things one needs. Prayer is about turning to God and opening up our hearts to express what we lack and desire.

שמות | פרק ח

יב וַיֹּאמֶר יהוה אֶל־מֹשֶׁה אֱמֹר אֶל־אַהֲרֹן נְטֵה אֶת־מַטְּךָ וְהַךְ אֶת־עֲפַר הָאָרֶץ וְהָיָה לְכִנִּם בְּכָל־אֶרֶץ מִצְרָיִם: יג וַיַּעֲשׂוּ־כֵן וַיֵּט אַהֲרֹן אֶת־יָדוֹ בְמַטֵּהוּ וַיַּךְ אֶת־עֲפַר הָאָרֶץ וַתְּהִי הַכִּנָּם בָּאָדָם וּבַבְּהֵמָה כָּל־עֲפַר הָאָרֶץ הָיָה כִנִּים בְּכָל־אֶרֶץ מִצְרָיִם: יד וַיַּעֲשׂוּ־כֵן הַחַרְטֻמִּים בְּלָטֵיהֶם לְהוֹצִיא אֶת־הַכִּנִּים וְלֹא יָכֹלוּ וַתְּהִי הַכִּנָּם בָּאָדָם וּבַבְּהֵמָה: טו וַיֹּאמְרוּ הַחַרְטֻמִּם אֶל־פַּרְעֹה אֶצְבַּע אֱלֹהִים הִוא וַיֶּחֱזַק לֵב־ כַּאֲשֶׁר דִּבֶּר יהוה:

CLASSIC COMMENTATORS

What did the sorcerers mean when they declared the plague of lice to be the "finger of God"?

RASHI — רש״י

Pharaoh's sorcerers acknowledged that the lice plague had not been effected through witchcraft but orchestrated by God.

מכה זו אינה על ידי כשפים, מאת הקב״ה היא.

IBN EZRA — אבן עזרא

They informed Pharaoh: This plague is not meant to force you to release Israel. This torment from God merely reflects Egypt's astrological fate.

אמרו לפרעה: לא באה זאת המכה בעבור ישראל לשלחם, רק מכת אלהים היא כפי מערכת הכוכבים על מזל ארץ מצרים.

RAMBAN — רמב״ן

When the magicians realized their inability to repeat Aharon's action of calling lice out of the dust, they understood that he was channeling the power of God. Therefore, Pharaoh did not again summon his magicians from this point onward.

בראות החרטומים שלא יכלו להוציא את הכנים הודו במעשה אהרן שהיה מאת האלהים, ולכן לא קרא להם פרעה מן העת הזאת והלאה.

QUESTIONS FOR THOUGHT

- Which of the commentaries understands that the sorcerers learned from this that all of the wonders produced by Aharon were of divine origin?
- Which of the commentaries understands that the sorcerers concluded that this particular plague was not done through magic?

Once again, Moshe is instructed to meet Pharaoh down by the water to warn him about an upcoming plague, the עָרוֹב. This time, God emphasizes, the plague will spare Benei Yisrael so that Pharaoh recognizes that God is "in the midst of the land." Indeed, a very heavy עָרוֹב invades the homes of Pharaoh, his servants, and the rest of the Egyptians.

16 would not listen to them. Then the LORD said to Moshe, "Rise up early in the morning and confront Pharaoh as he goes out to the water; tell him: This is what the LORD says:
17 Send My people forth, so that they may serve Me. If you refuse to send them forth, I will send swarms of insects onto you, your officials, your people and your houses. The Egyptians' houses will be filled with swarms of insects; the ground they stand upon will
18 be covered by them. On that day, I will set the land of Goshen, where My people live, apart – there, there will be no swarms – and then you will know that I am the LORD,
19 here on earth. Between My people and yours I will mark out a separation; tomorrow,
20 this sign will come to be." The LORD did so. Great swarms of insects infested Pharaoh's palace and the houses of his officials. All across Egypt, swarms of insects devastated the

QUESTIONS FOR THOUGHT

- Rashi explains that the word עָרוֹב means a "mixture," but Rashbam disagrees. How does he understand the meaning of that word?
- Rashi and Rashbam agree that the עָרוֹב involved predatory land animals, but Rashbam thinks that it is one specific land animal. Which animal is that?
- What reasoning does R. David Tzvi Hoffman provide for preferring the alternative explanation of עָרוֹב?

TEXTUAL SKILLS

1. In verse 8:18, God reveals the purpose of the plagues. In what way is it different, and in what way is it similar, to the purpose He identified in 7:16?
2. This is the first of the plagues which is not implemented immediately; rather, it will only come into effect on the following day (לְמָחָר). Look back at the previous plague to suggest an explanation.

WISDOM OF THE HEART

How are we to understand the word וְהִפְלֵיתִי in verse 18? The Ḥozeh of Lublin taught that it derives from the root פלא, meaning "wonder." Specifically, this refers to a wondrous point where heaven and earth can meet. In this instance, the Israelites would be able to raise the land of Goshen (known for nothing spiritual) and connect it to spiritual life. Rav Hutner, in his essays on Pesaḥ, makes use of this idea to explore other instances where a nexus is achieved between the physical and spiritual. One example is at the end of the blessing we say after using the restroom – there we bless God who "acts wondrously." Immediately following that blessing in the morning, many say the prayer אֱלֹהַי נְשָׁמָה, where we recognize the gift of having a soul. The word פלא, then, is used to express the link between the physical (e.g. going to the restroom) and the spiritual (our soul). Judaism uniquely celebrates the physical when it is in context of a physical pursuit. Soul without body or body without soul would undercut our purpose on earth.

שמות | פרק ח

טז פַּרְעֹה וְלֹא־שָׁמַע אֲלֵהֶם כַּאֲשֶׁר דִּבֶּר יְהוָה: וַיֹּאמֶר יְהוָה אֶל־מֹשֶׁה הַשְׁכֵּם בַּבֹּקֶר וְהִתְיַצֵּב לִפְנֵי פַרְעֹה הִנֵּה יוֹצֵא הַמָּיְמָה וְאָמַרְתָּ אֵלָיו כֹּה אָמַר יְהוָה שַׁלַּח עַמִּי וְיַעַבְדֻנִי: יז כִּי אִם־אֵינְךָ מְשַׁלֵּחַ אֶת־עַמִּי הִנְנִי מַשְׁלִיחַ בְּךָ וּבַעֲבָדֶיךָ וּבְעַמְּךָ וּבְבָתֶּיךָ אֶת־הֶעָרֹב וּמָלְאוּ בָּתֵּי מִצְרַיִם אֶת־הֶעָרֹב וְגַם הָאֲדָמָה אֲשֶׁר־הֵם עָלֶיהָ: יח וְהִפְלֵיתִי בַיּוֹם הַהוּא אֶת־אֶרֶץ גֹּשֶׁן אֲשֶׁר עַמִּי עֹמֵד עָלֶיהָ לְבִלְתִּי הֱיוֹת־שָׁם עָרֹב לְמַעַן תֵּדַע כִּי אֲנִי יְהוָה בְּקֶרֶב הָאָרֶץ: וְשַׂמְתִּי פְדֻת בֵּין עַמִּי וּבֵין עַמֶּךָ לְמָחָר ששי יִהְיֶה הָאֹת הַזֶּה: כ וַיַּעַשׂ יְהוָה כֵּן וַיָּבֹא עָרֹב כָּבֵד בֵּיתָה פַרְעֹה וּבֵית עֲבָדָיו וּבְכָל־אֶרֶץ מִצְרַיִם תִּשָּׁחֵת הָאָרֶץ מִפְּנֵי הֶעָרֹב:

CLASSIC COMMENTATORS

Although many versions of the Haggada translate ערוב as a mixture of wild animals, and provide graphic pictures to illustrate it, not all of the commentaries agree.

RASHI

A violent mixture of wild beasts, snakes, and scorpions, who set about killing the Egyptians.

רש"י

כל מיני חיות רעות ונחשים ועקרבים בעירבוביא, והיו משחיתים בהם.

RAMBAN

In my opinion this refers to packs of wolves God mustered to attack the Egyptians. The plague is referred to as ערוב because the wolf is a nocturnal hunter [the term ערוב being associated with the word ערב – "evening"]. Thus it is written, "A wolf of the evening shall rob them" (Jer. 5:6), and "Jerusalem's judges are wolves of the evening" (Zeph. 3:3).

רשב"ם

אומר אני כי מיני זאבים הם שנקראים ערוב על שם שדרכם לטרוף בלילות, כדכתיב: זאב ערבות ישדדם (ירמיהו ה ו). וכת': זאבי ערב לא גרמו לבקר (צפניה ג ג).

RABBI DAVID TZVI HOFFMAN

According to one interpretation the ערוב were carnivorous beasts, while another approach sees them as tiny parasites. Now, the second idea appears to be more accurate because Moshe threatens to send the ערוב to afflict the Egyptian people and to invade their houses.

ר' דוד צבי הופמן

חיות טורפות לפי פירוש אחד, טפילים זעירים לפי פירוש אחר. מכיון שנאמר אחר כך שישלחה' הערוב בבני אדם ובבתים, ויהיו הבתים מלאים ערוב, נראה יותר הפירוש השני.

Shemot | Chapter 8   Va'era | 64

> *With the arrival of the* עָרוֹב, *Pharaoh summons Moshe and Aharon and grants them permission to offer sacrifices to their God, but only in Egypt. Moshe insists that they need to go into the wilderness, and Pharaoh agrees, adding a request that they pray on his behalf. Moshe agrees to Pharaoh's request, but adds that Pharaoh needs to stop playing the game of changing his mind about letting the people worship. Moshe prays to God and the plague is removed, but Pharaoh's heart grows heavy again and he does not let them go.*

21 land. Pharaoh called for Moshe and Aharon; "Go," he said, "and sacrifice to your God
22 here in the land." But Moshe replied, "That would not be right for us to do; our sacrifice to the Lord our God is an abomination to the Egyptians. If, before the Egyptians' eyes, we offer the sacrifice they consider an abomination, will they not stone us to death?
23 Send us forth, three days' journey into the wilderness, to sacrifice there to the Lord
24 our God, as He will instruct us." Pharaoh said, "I will send you forth; you shall sacrifice
25 to the Lord your God in the wilderness. Just do not go far away. Pray for me." Moshe said, "I am going to leave you and pray to the Lord. Tomorrow, the swarms of insects will move on from Pharaoh, his officials and his people. But let Pharaoh no more deceive
26 us, refusing to send the people forth to make their sacrifice to the Lord." Moshe left
27 Pharaoh and prayed to the Lord. And the Lord did what Moshe asked. He diverted the swarms of insects from Pharaoh, his officials, his people – not one was left behind.
28 But this time too, Pharaoh hardened his heart and did not send the people forth.

QUESTIONS FOR THOUGHT

- Rashi brings both possibilities of interpreting the verse. Ibn Ezra quotes R. Yeshua, who presents a startling suggestion. What is that suggestion, and what forced him to suggest it?
- Look at verse 22 and notice that the phrase תוֹעֲבַת מִצְרַיִם is used twice. Is it possible that two different meanings are implied in the verse itself?

TEXTUAL SKILLS

1. Pharaoh expresses a hesitant trust in *Benei Yisrael*, allowing them to go but requesting that they not go too far. Where do we see in this passage that Moshe expresses a hesitant trust in Pharaoh?

2. The root ע-ת-ר appears seven times in the Torah, four of which are in this chapter(!) and relate to two of the plagues. Which plagues are those? (The first time it appears is twice in the same verse in Genesis. Can you find it?)

כא וַיִּקְרָ֤א פַרְעֹה֙ אֶל־מֹשֶׁ֣ה וּֽלְאַהֲרֹ֔ן וַיֹּ֕אמֶר לְכ֛וּ זִבְח֥וּ לֵֽאלֹהֵיכֶ֖ם
בָּאָֽרֶץ: כב וַיֹּ֣אמֶר מֹשֶׁ֗ה לֹ֤א נָכוֹן֙ לַֽעֲשׂ֣וֹת כֵּ֔ן כִּ֚י תּֽוֹעֲבַ֣ת מִצְרַ֔יִם
נִזְבַּ֖ח לַיהֹוָ֣ה אֱלֹהֵ֑ינוּ הֵ֣ן נִזְבַּ֞ח אֶת־תּֽוֹעֲבַ֥ת מִצְרַ֛יִם לְעֵֽינֵיהֶ֖ם
וְלֹ֥א יִסְקְלֻֽנוּ: כג דֶּ֚רֶךְ שְׁלֹ֣שֶׁת יָמִ֔ים נֵלֵ֖ךְ בַּמִּדְבָּ֑ר וְזָבַ֨חְנוּ֙ לַֽיהֹוָ֣ה
אֱלֹהֵ֔ינוּ כַּֽאֲשֶׁ֖ר יֹאמַ֥ר אֵלֵֽינוּ: כד וַיֹּ֣אמֶר פַּרְעֹ֗ה אָֽנֹכִ֞י אֲשַׁלַּ֤ח אֶתְכֶם֙
וּזְבַחְתֶּ֞ם לַֽיהֹוָ֤ה אֱלֹֽהֵיכֶם֙ בַּמִּדְבָּ֔ר רַ֛ק הַרְחֵ֥ק לֹֽא־תַרְחִ֖יקוּ לָלֶ֑כֶת
הַעְתִּ֖ירוּ בַּֽעֲדִֽי: כה וַיֹּ֣אמֶר מֹשֶׁ֗ה הִנֵּ֨ה אָֽנֹכִ֜י יוֹצֵ֤א מֵֽעִמָּךְ֙ וְהַעְתַּרְתִּ֣י
אֶל־יְהֹוָ֔ה וְסָ֣ר הֶֽעָרֹ֗ב מִפַּרְעֹ֛ה מֵֽעֲבָדָ֥יו וּמֵֽעַמּ֖וֹ מָחָ֑ר רַ֗ק אַל־
יֹסֵ֤ף פַּרְעֹה֙ הָתֵ֔ל לְבִלְתִּי֙ שַׁלַּ֣ח אֶת־הָעָ֔ם לִזְבֹּ֖חַ לַֽיהֹוָֽה: כו וַיֵּצֵ֥א
מֹשֶׁ֖ה מֵעִ֣ם פַּרְעֹ֑ה וַיֶּעְתַּ֖ר אֶל־יְהֹוָֽה: כז וַיַּ֤עַשׂ יְהֹוָה֙ כִּדְבַ֣ר מֹשֶׁ֔ה
כח וַיָּ֨סַר֙ הֶֽעָרֹ֔ב מִפַּרְעֹ֖ה מֵֽעֲבָדָ֣יו וּמֵֽעַמּ֑וֹ לֹ֥א נִשְׁאַ֖ר אֶחָֽד: וַיַּכְבֵּ֤ד
פַּרְעֹה֙ אֶת־לִבּ֔וֹ גַּ֖ם בַּפַּ֣עַם הַזֹּ֑את וְלֹ֥א שִׁלַּ֖ח אֶת־הָעָֽם:

CLASSIC COMMENTATORS

When Moshe asks to go on a three-day journey, he justifies the request with the rhetorical question: "If, before the Egyptians' eyes, we offer תועבת מצרים, will they not stone us to death?" The phrase תועבת מצרים puzzled many commentaries – does it refer to the Egyptian gods (i.e., the sheep), implying that the Egyptians would not tolerate it if *Benei Yisrael* were to slaughter those gods in front of them, or does it refer to the Egyptian reaction to witnessing *Benei Yisrael* worship?

RASHI

The abomination of Egypt – i.e., the gods of Egypt.
Another way of understanding this phrase is that it would be abominable In the eyes of the Egyptians to witness Israel sacrificing animals that they deem sacred.

רש"י

תועבת מצרים – יראת מצרים...
ועוד יש לומר בלשון אחר: תועבת מצרים – דבר שנאוי הוא למצרים זביחה שאנו זובחים.

IBN EZRA

According to Rabbi Yeshua, Moshe used the word "abomination" in the Torah as a slight to idolatry, but what he really said in his conversation with Pharaoh was "our sacrifice to the L ORD our God is a *god* to the Egyptians."

אבן עזרא

אמר ר' ישועה: כי פירוש תועבת מצרים – משה כתב כן לגנות עבודה זרה, כי לא אמר לפרעה רק "אלהי מצרים".

For the second time, God tells Moshe to go to Pharaoh in his palace and warn him about an upcoming plague. This time the plague is a disease that will kill the Egyptian livestock – sheep, cows, horses, donkeys, and camels – but leave the livestock of Benei Yisrael untouched. The plague comes and Pharaoh's investigation reveals that indeed, nothing happened to the livestock of Benei Yisrael, but his heart was heavy and he refused to send out Benei Yisrael.

9 1 Then the LORD said to Moshe, "Go to Pharaoh. Tell him: This is what the LORD, God 2 of the Hebrews, says: Send My people forth to serve Me. If you refuse to send them 3 forth, if you continue to hold them back, the LORD's hand will turn against your livestock in the field. A deadly epidemic will strike horses, donkeys, and camels, cattle and 4 flocks. But the LORD will set Israel's livestock apart from Egypt's; none belonging to the 5 Israelites will die. The LORD has set His appointed time; tomorrow the LORD will bring 6 this about in the land." And the next day, the LORD brought it to be. All the livestock of 7 the Egyptians perished, but of the Israelites' livestock, not one creature died. Pharaoh investigated the matter and discovered that not one among Israel's livestock had died. But still Pharaoh's heart remained hard, and he would not send the people forth.

QUESTIONS FOR THOUGHT

- According to Bekhor Shor, what is the significance of the fact that the livestock are in the field?
- Ramban offers two insights. In the first, he claims that there is no significance to the livestock being in the field – that's simply where livestock usually spend time. But then he offers an additional possibility, in which the livestock being in the field is a very important part of description because it sharpens the impact of what happens afterward. What is the insight he offers?

TEXTUAL SKILLS

1. Look carefully at verse 3, where the Torah describes what God will do to the Egyptians. Find two adjacent words in which the second one is a play on the first.

2. This plague is called דֶּבֶר. When the Torah describes that the livestock of *Benei Yisrael* will be left untouched, it uses a word which is a play on this. Find it!

WISDOM OF THE HEART

Ultimately, *Benei Yisrael* leave Egypt and cross the Sea of Reeds to freedom. The joy of liberation is mixed with the fear of the unknown; the closing of the sea behind them serves as a powerful symbol that there is no turning back. What do they do now?

Freedom is not the ultimate goal, but an important means to attaining that goal. God's message to Pharaoh is not merely "Let My people go," but "Let My people go so that they may serve Me." True freedom is not merely a freedom to escape from, but a freedom that enables us to pursue what we really want to do – and in the case of *Benei Yisrael*, freedom to worship God.

As part of healthy maturation we leave our parents' homes to pursue our own lives. That step can be both terrifying and exhilarating. What will you pursue when granted that freedom?

שמות | פרק ט

א וַיֹּאמֶר יְהוָה אֶל־מֹשֶׁה בֹּא אֶל־פַּרְעֹה וְדִבַּרְתָּ אֵלָיו כֹּה־אָמַר
ב יְהוָה אֱלֹהֵי הָעִבְרִים שַׁלַּח אֶת־עַמִּי וְיַעַבְדֻנִי: כִּי אִם־מָאֵן
ג אַתָּה לְשַׁלֵּחַ וְעוֹדְךָ מַחֲזִיק בָּם: הִנֵּה יַד־יְהוָה הוֹיָה בְּמִקְנְךָ
  אֲשֶׁר בַּשָּׂדֶה בַּסּוּסִים בַּחֲמֹרִים בַּגְּמַלִּים בַּבָּקָר וּבַצֹּאן דֶּבֶר
ד כָּבֵד מְאֹד: וְהִפְלָה יְהוָה בֵּין מִקְנֵה יִשְׂרָאֵל וּבֵין מִקְנֵה מִצְרָיִם
ה וְלֹא יָמוּת מִכָּל־לִבְנֵי יִשְׂרָאֵל דָּבָר: וַיָּשֶׂם יְהוָה מוֹעֵד לֵאמֹר
  מָחָר יַעֲשֶׂה יְהוָה הַדָּבָר הַזֶּה בָּאָרֶץ: וַיַּעַשׂ יְהוָֹה אֶת־הַדָּבָר
ו הַזֶּה מִמָּחֳרָת וַיָּמָת כֹּל מִקְנֵה מִצְרָיִם וּמִמִּקְנֵה בְנֵי־יִשְׂרָאֵל
ז לֹא־מֵת אֶחָד: וַיִּשְׁלַח פַּרְעֹה וְהִנֵּה לֹא־מֵת מִמִּקְנֵה יִשְׂרָאֵל
  עַד־אֶחָד וַיִּכְבַּד לֵב פַּרְעֹה וְלֹא שִׁלַּח אֶת־הָעָם:

CLASSIC COMMENTATORS

Moshe warns Pharaoh that the "livestock in the field" will be killed with the plague of דבר. Is there any significance to the identification of the livestock being in the field?

RABBI YOSEF BEKHOR SHOR
The victims of this fifth plague had survived the onslaught of the swarms by hiding in towers and fortresses during that attack. But now there would be no escape from the cattle plague, which was airborne.

ר׳ יוסף בכור שור
מן הערוב הייתה ניצול במגדלים ובמבצרים, אבל עתה לא תוכל להציל בהמתך מן הדבר, שהוא בידי שמים.

RAMBAN
The warning was issued regarding the livestock in the field because that is where most herds are located. Even so, the plague also struck beasts which the Egyptians sequestered inside their homes.

Now, it is likely that because "every shepherd is an abomination to Egypt" (Genesis 46:34), the people removed these beasts from their cities, save those horses they maintained for riding and donkeys they used to transport goods. What emerged was that most of the cattle were distant from Egypt proper, and were led to graze in pastures bordering the area of Goshen. Consequently, the animals belonging to Egyptians mixed with those owned by Israelites, necessitating Moshe's declaration: "The Lord will set Israel's livestock apart from Egypt's" (9:4).

רמב"ן
התרה אותם בהווה, כי רוב המקנה בשדה, אבל היה הדבר גם במקנה אשר בבית
ויתכן כי בעבור היות תועבה למצרים כל רועה צאן היו מפרישים אותם מן הערים, בלתי בעת השתמשם בסוסים לרכוב ובחמורים במשא, והנה היה המקנה רחוק ממצרים בשדה גבול גשן, ויתערב במקום המרעה מקנה מצרים ומקנה ישראל, ועל כן הוצרך לומר והפלה ה׳ בין מקנה מצרים ובין מקנה ישראל.

God instructs Moshe and Aharon to each take a fistful of soot (but no staff!) and, in front of Pharaoh, throw it heavenward. That dust-like soot will spread throughout Egypt and cause boils on the skin of people and domesticated animals. Moshe and Aharon do as told, and the boils affect the people and animals – even Pharaoh's sorcerers cannot stand before Moshe.

8 Then the LORD said to Moshe and Aharon, "Take a handful of soot from a furnace
9 and throw it up in the air before Pharaoh's eyes. It will become a cloud of dust over all the land of Egypt, and on people and animals it will become a rash, breaking out into
10 boils on people and animals throughout the land of Egypt." So they took soot from the furnace and stood before Pharaoh. Moshe threw it up in the air, and it became a rash
11 that broke into boils on people and animals. The magicians could not stand before Moshe because of their boils; for the boils had affected them as they had the rest of the
12 Egyptians. But the LORD strengthened Pharaoh's heart, and he would not listen to them,

---

QUESTIONS FOR THOUGHT

- Rabbi David Tzvi Hoffman and Meshekh Ḥokhma seem to agree that the sorcerers were able to replicate the ערוב and the דבר, even though the Torah doesn't mention it. According to Meshekh Ḥokhma, what were the sorcerers trying to do in this particular plague, which ultimately left them humiliated?
- The conclusion of this plague is the first time that the Torah describes God as making Pharaoh obstinate (until now Pharaoh did it himself). Which of the commentaries suggests why it was necessary for God to do it this time?

TEXTUAL SKILLS

1. Aharon brought the first three plagues with his staff. Who brings the second three?
2. This plague can be described as blisters resulting from a burn. Notice what is used to bring those blisters.

QUICK BITE

- Moshe and Aharon perform wondrous feats, as do Pharaoh's sorcerers. Rav Yaakov Kamenetsky explains that the same forces that can be used for positive purposes can be used for negative purposes. The same is true with each and every one of us. We all have talents, character traits, and power deep in our souls. We can choose to use these same powers to do good or evil – in fact, without the capacity for bad, the good is meaningless. The concept of free will means that ultimately, the choice of how to use our capabilities is in our hands.

ח וַיֹּ֣אמֶר יְהֹוָה֮ אֶל־מֹשֶׁ֣ה וְאֶֽל־אַהֲרֹן֒ קְח֤וּ לָכֶם֙ מְלֹ֣א חָפְנֵיכֶ֔ם פִּ֖יחַ
ט כִּבְשָׁ֑ן וּזְרָק֥וֹ מֹשֶׁ֛ה הַשָּׁמַ֖יְמָה לְעֵינֵ֥י פַרְעֹֽה: וְהָיָ֣ה לְאָבָ֔ק עַ֖ל
כָּל־אֶ֣רֶץ מִצְרָ֑יִם וְהָיָ֨ה עַל־הָאָדָ֜ם וְעַל־הַבְּהֵמָ֗ה לִשְׁחִ֥ין פֹּרֵ֛חַ
י אֲבַעְבֻּעֹ֖ת בְּכָל־אֶ֥רֶץ מִצְרָֽיִם: וַיִּקְח֞וּ אֶת־פִּ֣יחַ הַכִּבְשָׁ֗ן וַיַּֽעַמְדוּ֙
לִפְנֵ֣י פַרְעֹ֔ה וַיִּזְרֹ֥ק אֹת֛וֹ מֹשֶׁ֖ה הַשָּׁמָ֑יְמָה וַיְהִ֕י שְׁחִין֙ אֲבַעְבֻּעֹ֔ת
יא פֹּרֵ֔חַ בָּאָדָ֖ם וּבַבְּהֵמָֽה: וְלֹֽא־יָכְל֣וּ הַֽחַרְטֻמִּ֗ים לַעֲמֹ֛ד לִפְנֵ֥י מֹשֶׁ֖ה
מִפְּנֵ֣י הַשְּׁחִ֑ין כִּֽי־הָיָ֣ה הַשְּׁחִ֔ין בַּֽחֲרְטֻמִּ֖ם וּבְכָל־מִצְרָֽיִם: וַיְחַזֵּ֤ק
יב יְהֹוָה֙ אֶת־לֵ֣ב פַּרְעֹ֔ה וְלֹ֥א שָׁמַ֖ע אֲלֵהֶ֑ם כַּאֲשֶׁ֛ר דִּבֶּ֥ר יְהֹוָ֖ה אֶל־

CLASSIC COMMENTATORS

Pharaoh's sorcerers, who were so prominent before and through the first three plagues, have not been mentioned since they acknowledged to Pharaoh that the lice were the "finger of God." They reappear for the last time in this plague but with an odd twist – they cannot stand before Moshe. What made this plague unique so that it effectively finished them off as important actors in the story?

RAMBAN

It is possible that during the initial plagues Pharaoh's sorcerers supported their king and encouraged his recalcitrance… Their absence at this point suggests that there was nobody to help the monarch.

רמב"ן

ויתכן שבמכות הראשונות היו החרטומים מחזיקים את לבו … ועתה לא באו לפניו, ואין עוזר לו.

RABBI DAVID TZVI HOFFMAN

Once again Pharaoh demanded that his sorcerers mimic the miracle that the Hebrews had perpetrated, but saw that his servants could not even stand before Moshe since they too had been stricken with the boils. This circumstance really should have convinced the king to revere God… Nevertheless, the text reports that "the Lord strengthened Pharaoh's heart and he would not listen to them." What this means is that the Lord strengthened Pharaoh's heart in order to make him fearless of God.

ר' דוד צבי הופמן

שוב ביקש פרעה שגם חרטומיו יעשו כנס הזה, אלא שהם אפילו לא יכלו לעמוד לפני משה, מפני שגם הם עצמם לקו במכה זו. דבר זה צריך היה להביא את פרעה ליראה את האלהים – … ואולם, "ויחזק ה' את-לב פרעה ולא שמע אליהם", ה' חיזק את לבו כך, ששום יראה לא תחדור בו.

MESHEKH ḤOKHMA

Pharaoh's henchmen were unable to afflict Moshe with boils and were ashamed at their failure. It was an additional degradation to them that they were the plague's initial victims.

משך חכמה

לא יכלו להפוך בשרו [של משה] לשחין ולכן נכלמו מפניו מאד ואדרבא מהם התחילה מכת השחין.

13 just as the Lord had told Moshe. Then the Lord said to Moshe, "Rise up early in the morning and confront Pharaoh. Tell him: This is what the Lord, God of the Hebrews,
14 says: Send My people forth to serve Me, or this time I will set the full force of My plagues upon you, your officials, and your people so that you will know that there is none like
15 Me in all the world. By now I could have stretched out My hand and struck you and your
16 people with an epidemic that would have wiped you off the face of the earth. But I have let you survive for this purpose – to show you My power, and to have My name known
17 throughout the land. You are still abusing your power over My people, refusing to let
18 them go. And so this time tomorrow I will bring a hail storm on Egypt heavier than any
19 it has suffered, from the day Egypt was established until now. Give an order now to bring in your livestock and all else you have in the field. Anyone or any animal in the open,
20 any not brought under shelter, will die when the hail beats down." Those of Pharaoh's
21 officials who feared the Lord's word hurried to bring in their slaves and livestock. And those who set no stock by the Lord's word kept their slaves and livestock where they

---

MALBIM

Moshe informed Pharaoh that this would begin the third set of plagues to be inflicted on him.

מלבי״ם

הודיע לו שזה הסדר השלישי של המכות שיביא עליו.

QUESTIONS FOR THOUGHT

- Which commentary understands that the hail is more terrifying psychologically, but not in terms of the actual damage it will inflict?
- Which commentary suggests that the plague of hail is truly more devastating than any of the prior ones – in fact, as devastating as many of the previous ones combined?
- In what way is Malbim's explanation completely different from the other two?

TEXTUAL SKILLS

1. This plague is the beginning of the third set of three plagues. What is its purpose, and how is that different from the purposes of the first two sets?
2. While this passage is focused on the hail, it teaches something about an earlier plague. Which plague is that, and what does it teach us about it?
3. God suggests to Pharaoh: שלח העז את מקנך, "Bring in your livestock" to safety. The word העז, meaning "bring to safety," appears only here in all of the Torah (and only four other times in the rest of Tanakh). Find a "punny" reason that the Torah chooses to use that word here.

שמות | פרק ט

יג וַיֹּאמֶר יהוה אֶל־מֹשֶׁה הַשְׁכֵּם בַּבֹּקֶר וְהִתְיַצֵּב לִפְנֵי פַרְעֹה וְאָמַרְתָּ אֵלָיו כֹּה־אָמַר יהוה אֱלֹהֵי הָעִבְרִים שַׁלַּח אֶת־עַמִּי וְיַעַבְדֻנִי: יד כִּי ׀ בַּפַּעַם הַזֹּאת אֲנִי שֹׁלֵחַ אֶת־כָּל־מַגֵּפֹתַי אֶל־לִבְּךָ וּבַעֲבָדֶיךָ וּבְעַמֶּךָ בַּעֲבוּר תֵּדַע כִּי אֵין כָּמֹנִי בְּכָל־הָאָרֶץ: טו כִּי עַתָּה שָׁלַחְתִּי אֶת־יָדִי וָאַךְ אוֹתְךָ וְאֶת־עַמְּךָ בַּדָּבֶר וַתִּכָּחֵד מִן־הָאָרֶץ: טז וְאוּלָם בַּעֲבוּר זֹאת הֶעֱמַדְתִּיךָ בַּעֲבוּר הַרְאֹתְךָ אֶת־כֹּחִי וּלְמַעַן סַפֵּר שְׁמִי בְּכָל־הָאָרֶץ: יז עוֹדְךָ מִסְתּוֹלֵל בְּעַמִּי לְבִלְתִּי שַׁלְּחָם: יח הִנְנִי מַמְטִיר כָּעֵת מָחָר בָּרָד כָּבֵד מְאֹד אֲשֶׁר לֹא־הָיָה כָמֹהוּ בְּמִצְרַיִם לְמִן־הַיּוֹם הִוָּסְדָה וְעַד־עָתָּה: יט וְעַתָּה שְׁלַח הָעֵז אֶת־מִקְנְךָ וְאֵת כָּל־אֲשֶׁר לְךָ בַּשָּׂדֶה כָּל־הָאָדָם וְהַבְּהֵמָה אֲשֶׁר־יִמָּצֵא בַשָּׂדֶה וְלֹא יֵאָסֵף הַבַּיְתָה וְיָרַד עֲלֵהֶם הַבָּרָד וָמֵתוּ: כ הַיָּרֵא אֶת־דְּבַר יהוה מֵעַבְדֵי פַּרְעֹה הֵנִיס אֶת־עֲבָדָיו וְאֶת־מִקְנֵהוּ אֶל־הַבָּתִּים: כא וַאֲשֶׁר לֹא־שָׂם לִבּוֹ אֶל־דְּבַר יהוה וַיַּעֲזֹב אֶת־עֲבָדָיו וְאֶת־מִקְנֵהוּ בַּשָּׂדֶה:

שביעי

CLASSIC COMMENTATORS

In introducing the hail, God instructs Moshe to warn Pharaoh that this time He will send "the full force of My plagues" to afflict Egypt. What is it about the hail that God indicates will be so terrifying for Egypt?

IBN EZRA
The term מַגֵּפֹתַי ["My plagues"] appears in the plural because God was planning to unleash a punishing mixture of thunder, hail, rain, and fire.

אבן עזרא
הזכיר מגפותי בעבור הקולות והברד והמטר והאש שהתחברו

RABBI AVRAHAM BEN HARAMBAM
This plague struck different elements within the country, and was to rain destruction upon flora and fauna alike, decimating animals and people indiscriminately. For while the *arov* attacked the Egyptian populace, the *dever* plague wiped out the livestock, and the locusts were to devour the vegetation, the hail was to target all three groups – humans, cattle, and produce.

ר' אברהם בן הרמב"ם
במכה זו נאספו יחד הנפרדים בזולתה וזה כי היא השחיתה את הצמח ואת החי שאינו מדבר ואת המדבר הערוב השחית את בני האדם והדבר איבד את החי שאינו מדבר והברד איבד את שניהם והארבה איבד את הצמח כמבואר והברד [גם כן כמו שאמר בברד] ואת כל עץ השדה שבר.

Shemot | Chapter 9   va'era | 72

> *God instructs Moshe, who waves his staff toward the sky to begin the hail. The hail, which impacted people, animals, and plants and was unusually intense, was accompanied by thunder and lightning. Even more terrifying was that fires blazed amidst the hailstones.*
> *But the land of Goshen, where Benei Yisrael lived, was spared.*

22 were in the fields. The Lord said to Moshe, "Reach your hand out to the sky, that hail may fall on all the land of Egypt, on the people and the animals and everything growing
23 in Egypt's fields." Moshe raised his staff toward the sky: the Lord sent thunderclaps and hail. Fire struck the ground, and the Lord rained down hail on the land of Egypt.
24 The hail, with fire blazing inside it, battered so hard that there had been nothing like it
25 anywhere in Egypt since it first became a nation. The hail struck everything in the open field throughout all Egypt: people, animals and everything growing in the fields, and
26 it smashed asunder every tree. Only in Goshen, where the Israelites lived, no hail fell.

QUESTIONS FOR THOUGHT

- In the warning about the hail, no fire was mentioned, and it seems like the hail alone did enormous damage. According to the different commentaries, why did God add fire to the hail?
- Which of the commentaries try to explain the fire as an expression of an even greater miracle? Which try to minimize the miracle?
- Which of the commentaries seems to suggest that fire and ice have free will?

TEXTUAL SKILLS

1. Notice the similarities between the way the hail is described in verses 24–25 and the descriptions in Genesis 19:24–25 and 7:21–23. Notice also that in each, someone is spared.
2. Both in the warning (v. 18) and in describing the actual plague (v. 24), the Torah indicates that this hail was unlike any other hail which ever befell Egypt. There is only one other plague which the Torah describes similarly. Find it!

QUICK BITE

This hail was quite amazing. Besides beng a fusion of fire and ice, it had another incredible quality: A few verses later, Pharaoh summons Moshe and Aharon and confesses to having sinned. He promises to let them go. So Moshe leaves the city and prays to God, and then: "The thunder and hail stopped, the rain did not pound the earth any more." Rashi explains that even those hailstones that were already falling were suspended in the air and never reached the ground. What was the significance of this miracle? The Lubavitcher Rebbe argues that it wasn't really a miracle in the classic sense. It was our world obeying God's spiritual principles. The moment that Pharoah acknowledged that he had sinned – the power of his *teshuva* stopped the hail. It no longer had any reason to destroy.

כב וַיֹּ֨אמֶר יְהֹוָ֜ה אֶל־מֹשֶׁ֗ה נְטֵ֤ה אֶת־יָֽדְךָ֙ עַל־הַשָּׁמַ֔יִם וִיהִ֥י בָרָ֖ד בְּכָל־אֶ֣רֶץ מִצְרָ֑יִם עַל־הָֽאָדָ֣ם וְעַל־הַבְּהֵמָ֗ה וְעַ֛ל כָּל־עֵ֥שֶׂב הַשָּׂדֶ֖ה בְּאֶ֥רֶץ מִצְרָֽיִם׃

כג וַיֵּ֨ט מֹשֶׁ֣ה אֶת־מַטֵּהוּ֮ עַל־הַשָּׁמַיִם֒ וַֽיהֹוָ֗ה נָתַ֤ן קֹלֹת֙ וּבָרָ֔ד וַתִּ֥הֲלַךְ אֵ֖שׁ אָ֑רְצָה וַיַּמְטֵ֧ר יְהֹוָ֛ה בָּרָ֖ד עַל־אֶ֥רֶץ מִצְרָֽיִם׃

כד וַיְהִ֣י בָרָ֔ד וְאֵ֕שׁ מִתְלַקַּ֖חַת בְּת֣וֹךְ הַבָּרָ֑ד כָּבֵ֣ד מְאֹ֔ד אֲ֠שֶׁ֠ר לֹֽא־הָיָ֤ה כָמֹ֙הוּ֙ בְּכָל־אֶ֣רֶץ מִצְרַ֔יִם מֵאָ֖ז הָיְתָ֥ה לְגֽוֹי׃

כה וַיַּ֨ךְ הַבָּרָ֜ד בְּכָל־אֶ֣רֶץ מִצְרַ֗יִם אֵ֚ת כָּל־אֲשֶׁ֣ר בַּשָּׂדֶ֔ה מֵאָדָ֖ם וְעַד־בְּהֵמָ֑ה וְאֵ֨ת כָּל־עֵ֤שֶׂב הַשָּׂדֶה֙ הִכָּ֣ה הַבָּרָ֔ד וְאֶת־כָּל־עֵ֥ץ הַשָּׂדֶ֖ה שִׁבֵּֽר׃

כו רַ֚ק בְּאֶ֣רֶץ גֹּ֔שֶׁן אֲשֶׁר־שָׁ֖ם בְּנֵ֣י יִשְׂרָאֵ֑ל לֹ֥א הָיָ֖ה בָּרָֽד׃

CLASSIC COMMENTATORS

The fires blazing amidst the hailstones drew great attention from the commentaries.

RASHI
רש"י

The mixture of fire and hail represented a miracle within a miracle. Because although hail is made of water, now, the two elements made peace and banded together to carry out the will of their Creator.

נס בתוך נס, האש והברד מעורבין, והברד מים הוא. ולעשות רצון קונם עשו שלום ביניהם.

RABBI AVRAHAM BEN HARAMBAM
ר' אברהם בן הרמב"ם

The hail represented a miracle within a miracle – for fire was blazing within a housing of water! These ice and fire balls, which torpedoed the earth like rocks from the sky, exploded upon impact. And when these missiles smashed into their targets, their fire burst forth and set alight the shattered remnants of what the hail had just broken.

נס בתוך נס אש שורפת בתוך מים מוגבשים כאבנים יורדת אבן הברד מן השמים מנפצת בחוזק ובעת ניפוצה היא נשברת ונקדחת ממנה אש לוהטת ושורפת ובכן שיבר הברד ושרפה האש את מה שנשבר.

MALBIM
מלבי"ם

Under normal conditions the lightning accompanying the storm would have struck the earth before the hail, since electricity travels faster than ice pellets. However, in the current plague, the hail fell with the fire burning inside of it, and hence both elements struck simultaneously.

היה ראוי שיקדים האש העלעקטרי קודם הברד כי הוא ממהר בהליכתו מן הברד, בכ"ז בכאן היה אש מתלקחת ... וירד עמו בשוה מבלי קדימת זמן.

RABBI SAMSON RAPHAEL HIRSCH
ר' שמשון רפאל הירש

The fire did not affect anything outside of itself, for otherwise it would have melted the hail.

האש נשארה מכונסת בעצמה בתוך סערת הברד; אם לא כן היה הברד נמס.

27 Then Pharaoh sent for Moshe and Aharon and said to them, "This time I have sinned.
28 The Lord is in the right, and I and my people are guilty. Pray to the Lord. Enough of
29 God's thunder and hail – I will send you forth. You need not wait any longer." Moshe said to him, "As I leave the city, I will spread out my hands to the Lord. The thunder will stop and there will be no more hail. You will then know that the world belongs to the
30/31 Lord. But I know that you and your officials still do not hold the Lord God in awe." By then the flax and barley had been destroyed, because the barley was ripe and the flax in
32/33 bud. But the wheat and spelt had not been destroyed, because they ripen later. Moshe left Pharaoh and the city and spread out his hands to the Lord. The thunder and hail
34 stopped, the rain did not pound the earth any more. But when Pharaoh saw that the rain, hail and thunder had stopped, he once more turned to sinfulness. He hardened
35 his heart; his officials likewise. Pharaoh's heart was strengthened and he refused to send the Israelites forth, just as the Lord had predicted at Moshe's hand.

ר' דוד צבי הופמן

פסוקינו נחוצים כדי להבין, מניין היה לו לארבה מה להשחית, ולכאורה היה מקומם בסוף הפרשה, אחר פסוק לה. אלא שהתורה ביקשה לקשור את עיקשותו של פרעה עם דברי ה' בראשית פרק י, משום ששם מוסברת עיקשות זו.

RABBI DAVID TZVI HOFFMAN

The verse describing which crops were destroyed by the hail and which survived is necessary in order to explain what vegetation remained for the locusts to devour when they arrived. Indeed, it seems that this information should have been provided at the end of the current passage, following verse 35. However, the Torah wished to juxtapose Pharaoh's stubbornness as expressed at the end of our chapter with the Lord's pronouncement at the start of chapter 10. In those opening verses God makes reference to the king's obstinacy.

QUESTIONS FOR THOUGHT

- Which of the commentaries understands that the Torah's information helps us figure out what time of year this plague occurred?
- According to Ramban, the information about the plants is not what the Torah is telling us, but part of what Moshe is telling Pharaoh. How does this help Ramban understand the flow of the verses?
- According to Rabbi David Tzvi Hoffman, this information belongs at the end of the chapter. Why is this information necessary? Why is it not at the end of the chapter?
- Can you find a hidden message in Moshe's words to Pharaoh about the destruction of the inflexible plants and the survival of those which can bend?

TEXTUAL SKILLS

1. For the first time, Moshe says that he needs to do something before praying on Pharaoh's behalf. What is it?
2. Notice that Pharaoh says two things to Moshe: (A) who is righteous and who is wrong; (B) a request for Moshe to pray. Moshe responds to both of those, but in reverse order: A-B-B-A. Notice also that in part A, Pharaoh says one thing about the Egyptians and another about God. What does Moshe say about Pharaoh's two claims?
3. Pharaoh speaks about צדיק and רשע. Who introduces those two terms as a pair into the Torah?

כז וַיִּשְׁלַ֣ח פַּרְעֹ֗ה וַיִּקְרָא֙ לְמֹשֶׁ֣ה וּלְאַהֲרֹ֔ן וַיֹּ֥אמֶר אֲלֵהֶ֖ם חָטָ֣אתִי
כח הַפָּ֑עַם יְהוָה֙ הַצַּדִּ֔יק וַאֲנִ֥י וְעַמִּ֖י הָרְשָׁעִֽים: הַעְתִּ֙ירוּ֙ אֶל־יְהוָ֔ה
וְרַ֕ב מִֽהְיֹ֛ת קֹלֹ֥ת אֱלֹהִ֖ים וּבָרָ֑ד וַאֲשַׁלְּחָ֣ה אֶתְכֶ֔ם וְלֹ֥א תֹסִפ֖וּן
כט לַעֲמֹֽד: וַיֹּ֤אמֶר אֵלָיו֙ מֹשֶׁ֔ה כְּצֵאתִי֙ אֶת־הָעִ֔יר אֶפְרֹ֥שׂ אֶת־כַּפַּ֖י
אֶל־יְהוָ֑ה הַקֹּל֣וֹת יֶחְדָּל֗וּן וְהַבָּרָד֙ לֹ֣א יִֽהְיֶה־ע֔וֹד לְמַ֣עַן תֵּדַ֔ע
ל כִּ֥י לַיהוָ֖ה הָאָֽרֶץ: וְאַתָּ֖ה וַעֲבָדֶ֑יךָ יָדַ֕עְתִּי כִּ֚י טֶ֣רֶם תִּֽירְא֔וּן מִפְּנֵ֖י
לא יְהוָ֥ה אֱלֹהִֽים: וְהַפִּשְׁתָּ֥ה וְהַשְּׂעֹרָ֖ה נֻכָּ֑תָה כִּ֤י הַשְּׂעֹרָה֙ אָבִ֔יב
לב וְהַפִּשְׁתָּ֖ה גִּבְעֹֽל: וְהַחִטָּ֥ה וְהַכֻּסֶּ֖מֶת לֹ֣א נֻכּ֑וּ כִּ֥י אֲפִילֹ֖ת הֵֽנָּה:
לג וַיֵּצֵ֨א מֹשֶׁ֜ה מֵעִ֤ם פַּרְעֹה֙ אֶת־הָעִ֔יר וַיִּפְרֹ֥שׂ כַּפָּ֖יו אֶל־יְהוָ֑ה וַֽיַּחְדְּל֤וּ מפטיר
הַקֹּלוֹת֙ וְהַבָּרָ֔ד וּמָטָ֖ר לֹא־נִתַּ֥ךְ אָֽרְצָה:
לד וַיַּ֣רְא פַּרְעֹ֗ה כִּֽי־חָדַ֨ל
הַמָּטָ֧ר וְהַבָּרָ֛ד וְהַקֹּלֹ֖ת וַיֹּ֣סֶף לַחֲטֹ֑א וַיַּכְבֵּ֥ד לִבּ֖וֹ ה֥וּא וַעֲבָדָֽיו:
לה וַֽיֶּחֱזַק֙ לֵ֣ב פַּרְעֹ֔ה וְלֹ֥א שִׁלַּ֖ח אֶת־בְּנֵ֣י יִשְׂרָאֵ֑ל כַּאֲשֶׁ֛ר דִּבֶּ֥ר יְהוָ֖ה
בְּיַד־מֹשֶֽׁה:

CLASSIC COMMENTATORS

Seemingly out of nowhere, the Torah describes the damage to the flax and the barley, distinguishing them from the wheat and the spelt, which were not affected by the hail. Why is that description meaningful?

RAMBAN
In my opinion this is in fact part of Moshe's speech to Pharaoh, as follows: I know that although you always fear God somewhat before the plagues are removed, after the relief is granted you revert to your foolish ways. But recognize that even though the wheat and spelt have not yet been destroyed, leaving you with food to carry on, still, should you sin again, it is no matter for God to eradicate those grains as well.

RABBI YOSEF IBN KASPI
By reporting the effects of the hail storm, the Torah informs us that the plague took place in the month of Adar or close to it. That season represents the harvest time for barley in Egypt, whose agriculture is primarily wheat–based.

רמב״ן
ועל דעתי: שהם דברי משה אל פרעה, שאמר להם ידעתי כי טרם סור המכות תיראון, ואחרי כן תשנו באולתכם, אבל הפשתה והשעורה נכתה והחטה והכסמת – שהן לכל חיתכם לא נכו במכה הזאת, והן ביד האלהים לאבד אותם מכם אם תשובו ותחטאו לפניו.

ר׳ יוסף אבן כספי
ספרה התורה מה שאירע, א״כ זאת המכה היתה קרוב לאדר או באדר, כי אז הוא אביב לקציר שעורים במצרים שהיא ארץ חטה.

MORE QUICK BITES

- **6:12** The Jerusalem Talmud suggests that while *Benei Yisrael* were still slaves in Egypt, Moshe taught them the mitzva to free slaves in the seventh year. Rav Mordechai Weinberg suggests that this was the perfect time for them to study this mitzva. As slaves, they would understand the value of freedom and the compassion necessary to allow one to let their servants go.

- **9:2** Commenting on Psalms 37:10, Rabbi Moshe Leib of Sassov suggests that even the most evil of people has a core of goodness – an עוֹד – buried deep down inside. If the evil person seeks and finds that hidden core, he will discover that he is not evil at all.

The Nikolsburg Rebbe suggests that this is the essence of Moshe's comment to Pharaoh (9:2): "You are trying to hold onto the עוֹד of my people" – you are trying to tear the goodness of the people away from God. But you will never be successful – God will afflict you until you release them!

EXPLORING HASHKAFA
Arguing with God

God commands; we are obligated to follow. Should we choose not to follow, we bear the responsibility for the consequences. This is one of the foundational principles in Judaism. He is the Creator and we are bound by His instructions; He established a covenant with us and we are obligated to adhere to it.

On the flip side, we find some of our most important figures challenging God, His decisions, and His actions. Most famously, Avraham confronts God over the destruction of Sedom, and Moshe argues with God from the meeting at the burning bush until just before his death. Many others argue with God as well – Yehoshua does so after the defeat at the Ai; Ḥavakuk (1:13) challenges God on standing by while the wicked devour the righteous; Yona challenges God's justice; not to mention Iyov, whose entire book questions God. Rabbi Joseph B. Soloveitchik regularly pointed to Yirmiyahu, who in the book of Lamentations opens the floodgates of challenge and becomes the paradigm for the *kinnot* of Tisha BeAv. And, of course, there are the many figures from the Talmud and throughout history, up to our contemporary era.

Some people are surprised by God's tolerance of this insolent behavior. Isn't God the Supreme Being? Shouldn't we be fearful of speaking so brazenly?

Apparently, not only does God tolerate this behavior, He welcomes it and even invites it. When God tells Avraham about the impending destruction of Sedom, He is inviting Avraham to intervene. When He informs Moshe of His intent to destroy *Benei Yisrael* after the sins of the Golden Calf and of the spies, He is opening the door for Moshe's vigorous defense of the people. When it comes to explicit commands, God expects us to follow. Beyond that, however, He hopes that as His chosen partners we will stand up for the core values of justice and righteousness, no matter who is on the other end. In doing so, we offer the greatest possible tribute to God.

PARASHAT BO

> "And now the end is near, and so I face the final curtain."
> Frank Sinatra

The end is in sight. Seven plagues in and Pharaoh isn't broken, but the cracks in his resolve are appearing. It seems that without being artificially propped up by divine support, he would fall much quicker. Moshe senses Pharaoh's weakness and becomes emboldened, asking for more, and then even more, leading up to a final showdown. The tension builds. Will *Benei Yisrael* leave? Will they return? What surprises await?

PARASHAT BO

10 1 Then the Lord said to Moshe, "Go to Pharaoh. I have hardened his heart and his offi-
2 cials', that I may display these My signs before him, and so that you may tell your children
and grandchildren how I made the Egyptians a laughing stock by the signs I revealed
3 among them; and know that I am the Lord." Moshe and Aharon came to Pharaoh and
said to him, "Thus says the Lord, God of the Hebrews: How much longer will you
4 refuse to submit to Me? Send My people forth to serve Me. For if you refuse to send
5 My people forth, tomorrow I bring locusts to your land. They will cover the landscape
so that you will not be able to see the ground. They will eat what little remains after the
6 hail, including all the trees that grow up from your soil. They will fill your palaces, your
officials' houses and all the houses of Egypt. Your parents and grandparents never saw
anything like this, from the day they arrived upon this earth until today." Then Moshe
7 turned and left Pharaoh. Pharaoh's officials then said to him, "How long must we leave
this man to ensnare us? Send the people forth to serve the Lord their God. Do you not
8 yet know that Egypt is being destroyed?" Moshe and Aharon were summoned back to
Pharaoh, and he said to them, "Go and serve the Lord your God. Who exactly will be
9 going?" "With our youths and our elderly folk we will go," said Moshe, "with our sons
and our daughters, our sheep and our cattle, we all must go, for it will be our festival of
10 the Lord." He replied, "The Lord be with you if I let you and your children go! Look –
11 evil is staring you in the face. No! Let the men go and serve the Lord. That is what you

---

RASHI
התעללתי means "I have toyed with him."

RABBI SAMSON RAPHAEL HIRSCH
The term **התעלל** connotes a step-by-step progression through which a goal is achieved. Meanwhile, the addition of the prefix letter **ב**, as in the phrase **התעללתי ב-**, suggests the usage of an individual as a passive object upon which those series of actions are forced in order to accomplish the actor's purpose.

RABBI DAVID TZVI HOFFMAN
התעללתי means "I have performed great feats."

רש"י
התעללתי - שיחקתי.

ר' שמשון רפאל הירש
"התעלל": להתגלות על ידי סידרת פעולות הולכת ומתקדמת. "להתעלל ב-" פירושו: להראות את כוחו וכדומה דרך אדם המשמש לו כחומר גרידא, על ידי סידרת פעולות או מעשים הולכת ומתקדמת.

ר' דוד צבי הופמן
התעללתי - עשיתי מעשים גדולים.

QUESTIONS FOR THOUGHT

- The explanation offered by Rashi describes God's actions as intended to mock or humiliate Egypt. Do you think that God's intentions were truly to mock and humiliate Egypt, or is that simply the way He understands that the story will be told to future generations?
- In modern Hebrew, the word **עלילה** is used to describe the plot of a story. Which commentary comes closest to that interpretation?
- Do you find any of the commentaries troubling?

פרשת בא

וַיֹּ֤אמֶר יְהֹוָה֙ אֶל־מֹשֶׁ֔ה בֹּ֖א אֶל־פַּרְעֹ֑ה כִּֽי־אֲנִ֞י הִכְבַּ֤דְתִּי אֶת־לִבּוֹ֙ א
וְאֶת־לֵ֣ב עֲבָדָ֔יו לְמַ֗עַן שִׁתִ֛י אֹתֹתַ֥י אֵ֖לֶּה בְּקִרְבּֽוֹ: וּלְמַ֡עַן תְּסַפֵּר֩ ב
בְּאׇזְנֵ֨י בִנְךָ֜ וּבֶן־בִּנְךָ֗ אֵ֣ת אֲשֶׁ֤ר הִתְעַלַּ֙לְתִּי֙ בְּמִצְרַ֔יִם וְאֶת־אֹתֹתַ֖י
אֲשֶׁר־שַׂ֣מְתִּי בָ֑ם וִֽידַעְתֶּ֖ם כִּי־אֲנִ֥י יְהֹוָֽה: וַיָּבֹ֨א מֹשֶׁ֤ה וְאַהֲרֹן֙ אֶל־ ג
פַּרְעֹ֔ה וַיֹּאמְר֣וּ אֵלָ֗יו כֹּֽה־אָמַ֤ר יְהֹוָה֙ אֱלֹהֵ֣י הָֽעִבְרִ֔ים עַד־מָתַ֣י
מֵאַ֔נְתָּ לֵעָנֹ֖ת מִפָּנָ֑י שַׁלַּ֥ח עַמִּ֖י וְיַֽעַבְדֻֽנִי: כִּ֛י אִם־מָאֵ֥ן אַתָּ֖ה ד
לְשַׁלֵּ֣חַ אֶת־עַמִּ֑י הִנְנִ֨י מֵבִ֥יא מָחָ֛ר אַרְבֶּ֖ה בִּגְבֻלֶֽךָ: וְכִסָּה֙ אֶת־עֵ֣ין ה
הָאָ֔רֶץ וְלֹ֥א יוּכַ֖ל לִרְאֹ֣ת אֶת־הָאָ֑רֶץ וְאָכַ֣ל ׀ אֶת־יֶ֣תֶר הַפְּלֵטָ֗ה
הַנִּשְׁאֶ֤רֶת לָכֶם֙ מִן־הַבָּרָ֔ד וְאָכַל֙ אֶת־כׇּל־הָעֵ֔ץ הַצֹּמֵ֥חַ לָכֶ֖ם מִן־
הַשָּׂדֶֽה: וּמָלְא֨וּ בָתֶּ֜יךָ וּבָתֵּ֣י כׇל־עֲבָדֶ֘יךָ֮ וּבָתֵּ֣י כׇל־מִצְרַ֒יִם֒ אֲשֶׁ֨ר ו
לֹֽא־רָא֤וּ אֲבֹתֶ֙יךָ֙ וַאֲב֣וֹת אֲבֹתֶ֔יךָ מִיּ֗וֹם הֱיוֹתָם֙ עַל־הָ֣אֲדָמָ֔ה עַ֖ד
הַיּ֣וֹם הַזֶּ֑ה וַיִּ֥פֶן וַיֵּצֵ֖א מֵעִ֥ם פַּרְעֹֽה: וַיֹּאמְרוּ֩ עַבְדֵ֨י פַרְעֹ֜ה אֵלָ֗יו ז
עַד־מָתַי֙ יִהְיֶ֨ה זֶ֥ה לָ֙נוּ֙ לְמוֹקֵ֔שׁ שַׁלַּח֙ אֶת־הָ֣אֲנָשִׁ֔ים וְיַֽעַבְד֖וּ
אֶת־יְהֹוָ֣ה אֱלֹהֵיהֶ֑ם הֲטֶ֣רֶם תֵּדַ֔ע כִּ֥י אָבְדָ֖ה מִצְרָֽיִם: וַיּוּשַׁ֞ב ח
אֶת־מֹשֶׁ֤ה וְאֶֽת־אַהֲרֹן֙ אֶל־פַּרְעֹ֔ה וַיֹּ֣אמֶר אֲלֵהֶ֔ם לְכ֥וּ עִבְד֖וּ
אֶת־יְהֹוָ֣ה אֱלֹהֵיכֶ֑ם מִ֥י וָמִ֖י הַהֹלְכִֽים: וַיֹּ֣אמֶר מֹשֶׁ֔ה בִּנְעָרֵ֥ינוּ ט
וּבִזְקֵנֵ֖ינוּ נֵלֵ֑ךְ בְּבָנֵ֨ינוּ וּבִבְנוֹתֵ֜נוּ בְּצֹאנֵ֤נוּ וּבִבְקָרֵ֙נוּ֙ נֵלֵ֔ךְ כִּ֥י חַג־
יְהֹוָ֖ה לָֽנוּ: וַיֹּ֣אמֶר אֲלֵהֶ֗ם יְהִ֨י כֵ֤ן יְהֹוָה֙ עִמָּכֶ֔ם כַּאֲשֶׁ֛ר אֲשַׁלַּ֥ח י
אֶתְכֶ֖ם וְאֶֽת־טַפְּכֶ֑ם רְא֕וּ כִּ֥י רָעָ֖ה נֶ֣גֶד פְּנֵיכֶֽם: לֹ֣א כֵ֗ן לְכוּ־נָ֤א יא

CLASSIC COMMENTATORS

God informs Moshe that it was He who caused Pharaoh to change his mind after Pharaoh acknowledged his own sin in the plague of the hail. The reason, He explains, is so that Israel could later tell the tale of how God was מתעולל with the Egyptians. The precise translation of this word is a subject of debate, with serious implications.

Shemot | Chapter 10 — Bo

Following God's instruction, Moshe waves his staff and the locusts descend upon Egypt, wreaking great destruction on the remaining crops. Pharaoh hurriedly calls Moshe and Aharon, confessing his sin and requesting to have the plague removed – but without promising to accede to Moshe's request. Moshe prays immediately upon exiting his meeting with Pharaoh, and the locusts blow out to sea – but Pharaoh stubbornly refuses to send Benei Yisrael out.

12 are asking for." Then Pharaoh had Moshe and Aharon expelled from his presence. The Lord said to Moshe, "Reach out your hand over Egypt so that locusts swarm over the
13 land and eat everything growing there; all that is left after the hail." So Moshe stretched out his staff over Egypt, and the Lord caused an east wind to blow across the land all
14 that day and night. By morning, the east wind had brought the locusts. They invaded all of Egypt and settled throughout its land in a dense swarm. Never before had there been
15 such a plague of locusts, nor will there ever be again. They covered all the landscape until the ground was black. They ate all that was left after the hail: all the plants and
16 all the fruit. Nothing green remained on trees or plants throughout all Egypt. In haste, Pharaoh summoned Moshe and Aharon and said, "I have sinned against the Lord your
17 God and you. Forgive my sin now, one more time. Pray to the Lord your God to take
18 this death away from me." Moshe left Pharaoh's presence and prayed to the Lord. And
19 the Lord turned the wind, westerly and very strong, and lifted the locusts and swept
20 them into the Sea of Reeds. Not one locust remained anywhere in Egypt. But the Lord toughened Pharaoh's heart and he would not send the Israelites forth.

רבינו בחיי
למדך שהיו בני אדם מתים במכת הארבה... ואולי היה הארבה מסמא את עיניהם כענין הצרעה בזמן יהושע.

RABBEINU BAḤYA
We learn from here that Egyptian people were actually dying as a result of the locust plague… It is also possible that the oppressors were blinded by the locusts, as the Canaanites were when hornets attacked their eyes during the time of Yehoshua.

ר' שמשון רפאל הירש
פרעה נוכח לדעת, שהשמדת עושרה החקלאי של מצרים כמוהו כחורבן הארץ.

RABBI SAMSON RAPHAEL HIRSCH
Pharaoh realized that the devastation of Egypt's agricultural wealth was tantamount to the destruction of the whole country.

ר' דוד צבי הופמן
מסתבר, שהכוונה למיתה ברעב, שצפוי בעקבות מכת הארבה.

RABBI DAVID TZVI HOFFMAN
It seems that Pharaoh was referring to the inevitable famine resulting from the locust attack that would starve the Egyptian populace.

QUESTIONS FOR THOUGHT

- In what way is the explanation of Rabbeinu Baḥya dramatically different from the other two?
- Which of the other two understands the plague as being more damaging to Egypt than had it happened other nations?
- Which explanation do you think best captures why Pharaoh panics more in response to this plague than in response to any of the previous ones?

שמות | פרק י

הַגְּבָרִים וְעִבְדוּ אֶת־יהוה כִּי אֹתָהּ אַתֶּם מְבַקְשִׁים וַיְגָרֶשׁ אֹתָם מֵאֵת פְּנֵי פַרְעֹה׃

יב וַיֹּאמֶר יהוה אֶל־מֹשֶׁה נְטֵה יָדְךָ עַל־אֶרֶץ מִצְרַיִם בָּאַרְבֶּה וְיַעַל עַל־אֶרֶץ מִצְרָיִם וְיֹאכַל אֶת־כָּל־עֵשֶׂב הָאָרֶץ אֵת כָּל־אֲשֶׁר הִשְׁאִיר הַבָּרָד׃

יג וַיֵּט מֹשֶׁה אֶת־מַטֵּהוּ עַל־אֶרֶץ מִצְרַיִם וַיהוה נִהַג רוּחַ־קָדִים בָּאָרֶץ כָּל־הַיּוֹם הַהוּא וְכָל־הַלָּיְלָה הַבֹּקֶר הָיָה וְרוּחַ הַקָּדִים נָשָׂא אֶת־הָאַרְבֶּה׃

יד וַיַּעַל הָאַרְבֶּה עַל כָּל־אֶרֶץ מִצְרַיִם וַיָּנַח בְּכֹל גְּבוּל מִצְרָיִם כָּבֵד מְאֹד לְפָנָיו לֹא־הָיָה כֵן אַרְבֶּה כָּמֹהוּ וְאַחֲרָיו לֹא יִהְיֶה־כֵּן׃

טו וַיְכַס אֶת־עֵין כָּל־הָאָרֶץ וַתֶּחְשַׁךְ הָאָרֶץ וַיֹּאכַל אֶת־כָּל־עֵשֶׂב הָאָרֶץ וְאֵת כָּל־פְּרִי הָעֵץ אֲשֶׁר הוֹתִיר הַבָּרָד וְלֹא־נוֹתַר כָּל־יֶרֶק בָּעֵץ וּבְעֵשֶׂב הַשָּׂדֶה בְּכָל־אֶרֶץ מִצְרָיִם׃

טז וַיְמַהֵר פַּרְעֹה לִקְרֹא לְמֹשֶׁה וּלְאַהֲרֹן וַיֹּאמֶר חָטָאתִי לַיהוה אֱלֹהֵיכֶם וְלָכֶם׃

יז וְעַתָּה שָׂא נָא חַטָּאתִי אַךְ הַפַּעַם וְהַעְתִּירוּ לַיהוה אֱלֹהֵיכֶם וְיָסֵר מֵעָלַי רַק אֶת־הַמָּוֶת הַזֶּה׃

יח וַיֵּצֵא מֵעִם פַּרְעֹה וַיֶּעְתַּר אֶל־יהוה׃

יט וַיַּהֲפֹךְ יהוה רוּחַ־יָם חָזָק מְאֹד וַיִּשָּׂא אֶת־הָאַרְבֶּה וַיִּתְקָעֵהוּ יָמָּה סּוּף לֹא נִשְׁאַר אַרְבֶּה אֶחָד בְּכֹל גְּבוּל מִצְרָיִם׃

כ וַיְחַזֵּק יהוה אֶת־לֵב פַּרְעֹה וְלֹא שִׁלַּח אֶת־בְּנֵי יִשְׂרָאֵל׃

CLASSIC COMMENTATORS

Of all the plagues until now, Pharaoh identifies specifically this one as deathly.

Shemot | Chapter 10

21 Then the Lord said to Moshe, "Reach out your hand toward the sky to bring darkness
22 down over Egypt – darkness so deep it can be felt." Moshe reached out his hand toward
23 the sky, and all across Egypt it was pitch dark for three days. For three days, no one could
24 see anyone else or even move. But in the Israelites' homes, they had light. Then Pharaoh
    summoned Moshe and said, "Go, serve the Lord. Just leave your flocks and herds. Your
25 children may go with you." "Then give us sacrifices and burnt offerings to present to
26 the Lord our God," said Moshe. "Our livestock must go with us. Not a hoof can be left
    behind. We must take them to serve the Lord our God, for until we arrive, we will not
27 know what we must use to serve the Lord." But the Lord toughened Pharaoh's heart,
28 and he would not agree to send the people forth. "Leave my presence," said Pharaoh.
    "Take care never to see my face again, because on the day you do, that day you will die!"
29 Moshe replied, "As you say: I will not see your face again."

RABBI DAVID TZVI HOFFMAN

On the one hand, it is possible that the Israelites lived completely apart from the Egyptian population, and hence the verse describes that while one area was plunged into darkness, the other enjoyed sunlight as usual. Hence the term "in their dwelling places" connotes Israel's region…On the other hand, perhaps the Hebrew homes stood in the same neighborhoods as the Egyptian communities. In that case the Torah means that inside Israelite homes candlelight continued to operate normally, while in the Egyptian houses next door, no light could be generated. Thus the term "in their dwelling places" refers to the actual houses.

ר' דוד צבי הופמן

במושבתם - אם נאמר שבני ישראל התגוררו בנפרד מן המצרים, כי אז אפשר לומר ש"במושבתם" פירושו באזור מגוריהם, ... ואם נניח, שגרו במעורב בין המצרים, צריך לומר שבבתיהם היה להם אור, בעוד שאצל שכניהם המצרים היה חושך, ו"במושבתם" פירושו "בבתיהם".

QUESTIONS FOR THOUGHT

- Which of the commentaries understands that *Benei Yisrael* was spared this plague only as long as they stayed in Goshen?
- Which understands that each individual member of *Benei Yisrael* had an individual, miraculous beam of light accompany him or her wherever he or she went?
- What middle position does R. David Tzvi Hoffman suggest? What important question about the nature of the Israelites' life in Egypt does he raise in the process of the discussion?

TEXTUAL SKILLS

1. Notice the irony in the parallel between the language used to describe the onset of the plague of darkness (...יהי חושך ויהי חושך) and the language used in Genesis 1:3.

2. Pharaoh declares to Moshe: "Take care never to see my face again, because on the day you do, that day you will die!" This sounds similar to God's statement in 33:20: "Nor can you see My face, for no one can see Me and live." What might the Torah be hinting at?

3. In verse 23, how would you translate the *vav* at the beginning of the phrase ולכל בני ישראל היה אור במושבתם?

שמות | פרק י

כא וַיֹּאמֶר יְהוָה אֶל־מֹשֶׁה נְטֵה יָדְךָ עַל־הַשָּׁמַיִם וִיהִי חֹשֶׁךְ עַל־
אֶרֶץ מִצְרָיִם וְיָמֵשׁ חֹשֶׁךְ: כב וַיֵּט מֹשֶׁה אֶת־יָדוֹ עַל־הַשָּׁמָיִם וַיְהִי
חֹשֶׁךְ־אֲפֵלָה בְּכָל־אֶרֶץ מִצְרַיִם שְׁלֹשֶׁת יָמִים: כג לֹא־רָאוּ אִישׁ
אֶת־אָחִיו וְלֹא־קָמוּ אִישׁ מִתַּחְתָּיו שְׁלֹשֶׁת יָמִים וּלְכָל־בְּנֵי
יִשְׂרָאֵל הָיָה אוֹר בְּמוֹשְׁבֹתָם: כד וַיִּקְרָא פַרְעֹה אֶל־מֹשֶׁה וַיֹּאמֶר *שלישי*
לְכוּ עִבְדוּ אֶת־יְהוָה רַק צֹאנְכֶם וּבְקַרְכֶם יֻצָּג גַּם־טַפְּכֶם יֵלֵךְ
עִמָּכֶם: כה וַיֹּאמֶר מֹשֶׁה גַּם־אַתָּה תִּתֵּן בְּיָדֵנוּ זְבָחִים וְעֹלֹת וְעָשִׂינוּ
לַיהוָה אֱלֹהֵינוּ: כו וְגַם־מִקְנֵנוּ יֵלֵךְ עִמָּנוּ לֹא תִשָּׁאֵר פַּרְסָה כִּי
מִמֶּנּוּ נִקַּח לַעֲבֹד אֶת־יְהוָה אֱלֹהֵינוּ וַאֲנַחְנוּ לֹא־נֵדַע מַה־נַּעֲבֹד
אֶת־יְהוָה עַד־בֹּאֵנוּ שָׁמָּה: כז וַיְחַזֵּק יְהוָה אֶת־לֵב פַּרְעֹה וְלֹא
אָבָה לְשַׁלְּחָם: כח וַיֹּאמֶר־לוֹ פַרְעֹה לֵךְ מֵעָלָי הִשָּׁמֶר לְךָ אַל־תֹּסֶף
רְאוֹת פָּנַי כִּי בְּיוֹם רְאֹתְךָ פָנַי תָּמוּת: כט וַיֹּאמֶר מֹשֶׁה כֵּן דִּבַּרְתָּ
לֹא־אֹסִף עוֹד רְאוֹת פָּנֶיךָ:

CLASSIC COMMENTATORS

Benei Yisrael had light in their dwelling places. How extreme were the effects of that miracle within a miracle?

RASHBAM — רשב״ם

Even Hebrews who entered Egyptian homes were able to see.

היה אור במושבותם – אפילו שהוא יושב אצל בית המצרי.

RABBI YOSEF BEKHOR SHOR — ר' יוסף בכור שור

Light shone in the Goshen region where the Israelites lived, whereas the land of Egypt proper was enveloped by darkness that blinded everybody there, including Hebrews.

היה אור במושבותם – בארץ גושן שהם יושבין שם. אבל ארץ מצרים היתה חשוכה לכל העולם, אפילו לישראל.

SHEMOT | CHAPTER 11

For the first time since Moshe was challenged by the elders of Israel, the focus shifts back to the people of Israel. As part of their preparation to leave, they are instructed to ask their Egyptian neighbors for vessels of gold and silver. When they do so, they are showered with gifts by the Egyptians, who find them favorable. Even Moshe, who brought much suffering upon the Egyptians, is well respected by the Egyptian people and Pharaoh's staff.

11 1 Then the LORD said to Moshe, "One last plague will I send against Pharaoh, against Egypt. After that, he will send you forth from here, and when he does, he will drive you 2 out completely. Now tell the people, men and women, to ask of their neighbors articles 3 of silver and of gold." The LORD granted the people favor in the eyes of the Egyptians. And the man Moshe, too, was held in high regard in the land of Egypt, among both

TEXTUAL SKILLS

1. The instructions to *Benei Yisrael* here should sound familiar – they are very similar to a promise God made to Moshe at the burning bush (3:22). But there are some important differences. Can you find them?

2. Notice the contrast between the way Pharaoh related to Moshe and the way the rest of Egypt related to him as indicated in this passage.

WISDOM OF THE HEART

The people are encouraged to ask for gold and silver from their Egyptian neighbors and acquaintances. The same word in Hebrew, לשאול, is used to mean "ask" and "borrow," leading to discomfort among many readers, who wonder: "Did God tell the people to borrow things that they had no intention of returning?"

This "borrowing" has bothered a lot of commentaries. Ibn Ezra says that since God created everything, He chooses how to divide and re-divide that wealth. Rabbi Samson Raphael Hirsch, however, understands the word as meaning "to ask," and he flips this on its head: during the three days of darkness, the Egyptians' possessions lay unprotected in their home, yet none of the Israelites took advantage of them, despite the temptation for revenge. When the darkness ended and the Egyptians realized how ethical their former slaves were, they gladly acceded to their requests for parting gifts.

What does it say about us as a people that we resisted doing something unethical (that we could have rationalized) even though we could have gotten away with it? How does it make you feel when you do the right thing even though nobody else will know?

QUICK BITE

There is a divine symmetry to our world. Everything runs with powerful precision. Even when some outlying force seems to disrupt the awesome patterns of creation, we can look closely and realize that that it too is part of the grand, graceful production orchestrated by God. There is a teaching of Ḥasidei Breslov that every time the Torah focuses on some mundane behavior it is providing an opportunity to rescue חן. The word חן literally means "grace," but in this context it refers to the recognition of God's elegant manifestation in a world that often seems to hide it. Rabbi Natan of Breslov reads these verses as follows: "Go. Go and engage with the material possessions of the Egyptian people. Find חן there." If you can find God in silver and gold, then you can find God anywhere.

שמות | פרק יא

יא א וַיֹּ֨אמֶר יְהוָ֜ה אֶל־מֹשֶׁ֗ה ע֣וֹד נֶ֤גַע אֶחָד֙ אָבִ֤יא עַל־פַּרְעֹה֙ וְעַל־מִצְרַ֔יִם אַֽחֲרֵי־כֵ֕ן יְשַׁלַּ֥ח אֶתְכֶ֖ם מִזֶּ֑ה כְּשַׁ֨לְּח֔וֹ כָּלָ֕ה גָּרֵ֛שׁ יְגָרֵ֥שׁ אֶתְכֶ֖ם מִזֶּֽה: ב דַּבֶּר־נָ֖א בְּאָזְנֵ֣י הָעָ֑ם וְיִשְׁאֲל֞וּ אִ֣ישׁ ׀ מֵאֵ֣ת רֵעֵ֗הוּ וְאִשָּׁה֙ מֵאֵ֣ת רְעוּתָ֔הּ כְּלֵי־כֶ֖סֶף וּכְלֵ֥י זָהָֽב: ג וַיִּתֵּ֧ן יְהוָ֛ה אֶת־חֵ֥ן הָעָ֖ם בְּעֵינֵ֣י מִצְרָ֑יִם גַּ֣ם ׀ הָאִ֣ישׁ מֹשֶׁ֗ה גָּד֤וֹל מְאֹד֙ בְּאֶ֣רֶץ מִצְרַ֔יִם

CLASSIC COMMENTATORS

This passage seems to interrupt between Pharaoh's decree that Moshe will not be granted any further audiences and Moshe's parting words. When was this message from God delivered to Moshe, and why is that important?

ר' יוסף בכור שור

ויאמר ה' אל משה – שם דיבר אליו מיד, ושם הזהירו על מכת בכורות, ואחר כך יצא בכעס על שאמר לו ביום ראותך פני תמות.

RABBI YOSEF BEKHOR SHOR

It was right then that God informed Moshe about the final plague of the firstborns, whereupon Moshe immediately warned Pharaoh regarding what was about to happen. Then Moshe stormed out of the palace, angry at Pharaoh for having said: "Take care never to see my face again, because on the day that you do, that day you will die."

ר' דוד צבי הופמן

משה יכול היה לדבר בלשון בוטח ואמיץ מכיוון שכבר שמע מפי ה' על מכת בכורות, ומכיוון שבני ישראל מצאו חן בעיני המצרים, והוא עצמו נחשב ביותר אצל עבדי פרעה וגם אצל העם המצרי.

RABBI DAVID TZVI HOFFMAN

There are two reasons why Moshe could address Pharaoh and speak with confidence and assurance. Firstly, the Lord had told the leader about the impending death of the firstborns. Secondly, the people of Israel had found favor in the eyes of the Egyptian populace, while Moshe himself was held in high esteem by Pharaoh's officials and the common masses alike.

QUESTIONS FOR THOUGHT

- According to Rabbi David Tzvi Hoffman, why was it important for us to understand that this passage preceded Moshe's discussion with Pharaoh?
- According to Bekhor Shor, in what way is this passage linked to both the one that came before and the one that comes afterward?
- According to which opinion is God's message to Moshe about asking the Egyptians for gold and silver a reaction to Pharaoh's threat to Moshe?

4 Pharaoh's officials and the people. Moshe said, "This is what the LORD says: Around
5 midnight I will move throughout Egypt, and every firstborn son in Egypt will die, from Pharaoh's firstborn presiding on his throne to the firstborn of the slave girl at her hand
6 mill; the firstborn of the cattle as well. A scream will ring out across Egypt, unlike any
7 that has been before, or any that will be again. But among the Israelites not a dog will bare its tongue at man or beast. Then you will know that the LORD is setting Israel apart
8 from Egypt. And all these officials of yours will come and bow down to me, saying, 'Leave, you and all the people behind you.' After that, I will leave." He turned and left
9 Pharaoh, blazing with anger. The LORD said to Moshe, "Pharaoh will not listen to you,
10 that My wonders may be multiplied in Egypt." Moshe and Aharon had produced all these wonders before Pharaoh, but the LORD toughened Pharaoh's heart, and he did not

QUESTIONS FOR THOUGHT

- Which of the commentaries suggests that, despite Moshe's frustration and anger with Pharaoh, he still treats him with the dignity appropriate for a king?
- Which of the commentaries suggests that Pharaoh will be so humiliated that his servants, on their own, will bow and plead with Moshe to spare Pharaoh?
- Which of the commentaries suggests that Pharaoh will try to maintain his dignity by sending his servants to concede defeat?

TEXTUAL SKILLS

1. Verses 9–10 bring us full circle back to just before the plagues began, in 7:3–5. This is sometimes called a literary envelope, or an *inclusio*, in which a passage opens and closes with words, phrases, or an idea that indicates that the unit is now complete.

2. The bizarre expression (11:7) חרץ לשון, translated here as "bare its tongue," appears only twice in all of Tanakh: here and in Joshua 10:21. Can you find any similarities between the two contexts in which this phrase appears that may help explain its meaning?

WISDOM OF THE HEART

There is a theory that each of the plagues was designed to counteract some erroneous mythological belief that the Egyptians held. Here's how Rabbi Alec Goldstein presents this theory in relation to some of the plagues:

Blood: The Egyptians turned the Nile into a god; the plague of blood had to be locally interpreted as a weakening of the Egyptian god.

Frogs: Many sources say this is an attack against the fertility god Heqt, who had the head of a frog.

Lice: The lice came forth from the dust of the earth, demonstrating the powerlessness of Geb, the Egyptian god of the earth.

Pestilence: This plague killed the domestic animals and was directed against Hathor, the primeval goddess from which all other gods derived, who was depicted with the head of a cow.

Boils: This was interpreted as a challenge to the gods of healing, Sekhmet and Isis.

Hail & Locusts: According to Prof. Ziony Zevit, hail and locusts undermined the god Seth, who manifests himself in winds and storms; Isis, goddess of life (who spins flax, which was affected); and Min, who was worshiped as a protector of crops.

When God performs wonders, what do you think He is trying to accomplish?

בְּעֵינֵי עַבְדֵי־פַרְעֹה וּבְעֵינֵי הָעָם: וַיֹּאמֶר מֹשֶׁה כֹּה ד
אָמַר יהוה כַּחֲצֹת הַלַּיְלָה אֲנִי יוֹצֵא בְּתוֹךְ מִצְרָיִם: וּמֵת כָּל־ ה
בְּכוֹר בְּאֶרֶץ מִצְרַיִם מִבְּכוֹר פַּרְעֹה הַיֹּשֵׁב עַל־כִּסְאוֹ עַד בְּכוֹר
הַשִּׁפְחָה אֲשֶׁר אַחַר הָרֵחָיִם וְכֹל בְּכוֹר בְּהֵמָה: וְהָיְתָה צְעָקָה ו
גְדֹלָה בְּכָל־אֶרֶץ מִצְרָיִם אֲשֶׁר כָּמֹהוּ לֹא נִהְיָתָה וְכָמֹהוּ לֹא ז
תֹסִף: וּלְכֹל ׀ בְּנֵי יִשְׂרָאֵל לֹא יֶחֱרַץ־כֶּלֶב לְשֹׁנוֹ לְמֵאִישׁ וְעַד־
בְּהֵמָה לְמַעַן תֵּדְעוּן אֲשֶׁר יַפְלֶה יהוה בֵּין מִצְרַיִם וּבֵין יִשְׂרָאֵל: ח
וְיָרְדוּ כָל־עֲבָדֶיךָ אֵלֶּה אֵלַי וְהִשְׁתַּחֲווּ־לִי לֵאמֹר צֵא אַתָּה וְכָל־
הָעָם אֲשֶׁר־בְּרַגְלֶיךָ וְאַחֲרֵי־כֵן אֵצֵא וַיֵּצֵא מֵעִם־פַּרְעֹה בָּחֳרִי־ ט
אָף: וַיֹּאמֶר יהוה אֶל־מֹשֶׁה לֹא־יִשְׁמַע אֲלֵיכֶם פַּרְעֹה
לְמַעַן רְבוֹת מוֹפְתַי בְּאֶרֶץ מִצְרָיִם: וּמֹשֶׁה וְאַהֲרֹן עָשׂוּ אֶת־כָּל־ י
הַמֹּפְתִים הָאֵלֶּה לִפְנֵי פַרְעֹה וַיְחַזֵּק יהוה אֶת־לֵב פַּרְעֹה וְלֹא־שִׁלַּח

רביעי

CLASSIC COMMENTATORS

In his parting words Moshe tells Pharaoh that ultimately, Pharaoh's servants will bow down to Moshe and request that he and *Benei Yisrael* leave. Why, in this battle of wills between Moshe and Pharaoh, does Moshe suddenly invoke Pharaoh's servants?

רש״י / RASHI

וירדו כל עבדיך וגו' – חלק כבוד למלכות, שהרי סוף שירד פרעה בעצמו אליו בלילה, ויאמר: קומו צאו מתוך עמי.

Moshe paid respect to Pharaoh by suggesting that his ministers would bow and beg Israel to leave, rather than the king. In the end it was Pharaoh himself who came to appeal to Moshe during the plague of the firstborn, as the verse states: "That night, Pharaoh summoned Moshe and Aharon and said, 'Get up, get out from among my people'" (12:31).

אבן עזרא / IBN EZRA

וירדו [וגו'] והשתחוו לי לאמר – על פיך.

Your servants will actually bow down to me at your request.

ר' יוסף אבן כספי / RABBI YOSEF IBN KASPI

כל עבדיך – אלה הם השרים היותר גדולים שלו היושבים אצלו תמיד כמו שבארנו כי הם עבד פרעה החשובים. והשתחוו לי – הטעם כי יחלו פני שלא אשטמך, להשיב לך רעה כאשר גמלתני.

Moshe here refers to Pharaoh's closest and most important advisers, who were permanent fixtures in the king's throne room. These ministers will beg the Israelite not to hate Pharaoh nor to repay his wickedness with further suffering.

The story of Moshe and Pharaoh is dramatically interrupted by the instruction of the first mitzvot given to Benei Yisrael: establishing the lunar calendar beginning with Nisan and preparing for the first Pesaḥ. That preparation includes getting the sheep ready four days in advance and assembling a group – not too large but also not too small – that will gather to eat the Pesaḥ.

12 1 let the Israelites leave his land. Then the LORD spoke to Moshe and Aharon in the land 2 of Egypt; He said, "This month shall be to you the beginning of months; the opening 3 of the year, this month will be for you. Speak to the entire community of Israel and say: On the tenth of this month each man must take a lamb for his family; one for every 4 household. If the household is too small for a lamb, let him and a close neighbor take a lamb together, to suit the number of people involved; they shall be counted for the 5 lamb in proportion with their eating. A one-year-old male shall you take, flawless, from 6 among the sheep or goats. You shall guard it until the fourteenth day of this month. And

---

QUESTIONS FOR THOUGHT
- According to Rashi, which two factors were preventing God from taking *Benei Yisrael* out of Egypt? How did bringing the Pesaḥ address both of those factors?
- According to Rabbi Hirsch, what did bringing the Pesaḥ achieve?
- In your life, do you sometimes feel like there are things preventing you from moving forward? What do you think you can do to overcome or bypass them?

TEXTUAL SKILLS

1. Based on these verses, does the Pesaḥ seem to be a group command or an individual one? Which words in the Torah would strengthen each of those positions?
2. What is the key word of verse 2?

WISDOM OF THE HEART

The Hebrew word for month is חודש, meaning "renewal," because the moon renews itself every month. According to rabbinic tradition, the first mitzva commanded to *Benei Yisrael* – an essential part of the preparation to leave Egypt – is to establish a lunar calendar, one which puts renewal at its core.

Maharal of Prague explains that the annual calendar contains unique kernels of potential embedded in each of the days. Tisha Be'Av has the potential for tragedy, Ḥanukka the potential for light, Pesaḥ the potential for liberation. Every year, when we cycle through the various days, we can renew ourselves by activating the unique potential of each of these days.

The history of Israel is linked to this cycle of renewal. The moon waxes and wanes each month, gaining strength and then disappearing, only to reappear and restart the cycle. So too Israel goes through ups and downs, sometimes seeming to fade away from history only to bounce back and shine brightly all over again.

Do you ever wish you could just start all over again? What would you do differently? What stops you?

שמות | פרק יב

יב א וַיֹּאמֶר יהוה אֶל־מֹשֶׁה אֶת־בְּנֵי־יִשְׂרָאֵל מֵאַרְצוֹ:
ב וְאֶל־אַהֲרֹן בְּאֶרֶץ מִצְרַיִם לֵאמֹר: הַחֹדֶשׁ הַזֶּה לָכֶם רֹאשׁ
ג חֳדָשִׁים רִאשׁוֹן הוּא לָכֶם לְחָדְשֵׁי הַשָּׁנָה: דַּבְּרוּ אֶל־כָּל־עֲדַת
יִשְׂרָאֵל לֵאמֹר בֶּעָשֹׂר לַחֹדֶשׁ הַזֶּה וְיִקְחוּ לָהֶם אִישׁ שֶׂה לְבֵית־
ד אָבֹת שֶׂה לַבָּיִת: וְאִם־יִמְעַט הַבַּיִת מִהְיוֹת מִשֶּׂה וְלָקַח הוּא
וּשְׁכֵנוֹ הַקָּרֹב אֶל־בֵּיתוֹ בְּמִכְסַת נְפָשֹׁת אִישׁ לְפִי אָכְלוֹ תָּכֹסּוּ
ה עַל־הַשֶּׂה: שֶׂה תָמִים זָכָר בֶּן־שָׁנָה יִהְיֶה לָכֶם מִן־הַכְּבָשִׂים
ו וּמִן־הָעִזִּים תִּקָּחוּ: וְהָיָה לָכֶם לְמִשְׁמֶרֶת עַד אַרְבָּעָה עָשָׂר יוֹם
לַחֹדֶשׁ הַזֶּה וְשָׁחֲטוּ אֹתוֹ כֹּל קְהַל עֲדַת־יִשְׂרָאֵל בֵּין הָעַרְבָּיִם:

CLASSIC COMMENTATORS

The command of the first Pesaḥ sacrifice puzzled many of the commentaries – why was this necessary?

RASHI

רש״י

Rabbi Matya ben Ḥarash taught: God said: "The time has arrived for Me to fulfill the oath I made to Avraham to redeem his sons, but alas, Israel possesses no commandment they can fulfill to deserve redemption." Hence God provided the people with two commandments to observe: the blood of the Passover sacrifice, and the blood of circumcision. Another reason that Israel were asked to select their sacrificial animals four days early was that the nation was accustomed to worshipping idols, which is why Moshe said to them: "Each select [*mishkhu*] or acquire one of the flock for yourselves" (12:21). What he demanded was: *mishkhu* [also: withdraw] your hands from idolatry and instead take hold of a sheep of commandment.

היה ר׳ מתיא בן חרש אומר: ...הגיעה שבועה שנשבעתי לאברהם שאגאל את בניו, ולא היו בידן מצות להתעסק בהן כדי שיגאלו, ... ונתן להם שתי מצות דם פסח ודם מילה, . . ושהיו שטופין בעבודה זרה, אמר להם: משכו ידיכם מעבודה זרה, וקחו לכם צאן של מצוה.

RABBI SAMSON RAPHAEL HIRSCH

ר׳ שמשון רפאל הירש

Consumption of the Passover sacrifice symbolized the freedom and the independence that Israel acquired through their submission and devotion to the Lord.

אכילת הפסח מסמלת את החירות והעצמאות שעם ישראל משיג על ידי התמסרותו לה׳.

Special rules apply to the first Pesaḥ. It must be fire-broiled, not cooked; eaten with matza and bitter things; consumed completely before morning; eaten quickly with a readiness to leave at a moment's notice – belts fastened, shoes on, and walking sticks ready. Furthermore, the blood from the slaughtered animal needs to be dabbed on the door frame to ensure that the calamity befalling the Egyptians not affect the Israelites.

7 then, in the afternoon, all the community of Israel shall slaughter it. They shall then take some of the blood and put it on the two sides and top of the doorframes of the houses
8 where they are to eat the lamb. They shall eat the meat that night, roasted over a fire; with
9 unleavened bread and bitter herbs they shall eat it. Do not eat it raw or boiled in water;
10 it must be roasted over fire with its head, its legs and its inner parts. Do not leave any of
11 it until morning; any left over until morning, you shall burn with fire. This is how you shall eat it: your belt secured, the sandals on your feet, your staff in your hand. Eat it in
12 haste. It is the LORD's Passover. I will pass through the land of Egypt that night, and will kill every firstborn in Egypt, man and beast. Against all the gods of Egypt I will bring
13 judgment. I am the LORD. The blood will be your sign on the houses where you are. I will see the blood and I will pass over you. No deadly plague will touch you when

RAMBAM (GUIDE FOR THE PERPLEXED)
Because the Egyptians worshipped the constellation Aries [represented by a ram] their culture forbade the slaughter of sheep… This was the very reason why Israel was commanded to kill a sheep for the Passover sacrifice… The blood of the offering was spread on the outside of the Israelite gateways in order to make a definitive statement that the nation dissociated themselves from the Egyptian cultic beliefs. They simultaneously declared the opposite philosophy – that that which was considered the cause of death, actually brought deliverance from death.

רמב״ם (מורה נבוכים)
שהמצרים היו עובדים מזל טלה, מפני זה היו אוסרים לשחוט הצאן, ... ומפני זאת הכונה בעצמה ציונו לשחוט כבש בפסח ולהזות ... על השערים מבחוץ, לנקות עצמנו מן הדעות ההם ולפרסם שכנגדם, ולהביא להאמין שהמעשה אשר יחשבו בו שהוא סיבה ממיתה, הוא המציל מן המות.

QUESTIONS FOR THOUGHT
- Both Bekhor Shor and Rambam believe that the blood is to be seen on the outside, but they apparently disagree on why it needs to be there. Try to explain the difference between them.
- According to Ibn Ezra, what's the purpose of putting the blood on the inside of the door?
- Do you know of other mitzvot which involve symbols placed at the doorway? Do those symbols belong on the outside or the inside? Do you think they are connected to this mitzva?

TEXTUAL SKILLS

1. Most people assume that the root פ-ס-ח means "to skip" (or "pass) over," yet there are many indications in our sources that it can mean "to have compassion," or even "to love." Based on that alternate explanation, how would describe the meaning of the holiday named Pesaḥ?

2. Since the fourth plague, God automatically spared *Benei Yisrael*. Notice how this one is different!

3. Based on the description of the way this meal needs to be eaten, what name might you give the meal?

וְלָקְחוּ מִן־הַדָּם וְנָתְנוּ עַל־שְׁתֵּי הַמְּזוּזֹת וְעַל־הַמַּשְׁקוֹף עַל
הַבָּתִּים אֲשֶׁר־יֹאכְלוּ אֹתוֹ בָּהֶם: וְאָכְלוּ אֶת־הַבָּשָׂר בַּלַּיְלָה
הַזֶּה צְלִי־אֵשׁ וּמַצּוֹת עַל־מְרֹרִים יֹאכְלֻהוּ: אַל־תֹּאכְלוּ מִמֶּנּוּ
נָא וּבָשֵׁל מְבֻשָּׁל בַּמָּיִם כִּי אִם־צְלִי־אֵשׁ רֹאשׁוֹ עַל־כְּרָעָיו וְעַל־
קִרְבּוֹ: וְלֹא־תוֹתִירוּ מִמֶּנּוּ עַד־בֹּקֶר וְהַנֹּתָר מִמֶּנּוּ עַד־בֹּקֶר בָּאֵשׁ
תִּשְׂרֹפוּ: וְכָכָה תֹּאכְלוּ אֹתוֹ מָתְנֵיכֶם חֲגֻרִים נַעֲלֵיכֶם בְּרַגְלֵיכֶם
וּמַקֶּלְכֶם בְּיֶדְכֶם וַאֲכַלְתֶּם אֹתוֹ בְּחִפָּזוֹן פֶּסַח הוּא לַיהוה:
וְעָבַרְתִּי בְאֶרֶץ־מִצְרַיִם בַּלַּיְלָה הַזֶּה וְהִכֵּיתִי כָל־בְּכוֹר בְּאֶרֶץ
מִצְרַיִם מֵאָדָם וְעַד־בְּהֵמָה וּבְכָל־אֱלֹהֵי מִצְרַיִם אֶעֱשֶׂה שְׁפָטִים
אֲנִי יהוה: וְהָיָה הַדָּם לָכֶם לְאֹת עַל הַבָּתִּים אֲשֶׁר אַתֶּם שָׁם
וְרָאִיתִי אֶת־הַדָּם וּפָסַחְתִּי עֲלֵכֶם וְלֹא־יִהְיֶה בָכֶם נֶגֶף לְמַשְׁחִית

CLASSIC COMMENTATORS

It is unclear whether the blood on the door frame was on the inside of the house or the outside. The implication is clear – who is to see that blood, and why?

ר' יוסף בכור שור

ונתנו על שתי המזוזות – שהם מזה ומזה לפתח, ונראה מבחוץ. כדי שיראה אותו המשחית, ויהיה אותו דם סימן לכפרה על דמכם.

RABBI YOSEF BEKHOR SHOR

Israel was to apply the animal's blood to the doorposts – that is, the two vertical parts of the doorframe standing on either side of the door, such that the blood would be visible on the outside of the house. In that way the destroyer would be able to see the sign of the blood. The blood in turn would serve as atonement for the Israelites' blood.

אבן עזרא

והיה [וגו'] לאת – טעם לאות: שיחזק לבבכם, ולא ירך בשמעכם צעקת המצרים במות בכוריהם בעבור המשחית.

IBN EZRA

The purpose of dabbing the blood as a sign was to embolden the Israelites lest they panic at the sound of the Egyptians screaming when they discover their dead firstborns.

14 I strike the land of Egypt. This day will become a memorial for you; you will celebrate it as a festival to the Lord for all generations, a celebration that will be an everlasting law.
15 For seven days you shall eat unleavened bread. By the first day you shall have removed leaven dough from your houses, for the soul of anyone who eats leavened bread from
16 the first day to the seventh will be severed from Israel. The first day shall be a sacred assembly and the seventh day shall be a sacred assembly. On them no work may be
17 done but preparing the food for everyone to eat. That alone may you do. Safeguard the unleavened bread, because on this very day I will have brought your battalions out of
18 Egypt. You shall observe this day for all generations; it is an everlasting law. From the fourteenth day of the first month in the evening until the twenty-first day of the month
19 in the evening, you may eat only unleavened bread. During these seven days, leaven must not be found in your houses. Anyone, whether newcomer or native-born, who
20 eats leavened food will have his soul severed from the community of Israel. Eat nothing leavened. Wherever you may live, you shall eat unleavened bread."

RABBI DAVID TZVI HOFFMAN

The fact that here, as well as in other places in Tanakh, the evening seems to follow the day that precedes it should not surprise us. For actually, in the Temple procedures the day began in the morning and continued to the next morning. Incidentally, we should point out that in all places, including the current instance, where the evening is considered to follow the day, the day is mentioned first.

ר׳ דוד צבי הופמן

העובדה שכאן, וגם במקומות נוספים במקרא, נמשך הערב אחרי היום שקדם לו ("בראשון בארבעה עשר יום לחודש בערב") אינה צריכה להתמיה, שהרי במקדש אמנם נמנו הימים מבוקר עד בוקר, ובדרך אגב יצוין, כי כאן ובכל המקומות שבהם הערב נמשך אחר היום הקודם, נאמר היום תחילה.

QUESTIONS FOR THOUGHT

- Bekhor Shor offers a practical solution as to why the Torah describes the onset of the holiday as the fourteenth in the evening. What is his explanation?
- Rabbi David Tzvi Hoffman suggests that the cycle of the day in the Temple is different from the cycle outside the Temple. Do you know any other examples of the day in the Temple beginning in the morning?
- Look at Leviticus 23:32. In what way is the Torah's description of Yom Kippur similar to the description here?

WISDOM OF THE HEART

The Torah says that we are to guard the matzot. Given that there are no vowels written in the Torah, the word matzot could be read midrashically as mitzvot. Guard the mitzvot; protect them.

We protect things that are precious, special, important to us. The mitzvot we have been given are a treasure: they present us with numerous opportunities to engage in practices that will utterly change our lives. Giving charity, for example, isn't just something on a to-do list – it's transformative. It changes both the recipient and giver. Rather than viewing the mitzvot as chores, we could view them as gifts: opportunities to transform ourselves, others, and the entire world.

Which mitzvot do you see as a privilege?

שמות | פרק יב

יד בְּהַכֹּתִי בְּאֶרֶץ מִצְרָיִם: וְהָיָה הַיּוֹם הַזֶּה לָכֶם לְזִכָּרוֹן וְחַגֹּתֶם
טו אֹתוֹ חַג לַיהוה לְדֹרֹתֵיכֶם חֻקַּת עוֹלָם תְּחָגֻּהוּ: שִׁבְעַת יָמִים
מַצּוֹת תֹּאכֵלוּ אַךְ בַּיּוֹם הָרִאשׁוֹן תַּשְׁבִּיתוּ שְּׂאֹר מִבָּתֵּיכֶם כִּי ׀
כָּל־אֹכֵל חָמֵץ וְנִכְרְתָה הַנֶּפֶשׁ הַהִוא מִיִּשְׂרָאֵל מִיּוֹם הָרִאשֹׁן
טז עַד־יוֹם הַשְּׁבִעִי: וּבַיּוֹם הָרִאשׁוֹן מִקְרָא־קֹדֶשׁ וּבַיּוֹם הַשְּׁבִיעִי
מִקְרָא־קֹדֶשׁ יִהְיֶה לָכֶם כָּל־מְלָאכָה לֹא־יֵעָשֶׂה בָהֶם אַךְ אֲשֶׁר
יז יֵאָכֵל לְכָל־נֶפֶשׁ הוּא לְבַדּוֹ יֵעָשֶׂה לָכֶם: וּשְׁמַרְתֶּם אֶת־הַמַּצּוֹת
כִּי בְּעֶצֶם הַיּוֹם הַזֶּה הוֹצֵאתִי אֶת־צִבְאוֹתֵיכֶם מֵאֶרֶץ מִצְרָיִם
יח וּשְׁמַרְתֶּם אֶת־הַיּוֹם הַזֶּה לְדֹרֹתֵיכֶם חֻקַּת עוֹלָם: בָּרִאשֹׁן
בְּאַרְבָּעָה עָשָׂר יוֹם לַחֹדֶשׁ בָּעֶרֶב תֹּאכְלוּ מַצֹּת עַד יוֹם הָאֶחָד
יט וְעֶשְׂרִים לַחֹדֶשׁ בָּעָרֶב: שִׁבְעַת יָמִים שְׂאֹר לֹא יִמָּצֵא בְּבָתֵּיכֶם
כִּי ׀ כָּל־אֹכֵל מַחְמֶצֶת וְנִכְרְתָה הַנֶּפֶשׁ הַהִוא מֵעֲדַת יִשְׂרָאֵל
כ בַּגֵּר וּבְאֶזְרַח הָאָרֶץ: כָּל־מַחְמֶצֶת לֹא תֹאכֵלוּ בְּכֹל מוֹשְׁבֹתֵיכֶם
תֹּאכְלוּ מַצּוֹת:

CLASSIC COMMENTATORS

Verse 18 presents something of a puzzle. Other places in the Torah indicate that this holiday begins on the fifteenth of the first month, but here the Torah says that it begins on the fourteenth in the evening.

RABBI YOSEF IBN KASPI

ר׳ יוסף אבן כספי

This evening represents the end of the fourteenth of the month and the start of the fifteenth. But because no one can pinpoint the precise time that one day transitions into the next and we can only estimate, it is better to err on the early side than on the late.

בארבעה עשר יום לחדש בערב - זה הערב הוא תכלית ארבעה עשר והתחלת חמשה עשר, והנה אלו הנקודות בזמן אי אפשר לעמוד על אמתתם חוץ לנפש בעצמום, לכן טובה בזה הקדימה מן האחור.

RALBAG

רלב״ג

We learn from this verse that the Jewish day begins in the evening and not in the morning.

למדנו מזה שימינו הם מתחילים מהערב, לא מהבקר.

Shemot | Chapter 12

Moshe conveys to the elders of Israel the instructions he received from God, both regarding the preparations to leave Egypt as well as the reenactment of those events in future years, and the explanation to future generations. The Israelites then did as commanded.

21 Then Moshe called together all the elders of Israel and instructed them, "Each select or acquire one of the flock for yourselves, for your families and slaughter the Passover
22 sacrifice. Take a bunch of hyssop, dip it in the blood in the bowl, and put some of the blood on the top and two sides of the doorframe. None of you shall leave by the doors
23 of your houses until morning. When the Lord passes through to strike Egypt and sees the blood on the top and sides of a doorframe, He will pass over that doorway and will
24 not let the destroyer enter your houses to strike you down. Keep this as a law for you
25 and for your children forever. When you enter the land the Lord will give you as He
26 has promised, you shall keep this ceremony. And when your children say to you, 'What
27 does this ceremony mean to you?' you shall say, 'It is the Passover sacrifice to the Lord who passed over the houses of the Israelites in Egypt, for He struck the Egyptians; but
28 our homes, He spared.'" Then the people bowed down and prostrated themselves. The Israelites proceeded to do exactly as the Lord had commanded Moshe and Aharon.

ר' שמשון רפאל הירש

קרבן הפסח היה הדרך שעל ידה נכנסו בתחילה, האדם היהודי, הבית היהודי והמדינה היהודית, לעבודת ה'; וקרבן הפסח הוא גם הפעולה המסמלת תמיד כניסה מחודשת לעבודה זו.

RABBI SAMSON RAPHAEL HIRSCH

The Passover ritual acted as an initiation of the Jewish individual, the Jewish home, and the Jewish state into the service of the Lord. It is the practice that repeatedly symbolizes the annual renewal into the national membership of Israel.

QUESTIONS FOR THOUGHT

- Which of the commentaries indicates that the primary value of this commandment is to spark questions?
- Which commentary tries to bridge the other two positions?
- What value do commemorative ceremonies have even when not explicitly geared toward passing on collective memories to another generation?

WISDOM OF THE HEART

The instruction of משכו וקחו – translated here as "select or acquire" – can be understood to mean "draw yourself away and take." These words are amazingly powerful, especially when combined. "Draw yourself away" from idolatry and your old pagan practices – this is an important step, but simply rejecting parts of the past is not enough. It must be coupled with a positive move into a new future: "and take" the steps necessary to move forward. Replace the negative of what once was the past with the positive of what could be; abandon that which held you back and embrace the Torah that will empower you.

Which parts of your past do you think Judaism would encourage you to leave? What would you replace them with?

כא *חמישי* וַיִּקְרָ֥א מֹשֶׁ֛ה לְכָל־זִקְנֵ֥י יִשְׂרָאֵ֖ל וַיֹּ֣אמֶר אֲלֵהֶ֑ם מִֽשְׁכ֗וּ וּקְח֨וּ
כב לָכֶ֥ם צֹ֛אן לְמִשְׁפְּחֹתֵיכֶ֖ם וְשַׁחֲט֥וּ הַפָּֽסַח: וּלְקַחְתֶּ֞ם אֲגֻדַּ֣ת אֵז֗וֹב
וּטְבַלְתֶּם֮ בַּדָּ֣ם אֲשֶׁר־בַּסַּף֒ וְהִגַּעְתֶּ֤ם אֶל־הַמַּשְׁקוֹף֙ וְאֶל־שְׁתֵּ֣י
הַמְּזוּזֹ֔ת מִן־הַדָּ֖ם אֲשֶׁ֣ר בַּסָּ֑ף וְאַתֶּ֗ם לֹ֥א תֵצְא֛וּ אִ֥ישׁ מִפֶּֽתַח־
כג בֵּית֖וֹ עַד־בֹּֽקֶר: וְעָבַ֣ר יְהוָה֮ לִנְגֹּ֣ף אֶת־מִצְרַיִם֒ וְרָאָ֤ה אֶת־
הַדָּם֙ עַל־הַמַּשְׁק֔וֹף וְעַ֖ל שְׁתֵּ֣י הַמְּזוּזֹ֑ת וּפָסַ֤ח יְהוָה֙ עַל־הַפֶּ֔תַח
כד וְלֹ֤א יִתֵּן֙ הַמַּשְׁחִ֔ית לָבֹ֥א אֶל־בָּתֵּיכֶ֖ם לִנְגֹּֽף: וּשְׁמַרְתֶּ֖ם אֶת־
כה הַדָּבָ֣ר הַזֶּ֑ה לְחָק־לְךָ֥ וּלְבָנֶ֖יךָ עַד־עוֹלָֽם: וְהָיָ֞ה כִּֽי־תָבֹ֣אוּ אֶל־
הָאָ֗רֶץ אֲשֶׁ֨ר יִתֵּ֧ן יְהוָ֛ה לָכֶ֖ם כַּאֲשֶׁ֣ר דִּבֵּ֑ר וּשְׁמַרְתֶּ֖ם אֶת־הָעֲבֹדָ֥ה
כו הַזֹּֽאת: וְהָיָ֕ה כִּֽי־יֹאמְר֥וּ אֲלֵיכֶ֖ם בְּנֵיכֶ֑ם מָ֛ה הָעֲבֹדָ֥ה הַזֹּ֖את
כז לָכֶֽם: וַאֲמַרְתֶּ֡ם זֶֽבַח־פֶּ֨סַח ה֜וּא לַֽיהוָ֗ה אֲשֶׁ֣ר פָּ֠סַח עַל־בָּתֵּ֤י
בְנֵֽי־יִשְׂרָאֵל֙ בְּמִצְרַ֔יִם בְּנָגְפּ֥וֹ אֶת־מִצְרַ֖יִם וְאֶת־בָּתֵּ֣ינוּ הִצִּ֑יל
כח וַיִּקֹּ֥ד הָעָ֖ם וַיִּֽשְׁתַּחֲוֽוּ: וַיֵּלְכ֥וּ וַיַּעֲשׂ֖וּ בְּנֵ֣י יִשְׂרָאֵ֑ל כַּאֲשֶׁ֨ר צִוָּ֧ה יְהוָ֛ה

CLASSIC COMMENTATORS

Does the reenactment of the Pesaḥ have its own intrinsic value, or is it meaningful only as a spark for the questions of future generations?

RABBI YOSEF BEKHOR SHOR

The Passover ceremony was instituted in order to educate the nation's children, as the text proceeds to state: "And when your children say to you," etc.

ר׳ יוסף בכור שור

לחוק לך ולבניך – חוק יהיה לך לצורך בניך, כדמפרש ואזיל: והיה כי יאמרו אליכם בניכם.

RALBAG

We have been commanded to recall the exodus from Egypt on the night of the fifteenth, and to describe to our children the miracles that were performed on behalf of our nation. It is because of those wonders which the Lord executed for us that He subsequently ordered us to commemorate the events of the fifteenth of Nisan.

רלב״ג

ציוונו לזכור יציאת מצרים בליל חמישה עשר, ולפרסם לבנינו הנפלאות אשר בעבורם ציוונו ה׳ יתעלה לעשות מה שנעשהו בליל חמישה עשר.

Shemot | Chapter 12

At midnight, God strikes all the Egyptian firstborns – not a single home is spared. Amidst the anguished cries of the Egyptians Pharaoh sends out all of Israel, as per Moshe's last demand, to worship God, with a request that they bless him too. The rest of the Egyptians give Israel parting gifts of gold, silver, and clothes, and hurry to usher Israel out of their land – to the point that there is no time for the Israelites' bread to rise.

29 It happened at midnight: the LORD struck down all the firstborn in Egypt, from the firstborn of Pharaoh, presiding on his throne, to the firstborns of the prison captives, and
30 all the firstborn cattle. Pharaoh arose that night, he and all his officials and all Egypt –
31 for a great scream rang out across Egypt, for there was no house without its dead. That night, Pharaoh summoned Moshe and Aharon and said, "Get up, get out from among
32 my people, you and the Israelites. Go. Serve the LORD exactly as you requested; take
33 your sheep and cattle also, just as you said. Just go. But bless me too." The Egyptians
34 too urged the people to make haste and leave the land. "All of us will die," they said. The people took their dough before it could rise, carrying it on their shoulders in kneading
35 pans wrapped in their clothing. As Moshe had told them, the Israelites had requested
36 items of silver and gold, and clothing, of the Egyptians, and the LORD had given the people favor in the eyes of the Egyptians and they had granted their request. Thus they despoiled Egypt.

QUESTIONS FOR THOUGHT

- According to both Rashi and Ramban, Pharaoh is asking Moshe to pray that nothing else bad happen, but they disagree about what bad thing that is. Which of those makes better sense in the context of this passage of the Torah?
- Which of those makes better sense in the broader context of the entire series of plagues?
- According to Ralbag, what is Pharaoh actually asking *Benei Yisrael* to do for him? Which verses establish the context for his comment to make sense?

TEXTUAL SKILLS

1. The key word of verses 31–32 is small and seemingly insignificant, yet it appears five times. What purpose does it serve? What is the surprising twist in the last time it is used?
2. Note the dramatic contrast between the two opening verses of this passage and the two closing verses.
3. The root נ-צ-ל, as used in verse 36, appears five times in the Torah: twice in reference to what God gave Yaakov from Lavan's wealth after twenty years of work (Gen. 31:9, 16), twice in reference to what Israel received from Egypt after an extended enslavement (Ex. 3:22, 12:36), and once to describe what Israel gave up after the sin of the Golden Calf (Ex. 33:6). Is there a connection between them?

אֶת־מֹשֶׁה וְאַהֲרֹן כֵּן עָשֽׂוּ: וַיְהִ֣י ׀ בַּחֲצִ֣י הַלַּ֗יְלָה כט ששי
וַיהוָה֮ הִכָּ֣ה כָל־בְּכוֹר֮ בְּאֶ֣רֶץ מִצְרַיִם֒ מִבְּכֹ֤ר פַּרְעֹה֙ הַיֹּשֵׁ֣ב עַל־
כִּסְא֔וֹ עַ֚ד בְּכ֣וֹר הַשְּׁבִ֔י אֲשֶׁ֖ר בְּבֵ֣ית הַבּ֑וֹר וְכֹ֖ל בְּכ֥וֹר בְּהֵמָֽה:
וַיָּ֨קָם פַּרְעֹ֜ה לַ֗יְלָה ה֤וּא וְכָל־עֲבָדָיו֙ וְכָל־מִצְרַ֔יִם וַתְּהִ֛י צְעָקָ֥ה ל
גְדֹלָ֖ה בְּמִצְרָ֑יִם כִּֽי־אֵ֣ין בַּ֔יִת אֲשֶׁ֥ר אֵֽין־שָׁ֖ם מֵֽת: וַיִּקְרָא֩ לְמֹשֶׁ֨ה לא
וּלְאַהֲרֹ֜ן לַ֗יְלָה וַיֹּ֨אמֶר֙ ק֤וּמוּ צְּאוּ֙ מִתּ֣וֹךְ עַמִּ֔י גַּם־אַתֶּ֖ם גַּם־בְּנֵ֣י
יִשְׂרָאֵ֑ל וּלְכ֛וּ עִבְד֥וּ אֶת־יְהוָ֖ה כְּדַבֶּרְכֶֽם: גַּם־צֹאנְכֶ֨ם גַּם־בְּקַרְכֶ֥ם לב
קְח֛וּ כַּאֲשֶׁ֥ר דִּבַּרְתֶּ֖ם וָלֵ֑כוּ וּבֵרַכְתֶּ֖ם גַּם־אֹתִֽי: וַתֶּחֱזַ֤ק מִצְרַ֨יִם֙ לג
עַל־הָעָ֔ם לְמַהֵ֖ר לְשַׁלְּחָ֣ם מִן־הָאָ֑רֶץ כִּ֥י אָמְר֖וּ כֻּלָּ֥נוּ מֵתִֽים:
וַיִּשָּׂ֥א הָעָ֛ם אֶת־בְּצֵק֖וֹ טֶ֣רֶם יֶחְמָ֑ץ מִשְׁאֲרֹתָ֛ם צְרֻרֹ֥ת בְּשִׂמְלֹתָ֖ם לד
עַל־שִׁכְמָֽם: וּבְנֵי־יִשְׂרָאֵ֥ל עָשׂ֖וּ כִּדְבַ֣ר מֹשֶׁ֑ה וַֽיִּשְׁאֲלוּ֙ מִמִּצְרַ֔יִם לה
כְּלֵי־כֶ֛סֶף וּכְלֵ֥י זָהָ֖ב וּשְׂמָלֹֽת: וַֽיהוָ֞ה נָתַ֨ן אֶת־חֵ֥ן הָעָ֛ם בְּעֵינֵ֥י לו
מִצְרַ֖יִם וַיַּשְׁאִל֑וּם וַֽיְנַצְּל֖וּ אֶת־מִצְרָֽיִם:

CLASSIC COMMENTATORS

Pharaoh asks that *Benei Yisrael*, as they go to worship God, bless him as well. How did he want them to do this?

RASHI
רש״י

Pray for me that I not die, for I too am a firstborn.

התפללו עלי שלא אמות, שאני בכור.

RALBAG
רלב״ג

But bless me too – Pharaoh wanted the Israelites' blessing to come upon him as well. He meant: Not only will you release you and your animals, but I will give you of my own property as well, so that you will cause me to be blessed. Moshe had already raised this idea when he said: "Then give us sacrifices and burnt offerings to present to the LORD our God" (10:25).

וברכתם גם אתי – רוצה לומר שבברכתכם תבוא עלי; והרצון בזה: לא די שאשלח אתכם עם כל אשר לכם, אבל איטיב לכם משלי, ואתן לכם, באופן שתברכוני. וכבר שאל ממנו זה משה באומרו: 'גם אתה תתן בידנו זבחים ועלת' (י, כה).

RAMBAN
רמב״ן

He asked Moshe to keep him in mind when the nation offered their sacrifices to the LORD and prayed that they not be stricken with the plague or the sword. The king wanted to be included with Israel in that plea.

וטעם וברכתם גם אותי – כאשר תזבחו לי״י אלהיכם כאשר דברתם, ותתפללו על נפשותיכם שלא יפגע אתכם בדבר או בחרב, תזכירו גם אותי עמכם.

After 430 years in Egypt, the Israelites finally leave – some 600,000 men, not including the women and children – joined by an assortment of other peoples who left with them. Journeying from Ramesses to Sukkot, they finally bake the dough that they brought with them.

37 The Israelites traveled from Ramesses to Sukkot. There were about six hundred thou-
38 sand men on foot, quite apart from the children. And a great variety of other people
39 went up with them, as well as large droves of livestock; flocks and cattle. With the dough they had brought from Egypt, they baked cakes of unleavened bread, not risen. They had been driven out of Egypt and could not delay, and had prepared no other
40 provisions. The Israelites had lived in Egypt for 430 years. At the end of 430 years, to
41
42 the very day, all the Lord's battalions left Egypt. All that night, the Lord watched over them to bring them out of Egypt; and still this night is kept as one of watchfulness for the Lord throughout the generations of Israel.

QUESTIONS FOR THOUGHT

- Rashi and Bekhor Shor agree on the meaning of the first time the phrase is used, but they disagree dramatically regarding the second time. According to one, the second שמורים means "protecting," while the other understands it to mean "waiting." To what "protecting" and "waiting" are they referring?
- Ibn Ezra understands that the first שמורים refers to the past while the second refers to the future. In doing so, he sets up a beautiful parallel between God and Israel. Explain that parallel.
- In what way is Ibn Ezra's comment similar to Rashi's? In what way is his comment similar to Bekhor Shor's?
- Think about each of those comments and how they may affect your experience at the seder.

TEXTUAL SKILLS

1. The strange phrase בעצם היום הזה appears eleven times in the Torah – once as Noaḥ enters the ark (Gen. 6:13), twice in the context of Avraham's circumcision (Gen. 17), three times in the context of the exodus (all in Ex. 12), and four times in the context of the holidays (Lev. 23).

2. The first time that Ramesses is mentioned is in Genesis 47:11. What might be the significance of that in context of the appearance of Ramesses here? Note that Ramesses is also mentioned in Exodus chapter 1 – is that important?

WISDOM OF THE HEART

At the moment of the exodus, the Torah recounts that *Benei Yisrael* lived in Egypt for 430 years. When one does the math, it turns out that that number is impossible. *Ketav Sofer* offers a meaningful insight. Our ancestors, beginning with Avram and Sarai, began anticipating the exile and worrying about its consequences as soon as they were told about it – long before the family actually moved to Egypt. The pain experienced by parents knowing that their children will suffer is incomparable, so that the suffering of the exile began as soon as Avram was told about it in the Covenant between the Pieces.

Is there someone you care about so much that you can feel their pain?

לז וַיִּסְע֧וּ בְנֵֽי־יִשְׂרָאֵ֛ל מֵרַעְמְסֵ֖ס סֻכֹּ֑תָה כְּשֵׁשׁ־מֵא֨וֹת אֶ֧לֶף רַגְלִ֛י
לח הַגְּבָרִ֖ים לְבַ֥ד מִטָּֽף: וְגַם־עֵ֥רֶב רַ֖ב עָלָ֣ה אִתָּ֑ם וְצֹ֣אן וּבָקָ֔ר מִקְנֶ֖ה
לט כָּבֵ֥ד מְאֹֽד: וַיֹּאפ֨וּ אֶת־הַבָּצֵ֜ק אֲשֶׁ֨ר הוֹצִ֧יאוּ מִמִּצְרַ֛יִם עֻגֹ֥ת
מַצּ֖וֹת כִּ֣י לֹ֣א חָמֵ֑ץ כִּֽי־גֹרְשׁ֣וּ מִמִּצְרַ֗יִם וְלֹ֤א יָֽכְלוּ֙ לְהִתְמַהְמֵ֔הַּ וְגַם־
מ צֵדָ֖ה לֹא־עָשׂ֥וּ לָהֶֽם: וּמוֹשַׁב֙ בְּנֵ֣י יִשְׂרָאֵ֔ל אֲשֶׁ֥ר יָֽשְׁב֖וּ בְּמִצְרָ֑יִם
מא שְׁלֹשִׁ֣ים שָׁנָ֔ה וְאַרְבַּ֥ע מֵא֖וֹת שָׁנָֽה: וַיְהִ֗י מִקֵּץ֙ שְׁלֹשִׁ֣ים שָׁנָ֔ה
וְאַרְבַּ֥ע מֵא֖וֹת שָׁנָ֑ה וַֽיְהִ֗י בְּעֶ֨צֶם֙ הַיּ֣וֹם הַזֶּ֔ה יָ֥צְא֛וּ כָּל־צִבְא֥וֹת
מב יְהוָ֖ה מֵאֶ֥רֶץ מִצְרָֽיִם: לֵ֣יל שִׁמֻּרִ֥ים הוּא֙ לַֽיהוָ֔ה לְהוֹצִיאָ֖ם מֵאֶ֣רֶץ
מִצְרָ֑יִם הֽוּא־הַלַּ֤יְלָה הַזֶּה֙ לַֽיהוָ֔ה שִׁמֻּרִ֛ים לְכָל־בְּנֵ֥י יִשְׂרָאֵ֖ל
לְדֹרֹתָֽם:

CLASSIC COMMENTATORS

The phrase ליל שמורים, "night of watchfulness," appears twice in verse 42. To what "watching" is it referring, and why is it mentioned twice?

רש״י

ליל שימורים הוא ליה׳ הזה לי״י - הוא הלילה שאמר לאברהם: בלילה הזה אני גואל את בניך. שמורים לכל בני ישראל לדורותם - משומר ובא מן המזיקין.

RASHI

That is the night regarding which God said to Avraham: I will redeem your descendants on this night. This night provides protection for Israel from the damage of evil forces.

ר׳ יוסף בכור שור

ליל שמורים הוא לה׳ - שהקב״ה היה שומר וממתין לילה זה להוציא את בני ישראל. הוא הלילה הזה לה׳ לכל בני ישראל - שיהיו בני ישראל שומרים וממתינים לילה זה בכל שנה, לקיים מצות הללו לשם הקב״ה שגאלם.

RABBI YOSEF BEKHOR SHOR

The Holy One, blessed be He, watched and waited for the night when He would rescue Israel from Egypt. And hence the Jewish people wait all year for this night in order to observe its commandments for the Holy One, blessed be He, who redeemed them.

אבן עזרא

בעבור שהשם שמרם, ולא יתן המשחית לבוא אל בתיהם לנגף (שמות י״ב:כ״ג), צוה שיהיה זה הלילה שמורים לישראל לדורותם. והטעם שלא ישנו, רק יודו ויספרו גבורות השם בצאתם ממצרים.

IBN EZRA

Because it was on the fifteenth of the month that the Lord watched over Israel and prevented the destroyer from entering their homes to strike them, that He commanded His people to watch [observe] this night in all future generations. This means that the nation should not sleep on this night but pass the hours relating and discussing the mighty acts of God that He performed when taking Israel out of Egypt.

43 The Lord said to Moshe and Aharon, "This is the law of the Passover sacrifice. No
44 foreigner may eat of it. But any slave who has been acquired for money and circum-
45 cised, may eat it. No gentile resident or hired laborer may eat of it. It should be eaten
46 in a single house; bring none of the meat outside the house. Do not break any of its
47 bones. All the community of Israel shall observe this. If a stranger lives among you and
48 wishes to offer a Passover sacrifice to the Lord, every male in his household must be
circumcised. Then he may join in observing it and be like a native-born. But no uncir-
49 cumcised man may eat of it. There shall be one and the same law for the native-born
50 and the stranger who lives among you." All the Israelites did exactly as the Lord had
51 commanded Moshe and Aharon. And on that very day the Lord brought the Israelites
out of Egypt in their battalions.

רמב״ן

טעם, כי פרשת החדש הזה לכם נאמרה בראש חדש, ובו ביום מיד עשה משה שליחותו: ויקרא משה לכל זקני ישראל ויאמר אליהם – צוה אותם בחקת הפסח והבטיחם שיגאלו בליל חמשה עשר. והם האמינו: ויקוד העם וישתחוו. וסמך הכתוב לזה: ויהי בחצי הלילה, לומר שקיים להם הבטחתם, וכשהשלים זה, חזר לעניין ראשון להשלים חקת הפסח.

RAMBAN

The reason that the text returns now to discuss details of the Passover sacrifice is as follows. The introduction of the topic which starts with the verse "This month shall be to you the beginning of months" (12:2) was originally stated by God to Moshe on the first of the month of Nisan. The latter immediately fulfilled God's command as the verse states, "Then Moshe called together all the elders of Israel and instructed them" etc. (12:21). Hence as soon as Moshe received God's instructions, he conveyed them to the people, commanding them in the laws of the Passover sacrifice. It was also then that Moshe promised the nation that they would be redeemed from Egypt on the night of the fifteenth. Israel trusted in Moshe's assurance, as we read, "Then the people bowed down and prostrated themselves" (12:27). The text thereafter recounts how this promise was fulfilled: "It happened at midnight; the Lord struck down all the firstborn in Egypt" (12:29) – and only afterward returns to finish its outline of the Passover sacrifice's laws.

ר' שמשון רפאל הירש

מפסוק ל״ח נמצאנו למדים, שערב רב של זרים הצטרף אל בני ישראל ביציאתם ממצרים. בהקשר לכך באה עתה "חקת הפסח" הזאת, "חוקה" הכוללת את הדרישות שמעמיד קרבן הפסח בנוגע לאישיות המשתתפים בו.

RABBI SAMSON RAPHAEL HIRSCH

Verse 38 in this chapter informs us that "a great variety of other people," that is, foreigners who were not of Israel, joined the nation on their exodus out of the Egyptian bondage. It is in association with that fact that the Torah commands the law regarding the Passover sacrifice, defining the characteristics necessary for any participants in this ceremony.

QUESTIONS FOR THOUGHT

- Ibn Ezra and R. Hirsch both argue that this passage fits here because of the context. Look at the previous passage and at those two commentaries – how does each of them see this passage fitting in?
- Ramban does not think that this passage fits particularly well here, but the Torah had little choice but to put it here. Why does he think he the Torah needed to delay writing this passage until here?
- How do you think that context could or should affect the way we understand things?

שמות | פרק יב

מג וַיֹּאמֶר יהוה אֶל־מֹשֶׁה וְאַהֲרֹן זֹאת חֻקַּת הַפָּסַח כָּל־בֶּן־נֵכָר
מד לֹא־יֹאכַל בּוֹ: וְכָל־עֶבֶד אִישׁ מִקְנַת־כָּסֶף וּמַלְתָּה אֹתוֹ אָז
מה יֹאכַל בּוֹ: תּוֹשָׁב וְשָׂכִיר לֹא־יֹאכַל בּוֹ: בְּבַיִת אֶחָד יֵאָכֵל לֹא־
מו תוֹצִיא מִן־הַבַּיִת מִן־הַבָּשָׂר חוּצָה וְעֶצֶם לֹא תִשְׁבְּרוּ־בוֹ:
מז כָּל־עֲדַת יִשְׂרָאֵל יַעֲשׂוּ אֹתוֹ: וְכִי־יָגוּר אִתְּךָ גֵּר וְעָשָׂה פֶסַח
מח לַיהוה הִמּוֹל לוֹ כָל־זָכָר וְאָז יִקְרַב לַעֲשֹׂתוֹ וְהָיָה כְּאֶזְרַח
מט הָאָרֶץ וְכָל־עָרֵל לֹא־יֹאכַל בּוֹ: תּוֹרָה אַחַת יִהְיֶה לָאֶזְרָח
נ וְלַגֵּר הַגָּר בְּתוֹכְכֶם: וַיַּעֲשׂוּ כָּל־בְּנֵי יִשְׂרָאֵל כַּאֲשֶׁר צִוָּה יהוה
נא אֶת־מֹשֶׁה וְאֶת־אַהֲרֹן כֵּן עָשׂוּ: וַיְהִי בְּעֶצֶם הַיּוֹם
הַזֶּה הוֹצִיא יהוה אֶת־בְּנֵי יִשְׂרָאֵל מֵאֶרֶץ מִצְרַיִם עַל־
צִבְאֹתָם:

QUICK BITE

An interesting feature of the Passover sacrifice is that it is supposed to be eaten in one house, or more specifically in one group. This component turns the home into an altar, a place that is sanctified to God. The altar is a place of protection, as implied elsewhere in Tanakh (see 21:14, I Kings 1:50, 2:28). So too here, the Torah calls this night of the Passover offering ליל שימורים – a night of guarding. The power of the home to protect us is that we have converted it to an altar.

CLASSIC COMMENTATORS

We would have expected this passage to appear at the beginning of the chapter 12, together with the other instructions regarding the Pesaḥ. Why does it appear only now, after Israel has left Egypt?

IBN EZRA אבן עזרא

The previous verses speak about the fifteenth of Nisan as the night of watchfulness, and state that the night is to be observed for evermore by the consumption of the Passover sacrifice. Thus the text now returns to complete its discussion of how Passover is to be celebrated through the generations.

ויאמר י"י – בעבור שהזכיר: ליל שמורים שהוא ליל חמשה עשר שבו יאכל הפסח, השלים לפרש חוקות פסח דורות.

Shemot | Chapter 13

> *God tells Moshe that from this point onward, firstborns would have a special status of being dedicated to God. Interestingly, Moshe uses this opportunity to teach Israel about the commandment of the seven-day holiday revolving around matza (and the prohibition of ḥametz), which they will begin observing when they enter the Promised Land.*

13 1-2 The Lord said to Moshe, "Consecrate every firstborn to Me. Man and beast, the first 3 to emerge from every womb among the Israelites is Mine." Moshe said to the people, "Remember this day, the day you left Egypt, the house of slaves, when with a mighty 4 hand the Lord rescued you from here. No leaven may be eaten. Today, in the month of 5 Aviv, you are leaving. And when the Lord brings you into the land of the Canaanites, Hittites, Amorites, Hivites, and Jebusites, the land that He promised your ancestors He would give you – one flowing with milk and with honey – you shall keep this ceremony 6 in this month. For seven days you shall eat unleavened bread; the seventh day shall be 7 a festival to the Lord. Unleavened bread shall be eaten for those seven days; no bread 8 or leavening shall be seen in all your land. On that day you must tell your child, 'This is 9 because of what the Lord did for me when I left Egypt.' It shall be a sign on your arm, a reminder between your eyes, so that the Lord's teaching be on your tongue, for with 10 a mighty hand the Lord brought you out of Egypt. Celebrate this law each year at its set time.

RASHBAM / רשב״ם

I am performing this service because the Lord performed miracles in Egypt on my behalf.

בעבור זה – שעשה י״י לי ניסים במצרים אני עובד עבודה הזאת.

QUESTIONS FOR THOUGHT

- Three options are presented here regarding the message being delivered to the child:
  o I am doing this because of what God did for me in Egypt
  o God saved me from Egypt because I performed this very same service in Egypt
  o God saved me from Egypt so that I could perform this service tonight
- Which of the above belongs to which of the commentaries?
- Which of these explanations would be more meaningful to you? Why?

שמות | פרק יג

שביעי

יג א וַיְדַבֵּ֥ר יְהוָ֖ה אֶל־מֹשֶׁ֥ה לֵּאמֹֽר: ב קַדֶּשׁ־לִ֨י כָל־בְּכ֜וֹר פֶּ֤טֶר כָּל־רֶ֨חֶם֙ בִּבְנֵ֣י יִשְׂרָאֵ֔ל בָּאָדָ֖ם וּבַבְּהֵמָ֑ה לִ֖י הֽוּא: ג וַיֹּ֨אמֶר מֹשֶׁ֜ה אֶל־הָעָ֗ם זָכ֞וֹר אֶת־הַיּ֤וֹם הַזֶּה֙ אֲשֶׁ֨ר יְצָאתֶ֤ם מִמִּצְרַ֨יִם֙ מִבֵּ֣ית עֲבָדִ֔ים כִּ֚י בְּחֹ֣זֶק יָ֔ד הוֹצִ֧יא יְהוָ֛ה אֶתְכֶ֖ם מִזֶּ֑ה וְלֹ֥א יֵאָכֵ֖ל חָמֵֽץ: ד הַיּ֖וֹם אַתֶּ֣ם יֹצְאִ֑ים בְּחֹ֖דֶשׁ הָאָבִֽיב: ה וְהָיָ֣ה כִֽי־יְבִיאֲךָ֣ יְהוָ֡ה אֶל־אֶ֣רֶץ הַֽכְּנַעֲנִ֣י וְהַחִתִּ֡י וְהָאֱמֹרִי֩ וְהַחִוִּ֨י וְהַיְבוּסִ֜י אֲשֶׁ֨ר נִשְׁבַּ֤ע לַאֲבֹתֶ֨יךָ֙ לָ֣תֶת לָ֔ךְ אֶ֛רֶץ זָבַ֥ת חָלָ֖ב וּדְבָ֑שׁ וְעָבַדְתָּ֛ אֶת־הָעֲבֹדָ֥ה הַזֹּ֖את בַּחֹ֥דֶשׁ הַזֶּֽה: ו שִׁבְעַ֥ת יָמִ֖ים תֹּאכַ֣ל מַצֹּ֑ת וּבַיּוֹם֙ הַשְּׁבִיעִ֔י חַ֖ג לַיהוָֽה: ז מַצּוֹת֙ יֵֽאָכֵ֔ל אֵ֖ת שִׁבְעַ֣ת הַיָּמִ֑ים וְלֹֽא־יֵרָאֶ֨ה לְךָ֜ חָמֵ֗ץ וְלֹֽא־יֵרָאֶ֥ה לְךָ֛ שְׂאֹ֖ר בְּכָל־גְּבֻלֶֽךָ: ח וְהִגַּדְתָּ֣ לְבִנְךָ֔ בַּיּ֥וֹם הַה֖וּא לֵאמֹ֑ר בַּעֲב֣וּר זֶ֗ה עָשָׂ֤ה יְהוָה֙ לִ֔י בְּצֵאתִ֖י מִמִּצְרָֽיִם: ט וְהָיָה֩ לְךָ֨ לְא֜וֹת עַל־יָדְךָ֗ וּלְזִכָּרוֹן֙ בֵּ֣ין עֵינֶ֔יךָ לְמַ֗עַן תִּהְיֶ֛ה תּוֹרַ֥ת יְהוָ֖ה בְּפִ֑יךָ כִּ֚י בְּיָ֣ד חֲזָקָ֔ה הוֹצִֽאֲךָ֥ יְהוָ֖ה מִמִּצְרָֽיִם: י וְשָׁמַרְתָּ֛ אֶת־הַחֻקָּ֥ה הַזֹּ֖את לְמוֹעֲדָ֑הּ מִיָּמִ֖ים יָמִֽימָה:

CLASSIC COMMENTATORS

In a line made famous by the Haggada, Moshe instructs Israel to tell their children at some future date: בעבור זה עשה ה׳ לי בצאתי ממצרים, translated here as: "This is because of what the Lord did for me when I left Egypt." However, the precise meaning of this phrase – the essence of the message to the children – is the subject of debate.

RASHI
רש״י

בעבור זה – בעבור שאקיים מצוותיו, כגון פסח מצה ומרור הללו.

God redeemed me from Egypt so that I would fulfill His commandments, such as eating these festival foods of the Passover sacrifice, matza, and the bitter herbs.

IBN EZRA
אבן עזרא

ועבדת את העבודה הזאת – היא עבודת הפסח, ותאמר לבנך כי בעבור זאת העבודה שעשיתי, עשה לי האות שעשה, עד שיצאתי ממצרים.

The service in question is that of the Passover sacrifice. Tell your children that it was thanks to this ceremony that you first performed, that God performed this sign for you, until you left Egypt.

Moshe finally delivers the instruction to Israel about firstborn males, both among people and amongst the animals, "belonging" to God. Here, again, there is an anticipated question from the following generation regarding this mitzva, and the response is a short version of the story of the exodus culminating with the plague of the firstborns.

11 When the Lord brings you to the land of the Canaanites, as He promised you and your
12 ancestors, and He gives it to you, you shall give over to the Lord the first to emerge
13 from every womb. Every male firstborn of your animals shall be His. You shall redeem every firstborn donkey with a lamb; otherwise, you must break the donkey's neck. You
14 must redeem every firstborn among your sons. And in the future, when your children ask, 'What is this?' you shall answer, 'With a mighty hand the Lord brought us out
15 of Egypt, the house of slaves. And when Pharaoh was obstinate and refused to set us free, the Lord killed all the firstborn sons in Egypt, man and beast alike. That is why I sacrifice every male firstborn animal to the Lord, and redeem all my firstborn sons.'
16 It shall be a sign on your arm and an emblem between your eyes – with a mighty hand the Lord rescued us from Egypt."

QUESTIONS FOR THOUGHT

- In what way is Sforno's understanding of the question very different from that of Haamek Davar and R. Hirsch?
- For a variety of halakhic and medical reasons, the mitzva of *pidyon haben* (redeeming the firstborn) is not so commonly performed. How would you explain the meaning of this mitzva to someone who is unfamiliar with it?

TEXTUAL SKILLS

1. Once again, God's name appears seven times in this passage. What do you think the Torah is trying to say by having God's name as the theme word in two consecutive passages?
2. As Moshe conveys God's command to the people, he expands on what was said earlier. In that expansion, an idea is introduced through the use of a single word, which appears three times in verse 13 and one additional time later in this passage. Find the word and explain why it is so essential!

WISDOM OF THE HEART

Rabbi Tzadok HaKohen of Lublin says that when a person wants to start serving God, the evil inclination tries to interfere. The dark side in each of us starts asking questions, such as: "Who do you think you are that you can serve God? Do you know how lowly and unimportant you are?" The appropriate response to this, says Rabbi Tzadok, is to remember that God took Israel out of Egypt – not because of how exalted they were, but despite how low they were. If Israel, in a period of seven weeks, could raise themselves from being as low as one could go to receiving the Torah at Mount Sinai, then surely any Jew can become a true servant of God.

Which do you think is a greater challenge to achieving great things – excessive humility or excessive arrogance?

יא וְהָיָ֞ה כִּֽי־יְבִאֲךָ֣ יְהוָ֗ה אֶל־אֶ֤רֶץ הַֽכְּנַעֲנִי֙ כַּאֲשֶׁ֨ר נִשְׁבַּ֥ע לְךָ֖
וְלַאֲבֹתֶ֑יךָ וּנְתָנָ֖הּ לָֽךְ: וְהַעֲבַרְתָּ֥ כָל־פֶּֽטֶר־רֶ֖חֶם לַֽיהוָ֑ה וְכָל־
יב
יג פֶּ֣טֶר ׀ שֶׁ֣גֶר בְּהֵמָ֗ה אֲשֶׁ֨ר יִהְיֶ֥ה לְךָ֛ הַזְּכָרִ֖ים לַיהוָֽה: וְכָל־פֶּ֣טֶר
חֲמֹר֮ תִּפְדֶּ֣ה בְשֶׂה֒ וְאִם־לֹ֥א תִפְדֶּ֖ה וַעֲרַפְתּ֑וֹ וְכֹ֨ל בְּכ֥וֹר אָדָ֛ם
יד בְּבָנֶ֖יךָ תִּפְדֶּֽה: וְהָיָ֞ה כִּֽי־יִשְׁאָלְךָ֥ בִנְךָ֛ מָחָ֖ר לֵאמֹ֣ר מַה־זֹּ֑את מפטיר
וְאָמַרְתָּ֣ אֵלָ֔יו בְּחֹ֣זֶק יָ֗ד הוֹצִיאָ֧נוּ יְהוָ֛ה מִמִּצְרַ֖יִם מִבֵּ֥ית עֲבָדִֽים:
וַיְהִ֗י כִּֽי־הִקְשָׁ֣ה פַרְעֹה֮ לְשַׁלְּחֵנוּ֒ וַיַּהֲרֹ֨ג יְהוָ֤ה כָּל־בְּכוֹר֙ בְּאֶ֣רֶץ
מִצְרַ֔יִם מִבְּכֹ֥ר אָדָ֖ם וְעַד־בְּכ֣וֹר בְּהֵמָ֑ה עַל־כֵּן֩ אֲנִ֨י זֹבֵ֜חַ לַֽיהוָ֗ה
טז כָּל־פֶּ֤טֶר רֶ֨חֶם֙ הַזְּכָרִ֔ים וְכָל־בְּכ֥וֹר בָּנַ֖י אֶפְדֶּֽה: וְהָיָ֤ה לְאוֹת֙
עַל־יָ֣דְכָ֔ה וּלְטוֹטָפֹ֖ת בֵּ֣ין עֵינֶ֑יךָ כִּ֚י בְּחֹ֣זֶק יָ֔ד הוֹצִיאָ֥נוּ יְהוָ֖ה
מִמִּצְרָֽיִם:

CLASSIC COMMENTATORS

In the Haggada, the question asked in verse 14 is ascribed to the simple child. In the context of this passage, however, it is a question sparked by something the child witnesses. Identifying the trigger for this question is not so simple.

RABBI OVADYA SFORNO
ר׳ עובדה ספורנו

Your children are bound to ask you about the practice of redeeming your firstborn donkeys. After all, that animal is an impure [non-kosher] beast whose body cannot be considered holy.

מה זאת – פדיון פטר חמור, שהוא בהמה טמאה ולא תחול עליה קדושת הגוף.

RABBI SAMSON RAPHAEL HIRSCH
ר׳ שמשון רפאל הירש

Your children will wonder about the added sanctity that is attributed to firstborns.

מה זאת – מהי משמעותו של קידוש זה, המעניק יתרון בבכורים?

HAAMEK DAVAR
העמק דבר

"What", they will ask, "is the point of assigning holiness to the firstborns?"

מה זאת – מה תועלת לנו בקדושת בכורים.

QUICK BITES

- **10:1** Rabbi Kalonymous Kalman Shapira of Piaseczno is also known as the *Aish Kodesh* – the Holy Fire, based on the name of one his well-known books. The *Aish Kodesh* was killed by the Nazis in Auschwitz. Many of his writings were found by an American soldier with a note that said, "By the time you find these books there may be no more Jews left in the world. But there will be a Jew left in Israel; bring him my writings and I promise you a spot in the World to Come."

  Near the end of his life, he asked: how could God harden Pharaoh's heart and take away his free will? After offering some initial thoughts, he wrote: "And more of my thoughts on this I don't remember." That was his unfinished symphony.

  The rest of the Piaseczno Rebbe's Torah was lost, but his impact on his own generation and those to come radiates like a bright light. God led Moshe through the darkness of Egypt, even into Pharaoh's palace, to bring him and the rest of *Benei Yisrael* into a place of brilliant light. If we let the goodness of God shine, we can overcome the darkness that clouds our world.

- **10:11** A midrash explains that when Pharaoh tells Moshe that "evil is staring you in the face," he is referring to a star named Evil, symbolized by blood, which his astrologers informed him would mark the fate of *Benei Yisrael* when they left Egypt. The astrological sign of blood was later transformed into a positive event when it was reinterpreted as representing the blood of circumcision. The *Zohar Ḥadash* comments that God didn't cancel the bloody astrological sign; rather, He converted it to something positive.

  The same may be true of people. We may be predisposed to certain behaviors and attitudes – social or anti-social behavior, depressive or happy personalities, even preferences for chocolate or vanilla ice cream. But being predisposed should not be confused with predetermined. Each of us can take control of our actions and behaviors and transform those predispositions into positive forces.

- **10:29** After the plague of darkness, Moshe insists that all the people go to worship – men, women, and children. Furthermore, not only will they take all of their sheep and cattle with them, but Pharaoh must send some as well. Pharaoh is enraged and tells Moshe that the next time Moshe sees Pharaoh he will die. Moshe responds that, indeed, he will not see Pharaoh's face again. Despite this, after the plague of the firstborn, Pharaoh summons Moshe to tell *Benei Yisrael* to leave!

  Some would argue that Pharaoh did not actually meet Moshe personally, but sent a messenger. Perhaps more meaningfully we could say that the face Moshe saw earlier, the face of the mighty Pharaoh, was not present when they met after the death of Pharaoh's son. The tables have turned, and Pharaoh is no longer the almighty ruler he once was.

  Ironically, the Hebrew word for face, *panim*, can also be read as *penim*, what is inside of us. Ideally, the face we show to the world outside of ourselves is a reflection of our inner selves. Moshe understood that if he did see Pharaoh again, he would no longer be the Pharaoh who held the fate of Israel in his hand, nor would he be the Pharaoh who decided whose face would be granted an audience.

- **12:22** Sometimes, a task at hand seems to be too big, a challenge insurmountable. It is for circumstances like these that the Midrash says that all we need to do is begin, opening the tiniest of openings, and God will step in to make that opening large enough and more. *Benei Yisrael* were asked to declare their freedom by painting their door frames with the blood of the Pesaḥ sacrifice. Once they did that, God threw open the gates to their freedom.

- According to the mishna in Avot, the world was created through ten divine pronouncements. *Sefat Emet* suggests that in the generations following the Creation, the world created by those ten utterances had become defiled, and the ten plagues represent a process of purification. The net result of that purification was that the ten pronouncements could now be reformulated as the Ten Commandments.

Exploring Hashkafa
The Purpose of the Plagues

Children take delight in hearing about the plagues. The combination of watching the bad guy suffer and the almost comic nature of the events make for a delightful, albeit simplistic, feel-good story about us vs. them, and how in the end it was "us" who won and "them" who lost. But when we grow past that childish stage, the plagues raise troubling – even uncomfortable – questions. If God wanted Israel to leave Egypt, He could have magically airlifted them on eagles' wings, as the Torah later describes. Why was it necessary to bring so much pain to the Egyptians in the process, playing with Pharaoh's free will to inflict yet another round?

To watch the Amshinover Rebbe during the reading of the Torah was to watch the Torah come alive – it seemed that the Rebbe was not just listening, but experiencing what was being read. The pain – even horror – on his face as he heard the story of the plagues was a dramatic expression of the difficulty raised by the Torah.

There are many ways to grapple with the question, and the fact that there are many approaches suggests that none of them are completely satisfying. A mystical approach suggests that the ten plagues parallel the ten statements of Creation and are designed to somehow, mystically, repair the damage done to the world as reflected in the multiple expressions of Egyptian culture. Another approach, based on Exodus 12:12 and Numbers 33:4, suggests that it was necessary for God to demonstrate the worthlessness of the Egyptian deities.

Some suggest psychological explanations. The plagues were necessary to help Israel begin to think like free people so that they could be prepared to leave when the moment came. Or, perhaps, the plagues' purpose was to break them free from identifying with their captors/ masters – a phenomenon known as Stockholm syndrome. Maybe it was to help restore their self-esteem after generations of crushing servitude, or even for them to feel like they marched proudly out of Egypt rather than sneaking away like thieves in the middle of the night.

All of the above make sense, to some extent, yet a careful look at the text of the Torah reveals one more idea: The purpose was to help restore God's position as the sole divine force to reckon with. This idea is repeated so frequently in the text that it is difficult to overlook: in Exodus 7:5, 7:17, 8:7, 8:18, 9:14, 10:2, and many more. For whom was this message intended – for Egypt? For Israel? For everyone else in the world? That depends which verses you are looking at. Why was this so important? Did God need this? Did the people need this? It depends who you ask, and the sheer number of great thinkers who have proposed brilliant and creative ideas is impressive.

The multitude of answers don't make the question go away; they indicate just how important that question has been for thousands of years. They also reflect just how seriously we take our moral compass and tradition, and they suggest that underlying all this is a deep understanding still waiting to be discovered.

פרשת בשלח
PARASHAT BESHALAḤ

"I'll be the roundabout, the words will make you out 'n' out."
— Yes

Out at last. The light at the end of the tunnel is real and approaching fast. Suddenly, as Israel inches closer to a promising new beginning, they run into a proverbial wall – or a literal great body of water. "Wait – Moshe, what was the plan with this? You didn't tell us we would go through all of this excitement just to die by drowning in the Sea of Reeds!" What do you do when your hope seems to fade in the face of a new obstacle? The people will soon learn one of the greatest lessons of all: the obstacle is the way.

PARASHAT BESHALAḤ

13 17 When Pharaoh let the people go, the Lord did not lead them through the land of the Philistines, though it was the shorter way; "If the people face war," thought God, "they 18 will change their minds and go back to Egypt." So He led them on a roundabout course, by way of the wilderness, to the Sea of Reeds. The Israelites left Egypt armed for battle. 19 And Moshe took with him the remains of Yosef, who had bound the Israelites by oath: 20 "When God comes to your aid, bring my remains with you out of here." They set out 21 from Sukkot and camped at Etam, at the edge of the desert. The Lord went ahead of them by day in a column of cloud to guide them, and at night in a column of fire to give 22 them light, so that they might travel day and night. Neither the column of cloud by day nor that of fire by night once departed from the people.

RAMBAN
Even though God protected Israel from war by leading them into the wilderness, the nation was still afraid that the Philistines who lived in nearby settlements would attack them. They were therefore armed just in case they had to engage the enemy.

רמב״ן
וטעם וחמושים עלו בני ישראל - לומר כי אף על פי שהסב י"י אותם דרך המדבר היו יראים פן יבאו עליהם פלשתים יושבי הערים הקרובות להם, והיו חלוצים כמו היוצאים למלחמה.

QUESTIONS FOR THOUGHT
- The opinions of Rashbam and Ramban seem very similar, but as they explain themselves it turns out that they have dramatically different ideas about the state of mind of *Benei Yisrael* at this moment. How does each explain the state of mind of *Benei Yisrael*?
- In what way is Bekhor Shor's position very different from the other two? Look back at 12:39. Does this support or pose a challenge to Bekhor Shor's position?
- Do you think that it is possible for all of the opinions to be correct?

WISDOM OF THE HEART

God did not lead *Benei Yisrael* on the road through the land of the Philistines, even though it was shorter. "If the people face war," thought God, "they will change their minds and go back to Egypt."

According to Rashi, taking the "shorter way" could lead to problems, since it was also a shorter trip back to Egypt should the people get discouraged. Rashbam understands that the shorter way would have brought them more quickly to Canaan, to the wars necessary for conquest. Delaying the Canaanite wars would give the people a chance to prepare.

Rav Yoel Bin Nun points out that the engravings on the walls of the temple at Karnak in Egypt show that the entire northern Sinai coastal region was under direct Egyptian sovereignty, with Egyptian military outposts all along the way. The shorter way would also have more obstacles to overcome, but those would be small skirmishes. Rather than the small, nagging battles with military outposts, God wanted to bring the nation into a face-to-face confrontation at the Sea of Reeds with their former oppressors in order to help them break the mental shackles of slavery to Pharaoh. They needed to be liberated not only politically and economically, but also psychologically.

פרשת בשלח

יג ‎ יז וַיְהִ֗י בְּשַׁלַּ֣ח פַּרְעֹה֮ אֶת־הָעָם֒ וְלֹא־נָחָ֣ם אֱלֹהִ֗ים דֶּ֚רֶךְ אֶ֣רֶץ פְּלִשְׁתִּ֔ים כִּ֥י קָר֖וֹב ה֑וּא כִּ֣י ׀ אָמַ֣ר אֱלֹהִ֗ים פֶּן־יִנָּחֵ֥ם הָעָ֛ם בִּרְאֹתָ֥ם מִלְחָמָ֖ה וְשָׁ֥בוּ מִצְרָֽיְמָה: יח וַיַּסֵּ֨ב אֱלֹהִ֧ים ׀ אֶת־הָעָ֛ם דֶּ֥רֶךְ הַמִּדְבָּ֖ר יַם־ס֑וּף וַחֲמֻשִׁ֛ים עָל֥וּ בְנֵי־יִשְׂרָאֵ֖ל מֵאֶ֥רֶץ מִצְרָֽיִם: יט וַיִּקַּ֥ח מֹשֶׁ֛ה אֶת־עַצְמ֥וֹת יוֹסֵ֖ף עִמּ֑וֹ כִּי֩ הַשְׁבֵּ֨עַ הִשְׁבִּ֜יעַ אֶת־בְּנֵ֤י יִשְׂרָאֵל֙ לֵאמֹ֔ר פָּקֹ֨ד יִפְקֹ֤ד אֱלֹהִים֙ אֶתְכֶ֔ם וְהַעֲלִיתֶ֧ם אֶת־עַצְמֹתַ֛י מִזֶּ֖ה אִתְּכֶֽם: כ וַיִּסְע֖וּ מִסֻּכֹּ֑ת וַיַּחֲנ֣וּ בְאֵתָ֔ם בִּקְצֵ֖ה הַמִּדְבָּֽר: כא וַֽיהוָ֡ה הֹלֵךְ֩ לִפְנֵיהֶ֨ם יוֹמָ֜ם בְּעַמּ֤וּד עָנָן֙ לַנְחֹתָ֣ם הַדֶּ֔רֶךְ וְלַ֛יְלָה בְּעַמּ֥וּד אֵ֖שׁ לְהָאִ֣יר לָהֶ֑ם לָלֶ֖כֶת יוֹמָ֥ם וָלָֽיְלָה: כב לֹֽא־יָמִ֞ישׁ עַמּ֤וּד הֶֽעָנָן֙ יוֹמָ֔ם וְעַמּ֥וּד הָאֵ֖שׁ לָ֑יְלָה לִפְנֵ֖י הָעָֽם:

CLASSIC COMMENTATORS

The Torah makes of point of indicating that *Benei Yisrael* left Egypt חמושים, "equipped" (translated here as "armed"). What were they equipped for?

RASHBAM

רשב"ם

Israel left Egypt armed with weapons of war. The nation, after all, was headed toward a military confrontation with the Canaanites, as they sought to conquer their land. For so had God informed Moshe, "And I promise to bring you out of the misery of Egypt to the land of the Canaanites" (3:17). And thus does Yehoshua declare, "But all your warriors shall cross over [into Canaan] armed (Josh. 1:14).

וחמושים - בכלי זיין, שהיו הולכים לירש את ארץ כנען, כמו שכתוב למעלה: ואומר אעלה אתכם מעני מצרים אל ארץ הכנעני וגו׳: וכן: תעברו חמושים דיהושע (יהושע א׳:י"ד).

RABBI YOSEF BEKHOR SHOR

ר' יוסף בכור שור

The term חמושים is similar to how the root is used in the verse: "Take up a fifth part [וחמש] of the land of Egypt" (Gen. 41:34, a statement Yosef makes in advising Pharaoh to prepare for the years of famine). That is, Israel left Egypt well stocked with provisions for a lengthy journey. Evidence for this is the fact that they managed just fine for a full month until the manna began to fall on the fifteenth of Iyar.

חמושים עלו בני ישראל - כמו וחמש את ארץ מצרים (בראשית מ"א:ל"ד), שהיו עמהם מזונות כדי להספיק אותם דרך רחוק, שהרי ניזונו חודש אחד במזון שעמהם, שלא שאלו מן עד חמשה עשר באייר.

Shemot | Chapter 14

14 ¹ Then the Lord said to Moshe, "Speak to the Israelites and tell them to turn back and ² camp in front of Pi Haḥirot, between Migdol and the sea, before Baal Tzefon. Encamp ³ facing it, by the sea. Pharaoh will think that the Israelites are lost across the land, that ⁴ they are trapped in the desert. I will toughen Pharaoh's heart, and he will pursue them. I will be glorified over Pharaoh and all his force, and the Egyptians will know that I am the ⁵ Lord." And so they did. When the king of Egypt was told that the Israelites had escaped, he and his officials changed their minds about the people: "What have we done, releas- ⁶ ing the Israelites from serving us?" So the king harnessed his chariot and brought out ⁷ his army. He took six hundred elite chariots and all the other chariots of Egypt, with ⁸ officers over them all. The Lord strengthened the heart of Pharaoh King of Egypt, and ⁹ he pursued the Israelites, who were leaving in defiance of them. The Egyptians, with all the king's horses and chariots, cavalry and infantry, chased and caught up with them as

---

רמב״ן

הוגד זה למלך מצרים ואמר: כי ברח העם והם נבוכים במדבר, ואינם הולכים אל מקום ידוע לזבוח. וזה טעם: ובני ישראל יוצאים ביד רמה – שעשו להם דגל ונס להתנוסס, ויוצאים בשמחה ובשירים בתוף ובכנור כדמות הנגאלים מעבדות לחירות, לא כעבדים העתידים לשוב לעבודתם, וכל זה הוגד לו.

RAMBAN

The king of Egypt was informed that Israel had escaped and that rather than heading toward a well-known site to offer their sacrifices, they were wandering aimlessly in the wilderness. And this is the sense of the verse which states, "The Israelites were leaving in defiance of them" – the nation fashioned a flag which they flew proudly and a banner that they waved triumphantly. Israel thus left Egypt joyfully, accompanied by song and the playing of tambourines and harps. They behaved just like one would expect to see people acting who had been released from bondage into freedom; they had no fear that their slavery would be reimposed upon them. All of this was related to Pharaoh.

QUESTIONS FOR THOUGHT

- Both Rashbam and Ramban connect this statement to the context in which it is written. Which commentary connects it to what came before, and which connects it to what comes afterward?
- Bekhor Shor doesn't explicitly connect this to a context, but when you read his explanation carefully you realize that he is also doing that. To what context is he relating this statement?
- Based on what you know about the story, which of these do you think most accurately describes Israel's state of mind?

TEXTUAL SKILLS

1. It is unusual to hear that a king personally prepares his horse or his chariot, yet Pharaoh does. Do you know of other significant figures in Tanakh who saddle up their own animals even though they have servants who usually do it for them?

2. Baal Tzefon is mentioned twice in this passage and only one more time in the rest of Tanakh (referring back to this scene). What significance do you think Baal Tzefon has in this scene?

3. Notice the number of the best chariots Pharaoh takes. Do you remember where you saw this number earlier in the story of the exodus?

שמות | פרק יד

יד א וַיְדַבֵּר יהוה אֶל־מֹשֶׁה לֵּאמֹר: דַּבֵּר אֶל־בְּנֵי יִשְׂרָאֵל וְיָשֻׁבוּ וְיַחֲנוּ לִפְנֵי פִּי הַחִירֹת בֵּין מִגְדֹּל וּבֵין הַיָּם לִפְנֵי בַּעַל צְפֹן נִכְחוֹ תַחֲנוּ עַל־הַיָּם: ג וְאָמַר פַּרְעֹה לִבְנֵי יִשְׂרָאֵל נְבֻכִים הֵם בָּאָרֶץ סָגַר עֲלֵיהֶם הַמִּדְבָּר: ד וְחִזַּקְתִּי אֶת־לֵב־פַּרְעֹה וְרָדַף אַחֲרֵיהֶם וְאִכָּבְדָה בְּפַרְעֹה וּבְכָל־חֵילוֹ וְיָדְעוּ מִצְרַיִם כִּי־אֲנִי יהוה וַיַּעֲשׂוּ־כֵן: ה וַיֻּגַּד לְמֶלֶךְ מִצְרַיִם כִּי בָרַח הָעָם וַיֵּהָפֵךְ לְבַב פַּרְעֹה וַעֲבָדָיו אֶל־הָעָם וַיֹּאמְרוּ מַה־זֹּאת עָשִׂינוּ כִּי־שִׁלַּחְנוּ אֶת־יִשְׂרָאֵל מֵעָבְדֵנוּ: ו וַיֶּאְסֹר אֶת־רִכְבּוֹ וְאֶת־עַמּוֹ לָקַח עִמּוֹ: ז וַיִּקַּח שֵׁשׁ־מֵאוֹת רֶכֶב בָּחוּר וְכֹל רֶכֶב מִצְרָיִם וְשָׁלִשִׁם עַל־כֻּלּוֹ: ח וַיְחַזֵּק יהוה אֶת־לֵב פַּרְעֹה מֶלֶךְ מִצְרַיִם וַיִּרְדֹּף אַחֲרֵי בְּנֵי יִשְׂרָאֵל וּבְנֵי יִשְׂרָאֵל יֹצְאִים בְּיָד רָמָה: ט וַיִּרְדְּפוּ מִצְרַיִם אַחֲרֵיהֶם וַיַּשִּׂיגוּ שני אוֹתָם חֹנִים עַל־הַיָּם כָּל־סוּס רֶכֶב פַּרְעֹה וּפָרָשָׁיו וְחֵילוֹ עַל־

CLASSIC COMMENTATORS

Benei Yisrael are described in this passage as leaving ביד רמה, "in defiance." What is that referring to, and why are we told that at this point in the Torah?

RASHBAM

At first the Israelites marched out of Egypt with no worries on their minds. But then, when they saw Pharaoh and his nation chasing after them, they grew terrified.

רשב״ם

יוצאים ביד רמה – לא היו דואגים כלל עד שראו פרעה ועמו רודפים אחריהם, אז וייראו מאד.

RABBI YOSEF BEKHOR SHOR

The Israelites allowed nothing to hinder their departure. For the nation was marching out of Egypt with the king's permission. And so they left with open defiance; not stealthily like thieves in the night.

ר׳ יוסף בכור שור

ובני ישראל יוצאים – לא היו נותנים לב לשום דבר, כי ברשות יצאו, ויוצאים בפרהסיא, ולא כגנבים.

> *When the Israelites see Pharaoh approaching, they both call out to God and complain to Moshe, claiming that they had told him in Egypt to leave them and let them continue as slaves. Moshe is unfazed, calmly responding that they have nothing to fear because God will deal with the Egyptians.*

10 they were encamped by the sea near Pi Haḥirot, before Baal Tzefon. Pharaoh drew near – the Israelites looked up: there were the Egyptians thundering after them. They were
11 terrified and cried to the Lord for help. "Were there no graves in Egypt?" they asked Moshe; "Is that why you brought us here to die in the desert? What have you done to
12 us, bringing us out of Egypt? Did we not tell you in Egypt: Leave us alone – let us serve
13 the Egyptians. Better a life in servitude to Egypt than death in the desert." But Moshe told the people, "Fear not. Stand firm and see the deliverance the Lord will bring you
14 today. The Egyptians you see today, you shall never see again. The Lord will fight for you. You stay silent."

QUESTIONS FOR THOUGHT

- Ibn Ezra introduces psychology to explain Israel's fear. What is his explanation?
- Ramban distinguishes between the crying out to God and the complaining to Moshe – one is likely more legitimate and the other less so. How does his explanation help to answer why they would be so fearful after witnessing God's power?
- Which of these explanations works better with Moshe's response (v. 13)?

TEXTUAL SKILLS

1. Notice the play on two very different roots – י-ר-א (to fear) and ר-א-ה (to see). Who sees and fears, and what does Moshe suggest that they see so that they no longer fear?

2. Where in Exodus did we previously encounter a phrase which indicates that "you will no longer see again"?

WISDOM OF THE HEART

Benei Yisrael ask Moshe rhetorically, "Were there no graves in Egypt? Is that why you brought us here to die in the desert?" That mocking tone could be understood as a negative trait, but Rabbi Samson Raphael Hirsch sees that as an early version of classic Jewish humor – invented to be able to laugh at a dark reality and help elevate the people beyond it.

QUICK BITE

What beautiful words: "Fear not. Stand firm and see the deliverance the Lord will bring you today." This moment of trepidation for the Israelites is really an analogy for any fear we may have in our lives. We fear failure. We fear being irrelevant. We fear not being enough. In all of these scenarios, God tells us: "I've got you. Don't fear. You thought you were stuck, with no way out. But just watch what I can do in your life." There is no dilemma in our existence that God cannot solve.

שמות | פרק יד

פִּי הַחִירֹת לִפְנֵי בַּעַל צְפֹן: וּפַרְעֹה הִקְרִיב וַיִּשְׂאוּ בְנֵי־יִשְׂרָאֵל אֶת־עֵינֵיהֶם וְהִנֵּה מִצְרַיִם ׀ נֹסֵעַ אַחֲרֵיהֶם וַיִּירְאוּ מְאֹד וַיִּצְעֲקוּ בְנֵי־יִשְׂרָאֵל אֶל־יהוה: וַיֹּאמְרוּ אֶל־מֹשֶׁה הֲמִבְּלִי אֵין־קְבָרִים בְּמִצְרַיִם לְקַחְתָּנוּ לָמוּת בַּמִּדְבָּר מַה־זֹּאת עָשִׂיתָ לָּנוּ לְהוֹצִיאָנוּ מִמִּצְרָיִם: הֲלֹא־זֶה הַדָּבָר אֲשֶׁר דִּבַּרְנוּ אֵלֶיךָ בְמִצְרַיִם לֵאמֹר חֲדַל מִמֶּנּוּ וְנַעַבְדָה אֶת־מִצְרָיִם כִּי טוֹב לָנוּ עֲבֹד אֶת־מִצְרַיִם מִמֻּתֵנוּ בַּמִּדְבָּר: וַיֹּאמֶר מֹשֶׁה אֶל־הָעָם אַל־תִּירָאוּ הִתְיַצְּבוּ וּרְאוּ אֶת־יְשׁוּעַת יהוה אֲשֶׁר־יַעֲשֶׂה לָכֶם הַיּוֹם כִּי אֲשֶׁר רְאִיתֶם אֶת־מִצְרַיִם הַיּוֹם לֹא תֹסִפוּ לִרְאֹתָם עוֹד עַד־עוֹלָם: יהוה יִלָּחֵם לָכֶם וְאַתֶּם תַּחֲרִישׁוּן:

CLASSIC COMMENTATORS

Fearful that they are going to die at the hands of the Egyptians, *Benei Yisrael* complain to Moshe that being taken out of Egypt was the worst thing that could have happened to them. How could they be so fearful after witnessing God's power throughout the plagues?

IBN EZRA

The Egyptians had been masters over Israel for centuries, and the generation of slaves that escaped from Egypt had been raised to suffer the lash of their overlords. Naturally, this meant that Israel felt low and downtrodden – how could they possibly take up arms against their masters? Furthermore, the Israelites were weak and had no training in warfare whatsoever.

אבן עזרא

המצרים היו אדונים לישראל, וזה הדור היוצא ממצרים למד מנעוריו לסבול עול מצרים ונפשו שפלה, ואיך יוכל עתה להלחם עם אדוניו? והיו ישראל נרפים ואינם מלומדים למלחמה.

RAMBAN

Israel was divided into different factions, and our text reports the attitudes of each group. The first approach to the crisis was adopted by the faithful who cried to the Lord for assistance. Next to those people were others who denied the agency of God's prophet and refused to acknowledge the deliverance that had been executed on their behalf. Those were the individuals who complained, "Better a life in servitude to Egypt than death in the desert!" (14:12).

רמב״ן

אבל הנכון שנפרש שהם כתות והכתוב יספר כל מה שעשו כולם: אמר, כי הכת האחת צועקת אל ה' והאחרת מכחשת בנביאים ואינה בוחרת בישועה הנעשית להם, ויאמרו כי טוב להם לו לא הצילם.

SHEMOT | CHAPTER 14

BESHALAḤ

The divine cloud, which had been leading the way for Israel, moves behind them to protect them from the Egyptians. Acting upon God's instruction, Moshe raises his staff over the waters. Throughout the night a strong easterly wind blows, splitting the waters of the Sea of Reeds and leaving a trail of dry land. As Israel crosses through, the Egyptians pursue them, but toward morning they realize that the cloud and the fire – which had been keeping them from Israel – have turned on them, causing the chariots to become stuck and generating panic amongst the Egyptians, who realize that God is fighting Israel's battle.

15 The Lord said to Moshe, "Why are you crying out to Me? Speak to the Israelites; have
16 them move forward. Raise your staff, stretch out your hand over the sea and divide it,
17 and the Israelites will walk through the sea on dry land. I will strengthen the Egyptians' hearts and they will go after them. Then will My glory bear down hard upon Pharaoh
18 and his entire army, his chariots and cavalry. And when My glory bears down upon
19 Pharaoh, his chariots and cavalry, the Egyptians will know that I am the Lord." Then the angel of God who had been traveling ahead of the Israelite camp moved and went
20 behind them, and the column of cloud moved from in front of them to their rear. It came between the Egyptian and Israelite camps, as cloud and darkness for one, but lighting
21 the night for the other, keeping the two apart all night. Then Moshe stretched out his hand over the sea, and the Lord drove the sea back by a strong east wind all night,
22 turning it to dry land and dividing the waters. So the Israelites walked through the sea

---

RASHBAM

רשב״ם

ויסע מלאך האלהים - המוליך את עמוד הענן לפני מחנה ישראל, וילך - המלאך מאחריהם, ומתוך כך: ויסע עמוד {הענן} מפניהם ויעמוד מאחריהם.

"The מלאך האלהים" – which had been leading the column of cloud in front of Israel's camp – "moved and went behind them," and therefore "the column of cloud moved from in front of them to their rear."

IBN EZRA

אבן עזרא

מלאך האלהים - הוא השר הגדול ההולך בענן, והוא הכתוב עליו: וה׳ הולך לפניהם יומם. וכאשר נסע זה המלאך ההולך לפני מחנה ישראל והלך מאחריהם, נסע עמוד הענן עמו. והאומר: מלאך האלהים - הוא הענן, יראה לנו אנה מצאנו עמוד הענן נקרא מלאך ה׳.

This מלאך האלהים is the great prince [the angel Michael, referred to in Daniel 12:1 as the "great chief angel who stands for the children of Your people"]. This is the figure about whom the verse states, "The Lord went ahead of them by day in a column of cloud to guide them" (13:21). Subsequently, when this מלאך אלהים relocated to protect Israel from behind, the cloud accompanying him moved as well. As for those commentaries who claim that the cloud itself is the מלאך אלהים referred to in this verse, I challenge them to find any verse which refers to the cloud as a מלאך of the Lord.

QUESTIONS FOR THOUGHT

- What in the text may have caused Rashi to suggest that the מלאך אלהים and the cloud were one and the same?
- Why does Ibn Ezra absolutely reject Rashi?
- Rashi disagrees with both Rashbam and Ibn Ezra! How does he understand what is happening here?
- What difference would it have made to Israel, who experienced this, which of these is correct?

שמות | פרק יד

טו וַיֹּאמֶר יְהֹוָה אֶל־מֹשֶׁה מַה־תִּצְעַק אֵלָי דַּבֵּר אֶל־בְּנֵי־יִשְׂרָאֵל **יא** שלישי
טז וְיִסָּעוּ: וְאַתָּה הָרֵם אֶת־מַטְּךָ וּנְטֵה אֶת־יָדְךָ עַל־הַיָּם וּבְקָעֵהוּ
יז וְיָבֹאוּ בְנֵי־יִשְׂרָאֵל בְּתוֹךְ הַיָּם בַּיַּבָּשָׁה: וַאֲנִי הִנְנִי מְחַזֵּק אֶת־לֵב
מִצְרַיִם וְיָבֹאוּ אַחֲרֵיהֶם וְאִכָּבְדָה בְּפַרְעֹה וּבְכָל־חֵילוֹ בְּרִכְבּוֹ
יח וּבְפָרָשָׁיו: וְיָדְעוּ מִצְרַיִם כִּי־אֲנִי יְהֹוָה בְּהִכָּבְדִי בְּפַרְעֹה בְּרִכְבּוֹ
יט וּבְפָרָשָׁיו: וַיִּסַּע מַלְאַךְ הָאֱלֹהִים הַהֹלֵךְ לִפְנֵי מַחֲנֵה יִשְׂרָאֵל וַיֵּלֶךְ
מֵאַחֲרֵיהֶם וַיִּסַּע עַמּוּד הֶעָנָן מִפְּנֵיהֶם וַיַּעֲמֹד מֵאַחֲרֵיהֶם: וַיָּבֹא
כ בֵּין ׀ מַחֲנֵה מִצְרַיִם וּבֵין מַחֲנֵה יִשְׂרָאֵל וַיְהִי הֶעָנָן וְהַחֹשֶׁךְ וַיָּאֶר
אֶת־הַלָּיְלָה וְלֹא־קָרַב זֶה אֶל־זֶה כָּל־הַלָּיְלָה: וַיֵּט מֹשֶׁה אֶת־יָדוֹ
כא עַל־הַיָּם וַיּוֹלֶךְ יְהֹוָה ׀ אֶת־הַיָּם בְּרוּחַ קָדִים עַזָּה כָּל־הַלַּיְלָה
כב וַיָּשֶׂם אֶת־הַיָּם לֶחָרָבָה וַיִּבָּקְעוּ הַמָּיִם: וַיָּבֹאוּ בְנֵי־יִשְׂרָאֵל
בְּתוֹךְ הַיָּם בַּיַּבָּשָׁה וְהַמַּיִם לָהֶם חוֹמָה מִימִינָם וּמִשְּׂמֹאלָם:

CLASSIC COMMENTATORS

Verse 19 has two halves that seem to parallel each other:

וַיִּסַּע מַלְאַךְ הָאֱלֹהִים	וַיִּסַּע עַמּוּד הֶעָנָן
הַהֹלֵךְ לִפְנֵי מַחֲנֵה יִשְׂרָאֵל	מִפְּנֵיהֶם
וַיֵּלֶךְ מֵאַחֲרֵיהֶם	וַיַּעֲמֹד מֵאַחֲרֵיהֶם

Are the מַלְאַךְ הָאֱלֹהִים and the column of cloud the same thing or two different things?

RASHI — רש"י

"The column of cloud moved" – The cloud only moved once it had become dark, and then it handed over responsibility for Israel's protection to the column of fire. But the cloud did not dissipate completely like it usually did in the evenings, but moved behind Israel in order to create darkness for the Egyptians.

ויסע עמוד הענן - כשחשכה והשלים עמוד הענן את המחנה לעמוד האש, לא נסתלק הענן כמו שהיה רגיל להסתלק ערבית לגמרי, אלא נסע והולך לו מאחוריהם להחשיך למצרים.

23 on dry land. To their right and left, the water was like a wall. The Egyptians chased after
24 them. All Pharaoh's horses, chariots and cavalry followed them into the sea. During the last watch of the night, the LORD looked down at the Egyptian army from a column of
25 fire and cloud and threw them into a panic, clogging their chariot wheels so that it was hard for them to move. The Egyptians said, "Let us flee from the Israelites. The LORD is fighting for them against Egypt."

us to move forward and can set up virtual walls between us and others, or between us and our goals. But that cloud is not a divine blockage, as it was with the Egyptians – it is our own. Our sole task under those circumstances is to recognize that the other side of the cloud is filled with radiant light, which will help us to see clearly and get back on track.

The Baal HaTanya reflects on the deeper image here. On the most simple level, the water pooled to the sides and bared the dry land. But the deeper reading of these words is that the ocean itself became dry land – the water turned to earth. At first, this might seem like an even bigger miracle, but the Baal HaTanya argues that it isn't necessarily. Many of the properties dry land possesses are present in the ocean as well. Just look at your own body, think of how it is made up both of carbon, vitamins and minerals, and also water. By extension we can recognize that the whole of this very mundane world of ours masks a deeper spiritual blueprint; every piece of it contains the DNA of the entire universe.

WISDOM OF THE HEART

Professional sports players become even more memorable when they turn out to be good, decent people. That is inspiring. For example, NFL player John Frank (an Orthodox Jew!) is inspiring because he combines great talent with being a good human being. Mike Devereaux, a former Dodger who also had a brilliant season with Baltimore, was always known for being a great person. In a private conversation with a fan, who happened to be a rabbi, Devereaux discussed the question of praying for victory. Isn't that problematic? Praying for our victory also means praying for the other team to lose, and that just doesn't seem right. And what about when Moshe cries out to God? Doesn't that imply asking that the Egyptians be harmed?

Perhaps the two aren't the same at all. First, Israel needs to be saved from death or slavery; there is no comparison to a baseball game! Second, it didn't have to be a zero-sum game. It certainly was possibly for Israel to be saved without harm coming to Egypt. Sometimes we think that we know what the only answer is, but in fact God knows many ways to resolve crises, and it is not our place to second-guess which of those He will choose to use.

כג וַיִּרְדְּפוּ מִצְרַיִם וַיָּבֹאוּ אַחֲרֵיהֶם כֹּל סוּס פַּרְעֹה רִכְבּוֹ וּפָרָשָׁיו אֶל־תּוֹךְ הַיָּם: כד וַיְהִי בְּאַשְׁמֹרֶת הַבֹּקֶר וַיַּשְׁקֵף יְהוָה אֶל־מַחֲנֵה מִצְרַיִם בְּעַמּוּד אֵשׁ וְעָנָן וַיָּהָם אֵת מַחֲנֵה מִצְרָיִם: כה וַיָּסַר אֵת אֹפַן מַרְכְּבֹתָיו וַיְנַהֲגֵהוּ בִּכְבֵדֻת וַיֹּאמֶר מִצְרַיִם אָנוּסָה מִפְּנֵי יִשְׂרָאֵל כִּי יְהוָה נִלְחָם לָהֶם בְּמִצְרָיִם:

TEXTUAL SKILLS

1. Find the internal contradiction in verse 20.
2. The word ויהם means "to cause great turmoil." It appears thirteen times in Tanakh. Of those, eleven times it describes God causing turmoil to Israel's enemies.
3. Notice that verse 16 begins with ואתה ("and you…") while verse 17 begins with ואני ("and I…"). Look at the verses. What message is God sending to Moshe?

QUICK BITES

This teaching of Rav Shimshon Ostropoli is one of the most extraordinary and complex *gematrias* you'll ever encounter, but it is worth it! According to a mystical tradition, Moshe used two names of God, אדני and יהוה, to split the sea. The *gematria* of those two together totals 91. Remember that – we'll come back it later.

The verse where God tells Moshe to lift his staff could also be read as to lift up each letter of the word for staff – מ-ט-ך – and "raise" each one to the next letter of the *alef-beit*, so that the מ becomes a נ, the ט becomes a י, and the ך becomes a ל. That totals 90 (close, but not quite!). Similarly, later on, God tells Moshe to lower his hand, or lower each letter of the word י-ד-ך one letter in the *alef-beit*. So the י becomes ט, the ד becomes ג, and the ך becomes י, yielding 22. The third part of God's instruction is that this should be done over the sea, suggesting the letters י-ם are each raised: י becomes כ, and ם becomes נ, yielding 70. Add all of those together (90+22+70) and you have 182.

God's final instruction is to split it (the sea) – and when we split 182 we get 91, the *gematria* of the names of God!

Sandwiched between the terrifying sea and the threatening Egyptian military, Benei Yisrael are gripped by fear. Suddenly, a mysterious cloud comes between them and the Egyptians, providing light for Israel and darkening Egypt's way. As Sforno says, the complete darkness faced by the Egyptians slowed their path because they could not see where they were going. This served as a virtual wall separating Israel from Egypt.

Sforno's message can be read on a deeper level too. There are many kinds of darkness in our lives – physical, emotional, psychological, religious – each of which can make it difficult for

As the Egyptians prepare to flee, God instructs Moshe to once again wave his hands over the waters, this time to bring them crashing down upon the Egyptians. There are no survivors. The magnitude of what has just happened dawns upon Israel, who crossed the sea on dry land. As they watch from the safety of the shore, they stand in awe of God – they believe in the truth of God and that Moshe is His servant.

26 Then the LORD said to Moshe, "Stretch out your hand over the sea. The waters will flow
27 back over the Egyptians and their chariots and cavalry." Moshe stretched out his hand over the sea, and at daybreak the water came back in full force. The Egyptians fled at
28 its approach but the LORD swept them into the sea. The waters returned, covering the chariots, the cavalry and the whole Egyptian army that had followed the Israelites into
29 the sea. Not one of them remained. But the Israelites had walked through the sea on dry
30 land, with a wall of water to their right and left. That day, the LORD saved the Israelites from the Egyptians. And when the Israelites saw the Egyptians dead on the seashore,
31 and witnessed the wondrous power the LORD had unleashed against the Egyptians, the people were in awe of the LORD, and they believed in Him and in Moshe His servant.

QUESTIONS FOR THOUGHT

- What textual evidence does Ralbag bring to support his position? What part of the text presents a problem to Ralbag's explanation?
- Ibn Ezra emphasizes how supernatural this event is. Why do you think that was so important?
- Which would you find more religiously significant – citing natural explanations for miracles described in the Torah or emphasizing the supernatural to demonstrate that these are divine acts?

TEXTUAL SKILLS

1. Notice that here God tells Moshe to wave his hand, while earlier He told him to wave his staff. Where else in Exodus does such a distinction appear?

2. Earlier we noticed a play on two roots, י-ר-א (fear) and ר-א-ה (see). Look in this passage to see how that wordplay continues and reverses the earlier pattern!

WISDOM OF THE HEART

When Psalms 106, which poetically retells many of the stories from the Torah, describes the scene at the sea, it says that *Benei Yisrael* rebelled against God. The word וַיַּמְרוּ, which can be understood as meaning "rebelled," could also be translated as "exchanged." The Midrash elaborates: When *Benei Yisrael* descended into the sea and found themselves walking in mud, they said to each other, "We left the mud of Egypt to come to this mud?" At the greatest moment in their lives, at one of the most dramatic events in human history, all they could think about was the mud? And worse, comparing the mud of freedom to the mud of slavery?

Have you overlooked great moments, getting stuck on the small problems?

שמות | פרק יד

כו וַיֹּאמֶר יהוה אֶל־מֹשֶׁה נְטֵה אֶת־יָדְךָ עַל־הַיָּם וְיָשֻׁבוּ הַמַּיִם רביעי
עַל־מִצְרַיִם עַל־רִכְבּוֹ וְעַל־פָּרָשָׁיו: כז וַיֵּט מֹשֶׁה אֶת־יָדוֹ עַל־הַיָּם
וַיָּשָׁב הַיָּם לִפְנוֹת בֹּקֶר לְאֵיתָנוֹ וּמִצְרַיִם נָסִים לִקְרָאתוֹ וַיְנַעֵר
יהוה אֶת־מִצְרַיִם בְּתוֹךְ הַיָּם: כח וַיָּשֻׁבוּ הַמַּיִם וַיְכַסּוּ אֶת־הָרֶכֶב
וְאֶת־הַפָּרָשִׁים לְכֹל חֵיל פַּרְעֹה הַבָּאִים אַחֲרֵיהֶם בַּיָּם לֹא־נִשְׁאַר
בָּהֶם עַד־אֶחָד: כט וּבְנֵי יִשְׂרָאֵל הָלְכוּ בַיַּבָּשָׁה בְּתוֹךְ הַיָּם וְהַמַּיִם
לָהֶם חֹמָה מִימִינָם וּמִשְּׂמֹאלָם: ל וַיּוֹשַׁע יהוה בַּיּוֹם הַהוּא אֶת־
יִשְׂרָאֵל מִיַּד מִצְרָיִם וַיַּרְא יִשְׂרָאֵל אֶת־מִצְרַיִם מֵת עַל־שְׂפַת
הַיָּם: לא וַיַּרְא יִשְׂרָאֵל אֶת־הַיָּד הַגְּדֹלָה אֲשֶׁר עָשָׂה יהוה בְּמִצְרַיִם
וַיִּירְאוּ הָעָם אֶת־יהוה וַיַּאֲמִינוּ בַּיהוה וּבְמֹשֶׁה עַבְדּוֹ:

CLASSIC COMMENTATORS

Was the splitting of the sea a completely supernatural event, or could it be explained naturally?

IBN EZRA
God at that time performed a miracle within a miracle. In the very place where the Egyptians were drowning, Israel was crossing on dry land. For there were a great many Israelites, and although a good number of the Hebrews had already succeeded in crossing the sea when the Egyptians began to drown, some of them had yet to complete the trek.

אבן עזרא
עשה השם פלא בתוך פלא, כי זה טובע וזה עובר ביבשה, וזה קרוב מזה בים אחד. כי ישראל היו רבים, ויש רבים מהם שכבר עבר בעת טבוע מצרים, ויש מהם שהיו אז עוברים.

RALBAG
It is important for you to know that when the Lord, may He be exalted, performs miracles, He strives to execute them in a way that works within the boundaries of nature and which causes little interruption to the normal workings of the world... This explains why the Lord, may He be exalted, employed a strong east wind to dry out the sea and to push its waters to the west. This resulted in an exposed area of the sea bed where the Israelites could cross. The water stood to the left and to the right of the nation because the path upon which the nation crossed was at a higher elevation than the water. That is, the people walked on the land that formed a causeway through the sea. The water did not pile up above them on their right and their left. Even though the water did not stand high and upright on either side of the nation, it was nevertheless referred to as a wall because it prevented the Egyptians from approaching Israel from the right and from the left.

רלב״ג
ראוי שתדע כי ה' יתעלה כשיעשה המופתים ישתדל להמציא להם הסיבות אשר בהם יהיה בחידושם יותר מעט מהזרות אצל הטבע, ... ולזאת הסיבה המציא ה'יתעלה על דרך מופת רוח קדים עזה, אשר היא מנגבת ומעתיקה המים אל הצד המערבי, באופן שחידש להם מקום מגולה בים, והיו מי הים מימינו ומשמאלו, כי המקום ההוא היה יותר גבוה,... לא שיהיו המים גבוהים מימין ומשמאל ...ולזה הוליך ה' יתעלה רוח קדים עזה כל הלילה. והנה קרא המים 'חומה', ואם אינם גבוהים, לפי שהם היו מונעים המצרים מלבוא עליהם מימינם ומשמאלם.

SHEMOT | CHAPTER 15   BESHALAH | 124

> *Witnessing their great salvation from the Egyptians, Moshe and the Israelites burst out in song. The song has three parts, the first of which is a reaction to God's power and decisive victory over Egypt.*

15 1 And then, Moshe and the Israelites sang this song to the Lord: I will sing to the Lord, for He has triumphed in glory; / horse and horseman He hurled 2 into the sea. The Lord is my strength and song – / and now my salvation. This is my 3 God, I will glorify Him, / my father's God, I will exalt Him. The Lord is a Master of 4 war; / the Lord is His name. Pharaoh's chariots and army / He hurled into the sea; / the 5 best of his officers / drowned in the Sea of Reeds. The deep waters covered them; / they 6 sank to the depths like a stone. Your right hand, Lord, majestic in power, / Your right

---

QUESTIONS FOR THOUGHT

- Which one of the commentaries understands this as mocking Pharaoh (as opposed to making a statement about God's nature)? What about this is this odd?
- Which of these commentaries offers an answer to the meaning of איש but does not explain what Moshe is adding to our understanding of God?
- Given that Moshe is reacting to the events at the splitting of the sea, how would you challenge the comment of Haamek Davar?

TEXTUAL SKILLS

1. Notice that this passage ends with a double exclamation of ימינך ה׳. The second passage will also close with a double exclamation.
2. Find the introductory phrase that is included in the song but is not written as poetry. Find the parallel concluding phrase at the end of the song, which is also not written as poetry.
3. Notice that some of the verses are divided into two parallel sections, while others are broken into four phrases.

WISDOM OF THE HEART

The description of God as a "man of war" bothers some people; they would be more comfortable describing Him as the God of peace and harmony. Apparently, sometimes the only way to reach a world of love is by fighting the darkness. God is acting as a "man of war" for us.

According to the Mekhilta, even a maidservant saw at the sea what the prophet Yeḥezkel could not see in his great vision of the divine chariot. Rav Chaim Shmuelevitz asks, "What became of those maidservants that had such amazing experiences at the sea?" Nothing. Life is not about what you see; it's about what you do with that which you can see. Seize the moment and act upon it – don't wait for the next day to act on your inspiration.

Are you the type of person that delays changing your life for the better?

שמות | פרק טו

טו א אָ֣ז יָשִֽׁיר־מֹשֶׁה֩ וּבְנֵ֨י יִשְׂרָאֵ֜ל אֶת־הַשִּׁירָ֤ה הַזֹּאת֙ לַֽיהוָ֔ה וַיֹּאמְר֖וּ
לֵאמֹ֑ר אָשִׁ֤ירָה לַֽיהוָה֙ כִּֽי־גָאֹ֣ה גָּאָ֔ה ס֥וּס

ב וְרֹכְב֖וֹ רָמָ֥ה בַיָּֽם: עָזִּ֤י וְזִמְרָת֙ יָ֔הּ וַֽיְהִי־לִ֖י
לִֽישׁוּעָ֑ה זֶ֤ה אֵלִי֙ וְאַנְוֵ֔הוּ אֱלֹהֵ֥י

ג אָבִ֖י וַאֲרֹמְמֶֽנְהוּ: יְהוָ֖ה אִ֣ישׁ מִלְחָמָ֑ה יְהוָ֖ה

ד שְׁמֽוֹ: מַרְכְּבֹ֥ת פַּרְעֹ֛ה וְחֵיל֖וֹ יָרָ֣ה בַיָּ֑ם וּמִבְחַ֥ר

ה שָֽׁלִשָׁ֖יו טֻבְּע֥וּ בְיַם־סֽוּף: תְּהֹמֹ֖ת יְכַסְיֻ֑מוּ יָרְד֥וּ בִמְצוֹלֹ֖ת

ו כְּמוֹ־אָֽבֶן: יְמִֽינְךָ֣ יְהוָ֔ה נֶאְדָּרִ֖י בַּכֹּ֑חַ יְמִֽינְךָ֥

CLASSIC COMMENTATORS

In verse 3 God is described as an איש מלחמה – literally, "a man of war." Describing God as a "man" in any way is troubling.

רש״י
איש מלחמה – בעל מלחמות, כגון: איש נעמי.

RASHI
The word איש [does not connote "man" but] "Master" – God is Master of war. We find a similar usage in the verse, "And Elimelekh, Naomi's husband [איש, alternately: 'lord'] died" (Ruth 1:3).

אברבנאל
בעבור שפרעה אמר במצרים ..."לא ידעתי את ה'", אמר משה כאן כמתהתל ממנו: "ה' איש מלחמה ה' שמו" ו"איש מלחמה" הוא תואר לפרעה. אמר כנגדו: אתה, איש מלחמה וחפץ רע שבאת לרדוף אחרי בני ישראל להלחם בם, זהו ה' אשר לא ידעת "ה' שמו", עתה תדעהו מפאת פעולותיו.

ABARBANEL
As Pharaoh had declared in Egypt: "…I do not know the Lord" (5:2). Now, Moshe mocks Pharaoh, saying: Do you not know who the Lord is? Why, He is a Man of war; the Lord is His name! Pharaoh, you fancied yourself a capable warrior, seeking to pursue Israel and destroy them. But now – the Lord, whom you claimed not to recognize, He is the One who has bested you. Now you will surely know the wonders of His actions.

אור החיים
פירוש גם במדת הרחמים עשה מלחמה, ולא שישתנה מפני זה חס ושלום אלא ה' שמו.

OR HAHAYYIM
Even while He wages war, God acts compassionately. Because His attribute of mercy is not suppressed, heaven forbid, He is still called "Lord."

העמק דבר
ה' איש מלחמה – נראה שהוא נלחם כאיש בדרך הטבע ה' שמו – למעלה מן הטבע.

HAAMEK DAVAR
God is referred to as a man because He appears to use human-like – that is, natural – techniques when fighting His battles. And yet, His name is "Lord," for He acts above the laws of nature.

> *God's power is unparalleled. The mighty Egyptians and their supposed god of the water are easily shown to be powerless by just a breath of the true God.*

7 hand, LORD, shatters the enemy. In the greatness of Your majesty, You overthrew those
8 who rose against You. / You sent forth Your rage; it consumed them like stubble. By the blast of Your nostrils the waters heaped; / the surge stood upright as a wall; / the deeps
9 congealed at the heart of the sea. The enemy said, "I will give chase, will overtake, / I will divide the spoils. / My desire shall gorge its fill of them. I will draw my sword, /
10 and my hand destroy them." You blew with Your wind; the sea covered over them. /
11 They sank like lead in mighty waters. Who is like You, LORD, among the mighty? / Who

---

QUESTIONS FOR THOUGHT

- Both Rashi and Ramban understand these words as reflecting someone luring someone else into doing something (which will end up not as expected), but they disagree as to who is luring whom! Who is luring whom according to each of those two commentaries?
- According to Ramban, why was this important to include in the poem? How does this connect with the opening of *Parashat Beshallaḥ*?

TEXTUAL SKILLS

1. We saw earlier that the text of the song sometimes contains verses with two parts and sometimes with four parts. Most of the verses in this passage have three parts!

2. Notice how many times in this passage God's power over the water is mentioned.

WISDOM OF THE HEART

Rav Kook writes that there are four songs that are sung by human beings: the song of the soul, the song of the nation, the song of humanity, and the song of the world.

The song of the soul is essentially the song we sing when searching for the reason for our existence. Why are we here? Who am I, truly?

The song of the nation is for those who have not been able to find themselves and whose personal lives are often in shambles, but who are able to tap into the song of our people's history, culture, and our survival.

The next level is the song of humanity. This is the song of the one who may not understand his or her personal mission and may not know what his or her people are about, but who believes in humanity, or *tikkun olam* – repairing the world.

But the highest level is the song of the ones who rise above it all and see how their souls' purpose, their nation's destiny, and humanity's betterment are all bound together with the purpose of creation. This last movement is what the Song at the Sea was all about: the great realization that there aren't four separate songs, but one magnificent symphony.

If your life had a soundtrack, what would it sound like?

ז	יְהוָה תִּרְעַץ אוֹיֵב: וּבְרֹב גְּאוֹנְךָ תַּהֲרֹס
ח	קָמֶיךָ תְּשַׁלַּח חֲרֹנְךָ יֹאכְלֵמוֹ כַּקַּשׁ: וּבְרוּחַ אַפֶּיךָ נֶעֶרְמוּ מַיִם נִצְּבוּ
ט	כְמוֹ־נֵד נֹזְלִים קָפְאוּ תְהֹמֹת בְּלֶב־יָם: אָמַר אוֹיֵב אֶרְדֹּף אַשִּׂיג אֲחַלֵּק שָׁלָל תִּמְלָאֵמוֹ
י	נַפְשִׁי אָרִיק חַרְבִּי תּוֹרִישֵׁמוֹ יָדִי: נָשַׁפְתָּ בְרוּחֲךָ כִּסָּמוֹ יָם צָלֲלוּ כַּעוֹפֶרֶת בְּמַיִם
יא	אַדִּירִים: מִי־כָמֹכָה בָּאֵלִם יְהוָה מִי כָּמֹכָה נֶאְדָּר בַּקֹּדֶשׁ נוֹרָא תְהִלֹּת עֹשֵׂה

CLASSIC COMMENTATORS

Verse 9 contrasts Pharaoh's intentions with the reality that he met. The statement attributed to Pharaoh seems out of place, as it would have fit better in the opening of the song.

RASHI

In order to persuade his nation to follow him into battle, Pharaoh promised his army: "I will give chase, will overtake, I will divide the spoils" with my officers and my servants.

רש״י

אמר אויב - לעמו, כשפיתן בדברים: ארדוף ואשיגם ואחלק שללם עם שריי ועבדי.

RAMBAN

"By the blast of Your nostrils" – that is the strong east wind – "the waters heaped…the deeps congealed." When the enemy saw that, they thought: "I will give chase, will overtake" Israel in the midst of the sea; "I will divide the spoils. My desire shall gorge its fill of them." However, God "blew with [His] wind; the sea covered them." Moshe found it appropriate to mention the Egyptians' scheme in order to draw attention to God's wonders. For it was He who strengthened the oppressors' resolve and turned their wisdom to the foolishness that lured them into the water.

רמב״ן

כי ברוח אפך, היא רוח קדים עזה נערמו מים מתחלה וקפאו התהומות, ומפני זה חשב האויב שירדוף וישיגם בים ויחלק שלל ותמלא נפשו מהם, ונשפת עליהם ברוחך וכסמו הים. והזכיר זה כי גם במחשבתו זאת סבה ופלא מאת השם שחזק לבם וסכל עצתם לבא בים.

> It is not enough to proclaim God's wonders in the present or His almighty power as witnessed at one moment – it is also essential to understand the long-term impact of the events being witnessed. That impact includes the fear imposed upon all the surrounding nations, which will enable Israel to march triumphantly (and bloodlessly) into their Promised Land, where they will dwell eternally and establish a center for God's divine throne for all people and for all time.

12 is like You – majestic in holiness, / awesome in glory, working wonders? You reached
13 out Your right hand – / the earth swallowed them up. In Your love, You guided out the
14 people You redeemed. / In Your strength, You led them to Your holy abode. Nations
15 heard and they trembled; / terror seized the Philistines. The chiefs of Edom were dismayed, then, / Moab's leaders were seized with trembling, / the people of Canaan
16 melted away. Dread, terror fell upon them; / by Your arm's power they were stilled as stone – until Your people crossed, Lord, / until the people You acquired crossed over.
17 You will bring them, You will plant them on the mountain, Your heritage – / the place, Lord, that You made for Your dwelling, / the sanctuary, Lord, that Your hands estab-
18 lished. The Lord will reign for ever and all time. This they sang when Pharaoh's horses,
19 chariots and cavalry had gone into the sea / and the Lord had brought the waters of the sea back over them / while the Israelites had walked on dry land through the sea.

QUESTIONS FOR THOUGHT
- Which of the commentaries understand this as a prayer?
- Which of the commentaries understands that this actually came true – relatively soon (from a historical perspective) after the exodus?
- Which of these commentaries understands that establishing God as king is in our hands?

TEXTUAL SKILLS

1. The first two sections of the song closed with a double phrase (vv. 6, 11). The third section also has a double phrase, but in the middle (v. 16). Take a look at the way this song appears in the siddur – notice what the authors of the siddur did to match the style of the siddur to the Torah!
2. Notice how many words are used in this third passage to describe the fear experienced by the other nations.

WISDOM OF THE HEART

The Gemara says that when *Benei Yisrael* began singing, the angels wanted to join and rejoice in the downfall of the Egyptians. God stopped them, saying, "Those whom I created are drowning in the sea, and you sing songs?" Interestingly, God did not stop *Benei Yisrael* from singing, and even included their song in the Torah! Apparently, for *Benei Yisrael*, who suffered terrible oppression at the hands of the Egyptians, it was entirely appropriate – even praiseworthy – to acknowledge that God had saved them and burst out in song at the downfall of their mortal enemies. The angels, however, were bystanders, and should have been horrified by the deaths of any of God's creations.

שמות | פרק טו

יג נָחִיתָ נָטִיתָ יְמִינְךָ תִּבְלָעֵמוֹ אָרֶץ: פֶּלֶא:
בְחַסְדְּךָ עַם־זוּ גָּאָלְתָּ נֵהַלְתָּ בְעָזְּךָ אֶל־נְוֵה
יד קָדְשֶׁךָ: שָׁמְעוּ עַמִּים יִרְגָּזוּן חִיל
טו אָחַז יֹשְׁבֵי פְּלָשֶׁת: אָז נִבְהֲלוּ אַלּוּפֵי
אֱדוֹם אֵילֵי מוֹאָב יֹאחֲזֵמוֹ רָעַד נָמֹגוּ
טז כֹּל יֹשְׁבֵי כְנָעַן: תִּפֹּל עֲלֵיהֶם אֵימָתָה
וָפַחַד בִּגְדֹל זְרוֹעֲךָ יִדְּמוּ כָּאָבֶן עַד־
יַעֲבֹר עַמְּךָ יְהוָה עַד־יַעֲבֹר עַם־זוּ
יז קָנִיתָ: תְּבִאֵמוֹ וְתִטָּעֵמוֹ בְּהַר נַחֲלָתְךָ מָכוֹן
לְשִׁבְתְּךָ פָּעַלְתָּ יְהוָה מִקְּדָשׁ אֲדֹנָי כּוֹנְנוּ
יח יָדֶיךָ: יְהוָה ׀ יִמְלֹךְ לְעֹלָם וָעֶד: כִּי
בָא סוּס פַּרְעֹה בְּרִכְבּוֹ וּבְפָרָשָׁיו בַּיָּם וַיָּשֶׁב יְהוָה עֲלֵהֶם אֶת־מֵי
הַיָּם וּבְנֵי יִשְׂרָאֵל הָלְכוּ בַיַּבָּשָׁה בְּתוֹךְ הַיָּם:

CLASSIC COMMENTATORS

The close of the poem is ה' ימלוך לעולם ועד: God is, or will hopefully be, or will eventually be, king forever. Which is the proper understanding?

RASHI **רש״י**
This expresses the hope for the future when the kingdom of the world will belong to God alone [that is, it will be recognized as such].

לעתיד לבא שכל המלוכה שלו.

IBN EZRA **אבן עזרא**
When the Temple is built in God's name, His reign will be acknowledged across the land.

כאשר יבנה בית המקדש לשמו, אז תראה מלכותו בארץ.

RAMBAN **רמב״ן**
God has now convincingly demonstrated that He is King and ruler over everything by saving His servants and vanquishing those who rebelled against him. So may it remain God's will to maintain these practices across the generations.

כי הראה עתה כי הוא מלך ושלטון על הכל, שהושיע את עבדיו ואבד את מורדיו, כן יהי הרצון מלפניו לעשות בכל הדורות לעולם.

Miriam the prophetess leads the women in song as well, accompanied by musical instruments.

20 Then Miriam, the prophetess, sister of Aharon, took a tambourine in her hand, and all
21 the women followed her with tambourines and dance. And Miriam led them in song: Sing to the Lord, for He has triumphed in glory; / horse and horseman He hurled into

---

TEXTUAL SKILLS

1. Miriam's song is almost identical to the first line of Moshe's. Find the main difference!

2. Compare verse 20 to the opening of Moshe's poem. What other differences can you find?

WISDOM OF THE HEART

The *Keli Yakar* argues that Miriam truly became a prophet now, for the first time. The sheer energy and joy of this moment allowed her to unleash a power she had never known was in her. Her use of musical instruments helped her further channel this jubilation into even more powerful levels of prophecy. Try something: Take a pen and paper. Pause and close your eyes and think of something amazing in your life. Let the feeling of bliss sink in. Feel the enjoyment of life flowing through you and the consciousness of truly being yourself. Write a one-sentence description of that memory. Fold the paper and put it in your pocket. Moving forward, whenever you feel powerless, take it out and read it. Your positive consciousness is the source of tremendous potential power.

Of course Miriam would lead the celebration. The Yalkut Shimoni teaches us that we were redeemed from Egypt because of the acts of righteous women. Their commitment throughout the ages – in the face of tremendous adversity and discrimination – has sustained our people. The Lubavitcher Rebbe, Rav Menachem Mendel Schneerson, would often say that just as the righteousness of women brought us out of Egypt, it will also bring us the future redemption. Miriam's tambourine is the celebration of this innate female power. It is the weapon used to bring down the enemy when violent force is useless – it is her music that will vanquish the darkness. See Isaiah 30:32 – "In every passage where the Lord plants down the staff, firmly, drums will sound, and lutes, and the brandished hands of warfare: so will He fight them."

QUICK BITES

What was different about the splitting of the sea that caused Israel to sing? Were there no great miracles in Egypt? The Talmud Yerushalmi suggests that the song is only appropriate when the redemption climaxes, not at the intermediary stages. And how did they know that this was the climax? Rabbi Betzalel Zolti says that that when they reached a moment of genuine belief in God – "they believed in the Lord and in Moshe His servant" – that was itself the climax of redemption.

כ וַתִּקַּח מִרְיָם הַנְּבִיאָה אֲחוֹת אַהֲרֹן אֶת־הַתֹּף בְּיָדָהּ וַתֵּצֶאןָ
כא כָל־הַנָּשִׁים אַחֲרֶיהָ בְּתֻפִּים וּבִמְחֹלֹת: וַתַּעַן לָהֶם מִרְיָם שִׁירוּ

CLASSIC COMMENTATORS

Moshe's poem is quite long while Miriam's is very brief. Was her poem really so short?

RASHBAM

Miriam and the women repeated the entire song that had just been recited by Moshe. However, the Torah saw no need to repeat the whole text again, but sufficed with a single verse.

רשב״ם

ואמרו כל השירה. אלא מאחר שכתב למעלה כל השירה, לא הזכיר כאן רק פסוק אחד.

HAAMEK DAVAR

Although the Torah cites just a single verse of the song offered by Miriam, in fact the women recited a lengthy poem. Nevertheless, because their words were not spoken with divine inspiration, they are not included in the Torah text. On the other hand, Miriam was directed by divine inspiration to sing the closing statement in each stanza.

העמק דבר

אלא הנשים עשו להן שיר ארוך שלא היה ראוי לכתוב זאת בספר תורה, שלא היה בא בשפע רוח הקודש, אבל הסוגר מכל בית היה על פי מרים ברוח הקודש.

HO'IL MOSHE

Note that even though Miriam was conducting a chorus of women in song, the verse states, "And Miriam led them [לָהֶם] in song," where the term לָהֶם is masculine. When Moshe led the men, the latter responded to each of his pronouncements with the declaration "I will sing to the Lord, for He has triumphed in glory" (15:1), whereas the women would answer, "Sing to the Lord, for He has triumphed in glory" (15:21). In other words, the women were advising the men that it behooved them to sing God's praises.

הואיל משה

שירו לה' – תיבת להם במ״ם, ושירו בלשון זכר; האנשים היו עונים על דברי משה אחר כל פסוק ופסוק: "אשירה לה' וגו'" והנשים עונות לעומתם: שירו לה', כלומר כדאי לכם לשיר.

QUESTIONS FOR THOUGHT

- According to Rashbam, Miriam led exactly the same poem that Moshe did. If so, why did the Torah record a short version?
- In what way is the explanation of Ho'il Moshe the same as that of Rashbam? In what way is his explanation very different?
- According to Haamek Davar, why is Miriam's poem so short?
- Which of the above comments do you think fits best with the words of the Torah?

22 the sea. Moshe then led the Israelites from the Sea of Reeds out into the desert of Shur.
23 For three days, they journeyed across the desert without finding water. Eventually they came to Mara, but they could not drink the water there because it was bitter; because
24 of this it was named Mara. The people railed against Moshe – "What are we to drink?"
25 Moshe cried out to the Lord. And the Lord showed him a piece of wood, which he threw into the water – and the water became sweet. It was there that the Lord gave His
26 people decree and law; it was there that He put them to the test. He said, "If you listen faithfully to the voice of the Lord your God, doing what is right in His eyes, heeding His commands and keeping His decrees, I will not bring on you any of the sicknesses I
27 brought on the Egyptians, for I am the Lord – your Healer." And then they arrived at Elim, where there were twelve springs and seventy date palms. They encamped there

TUR
טור

God now began to afflict Israel with the difficulties of the wilderness, the thirst and the hunger that are present there, so that the people would learn to cry to the Lord for assistance rather than complain.

ליסרם בחוקי המדבר לסבול הרעב והצמא לקרוא
לה' ולא דרך תלונה.

QUESTIONS FOR THOUGHT

- Rashi seems to understand נסיון as test. Who tested whom, and did the one being tested pass the test?
- The other three commentaries understand this נסיון as an attempt by God to bring positive change to Israel. According to each of them, what kind of positive change is God trying to bring about?
- Which of the above ideas would you see as appropriate for you to try to implement in your own relationships?

WISDOM OF THE HEART

Three days into the wilderness. The merciless sun is beating down; no water, mouths parched. Can you imagine? *Benei Yisrael* murmured against Moshe. Finally, on the third day, they found water! But just as fast as they run to drink it, they spit it out – it's bitter. Undrinkable. The ultimate insult: just when you think the worst is over, it gets worse.

God shows Moshe the tree. "Take a branch and throw it into the water. The water will become sweet."

Trees don't grow overnight. Somewhere in the past, God directed a seed to fall into the thirsty ground of the wilderness and cultivated it, with just enough moisture in this unlikely place, waiting for the day that *Benei Yisrael* would need it.

Bitter water is part of life. You were expecting to get into College X, and suddenly the letter comes in the mail: "You've been deferred." You thought your family would last forever, but one day your parents tell you, "We're getting divorced."

Little do we know, but for the very bitter water we encounter, somewhere God has planted a tree – a tree of life for us – waiting for the day when we can finally open our eyes and see how to use it to sweeten our lives.

Are there things you can look at in hindsight and say, "Wow, that really was for my benefit?"

כב לַיהוה כִּי־גָאֹה גָּאָה סוּס וְרֹכְבוֹ רָמָה בַיָּם׃ וַיַּסַּע מֹשֶׁה אֶת־יִשְׂרָאֵל מִיַּם־סוּף וַיֵּצְאוּ אֶל־מִדְבַּר־שׁוּר וַיֵּלְכוּ
כג שְׁלֹשֶׁת־יָמִים בַּמִּדְבָּר וְלֹא־מָצְאוּ מָיִם׃ וַיָּבֹאוּ מָרָתָה וְלֹא יָכְלוּ לִשְׁתֹּת מַיִם מִמָּרָה כִּי מָרִים הֵם עַל־כֵּן קָרָא־שְׁמָהּ
כד מָרָה׃ וַיִּלֹּנוּ הָעָם עַל־מֹשֶׁה לֵּאמֹר מַה־נִּשְׁתֶּה׃ וַיִּצְעַק אֶל־
כה יהוה וַיּוֹרֵהוּ יהוה עֵץ וַיַּשְׁלֵךְ אֶל־הַמַּיִם וַיִּמְתְּקוּ הַמָּיִם שָׁם שָׂם לוֹ חֹק וּמִשְׁפָּט וְשָׁם נִסָּהוּ׃ וַיֹּאמֶר אִם־שָׁמוֹעַ תִּשְׁמַע
כו לְקוֹל ׀ יהוה אֱלֹהֶיךָ וְהַיָּשָׁר בְּעֵינָיו תַּעֲשֶׂה וְהַאֲזַנְתָּ לְמִצְוֺתָיו וְשָׁמַרְתָּ כָּל־חֻקָּיו כָּל־הַמַּחֲלָה אֲשֶׁר־שַׂמְתִּי בְמִצְרַיִם לֹא־
כז אָשִׂים עָלֶיךָ כִּי אֲנִי יהוה רֹפְאֶךָ׃ חמישי וַיָּבֹאוּ אֵילִמָה וְשָׁם שְׁתֵּים עֶשְׂרֵה עֵינֹת מַיִם וְשִׁבְעִים תְּמָרִים וַיַּחֲנוּ־שָׁם

CLASSIC COMMENTATORS

When the Torah tells us that God gave the Israelites some instructions, it adds that He also gave them a נִסָּיוֹן. This word has been translated many different ways, especially in the Torah, since the conventional translation – "test" – is problematic: God doesn't need to test us to find out things about us.

RASHI / רש״י

The nation was tested at Mara, and that revealed their stubbornness. For rather than consulting with Moshe and politely asking for water, Israel complained about the situation.

ושם נסהו – לעם, וראה קשי ערפו, שלא נמלכו ממשה בלשון יפה: בקש עלינו שיהיו לנו מים לשתות, אלא נתלוננו.

RABBI YOSEF BEKHOR SHOR / ר' יוסף בכור שור

He acted like someone who tries to please a difficult person in an attempt to win him over and return him to a proper path.

ושם ניסהו – כאדם שעושה לאדם קשה רצונו, לנסות אם יכול לפתותו על ידי שעושה לו רצונו, להחזירו למוטב.

RABBI AVRAHAM BEN HARAMBAM / ר' אברהם בן הרמב״ם

God was training Israel to become accustomed to uncertainty. This in turn would lead to patience and trust in Him.

יהיה נסהו מן ענין "ההרגל", הטעם כי שם הורגלו בהתלבטות והסבלנות והבטחון.

Shemot | Chapter 16   Beshalaḥ

16 1 by the water. They set out from Elim, and on the fifteenth day of the second month after leaving Egypt, the congregation of Israel all arrived at the desert of Sin, between Elim
2 and Sinai. In the desert, all the community started railing against Moshe and Aharon.
3 The Israelites said to them, "If only we had died by the Lord's hand in Egypt, when we sat by the fleshpots and ate our fill of bread. Instead, you have brought us out into this desert to kill the entire assembly by starvation."
4 Then the Lord said to Moshe, "I am going to rain down bread from heaven. Let the people go out and gather enough for each
5 day; I will test them to see whether they will follow My law or not. On the sixth day, they will have to prepare what they bring in. It will be twice as much as they gather on
6 all other days." So Moshe and Aharon told all the Israelites, "At evening you will know
7 that it was the Lord who brought you out of Egypt, and by morning you shall see the Lord's glory, for He has heard you railing against Him. As for us, what are we that you
8 rail against us?" Then Moshe said, "In the evening, the Lord will give you meat to eat, and in the morning bread to fill you, for He has heard you railing against Him. We – what
9 are we? It is not us you rail against, but the Lord." Then Moshe said to Aharon, "Tell all the community of Israel to come before the Lord, because He has heard your railing."
10 As soon as Aharon had spoken to the whole community of Israel, they looked toward the desert – and the glory of the Lord appeared in the midst of cloud.

CLASSIC COMMENTATORS

In response to the people's complaint for food, aside from responding to the substance of the complaint itself, Moshe twice (v. 8 and v. 9) makes the point that their complaint is misplaced – they should not be complaining about him and Aharon but about God Himself. This made the commentaries uncomfortable.

ר' יוסף בכור שור
אתם מראים עצמיכם כאילו אין אתם מתלוננים כי אם עלינו, ותלונותיכם אינם כי (אם) על הקב"ה, כי אין בידינו לעשות עמכם כלום.

RABBI YOSEF BEKHOR SHOR
You people pretend that you are only complaining against us, but in fact it is the Holy One, blessed be He, whom you are blaming for your situation. For we lack the ability to do anything for you.

רשב"ם
כי י"י הוציא אתכם – ולא כמה שאמרתם: כי הוצאתם אותנו.

RASHBAM
For it is the Lord who brought you out of Egypt, and not us as you claim.

QUESTIONS FOR THOUGHT
- Which of the commentaries seems to suggest that Moshe is looking to deflect responsibility away from himself and toward God, as He is the One who actually took them out of Egypt?
- How do you think Moshe felt, receiving complaints from the people about something over which he had no control?
- God could have easily provided them with food and water before the crises hit. Why do you think that He waited until after they complained to provide them with their basic, legitimate needs?

טז א עַל־הַמָּיִם: וַיִּסְעוּ מֵאֵילִם וַיָּבֹאוּ כָּל־עֲדַת בְּנֵי־יִשְׂרָאֵל אֶל־מִדְבַּר־סִין אֲשֶׁר בֵּין־אֵילִם וּבֵין סִינָי בַּחֲמִשָּׁה עָשָׂר יוֹם לַחֹדֶשׁ
ב הַשֵּׁנִי לְצֵאתָם מֵאֶרֶץ מִצְרָיִם: וַיִּלּוֹנוּ כָּל־עֲדַת בְּנֵי־יִשְׂרָאֵל וַיִּלּוֹנוּ
ג עַל־מֹשֶׁה וְעַל־אַהֲרֹן בַּמִּדְבָּר: וַיֹּאמְרוּ אֲלֵהֶם בְּנֵי יִשְׂרָאֵל מִי־יִתֵּן מוּתֵנוּ בְיַד־יְהוָה בְּאֶרֶץ מִצְרַיִם בְּשִׁבְתֵּנוּ עַל־סִיר הַבָּשָׂר בְּאָכְלֵנוּ לֶחֶם לָשֹׂבַע כִּי־הוֹצֵאתֶם אֹתָנוּ אֶל־הַמִּדְבָּר הַזֶּה
ד לְהָמִית אֶת־כָּל־הַקָּהָל הַזֶּה בָּרָעָב: יב וַיֹּאמֶר יְהוָה אֶל־מֹשֶׁה הִנְנִי מַמְטִיר לָכֶם לֶחֶם מִן־הַשָּׁמָיִם וְיָצָא הָעָם וְלָקְטוּ דְּבַר־יוֹם בְּיוֹמוֹ לְמַעַן אֲנַסֶּנּוּ הֲיֵלֵךְ בְּתוֹרָתִי אִם־לֹא: וְהָיָה
ה בַּיּוֹם הַשִּׁשִּׁי וְהֵכִינוּ אֵת אֲשֶׁר־יָבִיאוּ וְהָיָה מִשְׁנֶה עַל אֲשֶׁר־
ו יִלְקְטוּ יוֹם ׀ יוֹם: וַיֹּאמֶר מֹשֶׁה וְאַהֲרֹן אֶל־כָּל־בְּנֵי יִשְׂרָאֵל
ז עֶרֶב וִידַעְתֶּם כִּי יְהוָה הוֹצִיא אֶתְכֶם מֵאֶרֶץ מִצְרָיִם: וּבֹקֶר וּרְאִיתֶם אֶת־כְּבוֹד יְהוָה בְּשָׁמְעוֹ אֶת־תְּלֻנֹּתֵיכֶם עַל־יְהוָה
ח וְנַחְנוּ מָה כִּי תלונו עָלֵינוּ: וַיֹּאמֶר מֹשֶׁה בְּתֵת יְהוָה לָכֶם תְּלִינוּ בָּעֶרֶב בָּשָׂר לֶאֱכֹל וְלֶחֶם בַּבֹּקֶר לִשְׂבֹּעַ בִּשְׁמֹעַ יְהוָה אֶת־תְּלֻנֹּתֵיכֶם אֲשֶׁר־אַתֶּם מַלִּינִם עָלָיו וְנַחְנוּ מָה לֹא־עָלֵינוּ
ט תְלֻנֹּתֵיכֶם כִּי עַל־יְהוָה: וַיֹּאמֶר מֹשֶׁה אֶל־אַהֲרֹן אֱמֹר אֶל־כָּל־עֲדַת בְּנֵי יִשְׂרָאֵל קִרְבוּ לִפְנֵי יְהוָה כִּי שָׁמַע אֵת תְּלֻנֹּתֵיכֶם:
י וַיְהִי כְּדַבֵּר אַהֲרֹן אֶל־כָּל־עֲדַת בְּנֵי־יִשְׂרָאֵל וַיִּפְנוּ אֶל־הַמִּדְבָּר וְהִנֵּה כְּבוֹד יְהוָה נִרְאָה בֶּעָנָן:

That evening the quails arrived and covered the encampment. The next morning, when the dew evaporates, there is a thin substance on the ground. The people have no idea what it is and ask, "מן הוא?" Moshe responds that it is the bread that God is providing, and that there are instructions which accompany it: each family should gather one omer per household member. When they measure, it turns out that each household has exactly one omer per family member.

11
12 The Lord spoke to Moshe and said, "I have heard the Israelites' railing. Tell them: At twilight you shall eat meat, and in the morning your fill of bread. Then you will know
13 that I am the Lord your God." That evening a flock of quail flew in and covered the
14 camp; next morning a layer of dew surrounded the camp. When the dew covering
15 lifted, fine flakes covered the floor of the desert like fine frost on the ground. When the Israelites saw it, they asked one another, "What is it?" for they did not recognize
16 it. Moshe said to them, "This is the bread the Lord has given you to eat. This is what the Lord has instructed: Each of you gather as much as you need, an omer for every
17 person; each take enough for all the people in your tent." The people of Israel did so.
18 Some gathered more, others less. But when they measured it with an omer measure, those who had gathered much had none left over, and those who gathered but little did

---

QUESTIONS FOR THOUGHT

- Regarding the definition of the word מן, look at the entire verse. Do you think that Rashi or Rashbam fits better based on what the Torah describes?
- Rashi and Ibn Ezra disagree as to whether the Torah means to say that Israel did as instructed or that they did not do as instructed but that a miracle happened. Based on verse 17, which explanation would seem to fit the text of the Torah better?
- Why might Rashi insist on suggesting that a miracle happened with the manna when it would make more sense, based on the text, to not suggest that?

TEXTUAL SKILLS

1. Is what God tells Moshe here a repetition of what was said earlier, a longer version of it, or is this something different?
2. Notice the difference between the verbs used to describe the eating of the meat and of the manna.
3. One of the words used to describe the manna is מחספס. This is the only place in Tanakh that the word appears.

שמות | פרק טז

יא וַיְדַבֵּר יְהֹוָה אֶל־מֹשֶׁה לֵּאמֹר: שָׁמַעְתִּי אֶת־תְּלוּנֹּת בְּנֵי יִשְׂרָאֵל ששי
דַּבֵּר אֲלֵהֶם לֵאמֹר בֵּין הָעַרְבַּיִם תֹּאכְלוּ בָשָׂר וּבַבֹּקֶר תִּשְׂבְּעוּ־
לָחֶם וִידַעְתֶּם כִּי אֲנִי יְהֹוָה אֱלֹהֵיכֶם: וַיְהִי בָעֶרֶב וַתַּעַל הַשְּׂלָו יג
וַתְּכַס אֶת־הַמַּחֲנֶה וּבַבֹּקֶר הָיְתָה שִׁכְבַת הַטָּל סָבִיב לַמַּחֲנֶה:
יד וַתַּעַל שִׁכְבַת הַטָּל וְהִנֵּה עַל־פְּנֵי הַמִּדְבָּר דַּק מְחֻסְפָּס דַּק כַּכְּפֹר
עַל־הָאָרֶץ: וַיִּרְאוּ בְנֵי־יִשְׂרָאֵל וַיֹּאמְרוּ אִישׁ אֶל־אָחִיו מָן הוּא טו
כִּי לֹא יָדְעוּ מַה־הוּא וַיֹּאמֶר מֹשֶׁה אֲלֵהֶם הוּא הַלֶּחֶם אֲשֶׁר נָתַן
יְהֹוָה לָכֶם לְאָכְלָה: זֶה הַדָּבָר אֲשֶׁר צִוָּה יְהֹוָה לִקְטוּ מִמֶּנּוּ אִישׁ טז
לְפִי אָכְלוֹ עֹמֶר לַגֻּלְגֹּלֶת מִסְפַּר נַפְשֹׁתֵיכֶם אִישׁ לַאֲשֶׁר בְּאָהֳלוֹ
יז תִּקָּחוּ: וַיַּעֲשׂוּ־כֵן בְּנֵי יִשְׂרָאֵל וַיִּלְקְטוּ הַמַּרְבֶּה וְהַמַּמְעִיט:
יח וַיָּמֹדּוּ בָעֹמֶר וְלֹא הֶעְדִּיף הַמַּרְבֶּה וְהַמַּמְעִיט לֹא הֶחְסִיר אִישׁ

CLASSIC COMMENTATORS

Two questions bothered the commentaries about the manna.
1. When *Benei Yisrael* said מן הוא, what did they mean?
2. The Torah describes that some collected a lot and some a little of manna, but they still all end up with one omer per person. What does that mean?

RASHI — רש"י

The term מן refers to food preparation.

מן הוא - הכנת מזון הוא.

RASHBAM — רשב"ם

The phrase "מן הוא" means "what [מה] is it?"

מן הוא - כמו: מה הוא.

RASHI — רש"י

When everyone got home and measured what they had collected, they found that people who had brought home an excess amount now had exactly an omer of manna for each individual in his tent…And this was a great miracle of the manna.

כשבאו לביתם מדדו בעומר איש איש מה שליקטו, מצאו שהמרבה ללקוט לא העדיף על עומר לגלגלת, וזה נס גדול שנעשה בו.

IBN EZRA — אבן עזרא

Some Israelites gathered more manna, and others collected less – it all depended on the number of people living in each household. Still, our Sages say that this verse reflects a miracle.

המרבה והממעיט לפי מספר נפשות אהלו. וקדמונינו אמרו: כי הוא דבר פלא.

Despite very clear instructions from Moshe not to leave any manna overnight, some people do so and find it rotten in the morning. On the sixth day Moshe tells the nation that they should save some for the next day, as the manna will not be coming on Shabbat. Sure enough, they leave it overnight and it does not spoil – but some people go out to look for manna anyway. God expresses His displeasure, explaining that He is giving them a day to rest from collecting, which is why they received double on the sixth day. The next week, no one goes out to collect on Shabbat.

19 not fall short. All had gathered as much as they could eat. "Let no one leave any over
20 for the morning," said Moshe; but they did not listen to Moshe. Some of them left part of it till morning, and it became worm-infested and stank. Moshe was enraged with
21 them. Every morning they gathered it, all as much as they could eat, and when the sun
22 grew hot, it melted away. When the sixth day came, they gathered a double portion, two
23 omers each. All the leaders of the community came and reported this to Moshe. "This" he told them, "is what the LORD has said: Tomorrow is a day of rest, a holy Sabbath to the LORD. Bake now what you need to bake and cook what you need to cook. Whatever
24 is left, keep carefully aside for the morning." So they put it aside until the morning, as

---

אבן עזרא

וישראל לקטו לחם משנה – כי משה צוה להם לעשות ככה, והם לא ידעו למה. והעד, שהכתוב אמר: לקטו – ולא אמר: מצאו. ובאו הנשיאים והגידו למשה כי ישראל עשו כאשר צום. ושאלוהו מה יעשו.

IBN EZRA

"They gathered a double portion" – on this day Moshe commanded Israel to collect twice as much food as before, but he did not explain why. Furthermore, the verse states that "they gathered a double portion," not that they found they had twice as much as usual. [Ibn Ezra thereby rejects the idea that Israel took home as much as during the rest of the week, and that when they measured their take they miraculously found enough to eat for two days.] Meanwhile, "the leaders of the community came and reported this to Moshe" that the people had done as they were told. The point of their mission was to ask why the nation was instructed to double their collection efforts, and how the people could possibly consume so much food in one day.

QUESTIONS FOR THOUGHT

- Rashi and Bekhor Shor have similar positions. They disagree on the reaction of the leaders to the realization that the people had double. What does each of them think that reaction was?
- What was God trying to teach the people by having them collect double on the sixth day and nothing on the seventh?
- Do you think that would be better accomplished if they had been told in advance or if they were surprised to discover the extra portions when they got home?

יט לְפִי־אָכְלוֹ לָקָטוּ: וַיֹּאמֶר מֹשֶׁה אֲלֵהֶם אִישׁ אַל־יוֹתֵר מִמֶּנּוּ עַד־
כ בֹּקֶר: וְלֹא־שָׁמְעוּ אֶל־מֹשֶׁה וַיּוֹתִרוּ אֲנָשִׁים מִמֶּנּוּ עַד־בֹּקֶר וַיָּרֻם
כא תּוֹלָעִים וַיִּבְאַשׁ וַיִּקְצֹף עֲלֵהֶם מֹשֶׁה: וַיִּלְקְטוּ אֹתוֹ בַּבֹּקֶר
בַּבֹּקֶר אִישׁ כְּפִי אָכְלוֹ וְחַם הַשֶּׁמֶשׁ וְנָמָס: וַיְהִי ׀ בַּיּוֹם הַשִּׁשִּׁי לָקְטוּ
כב לֶחֶם מִשְׁנֶה שְׁנֵי הָעֹמֶר לָאֶחָד וַיָּבֹאוּ כָּל־נְשִׂיאֵי הָעֵדָה וַיַּגִּידוּ
כג לְמֹשֶׁה: וַיֹּאמֶר אֲלֵהֶם הוּא אֲשֶׁר דִּבֶּר יְהוָה שַׁבָּתוֹן שַׁבַּת־קֹדֶשׁ
לַיהוָה מָחָר אֵת אֲשֶׁר־תֹּאפוּ אֵפוּ וְאֵת אֲשֶׁר־תְּבַשְּׁלוּ בַּשֵּׁלוּ
כד וְאֵת כָּל־הָעֹדֵף הַנִּיחוּ לָכֶם לְמִשְׁמֶרֶת עַד־הַבֹּקֶר: וַיַּנִּיחוּ אֹתוֹ
עַד־הַבֹּקֶר כַּאֲשֶׁר צִוָּה מֹשֶׁה וְלֹא הִבְאִישׁ וְרִמָּה לֹא־הָיְתָה־

CLASSIC COMMENTATORS

The people collected double on the sixth day, and their leaders came to consult with Moshe. Did they purposely collect double, or did they gather the usual amount and were then surprised to discover that they miraculously had double?

RASHI

רש"י

"They gathered a double portion" – when the Israelites measured their manna haul in their tents they found that the yield was twice as much as before.

"They reported this to Moshe" – the nation's elders asked their leader why this day was different than any other. The fact that the people inquired about the matter shows that Moshe had yet to describe the alternative protocol for Shabbat detailed earlier in the text: "On the sixth day, they will have to prepare what they bring in" (16:5). The explanation was provided only when the people realized something had changed.

לקטו לחם משנה - כשמדדו את לקיטתם באהליהם, מצאו כפלים.

ויגידו למשה - שאלוהו מה היום מימים. ומכאן יש ללמוד שעדיין לא הגיד משה להם פרשת שבת, שנצטווה לומר להם: והיה ביום הששי והכינו וגו' (שמות ט"ז:ה'), עד ששאלוהו את זאת.

RABBI YOSEF BEKHOR SHOR

ר' יוסף בכור שור

"All the leaders of the community came" – they were afraid to leave the uneaten food for the next day, for they had seen Moshe's displeasure when some individuals had previously left manna overnight.

ויבאו כל נשיאי העדה - כי היו יראים להניחו עד למחר, לפי שקצף משה על המותירים.

25 Moshe had instructed them, and it did not stink, nor did worms infest it. And Moshe said, "Today, eat this, for today is a Sabbath to the Lord; today you will not find it on
26 the ground. Six days shall you gather it, but on the seventh day, the Sabbath, it will not
27 be there." Some people did go out to gather it on the seventh day; but they found none.
28 Then the Lord said to Moshe, "How long will you refuse to keep My commandments
29 and laws? Understand that the Lord has given you a Sabbath – that is why He gave you two days' bread on the sixth day. You shall each rest where you are: let no man
30 depart from where he is on the seventh day." So the people rested on the seventh day.

WISDOM OF THE HEART

Each of the three Shabbat meals are required to begin with *leḥem mishneh*, two loaves of bread. There is some discussion of leniency in respect to the third meal. Why do we insist on *leḥem mishneh*? It is to commemorate the double portion of manna that would come down on Friday morning when *Benei Yisrael* were in the desert, so that the people would have enough for Shabbat. Shabbat reflects a taste of the world to come. We come into it complete, with all our needs taken care of, and nothing more to look for or want. People mistakenly think that all labor is prohibited on Shabbat. But it is really only creative labor that is forbidden: To cook a new dish is forbidden but to schlep a couch is not. The underlying idea is that one shouldn't feel any need on Shabbat to produce anything more. We have everything we need.

God has told Moshe about this miraculous food from the sky. He has informed him he will be sending the people a double portion on Friday. But God hasn't mentioned anything about not leaving manna over. How did Moshe guess this requirement in verse 19? Perhaps he invented it in order to help Benei Yisrael build their trust in God. God then caused all the leftovers to spoil in order to strengthen Moshe's authority. Rav Yaakov Asher Weisfish uses this thesis to explain another element of the story. On Shabbat morning, several Israelites left the camp to look for the manna, even though they were told that no manna would fall on Shabbat. Rashi says that God's indignant response in verse 28, "How long will you refuse to keep My commandments," was directed at Moshe as well. Perhaps this was a rebuke for having introduced the prohibition in the first place. Being strict can sometimes establish a healthy boundary, but one needs to be careful that it doesn't overreach.

כה בֹּאוּ: וַיֹּאמֶר מֹשֶׁה אִכְלֻהוּ הַיּוֹם כִּי־שַׁבָּת הַיּוֹם לַיהוה הַיּוֹם לֹא
כו תִמְצָאֻהוּ בַּשָּׂדֶה: שֵׁשֶׁת יָמִים תִּלְקְטֻהוּ וּבַיּוֹם הַשְּׁבִיעִי שַׁבָּת
כז לֹא יִהְיֶה־בּוֹ: וַיְהִי בַּיּוֹם הַשְּׁבִיעִי יָצְאוּ מִן־הָעָם לִלְקֹט וְלֹא
כח מָצָאוּ: וַיֹּאמֶר יהוה אֶל־מֹשֶׁה עַד־אָנָה מֵאַנְתֶּם יג
כט לִשְׁמֹר מִצְוֺתַי וְתוֹרֹתָי: רְאוּ כִּי־יהוה נָתַן לָכֶם הַשַּׁבָּת עַל־כֵּן
הוּא נֹתֵן לָכֶם בַּיּוֹם הַשִּׁשִּׁי לֶחֶם יוֹמָיִם שְׁבוּ ׀ אִישׁ תַּחְתָּיו אַל־
ל יֵצֵא אִישׁ מִמְּקֹמוֹ בַּיּוֹם הַשְּׁבִיעִי: וַיִּשְׁבְּתוּ הָעָם בַּיּוֹם הַשְּׁבִיעִי:

TEXTUAL SKILLS

1. Of the twelve verses in this passage, the first six focus on leaving the manna from one day to the next – when the people are supposed to, when they are not allowed to, and what happens when people disobey. The word בֹּקֶר is the most frequent word in these verses (appearing six times).
2. The second six verses focus on introducing Shabbat as a day of non-collection. The word יוֹם is the most frequent word here (ten times), and the roots ש-ב-ע and ש-ב-ת appear four times each.
3. Note: This is the second time that Israel was given an instruction not to leave something over until the morning.

QUICK BITE

According to the Gemara in Massekhet Yoma, the manna could taste like whatever you wanted. But could it also change its shape? According to one midrash that Rashi cites (Num. 11:5), the manna could not change into onions, for example, since this would be harmful to nursing mothers. Might this be a hint that the physical nature of the food would change? Hypothetically, would it be a problem to have the manna taste like a cheeseburger? According to the Ritva, Benei Yisrael fulfilled the mitzva of matza in the desert by eating the manna!

Following God's instruction, Moshe tells Aharon to fill a jar with one omer of manna as an everlasting testimony of the unique food God provided for the forty years of Israel's stay in the wilderness.

31 The house of Israel named it manna. It looked like white coriander seeds, and tasted
32 like wafers made with honey. Moshe said, "This is what the LORD commands: Let an omer of it be kept carefully aside for your descendants, that they may see the bread I
33 fed you in the desert when I brought you out of Egypt." Moshe said to Aharon, "Take an urn, put an omer of manna in it, and place it before the LORD to be kept for future
34 generations." As the LORD commanded Moshe, so Aharon placed it before the Ark of
35 Testimony to be kept with care. The Israelites ate manna for forty years, until they came to the land where they could settle down. They ate the manna until they came to the
36 border of Canaan. (An omer is a tenth of an ephah.)

QUESTIONS FOR THOUGHT

- According to Rashi and R. Hirsch, for whom was the jar of manna intended?
- R. Hirsch actually describes two different answers identifying the intended audience for the jar of manna. What two audiences does he see, and how do those answers complement each other?
- Supposing that jar were found today, what impact do you think it would have on people's religious lives?

TEXTUAL SKILLS

1. The description of the manna in verse 31 contains words that we don't really understand. Why might the Torah use unintelligible words to describe the manna?
2. It is evident from the text of the Torah that some of these verses could not have been written at the time that this story happened. Which verses are those, and why could they not have been written then?

WISDOM OF THE HEART

Rav Shimon Schwab once had the opportunity to eat at the house of the Ḥafetz Ḥayyim, where his host asked the following question: there is a midrashic teaching that the manna would taste like whatever flavor you would think of. You could imagine the taste of a hamburger, and that's what it would it taste like. But what if you had no thought whatsoever?

This question becomes more powerful when we imagine that the manna was an otherworldly, spiritual food, meant to sustain our souls alongside our bodies. Just as manna without intention can become tasteless, so too can religious acts become meaningless if they are performed by rote without a soul.

What kind of religious intention is possible with different mitzvot?

שמות | פרק טז

לא וַיִּקְרְא֧וּ בֵית־יִשְׂרָאֵ֛ל אֶת־שְׁמ֖וֹ מָ֑ן וְה֗וּא כְּזֶ֤רַע גַּד֙ לָבָ֔ן וְטַעְמ֖וֹ
לב כְּצַפִּיחִ֥ת בִּדְבָֽשׁ: וַיֹּ֣אמֶר מֹשֶׁ֗ה זֶ֤ה הַדָּבָר֙ אֲשֶׁ֣ר צִוָּ֣ה יְהֹוָ֔ה מְלֹ֤א
הָעֹ֙מֶר֙ מִמֶּ֔נּוּ לְמִשְׁמֶ֖רֶת לְדֹרֹֽתֵיכֶ֑ם לְמַ֣עַן ׀ יִרְא֣וּ אֶת־הַלֶּ֗חֶם
אֲשֶׁ֨ר הֶאֱכַ֤לְתִּי אֶתְכֶם֙ בַּמִּדְבָּ֔ר בְּהוֹצִיאִ֥י אֶתְכֶ֖ם מֵאֶ֥רֶץ מִצְרָֽיִם:
לג וַיֹּ֨אמֶר מֹשֶׁ֜ה אֶֽל־אַהֲרֹ֗ן קַ֚ח צִנְצֶ֣נֶת אַחַ֔ת וְתֶן־שָׁ֥מָּה מְלֹֽא־
הָעֹ֖מֶר מָ֑ן וְהַנַּ֤ח אֹתוֹ֙ לִפְנֵ֣י יְהֹוָ֔ה לְמִשְׁמֶ֖רֶת לְדֹרֹֽתֵיכֶֽם: כַּאֲשֶׁ֛ר
לד צִוָּ֥ה יְהֹוָ֖ה אֶל־מֹשֶׁ֑ה וַיַּנִּיחֵ֧הוּ אַהֲרֹ֛ן לִפְנֵ֥י הָעֵדֻ֖ת לְמִשְׁמָֽרֶת:
לה וּבְנֵ֣י יִשְׂרָאֵ֗ל אָֽכְל֤וּ אֶת־הַמָּן֙ אַרְבָּעִ֣ים שָׁנָ֔ה עַד־בֹּאָ֖ם אֶל־אֶ֣רֶץ
לו נוֹשָׁ֑בֶת אֶת־הַמָּן֙ אָֽכְל֔וּ עַד־בֹּאָ֕ם אֶל־קְצֵ֖ה אֶ֥רֶץ כְּנָֽעַן: וְהָעֹ֕מֶר
עֲשִׂרִ֥ית הָאֵיפָ֖ה הֽוּא:

CLASSIC COMMENTATORS

Although the Torah explicitly describes the purpose of the omer of manna in the jar (v. 32), many of the commentaries looked for additional meaning. What was the purpose of putting a portion of the manna into a jar?

רש"י

לדרתיכם - בימי ירמיהו. כשהיה ירמיהו מוכיחן: למה אין אתם עוסקין בתורה, והם אומרים: נניח מלאכתנו ונעסוק בתורה, מהיכן נתפרנס? הוציא להם צנצנת המן, אמר להם: הדור אתם ראו את דבר י"י ... בזה נתפרנסו אבותיכם.

RASHI

"For your descendants" – in the time of the prophet Yirmiyahu. When Yirmiyahu rebuked the nation for their lack of Torah study, the people responded: If we quit our jobs and occupy ourselves with learning Torah, how will we live? Yirimiyahu took out the jar of manna and, showing it to the Israelites, declared, "O generation, see the word of the Lord" (Jer. 2:31)… Look, he said, this is how your ancestors subsisted.

ר' שמשון רפאל הירש

למשמרת לדרתיכם וגו' - ציווי זה בישר לדור המדבר שנדודיהם במדבר יגיעו לקיצם, ושבסופו של דבר יוכלו להשיג את פרנסתם במצב הרגיל. אך גם במצב הרגיל, ... עליהם לראות את מזונם כ"מן" בלבד, כמתנה שה' מעניק ומחלק להם למנה.

RABBI SAMSON RAPHAEL HIRSCH

This commandment informed the generation of the wilderness that eventually their wanderings would come to an end, and that in time they would be able to earn their livelihood by natural means…Nevertheless, Israel was meant to believe that even when they were able to feed their families by virtue of their own efforts, the food that they served should be viewed as manna, as a present from the Lord. That is, God will consistently and constantly provide the gift of sustenance to the nation.

Shemot | Chapter 17 — Beshalaḥ

At Refidim, the next stop, Israel finds itself again without water. The people quarrel with Moshe, who accuses them of testing God. Moshe turns to God, frustrated by the people, who seem to never be satisfied. God instructs Moshe to take his staff and, in front of the elders of the camp, hit a rock. Moshe does as instructed, and water flows from the rock for the people. Moshe names the place Masa and Meriva (literally, "Testing and Quarreling"), for the people's testing of God and quarreling with him.

17 1 All the community of Israel moved on after that from the desert of Sin, traveling from place to place as the Lord guided them, and they camped at Refidim, but there was no 2 water there for the people to drink. The people started to wrangle with Moshe. "Give us water to drink," they raged. "Why do you wrangle with me?" asked Moshe. "Why 3 are you testing the Lord?" But the people were thirsty for water. They railed against Moshe, "Why did you bring us out of Egypt? Was it to kill me, my children and all my 4 livestock by thirst?" "What shall I do with this people?" Moshe cried to the Lord – 5 "another moment and they will stone me." The Lord answered Moshe, "Walk out to face the people taking some of the elders of Israel with you. Take the staff with which 6 you struck the Nile in your hand, and go. I will be there before you by the rock at Ḥorev. Strike the rock, water will come out of it and the people will drink." And that is what 7 Moshe did, before the eyes of the elders of Israel. He named the place Masa and Meriva, because the people had quarreled and had tested the Lord, demanding, "Is the Lord among us or not?"

HAAMEK DAVAR / העמק דבר

They really were not yet thirsty at all, but they said that there was no water to drink. Moshe understood what was happening, which is why he retorted, "Why do you wrangle with me?"

באמת עוד לא צמאו כלל, אבל העם אמרו, כי אין מים לשתות. ומשה הבין הדבר, על כן אמר "מה תריבון עמדי".

QUESTIONS FOR THOUGHT

- Which of the above opinions fits best with verse 3?
- Based on God's reaction, which of the above opinions makes the most sense?
- When you are faced with frustration, how can you avoid taking it out on someone who is not directly responsible?

TEXTUAL SKILLS

1. This is the third story in a row where the concept of "testing" appears. What are the two kinds of testing in these three stories?

2. Under what circumstances do God and Moshe each become angry in these three stories?

שמות | פרק יז | בשלח

יז א וַיִּסְעוּ כָּל־עֲדַת בְּנֵי־יִשְׂרָאֵל מִמִּדְבַּר־סִין לְמַסְעֵיהֶם עַל־פִּי שביעי
יְהוָה וַיַּחֲנוּ בִּרְפִידִים וְאֵין מַיִם לִשְׁתֹּת הָעָם: ב וַיָּרֶב הָעָם עִם־
מֹשֶׁה וַיֹּאמְרוּ תְּנוּ־לָנוּ מַיִם וְנִשְׁתֶּה וַיֹּאמֶר לָהֶם מֹשֶׁה מַה־
תְּרִיבוּן עִמָּדִי מַה־תְּנַסּוּן אֶת־יְהוָה: ג וַיִּצְמָא שָׁם הָעָם לַמַּיִם וַיָּלֶן
הָעָם עַל־מֹשֶׁה וַיֹּאמֶר לָמָּה זֶּה הֶעֱלִיתָנוּ מִמִּצְרַיִם לְהָמִית אֹתִי
וְאֶת־בָּנַי וְאֶת־מִקְנַי בַּצָּמָא: ד וַיִּצְעַק מֹשֶׁה אֶל־יְהוָה לֵאמֹר מָה
אֶעֱשֶׂה לָעָם הַזֶּה עוֹד מְעַט וּסְקָלֻנִי: ה וַיֹּאמֶר יְהוָה אֶל־מֹשֶׁה
עֲבֹר לִפְנֵי הָעָם וְקַח אִתְּךָ מִזִּקְנֵי יִשְׂרָאֵל וּמַטְּךָ אֲשֶׁר הִכִּיתָ
בּוֹ אֶת־הַיְאֹר קַח בְּיָדְךָ וְהָלָכְתָּ: ו הִנְנִי עֹמֵד לְפָנֶיךָ שָּׁם ׀ עַל־
הַצּוּר בְּחֹרֵב וְהִכִּיתָ בַצּוּר וְיָצְאוּ מִמֶּנּוּ מַיִם וְשָׁתָה הָעָם וַיַּעַשׂ
כֵּן מֹשֶׁה לְעֵינֵי זִקְנֵי יִשְׂרָאֵל: ז וַיִּקְרָא שֵׁם הַמָּקוֹם מַסָּה וּמְרִיבָה
עַל־רִיב ׀ בְּנֵי יִשְׂרָאֵל וְעַל נַסֹּתָם אֶת־יְהוָה לֵאמֹר הֲיֵשׁ יְהוָה
בְּקִרְבֵּנוּ אִם־אָיִן:

CLASSIC COMMENTATORS

Twice earlier in this *parasha* we find that Israel is lacking water, but this third time their complaint is more intense, and they even feud with Moshe. Was this case of thirst different than the previous two?

RABBI AVRAHAM BEN HARAMBAM

ר׳ אברהם בן הרמב״ס

Israel's discontent was stronger here than it had been at Mara because the level of thirst was more severe…Indeed, even though the water the nation found at Mara had been bitter, they still had managed to locate water! At that point the people were certain that Moshe would be able to make the water drinkable…At Refidim, however, there was not even any water to work with.

כאן חזקה תסיסתם יותר מבמרה, מפני שהצמא חזק עליהם כאן יותר… וגם מפני שבמרה מצאו מים, אלא שהיו מרים, וכאילו הונחה דעתם שמשה יהפוך אותם למים מתוקים… אבל כאן חסרו המים לגמרי.

HAKETAV VEHAKABBALA

הכתב והקבלה

Israel lacked an abundance of water that would have allowed the people to drink to their satisfaction. Nevertheless, there was a small amount of water there.

לא היה להם מים בשפע, כדי שיוכל כל אחד לשתות בכל עת שירצה, אבל לשתיה מצומצמת היה.

Shemot | Chapter 17 — Beshalaḥ

8 Then, at Refidim, Amalek came and attacked Israel. Moshe said to Yehoshua, "Choose
9 men for us, and go out and do battle against Amalek. Tomorrow I will stand on top of
10 the hill with the staff of God in my hand." Yehoshua fought the Amalekites as Moshe had
11 directed him, while Moshe, Aharon, and Ḥur climbed to the top of the hill. Whenever
Moshe held his hand high, the Israelites prevailed, but whenever he let his hand drop,
12 the Amalekites prevailed. But Moshe's hands grew heavy. So they took a stone and
placed it under him and he sat, while Aharon and Ḥur held up his hands, one on each
13 side, so that his hands held true until sunset. And Yehoshua overcame Amalek and his
14 people by the sword. Then the Lord said to Moshe, "Write this as a memorial on a
scroll, and commit it to Yehoshua's ears: I will erase the memory of Amalek, utterly,
15 from under the heavens." Moshe built an altar and named it, "The Lord Is My Banner,"
16 saying, "There is a hand on the Lord's throne. The Lord will be at war with Amalek
throughout the ages."

ר׳ אברהם בן הרמב״ם
בהרימו את ידיו דוגמת ויפרש כפיו השמימה היו מתגברים על ידי תחינתו וכאשר הניח אותן חלשו על ידי התרשלות כוונתו.

RABBI AVRAHAM BEN HARAMBAM
When Moshe raised his hands toward heaven, that represented the leader's petition to God for salvation, and Israel therefore succeeded. However, when Moshe lowered his hands, that signified that his concentration had lapsed, and the army was beaten back.

ר׳ דוד צבי הופמן
דומה שמטה האלוהים כשלעצמו הוסיף גם הוא בהרמתו זו הן לעידודם של ישראל הן להשגת הנס האלוהי, שאם לא כן, תהיה נטילת המטה ביד משה המוזכרת בפסוק ט – מיותרת.

RABBI DAVID TZVI HOFFMANN
It seems that Moshe raising the staff of God here contributed in and of itself both to encouraging the Israelites and to bringing about the divine miracle – for were it not so, Moshe taking the staff in his hand, as mentioned in verse 9, would be superfluous.

QUESTIONS FOR THOUGHT

- Two of the commentaries say that Moshe's hands are related to prayer and that the prayer affected the course of the battle. Which two commentaries are those, and whose prayer does each of them talk about?
- A third commentary says that Moshe's hands are giving signals to the warriors on how to conduct the battle, while a fourth suggests that Moshe is performing miracles. Which commentaries express each of these opinions?
- Of the three basic approaches outlined above (rational, miraculous, prayer), which do you think makes the most sense in the context of these verses? Why?
- Which do you think is the most meaningful? Why?

TEXTUAL SKILLS

1. Earlier in this *parasha* there was a series of four two-letter words. In this passage there is a string of five two-letter words – the longest such string in the Torah.

2. The names "Amalek" and "Moshe" each appear seven times in this passage. Find the one other word which also appears seven times. Why is it important?

שמות | פרק יז

ח וַיָּבֹא עֲמָלֵק וַיִּלָּחֶם עִם־יִשְׂרָאֵל בִּרְפִידִם: וַיֹּאמֶר מֹשֶׁה אֶל־
יְהוֹשֻׁעַ בְּחַר־לָנוּ אֲנָשִׁים וְצֵא הִלָּחֵם בַּעֲמָלֵק מָחָר אָנֹכִי נִצָּב
י עַל־רֹאשׁ הַגִּבְעָה וּמַטֵּה הָאֱלֹהִים בְּיָדִי: וַיַּעַשׂ יְהוֹשֻׁעַ כַּאֲשֶׁר
אָמַר־לוֹ מֹשֶׁה לְהִלָּחֵם בַּעֲמָלֵק וּמֹשֶׁה אַהֲרֹן וְחוּר עָלוּ רֹאשׁ
יא הַגִּבְעָה: וְהָיָה כַּאֲשֶׁר יָרִים מֹשֶׁה יָדוֹ וְגָבַר יִשְׂרָאֵל וְכַאֲשֶׁר
יב יָנִיחַ יָדוֹ וְגָבַר עֲמָלֵק: וִידֵי מֹשֶׁה כְּבֵדִים וַיִּקְחוּ־אֶבֶן וַיָּשִׂימוּ
תַחְתָּיו וַיֵּשֶׁב עָלֶיהָ וְאַהֲרֹן וְחוּר תָּמְכוּ בְיָדָיו מִזֶּה אֶחָד וּמִזֶּה
יג אֶחָד וַיְהִי יָדָיו אֱמוּנָה עַד־בֹּא הַשָּׁמֶשׁ: וַיַּחֲלֹשׁ יְהוֹשֻׁעַ אֶת־
עֲמָלֵק וְאֶת־עַמּוֹ לְפִי־חָרֶב:
יד וַיֹּאמֶר יְהֹוָה אֶל־מֹשֶׁה כְּתֹב זֹאת זִכָּרוֹן בַּסֵּפֶר וְשִׂים בְּאָזְנֵי מפטיר
יְהוֹשֻׁעַ כִּי־מָחֹה אֶמְחֶה אֶת־זֵכֶר עֲמָלֵק מִתַּחַת הַשָּׁמָיִם: וַיִּבֶן
טו מֹשֶׁה מִזְבֵּחַ וַיִּקְרָא שְׁמוֹ יְהֹוָה | נִסִּי: וַיֹּאמֶר כִּי־יָד עַל־כֵּס יָהּ
טז מִלְחָמָה לַיהֹוָה בַּעֲמָלֵק מִדֹּר דֹּר:

CLASSIC COMMENTATORS

What is the connection between Moshe's hands at the top of the hill and the battle taking place below?

MISHNA ROSH HASHANA 3:8

"Whenever Moshe held his hand high the Israelites prevailed" – is it the hands of Moshe held aloft that win a battle or lose it? Rather, the episode teaches that when Israel [saw Moshe on the hill and then] looked upward, they directed their hearts to their Father in heaven. That in turn helped them to prevail against the enemy. But when they did not submit to the authority of God, they stumbled in the conflict.

משנה ראש השנה ג:ח

וְהָיָה כַּאֲשֶׁר יָרִים מֹשֶׁה אֶת יָדוֹ וְגָבַר יִשְׂרָאֵל: וְכִי יָדָיו של משה עושות מלחמה או שוברות מלחמה? אלא לומר לך שכל זמן שהיו ישראל מסתכלין כלפי מעלה ומשעבדין את לבם לאביהן שבשמים היו מתגברים ואם לאו – היו נופלים.

RABBI YOSEF BEKHOR SHOR

Moshe's hands held high were a substitute for a war banner...for it is customary that when armies march into battle they raise a flag to signal to their soldiers that victory is at hand, and lower the flag in moments of distress. Thus fighters who are behind the action are informed that their brethren are being beaten and that they should rush to the front to assist them.

ר' יוסף בכור שור

במקום נס [=דגל]... שדרך לזקוף במלחמה. וכשמתגברין, זוקפין אותה ויודעין שהם נוצחין, וכשאין מתגברין משפילין אותה, כדי שידעו אותם של אחריהם שאותם שבתוך המלחמה צריכין סיועא.

MORE QUICK BITES

- **13:19** There is a midrash which says that *Benei Yisrael* carried two special boxes during their wanderings: one held the tablets from Sinai, the other contained Yosef's bones. The nations they encountered were puzzled by the juxtaposition of these two vessels – the Covenant and…Yosef's bones? *Benei Yisrael* responded: "This man fulfilled the essence of what was in the other ark." What greater legacy could there be than to be identified as an embodiment of Torah? That is within the grasp of every one of us.

- **15:1** Rav Kook explains that the song refers to two types of love of God. The first is an innate love and appreciation of God as our Creator and Provider, the Source of all life. All things are inherently drawn to their source, and this love of God is natural – involuntary – like the innate feelings of love and respect for one's parents.

  The second love of God is one that we need to work for. It is acquired through reflecting on God's actions – His creation of the world and guiding hand in the unfolding of history. As we recognize the sometimes-hidden Divine Providence in the world, we experience this contemplative love.

EXPLORING HASHKAFA
Thinking about the Egyptians

Benei Yisrael finally leave Egypt, loaded with sheep and cattle, gold and silver, but also carrying a heavy burden: the memory of what must have felt like endless misery. With each step that burden may have lifted slightly, and there must have been a great collective relief when they stood by the seashore watching their oppressors be destroyed – so much so that they burst into song.

For the rest of time they are commanded to regularly remember that exodus and, once a year, to retell the story – in all its gory details, beginning with the bad years. What about all of those negative feelings toward the Egyptians? Were they supposed to hold on to those feelings or let them fade away with time?

On the one hand, we are expected to retell and relive the misery at the Seder and are commanded to never return to Egypt; on the other hand, the Torah also commands us to not bear a grudge or distance the Egyptian, for he hosted us when we were living away from our home (Deut. 23:8). Even our understanding of the immediate reaction to the demise of the Egyptians is no so clear. One the one hand, *Benei Yisrael* sing in joy, and that song is not only in the Torah but recited daily in *tefilla*; on the other hand, the book of Proverbs (24:17) instructs us not to rejoice at the downfall of our enemies, which became the motto of the mishnaic Sage Shmuel HaKatan (Avot 4:19).

The fact that the Egyptians were evil does not necessarily affect our calculations on this. The Talmud (Sanhedrin 96b) lists descendants of evil people who became great Torah scholars, and the following famous story is related about Rabbi Meir (Berakhot 10a): Rabbi Meir was repeatedly victimized by local gangsters, but he nonetheless prayed for them. When he was questioned about his bizarre behavior he cited the verse from Psalms (104:35), "The sins will be erased from the land," noting that the verse talks about the sins, not the sinners. He prayed for their sins to disappear so that they would become righteous.

Maybe Rabbi Meir and Shmuel HaKatan are examples of extremely pious and tolerant people and should not set the standard for the rest of us. The fact that they are mentioned at all could be evidence of this – the exceptions that prove the rule. Nevertheless, it is still unclear how we should handle those feelings of bitterness.

Perhaps there is, and should be, a difference between our immediate reaction and our long-term attitude. In the short term it is normal and natural to bear bad feelings toward someone who harmed you, but in the long term, who wants to live their entire life consumed by anger and hatred, bearing grudges? As Rabbi Jonathan Sacks explains – to truly be free you have to let go of hate, otherwise you are still enslaved to that hatred.

While it is not crystal clear exactly how the Torah expects us to react in the long term to the downfall of our enemies, perhaps we can nonetheless learn an important lesson. The verse from Proverbs about not rejoicing at an adversary's downfall may be pointing to a deep message. If the only reason for your success is that your opponent made a mistake, that is no cause to rejoice. You should rise to the top on your own merits, not on the weaknesses of others. A real reason to rejoice would be rising to the top regardless of what your adversaries do.

The defeat of the Egyptians generates immediate song – and that is appropriate. But we dare not think that we have achieved something just because they lost. Our achievements are yet to come, and they will take work – a lot of it.

פרשת יתרו
PARASHAT YITRO

"Who is wise? It is one who learns from all people."
Pirkei Avot

One amazing miracle set *Benei Yisrael* free of Egypt forever. That miracle was followed by something even more amazing – daily food and water provided directly from Heaven. But what's next? Where do we go from here? Is this really the Promised Land? Was all of this so that Israel could live a pure life in the wilderness nourished by divine support?

PARASHAT YITRO

Moshe's father-in-law Yitro, having heard about what God did for Moshe and Israel, comes to visit Moshe in the wilderness. He brings with him Moshe's wife and two sons, who had been left in Midian.

18 1 Moshe's father-in-law Yitro, priest of Midian, heard about all that God had done for
2 Moshe and for His people Israel when the Lord brought Israel out of Egypt. Yitro had
3 received Moshe's wife Tzipora after he had sent her home, together with her two sons. One was named Gershom, for Moshe had said, "I have been a stranger in a foreign land,"
4 and the other, Eliezer, for he had said, "My father's God has helped me, saving me from
5 Pharaoh's sword." And now Moshe's father-in-law Yitro came to Moshe in the desert, bringing his sons and his wife, to where he was encamped by the mountain of God.
6 Yitro sent word to Moshe, "I am coming to you – your father-in-law Yitro – together

רמב״ן

והקרוב אלי לתפוש סדר התורה, שבא קודם מתן תורה בהיותם ברפידים... והנה יהיה פירוש הכתוב: ויבא יתרו חותן משה ובניו ואשתו אל משה אל המדבר אשר הוא חונה שם ויבא אל הר האלהים... ומן ההר שלח אליו: אני חותנך יתרו בא אליך, ויצא אליו משה

RAMBAN

It seems most reasonable to me to accept the sequence of events as they appear in the Torah, meaning that Yitro traveled toward Israel when the nation was still stationed at Refidim, before the Torah was given... Thus, when the verse states, "And now Moshe's father-in-law Yitro came to Moshe in the desert, bringing his sons and his wife, to where he was encamped by the mountain of God," what the text means is that the man came to the mountain and stopped. From Mount Sinai he dispatched a message to Moshe [who was still at Refidim] saying, "I am coming to you – your father-in-law Yitro." Whereupon Moshe went out to greet him.

QUESTIONS FOR THOUGHT

- What proofs does Ibn Ezra bring here to support his assertion that this story took place after the giving of the Torah?
- Ibn Ezra needs to find a reason why this story would appear out of chronological order in the Torah. What explanation does he offer?
- For Ramban, keeping the Torah in order is very important. What problems must he deal with?
- What difference would it make if Yitro (and his daughter and grandsons) arrived prior to or only after the giving of the Torah?

WISDOM OF THE HEART

Yitro brings Moshe's wife and children. Wait a minute – that means that Moshe did not bring them to Egypt, that they did not experience the great miracles of the exodus and may not even have experienced the giving of the Torah! Could it be that in Moshe's desire to spare them the pain of slavery in Egypt he inadvertently denied them participation in the most critical moments of Jewish history, the very moments that became the cornerstones of our identity as a people?

What price do we pay when we take the safe route?

פרשת יתרו

יח א וַיִּשְׁמַ֞ע יִתְר֨וֹ כֹהֵ֤ן מִדְיָן֙ חֹתֵ֣ן מֹשֶׁ֔ה אֵת֩ כָּל־אֲשֶׁ֨ר עָשָׂ֤ה אֱלֹהִים֙ לְמֹשֶׁ֔ה וּלְיִשְׂרָאֵ֖ל עַמּ֑וֹ כִּֽי־הוֹצִ֧יא יְהֹוָ֛ה אֶת־יִשְׂרָאֵ֖ל מִמִּצְרָֽיִם: ב וַיִּקַּ֗ח יִתְרוֹ֙ חֹתֵ֣ן מֹשֶׁ֔ה אֶת־צִפֹּרָ֖ה אֵ֣שֶׁת מֹשֶׁ֑ה אַחַ֖ר שִׁלּוּחֶֽיהָ: ג וְאֵ֖ת שְׁנֵ֣י בָנֶ֑יהָ אֲשֶׁ֨ר שֵׁ֤ם הָֽאֶחָד֙ גֵּֽרְשֹׁ֔ם כִּ֣י אָמַ֔ר גֵּ֣ר הָיִ֔יתִי בְּאֶ֖רֶץ נָכְרִיָּֽה: ד וְשֵׁ֥ם הָאֶחָ֖ד אֱלִיעֶ֑זֶר כִּֽי־אֱלֹהֵ֤י אָבִי֙ בְּעֶזְרִ֔י וַיַּצִּלֵ֖נִי מֵחֶ֥רֶב פַּרְעֹֽה: ה וַיָּבֹ֞א יִתְר֨וֹ חֹתֵ֥ן מֹשֶׁ֛ה וּבָנָ֥יו וְאִשְׁתּ֖וֹ אֶל־מֹשֶׁ֑ה אֶל־הַמִּדְבָּ֕ר אֲשֶׁר־ה֛וּא חֹנֶ֥ה שָׁ֖ם הַ֥ר הָאֱלֹהִֽים: ו וַיֹּ֙אמֶר֙ אֶל־

CLASSIC COMMENTATORS

The timing of Yitro's visit is the subject of intense debate. The Torah places it before the events at Mount Sinai, even though some of the descriptions of the visit make more sense only after the giving of the Torah.

IBN EZRA

I maintain that Yitro joined the nation only in its second year following the construction of the Tabernacle. For the text states, "Then Yitro brought a burnt offering and sacrifices to God" (18:12), and yet it does not report that the man first built a new altar [suggesting that he used the national altar that Moshe had fashioned]. Furthermore, Moshe tells Yitro that "when they have a dispute, they come to me and I judge between one neighbor and another, and I make God's laws and teachings known" (18:16), a statement which makes sense only after the giving of the Torah. Finally, the language of the text supports my contention, for it states, "And now Moshe's father-in-law Yitro came to Moshe in the desert, bringing his sons and his wife, to where he was encamped by the mountain of God" (18:5; this verse implies that Moshe had long been situated next to Sinai, not that he had recently set up camp there)... I will now explain why this episode of Yitro's visit was inserted into the text at this point: namely, in order to balance the Torah's previous account of the evil that Amalek exercised against Israel, we now read about the good turn that Yitro performed on behalf of the nation.

אבן עזרא

ולפי דעתי: שלא בא רק בשנה השנית אחר שהוקם המשכן, כי כתוב בפרשה: עולה וזבחים לאלהים ולא הזכיר שבנה מזבח חדש ועוד כתוב: והודעתי את חקי האלהים ואת תורותיו, והנה זה אחר מתן תורה. והעד הנאמן על דברי, כי כתב: אל המדבר אשר הוא חונה שם הר האלהים ... ועתה אפרש למה נכנסה פרשת יתרו במקום הזה. בעבור שהזכיר למעלה הרעה שעשה עמלק לישראל, הזכיר כנגדה הטובה שעשה יתרו לישראל.

Moshe prepares a grand welcome for Yitro. Even though Yitro has heard some of what happened to Moshe and Israel, Moshe nonetheless fills Yitro in on additional details, and Yitro is overjoyed at what he hears. "Blessed be the Lord!" he exclaims, adding that it is now clear to him that God is greater than all the other gods. Moshe and Yitro bring sacrifices and sit down to a meal "before God."

7 with your wife and both of your sons." Moshe went out to greet his father-in-law and bowed down and kissed him. Each asked after the other's welfare, and they went inside
8 the tent. And Moshe told his father-in-law all that the Lord had done to Pharaoh and the Egyptians for Israel's sake, all the hardship they had encountered along the way,
9 and how the Lord had rescued them. Yitro delighted in all the good that the Lord had
10 done for Israel, in His liberating them from the Egyptians – and said, "Blessed be the Lord who has rescued you from Egypt and Pharaoh and liberated the people from the
11 Egyptians' hands. Now I know that the Lord is greater than all gods – for He brought
12 upon them what they schemed against others." Then Yitro brought a burnt offering and sacrifices to God. And Aharon and all the elders of Israel came to break bread with

---

QUESTIONS FOR THOUGHT

- According to Ramban, what aspect of God's justice inspired Yitro to believe in Him?
- How does Sforno understand the idea of "a measure for a measure" (מידה כנגד מידה) and why did that inspire Yitro to believe in God?
- Many people are bothered by injustice at all levels – whether at home, in school, in society at large, or on the international stage. Hypocrisy and abuse of power undermine our sense of fairness, and we pray for the restoration of justice thrice daily in the *Amida*. What injustices would you like to see fixed?

TEXTUAL SKILLS

1. What key word appears four times in verses 8–10?
2. In verse 10, Yitro seems to be saying the same thing twice. Find differences between the first half and the second half of this verse.

WISDOM OF THE HEART

The word used to describe Yitro's reaction to the news, וַיִּחַדְּ, means more than rejoicing – its meaning is closer to "thrilled." Rebbe Nachman of Breslov notes the rest of this verse – that he was thrilled about all the good that God did for Israel – and comments that Yitro's excitement was in that he saw all the pieces come together. There is a huge difference between individual things working out well and having all the parts work in harmony to produce something even greater. Like a great band or team, there is a huge difference between having a single star and having a group working together to produce something greater than the sum of their parts.

ז מֹשֶׁה אֲנִי חֹתֶנְךָ יִתְרוֹ בָּא אֵלֶיךָ וְאִשְׁתְּךָ וּשְׁנֵי בָנֶיהָ עִמָּהּ: וַיֵּצֵא
מֹשֶׁה לִקְרַאת חֹתְנוֹ וַיִּשְׁתַּחוּ וַיִּשַּׁק־לוֹ וַיִּשְׁאֲלוּ אִישׁ־לְרֵעֵהוּ
ח לְשָׁלוֹם וַיָּבֹאוּ הָאֹהֱלָה: וַיְסַפֵּר מֹשֶׁה לְחֹתְנוֹ אֵת כָּל־אֲשֶׁר עָשָׂה
יהוה לְפַרְעֹה וּלְמִצְרַיִם עַל אוֹדֹת יִשְׂרָאֵל אֵת כָּל־הַתְּלָאָה
ט אֲשֶׁר מְצָאָתַם בַּדֶּרֶךְ וַיַּצִּלֵם יהוה: וַיִּחַדְּ יִתְרוֹ עַל כָּל־הַטּוֹבָה
י אֲשֶׁר־עָשָׂה יהוה לְיִשְׂרָאֵל אֲשֶׁר הִצִּילוֹ מִיַּד מִצְרָיִם: וַיֹּאמֶר
יִתְרוֹ בָּרוּךְ יהוה אֲשֶׁר הִצִּיל אֶתְכֶם מִיַּד מִצְרַיִם וּמִיַּד פַּרְעֹה
יא אֲשֶׁר הִצִּיל אֶת־הָעָם מִתַּחַת יַד־מִצְרָיִם: עַתָּה יָדַעְתִּי כִּי־גָדוֹל
יב יהוה מִכָּל־הָאֱלֹהִים כִּי בַדָּבָר אֲשֶׁר זָדוּ עֲלֵיהֶם: וַיִּקַּח יִתְרוֹ
חֹתֵן מֹשֶׁה עֹלָה וּזְבָחִים לֵאלֹהִים וַיָּבֹא אַהֲרֹן וְכֹל ׀ זִקְנֵי יִשְׂרָאֵל

CLASSIC COMMENTATORS

In verse 11 we hear Yitro's exclamation that God is greater than all other gods, and he explains: כי בדבר אשר זדו עליהם (translated here as: "For He brought upon them what they schemed against others"). What was it that convinced Yitro that Moshe's God was the greatest of all?

RAMBAN

רמב״ן

Now, since it was God who had decreed that Israel should be oppressed, as He says to Avraham, "Your seed shall be a stranger in a land that is not theirs, and shall serve them; and they shall afflict them four hundred years" (Gen. 15:13), it surely would have been reasonable for the Egyptians to escape any punishment whatsoever. And yet, the Egyptians exceeded God's mission and acted maliciously, plotting to commit genocide against Israel...as Pharaoh commanded to the midwives to strangle the Hebrew boys at birth (1:16), followed by the order to the entire Egyptian nation: "throw every boy that is born into the Nile" (1:22). Because of these actions against Israel, Egypt deserved to be utterly annihilated.

מפני שהשם גזר על ישראל: ועבדום וענו אותם, ולא היה על המצרים בזה העונש הגדול, אבל הזידו עליהם וחשבו להכרית אותם מן העולם, וצוה למילדות להמית הבנים, וגזר עליהם: כל הבן הילוד היאורה תשליכהו ומפני זה היה עליהם העונש המשחית אותם לגמרי.

RABBI OVADYA SFORNO

ר׳ עובדיה ספורנו

Yitro was impressed by Moshe's account of God slaying the Egyptian firstborns, as punishment for the oppressors' murder of the Israelites' baby boys. He was further moved by the drowning of the cavalry in the sea, corresponding to the enemy's program of drowning the Hebrew children in the Nile. Yitro noted that God killed the Egyptian firstborns as a parallel to God's claim that Israel was His firstborn. Finally, the father-in-law learned that God hardened the Egyptians' hearts after they themselves refused to yield.

שהרג בכוריהם כמו שהרגו המצרים כל הבן הילוד לישראל, והטביעם בים כדרך שהטביעו הם הבנים ביאור, והרג את הבכורות כנגד "בני בכרי ישראל" ... והקשה את לבם אחרי שלא שמעו ברצונם.

SHEMOT | CHAPTER 18   YITRO | 156

The next day, Moshe is busy dealing with cases brought before him. Yitro notices that Moshe is handling the load all by himself and expresses his distress at the toll this will take on Moshe, and ultimately, on the people.

13 Moshe's father-in-law before God. The next day Moshe sat to serve the people as judge.
14 From morning to evening the people stood before him. When Moshe's father-in-law saw everything Moshe did for the people, he asked, "What is this that you do for the people? Why do you sit alone while all the people stand over you from morning to
15 evening?" "The people come to me to inquire of God," Moshe replied. "When they
16 have a dispute, they come to me and I judge between one neighbor and another, and I
17 make God's laws and teachings known." Moshe's father-in-law said to him, "What you
18 are doing is not good. You will be worn away, and this people along with you. It is too

---

QUESTIONS FOR THOUGHT

- Which of the above opinions seems most reasonable to you?
- Try to find words in the Torah that support some of the suggestions raised.
- Which of these would make sense if we assume that the story happened before the giving of the Torah?
- If you had the opportunity to ask Moshe one question, what would it be?

TEXTUAL SKILLS

1. Notice the verbs used to describe the physical positions of both Moshe and the people (v. 13–14). How does that add to your understanding of what Yitro saw as the problem?
2. Yitro tells Moshe (in the beginning of v. 18) נָבֹל תִּבֹּל, although it is not clear if the root of that phrase is ב-ל-ה, נ-ב-ל, or ב-ל-ל! What would each of those mean, and how would that affect our understanding of Yitro's concern?

WISDOM OF THE HEART

Why did God not set up the judicial system in advance? Did He not anticipate how overwhelming it would be for Moshe to deal with it alone? Rabbi Samson Raphael Hirsch suggests that God wanted everyone to see that Moshe was incapable of dealing with this, so that nobody could claim that Moshe had invented the entire system. Or HaḤayyim understands this completely differently: after Israel's horrific experience with Egypt, God wanted them to understand that they could still learn to appreciate and trust the advice of gentiles when appropriate.

יג לֶאֱכָל־לֶחֶם עִם־חֹתֵן מֹשֶׁה לִפְנֵי הָאֱלֹהִים: וַיְהִי מִמָּחֳרָת
וַיֵּשֶׁב מֹשֶׁה לִשְׁפֹּט אֶת־הָעָם וַיַּעֲמֹד הָעָם עַל־מֹשֶׁה מִן־הַבֹּקֶר
יד עַד־הָעָרֶב: וַיַּרְא חֹתֵן מֹשֶׁה אֵת כָּל־אֲשֶׁר־הוּא עֹשֶׂה לָעָם
וַיֹּאמֶר מָה־הַדָּבָר הַזֶּה אֲשֶׁר אַתָּה עֹשֶׂה לָעָם מַדּוּעַ אַתָּה
טו יוֹשֵׁב לְבַדֶּךָ וְכָל־הָעָם נִצָּב עָלֶיךָ מִן־בֹּקֶר עַד־עָרֶב: וַיֹּאמֶר
טז מֹשֶׁה לְחֹתְנוֹ כִּי־יָבֹא אֵלַי הָעָם לִדְרֹשׁ אֱלֹהִים: כִּי־יִהְיֶה לָהֶם
דָּבָר בָּא אֵלַי וְשָׁפַטְתִּי בֵּין אִישׁ וּבֵין רֵעֵהוּ וְהוֹדַעְתִּי אֶת־חֻקֵּי
יז הָאֱלֹהִים וְאֶת־תּוֹרֹתָיו: וַיֹּאמֶר חֹתֵן מֹשֶׁה אֵלָיו לֹא־טוֹב הַדָּבָר
יח אֲשֶׁר אַתָּה עֹשֶׂה: נָבֹל תִּבֹּל גַּם־אַתָּה גַּם־הָעָם הַזֶּה אֲשֶׁר

CLASSIC COMMENTATORS

What kinds of questions were people asking Moshe?

רשב״ם
אני לבדי צריך לשפטם שהרי באים אלי העם לדרוש דינים שאני צריך לשאל אל אלהים, ואין בהם רגיל לדבר אל אלהים כי אם אני לבדי.

RASHBAM
The people come to me alone because I am the only individual with direct access to God. Hence I remain the sole judge who can seek God's advice on Israel's behalf.

רמב״ן
להתפלל על חוליהם ולהודיעם מה שיאבד להם, כי זה יקרא 'דרישת אלהים' ... ועוד, שאני שופט אותם ... ועוד אני מלמד אותם תורה.

RAMBAN
The Israelites appealed to Moshe to pray to God on behalf of their sick relatives. They also sought divine guidance in locating misplaced objects. This is what it means that the people came "to inquire of God"…Moshe further used his meetings with the nation to judge them and to teach them Torah.

ר׳ יצחק רג׳יו
משפטים רבים יש שדעת האדם מכריעתן אף אם לא נטתו, כגון הגזל והחמס ושבועת שקר.

RABBI ISAAC SAMUEL REGGIO
There are plenty of disputes that an intelligent individual can resolve even outside the framework of revealed law. I refer to cases of theft, fraud, and false testimony.

> Yitro suggests establishing a system comprising lower-level courts dealing with small local issues as well as progressively higher courts, with Moshe at the top of the pyramid. That would free up Moshe to deal with only the most difficult questions, and would establish an entire hierarchy to deal with everything else. Of course, the people staffing these courts would have to have high moral character and be recognized for their honesty. Moshe accepts his father-in-law's advice and sets up the system, after which Moshe sends Yitro home.

19 heavy a burden for you. You cannot carry it alone. Now listen to me, let me advise you; and may God be with you. You speak for the people before God, and their concerns
20 to Him. And you must acquaint them with His precepts and laws, and make known to
21 them the path they are to walk and the way they must act. You, as well, must seek out among the people, capable men – God-fearing, trustworthy men, who despise corruption; and appoint them over the people as leaders of thousands, hundreds, fifties, and

HIZKUNI
חזקוני

אנשי חיל: אלו יכול היה משה להכיר, אבל מידת הלב כגון יראי אלהים אנשי אמת שונאי בצע אין בשר ודם יכול לראות, רק לפי אומד הדעת, לפיכך לא הזכירם כאן.

Although it would have been possible for Moshe to detect whether an aspirant to the job was a "capable man", he would have been unable to determine whether the individual was truly a God-fearing and trustworthy man who despised corruption. For no one can truly know the contents of another's heart. Hence [although Yitro suggested that such men be found] the Torah does not report that Moshe selected only men who possessed such qualities. Moshe could only guess whether the men he selected were as superlative as he hoped.

RABBI OVADYA SFORNO
ר' עובדיה ספורנו

אחר שביקש ולא מצא אנשים שיהיו בהם כל המעלות שהזכיר יתרו, בחר באנשי חיל בקיאים וחרוצים לברר וללבן אמיתות דבר ולהביאו אל תכלית יותר מיראי אלהים בלתי אנשי חיל.

Actually, Moshe tried in vain to locate men who possessed all of the characteristics Yitro listed. And so he settled for individuals who were capable men, people who were experts in the law, those who were diligent, and who were committed to getting at the heart of a matter as they reached an equitable solution. Such minds were preferable over those that were God-fearing and yet were less capable.

QUESTIONS FOR THOUGHT

- Which of the commentaries believes that Moshe implemented Yitro's idea as planned?
- According to the other two commentaries, why did Moshe not implement the plan all the way?
- According to Sforno, what became the most important criteria for choosing judges?
- If you were sitting on a panel selecting judges and had to choose between one candidate with street smarts, one with a deep understanding of the law, and a third with a reputation for honesty, which would you choose?

יט עַמָּךְ כִּי־כָבֵד מִמְּךָ הַדָּבָר לֹא־תוּכַל עֲשֹׂהוּ לְבַדֶּךָ: עַתָּה שְׁמַע בְּקֹלִי אִיעָצְךָ וִיהִי אֱלֹהִים עִמָּךְ הֱיֵה אַתָּה לָעָם מוּל הָאֱלֹהִים כ וְהֵבֵאתָ אַתָּה אֶת־הַדְּבָרִים אֶל־הָאֱלֹהִים: וְהִזְהַרְתָּה אֶתְהֶם אֶת־הַחֻקִּים וְאֶת־הַתּוֹרֹת וְהוֹדַעְתָּ לָהֶם אֶת־הַדֶּרֶךְ יֵלְכוּ בָהּ כא וְאֶת־הַמַּעֲשֶׂה אֲשֶׁר יַעֲשׂוּן: וְאַתָּה תֶחֱזֶה מִכָּל־הָעָם אַנְשֵׁי־ חַיִל יִרְאֵי אֱלֹהִים אַנְשֵׁי אֱמֶת שֹׂנְאֵי בָצַע וְשַׂמְתָּ עֲלֵהֶם שָׂרֵי

CLASSIC COMMENTATORS

Did Moshe actually follow Yitro's advice? Yitro had identified four characteristics to look for (see v. 21) yet only one of those is listed in the description of the people Moshe actually appoints (v. 25).

RAMBAN

"Capable men" – men who were capable of leading large numbers of people...Now Yitro expressed his advice to Moshe in terms combining a general statement with particular details. Firstly, he suggested to his son-in-law that when he sought judges to assist him, he should locate individuals who were capable of leading large numbers of people – that represented the overall characteristic of the new officers. But specifically, these individuals must be "God-fearing, trustworthy men, who despise corruption." For judges who lack these attributes could clearly not be defined as "capable men". And it went without saying that any candidates Moshe found would have to be intelligent and understanding characters – obviously only wise men could be termed capable. Thus when the Torah subsequently reports that "Moshe chose capable men" [without listing all of the requirements Yitro had described] it is understood that the assistants he tapped possessed all of the necessary features Yitro and Moshe had discussed. They were surely "capable men – God-fearing, trustworthy men, who despised corruption," smart and of acute discernment.

רמב״ן

אנשי חיל: אנשים ראויים להנהיג עם גדול ... והנה יתרו דיבר בכלל ופרט, אמר שיחזה אנשים ראויים להנהיג העם הגדול במשפטים, ופרט, שיהיו יראי אלהים אנשי אמת ושונאי בצע, כי לא יהיו אנשי חיל במשפט בלי מידות הללו. ולא הוצרך להזכיר חכמתם ובינתם, כי הדבר ברור שהוא בכלל אנשי חיל.

וכאשר נאמר למטה ויבחר משה אנשי חיל, הנה הכל בכלל, שהיו יראי אלהים אנשי אמת שונאי בצע וחכמים ונבונים.

22 tens. Have them serve as daily judges for the people; let them bring the major cases to you, but judge the minor ones themselves. In this way they will lighten your load, and
23 bear it together with you. If you do this, and God so commands, then you will endure,
24 and all these people will be able to go home in peace." Moshe listened to his father-in-
25 law and did all that he said. Moshe chose capable men from all Israel and made them
26 chiefs over the people, leaders of thousands, hundreds, fifties, and tens. They judged the people every day. Any major case they brought to Moshe, but they decided every
27 minor matter themselves. Then Moshe parted from his father-in-law, and the latter went forth, back to his own land.

WISDOM OF THE HEART

Rabbi Naḥman of Breslov understood the phrase אנשי אמת to mean "people who search for the truth." He meant that the leaders of the nation must be people who are never content with what they know. Our life's journey is just that – a constant movement in pursuit of understanding. The world is a mysterious web that must constantly seek to unravel; ignorance may be easy, but it is not bliss.

From the very first moment Avraham our forefather opened his eyes and knew there must be more to life, to the time that Queen Esther had a feeling that she was being called to something more – the Jewish people's founding ancestors have always endlessly sought after truth. The Talmud says that the insignia of Hashem is truth – אמת. The Dinnover Rebbe says that truth is a perfect word: In gematria it adds up to 441. Add its digits and to get 9. Multiply 9, by any number from 1 to 10 – for example by 2, and get 18. Add its digits: 1+8 = 9. Multiply 9 again, for example by 3 = 36. Add its digits: 3+6 = 9. The truth is perfect, at times elusive, and your search for it may keep you up at night. But that truth is worth it.

The end of this parasha bookends its message. *Parashat Yitro* began with "Yitro heard." It ends with the voice of God through thunder and lighting. The message therefore, is that be open to hear God speaking to us.

Up until World War II the Swiss Watch Company was the largest watch company in the world. They controlled 90% of the market. In the late 1960s, researchers presented them with an idea for a new electronic watch. However, the managers at Swiss wouldn't give them the time of day. The inventors took their concept to a watch fair where two small vendors bought the rights to it and cornered the market. When something great comes your way – don't close your mind. God wants us to always be open to new possibilities.

The first word the Torah uses to describe Yitro in this story is "heard." According to Stephen Covey's *The 7 Habits of Highly Effective People*, habit number five is that one must first try to listen to others – to understand – and only afterward to be understood.

What are some ways in which you can make people feel they have been heard?

כב אֲלָפִים שָׂרֵי מֵאוֹת שָׂרֵי חֲמִשִּׁים וְשָׂרֵי עֲשָׂרֹת: וְשָׁפְטוּ אֶת־
הָעָם בְּכָל־עֵת וְהָיָה כָּל־הַדָּבָר הַגָּדֹל יָבִיאוּ אֵלֶיךָ וְכָל־הַדָּבָר
כג הַקָּטֹן יִשְׁפְּטוּ־הֵם וְהָקֵל מֵעָלֶיךָ וְנָשְׂאוּ אִתָּךְ: אִם אֶת־הַדָּבָר
הַזֶּה תַּעֲשֶׂה וְצִוְּךָ אֱלֹהִים וְיָכָלְתָּ עֲמֹד וְגַם כָּל־הָעָם הַזֶּה עַל־
כד מְקֹמוֹ יָבֹא בְשָׁלוֹם: וַיִּשְׁמַע מֹשֶׁה לְקוֹל חֹתְנוֹ וַיַּעַשׂ כֹּל אֲשֶׁר שלישי
כה אָמָר: וַיִּבְחַר מֹשֶׁה אַנְשֵׁי־חַיִל מִכָּל־יִשְׂרָאֵל וַיִּתֵּן אֹתָם רָאשִׁים
עַל־הָעָם שָׂרֵי אֲלָפִים שָׂרֵי מֵאוֹת שָׂרֵי חֲמִשִּׁים וְשָׂרֵי עֲשָׂרֹת:
כו וְשָׁפְטוּ אֶת־הָעָם בְּכָל־עֵת אֶת־הַדָּבָר הַקָּשֶׁה יְבִיאוּן אֶל־מֹשֶׁה
כז וְכָל־הַדָּבָר הַקָּטֹן יִשְׁפּוּטוּ הֵם: וַיְשַׁלַּח מֹשֶׁה אֶת־חֹתְנוֹ וַיֵּלֶךְ
לוֹ אֶל־אַרְצוֹ:

TEXTUAL SKILLS

1. According to Yitro's plan, aside from Moshe being the highest authority in the justice system, he was to play another very significant role. What role is that?

2. The phrase בכל עת appears both in Yitro's plan (v. 22) and in Moshe's implementation (v. 26). Why is this phrase important in this context?

QUICK BITE

According to Rashi, one of the things that piqued Yitro's curiosity was the battle with Amalek. Rav Yechiel Mordechai Gordon notes that Rashi does not say the victory over Amalek, but the battle – the one initiated by Amalek despite God's obvious intervention on Israel's behalf. Amalek's brazenness got Yitro thinking that there must be something special about Israel, and that he needed to find out more.

Having left Refidim, Benei Yisrael camp at the foot of Mount Sinai. Moshe ascends the mountain, where God speaks with him and asks him to present an offer to the people. Now that they know what He has done for them, they are given the option of becoming God's special people. That new status, however, is bound to their commitment to adhere to God's laws.

19 1 On the first day of the third month after the Israelites had left Egypt they came to the
2 Sinai Desert. Setting out from Refidim they had arrived at the Sinai Desert, encamping
3 in the wilderness, and there Israel camped, facing the mountain, while Moshe went up to God. And the Lord called to him from the mountain: "This is what you shall say to
4 the house of Yaakov, what you shall tell the people of Israel: You yourselves have seen what I did to the Egyptians: how I lifted you up on eagles' wings and brought you to Me.
5 Now, if you faithfully heed My voice and keep My covenant, you will be My treasure
6 among all the peoples, although the whole earth is Mine. A kingdom of priests and a holy nation you shall be to Me. These are the words you must speak to the Israelites."

QUESTIONS FOR THOUGHT

- According to which commentary is the mention of the rest of the nations as belonging to God designed to let Israel know just how special it is?
- Which of the commentaries understands that mentioning that the whole world belongs to God is God justifying His right to choose anyone He pleases?
- Which of the commentaries understands that mentioning that the whole world belongs to God defines the purpose of the choice of one nation?
- According to Sforno, when the Torah describes Israel as the Chosen People, for what are they chosen?

TEXTUAL SKILLS

1. According to the Torah, what will happen to Israel if it does not accept God's offer?

2. In verse 5, what is the difference between "faithfully heeding God's voice" and "keeping His covenant?"

WISDOM OF THE HEART

According to the Midrash, *Benei Yisrael* camped at the foot of Mount Sinai "as one person with one heart." Rav Yitzchok Hutner noticed that when describing the Egyptian camp chasing Israel earlier, the Midrash uses the same terms but in reverse order: "as one heart, like a single person." He offers the following explanation. The Egyptians were united by a single, negative cause: to bring harm to Israel. By contrast, when Israel arrived at Sinai they were committed to being a single nation, and it was that unity which made them ready to receive the Torah.

What would have to change for *Benei Yisrael* to be united in this era?

שמות | פרק יט

יט א בַּחֹ֙דֶשׁ֙ הַשְּׁלִישִׁ֔י לְצֵ֥את בְּנֵֽי־יִשְׂרָאֵ֖ל מֵאֶ֣רֶץ מִצְרָ֑יִם בַּיּ֣וֹם
ב הַזֶּ֔ה בָּ֖אוּ מִדְבַּ֥ר סִינָֽי: וַיִּסְע֣וּ מֵרְפִידִ֗ים וַיָּבֹ֙אוּ֙ מִדְבַּ֣ר סִינַ֔י
ג וַֽיַּחֲנ֖וּ בַּמִּדְבָּ֑ר וַיִּֽחַן־שָׁ֥ם יִשְׂרָאֵ֖ל נֶ֥גֶד הָהָֽר: וּמֹשֶׁ֥ה עָלָ֖ה אֶל־
הָאֱלֹהִ֑ים וַיִּקְרָ֨א אֵלָ֤יו יְהוָה֙ מִן־הָהָ֣ר לֵאמֹ֔ר כֹּ֤ה תֹאמַר֙ לְבֵ֣ית
ד יַעֲקֹ֔ב וְתַגֵּ֖יד לִבְנֵ֥י יִשְׂרָאֵֽל: אַתֶּ֣ם רְאִיתֶ֔ם אֲשֶׁ֥ר עָשִׂ֖יתִי לְמִצְרָ֑יִם
ה וָאֶשָּׂ֤א אֶתְכֶם֙ עַל־כַּנְפֵ֣י נְשָׁרִ֔ים וָאָבִ֥א אֶתְכֶ֖ם אֵלָֽי: וְעַתָּ֗ה אִם־
שָׁמ֤וֹעַ תִּשְׁמְעוּ֙ בְּקֹלִ֔י וּשְׁמַרְתֶּ֖ם אֶת־בְּרִיתִ֑י וִהְיִ֨יתֶם לִ֤י סְגֻלָּה֙
ו מִכָּל־הָ֣עַמִּ֔ים כִּי־לִ֖י כָּל־הָאָֽרֶץ: וְאַתֶּ֧ם תִּהְיוּ־לִ֛י מַמְלֶ֥כֶת
כֹּהֲנִ֖ים וְג֣וֹי קָד֑וֹשׁ אֵ֚לֶּה הַדְּבָרִ֔ים אֲשֶׁ֥ר תְּדַבֵּ֖ר אֶל־בְּנֵ֥י יִשְׂרָאֵֽל:

CLASSIC COMMENTATORS

As God makes His offer for Israel to become His special people, He adds, "the whole earth is Mine." This sound like a contradiction – either Israel is chosen to be unique amongst the nations or God cares about all the nations.

רשב"ם

וכל העמים שלי, ולא בחרתי כי אם אתכם לבדכם.

RASHBAM

Although I have created and possess all of the world's nations, yours is the only one I have chosen.

ר' עובדיה ספורנו

אף על פי שכל המין האנושי יקר אצלי מכל יתר הנמצאים השפלים ... מכל מקום אתם תהיו לי סגולה מכולם. ...ובזה תהיו סגולה מכולם כי תהיו ממלכת כהנים להבין ולהורות לכל המין האנושי לקרוא כלם בשם ה', ולעבדו שכם אחד.

RABBI OVADYA SFORNO

Now, the entire human race is beloved to Me, and more important than the rest of the animal kingdom…nevertheless you, Israel, will be even more special to Me…In this way you will be a treasured people to me, for you will become "a kingdom of priests and a holy nation." The responsibility will then devolve upon you to understand God's law and to teach it to the entire human race. As a consequence, all nations of the world will acknowledge the name of the Lord and serve Him uniformly.

ר' יצחק רג'יו

מי שהוא בקהל גוים נבזים וחסרים ואומרים לו אתה תהיה הסגולה שבכולם, אין יתרונו יתרון. אבל בהיותו בקהל נכברים וגדולים, ועם כל זה עושים אותו סגולה מכולם, זאת אות על יתרונו וגדולתו.

RABBI ISAAC SAMUEL REGGIO

When someone is part of a despised and lowly group, being told that he is the best of the lot is not very encouraging. However, when someone is already part of an exalted and respected group, and is then promoted to the top of that group, it surely signifies that person's greatness and achievement.

7 So Moshe came and summoned the elders of the people, and set before them all that the
8 Lord had commanded him. And the people answered as one – "All that the Lord has
9 spoken we will do." Moshe brought their answer back to the Lord. Then the Lord said to Moshe, "I will come to you in a dense cloud, that the people may hear Me speaking to you. They will then believe you forever." When Moshe reported the words of the
10 people to the Lord, the Lord said to Moshe, "Go to the people and consecrate them
11 today and tomorrow; let them wash their clothes and be ready for the third day, for on
12 that third day the Lord will descend on Mount Sinai before all the peoples' eyes. Set a boundary for the people around the mountain; tell them to take care not to ascend to it, not even touch its edge. Anyone who touches the mountain must be put to death.
13 No hand shall touch him: he shall be stoned or shot with arrows; beast or man, he shall not live. When the ram's horn sounds a long blast – only then may they go up on the
14 mountain." So Moshe came down from the mountain to the people; he consecrated
15 them and they cleansed their clothes. "Be ready for the third day," he told them, "and do

---

RAMBAN
The method for Israel to reach a state of sanctity was for them to refrain from relations with their wives and to avoid all sources of impurity. For one who has no contact with impurity is termed "consecrated."

רמב״ן
והנכון שיהיו קדושים, שלא יגשו אל אשה ואל כל טומאה, כי הנשמר מן הטומאה יקרא מקודש.

QUESTIONS FOR THOUGHT
- Which of the commentaries believes that the "consecration" involves doing some action?
- Which of the commentaries understands that the "consecration" is some kind of mental/spiritual readiness?
- Are **קדושה** (translated here as "consecration") and **טומאה** (translated here as "impurity") two ends of the same spectrum, or two different things completely?
- Imagine that you were getting ready for the most important meeting in your life. What kinds of preparation would you do?

WISDOM OF THE HEART

The command that the people be very careful not to touch the mountain is mentioned twice in this passage. Rav Soloveitchik explains that there are two types of boundaries. One is a physical border, like a fence around a yard. The other is a conceptual boundary – the line that we just don't cross. The first time God instructed Moshe to make a boundary that the people wouldn't physically cross, but the second time His instruction was to let the people know that the mountain was holy, and that holiness would automatically create for them the lines that they are not to cross.

What happens to our concept of sanctity or specialness when we cross lines?

שמות | פרק יט

ז וַיָּבֹא מֹשֶׁה וַיִּקְרָא לְזִקְנֵי הָעָם וַיָּשֶׂם לִפְנֵיהֶם אֵת כָּל־הַדְּבָרִים חמישי
ח הָאֵלֶּה אֲשֶׁר צִוָּהוּ יְהֹוָה: וַיַּעֲנוּ כָל־הָעָם יַחְדָּו וַיֹּאמְרוּ כֹּל אֲשֶׁר־
ט דִּבֶּר יְהֹוָה נַעֲשֶׂה וַיָּשֶׁב מֹשֶׁה אֶת־דִּבְרֵי הָעָם אֶל־יְהֹוָה: וַיֹּאמֶר
יְהֹוָה אֶל־מֹשֶׁה הִנֵּה אָנֹכִי בָּא אֵלֶיךָ בְּעַב הֶעָנָן בַּעֲבוּר יִשְׁמַע
הָעָם בְּדַבְּרִי עִמָּךְ וְגַם־בְּךָ יַאֲמִינוּ לְעוֹלָם וַיַּגֵּד מֹשֶׁה אֶת־דִּבְרֵי
י הָעָם אֶל־יְהֹוָה: וַיֹּאמֶר יְהֹוָה אֶל־מֹשֶׁה לֵךְ אֶל־הָעָם וְקִדַּשְׁתָּם
יא הַיּוֹם וּמָחָר וְכִבְּסוּ שִׂמְלֹתָם: וְהָיוּ נְכֹנִים לַיּוֹם הַשְּׁלִישִׁי כִּי |
יב בַּיּוֹם הַשְּׁלִשִׁי יֵרֵד יְהֹוָה לְעֵינֵי כָל־הָעָם עַל־הַר סִינָי: וְהִגְבַּלְתָּ
אֶת־הָעָם סָבִיב לֵאמֹר הִשָּׁמְרוּ לָכֶם עֲלוֹת בָּהָר וּנְגֹעַ בְּקָצֵהוּ
יג כָּל־הַנֹּגֵעַ בָּהָר מוֹת יוּמָת: לֹא־תִגַּע בּוֹ יָד כִּי־סָקוֹל יִסָּקֵל
אוֹ־יָרֹה יִיָּרֶה אִם־בְּהֵמָה אִם־אִישׁ לֹא יִחְיֶה בִּמְשֹׁךְ הַיֹּבֵל
יד הֵמָּה יַעֲלוּ בָהָר: וַיֵּרֶד מֹשֶׁה מִן־הָהָר אֶל־הָעָם וַיְקַדֵּשׁ אֶת־
טו הָעָם וַיְכַבְּסוּ שִׂמְלֹתָם: וַיֹּאמֶר אֶל־הָעָם הֱיוּ נְכֹנִים לִשְׁלֹשֶׁת

CLASSIC COMMENTATORS

God tells Moshe to consecrate the people. What does that mean?

IBN EZRA — אבן עזרא
The people are told to avoid any contact with impure items that might convey impurity to them.
שישמרו מכל טמא ומטמא.

RABBI YOSEF BEKHOR SHOR — ר' יוסף בכור שור
Moshe is meant to prepare the people psychologically to hear and accept the word of God.
הזמין שיהו מזומנים לשמוע דברי ולקבלם.

RASHBAM — רשב״ם
The instruction here to consecrate the people means to prepare them, as in the verse, "Consecrate yourselves for tomorrow; you will then have meat to eat" (Num. 11:18).
לשון הזמנה, כמו: התקדשו למחר ואכלתם בשר.

SHEMOT | CHAPTER 19   YITRO | 166

16 not draw close to your wives." The third day came; and that morning there was thunder and lightning and a dense cloud on the mountain and the sound of a ram's horn,
17 intensely loud, and all the people in the camp shook. Then Moshe led the people out
18 of the camp to meet God, and they stood at the foot of the mountain. Mount Sinai was enveloped in smoke because the LORD had descended on it in fire. Smoke billowed up
19 from it as if from a furnace, and the mountain shook violently as one. As the sound of
20 the ram's horn grew louder and louder, Moshe spoke and God answered him aloud. And the LORD descended on Mount Sinai, to the top of the mountain, and called Moshe
21 to the mountain top, and Moshe ascended. The LORD told Moshe, "Go back down – warn the people not to force their way through to look at the LORD, or many will die.
22 Even priests who come near to the LORD must first consecrate themselves, or the LORD
23 will break out against them." Moshe replied to the LORD, "The people cannot climb Mount Sinai. You Yourself warned us to set a boundary around the mountain and con-
24 secrate it." The LORD said to him, "Go down, and come back together with Aharon. But do not let the priests or people force their way through to come up to the LORD,
25 or He will break out against them." So Moshe went down to the people and told them.

אבן עזרא
וירד משה אל העם ויאמר אליהם – פירושו: שהעיד בהם ובכהנים שלא יהרסו לראות. ולא הזכיר הכתוב: ויעל משה ואהרן, כי איננו צריך. כי אחר שאמר לו השם שיעלו, ידענו שעלו.

IBN EZRA
Moshe warned the nation and the priests not to force their way through to view the revelation. But there was no need for the text to report that Moshe and Aharon ascended the mountain, for since the verse relates God's command that they climb up, the men surely obeyed that order.

ר' שמשון רפאל הירש
גם משה עצמו נצטווה לעמוד עם העם למטה, בשעה שידבר אל ישראל מראש ההר. "וירד משה אל העם ויאמר אלהם" (פסוק כה), ואז ה' דיבר את הדברים הבאים (להלן כ, א והלאה). התורה תינתן לא רק על ידי משה אלא אל משה, כשם שניתנה אל העם.

RABBI SAMSON RAPHAEL HIRSCH
Moshe was instructed to stand at the foot of the mountain along with the rest of the nation, while the LORD addressed Israel from its peak. Thus the text relates that "Moshe went down to the people and told them" (19:25), whereupon "God spoke all these words" (20:1). What this means is that the Torah was not only given through Moshe, but to Moshe, just like it was delivered to the rest of Israel.

QUESTIONS FOR THOUGHT
- Which commentaries understand that Moshe was on the top of the mountain when God said the Ten Commandments?
- Who says that Moshe was down with the people when God said the Ten Commandments?
- What difference does it make whether Moshe was on top of the mountain or together with the people?

שמות | פרק יט

טז יָמִ֔ים אַֽל־תִּגְּשׁ֖וּ אֶל־אִשָּֽׁה: וַיְהִי֩ בַיּ֨וֹם הַשְּׁלִישִׁ֜י בִּֽהְיֹ֣ת הַבֹּ֗קֶר וַיְהִי֩ קֹלֹ֨ת וּבְרָקִ֜ים וְעָנָ֤ן כָּבֵד֙ עַל־הָהָ֔ר וְקֹ֥ל שֹׁפָ֖ר חָזָ֣ק מְאֹ֑ד

יז וַיֶּחֱרַ֥ד כָּל־הָעָ֖ם אֲשֶׁ֥ר בַּֽמַּחֲנֶֽה: וַיּוֹצֵ֨א מֹשֶׁ֧ה אֶת־הָעָ֛ם לִקְרַ֥את

יח הָֽאֱלֹהִ֖ים מִן־הַֽמַּחֲנֶ֑ה וַיִּֽתְיַצְּב֖וּ בְּתַחְתִּ֥ית הָהָֽר: וְהַ֤ר סִינַי֙ עָשַׁ֣ן כֻּלּ֔וֹ מִ֠פְּנֵ֠י אֲשֶׁ֨ר יָרַ֥ד עָלָ֛יו יְהֹוָ֖ה בָּאֵ֑שׁ וַיַּ֤עַל עֲשָׁנוֹ֙ כְּעֶ֣שֶׁן הַכִּבְשָׁ֔ן

יט וַיֶּחֱרַ֥ד כָּל־הָהָ֖ר מְאֹֽד: וַיְהִי֙ ק֣וֹל הַשֹּׁפָ֔ר הוֹלֵ֖ךְ וְחָזֵ֣ק מְאֹ֑ד מֹשֶׁ֣ה

כ יְדַבֵּ֔ר וְהָאֱלֹהִ֖ים יַעֲנֶ֥נּוּ בְקֽוֹל: וַיֵּ֧רֶד יְהֹוָ֛ה עַל־הַ֥ר סִינַ֖י אֶל־רֹ֣אשׁ ששי

הָהָ֑ר וַיִּקְרָ֨א יְהֹוָ֧ה לְמֹשֶׁ֛ה אֶל־רֹ֥אשׁ הָהָ֖ר וַיַּ֥עַל מֹשֶֽׁה: וַיֹּ֤אמֶר

כא יְהֹוָה֙ אֶל־מֹשֶׁ֔ה רֵ֖ד הָעֵ֣ד בָּעָ֑ם פֶּן־יֶהֶרְס֤וּ אֶל־יְהֹוָה֙ לִרְא֔וֹת וְנָפַ֥ל

כב מִמֶּ֖נּוּ רָֽב: וְגַ֧ם הַכֹּהֲנִ֛ים הַנִּגָּשִׁ֥ים אֶל־יְהֹוָ֖ה יִתְקַדָּ֑שׁוּ פֶּן־יִפְרֹ֥ץ

כג בָּהֶ֖ם יְהֹוָֽה: וַיֹּ֤אמֶר מֹשֶׁה֙ אֶל־יְהֹוָ֔ה לֹא־יוּכַ֣ל הָעָ֔ם לַעֲלֹ֖ת אֶל־הַ֣ר סִינָ֑י כִּֽי־אַתָּ֞ה הַעֵדֹ֤תָה בָּ֨נוּ֙ לֵאמֹ֔ר הַגְבֵּ֥ל אֶת־הָהָ֖ר וְקִדַּשְׁתּֽוֹ:

כד וַיֹּ֨אמֶר אֵלָ֤יו יְהֹוָה֙ לֶךְ־רֵ֔ד וְעָלִ֥יתָ אַתָּ֖ה וְאַהֲרֹ֣ן עִמָּ֑ךְ וְהַכֹּהֲנִ֣ים

כה וְהָעָ֗ם אַל־יֶֽהֶרְס֛וּ לַעֲלֹ֥ת אֶל־יְהֹוָ֖ה פֶּן־יִפְרָץ־בָּֽם: וַיֵּ֥רֶד מֹשֶׁ֖ה

CLASSIC COMMENTATORS

Where was Moshe during the giving of the Ten Commandments?

RASHI

The people heard only the first two precepts directly from God – "I am the Lord your God who brought you out of the land of Egypt, out of the house of slaves," and "Have no other gods than Me" (20:2–3). The other statements were first conveyed to Moshe, who then repeated the information to the nation. Meanwhile, the Holy One, blessed be He, amplified Moshe's voice when he addressed Israel so that everyone could hear him.

רש"י

משה ידבר – כשהיה משה מדבר ומשמיע הדברות לישראל, שהרי לא שמעו מפי הגבורה אלא אנכי ולא יהיה לך הקב"ה מסייעו לתת בו כח, להיות קולו מגביר ונשמע.

Shemot | Chapter 20 — Yitro

The first three commandments focus our attention on God's uniqueness. God is the One who redeemed us from Egypt, we may not worship any other gods, and we may not speak God's name without purpose.

20 ¹ ² ³ ⁴ Then God spoke all these words: "I am the Lord your God who brought you out of the land of Egypt, out of the house of slaves. Have no other gods than Me. Do not make for yourself any carved image or likeness of any creature in the heavens above or the earth ⁵ beneath or the water beneath the earth. Do not bow down to them or worship them, for I the Lord your God demand absolute loyalty. For those who hate Me, I hold the ⁶ descendants to account for the sins of the fathers to the third and fourth generation, ⁷ but to those who love Me and keep My commands – I shall act with faithful love for thousands. Do not speak the name of the Lord your God in vain, for the Lord will not hold guiltless those who speak His name in vain.

RABBI ELIYAHU BEN AMOZEGH — בן אמוזג

The Torah represents an inheritance of the congregation of Yaakov, not a set of obligations for all of humanity. That is the reason that God describes Himself as the God of Israel who brought them out of Egypt, an event that defined the birth of the nation. He does not characterize Himself as the God who created the world, a fact which relates equally to all of the planet's peoples.

כי להיות שהתורה מורשה קהילת יעקב ואינה חובה לכל בני האדם, על כן תיאר עצמו ברוך הוא באלקי ישראל שהוציאנו מארץ מצרים, שהיא בריאת ישראל, ולא בריאת העולם שהוא דבר השוה לגוי וליהודי.

QUESTIONS FOR THOUGHT

- Which of the explanations makes sense mostly for the generation that stood at Mount Sinai?
- If there were to be a divine revelation today, and it would start with the words, "I am your God who…" how do you think that statement would end?

TEXTUAL SKILLS

1. Notice the similarity between God's opening words here and His opening words to Avram (Gen. 15:7)!
2. Who is doing the talking in the first two Commandments? Who is doing the talking in the third?

WISDOM OF THE HEART

The Torah describes God as jealous. Really?

We already know that the Torah uses human features to describe God – His hand, nose, etc. – and these are used to help us understand, in our terms, God's actions. God's jealousy is similar, as it conveys the level of intensity of His love for us.

שמות | פרק כ

כ א וַיְדַבֵּר אֱלֹהִים אֵת כָּל־הַדְּבָרִים הָאֵלֶּה לֵאמֹר׃ ב אָנֹכִי יְהֹוָה אֱלֹהֶיךָ אֲשֶׁר הוֹצֵאתִיךָ מֵאֶרֶץ מִצְרַיִם מִבֵּית עֲבָדִים׃ ג לֹא־יִהְיֶה לְךָ אֱלֹהִים אֲחֵרִים עַל־פָּנָי׃ ד לֹא־תַעֲשֶׂה־לְךָ פֶסֶל וְכָל־תְּמוּנָה אֲשֶׁר בַּשָּׁמַיִם מִמַּעַל וַאֲשֶׁר בָּאָרֶץ מִתַּחַת וַאֲשֶׁר בַּמַּיִם מִתַּחַת לָאָרֶץ׃ ה לֹא־תִשְׁתַּחֲוֶה לָהֶם וְלֹא תָעָבְדֵם כִּי אָנֹכִי יְהֹוָה אֱלֹהֶיךָ אֵל קַנָּא פֹּקֵד עֲוֹן אָבֹת עַל־בָּנִים עַל־שִׁלֵּשִׁים וְעַל־רִבֵּעִים לְשֹׂנְאָי׃ ו וְעֹשֶׂה חֶסֶד לַאֲלָפִים לְאֹהֲבַי וּלְשֹׁמְרֵי מִצְוֹתָי׃ ז לֹא תִשָּׂא אֶת־שֵׁם־יְהֹוָה אֱלֹהֶיךָ לַשָּׁוְא כִּי לֹא יְנַקֶּה יְהֹוָה אֵת אֲשֶׁר־יִשָּׂא אֶת־שְׁמוֹ לַשָּׁוְא׃

CLASSIC COMMENTATORS

Why do the Ten Commandments begin with God identifying Himself as the One who redeemed them from Egypt and not as the One who created heaven and earth?

אבן עזרא
IBN EZRA

שה' עשה לישראל מה שלא לכל גוי ... והנה בעבור האות שעשה ה' במצרים אמר משה "אתה הראית לדעת כי ה' הוא האלהים!", שהכל ראו זה, חכמים ושאינן חכמים, גדולים וקטנים.

The Lord had done for Israel things that no other nation on earth had merited… Based on the wonders that Israel witnessed in Egypt, Moshe later told the people, "To you this was shown so that you would know that the Lord is God" (Deut. 4:35). For the entire populace had seen the manifestation of God in Egypt – the wise individuals and the simple folk, the adults along with the children.

ר' יוסף אבן כספי
RABBI YOSEF IBN KASPI

אין לשאול: למה אמר "הוצאתיך מארץ מצרים" ולא אמר "אשר עשיתי שמים וארץ", כי הוא זכר להם החביב להם עתה.

Do not ask why God at this point declares that He had brought them out of Egypt instead of emphasizing that He had created the heavens and the earth. For God mentioned to them the event that at that moment was dearest to their hearts.

אברבנאל
ABARBANEL

לפי שאני הוצאתיך מארץ מצרים, שהיתה ארץ קשה למלך קשה, ולכך קראה "בית עבדים" שהאסירים בתוכה לא יכולו לצאת משם. ומפני החסד וההטבה הזאת שעשיתי לך בהוציאי אותך משם, ראוי שתעשו מצוותי ותשמרו דרכי.

God introduces Himself to the people as the One who brought the nation out of the land of Egypt, a place ruled by a cruel monarch. The state was therefore called a "house of slaves" because the prisoners it held had no chance of leaving. Now, in response to the kindness and compassion that God demonstrated by emancipating Israel from that land, God expected the people to observe His commandments and to follow His ways.

Shemot | Chapter 20 — Yitro | 170

The fourth commandment contains many mitzvot related to Shabbat, including things we are obligated to do and things we are prohibited from doing. The fifth commandment, showing respect for one's parents, is the first that seems to offer reward for its fulfillment.

8 Remember the Sabbath to keep it holy. Six days you shall work, and carry out all your
9
10 labors, but the seventh is a Sabbath to the Lord your God. On it, you shall perform no work at all – neither you, nor your son or daughter, your male or female servant, your
11 livestock, or the stranger within your gates. For in six days the Lord made heaven and earth, the sea, and all that they contain, and He rested on the seventh day. And so the
12 Lord blessed the Sabbath day and made it holy. Honor your father and mother. Then

---

TEXTUAL SKILLS

1. Verbs with the roots ב-ר-ך and ק-ד-ש appear together only twice in the entire Tanakh! Once is in these verses; the other time is in the story of creation (Gen. 2:3).

2. What theme word appears eight times in the first five commandments but not a single time in the last five?

WISDOM OF THE HEART

Notice that the Torah commands us to honor our parents. Elsewhere it commands us to revere them. But nowhere does it say that we have to love them. We certainly should love them, and perhaps the Torah considered that so basic that it did not mandate it. Or perhaps the Torah understands that relationships between parents and children can get complicated, with lots of conflicting emotions, so the Torah requires certain behaviors that show honor or reverence but does not make demands of one's emotions.

QUICK BITE

Here God commands: "remember the Sabbath." But the version of the Ten Commandments given in the book of Devarim (5:12) uses slightly different language: **שמור את יום השבת** – "guard the Sabbath." These are two sides of the same coin. There is a positive aspect to Shabbat. We often associate it with behaviors such as lighting candles or having Shabbat meals. This is "remembering." "Guarding" is avoiding transgressions, such as trapping on Shabbat, for example. But there is more to this dynamic. Our tradition tells us that **שמור וזכור בדבור אחד נאמרו** – *shamor* and *zakhor* were said in the same "breath." Perhaps this means that the positive and negative aren't two separate worlds within Shabbat. One cannot "choose" which aspect one connects to more. Rather, the two values are intertwined. As the Kedushat Levi puts it: Although each mitzvah has an outer body and also an inner dimension, when it comes to Shabbat the two layers are one entity. The full scope of Shabbat can't be experienced simply through the beautiful meal with singing. It depends at the same time on the potent energy that is claimed when we are careful about how we prepare that meal.

שמות | פרק כ | יתרו

ט זָכוֹר אֶת־יוֹם הַשַּׁבָּת לְקַדְּשׁוֹ: שֵׁשֶׁת יָמִים תַּעֲבֹד וְעָשִׂיתָ כָּל־
י מְלַאכְתֶּךָ: וְיוֹם הַשְּׁבִיעִי שַׁבָּת לַיהוָה אֱלֹהֶיךָ לֹא־תַעֲשֶׂה כָל־
מְלָאכָה אַתָּה ׀ וּבִנְךָ־וּבִתֶּךָ עַבְדְּךָ וַאֲמָתְךָ וּבְהֶמְתֶּךָ וְגֵרְךָ אֲשֶׁר
יא בִּשְׁעָרֶיךָ: כִּי שֵׁשֶׁת־יָמִים עָשָׂה יְהוָה אֶת־הַשָּׁמַיִם וְאֶת־הָאָרֶץ
אֶת־הַיָּם וְאֶת־כָּל־אֲשֶׁר־בָּם וַיָּנַח בַּיּוֹם הַשְּׁבִיעִי עַל־כֵּן בֵּרַךְ
יב יְהוָה אֶת־יוֹם הַשַּׁבָּת וַיְקַדְּשֵׁהוּ: כַּבֵּד אֶת־אָבִיךָ
וְאֶת־אִמֶּךָ לְמַעַן יַאֲרִכוּן יָמֶיךָ עַל הָאֲדָמָה אֲשֶׁר־יְהוָה אֱלֹהֶיךָ

CLASSIC COMMENTATORS

When and how are we supposed to remember the Shabbat?

RASHI
רש״י

Take note to always have the Sabbath on your mind, even during the week. If you perchance come across a choice food item in the market – buy it in anticipation of your Sabbath meal.

תנו לב לזכור תמיד את יום השבת, שאם נזדמן לך חפץ יפה, תהא מזמינו לשבת.

RASHBAM
רשב״ם

The term "remember" always refers to some past event…Here too, Israel is instructed to remember the six days of creation, as the text proceeds to elaborate, "For in six days the Lord made heaven and earth" (20:11). The command here is to remember the history of the world's creation in order to sanctify the day through abstention of labor.

כל זכירה הכוונה על ימים שעברו … אף כאן זכור את יום השבת של ששת ימי בראשית, כמו שמפרש והולך "כי ששת ימים עשה ה'" – ולפיכך נכתב כאן "זכור" כדי לקדשו, להיות שובת ממלאכה.

RABBI OVADYA SFORNO
ר' עובדיה ספורנו

As you toil through your daily business you must always keep the Sabbath day in mind…You shall do this in order to make the day holy. In other words, in anticipation of Shabbat, the individual should arrange and complete all of his affairs during the week, such that his mind is not troubled by financial issues when the Sabbath arrives.

היה תמיד זוכר את יום השבת בעסקיך בימי המעשה … וזה תעשה, כדי שתוכל לקדשו. הזהיר שיסדר האדם עסקיו בימי המעשה, באופן שיוכל להסיח דעתו מהם ביום השבת.

QUESTIONS FOR THOUGHT
- Are we supposed to remember the Shabbat of creation or the Shabbat we encounter each week?
- What is the purpose of remembering the Shabbat?
- When does the sanctification of Shabbat happen?
- How can you apply any of these opinions into enhancing your own Shabbat experience?

> *The last four commandments – which all deal with respecting other people and their possessions – are presented in rapid-fire fashion.*

13 you will live long in the land that the LORD your God is giving you. Do not murder. Do
14 not commit adultery. Do not steal. Do not bear false witness against your neighbor. Do not crave your neighbor's house. Do not crave your neighbor's wife, his male or female servant, his ox, his donkey, or anything else that is your neighbor's."

QUESTIONS FOR THOUGHT

- According to Ralbag, what does the Torah actually prohibit?
- How do you think the people making Hollywood movies would react to Ibn Ezra's idea?
- Are you aware of other mitzvot in which the Torah commands an emotion?

TEXTUAL SKILLS

1. What theme word appears four times in these last commandments?

2. Find the similarities in the language used in the commandment of Shabbat and the final commandment.

WISDOM OF THE HEART

Rav Yechiel Michel, the Maggid of Zlotchov, suggests there is a link between the first and the last commandments. Someone who truly lives with the message of the first commandment, accepting God completely, will understand that whatever they truly deserve they will get from God. If so, they will have no need for jealousy; in fact, the lack of jealousy in their lives is the reward for accepting God.

QUICK BITES

At the end of 19:19 we see that when Moshe spoke, "God answered him aloud." *HaKetav VehaKabbala* notes that no specific answer of God is provided here. It relates the word יעננו, "answered him" as related to עיון, meaning "deep understanding." In this context, God responded to Moshe's words with depth, giving him the ability to reach the deepest levels of clarity. Moshe wasn't just charged with passing on God's words to the people, but also the meaning and intent behind them. Learning Torah is in part about studying what God says, but it is more truly about what He means to say.

Sforno explains that the commandment "Do not steal" includes even the prohibition of stealing intellectually. Each of us comes into the world with certain natural gifts. We also pick up different inspirations and ideas along the way. By combining those various experiences, feelings, and ideas at certain opportunities we give birth to new, original insights. Sometimes it can be a new medical breakthrough, and sometimes it can be lyrics to a song. But it's yours, uniquely yours, and nobody can take that from you. In the same way, the work someone puts in to study for a test is theirs. It is their labor and time spent. To take that from them by cheating is no less immoral than stealing their money.

שמות | פרק כ

יג נָתַן לָֽךְ: לֹ֥א תִּרְצָ֖ח׃ לֹ֥א
תִּנְאָ֑ף לֹ֥א תִּגְנֹ֖ב לֹֽא־
יד תַעֲנֶ֥ה בְרֵעֲךָ֖ עֵ֥ד שָֽׁקֶר׃ לֹ֥א
תַחְמֹ֖ד בֵּ֣ית רֵעֶ֑ךָ לֹֽא־
תַחְמֹ֞ד אֵ֣שֶׁת רֵעֶ֗ךָ וְעַבְדּ֤וֹ וַאֲמָתוֹ֙ וְשׁוֹר֣וֹ וַחֲמֹר֔וֹ וְכֹ֖ל אֲשֶׁ֥ר
לְרֵעֶֽךָ׃

CLASSIC COMMENTATORS

The last of the commandments prohibits craving what is someone else's. How can the Torah legislate an emotion?

IBN EZRA   **אבן עזרא**

Consider a simple yet sound-minded farm boy who catches a glimpse of a gorgeous princess. Such a man will not dream about sleeping with that woman, since he knows in his heart that such a union is out of the question. This rustic will not dream of being with the princess like the delusional individual who fantasizes about growing wings and taking to flight, since he is well aware of his limitations. Similarly, a normal male does not desire relations with his mother, attractive though she may be, since he has been conditioned from childhood to understand that that woman is forbidden to him. In the same manner, every intelligent person must train himself to acknowledge that it is not his brains nor his wisdom that will aid him in acquiring money or a good-looking woman, but that he will receive only what the Lord allots to him.

דע, כי איש כפרי שיש לו דעת נכונה, והוא ראה בת מלך שהיא יפה, לא יחמוד אותה בלבו שישכוב עמה, כי ידע כי זה לא יתכן. ואל תחשוב זה הכפרי שהוא כאחד מן המשוגעים, שיתאוה שיהיו לו כנפים לעוף השמים, ולא יתכן להיות, כאשר אין אדם מתאוה לשכב עם אמו, אף על פי שהיא יפה, כי הרגילוהו מנעוריו לדעת שהיא אסורה לו. ככה כל משכיל צריך שידע, כי אשה יפה או ממון, לא ימצאנו אדם בעבור חכמתו ודעתו, רק כאשר חלק לו ה׳.

RALBAG   **רלב״ג**

Once an individual craves something that belongs to another he will devise methods of procuring it. He will attempt to obtain the wealth of his neighbor in some manner, or he will scheme to have his fellow divorce his wife so that he can marry the woman he desires. Similarly, he who covets the slave, the maidservant, the ox, the donkey, or any other possession belonging to his fellow Israelite will pressure the other to sell him his property. And it is a very evil posture to try to separate a person from his holdings if that person has no interest in selling what he owns.

ענין החמדה הוא שישתדל שיהיו לו, כאילו תאמר שיתן ממון לרעהו, שיגרש אשתו כדי שישאנה, או שימכור לו עבדו ואמתו ושורו וחמורו או אחד משאר קנייניו, כי זאת היא תכונה רעה מאד להשתדל שיצאו קנייני רעהו מתחת ידו אם לא יתרצה מעצמו למוכרם ולהוציאם מתחת ידו.

The scene at Mount Sinai was terrifying – thunder and lightning, shofar blasting, the mountain billowing smoke – so much so that Benei Yisrael pulled back from the scene and asked Moshe to be their intermediary with God. Moshe tries to reassure them, indicating that God was merely trying to prevent them from sinning in the future. Nonetheless, the people pulled back as Moshe approached the dark cloud on the mountain.

15 Every one of the people witnessed the thunder and lightning and the sound of the ram's horn and the smoke-covered mountain; they saw and they shook – and they stood at a
16 distance, and said to Moshe, "Speak to us yourself and we will listen, but let not God say
17 any more to us, or we will die." "Do not be afraid," said Moshe to the people, "God has come to lift you up, so that the awe of Him will be with you always, keeping you from
18 sin." But the people remained at a distance while Moshe approached the thick darkness

QUESTIONS FOR THOUGHT

- According to each of the commentaries above, how much of the Ten Commandments did Israel hear directly from God?
- Why should it make a difference how much they heard directly?
- Prior to the scene at Mount Sinai, God tells Moshe, "I will come to you in a dense cloud, that the people may hear Me speaking to you. They will then believe you forever" (19:9). According to which of the commentaries is this verse fulfilled best here?

TEXTUAL SKILLS

1. In verse 17 Moshe tells the people not to fear: כי לבעבור נסות אתכם בא האלהים, "God has come to lift you up." The word נסות, translated here as "lift up," is often translated as God "testing" *Benei Yisrael*. If we follow this understanding, this is not the first time that we read that God is doing something to test Israel – where did we read about it earlier?
2. What is added in this "test" of Israel that we did not hear about earlier?

WISDOM OF THE HEART

Moshe approaches the dark cloud. For him, the dark cloud was where he could find God. When life begins to get foggy, when the world doesn't seem to make sense, when we feel surrounded by darkness – we can embrace it. Take a bold step forward, like Moshe did. God will be there for you.

QUICK BITE

The people "wintessed the thunder"? How can you see sounds? The *Keli Yakar* says that any word of God uttered into the universe becomes a physical reality. Think of creation – God said: "Let there be light," and there was light. The words themselves become a tangible aspect of our world. The Baal HaTanya adds a more mystical element to this conversation, arguing that letters are the DNA of the universe. When he was on his deathbed, they asked him what he saw. He said: "Above my bed there used to be a beam (קורה), but now I see only letters – ק-ו-ר-ה."

טו וְכָל־הָעָם רֹאִים אֶת־הַקּוֹלֹת וְאֶת־הַלַּפִּידִם וְאֵת קוֹל הַשֹּׁפָר *שביעי*
וְאֶת־הָהָר עָשֵׁן וַיַּרְא הָעָם וַיָּנֻעוּ וַיַּעַמְדוּ מֵרָחֹק: וַיֹּאמְרוּ אֶל־
טז מֹשֶׁה דַּבֵּר־אַתָּה עִמָּנוּ וְנִשְׁמָעָה וְאַל־יְדַבֵּר עִמָּנוּ אֱלֹהִים פֶּן־
יז נָמוּת: וַיֹּאמֶר מֹשֶׁה אֶל־הָעָם אַל־תִּירָאוּ כִּי לְבַעֲבוּר נַסּוֹת
אֶתְכֶם בָּא הָאֱלֹהִים וּבַעֲבוּר תִּהְיֶה יִרְאָתוֹ עַל־פְּנֵיכֶם לְבִלְתִּי
יח תֶחֱטָאוּ: וַיַּעֲמֹד הָעָם מֵרָחֹק וּמֹשֶׁה נִגַּשׁ אֶל־הָעֲרָפֶל אֲשֶׁר־

CLASSIC COMMENTATORS

Before the Ten Commandments we learned that Israel was afraid and pulled back, and in this passage we read a similar description. Is this a repeat of what happened earlier? Perhaps even more importantly, how much of the Ten Commandments did Israel hear directly from God?

רש״י

כשהיה משה מדבר ומשמיע הדברות לישראל, שהרי לא שמעו *מפי* הגבורה אלא אנכי ולא יהיה לך, הקב״ה מסייעו לתת בו כח, להיות קולו מגביר ונשמע.

RASHI

The people heard only the first two precepts directly from God – "I am the Lord your God who brought you out of the land of Egypt, out of the house of slaves," and "Have no other gods than Me" (20:2–3). The other statements were first conveyed to Moshe, who then repeated the information to the nation. Meanwhile, the Holy One, blessed be He, amplified Moshe's voice when he addressed Israel so that everyone could hear him.

רשב״ם

ויאמרו אל משה - לאחר ששמעו עשרת הדברים.

RASHBAM

"And they said to Moshe" – after they heard the Ten Commandments.

רמב״ן

והנכון בעיני בפרשה ובסידור העניין, כי "וכל העם רואים ... ויאמרו אל משה" היה קודם מתן תורה, ומתחילה הזכיר כסדר כל דברי האלהים מה שציווה למשה בהגבלת ההר ואזהרת העם ועשרת הדברות, ועתה חזר והזכיר דברי העם אל משה ואמר כי מעת שראו את הקולות ואת הלפידים נעו לאחור ועמדו מרחוק יותר מגבול ההר אשר הגביל משה.

RAMBAN

I will now offer my own interpretation of this passage and the sequence of events appearing in this and the previous chapter. Firstly, the statements that "every one of the people witnessed the thunder and lightning" (20:15) and "said to Moshe, 'Speak to us yourself'" (20:16) occurred before the giving of the Torah. Initially [in chapter 19], the Torah describes the preparatory instructions that God issued to Moshe regarding establishing a boundary around the mountain and warning the nation not to climb the hill. After that, God pronounced the Ten Commandments to the nation [in the first half of chapter 20]. Following that text, the Torah returns to describe Israel's reaction upon seeing the thunder and lightning [phenomena first mentioned in 19:16]. Fear struck Israel's hearts at that time, and "they shook – and they stood at a distance" (20:15), moving even further beyond the boundary that Moshe had marked out for them.

Shemot | Chapter 20 — Yitro

> *In the first instructions following the great divine revelation at Mount Sinai, God warns Israel how not to remember the event (no physical images) but also provides them with a positive way to recreate the experience of being in God's presence (how to build an altar). This passage can also be understood as an expanded version of the first two commandments.*

19 where God was. Then the Lord said to Moshe, "This is what you shall tell the Israelites:
20 You yourselves have seen that I, from the heavens, have spoken to you. Have no others
21 alongside Me; make yourselves no silver gods, no golden gods. Make for Me an altar of earth and on that sacrifice your burnt offerings and peace offerings, your sheep and your cattle. Wherever I cause My name to be invoked, I will come to you and I will bless
22 you. If you make Me an altar of stones, do not build it of hewn stone, for in wielding a
23 sword upon it, you profane it. Do not ascend to My altar with steps, for your nakedness must not be exposed on it.

RAMBAM (GUIDE FOR THE PERPLEXED)

Those peoples who worship idolatry build their altars out of hewn stones. And hence the Torah warns its practitioners not to mimic the behavior of such nations, but to construct their altar out of earth. Thus does the verse command, "Make for Me an altar of earth." And should it not be possible to fashion an altar without using stones, the materials should be assembled as they are – in their natural state; they must not be quarried. In addition, the stones employed for the altar should not be dressed, nor should any trees be planted near the altar of the Lord. For a single principle governs all of these laws, namely that our service of God should in no way resemble the manner in which the heathens worship their idols.

רמב״ם (מורה נבוכים)

שעובדי עבודה זרה היו בונים מזבחות באבני גזית, והזהיר מלהידמות להם ושיהיה המזבח מאדמה - הרחקה מלהידמות להם, ואמר "מזבח אדמה תעשה לי" ואם אי אפשר לעשותו מבלי אבנים - יהיו בצורתם הטבעית, לא יחצבו, כמו שהזהיר מאבן משכית ומנטוע כל עץ אצל מזבח ה', והכוונה כולה אחת, והיא: שלא נעבוד ה' כדמות עבודתם החלקית אשר היו עושים אותה לנעבדים.

QUESTIONS FOR THOUGHT

- Which word in verse 22 seems to have inspired Rashi's opinion?
- If we understand this requirement as part of the Torah's expanded prohibition of idolatry, which of the commentaries fits best?
- Which commentator suggests that the Torah is concerned about people turning "holy souvenirs" into objects of worship?

TEXTUAL SKILLS

1. This is the second time in two chapters that God introduces His comments to Israel by saying, "You yourselves have seen…" Where is the first?

2. What is strange about the use of singular and plural in verse 22?

שמות | פרק כ

יט שֵׁם הָאֱלֹהִֽים: וַיֹּ֤אמֶר יְהֹוָה֙ אֶל־מֹשֶׁ֔ה כֹּ֥ה תֹאמַ֖ר מפטיר
אֶל־בְּנֵ֣י יִשְׂרָאֵ֑ל אַתֶּ֣ם רְאִיתֶ֔ם כִּ֚י מִן־הַשָּׁמַ֔יִם דִּבַּ֖רְתִּי עִמָּכֶֽם:
כ לֹ֥א תַעֲשׂ֖וּן אִתִּ֑י אֱלֹ֤הֵי כֶ֙סֶף֙ וֵאלֹהֵ֣י זָהָ֔ב לֹ֥א תַעֲשׂ֖וּ לָכֶֽם: מִזְבַּ֣ח
אֲדָמָה֮ תַּעֲשֶׂה־לִּי֒ וְזָבַחְתָּ֣ עָלָ֗יו אֶת־עֹלֹתֶ֙יךָ֙ וְאֶת־שְׁלָמֶ֔יךָ אֶת־
צֹאנְךָ֖ וְאֶת־בְּקָרֶ֑ךָ בְּכָל־הַמָּקוֹם֙ אֲשֶׁ֣ר אַזְכִּ֣יר אֶת־שְׁמִ֔י אָב֥וֹא
אֵלֶ֖יךָ וּבֵרַכְתִּֽיךָ: כא וְאִם־מִזְבַּ֤ח אֲבָנִים֙ תַּֽעֲשֶׂה־לִּ֔י לֹֽא־תִבְנֶ֥ה אֶתְהֶ֖ן
גָּזִ֑ית כִּ֧י חַרְבְּךָ֛ הֵנַ֥פְתָּ עָלֶ֖יהָ וַתְּחַֽלְלֶֽהָ: כב וְלֹֽא־תַעֲלֶ֥ה בְמַעֲלֹ֖ת
עַֽל־מִזְבְּחִ֑י אֲשֶׁ֛ר לֹֽא־תִגָּלֶ֥ה עֶרְוָתְךָ֖ עָלָֽיו:

CLASSIC COMMENTATORS

The Torah forbids using chiseled stones to build an altar – only stones in their natural form are permitted. Why?

RASHI

We learn from here that placing an iron tool upon the altar will profane it. Why should this be so? Because the purpose of the altar is to extend the individual's life [a person's life is spared by bringing a sacrifice that atones for his sin], whereas the nature of iron [a sword] is to shorten a person's life. Hence these two items are incompatible, and it is inappropriate for the latter to be placed upon the former.

רש״י

אם הנפת עליה ברזל חללתה, שהמזבח נברא להאריך ימיו של אדם, והברזל נברא לקצר ימיו של אדם, אין זה בדין שיניף המקצר על המאריך.

IBN EZRA

Perhaps the text here is forbidding the usage of hewn stones in a way akin to the philosophy of *piggul*. [If the priest, while offering an animal as a sacrifice, intended for it to be eaten after the allowed time, the entire sacrifice is called *piggul* and is rendered invalid.] For even after an animal has been sacrificed on the altar, if the meat is left over [and the priest intended that] then it will turn out that an inappropriate sacrifice had been brought to the altar. In like manner, should stones be cut in order to fashion the proper building blocks for the altar, it is possible that the leftover stone chips would be used for a profane purpose, such as the celebration of idolatry or disgraced by being discarded in a foul place. This in turn would not be respectful to the stones used to construct the altar.

אבן עזרא

אולי היה כן כדרך הפיגול, בעבור שהיה קרב על גבי המזבח, אין ראוי להיות הנשאר פיגול, כי יחלל הקודש שהקדיש, אם ישאירו ממנו עד שיהיה פיגול. וככה זה, אם יכרתו האבנים לבנות מזבח, אולי יחולל הנכרת מהאבנים לעבודה זרה או אל מקום מטונף, וזה איננו כבוד.

MORE QUICK BITES

- **19:2** R. Yitzḥak Meir Alter points out that when *Benei Yisrael* camped facing the mountain, they were also turning their backs on the wilderness. Turning to embrace God, they turned their backs on their frustrations with life in the wilderness – and that was a truly great act.

- **19:17** The verse states: "Moshe led the people out of the camp to meet God, and they stood at the foot of the mountain" (19:17) (בְּתַחְתִּית הָהָר). The Midrash interprets the phrase תחתית ההר literally, the people were standing not at the foot of the mountain, but underneath it. The Gemara explains in Shabbat 88a: "The Holy One, blessed be He, overturned the mountain above them like a tub and warned them: If you accept the Torah – excellent. And if not – here you will be buried." This sounds like we didn't have much of a choice. Wouldn't free will have been better?

  Rav Kook tackles this dilemma head on: Yes, it is essential that we have the ability to choose between right and wrong. It is through our free will that we develop spiritually and refine out ethical qualities. And if the Torah were just a moral guidebook, then all of it would need to be accepted freely. But the Torah is much more than that – the Torah expresses our inner essence. When we violate the Torah's teachings, we become estranged from our own true selves. The image of the mountain over our heads symbolizes that this Torah is so necessary to our survival. Life could not be without it.

EXPLORING HASHKAFA
Israel as the Chosen People

The chosenness of Israel – one of the key elements of the events at Mount Sinai – has been the subject of many discussions and debates. For some, it is a source of great pride; for others, it is understood as one the roots of anti-Semitism; and Tevye of *Fiddler on the Roof* wishes that God would choose someone else once in a while.

There are Jewish sages – from R. Yehuda Halevi to Maharal of Prague – who believed that chosenness implies inherent superiority. R. Yehuda Halevi, for example, believed that only natural-born members of *Benei Yisrael* can achieve prophecy – converts are ineligible forever. Maharal believed that *Benei Yisrael* possess a special soul that non-Jews don't have.

Others, however, believe that chosenness is not about superiority, natural or otherwise, but about a mission. God did not create *Benei Yisrael* first; He created humanity, and He wanted a relationship with all of humanity. The first human was not a Jew, Noaḥ was not a Jew, and even Avraham was not a Jew. But when it became clear that the attempt to reach all of humanity directly was not working – whether we're talking about the story of the Flood or of the Tower of Bavel – He changed course and chose Israel as the vehicle through which He would spread His message to the rest of humanity.

This message is part of the framework of our daily prayers. The first part of *Pesukei DeZimra* focuses on God's relationship with the entire world; it is not until after the chapters from Psalms that we focus on God's unique relationship with Israel. The same is true in the blessings leading up to *Shema*. The first is a celebration of God as Creator – not creator of Israel, but of the entire world. It is not until the second blessing that we speak about God's unique love for Israel.

God's unique love for Israel is because they are his *kohanim* – the ones He chose to be the bridge between Him and the rest of humanity. This is one of the central messages of the prayers on Rosh Hashanah and Yom Kippur, and is repeated three times every day in *Aleinu*. The first paragraph of *Aleinu* celebrates the uniqueness of Israel, but the second expresses our deepest desire that everyone else in the world get to share in what we have.

Chosenness, in this light, is not about superiority at all. It is about humbling ourselves for an endless task to spread Godliness without imposing it, about setting a model for others without being arrogant, about earning dignity for ourselves and the God we represent despite the seemingly infinite challenges placed in our way.

פרשת משפטים
PARASHAT MISHPATIM

> "The Bible is about the priority of the other in relation to the I."
> Emmanuel Levinas

Societies based on rigid class systems have been around for a very long time. In a typical ancient river valley civilization like Mesopotamia and Egypt, the king was regarded as either a god or the delegate of a god. A complex class system developed around him: beneath the monarch was a class of hereditary military aristocrats and a powerful priesthood, below them were several kinds of freemen (mostly peasants) and at the bottom were many slaves. Numerous cultures and religions throughout history have been defined by their class system. Does the Torah suggest such systems for *Benei Yisrael* or is our nation meant to be organized differently? Look at the text of this *parasha* with a watchful eye. Our system may seem similar in some ways to other ancient cultures, yet careful attention will show you many differences. As Ibn Ezra points out, the *parasha* begins with great detail about how to treat servants, because the moral litmus test of any ideal society is how it protects its weakest element.

PARASHAT MISHPATIM

21 ¹ "And these are the laws that you shall set before them. ² If you buy a Hebrew slave, he shall serve for six years, but in the seventh he shall go forth free, without paying anything. ³ If he came alone, he shall leave alone. But if he was a married man, his wife shall leave with him. ⁴ If his master gave him a wife and she bore him sons or daughters, the woman and her children shall remain her master's, while he shall leave alone. ⁵ But if the slave declares, 'I love my master, my wife and my children; I do not want to go free,' ⁶ then his master shall bring him before the judges. He shall take him to the door or to the doorpost and pierce his ear with an awl; after that he shall then remain his slave forever. ⁷ If a man sells his daughter as a maidservant, she does not go free in the usual way of slaves. ⁸ If her master, who intended to wed her, finds that he dislikes her, he must let her be redeemed. He has no right to sell her to foreigners, because he has broken faith with her. ⁹,¹⁰ If he intends her for his son, he shall grant her all the rights of a daughter. If he marries another woman alongside her, he shall not reduce her food, her clothing, or marital ¹¹ rights. If he fails her in any of these three things, she shall go forth free without paying

---

RABBI SAMSON RAPHAEL HIRSCH

Consider the slave who enjoys the life and security that his state of servitude provides. He no longer has the worries and the troubles that plagued him as a free person. And hence this individual decides that he would prefer to remain where he is, rather than be released into a life of responsibility. In response to this rejection of freedom, his master brings the slave to the door and to the doorpost where his ear is pierced. This is done by puncturing the man's ear through to the door itself – not to the door frame. That distinction is significant because the doorway of a Jewish home symbolizes independence as we note in the role this architectural element plays in the redemption of Israel from Egypt. At the moment that God raised the slave community out of their oppression and transformed the people into a liberated nation, he restored to them the right, nay the obligation, to establish free and individual households.

ר' שמשון רפאל הירש

עבד הרוצה יותר בביטחון ובחיים הנוחים חסרי הדאגה שבמצב העבדות, ומואס בחיי המשפחה העצמאיים שלו על כל דאגותיהם וטרחותיהם, מובא על ידי אדוניו אל הדלת או אל המזוזה, ואדוניו רוצע את אזנו במרצע על הדלת, ולא על המזוזה.

המזוזות הינן נציגויותיו של הבית העצמאי, וככאלה הן מופיעות בשעת הגאולה, עת העלה ה' את עבדי המצרים, עשה אותם לבני חורין, והשיב להם את הזכות – ועל ידי כך את החובה – להקים את בתיהם העצמאיים שלהם.

QUESTIONS FOR THOUGHT

- R. Hirsch understands that the process symbolizes a critique of the servant. What is the critique?
- The other two agree that the point of the door is that it is public, but they disagree on the point of it being public. What does each of them say?
- Can you imagine anyone standing at Mount Sinai, who had just left Egypt a few weeks earlier, wanting to go back into a situation of servitude?

פרשת משפטים

כא וְאֵלֶּה הַמִּשְׁפָּטִים אֲשֶׁר תָּשִׂים לִפְנֵיהֶם: כִּי תִקְנֶה עֶבֶד עִבְרִי שֵׁשׁ שָׁנִים יַעֲבֹד וּבַשְּׁבִעִת יֵצֵא לַחָפְשִׁי חִנָּם: אִם־בְּגַפּוֹ יָבֹא בְּגַפּוֹ יֵצֵא אִם־בַּעַל אִשָּׁה הוּא וְיָצְאָה אִשְׁתּוֹ עִמּוֹ: אִם־אֲדֹנָיו יִתֶּן־לוֹ אִשָּׁה וְיָלְדָה־לּוֹ בָנִים אוֹ בָנוֹת הָאִשָּׁה וִילָדֶיהָ תִּהְיֶה לַאדֹנֶיהָ וְהוּא יֵצֵא בְגַפּוֹ: וְאִם־אָמֹר יֹאמַר הָעֶבֶד אָהַבְתִּי אֶת־אֲדֹנִי אֶת־אִשְׁתִּי וְאֶת־בָּנָי לֹא אֵצֵא חָפְשִׁי: וְהִגִּישׁוֹ אֲדֹנָיו אֶל־הָאֱלֹהִים וְהִגִּישׁוֹ אֶל־הַדֶּלֶת אוֹ אֶל־הַמְּזוּזָה וְרָצַע אֲדֹנָיו אֶת־אָזְנוֹ בַּמַּרְצֵעַ וַעֲבָדוֹ לְעֹלָם: וְכִי־יִמְכֹּר אִישׁ אֶת־בִּתּוֹ לְאָמָה לֹא תֵצֵא כְּצֵאת הָעֲבָדִים: אִם־רָעָה בְּעֵינֵי אֲדֹנֶיהָ אֲשֶׁר־לֹא יְעָדָהּ וְהֶפְדָּהּ לְעַם נָכְרִי לֹא־יִמְשֹׁל לְמָכְרָהּ בְּבִגְדוֹ־בָהּ: וְאִם־לִבְנוֹ יִיעָדֶנָּה כְּמִשְׁפַּט הַבָּנוֹת יַעֲשֶׂה־לָּהּ: אִם־אַחֶרֶת יִקַּח־לוֹ שְׁאֵרָהּ כְּסוּתָהּ וְעֹנָתָהּ לֹא יִגְרָע: וְאִם־שְׁלָשׁ־

CLASSIC COMMENTATORS

The Hebrew servant who desires to stay with his master must undergo a procedure in which his ear is pierced next to a door. Why?

RABBI YOSEF KARA — ר' יוסף קרא

The purpose of piercing the slave's ear into a door is to attract the attention of the public who are passing by on the street. It will thereby become known to all that the slave has made this poor decision to prolong his servitude.

שיראו בני רשות הרבים שעוברים שם בהרצעו ויודע הדבר לרבים.

TUR — טור

The reason the slave's ear is pierced at the door is as follows. The perforation is intended to serve as a sign for the perpetual servitude this man has signed onto. To inflict this mark on him, the slave is first held against the door which has the effect of creating matching holes in the individual's ear and on the wood door itself. Thus, if the slave subsequently argues that his injury was self-inflicted [and does not indicate his extended slave status] he can be brought to the door which bears the corresponding perforation to that which he carries.

לפי שהרציעה היא סימן לעבדות ורוצעו אוחז אותו אל הדלת רוצה לומר מעצמי נגפתי יקרבנו אל הדלת וימצא שרצועת אזנו מכוון למקום הדלת שנרצע שם.

> *For the most serious interpersonal offenses, those that threaten the fabric of society and destabilize civil life, the Torah prescribes the death penalty. These include murder, kidnapping, and cursing or hitting one's parents.*

12 anything. One person who strikes another so that he dies shall be put to death. If he did
13 not lie in wait to harm him, but it came about by an act of God – I am setting apart a
14 place where he may find refuge. But if someone schemes against another and kills him
15 by stealth, you shall take him even from My altar and he shall die. One who wounds his
16 father or mother shall be put to death. One who kidnaps a person shall be put to death,
17 whether the victim is sold on or found in his possession. One who curses his father or

QUESTIONS FOR THOUGHT

- What three different opinions are suggested in response to the question posed above?
- All three opinions above understand that the Torah intends to say that the incident was a form of divine justice. Can you imagine an alternative way of understanding the term, "an act of God?"
- Do you believe that everything that happens to us is the result of divine intervention in the world?

TEXTUAL SKILLS

1. Do you recall a story in Genesis in which people preferred to kidnap-sell someone rather than kill him? What commentary might the Torah be offering here on the morality of that choice?

2. Find the word in verse 14 which has a similar sound (and even a similar meaning) to a word in verse 13. Can you find a place in Genesis where these words are also used to play off each other?

WISDOM OF THE HEART

The consequence for a person who kills someone accidentally is that he has to go into exile, much like Kayin had to become a wanderer for killing his brother. Rav Tzadok HaKohen of Lublin says that the hustle and bustle of the modern world suggests that in some way we are all murderers. Perhaps not in the literal sense, but when we embarrass people, bad-mouth them, harm them in their personal or professional relationships, or create social havoc, we destroy people's lives. And the price we pay is that we lose our sense of security and are always in flux.

QUICK BITE

Rabbi Avraham ben HaRambam teaches that when something goes wrong in our lives, we shouldn't beat ourselves up over it. Lines like "If I had only listened to his advice, I wouldn't be in trouble now" may be useful to guide us in future decision-making, but dwelling on them is counterproductive. At the end of the day, many things that happen to us are "acts of God." God wants it to be this way. We must accept that אשר לא צדה – there is no real "side" [צד], no argument as to why this is the case. But we simultaneously have faith that there is a bigger plan for us. And once we accept the power of the present moment, we will find: "I am setting apart a place where he may find refuge" – God has made us space to find our way out of this ordeal.

אֵ֫לֶּה לֹ֣א יַעֲשֶׂ֣ה לָ֑הּ וְיָצְאָ֥ה חִנָּ֖ם אֵ֥ין כָּֽסֶף׃ מַכֵּ֥ה יב

אִ֛ישׁ וָמֵ֖ת מ֥וֹת יוּמָֽת׃ וַאֲשֶׁר֙ לֹ֣א צָדָ֔ה וְהָאֱלֹהִ֖ים אִנָּ֣ה יג

לְיָד֑וֹ וְשַׂמְתִּ֤י לְךָ֙ מָק֔וֹם אֲשֶׁ֥ר יָנ֖וּס שָֽׁמָּה׃ וְכִֽי־ יד

יָזִ֥ד אִ֛ישׁ עַל־רֵעֵ֖הוּ לְהׇרְג֣וֹ בְעׇרְמָ֑ה מֵעִ֣ם מִזְבְּחִ֔י תִּקָּחֶ֖נּוּ

לָמֽוּת׃ וּמַכֵּ֥ה אָבִ֛יו וְאִמּ֖וֹ מ֥וֹת יוּמָֽת׃ וְגֹנֵ֨ב טו

אִ֧ישׁ וּמְכָר֛וֹ וְנִמְצָ֥א בְיָד֖וֹ מ֥וֹת יוּמָֽת׃ וּמְקַלֵּ֥ל אָבִ֖יו יז

CLASSIC COMMENTATORS

If someone kills another by accident there is no death penalty, rather, the Torah provides a safe haven for the perpetrator. The language used by the Torah to describe the accident – it was an act of God – is vague. Did God bring about that the person be killed by accident, or that the perpetrator would kill by accident?

RASHI

רש"י

Consider a situation of two individuals, one of whom killed somebody inadvertently, while the other one killed somebody else intentionally. Now in neither case were there witnesses who could testify and thereby prosecute the killers, meaning that the one who committed murder cannot be executed and the one who committed manslaughter cannot be exiled [to a city of refuge, akin to a minimum security prison]. In order to set things straight, the Holy One, blessed be He, arranges for both men to convene at the same inn. The one who killed somebody unintentionally finds himself climbing a ladder and then falling onto and killing the murderer seated below. Subsequently, witnesses testify that the survivor killed his victim [the murderer] unintentionally and so he is sentenced to exile. Thus, the one who originally killed somebody unintentionally does indeed end up being exiled [for his second act rather than his first], while the one who murdered with intent is dispatched.

במה הכתוב מדבר? בשני בני אדם, אחד הרג שוגג, ואחד הרג מזיד, ולא היו עדים בדבר שיעידו – זה לא נהרג, וזה לא גלה. הקב"ה מזמנן לפונדוק אחד, זה שהרג שוגג עולה בסלם ונופל על זה שהרג מזיד והורגו, ועדים מעידין אותו ומחייבין אותו לגלות. נמצא זה שהרג שוגג גולה, וזה שהרג מזיד נהרג.

RASHBAM

רשב"ם

This confrontation was arranged by God because the victim deserved to die at the hand of heaven.

אנה לידו – כי חייב מיתה בידי שמים היה.

RABBI OVADYA SFORNO

ר' עובדיה ספורנו

The perpetrator in this episode did not act negligently to cause this event. However, [it was God's will that the victim would die, and] a punishment is effected in this world by those who are guilty.

והאלהים אנה לידו – שלא פשע לעשות דבר גורם זה, אלא שמגלגלין חובה על ידי חייבים.

18 mother shall be put to death. If two people fight and one strikes another with a stone
19 or with his fist – if the victim does not die but is confined to bed, and afterward he gets
up and walks outdoors even leaning on a cane, the assailant is absolved, but he must
20 pay for the victim's loss of time and provide for his cure. If a man strikes his slave, male
21 or female, with a rod and the slave dies there and then, the death shall be avenged. But
if the slave survives a day, two days – since the money lost is the master's, the death
22 shall not be avenged. If two men fight and one of them hits a pregnant woman, and
she miscarries but suffers no irreparable injury herself, the offender must be fined, as
23 the woman's husband demands and as the judges rule. But if she suffers an irreparable
24 injury, he must compensate life for life, eye for eye, tooth for tooth, hand for hand, foot
25 for foot, burn for burn, wound for wound, bruise for bruise. If a man should strike the
26 eye of his slave, male or female, and maim it, he must send the slave out free on account
27 of his eye. If he knocks out the tooth of his slave, male or female, he must send the slave
out free on account of his tooth.

ר' יוסף בכור שור

כשאדם ממית אדם, אין לפייסו בממון, ומשום הכי נהרג, אבל באיבריו מה יועיל אם יטלו כמו כן מום בחבירו, מוטב לו שיתן לו ממון לפרנס את עצמו.

RABBI YOSEF BEKHOR SHOR

When an individual murders another person it is impossible to compensate the victim by paying him a sum of money. And that is why the killer's own life is taken. But if an attacker injures his fellow, how will wounding the criminal in a similar manner benefit the victim? It is far better that the thug pay the other money which he can use to support himself.

QUESTIONS FOR THOUGHT

- Which of the commentaries seems to suffice with the fact that the rabbis in the Talmud understood it non-literally?
- Which of the commentaries uses practical reasoning to explain why it wouldn't make sense to read it literally?
- Which of the commentaries explains why the Torah used language that could easily have been understood as literally taking an eye for an eye?

TEXTUAL SKILLS

1. Notice that from verse 12 through verse 35, each new case is introduced with a connecting letter *vav*. Why do you think that is?

2. Notice that verses 26–27 are meant to parallel verses 22–25. What message do you think this is meant to convey?

WISDOM OF THE HEART

The verse that commands one to pay for healing one who he wounded is used by the Gemara (Bava Kama 85a) as a source granting permission to doctors to heal. In many religions this idea is not self-evident, as they believe that humans have no right to interfere in God's work; rather people should simply trust in God. The Gemara teaches us that God works in many ways and through many messengers; doctors who heal the sick are among these divine messengers.

שמות | פרק כא

יח וְכִי־יְרִיבֻן אֲנָשִׁים וְהִכָּה־אִישׁ אֶת־ רֵעֵהוּ בְּאֶבֶן אוֹ בְאֶגְרֹף וְלֹא יָמוּת וְנָפַל לְמִשְׁכָּב: אִם־יָקוּם וְהִתְהַלֵּךְ בַּחוּץ עַל־מִשְׁעַנְתּוֹ וְנִקָּה הַמַּכֶּה רַק שִׁבְתּוֹ יִתֵּן וְרַפֹּא יְרַפֵּא: ס

שני כ וְכִי־יַכֶּה אִישׁ אֶת־עַבְדּוֹ אוֹ אֶת־אֲמָתוֹ בַּשֵּׁבֶט וּמֵת תַּחַת יָדוֹ נָקֹם יִנָּקֵם: אַךְ אִם־יוֹם אוֹ יוֹמַיִם יַעֲמֹד כא לֹא יֻקַּם כִּי כַסְפּוֹ הוּא: ס כב וְכִי־יִנָּצוּ אֲנָשִׁים וְנָגְפוּ אִשָּׁה הָרָה וְיָצְאוּ יְלָדֶיהָ וְלֹא יִהְיֶה אָסוֹן עָנוֹשׁ יֵעָנֵשׁ כַּאֲשֶׁר יָשִׁית עָלָיו בַּעַל הָאִשָּׁה וְנָתַן בִּפְלִלִים: וְאִם־אָסוֹן יִהְיֶה וְנָתַתָּה כג נֶפֶשׁ תַּחַת נָפֶשׁ: עַיִן תַּחַת עַיִן שֵׁן תַּחַת שֵׁן יָד תַּחַת יָד רֶגֶל כד תַּחַת רָגֶל: כְּוִיָּה תַּחַת כְּוִיָּה פֶּצַע תַּחַת פָּצַע חַבּוּרָה תַּחַת כה חַבּוּרָה: ס כו וְכִי־יַכֶּה אִישׁ אֶת־עֵין עַבְדּוֹ אוֹ־אֶת־עֵין אֲמָתוֹ וְשִׁחֲתָהּ לַחָפְשִׁי יְשַׁלְּחֶנּוּ תַּחַת עֵינוֹ: ס וְאִם־שֵׁן עַבְדּוֹ כז אוֹ־שֵׁן אֲמָתוֹ יַפִּיל לַחָפְשִׁי יְשַׁלְּחֶנּוּ תַּחַת שִׁנּוֹ: ס

CLASSIC COMMENTATORS

There is universal agreement amongst the commentaries that the expression "eye for an eye" does not indicate that a court would actually poke out the eye of the offender. Nevertheless, they disagree about how that conclusion is derived.

RASHI — רש״י

If an attacker blinds his fellow person, he pays him for the value of his eye. This is assessed according to the reduction in the individual's worth as a slave. And such is the consequence of all inflicted injuries listed here – the Torah does not mean for us to follow the law of retaliation on a physical level.

סימא את עין חברו, נותן לו דמי עינו כמה שפחתתו דמיו לימכר בשוק, וכן כולם. ולא נטילת אבר ממש.

IBN EZRA — אבן עזרא

If the perpetrator does not pay for the damage he has inflicted, he deserves to have his own eye removed.

ראוי להיותו עינו תחת עינו, אם לא יתן כפרו.

28 If an ox gores a man or a woman to death, the ox shall be stoned, and its flesh not eaten,
29 but the owner of the ox shall not be liable. But if the ox has already gored in the past, and its owner was warned but failed to guard it, and it kills a man or a woman, the ox
30 shall be stoned, and its owner also shall be put to death. If a ransom is imposed on his
31 life, then he shall pay whatever is imposed on him and redeem his life. This rule also
32 applies if the ox gores a minor son or daughter, but if the ox gores a slave, male or female,
33 the owner shall give thirty shekels of silver to the master, and the ox must be stoned. If a man uncovers a hole or digs one and fails to cover it, and an ox or a donkey falls into
34 it, the one responsible for the pit shall make restitution. He shall give its owner its full
35 value, and the dead animal shall be his. If one man's ox injures another's so that it dies,
36 they shall sell the live ox and share the money. The dead animal they shall also share. If, however, it is known that the ox had gored in the past, and still the owner failed to guard

HAAMEK DAVAR

It seems to me that the straightforward meaning of the phrase "and its owner also shall be put to death" should not be ignored. The verse means that the farmer is expected to be put to death by the court. Since he did not restrain his animal which was a forewarned beast, he has thereby demonstrated that he takes the shedding of human blood to be a trivial matter. As such, it is likely that this brute will eventually kill somebody himself. [Thus when the verse states "and its owner also shall be put to death" it does indicate direct retribution for the animal's behavior, but predicts that this will happen in the future, as a consequence of what the owner will likely do.]

העמק דבר

נראה שלא להוציא משמעות "יומת" מידי פשוטו גם כן, והכא פירושו שהוא מיועד לבוא לידי מיתה בבית דין, שאחר שלא שמר שורו המועד לכך, ניכר שקל עליו חומר שפיכת דמים וסופו שיהרוג הוא את האדם.

QUESTIONS FOR THOUGHT

- Which of the commentaries thinks that it may be possible to execute the owner under certain circumstances? Does that sound reasonable to you?
- *Haamek Davar* argues that the Torah is making an important statement about the morality of the owner. What is that statement?
- One can imagine a wide range of circumstances, ranging from a person who has a dangerous dog that gets agitated easily to one who owns a trained attack dog that he sets against other people. How different are these cases from one another, especially if the owner doesn't keep his animal properly restrained?

TEXTUAL SKILLS

1. Notice that the Torah's discussion of an ox which damages (vv. 28–32 and vv. 35–36) is interrupted by a discussion of a person who caused damage by opening a pit. Try to explain that interruption.

2. The phrase ולא ישמרנו, "he did not guard it," appears twice in this section. What does it refer to in both cases?

כח וְכִי־יִגַּח שׁוֹר אֶת־אִישׁ אוֹ אֶת־אִשָּׁה וָמֵת סָקוֹל יִסָּקֵל הַשּׁוֹר
כט וְלֹא יֵאָכֵל אֶת־בְּשָׂרוֹ וּבַעַל הַשּׁוֹר נָקִי: וְאִם שׁוֹר נַגָּח הוּא מִתְּמֹל שִׁלְשֹׁם וְהוּעַד בִּבְעָלָיו וְלֹא יִשְׁמְרֶנּוּ וְהֵמִית אִישׁ
ל אוֹ אִשָּׁה הַשּׁוֹר יִסָּקֵל וְגַם־בְּעָלָיו יוּמָת: אִם־כֹּפֶר יוּשַׁת
לא עָלָיו וְנָתַן פִּדְיֹן נַפְשׁוֹ כְּכֹל אֲשֶׁר־יוּשַׁת עָלָיו: אוֹ־בֵן יִגָּח אוֹ־
לב בַת יִגָּח כַּמִּשְׁפָּט הַזֶּה יֵעָשֶׂה לּוֹ: אִם־עֶבֶד יִגַּח הַשּׁוֹר אוֹ אָמָה כֶּסֶף ׀ שְׁלֹשִׁים שְׁקָלִים יִתֵּן לַאדֹנָיו וְהַשּׁוֹר יִסָּקֵל: וְכִי־
לג יִפְתַּח אִישׁ בּוֹר אוֹ כִּי־יִכְרֶה אִישׁ בֹּר וְלֹא יְכַסֶּנּוּ וְנָפַל־שָׁמָּה שּׁוֹר
לד אוֹ חֲמוֹר: בַּעַל הַבּוֹר יְשַׁלֵּם כֶּסֶף יָשִׁיב לִבְעָלָיו וְהַמֵּת יִהְיֶה־
לה לּוֹ: וְכִי־יִגֹּף שׁוֹר־אִישׁ אֶת־שׁוֹר רֵעֵהוּ וָמֵת וּמָכְרוּ
לו אֶת־הַשּׁוֹר הַחַי וְחָצוּ אֶת־כַּסְפּוֹ וְגַם אֶת־הַמֵּת יֶחֱצוּן: אוֹ נוֹדַע כִּי שׁוֹר נַגָּח הוּא מִתְּמוֹל שִׁלְשֹׁם וְלֹא יִשְׁמְרֶנּוּ בְּעָלָיו שַׁלֵּם יְשַׁלֵּם

CLASSIC COMMENTATORS

If someone's ox kills a person, the ox is killed. In addition, if the ox has killed multiple individuals and the owner has been warned, the Torah indicates that the owner also ought to be killed but allows him to pay ransom money instead. The commentaries debate the meaning of the Torah's statement regarding a death penalty for the owner.

ר' יוסף בכור שור
לפי הפשט פעמים שהוא חייב מיתה, כגון שהניח אותו לילך לדעת, כדי שיהרוג אדם שהוא שונא והרגו, ואז חייב מיתה, דהוה ליה כמו שהרגו בידיים.

RABBI YOSEF BEKHOR SHOR
According to the straightforward meaning of the text, there are times when the murderous ox's owner deserves to die. For example, consider a case where a farmer allows his ox to roam free in the hope that the beast will end up killing the owner's enemy. In such a circumstance the farmer should receive the death penalty, because his actions are equivalent to killing his foe with his own hands.

רמב״ן
קיבלו רבותינו ז״ל שהיא מיתה בידי שמים.

RAMBAN
Although the verse rules that the owner of a murderous animal shall be put to death, the tradition conveyed by our Rabbis, of blessed memory, is that the individual is killed by the hand of heaven [and not by a human court].

> *The Torah continues its discussion of various forms of property damage: unrestrained animals that damage property, uncontrolled fires that spread to other people's property, and theft. All of these situations generate a financial obligation on the responsible party to compensate the victim for the loss.*

37 it, he shall pay an ox for an ox, and the dead animal shall be his. If a man steals an ox or a sheep and kills it or sells it, he shall pay five oxen for an ox, four sheep for a sheep.

22 1 If a burglar is caught tunneling in, and is struck and killed, there is no blood-guilt on his account. But if the sun has risen on him, there is blood-guilt on his account. A thief must make restitution; if he lacks the means, he shall be sold as a slave to repay his debt. If what he stole – an ox, ass or sheep – is found alive in his possession, he shall pay double.

4 If a person lets a field or vineyard be damaged, either by letting his livestock loose or by letting them graze in someone else's field, he must repay the best of his field or vineyard.

5 If a fire is started and spreads to thorns, so that grain is destroyed, stacked or standing or growing in the field, the person who started the fire must redress the damage.

QUESTIONS FOR THOUGHT

- How do the different commentaries understand the word דמים?
- Abarbanel and Ibn Ezra say similar things, but there is one major difference between them. What is that difference?
- Rashbam offers a psychological reason to explain the Torah's ruling. Try to think of an alternate rationale for this law.

TEXTUAL SKILLS

1. What single word appears four times in verses 4 and 5, but with two very different meanings? What are the two meanings?
2. Notice the lack of connecting "*vav*"s in this section. Why do you think that they are absent?

WISDOM OF THE HEART

According to Jewish mystics, fire can sometimes refer to discord. Just like a fire can suddenly burn out of control, arguments can also spin out of control – and then, just like fires, they consume everything and everyone in their path. Sadly, once they've done their damage, we often cannot even remember how it started.

Do you ever look back at your fights and wonder what you were really fighting about?

שמות | פרק כא

לו שׁוֹר תַּחַת הַשּׁוֹר וְהַמֵּת יִהְיֶה־לּוֹ: כִּי יִגְנֹב־אִישׁ
שׁוֹר אוֹ־שֶׂה וּטְבָחוֹ אוֹ מְכָרוֹ חֲמִשָּׁה בָקָר יְשַׁלֵּם תַּחַת הַשּׁוֹר
כב א וְאַרְבַּע־צֹאן תַּחַת הַשֶּׂה: אִם־בַּמַּחְתֶּרֶת יִמָּצֵא הַגַּנָּב וְהֻכָּה
ב וָמֵת אֵין לוֹ דָּמִים: אִם־זָרְחָה הַשֶּׁמֶשׁ עָלָיו דָּמִים לוֹ שַׁלֵּם יְשַׁלֵּם
ג אִם־אֵין לוֹ וְנִמְכַּר בִּגְנֵבָתוֹ: אִם־הִמָּצֵא תִמָּצֵא בְיָדוֹ הַגְּנֵבָה
ד מִשּׁוֹר עַד־חֲמוֹר עַד־שֶׂה חַיִּים שְׁנַיִם יְשַׁלֵּם: שלישי כִּי
יַבְעֶר־אִישׁ שָׂדֶה אוֹ־כֶרֶם וְשִׁלַּח אֶת־בְּעִירֹה וּבִעֵר בִּשְׂדֵה
ה אַחֵר מֵיטַב שָׂדֵהוּ וּמֵיטַב כַּרְמוֹ יְשַׁלֵּם: כִּי־תֵצֵא
אֵשׁ וּמָצְאָה קֹצִים וְנֶאֱכַל גָּדִישׁ אוֹ הַקָּמָה אוֹ הַשָּׂדֶה שַׁלֵּם

CLASSIC COMMENTATORS

The Torah says that if someone found a thief sneaking around his house and he kills the thief, אין לו דמים. This odd statement caught the attention of the commentaries, who offer very different opinions about its meaning.

IBN EZRA   אבן עזרא

The homeowner who slays the intruder is not guilty of shedding blood.

אין על הורגו שפיכות דמים.

RASHBAM   רשב״ם

When the burglar enters the home, he recognizes the possibility that he will either have to kill the homeowner or that the latter will kill him. And hence the homeowner shall not be required to pay any money [*damim*] if he kills the thief.

אם במחתרת: ובלילה – או להרוג או ליהרג בא. לפיכך אין לו דמים – תשלומי דמים, אלא פטור ההורגו.

ABARBANEL   אברבנאל

The homeowner shall receive no punishment [*damim*] if he kills the trespasser.

אין לבעל הבית דמים, רצוני לומר, שלא ייענש בהריגתו.

6 If one person entrusts another with money or goods, and they are stolen from his house,
7 then if the thief is found he must pay double. If the thief is not found, then the owner of the house must swear before the court that he has not laid hands on his neighbor's
8 goods himself. In every case of betrayal of trust, whether concerning an ox, donkey or sheep, clothing, or any loss that one can point to and say, 'This is it,' – both parties' claims shall be brought to the court. The one the court finds guilty shall pay the other double.
9 If one person entrusts another with a donkey, ox, sheep or any animal, for safekeeping,
10 and it dies or is injured or is carried away unseen, an oath before the Lord shall settle between them; if the second man swears that he did not lay his hands on his charge,
11 then the owner must accept this, and no restitution need be made. But if the charge was
12 stolen from him, he must make restitution to the owner. If it was torn by a wild animal and the second man brings the remains as evidence, he need not make good the loss.
13 If one person borrows a creature from his neighbor, and it is injured or dies while the
14 owner is not there, he must make restitution. But if the owner was present, he need not

---

RASHBAM

Our Rabbis have explained that the first case deals with an unpaid watchman, while the second case describes one who is paid.

However, according to the straightforward meaning of the text, the distinction between the passages is as follows. At first, the Torah is describing movable objects when it states, "If one person entrusts another with money or goods." Thus, the guard is given the owner's possessions which he is tasked with taking home and protecting just like he guards his own possessions. Hence if the watchman's home is robbed, he is exempt, since he extended the same sort of care to the owner's items as he did to his own home. However, when the text states, "If one person entrusts another with a donkey, ox, sheep or any animal" it is now describing the transfer of beasts, which are normally allowed out to the fields in order to graze. Under such circumstances it is obvious that the watchman must keep a greater eye on the property he has been given in order to prevent theft.

רשב״ם

פירשו רבותינו ראשונה בשומר חנם, שנייה בשומר שכר.

ולפי פשוטו של מקרא: פרשה ראשונה שכתוב בה: כי יתן איש אל רעהו כסף או כלים לשמור, מטלטלין הם ולשומרם בתוך ביתו כשאר חפציו נתן לו. לפיכך אם נגנבו בביתו פטור, כי שמרן כשמירת חפציו. אבל פרשה שנייה שכתוב בה:

כי יתן איש אל רעהו חמור או שור או שה וכל בהמה לשמור, ודרך בהמות לרעות בשדה, וודאי כשהפקידם, על מנת לשומרם מגנבים הפקידם.

QUESTIONS FOR THOUGHT

- Rashbam is aware of the Gemara's interpretation and accepts it as halakha, yet he offers an alternative interpretation based on a careful reading of the text. Why do you think he feels the need to offer that second interpretation?
- Ramban sticks with the Gemara's interpretation. How does Ramban try to take address Rashbam's concerns?

TEXTUAL SKILLS

1. Can you find evidence from within the text that challenges Rashbam's interpretation? How do you think Rashbam might respond?

2. There is a three-word phrase in the opening of the first case that is missing in the second one. What is that phrase, and does it support Rashbam's reading or Ramban's?

וְ כִּי־יִתֵּ֨ן אִ֜ישׁ אֶל־רֵעֵ֗הוּ   יְשַׁלֵּ֥ם הַמַּבְעִ֖ר אֶת־הַבְּעֵרָֽה׃
כֶּ֤סֶף אֽוֹ־כֵלִים֙ לִשְׁמֹ֔ר וְגֻנַּ֖ב מִבֵּ֣ית הָאִ֑ישׁ אִם־יִמָּצֵ֥א הַגַּנָּ֖ב
ז יְשַׁלֵּ֥ם שְׁנָֽיִם׃ אִם־לֹ֤א יִמָּצֵא֙ הַגַּנָּ֔ב וְנִקְרַ֥ב בַּֽעַל־הַבַּ֖יִת אֶל־
ח הָֽאֱלֹהִ֑ים אִם־לֹ֛א שָׁלַ֥ח יָד֖וֹ בִּמְלֶ֥אכֶת רֵעֵֽהוּ׃ עַֽל־כָּל־דְּבַר־
פֶּ֡שַׁע עַל־שׁ֡וֹר עַל־֠חֲמ֠וֹר עַל־שֶׂ֨ה עַל־שַׂלְמָ֜ה עַל־כָּל־אֲבֵדָ֗ה
אֲשֶׁ֤ר יֹאמַר֙ כִּי־ה֣וּא זֶ֔ה עַ֚ד הָֽאֱלֹהִ֔ים יָבֹ֖א דְּבַר־שְׁנֵיהֶ֑ם אֲשֶׁ֤ר
ט יַרְשִׁיעֻ֣ן אֱלֹהִ֔ים יְשַׁלֵּ֥ם שְׁנַ֖יִם לְרֵעֵֽהוּ׃ כִּֽי־יִתֵּן֩ אִ֨ישׁ
אֶל־רֵעֵ֜הוּ חֲמ֨וֹר אוֹ־שׁ֥וֹר אוֹ־שֶׂ֛ה וְכָל־בְּהֵמָ֖ה לִשְׁמֹ֑ר וּמֵ֛ת
י אוֹ־נִשְׁבַּ֥ר אוֹ־נִשְׁבָּ֖ה אֵ֥ין רֹאֶֽה׃ שְׁבֻעַ֣ת יְהוָ֗ה תִּהְיֶה֙ בֵּ֣ין שְׁנֵיהֶ֔ם
אִם־לֹ֥א שָׁלַ֛ח יָד֖וֹ בִּמְלֶ֣אכֶת רֵעֵ֑הוּ וְלָקַ֥ח בְּעָלָ֖יו וְלֹ֥א יְשַׁלֵּֽם׃
יא וְאִם־גָּנֹ֥ב יִגָּנֵ֖ב מֵעִמּ֑וֹ יְשַׁלֵּ֖ם לִבְעָלָֽיו׃ אִם־טָרֹ֥ף יִטָּרֵף֙ יְבִאֵ֣הוּ
עֵ֔ד הַטְּרֵפָ֖ה לֹ֥א יְשַׁלֵּֽם׃
יב וְכִֽי־יִשְׁאַ֥ל אִ֛ישׁ מֵעִ֥ם רֵעֵ֖הוּ וְנִשְׁבַּ֣ר אוֹ־מֵ֑ת בְּעָלָ֥יו אֵין־עִמּ֖וֹ
יג שַׁלֵּ֣ם יְשַׁלֵּֽם׃ אִם־בְּעָלָ֥יו עִמּ֖וֹ לֹ֣א יְשַׁלֵּ֑ם אִם־שָׂכִ֣יר ה֔וּא בָּ֖א

CLASSIC COMMENTATORS

The first two cases of watchmen presented by the Torah sound (vv. 6–8 and 9–12) very similar, but their laws are different.

RAMBAN

This first section deals with an unpaid watchman, which is why he is exempt if the item entrusted to his care is stolen, as our Rabbis understood. The text does not specify that the watchman is not being paid for his duty, because it is simply not customary to compensate a person who is given money or utensils to watch. However, the second passage describes a guard who is hired to watch a donkey, an ox, a sheep, or any other animal. We can understand that this individual is being paid, since it is common practice for shepherds and cowherds to take money for their services.

רמב״ן

פרשה זו נאמרה בשומר חנם, ולפיכך פטר בו את הגניבה, כפי קבלת רבותינו. ונזכר סתם בכתוב, מפני שדרך שומרי כסף או כלים לשמרם בחנם. והפרשה השניה שבשומר שכר הזכירה חמור או שור או שה וכל בהמה, ודרך הבהמות לתת ביד רועים לשמור, וידעו אותם בשכר.

15 make restitution; if the animal was hired, only the hiring fee is due. If a man seduces a
virgin who is not betrothed, and lies with her, he must pay her bride-price and marry
16 her. If her father refuses to let him marry her, he must still pay out the full bride-price for
17 virgins. Do not allow a witch to live. And any person who lies with an animal shall be put
18
19 to death. Whoever sacrifices to any deity other than the Lord shall be utterly destroyed.
20 Do not oppress a stranger or exploit him, for you yourselves were strangers in the land
21 of Egypt. Do not abuse a widow or an orphan. For if you do abuse them, if they cry out
22
23 to Me, I will unquestionably heed their cry. My anger will flare and I will kill you by
24 the sword – and then your wives will be widows and your children orphans. If you lend
money to one of My people who is poor, do not act with him as a harsh creditor, and do
25 not charge him interest. If you take your neighbor's garment as collateral, return it to him
26 before the sun sets, because it is his only clothing, the sole covering for his skin. What
else does he have in which to sleep? And if he cries out to Me, I will be listening: I am

---

RABBI OVADYA SFORNO

The Torah provides the nation with two possibilities. On the one hand it states, "There will be no poor among you" (Deut. 15:4), while on the other hand it warns Israel that, "There will always be poor people in the land" (Deut. 15:11). And now the text states that *if* the former promise does not come true, but the latter description is fulfilled, then the people will be required to lend money to the needy.

ר׳ עובדיה ספורנו

אם יהיה זה שלא יתקיים בישראל מה שנאמר "אפס כי לא יהיה בך אביון" (דברים ט״ו:ד׳), אבל יתקיים בהם "כי לא יחדל אביון" (שם ט״ו:י״א), ואז יקרה שתלוה.

QUESTIONS FOR THOUGHT

- How would Rashi translate the word אם?
- Ibn Ezra and Sforno seemingly agree that אם should be understood as "if," but they disagree regarding the focus of that word. Who does each of them think is the focus of the "if," which would then trigger the obligation to lend?
- Most of the mitzvot in this *parasha* focus on the consequence of doing something bad to someone else. This mitzva requires us to do something positive for someone in need even though we had no hand in causing their predicament. What value do you think the Torah is trying to promote here, especially considering that this is the first full set of instructions the nation receives after leaving Egypt?

WISDOM OF THE HEART

Notice that when describing how we should not mistreat a stranger, the Torah uses multiple doubled phrases – ענה תענה and שמע אשמע. The Kotzker Rebbe explains that when somebody hurts an orphan or a widow it really is a double blow. The first wound refers to what was said or done. The second wound is the additional suffering caused by the victim who is forced to confront the objective difficulties caused by his or her unfortunate situation. This dual pain evokes a dual cry to God, and the dual promise that God will listen.

שמות | פרק כב — משפטים | 195

טו בְּשִׁכְרוֹ: וְכִי־יְפַתֶּה אִישׁ בְּתוּלָה אֲשֶׁר לֹא־אֹרָשָׂה
טז וְשָׁכַב עִמָּהּ מָהֹר יִמְהָרֶנָּה לּוֹ לְאִשָּׁה: אִם־מָאֵן יְמָאֵן אָבִיהָ
יז לְתִתָּהּ לוֹ כֶּסֶף יִשְׁקֹל כְּמֹהַר הַבְּתוּלֹת: מְכַשֵּׁפָה
יח לֹא תְחַיֶּה: כָּל־שֹׁכֵב עִם־בְּהֵמָה מוֹת יוּמָת: זֹבֵחַ
יט לָאֱלֹהִים יָחֳרָם בִּלְתִּי לַיהוה לְבַדּוֹ: וְגֵר לֹא־תוֹנֶה וְלֹא תִלְחָצֶנּוּ
כ כִּי־גֵרִים הֱיִיתֶם בְּאֶרֶץ מִצְרָיִם: כָּל־אַלְמָנָה וְיָתוֹם לֹא תְעַנּוּן:
כא אִם־עַנֵּה תְעַנֶּה אֹתוֹ כִּי אִם־צָעֹק יִצְעַק אֵלַי שָׁמֹעַ אֶשְׁמַע
כב צַעֲקָתוֹ: וְחָרָה אַפִּי וְהָרַגְתִּי אֶתְכֶם בֶּחָרֶב וְהָיוּ נְשֵׁיכֶם אַלְמָנוֹת
כג וּבְנֵיכֶם יְתֹמִים:
כד אִם־כֶּסֶף ׀ תַּלְוֶה אֶת־עַמִּי אֶת־הֶעָנִי עִמָּךְ לֹא־תִהְיֶה לוֹ כְּנֹשֶׁה יז
כה לֹא־תְשִׂימוּן עָלָיו נֶשֶׁךְ: אִם־חָבֹל תַּחְבֹּל שַׂלְמַת רֵעֶךָ עַד־
כו בֹּא הַשֶּׁמֶשׁ תְּשִׁיבֶנּוּ לוֹ: כִּי הִוא כְסוּתֹה לְבַדָּהּ הִוא שִׂמְלָתוֹ
לְעֹרוֹ בַּמֶּה יִשְׁכָּב וְהָיָה כִּי־יִצְעַק אֵלַי וְשָׁמַעְתִּי כִּי־חַנּוּן

CLASSIC COMMENTATORS

The Torah introduces the idea of loans with the phrase, "If you lend money …," suggesting that one can choose whether or not to lend money to a poor person. Yet Leviticus 25:35 indicates that it is an obligation. How can we resolve this apparent contradiction?

רש"י — **RASHI**

רבי ישמעאל אומר: כל אם ואם שבתורה רשות חוץ מג', וזה אחד מהן.

Rabbi Yishmael teaches: Whenever the Torah uses the word "if" [אם] it connotes an optional action, except for three cases, and this is one of them [as the Torah really means: *when* you lend money, since charity is an obligation – not a choice].

אבן עזרא — **IBN EZRA**

אם נתן לך השם הון שתוכל להלוות העני.

When the Torah states "If you lend money" what it means is: If God has graced you with enough wealth to be able to help the poor.

²⁷ gracious. Do not curse a judge, and do not deride a leader of your people. Do not delay
²⁸ offerings from your harvest of grain or wine. The firstborn of your sons you must give
²⁹ to Me. Likewise with your oxen and sheep; let them stay with their mothers for seven
³⁰ days, and on the eighth, give them over to Me. You are to be My holy people. Do not eat
23 ¹ flesh torn by beasts in the wild. Throw it to the dogs. Do not accept a false report. Do
² not join with an unscrupulous person to bear corrupt witness. Do not follow the crowd
to do evil. When you give testimony in a lawsuit, do not pervert justice by siding with
³ the crowd. Do not show favoritism even to a poor man in a dispute. If you come across
⁴
⁵ your enemy's ox or donkey going astray – bring it back to him. If you see the donkey of
someone who hates you, fallen under its load, resist the impulse to leave it there. Help
⁶ him to release it. Do not subvert the rights of the needy when they come to court. Keep
⁷ far from a false charge. Do not bring death on the innocent and righteous, for I will
⁸ not acquit the wrongdoer. Take no bribe, for bribes blind the sighted and subvert the
⁹ cause of the just. Do not oppress a stranger. You know what it is to be a stranger, for you

---

RAMBAN

It seems to me that when the Torah warns its adherents not to "oppress a stranger or exploit him" it anticipates the Israelite believing that he can take advantage of the outsider because the latter has no rescuer to whom he can turn. To counter this, the verse reminds us that when *Benei Yisrael* were foreigners in Egypt, God witnessed the abuse they suffered and avenged that injustice. For the Lord sees all, especially "the victims' tears with none to console them from their oppressors" (Eccl. 4:1). Thus, God vows to rescue all the powerless individuals from those who are stronger than they.

רמב״ן

והנכון בעיני, כי יאמר לא תונה את הגר ולא תלחצנו, ותחשוב שאין לו מציל מידך, כי אתה ידעת שהייתם גרים במצרים, וראיתי את הלחץ אשר מצרים לוחצים אתכם, ועשיתי בהם נקמה, כי אני ה' רואה את "דמעות העשוקים אשר אין להם מנחם מיד עושקיהם" (קהלת ד' א') ואני מציל כל אדם מיד חזק ממנו.

SEFER HAḤINUCH

The Torah mentions Israel's history to remind us that we have been burned with this great suffering of oppression. Thus, whenever one sees a foreigner, he must recall what it is like to be an outsider in a strange land. On a national level we can empathize with such a class of people, since we recall the Egyptian slavery. How fortunate were we that in His compassion and righteousness God rescued us from that abuse. We should therefore learn from God's example and demonstrate understanding toward all individuals.

ספר החינוך

הזכיר לנו שכבר נכווינו בצער הגדול הזה, שיש לכל איש הרואה את עצמו בתוך אנשים זרים בארץ נכריה, ובזכרונו גודל דאגת הלב שיש בדבר, וכי כבר עבר עלינו והשם יתברך ברחמיו ובחסדיו הוציאנו משם, יכמרו רחמינו על כל אדם שהוא כן.

QUESTIONS FOR THOUGHT

- Which of the commentaries presents this rationale from a purely practical perspective?
- Which understands it as presenting a moral imperative?
- Which understands it as a reminder of universal divine protection for the unprotected?
- Which of these approaches would you use to explain this mitzva to someone else?

שמות | פרק כב | משפטים | 197

כז אֱלֹהִ֖ים לֹ֣א תְקַלֵּ֑ל וְנָשִׂ֥יא בְעַמְּךָ֖ לֹ֥א תָאֹֽר׃ אֲנִ֥י׃ רביעי

כח מְלֵאָתְךָ֥ וְדִמְעֲךָ֖ לֹ֣א תְאַחֵ֑ר בְּכ֥וֹר בָּנֶ֖יךָ תִּתֶּן־לִֽי׃ כֵּֽן־תַּעֲשֶׂ֥ה לְשֹׁרְךָ֖ לְצֹאנֶ֑ךָ שִׁבְעַ֤ת יָמִים֙ יִהְיֶ֣ה עִם־אִמּ֔וֹ בַּיּ֥וֹם הַשְּׁמִינִ֖י

ל תִּתְּנוֹ־לִֽי׃ וְאַנְשֵׁי־קֹ֖דֶשׁ תִּהְי֣וּן לִ֑י וּבָשָׂ֨ר בַּשָּׂדֶ֤ה טְרֵפָה֙ לֹ֣א

כג א תֹאכֵ֔לוּ לַכֶּ֖לֶב תַּשְׁלִכ֥וּן אֹתֽוֹ׃ לֹ֥א תִשָּׂ֖א שֵׁ֣מַע שָׁ֑וְא

ב אַל־תָּ֤שֶׁת יָֽדְךָ֙ עִם־רָשָׁ֔ע לִהְיֹ֖ת עֵ֥ד חָמָֽס׃ לֹֽא־תִהְיֶ֥ה אַחֲרֵי־רַבִּ֖ים לְרָעֹ֑ת וְלֹא־תַעֲנֶ֣ה עַל־רִ֔ב לִנְטֹ֛ת אַחֲרֵ֥י רַבִּ֖ים לְהַטֹּֽת׃

ג וְדָ֕ל לֹ֥א תֶהְדַּ֖ר בְּרִיבֽוֹ׃ כִּ֣י תִפְגַּ֞ע שׁ֧וֹר אֹֽיִבְךָ֛ א֥וֹ חֲמֹר֖וֹ

ד תֹּעֶ֑ה הָשֵׁ֥ב תְּשִׁיבֶ֖נּוּ לֽוֹ׃ כִּֽי־תִרְאֶ֞ה חֲמ֣וֹר שֹׂנַאֲךָ֗ רֹבֵץ֙

ה תַּ֣חַת מַשָּׂא֔וֹ וְחָדַלְתָּ֖ מֵעֲזֹ֣ב ל֑וֹ עָזֹ֥ב תַּעֲזֹ֖ב עִמּֽוֹ׃ לֹ֥א חמישי

ו תַטֶּ֛ה מִשְׁפַּ֥ט אֶבְיֹנְךָ֖ בְּרִיבֽוֹ׃ מִדְּבַר־שֶׁ֖קֶר תִּרְחָ֑ק וְנָקִ֤י וְצַדִּיק֙

ז אַֽל־תַּהֲרֹ֔ג כִּ֥י לֹא־אַצְדִּ֖יק רָשָֽׁע׃ וְשֹׁ֖חַד לֹ֣א תִקָּ֑ח כִּ֤י הַשֹּׁ֨חַד֙ יְעַוֵּ֣ר

ח פִּקְחִ֔ים וִֽיסַלֵּ֖ף דִּבְרֵ֥י צַדִּיקִֽים׃ וְגֵ֖ר לֹ֣א תִלְחָ֑ץ וְאַתֶּ֗ם יְדַעְתֶּם֙ אֶת־

CLASSIC COMMENTATORS

The Torah repeatedly (at least thirty-six times!) warns that we must treat a foreigner fairly, sometimes adding the explanation that we too were foreigners in Egypt. This reasoning can be understood in many ways.

RASHI — רש״י

If you disparage the stranger [by mocking his origins], he can turn the tables on you and say: You are also descended from strangers. Such is the common proverb: Do not point out a blemish in your fellow that you also share.

אם הוניתו, אף הוא יכול להונותך ולומר: אף אתה מגרים באת, מום שבך אל תאמר לחבירך.

10 yourselves were strangers in the land of Egypt. For six years, sow your land and gather its
11 crops, but in the seventh let it rest and lie fallow. Let the needy of your people eat from it, and what they leave, let the wild animals eat. Do the same with your vineyards and
12 olive groves. For six days carry out your work, but on the seventh you must cease, so that your ox and donkey may rest, and even the children of maidservants and strangers be
13 revived. Take care in all that I have said to you. Never invoke the names of other gods;
14 let them never pass your lips. Three times a year, celebrate a festival for Me. Keep the
15 Festival of Unleavened Bread. For seven days, eat unleavened bread as I commanded you, at the time appointed, in the month of Aviv, for at that time you left Egypt. Do not
16 appear before Me empty-handed. Likewise, keep the Festival of the Harvest, of the first fruits of the produce that you sowed in the field. Keep the Festival of Ingathering at the
17 end of the year, when you gather in the fruit of your labor from the field. Three times a
18 year, all the males among you shall appear before the Master, the Lord. Do not offer the blood of my sacrifice together with anything leavened. Do not let the fat of My festive
19 offering remain until morning. Bring the best first fruits of your land to the house of the Lord your God. Do not boil a kid in the milk of its mother.

RABBI OVADYA SFORNO

If you allow the children of your maidservants and the strangers to rest on the seventh day, you will be acting in a manner opposite to the way you were treated in Egypt. For when Israel were slaves there, they were given no respite from their labors, as the verse states, "Make the work harder for the people" (5:9). Such graciousness will compel the nation to recall the exodus from Egypt, just as the text of the Ten Commandments directs, when it states [in the context of the Sabbath], "Remember that you were slaves in Egypt" (Deut. 5:15).

ר׳ עובדיה ספורנו

ומזה ימשך שינפש גם בן אמתך הגר, על היפך מה שקרה לך במצרים כשהיית שם עבד, שלא היתה לך מנוחה, כאמרו "תכבד העבדה על האנשים" (שמות ה׳:ט׳), ובזה תזכור יציאת מצרים, כמו שאמר בדברות משנה תורה "וזכרת כי עבד היית".

RABBI DAVID TZVI HOFFMAN

The rest that the Sabbath provides must be extended even to our servants and to our cattle. We must not allow these people and beasts to labor away on this day for our profit. Israel is called upon to demonstrate that our help and our animals were not created for our sake. Rather, we must acknowledge that all creatures were made for the purpose of serving God and exalting Him. This is why we are obligated to treat them well and grant them time to rest.

ר׳ דוד צבי הופמן

על מנוחה זו להתפשט גם על עבדינו ובהמתנו, אל לנו להניח להם לעבוד ביום זה להביא לנו תועלת, כדי להפגין שברואים אלה אינם עלי אדמות בשבילנו, אלא גם אנחנו וגם הם נבראו לעבוד את ה׳ ולפארו, ולכן אנו חייבים להיטיב עמהם וליתן להם מנוחה.

QUESTIONS FOR THOUGHT

- On what point do Ramban and Sforno agree? Regarding what do they disagree?
- According to Sforno's understanding, how does this mitzva connect back to the beginning of *Parashat Mishpatim*?
- What is the great innovation in R. David Tzvi Hoffman's explanation?

שמות | פרק כג

י נֶפֶשׁ הַגֵּר כִּי־גֵרִים הֱיִיתֶם בְּאֶרֶץ מִצְרָיִם: וְשֵׁשׁ שָׁנִים תִּזְרַע אֶת־
יא אַרְצֶךָ וְאָסַפְתָּ אֶת־תְּבוּאָתָהּ: וְהַשְּׁבִיעִת תִּשְׁמְטֶנָּה וּנְטַשְׁתָּהּ
וְאָכְלוּ אֶבְיֹנֵי עַמֶּךָ וְיִתְרָם תֹּאכַל חַיַּת הַשָּׂדֶה כֵּן־תַּעֲשֶׂה לְכַרְמְךָ
יב לְזֵיתֶךָ: שֵׁשֶׁת יָמִים תַּעֲשֶׂה מַעֲשֶׂיךָ וּבַיּוֹם הַשְּׁבִיעִי תִּשְׁבֹּת
יג לְמַעַן יָנוּחַ שׁוֹרְךָ וַחֲמֹרֶךָ וְיִנָּפֵשׁ בֶּן־אֲמָתְךָ וְהַגֵּר: וּבְכֹל אֲשֶׁר־
אָמַרְתִּי אֲלֵיכֶם תִּשָּׁמֵרוּ וְשֵׁם אֱלֹהִים אֲחֵרִים לֹא תַזְכִּירוּ לֹא
יד יִשָּׁמַע עַל־פִּיךָ: שָׁלֹשׁ רְגָלִים תָּחֹג לִי בַּשָּׁנָה: אֶת־חַג הַמַּצּוֹת
תִּשְׁמֹר שִׁבְעַת יָמִים תֹּאכַל מַצּוֹת כַּאֲשֶׁר צִוִּיתִךָ לְמוֹעֵד חֹדֶשׁ
הָאָבִיב כִּי־בוֹ יָצָאתָ מִמִּצְרָיִם וְלֹא־יֵרָאוּ פָנַי רֵיקָם: וְחַג הַקָּצִיר
טז בִּכּוּרֵי מַעֲשֶׂיךָ אֲשֶׁר תִּזְרַע בַּשָּׂדֶה וְחַג הָאָסִף בְּצֵאת הַשָּׁנָה
יז בְּאָסְפְּךָ אֶת־מַעֲשֶׂיךָ מִן־הַשָּׂדֶה: שָׁלֹשׁ פְּעָמִים בַּשָּׁנָה יֵרָאֶה
יח כָּל־זְכוּרְךָ אֶל־פְּנֵי הָאָדֹן ׀ יְהֹוָה: לֹא־תִזְבַּח עַל־חָמֵץ דַּם־זִבְחִי
יט וְלֹא־יָלִין חֵלֶב־חַגִּי עַד־בֹּקֶר: רֵאשִׁית בִּכּוּרֵי אַדְמָתְךָ תָּבִיא
בֵּית יְהֹוָה אֱלֹהֶיךָ לֹא־תְבַשֵּׁל גְּדִי בַּחֲלֵב אִמּוֹ:

CLASSIC COMMENTATORS

When discussing Shabbat, the verse states, "... so that your ox and donkey may rest, and even the children of maidservants and strangers be revived." Is the purpose of Shabbat only to provide time for workers to rest? What about the other reasons mentioned in the Ten Commandments in Exodus (20:8–11) and Deuteronomy (5:12–15)?

RAMBAN רמב״ן

The Torah commands, "For six days carry out your work" in your house and in your fields so that on the seventh day "the children of maidservants and strangers" can rest. If you do that, all people will be able to testify to the creation of the world.

ששת ימים תעשה כל מעשיך בבית ובשדה בעבור שינוח בשביעי בן אמתך והגר, להיות כלם עדים במעשה בראשית.

> God promises to send His messenger to bring Benei Yisrael to their promised land, where they are instructed to destroy the institutions of idolatry established by the nations who preceded them. They need to be careful, however, because that divine messenger will not tolerate Israel's straying from the proper behavior.

20 I am sending a messenger ahead of you to guard you on the way and to bring you to
21 the place that I have prepared. Heed his presence and listen to his voice. Do not rebel against him, for he will not let your transgression pass, because My name is with him.
22 But if you listen carefully to him and do all that I tell you, then I will be an Enemy to
23 your enemies, a Foe to your foes. When My messenger goes ahead of you and brings you to the Amorites, Hittites, Perizzites, Canaanites, Hivites and Jebusites, and I wipe
24 them out, do not bow down to their gods or worship them, and do not do as they do.
25 Demolish their gods and shatter their worship pillars. Serve the LORD your God, and He

---

QUESTIONS FOR THOUGHT

- According to Rashbam, when did this מלאך actually come to help *Benei Yisrael*? Which parts of our text would be challenging for Rashbam to explain?
- Ralbag understands that we are not talking about a supernatural being, but a prophet. Which parts of our text would Ralbag have a difficult time explaining?
- How does R. Avraham ben HaRambam try to avoid the problems faced by the other two commentaries? What difficulty will he face in explaining this section?

TEXTUAL SKILLS

1. After the sin of the golden calf (33:2–3), God threatens to send a מלאך instead of His presence. Could these verses be referring to the same מלאך mentioned there?

2. In verse 25 God promises to banish all sickness from their midst. Where have you seen a similar message earlier in Exodus?

QUICK BITE

Rabbi Natan of Breslov teaches that even when we are the darkest of places, God sends an angel there with us to assist our prayers in reaching His holy throne. The Talmud identifies this angel as Metatron. The Ramban, citing Rashi, points out that the numerical value of מטטרון is equal to God's name שדי. This emissary is carrying out God's will for us – "My name is with him" (verse 21). But sometimes we need to do this on our own. Earlier in Bereshit (32:24) we find that "Yaakov was left alone." The Koidenover Rebbe teaches that at a certain point we have to take leave of our angels and fend for ourselves. At the end of the day, we cannot expect anything or anyone outside of ourselves to do the work for us.

כ הִנֵּ֨ה אָנֹכִ֜י שֹׁלֵ֤חַ מַלְאָךְ֙ לְפָנֶ֔יךָ לִשְׁמָרְךָ֖ בַּדָּ֑רֶךְ וְלַהֲבִ֣יאֲךָ֔ אֶל־ ששי

כא הַמָּק֖וֹם אֲשֶׁ֥ר הֲכִנֹֽתִי׃ הִשָּׁ֧מֶר מִפָּנָ֛יו וּשְׁמַ֥ע בְּקֹל֖וֹ אַל־תַּמֵּ֣ר בּ֑וֹ כִּ֣י

כב לֹ֤א יִשָּׂא֙ לְפִשְׁעֲכֶ֔ם כִּ֥י שְׁמִ֖י בְּקִרְבּֽוֹ׃ כִּ֣י אִם־שָׁמ֤וֹעַ תִּשְׁמַע֙ בְּקֹל֔וֹ וְעָשִׂ֕יתָ כֹּ֖ל אֲשֶׁ֣ר אֲדַבֵּ֑ר וְאָֽיַבְתִּי֙ אֶת־אֹ֣יְבֶ֔יךָ וְצַרְתִּ֖י אֶת־צֹרְרֶֽיךָ׃

כג כִּֽי־יֵלֵ֣ךְ מַלְאָכִי֮ לְפָנֶיךָ֒ וֶהֱבִֽיאֲךָ֗ אֶל־הָֽאֱמֹרִי֙ וְהַ֣חִתִּ֔י וְהַפְּרִזִּ֔י

כד וְהַֽכְּנַעֲנִ֔י הַחִוִּ֖י וְהַיְבוּסִ֑י וְהִכְחַדְתִּֽיו׃ לֹֽא־תִשְׁתַּחֲוֶ֤ה לֵאלֹֽהֵיהֶם֙ וְלֹ֣א תָֽעָבְדֵ֔ם וְלֹ֥א תַעֲשֶׂ֖ה כְּמַעֲשֵׂיהֶ֑ם כִּ֤י הָרֵס֙ תְּהָ֣רְסֵ֔ם וְשַׁבֵּ֥ר

כה תְּשַׁבֵּ֖ר מַצֵּבֹתֵיהֶֽם׃ וַעֲבַדְתֶּ֗ם אֵ֚ת יְהֹוָ֣ה אֱלֹֽהֵיכֶ֔ם וּבֵרַ֥ךְ אֶת־

CLASSIC COMMENTATORS

The Hebrew word מלאך can be translated as "messenger" or as "angel", which is a messenger of God. In verse 20 God says that He will send a מלאך to protect *Benei Yisrael*, bring them to the land, and help them conquer it. The Torah adds that this מלאך will have God's name "with him" and will not tolerate deviation from God's laws. What kind of מלאך is this?

RASHBAM — רשב״ם

The messenger mentioned here is similar to the figure Yehoshua encounters, who states that he has arrived to rescue Israel: "I am the commander of the Lord's hosts. Now I have come!" (Josh. 5:14).

כדכתיב ביהושע (ה:יד) "כי אני שר צבא ה' עתה באתי" להושיע את ישראל.

RABBI AVRAHAM BEN HARAMBAM — ר' אברהם בן הרמב״ם

The verse relates back to an earlier description of Israel's departure from Egypt about which the verse states, "Then the angel of God who had been traveling ahead of the Israelite camp moved and went behind them" (14:19).

כמו שביאר ביציאתם ממצרים (שמות יד:יט) "ויסע מלאך האלהים וגו'".

RALBAG — רלב״ג

The messenger who is introduced here is a human prophet, a personality who is sometimes called a *malakh*. Now when God states that "My name is with him" what God means is that His communication is being conveyed through the prophet. For God's message is what a prophet takes away from his encounter with the Almighty. And hence the word of the prophet represents the word of the Lord, may He be blessed.

מלאך הוא נביא, כי הנביא יקרא "מלאך". כי שמי בקרבו: הנה קרא דברו "שמו", כי דבר ה' לנביא הוא מה שהגיע לנו מהידיעה בנימוסים הנמצאות ולזה היה המימרה בנביא – ממרה בה' יתברך.

> God will send terrifying forces to remove the obstacles that might make it difficult for Benei Yisrael to conquer and settle the land. He promises them long and fruitful lives in the promised land, but they need to be careful, to avoid getting too friendly with the locals, lest they be influenced to worship their gods.

26 will bless your bread, your water. I will banish all sickness from your midst. No woman in your land will suffer miscarriage or barrenness. I will fill out the full measure of your
27 years. I will send My terror before you, throwing into panic all the people you come
28 upon. All you will see of your enemies will be their fleeing backs. I will send hornets ahead of you, and they will drive the Hivites, Canaanites and Hittites out before you.
29 I will not drive them out in a single year, lest the land become desolate and the wild
30 animals too numerous for you. No – little by little I will drive them out before you, as
31 you burgeon and come to take possession of the land. I will set your borders from the Sea of Reeds to the Sea of the Philistines, and from the wilderness to the Euphrates, for I will deliver the inhabitants of the land into your hands: you will drive them out before
32/33 you. Make no covenant with them and their gods. They must not stay in your land, for they would make you sin against Me. If you worship their gods, it will be a trap for you."

RABBI YOSEF IBN KASPI
ר׳ יוסף אבן כספי

The *tzir'a* is like the bee, only more dangerous.

הוא מין הדבורים היותר רע.

ḤIZKUNI
חזקוני

God here presents a message: I do not require the sword nor do I need bows and arrows to drive the Canaanites from the land. Rather, I can achieve that with something small like the *tzir'a*.

משל הוא: לא בחרב ולא בקשת אני מגרשם אלא בדבר קל.

QUESTIONS FOR THOUGHT

- According to the various explanations, is the צרעה something powerful or weak? Which makes sense to you in the text of the Torah?
- According to the various explanations, is verse 28 linked to or separate from the verse that precedes it?

TEXTUAL SKILLS

1. The word צרעה appears only three times in all of Tanakh, and all refer to what God sends in advance of *Benei Yisrael*'s capture of the land.
2. In verse 29 God says that He will not chase out all the enemies at once, lest wild animals fill the vacuum left by their departure. Where else in the Torah do we find a concern about wild animals displacing people?

לַחְמְךָ וְאֶת־מֵימֶיךָ וַהֲסִרֹתִי מַחֲלָה מִקִּרְבֶּךָ: לֹא
תִהְיֶה מְשַׁכֵּלָה וַעֲקָרָה בְּאַרְצֶךָ אֶת־מִסְפַּר יָמֶיךָ אֲמַלֵּא:
אֶת־אֵימָתִי אֲשַׁלַּח לְפָנֶיךָ וְהַמֹּתִי אֶת־כָּל־הָעָם אֲשֶׁר תָּבֹא
בָּהֶם וְנָתַתִּי אֶת־כָּל־אֹיְבֶיךָ אֵלֶיךָ עֹרֶף: וְשָׁלַחְתִּי אֶת־הַצִּרְעָה
לְפָנֶיךָ וְגֵרְשָׁה אֶת־הַחִוִּי אֶת־הַכְּנַעֲנִי וְאֶת־הַחִתִּי מִלְּפָנֶיךָ: לֹא
אֲגָרְשֶׁנּוּ מִפָּנֶיךָ בְּשָׁנָה אֶחָת פֶּן־תִּהְיֶה הָאָרֶץ שְׁמָמָה וְרַבָּה
עָלֶיךָ חַיַּת הַשָּׂדֶה: מְעַט מְעַט אֲגָרְשֶׁנּוּ מִפָּנֶיךָ עַד אֲשֶׁר תִּפְרֶה
וְנָחַלְתָּ אֶת־הָאָרֶץ: וְשַׁתִּי אֶת־גְּבֻלְךָ מִיַּם־סוּף וְעַד־יָם פְּלִשְׁתִּים
וּמִמִּדְבָּר עַד־הַנָּהָר כִּי ׀ אֶתֵּן בְּיֶדְכֶם אֵת יֹשְׁבֵי הָאָרֶץ וְגֵרַשְׁתָּמוֹ
מִפָּנֶיךָ: לֹא־תִכְרֹת לָהֶם וְלֵאלֹהֵיהֶם בְּרִית: לֹא יֵשְׁבוּ בְּאַרְצְךָ
פֶּן־יַחֲטִיאוּ אֹתְךָ לִי כִּי תַעֲבֹד אֶת־אֱלֹהֵיהֶם כִּי־יִהְיֶה לְךָ
לְמוֹקֵשׁ:

CLASSIC COMMENTATORS

God promises to send the צרעה to chase away the Canaanite nations. What is this צרעה?

IBN EZRA
אבן עזרא
מכה בגוף מגזרת "צרעת" שתחלש כוח הגוף.

The *tzir'a* with which God threatens to strike the Canaanites is a plague that weakens the body. The term is related to the term *tza'ra'at* [leprosy].

RAMBAN
רמב״ן
הוא מין ידוע כגון הדבורה ... והענין, כי ישלח המכה הזו באויר ארצם כמו הארבה, ששלח במצרים והילק החסיל והגזם חילו הגדול בימי יואל. וטעם "וגרשה", כי הוא סיבה בהם לגרשה מן הארץ, כי תכסה את עין הארץ ותחשך ולא יוכלו לבוא במלחמה, ועוד כי תאכל כל יגיעם בשדה.

The *tzir'a* is a well-known species of the bee family… God informs Israel that He will send this plague across the land, through the air like the locust infestation He dispatched to Egypt, and the canker-worm, the caterpillar, and the palmer-worm which arrived in the times of Yoel. These hornets will act to drive out the Canaanites from the land by virtue of the fact that they will completely obscure the earth. It will then become so dark that the enemy will be unable to field an army. Furthermore, these hordes of insects will devour the crops of the fields.

SHEMOT | CHAPTER 24 — MISHPATIM

24 ¹ Then He said to Moshe, "Ascend to the Lord, you and Aharon, Nadav and Avihu, and ² seventy of Israel's elders and bow down from afar. Moshe alone shall approach the ³ Lord. The others must not come close, nor shall the people come up with him." Moshe came and told the people all the Lord's words and laws, and the people all responded ⁴ with one voice, "All that the Lord has spoken we shall do." Then Moshe wrote down all the Lord's words. Early the next morning he rose and built an altar at the base of ⁵ the mountain, and also twelve pillars for the twelve tribes of Israel. Then he sent young men of Israel, and they sacrificed bulls as burnt offerings and peace offerings to the ⁶ Lord. Moshe took half the blood and put it in bowls. The other half he sprinkled on ⁷ the altar. Then he took the book of the covenant and read it aloud to the people. They ⁸ replied, "All that the Lord has spoken we shall do and we shall heed." Then Moshe took the blood, sprinkled it on the people, and said, "This is the blood of the covenant that ⁹ the Lord is making with you regarding all these words." Then Moshe went up with ¹⁰ Aharon, Nadav, Avihu, and seventy of Israel's elders. They saw a vision of the God of Israel, and beneath his feet what looked like a lapis lazuli pavement as clear as the sky ¹¹ itself. And He did the leaders of Israel no harm – and they looked upon God and they

---

אבן עזרא

לא שלח ידו - כי ראו השם הנכבד ולא מתו, כאשר אפרש בפסוק: "כי לא יראני האדם וחי. ויאכלו וישתו - שירדו שמחים מהר, ויאכלו - זבחי שלמים שזבחו נעריהם, וישתו - בשמחה."

IBN EZRA

The verse points out that these individuals saw the glory of God but did not die, as I will explain in my commentary to the verse, "For no one can see Me and live" (33:20). Meanwhile, when our verse states that "they ate and they drank", it means that that they descended the mountain in a happy mood. What they ate were the peace offerings that the young men had sacrificed, while they drank in happiness.

רמב״ן

לא שלח ידו - בעבור שאמר: "והכהנים והעם אל יהרסו לעלות אל ה' פן יפרץ בם" (שמות י״ט:כ״ד), הודיע בכאן שנזהרו בכך ולא פרץ בהם פרץ, כי היו אצילי בני ישראל ראויים למה שחזו במחזה הזה, והטעם כי חזו את האלהים, ולא הרסו לעלות אל ה'. וטעם ויאכלו וישתו - שאכלו שם השלמים בתחתית ההר לפני האלהים טרם שישובו אל אהליהם.

RAMBAN

Earlier God had warned Israel not to approach the mountain stating, "Do not let the priests or people force their way through to come up to the Lord, or He will break out against them" (19:24). And now God declares that indeed the people had taken care to follow this order, and as such God had not broken out against them. Thus, the nobles of Israel remained worthy of seeing the vision of God. This means that these individuals "looked upon God" but they did not "force their way through to come up to the Lord." As for the clause stating that the men "ate and they drank", that means that they consumed the peace offerings at the foot of the mountain before God, prior to returning to their tents.

QUESTIONS FOR THOUGHT

- According to the different commentaries, did these people do something wrong or something right?
- Each of the commentaries quoted here suggests that God "not sending His hand" meant that they did not die, but they differ greatly on why we would have thought that they should die. What are their different positions?

שמות | פרק כד | משפטים

כד א וְאֶל־מֹשֶׁה אָמַר עֲלֵה אֶל־יהוה אַתָּה וְאַהֲרֹן נָדָב וַאֲבִיהוּא
ב וְשִׁבְעִים מִזִּקְנֵי יִשְׂרָאֵל וְהִשְׁתַּחֲוִיתֶם מֵרָחֹק: וְנִגַּשׁ מֹשֶׁה
ג לְבַדּוֹ אֶל־יהוה וְהֵם לֹא יִגָּשׁוּ וְהָעָם לֹא יַעֲלוּ עִמּוֹ: וַיָּבֹא מֹשֶׁה
וַיְסַפֵּר לָעָם אֵת כָּל־דִּבְרֵי יהוה וְאֵת כָּל־הַמִּשְׁפָּטִים וַיַּעַן
כָּל־הָעָם קוֹל אֶחָד וַיֹּאמְרוּ כָּל־הַדְּבָרִים אֲשֶׁר־דִּבֶּר יהוה
ד נַעֲשֶׂה: וַיִּכְתֹּב מֹשֶׁה אֵת כָּל־דִּבְרֵי יהוה וַיַּשְׁכֵּם בַּבֹּקֶר וַיִּבֶן
מִזְבֵּחַ תַּחַת הָהָר וּשְׁתֵּים עֶשְׂרֵה מַצֵּבָה לִשְׁנֵים עָשָׂר שִׁבְטֵי
ה יִשְׂרָאֵל: וַיִּשְׁלַח אֶת־נַעֲרֵי בְּנֵי יִשְׂרָאֵל וַיַּעֲלוּ עֹלֹת וַיִּזְבְּחוּ זְבָחִים
ו שְׁלָמִים לַיהוה פָּרִים: וַיִּקַּח מֹשֶׁה חֲצִי הַדָּם וַיָּשֶׂם בָּאַגָּנֹת
ז וַחֲצִי הַדָּם זָרַק עַל־הַמִּזְבֵּחַ: וַיִּקַּח סֵפֶר הַבְּרִית וַיִּקְרָא בְּאָזְנֵי
ח הָעָם וַיֹּאמְרוּ כֹּל אֲשֶׁר־דִּבֶּר יהוה נַעֲשֶׂה וְנִשְׁמָע: וַיִּקַּח מֹשֶׁה
אֶת־הַדָּם וַיִּזְרֹק עַל־הָעָם וַיֹּאמֶר הִנֵּה דַם־הַבְּרִית אֲשֶׁר כָּרַת
ט יהוה עִמָּכֶם עַל כָּל־הַדְּבָרִים הָאֵלֶּה: וַיַּעַל מֹשֶׁה וְאַהֲרֹן נָדָב
י וַאֲבִיהוּא וְשִׁבְעִים מִזִּקְנֵי יִשְׂרָאֵל: וַיִּרְאוּ אֵת אֱלֹהֵי יִשְׂרָאֵל
וְתַחַת רַגְלָיו כְּמַעֲשֵׂה לִבְנַת הַסַּפִּיר וּכְעֶצֶם הַשָּׁמַיִם לָטֹהַר:
יא וְאֶל־אֲצִילֵי בְּנֵי יִשְׂרָאֵל לֹא שָׁלַח יָדוֹ וַיֶּחֱזוּ אֶת־הָאֱלֹהִים

CLASSIC COMMENTATORS

The end of this section describes the unique revelation experienced by the elders along with Nadav and Avihu and adds that "God did not send His hand." This strange description raised the curiosity of the commentaries, who offer dramatically different explanations.

RASHI

The term *atzilei* refers to Nadav, Avihu, and the elders.
When the verse states that "He did not send His hand" it means he did not harm them, implying that they indeed deserved to be harmed. These men looked upon God with arrogance while they were still eating and drinking.

רש״י

ואל אצילי – הם נדב ואביהוא והזקנים.
לא שלח ידו – מכאן שהיו ראויין להשלחת יד.
ויחזו את האלהים – היו מסתכלין בו בלב גס
מתוך אכילה ושתיה.

12 ate and they drank. The LORD said to Moshe, "Ascend to Me on the mountain, and as you stand there I will give you the stone tablets with the teaching and commandments
13 that I have written to instruct the people." So Moshe set out with Yehoshua, his disciple,
14 and ascended the mountain of God. He told the elders, "Wait for us here until we return to you. Aharon and Ḥur will stay here with you; whoever has a dispute shall go to them."
15/16 As Moshe climbed the mountain, it was covered in a cloud. The glory of the LORD rested on Mount Sinai, and the cloud covered it for six days. On the seventh, He called
17 to Moshe from within the cloud. To the Israelites the appearance of the LORD's glory
18 on the mountaintop was like consuming fire. Moshe entered the cloud and climbed the mountain, and he stayed there for forty days and forty nights.

RABBI OVADYA SFORNO

ר' עובדיה ספורנו

והתורה – החלק העיוני ממנה.
והמצוה – הוא חלק המעשי ממנה.
אשר כתבתי – כי לולא חטאו בעגל היתה כל התורה נתונה חתומה מיד הבורא יתברך כמו הלוחות ... ומאז שחטאו בעגל לא זכו לכך, אבל כתבה משה במצותו.

The term "Torah" in this verse refers to the theoretical dimension of the law, while the word "mitzva" relates to the practical applications of the commandments. Had Israel not sinned by fashioning the golden calf, the entire Torah would have been given to the nation as a signed document from the Creator, may He be blessed, just as the tablets were... However, because the people did commit this grievous sin, they did not merit such a gift. Instead, Moshe recorded the Torah at God's command.

QUESTIONS FOR THOUGHT

- Rashi believes that the Torah and the mitzva are the same thing as the tablets. What letter in the Hebrew text challenges Rashi's explanation?
- According to Ramban, the tablets were what was written by God, while "the Torah and the mitzva" refer to the rest of the commandments, that were taught to Moshe orally. What creative work does Ramban need to do with the text of the verse to make this work?
- Sforno distinguishes between two different parts of the Torah – one is designed to spark thought while the other is designed to instruct practice. He continues with a radical idea. What is that radical idea?

TEXTUAL SKILLS

1. For how long was Moshe supposed to be on the mountain? (Hint: read the text carefully!)
2. What two contrasting images did the people see at the top of the mountain?

WISDOM OF THE HEART

Moshe's time on the mountain sets an example for immersion in Torah study. The ways in which people have studied Torah since then have varied widely. Rabbi Yaakov Kamenetsky points out that according to the Gemara, the most important expression of Torah study is when it impacts on our actions. But since how this plays out in practice changes in every generation, each generation needs to find the kind of Torah study which will most meaningfully affect our behavior.

שמות | פרק כד   משפטים | 207

יב וַיֹּאכְלוּ וַיִּשְׁתּוּ: וַיֹּאמֶר יהוה אֶל־מֹשֶׁה עֲלֵה אֵלַי הָהָרָה וֶהְיֵה־שָׁם וְאֶתְּנָה לְךָ אֶת־לֻחֹת הָאֶבֶן וְהַתּוֹרָה וְהַמִּצְוָה
יג אֲשֶׁר כָּתַבְתִּי לְהוֹרֹתָם: וַיָּקָם מֹשֶׁה וִיהוֹשֻׁעַ מְשָׁרְתוֹ וַיַּעַל
יד מֹשֶׁה אֶל־הַר הָאֱלֹהִים: וְאֶל־הַזְּקֵנִים אָמַר שְׁבוּ־לָנוּ בָזֶה עַד אֲשֶׁר־נָשׁוּב אֲלֵיכֶם וְהִנֵּה אַהֲרֹן וְחוּר עִמָּכֶם מִי־בַעַל דְּבָרִים
טו יִגַּשׁ אֲלֵהֶם: וַיַּעַל מֹשֶׁה אֶל־הָהָר וַיְכַס הֶעָנָן אֶת־הָהָר: וַיִּשְׁכֹּן מפטיר
כְּבוֹד־יהוה עַל־הַר סִינַי וַיְכַסֵּהוּ הֶעָנָן שֵׁשֶׁת יָמִים וַיִּקְרָא אֶל־
יז מֹשֶׁה בַּיּוֹם הַשְּׁבִיעִי מִתּוֹךְ הֶעָנָן: וּמַרְאֵה כְּבוֹד יהוה כְּאֵשׁ
יח אֹכֶלֶת בְּרֹאשׁ הָהָר לְעֵינֵי בְּנֵי יִשְׂרָאֵל: וַיָּבֹא מֹשֶׁה בְּתוֹךְ הֶעָנָן וַיַּעַל אֶל־הָהָר וַיְהִי מֹשֶׁה בָּהָר אַרְבָּעִים יוֹם וְאַרְבָּעִים לָיְלָה:

CLASSIC COMMENTATORS

In verse 12, God calls Moshe up to the mountain to receive the tablets, the Torah, and the mitzva that He wrote to teach *Benei Yisrael*. What are the "Torah" and the "mitzva" to which the verse refers?

RASHI

All six hundred and thirteen mitzvot are included in the Ten Commandments.

רש"י

כל שש מאות ושלש עשרה מצוות בכלל עשרת הדברות הן.

RAMBAN

The phrase "that I have written" in this verse refers to the tablets that Moshe received, while the clause "to instruct the people" relates to the teaching and commandments. Thus the meaning of this text is: I will give you the stone tablets that I have written, and the teaching and the commandment to instruct the people, as God gave Moshe all six hundred and thirteen commandments [at that time].

רמב"ן

ואשר כתבתי - יחזור על הלוחות, ולהורותם - על התורה והמצוה. ושיעור הכתוב: ואתנה לך את לוחות האבן אשר כתבתי, והתורה והמצוה להורותם - שכל שש מאות ושלש עשרה מצות נתן לו.

QUICK BITES

- **21:6** If a slave wants to stay longer than six years he must get his ear pierced. According to a midrash cited by Rashi, "the ear that heard at Sinai 'to Me you are slaves' decided to become a slave to another." If we truly listen for the purpose of knowing what God wants of us, then His word enters into all of our limbs. But if we're not paying attention, then it "goes in one ear and out the other."

- **22:20** We are commanded to not denigrate the convert. It is well known that victims often become oppressors themselves; for example, sons who were abused by their fathers frequently remember what their father did and repeat this vicious behavior with their own children. Remembering what happened to us as strangers in Egypt is not sufficient. Rather, we are called upon to take it one step further: we must reexperience the pain with the intent to turn it into a force to stop the cycle of abuse rather than continue it.

- **24:7** According to Rabbeinu Yona, *Benei Yisrael*'s declaration "we shall do and we shall heed" is best understood in light of a mishna in *Pirkei Avot* (3:22), which states that one whose actions are greater than his wisdom, his wisdom has a solid foundation, whereas one whose wisdom is more than his actions, his wisdom fades away. Rabbeinu Yona understands the mishna to mean that one must commit to act before he understands everything.

- Rabbi Avigdor Nevenzahl suggests a creative alternate explanation. The placing of "we shall do and we shall heed" indicates a desire by *Benei Yisrael* to be able to intuit the mitzvot prior to being commanded, much like the tradition which suggests that the matriarchs and patriarchs intuited the mitzvot long before the Torah was given.

EXPLORING HASHKAFA
THE TORAH AND ANCIENT LEGAL CODES

It is now well-known that in ancient Near East (the area in which most of the narratives of the Tanakh happened) there were various collections of legal codes, some of which were written long before the revelation on Mount Sinai. The most famous of those was the Code of Hammurabi, written by a Babylonian king around the time of Avraham, but there are others as well (such as Hittite laws, the laws of Lipit-Ishtar, and the Middle Assyrian laws). These written codes contain laws which sound remarkably similar to those listed in *Parashat Mishpatim*. For example, the code of Hammurabi includes laws about stealing, business dealings, retribution against those guilty of wounding and killing people, and marriage and inheritance, and spells out punishments for violations including those which sound like "an eye for an eye."

The discovery of these codes caused great anxiety for some Jews. After all, the existence of legal texts containing material very similar to the Torah but written long before it was given raised questions about whether the Torah is truly original or unique.

One of the first people to grapple with these issues was Rabbi Dr. J. H. Hertz, the Chief Rabbi of the United Kingdom from 1913 to 1946. In his commentary to the Torah, which was used in many Orthodox synagogues throughout the second half of the twentieth century, he delves beyond the surface to demonstrate that while the style of presentation and formulation of the laws is similar, there are dramatic differences between the Torah's laws and those found in other societies of that time.

Since then, multiple scholars have analyzed these legal codes and noted significant differences. For example, the Torah's laws insist that the violator be punished, and no one else can be punished on behalf of that person. Also, in the Torah, with the partial exception of the slave, there are no separate rules for people of different classes – justice remains blind to the class of both the perpetrator and the victim and many of the mitzvot are designed specifically to promote equality amongst people. Perhaps most important, the Torah's value system places the value and sacredness of human life as the highest value, whereas most of the ancient codes place high value on property.

Context is also very important. The Torah's laws are presented as divine, not the innovation of a human. Even more significantly, the laws of the Torah are not designed to promote the establishment of a functioning society (which is certainly valuable) but are part of a covenant established between God and His people. Everyone has access to the laws, and study of the laws – including their details – is considered a religious obligation and an expression of dedication to God.

Perhaps the most radical idea is that the laws are presented in the context of a historical story, in which God redeemed His people as part of His covenant with them. The story and the laws are inseparable – the number of laws established to help us remember the exodus from Egypt is staggering. And since the laws are part of a covenant, they obligate not only the people, but God Himself.

As always, when we find things that seem similar it presents a dual challenge. The first part of that challenge is what can we learn from the similarity. Why was the later text written in ways that are like the earlier one? Even more important, however, is to dig deeper to uncover just how different the two texts are. It is that exploration which will help uncover the *ḥiddush*, the meaningful innovation being introduced.

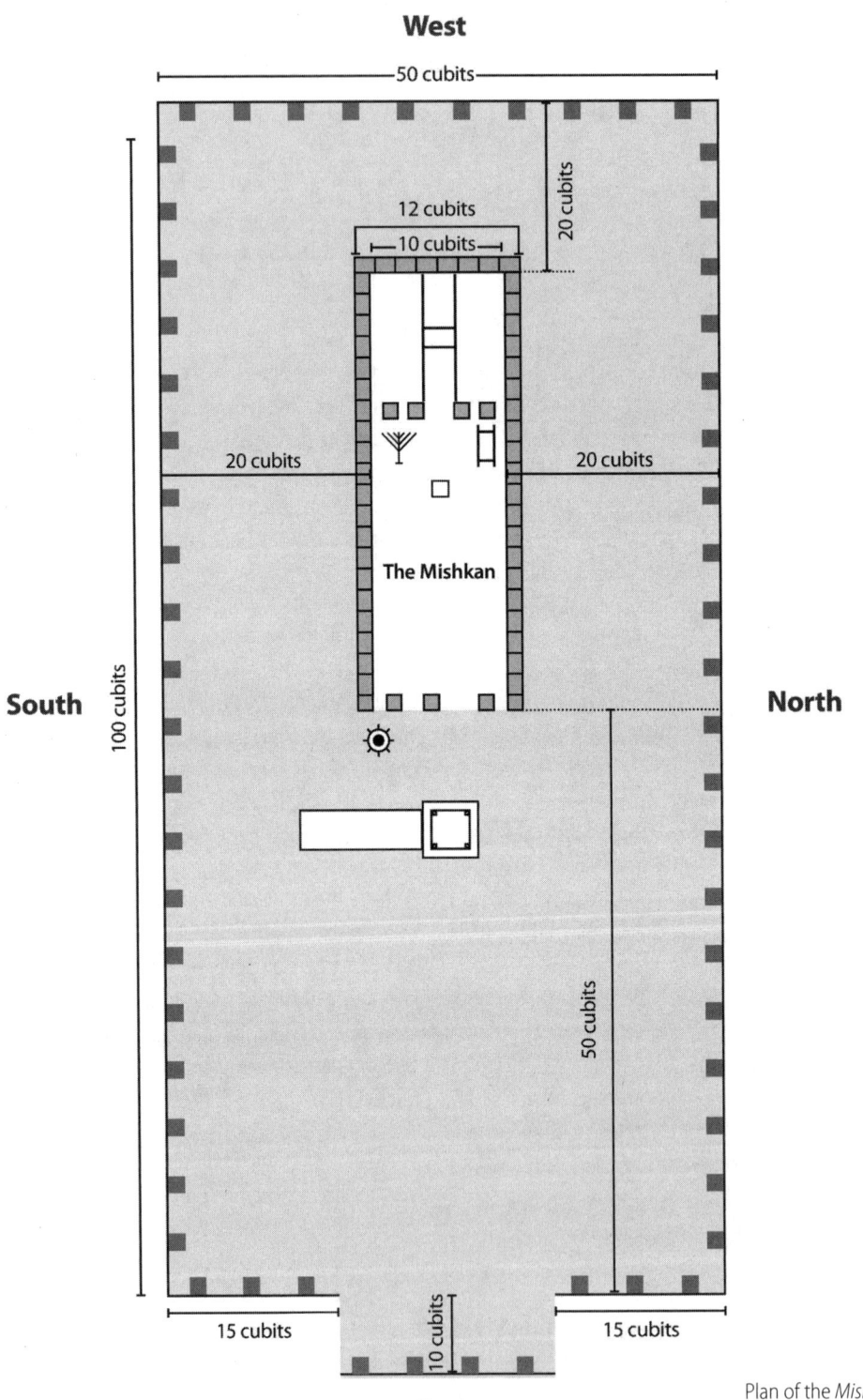

Plan of the *Mishkan*

פרשת תרומה
PARASHAT TERUMA

"For every setback, God has a major comeback."
Jaylen Taylor

Some say that the *Mishkan* was part of God's response to the sin of the golden calf, after *Benei Yisrael* demonstrated that they needed something concrete to focus on in their worship of the Divine. Others argue that the *Mishkan* is not meant to compensate for human weakness but is an essential part of the divine plan – a central place to experience God's presence; a focal point for awakening the soul. Indeed, the *Beit HaMikdash*, built on the model of the *Mishkan*, even in its absence has been a core symbol of the relationship between God and Israel for three thousand years.

This is true both on the national level and on the individual level. A careful look at God's instruction reveals a beautiful insight. God says, "They shall make Me a sanctuary and I will dwell in their midst" (25:8). It does not say, "I will dwell in it," but "in their midst." The existence of that central place means that God can dwell in the community of Israel, and in the hearts and souls of every individual member of Israel.

PARASHAT TERUMA

25 ¹ The Lord spoke to Moshe, saying, "Tell the Israelites to take an offering for Me; take
² My offering from all whose heart moves them to give. These are the offerings you shall
³ receive from them: gold, silver and bronze; sky-blue, purple, and scarlet wool; linen
⁴ and goats' hair; rams' hides dyed red and fine leather; acacia wood; oil for the lamps;
⁵ spices for the anointing oil and the fragrant incense; and onyx together with other
⁶ precious stones for the ephod and breast piece. They shall make Me a sanctuary and I
⁷ will dwell in their midst. Form the Tabernacle and form all of its furnishings following
⁸
⁹

RAMBAN

After the Lord had spoken to Israel face to face in order to pronounce the Ten Commandments to them, Moshe was directed to command them in several principles that would serve as general principles to the Torah's law system. And just as Israel then agreed to observe everything that Moshe would subsequently demand of them, in later generations, gentiles undergoing conversion to Judaism are first taught the basic rules of our religion, and following their declared commitment to accept the Torah, they are guided in the full gamut of the law. From this point on the people would be God's nation, and He would be their God….Now, since Israel was to be a holy nation, they deserved to have a *mikdash* so that the Divine Presence could dwell amongst them. God therefore first commanded the people to construct a Tabernacle to serve as a house dedicated to His name where His manifestation could dwell. It is at that site where God would continue to speak to Moshe and inform him just what he should relate to the people of Israel. Thus the main function of the Tabernacle was to provide a place for the Divine Presence to rest, that being the Ark.

רמב״ן

כאשר דבר השם עם ישראל פנים בפנים עשרת הדברות, וצוה אותם על ידי משה קצת מצות שהם כמו אבות למצותיה של תורה, כאשר הנהיגו רבותינו עם הגרים שבאים להתיהד, וישראל קבלו עליהם לעשות כל מה שיצום על ידו של משה, וכרת עמהם ברית על כל זה, מעתה הנה הם לו לעם והוא להם לאלהים ... והנה הם קדושים, ראוים שיהיה בהם מקדש להשרות שכינתו ביניהם ולכן צוה תחלה על דבר המשכן שיהיה לו בית בתוכם מקודש לשמו, ושם ידבר עם משה ויצוה את בני ישראל.
והנה עיקר החפץ במשכן הוא מקום מנוחת השכינה שהוא הארון.

QUESTIONS FOR THOUGHT

- According to Rashi, had *Benei Yisrael* not have sinned with the golden calf, would there have been a *Mishkan*?
- According to Ramban, what was the primary function of the *Mishkan*?
- When someone wants to argue that the Torah is not in chronological order, what is an appropriate follow-up question?

WISDOM OF THE HEART

The conversation about the *Mishkan* begins with the commandment to donate to the construction: "Take an offering for Me" (25:2). If we are talking about donations, shouldn't the Torah have written: "Give an offering"? Or HaḤayyim suggests that the language was chosen deliberately to indicate that this is not optional – that giving to the *Mishkan* is obligatory.

What do we gain when we give to others?

פרשת תרומה

כה

א וַיְדַבֵּר יְהוָה אֶל־מֹשֶׁה לֵּאמֹר: ב דַּבֵּר אֶל־בְּנֵי יִשְׂרָאֵל וְיִקְחוּ־לִי תְּרוּמָה מֵאֵת כָּל־אִישׁ אֲשֶׁר יִדְּבֶנּוּ לִבּוֹ תִּקְחוּ אֶת־תְּרוּמָתִי: ג וְזֹאת הַתְּרוּמָה אֲשֶׁר תִּקְחוּ מֵאִתָּם זָהָב וָכֶסֶף וּנְחֹשֶׁת: ד וּתְכֵלֶת וְאַרְגָּמָן וְתוֹלַעַת שָׁנִי וְשֵׁשׁ וְעִזִּים: ה וְעֹרֹת אֵילִם מְאָדָּמִים וְעֹרֹת תְּחָשִׁים וַעֲצֵי שִׁטִּים: ו שֶׁמֶן לַמָּאֹר בְּשָׂמִים לְשֶׁמֶן הַמִּשְׁחָה וְלִקְטֹרֶת הַסַּמִּים: ז אַבְנֵי־שֹׁהַם וְאַבְנֵי מִלֻּאִים לָאֵפֹד וְלַחֹשֶׁן: ח וְעָשׂוּ לִי מִקְדָּשׁ וְשָׁכַנְתִּי בְּתוֹכָם: ט כְּכֹל אֲשֶׁר אֲנִי מַרְאֶה אוֹתְךָ אֵת תַּבְנִית הַמִּשְׁכָּן וְאֵת תַּבְנִית כָּל־כֵּלָיו:

CLASSIC COMMENTATORS

There is a great debate about the timing of the construction of the *Mishkan*.

RASHI

The Torah does not insist on presenting events precisely in the sequence that they occurred. Case in point: the debacle of the golden calf actually took place long before God commanded Israel to build the Tabernacle. We know this to be true because Moshe smashed the tablets of the law on the seventeenth of the month of Tamuz [the fourth month of the calendar, in the first year], and the Holy One, blessed be He, forgave Israel for that sin on Yom Kippur [in the seventh month]. On the day after that, Israel began to provide their donations for the national project. The construction began then and culminated on the first of Nisan [the first month, in the second year. According to this schedule the instructions for the Tabernacle – which appear in chapters 25–31 – were issued after the people sinned even though that episode is described in chapter 32.]

רש"י

אין מוקדם ומאוחר בתורה. מעשה העגל קודם לציווי מלאכת המשכן ימים רבים היה, שהרי בי"ז בתמוז נשתברו הלוחות וביום הכיפורים נתרצה הקב"ה לישראל ולמחרת התחילו בנדבת המשכן והוקם באחד בניסן.

10 the patterns that I show you. Make an Ark of acacia wood, two and a half cubits long, a
11 cubit and a half wide, and a cubit and a half high. Overlay it with pure gold, inside and
12 out, and around it make a gold rim. Cast four gold rings for it and place them on its four
13 corners, two rings on one side and two on the other. Make staves of acacia wood and
14 overlay them with gold; place these staves in the rings on the sides of the Ark so that

The Ark

QUESTIONS FOR THOUGHT

- Ibn Ezra offers two textual sources as well as a logical reason for suggesting that the Ark of the Covenant sat on legs (or a stand). What is the logical reason he offers?
- Rashi and Ralbag apparently disagree with Ibn Ezra. How would they each respond to his textual proofs?

שמות | פרק כה | תרומה

י וְכֵ֖ן תַּעֲשֽׂוּ׃ וְעָשׂ֥וּ אֲר֖וֹן עֲצֵ֣י שִׁטִּ֑ים אַמָּתַ֨יִם וָחֵ֜צִי

יא אָרְכּ֗וֹ וְאַמָּ֤ה וָחֵ֨צִי֙ רָחְבּ֔וֹ וְאַמָּ֥ה וָחֵ֖צִי קֹמָת֑וֹ׃ וְצִפִּיתָ֤ אֹתוֹ֙

זָהָ֣ב טָה֔וֹר מִבַּ֥יִת וּמִח֖וּץ תְּצַפֶּ֑נּוּ וְעָשִׂ֧יתָ עָלָ֛יו זֵ֥ר זָהָ֖ב סָבִֽיב׃

יב וְיָצַ֣קְתָּ לּ֗וֹ אַרְבַּע֙ טַבְּעֹ֣ת זָהָ֔ב וְנָ֣תַתָּ֔ה עַ֖ל אַרְבַּ֣ע פַּעֲמֹתָ֑יו וּשְׁתֵּ֣י

טַבָּעֹ֗ת עַל־צַלְעוֹ֙ הָֽאֶחָ֔ת וּשְׁתֵּי֙ טַבָּעֹ֔ת עַל־צַלְע֖וֹ הַשֵּׁנִֽית׃

יג וְעָשִׂ֥יתָ בַדֵּ֖י עֲצֵ֣י שִׁטִּ֑ים וְצִפִּיתָ֥ אֹתָ֖ם זָהָֽב׃ וְהֵבֵאתָ֤ אֶת־הַבַּדִּים֙

CLASSIC COMMENTATORS

Did the Ark of the Covenant sit on the floor of the *Mishkan*?

RASHI

רש״י

ושתי טבעות – מן הארבע טבעות.

"And two rings" – of the four rings [mentioned at the start of the verse].

IBN EZRA

אבן עזרא

חפשתי בכל המקרא ולא מצאתי פעם שהוא זוית, רק רגל: רגלי עני פעמי דלים (ישעיהו כ״ו:ו׳), וישם לדרך פעמיו (תהלים פ״ה:י״ד), מה יפו פעמיך (שיר השירים ז׳:ב׳), ורבים ככה. על כן הוצרכתי לפרש כי רגלים היו לארון, כי דרך בזיון הוא שישב הארון בארץ. ועוד: מה טעם לומר ושתי טבעות בתוספת הו״ו, ואלו היו הראשונות היה כתוב: שתי טבעות, להודיע שהם ארבע טבעות זהב, שהזכיר כמשפט הלשון.

I have searched all of Scripture and I have been unable to find the term **פעם** used to connote corners [as Rashi and others interpret the word]. Rather, the word is always used to mean a foot, as in the verse: "The foot shall trample it down, even the feet of the poor, and the steps [**פעמי**] of the needy" (Is. 26:6); in the verse: "Righteousness shall go before Him, and walk in the way of His steps [**פעמיו**]" (Ps. 85:14); in the verse: "How beautiful are your feet [**פעמיך**] in sandals, O prince's daughter!" (Song. 7:2), and many other instances. I am therefore forced to conclude that the Ark had feet, for it would certainly have been disgraceful to place this holy object directly on the ground. Furthermore, why does the verse need to state: "And two [**ושתי**] rings on one side," with the added prefix ו? If the second part of the verse referred to the four rings mentioned at the start, it could have just said [as the translation here renders the verse]: "Two rings on one side and two on the other," and we would know that this means the four gold rings introduced in the verse's first clause.

RALBAG

רלב״ג

הנה הארון לא היו לו רגלים, לפי הנראה מהפשט.

According to the straightforward understanding of the text the Ark was not fitted with feet.

15 the Ark may be carried. The staves must stay in the rings of the Ark; they must not be
16 removed. Inside the Ark, place the tablets of the covenant that I will give you. Make an
17 Ark cover of pure gold, two and a half cubits long and a cubit and a half wide. Make two
18 cherubim of beaten gold and place them at the two ends of the cover: one cherub at one
19 end and one at the other; the cherubim shall be made of one piece with the cover. These
20 cherubim should have wings spread upward, sheltering the cover. They should face one
21 another, and look toward the cover. Place the cover on top of the Ark, and inside the
22 Ark place the tablets of the covenant that I will give you. There, from above the cover, between the two cherubim, above the Ark of the Testimony, I will meet with you and speak with you, and give you all My commands to the Israelites.

WISDOM OF THE HEART

The centerpiece of the *Mishkan* was undoubtedly the Ark of the Covenant. That Ark held the tablets that God gave to Moshe, but – according to our Sages – also the broken tablets, the ones that Moshe smashed when he saw the golden calf. Why would the broken tablets be there with the unbroken ones?

All of us fulfill and sometimes violate commandments. All of us sometimes embody what our tradition teaches us and sometimes shatter what we know is good. Fundamentally, each one of us has a heart that is both whole and broken. Our hearts aren't sculptures, pure and complete – they are mosaics, made up of the pieces of our experiences. The broken tablets in the Ark, like the broken parts of our souls, add a new dimension to the wholeness that we strive for.

Do you embrace your imperfections or try to hide them?

QUICK BITE

Cherubim first make their appearance in the Torah in Genesis – they are the guards blocking the path to the Tree of Life, creating distance between us and an ideal existence in the Garden. By contrast, the cherubim in the *Mishkan* were the seat of God's communication with Moshe, generating closeness between God and Israel. Everything in this world – every emotion, every talent, every force – can be used for positive or for negative. It is our choices, and sometimes our perspective, that determine whether it will be used constructively or not.

שמות | פרק כה

טו בַּטַּבָּעֹת עַל צַלְעֹת הָאָרֹן לָשֵׂאת אֶת־הָאָרֹן בָּהֶם: בְּטַבְּעֹת
טז הָאָרֹן יִהְיוּ הַבַּדִּים לֹא יָסֻרוּ מִמֶּנּוּ: וְנָתַתָּ אֶל־הָאָרֹן אֵת הָעֵדֻת
יז אֲשֶׁר אֶתֵּן אֵלֶיךָ: ◦ וְעָשִׂיתָ כַפֹּרֶת זָהָב טָהוֹר אַמָּתַיִם וָחֵצִי   שני
יח אָרְכָּהּ וְאַמָּה וָחֵצִי רָחְבָּהּ: וְעָשִׂיתָ שְׁנַיִם כְּרֻבִים זָהָב מִקְשָׁה
יט תַּעֲשֶׂה אֹתָם מִשְּׁנֵי קְצוֹת הַכַּפֹּרֶת: וַעֲשֵׂה כְּרוּב אֶחָד מִקָּצָה
מִזֶּה וּכְרוּב־אֶחָד מִקָּצָה מִזֶּה מִן־הַכַּפֹּרֶת תַּעֲשׂוּ אֶת־הַכְּרֻבִים
כ עַל־שְׁנֵי קְצוֹתָיו: וְהָיוּ הַכְּרֻבִים פֹּרְשֵׂי כְנָפַיִם לְמַעְלָה סֹכְכִים
בְּכַנְפֵיהֶם עַל־הַכַּפֹּרֶת וּפְנֵיהֶם אִישׁ אֶל־אָחִיו אֶל־הַכַּפֹּרֶת
כא יִהְיוּ פְּנֵי הַכְּרֻבִים: וְנָתַתָּ אֶת־הַכַּפֹּרֶת עַל־הָאָרֹן מִלְמָעְלָה
כב וְאֶל־הָאָרֹן תִּתֵּן אֶת־הָעֵדֻת אֲשֶׁר אֶתֵּן אֵלֶיךָ: וְנוֹעַדְתִּי לְךָ שָׁם
וְדִבַּרְתִּי אִתְּךָ מֵעַל הַכַּפֹּרֶת מִבֵּין שְׁנֵי הַכְּרֻבִים אֲשֶׁר עַל־אֲרֹן
הָעֵדֻת אֵת כָּל־אֲשֶׁר אֲצַוֶּה אוֹתְךָ אֶל־בְּנֵי יִשְׂרָאֵל:

TEXTUAL SKILLS

1. The command to build the Ark (25:10) is different from the commands to build all of the other internal vessels. What is the difference?
2. What two essential purposes does the Ark serve?
3. Where else in the Torah do we find כרובים?

23 Make a table of acacia wood, two cubits long, a cubit wide and a cubit and a half high.
24 Overlay it with pure gold and around it make a gold rim. Make a frame a handbreadth
25
26 wide all around, and around the frame also make a gold rim. Make for it four gold rings,
27 and place the rings on the four corners where the four legs are. The rings should be
28 attached next to the frame as holders for staves to carry the table. Make the staves of
29 acacia wood and overlay them with gold; by these the table shall be carried. You must also make, out of pure gold, its bowls, spoons, pitchers and jars for pouring libations.
30 On this table the showbread must be placed before Me at all times.

The table

QUESTIONS FOR THOUGHT

- Match up the following explanations with the commentaries above:
  Since the *Mishkan* is God's house (so to speak), it is only appropriate that it be properly furnished, and every house needs a table.
  Since the priests are the royal workers in the divine palace, God wants to make sure that they eat from the King's table.
  Since God wants to bring blessing to all of Israel, and blessing can only expand that which already exists, it is important to bring the bread into the *Mishkan* so that God's blessing can work.
- Which explanation sees the *Mishkan* as serving a practical purpose? Which see the *Mishkan* as serving a symbolic purpose?
- Which explanation do you think would be most easily understood in the twenty-first century? Why?

WISDOM OF THE HEART

The instruction to build the *Mishkan* focuses on the construction of the vessels – the Ark, the table, the *menora*, etc. Why does the Torah suddenly talk about the bread that is to be placed on the table? The Gaon of Rogachov suggests that placing the bread on the table is actually the completion of the construction of the table. This is similar to the *menora*, where the Torah includes a line about lighting the flames. The existence of an object, whether in the *Mishkan* or in our home, is insufficient to transform it into a holy object. Only when it is used properly it becomes a holy object, and each time we use it, it is recreated so that it is fresh and new, again and again.

How can you make space for God at your own dinner table?

שמות | פרק כה

כג וְעָשִׂיתָ שֻׁלְחָן עֲצֵי שִׁטִּים אַמָּתַיִם אָרְכּוֹ וְאַמָּה רָחְבּוֹ וְאַמָּה וָחֵצִי קֹמָתוֹ: כד וְצִפִּיתָ אֹתוֹ זָהָב טָהוֹר וְעָשִׂיתָ לּוֹ זֵר זָהָב סָבִיב: כה וְעָשִׂיתָ לּוֹ מִסְגֶּרֶת טֹפַח סָבִיב וְעָשִׂיתָ זֵר־זָהָב לְמִסְגַּרְתּוֹ סָבִיב: כו וְעָשִׂיתָ לּוֹ אַרְבַּע טַבְּעֹת זָהָב וְנָתַתָּ אֶת־הַטַּבָּעֹת עַל אַרְבַּע הַפֵּאֹת אֲשֶׁר לְאַרְבַּע רַגְלָיו: כז לְעֻמַּת הַמִּסְגֶּרֶת תִּהְיֶיןָ הַטַּבָּעֹת לְבָתִּים לְבַדִּים לָשֵׂאת אֶת־הַשֻּׁלְחָן: כח וְעָשִׂיתָ אֶת־הַבַּדִּים עֲצֵי שִׁטִּים וְצִפִּיתָ אֹתָם זָהָב וְנִשָּׂא־בָם אֶת־הַשֻּׁלְחָן: כט וְעָשִׂיתָ קְּעָרֹתָיו וְכַפֹּתָיו וּקְשׂוֹתָיו וּמְנַקִּיֹּתָיו אֲשֶׁר יֻסַּךְ בָּהֵן זָהָב טָהוֹר תַּעֲשֶׂה אֹתָם: ל וְנָתַתָּ עַל־הַשֻּׁלְחָן לֶחֶם פָּנִים לְפָנַי תָּמִיד:

CLASSIC COMMENTATORS

Why does the *Mishkan* need a table with bread on display?

RABBI YOSEF BEKHOR SHOR

It is an honor for the king when his servants and his priests share food off his table.

ר׳ יוסף בכור שור

דרך כבוד הוא שיהו עבדיו וכהניו אוכלים משולחנו.

RAMBAN

For since the dawn of time, God has never again created anything *ex nihilo*… However, when the basic item already exists, God's blessing can descend upon the object and make it grow, as in the episode where Elisha said: "Tell me, what do you have in the house?" (II Kings 4:2), and the blessing descended upon the jar of oil and filled all of the vessels; and the episode of Eliyahu: "The jar of flour did not run out, and the jug of oil was never empty" (I Kings 17:15). This was so with the showbread that sat on the table – God's blessing infused these loaves, and from them plenitude extended to all of Israel.

רמב״ן

מעת היות העולם לא נברא יש מאין… אבל כאשר יהיה שם שרש דבר תחול עליו הברכה ותוסיף בו, כאשר אמר אלישע: הגידי לי מה יש לך בבית (מלכים ב ד׳:ב׳), וחלה הברכה על אסוך שמן ומלאה כל הכלים, ובאליהו: כד הקמח לא כלתה וצפחת השמן לא חסר (מלכים א י״ז:ט״ז). וכן השולחן בלחם הפנים, בו תחול הברכה, וממנו יבא השובע לכל ישראל.

RABBI OVADYA SFORNO

God commanded Israel to fashion a table and a candelabrum for the *Mishkan* since these decorative items adorn an important personage's home. Thus the woman from Shunem suggests to her husband, "Let us make him a small enclosed upper chamber and provide him with a bed, table, chair, and lamp there, so that whenever he comes to us, he can turn in there" (II Kings 4:10).

ר׳ עובדיה ספורנו

צוה על שולחן ומנורה, כמנהגם לפני השרים, כענין השונמית באמרה "ונשים לו שם מטה ושלחן וכסא ומנורה" (מלכים ב ד׳:י׳).

Shemot | Chapter 25

31 Make a candelabrum of pure gold. Its base and shaft, cups, knobs and flowers shall be
32 hammered from a single piece. Six branches shall extend from its sides, three on one
33 side, three on the other. On each branch there shall be three finely crafted cups, each
with a knob and a flower. All six branches extending from the candelabrum shall be
34 like this. The shaft of the candelabrum shall have four finely-crafted cups, each with a
35 knob and a flower. For the six branches that extend from the candelabrum, there must
36 be a knob at the base of each pair of branches. The knobs and their branches shall be
37 of one piece with it, the whole of it a single, hammered piece of pure gold. Make its
38 seven lamps and mount them so that they light the space in front of it. Make its tongs
39 and pans of pure gold. All these items shall be made from a talent of pure gold. Take
40 care to make them according to that design that is shown to you on the mountain.

The *menora*

QUESTIONS FOR THOUGHT

- According to Rashi, what is the focus of the lighting of the *menora*?
- According to Rashbam, what is the focus of the lighting of the *menora*?
- Which of these commentaries understands that the Torah is setting up a connection between the *menora* and the table? Try to suggest what the meaning of that connection might be.

תרומה | פרק כה

לא וְעָשִׂיתָ מְנֹרַת זָהָב טָהוֹר מִקְשָׁה תֵּיעָשֶׂה הַמְּנוֹרָה יְרֵכָהּ וְקָנָהּ ‎*שלישי*

לב גְּבִיעֶיהָ כַּפְתֹּרֶיהָ וּפְרָחֶיהָ מִמֶּנָּה יִהְיוּ: וְשִׁשָּׁה קָנִים יֹצְאִים מִצִּדֶּיהָ שְׁלֹשָׁה ׀ קְנֵי מְנֹרָה מִצִּדָּהּ הָאֶחָד וּשְׁלֹשָׁה קְנֵי מְנֹרָה

לג מִצִּדָּהּ הַשֵּׁנִי: שְׁלֹשָׁה גְבִעִים מְשֻׁקָּדִים בַּקָּנֶה הָאֶחָד כַּפְתֹּר וָפֶרַח וּשְׁלֹשָׁה גְבִעִים מְשֻׁקָּדִים בַּקָּנֶה הָאֶחָד כַּפְתֹּר וָפָרַח כֵּן

לד לְשֵׁשֶׁת הַקָּנִים הַיֹּצְאִים מִן־הַמְּנֹרָה: וּבַמְּנֹרָה אַרְבָּעָה גְבִעִים

לה מְשֻׁקָּדִים כַּפְתֹּרֶיהָ וּפְרָחֶיהָ: וְכַפְתֹּר תַּחַת שְׁנֵי הַקָּנִים מִמֶּנָּה וְכַפְתֹּר תַּחַת שְׁנֵי הַקָּנִים מִמֶּנָּה וְכַפְתֹּר תַּחַת־שְׁנֵי הַקָּנִים

לו מִמֶּנָּה לְשֵׁשֶׁת הַקָּנִים הַיֹּצְאִים מִן־הַמְּנֹרָה: כַּפְתֹּרֵיהֶם וּקְנֹתָם

לז מִמֶּנָּה יִהְיוּ כֻּלָּהּ מִקְשָׁה אַחַת זָהָב טָהוֹר: וְעָשִׂיתָ אֶת־נֵרֹתֶיהָ שִׁבְעָה וְהֶעֱלָה אֶת־נֵרֹתֶיהָ וְהֵאִיר עַל־עֵבֶר פָּנֶיהָ: וּמַלְקָחֶיהָ

לח

לט וּמַחְתֹּתֶיהָ זָהָב טָהוֹר: כִּכָּר זָהָב טָהוֹר יַעֲשֶׂה אֹתָהּ אֵת כָּל־

מ הַכֵּלִים הָאֵלֶּה: וּרְאֵה וַעֲשֵׂה בְּתַבְנִיתָם אֲשֶׁר־אַתָּה מָרְאֶה

CLASSIC COMMENTATORS

The Torah says that the lamps on the *menora* should be lit so that "וְהֵאִיר עַל עֵבֶר פָּנֶיהָ", translated here as "they light the space in front of it." This strange phrase is addressed by the commentaries.

רש״י

והאיר על עבר פניה – עשה פי ששת הנרות שבראשי הקנים היוצאים מצדיה מסובים כלפי האמצעי כדי שיהיו הנרות כשתדליקם מאירים אל עבר פניה מוסב אורם אל צד פני הקנה האמצעי שהוא גוף המנורה.

רשב״ם

והאיר על עבר פניה – ידליק הפתילות אל מול המנורה שזהו לצד השולחן שכנגדו כדכתיב ואת המנורה נוכח השולחן, וכן כתב אל מול פני המנורה יאיר שבעת הנרות (במדבר ח׳:ב׳), שכל שבעתן מאירין לצד השולחן שכנגדו לפניה.

RASHI

Fashion the six lamps at the tops of the candelabrum's six branches so that they point toward the middle shaft. In this way, when the lamps are lit, they will "light the space in front of it" – that is, toward the direction of the face of the central branch, which forms the body of the candelabrum.

RASHBAM

The wicks of the lamps should be lit such that they are facing the front of the candelabrum – that is, toward the table, which stands on the opposite wall, as the verse states: "And the candelabrum [shall be placed] on the south side, opposite the table" (26:35). Similarly, it is written, "When you light the lamps, the seven lamps shall give light toward the body of the candelabrum" (Num. 8:2), meaning that all seven lamps should be turned to light up the table facing the candelabrum.

26 1 As for the Tabernacle itself, make it with ten sheets of finely spun linen and sky-blue,
2 purple, and scarlet wool, with a design of cherubim worked into them. Each sheet shall be twenty-eight cubits long and four cubits wide; all the sheets should be the same size.
3 Five of the sheets should be sewn together; the other five likewise. Make loops of sky-
4 blue wool on the upper edge of the end sheet in the first set, and likewise on the upper
5 edge of the outermost sheet in the second set. Make fifty loops on each sheet on one side and fifty on the upper edge of the corresponding sheets in the other set, with the

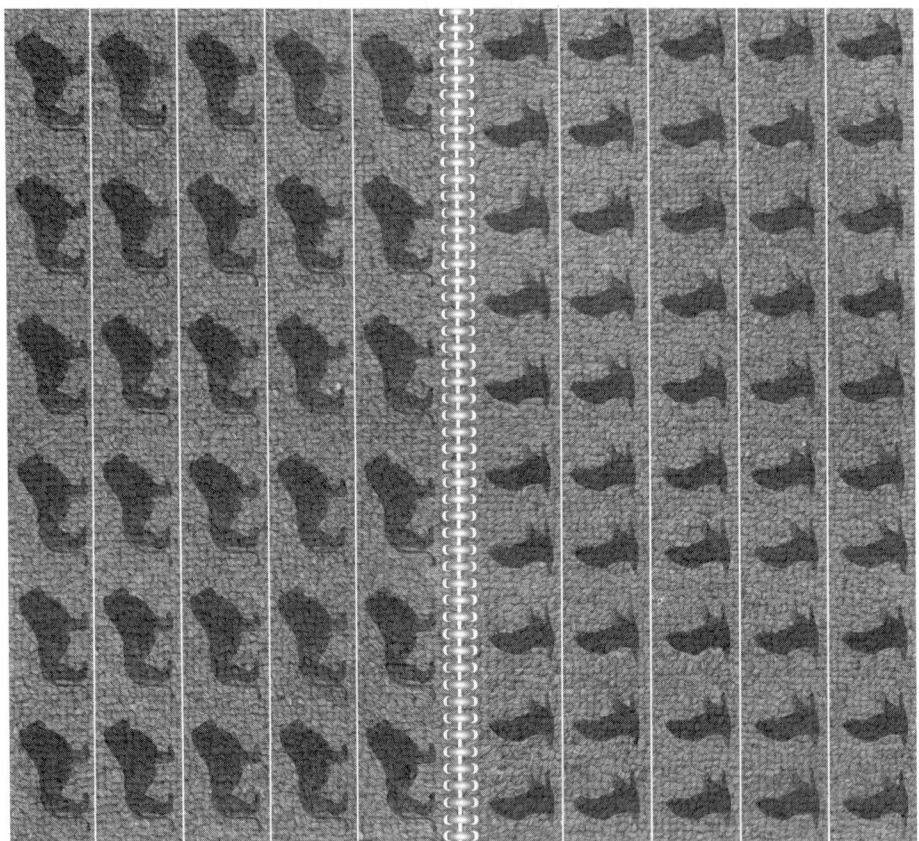

The sheets

QUESTIONS FOR THOUGHT

- The debate between Rashbam and Sforno seems like a minor technicality, but actually reveals something deeper about their understanding of the *Mishkan*. What is that understanding?
- Rashi takes a different approach than Rashbam and Sforno. How does he suggest we understand the first two words of verse 1?

שמות | פרק כו

כו א וְאֶת־הַמִּשְׁכָּן תַּעֲשֶׂה עֶשֶׂר יְרִיעֹת שֵׁשׁ מָשְׁזָר בָּדָד: יט
וּתְכֵלֶת וְאַרְגָּמָן וְתוֹלַעַת שָׁנִי כְּרֻבִים מַעֲשֵׂה חֹשֵׁב תַּעֲשֶׂה
אֹתָם: ב אֹרֶךְ ׀ הַיְרִיעָה הָאַחַת שְׁמֹנֶה וְעֶשְׂרִים בָּאַמָּה וְרֹחַב
אַרְבַּע בָּאַמָּה הַיְרִיעָה הָאֶחָת מִדָּה אַחַת לְכָל־הַיְרִיעֹת: ג חֲמֵשׁ
הַיְרִיעֹת תִּהְיֶיןָ חֹבְרֹת אִשָּׁה אֶל־אֲחֹתָהּ וְחָמֵשׁ יְרִיעֹת חֹבְרֹת
אִשָּׁה אֶל־אֲחֹתָהּ: ד וְעָשִׂיתָ לֻלְאֹת תְּכֵלֶת עַל שְׂפַת הַיְרִיעָה
הָאֶחָת מִקָּצָה בַּחֹבָרֶת וְכֵן תַּעֲשֶׂה בִּשְׂפַת הַיְרִיעָה הַקִּיצוֹנָה
בַּמַּחְבֶּרֶת הַשֵּׁנִית: ה חֲמִשִּׁים לֻלָאֹת תַּעֲשֶׂה בַּיְרִיעָה הָאֶחָת
וַחֲמִשִּׁים לֻלָאֹת תַּעֲשֶׂה בִּקְצֵה הַיְרִיעָה אֲשֶׁר בַּמַּחְבֶּרֶת הַשֵּׁנִית

CLASSIC COMMENTATORS

A careful look at verse 1 reveals that the elaborate, multicolored cloths with the woven designs are referred to as the משכן. Why?

RASHI
רש"י

These ten sheets will serve as a roof for the structure, as well as for coverings outside the boards [that formed the walls]. For the sheets were hung behind the boards to cover them.

להיות לו לגג ולמחיצות מחוץ לקרשים, שהיריעות תלויים מאחריהם לכסותם.

RASHBAM
רשב"ם

The first, lower, set of sheets was called the משכן. [The sheets that covered the structure thereby serve as a synecdoche for the building.] These sheets deserved that title because the Ark stood directly beneath them, and the Ark was the spot where the Divine Presence [שכינה] rested.

התחתונות קרויין "משכן", כי תחותיהם הארון מקום שהשכינה שורה.

RABBI OVADYA SFORNO
ר' עובדיה ספורנו

The sheets covering the structure were also called משכן, since the structure contained a throne [the incense altar], a table, and a candelabrum to host [למשכן] the Divine Presence [שכינה].

קרא היריעות בשם משכן, כי בתוכם היו כסא שולחן ומנורה למשכן שכינה.

6 loops opposite one another. And make fifty gold clasps. With the clasps, join the sheets
7 together so that the Tabernacle becomes one whole. Make sheets of goats' hair as a tent
8 over the Tabernacle; make eleven of these sheets. Each sheet shall be thirty cubits long
9 and four cubits wide, all eleven sheets the same size. Join five of the sheets by themselves, and the other six by themselves. Fold the sixth sheet over the front of the tent. Make
10 fifty loops on the edge of the end sheet of one set, and fifty on the edge of the end sheet
11 of the other. Make, also, fifty bronze clasps. Put the clasps through the loops, joining
12 the tent together so that becomes one whole. As for the additional length of the tent sheets, the extra half sheet is to hang down at the rear of the Tabernacle. The extra cubit
13 at either end of each of the tent sheets should hang over the sides of the Tabernacle to
14 cover it on both sides. Make a covering for the tent from rams' hides dyed red. Above it make a covering of fine leather.

WISDOM OF THE HEART

The Torah describes the process of weaving the special cloths as מעשה חשב. That term refers to a specific type of creative workmanship, but the commentaries debate what the nature of it is. One even suggests that it is a technique whereby the designer would create one design that would appear differently on both sides of the item. Introducing this level of artistry into the *Mishkan* both elevates the artistic process, declaring it as a holy pursuit, and enhances the status of the *Mishkan* as a place of extraordinary beauty and sophistication.

Do you see your creativity as a gift from God? What would be an appropriate way to show gratitude to God through that gift?

QUICK BITE

Rav Shimon Schwab, in his commentary on *tefilla*, explains that the structure of the siddur echoes the process of entering the *Beit HaMikdash* – something we can try to visualize as we move through the parts of the prayer. The morning begins with fifteen blessings (*birkot hashaḥar*), mirroring the fifteen steps that led up to the gate of the courtyard. Following that is the section about the sacrifices (*korbanot*), which is what we would see next after ascending the steps. As we arrive at the building of the *Beit HaMikdash*, we enter the entrance hall through two large doors, represented in the siddur by the two long blessings of *Barukh SheAmar* and *Yishtabaḥ*. The blessings prior to *Shema* represent the table and the *menora*, and they are followed by *Shema*, representing the beautiful scent rising from the golden altar of incense. It is only then, after this entire progression, that we reach the Holy of Holies – the private, intense encounter with God in the *Amida*.

ו מַקְבִּילֹת הַלֻּלָאֹת אִשָּׁה אֶל־אֲחֹתָהּ: וְעָשִׂיתָ חֲמִשִּׁים קַרְסֵי זָהָב
וְחִבַּרְתָּ אֶת־הַיְרִיעֹת אִשָּׁה אֶל־אֲחֹתָהּ בַּקְּרָסִים וְהָיָה הַמִּשְׁכָּן
ז אֶחָד: וְעָשִׂיתָ יְרִיעֹת עִזִּים לְאֹהֶל עַל־הַמִּשְׁכָּן עַשְׁתֵּי־עֶשְׂרֵה
ח יְרִיעֹת תַּעֲשֶׂה אֹתָם: אֹרֶךְ ׀ הַיְרִיעָה הָאַחַת שְׁלֹשִׁים בָּאַמָּה
וְרֹחַב אַרְבַּע בָּאַמָּה הַיְרִיעָה הָאֶחָת מִדָּה אַחַת לְעַשְׁתֵּי עֶשְׂרֵה
ט יְרִיעֹת: וְחִבַּרְתָּ אֶת־חֲמֵשׁ הַיְרִיעֹת לְבָד וְאֶת־שֵׁשׁ הַיְרִיעֹת
י לְבָד וְכָפַלְתָּ אֶת־הַיְרִיעָה הַשִּׁשִּׁית אֶל־מוּל פְּנֵי הָאֹהֶל: וְעָשִׂיתָ
חֲמִשִּׁים לֻלָאֹת עַל שְׂפַת הַיְרִיעָה הָאֶחָת הַקִּיצֹנָה בַּחֹבָרֶת
יא וַחֲמִשִּׁים לֻלָאֹת עַל שְׂפַת הַיְרִיעָה הַחֹבֶרֶת הַשֵּׁנִית: וְעָשִׂיתָ
קַרְסֵי נְחֹשֶׁת חֲמִשִּׁים וְהֵבֵאתָ אֶת־הַקְּרָסִים בַּלֻּלָאֹת וְחִבַּרְתָּ
יב אֶת־הָאֹהֶל וְהָיָה אֶחָד: וְסֶרַח הָעֹדֵף בִּירִיעֹת הָאֹהֶל חֲצִי
יג הַיְרִיעָה הָעֹדֶפֶת תִּסְרַח עַל אֲחֹרֵי הַמִּשְׁכָּן: וְהָאַמָּה מִזֶּה
וְהָאַמָּה מִזֶּה בָּעֹדֵף בְּאֹרֶךְ יְרִיעֹת הָאֹהֶל יִהְיֶה סָרוּחַ עַל־צִדֵּי
יד הַמִּשְׁכָּן מִזֶּה וּמִזֶּה לְכַסֹּתוֹ: וְעָשִׂיתָ מִכְסֶה לָאֹהֶל עֹרֹת אֵילִם
מְאָדָּמִים וּמִכְסֵה עֹרֹת תְּחָשִׁים מִלְמָעְלָה:

TEXTUAL SKILLS

1. Three different coverings are discussed in this passage, one on top of the other. The innermost one is called the משכן. What are the other two called?

2. What unusual word appears three times in this passage and nowhere else in the Torah?

3. The phrase אשה אל אחותה is used four times in this passage and once more in the following one. Aside from these, it is used three other times in Tanakh with the same meaning (all in the beginning of Ezekiel). It appears only once more in the entire Torah (in Leviticus), but with a very different meaning. Find it!

¹⁵₁₆ Make the upright boards for the Tabernacle of acacia wood. Each board shall be ten
17 cubits long and one and a half cubits wide. Each board should have two matching

The beams

ABARBANEL

According to the midrash, when Yaakov came down to Egypt, he planted the acacia trees that his descendants would eventually use for constructing the Tabernacle. But it seems exceedingly unlikely that Israel hauled this timber with them out of slavery and crossed the sea while transporting all of this wood. Meanwhile, Rabbi Avraham Ibn Ezra explains that a grove of acacia trees grew next to Mount Sinai, and it was that grove which supplied material for the nation's courtyards and commerce. When the Tabernacle project commenced, those individuals who possessed the necessary wood were asked to donate it. Still, it seems more reasonable to suggest that traveling merchants from neighboring nations arrived at the Israelite camp to sell their wares. This is how the nation procured oil for the candelabrum and for anointing the Tabernacle, and the incense [ingredients] – do not imagine that the people took these items with them when they left Egypt. Similarly, in this manner the Israelites were able to obtain acacia wood.

אברבנאל

ובדרש אמרו שנטעם יעקב במצרים, אבל רחוק הוא שנאמר שהוציאום עמהם והעבירום בים, והראב"ע כתב שיער היה סמוך להר סיני ומשה כרתו אותם לחצריהם ולסחורותיהם. והתנדבו כל מי שנמצא אתו הראויים לקרשים.
והיותר נכון הוא, שהיו באים עמים מכל הסביבות אל מחנה ישראל למכור כל מיני סחורות, ומשם קנו שמן למאור והבשמים ושמן למשחה ולקטורת, כי אין לחשוב שהוציאו כל זה ממצרים. ומשם קנו גם כן עצי שטים.

QUESTIONS FOR THOUGHT

- How do you think Rashi would respond to the challenges presented by Ibn Ezra and Abarbanel?
- Both Ibn Ezra and Abarbanel offer rational alternatives to the midrash quoted by Rashi. Which of those do you think is more realistic and reasonable?

שמות | פרק כו | תרומה

טו וְעָשִׂיתָ אֶת־הַקְּרָשִׁים לַמִּשְׁכָּן עֲצֵי שִׁטִּים עֹמְדִים: עֶשֶׂר אַמּוֹת *רביעי*
טז אֹרֶךְ הַקָּרֶשׁ וְאַמָּה וַחֲצִי הָאַמָּה רֹחַב הַקֶּרֶשׁ הָאֶחָד: שְׁתֵּי
יָדוֹת לַקֶּרֶשׁ הָאֶחָד מְשֻׁלָּבֹת אִשָּׁה אֶל־אֲחֹתָהּ כֵּן תַּעֲשֶׂה

CLASSIC COMMENTATORS

While the acacia wood was necessary for the Ark and the table, nowhere was it as essential as for the beams that made up the walls of the *Mishkan*. The size of each board (ten cubits long and one and a half cubits wide) required a great number of very large trees, the kind that are not usually found in dry wilderness areas. From where did they get so much wood?

רש״י
מאין היו להם במדבר? פירש ר׳ תנחומא: יעקב אבינו צפה ברוח הקודש שעתידים ישראל לבנות משכן במדבר והביא ארזים למצרים ונטעם וציוה לבניו ליטלם עמהם כשיצאו ממצרים.

RASHI
Where did the Israelites find acacia trees in the middle of the wilderness? Rabbi Tanhuma explains: Through divine inspiration our patriarch Yaakov saw that his descendants were destined to construct a Tabernacle in the desert [and that they would require timber to build it]. Hence, when he left Canaan, Yaakov took cedar trees [of which the acacia is a variety according to the Talmud; see Rosh HaShana 23a] with him and planted them in Egypt centuries earlier. He then commanded his descendants to uproot the trees and take them along when they escaped from Egypt.

אבן עזרא
יש מקדמונינו שאמרו שיעקב אבינו נטע וישראל הוציאו ממצרים במצוות משה, ... ויש לתמוה: ... הנה המצרים חושבים כי לזבוח הם הולכים ואחר כך ישובו ... ומה היתה תשובה לשואליהם, למה יוליכו עצי שטים והם הולכים לזבוח דרך שלושת ימים?
והנה לא ידענו, אם קבלה היתה ביד אבותינו שממצרים הוציאום, גם אנחנו נסור אל משמעתם, ואם סברא היא, יש לבקש דרך אחרת. ונאמר, כי היה סמוך אל הר סיני יער עצי שטים, ובבואם שם, אמר להם ששם יעכבו הרבה ... וכרתו כל היער.

IBN EZRA
Some of our early scholars have argued that the patriarch Yaakov planted these trees in Egypt after his descent to that land. Centuries later Moshe commanded Israel to chop down the timber and cart the wood with them upon leaving slavery…And yet, consider the fact that the Egyptians were led to believe that the nation was setting out for a brief furlough in the desert where they would offer sacrifices to their God, whereupon they would return to slavery…Why and how could the Israelites have snuck out such an excess of lumber for private usage? What answer could they have given to someone who asked them why they were transporting acacia trees if they were merely leaving the country for a three-day journey to offer sacrifices? Now, the truth is, we do not know whether or not our ancestors held the tradition that their forebears took the wood with them when they left the land of their oppression, and if such an explanation is a tradition, then we should accept it. However, if the theory is based on reasoning, then we should seek a different approach to the problem, and suggest that next to Mount Sinai grew a grove of acacia trees. When Israel arrived at that location Moshe informed the people that they would be remaining there for some time. And since the protective cloud was absent for that period, as I have already explained [in commentary on 15:22], each individual fashioned a booth for his family to live in.

18 tenons; all the Tabernacle's boards should be made in this way. Make twenty boards for
19 the southern side of the Tabernacle, and forty silver sockets under the twenty boards,
20 two sockets under the first board for its two tenons, and two under the next. For the sec-
21 ond side of the Tabernacle, the northern side, there should be twenty boards, along with their forty silver sockets, two under the first board and two under each of the others.
22
23 Make six boards for the west side of the Tabernacle, and two additional boards for the
24 Tabernacle's rear corners. These should adjoin each other at the bottom, and be joined together at the top by a ring. So it should be for both sides; they shall form the two
25 corners. So there should be eight boards and sixteen silver sockets, two sockets under
26 each board. Make crossbars, too, of acacia wood, five for the boards of the first side of
27 the Tabernacle, five for the boards of the second side of the Tabernacle, and five for the
28 boards of the western side of the Tabernacle at the rear. The central crossbar should go
29 through the middle of the boards from one end to the other. Overlay the boards with gold, and make gold rings for the crossbars. The crossbars too should be overlaid with
30 gold. So shall you set up the Tabernacle, according to the plan you were shown on the

WISDOM OF THE HEART

The upright beams were joined to make the walls and were held together in multiple ways, including by a central rod that went through them all. Targum Yerushalmi states that this center rod was made of wood from the tree that Avraham had planted in Beersheba, while the Zohar suggests that the center beam is from Yaakov's plantings. Avraham and Yaakov each represented values: Avraham represented kindness while Yaakov represented truth. Kindness demands flexibility; truth demands rigidity. These two explanations of the rod's origins are in fact a debate about which value was more representative of the *Mishkan*. Does the *Mishkan* represent the ultimate truth of God in this world, or does it represent the presence of God's infinite kindness?

Which do you think is more important – kindness or truth?

QUICK BITE

A riddle: The boards of the walls of the *Mishkan* seem to have been freestanding. There were rings at the top to bind them to each other and there were also two external bars and one internal bar that served as support, but nothing attaching them firmly to the ground. Consider that there were weighty roof coverings that would have pushed them inward – how did all these boards stay upright and not collapse?

Possible Approaches: 1) A miracle. But no such miracle is mentioned in the Torah or by the Sages. 2) Ropes might have been attached to the boards to hold them in place. The problem with this approach is that the Torah doesn't mention any ropes. 3) Additional boards serving as a roof for the *Mishkan* could have stabilized the weight. But this too isn't mentioned.

A certain architect has suggested that the wood from which the beams were formed were not very dense. The boards were set into solid silver sockets, which would have been very weighty – much denser than the boards. This would have made the boards very bottom-heavy, stabilizing them and allowing them to remain upright.

שמות | פרק כו

יח לְכֹ֖ל קַרְשֵׁ֥י הַמִּשְׁכָּֽן: וְעָשִׂ֥יתָ אֶת־הַקְּרָשִׁ֖ים לַמִּשְׁכָּ֑ן עֶשְׂרִ֣ים
יט קֶ֔רֶשׁ לִפְאַ֖ת נֶ֥גְבָּה תֵימָֽנָה: וְאַרְבָּעִים֙ אַדְנֵי־כֶ֔סֶף תַּעֲשֶׂ֕ה תַּ֖חַת
עֶשְׂרִ֣ים הַקָּ֑רֶשׁ שְׁנֵ֨י אֲדָנִ֜ים תַּֽחַת־הַקֶּ֤רֶשׁ הָֽאֶחָד֙ לִשְׁתֵּ֣י יְדֹתָ֔יו
כ וּשְׁנֵ֧י אֲדָנִ֛ים תַּֽחַת־הַקֶּ֥רֶשׁ הָאֶחָ֖ד לִשְׁתֵּ֥י יְדֹתָֽיו: וּלְצֶ֥לַע הַמִּשְׁכָּ֖ן
כא הַשֵּׁנִ֣ית לִפְאַ֣ת צָפ֑וֹן עֶשְׂרִ֖ים קָֽרֶשׁ: וְאַרְבָּעִ֥ים אַדְנֵיהֶ֖ם כָּ֑סֶף שְׁנֵ֣י
אֲדָנִ֗ים תַּ֚חַת הַקֶּ֣רֶשׁ הָֽאֶחָ֔ד וּשְׁנֵ֣י אֲדָנִ֔ים תַּ֖חַת הַקֶּ֥רֶשׁ הָאֶחָֽד:
כב וּלְיַרְכְּתֵ֥י הַמִּשְׁכָּ֖ן יָ֑מָּה תַּעֲשֶׂ֖ה שִׁשָּׁ֥ה קְרָשִֽׁים: וּשְׁנֵ֤י קְרָשִׁים֙
כג תַּעֲשֶׂ֔ה לִמְקֻצְעֹ֖ת הַמִּשְׁכָּ֑ן בַּיַּרְכָתָֽיִם: וְיִֽהְי֣וּ תֹֽאֲמִם֮ מִלְּמַ֒טָּה֒
כד וְיַחְדָּ֗ו יִהְי֤וּ תַמִּים֙ עַל־רֹאשׁ֔וֹ אֶל־הַטַּבַּ֖עַת הָאֶחָ֑ת כֵּ֚ן יִֽהְיֶ֣ה
לִשְׁנֵיהֶ֔ם לִשְׁנֵ֥י הַמִּקְצֹעֹ֖ת יִֽהְיֽוּ: וְהָיוּ֙ שְׁמֹנָ֣ה קְרָשִׁ֔ים וְאַדְנֵיהֶ֣ם
כה כֶּ֔סֶף שִׁשָּׁ֥ה עָשָׂ֖ר אֲדָנִ֑ים שְׁנֵ֣י אֲדָנִ֗ים תַּ֚חַת הַקֶּ֣רֶשׁ הָֽאֶחָ֔ד וּשְׁנֵ֣י
כו אֲדָנִ֔ים תַּ֖חַת הַקֶּ֥רֶשׁ הָאֶחָֽד: וְעָשִׂ֥יתָ בְרִיחִ֖ם עֲצֵ֣י שִׁטִּ֑ים חֲמִשָּׁ֕ה
כז לְקַרְשֵׁ֥י צֶֽלַע־הַמִּשְׁכָּ֖ן הָאֶחָֽד: וַחֲמִשָּׁ֣ה בְרִיחִ֔ם לְקַרְשֵׁ֥י צֶֽלַע־
הַמִּשְׁכָּ֖ן הַשֵּׁנִ֑ית וַחֲמִשָּׁ֤ה בְרִיחִם֙ לְקַרְשֵׁי֙ צֶ֣לַע הַמִּשְׁכָּ֔ן לַיַּרְכָתַ֖יִם
כח יָֽמָּה: וְהַבְּרִ֥יחַ הַתִּיכֹ֖ן בְּת֣וֹךְ הַקְּרָשִׁ֑ים מַבְרִ֕חַ מִן־הַקָּצֶ֖ה אֶל־
כט הַקָּצֶֽה: וְֽאֶת־הַקְּרָשִׁ֞ים תְּצַפֶּ֣ה זָהָ֗ב וְאֶת־טַבְּעֹתֵיהֶם֙ תַּעֲשֶׂ֣ה
ל זָהָ֔ב בָּתִּ֖ים לַבְּרִיחִ֑ם וְצִפִּיתָ֥ אֶת־הַבְּרִיחִ֖ם זָהָֽב: וַהֲקֵמֹתָ֖ אֶת־

TEXTUAL SKILLS

1. In verse 24 there are two words which are nearly twins. Those same words appear in Genesis to describe twins (Gen. 25:24, 38:27).

2. Note that in this passage, for the first time the Torah describes the physical orientation of the *Mishkan*.

31 mountain. Make a curtain of sky-blue, purple, and scarlet wool, and finely spun linen
32 with a design of cherubim worked into it. Hang it on four gold-covered posts of acacia
33 wood with gold hooks, set on four sockets of silver. Hang the curtain under the clasps
and bring the Ark of the Testimony behind it, so that the curtain separates the holy
34 place from the Holy of Holies. Put the cover on the Ark of the Testimony in the Holy
35 of Holies. The table shall be placed on the north side of the Tabernacle outside the cur-
36 tain, and the candelabrum on the south side, opposite the table. Make a screen for the
entrance to the tent, embroidered with sky-blue, purple and scarlet wool and finely spun
37 linen. Make five posts of acacia wood for the screen and overlay them with gold; their

---

RAMBAN / רמב״ן

This does not mean that the Ark's cover was to be adjusted into position only after the Ark was placed inside its chamber as described in the previous verse. Rather, the purpose of our verse was to explain to Moshe that the curtain should be hung directly beneath the row of clasps such that the Ark should be on the inside of the partition, "so that the curtain separates the holy place from the Holy of Holies." Thus we are informed that the Ark cover with its attendant cherubim should be situated within the aforementioned Holy of Holies, which in turn is located behind the curtain.

אין פירושו שיתן הכפורת על ארון העדות כשהארון שם בקדש הקדשים, אבל העניין שיצוה אותו הכתוב שישים הפרכת תחת הקרסים כדי שיהא הארון שמה מבית לפרכת, ותבדיל הפרכת בין הקדש ובין קדש הקדשים. וכן אמר: "ונתת את הכפורת על ארון העדות בקדש הקדשים" – להודיע שהכפרת עם כרוביו על הארון יהיו כלם שם בקדש הקדשים הנזכר, שהוא מבית לפרכת.

HAAMEK DAVAR / העמק דבר

Ramban has already addressed this difficulty, but in my opinion his resolution is unsatisfactory… What Moshe learned was that he was meant to bring the cover of the Ark into the chamber at the same time as he positioned the Ark itself in the room. Nevertheless, initially the cover was not to be put in its proper place and adjusted to sit atop the Ark where it served as a testament. Rather, at first the cover was to be set down randomly on the Ark as the two items were brought in together. This is what the verse means when it states, "Place the cover on top of the Ark" (25:21), without specifying, as the text later does, "Put the cover on the Ark of the Testimony" (26:34). This is so even though when the cover was placed haphazardly on top of the Ark, the testimony had already been placed inside the vessel, as I have written above… For the Ark was only referred to as the "Ark of the Testimony" once it was situated in the Holy of Holies.

כבר עמד על זה הרמב״ן, ולא אמר בזה ישוב נכון... למד משה שבעוד שיביא את הארון לפנים יביא את הכפורת עמו, אבל לא שיהא מונח יפה ומתוקן כל צרכו שיהא ראוי לעדות, אלא להניח את הכפורת על הארון איך שהוא ולהביאם יחד, ועל זו הנתינה כתיב לעיל "ונתת את הכפורת על הארון מלמעלה" ולא כתיב 'על ארון העדות', אע״ג שכבר הניח שם את העדות כמו שכתבתי... לא נקרא עדיין "ארון העדות" עד שיהיה נתון בקודש הקדשים.

QUESTIONS FOR THOUGHT

- It seems like an insignificant detail – whether the Ark was placed in the Holy of Holies with its cover already in place or with its cover ready to be put into place. Aside from the desire to understand this properly, what might have motivated the *Haamek Davar* to argue and take such a strong stand against Ramban?
- According to *Haamek Davar*, what is the impact of placing the *kaporet* onto the Ark?

שמות | פרק כו

לא הַמִּשְׁכָּן כְּמִשְׁפָּט֕וֹ אֲשֶׁ֥ר הָרְאֵ֖יתָ בָּהָֽר׃ וְעָשִׂ֣יתָ פָרֹ֗כֶת ב חמישי
תְּכֵ֧לֶת וְאַרְגָּמָ֛ן וְתוֹלַ֥עַת שָׁנִ֖י וְשֵׁ֣שׁ מָשְׁזָ֑ר מַעֲשֵׂ֥ה חֹשֵׁ֛ב יַעֲשֶׂ֥ה
אֹתָ֖הּ כְּרֻבִֽים׃ לב וְנָתַתָּ֣ה אֹתָ֗הּ עַל־אַרְבָּעָה֙ עַמּוּדֵ֣י שִׁטִּ֔ים מְצֻפִּ֣ים
זָהָ֔ב וָוֵיהֶ֖ם זָהָ֑ב עַל־אַרְבָּעָ֖ה אַדְנֵי־כָֽסֶף׃ לג וְנָתַתָּ֣ה אֶת־הַפָּרֹ֘כֶת֮
תַּ֣חַת הַקְּרָסִים֒ וְהֵבֵאתָ֤ שָׁ֙מָּה֙ מִבֵּ֣ית לַפָּרֹ֔כֶת אֵ֖ת אֲר֣וֹן הָעֵד֑וּת
וְהִבְדִּילָ֤ה הַפָּרֹ֙כֶת֙ לָכֶ֔ם בֵּ֣ין הַקֹּ֔דֶשׁ וּבֵ֖ין קֹ֥דֶשׁ הַקֳּדָשִֽׁים׃ לד וְנָתַתָּ֣
אֶת־הַכַּפֹּ֕רֶת עַ֖ל אֲר֣וֹן הָעֵדֻ֑ת בְּקֹ֖דֶשׁ הַקֳּדָשִֽׁים׃ לה וְשַׂמְתָּ֤ אֶת־
הַשֻּׁלְחָן֙ מִח֣וּץ לַפָּרֹ֔כֶת וְאֶת־הַמְּנֹרָה֙ נֹ֣כַח הַשֻּׁלְחָ֔ן עַ֖ל צֶ֣לַע
הַמִּשְׁכָּ֖ן תֵּימָ֑נָה וְהַ֨שֻּׁלְחָ֔ן תִּתֵּ֖ן עַל־צֶ֥לַע צָפֽוֹן׃ לו וְעָשִׂ֤יתָ מָסָךְ֙ לְפֶ֣תַח
הָאֹ֔הֶל תְּכֵ֧לֶת וְאַרְגָּמָ֛ן וְתוֹלַ֥עַת שָׁנִ֖י וְשֵׁ֣שׁ מָשְׁזָ֑ר מַעֲשֵׂ֖ה רֹקֵֽם׃
לז וְעָשִׂ֣יתָ לַמָּסָ֗ךְ חֲמִשָּׁה֙ עַמּוּדֵ֣י שִׁטִּ֔ים וְצִפִּיתָ֤ אֹתָם֙ זָהָ֔ב וָוֵיהֶ֖ם

The curtain and the screen

CLASSIC COMMENTATORS

Most people think of the Ark and its cover, the *kaporet*, as one unit. A careful look at the earlier verses (25:10–22) reveals that they are two separate things which are joined. This passage highlights that distinction, as verse 33 mentions bringing in the Ark, but its cover, the *kaporet*, is mentioned separately in the following verse. This raised the eyebrows of some of the careful readers of the Torah.

27 1 hooks, also, shall be of gold. Cast for them, too, five sockets of bronze. Make the altar from acacia wood. It should be square, five cubits long, five cubits wide and three cubits
2 high. Make horns for it on its four corners, the horns being of one piece with it, and
3 overlay it with bronze. Make pots for removing its ashes, together with shovels, basins,
4 forks and pans. Make all of these of bronze. Make a grate of bronze mesh for it, and on
5 the mesh make four bronze rings at its four corners. The grate should be set below, under
6 the ledge of the altar, so that the mesh reaches the middle of the altar. And make staves
7 of acacia wood for the altar, and overlay them with bronze. Place the poles in the rings,
8 so that the poles will be on the two sides of the altar when it is carried. Make it hollow,

The bronze altar

QUESTIONS FOR THOUGHT

- According to each of the commentaries above, did the כרוב serve a function or was it decorative?
- For those who think that it served a function, what are the ideas represented by the functions that they suggest?

WISDOM OF THE HEART

Midrash Yalkut Shimoni says that all of the vessels in the *Mishkan* required immersion in a *mikve* except for the two altars – one made of bronze filled with earth and the other made of wood plated in gold. According to tradition, the altar is compared to our hearts. Rav Itche Meir Morgenstern says that there are two ways to guard the heart from impurity: there is the path of humility, like the earth of the bronze altar, and the path of having a heart of gold.

שמות | פרק כז

כז א זָהָב וְיָצַקְתָּ לָהֶם חֲמִשָּׁה אַדְנֵי נְחֹשֶׁת: וְעָשִׂיתָ אֶת־ ששי
הַמִּזְבֵּחַ עֲצֵי שִׁטִּים חָמֵשׁ אַמּוֹת אֹרֶךְ וְחָמֵשׁ אַמּוֹת רֹחַב
ב רָבוּעַ יִהְיֶה הַמִּזְבֵּחַ וְשָׁלֹשׁ אַמּוֹת קֹמָתוֹ: וְעָשִׂיתָ קַרְנֹתָיו עַל
ג אַרְבַּע פִּנֹּתָיו מִמֶּנּוּ תִּהְיֶיןָ קַרְנֹתָיו וְצִפִּיתָ אֹתוֹ נְחֹשֶׁת: וְעָשִׂיתָ
סִּירֹתָיו לְדַשְּׁנוֹ וְיָעָיו וּמִזְרְקֹתָיו וּמִזְלְגֹתָיו וּמַחְתֹּתָיו לְכָל־כֵּלָיו
ד תַּעֲשֶׂה נְחֹשֶׁת: וְעָשִׂיתָ לּוֹ מִכְבָּר מַעֲשֵׂה רֶשֶׁת נְחֹשֶׁת וְעָשִׂיתָ
ה עַל־הָרֶשֶׁת אַרְבַּע טַבְּעֹת נְחֹשֶׁת עַל אַרְבַּע קְצוֹתָיו: וְנָתַתָּה
אֹתָהּ תַּחַת כַּרְכֹּב הַמִּזְבֵּחַ מִלְּמָטָּה וְהָיְתָה הָרֶשֶׁת עַד חֲצִי
ו הַמִּזְבֵּחַ: וְעָשִׂיתָ בַדִּים לַמִּזְבֵּחַ בַּדֵּי עֲצֵי שִׁטִּים וְצִפִּיתָ אֹתָם
ז נְחֹשֶׁת: וְהוּבָא אֶת־בַּדָּיו בַּטַּבָּעֹת וְהָיוּ הַבַּדִּים עַל־שְׁתֵּי צַלְעֹת
ח הַמִּזְבֵּחַ בִּשְׂאֵת אֹתוֹ: נְבוּב לֻחֹת תַּעֲשֶׂה אֹתוֹ כַּאֲשֶׁר הֶרְאָה

CLASSIC COMMENTATORS

The bronze altar had some something called a **כרכב**, but it is not at all clear what that is.

RASHI
The **כרכב** mentioned in this verse is also known as the **סובב**, for anything that encircles around [**סביב**] is called a **כרכב**...On the altar a groove was made all around its walls for decorative purposes.

רש״י
סובב, כל דבר המקיף סביב בעוגל קרוי כרכב, ... למזבח עשו חריץ סביבו בדופנו לנוי.

RASHBAM
This refers to the entrance of the altar, for it provided a shortcut to move around the periphery on top of the altar.

רשב״ם
כניסת המזבח שמתקצר למעלה, ללכת על אותה הכניסה סביב המזבח.

RABBI SAMSON RAPHAEL HIRSCH
It seems to me that the term **כרכב** derives from the root **ר-כ-ב**, in the same way that the word **קרקע** is derived from the root **ר-ק-ע**. Meanwhile, the term **רכב** connotes a base or a foundation of some kind.

ר' שמשון רפאל הירש
נגור כנראה מ"רכב", כדרך ש"קרקע" נגור מ"רקע". "רכב" פירושו: להיות מונח על בסיס או סומך כל שהוא, ובסיס, או סומך זה נקרא "רֶכֶב".

9 with planks; make it as it was shown to you on the mountain. Make the courtyard of the Tabernacle thus: on the south side there should be hangings a hundred cubits long
10 of finely spun linen, all the length of the courtyard on that side, with twenty posts and
11 their twenty bronze sockets. The hooks and bands of the posts shall be of silver. Likewise on the north side; the hangings shall be a hundred cubits long, with twenty posts and
12 their twenty corresponding bronze sockets, with hooks and bands of silver. The width of the hangings at the western end of the courtyard shall be fifty cubits, and it should

The courtyard

QUESTIONS FOR THOUGHT

- According to which commentaries was the purpose of those חשוקים exclusively decorative?
- According to the one who says that they served a function, what was that function?
- Think about those commentaries which say that they were purely decorative. Why would God care about the small, decorative details of the *Mishkan*?
- Can you imagine a purpose that was neither decorative nor functional?

TEXTUAL SKILLS

1. At the entrance to the courtyard was a curtain (v. 16), which is described in ways that are very similar to the curtains at the entrance to the *Mishkan* and the Holy of Holies. In what way(s) are they similar? In what way(s) are they different?

2. The dimensions of the courtyard are described as being one hundred cubits long and fifty cubits wide (v. 11–12). Later, however (v. 18), the width is described as being fifty cubits by fifty cubits. Try to find an answer to this contradiction!

ט וְעָשִׂיתָ אֵת חֲצַר הַמִּשְׁכָּן לִפְאַת אֹתְךָ בָּהָר כֵּן יַעֲשׂוּ: *שביעי*
נֶגֶב־תֵּימָנָה קְלָעִים לֶחָצֵר שֵׁשׁ מָשְׁזָר מֵאָה בָאַמָּה אֹרֶךְ לַפֵּאָה
הָאֶחָת: י וְעַמֻּדָיו עֶשְׂרִים וְאַדְנֵיהֶם עֶשְׂרִים נְחֹשֶׁת וָוֵי הָעַמֻּדִים
וַחֲשֻׁקֵיהֶם כָּסֶף: יא וְכֵן לִפְאַת צָפוֹן בָּאֹרֶךְ קְלָעִים מֵאָה אֹרֶךְ
וְעַמֻּדָו עֶשְׂרִים וְאַדְנֵיהֶם עֶשְׂרִים נְחֹשֶׁת וָוֵי הָעַמֻּדִים וַחֲשֻׁקֵיהֶם
כָּסֶף: יב וְרֹחַב הֶחָצֵר לִפְאַת־יָם קְלָעִים חֲמִשִּׁים אַמָּה עַמֻּדֵיהֶם

CLASSIC COMMENTATORS

The courtyard of the *Mishkan* was delineated by plain white linen curtains supported by upright pillars. Those pillars had what the Torah calls חשוקים made of silver. What are those חשוקים, and what was their purpose?

RABBI AVRAHAM BEN HARAMBAM

The term חשקיהם refers to ornamental coverings, and the term derives from the same root as חשקה ["longing" or "desire"].. Thus this beautifying feature clung to the pillars they adorned.

ר' אברהם בן הרמב"ם

ופירוש חשקיהם כיסוייהם וציפוייהם נגזר מן דעתי מן חשקה נפשו מפני שהוא (הציפוי) הנראה יפה בהם (בעמודים).

RALBAG

These pillars were supported by bronze sockets, and they bore silver hooks at their tops to which the hangings were attached. Additionally, silver threads were affixed to the posts that were in turn tied to the hangings to prevent them from separating with the wind. In my estimation there were more of these threads than there were posts, such that the hangings were tied tightly to the pillars and were maintained there.

רלב"ג

והעמודים ההם היו נסמכים על אדני נחושת, ובראשם היו ווים של כסף להחזיק בקלעים. ואחר כן היו חוטי כסף דבקים בעמודים, לקשור בהם הקלעים לעמודים בדרך שלא תפרידם הרוח מהם, ואלו החוטים היו במקומות רבים מן העמודים, לפי מה שאחשוב, באופן שיקשרו הקלעים בעמודים ויתקיימו בהם.

RABBI OVADYA SFORNO

These were circular pieces of silver that encompassed the pillars for ornamentation.

ר' עובדיה ספורנו

וחשקיהם - עגולים סובבים העמוד באמצעו לנוי.

13 have ten posts and their ten corresponding sockets. The width of the courtyard at the
14 front, facing east, shall be fifty cubits: fifteen cubits of hangings with three posts and
15 three sockets on one side, and fifteen cubits of hangings with three posts and three
16 sockets on the other, and for the gate of the courtyard there shall be an embroidered screen of twenty cubits of sky-blue, purple and scarlet wool and finely spun linen, with
17 four posts and four sockets. All the posts around the courtyard should be banded with
18 silver. Their hooks shall be of silver, and their sockets of bronze. The courtyard shall be a hundred cubits long, fifty cubits wide, and five cubits high, with hangings of finely
19 spun linen and sockets of bronze. All the Tabernacle utensils, for every use, as well as all its tent pegs and the tent pegs of the courtyard, shall be of bronze."

יג עֶשְׂרָ֖ה וְאַדְנֵיהֶ֣ם עֲשָׂרָֽה: וְרֹ֣חַב הֶֽחָצֵר֩ לִפְאַ֨ת קֵ֜דְמָה מִזְרָ֗חָה
חֲמִשִּׁ֣ים אַמָּ֑ה: וַחֲמֵ֨שׁ עֶשְׂרֵ֥ה אַמָּ֛ה קְלָעִ֖ים לַכָּתֵ֑ף עַמֻּדֵיהֶ֣ם
יד שְׁלֹשָׁ֔ה וְאַדְנֵיהֶ֖ם שְׁלֹשָֽׁה: וְלַכָּתֵף֙ הַשֵּׁנִ֔ית חֲמֵ֥שׁ עֶשְׂרֵ֖ה קְלָעִ֑ים
טו עַמֻּדֵיהֶ֣ם שְׁלֹשָׁ֔ה וְאַדְנֵיהֶ֖ם שְׁלֹשָֽׁה: וּלְשַׁ֨עַר הֶֽחָצֵ֜ר מָסָ֣ךְ ׀
טז עֶשְׂרִ֣ים אַמָּ֗ה תְּכֵ֨לֶת וְאַרְגָּמָ֜ן וְתוֹלַ֧עַת שָׁנִ֛י וְשֵׁ֥שׁ מָשְׁזָ֖ר מַעֲשֵׂ֣ה
רֹקֵ֑ם עַמֻּֽדֵיהֶם֙ אַרְבָּעָ֔ה וְאַדְנֵיהֶ֖ם אַרְבָּעָֽה: כָּל־עַמּוּדֵ֨י הֶֽחָצֵ֤ר מפטיר
יז סָבִיב֙ מְחֻשָּׁקִ֣ים כֶּ֔סֶף וָוֵיהֶ֖ם כָּ֑סֶף וְאַדְנֵיהֶ֖ם נְחֹֽשֶׁת: אֹ֣רֶךְ הֶֽחָצֵ֞ר
יח מֵאָ֣ה בָֽאַמָּ֗ה וְרֹ֣חַב ׀ חֲמִשִּׁ֣ים בַּחֲמִשִּׁ֔ים וְקֹמָ֖ה חָמֵ֣שׁ אַמּ֑וֹת
יט שֵׁ֣שׁ מָשְׁזָ֔ר וְאַדְנֵיהֶ֖ם נְחֹֽשֶׁת: לְכֹל֙ כְּלֵ֣י הַמִּשְׁכָּ֔ן בְּכֹ֖ל עֲבֹדָת֑וֹ
וְכָל־יְתֵדֹתָ֛יו וְכָל־יִתְדֹ֥ת הֶחָצֵ֖ר נְחֹֽשֶׁת:

פרשת תצוה
PARASHAT TETZAVEH

> "To me, clothing is a form of self-expression – there are hints about who you are in what you wear."
> — Marc Jacobs

According to *Sefer HaḤinukh*, the commandment that the priests wear special clothing is based on the idea that people are changed by their behaviors. When we dress differently, we act differently; when we are wearing our fine clothes we behave differently than when we are wearing work clothes. There is an entire section in *Shulḥan Arukh* dedicated to the preparations for Shabbat, including what to wear, because what we wear makes a difference.

PARASHAT TETZAVEH

27 20 "Command the Israelites to bring you pure oil from crushed olives for light, to kindle
21 the lamp, every night. From evening to morning, before the Lord, Aharon and his sons shall set the lamp to burn in the Tent of Meeting, outside the curtain that veils the Ark of the Testimony. This shall be a rule for all time for the Israelites, throughout their
28 1 generations. From among the Israelites, draw your brother Aharon and his sons close to you to serve Me as priests – Aharon and his sons Nadav and Avihu, Elazar and Itamar.
2/3 Make sacred vestments for your brother Aharon, for glory and for splendor. Speak to all the skilled craftsmen whom I have endowed with a spirit of wisdom, and have them
4 make Aharon's vestments; these will consecrate him to serve Me as priest. These are the garments they shall make: a breast piece, an ephod, a robe, a quilted tunic, a miter and a sash; sacred vestments shall they make, for your brother Aharon and his sons to
5 serve Me in. They should use gold, and sky-blue, purple and scarlet wool, and fine linen.

מלבי״ם

הנה הבגדים שציוה לעשות היו כפי הגלוי בגדים חיצוניים ... אבל באמת היו מורים על בגדים פנימיים שיעשו כהני ה' להלביש בם את נפשותיהם בדעות ובמידות ובתכונות טובות שהם מלבושי הנפש ... וציוה ה' אל משה שהוא יעשה בגדי קודש אלה, היינו ללמדם תיקון נפשותיהם ומידותיהם באופן שילבישו הוד והדר את נפשם הפנימית.

MALBIM

The first level of clothing comprised the external garments... But in truth of fact, these articles of clothing only symbolized the true inner wardrobe that defined the priests of the Lord. For these men had to garb themselves in the appropriate beliefs and the proper personality attributes suitable to their office. Those are the real elements that dress the individual... Thus the Lord commanded Moshe to "make sacred vestments" for the priests. That is, it was Moshe's responsibility to guide his brother and nephews in perfecting their souls and their behavior so that the image of their character that they presented to the nation would be one of glory and splendor.

QUESTIONS FOR THOUGHT

- Does wearing different clothes change who we are, or do we wear different clothes to reflect what is happening inside of us? Find both opinions in the commentaries above.
- Ramban doesn't relate to the above question at all, but presents a different position about why the priests need to wear special clothes. According to Ramban's opinion, who do you think the special clothes are meant to affect?

TEXTUAL SKILLS

1. Three verses in this passage begin with the same word. What is that word and why is it surprising?
2. Note: this is the first time in the Torah that we hear of a special status for Aharon, and his name is mentioned seven times. In three of those instances, he is specifically identified as Moshe's brother.

The clothes of the High Priest

פרשת תצוה

כז
כ וְאַתָּה תְּצַוֶּה ׀ אֶת־בְּנֵי יִשְׂרָאֵל וְיִקְחוּ אֵלֶיךָ שֶׁמֶן זַיִת זָךְ כָּתִית לַמָּאוֹר לְהַעֲלֹת נֵר תָּמִיד: כא בְּאֹהֶל מוֹעֵד מִחוּץ לַפָּרֹכֶת אֲשֶׁר עַל־הָעֵדֻת יַעֲרֹךְ אֹתוֹ אַהֲרֹן וּבָנָיו מֵעֶרֶב עַד־בֹּקֶר לִפְנֵי יהוה חֻקַּת עוֹלָם לְדֹרֹתָם מֵאֵת בְּנֵי יִשְׂרָאֵל:

כח
א וְאַתָּה הַקְרֵב אֵלֶיךָ אֶת־אַהֲרֹן אָחִיךָ וְאֶת־בָּנָיו אִתּוֹ מִתּוֹךְ בְּנֵי יִשְׂרָאֵל לְכַהֲנוֹ־לִי אַהֲרֹן נָדָב וַאֲבִיהוּא אֶלְעָזָר וְאִיתָמָר בְּנֵי אַהֲרֹן: ב וְעָשִׂיתָ בִגְדֵי־קֹדֶשׁ לְאַהֲרֹן אָחִיךָ לְכָבוֹד וּלְתִפְאָרֶת: ג וְאַתָּה תְּדַבֵּר אֶל־כָּל־חַכְמֵי־לֵב אֲשֶׁר מִלֵּאתִיו רוּחַ חָכְמָה וְעָשׂוּ אֶת־בִּגְדֵי אַהֲרֹן לְקַדְּשׁוֹ לְכַהֲנוֹ־לִי: ד וְאֵלֶּה הַבְּגָדִים אֲשֶׁר יַעֲשׂוּ חֹשֶׁן וְאֵפוֹד וּמְעִיל וּכְתֹנֶת תַּשְׁבֵּץ מִצְנֶפֶת וְאַבְנֵט וְעָשׂוּ בִגְדֵי־קֹדֶשׁ לְאַהֲרֹן אָחִיךָ וּלְבָנָיו לְכַהֲנוֹ־לִי: ה וְהֵם יִקְחוּ אֶת־הַזָּהָב וְאֶת־הַתְּכֵלֶת וְאֶת־הָאַרְגָּמָן וְאֶת־תּוֹלַעַת הַשָּׁנִי וְאֶת־הַשֵּׁשׁ:

CLASSIC COMMENTATORS

Why do the priests have to wear special clothes?

רמב״ן
כי אלה הבגדים לבושי מלכות הן, כדמותן ילבשו המלכים בזמן התורה.

RAMBAN
For the clothes being described now are royal garments, and are similar to those favored by kings in the time of the Torah.

עקדת יצחק
וכמו שאדם ניכר בלבושו הכרה חיצונית אם סוחר אם פרש, אם פרוש (נזיר), כן התחלת הכרת נפשותינו הנעלמות היא בפעולותיהן החיצוניות, כי ודאי מהפעולות ייוודעו הכוחות.

AKEDAT YITZHAK
The uniform that an individual wears and the appearance he presents identify the office that he holds – be he merchant, horseman, or Nazirite. In a similar manner, a clue to a person's character is first broadcast by his behavior, for one's actions certainly betray the nature of his personality.

6 They are to make the ephod of finely spun linen embroidered with gold,
7 and sky-blue, purple and scarlet wool. It should have two shoulder pieces
8 attached to its two edges so that it can be joined together. The decorated waistband on it shall be like it and of one piece with it, made of gold, of
9 sky-blue, purple, and scarlet wool and finely spun linen. Take two onyx
10 stones and engrave on them the names of Yisrael's sons: six names on one stone and the remaining six names on the other, in the order of their birth.
11 Engrave the two stones with the names of Yisrael's sons as a gem cutter
12 engraves a seal, then mount them in gold filigree settings. Place the two stones on the shoulder-pieces of the ephod as remembrance stones for the sons of Yisrael. Thus will Aharon carry their names on his shoulders
13 as a remembrance before the Lord. Make gold filigree settings and two
14

The ephod

אבן עזרא

והנה על האבן האחת: ראובן שמעון לוי ויהודה דן ונפתלי. ועל האבן השנית: גד אשר יששכר זבולון יוסף ובנימין. וזה טעם: כתולדתם.

ר' אברהם בן הרמב"ם

ששה משמותם וג' – למדה הקבלה שהשחרות אל האבן הימנית "ראובן לוי יששכר נפתלי גד יהוסף" ועל האבן השמאלית "שמעון יהודה זבולון דן אשר בנימן".

ר' שמשון רפאל הירש

לגבי סדר השמות בשתי האבנים, אומרת הגמרא (שם): "בני לאה כסידרן בני רחל אחד מכאן ואחד מכאן ובני שפחות באמצע", ומפרש רש"י (שם): ששת בני לאה – ראובן, שמעון, לוי, יהודה, יששכר וזבולון – על האבן האחת; ועל האבן השנייה שני בני רחל – בנימין ויוסף, וביניהם בני השפחות – דן, נפתלי, גד ואשר. זהו גם הסדר בו נמנו לעיל (א, ב-ד).

IBN EZRA

The first stone held the names: Reuven, Shimon, Levi, Yehuda, Dan, and Naftali, while on the second stone were engraved the names of the other six tribes: Gad, Asher, Yissakhar, Zevulun, Yosef, and Binyamin. Thus were the names presented in chronological order of their bearers' births.

RABBI AVRAHAM BEN HARAMBAM

Our tradition teaches that the right hand stone held the names: Reuven, Levi, Yissakhar, Naftali, Gad, and Yosef. And the left hand stone bore the names: Shimon, Yehuda, Zevulun, Dan, Asher, and Binyamin.

RABBI SAMSON RAPHAEL HIRSCH

According to the Talmud, the names of the tribes were presented as follows: The names of Leah's sons appeared in sequence, the names of Raḥel's sons were here and there, and the names of the maidservants' sons were in the middle. Commenting on this, Rashi explains: The names of Leah's six sons – Reuven, Shimon, Levi, Yehuda, Yissakhar, and Zevulun – were engraved on one stone. On the second stone the names of Raḥel's two sons were split up: Yosef was at the top of the list, and Binyamin was at the bottom. In between those two brothers' names were those of the maidservants' sons: Dan, Naftali, Gad, and Asher. Indeed, this is the sequence by which all twelve sons are mentioned at the start of the book (Ex. 1:2–4).

QUESTIONS FOR THOUGHT

- Each of the opinions above has a rational explanation. Try to figure out the rationale for each.
- Which explanation do you think fits the words of the Torah best?
- Which rationale do you think is most appropriate for the ephod?

ו וְעָשׂוּ אֶת־הָאֵפֹד זָהָב תְּכֵלֶת וְאַרְגָּמָן תּוֹלַעַת שָׁנִי וְשֵׁשׁ מָשְׁזָר
מַעֲשֵׂה חֹשֵׁב: ז שְׁתֵּי כְתֵפֹת חֹבְרֹת יִהְיֶה־לּוֹ אֶל־שְׁנֵי קְצוֹתָיו
וְחֻבָּר: ח וְחֵשֶׁב אֲפֻדָּתוֹ אֲשֶׁר עָלָיו כְּמַעֲשֵׂהוּ מִמֶּנּוּ יִהְיֶה זָהָב
תְּכֵלֶת וְאַרְגָּמָן וְתוֹלַעַת שָׁנִי וְשֵׁשׁ מָשְׁזָר: ט וְלָקַחְתָּ אֶת־שְׁתֵּי
אַבְנֵי־שֹׁהַם וּפִתַּחְתָּ עֲלֵיהֶם שְׁמוֹת בְּנֵי יִשְׂרָאֵל: י שִׁשָּׁה
מִשְּׁמֹתָם עַל הָאֶבֶן הָאֶחָת וְאֶת־שְׁמוֹת הַשִּׁשָּׁה הַנּוֹתָרִים
עַל־הָאֶבֶן הַשֵּׁנִית כְּתוֹלְדֹתָם: יא מַעֲשֵׂה חָרַשׁ אֶבֶן פִּתּוּחֵי חֹתָם
תְּפַתַּח אֶת־שְׁתֵּי הָאֲבָנִים עַל־שְׁמֹת בְּנֵי יִשְׂרָאֵל מֻסַבֹּת
מִשְׁבְּצוֹת זָהָב תַּעֲשֶׂה אֹתָם: יב וְשַׂמְתָּ אֶת־שְׁתֵּי הָאֲבָנִים עַל
כִּתְפֹת הָאֵפֹד אַבְנֵי זִכָּרֹן לִבְנֵי יִשְׂרָאֵל וְנָשָׂא אַהֲרֹן אֶת־שְׁמוֹתָם
לִפְנֵי יְהוָה עַל־שְׁתֵּי כְתֵפָיו לְזִכָּרֹן: יג וְעָשִׂיתָ [שני]
מִשְׁבְּצֹת זָהָב: יד וּשְׁתֵּי שַׁרְשְׁרֹת זָהָב טָהוֹר מִגְבָּלֹת תַּעֲשֶׂה
אֹתָם מַעֲשֵׂה עֲבֹת וְנָתַתָּה אֶת־שַׁרְשְׁרֹת הָעֲבֹתֹת עַל־

CLASSIC COMMENTATORS

The two stones on the shoulder straps of the ephod had the names of the twelve tribes engraved in them. While the Torah says that they should be listed with "six names on one stone and the remaining six names on the other, in the order of their birth," there is great discussion about what the order actually is.

RASHI

The names are to be inscribed in the order in which their original bearers were born. Thus the words inscribed on the first stone were: Reuven, Shimon, Levi, Yehuda, Dan, Naftali. The second stone featured the names: Gad, Asher, Yissakhar, Zevulun, Yosef, Binyamin. The last name was written with its full spelling [with a *yod* appearing as the penultimate letter], for that is the form used in the verse reporting that individual's birth [see Gen. 35:18; this second *yod* is often absent when the name Binyamin is mentioned]. Each stone bore a total of twenty-five letters each.

רש״י

כסדר שנולדו: ראובן שמעון לוי יהודה דן נפתלי על האחת, ועל השנית: גד אשר יששכר זבולן יוסף בנימין מלא, שכך הוא כתוב מלא במקום תולדותיו, עשרים וחמש אותיות בכל אחת ואחת.

sets of pure gold chains braided into cords, and attach the cords of chains to the settings.
15 Make a breast piece for judgment. Make it with the same skilled craftsmanship as the
16 ephod: of gold, of sky-blue, purple and scarlet wool, and of finely spun linen. It shall be
17 square and folded double, a span long and a span wide. Mount four rows of precious
18 stones onto it: the first row a ruby, a peridot and an emerald; the second row a carbuncle,
19 a lapis lazuli and a clear quartz; the third row a jacinth, an agate and an amethyst; and
20
21 the fourth a beryl, an onyx and a chalcedony. Mount them in gold filigree settings. The
stones shall correspond to the names of Yisrael's sons. Each stone should be engraved

The ḥoshen

QUESTIONS FOR THOUGHT
- According to the different commentaries, was the ḥoshen meant for individuals or for the nation as whole?
- According to the different commentaries, is the ḥoshen meant to relate things that happened in the past, that are happening the present, or that are going to happen in the future?

שמות | פרק כח

טו וְעָשִׂיתָ חֹשֶׁן מִשְׁפָּט מַעֲשֵׂה חֹשֵׁב כְּמַעֲשֵׂה אֵפֹד תַּעֲשֶׂנּוּ זָהָב תְּכֵלֶת וְאַרְגָּמָן וְתוֹלַעַת שָׁנִי וְשֵׁשׁ מָשְׁזָר תַּעֲשֶׂה אֹתוֹ:
טז רָבוּעַ יִהְיֶה כָּפוּל זֶרֶת אָרְכּוֹ וְזֶרֶת רָחְבּוֹ:
יז וּמִלֵּאתָ בוֹ מִלֻּאַת אֶבֶן אַרְבָּעָה טוּרִים אָבֶן טוּר אֹדֶם פִּטְדָה וּבָרֶקֶת הַטּוּר הָאֶחָד:
יח וְהַטּוּר הַשֵּׁנִי נֹפֶךְ סַפִּיר וְיָהֲלֹם:
יט וְהַטּוּר הַשְּׁלִישִׁי לֶשֶׁם שְׁבוֹ וְאַחְלָמָה:
כ וְהַטּוּר הָרְבִיעִי תַּרְשִׁישׁ וְשֹׁהַם וְיָשְׁפֵה מְשֻׁבָּצִים זָהָב יִהְיוּ בְּמִלּוּאֹתָם:
כא וְהָאֲבָנִים תִּהְיֶיןָ עַל־שְׁמֹת בְּנֵי־יִשְׂרָאֵל שְׁתֵּים עֶשְׂרֵה עַל־שְׁמֹתָם פִּתּוּחֵי חוֹתָם

CLASSIC COMMENTATORS

What was the purpose of the *ḥoshen* with its Urim and Tumim?

RASHI
רש"י

It serves to atone for faulty rulings [perpetrated by careless judges]. Another interpretation for the term **משפט** ("judgment") here: The breast piece can be employed to clarify the words of the inquirer, and his actions are guaranteed to be correct [when he follows the received communication]… For the term **משפט** has three connotations. Firstly, it can refer to a claim brought by litigants [that is, the demand for a trial]; secondly, it can mean the verdict given in a court case; thirdly, **משפט** might refer to the actual punishment – capital punishment, lashes, or a monetary fine. In our verse, the term is used to indicate the clarification of a matter [i.e., the verdict] where an individual's words are made intelligible.

שמכפר על קילקול הדין. דבר אחר: משפט - שמברר דבריו והבטחתו אמת ... שהמשפט משמש שלשה לשונות - דברי טענות הדיינין, וגמר דין, ועונש הדין, אם עונש מיתה, אם עונש מכות, אם עונש ממון. וזה משמש לשון דברים, שמפרש ומברר דבריו.

RASHBAM
רשב"ם

With the Urim and Tumim inside it, the item served to determine justice for Israel, and to express the nation's needs. Thus the verse states, "And he [Yehoshua, upon taking office] shall stand before Elazar the priest, who shall ask counsel for him after the judgment of the Urim before the Lord" (Num. 27:21). Therefore it is called "judgment."

לפי שנתנו בחשוב האורים והתומים שמגידין משפט ישראל וצורכיהם, כדכתיב: "ושאל לו במשפט האורים לכן קרוי: משפט".

RALBAG
רלב"ג

The breast piece of judgment was so called because the High Priest was meant to use this utensil to judge [gauge] the future based on questions posed to him.

נקרא כן בעבור כי בו ישפוט הכהן על העתידות שישאלוהו מהם.

22 like a seal, with one of the names of the twelve tribes. Make chains of pure gold, braided
23 into cords, for the breast piece. Make the breast piece two gold rings and attach them
24 to its two corners. Then fasten the two gold chains to the two gold rings at the corners
25 of the breast piece. Attach the other ends of the chains to the two settings. Thus they
26 will be joined to the ephod's shoulder pieces at the front. Make two gold rings and place
them at the two other corners of the breast piece on the edge, inside, next to the ephod.
27 Make two more gold rings and attach them to the bottom of the ephod's two shoulder
28 pieces facing its front, close to its seam and above the ephod's woven waistband. The
breast piece shall be held in place by a cord of sky-blue from its rings to the rings of the
ephod, so that the breast piece remains secured above the ephod's waistband, and does
29 not come loose from the ephod. Thus will Aharon carry the names of Yisrael's sons on
the breast piece of judgment at his heart whenever he enters the sanctuary, as a remem-
30 brance before the LORD at all times. Place the Urim and Tumim in the breast piece of
judgment so that they too will be at Aharon's heart when he comes before the LORD.
Aharon will then always be carrying at his heart Israel's means of judgment, before the

---

WISDOM OF THE HEART

Rav Mosheh Lichtenstein shares such a wonderful teaching on the Torah's insistence that the *ḥoshen* be attached firmly to the ephod. The shoulder straps of the ephod, which link it to the *ḥoshen*, have two identical onyx stones. This is contrasted to the *ḥoshen*, which has twelve distinctive stones. The stones on the *ḥoshen* reflect individuality and creativity, while those on the ephod's shoulder straps symbolize uniformity and the collective. The *ḥoshen* is worn on the heart, reflecting the uniqueness of every individual; the ephod straps sit on the shoulders, signifying the burden of the community. In the end, the Torah insists that they be connected. Being part of a community should not stifle individual expression, but that individuality should not imply divorcing oneself from the community.

Can you imagine situations in which it would be difficult to balance individuality and commitment to community?

QUICK BITE

The last of the stones in the breast piece of the High Priest is the ישפה, translated here as chalcedony. There is a story told in Kiddushin (31a), as well as in the Talmud Yerushalmi (Kiddushin 1:7), in which this stone needed to be replaced. The rabbis' search brought them to a non-Jew named Dama son of Netina, whose father had such a stone. When the rabbis arrived, his father was asleep and the key to the safety box in which the precious stones were kept was resting under his father's head. Retrieving the key would require waking his father, and Dama, out of respect for his father, refrained from waking him and lost the deal. *Meshekh Ḥokhma* notes that the ישפה was the stone representing the tribe of Binyamin, who was the only one of Yosef's brothers who did not participate in the selling of Yosef and the deception of their father. In that light, he was the only one who showed respect for his father. How appropriate it is that the story in the Gemara about honoring one's father was about the ישפה stone!

כב אִ֗ישׁ עַל־שְׁמ֛וֹ תִּהְיֶ֖יןָ לִשְׁנֵ֥י עָשָׂ֖ר שָֽׁבֶט: וְעָשִׂ֧יתָ עַל־הַחֹ֛שֶׁן
כג שַׁרְשֹׁ֥ת גַּבְלֻ֖ת מַעֲשֵׂ֣ה עֲבֹ֑ת זָהָ֖ב טָהֽוֹר: וְעָשִׂ֗יתָ עַל־הַחֹ֔שֶׁן שְׁתֵּ֖י טַבְּע֣וֹת זָהָ֑ב וְנָתַתָּ֗ אֶת־שְׁתֵּי֙ הַטַּבָּע֔וֹת עַל־שְׁנֵ֖י קְצ֥וֹת
כד הַחֹֽשֶׁן: וְנָתַתָּ֗ה אֶת־שְׁתֵּי֙ עֲבֹתֹ֣ת הַזָּהָ֔ב עַל־שְׁתֵּ֖י הַטַּבָּעֹ֑ת אֶל־
כה קְצ֖וֹת הַחֹֽשֶׁן: וְאֵ֗ת שְׁתֵּי֙ קְצ֣וֹת שְׁתֵּ֣י הָעֲבֹתֹ֔ת תִּתֵּ֖ן עַל־שְׁתֵּ֣י הַֽמִּשְׁבְּצ֑וֹת וְנָתַתָּ֛ה עַל־כִּתְפ֥וֹת הָאֵפֹ֖ד אֶל־מ֥וּל פָּנָֽיו: וְעָשִׂ֗יתָ
כו שְׁתֵּי֙ טַבְּע֣וֹת זָהָ֔ב וְשַׂמְתָּ֣ אֹתָ֔ם עַל־שְׁנֵ֖י קְצ֣וֹת הַחֹ֑שֶׁן עַל־שְׂפָת֕וֹ אֲשֶׁ֛ר אֶל־עֵ֥בֶר הָאֵפ֖וֹד בָּֽיְתָה: וְעָשִׂ֗יתָ שְׁתֵּ֣י טַבְּע֣וֹת זָהָב֮ וְנָתַתָּ֣ה
כז אֹתָ֡ם עַל־שְׁתֵּי֩ כִתְפ֨וֹת הָאֵפ֤וֹד מִלְּמַ֨טָּה֙ מִמּ֣וּל פָּנָ֔יו לְעֻמַּ֖ת מֶחְבַּרְתּ֑וֹ מִמַּ֕עַל לְחֵ֖שֶׁב הָאֵפֽוֹד: וְיִרְכְּס֣וּ אֶת־הַ֠חֹ֠שֶׁן מִטַּבְּעֹתָ֞ו
כח אֶל־טַבְּעֹ֤ת הָֽאֵפֹד֙ בִּפְתִ֣יל תְּכֵ֔לֶת לִֽהְי֖וֹת עַל־חֵ֣שֶׁב הָאֵפ֑וֹד
כט וְלֹֽא־יִזַּ֣ח הַחֹ֔שֶׁן מֵעַ֖ל הָאֵפֽוֹד: וְנָשָׂ֣א אַ֠הֲרֹ֠ן אֶת־שְׁמ֨וֹת בְּנֵֽי־יִשְׂרָאֵ֜ל בְּחֹ֧שֶׁן הַמִּשְׁפָּ֛ט עַל־לִבּ֖וֹ בְּבֹא֣וֹ אֶל־הַקֹּ֑דֶשׁ
ל לְזִכָּרֹ֥ן לִפְנֵֽי־יְהוָֹ֖ה תָּמִֽיד: וְנָתַתָּ֞ אֶל־חֹ֣שֶׁן הַמִּשְׁפָּ֗ט אֶת־הָֽאוּרִים֙ וְאֶת־הַתֻּמִּ֔ים וְהָיוּ֙ עַל־לֵ֣ב אַהֲרֹ֔ן בְּבֹא֖וֹ לִפְנֵ֣י יְהוָ֑ה וְנָשָׂ֣א אַ֠הֲרֹ֠ן אֶת־מִשְׁפַּ֨ט בְּנֵֽי־יִשְׂרָאֵ֧ל עַל־לִבּ֛וֹ לִפְנֵ֥י יְהוָ֖ה

TEXTUAL SKILLS

1. Notice the similarity between verse 29 and the end of verse 30.
2. Notice the similarity in the language at the beginning of verse 30 and at the beginning of 25:21. Can you find other parallels between the construction of the Ark and that of the ḥoshen?
3. Notice the language at the beginning of verse 30. Are the Urim and Tumim one thing or two different things?

31
32 Lord. Make the robe of the ephod entirely of sky-blue wool. It should have an opening for the head in the middle with a woven border around it like the neck of a coat of mail,
33 so that it does not tear. Around the hem of the robe make pomegranates of sky-blue, purple and scarlet wool, and between them put gold bells, so that gold bells and pome-
34
35 granates alternate around the hem of the robe. Aharon shall wear this robe whenever he ministers, and its sound will be heard when he enters the sanctuary before the Lord

The robe

QUESTIONS FOR THOUGHT

- The commentaries on this fall into two general categories – those who see the bells as serving a practical purpose and those who see them as serving a symbolic one. Into which category does each of the commentaries above fit?
- For whose "benefit" are the bells?

TEXTUAL SKILLS

1. The phrase **כפי תחרא** (v. 32) appears only twice in all of Tanakh, both as part of the description of the priestly robe.
2. Verse 33 describes golden bells and woven pomegranates on the bottom of the robe. Are the bells inside the pomegranates or interspersed between them?

שמות | פרק כח

לא וְעָשִׂיתָ אֶת־מְעִיל הָאֵפוֹד כְּלִיל תְּכֵלֶת: *שלישי*
תָּמִיד:
לב וְהָיָה פִי־רֹאשׁוֹ בְּתוֹכוֹ שָׂפָה יִהְיֶה לְפִיו סָבִיב מַעֲשֵׂה אֹרֵג כְּפִי
תַחְרָא יִהְיֶה־לּוֹ לֹא יִקָּרֵעַ: לג וְעָשִׂיתָ עַל־שׁוּלָיו רִמֹּנֵי תְּכֵלֶת
וְאַרְגָּמָן וְתוֹלַעַת שָׁנִי עַל־שׁוּלָיו סָבִיב וּפַעֲמֹנֵי זָהָב בְּתוֹכָם
סָבִיב: לד פַּעֲמֹן זָהָב וְרִמּוֹן פַּעֲמֹן זָהָב וְרִמּוֹן עַל־שׁוּלֵי הַמְּעִיל
סָבִיב: לה וְהָיָה עַל־אַהֲרֹן לְשָׁרֵת וְנִשְׁמַע קוֹלוֹ בְּבֹאוֹ אֶל־הַקֹּדֶשׁ

CLASSIC COMMENTATORS

The robe had bells on it which were supposed to be heard. This was so significant that the verse states: "Its sound will be heard when he enters the sanctuary before the Lord and when he leaves, so that he will not die." Why was it so important for the High Priest to make noise in the sanctuary?

רשב״ם

לפי שציוה הקב״ה: וכל אדם לא יהיה באהל מועד בבאו לכפר בקדש עד צאתו כך ציוה הקב״ה: ונשמע קולו בבאו, ויתרחקו השומעים משם.

RASHBAM

Now since the Holy One, blessed be He, commanded, "And there shall be no man in the Tent of Meeting when he goes in to make atonement in the holy place, until he comes out" (Lev. 16:17), God also ordered that "its sound will be heard when he enters the sanctuary." In other words, when the attendant priests hear Aharon approaching, they will be signaled to leave the site.

רמב״ן

בעבור שישמע קולו בקדש, ויכנס לפני אדוניו כאלו ברשות, כי הבא בהיכל מלך פתאום חייב מיתה בטכסיסי המלכות... וכן בצאתו, לצאת ברשות, ושיודע הדבר כדי שיוכלו משרתי המלך לשוב לפניו.

RAMBAN

When the High Priest walked through the sanctuary, the bells on his robe would signal his approach toward the Holy of Holies and serve as a sort of request to advance toward his Master. For it is a universal rule that one does not intrude upon the presence of a king suddenly and without being announced... Similarly, the ringing of the garment's ornaments indicated the man's departure from the presence of the King, thereby allowing His other servants to return.

רלב״ג

וזה היה סיבה אל שישמע קול אהרן בבואו אל הקודש, ויעירהו להתבונן במה שהיה בקודש ובמה שהיה עליו מהבגדים לאי־זה תכלית היה... ולזאת הסיבה בעינה לא היה אפשר שיכנס שם הכהן אם היה שתוי יין, כמו שיתבאר במה שיבוא, כי היין ימנעהו מהתבונן באלו הדברים כראוי.

RALBAG

It was these ornaments which created the sounds that accompanied Aharon when he entered the sanctuary. The ringing of the bells is intended to focus the High Priest's thoughts upon the purpose of his presence in the sanctuary, and the reason he is wearing the sacred vestments... In similar fashion, we find that it was forbidden for a priest to enter the sacred precincts if he was inebriated, as I will explain below [in comments on Leviticus 10:9–10], for alcohol consumption would prevent the individual from concentrating his thoughts in the appropriate manner.

36 and when he leaves, so that he will not die. Make a headplate of pure gold and engrave
37 on it, as on a seal: Holy to the Lord. Attach a cord of sky-blue to it, so that it can be
38 fixed to the miter, affixed to the miter's front. It shall remain on Aharon's forehead, that Aharon may bear away all guilt that arises from the holy offerings the Israelites consecrate, from all their sacred gifts; it shall be on his forehead always, that they may find

The headplate

QUICK BITE

The Ari z"l explains that the High Priest represented the best version of ourselves. He was an image of the piety and love that we all are capable of. On this gold plate on his forehead were inscribed the words קדש לה׳. When a good and decent person gazed at it, these words would inspire them to higher levels of growth. And when people who had sinned gazed at it, it would move them to do *teshuva*. The potency and power of seeing the name of God on the head of the High Priest is something we cannot directly relate to in our time. However, think about what it means to look at something or someone that inspires you to be better.

לו לִפְנֵי יְהוָה וּבְצֵאתוֹ וְלֹא יָמוּת: וְעָשִׂיתָ צִּיץ זָהָב
לז טָהוֹר וּפִתַּחְתָּ עָלָיו פִּתּוּחֵי חֹתָם קֹדֶשׁ לַיהוָה: וְשַׂמְתָּ אֹתוֹ
עַל־פְּתִיל תְּכֵלֶת וְהָיָה עַל־הַמִּצְנָפֶת אֶל־מוּל פְּנֵי־הַמִּצְנֶפֶת
לח יִהְיֶה: וְהָיָה עַל־מֵצַח אַהֲרֹן וְנָשָׂא אַהֲרֹן אֶת־עֲוֹן הַקֳּדָשִׁים
אֲשֶׁר יַקְדִּישׁוּ בְּנֵי יִשְׂרָאֵל לְכָל־מַתְּנֹת קָדְשֵׁיהֶם וְהָיָה עַל־

CLASSIC COMMENTATORS

Engraved on the headplate were the words קודש לה׳, "Holy to the Lord." To what do these words refer?

RASHBAM
רשב״ם

These served as a remembrance to the Holy One, blessed be He, to atone for sins that might be committed during Israel's sacrificial service.

כלומר: הקב״ה מרצה עון הקדשים.

RABBI AVRAHAM BEN HARAMBAM
ר' אברהם בן הרמב״ם

The phrase "Holy to the Lord" implied that the bearer of these words – Aharon and every descendant of his who served as High Priest – was sanctified to God.

הכינוי והכוונה כאן בקדש על הלובש היינו אהרן וכל כהן גדול מבניו.

QUESTIONS FOR THOUGHT

- According to Rashbam, to *what* does "Holy to the Lord" refer?
- According to R. Avraham ben HaRambam, *who* is "Holy to the Lord"?
- Can you think of another possibility as to what those words are referring to?

TEXTUAL SKILLS

1. Think back to a special feature that the Ark and the table both have. To what special feature could the headplate be compared?
2. Notice that this is the second of the articles of clothing for the High Priest for which the word תמיד is used. Do you recall where that word was very prominent in the description of the *Mishkan* vessels?

WISDOM OF THE HEART

On his forehead the High Priest wore a golden band with God's four-letter name engraved upon it, and he was not permitted to raise his hands above his head lest it appear that he was suggesting that something was higher than God. Perhaps there is something we can learn from this: we, too, should not raise our hands above God's name – meaning, we should not decide on our own how we access spirituality. The Torah provides the guidance and the means necessary for that.

39 favor in the LORD's sight. Quilt the tunic of fine linen. Make a miter out of fine linen,
40 and an embroidered sash. Make tunics, sashes and caps for Aharon's sons, for glory and
41 for splendor. Put these on your brother Aharon and his sons; then anoint, ordain and
42 consecrate them to serve Me as priests. Make them linen trousers to cover their naked-
43 ness, reaching from waist to thigh. They must be worn by Aharon and his sons whenever they enter the Tent of Meeting or approach the altar to minister in the sanctuary so that they do not incur guilt and die. This shall be a law for Aharon and his descendants for

The clothes of the ordinary priests

TEXTUAL SKILLS

1. The trousers seem to be listed as an afterthought. Based on what the Torah describes as their function, why are they separated from the other clothes of the priests?
2. The Torah does not separate between this passage and the one which precedes it, the one that describes the headplate worn by the High Priest. On the surface there seems to be no connection between them. Find the phrase that appears in both halves of the passage which links them.

WISDOM OF THE HEART

There is a strange phrase used to describe the inauguration of the priests: "מלאת את ידם" (translated here as "ordain them"), literally meaning "fill their hands". Many explanations have been offered to explain it. Or HaHayyim suggests that this means we should enable them to have an impact beyond the walls of the Mishkan. Our religious work is important – but it truly gains significance only when the work and strides we make affect the people outside of our inner sphere. "Fill their hands" – for the hands to reach out and touch others.

How do we share our special experiences with others and draw them in, rather than push them away?

מִצְחוֹ תָּמִיד לְרָצוֹן לָהֶם לִפְנֵי יְהוָה: וְשִׁבַּצְתָּ הַכְּתֹנֶת שֵׁשׁ לט
וְעָשִׂיתָ מִצְנֶפֶת שֵׁשׁ וְאַבְנֵט תַּעֲשֶׂה מַעֲשֵׂה רֹקֵם: וְלִבְנֵי אַהֲרֹן מ
תַּעֲשֶׂה כֻתֳּנֹת וְעָשִׂיתָ לָהֶם אַבְנֵטִים וּמִגְבָּעוֹת תַּעֲשֶׂה לָהֶם
לְכָבוֹד וּלְתִפְאָרֶת: וְהִלְבַּשְׁתָּ אֹתָם אֶת־אַהֲרֹן אָחִיךָ וְאֶת־בָּנָיו מא
אִתּוֹ וּמָשַׁחְתָּ אֹתָם וּמִלֵּאתָ אֶת־יָדָם וְקִדַּשְׁתָּ אֹתָם וְכִהֲנוּ־לִי:
וַעֲשֵׂה לָהֶם מִכְנְסֵי־בָד לְכַסּוֹת בְּשַׂר עֶרְוָה מִמָּתְנַיִם וְעַד־יְרֵכַיִם מב
יִהְיוּ: וְהָיוּ עַל־אַהֲרֹן וְעַל־בָּנָיו בְּבֹאָם ׀ אֶל־אֹהֶל מוֹעֵד אוֹ מג
בְגִשְׁתָּם אֶל־הַמִּזְבֵּחַ לְשָׁרֵת בַּקֹּדֶשׁ וְלֹא־יִשְׂאוּ עָוֺן וָמֵתוּ חֻקַּת

CLASSIC COMMENTATORS

In verse 40, the Torah describes the clothing as being for "glory" and "splendor." Does this refer to all the clothes worn by the priest or only to the special caps?

RASHBAM

Because the caps were worn on the priests' heads they had to be particularly beautiful.

רשב״ם

לפי שהמגבעות על הראש צריכים יפוי נאה ביותר.

RABBI AVRAHAM BEN HARAMBAM

The reason that the vestments of the ordinary priests – that is, the sons of Aharon – had to be fashioned as beautiful garments of quality material, made with craftsmanship, was so that they would provide a sense of glory and splendor to the men who wore them.

ר' אברהם בן הרמב״ם

הטעם שגם בבגדי כהונה, (אלה) שהם בגדי בני אהרן יהיה שיפור ויופי וטובת החומר ומעשה אומן כדי שיהיה בלבישתם כבוד ותפארת.

QUESTIONS FOR THOUGHT

- If only the caps are for glory and splendor, what are the other clothes for?
- Why might it be valuable for all the priests to wear standardized clothes?
- Do the *taamei hamikra* (the "*trop*") seem to support the position of Rashbam or that of Rabbi Avraham ben HaRambam?

SHEMOT | CHAPTER 29   TETZAVEH | 254

> With the close of the description of how to build the Mishkan, its vessels, and the clothes for the priests, Moshe is instructed to begin the process of consecrating the priests. It begins with preparing certain offerings, including both animals and grain products, anointing Aharon as High Priest, and dressing Aharon and his sons in the priestly clothes.

29 1 all time. This is what you must do to consecrate them to serve Me as priests. Take a
2 young bull, two unblemished rams, and unleavened bread, unleavened loaves mixed with oil, and unleavened wafers brushed with oil – all made of fine wheat flour. Place
3 these in a basket and bring them in the basket together with the young bull and two
4 rams. Bring Aharon and his sons to the entrance of the Tent of Meeting, and you shall
5 wash them with water. Then take the vestments and dress Aharon in the tunic, the robe of the ephod, the ephod itself and the breast piece. Fasten the ephod on him by its woven
6 waistband. Put the miter on his head and on the miter place the sacred diadem. Take
7 the anointing oil, pour it on his head and anoint him. Then bring his sons forward and
8 dress them with the tunics. Gird Aharon and his sons with the sashes and fasten their
9 headdresses. The priesthood shall be theirs as a law for all time. Thus you shall ordain

---

QUESTIONS FOR THOUGHT

- According to the order in the Torah, the anointing is the last item on this list of things to do. Why would Ibn Ezra insist that the anointing happened earlier than when the Torah describes?
- How does Rabbi Isaac Samuel Reggio address Ibn Ezra's concern?
- Which of those two do you think Rashi agrees with?
- If Ibn Ezra is correct, why would the Torah have written to anoint the High Priest only after he is fully dressed?

TEXTUAL SKILLS

1. Moshe is commanded to dress Aharon and his sons in the special clothing made for them. Which article of clothing is absent? Why?

2. The ציץ ("headplate") is called by a different name or description here. What is it?

QUICK BITE

Before our many collective sins as a people, *Benei Yisrael* were like angels. After the episodes of the golden calf and the spies, and everything else that happened along their journey, we had been reminded just how mortal we really are. Still, the *Sefat Emet* adds that Aharon the High Priest and, by extension, the many great figures of Jewish history can show us what it is like to live as an angel. For example, the great *tzaddik* of Jerusalem at the beginning of the twentieth century – Rav Aryeh Levin – was said to have had a personality like that of an angel. He would visit broken Jews imprisoned in the jails of the British Mandate. There was no beggar who could walk by him without him showing empathy and care. Sometimes the greatness of angels can be found just one small act of *ḥesed* away. This, says the *Sefat Emet*, was the job of the High Priest – "לקדש אתם לכהן לי" (29:1).

שמות | פרק כט

כט א וְזֶ֨ה הַדָּבָ֜ר אֲשֶֽׁר־תַּעֲשֶׂ֤ה כב רביעי עוֹלָ֖ם ל֑וֹ וּלְזַרְע֖וֹ אַחֲרָֽיו:
לָהֶ֛ם לְקַדֵּ֥שׁ אֹתָ֖ם לְכַהֵ֣ן לִ֑י לְקַ֣ח פַּ֣ר אֶחָ֧ד בֶּן־בָּקָ֛ר וְאֵילִ֥ם שְׁנַ֖יִם
ב תְּמִימִֽם: וְלֶ֣חֶם מַצּ֗וֹת וְחַלֹּ֤ת מַצֹּת֙ בְּלוּלֹ֣ת בַּשֶּׁ֔מֶן וּרְקִיקֵ֥י מַצּ֖וֹת
ג מְשֻׁחִ֣ים בַּשָּׁ֑מֶן סֹ֥לֶת חִטִּ֖ים תַּעֲשֶׂ֥ה אֹתָֽם: וְנָתַתָּ֤ אוֹתָם֙ עַל־סַ֣ל
ד אֶחָ֔ד וְהִקְרַבְתָּ֥ אֹתָ֖ם בַּסָּ֑ל וְאֶ֨ת־הַפָּ֔ר וְאֵ֖ת שְׁנֵ֥י הָאֵילִֽם: וְאֶת־
אַהֲרֹ֤ן וְאֶת־בָּנָיו֙ תַּקְרִ֔יב אֶל־פֶּ֖תַח אֹ֣הֶל מוֹעֵ֑ד וְרָחַצְתָּ֥ אֹתָ֖ם
ה בַּמָּֽיִם: וְלָקַחְתָּ֣ אֶת־הַבְּגָדִ֗ים וְהִלְבַּשְׁתָּ֤ אֶֽת־אַהֲרֹן֙ אֶת־הַכֻּתֹּ֔נֶת
וְאֵת֙ מְעִ֣יל הָאֵפֹ֔ד וְאֶת־הָאֵפֹ֖ד וְאֶת־הַחֹ֑שֶׁן וְאָפַדְתָּ֣ ל֔וֹ בְּחֵ֖שֶׁב
ו הָאֵפֹֽד: וְשַׂמְתָּ֥ הַמִּצְנֶ֖פֶת עַל־רֹאשׁ֑וֹ וְנָתַתָּ֛ אֶת־נֵ֥זֶר הַקֹּ֖דֶשׁ עַל־
ז הַמִּצְנָֽפֶת: וְלָֽקַחְתָּ֙ אֶת־שֶׁ֣מֶן הַמִּשְׁחָ֔ה וְיָצַקְתָּ֖ עַל־רֹאשׁ֑וֹ
ח וּמָשַׁחְתָּ֖ אֹתֽוֹ: וְאֶת־בָּנָ֖יו תַּקְרִ֑יב וְהִלְבַּשְׁתָּ֖ם כֻּתֳּנֹֽת: וְחָגַרְתָּ֩
אֹתָ֨ם אַבְנֵ֜ט אַהֲרֹ֣ן וּבָנָ֗יו וְחָבַשְׁתָּ֤ לָהֶם֙ מִגְבָּעֹ֔ת וְהָיְתָ֥ה לָהֶ֛ם

CLASSIC COMMENTATORS

Moshe is told to anoint Aharon. There is a debate about when that anointment happened.

RASHI — רש״י

Moshe was to apply oil to Aharon's head and between his eyebrows, joining the oil in these two spots with his finger.

נותן שמן על ראשו ובין ריסי עיניו, ומחברן באצבעו.

IBN EZRA — אבן עזרא

The oil was applied to Aharon's head before the miter was placed upon him, for Moshe poured the oil only onto his brother's head [and not upon the miter itself].

והנה זה היה לפני שומו המצנפת על ראשו, כי על הראש יצוק לבדו.

RABBI ISAAC SAMUEL REGGIO — ר׳ יצחק שמואל רג׳יו

Moshe anointed Aharon after the miter was placed on the High Priest. For the miter was wrapped around Aharon's head and the oil was applied to the middle of the head which was exposed.

אחרי ששם המצנפת, כי הצניפה היתה סביב ואמצע הראש מגולה ועליו יצק השמן.

Shemot | Chapter 29

There are three sacrifices brought as part of the inauguration of the priests – one bull and two rams. Each of those is a different kind of sacrifice: the bull is a one-of-a-kind חטאת used only for the inauguration of the priests, while the first ram is an עולה, completely burnt on the altar. Both include the requirement that Aharon and his sons "lay their hands upon its head" – an action known as סמיכה, in which the person for whom the offering is being brought rests his entire body weight on the animal prior to the slaughtering.

10 Aharon and his sons. Then bring the young bull in front of the Tent of Meeting, and have Aharon and his sons lay their hands on its head. Slaughter the bull before the Lord
11,12 at the entrance of the Tent of Meeting. Take some of the bull's blood and put it on the horns of the altar with your finger. Pour out the rest of the blood at the base of the altar.
13 Take all the fat that covers the entrails, the diaphragm of the liver, and the two kidneys with the fat around them, and burn them on the altar. Burn the bull's flesh, its hide and
14,15 its waste outside the camp; it is a sin offering. Then take one of the rams and have
16 Aharon and his sons lay their hands upon its head, then slaughter it; let them take its
17 blood and sprinkle it on all the sides of the altar. Cut the ram into pieces, wash its entrails and legs, and put them with its pieces and its head. Burn the entire ram on the altar. It
18 is a burnt offering to the Lord, a pleasing aroma, a fire-offering to the Lord. Then take

---

QUESTIONS FOR THOUGHT

- One of the opinions is that the חטאת is to atone for past sins, while the other understands that it is an attempt to keep away from sin in the future. How does each of those make sense in the context of the inauguration of the priests?
- Rambam, in his discussion on repentance, describes the stages of the process of repentance (Laws of Repentance 2:2). How do these two opinions relate to the stages in Rambam's description?

TEXTUAL SKILLS

1. For the bull, notice where the animal is actually burned.
2. Notice the difference between the bull and the ram regarding where the blood is placed.

QUICK BITE

This מילואים ceremony was an elaborate process that served to induct the new High Priest and subsequent priests. Why does the Torah give us so much detail about this process? Rabbi Menachem Leibtag teaches that the care and attention given to the inauguration was similar in many ways to the warning given to *Benei Yisrael* in how they were to prepare for the approach to Mount Sinai. One cannot just barge into the service of the *Mishkan*. The *avoda* demands real reverence. The Zohar teaches us that all matters of sanctity require preparation and readying oneself – כל מילי דקדושה צריך הכנה והזמנה. This would also explain why the story of the binding of Yitzhak focuses on Avraham's actions. Avraham devoted two whole days to preparation before Yitzhak even knew what was happening.

כְּהֻנָּה לְחֻקַּת עוֹלָם וּמִלֵּאתָ יַד־אַהֲרֹן וְיַד־בָּנָיו: וְהִקְרַבְתָּ אֶת־
הַפָּר לִפְנֵי אֹהֶל מוֹעֵד וְסָמַךְ אַהֲרֹן וּבָנָיו אֶת־יְדֵיהֶם עַל־רֹאשׁ
הַפָּר: וְשָׁחַטְתָּ אֶת־הַפָּר לִפְנֵי יְהוָה פֶּתַח אֹהֶל מוֹעֵד: וְלָקַחְתָּ
מִדַּם הַפָּר וְנָתַתָּה עַל־קַרְנֹת הַמִּזְבֵּחַ בְּאֶצְבָּעֶךָ וְאֶת־כָּל־הַדָּם
תִּשְׁפֹּךְ אֶל־יְסוֹד הַמִּזְבֵּחַ: וְלָקַחְתָּ אֶת־כָּל־הַחֵלֶב הַמְכַסֶּה
אֶת־הַקֶּרֶב וְאֵת הַיֹּתֶרֶת עַל־הַכָּבֵד וְאֵת שְׁתֵּי הַכְּלָיֹת וְאֶת־
הַחֵלֶב אֲשֶׁר עֲלֵיהֶן וְהִקְטַרְתָּ הַמִּזְבֵּחָה: וְאֶת־בְּשַׂר הַפָּר וְאֶת־
עֹרוֹ וְאֶת־פִּרְשׁוֹ תִּשְׂרֹף בָּאֵשׁ מִחוּץ לַמַּחֲנֶה חַטָּאת הוּא:
וְאֶת־הָאַיִל הָאֶחָד תִּקָּח וְסָמְכוּ אַהֲרֹן וּבָנָיו אֶת־יְדֵיהֶם עַל־
רֹאשׁ הָאָיִל: וְשָׁחַטְתָּ אֶת־הָאָיִל וְלָקַחְתָּ אֶת־דָּמוֹ וְזָרַקְתָּ עַל־
הַמִּזְבֵּחַ סָבִיב: וְאֶת־הָאַיִל תְּנַתֵּחַ לִנְתָחָיו וְרָחַצְתָּ קִרְבּוֹ וּכְרָעָיו
וְנָתַתָּ עַל־נְתָחָיו וְעַל־רֹאשׁוֹ: וְהִקְטַרְתָּ אֶת־כָּל־הָאַיִל הַמִּזְבֵּחָה

CLASSIC COMMENTATORS

There are two very different understandings of the sacrifice called חטאת.

IBN EZRA

This sacrifice is called a חטאת because it was meant to atone for the sins [חטאת] of Aharon and his sons.

RABBI SAMSON RAPHAEL HIRSCH

It is my understanding that the term חטאת derives from the root ח-ט-א in the *pi'el* construction [the form which indicates an action that is performed with greater focus and intensity]. Hence the word חטאת need not necessarily connote a sacrifice brought to atone for sin that has already been committed [חָטָא], but to cleanse [לְחַטֵּא] oneself from sinning. That is, offering such a sacrifice reflects the donor's will to distance himself or herself from future transgression.

אבן עזרא

וטעם חטאת, כפור חטאת אהרן ובניו.

ר' שמשון רפאל הירש

מתקבל על הדעת ש"חטאת" נגזרת משורש "חטא" בבניין פיעל, "חִטֵּא", [הצורה המורה שהפעולה נעשית באופן מכוון וחזק יותר] לפיכך קרבן זה לא בא לכפר בהכרח על חטא שכבר נעשה [חָטָא], אלא בא "לְחַטֵּא": הוא מביע את רצונו של בעל הקרבן להתרחק מכל חטא בעתיד.

19 the second ram, and have Aharon and his sons lay their hands on its head. Slaughter the
20 ram, take some of its blood and put it on the ridges of the right ears of Aharon and his sons, and on the thumbs of their right hands and on the big toes of their right feet. Sprinkle the rest of the blood on the sides of the altar. Collect some of the blood on the
21 altar and some of the anointing oil and sprinkle it on Aharon and his vestments, and on his sons and his sons' vestments. Then he, and his sons with him, and their vestments,
22 will be consecrated. From the ram take its fat parts – the broad tail, the fat that covers the entrails, the diaphragm of the liver and the two kidneys with the fat on them – and the right thigh, for this is the ram of ordination. From the basket of unleavened bread
23 before the Lord, take one loaf of bread, one loaf of oil bread and one wafer. Place all of
24 these on the palms of Aharon and his sons, and have them wave them as a wave offering
25 before the Lord. Then take them from their hands and burn them on the altar with the burnt offering, for a pleasing aroma before the Lord. It is a fire offering to the Lord.
26 Take the breast of Aharon's ram of ordination and wave it as a wave offering before the
27 Lord; it shall be your portion. From Aharon and his sons' ram of ordination, consecrate the breast, the wave offering and the thigh, the upraised gift. These parts shall be the
28 Israelites' due to Aharon and his sons for all time. They are the Israelites' gift from their

---

RALBAG

רלב״ג

הנה זה היה באופן כריתת ברית. והנה היתה זאת הנתינה באלו המקומות הנזכרים, כי האוזן הוא כלי השמיעה, והידים והרגלים – כלי העשייה, כי ברגלים תהיה ההליכה ובידים תֵּעָשׂינה העבודות.

Placing blood on these body parts of the priests signaled that a covenant had been forged. Specifically, blood was dabbed on the priests' ears because that is the organ of hearing. Blood was put on the hands because these limbs are employed in the Tabernacle services, and on the feet because they convey the priests through the compound while they execute their holy duties.

RABBI SAMSON RAPHAEL HIRSCH

ר' שמשון רפאל הירש

יש לתת מן הדם, שהתקבל בכלי קודש, על אוזנם, ידם ורגלם של הכהנים, כדי שיתבוננו בכבוד ובעיקר שייתנו להם. האוזן (שמיעה והבנה), היד (עבודה יוצרת), והרגל (שאיפת התקדמות) – אלה הם התחומים העיקריים שבהם צריכה להוכיח את עצמה, האישיות שניתן לה כבוד הנהגת הציבור כאיל בראש הצאן.

This ritual was intended to focus the men on the gravity of the position they had acquired. The symbolism of the three organs is as follows. An individual's ear absorbs spiritual messages through word; his hands translate that communication into sacred service; and the feet lead the man forward in pursuit of his goals. It is in these three areas that the priest has to prove his mettle and demonstrate his character within the capacity of his leadership role. For the priests are the religious guides for the people of Israel, akin to the ram who walks in the front of his flock.

QUESTIONS FOR THOUGHT

- Regarding what do these two commentaries seem to agree?
- What led Ralbag to suggest that this blood is a sign of a covenant? What is the weakness in Ralbag's explanation?
- What do you see as the strength and weakness of the explanation offered by R. Hirsch?
- In Leviticus 14 the process of purification from *tzara'at* involves a similar process of placing blood on the right earlobe, thumb, and big toe. Do the explanations offered here make sense in that context as well?

שמות | פרק כט | תצוה

יט עֹלָ֥ה ה֖וּא לַֽיהוָ֑ה רֵ֣יחַ נִיח֗וֹחַ אִשֶּׁ֛ה לַֽיהוָ֖ה הֽוּא: וְלָ֣קַחְתָּ֔ אֵ֖ת הָאַ֣יִל הַשֵּׁנִ֑י וְסָמַ֨ךְ אַהֲרֹ֧ן וּבָנָ֛יו אֶת־יְדֵיהֶ֖ם עַל־רֹ֥אשׁ הָאָֽיִל:

כ וְשָֽׁחַטְתָּ֣ אֶת־הָאַ֗יִל וְלָֽקַחְתָּ֣ מִדָּמ֔וֹ וְנָֽתַתָּ֡ה עַל־תְּנוּךְ֩ אֹ֨זֶן אַֽהֲרֹ֜ן וְעַל־תְּנ֨וּךְ אֹ֤זֶן בָּנָיו֙ הַיְמָנִ֔ית וְעַל־בֹּ֤הֶן יָדָם֙ הַיְמָנִ֔ית וְעַל־בֹּ֥הֶן רַגְלָ֖ם הַיְמָנִ֑ית וְזָֽרַקְתָּ֧ אֶת־הַדָּ֛ם עַל־הַמִּזְבֵּ֖חַ סָבִֽיב:

כא וְלָֽקַחְתָּ֞ מִן־הַדָּ֨ם אֲשֶׁ֥ר עַל־הַמִּזְבֵּ֘חַ֮ וּמִשֶּׁ֣מֶן הַמִּשְׁחָה֒ וְהִזֵּיתָ֤ עַל־אַהֲרֹן֙ וְעַל־בְּגָדָ֔יו וְעַל־בָּנָ֛יו וְעַל־בִּגְדֵ֥י בָנָ֖יו אִתּ֑וֹ וְקָדַ֥שׁ הוּא֙ וּבְגָדָ֔יו וּבָנָ֛יו וּבִגְדֵ֥י בָנָ֖יו אִתּֽוֹ:

כב וְלָֽקַחְתָּ֣ מִן־הָ֠אַ֠יִל הַחֵ֨לֶב וְהָֽאַלְיָ֜ה וְאֶת־הַחֵ֣לֶב | הַֽמְכַסֶּ֣ה אֶת־הַקֶּ֗רֶב וְאֵ֨ת יֹתֶ֤רֶת הַכָּבֵד֙ וְאֵ֣ת | שְׁתֵּ֣י הַכְּלָיֹ֗ת וְאֶת־הַחֵ֨לֶב֙ אֲשֶׁ֣ר עֲלֵיהֶ֔ן וְאֵ֖ת שׁ֣וֹק הַיָּמִ֑ין כִּ֛י אֵ֥יל מִלֻּאִ֖ים הֽוּא:

כג וְכִכַּ֨ר לֶ֜חֶם אַחַ֗ת וְֽחַלַּ֨ת לֶ֥חֶם שֶׁ֛מֶן אַחַ֖ת וְרָקִ֣יק אֶחָ֑ד מִסַּל֙ הַמַּצּ֔וֹת אֲשֶׁ֖ר לִפְנֵ֥י יְהוָֽה:

כד וְשַׂמְתָּ֣ הַכֹּ֔ל עַ֚ל כַּפֵּ֣י אַהֲרֹ֔ן וְעַ֖ל כַּפֵּ֣י בָנָ֑יו וְהֵנַפְתָּ֥ אֹתָ֛ם תְּנוּפָ֖ה לִפְנֵ֥י יְהוָֽה:

כה וְלָֽקַחְתָּ֤ אֹתָם֙ מִיָּדָ֔ם וְהִקְטַרְתָּ֥ הַמִּזְבֵּ֖חָה עַל־הָעֹלָ֑ה לְרֵ֤יחַ נִיחוֹחַ֙ לִפְנֵ֣י יְהוָ֔ה אִשֶּׁ֥ה ה֖וּא לַיהוָֽה:

כו וְלָֽקַחְתָּ֣ אֶת־הֶֽחָזֶ֗ה מֵאֵ֤יל הַמִּלֻּאִים֙ אֲשֶׁ֣ר לְאַֽהֲרֹ֔ן וְהֵנַפְתָּ֥ אֹת֛וֹ תְּנוּפָ֖ה לִפְנֵ֣י יְהוָ֑ה וְהָיָ֥ה לְךָ֖ לְמָנָֽה:

כז וְקִדַּשְׁתָּ֞ אֵ֣ת | חֲזֵ֣ה הַתְּנוּפָ֗ה וְאֵת֙ שׁ֣וֹק הַתְּרוּמָ֔ה אֲשֶׁ֥ר הוּנַ֖ף וַאֲשֶׁ֣ר הוּרָ֑ם מֵאֵיל֙ הַמִּלֻּאִ֔ים מֵאֲשֶׁ֥ר לְאַהֲרֹ֖ן וּמֵאֲשֶׁ֥ר לְבָנָֽיו:

כח וְהָיָה֩ לְאַהֲרֹ֨ן וּלְבָנָ֜יו לְחָק־עוֹלָ֗ם מֵאֵת֙ בְּנֵ֣י יִשְׂרָאֵ֔ל כִּ֥י תְרוּמָ֖ה ה֑וּא וּתְרוּמָ֨ה

חמישי

CLASSIC COMMENTATORS

The Torah instructs Moshe to take the blood of the second ram and place some of it on the altar and some on the right earlobes, thumbs, and big toes of the priests. What does this unusual process represent?

> *Three topics are addressed briefly in this passage:*
>
> 1. *Aharon and his sons are to eat from the ram of ordination as well as from the bread that was brought. This eating is an essential part of their ordination as priests performing the service in the Mishkan.*
>
> 2. *The entire process described earlier is repeated daily for seven days and is to be done every time there is an installation of a new High Priest.*
>
> 3. *There is an additional* חטאת *sacrifice brought daily during the seven-day period, not for the purpose of inaugurating the priests but to purify and inaugurate the altar.*

peace offerings, their gift to the LORD. Aharon's sacred vestments shall pass on to his
29 sons after him. In them they shall be anointed and ordained. The son who succeeds him
30 as priest, entering the Tent of Meeting to minister in the sanctuary, shall wear them for
31 seven days. Take the ram of ordination and, in the sacred precinct, cook its flesh. Aharon
32 and his sons shall eat the meat of the ram, and the bread in the basket, near the entrance
of the Tent of Meeting. They shall eat these things, through which atonement will be
33 made, to be ordained and consecrated. Because they are consecrated no layman may
34 eat of them. If any of the meat of the ordination ram or any of the bread is left over until
morning, you shall burn what remains with fire. It must not be eaten, for it is conse-
35 crated. This is what you must do for Aharon and his sons, just as I have commanded
you. Their ordination shall take seven days. Each day, offer a bull as a sin offering for
36 atonement. Purify the altar by making atonement for it, and consecrate it by anointing
37 it. For seven days, make atonement for the altar and consecrate it, so that the altar
becomes holy of holies – and anything that touches it will become holy. This is what

---

QUESTIONS FOR THOUGHT

- Rashi's understanding is that as a result of the status of the altar, anything that touches it becomes sacred, almost magically. Ibn Ezra understands that the status of the altar limits those who may approach it. Which of those served as the basis of the translation that appears here?
- With whom does Bekhor Shor seem to agree?
- Which explanation do you think fits better with the context of the entire chapter leading up to this statement?

TEXTUAL SKILLS

1. The entire process described from the beginning of chapter 29 is called the מילואים. The root מ-ל-א appears nine times in this passage, and another eleven times in Leviticus 8–9 where the process is actually implemented.

2. There are three verbs used throughout this process which mean very different things: לְחַטֵּא, לְקַדֵּשׁ, and לְכַפֵּר.

שמות | פרק כט

יִהְיֶ֔ה מֵאֵ֖ת בְּנֵ֣י־יִשְׂרָאֵ֑ל מִזִּבְחֵ֣י שַׁלְמֵיהֶ֔ם תְּרוּמָתָ֖ם לַיהוָֽה׃

כט וּבִגְדֵ֤י הַקֹּ֙דֶשׁ֙ אֲשֶׁ֣ר לְאַהֲרֹ֔ן יִהְי֥וּ לְבָנָ֖יו אַחֲרָ֑יו לְמָשְׁחָ֣ה בָהֶ֔ם

ל וּלְמַלֵּא־בָ֖ם אֶת־יָדָֽם׃ שִׁבְעַ֣ת יָמִ֗ים יִלְבָּשָׁ֧ם הַכֹּהֵ֛ן תַּחְתָּ֖יו מִבָּנָ֑יו

לא אֲשֶׁ֥ר יָבֹ֛א אֶל־אֹ֥הֶל מוֹעֵ֖ד לְשָׁרֵ֥ת בַּקֹּֽדֶשׁ׃ וְאֵ֛ת אֵ֥יל הַמִּלֻּאִ֖ים

לב תִּקָּ֑ח וּבִשַּׁלְתָּ֥ אֶת־בְּשָׂר֖וֹ בְּמָקֹ֥ם קָדֹֽשׁ׃ וְאָכַ֨ל אַהֲרֹ֤ן וּבָנָיו֙ אֶת־

לג בְּשַׂ֣ר הָאַ֔יִל וְאֶת־הַלֶּ֔חֶם אֲשֶׁ֖ר בַּסָּ֑ל פֶּ֖תַח אֹ֥הֶל מוֹעֵֽד׃ וְאָכְל֤וּ

אֹתָם֙ אֲשֶׁ֣ר כֻּפַּ֣ר בָּהֶ֔ם לְמַלֵּ֥א אֶת־יָדָ֖ם לְקַדֵּ֣שׁ אֹתָ֑ם וְזָ֥ר לֹא־

לד יֹאכַ֖ל כִּי־קֹ֥דֶשׁ הֵֽם׃ וְֽאִם־יִוָּתֵ֞ר מִבְּשַׂ֧ר הַמִּלֻּאִ֛ים וּמִן־הַלֶּ֖חֶם

עַד־הַבֹּ֑קֶר וְשָׂרַפְתָּ֤ אֶת־הַנּוֹתָר֙ בָּאֵ֔שׁ לֹ֥א יֵאָכֵ֖ל כִּי־קֹ֥דֶשׁ הֽוּא׃

לה וְעָשִׂ֜יתָ לְאַהֲרֹ֤ן וּלְבָנָיו֙ כָּ֔כָה כְּכֹ֥ל אֲשֶׁר־צִוִּ֖יתִי אֹתָ֑כָה שִׁבְעַ֥ת

לו יָמִ֖ים תְּמַלֵּ֥א יָדָֽם׃ וּפַ֨ר חַטָּ֜את תַּעֲשֶׂ֤ה לַיּוֹם֙ עַל־הַכִּפֻּרִ֔ים

וְחִטֵּאתָ֙ עַל־הַמִּזְבֵּ֔חַ בְּכַפֶּרְךָ֖ עָלָ֑יו וּמָשַׁחְתָּ֥ אֹת֖וֹ לְקַדְּשֽׁוֹ׃

לז שִׁבְעַ֣ת יָמִ֗ים תְּכַפֵּר֙ עַל־הַמִּזְבֵּ֔חַ וְקִדַּשְׁתָּ֖ אֹת֑וֹ וְהָיָ֤ה הַמִּזְבֵּ֙חַ֙

CLASSIC COMMENTATORS

The phrase כל הנוגע במזבח יקדש (v. 37) is a source of controversy.

RASHI

רש״י

"Anything that touches it will become holy" – this means that even a sacrifice that has become invalid that has nevertheless been raised to the altar thereby becomes holy and may not be removed.

כל הנוגע במזבח יקדש - אפילו קרבן פסול שעלה עליו קידשו המזבח להכשירו שלא ירד.

IBN EZRA

אבן עזרא

No foreigner [non-priest] shall touch the altar. Only the priest who is holy may do so.

טעמו: שלא יגע בו זר, כי אם הכהן שהוא קדוש.

RABBI YOSEF BEKHOR SHOR

ר' יוסף בכור שור

"Anything that touches it will become holy" – the straightforward meaning of this verse is that anyone who touches the altar should be holy – that is, he must sanctify and purify himself first, since the altar represents the holy of holies.

כל הנוגע במזבח יקדש - לפי פשוטו: יהיה קדוש שצריך לקדש ולטהר, מפני שמזבח קדש קדשים.

38 you shall offer on the altar: two yearling lambs each day, with constancy. Offer one lamb
39 in the morning, and the other in the afternoon. With the first lamb offer a tenth measure
40 of fine flour mixed with a quarter of a hin of beaten oil, and a quarter of a hin of wine
41 as a libation. Offer the other lamb in the afternoon together with a grain offering and
   libation as in the morning, as a pleasing aroma, a fire offering to the Lord. This shall
42 be the regular burnt offering throughout your generations at the entrance of the Tent
   of Meeting before the Lord. There I will meet with you, there I will speak to you, and
43 there I will meet with the Israelites. It will be sanctified by My glory. I will consecrate
44 the Tent of Meeting and the altar. I will also consecrate Aharon and his sons to serve
45 Me as priests. I will have My Presence dwell among the Israelites and I shall be their
46 God. Then they will know that I am the Lord their God, who brought them out of
   Egypt to dwell among them. I am the Lord their God.

RABBI OVADYA SFORNO — ר' עובדיה ספורנו

לקבל עבודתם ברצון ולשמוע תפילתם.

By dwelling among the Israelites God was present to receive their services with favor and to hear their prayers.

RABBI SAMSON RAPHAEL HIRSCH — ר' שמשון רפאל הירש

גילוי שכינת ה' בקרב האומה לא יישאר רעיון מופשט, אלא האומה תדע בחוש שה' שוכן בתוכה. כל אופי חייהם הפנימיים והחיצוניים יוכיח להם שה' בקרבם.

The revelation of the Lord's presence in the midst of the nation would now not remain an abstract claim. Rather, the people would know; they would sense that the Lord dwelled among them. Every internal and external facet of their lives would prove to them that the Lord was present within Israel.

QUESTIONS FOR THOUGHT

- Is God's dwelling amongst the people meant to convey a theoretical idea to the people, to generate an unambiguous experience of God's presence, or to provide a visible sign that God accepts our prayers? Match these three ideas with the three commentaries above.
- Which of the above explanations applies universally to all people and which speaks about God's unique, particular relationship with Israel?
- Which of those is most meaningful for you?

WISDOM OF THE HEART

It seems like the תמיד sacrifice is included as part of the construction of the *Mishkan*, and only after the Torah tells us about it does it say that God's presence will dwell among *Benei Yisrael*. Why is this mentioned right after the תמיד? Rabbi Samson Raphael Hirsch explains that the promised goal of the *Mishkan* – which is God's presence in the nation – is achieved only by daily, constant devotion and dedication, not occasional, spontaneous religious outpouring.

לח קֹ֣דֶשׁ קָֽדָשִׁ֑ים כָּל־הַנֹּגֵ֥עַ בַּמִּזְבֵּ֖חַ יִקְדָּֽשׁ: וְזֶ֖ה אֲשֶׁ֣ר ששי
לט תַּעֲשֶׂ֖ה עַל־הַמִּזְבֵּ֑חַ כְּבָשִׂ֧ים בְּנֵֽי־שָׁנָ֛ה שְׁנַ֥יִם לַיּ֖וֹם תָּמִֽיד: אֶת־
הַכֶּ֥בֶשׂ הָאֶחָ֖ד תַּעֲשֶׂ֣ה בַבֹּ֑קֶר וְאֵת֙ הַכֶּ֣בֶשׂ הַשֵּׁנִ֔י תַּעֲשֶׂ֖ה בֵּ֥ין
מ הָעַרְבָּֽיִם: וְעִשָּׂרֹ֨ן סֹ֜לֶת בָּל֨וּל בְּשֶׁ֤מֶן כָּתִית֙ רֶ֣בַע הַהִ֔ין וְנֵ֕סֶךְ
מא רְבִיעִ֥ת הַהִ֖ין יָ֑יִן לַכֶּ֖בֶשׂ הָאֶחָֽד: וְאֵת֙ הַכֶּ֣בֶשׂ הַשֵּׁנִ֔י תַּעֲשֶׂ֖ה בֵּ֣ין
הָעַרְבָּ֑יִם כְּמִנְחַ֨ת הַבֹּ֤קֶר וּכְנִסְכָּהּ֙ תַּעֲשֶׂה־לָּ֔הּ לְרֵ֣יחַ נִיחֹ֔חַ אִשֶּׁ֖ה
מב לַיהוָֽה: עֹלַ֤ת תָּמִיד֙ לְדֹרֹ֣תֵיכֶ֔ם פֶּ֥תַח אֹֽהֶל־מוֹעֵ֖ד לִפְנֵ֣י יְהוָ֑ה
מג אֲשֶׁ֨ר אִוָּעֵ֥ד לָכֶ֛ם שָׁ֖מָּה לְדַבֵּ֥ר אֵלֶ֖יךָ שָֽׁם: וְנֹעַדְתִּ֥י שָׁ֖מָּה לִבְנֵ֣י
מד יִשְׂרָאֵ֑ל וְנִקְדַּ֖שׁ בִּכְבֹדִֽי: וְקִדַּשְׁתִּ֛י אֶת־אֹ֥הֶל מוֹעֵ֖ד וְאֶת־הַמִּזְבֵּ֑חַ
מה וְאֶת־אַהֲרֹ֧ן וְאֶת־בָּנָ֛יו אֲקַדֵּ֖שׁ לְכַהֵ֥ן לִֽי: וְשָׁ֣כַנְתִּ֔י בְּת֖וֹךְ בְּנֵ֣י
מו יִשְׂרָאֵ֑ל וְהָיִ֥יתִי לָהֶ֖ם לֵֽאלֹהִֽים: וְיָדְע֗וּ כִּ֣י אֲנִ֤י יְהוָה֙ אֱלֹ֣הֵיהֶ֔ם
אֲשֶׁ֨ר הוֹצֵ֧אתִי אֹתָ֛ם מֵאֶ֥רֶץ מִצְרַ֖יִם לְשָׁכְנִ֣י בְתוֹכָ֑ם אֲנִ֖י יְהוָ֥ה
אֱלֹהֵיהֶֽם:

CLASSIC COMMENTATORS

What does it mean for God to "dwell" amongst the people?

ABARBANEL

It was critical for the nation to understand that the Lord had not abandoned the earth to its own devices while He repaired to His celestial throne far from humanity. In order to dispel this false belief from the hearts of the people, God commanded that Israel construct a Tabernacle for Him, to make it seem as if He dwelled among them. In this way the Israelites would feel that God lived with them, and that His supreme providence hovered over the nation. This is what God meant when He stated, "I will have My presence dwell among the Israelites" (v. 45)…"with them in the midst of their impurity" (Lev. 16:16).

אברבנאל

שלא יחשבו שעזב ה' את הארץ ויאמרו שבשמים כסאו והוא מרוחק מבני אדם. וכדי להסיר בלבם האמונה הכוזבת הזאת ציוה שיעשו לו משכן כאילו הוא ישכן בתוכם שיאמינו כי אל חי בקרבם והשגחתו העליונה דבקה עמהם. וזה ענין "ושכנתי בתוך בני ישראל"… "השוכן אתם בתוך טמאתם"…

30 1 Make an altar on which to burn incense; make it of acacia wood. It shall be square, a
   2 cubit long, a cubit wide and two cubits high, its horns of one piece with it. Overlay it
      with pure gold on its top, all around its sides and on its horns, and around it make a
   4 gold molding. Make two gold rings for it under its molding on both sides to hold the

MESHEKH ḤOKHMA

With regard to all of the matters heretofore described, the accompanying vessels are critical to performance of the rituals. For example, in the absence of the Ark of the Covenant, the tablets that vessel is meant to hold are not simply set down upon the ground. Similarly, should the burnt offering altar be unavailable, no daily sacrifices are brought. In addition, no priest is permitted to serve in the Tabernacle if he is not wearing his sacred vestments, he may not light the lamps if they are not positioned inside the candelabrum, and he may not set the loaves of bread anywhere but in the table built for that purpose. Nevertheless, incense may be burned even when the altar that is specially designed and made for that activity is not present… Thus despite the fact that sole function of this altar is to host the burning incense, its use is considered desirable but not indispensable. As Rav stated (Zevaḥim 59a): If the altar is uprooted from its place, one may burn the incense in its place.

משך חכמה

והעיקר כי כל הצוויים כמו אם אין ארון אין מניחים לוחות, וכן בלא מזבח אין מקריבין עולת תמיד, וכן בלא בגדים אין כהן רשאי לעבוד, ובלא מנורה אינו רשאי להדליק נרות, ובלא שולחן אין מניחין לחם הפנים, אבל מזבח מקטר קטרת... הלא קיימא לן דהקטרת נקטר אף אם אין מזבח וכמו דאמר רב בזבחים דף נ"ט דמזבח שנעקר מקטירין קטרת במקומו.

QUESTIONS FOR THOUGHT

- Which of the above explanations implies that the golden altar was less critical than any of the previously mentioned items in the *Mishkan*?
- Which of the above explanations believes that the golden altar served a different function than the other vessels of the *Mishkan*?
- What is the main difference between the explanations of Sforno and *HaKetav VehaKabbala*?

TEXTUAL SKILLS

1. Notice that the Torah emphasizes what we are not allowed to do on the golden altar – the word לא appears twice in verse 9. This was not mentioned regarding any of the other vessels of the *Mishkan*.

2. Notice that the ritual performed on the golden altar is linked with the ritual of one of the other vessels of the *Mishkan*. Which vessel is that?

שמות | פרק ל

תצוה

לׁ א וְעָשִׂ֥יתָ מִזְבֵּ֖חַ מִקְטַ֣ר קְטֹ֑רֶת עֲצֵ֥י שִׁטִּ֖ים תַּעֲשֶׂ֥ה אֹתֽוֹ: אַמָּ֨ה ‎‏כג שביעי‏‎
אָרְכּ֜וֹ וְאַמָּ֤ה רָחְבּוֹ֙ רָב֣וּעַ יִהְיֶ֔ה וְאַמָּתַ֖יִם קֹמָת֑וֹ מִמֶּ֖נּוּ קַרְנֹתָֽיו:
ג וְצִפִּיתָ֨ אֹת֜וֹ זָהָ֣ב טָה֗וֹר אֶת־גַּגּ֧וֹ וְאֶת־קִירֹתָ֛יו סָבִ֖יב וְאֶת־קַרְנֹתָ֑יו
ד וְעָשִׂ֥יתָ לּ֛וֹ זֵ֥ר זָהָ֖ב סָבִֽיב: וּשְׁתֵּי֩ טַבְּעֹ֨ת זָהָ֜ב תַּֽעֲשֶׂה־לּ֣וֹ ׀ מִתַּ֣חַת
לְזֵר֗וֹ עַ֚ל שְׁתֵּ֣י צַלְעֹתָ֔יו תַּעֲשֶׂ֖ה עַל־שְׁנֵ֣י צִדָּ֑יו וְהָיָה֙ לְבָתִּ֣ים לְבַדִּ֔ים

CLASSIC COMMENTATORS

The presentation of the golden incense altar here is quite puzzling. Why was it not presented together with the *menora* and the table, which are similar in their construction and which are placed in the same area as the incense altar? And why was it presented only after what seems like the conclusion of the construction of the *Mishkan* and its purpose?

RABBI OVADYA SFORNO

Now, the reason why the incense altar is not mentioned alongside its fellow inner utensils [the candelabrum and the table] in *Parashat Teruma* [in chapter 25] is that this altar was never intended to assist in drawing the Divine Presence into the nation's midst, which was the function of the other objects… Instead, the purpose of the incense altar was to honor God, may He be blessed, after He had accepted Israel's sacrifices morning and evening.

HAKETAV VEHAKABBALA

It was not mentioned in the section that describes the construction of the other Tabernacle vessels: at first the Torah demands that the Tabernacle itself be built, its vessels be crafted, and the priestly vestments be fashioned. Following that, the text instructs that Aharon be drawn near to the burnt offering altar to initiate his service there, with the Torah continuing to describe the twice daily offerings that the High Priest will be required to sacrifice. As a result of those activities the presence of the Lord will dwell among Israel. And now the Torah turns its attention to the creation of the incense altar and the collection of the atonement silver [that is, the half shekel that each Israelite male was commanded to supply, as stated in the current chapter]. What this means is that the manifestation of the Divine Presence among the people did not depend on this, but these were strictly intended to expiate the sins of the nation.

ר' עובדיה ספורנו

ולא הוזכר זה המזבח עם שאר הכלים בפרשת תרומה, כי לא היתה הכוונה בו להשכין האל יתברך בתוכנו, כמו שהיה הענין בשאר הכלים... אבל היה ענין זה המזבח לכבד את האל יתברך אחרי בואו לקבל ברצון עבודת עמו בקרבנות הבוקר והערב.

הכתב והקבלה

לא הוזכר בעשיית כלי המשכן, כי הזהיר תחילה על המשכן וכליו והבגדים וקריבת אהרן למזבח ואחר כך אמר עשיית התמיד ואמר בזה אשכון בתוככם. ואחר כך הזכיר מזבח הקטורת וכסף הכיפורים, יורה שזה לא היה מעכב להשראת שכינה, רק אלו היו לכפרת ישראל.

5 staves used to carry it. Make the staves of acacia wood and overlay them with gold. Put
6 it in front of the screen that veils the Ark of the Testimony, in front of the cover above
7 the Ark, where I will meet with you. Aharon should burn incense on it every morning
8 when he tends the lamps, and before evening when he lights the lamps. It shall be a
9 perpetual incense offering before the Lord throughout your generations. Offer no
10 unauthorized incense on it, or any burnt offering, grain offering or libation. Once a year Aharon shall make atonement on its horns; once a year, with the blood of the sin offering of atonement, he shall make atonement on it; throughout your generations. It is holy of holies to the Lord."

The golden altar

ה לָשֵׂאת אֹתוֹ בָּהֵמָּה: וְעָשִׂיתָ אֶת־הַבַּדִּים עֲצֵי שִׁטִּים וְצִפִּיתָ
ו אֹתָם זָהָב: וְנָתַתָּה אֹתוֹ לִפְנֵי הַפָּרֹכֶת אֲשֶׁר עַל־אֲרֹן הָעֵדֻת
ז לִפְנֵי הַכַּפֹּרֶת אֲשֶׁר עַל־הָעֵדֻת אֲשֶׁר אִוָּעֵד לְךָ שָׁמָּה: וְהִקְטִיר
עָלָיו אַהֲרֹן קְטֹרֶת סַמִּים בַּבֹּקֶר בַּבֹּקֶר בְּהֵיטִיבוֹ אֶת־הַנֵּרֹת
ח יַקְטִירֶנָּה: וּבְהַעֲלֹת אַהֲרֹן אֶת־הַנֵּרֹת בֵּין הָעַרְבַּיִם יַקְטִירֶנָּה מפטיר
ט קְטֹרֶת תָּמִיד לִפְנֵי יהוה לְדֹרֹתֵיכֶם: לֹא־תַעֲלוּ עָלָיו קְטֹרֶת זָרָה
י וְעֹלָה וּמִנְחָה וְנֵסֶךְ לֹא תִסְּכוּ עָלָיו: וְכִפֶּר אַהֲרֹן עַל־קַרְנֹתָיו
אַחַת בַּשָּׁנָה מִדַּם חַטַּאת הַכִּפֻּרִים אַחַת בַּשָּׁנָה יְכַפֵּר עָלָיו
לְדֹרֹתֵיכֶם קֹדֶשׁ־קָדָשִׁים הוּא לַיהוה:

QUICK BITE

This *parasha* closes with the role of the incense altar. Why does the Torah wait to address the role of this altar, rather than discussing it in *Parashat Teruma* together with the other parts of the *Mishkan*? The Talmud (Zevachim 59a) teaches that the incense could continue to be offered on that spot even if the altar itself were gone. The *Meshekh Ḥokhma* points out that this might explain the odd placing of this teaching: It was stated separately because there are scenarios where we simply don't need it.

On the other hand, and in an almost contradictory way – this altar was more special. Unlike the large altar in the courtyard, this smaller altar was made of pure gold. It is called "holy of holies" in verse 10. So which is it – is it holier or less holy?

Rabbi Samson Raphael Hirsch sees this altar as a force that harmonizes the *menora*, which symbolizes spirituality, and the table, which stands for physicality. In this way it was unique. It was a bridge between worlds, bringing balance between opposing energies in the *Mishkan*.

פרשת כי תשא
PARASHAT KI TISA

> "If I weren't a Jew, then I wouldn't be an artist."
> Marc Chagall

It does not take long after God prohibits graven images for the people to make the golden calf. The Kotzker Rebbe says that this was ultimately a forgivable sin, because at least making the golden calf had a spark of spirituality, a desire to cleave to something bigger. They wanted to worship, but their worship was simply misdirected.

Perhaps the golden calf was not just about worship, but also about beauty. Judaism is not opposed to beauty – David created beautiful poetry, Betzalel used his artistic talent to make the breathtaking *Mishkan* even more spectacular, and beautifying one's religious performance [*hiddur mitzva*] is applauded. But there is a fine line between admiring beauty and worshipping it. *Benei Yisrael* were exposed to man-made beauty in Egypt and natural beauty in the wilderness, but in worshipping an object of their own creation, they crossed the line.

PARASHAT KI TISA

30 ¹¹ The LORD said to Moshe, "When you take the census of the Israelites, as you count,
¹² each must give ransom for his life to the LORD, so that no plague strikes them when
¹³ you count them. Everyone numbered in the census shall give half a shekel according to the sanctuary weight, where the shekel is twenty gerahs. This half shekel is an offering
¹⁴ to the LORD. Every male over twenty is to be included in the census and must give the
¹⁵ LORD's offering. The rich shall not give more, and the poor shall not give less, than this
¹⁶ half shekel. It is an offering to the LORD to redeem your lives. Take this redemption money from the Israelites and assign it for the service of the Tent of Meeting. It shall be a remembrance for the Israelites before the LORD, to redeem your lives."

רלב״ג

וכבר נתבאר בפרשת אלה פקודי (לח, כו) שבזה המספר הראשון נהג זה; ואולם בשאר המנינים שנמנו בימי משה לא נתנו חצאי שקלים, כי תמצא בהם שלא נמנו כי אם במספר שמות, רוצה לומר שהשמות לבד נמנו, לא האנשים.

RALBAG

The Torah makes clear in *Parashat Pekudei* (38:26) that indeed this first census was conducted by the donation of *shekalim*. However, other tallies that were undertaken during Moshe's leadership did not involve the accumulation of half-*shekalim*. For the text's descriptions show that the census-takers merely counted the Israelites' names and not the individuals.

QUESTIONS FOR THOUGHT

- Is taking a census of the people positive, negative, or neutral?
- The Torah says that counting using the half-shekel would prevent something bad – *negef* – from happening. Is that *negef* something that would have resulted from the counting? Or from some other cause?
- The Torah refers to the half-shekel multiple times as enabling atonement [*kapara*]. For what does it atone? Is there a connection between this atonement and the one mentioned three times at the end of the previous section (30:10)?

TEXTUAL SKILLS

1. Notice how many times the roots פ-ק-ד, כ-פ-ר, נ-ת-ן, and מעט are used in contrast with each other. Where is the first? Notice also that in both instances, the רב and the מעט are replaced by equality for all.
2. This is the second time in Exodus that the words רב and

WISDOM OF THE HEART

Benei Yisrael are commanded to bring the half-shekel as a donation to the construction of the *Mishkan*. Every individual, whether wealthy or poor, was required to bring this donation. There's something powerful of each person only bringing half. Perhaps the message is, "I only have part of the story, I need to hear my brother out to complete the story."

How can you bring yourself to hear what others have to say and not just see them as annoyances?

פרשת כי תשא

וַיְדַבֵּ֥ר יְהוָ֖ה אֶל־מֹשֶׁ֥ה לֵּאמֹֽר: כִּ֣י תִשָּׂ֞א אֶת־רֹ֥אשׁ בְּנֵֽי־יִשְׂרָאֵ֘ל לִפְקֻדֵיהֶם֒ וְנָ֨תְנ֜וּ אִ֣ישׁ כֹּ֧פֶר נַפְשׁ֛וֹ לַֽיהוָ֖ה בִּפְקֹ֣ד אֹתָ֑ם וְלֹא־יִֽהְיֶ֥ה בָהֶ֛ם נֶ֖גֶף בִּפְקֹ֥ד אֹתָֽם: זֶ֣ה ׀ יִתְּנ֗וּ כָּל־הָעֹבֵר֙ עַל־הַפְּקֻדִ֔ים מַחֲצִ֥ית הַשֶּׁ֖קֶל בְּשֶׁ֣קֶל הַקֹּ֑דֶשׁ עֶשְׂרִ֤ים גֵּרָה֙ הַשֶּׁ֔קֶל מַחֲצִ֣ית הַשֶּׁ֔קֶל תְּרוּמָ֖ה לַֽיהוָֽה: כֹּ֗ל הָעֹבֵר֙ עַל־הַפְּקֻדִ֔ים מִבֶּ֛ן עֶשְׂרִ֥ים שָׁנָ֖ה וָמָ֑עְלָה יִתֵּ֖ן תְּרוּמַ֥ת יְהוָֽה: הֶֽעָשִׁ֣יר לֹֽא־יַרְבֶּ֗ה וְהַדַּל֙ לֹ֣א יַמְעִ֔יט מִֽמַּחֲצִ֖ית הַשָּׁ֑קֶל לָתֵת֙ אֶת־תְּרוּמַ֣ת יְהוָ֔ה לְכַפֵּ֖ר עַל־נַפְשֹֽׁתֵיכֶֽם: וְלָקַחְתָּ֞ אֶת־כֶּ֣סֶף הַכִּפֻּרִ֗ים מֵאֵת֙ בְּנֵ֣י יִשְׂרָאֵ֔ל וְנָתַתָּ֣ אֹת֔וֹ עַל־עֲבֹדַ֖ת אֹ֣הֶל מוֹעֵ֑ד וְהָיָה֩ לִבְנֵ֨י יִשְׂרָאֵ֤ל לְזִכָּרוֹן֙ לִפְנֵ֣י יְהוָ֔ה לְכַפֵּ֖ר עַל־נַפְשֹֽׁתֵיכֶֽם:

CLASSIC COMMENTATORS

Is there a mitzva to count the people? Is the Torah telling *how* to count the people only if there is a decision to count them? Were God's instructions to Moshe meant for this time only, or were they intended to be permanent guidelines for whenever a census would be conducted?

RASHI

Should you wish to tally the number of Israelites in the nation, do not count the people directly. Rather, instruct each individual to donate half a shekel; count these half *shekalim*, and that will tell you how many men are in the nation.

רש״י

כשתחפוץ לקבל סכום מניינם לדעת כמה הם, אל תמנם לגולגולת אלא יתנו כל אחד מחצית השקל, ותמנה את השקלים ותדע מניינם.

RAMBAN

The Torah does not make explicit whether this method of counting Israelites was to be used whenever a census was undertaken throughout the generations, or whether the instruction to collect *shekalim* to tally the people was a one-time command. Because of this vagueness, King David erred when he counted the nation without collecting *shekalim* from Israel (as reported in II Samuel chapter 24). This resulted in a plague striking the nation as punishment.

רמב״ן

ומפני שלא נתפרש כאן אם היא מצות דורות, או לשעה למשה במדבר, טעה דוד ומנה אותם בלא שקלים (שמואל ב כ״ד), והיה הנגף בהם.

Shemot | Chapter 30

17
18 The Lord said to Moshe, "Make a bronze laver with a bronze base for washing. Place it
19 between the Tent of Meeting and the altar, and put water in it, for Aharon and his sons
20 to wash their hands and feet. When they enter the Tent of Meeting or approach the altar
to minister by presenting a food offering to the Lord, they must wash with water, so
21 that they do not die. They must wash their hands and feet so that they do not die; it shall
be an eternal law for them, for Aharon and his offspring, throughout the generations."

The laver

TEXTUAL SKILLS

1. The laver was located between the altar and the *Mishkan*. Wouldn't it make more sense to place it in a location where the priests would reach it *before* encountering the altar? Find an answer based on a close reading of verse 20.

2. Look at the word the Torah uses in verse 18 to describe where Moshe should put the water. What different word would you expect the Torah to use?

WISDOM OF THE HEART

The Torah gives precise sizes and measurements for all of the vessels of the *Mishkan*, with two exceptions: the *menora* and the laver. Even more striking is that when King Shlomo makes the laver for the first *Beit HaMikdash* we are provided with detailed measurements (I Kings 7:23–39). The *Musar* masters share the following explanation: the laver in the *Mishkan* was made from mirrors donated by women (38:8). These mirrors were sources of personal vanity, which the women shattered for the sake of the *Mishkan*. Every individual piece that was donated expressed immeasurable devotion, hence there is no measurement for this laver.

שמות | פרק ל

יח וַיְדַבֵּר יְהֹוָה אֶל־מֹשֶׁה לֵּאמֹר: וְעָשִׂיתָ כִּיּוֹר נְחֹשֶׁת וְכַנּוֹ נְחֹשֶׁת לְרָחְצָה וְנָתַתָּ אֹתוֹ בֵּין־אֹהֶל מוֹעֵד וּבֵין הַמִּזְבֵּחַ וְנָתַתָּ שָׁמָּה מָיִם: יט וְרָחֲצוּ אַהֲרֹן וּבָנָיו מִמֶּנּוּ אֶת־יְדֵיהֶם וְאֶת־רַגְלֵיהֶם: בְּבֹאָם אֶל־אֹהֶל מוֹעֵד יִרְחֲצוּ־מַיִם וְלֹא יָמֻתוּ אוֹ בְגִשְׁתָּם אֶל־הַמִּזְבֵּחַ לְשָׁרֵת לְהַקְטִיר אִשֶּׁה לַיהֹוָה: כא וְרָחֲצוּ יְדֵיהֶם וְרַגְלֵיהֶם וְלֹא יָמֻתוּ וְהָיְתָה לָהֶם חָק־עוֹלָם לוֹ וּלְזַרְעוֹ לְדֹרֹתָם: ‏

CLASSIC COMMENTATORS

Like the large altar for sacrifices, the laver was made of bronze and located in the courtyard. Why is it mentioned as an "afterthought" to the construction of the *Mishkan* and not together with the altar in the main section dealing with the *Mishkan*?

RABBI YOSEF BEKHOR SHOR

ר' יוסף בכור שור

The description of the laver is mentioned after the other utensils because it is merely a preparatory tool, and is not used to perform a service in the Tabernacle. Rather, the priests wash from the laver's water to enable them to participate in the services.

לפי שאינו אלא להכשר מצוה, לא מנה עשייתו למעלה עם שאר כלים, ולא היה אלא לרחוץ הכהנים ידיהם.

RABBI OVADYA SFORNO

ר' עובדיה ספורנו

The laver is not mentioned above with the other utensils because it did not contribute, as the other items did, to drawing the Divine Presence into the Tabernacle to dwell there. Rather, the purpose of the laver was merely to prepare the priests for their service.

גם זה הכלי לא הוזכר למעלה עם שאר הכלים, כי לא היתה הכוונה בו להשכין שכינה במקדש כענין הכוונה באותם הכלים, כמבואר למעלה.

QUESTIONS FOR THOUGHT

- There is a subtle difference between the explanations of Bekhor Shor and Sforno. What is it?
- What contemporary Jewish practices today seem to echo this command in the *Mishkan*?

SHEMOT | CHAPTER 30

The Mishkan, its vessels, and the priests are to be anointed with specially-prepared oil. Based on olive oil, it is mixed with a unique blend of spices. That recipe is reserved for use in the Mishkan and the future Beit HaMikdash – it may not be used for non-holy purposes or even made privately by anyone.

22-23 Then the LORD said to Moshe, "Take the finest spices: 500 shekels of liquid myrrh, and
24 half as much, 250, of fragrant cinnamon, as well as 250 of aromatic cane, and 500 shekels
25 of cassia – all according to the sanctuary weight – and a hin of olive oil. Make from these
26 a sacred anointing oil, blended as by a perfumer; it shall be a sacred anointing oil. With
27 it, anoint the Tent of Meeting and the Ark of the Testimony, the table and all its utensils,
28 the candelabrum and its utensils, the incense altar, the sacrificial altar with all its uten-
29 sils and the laver and its base. You shall consecrate them and they will become holy of
30 holies, and whatever touches them will become holy. You shall anoint Aharon and his
31 sons and consecrate them to serve Me as priests. And you shall tell the Israelites: This
32 shall be My sacred anointing oil throughout the generations. Do not pour it on anyone else's body, and do not make any other oil with the same formula. It is sacred, and shall
33 remain sacred to you. Whoever makes perfume like it or applies it to a layperson shall

ר' שמשון רפאל הירש

שמן המשחה הוא חותם ה' על קידוש והקדשת בני אדם וחפצים. מובן הדבר, שלעשיות כמתכונת "חותם" זה, או להשתמש בו לכל דבר זולת השימוש המקודש שנצטווה מאת ה', הוא בבחינת כפירה במציאותה של קדושת ה', או כחילול הקידוש האלקי.

RABBI SAMSON RAPHAEL HIRSCH

The anointing oil represents the seal of the LORD, to be used in the sanctification and dedication of individuals and objects which have been consecrated. It is obvious that the casual manufacture of this official stamp, or the usage of the sacred oil for anything but the holy purpose that the LORD has commanded, is tantamount to denying the sanctity of the LORD. Such behavior represents the utmost profanation of the divine holiness.

QUESTIONS FOR THOUGHT

- Whose uniqueness is challenged by non-sacred use of the anointing oil?
- Can you relate to the idea of sacred space (think about special places that you don't want outsiders coming into), sacred time (think about Shabbat, or about times when you just want to be left alone), sacred objects (think about trophies you worked hard for or family heirlooms), sacred music (think about tunes you associate with special events) – all of which have a special status that must not be violated? Or does that idea sound completely foreign to you?

WISDOM OF THE HEART

Special oil was reserved for anointing the High Priest, the priest who would lead the nation into battle, and the king. What was this oil supposed to symbolize? Rabbi Chaim Yaakov Goldvicht once suggested that each of these individuals has a very stressful leadership role, as they are always under the scrutiny of the people. They need the oil to learn to let the judgment and negativity slide right off of them.

How do we learn to listen to criticism and take it seriously without letting it get us down?

כג וַיְדַבֵּר יְהוָה אֶל־מֹשֶׁה לֵּאמֹר: וְאַתָּה קַח־לְךָ בְּשָׂמִים רֹאשׁ מָר־דְּרוֹר חֲמֵשׁ מֵאוֹת וְקִנְּמָן־בֶּשֶׂם מַחֲצִיתוֹ חֲמִשִּׁים וּמָאתָיִם

כד וּקְנֵה־בֹשֶׂם חֲמִשִּׁים וּמָאתָיִם: וְקִדָּה חֲמֵשׁ מֵאוֹת בְּשֶׁקֶל הַקֹּדֶשׁ וְשֶׁמֶן זַיִת הִין:

כה וְעָשִׂיתָ אֹתוֹ שֶׁמֶן מִשְׁחַת־קֹדֶשׁ רֹקַח מִרְקַחַת מַעֲשֵׂה רֹקֵחַ שֶׁמֶן מִשְׁחַת־קֹדֶשׁ יִהְיֶה:

כו וּמָשַׁחְתָּ בוֹ אֶת־אֹהֶל מוֹעֵד וְאֵת אֲרוֹן הָעֵדֻת:

כז וְאֶת־הַשֻּׁלְחָן וְאֶת־כָּל־כֵּלָיו וְאֶת־הַמְּנֹרָה וְאֶת־כֵּלֶיהָ וְאֵת מִזְבַּח הַקְּטֹרֶת:

כח וְאֶת־מִזְבַּח הָעֹלָה וְאֶת־כָּל־כֵּלָיו וְאֶת־הַכִּיֹּר וְאֶת־כַּנּוֹ:

כט וְקִדַּשְׁתָּ אֹתָם וְהָיוּ קֹדֶשׁ קָדָשִׁים כָּל־הַנֹּגֵעַ בָּהֶם יִקְדָּשׁ:

ל וְאֶת־אַהֲרֹן וְאֶת־בָּנָיו תִּמְשָׁח וְקִדַּשְׁתָּ אֹתָם לְכַהֵן לִי:

לא וְאֶל־בְּנֵי יִשְׂרָאֵל תְּדַבֵּר לֵאמֹר שֶׁמֶן מִשְׁחַת־קֹדֶשׁ יִהְיֶה זֶה לִי לְדֹרֹתֵיכֶם:

לב עַל־בְּשַׂר אָדָם לֹא יִיסָךְ וּבְמַתְכֻּנְתּוֹ לֹא תַעֲשׂוּ כָּמֹהוּ קֹדֶשׁ הוּא קֹדֶשׁ יִהְיֶה לָכֶם:

לג אִישׁ אֲשֶׁר יִרְקַח כָּמֹהוּ וַאֲשֶׁר יִתֵּן מִמֶּנּוּ עַל־זָר וְנִכְרַת

CLASSIC COMMENTATORS

Why is it forbidden to replicate the anointing oil by using the same recipe for private purposes?

RAMBAN

Note that our verse does not use the expected language: This shall be a sacred anointing oil for Aharon and his sons throughout the generations, an expression which would parallel the command regarding the garments, "Aharon's sacred vestments shall pass on to his sons after him" (29:29)... Such is the explanation of the matter: God commanded Moshe to anoint Aharon and his sons at that point, and added, "This shall be My sacred anointing oil throughout the generations" (30:31). This means that the oil was to be applied in the future to God's holy anointed ones whom He shall choose throughout the generations. The oil shall not be put onto people who are strangers, that is those who have not been drawn to God.

רמב״ן

היה ראוי שיאמר: שמן משחת קדש יהיה זה לאהרן ולבניו לדורותם, ראשר אמר בבגדים: "ובגדי הקדש אשר לאהרן יהיו לבניו אחריו" (שמות כ״ט:כ״ט) ... אבל כך הדבר: צוה שימשח בו עתה אהרן ובניו, ואמר: שמן משחת קדש יהיה זה לי – למשוח בו משיחי קדשי אשר אבחר בו 'לדורותיכם', ולא ינתן על זר שאיננו לי.

Shemot | Chapter 30

The recipe for the incense to be offered on the small altar is also unique. It is to be made using a special process, and it is forbidden to replicate it for private use.

34 be severed from his people." The LORD said to Moshe, "Take sweet spices, equal parts of
35 stacte, onycha, galbanum and pure frankincense and make them into incense, blended
36 as by a perfumer, salted, pure and sacred. Beat some of it into powder and put part of it before the covenant in the Tent of Meeting where I will meet with you. It shall be holy
37 of holies to you. Do not make any incense with this formula for yourselves. It must, for
38 you, remain sacred to the LORD. The person who makes any incense like it to use as

---

RABBI OVADYA SFORNO

The term *samim* refers to those substances listed in the text's description of the anointing oil in 30:23–24, which are: myrrh, aromatic cane, fragrant cinnamon, and cassia. Moshe is to mix with these the items mentioned our verse: stacte, onycha, galbanum, as well as other *samim* which are known to enhance the listed ingredients, as is known by perfumers.

ר' עובדיה ספורנו

קח לך סמים – הנזכרים בשמן המשחה (שמות ל':כ"ג-כ"ד), והם מור קנה וקנמון וקדה, ועם אלה נטף ושחלת וחלבנה, ועמהם "סמים" הנודעים לתקון הסמים הנזכרים, כמו שנודע אצל הרוקחים.

QUESTIONS FOR THOUGHT

- Rashbam suggests that the word *samim* is used to form a structure in the text. What structure is that? Does he understand the word to refer to specific spices? Or is it a generic term?
- What is very surprising about Ramban's interpretation?
- How does Sforno use context to solve the riddle of the *samim*? According to him, why does the Torah use the word twice?

TEXTUAL SKILLS

1. Notice how prominent the word קדש is in the previous passage and this one. What is being emphasized?
2. What other similarities can you find between this passage and the previous one?

WISDOM OF THE HEART

The incense was a very powerful sweet-smelling aromatic recipe with a particular mix of spices. It was prepared as a gift to God. However, one of the ingredients, galbanum [*ḥelbena*] had a particularly noxious odor. The Gemara (Karetot 6b) says, "Any public fast that does not include the sinners is not a [genuine] fast," and one of the proofs is from the incense, which included the foul-smelling galbanum. The Rebbe of Izhbitz takes this one step further, suggesting that just as the bad smell of the galbanum made the smell of the incense nicer, so too, bringing the sinner into the fold of *Benei Yisrael* makes the group even stronger.

מֵעַמָּיו: וַיֹּאמֶר יְהוָה אֶל־מֹשֶׁה קַח־לְךָ סַמִּים נָטָף ׀ לד
וּשְׁחֵלֶת וְחֶלְבְּנָה סַמִּים וּלְבֹנָה זַכָּה בַּד בְּבַד יִהְיֶה: וְעָשִׂיתָ אֹתָהּ לה
קְטֹרֶת רֹקַח מַעֲשֵׂה רוֹקֵחַ מְמֻלָּח טָהוֹר קֹדֶשׁ: וְשָׁחַקְתָּ מִמֶּנָּה לו
הָדֵק וְנָתַתָּה מִמֶּנָּה לִפְנֵי הָעֵדֻת בְּאֹהֶל מוֹעֵד אֲשֶׁר אִוָּעֵד
לְךָ שָׁמָּה קֹדֶשׁ קָדָשִׁים תִּהְיֶה לָכֶם: וְהַקְּטֹרֶת אֲשֶׁר תַּעֲשֶׂה לז
בְּמַתְכֻּנְתָּהּ לֹא תַעֲשׂוּ לָכֶם קֹדֶשׁ תִּהְיֶה לְךָ לַיהוָה: אִישׁ אֲשֶׁר־ לח

CLASSIC COMMENTATORS

The word "spices" [*samim*] appears twice in the same verse (34): once in God's general instruction to Moshe, and once among the list of specific ingredients. Does this word refer to particular spices, or is it a generic term? And why is it mentioned twice?

RASHBAM — רשב״ם

The verse mentions *samim* and then proceeds to define what that includes: stacte, onycha, and galbanum. These are the spices that Moshe is required to take; in addition, pure frankincense is to be used. Thus the straightforward meaning of the text is that frankincense is not considered a spice, and the second usage of the term *samim* refers to the same ingredients indicated by the first mention of *samim*. This is a standard biblical construction: a general term followed by an interpretation of that idea, followed by a summary that states: these particulars are what was intended by the earlier generality.

לפי הפשט: בתחילה כלל – קח לך סמים, ופירש מה הם סמים – נטף ושחלת וחלבנה, הרי אילו סמים שציויתי שתקח לך, ועוד קח לבונה זכה. ולפי הפשט: לבונה זכה אינה סמים. סמים אחרון הם "סמים" ראשון שבפסוק. וכן דרך מקראות: כולל, ומפרש, וחוזר ואומר: הרי לך כלל שאמרתי לך.

RAMBAN — רמב״ן

The second reference to *samim* indicates other spices which are not named here... And yet we must ask why the Torah does not list these additional ingredients. Perhaps the sense of the text is as follows. First it states, "Take sweet spices, equal parts of stacte, onycha, galbanum", then again *samim* [here untranslated], concluding with "and pure frankincense". The Torah thus only insists on the usage of these four items, because these substances have the effect of causing the cloud of incense smoke to rise up. As well, Moshe is commanded to mix in additional known aromatic spices to enhance the fragrance of the smoke.

יש לתמוה, ולמה לא יזכירם הכתוב. ואולי יאמר הכתוב: קח לך סמים נטף ושחלת וחלבנה, סמים רבים, ולבונה זכה, ולא יקפיד רק באלה הארבע, כי בהם ענן עשן הקטורת עולה, רק צוה שיתן עמהם סמים רבים אשר להן ריח טוב, כדי שיהיה בתמרות עשנו מבושם.

Shemot | Chapter 31

31 ¹ perfume shall be severed from his people." The Lord said to Moshe, "See, I have called ² by name Betzalel, son of Uri, son of Ḥur from the tribe of Yehuda, and I have filled ³ him with a divine spirit, with wisdom, understanding and knowledge in every craft. ⁴ He will fashion works of art in gold, silver, and bronze. He will cut stones for setting, ⁵ carve wood, and work in every craft. I have assigned to him Oholiav, son of Aḥisamakh ⁶ from the tribe of Dan. I have also put wisdom into the heart of all the wise-hearted, so ⁷ that they will be able to make all I have commanded you: the Tent of Meeting, the Ark ⁸ of the Testimony and its cover, and all other furnishings of the tent; the table and its ⁹ utensils, the pure candelabrum and all its utensils, the incense altar, the sacrificial altar ¹⁰ with all its utensils, the laver and its base, the service vestments, the sacred vestments ¹¹ for Aharon the priest and the vestments for his sons for when they serve as priests, the anointing oil and the fragrant incense for the sanctuary; they shall make them exactly as I have commanded you."

RALBAG

We learn an extraordinary matter from this episode. Namely, that although the Lord, may He be blessed, is willing to bestow His beneficence upon an individual, that person must first prepare himself to receive such a divine gift.

רלב״ג

העירנו על ענין נפלא; והוא, שזה השפע השופע לנו מה' יתעלה לא יגיע לנו אם לא הכננו עצמנו לקיבול השפע ההוא.

RABBI SAMSON RAPHAEL HIRSCH

The construction of the Tabernacle was never intended to be merely the artistic fashioning of physical materials. Rather, with the assembly of the project, each part contained symbolic significance. Thus the messages hidden within the details of the enterprise had to be known to and understood by the craftsman who were shaping the structure and its vessels. It is these ideas that served to guide the artisans as they went about their sacred labor.

ר' שמשון רפאל הירש

עשיית המשכן לא הייתה אמורה להיות מעשה אמנות חיצונית גרידא, אלא הקמת מבנה שלכל חלק וחלק בו תהיה משמעות סמלית. הרעיונות הבאים לידי ביטוי באמצעות המשכן ובאמצעות כל חלקיו צריכים להיות קבועים תמיד בליבם של האומנים, ולהדריך את מחשבותיהם וכוונותיהם כאשר הם עושים את המלאכה.

QUESTIONS FOR THOUGHT

- Which of the commentaries believe that the wisdom was an inborn, God-given gift?
- What different insight does R. Hirsch offering regarding this wisdom?
- Does everyone who has natural talent become great? Are all people who become great endowed with amazing natural talent? What is the relationship between natural talent and dedication, perseverance, and hard work?

TEXTUAL SKILLS

1. Look at the names (in Hebrew!) of the two people tasked with making the *Mishkan*, and try to break each of them into two words. What do their names say about them?
2. From which two tribes do Betzalel and Oholiav come?

Why might that be important? (Hint: look at Numbers chapter 2)

3. Where have we earlier seen the name of Betzalel's grandfather?

שמות | פרק לא

א יַעֲשֶׂה כָמוֹהָ לְהָרִיחַ בָּהּ וְנִכְרַת מֵעַמָּיו: וַיְדַבֵּר יהוה לא
ב אֶל־מֹשֶׁה לֵּאמְר: רְאֵה קָרָאתִי בְשֵׁם בְּצַלְאֵל בֶּן־אוּרִי בֶן־חוּר
ג לְמַטֵּה יְהוּדָה: וָאֲמַלֵּא אֹתוֹ רוּחַ אֱלֹהִים בְּחָכְמָה וּבִתְבוּנָה
ד וּבְדַעַת וּבְכָל־מְלָאכָה: לַחְשֹׁב מַחֲשָׁבֹת לַעֲשׂוֹת בַּזָּהָב וּבַכֶּסֶף
ה וּבַנְּחְשֶׁת: וּבַחֲרֹשֶׁת אֶבֶן לְמַלֹּאת וּבַחֲרֹשֶׁת עֵץ לַעֲשׂוֹת בְּכָל־
ו מְלָאכָה: וַאֲנִי הִנֵּה נָתַתִּי אִתּוֹ אֵת אָהֳלִיאָב בֶּן־אֲחִיסָמָךְ
לְמַטֵּה־דָן וּבְלֵב כָּל־חֲכַם־לֵב נָתַתִּי חָכְמָה וְעָשׂוּ אֵת כָּל־אֲשֶׁר
ז צִוִּיתִךָ: אֵת ׀ אֹהֶל מוֹעֵד וְאֶת־הָאָרֹן לָעֵדֻת וְאֶת־הַכַּפֹּרֶת אֲשֶׁר
ח עָלָיו וְאֵת כָּל־כְּלֵי הָאֹהֶל: וְאֶת־הַשֻּׁלְחָן וְאֶת־כֵּלָיו וְאֶת־הַמְּנֹרָה
ט הַטְּהֹרָה וְאֶת־כָּל־כֵּלֶיהָ וְאֵת מִזְבַּח הַקְּטֹרֶת: וְאֶת־מִזְבַּח הָעֹלָה
י וְאֶת־כָּל־כֵּלָיו וְאֶת־הַכִּיּוֹר וְאֶת־כַּנּוֹ: וְאֵת בִּגְדֵי הַשְּׂרָד וְאֶת־בִּגְדֵי
יא הַקֹּדֶשׁ לְאַהֲרֹן הַכֹּהֵן וְאֶת־בִּגְדֵי בָנָיו לְכַהֵן: וְאֵת שֶׁמֶן הַמִּשְׁחָה
וְאֶת־קְטֹרֶת הַסַּמִּים לַקֹּדֶשׁ כְּכֹל אֲשֶׁר־צִוִּיתִךָ יַעֲשׂוּ:

CLASSIC COMMENTATORS

When it comes to the choosing of the craftsmen, God tells Moshe: "I have also put wisdom into the heart of all the wise-hearted." Is the wisdom that they need an inborn gift from God, or did they learn it?

IBN EZRA — אבן עזרא

Some people have the innate ability to create complex figures. This is not a learned skill.

זה ימצא בתולדת האדם, שיוציא מלבו דברים עמוקים במלאכת המדות, והוא לא למד החכמה.

RAMBAN — רמב"ן

When Israel was toiling away in Egypt they were involved in construction with brick and mortar. These people had no opportunity to study silversmithing or the chance to learn to work with gold or precious jewels. Indeed, never would they have even glimpsed such treasures. Hence the Lord informed Moshe that when he sees that Betzalel is capable of multiple forms of artistry, he should understand that God has "filled him with a divine spirit, with wisdom" to perform all of the tasks necessary for the Tabernacle's construction.

ישראל במצרים פרוכים בעבודת חומר ולבנים, לא למדו מלאכת כסף וזהב וחרושת אבנים טובות ולכן אמר השם למשה שיראה הפלא הזה, וידע כי הוא מלא אותו רוח אלהים לדעת כל אלה בעבור שיעשה המשכן.

The seventh and final topic of the epilogue to the Mishkan is Shabbat. For the first time, Shabbat is identified as a sign given by God to Benei Yisrael indicating that He sanctified them and that when they observe the Shabbat it serves as their acknowledgment of God as Creator.

12
13 Then the Lord said to Moshe, "Speak to the Israelites and say: Nevertheless, you shall keep My Sabbaths. It is a sign between Me and you throughout the generations, that
14 you may know that I, the Lord, make you holy. Keep the Sabbath, for it is holy to you. Whoever profanes it shall be put to death. Whoever does work on it shall be severed
15 from his people. Six days through shall work be done, but the seventh day is a Sabbath of complete rest, sacred to the Lord. Whoever does any work on the Sabbath shall be
16 put to death. The Israelites shall keep the Sabbath, making it a day of rest throughout
17 their generations as a covenant forever. It is an eternal sign between Me and the Israelites that in six days the Lord made heaven and earth, and on the seventh day He ceased and

---

QUESTIONS FOR THOUGHT

- Which of the commentaries sounds similar to the story told in the Talmud of Shammai the Elder, who, when he went to the market on each day of the week would find something nice and buy it for Shabbat?
- Sforno and Rabbi Isaac Samuel Reggio each use context to explain the word לעשות. Which one looks at the words before it and which looks at the words which come after it?
- Which of the above interpretations do you think fits the text most closely? Which do you think has the most meaningful message?

TEXTUAL SKILLS

1. Notice which word appears seven times in this passage.
2. Notice that the word אות is used in the opening and closing verses of this section, but in apparently referring to two different things. Try to figure out how they are related.

WISDOM OF THE HEART

Many people experience Shabbat as a 25-hour period loaded with restrictions and limitations. When we look at it from a different perspective, though, Shabbat is a day on which we refrain from creative activity to reflect on what we did during the past week, so that we can do even better in the future. This kind of reflection – which in manufacturing might be called "quality control" – actually improves what we do on the other six days. What it also does is put us in control of our work. When we work without stop, our work controls us – we become slaves to our work, much as *Benei Yisrael* were slaves in Egypt. But Shabbat allows us to declare ourselves free from that work. Doing so enables us to find the Godliness in everything we do, and in the entirety of creation.

How can you transform your Shabbat into a day of pause and reflection on those things that are most important in your life?

שמות | פרק לא

יג וַיֹּאמֶר יְהֹוָה אֶל־מֹשֶׁה לֵּאמֹר: וְאַתָּה דַּבֵּר אֶל־בְּנֵי יִשְׂרָאֵל לֵאמֹר אַךְ אֶת־שַׁבְּתֹתַי תִּשְׁמֹרוּ כִּי אוֹת הִוא בֵּינִי וּבֵינֵיכֶם לְדֹרֹתֵיכֶם לָדַעַת כִּי אֲנִי יְהֹוָה מְקַדִּשְׁכֶם: יד וּשְׁמַרְתֶּם אֶת־הַשַּׁבָּת כִּי קֹדֶשׁ הִוא לָכֶם מְחַלְלֶיהָ מוֹת יוּמָת כִּי כָּל־הָעֹשֶׂה בָהּ מְלָאכָה וְנִכְרְתָה הַנֶּפֶשׁ הַהִוא מִקֶּרֶב עַמֶּיהָ: טו שֵׁשֶׁת יָמִים יֵעָשֶׂה מְלָאכָה וּבַיּוֹם הַשְּׁבִיעִי שַׁבַּת שַׁבָּתוֹן קֹדֶשׁ לַיהֹוָה כָּל־הָעֹשֶׂה מְלָאכָה בְּיוֹם הַשַּׁבָּת מוֹת יוּמָת: טז וְשָׁמְרוּ בְנֵי־יִשְׂרָאֵל אֶת־הַשַּׁבָּת לַעֲשׂוֹת אֶת־הַשַּׁבָּת לְדֹרֹתָם בְּרִית עוֹלָם: יז בֵּינִי וּבֵין בְּנֵי יִשְׂרָאֵל אוֹת הִוא לְעֹלָם כִּי־שֵׁשֶׁת יָמִים עָשָׂה יְהֹוָה אֶת־הַשָּׁמַיִם

CLASSIC COMMENTATORS

In verse 16 the Torah instructs *Benei Yisrael* to "make" the Shabbat. What does the Torah mean by the term to "make" (לעשות) the Shabbat?

IBN EZRA — אבן עזרא

The command here is for the Israelites to finish, on Friday, all of the arrangements that they will need in order to rest on the Sabbath, specifically the preparation of food. As well, one should not set out on a journey on Friday if he is not certain that he can reach his destination before the advent of the holy day.

שיעשה קודם השבת כל מה שהוא צריך כדי שישבות, כמו המאכל. ולא יכנס ביום ששי בדרך, אם ידע שהדרך בספק היא להגיע קודם השבת.

RABBI OVADYA SFORNO — ר' עובדיה ספורנו

When the verse states, "The Israelites shall keep the Sabbath", that refers to the observance of the day in this world as we currently know it. Whereas, the continuation which states, "Making it a day of rest" implies that eventually, we will enjoy an era which is entirely the Sabbath.

ושמרו בני ישראל את השבת - בעולם הזה, לעשות את השבת - ביום שכולו שבת.

RABBI ISAAC SAMUEL REGGIO — ר' יצחק שמואל ריג'יו

In the clause, "making it a day of rest" the word "making" refers to the words "a covenant forever", meaning that Israel should observe the Sabbath in such a way that the covenant between God and the nation of Israel endures forever.

מלת לעשות מוסב על ברית עולם, לעשות באופן שיהיה השבת ברית עולם, שעל ידי שמירתו יתקיים הברית שקיים ה' עם ישראל.

Shemot | Chapter 32

18 was revived." When he had finished speaking to Moshe on Mount Sinai, He gave him
32 1 the two tablets of the covenant, stone tablets, inscribed by the finger of God. When the people saw that Moshe was long delayed in coming down the mountain, they gathered around Aharon and said to him, "Get up, make us gods to go before us. This man Moshe
2 who brought us out of Egypt – we have no idea what has become of him." So Aharon said to them, "Remove the gold rings from the ears of your wives, your sons and your
3 daughters and bring them to me." So all the people took the gold rings from their ears
4 and brought them to Aharon. He took the gold from them and, fashioning it with a chisel, made a molten calf. And they said, "These, Israel, are your gods who brought
5 you out of Egypt!" Seeing this, Aharon built an altar in front of it and announced,
6 "Tomorrow will be a festival to the Lord." The next day, they rose early and sacrificed burnt offerings and brought peace offerings. The people sat down to eat and drink and then stood up to engage in revelry.

IBN EZRA

אבן עזרא

The golden calf was fashioned for the glory of God. This is why Aharon built an altar in front of it and announced that the next day sacrifices would be offered to God, an instruction that the people followed… There were only a few individuals among Israel who believed they were actually worshipping the idol. These were the ones who declared, "These, Israel, are your gods who brought you out of Egypt!" And do not argue against this point by citing God's statement, "Your people, whom you brought out of Egypt, are acting ruinously. They have deviated swiftly," for you will note that God does not say to Moshe, "Your entire people are acting ruinously."

והנה לכבוד השם נעשה. על כן בנה אהרן מזבח לפניו והכריז שיזבחו מחר לכבוד השם, וכן עשו כאשר ציום … וחשבו מעטים מישראל שהיתה עבודה זרה, והביאו זבחים והשתחוו לו ואמרו "אלה אלהיך ישראל". ואל תתמה בעבור שהכתוב אומר "כי שחת עמך סרו מהר". כי לא כתוב כל עמך.

RAMBAN

רמב"ן

The matter is as I have explained: Israel did not seek a god in the calf who would have the power to kill and to restore life, and whom they would serve as a deity. Rather, they sought a figure to take Moshe's place and to show them the way.

אבל העניין כמו שאמרתי, שלא ביקשו העגל להיות להם לאל ממית ומחיה … אבל ירצו שיהיה להם במקום משה מורה דרכם.

QUESTIONS FOR THOUGHT

- What do all three commentaries above have in common regarding the main question?
- How does each, in his own way, try to minimize the problematic nature of what transpired?
- Given the continuation of the story – God's anger, Moshe's smashing of the tablets, God's long-term reaction – what problem do all three commentaries above face?

TEXTUAL SKILLS

1. Look carefully at 32:1. Do the people relate to Moshe as a man or a god?
2. Look carefully this section and notice that the verses alternate between Aharon and the people as the primary actors. What differences can you find between what Aharon says and does, and what the people say and do?

שמות | פרק לב

וְאֶת־הָאָרֶץ וּבַיּוֹם הַשְּׁבִיעִי שָׁבַת וַיִּנָּפַשׁ: וַיִּתֵּן יח שני
אֶל־מֹשֶׁה כְּכַלֹּתוֹ לְדַבֵּר אִתּוֹ בְּהַר סִינַי שְׁנֵי לֻחֹת הָעֵדֻת לֻחֹת
אֶבֶן כְּתֻבִים בְּאֶצְבַּע אֱלֹהִים: וַיַּרְא הָעָם כִּי־בֹשֵׁשׁ מֹשֶׁה לָרֶדֶת לב א
מִן־הָהָר וַיִּקָּהֵל הָעָם עַל־אַהֲרֹן וַיֹּאמְרוּ אֵלָיו קוּם ׀ עֲשֵׂה־לָנוּ
אֱלֹהִים אֲשֶׁר יֵלְכוּ לְפָנֵינוּ כִּי־זֶה ׀ מֹשֶׁה הָאִישׁ אֲשֶׁר הֶעֱלָנוּ
מֵאֶרֶץ מִצְרַיִם לֹא יָדַעְנוּ מֶה־הָיָה לוֹ: וַיֹּאמֶר אֲלֵהֶם אַהֲרֹן ב
פָּרְקוּ נִזְמֵי הַזָּהָב אֲשֶׁר בְּאָזְנֵי נְשֵׁיכֶם בְּנֵיכֶם וּבְנֹתֵיכֶם וְהָבִיאוּ
אֵלָי: וַיִּתְפָּרְקוּ כָּל־הָעָם אֶת־נִזְמֵי הַזָּהָב אֲשֶׁר בְּאָזְנֵיהֶם וַיָּבִיאוּ ג
אֶל־אַהֲרֹן: וַיִּקַּח מִיָּדָם וַיָּצַר אֹתוֹ בַּחֶרֶט וַיַּעֲשֵׂהוּ עֵגֶל מַסֵּכָה ד
וַיֹּאמְרוּ אֵלֶּה אֱלֹהֶיךָ יִשְׂרָאֵל אֲשֶׁר הֶעֱלוּךָ מֵאֶרֶץ מִצְרָיִם:
וַיַּרְא אַהֲרֹן וַיִּבֶן מִזְבֵּחַ לְפָנָיו וַיִּקְרָא אַהֲרֹן וַיֹּאמַר חַג לַיהוה ה
מָחָר: וַיַּשְׁכִּימוּ מִמָּחֳרָת וַיַּעֲלוּ עֹלֹת וַיַּגִּשׁוּ שְׁלָמִים וַיֵּשֶׁב הָעָם ו
לֶאֱכֹל וְשָׁתוֹ וַיָּקֻמוּ לְצַחֵק:

CLASSIC COMMENTATORS

The commentaries are deeply troubled about how the people could worship a golden calf so soon after the great revelation at Sinai, and especially how the great Aharon could have been involved in such a travesty.

RASHI

Note that the people did not cry out: These are *our* gods who brought *us* out of Egypt! This betrays the fact that it was actually the interloping nations who had escaped slavery along with Israel, who ganged up on Aharon and fashioned the golden calf. Once the idol was created, these people enticed Israel into joining their worship of the object.

רש״י

ד״ה אלה אלהיך: ולא נאמר אלה אלוהינו. מכאן שערב רב שעלו ממצרים הם שנקהלו על אהרן, והם שעשאוהו, ואחר כך הטעו את ישראל אחריו.

In response to the golden calf, God threatens to destroy Benei Yisrael and start again with Moshe as the father of a new nation. Moshe argues that to do so would be a desecration of God's name – the Egyptians would claim that God took the people out of Egypt only to kill them in the mountains. God accepts Moshe's argument and agrees to spare them the worst.

7 The Lord said to Moshe, "Quick – go down. Your people, whom you brought out of
8 Egypt, are acting ruinously. They have deviated swiftly from the way I commanded them; they have made themselves a molten calf and are bowing down and sacrificing to
9 it, saying, 'These, Israel, are your gods who brought you out of Egypt!'" Then the Lord
10 said to Moshe, "I have seen this people; it is a stiff-necked people. So do not try to stop Me when My anger burns against them. I will put an end to them and make of you a
11 great nation." Moshe implored the Lord his God, "Why, O Lord, unleash Your anger against Your people, whom You brought out of Egypt with such vast power and mighty
12 force? Why should the Egyptians be able to say that You brought them out with evil intent, to kill them in the mountains and purge them from the face of the earth? Turn
13 from Your fierce anger and relent from doing evil to Your people. Remember Avraham, Yitzḥak, and Yisrael, Your servants, to whom You swore by Your very Self, telling them, 'I will make your descendants as many as the stars of heaven, and give them this land of
14 which I spoke, to inherit forever.'" Then the Lord relented from the evil He had spoken of doing to His people.

אברבנאל

הלוא ידעת שהוצאת אותם ממצרים, עיר מלאה גילולים, אשר שם היו מלומדים בכל התועבות האלה... והמצרים עובדי טלאים הם, ומהם למדו. לפיכך אמר: "אשר הוצאת ממצרים"... ואם הוצאת אותם מתוך הגילולים והעבודות הזרות, למה יחרה אפך, אם חזרו לעשותם, כי ההרגל נעשה בהם טבע שני.

ABARBANEL

Said Moshe to God: You know that You rescued Israel from Egypt – a land filled with idols, a place where Israel witnessed all manner of licentiousness… The Egyptians worshipped sheep, and the Hebrews learned this practice from them… This is why Moshe mentions the fact that He removed the nation from Egypt… Essentially Moshe argues to God: How can You blame Israel for returning to serve statues and foreign gods? Why unleash Your anger against them, when all they are doing is reverting to what they have been accustomed to?

QUESTIONS FOR THOUGHT

- Two of the commentaries suggest that Moshe is using a psychological reason for challenging God's anger. One of them seems to suggest that Moshe is explaining the psychology of the people, while the other suggests a psychology of God. Which of the commentaries takes each of those approaches?
- Which of the commentaries explains Moshe's argument in a way that is very much like Avraham's challenge to God as he tried to save Sedom?
- Why is it valuable for Moshe to argue with God – doesn't He know everything that Moshe says?

שמות | פרק לב

ז וַיְדַבֵּ֥ר יְהוָ֖ה אֶל־מֹשֶׁ֑ה לֶךְ־רֵ֕ד כִּ֚י שִׁחֵ֣ת עַמְּךָ֔ אֲשֶׁ֥ר הֶעֱלֵ֖יתָ
ח מֵאֶ֣רֶץ מִצְרָֽיִם: סָ֣רוּ מַהֵ֗ר מִן־הַדֶּ֙רֶךְ֙ אֲשֶׁ֣ר צִוִּיתִ֔ם עָשׂ֣וּ לָהֶ֔ם עֵ֖גֶל
מַסֵּכָ֑ה וַיִּֽשְׁתַּֽחֲווּ־לוֹ֙ וַיִּזְבְּחוּ־ל֔וֹ וַיֹּ֣אמְר֔וּ אֵ֤לֶּה אֱלֹהֶ֙יךָ֙ יִשְׂרָאֵ֔ל
ט אֲשֶׁ֥ר הֶעֱל֖וּךָ מֵאֶ֥רֶץ מִצְרָֽיִם: וַיֹּ֥אמֶר יְהוָ֖ה אֶל־מֹשֶׁ֑ה רָאִ֙יתִי֙
י אֶת־הָעָ֣ם הַזֶּ֔ה וְהִנֵּ֥ה עַם־קְשֵׁה־עֹ֖רֶף הֽוּא: וְעַתָּה֙ הַנִּ֣יחָה לִּ֔י
יא וְיִֽחַר־אַפִּ֥י בָהֶ֖ם וַאֲכַלֵּ֑ם וְאֶֽעֱשֶׂ֥ה אוֹתְךָ֖ לְג֥וֹי גָּדֽוֹל: וַיְחַ֣ל מֹשֶׁ֔ה
אֶת־פְּנֵ֖י יְהוָ֣ה אֱלֹהָ֑יו וַיֹּ֗אמֶר לָמָ֤ה יְהוָה֙ יֶחֱרֶ֤ה אַפְּךָ֙ בְּעַמֶּ֔ךָ אֲשֶׁ֤ר
יב הוֹצֵ֙אתָ֙ מֵאֶ֣רֶץ מִצְרַ֔יִם בְּכֹ֥חַ גָּד֖וֹל וּבְיָ֥ד חֲזָקָֽה: לָ֩מָּה֩ יֹאמְר֨וּ
מִצְרַ֜יִם לֵאמֹ֗ר בְּרָעָ֤ה הֽוֹצִיאָם֙ לַהֲרֹ֤ג אֹתָם֙ בֶּֽהָרִ֔ים וּ֨לְכַלֹּתָ֔ם
מֵעַ֖ל פְּנֵ֣י הָֽאֲדָמָ֑ה שׁ֚וּב מֵחֲר֣וֹן אַפֶּ֔ךָ וְהִנָּחֵ֥ם עַל־הָרָעָ֖ה לְעַמֶּֽךָ:
יג זְכֹ֡ר לְאַבְרָהָם֩ לְיִצְחָ֨ק וּלְיִשְׂרָאֵ֜ל עֲבָדֶ֗יךָ אֲשֶׁ֨ר נִשְׁבַּ֣עְתָּ לָהֶם֮ בָּךְ֒
וַתְּדַבֵּ֣ר אֲלֵהֶ֔ם אַרְבֶּה֙ אֶֽת־זַרְעֲכֶ֔ם כְּכוֹכְבֵ֖י הַשָּׁמָ֑יִם וְכָל־הָאָ֜רֶץ
יד הַזֹּ֗את אֲשֶׁ֤ר אָמַ֙רְתִּי֙ אֶתֵּ֣ן לְזַרְעֲכֶ֔ם וְנָחֲל֖וּ לְעֹלָֽם: וַיִּנָּ֖חֶם יְהוָ֑ה
עַל־הָ֣רָעָ֔ה אֲשֶׁ֥ר דִּבֶּ֖ר לַעֲשׂ֥וֹת לְעַמּֽוֹ:

CLASSIC COMMENTATORS

As part of Moshe's defense of the people, he asks God why He is so enraged at His people. That seems like an odd question, particularly in light of what they just did and God's explicit explanation of the reason for His rage (32:8).

רש"י
כלום מתקנא אלא חכם בחכם גיבור בגיבור.

RASHI
Moshe argued before God: A wise man is only jealous of another intellectual; a warrior only faces competition from another strong man.

ר' עובדיה ספורנו
באותם שלא חטאו בעגל.

RABBI OVADYA SFORNO
Moshe asks God how He can be angry at those individuals who did not sin with the golden calf.

Yehoshua, who had been waiting for Moshe, greets Moshe when he descends from the mountain, but it is clear that Yehoshua doesn't know what is happening inside the camp. Although Moshe does know, when he sees the celebration around the calf he throws the tablets down and smashes them, even though they were divinely made and divinely engraved. He then takes the calf, burns it, grinds it up, sprinkles the flakes into the nation's water, and makes them drink the tainted water.

15 Then Moshe turned and came down the mountain with the two tablets of testimony
16 in his hand, inscribed on both sides, front and back. The tablets were the work of God,
17 and the writing was God's writing, engraved on the tablets. When Yehoshua heard the noise of the people shouting, he said to Moshe, "The sound of war is coming from the
18 camp." But Moshe said, "It is neither the sound of triumph nor the wailing of defeat.
19 What I hear is the sound of revelry." As he approached the camp and saw the calf and the dancing, Moshe's anger blazed, and he flung the tablets from his hands and smashed
20 them at the foot of the mountain. Then he took the calf that they had made, burned it with fire, ground it to fine powder, scattered it on the water and made the Israelites

---

QUESTIONS FOR THOUGHT
- Which of the commentaries understands that Moshe *intentionally* waited to smash the tablets? Look at Deuteronomy 9:17 – does it support or contradict this position?
- According to *Haamek Davar*, Moshe is counting on the shock value of smashing the tablets. In modern terms, this is sometimes called "leadership by outrage." How do you react when people act this way? Do you think that the effects are strongest in the short term or the long term?

TEXTUAL SKILLS

1. In this section, the Torah offers a unique description of the tablets. Why does this description appear here, and not when the tablets are first mentioned (31:18)?

2. Moshe's conversation with Yehoshua seems to interrupt the flow of the story. Why is it here?

QUICK BITE

Aharon's role in the story (v. 21) of the golden calf is particularly disturbing. How could he justify making it? And even if his life was threatened, isn't idolatry one of the three cardinal sins for which we are obligated to sacrifice ourselves? Ḥatam Sofer suggests that what Aharon was concerned about was the internal debate that would erupt amongst the people – a debate that would be so intense it could lead to the destruction of the people. It wasn't his life that he was concerned about, but the future of the nation. For this reason, he tried to stall them until Moshe, who could handle the situation, would come and deal with it before it exploded beyond control.

שמות | פרק לב

טו וַיִּ֜פֶן וַיֵּ֤רֶד מֹשֶׁה֙ מִן־הָהָ֔ר וּשְׁנֵ֛י לֻחֹ֥ת הָעֵדֻ֖ת בְּיָד֑וֹ לֻחֹ֗ת כְּתֻבִים֙ מִשְּׁנֵ֣י עֶבְרֵיהֶ֔ם מִזֶּ֥ה וּמִזֶּ֖ה הֵ֥ם כְּתֻבִֽים׃
טז וְהַ֨לֻּחֹ֔ת מַעֲשֵׂ֥ה אֱלֹהִ֖ים הֵ֑מָּה וְהַמִּכְתָּ֗ב מִכְתַּ֤ב אֱלֹהִים֙ ה֔וּא חָר֖וּת עַל־הַלֻּחֹֽת׃
יז וַיִּשְׁמַ֧ע יְהוֹשֻׁ֛עַ אֶת־ק֥וֹל הָעָ֖ם בְּרֵעֹ֑ה וַיֹּ֙אמֶר֙ אֶל־מֹשֶׁ֔ה ק֥וֹל מִלְחָמָ֖ה בַּֽמַּחֲנֶֽה׃
יח וַיֹּ֗אמֶר אֵ֥ין קוֹל֙ עֲנ֣וֹת גְּבוּרָ֔ה וְאֵ֥ין ק֖וֹל עֲנ֣וֹת חֲלוּשָׁ֑ה ק֣וֹל עַנּ֔וֹת אָנֹכִ֖י שֹׁמֵֽעַ׃
יט וַיְהִ֗י כַּאֲשֶׁ֤ר קָרַב֙ אֶל־הַֽמַּחֲנֶ֔ה וַיַּ֥רְא אֶת־הָעֵ֖גֶל וּמְחֹלֹ֑ת וַיִּֽחַר־אַ֣ף מֹשֶׁ֗ה וַיַּשְׁלֵ֤ךְ מִיָּדָו֙ אֶת־הַלֻּחֹ֔ת וַיְשַׁבֵּ֥ר אֹתָ֖ם תַּ֥חַת הָהָֽר׃
כ וַיִּקַּ֞ח אֶת־הָעֵ֨גֶל אֲשֶׁ֤ר עָשׂוּ֙ וַיִּשְׂרֹ֣ף בָּאֵ֔שׁ וַיִּטְחַ֖ן עַ֣ד אֲשֶׁר־דָּ֑ק וַיִּ֙זֶר֙ עַל־פְּנֵ֣י הַמַּ֔יִם וַיַּ֖שְׁקְ אֶת־בְּנֵ֥י יִשְׂרָאֵֽל׃

CLASSIC COMMENTATORS

When Moshe first hears about the sin of the calf, he defends the people to God, but when he sees the calf he smashes the tablets. Why did Moshe not smash the tablets immediately?

AKEDAT YITZHAK
Moshe's behavior is actually not that surprising, for a person always reacts more strongly to something he sees with his eyes than to something he merely hears about. This is true even if the report he is told is undeniably true.

עקדת יצחק

ואינה שאלה חמורה כל כך, כי ברית כרותה לעינים שיתפעל האדם למראיהן יותר ממה שיתפעל למשמע אזניו, אף על פי שלא יהיה במה שישמע שום ספק.

RABBI OVADYA SFORNO
Moshe believed that when he returned to the Israelite camp, the people would repent. And if that did not happen, he planned to smash the tablets in front of them, a sight that would be so dramatic that the people would feel compelled to repent.

ר' עובדיה ספורנו

כי חשב שבשובו אליהם ישובו בתשובה, ואם אין ישברם לעיניהם לרלות עיניהם כדי שיחזרו בתשובה.

HAAMEK DAVAR
Moshe smashed the tablets because he wanted to break the hearts of the nation and arouse their emotions. For when the Israelites saw Moshe destroying this wonderful treasure that God had given them they would become so anguished, that they would be unable to criticize what he had done.

העמק דבר

משום שרצה משה לשבור את לב העם ולהסעיר דעתם בראותם, אשר משה משבר לעיניהם סגולה נפלאה כזו ויהיו נעצבים, עד שלא ימצאו ידיהם למחות על כל מה שעשה... שנשברה לעיניהם סגולה שאין כמוה בעולם.

> Moshe confronts Aharon regarding his role in this terrible sin. Aharon retells the story, blaming the people and their evil intentions for what happened.

21 drink it. "What did this people do to you," said Moshe to Aharon, "that you should have
22 brought so great a sin upon it?" Aharon replied, "Do not be angry with me. You know
23 that the people are set on evil. They said to me, 'Make us gods to go before us. This man
24 Moshe who brought us out of Egypt – we have no idea what has become of him.' So I
told them, 'Who has gold? Take it off.' They gave it to me, I threw it into the fire – and
25 out came this calf." Moshe saw that the people were running wild, for Aharon had let

---

RABBI SAMSON RAPHAEL HIRSCH
The fact that nobody objected to Moshe's decisive destruction of the golden calf demonstrates how much a strong leader is capable of accomplishing. There is, therefore, an underlying message in Moshe's question to Aharon, "What did this people do to you?" i.e., what force did they exert against you, "that you should have brought so great a sin upon it?" What could the Israelites have done to you to compel you to yield to their requests and allow them to continue with their error?

ר' שמשון רפאל הירש
העובדה שאף אחד לא התנגד למעשהו ההחלטי של משה באיבוד פסל העגל, הוכיחה מה מנהיג חזק מסוגל לעשות. לפיכך יש משנה תוקף בשאלת משה לאהרן: "מה עשה לך העם הזה" – איזה כח הם הפעילו נגדך; "כי הבאת עליו חטאה גדלה" – היינו, שהוכרחת להניח להם לעשות כרצונם ולהחזיק בטעותם?

QUESTIONS FOR THOUGHT
- Which of the commentaries understands that Moshe is not questioning Aharon at all, but rather sympathizing with him?
- One of the commentaries believes that Moshe understands that Aharon's action was not a moral or religious failure, but one of leadership. Which is that one?
- Which of the commentaries understands that Moshe is quite upset with Aharon and rebukes him, but withholds some of his criticism out of respect for his older brother?

TEXTUAL SKILLS
1. Compare the Torah's description of Aharon's role in this incident (32:1–5, 32:25, and 32:35) with his own retelling of the same scene (32:22–24).
2. Notice that in this section and the previous one the Torah plays on similar words in multiple ways. ברעה (v. 17), ברע (v. 22), פרע and פרעה (v. 25).

כא וַיֹּאמֶר מֹשֶׁה אֶל־אַהֲרֹן מֶה־עָשָׂה לְךָ הָעָם הַזֶּה כִּי־הֵבֵאתָ
כב עָלָיו חֲטָאָה גְדֹלָה: וַיֹּאמֶר אַהֲרֹן אַל־יִחַר אַף אֲדֹנִי אַתָּה
כג יָדַעְתָּ אֶת־הָעָם כִּי בְרָע הוּא: וַיֹּאמְרוּ לִי עֲשֵׂה־לָנוּ אֱלֹהִים
אֲשֶׁר יֵלְכוּ לְפָנֵינוּ כִּי־זֶה ׀ מֹשֶׁה הָאִישׁ אֲשֶׁר הֶעֱלָנוּ מֵאֶרֶץ
כד מִצְרַיִם לֹא יָדַעְנוּ מֶה־הָיָה לוֹ: וָאֹמַר לָהֶם לְמִי זָהָב הִתְפָּרָקוּ
כה וַיִּתְּנוּ־לִי וָאַשְׁלִכֵהוּ בָאֵשׁ וַיֵּצֵא הָעֵגֶל הַזֶּה: וַיַּרְא מֹשֶׁה
אֶת־הָעָם כִּי פָרֻעַ הוּא כִּי־פְרָעֹה אַהֲרֹן לְשִׁמְצָה בְּקָמֵיהֶם:

CLASSIC COMMENTATORS

Aharon's role and possible culpability in this incident are subjects of intense discussion that begin with Moshe's question, "What did this people do to you that you should have brought so great a sin upon it?" The precise thrust of Moshe's question is the subject of debate.

RASHI

רש"י

ד"ה מה עשה לך העם: כמה יסורים סבלת שיסרוך, עד שלא תביא עליהם חטא זה.

To how many torments did the nation subject you in forcing you to lead them into this sin?

RAMBAN

רמב"ן

מפני שהיה אהרן להם לאיש מוכיח ולמכפר, והיה ראוי שיחוס וירחם עליהם, אמר לו כן. כלומר, נהגת עמהם כאויב החפץ ברעתם, לא פשעו ולא חטאו לך. והנה היה ראוי משה להאשים אותו תחילה על חטאתו אשר חטא הוא, ואחרי כן יאשים אותו על אשמת העם, ויאמר, איך חטאת החטאה הגדולה הזאת לאלהים, וגם הכשלת רבים והבאת עליהם חטאה גדולה, אבל משה בענוותנותו נהג כבוד באחיו הגדול ולא הזכיר לו רק מכשול העם.

While the nation was still in Egypt it was Aharon's job to rebuke the people and to atone for their sins. Thus it was expected that when Israel embarked on the sin of the golden calf, Aharon should have had compassion for his people [and prevented them from transgressing]. So Moshe told his brother: You instead acted like an enemy of the nation who is eager for his foes to fail, whereas they had neither harmed you nor sinned against you. Now it would have been reasonable for Moshe to first accuse Aharon of the sin that he himself had perpetrated, and to then reprove him for leading Israel astray. Moshe should have said: How could you have committed this awful sin against God? And furthermore, how could you have caused the multitudes to fail in "that you have brought so great a sin upon [them]"? But because Moshe was exceedingly humble, he treated his older brother respectfully and only focused on Aharon's role in misleading the nation.

> *Moshe stands at the entrance to the camp of Benei Yisrael and calls out: "Who is for the Lord? Come to me." The tribe of Levi gathers, and Moshe instructs them, in the name of God, to go through and kill anyone involved with worshipping the calf, even if these were their family members. Three thousand people were killed that day.*

26 them run beyond control and become a laughingstock to their enemies. So Moshe stood at the gate of the camp and said, "Who is for the Lord? Come to me." All the
27 Levites rallied round him. He said to them, "This is what the Lord God of Israel says: Let each of you put sword on thigh and go back and forth from gate to gate throughout
28 the camp – slaying brother, neighbor, kinsman." The Levites did as Moshe had ordered.
29 Some three thousand people fell that day. Moshe said, "Dedicate yourselves to the Lord today. You have been willing to act even against your son or brother. May He bestow

---

QUESTIONS FOR THOUGHT

- One of the commentaries suggests that what distinguished the tribe of Levi was their unity while the other says that it was the purity of their intention. Which says which opinion?
- Why would a numerical distinction be important? Can you imagine a contemporary situation where that numerical distinctiveness would be so significant?
- Why is the purity of intention important? Isn't it enough to find the people who will get the job done?

TEXTUAL SKILLS

1. Some have suggested that the blessing Moshe gives to Levi before his death (Deut. 33:8–11) is connected to this incident. Try to find at least two connections that would justify such an explanation.

2. The phrase מלאו ידכם (v. 29) should remind you of a similar phrase which appeared four times in chapters 28–29. What might be the connection?

WISDOM OF THE HEART

Moshe calls out, "Who is for the Lord? Come to me." These very powerful words have resonated throughout the ages. Every generation has seen existential challenges for *Am Yisrael*, whether physical, spiritual, or ideological. And in every generation, some individuals shake themselves out of complacency and rise to answer the call. Yes, I am for God! Yes, I will give of myself for the greater good of *Am Yisrael* and humanity!

What do you believe in deeply enough that you would be willing to give up some of your comforts to "rise and answer the call?"

כו וַיַּעֲמֹ֤ד מֹשֶׁה֙ בְּשַׁ֣עַר הַֽמַּחֲנֶ֔ה וַיֹּ֕אמֶר מִ֥י לַיהוָ֖ה אֵלָ֑י וַיֵּאָסְפ֥וּ אֵלָ֖יו
כז כָּל־בְּנֵ֥י לֵוִֽי: וַיֹּ֣אמֶר לָהֶ֗ם כֹּֽה־אָמַ֤ר יְהוָה֙ אֱלֹהֵ֣י יִשְׂרָאֵ֔ל שִׂ֥ימוּ
אִישׁ־חַרְבּ֖וֹ עַל־יְרֵכ֑וֹ עִבְר֨וּ וָשׁ֜וּבוּ מִשַּׁ֤עַר לָשַׁ֙עַר֙ בַּֽמַּחֲנֶ֔ה וְהִרְג֧וּ
כח אִישׁ־אֶת־אָחִ֛יו וְאִ֥ישׁ אֶת־רֵעֵ֖הוּ וְאִ֥ישׁ אֶת־קְרֹבֽוֹ: וַיַּֽעֲשׂ֥וּ בְנֵֽי־
לֵוִ֖י כִּדְבַ֣ר מֹשֶׁ֑ה וַיִּפֹּ֤ל מִן־הָעָם֙ בַּיּ֣וֹם הַה֔וּא כִּשְׁלֹ֥שֶׁת אַלְפֵ֖י אִֽישׁ:
כט וַיֹּ֣אמֶר מֹשֶׁ֗ה מִלְא֨וּ יֶדְכֶ֤ם הַיּוֹם֙ לַֽיהוָ֔ה כִּ֛י אִ֥ישׁ בִּבְנ֖וֹ וּבְאָחִ֑יו

CLASSIC COMMENTATORS

When Moshe asks for people who are for God to step forward, the Torah indicates that the tribe of Levi stepped forward. Is it possible that no others were willing to take a stand against the worshippers of the calf? After all, only three thousand were killed. Where was everyone else?

ר׳ יוסף בכור שור

ודאי כל ישראל באו שם, כל אותם שלא פשעו בעגל, דהכי קאמר "מי לה׳" - מי שעמד ביראת ה׳, שלא פשע בעגל, ולא עשה מסכה, יבא אלי. אלא לא בא אלא שבט שלם שלא היה בהם מקצת פושעים, חוץ מבני לוי שבאו כולם, שלא פשעו אחד מהם בעגל. ולכך הוא אומר: "ויאספו אליו כל בני לוי".

RABBI YOSEF BEKHOR SHOR

Surely all of the Israelites who had not participated in the sin of the golden calf must have showed up when Moshe called for them. For the leader had declared, "Who is for the Lord?", meaning: whoever is imbued with the fear of God, those individuals who have not fashioned the idol, "come to me." But the Levites comprised the only tribe that was wholly devoted to God and from whom not a single person had joined in the debacle. Hence the entire tribe joined Moshe in punishing the idolators. This explains the verse which states, "All the Levites rallied around him."

העמק דבר

אין הכוונה מי הוא שלא עבד עבודת כוכבים, שהרי רוב ישראל לא עבדו עבודת כוכבים, אלא מי יודע בעצמו שהוא אך לה׳ למסור נפשו וכל אשר לו לאהבת ה׳ וכבודו.

HAAMEK DAVAR

Moshe's call here was not directed at all those people who had not worshipped idolatry, for clearly most of the nation had not participated in the sin. Rather, this is what Moshe meant when he announced, "Who is for the Lord?": Whoever knows, deep in his heart, that he would be willing to lay down his life and everything he has for the Lord, out of love and honor for God; it is those individuals who should step forward.

30 a blessing on you this day." On the following day, Moshe said to the people, "You have committed a grievous sin. Now I must go back up to the Lord. Perhaps I can secure
31 atonement for your sin." So Moshe went back to the Lord and said, "I beg of You. This
32 people has committed a grievous sin. They made gods of gold for themselves. But now, if only You would forgive their sin – but if not, please blot me out of the book You have
33 written." The Lord said to Moshe, "I will blot out of My book those who have sinned
34 against Me. Now go and lead the people to the place about which I have spoken to you. My messenger shall go before you. But when the time comes for Me to punish, I will
35 punish them for their sin." Thus the Lord struck the people with a plague for what

---

HO'IL MOSHE
הואיל משה

על דרך שאנו אומרים בתפלה כתבנו בספר צדיקים, כלומר אם תשא חטאתם, ואם אין אל אהי גם אני בחירך ואל תיטיב גם עמי, ואל תקיים בי דברך ואעשה אותך לגוי גדול.

This is similar to the expression we use in our prayers: "Inscribe us in the book of the righteous". What Moshe meant was, "If only You would forgive their sin – but if not," I do not wish to be inscribed in Your book as Your chosen one. Do not bless me, and do not fulfill Your statement "I will [put an end to them and] make of you a great nation."

QUESTIONS FOR THOUGHT

- Which commentaries believe that Moshe is referring to an actual book? Which believe that it is referring to a metaphorical book?
- Which of the commentaries understands that Moshe is challenging God's reputation of justice (as Avraham did to try to save Sedom)?
- Which of the commentaries understands that Moshe is threatening to thwart God's initial threat to start all over again with him as the father of a new nation?
- Which of the above arguments do you find the boldest? Which do you think involves the greatest sacrifice on Moshe's part? Which do you think provides the strongest indication of Moshe's qualification to lead *Benei Yisrael*?

TEXTUAL SKILLS

1. When Moshe describes to God what the people did (v. 31) he omits one word from the description used earlier (v. 4 and v. 8). Which word is it?

2. In the closing line of this chapter, who does the Torah seem to hold responsible for what the people did?

WISDOM OF THE HEART

Moshe storms the heavens in defense of his people: "If only You would forgive their sin – but if not, please blot me out of the book You have written." Rav Aharon of Karlin has a unique reading of the words "if not." He suggests that it means, "If I am nothing, and therefore You reject my prayer, You might as well delete me from Your story because the people will falsely say that you don't hear the prayers of all humanity, sinner or saint."

שמות | פרק לב

וּלָתֵת עֲלֵיכֶם הַיּוֹם בְּרָכָה: וַיְהִי מִמָּחֳרָת וַיֹּאמֶר מֹשֶׁה אֶל־ ל
הָעָם אַתֶּם חֲטָאתֶם חֲטָאָה גְדֹלָה וְעַתָּה אֶעֱלֶה אֶל־יהוה אוּלַי
אֲכַפְּרָה בְּעַד חַטַּאתְכֶם: וַיָּשָׁב מֹשֶׁה אֶל־יהוה וַיֹּאמַר אָנָּא לא
חָטָא הָעָם הַזֶּה חֲטָאָה גְדֹלָה וַיַּעֲשׂוּ לָהֶם אֱלֹהֵי זָהָב: וְעַתָּה לב
אִם־תִּשָּׂא חַטָּאתָם וְאִם־אַיִן מְחֵנִי נָא מִסִּפְרְךָ אֲשֶׁר כָּתָבְתָּ:
וַיֹּאמֶר יהוה אֶל־מֹשֶׁה מִי אֲשֶׁר חָטָא־לִי אֶמְחֶנּוּ מִסִּפְרִי: וְעַתָּה לג
לֵךְ ׀ נְחֵה אֶת־הָעָם אֶל אֲשֶׁר־דִּבַּרְתִּי לָךְ הִנֵּה מַלְאָכִי יֵלֵךְ לְפָנֶיךָ
וּבְיוֹם פָּקְדִי וּפָקַדְתִּי עֲלֵיהֶם חַטָּאתָם: וַיִּגֹּף יהוה אֶת־הָעָם עַל לה

CLASSIC COMMENTATORS

What did Moshe mean when he challenged God to erase him from His book if He does not forgive the people?

RASHI
רש״י

מכל התורה, שלא יאמרו עלי שלא הייתי כדיי לבקש עליהם רחמים.

Moshe requests that any mention of him be removed from the Torah so that people will be unable to claim that he lacked the merit to secure compassion for the nation.

RABBI YOSEF BEKHOR SHOR
ר׳ יוסף בכור שור

אין אתה מוחל על קילקולם, איך תמחול לי על ששברתי את הלוחות. שהרי בתחילה כתוב: ואכלם ואעשה אותך לגוי גדול אבל עכשיו גם אני קלקלתי ששברתי הלוחות. ואתה שופט צדק, אם תמחול לי - מחול להם, ואם לא תמחול להם - איך תמחול לי.

Moshe said to God: If You do not forgive Israel's sin, how can You excuse the fact that I smashed the tablets? For initially You threatened, "I will put an end to them and make of you a great nation", but behold I too have acted ruinously by destroying the tablets. And since You are a righteous Judge, if You pardon my behavior, You must forgive the people. Whereas if You refuse to pardon them, how can You forgive me?

RABBI OVADYA SFORNO
ר׳ עובדיה ספורנו

הן תרצה לשאת חטאתם והן שלא תרצה לשאת, מחה את הזכיות שלי מספרך ושים לחשבונם, כדי שיזכו לסליחה.

Moshe pleaded with God: Whether You agree to forgive the people's sin or not, I beseech You to erase from Your book any merits that I have accrued so that they may be added to Israel's account and help the nation be forgiven.

33 1 they had done with the calf Aharon had made. The Lord said to Moshe, "Go. Set out from here – you and the people you brought out of Egypt – to the land I promised to
2 Avraham, Yitzḥak, and Yaakov, saying, 'I will give this to your descendants.' I will send a messenger ahead of you and drive out the Canaanites and Amorites, the Hittites
3 and the Perizzites, the Hivites, and the Jebusites. You will come to a land flowing with milk and honey, but I will not go among you, because you are a stiff-necked people;
4 I might destroy you on the way." When the people heard this distressing news, they
5 were grief-stricken. None put on their finery; for the Lord had said to Moshe, "Tell the Israelites: You are a stiff-necked people. If for one moment I were to go among you, I might destroy you. So now take off your finery; and I will consider what to do with
6 you." So the Israelites stripped themselves of their finery from Mount Ḥorev onward.

RABBI AVRAHAM BEN HARAMBAM

At this point Israel did not adorn themselves, meaning did not arm themselves with weapons as they had previously done, as the verse states, "The Israelites left Egypt armed for battle" (13:18). Until now, God had led Israel with His direct providence, as the verse states, "and [Pharaoh] pursued the Israelites, who were leaving in defiance of them" (14:8). But now, when Israel heard that they would be directed by a messenger of God, they despaired and were crushed because they suddenly felt the absence of God's presence. Now when the nation was informed of this new and unfortunate development, some of the people refused to prepare for the continuation of their voyage by arming themselves. It is regarding those individuals that the verse states, "None put on their finery". However, other parts of the population did take up their weapons in readiness, until they were given the order, "So now take off your finery." Thus the following verse concludes, "So the Israelites stripped themselves of their finery." This explanation resolves the apparent contradiction within these verses.

ר׳ אברהם בן הרמב״ם

לא הזדיינו בנטילת כלי זיין כמו שהיו מזדיינים בתחילה ככתוב וחמשים עלו בני ישראל מפני שהיה מסעם בכח אשר רכשו נפשותיהם על ידי השגחתו יתעלה עליהם ככתוב ובני ישראל יצאים ביד רמה וכאן נתיאשו ונכנעו לפי ששמעו הודעת השליח ע״ה על גרעון אותה ההשגחה הנפלאה וחסרונה.
כאשר שמעו העם את הדבר הרע הזה קצתם לא התכוננו לנסיעה להזדיע בכלי זיין ונשארו במצבם ועליהם נאמר ולא שתו איש עדיו עליו. וקצתם התכוננו והזדיינו והם שנצטוו הורד עדיך וג׳ ועליהם נאמר גם כן ויתנצלו בני ישראל את עדים וג׳ – ונסתלקה הסתירה על ידי פתרון זה.

QUESTIONS FOR THOUGHT

- According to each of the commentaries, is the *adi* a physical ornament or a spiritual one?
- Was there one *adi* or two?
- How does each of the commentaries address the question about why God needed to tell them to take it off if they hadn't put it on?
- What do you think is the Torah trying to tell us about the reactions of both *Benei Yisrael* and God to the idea that God would not be in their midst?

שמות | פרק לג

לג א וַיְדַבֵּ֨ר יְהוָ֜ה אֲשֶׁ֤ר עָשׂוּ֙ אֶת־הָעֵ֔גֶל אֲשֶׁ֥ר עָשָׂ֖ה אַהֲרֹֽן׃
אֶל־מֹשֶׁ֜ה לֵ֣ךְ עֲלֵ֣ה מִזֶּ֗ה אַתָּה֙ וְהָעָ֔ם אֲשֶׁ֥ר הֶעֱלִ֖יתָ מֵאֶ֣רֶץ מִצְרָ֑יִם
אֶל־הָאָ֗רֶץ אֲשֶׁ֣ר נִ֠שְׁבַּ֠עְתִּי לְאַבְרָהָ֨ם לְיִצְחָ֤ק וּֽלְיַעֲקֹב֙ לֵאמֹ֔ר
ב לְזַרְעֲךָ֖ אֶתְּנֶֽנָּה׃ וְשָׁלַחְתִּ֥י לְפָנֶ֖יךָ מַלְאָ֑ךְ וְגֵֽרַשְׁתִּ֗י אֶת־הַֽכְּנַעֲנִי֙
ג הָֽאֱמֹרִ֔י וְהַֽחִתִּי֙ וְהַפְּרִזִּ֔י הַחִוִּ֖י וְהַיְבוּסִֽי׃ אֶל־אֶ֛רֶץ זָבַ֥ת חָלָ֖ב וּדְבָ֑שׁ
כִּי֩ לֹ֨א אֶֽעֱלֶ֜ה בְּקִרְבְּךָ֗ כִּ֤י עַם־קְשֵׁה־עֹ֨רֶף֙ אַ֔תָּה פֶּן־אֲכֶלְךָ֖ בַּדָּֽרֶךְ׃
ד וַיִּשְׁמַ֣ע הָעָ֗ם אֶת־הַדָּבָ֥ר הָרָ֛ע הַזֶּ֖ה וַיִּתְאַבָּ֑לוּ וְלֹא־שָׁ֛תוּ אִ֥ישׁ
ה עֶדְי֖וֹ עָלָֽיו׃ וַיֹּ֨אמֶר יְהוָ֜ה אֶל־מֹשֶׁ֗ה אֱמֹ֤ר אֶל־בְּנֵֽי־יִשְׂרָאֵל֙ אַתֶּ֣ם
עַם־קְשֵׁה־עֹ֔רֶף רֶ֧גַע אֶחָ֛ד אֶֽעֱלֶ֥ה בְקִרְבְּךָ֖ וְכִלִּיתִ֑יךָ וְעַתָּ֗ה הוֹרֵ֤ד
ו עֶדְיְךָ֙ מֵֽעָלֶ֔יךָ וְאֵדְעָ֖ה מָ֥ה אֶֽעֱשֶׂה־לָּֽךְ׃ וַיִּֽתְנַצְּל֧וּ בְנֵֽי־יִשְׂרָאֵ֛ל

CLASSIC COMMENTATORS

When *Benei Yisrael* heard that God would not accompany them to the Promised Land, the verse states that they did not put on some special item called עֲדִי [*adi*]. Immediately afterward God instructs Moshe to tell them to remove their *adi*, and in the following verse, we are told that they stripped themselves of the *adi* they had from Mount Ḥorev. This is a puzzling sequence of events. What is this *adi*? Why would God tell them to remove it if they did not put it on?

RABBI YOSEF KARA   ר' יוסף קרא

The verse reports that when Israel heard that God would not be accompanying them, "none put on their finery [*adi*]". This term refers to fancy clothing that the people wore to attend the revelation of God at Mount Sinai. For we see that the nation was told to wash their clothes in preparation for that event (19:10). However, when the Israelites were told "now take off your finery", this relates to the crowns that they were all given when they declared, "we shall do and we shall heed" (24:7). These ornaments were subsequently removed from the people's heads by the angels of destruction when the nation worshipped the golden calf.

הם בגדים חמודים ונאים שלבשו בשעת מתן תורה כדכתיב ויכבסו שמלותם, אבל הורד עדיך הם הכתרים שניתנו להם בשעה שאמרו נעשה ונשמע, ופרקו אותם מלאכי חבלה בשעה שעבדו לעגל.

RASHBAM   רשב"ם

The term *adi* in these verses refers to jewelry. The people refrained from putting on their adornments because they were mourning their condition, as the verse states, "They were grief-stricken. None put on their finery." This was because the Holy One, blessed be He, said to them, "So now take off your finery."

מיני תכשיטין, לפי שנהגו אבילות, כדכתיב: ויתאבלו ולא שתו איש עדיו עליו, שהרי אמר להן הקב"ה: הורד עדיך.

Moshe's tent – which he has taken far outside the camp – is the point of contact between God and the people. Anyone seeking God would have to go to Moshe's tent, now called the Ohel Moed, or Tent of Meeting. It was there that God spoke to Moshe face to face as the rest of the nation viewed from afar. By contrast, Yehoshua became a permanent fixture in the tent.

7 Moshe took the tent and pitched it at a distance outside the camp, calling it the Tent of Meeting. Whoever sought the Lord would go to the Tent of Meeting, outside the
8 camp. And when Moshe went out to the Tent, all the people would rise, standing at the
9 openings of their tents, and watch Moshe until he had entered the Tent. When Moshe entered the tent, the pillar of cloud would descend and stand at the Tent's opening while
10 He spoke with Moshe. When the people saw the pillar of cloud standing at the Tent's opening, all the people would rise and bow down, each at the opening of his own tent.
11 The Lord would speak to Moshe face to face, as one person speaks to his friend. And then Moshe would return to the camp, but his young disciple, Yehoshua son of Nun, did not leave the Tent.

QUESTIONS FOR THOUGHT

- Which of the commentaries suggests that Moshe moved his tent outside the camp because he was personally insulted?
- Which of the commentaries understands that Moshe moved his tent outside of the camp because God did not want to be amongst the people anymore?
- Which of the commentaries explains that Moshe's tent being outside of the camp is completely unrelated to the story of the golden calf?
- Which of the above interpretations do you think makes the most sense in the context where this scene is described in the Torah?

TEXTUAL SKILLS

1. Look at the opening four words of verse 7. Do they mean that this is what Moshe did *now* or that this *already was* Moshe's regular practice?
2. Notice how many times the word אהל appears in this section!
3. What is being emphasized in verse 7?
4. Why do you think that Yehoshua is mentioned in this context?

WISDOM OF THE HEART

After the sin of the golden calf, we read that Moshe pitched his tent outside the camp, after which, "The Lord would speak to Moshe face to face, as one person speaks to his friend." The Gemara (Berakhot 63b) says that God rebuked Moshe: If both you and I are angry with the people, what will become of them? The people must always know that someone in charge loves them and cares about them. The same is true with children who get their parents (or teachers) angry – there must always be someone to whom they can turn, who they know will stand by them. With that, they have hope for a better future.

אֶת־עֶדְיָם מֵהַר חוֹרֵב: וּמֹשֶׁה יִקַּח אֶת־הָאֹהֶל וְנָטָה־לוֹ ׀ מִחוּץ לַמַּחֲנֶה הַרְחֵק מִן־הַמַּחֲנֶה וְקָרָא לוֹ אֹהֶל מוֹעֵד וְהָיָה כָּל־מְבַקֵּשׁ יהוה יֵצֵא אֶל־אֹהֶל מוֹעֵד אֲשֶׁר מִחוּץ לַמַּחֲנֶה: וְהָיָה כְּצֵאת מֹשֶׁה אֶל־הָאֹהֶל יָקוּמוּ כָּל־הָעָם וְנִצְּבוּ אִישׁ פֶּתַח אָהֳלוֹ וְהִבִּיטוּ אַחֲרֵי מֹשֶׁה עַד־בֹּאוֹ הָאֹהֱלָה: וְהָיָה כְּבֹא מֹשֶׁה הָאֹהֱלָה יֵרֵד עַמּוּד הֶעָנָן וְעָמַד פֶּתַח הָאֹהֶל וְדִבֶּר עִם־מֹשֶׁה: וְרָאָה כָל־הָעָם אֶת־עַמּוּד הֶעָנָן עֹמֵד פֶּתַח הָאֹהֶל וְקָם כָּל־הָעָם וְהִשְׁתַּחֲווּ אִישׁ פֶּתַח אָהֳלוֹ: וְדִבֶּר יהוה אֶל־מֹשֶׁה פָּנִים אֶל־פָּנִים כַּאֲשֶׁר יְדַבֵּר אִישׁ אֶל־רֵעֵהוּ וְשָׁב אֶל־הַמַּחֲנֶה וּמְשָׁרְתוֹ יְהוֹשֻׁעַ בִּן־נוּן נַעַר לֹא יָמִישׁ מִתּוֹךְ הָאֹהֶל:

CLASSIC COMMENTATORS

The commentaries disagree about why Moshe's tent is outside the camp.

IBN EZRA

Moshe's tent was pitched apart from the rest of Israel's camp due to the glory of God that spoke with him. This shift happened after Moshe descended from the mountain with the second tablets and Israel began the construction of the Tabernacle. Moshe referred to his tent as "the tent of meeting" because God would commune with him there before the Tabernacle was completed. (The Torah does not insist on presenting events in strict chronological order.)

אבן עזרא

והנה משה נבדל מישראל בעבור הכבוד שידבר עמו, וזה היה אחר שהוריד הלוחות השניים כתובים, והחלו ישראל לעשות המשכן, שקרא לאהלו אהל מועד – כי השם נועד לו שם עד שנעשה המשכן. ואין מוקדם ומאוחר בתורה.

RABBI YOSEF BEKHOR SHOR

Moshe moved outside the camp because the nation had rebelled against him and wanted to replace him with a new leader.

ר' יוסף בכור שור

לפי שמרדו בו ורצו להעמיד ראש אחר פירש מהם.

RASHBAM

Moshe treated the nation as if they had been ostracized. For the Holy One, blessed be He, did not wish to speak with Moshe as long as he resided in Israel's camp.

רשב"ם

שניהג בהן כמנודים, שלא חפץ הקב"ה לדבר עם משה בתוך מחנה ישראל.

12 Moshe said to the Lord, "You told me to lead this people forth, but You have not let me know whom You will send with me. And You said, 'I have known you by name, and you
13 have found favor in My sight.' So now, if I have found favor in Your sight, please show me Your ways, so that I may know You and continue to find favor in Your sight. And
14 look upon this nation: it is Your people." "My Presence," He replied, "will go with you,
15 and I will grant you rest." Then Moshe said to Him, "If Your Presence does not go with
16 us, do not make us leave this place. For unless You go with us, how shall it be known that I and Your people have found favor in Your sight? That is how I and Your people are distinguished from every other people on the face of the earth."
17 Then the Lord said to Moshe, "In this too I will do what you ask, for you have found
18 favor in My sight; for I know you by name." Then Moshe said, "Show me, please, Your
19 glory." And He said, "I will cause all My goodness to pass before you and in your presence I will proclaim My name: The Lord. But I will be gracious to whom I choose to
20 be gracious, and will show mercy to whom I decide to show mercy. Nor," He said, "can
21 you see My face. For no one can see Me and live." Then the Lord said, "Look, there is
22 a place by Me where you may stand on the rock, and while My glory passes by I will put you in a cleft of the rock, and I will shield you with My hand until I have passed.
23 Then I will take My hand away, and you will see My back, but My face may not be seen."

RABBI YOSEF BEKHOR SHOR

ר' יוסף בכור שור

אמר בלבו: אשאל לפניו שיודיעני מדותיו, ולפי המדות אדע אם טוב לנו שילך עמנו, אם לא.

Said Moshe to himself: I will ask God to teach me His attributes, and based on that I will know whether it is to our advantage that God go with us, or to our detriment.

HO'IL MOSHE

הואיל משה

לפי שמדבריך ניכר שעתיד אתה לשנות מצב העם הזה ממה שהיה עד היום, ובכן צריך אתה גם כן לשנות חקיך ומצוותיך שהורית לו בהיותו עם סגולתך ממלכת כהנים וגוי קדוש, עתה הודיעני נא מה יהיה בהם ואדע אופן עבודתך מהיום והלאה.

Said Moshe to God: I can tell from the way You are speaking that You plan to alter the status of the nation from what it is today. As such, it makes sense that You must also replace the laws and the commandments that You issued when Israel was Your favored nation, a kingdom of priests and a holy people. So now, "please show me Your ways" so that I will know how to serve You from this point forward.

QUESTIONS FOR THOUGHT

- For each of the explanations above, which phrase serves as the context for understanding Moshe's request?
- In what way is Rashi's explanation dramatically different from all the others?
- Given what is happening at this point in the Torah, to what would you expect Moshe's request to be related?

שמות | פרק לג

שלישי יב וַיֹּאמֶר מֹשֶׁה אֶל־יְהוָֹה רְאֵה אַתָּה אֹמֵר אֵלַי הַעַל אֶת־הָעָם הַזֶּה וְאַתָּה לֹא הְוֹדַעְתַּנִי אֵת אֲשֶׁר־תִּשְׁלַח עִמִּי וְאַתָּה אָמַרְתָּ יְדַעְתִּיךָ בְשֵׁם וְגַם־מָצָאתָ חֵן בְּעֵינָי: יג וְעַתָּה אִם־נָא מָצָאתִי חֵן בְּעֵינֶיךָ הוֹדִעֵנִי נָא אֶת־דְּרָכֶךָ וְאֵדָעֲךָ לְמַעַן אֶמְצָא־חֵן בְּעֵינֶיךָ וּרְאֵה כִּי עַמְּךָ הַגּוֹי הַזֶּה: יד וַיֹּאמַר פָּנַי יֵלֵכוּ וַהֲנִחֹתִי לָךְ: טו וַיֹּאמֶר אֵלָיו אִם־אֵין פָּנֶיךָ הֹלְכִים אַל־תַּעֲלֵנוּ מִזֶּה: טז וּבַמֶּה ׀ יִוָּדַע אֵפוֹא כִּי־מָצָאתִי חֵן בְּעֵינֶיךָ אֲנִי וְעַמֶּךָ הֲלוֹא בְּלֶכְתְּךָ עִמָּנוּ וְנִפְלִינוּ אֲנִי וְעַמְּךָ מִכָּל־הָעָם אֲשֶׁר עַל־פְּנֵי הָאֲדָמָה:

רביעי יז וַיֹּאמֶר יְהוָֹה אֶל־מֹשֶׁה גַּם אֶת־הַדָּבָר הַזֶּה אֲשֶׁר דִּבַּרְתָּ אֶעֱשֶׂה כִּי־מָצָאתָ חֵן בְּעֵינַי וָאֵדָעֲךָ בְּשֵׁם: יח וַיֹּאמַר הַרְאֵנִי נָא אֶת־כְּבֹדֶךָ: יט וַיֹּאמֶר אֲנִי אַעֲבִיר כָּל־טוּבִי עַל־פָּנֶיךָ וְקָרָאתִי בְשֵׁם יְהוָֹה לְפָנֶיךָ וְחַנֹּתִי אֶת־אֲשֶׁר אָחֹן וְרִחַמְתִּי אֶת־אֲשֶׁר אֲרַחֵם: כ וַיֹּאמֶר לֹא תוּכַל לִרְאֹת אֶת־פָּנָי כִּי לֹא־יִרְאַנִי הָאָדָם וָחָי: כא וַיֹּאמֶר יְהוָֹה הִנֵּה מָקוֹם אִתִּי וְנִצַּבְתָּ עַל־הַצּוּר: כב וְהָיָה בַּעֲבֹר כְּבֹדִי וְשַׂמְתִּיךָ בְּנִקְרַת הַצּוּר וְשַׂכֹּתִי כַפִּי עָלֶיךָ עַד־עָבְרִי: כג וַהֲסִרֹתִי אֶת־כַּפִּי וְרָאִיתָ אֶת־אֲחֹרָי וּפָנַי לֹא יֵרָאוּ:

CLASSIC COMMENTATORS

One of Moshe's requests was to know God's ways (v. 13). What does that mean and why is he asking for that now? Many of the commentaries explore this as a philosophical question. The ones below seek to understand this request within the context of the text.

RASHI — רש"י

Show me what reward You bestow upon those who find favor in Your sight.

מה שכר אתה נותן למוצאי חן בעיניך.

RASHBAM — רשב"ם

Moshe requested that God Himself show the nation the path through the wilderness. Said Moshe: "Show me Your ways" so that I may walk after You.

אתה עצמך תהיה מודיע לנו את הדרך, שתראני דרכיך ואני אלך אחריך.

Shemot | Chapter 34   Ki Tisa

God instructs Moshe to carve two new tablets to replace the ones he had shattered, and bring them up the mountain where He will write on them the same words which were on the original ones. Moshe is to go alone – even the animals are not to graze on the mountain. Moshe does as instructed, God appears in a cloud, and when God passes by him, He proclaims the thirteen attributes of mercy.

34 1 The Lord said to Moshe, "Carve two tablets of stone like the first, and I will inscribe on 2 them the words that were on the first tablets that you broke. Be ready in the morning. Climb Mount Sinai in the morning and present yourself to Me there on the mountain 3 top. Let no one come up with you. No one else should be seen anywhere on the moun- 4 tain, nor may flocks or herds graze near the mountain." So Moshe carved two stone tablets like the first. He rose early in the morning and climbed Mount Sinai, as the Lord 5 had commanded him. In his hand he took the two tablets of stone. The Lord descended 6 in a cloud and stood with him there, and proclaimed the name: The Lord. And the Lord passed before him, and proclaimed, "The Lord, the Lord, God compassionate 7 and gracious, slow to anger, abounding in kindness and truth, extending kindness for thousands of generations, forgiving sin, rebellion and error, but who does not acquit the guilty, holding descendants to account for the sins of the fathers; children and

---

QUESTIONS FOR THOUGHT

- In what way does the Targum Yerushalmi differ from the later commentaries? What do you think drove the Targum to take that position?
- Both Rashbam and Bekhor Shor explain that God is announcing His name to Moshe, and they both agree that He is doing it to respond to something said in His earlier discussions with Moshe. They *disagree* on which discussion it is. Find the discussion that each thinks God is responding to.
- Do you recall the first time in Exodus that the specific name of God being used was significant?

TEXTUAL SKILLS

1. What are the similarities and differences between this revelation by God on Sinai and the first one, described back in chapter 19?

2. What is the difference between the first set of tablets (described in 32:15) and the second set (described here in 34:1–2)?

QUICK BITE

These amazing words – "God compassionate, etc." – are the essence of God's grace. We are the recipients of an incredible gift – *teshuva*. Our story illustrates just how powerful this gift is: The Israelites have hit rock bottom. They have betrayed God with the golden calf. They have sinned a "grievous sin" (22:30). But it is at this moment Moshe asks God: "Show me, please, Your glory" (33:18). It is an inconceivable time to ask for such a thing. And yet, God answers: Yes! The Lelover Rebbe teaches that specifically at a moment of forgiveness of sin, we experience God's true power.

שמות | פרק לד

חמישי
א וַיֹּ֤אמֶר יְהוָה֙ אֶל־מֹשֶׁ֔ה פְּסָל־לְךָ֛ שְׁנֵֽי־לֻחֹ֥ת אֲבָנִ֖ים כָּרִאשֹׁנִ֑ים וְכָתַבְתִּי֙ עַל־הַלֻּחֹ֔ת אֶת־הַדְּבָרִ֔ים אֲשֶׁ֥ר הָי֛וּ עַל־הַלֻּחֹ֥ת הָרִאשֹׁנִ֖ים אֲשֶׁ֥ר שִׁבַּֽרְתָּ׃ ב וֶהְיֵ֥ה נָכ֖וֹן לַבֹּ֑קֶר וְעָלִ֤יתָ בַבֹּ֙קֶר֙ אֶל־הַ֣ר סִינַ֔י וְנִצַּבְתָּ֥ לִ֛י שָׁ֖ם עַל־רֹ֥אשׁ הָהָֽר׃ ג וְאִישׁ֙ לֹֽא־יַעֲלֶ֣ה עִמָּ֔ךְ וְגַם־אִ֥ישׁ אַל־יֵרָ֖א בְּכָל־הָהָ֑ר גַּם־הַצֹּ֤אן וְהַבָּקָר֙ אַל־יִרְע֔וּ אֶל־מ֖וּל הָהָ֥ר הַהֽוּא׃ ד וַיִּפְסֹ֡ל שְׁנֵֽי־לֻחֹ֨ת אֲבָנִ֜ים כָּרִאשֹׁנִ֗ים וַיַּשְׁכֵּ֨ם מֹשֶׁ֤ה בַבֹּ֙קֶר֙ וַיַּ֙עַל֙ אֶל־הַ֣ר סִינַ֔י כַּאֲשֶׁ֛ר צִוָּ֥ה יְהוָ֖ה אֹת֑וֹ וַיִּקַּ֣ח בְּיָד֔וֹ שְׁנֵ֖י לֻחֹ֥ת אֲבָנִֽים׃ ה וַיֵּ֤רֶד יְהוָה֙ בֶּֽעָנָ֔ן וַיִּתְיַצֵּ֥ב עִמּ֖וֹ שָׁ֑ם וַיִּקְרָ֥א בְשֵׁ֖ם יְהוָֽה׃ ו וַיַּעֲבֹ֨ר יְהוָ֥ה ׀ עַל־פָּנָיו֮ וַיִּקְרָא֒ יְהוָ֣ה ׀ יְהוָ֔ה אֵ֥ל רַח֖וּם וְחַנּ֑וּן אֶ֥רֶךְ אַפַּ֖יִם וְרַב־חֶ֥סֶד וֶאֱמֶֽת׃ ז נֹצֵ֥ר חֶ֙סֶד֙ לָאֲלָפִ֔ים נֹשֵׂ֥א עָוֺ֛ן וָפֶ֖שַׁע וְחַטָּאָ֑ה וְנַקֵּה֙ לֹ֣א יְנַקֶּ֔ה פֹּקֵ֣ד ׀ עֲוֺ֣ן אָב֗וֹת עַל־בָּנִים֙ וְעַל־בְּנֵ֣י בָנִ֔ים

CLASSIC COMMENTATORS

In verse 5 the Torah says that God descended in a cloud and that He/he called out God's name. It is not clear who called out God's name. Perhaps even more importantly, why was God's name called out at all?

TARGUM YERUSHALMI
תרגום ירושלמי
וקרא משה בשום מימרא דיי.

Moshe proclaimed the name of God's statement.

RASHBAM
רשב״ם
הקב״ה קרא, כשהיה עובר, בשם, כמו שהולך ומפרש. שכן כתיב למעלה: וקראתי בשם י״י לפניך.

As He passed Moshe, the Holy One, blessed be He, called out, as the text proceeds to describe. For so does the verse state above, "And he said, 'I will cause all My goodness to pass before you and in your presence I will proclaim My name'" (33:19).

RABBI YOSEF BEKHOR SHOR
ר׳ יוסף בכור שור
ויקרא בשם ה׳ – בשם שהוא ילך עמו.

God declared the name which He will employ when accompanying Moshe.

8 grandchildren to the third and fourth generation." Moshe quickly bowed and prostrated
9 himself, and he said, "If now I have found favor in Your sight, O Lord, please, let the Lord go among us. Though this is a stiff-necked people, pardon our sins and errors,
10 and keep us as Your own." The Lord said, "Now am I hereby making a covenant. Before your entire people I will perform such wonders as never have been performed anywhere on earth, for any nation. All the peoples you live among shall see: how awe-inspiring
11 are the deeds that I the Lord will do for you. Be vigilant in what I am commanding you this day. I am going to drive out before you the Amorites, Canaanites, Hittites,
12 Perizzites, Hivites and Jebusites. Take care not to make a treaty with the inhabitants of
13 the land you are going to; for they would become a dangerous trap to you. Tear down
14 their altars, smash their worship pillars and cut down their sacred trees, for you must worship no other god. The Lord, known to demand absolute loyalty, is your God who
15 demands it indeed. You must not make a treaty with the inhabitants of the land, for they will lust after their gods and sacrifice to them; they will invite you to join them and you
16 will eat of their sacrifice, and you will take their daughters as wives for your sons, and
17 their daughters will lust after their gods and cause your sons to do as they do. Make for

---

RABBI YOSEF BEKHOR SHOR ר' יוסף בכור שור

God forges a covenant agreeing to travel with Moshe. הנה אנכי כורת ברית – שאלך עמך.

QUESTIONS FOR THOUGHT

- With whom does God promise to "travel?" Find the difference between Rashbam and Bekhor Shor.
- Ibn Ezra omits the idea of travel. According to him, does God respond to Moshe's request?
- Look carefully at verse 10. Whose status has changed as a result of the incident of the golden calf?

TEXTUAL SKILLS

1. Compare 34:11 (in this section) with 33:3. What seems to have changed?
2. The Torah has already mentioned the prohibition against idolatry many times. What new twist is added in 34:17? Can you figure out why that is added now?

WISDOM OF THE HEART

The renewed relationship between God and *Benei Yisrael* is concretized with mitzvot, detailed here and in the next section. Mitzvot provide a tangible way for us to experience God (who cannot be seen or touched) and enable us to keep our connection with Him, even though we cannot see Him.

ח עַל־שִׁלֵּשִׁים וְעַל־רִבֵּעִים: וַיְמַהֵר מֹשֶׁה וַיִּקֹּד אַרְצָה וַיִּשְׁתָּחוּ:
ט וַיֹּאמֶר אִם־נָא מָצָאתִי חֵן בְּעֵינֶיךָ אֲדֹנָי יֵלֶךְ־נָא אֲדֹנָי בְּקִרְבֵּנוּ כִּי עַם־קְשֵׁה־עֹרֶף הוּא וְסָלַחְתָּ לַעֲוֺנֵנוּ וּלְחַטָּאתֵנוּ וּנְחַלְתָּנוּ:
י וַיֹּאמֶר הִנֵּה אָנֹכִי כֹּרֵת בְּרִית נֶגֶד כָּל־עַמְּךָ אֶעֱשֶׂה נִפְלָאֹת אֲשֶׁר לֹא־נִבְרְאוּ בְכָל־הָאָרֶץ וּבְכָל־הַגּוֹיִם וְרָאָה כָל־הָעָם אֲשֶׁר־אַתָּה בְקִרְבּוֹ אֶת־מַעֲשֵׂה יְהוָה כִּי־נוֹרָא הוּא אֲשֶׁר אֲנִי עֹשֶׂה עִמָּךְ:
יא שְׁמָר־לְךָ אֵת אֲשֶׁר אָנֹכִי מְצַוְּךָ הַיּוֹם הִנְנִי גֹרֵשׁ מִפָּנֶיךָ אֶת־הָאֱמֹרִי וְהַכְּנַעֲנִי וְהַחִתִּי וְהַפְּרִזִּי וְהַחִוִּי וְהַיְבוּסִי:
יב הִשָּׁמֶר לְךָ פֶּן־תִּכְרֹת בְּרִית לְיוֹשֵׁב הָאָרֶץ אֲשֶׁר אַתָּה בָּא עָלֶיהָ פֶּן־יִהְיֶה לְמוֹקֵשׁ בְּקִרְבֶּךָ:
יג כִּי אֶת־מִזְבְּחֹתָם תִּתֹּצוּן וְאֶת־מַצֵּבֹתָם תְּשַׁבֵּרוּן וְאֶת־אֲשֵׁרָיו תִּכְרֹתוּן:
יד כִּי לֹא תִשְׁתַּחֲוֶה לְאֵל אַחֵר כִּי יְהוָה קַנָּא שְׁמוֹ אֵל קַנָּא הוּא:
טו פֶּן־תִּכְרֹת בְּרִית לְיוֹשֵׁב הָאָרֶץ וְזָנוּ ׀ אַחֲרֵי אֱלֹהֵיהֶם וְזָבְחוּ לֵאלֹהֵיהֶם וְקָרָא לְךָ וְאָכַלְתָּ מִזִּבְחוֹ:
טז וְלָקַחְתָּ מִבְּנֹתָיו לְבָנֶיךָ וְזָנוּ בְנֹתָיו אַחֲרֵי אֱלֹהֵיהֶן וְהִזְנוּ אֶת־בָּנֶיךָ אַחֲרֵי אֱלֹהֵיהֶן:
יז אֱלֹהֵי מַסֵּכָה לֹא תַעֲשֶׂה־לָּךְ:

CLASSIC COMMENTATORS

God doesn't explicitly respond to Moshe's request that God "travel" with the people, that is, restore His presence to their midst. Is that the intention of the renewal of the covenant or is God hinting that the relationship between Him and the people will not be as it was earlier? These three commentaries say things that at first seem very similar, but upon closer inspection reveal a subtle difference.

RASHBAM — רשב״ם

God states His willingness to make a covenant to accompany them all.

הנה אנכי כורת ברית - על זאת שאלך עמכם.

IBN EZRA — אבן עזרא

God is striking a covenant with Moshe and with Israel.

הנה אנכי כרת ברית - עמך ועם ישראל.

18 yourselves no molten gods. Keep the Festival of Unleavened Bread. For seven days, eat unleavened bread as I commanded you, at the time appointed, in the month of Aviv,
19 because in that month you left Egypt. The first to emerge from every womb is Mine;
20 among all your livestock, separate out the male firstborn cattle and sheep. Redeem each firstborn donkey with a sheep; if you do not redeem it, you must break its neck. Also
21 redeem all your firstborn sons. Do not appear before Me empty-handed. Six days you shall work, but on the seventh day you shall rest, ceasing from labor even at plowing time
22 and harvest time. Observe the Festival of Weeks, of the first fruits of wheat harvest, as
23 well as the Festival of Ingathering at the close of the year. Three times a year all the males
24 among you shall appear before the Master, the Lord, God of Israel. For I will banish nations before you and enlarge your territory. No one will covet your land when you
25 go up, three times a year, to appear before the Lord your God. Do not offer the blood of My sacrifice with anything leavened. Do not let any of the Passover festival sacrifice
26 remain until morning. Bring the best first fruits of your land to the house of the Lord your God. Do not cook a kid in the milk of its mother."

העמק דבר

ואחר מעשה העגל שנשתנה העניין ובאה קדושת שבט לוי תחתיהם, היה עולה על הדעת שיצאו קדושת בכורים לגמרי, משום הכי הוצרך לכפול דמ"מ "כל פטר רחם לי".

HAAMEK DAVAR

Following the sin of the golden calf the social structure of the nation changed, as the tribe of Levi became sanctified in place of Israel's firstborn. And because we might have thought that the firstborn thereby completely lost all measure of holiness, the Torah emphasizes that nevertheless, "The first to emerge from every womb is [God's]".

QUESTIONS FOR THOUGHT

- Rashbam, like many of his contemporaries (Ibn Ezra and Bekhor Shor), simply notes that the Torah here merges two different sections where it had earlier discussed mitzvot related to the exodus (ch. 13 and ch. 23). What does he *not* explain?
- R. Hirsch offers a philosophical explanation. According to him, why is this particular mitzva, amongst all the others which commemorate the exodus, joined to this discussion of the holidays?
- Netziv (Haamek Davar) offers a halakhic explanation. How does his explanation fit the context of the story of the golden calf? His explanation is based on an assumption that is not mentioned anywhere in the story of the golden calf. What is that assumption?

WISDOM OF THE HEART

We are commanded in verse 17 not to make a graven image. In the next verse we are asked to eat only matza for seven days. What is the connection between the two? The Gemara (Shabbat 105b) says that whenever we get angry, it is as though we have worshipped idols. Why? Because our anger says: "I am at the center"; "How dare you do that to me?" If instead we hold God at the center of our perspective, then we know that everything in life is happening *for* us, not *to* us. Idolatry is worship of the self. The commandment of matza reflects a similar teaching. On Pesaḥ we refrain from eating bread because leavened dough has puffed up. It conjures up an image of a puffed-up sense of self. When we humble ourselves, we prevent ourselves from being victims.

שמות | פרק לד

יח אֶת־חַג הַמַּצּוֹת תִּשְׁמֹר שִׁבְעַת יָמִים תֹּאכַל מַצּוֹת אֲשֶׁר צִוִּיתִךָ
יט לְמוֹעֵד חֹדֶשׁ הָאָבִיב כִּי בְּחֹדֶשׁ הָאָבִיב יָצָאתָ מִמִּצְרָיִם: כָּל־
כ פֶּטֶר רֶחֶם לִי וְכָל־מִקְנְךָ תִּזָּכָר פֶּטֶר שׁוֹר וָשֶׂה: וּפֶטֶר חֲמוֹר
תִּפְדֶּה בְשֶׂה וְאִם־לֹא תִפְדֶּה וַעֲרַפְתּוֹ כֹּל בְּכוֹר בָּנֶיךָ תִּפְדֶּה
כא וְלֹא־יֵרָאוּ פָנַי רֵיקָם: שֵׁשֶׁת יָמִים תַּעֲבֹד וּבַיּוֹם הַשְּׁבִיעִי תִּשְׁבֹּת
כב בֶּחָרִישׁ וּבַקָּצִיר תִּשְׁבֹּת: וְחַג שָׁבֻעֹת תַּעֲשֶׂה לְךָ בִּכּוּרֵי קְצִיר
כג חִטִּים וְחַג הָאָסִיף תְּקוּפַת הַשָּׁנָה: שָׁלֹשׁ פְּעָמִים בַּשָּׁנָה יֵרָאֶה
כד כָּל־זְכוּרְךָ אֶת־פְּנֵי הָאָדֹן ׀ יְהוָֹה אֱלֹהֵי יִשְׂרָאֵל: כִּי־אוֹרִישׁ גּוֹיִם
מִפָּנֶיךָ וְהִרְחַבְתִּי אֶת־גְּבֻלֶךָ וְלֹא־יַחְמֹד אִישׁ אֶת־אַרְצְךָ בַּעֲלֹתְךָ
כה לֵרָאוֹת אֶת־פְּנֵי יְהוָֹה אֱלֹהֶיךָ שָׁלֹשׁ פְּעָמִים בַּשָּׁנָה: לֹא־תִשְׁחַט
כו עַל־חָמֵץ דַּם־זִבְחִי וְלֹא־יָלִין לַבֹּקֶר זֶבַח חַג הַפָּסַח: רֵאשִׁית בִּכּוּרֵי
אַדְמָתְךָ תָּבִיא בֵּית יְהוָֹה אֱלֹהֶיךָ לֹא־תְבַשֵּׁל גְּדִי בַּחֲלֵב אִמּוֹ:

CLASSIC COMMENTATORS

Almost everything mentioned here appears earlier in 23:12–19 using almost the same language. The one mitzva which appears here and not in that section is the command to sanctify every firstborn. This has generated great interest in the nature of the commandment amongst the commentaries.

RASHBAM / רשב״ם

The slaying of the Egyptian firstborn effectively consecrated Israel's firstborn. And because that plague led directly to the nation's departure from Egypt, the matter of the firstborn's sanctification is discussed here [in conjunction with the festivals].

לפי שעל ידי מכת בכורות נתקדשו בכורות ביציאתן ממצרים נכתב כאן.

RABBI SAMSON RAPHAEL HIRSCH / ר׳ שמשון רפאל הירש

The Torah here juxtaposes the celebration of the holiday that commemorates the exodus from Egypt with the sanctification of the firstborn sons, a commandment which is rooted in the story of Israel's emancipation from slavery. God's message to the nation is therefore, "The first to emerge from every womb is Mine", meaning that every physical birth in the nation belongs to God. For it is thanks to God, and because of Israel's direct relationship with Him that the people of Israel merit all that lives among them. The lives of the nation are not merely a function of the powers of nature.

לפיכך מצרף כאן הכתוב את מצות החג שהוא זכר ליציאת מצרים למצות קידוש הבכור אשר טעמו אף הוא מושרש ביציאת מצרים. בהקשר הזה, "כל פטר רחם לי" פירושו: כל לידה גשמית בישראל, היא שלי. הודות לי, הודות לקשר הישיר שלך איתי, ולא הודות לחסדי כוחות הטבע, זכית לכל אשר חי אתכם.

27 Then the LORD said to Moshe, "Write down these words, for in accordance with
28 these words I have made a covenant with you and with Israel." He stayed there with the LORD for forty days and forty nights, eating no bread and drinking no water. And
29 on the tablets, he wrote the words of the covenant, the Ten Commandments. When Moshe came down from Mount Sinai with the two tablets of testimony in his hand, he was unaware that the skin of his face shone with light, because he had been speaking
30 with God. When Aharon and all the Israelites saw the light that shone from the skin
31 of Moshe's face, they were afraid to come close to him. But Moshe called them, and
32 Aharon and all the community leaders came back to him, and Moshe spoke. After that, all the Israelites approached, and he instructed them in all that the LORD had spoken
33 to him on Mount Sinai. And when Moshe had finished speaking to them, he veiled his
34 face. Whenever Moshe came before the LORD to speak with Him, he would remove the veil until he came out. When he came out and told the Israelites what he had been
35 commanded, the Israelites would see how the skin of Moshe's face shone with light, and he would veil his face again until he went back in to speak with Him.

ABARBANEL

אברבנאל

עניין המסוה אצלי הוא, שכאשר ידע כי קרן אור פניו, ידע שלא היה דבר הגון וראוי שישתמש בזוהר ההוא בדבר חולין, כמו בעת אכילה והמשתה והשינה, וגם בעת דברו לאשתו ובני ביתו בדברים שאינם מהתורה והמצוות, אבל בעת תתו השפע לבני ישראל ללמד אותם התורה והמצוות, לא היה נותן על פני המסוה, כדי שיהיו עיניהם רואות את מוריהם.

In my opinion, the meaning of the face covering is that once Moshe knew that his face shone with light, he understood that it would be inappropriate for him to make usage of the light for everyday purposes, such as to illuminate his food and his beverage when he dined. Similarly, it would have been wrong for Moshe to exude this light when conducting casual conversations with his wife and sons regarding household matters, things that were unconnected to the Torah and its commandments. [Thus, under those circumstances Moshe veiled his face.] However, when Moshe had occasion to share the divine bounty with the nation through the teaching of God's Torah, he removed the covering from his face so that the people would be able to see their teacher.

העמק דבר

ועניין המסוה שנתן על פניו, ולא רצה שיהיו מסתכלים על פניו תמיד, הוא כדי שיוכל להיות דבק במחשבתו באלוקות ולא יתבלבל על ידי כך.

HAAMEK DAVAR

Moshe covered his face with a veil because he did not want the Israelites to be looking at his face constantly. This allowed the leader to focus his thoughts on God without being distracted by the people's stares.

QUESTIONS FOR THOUGHT

- Three different answers are offered here. 1) To reserve the special glow for receiving and teaching God's commands. 2) So that Moshe wouldn't be distracted by people staring at him all the time. 3) To avoid frightening the people. Match up these opinions with the commentaries above.
- What do you think are the strengths and weaknesses of each of the opinions?
- Why do you think that God gave Moshe the special glow? Was it supposed to accomplish something? Was it supposed to symbolize something?

שמות | פרק לד

כז וַיֹּ֤אמֶר יְהוָה֙ אֶל־מֹשֶׁ֔ה כְּתָב־לְךָ֖ אֶת־הַדְּבָרִ֣ים הָאֵ֑לֶּה כִּ֞י עַל־ **כו** שביעי
כח פִּ֣י ׀ הַדְּבָרִ֣ים הָאֵ֗לֶּה כָּרַ֧תִּי אִתְּךָ֛ בְּרִ֖ית וְאֶת־יִשְׂרָאֵֽל: וַֽיְהִי־שָׁ֣ם עִם־יְהוָ֗ה אַרְבָּעִ֥ים יוֹם֙ וְאַרְבָּעִ֣ים לַ֔יְלָה לֶ֚חֶם לֹ֣א אָכַ֔ל וּמַ֖יִם לֹ֣א שָׁתָ֑ה וַיִּכְתֹּ֣ב עַל־הַלֻּחֹ֗ת אֵ֚ת דִּבְרֵ֣י הַבְּרִ֔ית עֲשֶׂ֖רֶת הַדְּבָרִֽים:
כט וַיְהִ֗י בְּרֶ֤דֶת מֹשֶׁה֙ מֵהַ֣ר סִינַ֔י וּשְׁנֵ֨י לֻחֹ֤ת הָֽעֵדֻת֙ בְּיַד־מֹשֶׁ֔ה בְּרִדְתּ֖וֹ מִן־הָהָ֑ר וּמֹשֶׁ֣ה לֹֽא־יָדַ֗ע כִּ֣י קָרַ֛ן ע֥וֹר פָּנָ֖יו בְּדַבְּר֥וֹ אִתּֽוֹ:
ל וַיַּ֨רְא אַהֲרֹ֜ן וְכָל־בְּנֵ֤י יִשְׂרָאֵל֙ אֶת־מֹשֶׁ֔ה וְהִנֵּ֥ה קָרַ֖ן ע֣וֹר פָּנָ֑יו וַיִּֽירְא֖וּ מִגֶּ֥שֶׁת אֵלָֽיו:
לא וַיִּקְרָ֤א אֲלֵהֶם֙ מֹשֶׁ֔ה וַיָּשֻׁ֧בוּ אֵלָ֛יו אַהֲרֹ֥ן וְכָל־הַנְּשִׂאִ֖ים בָּעֵדָ֑ה וַיְדַבֵּ֥ר מֹשֶׁ֖ה אֲלֵהֶֽם: וְאַחֲרֵי־כֵ֥ן נִגְּשׁ֖וּ כָּל־
לב בְּנֵ֣י יִשְׂרָאֵ֑ל וַיְצַוֵּ֕ם אֵת֩ כָּל־אֲשֶׁ֨ר דִּבֶּ֧ר יְהוָ֛ה אִתּ֖וֹ בְּהַ֥ר סִינָֽי: וַיְכַ֣ל מפטיר
לג מֹשֶׁ֔ה מִדַּבֵּ֖ר אִתָּ֑ם וַיִּתֵּ֥ן עַל־פָּנָ֖יו מַסְוֶֽה: וּבְבֹ֨א מֹשֶׁ֜ה לִפְנֵ֤י יְהוָה֙
לד לְדַבֵּ֣ר אִתּ֔וֹ יָסִ֥יר אֶת־הַמַּסְוֶ֖ה עַד־צֵאת֑וֹ וְיָצָ֗א וְדִבֶּר֙ אֶל־בְּנֵ֣י יִשְׂרָאֵ֔ל אֵ֖ת אֲשֶׁ֥ר יְצֻוֶּֽה: וְרָא֤וּ בְנֵֽי־יִשְׂרָאֵל֙ אֶת־פְּנֵ֣י מֹשֶׁ֔ה כִּ֣י
לה קָרַ֔ן ע֖וֹר פְּנֵ֣י מֹשֶׁ֑ה וְהֵשִׁ֨יב מֹשֶׁ֤ה אֶת־הַמַּסְוֶה֙ עַל־פָּנָ֔יו עַד־בֹּא֖וֹ לְדַבֵּ֥ר אִתּֽוֹ:

CLASSIC COMMENTATORS

If God wanted Moshe's face to radiate, why does he keep it covered?

RAV SE'ADYA GAON — ר' סעדיה גאון

Moshe covered his face with a veil to avoid frightening the people when they quarrel with each other. [That is, when disputants approach Moshe to hear their case, they might be startled by his appearance.]

טעם המסוה, בעבור שלא יפחדו ישראל בריבם זה עם זה.

MORE QUICK BITES

- **30:13** According to the Talmud Yerushalmi, Moshe had difficulty understanding the half-shekel, until God showed it to him. Rav Zevulun Charlop was perplexed by what could be so complicated about the half-shekel. He suggests that Moshe was concerned about the use of silver, which is so often connected with corruption and greed, as the primary medium of performing a mitzva. God showed him that, like anything else, the potential for misuse of money also means that there is great potential for using it positively. The same is true with any talent, skill, personal trait, etc. – the same potential that can be used for negative purposes can be used for positive ones, and it is up to us to decide how we are going to use them.

- **32:9** The label "stiff-necked" has stuck with *Am Yisrael* ever since God described us this way. Most people understand it to mean that we are stubborn, but Rashi has a different take. He understands that "stiff-necked" means that they turn their backs on those who try to rebuke them and help them get back on track. That's not stubbornness, but a characteristic which makes improvement impossible. Stubbornness is not a fatal flaw; it has its advantages also. But the inability to improve could condemn people to a life of mediocrity since they will never be open to critique. God is not interested in his human partners being mediocre; His representatives on earth need to display excellence if they are going to represent Him.

EXPLORING HASHAKAFA

The Thirteen attributes of God's Mercy – Understandable and Personalizable

The great kabbalist, Rabbi Moshe Cordovero, wrote a book called *Tomer Devora* in which he explains the thirteen attributes of God's mercy in a manner with practical application in our lives:

1) אל ה׳ ה׳ – signifies God's patience. We need to be patient with others and look past their flaws.

2) רחום – describes God's capacity to absorb the negative energy generated by sin as he waits for the person to restore himself. We need to be aware of, and sensitive to, the darkness which surrounds those who have erred.

3) וחנון – indicates God's commitment to cleanse the sinner Himself. We should help those who are struggling to wash themselves clean of the challenges that bring them down.

4) ארך – reflects God's compassion, as though we were a close member of His family. All of *Benei Yisrael* are responsible for one another and therefore we should extend a hand because we truly are related.

5) אפים – expresses God's commitment to allow His anger to dissipate over time. Preventing an immediate outburst and letting the anger melt away can be replaced by leaning in to love those who have angered us.

6) ורב חסד – portrays God as the master over a river of kindness, a record of good deeds from which He draws whenever He needs additional justification to judge us favorably. We need to look for the deep reservoir of whatever good someone may have done as an anchor for dealing with them positively.

7) ואמת – depicts God as closer to us after having sinned and repented than before. We need to try to accept those who are authentically remorseful as they will have learned from their mistakes.

8) נצר חסד – defines God's quality of not allowing our misdeeds to overshadow our good ones. We should not allow someone's bad behavior to ruin the many good memories we have of them.

9) לאלפים – refers to God's zealous defense of *Benei Yisrael* from those who try to hurt them. When we see that someone is in danger, even from themselves, we must zealously protect them, even if they have wronged us.

10) נשא עון – relates to God's appreciation of those who suffice with doing the bare minimum. We need to appreciate anything that is done for us, and even more so when people go beyond normal expectations.

11) ופשע – characterizes God as acting with abundant kindness to those who go beyond the letter of the law. We should treat those who are kind and compassionate with an extra dose of appreciation.

12) וחטאה – represents God as kind if only because the sinner has *zekhut avot*, ancestral merits. We must recognize that even the people we believe are the worst have someone in their past who was good and righteous, and if only as a recognition of the goodness of the ancestor we should be gracious to his descendant.

13) ונקה – indicates that when all else fails, God still is nostalgic in His love for us, remembering "the good old days" when we followed Him loyally. Try to hold onto any positive memory that you have of someone who is not currently your friend.

PARASHAT VAYAK-HEL

> "Art lies in both directions – the broad strokes, big picture but on the other hand the minute examination of the apparently mundane."
> Peter Hammill

The Lubavitcher Rebbe notes that Vayak-hel means "assembled," meaning that Moshe brought the people together and formed them into a single, united entity. Therefore, this *parasha* is a picture of the *Mishkan* in aggregate. The individual parts come together to forge a single structure. Perhaps for this reason, the *parasha* opens with a discussion of Shabbat. Shabbat is a time of unity – we eat together, pray together, study together and contemplate together.

PARASHAT VAYAK-HEL

35 1 Moshe assembled all the community of Israel and said to them, "These are the things
2 the Lord has commanded you to do. For six days, let work be done, but the seventh must be sacred to you. It is a Sabbath of complete rest dedicated to the Lord. Whoever
3 does work on it shall be put to death. Do not light a fire in any of your dwellings on the Sabbath day."

QUESTIONS FOR THOUGHT

- Two of the commentaries suggest that Moshe gathered the people to teach them about building the *Mishkan*, and not to teach them about Shabbat – even though that is what he did immediately after gathering them. What can you learn from that about the appearance of Shabbat here?
- How does verse 20 affect our understanding of the purpose of Moshe's gathering of the people?
- Both Rashbam and Or HaḤayyim suggest a context for this gathering, but they suggest very different contexts. What context does each suggest? What is the advantage of each of those contexts?
- It seems that Bekhor Shor does not offer a context at all, but the context for his explanation might come from later in the text rather than earlier. Find the context for Bekhor Shor.

TEXTUAL SKILLS

1. What one aspect of Shabbat is emphasized in this passage which has never appeared before?
2. Compare the description of the workweek as it is described in verse 2 to the description which appears earlier in the Ten Commandments (20:9). What small, but possibly significant difference can you find?
3. The word describing Moshe's gathering of the people (from the root ק-ה-ל) appears in a different form at the beginning of the story of the golden calf (32:1). How are the two words different? Can you find a connection between them?

WISDOM OF THE HEART

There is a deep connection between the *Mishkan* and Shabbat. First, the thirty-nine categories of of activities prohibited on Shabbat are derived from the construction of the *Mishkan*. Also, the *Mishkan* and Shabbat are paradoxically intertwined: on the one hand, it was forbidden to build the *Mishkan* on Shabbat, but certain sacrifices, such as the *tamid* and the *musaf*, are brought on Shabbat, involving activities that are otherwise prohibited. The *Mishkan* is the headquarters of God's presence amid Benei Yisrael. The outer manifestation of that, the building itself, is suspended on Shabbat, but the sacrifices that reflect the inner hidden world do operate on Shabbat.

There is a poem in *Sefer Haredim* that describes an individual yearning to build a *Mishkan* in his heart. What do you think that means? What do you think it feels like to have God dwell in that *Mishkan*?

פרשת ויקהל

לה א וַיַּקְהֵ֣ל מֹשֶׁ֗ה אֶֽת־כָּל־עֲדַ֛ת בְּנֵ֥י יִשְׂרָאֵ֖ל וַיֹּ֣אמֶר אֲלֵהֶ֑ם אֵ֚לֶּה
ב הַדְּבָרִ֔ים אֲשֶׁר־צִוָּ֥ה יְהֹוָ֖ה לַעֲשֹׂ֥ת אֹתָֽם׃ שֵׁ֣שֶׁת יָמִים֮ תֵּעָשֶׂ֣ה
מְלָאכָה֒ וּבַיּ֣וֹם הַשְּׁבִיעִ֗י יִהְיֶ֨ה לָכֶ֥ם קֹ֛דֶשׁ שַׁבַּ֥ת שַׁבָּת֖וֹן לַיהֹוָ֑ה
ג כָּל־הָעֹשֶׂ֥ה ב֛וֹ מְלָאכָ֖ה יוּמָֽת׃ לֹא־תְבַעֲר֣וּ אֵ֔שׁ בְּכֹ֖ל מֹשְׁבֹֽתֵיכֶ֑ם
בְּי֖וֹם הַשַּׁבָּֽת׃

CLASSIC COMMENTATORS

Moshe assembles the people, and then teaches them about Shabbat before commencing with the work for the *Mishkan*. This terminology, "assembling the people," is unique to this particular situation. What makes this different?

RASHBAM — רשב"ם

"Moshe assembled all the community of Israel" to collect the half-shekel from each male, and to direct the nation in the construction of the Tabernacle.

לקחת מכל אחד בקע לגלגלת, וגם להזהירם על מלאכת המשכן.

RABBI YOSEF BEKHOR SHOR — ר' יוסף בכור שור

Moshe made a public announcement ordering the people to donate funds for the building of the Tabernacle, to preclude subsequent complaints. For Moshe knew that unless they were invited to supply silver for the project, the Israelites might attack him later saying: The Holy One, blessed be He, commanded that we build Him a Tabernacle, but nobody told us that we could supply materials for that enterprise. We only became aware of that possibility once we saw those select individuals who always seem to know what's going on, bringing their valuables forward! Why weren't we given the chance to also contribute to this holy endeavor like they were? Thus Moshe assembled the entire congregation, to provide an equal opportunity to everybody to participate in the commandment.

כדי שלא יוכלו להתרעם לאמר: הקב"ה צוה לעשות לו משכן, ולא הודיענו שנביא תרומת המשכן, ולא ידענו עד שהביאו אותם שידעו הכל, ולא זכינו להתנדב כמו האחרים. לכך הקהילם והודיע לכולם כאחד.

OR HAḤAYYIM — אור החיים

It seems that once the people saw that Moshe's face shone and were afraid to approach him, Moshe assembled the entire nation lest some individuals avoid their leader altogether out of fear.

ונראה כי לצד שראו כי קרן עור פניו וייראו מגשת אליו, לזה הוצרך להקהיל את כולן לבל ימנעו קצת מהמורא.

4 Then Moshe said to all the community of Israel, "This is what the Lord has com-
5 manded. Bring of what is yours an offering to the Lord. Let everyone whose heart
6 moves him bring an offering to the Lord: gold, silver and bronze; sky-blue, purple, and
7 scarlet wool; linen and goats' hair; rams' hides dyed red and fine leather; acacia wood;
8 oil for the lamp; spices for the anointing oil and the fragrant incense; and onyx together
9
10 with other precious stones for the ephod and breast piece. And let all among you who
11 are skilled come and make the things that the Lord has commanded: the Tabernacle,
12 its tent and covering, its hooks and frames, its bars, posts and sockets; the Ark and its
13 staves, the cover and the curtain for the screen; the table, its staves and all its utensils,
14 and the showbread; the candelabrum for light, together with its utensils, lamps, and
15 the oil for lighting; the incense altar with its staves, the anointing oil and the fragrant
16 incense, and the entrance screen for the entrance of the Tabernacle; the sacrificial
17 altar, its bronze grate, its staves and all its utensils, the laver and its base; the hangings
18 of the courtyard, its posts and its sockets, and the screen for the gate of the court; the
19 tent pegs of the Tabernacle and of the courtyard and their ropes; the vestments for
ministering in the sanctuary, and the sacred vestments for Aharon the priest and for
20 his sons for their priestly service." So all the community of Israel left Moshe's presence.

CLASSIC COMMENTATORS

In verse 19 the Torah uses an unusual term, בגדי השרד, the meaning of which is not clear.

RASHI

רש"י

לכסות הארון, והשולחן, והמנורה, והמזבחות, בשעות סילוק המסעות.

This term refers to the coverings that were fashioned to enclose the Ark, the table, the candelabrum, and the two altars when these vessels were transported during the nation's journeys.

RABBI AVRAHAM BEN HARAMBAM

ר' אברהם בן הרמב"ם

כמו שביאר המתרגם "לבושי שמושא" והם כוללים לבגדי כהן גדול ובגדי כהן הדיוט."

The term *bigdei se'rad* should be understood as the Aramaic translation renders it: the service garments. These are the vestments which included the clothing of the High Priest and of the ordinary priests.

QUESTIONS FOR THOUGHT

- Looking at verse 19 itself, why would Rashi suggest that it refers to items which we are not told about until the book of Numbers (ch. 4)?
- How would Rabbi Avraham ben HaRambam explain verse 19 to avoid the problem that caused Rashi to search for an alternate interpretation?

ד וַיֹּאמֶר מֹשֶׁה אֶל־כָּל־עֲדַת בְּנֵי־יִשְׂרָאֵל לֵאמֹר זֶה הַדָּבָר
ה אֲשֶׁר־צִוָּה יְהֹוָה לֵאמֹר: קְחוּ מֵאִתְּכֶם תְּרוּמָה לַיהוָה כֹּל נְדִיב
לִבּוֹ יְבִיאֶהָ אֵת תְּרוּמַת יְהֹוָה זָהָב וָכֶסֶף וּנְחֹשֶׁת: וּתְכֵלֶת
ו וְאַרְגָּמָן וְתוֹלַעַת שָׁנִי וְשֵׁשׁ וְעִזִּים: וְעֹרֹת אֵילִם מְאָדָּמִים
ז וְעֹרֹת תְּחָשִׁים וַעֲצֵי שִׁטִּים: וְשֶׁמֶן לַמָּאוֹר וּבְשָׂמִים לְשֶׁמֶן
ח הַמִּשְׁחָה וְלִקְטֹרֶת הַסַּמִּים: וְאַבְנֵי־שֹׁהַם וְאַבְנֵי מִלֻּאִים לָאֵפוֹד
ט וְלַחֹשֶׁן: וְכָל־חֲכַם־לֵב בָּכֶם יָבֹאוּ וְיַעֲשׂוּ אֵת כָּל־אֲשֶׁר צִוָּה יְהֹוָה:
י
יא אֶת־הַמִּשְׁכָּן אֶת־אָהֳלוֹ וְאֶת־מִכְסֵהוּ אֶת־קְרָסָיו וְאֶת־קְרָשָׁיו
אֶת־בְּרִיחָו אֶת־עַמֻּדָיו וְאֶת־אֲדָנָיו: אֶת־הָאָרֹן וְאֶת־בַּדָּיו אֶת־
יב
הַכַּפֹּרֶת וְאֵת פָּרֹכֶת הַמָּסָךְ: אֶת־הַשֻּׁלְחָן וְאֶת־בַּדָּיו וְאֶת־כָּל־
יג
כֵּלָיו וְאֵת לֶחֶם הַפָּנִים: וְאֶת־מְנֹרַת הַמָּאוֹר וְאֶת־כֵּלֶיהָ וְאֶת־
יד
נֵרֹתֶיהָ וְאֵת שֶׁמֶן הַמָּאוֹר: וְאֶת־מִזְבַּח הַקְּטֹרֶת וְאֶת־בַּדָּיו
טו
וְאֵת שֶׁמֶן הַמִּשְׁחָה וְאֵת קְטֹרֶת הַסַּמִּים וְאֶת־מָסַךְ הַפֶּתַח
לְפֶתַח הַמִּשְׁכָּן: אֵת ׀ מִזְבַּח הָעֹלָה וְאֶת־מִכְבַּר הַנְּחֹשֶׁת אֲשֶׁר־
טז
לוֹ אֶת־בַּדָּיו וְאֶת־כָּל־כֵּלָיו אֶת־הַכִּיֹּר וְאֶת־כַּנּוֹ: אֵת קַלְעֵי
יז
הֶחָצֵר אֶת־עַמֻּדָיו וְאֶת־אֲדָנֶיהָ וְאֵת מָסַךְ שַׁעַר הֶחָצֵר: אֶת־
יח
יִתְדֹת הַמִּשְׁכָּן וְאֶת־יִתְדֹת הֶחָצֵר וְאֶת־מֵיתְרֵיהֶם: אֶת־בִּגְדֵי
יט
הַשְּׂרָד לְשָׁרֵת בַּקֹּדֶשׁ אֶת־בִּגְדֵי הַקֹּדֶשׁ לְאַהֲרֹן הַכֹּהֵן וְאֶת־
בִּגְדֵי בָנָיו לְכַהֵן: וַיֵּצְאוּ כָּל־עֲדַת בְּנֵי־יִשְׂרָאֵל מִלִּפְנֵי מֹשֶׁה:
כ

Benei Yisrael – both the women and the men – respond overwhelmingly to Moshe's call for donations. Those donations did not consist of money, but rather of precious metals, expensive dyed wool, and even the wooden boards; the tribal heads donated the precious stones and the spices. Beyond the material donations were donations of labor, particularly, skilled women who volunteered to spin the threads and weave the cloths.

21 And they came, everyone whose heart inspired him and whose spirit moved him, and brought an offering for the Lord, to be used for the Tent of Meeting and all its ser-
22 vice, and for the sacred vestments. All whose hearts moved them – the men with the women – brought brooches, earrings, signet rings and pendants, all kinds of gold orna-
23 ments; together with all those who gave gold as a wave offering to the Lord. Everyone who had sky-blue, purple, or scarlet wool, linen or goats' hair, rams' hides dyed red or
24 fine leather brought them. Whoever could make an offering of silver or bronze brought it as an offering to the Lord, as did everyone who had acacia wood that could be used
25 for the work. Every skilled woman spun with her own hands, and brought what she
26 had spun: sky-blue, purple and scarlet wool and fine linen. All the women whose hearts
27 inspired them used their skill to spin the goats' hair. The leaders brought onyx stones and
28 other precious stones for setting in the ephod and the breast piece, together with spices
29 and oil for the light, the anointing oil and the fragrant incense. So the Israelites – all the men and women whose hearts moved them to bring anything for the work that the Lord, through Moshe, had commanded – brought it as a freewill offering to the Lord.

HAAMEK DAVAR

There are two motivating factors that persuade people to donate to a cause. The first is guilt: individuals are afraid to be embarrassed by the fact that their neighbors have opened their wallets while they have ignored the call to contribute. This emotion that spurs one to give is what the text refers to as "All whose hearts moved them." On the other hand, some people are guided by nobility of character and the thought that donating is the right thing to do. These are individuals "whose spirit moved them". Nevertheless, verse 29 suggests that even those people who had initially contributed materials because their "hearts moved them" later brought their possessions "as a freewill offering [*nedava*] to the Lord".

העמק דבר

בשני אופנים נותן אדם נדבה, יש מנדב מחמת כי לבבו מכהו אם לא יתן כאחד מחבריו יהיה לחרפה או ישא עונש על העלמת עין, וזה נקרא "נשאו לבו". ויש מנדב משום ששכלו ורוחו הטובה מייעצוהו ליתן על זה, ועל זה כתיב "אשר נדבה רוחו". ובפסוק כ"ט פירש הכתוב דאפילו מי שנשאו לבו מתחילה, בא אח"כ בנדבה לה'.

QUESTIONS FOR THOUGHT

- Which of the above explanations fits the words of the Torah better?
- Which of the above explanations offers a psychological and moral insight?
- Which of these interpretations do you think accurately reflects what the Torah was trying to highlight? Why would that have been an important thing for the Torah to emphasize?

שמות | פרק לה

כא וַיָּבֹאוּ כָּל־אִישׁ אֲשֶׁר־נְשָׂאוֹ לִבּוֹ וְכֹל אֲשֶׁר נָדְבָה רוּחוֹ אֹתוֹ הֵבִיאוּ אֶת־תְּרוּמַת יהוה לִמְלֶאכֶת אֹהֶל מוֹעֵד וּלְכָל־עֲבֹדָתוֹ וּלְבִגְדֵי הַקֹּדֶשׁ: כב וַיָּבֹאוּ הָאֲנָשִׁים עַל־הַנָּשִׁים כֹּל ׀ נְדִיב לֵב הֵבִיאוּ חָח וָנֶזֶם וְטַבַּעַת וְכוּמָז כָּל־כְּלִי זָהָב וְכָל־אִישׁ אֲשֶׁר הֵנִיף תְּנוּפַת זָהָב לַיהוה: כג וְכָל־אִישׁ אֲשֶׁר־נִמְצָא אִתּוֹ תְּכֵלֶת וְאַרְגָּמָן וְתוֹלַעַת שָׁנִי וְשֵׁשׁ וְעִזִּים וְעֹרֹת אֵילִם מְאָדָּמִים וְעֹרֹת תְּחָשִׁים הֵבִיאוּ: כד כָּל־מֵרִים תְּרוּמַת כֶּסֶף וּנְחֹשֶׁת הֵבִיאוּ אֵת תְּרוּמַת יהוה וְכֹל אֲשֶׁר נִמְצָא אִתּוֹ עֲצֵי שִׁטִּים לְכָל־מְלֶאכֶת הָעֲבֹדָה הֵבִיאוּ: כה וְכָל־אִשָּׁה חַכְמַת־לֵב בְּיָדֶיהָ טָווּ וַיָּבִיאוּ מַטְוֶה אֶת־הַתְּכֵלֶת וְאֶת־הָאַרְגָּמָן אֶת־תּוֹלַעַת הַשָּׁנִי וְאֶת־הַשֵּׁשׁ: כו וְכָל־הַנָּשִׁים אֲשֶׁר נָשָׂא לִבָּן אֹתָנָה בְּחָכְמָה טָווּ אֶת־הָעִזִּים: כז וְהַנְּשִׂאִם הֵבִיאוּ אֵת אַבְנֵי הַשֹּׁהַם וְאֵת אַבְנֵי הַמִּלֻּאִים לָאֵפוֹד וְלַחֹשֶׁן: כח וְאֶת־הַבֹּשֶׂם וְאֶת־הַשָּׁמֶן לַמָּאוֹר וּלְשֶׁמֶן הַמִּשְׁחָה וְלִקְטֹרֶת הַסַּמִּים: כט כָּל־אִישׁ וְאִשָּׁה אֲשֶׁר נָדַב לִבָּם אֹתָם לְהָבִיא לְכָל־הַמְּלָאכָה אֲשֶׁר צִוָּה יהוה לַעֲשׂוֹת בְּיַד־מֹשֶׁה הֵבִיאוּ בְנֵי־יִשְׂרָאֵל נְדָבָה לַיהוה:

שני

CLASSIC COMMENTATORS

In verse 21 the Torah describes those who responded to Moshe's call with two descriptions – אשר נשאו לבו ("whose heart inspired him") and אשר נדבה רוחו אתו ("whose spirit moved him"). What is the difference between these two expressions?

RAMBAN

The phrase "everyone whose heart inspired him" refers to the wise individuals who would be performing the construction for the Tabernacle. For this description is not apt for those people who donated materials for the project; they are referred to instead as being generous.

רמב״ן

ויבאו כל איש אשר נשאו לבו – על החכמים העושים במלאכה יאמר כן, כי לא מצינו על המתנדבים נשיאות לב, אבל יזכיר בהם נדיבות.

Shemot | Chapter 35

שלישי / שני /

וַיֹּ֤אמֶר מֹשֶׁה֙ אֶל־בְּנֵ֣י יִשְׂרָאֵ֔ל רְא֛וּ קָרָ֥א יְהוָ֖ה בְּשֵׁ֑ם בְּצַלְאֵ֛ל בֶּן־ ל
אוּרִ֥י בֶן־ח֖וּר לְמַטֵּ֥ה יְהוּדָֽה: וַיְמַלֵּ֥א אֹת֖וֹ ר֣וּחַ אֱלֹהִ֑ים בְּחָכְמָ֖ה לא

30 Then Moshe said to the Israelites, "Know that the Lord has summoned by name
31 Betzalel, son of Uri, son of Ḥur, of the tribe of Yehuda, and has filled him with a divine
32 spirit of wisdom, understanding and knowledge in every craft, to devise designs, work-
33 ing in gold, silver and bronze, as well as cutting stones for setting, carving wood, and
34 working in every other craft. He has also given him the ability to teach others, together
35 with Oholiav, son of Aḥisamakh of the tribe of Dan. He has filled them with the skill to
do all kinds of work, as engravers, designers, embroiderers in sky-blue, purple or scarlet
wool or fine linen, and as weavers. They will be able to carry out all the necessary work
36 1 and design. And so Betzalel and Oholiav shall carry out everything the Lord has commanded, together with all the skilled people to whom the Lord has granted expertise
2 and acumen to do all the work necessary for the service of the sanctuary." Then Moshe
summoned Betzalel and Oholiav and all the skilled craftsmen to whom God had given
expertise and who were inspired to dedicate themselves and come to carry out the work.
3 From Moshe they received all the offerings the Israelites had brought for the work of
4 the sanctuary. And the people kept bringing him additional gifts every morning. So
5 all the craftsmen engaged in the work of the sanctuary left what they were doing, and
said to Moshe, "The people are bringing more than is necessary for the work God has

---

ר' יוסף בכור שור

מלאכה – שהיו טוות בביתם ומביאות.

ר' שמשון רפאל הירש

ה"מלאכה" שנעשתה על ידי העם – הוי אומר, החומרים שהביאו היה בה די לאלה שבנו את המשכן וכליו.

RABBI YOSEF BEKHOR SHOR
The term *melakha* refers to the woven work that the women did in their homes and then brought to the project.

RABBI SAMSON RAPHAEL HIRSCH
The work that the people did refers to the action of bringing the materials forward. These acts of donation were sufficient for the labor that those workmen who constructed the Tabernacle and its utensils did.

QUESTIONS FOR THOUGHT

- What three different opinions are there as to what the word מלאכה could mean?
- Are those opinions discussing the first instance of the word מלאכה in the verse or the second?
- Bekhor Shor's explanation has many interesting implications. Think about what some of them could be!

לב בִּתְבוּנָ֥ה וּבְדַ֖עַת וּבְכָל־מְלָאכָֽה: וְלַחְשֹׁ֖ב מַחֲשָׁבֹ֑ת לַעֲשֹׂ֥ת בַּזָּהָ֖ב
לג וּבַכֶּ֣סֶף וּבַנְּחֹֽשֶׁת: וּבַחֲרֹ֤שֶׁת אֶ֨בֶן֙ לְמַלֹּ֔את וּבַחֲרֹ֥שֶׁת עֵ֖ץ לַעֲשׂ֑וֹת
לד בְּכָל־מְלֶ֣אכֶת מַחֲשָֽׁבֶת: וּלְהוֹרֹ֖ת נָתַ֣ן בְּלִבּ֑וֹ ה֕וּא וְאָֽהֳלִיאָ֥ב
לה בֶּן־אֲחִיסָמָ֖ךְ לְמַטֵּה־דָֽן: מִלֵּ֨א אֹתָ֜ם חָכְמַת־לֵ֗ב לַעֲשׂוֹת֮ כָּל־
מְלֶ֣אכֶת חָרָ֣שׁ ׀ וְחֹשֵׁ֗ב וְרֹקֵ֞ם בַּתְּכֵ֣לֶת וּבָֽאַרְגָּמָ֗ן בְּתוֹלַ֧עַת
לו א הַשָּׁנִ֛י וּבַשֵּׁ֖שׁ וְאֹרֵ֑ג עֹשֵׂי֙ כָּל־מְלָאכָ֔ה וְחֹשְׁבֵ֖י מַחֲשָׁבֹֽת: וְעָשָׂ֣ה
בְצַלְאֵ֨ל וְאָהֳלִיאָ֜ב וְכֹ֣ל ׀ אִ֣ישׁ חֲכַם־לֵ֗ב אֲשֶׁר֩ נָתַ֨ן יְהֹוָ֜ה חָכְמָ֤ה
וּתְבוּנָה֙ בָּהֵ֔מָּה לָדַ֣עַת לַעֲשֹׂ֔ת אֶֽת־כָּל־מְלֶ֖אכֶת עֲבֹדַ֣ת הַקֹּ֑דֶשׁ
ב לְכֹ֥ל אֲשֶׁר־צִוָּ֖ה יְהֹוָֽה: וַיִּקְרָ֣א מֹשֶׁ֗ה אֶל־בְּצַלְאֵל֮ וְאֶל־אָֽהֳלִיאָב֒
וְאֶל֙ כָּל־אִ֣ישׁ חֲכַם־לֵ֔ב אֲשֶׁ֨ר נָתַ֧ן יְהֹוָ֛ה חָכְמָ֖ה בְּלִבּ֑וֹ כֹּ֚ל אֲשֶׁ֣ר
ג נְשָׂא֣וֹ לִבּ֔וֹ לְקָרְבָ֥ה אֶל־הַמְּלָאכָ֖ה לַעֲשֹׂ֥ת אֹתָֽהּ: וַיִּקְח֞וּ מִלִּפְנֵ֣י
מֹשֶׁ֗ה אֵ֤ת כָּל־הַתְּרוּמָה֙ אֲשֶׁ֨ר הֵבִ֜יאוּ בְּנֵ֣י יִשְׂרָאֵ֗ל לִמְלֶ֛אכֶת
עֲבֹדַ֥ת הַקֹּ֖דֶשׁ לַעֲשֹׂ֣ת אֹתָ֑הּ וְ֠הֵ֠ם הֵבִ֨יאוּ אֵלָ֥יו ע֛וֹד נְדָבָ֖ה בַּבֹּ֥קֶר
ד בַּבֹּֽקֶר: וַיָּבֹ֨אוּ֙ כָּל־הַ֣חֲכָמִ֔ים הָעֹשִׂ֕ים אֵ֖ת כָּל־מְלֶ֣אכֶת הַקֹּ֑דֶשׁ
ה אִ֥ישׁ אִ֖ישׁ מִמְּלַאכְתּ֑וֹ אֲשֶׁר־הֵ֖מָּה עֹשִֽׂים: וַיֹּאמְר֣וּ אֶל־מֹשֶׁ֗ה

CLASSIC COMMENTATORS

It is quite extraordinary that the people brought so much for the *Mishkan* that Moshe had to call for them to stop bringing. The last verse in this passage says that the מלאכה was more than sufficient for the מלאכה which needed to be done. It seems that the same word is used with two different meanings in the same verse. How can this be understood?

RASHI

רש״י

The *melakha* [activity] of donating materials sufficed for those individuals working on the Tabernacle, such that all of the *melakha* [work, construction] for the project could be performed, and could leave items unused.

ומלאכת ההבאה היתה דים של עושי המשכן, לכל המלאכה של משכן לעשות אותה.

Shemot | Chapter 36 — Vayak-hel

לֵאמֹר מַרְבִּים הָעָם לְהָבִיא מִדֵּי הָעֲבֹדָה לַמְּלָאכָה אֲשֶׁר־צִוָּה יְהוָה לַעֲשֹׂת אֹתָהּ: וַיְצַו מֹשֶׁה וַיַּעֲבִירוּ קוֹל בַּמַּחֲנֶה לֵאמֹר אִישׁ וְאִשָּׁה אַל־יַעֲשׂוּ־עוֹד מְלָאכָה לִתְרוּמַת הַקֹּדֶשׁ וַיִּכָּלֵא הָעָם מֵהָבִיא: וְהַמְּלָאכָה הָיְתָה דַיָּם לְכָל־הַמְּלָאכָה לַעֲשׂוֹת אֹתָהּ וְהוֹתֵר: וַיַּעֲשׂוּ

רביעי

6 commanded us to do." Moshe ordered an announcement to be made throughout the camp, "Let no man or woman make anything more as an offering for the sanctuary."
7 So the people brought no more; for what they already had was more than enough for
8 all the work that was to be done. All the skilled craftsmen among those engaged in the work made the Tabernacle with ten sheets of fine linen and sky-blue, purple and scarlet
9 wool, with a woven design of cherubim. All the sheets were of the same size: twenty-
10 eight cubits long and four cubits wide. Five sheets were sown together, and likewise
11 the second five. He made loops of sky-blue wool on the edge of the outermost sheet
12 of the first set and likewise on the outermost sheet of the second set: fifty loops on the first sheet and fifty on the edge of the end sheet of the other set, so that the loops were
13 opposite one another. He made fifty gold clasps and used them to fasten the two sets of sheets together so that the Tabernacle was all of one piece.
14 He made sheets of goats' hair for a tent over the Tabernacle. There were eleven
15 such sheets. All eleven were the same size: thirty cubits long and four cubits wide.
16/17 He joined five of the sheets into one set and six into another. He made fifty loops on the edge of the outermost sheet of the first set, and fifty loops on the edge of the second
18/19 set. He made fifty bronze clasps to join the tent together into a single piece. And for the tent he made a covering of rams' skins dyed red, with a covering of fine leather above.

WISDOM OF THE HEART

The Torah says that the materials that were brought for the *Mishkan* were "more than enough" (verse 7). The Midrash, noting that odd expression, suggests that Moshe turned to God for guidance about what do with the extra materials. God responded, "Make them a *Mishkan*." The Lelover Rebbe explains that the people were so driven by religious passion that they kept bringing materials even when no longer necessary. Moshe, recognizing that this zeal was in principle very positive but also potentially dangerous (after all, untamed passion led to the golden calf), turned to God for guidance. God responded that they should use it to make a *Mishkan* of themselves.

How can we make a *Mishkan* of ourselves?

שמות | פרק לו

כָּל־חֲכַם־לֵב בְּעֹשֵׂי הַמְּלָאכָה אֶת־הַמִּשְׁכָּן עֶשֶׂר יְרִיעֹת שֵׁשׁ מָשְׁזָר וּתְכֵלֶת וְאַרְגָּמָן וְתוֹלַעַת שָׁנִי כְּרֻבִים מַעֲשֵׂה חֹשֵׁב עָשָׂה אֹתָם: אֹרֶךְ הַיְרִיעָה הָאַחַת שְׁמֹנֶה וְעֶשְׂרִים בָּאַמָּה וְרֹחַב אַרְבַּע בָּאַמָּה הַיְרִיעָה הָאֶחָת מִדָּה אַחַת לְכָל־הַיְרִיעֹת: וַיְחַבֵּר אֶת־חֲמֵשׁ הַיְרִיעֹת אַחַת אֶל־אֶחָת וְחָמֵשׁ יְרִיעֹת חִבַּר אַחַת אֶל־אֶחָת: וַיַּעַשׂ לֻלְאֹת תְּכֵלֶת עַל שְׂפַת הַיְרִיעָה הָאֶחָת מִקָּצָה בַּמַּחְבָּרֶת כֵּן עָשָׂה בִּשְׂפַת הַיְרִיעָה הַקִּיצוֹנָה בַּמַּחְבֶּרֶת הַשֵּׁנִית: חֲמִשִּׁים לֻלָאֹת עָשָׂה בַּיְרִיעָה הָאֶחָת וַחֲמִשִּׁים לֻלָאֹת עָשָׂה בִּקְצֵה הַיְרִיעָה אֲשֶׁר בַּמַּחְבֶּרֶת הַשֵּׁנִית מַקְבִּילֹת הַלֻּלָאֹת אַחַת אֶל־אֶחָת: וַיַּעַשׂ חֲמִשִּׁים קַרְסֵי זָהָב וַיְחַבֵּר אֶת־הַיְרִיעֹת אַחַת אֶל־אַחַת בַּקְּרָסִים וַיְהִי הַמִּשְׁכָּן אֶחָד: וַיַּעַשׂ יְרִיעֹת עִזִּים לְאֹהֶל עַל־הַמִּשְׁכָּן עַשְׁתֵּי־עֶשְׂרֵה יְרִיעֹת עָשָׂה אֹתָם: אֹרֶךְ הַיְרִיעָה הָאַחַת שְׁלֹשִׁים בָּאַמָּה וְאַרְבַּע אַמּוֹת רֹחַב הַיְרִיעָה הָאֶחָת מִדָּה אַחַת לְעַשְׁתֵּי עֶשְׂרֵה יְרִיעֹת: וַיְחַבֵּר אֶת־חֲמֵשׁ הַיְרִיעֹת לְבָד וְאֶת־שֵׁשׁ הַיְרִיעֹת לְבָד: וַיַּעַשׂ לֻלָאֹת חֲמִשִּׁים עַל שְׂפַת הַיְרִיעָה הַקִּיצֹנָה בַּמַּחְבָּרֶת וַחֲמִשִּׁים לֻלָאֹת עָשָׂה עַל־שְׂפַת הַיְרִיעָה הַחֹבֶרֶת הַשֵּׁנִית: וַיַּעַשׂ קַרְסֵי נְחֹשֶׁת חֲמִשִּׁים לְחַבֵּר אֶת־הָאֹהֶל לִהְיֹת אֶחָד: וַיַּעַשׂ מִכְסֶה לָאֹהֶל עֹרֹת אֵילִם מְאָדָּמִים וּמִכְסֵה עֹרֹת תְּחָשִׁים

WISDOM OF THE HEART

The curtains were magnificently and intricately woven, with the images of the *keruvim* worked into the cloth, rather than sewn on. Abarbanel argues that the designs were woven into the fabric itself, while Ibn Ezra suggests a complex process similar to that used to make designs on silk.

Shemot | Chapter 36

חמישי מִלְמָעְלָה: וַיַּעַשׂ אֶת־הַקְּרָשִׁים לַמִּשְׁכָּן עֲצֵי שִׁטִּים עֹמְדִים: כ עֶשֶׂר אַמֹּת אֹרֶךְ הַקָּרֶשׁ וְאַמָּה וַחֲצִי הָאַמָּה רֹחַב הַקֶּרֶשׁ הָאֶחָד: שְׁתֵּי כא כב יָדֹת לַקֶּרֶשׁ הָאֶחָד מְשֻׁלָּבֹת אַחַת אֶל־אֶחָת כֵּן עָשָׂה לְכֹל קַרְשֵׁי הַמִּשְׁכָּן: וַיַּעַשׂ אֶת־הַקְּרָשִׁים לַמִּשְׁכָּן עֶשְׂרִים קְרָשִׁים לִפְאַת נֶגֶב כג תֵּימָנָה: וְאַרְבָּעִים אַדְנֵי־כֶסֶף עָשָׂה תַּחַת עֶשְׂרִים הַקְּרָשִׁים שְׁנֵי אֲדָנִים כד תַּחַת־הַקֶּרֶשׁ הָאֶחָד לִשְׁתֵּי יְדֹתָיו וּשְׁנֵי אֲדָנִים תַּחַת־הַקֶּרֶשׁ הָאֶחָד

20/21 Then he made the upright boards for the Tabernacle from acacia wood. Each was ten
22 cubits long and a cubit and a half wide. Each board had two matching tenons; all the
23 Tabernacle's boards were made in this way. He made twenty boards for the south side,
24 and forty silver sockets to go under them, two sockets under each board, one under each
25 tenon. For the second side of the Tabernacle, the north side, he made twenty boards
26/27 and their forty silver sockets, two under each board. For the rear of the Tabernacle on
28 the west side he made six boards, along with two boards for each of the rear corners of
29 the Tabernacle. They were even at the bottom, and joined at the top by a ring. This was
30 so for the other corner also. So there were eight boards and sixteen silver sockets, two
31 under each board. He made crossbars of acacia wood, five for the boards of the first side
32 of the Tabernacle, five for the boards of the second, and five for those of the rear of the
33 Tabernacle on the west side. He made the central crossbar to go across the middles of
34 the boards from one end to the other. He overlaid the boards with gold, and made gold
35 rings to hold the crossbars; he overlaid the crossbars themselves with gold. He made
   the curtain of sky-blue, purple and scarlet wool and finely spun linen, with a design of
36 cherubim worked into it. He also made four posts of acacia wood for it and overlaid
   them with gold. Their hooks were of gold, and he cast for them four sockets of silver.
37 He made an embroidered screen for the entrance of the tent, of sky-blue, purple and
38 scarlet wool and finely spun linen, as well as five posts with their hooks. He overlaid
   their tops and bands with gold, but their five sockets were of bronze.

37 1 Betzalel made the Ark of acacia wood, two and a half cubits long, a cubit and a half wide,
2 and a cubit and a half high. He overlaid it with pure gold inside and out, and encircled
3 it around with a gold rim. He cast four gold rings for its four corners, two rings on one

כה לִשְׁתֵּי יְדֹתָיו: וּלְצֶ֧לַע הַמִּשְׁכָּ֛ן הַשֵּׁנִ֖ית לִפְאַ֣ת צָפ֑וֹן עָשָׂ֖ה עֶשְׂרִ֥ים
כו קְרָשִֽׁים: וְאַרְבָּעִ֥ים אַדְנֵיהֶ֖ם כָּ֑סֶף שְׁנֵ֣י אֲדָנִ֗ים תַּ֚חַת הַקֶּ֣רֶשׁ
כז הָאֶחָ֔ד וּשְׁנֵ֣י אֲדָנִ֔ים תַּ֖חַת הַקֶּ֥רֶשׁ הָאֶחָֽד: וּֽלְיַרְכְּתֵ֥י הַמִּשְׁכָּ֖ן יָ֑מָּה
כח עָשָׂ֖ה שִׁשָּׁ֥ה קְרָשִֽׁים: וּשְׁנֵ֤י קְרָשִׁים֙ עָשָׂ֔ה לִמְקֻצְעֹ֖ת הַמִּשְׁכָּ֑ן
כט בַּיַּרְכָתָֽיִם: וְהָי֣וּ תוֹאֲמִם֮ מִלְּמַטָּה֒ וְיַחְדָּ֗ו יִהְי֤וּ תַמִּים֙ אֶל־רֹאשׁ֔וֹ
ל אֶל־הַטַּבַּ֖עַת הָאֶחָ֑ת כֵּ֚ן עָשָׂ֣ה לִשְׁנֵיהֶ֔ם לִשְׁנֵ֖י הַמִּקְצֹעֹֽת: וְהָיוּ֙
שְׁמֹנָ֣ה קְרָשִׁ֔ים וְאַדְנֵיהֶ֣ם כֶּ֔סֶף שִׁשָּׁ֥ה עָשָׂ֖ר אֲדָנִ֑ים שְׁנֵ֣י
לא אֲדָנִ֔ים שְׁנֵ֣י אֲדָנִ֔ים תַּ֖חַת הַקֶּ֥רֶשׁ הָאֶחָֽד: וַיַּ֥עַשׂ בְּרִיחֵ֖י עֲצֵ֣י שִׁטִּ֑ים חֲמִשָּׁ֕ה
לב לְקַרְשֵׁ֥י צֶֽלַע־הַמִּשְׁכָּ֖ן הָאֶחָֽת: וַחֲמִשָּׁ֣ה בְרִיחִ֔ם לְקַרְשֵׁ֥י צֶֽלַע־
הַמִּשְׁכָּ֖ן הַשֵּׁנִ֑ית וַחֲמִשָּׁ֤ה בְרִיחִם֙ לְקַרְשֵׁ֣י הַמִּשְׁכָּ֔ן לַיַּרְכָתַ֖יִם
לג יָֽמָּה: וַיַּ֖עַשׂ אֶת־הַבְּרִ֣יחַ הַתִּיכֹ֑ן לִבְרֹ֙חַ֙ בְּת֣וֹךְ הַקְּרָשִׁ֔ים מִן־הַקָּצֶ֖ה
לד אֶל־הַקָּצֶֽה: וְֽאֶת־הַקְּרָשִׁ֞ים צִפָּ֣ה זָהָ֗ב וְאֶת־טַבְּעֹתָם֙ עָשָׂ֣ה זָהָ֔ב
לה בָּתִּ֖ים לַבְּרִיחִ֑ם וַיְצַ֥ף אֶת־הַבְּרִיחִ֖ם זָהָֽב: וַיַּ֙עַשׂ֙ אֶת־הַפָּרֹ֔כֶת
תְּכֵ֧לֶת וְאַרְגָּמָ֛ן וְתוֹלַ֥עַת שָׁנִ֖י וְשֵׁ֣שׁ מָשְׁזָ֑ר מַעֲשֵׂ֥ה חֹשֵׁ֛ב עָשָׂ֥ה
לו אֹתָ֖הּ כְּרֻבִֽים: וַיַּ֣עַשׂ לָ֗הּ אַרְבָּעָה֙ עַמּוּדֵ֣י שִׁטִּ֔ים וַיְצַפֵּ֣ם זָהָ֔ב
וָוֵיהֶ֖ם זָהָ֑ב וַיִּצֹ֣ק לָהֶ֔ם אַרְבָּעָ֖ה אַדְנֵי־כָֽסֶף: וַיַּ֤עַשׂ מָסָךְ֙ לְפֶ֣תַח
לז הָאֹ֔הֶל תְּכֵ֧לֶת וְאַרְגָּמָ֛ן וְתוֹלַ֥עַת שָׁנִ֖י וְשֵׁ֣שׁ מָשְׁזָ֑ר מַעֲשֵׂ֖ה רֹקֵֽם:
לח וְאֶת־עַמּוּדָ֣יו חֲמִשָּׁ֗ה וְאֶת־וָֽוֵיהֶם֙ וְצִפָּ֤ה רָאשֵׁיהֶם֙ וַחֲשֻׁקֵיהֶ֖ם
זָהָ֑ב וְאַדְנֵיהֶ֥ם חֲמִשָּׁ֖ה נְחֹֽשֶׁת:

לז א וַיַּ֧עַשׂ בְּצַלְאֵ֛ל אֶת־הָאָרֹ֖ן עֲצֵ֣י שִׁטִּ֑ים אַמָּתַ֨יִם וָחֵ֜צִי אָרְכּ֗וֹ וְאַמָּ֤ה
ב וָחֵ֙צִי֙ רָחְבּ֔וֹ וְאַמָּ֥ה וָחֵ֖צִי קֹמָתֽוֹ: וַיְצַפֵּ֛הוּ זָהָ֥ב טָה֖וֹר מִבַּ֣יִת וּמִח֑וּץ
ג וַיַּ֥עַשׂ ל֛וֹ זֵ֥ר זָהָ֖ב סָבִֽיב: וַיִּצֹ֣ק ל֗וֹ אַרְבַּע֙ טַבְּעֹ֣ת זָהָ֔ב עַ֖ל אַרְבַּ֥ע

SHEMOT | CHAPTER 37   VAYAK-HEL | 324

פַּעֲמֹתָ֑יו וּשְׁתֵּ֣י טַבָּעֹ֗ת עַל־צַלְעוֹ֙ הָֽאֶחָ֔ת וּשְׁתֵּי֙ טַבָּעֹ֔ת עַל־צַלְע֖וֹ
הַשֵּׁנִֽית׃ וַיַּ֥עַשׂ בַּדֵּ֖י עֲצֵ֣י שִׁטִּ֑ים וַיְצַ֥ף אֹתָ֖ם זָהָֽב׃ וַיָּבֵ֤א אֶת־הַבַּדִּים֙
בַּטַּבָּעֹ֔ת עַ֖ל צַלְעֹ֣ת הָאָרֹ֑ן לָשֵׂ֖את אֶת־הָאָרֹֽן׃ וַיַּ֥עַשׂ כַּפֹּ֖רֶת זָהָ֣ב טָה֑וֹר
אַמָּתַ֤יִם וָחֵ֨צִי֙ אׇרְכָּ֔הּ וְאַמָּ֥ה וָחֵ֖צִי רׇחְבָּֽהּ׃ וַיַּ֛עַשׂ שְׁנֵ֥י כְרֻבִ֖ים זָהָ֑ב מִקְשָׁה֙
עָשָׂ֣ה אֹתָ֔ם מִשְּׁנֵ֖י קְצ֥וֹת הַכַּפֹּֽרֶת׃ כְּרוּב־אֶחָ֤ד מִקָּצָה֙ מִזֶּ֔ה וּכְרוּב־אֶחָ֥ד
מִקָּצָ֖ה מִזֶּ֑ה מִן־הַכַּפֹּ֛רֶת עָשָׂ֥ה אֶת־הַכְּרֻבִ֖ים מִשְּׁנֵ֥י קְצוֹתָֽו׃ וַיִּהְי֣וּ

4 side and two on the other. He made staves of acacia wood and overlaid them with gold.
5/6 He then placed the staves in the rings on the Ark's sides so that it could be carried. He
7 made a cover of pure gold, two and a half cubits long and a cubit and a half wide. He
8 made two cherubim of beaten gold for the two ends of the cover, one cherub at one
9 end and one at the other. He made them of one piece with the cover, and the wings of
the cherubim were spread upward, sheltering the cover. They faced each other, their
faces toward the cover.
10 He made a table of acacia wood, two cubits long, a cubit wide, and a cubit and a half
11/12 high. He overlaid it with pure gold and around it made a gold rim. He also made a frame
13 a handbreadth wide around it and made a gold rim for the frame. He cast four gold rings
14 and placed the rings on the corners of its four legs. The rings were close to the frame
15 to hold the staves used to carry the table. He made the staves for carrying the table of
16 acacia wood overlaid with gold. The articles for the table – the bowls, spoons, jars and
pitchers for pouring libations – he made of pure gold.
17 He made the candelabrum of pure beaten gold. Its base and shaft, cups, knobs and
18 flowers were hammered from a single piece. Six branches extended from its sides,
19 three on one side, three on the other. On each of the six branches extending from the
20 candelabrum were three finely crafted cups, each with a knob and a flower. On the candelabrum itself there were four finely crafted cups, each, also, with a knob and a flower.
21 At the base of each of the three pairs of branches extending from the candelabrum there
22 was a knob of one piece with it; their knobs and branches were of one piece with it, so
23 that the whole of it was a single piece of pure beaten gold. Its seven lamps and its tongs
24 and pans were of pure gold; it and all its utensils were made from a talent of pure gold.

הַכְּרֻבִים פֹּרְשֵׂי כְנָפַיִם לְמַעְלָה סֹכְכִים בְּכַנְפֵיהֶם עַל־הַכַּפֹּרֶת וּפְנֵיהֶם אִישׁ אֶל־אָחִיו אֶל־הַכַּפֹּרֶת הָיוּ פְּנֵי הַכְּרֻבִים:

י וַיַּעַשׂ אֶת־הַשֻּׁלְחָן עֲצֵי שִׁטִּים אַמָּתַיִם אָרְכּוֹ וְאַמָּה רָחְבּוֹ וְאַמָּה וָחֵצִי קֹמָתוֹ:

יא וַיְצַף אֹתוֹ זָהָב טָהוֹר וַיַּעַשׂ לוֹ זֵר זָהָב סָבִיב: וַיַּעַשׂ

יב לוֹ מִסְגֶּרֶת טֹפַח סָבִיב וַיַּעַשׂ זֵר־זָהָב לְמִסְגַּרְתּוֹ סָבִיב: וַיִּצֹק לוֹ

יג אַרְבַּע טַבְּעֹת זָהָב וַיִּתֵּן אֶת־הַטַּבָּעֹת עַל אַרְבַּע הַפֵּאֹת אֲשֶׁר לְאַרְבַּע רַגְלָיו:

יד לְעֻמַּת הַמִּסְגֶּרֶת הָיוּ הַטַּבָּעֹת בָּתִּים לַבַּדִּים לָשֵׂאת אֶת־הַשֻּׁלְחָן: וַיַּעַשׂ אֶת־הַבַּדִּים עֲצֵי שִׁטִּים וַיְצַף אֹתָם

טו זָהָב לָשֵׂאת אֶת־הַשֻּׁלְחָן: וַיַּעַשׂ אֶת־הַכֵּלִים ׀ אֲשֶׁר עַל־הַשֻּׁלְחָן

טז אֶת־קְעָרֹתָיו וְאֶת־כַּפֹּתָיו וְאֵת מְנַקִּיֹּתָיו וְאֶת־הַקְּשָׂוֺת אֲשֶׁר יֻסַּךְ בָּהֵן זָהָב טָהוֹר:

ששי /שלישי/

יז וַיַּעַשׂ אֶת־הַמְּנֹרָה זָהָב טָהוֹר מִקְשָׁה עָשָׂה אֶת־הַמְּנֹרָה יְרֵכָהּ וְקָנָהּ גְּבִיעֶיהָ כַּפְתֹּרֶיהָ וּפְרָחֶיהָ מִמֶּנָּה הָיוּ: וְשִׁשָּׁה קָנִים יֹצְאִים

יח מִצִּדֶּיהָ שְׁלֹשָׁה ׀ קְנֵי מְנֹרָה מִצִּדָּהּ הָאֶחָד וּשְׁלֹשָׁה קְנֵי מְנֹרָה

יט מִצִּדָּהּ הַשֵּׁנִי: שְׁלֹשָׁה גְבִעִים מְשֻׁקָּדִים בַּקָּנֶה הָאֶחָד כַּפְתֹּר וָפֶרַח וּשְׁלֹשָׁה גְבִעִים מְשֻׁקָּדִים בְּקָנֶה אֶחָד כַּפְתֹּר וָפָרַח כֵּן לְשֵׁשֶׁת

כ הַקָּנִים הַיֹּצְאִים מִן־הַמְּנֹרָה: וּבַמְּנֹרָה אַרְבָּעָה גְבִעִים מְשֻׁקָּדִים

כא כַּפְתֹּרֶיהָ וּפְרָחֶיהָ: וְכַפְתֹּר תַּחַת שְׁנֵי הַקָּנִים מִמֶּנָּה וְכַפְתֹּר תַּחַת שְׁנֵי הַקָּנִים מִמֶּנָּה וְכַפְתֹּר תַּחַת־שְׁנֵי הַקָּנִים מִמֶּנָּה לְשֵׁשֶׁת

כב הַקָּנִים הַיֹּצְאִים מִמֶּנָּה: כַּפְתֹּרֵיהֶם וּקְנֹתָם מִמֶּנָּה הָיוּ כֻּלָּהּ מִקְשָׁה

כג אַחַת זָהָב טָהוֹר: וַיַּעַשׂ אֶת־נֵרֹתֶיהָ שִׁבְעָה וּמַלְקָחֶיהָ וּמַחְתֹּתֶיהָ

כד זָהָב טָהוֹר: כִּכָּר זָהָב טָהוֹר עָשָׂה אֹתָהּ וְאֵת כָּל־כֵּלֶיהָ:

Shemot | Chapter 37 — Vayak-hel

כה וַיַּ֛עַשׂ אֶת־מִזְבַּ֥ח הַקְּטֹ֖רֶת עֲצֵ֣י שִׁטִּ֑ים אַמָּ֨ה אָרְכּ֜וֹ וְאַמָּ֤ה רָחְבּוֹ֙ רָב֔וּעַ
כו וְאַמָּתַ֖יִם קֹמָת֑וֹ מִמֶּ֖נּוּ הָי֥וּ קַרְנֹתָֽיו: וַיְצַ֨ף אֹת֜וֹ זָהָ֣ב טָה֗וֹר אֶת־גַּגּ֤וֹ וְאֶת־
כז קִירֹתָיו֙ סָבִ֔יב וְאֶת־קַרְנֹתָ֑יו וַיַּ֥עַשׂ ל֛וֹ זֵ֥ר זָהָ֖ב סָבִֽיב: וּשְׁתֵּי֩ טַבְּעֹ֨ת זָהָ֜ב
עָֽשָׂה־ל֣וֹ ׀ מִתַּ֣חַת לְזֵר֗וֹ עַ֚ל שְׁתֵּ֣י צַלְעֹתָ֔יו עַ֖ל שְׁנֵ֣י צִדָּ֑יו לְבָתִּ֣ים לְבַדִּ֔ים
כח לָשֵׂ֥את אֹת֖וֹ בָּהֶֽם: וַיַּ֥עַשׂ אֶת־הַבַּדִּ֖ים עֲצֵ֣י שִׁטִּ֑ים וַיְצַ֥ף אֹתָ֖ם זָהָֽב:

25 He made the incense altar of acacia wood, square, a cubit long, a cubit wide, and two
26 cubits high, with horns of one piece with it. He overlaid its top, its sides all around, and
27 its horns with pure gold and around it he made a gold molding. Under the molding he
28 made two gold rings on the two sides, to hold the staves by which it was carried. The
29 staves themselves were made of acacia wood, overlaid with gold. As well as this, with
the skill of a perfumer, he prepared the sacred anointing oil and the fragrant incense.
38 1 He made the sacrificial altar of acacia wood, square, five cubits long, five cubits wide
2 and three cubits high. He made horns on its four corners, of one piece with it, and then
3 overlaid it with bronze. He made all the altar's utensils: pots, shovels, basins, forks and
4 pans, out of bronze. He made a grate of bronze mesh beneath the ledge, extending
5 downward to the middle of the altar. Four rings were cast for the four corners of the

---

IBN EZRA
Among the women in Israel were pious individuals who removed themselves from the physical pleasures of this world to devote their lives to the service of God. These were the women who donated their mirrors to the construction of the laver, feeling that they no longer had any need to make themselves beautiful. Rather, every day they would arrive at the entrance to the Tent of Meeting to pray and to learn the lessons of the commandments.

אבן עזרא
והנה היו בישראל עובדות השם שסרו מתאוות זה העולם, ונתנו מראותיהן נדבה, כי אין להם צורך עוד להיות יפות, רק באות יום יום אל פתח אהל מועד להתפלל ולשמוע דברי המצות.

QUESTIONS FOR THOUGHT
- Rashi and Ibn Ezra present diametrically opposite positions about the value of female beauty. Explain the two ideas.
- How does Rashi support his interpretation from the passage of the Torah dealing with the *sota*?
- Which part of verse 8 would support Ibn Ezra's position?

כט וַיַּעַשׂ אֶת־שֶׁמֶן הַמִּשְׁחָה קֹדֶשׁ וְאֶת־קְטֹרֶת הַסַּמִּים טָהוֹר
מַעֲשֵׂה רֹקֵחַ: לח א וַיַּעַשׂ אֶת־מִזְבַּח הָעֹלָה עֲצֵי שִׁטִּים
חָמֵשׁ אַמּוֹת אָרְכּוֹ וְחָמֵשׁ־אַמּוֹת רָחְבּוֹ רָבוּעַ וְשָׁלֹשׁ אַמּוֹת
קֹמָתוֹ: ב וַיַּעַשׂ קַרְנֹתָיו עַל אַרְבַּע פִּנֹּתָיו מִמֶּנּוּ הָיוּ קַרְנֹתָיו וַיְצַף
אֹתוֹ נְחֹשֶׁת: ג וַיַּעַשׂ אֶת־כָּל־כְּלֵי הַמִּזְבֵּחַ אֶת־הַסִּירֹת וְאֶת־
הַיָּעִים וְאֶת־הַמִּזְרָקֹת אֶת־הַמִּזְלָגֹת וְאֶת־הַמַּחְתֹּת כָּל־כֵּלָיו
עָשָׂה נְחֹשֶׁת: ד וַיַּעַשׂ לַמִּזְבֵּחַ מִכְבָּר מַעֲשֵׂה רֶשֶׁת נְחֹשֶׁת תַּחַת
כַּרְכֻּבּוֹ מִלְּמַטָּה עַד־חֶצְיוֹ: ה וַיִּצֹק אַרְבַּע טַבָּעֹת בְּאַרְבַּע הַקְּצָוֹת
לְמִכְבַּר הַנְּחֹשֶׁת בָּתִּים לַבַּדִּים: ו וַיַּעַשׂ אֶת־הַבַּדִּים עֲצֵי שִׁטִּים

שביעי /רביעי

שמות | פרק לז | ויקהל | 327

CLASSIC COMMENTATORS

In verse 8, the bronze laver was made from the mirrors of the *tzoveot*, translated here as "the women who served at the entrance of the Tent of Meeting," but whose meaning is unclear.

RASHI

רש"י

בנות ישראל היו בידן מראות שרואות בהן כשהן מתקשטות, ואף אותן לא עזבו מלהביא למלאכת המשכן לנדבתו. והיה משה מואס בהם מפני שעשויין ליצר הרע. אמר לו הקב"ה: קבל, כי אילו חביבין עלי מן הכל, שעל ידיהם העמידו נשים הללו צבאות רבות במצרים. כשהיו בעליהם יגיעין מעבודת פרך בשדה, היו הולכות ומוליכות להם מאכל ומשתה ומאכילות אותם, ונוטלות המראות, וכל אחת ואחת רואה עצמה עם בעלה במראה, ומשדלתו בדברים אני נאה ממך. ומתוך כך מביאות אותם לידי תאוה ונזקקות להם, ומתעברות ויולדות ... ונעשה הכיור מהם, שהוא לשום שלום בין איש לאשתו להשקות ממים שבתוכו את שקינא לה בעלה.

The Israelite women owned mirrors that they used to look into when they adorned themselves, yet they did not hesitate to donate them to the Tabernacle. Now at first Moshe considered these mirrors distasteful and inappropriate for this holy purpose, as they were used to indulge the evil inclination. But the Holy One, blessed be He, said to him: You should accept these gifts, for the women's mirrors are more dear to me than any of the other donations the people have brought. Know that it is these mirrors that assisted Israel to burgeon to huge numbers [*tzevaot*] in Egypt. While the women's husbands were exhausting themselves with oppressive labor in the fields, their wives would bring them food and drink to sustain them. As they visited with their men, the women would invite them to gaze at their reflections in the mirrors. Flirting with her husband, a wife would say: You know I'm more beautiful than you are! This sort of talk had the effect of arousing the men who would sleep with their wives, who would conceive and give birth… And this is why the mirrors were repurposed to make the laver. For initially they were employed to forge peace between the husbands and the wives, and subsequently, water from the utensil was to be served to the woman whose husband suspected her of infidelity. [Rashi refers to the case of a *sota* whose ordeal is described in Numbers 5:11–31. Ultimately, the purpose of that ceremony is to repair the relationship between the couple.]

ז וַיְצַ֥ף אֹתָ֖ם נְחֹֽשֶׁת׃ וַיָּבֵ֤א אֶת־הַבַּדִּים֙ בַּטַּבָּעֹ֔ת עַ֖ל צַלְעֹ֣ת הַמִּזְבֵּ֑חַ

ח לָשֵׂ֥את אֹת֖וֹ בָּהֶ֑ם נְב֥וּב לֻחֹ֖ת עָשָׂ֥ה אֹתֽוֹ׃ וַיַּ֗עַשׂ אֵ֚ת

הַכִּיּ֣וֹר נְחֹ֔שֶׁת וְאֵ֖ת כַּנּ֣וֹ נְחֹ֑שֶׁת בְּמַרְאֹת֙ הַצֹּ֣בְאֹ֔ת אֲשֶׁ֣ר צָֽבְא֔וּ פֶּ֖תַח

ט אֹ֥הֶל מוֹעֵֽד׃ וַיַּ֖עַשׂ אֶת־הֶֽחָצֵ֑ר לִפְאַ֣ת ׀ נֶ֣גֶב תֵּימָ֗נָה קַלְעֵ֤י

6 bronze mesh, to hold the staves, which were made of acacia wood and overlaid with
7 bronze. He placed the staves in the rings on the sides of the altar so that it could be
8 carried. The altar itself was hollow, made of planks. He made the bronze laver and its
bronze base from the mirrors of the women who served at the entrance of the Tent of
9 Meeting. On the south side, the hangings were of finely spun linen, a hundred cubits
10 long, with twenty posts and their twenty bronze sockets. The posts' hooks and bands
11 were of silver. Likewise on the north side: the hangings were a hundred cubits long, with
12 twenty pillars and their bronze sockets, and hooks and bands of silver. On the west side
the hangings were fifty cubits long, with ten posts and ten sockets, and hooks and bands
13 of silver. The east side was also fifty cubits long: fifteen cubits of hangings with three
14
15 posts and three sockets on one side, and fifteen cubits of hangings with three posts and
16 three sockets on the other. All the hangings of the courtyard were of finely spun linen.
17 The sockets for the posts were of bronze, the posts' hooks and bands were of silver,
18 and their tops were overlaid with silver; all the posts had silver bands. At the entrance
of the courtyard there was an embroidered screen of sky-blue, purple and scarlet wool
and finely spun linen, twenty cubits long and five cubits wide, like the hangings of the
19 courtyard. It had four posts with four bronze sockets and with hooks and bands of
20 silver; their tops were overlaid with silver. All the tent pegs for the Tabernacle and the
surrounding courtyard were of bronze.

TEXTUAL SKILLS

2. The order of the construction is different from the sequence in which God instructed Moshe in *Parashat Teruma*. How many differences can you find?
3. Notice that sometimes it says that "they made" and sometimes that "he made." Who is the the person identified as "he?" Can you figure out why it switches from plural to singular?

שמות | פרק לח

י הֶחָצֵר שֵׁשׁ מָשְׁזָר מֵאָה בָאַמָּה: עַמּוּדֵיהֶם עֶשְׂרִים וְאַדְנֵיהֶם
יא עֶשְׂרִים נְחֹשֶׁת וָוֵי הָעַמֻּדִים וַחֲשֻׁקֵיהֶם כָּסֶף: וְלִפְאַת צָפוֹן
   מֵאָה בָאַמָּה עַמּוּדֵיהֶם עֶשְׂרִים וְאַדְנֵיהֶם עֶשְׂרִים נְחֹשֶׁת וָוֵי
יב הָעַמּוּדִים וַחֲשֻׁקֵיהֶם כָּסֶף: וְלִפְאַת־יָם קְלָעִים חֲמִשִּׁים בָּאַמָּה
   עַמּוּדֵיהֶם עֲשָׂרָה וְאַדְנֵיהֶם עֲשָׂרָה וָוֵי הָעַמֻּדִים וַחֲשׁוּקֵיהֶם
יג כָּסֶף: וְלִפְאַת קֵדְמָה מִזְרָחָה חֲמִשִּׁים אַמָּה: קְלָעִים חֲמֵשׁ־
יד עֶשְׂרֵה אַמָּה אֶל־הַכָּתֵף עַמּוּדֵיהֶם שְׁלֹשָׁה וְאַדְנֵיהֶם שְׁלֹשָׁה:
טו וְלַכָּתֵף הַשֵּׁנִית מִזֶּה וּמִזֶּה לְשַׁעַר הֶחָצֵר קְלָעִים חֲמֵשׁ עֶשְׂרֵה
טז אַמָּה עַמֻּדֵיהֶם שְׁלֹשָׁה וְאַדְנֵיהֶם שְׁלֹשָׁה: כָּל־קַלְעֵי הֶחָצֵר
יז סָבִיב שֵׁשׁ מָשְׁזָר: וְהָאֲדָנִים לָעַמֻּדִים נְחֹשֶׁת וָוֵי הָעַמּוּדִים
   וַחֲשׁוּקֵיהֶם כֶּסֶף וְצִפּוּי רָאשֵׁיהֶם כָּסֶף וְהֵם מְחֻשָּׁקִים כֶּסֶף כֹּל
יח עַמֻּדֵי הֶחָצֵר: וּמָסַךְ שַׁעַר הֶחָצֵר מַעֲשֵׂה רֹקֵם תְּכֵלֶת וְאַרְגָּמָן   מפטיר
   וְתוֹלַעַת שָׁנִי וְשֵׁשׁ מָשְׁזָר וְעֶשְׂרִים אַמָּה אֹרֶךְ וְקוֹמָה בָרֹחַב
יט חָמֵשׁ אַמּוֹת לְעֻמַּת קַלְעֵי הֶחָצֵר: וְעַמֻּדֵיהֶם אַרְבָּעָה וְאַדְנֵיהֶם
   אַרְבָּעָה נְחֹשֶׁת וָוֵיהֶם כֶּסֶף וְצִפּוּי רָאשֵׁיהֶם וַחֲשֻׁקֵיהֶם כָּסֶף:
כ וְכָל־הַיְתֵדֹת לַמִּשְׁכָּן וְלֶחָצֵר סָבִיב נְחֹשֶׁת:

TEXTUAL SKILLS

1. Notice that verse 8 has fourteen words, seven in each half. Also notice that in each half of the verse there is a word which repeats, reinforcing the sense of symmetry between the two halves. Which are these words, and how do they serve this function?

QUICK BITES

- **35:2** The activities performed for the construction of the *Mishkan* are sources of holiness. How then can these very same activities become the standard for violating Shabbat (the thirty-nine prohibited Shabbat activities are derived from the construction of the *Mishkan*)? Rabbi Mayer Twersky suggests that it is precisely because we refrain from these activities on Shabbat that we can imbue them with holiness and use them to construct something as holy as the *Mishkan*.

- **35:3** According to the Zohar, the tranquility, peace, and unity that is accessed on Shabbat enable our week to be blessed. This is why it is especially important to avoid the temptation to fight and tear each other apart on Shabbat. With this in mind, Ḥatam Sofer rereads the verses that discuss Shabbat: The six days of work are in the merit of the Shabbat, *therefore* don't allow the fire of conflict to burn in your homes.

- **38:8** Rabbi Samson Raphael Hirsch says that it was exceptionally significant that the laver of the *Mishkan*, which is used to sanctify hands – symbolizing our efforts and actions and thus representing the need for moral purity and sanctity our activities – was made of out of mirrors. Mirrors are used to check our physical body and appearance. By constructing the laver out of mirrors the Torah was illustrating that our sensual side is not excluded from the world of the holy – on the contrary, it is the gateway to finding sanctity.

פרשת פקודי
PARASHAT PEKUDEI

> "The wave does not need to die to become water. She already is water."
> Thich Nhat Hanh

The eastern philosopher Thich Nhat Hanh wrote about a concept called "interbeing." He explains, "Without a cloud, there will be no rain; without rain, trees cannot grow, and without trees, we cannot make paper. The cloud is essential for the paper to exist. If the cloud is not here, the sheet of paper cannot be here either. So we can say that the cloud and paper inter-are."

The *Mishkan* houses the tablets, the tablets are what we teach our children. According to the idea of interbeing, the children are by extension in the *Mishkan*! This is a powerful way of looking at the interconnectedness of all of existence. Looking at the *Mishkan* and its underlying message is about looking at the relationship between the disparate parts of our lives.

And when the pieces of life's puzzle don't seem to fit – that's when we unleash our finest art: broken tablets sitting next to the unbroken second ones.

PARASHAT PEKUDEI

38 21 These are the accounts of the Tabernacle, the Tabernacle of testimony, recorded at
22 Moshe's command by the Levites under Itamar, son of Aharon the priest. Betzalel, son of Uri, son of Ḥur, from the tribe of Yehuda made everything that the Lord had
23 commanded Moshe. He was assisted by Oholiav, son of Aḥisamakh, from the tribe of Dan, an engraver, designer and embroiderer in sky-blue, purple and scarlet wool and
24 fine linen. All the gold used in all the sacred work, donated as wave offerings, came to
25 twenty-nine talents and 730 shekels according to the sanctuary weight. The silver of those recorded in the census came to a hundred talents and 1775 shekels, according to
26 the sanctuary weight. One beka (half a shekel according to the sanctuary weight) was
27 given by each of the 603,550 men aged twenty or over included in the census. A hundred talents of silver were used for casting the sockets of the sanctuary and the curtain, one
28 talent for each socket: a hundred talents for the hundred sockets. Of 1775 shekels he

---

QUESTIONS FOR THOUGHT

- What would be the point of the Torah providing us with an accounting of the metals collected?
- What would be the message in the Torah providing an accounting of the vessels after it already described their creation in the previous chapters?
- Look at the opening verse of this *parasha*. Based on that verse, which of the above commentaries do you think is correct?

TEXTUAL SKILLS

1. Look throughout the Torah to see what the root פ-ק-ד means. Based on that, which of the above commentaries do you think is right?
2. It is well-known that the division of the Tanakh into chapters is not of Jewish origin, but the division into paragraphs (the open spaces in the Torah) reflects an ancient Jewish tradition. Notice that according to the non-Jewish chapter breaks, the last verse of this section is the beginning of the next section. But in Jewish tradition, this verse is connected to what came before it. Try to explain the rationale for each of those approaches to dividing the Torah into sections.

WISDOM OF THE HEART

In 38:21, as the Torah summarizes the donations made for the *Mishkan*, it says the word *Mishkan* twice in a row. Rashi quotes a midrash that says that the phrase is hinting to a future *Mishkan* – the *Beit HaMikdash*. Interestingly, the word *Mishkan* is similar to the word *mashkon*, meaning "collateral," a guarantee that a loan will be repaid. The midrash says that two temples that were destroyed are the collateral God took from the *Am Yisrael* for their sins, and He is waiting for them to demand them back.

Rav Zalmele of Volozhin notes that according to halakha if the debtor needs to use the collateral then the lender must return it to him. When we realize that we cannot live without the *Beit HaMikdash* God will be required to return it.

פרשת פקודי

לח א אֵלֶּה פְקוּדֵי הַמִּשְׁכָּן מִשְׁכַּן הָעֵדֻת אֲשֶׁר פֻּקַּד עַל־פִּי מֹשֶׁה
כב עֲבֹדַת הַלְוִיִּם בְּיַד אִיתָמָר בֶּן־אַהֲרֹן הַכֹּהֵן: וּבְצַלְאֵל בֶּן־אוּרִי
בֶן־חוּר לְמַטֵּה יְהוּדָה עָשָׂה אֵת כָּל־אֲשֶׁר־צִוָּה יְהוָה אֶת־מֹשֶׁה:
כג וְאִתּוֹ אָהֳלִיאָב בֶּן־אֲחִיסָמָךְ לְמַטֵּה־דָן חָרָשׁ וְחֹשֵׁב וְרֹקֵם
כד בַּתְּכֵלֶת וּבָאַרְגָּמָן וּבְתוֹלַעַת הַשָּׁנִי וּבַשֵּׁשׁ: כָּל־
הַזָּהָב הֶעָשׂוּי לַמְּלָאכָה בְּכֹל מְלֶאכֶת הַקֹּדֶשׁ וַיְהִי ׀ זְהַב
הַתְּנוּפָה תֵּשַׁע וְעֶשְׂרִים כִּכָּר וּשְׁבַע מֵאוֹת וּשְׁלֹשִׁים שֶׁקֶל
כה בְּשֶׁקֶל הַקֹּדֶשׁ: וְכֶסֶף פְּקוּדֵי הָעֵדָה מְאַת כִּכָּר וְאֶלֶף וּשְׁבַע
כו מֵאוֹת וַחֲמִשָּׁה וְשִׁבְעִים שֶׁקֶל בְּשֶׁקֶל הַקֹּדֶשׁ: בֶּקַע לַגֻּלְגֹּלֶת
מַחֲצִית הַשֶּׁקֶל בְּשֶׁקֶל הַקֹּדֶשׁ לְכֹל הָעֹבֵר עַל־הַפְּקֻדִים מִבֶּן
עֶשְׂרִים שָׁנָה וָמַעְלָה לְשֵׁשׁ־מֵאוֹת אֶלֶף וּשְׁלֹשֶׁת אֲלָפִים
כז וַחֲמֵשׁ מֵאוֹת וַחֲמִשִּׁים: וַיְהִי מְאַת כִּכַּר הַכֶּסֶף לָצֶקֶת אֵת
אַדְנֵי הַקֹּדֶשׁ וְאֵת אַדְנֵי הַפָּרֹכֶת מְאַת אֲדָנִים לִמְאַת הַכִּכָּר
כח כִּכָּר לָאָדֶן: וְאֶת־הָאֶלֶף וּשְׁבַע הַמֵּאוֹת וַחֲמִשָּׁה וְשִׁבְעִים

CLASSIC COMMENTATORS

What was being counted – the precious metals collected or the *Mishkan* with its vessels?

RASHBAM — רשב״ם

What is being tabulated here are the amounts of silver, gold, and bronze that the Israelites donated.

אלה פקודי – חשבון הכסף והזהב והנחשת.

IBN EZRA — אבן עזרא

These are the accounts of the Tabernacle utensils.

אלה פקודי כלי המשכן.

Shemot | Chapter 38

כט עָשָׂה וָוִים לָעַמּוּדִים וְצִפָּה רָאשֵׁיהֶם וְחִשַּׁק אֹתָם: וּנְחֹשֶׁת הַתְּנוּפָה
ל שִׁבְעִים כִּכָּר וְאַלְפַּיִם וְאַרְבַּע־מֵאוֹת שָׁקֶל: וַיַּעַשׂ בָּהּ אֶת־אַדְנֵי
פֶּתַח אֹהֶל מוֹעֵד וְאֵת מִזְבַּח הַנְּחֹשֶׁת וְאֶת־מִכְבַּר הַנְּחֹשֶׁת אֲשֶׁר־
לא לוֹ וְאֵת כָּל־כְּלֵי הַמִּזְבֵּחַ: וְאֶת־אַדְנֵי הֶחָצֵר סָבִיב וְאֶת־אַדְנֵי שַׁעַר
לט א הֶחָצֵר וְאֵת כָּל־יִתְדֹת הַמִּשְׁכָּן וְאֶת־כָּל־יִתְדֹת הֶחָצֵר סָבִיב: וּמִן־
הַתְּכֵלֶת וְהָאַרְגָּמָן וְתוֹלַעַת הַשָּׁנִי עָשׂוּ בִגְדֵי־שְׂרָד לְשָׁרֵת בַּקֹּדֶשׁ

29 made the hooks and bands of the posts and their silver-plated tops. The bronze given as
30 an offering came to seventy talents and 2400 shekels. With this were made the sockets for the entrance of the Tent of Meeting, the bronze altar with its bronze mesh, and all
31 the utensils of the altar, the sockets around the courtyard, the sockets at the courtyard
39 1 gate, and all the tent pegs for the Tabernacle and the surrounding courtyard. From the sky-blue, purple and scarlet wool they made woven garments for ministering in the sanctuary. They also made sacred vestments for Aharon, as the Lord commanded Moshe.
2 He made the ephod of gold, with sky-blue, purple and scarlet wool and finely spun linen.
3 They hammered out thin sheets of gold and cut strands to be worked into the sky-blue,
4 purple and scarlet wool and fine linen – highly skilled work. They made fixed shoulder
5 pieces for the ephod; these were affixed to its two ends. Its decorated waistband was like it and of one piece with the ephod, made with gold, with sky-blue, purple and scarlet
6 wool and finely spun linen, as the Lord commanded Moshe. They mounted the onyx stones in gold filigree settings and engraved them as a seal with the names of Yisrael's
7 sons. He fastened them on the shoulder-pieces of the ephod as remembrance stones for Yisrael's sons, as the Lord commanded Moshe.
8 He made the breast piece with the same skilled craftsmanship as the ephod: of gold,
9 of sky-blue, purple and scarlet wool, and of finely spun linen. It was square and folded
10 double, a span long and a span wide. Then they mounted four rows of precious stones on
11 it. The first row was a ruby, a peridot and an emerald; the second row was a carbuncle, a
12
13 lapis lazuli and a clear quartz; the third row was a jacinth, an agate and an amethyst; and the fourth was a beryl, an onyx and a chalcedony. They were mounted in gold filigree
14 settings. There were twelve stones, one for each of the names of Yisrael's sons. Each was

שמות | פרק לח

וַיַּעֲשׂוּ אֶת־בִּגְדֵי הַקֹּדֶשׁ אֲשֶׁר לְאַהֲרֹן כַּאֲשֶׁר צִוָּה יְהֹוָה אֶת־מֹשֶׁה׃

ב וַיַּעַשׂ אֶת־הָאֵפֹד זָהָב תְּכֵלֶת וְאַרְגָּמָן וְתוֹלַעַת שָׁנִי וְשֵׁשׁ מָשְׁזָר׃ *(שני /חמישי/)*

ג וַיְרַקְּעוּ אֶת־פַּחֵי הַזָּהָב וְקִצֵּץ פְּתִילִם לַעֲשׂוֹת בְּתוֹךְ הַתְּכֵלֶת וּבְתוֹךְ הָאַרְגָּמָן וּבְתוֹךְ תּוֹלַעַת הַשָּׁנִי וּבְתוֹךְ הַשֵּׁשׁ מַעֲשֵׂה חֹשֵׁב׃

ד כְּתֵפֹת עָשׂוּ־לוֹ חֹבְרֹת עַל־שְׁנֵי קְצוֹתָו חֻבָּר׃

ה וְחֵשֶׁב אֲפֻדָּתוֹ אֲשֶׁר עָלָיו מִמֶּנּוּ הוּא כְּמַעֲשֵׂהוּ זָהָב תְּכֵלֶת וְאַרְגָּמָן וְתוֹלַעַת שָׁנִי וְשֵׁשׁ מָשְׁזָר כַּאֲשֶׁר צִוָּה יְהֹוָה אֶת־מֹשֶׁה׃

ו וַיַּעֲשׂוּ אֶת־אַבְנֵי הַשֹּׁהַם מֻסַבֹּת מִשְׁבְּצֹת זָהָב מְפֻתָּחֹת פִּתּוּחֵי חוֹתָם עַל־שְׁמוֹת בְּנֵי יִשְׂרָאֵל׃

ז וַיָּשֶׂם אֹתָם עַל כִּתְפֹת הָאֵפֹד אַבְנֵי זִכָּרוֹן לִבְנֵי יִשְׂרָאֵל כַּאֲשֶׁר צִוָּה יְהֹוָה אֶת־מֹשֶׁה׃

ח וַיַּעַשׂ אֶת־הַחֹשֶׁן מַעֲשֵׂה חֹשֵׁב כְּמַעֲשֵׂה אֵפֹד זָהָב תְּכֵלֶת וְאַרְגָּמָן וְתוֹלַעַת שָׁנִי וְשֵׁשׁ מָשְׁזָר׃

ט רָבוּעַ הָיָה כָּפוּל עָשׂוּ אֶת־הַחֹשֶׁן זֶרֶת אָרְכּוֹ וְזֶרֶת רָחְבּוֹ כָּפוּל׃

י וַיְמַלְאוּ־בוֹ אַרְבָּעָה טוּרֵי אָבֶן טוּר אֹדֶם פִּטְדָה וּבָרֶקֶת הַטּוּר הָאֶחָד׃

יא וְהַטּוּר הַשֵּׁנִי נֹפֶךְ סַפִּיר וְיָהֲלֹם׃

יב וְהַטּוּר הַשְּׁלִישִׁי לֶשֶׁם שְׁבוֹ וְאַחְלָמָה׃ וְהַטּוּר הָרְבִיעִי תַּרְשִׁישׁ שֹׁהַם וְיָשְׁפֵה מוּסַבֹּת מִשְׁבְּצֹת זָהָב בְּמִלֻּאֹתָם׃

יד וְהָאֲבָנִים עַל־

TEXTUAL SKILLS

1. What essential components of the *ḥoshen* are missing in the description of how it was made?
2. What theme phrase concludes nearly every passage in this *parasha*? How many times does it appear altogether? Why does it appear so many times?

שְׁמֹת בְּנֵי־יִשְׂרָאֵל הֵנָּה שְׁתֵּים עֶשְׂרֵה עַל־שְׁמֹתָם פִּתּוּחֵי חֹתָם אִישׁ
עַל־שְׁמוֹ לִשְׁנֵים עָשָׂר שָׁבֶט: וַיַּעֲשׂוּ עַל־הַחֹשֶׁן שַׁרְשְׁרֹת גַּבְלֻת מַעֲשֵׂה
עֲבֹת זָהָב טָהוֹר: וַיַּעֲשׂוּ שְׁתֵּי מִשְׁבְּצֹת זָהָב וּשְׁתֵּי טַבְּעֹת זָהָב וַיִּתְּנוּ
אֶת־שְׁתֵּי הַטַּבָּעֹת עַל־שְׁנֵי קְצוֹת הַחֹשֶׁן: וַיִּתְּנוּ שְׁתֵּי הָעֲבֹתֹת הַזָּהָב
עַל־שְׁתֵּי הַטַּבָּעֹת עַל־קְצוֹת הַחֹשֶׁן: וְאֵת שְׁתֵּי קְצוֹת שְׁתֵּי הָעֲבֹתֹת

15 engraved like a seal with the name of one of the twelve tribes. For the breast piece they
16 made chains of pure gold, braided like cords. They made two gold filigree settings and
17 two gold rings, and attached the rings to two of the corners of the breast piece. They
18 fastened the two gold chains to the rings at the corners of the breast piece, and the other ends of the chains to the two settings, attaching them to the ephod's shoulder pieces at
19 the front. They made two gold rings and placed them at the two other corners of the
20 breast piece on the edge, inside, next to the ephod. Then they made two more gold rings and attached them to the bottom of the ephod's two shoulder pieces facing the
21 priest's front, close to the seam and above the ephod's woven waistband. They tied the rings of the breast piece to the rings of the ephod with a sky-blue cord, connecting it to the waistband so that the breastplate would remain secured to the ephod, as the Lord
22 had commanded Moshe. They made the robe of the ephod woven entirely of sky-blue
23 wool, with an opening in the center like the neck of a coat of mail, with a woven border
24 around it so that it would not tear. They made pomegranates of sky-blue, purple and
25 scarlet wool and finely spun linen around the hem of the robe. And they made bells of
26 pure gold and attached them around the hem between the pomegranates. The bells and pomegranates alternated around the hem of the robe worn for ministering, as the Lord
27 commanded Moshe. For Aharon and his sons, they made tunics woven from fine linen,
28 together with a linen miter, linen headdresses and trousers of finely spun linen. The sash
29 was embroidered out of finely spun linen and sky-blue, purple and scarlet wool, as the
30 Lord commanded Moshe. They made the headplate, the holy diadem, of pure gold and
31 engraved on it, as on a seal: Holy to the Lord. Then they attached a sky-blue cord to
32 it to affix it to the miter, as the Lord had commanded Moshe. Thus all the work on the Tabernacle, the Tent of Meeting, was completed. The Israelites did everything exactly as the Lord had commanded Moshe.

נָתְנ֗וּ עַל־שְׁתֵּי֙ הַֽמִּשְׁבְּצֹ֔ת וַֽיִּתְּנֻ֛ם עַל־כִּתְפֹ֥ת הָאֵפֹ֖ד אֶל־מ֥וּל
פָּנָֽיו: וַֽיַּעֲשׂ֗וּ שְׁתֵּי֙ טַבְּעֹ֣ת זָהָ֔ב וַיָּשִׂ֕ימוּ עַל־שְׁנֵ֖י קְצ֣וֹת הַחֹ֑שֶׁן
עַל־שְׂפָת֕וֹ אֲשֶׁ֛ר אֶל־עֵ֥בֶר הָאֵפֹ֖ד בָּֽיְתָה: וַֽיַּעֲשׂוּ֮ שְׁתֵּ֣י טַבְּעֹ֣ת
זָהָב֒ וַֽיִּתְּנ֗וּ עַל־שְׁתֵּ֛י כִתְפֹ֥ת הָאֵפֹ֖ד מִלְּמַ֣טָּה מִמּ֣וּל פָּנָ֔יו לְעֻמַּ֖ת
מֶחְבַּרְתּ֑וֹ מִמַּ֕עַל לְחֵ֖שֶׁב הָאֵפֹֽד: וַיִּרְכְּס֣וּ אֶת־הַחֹ֡שֶׁן מִטַּבְּעֹתָיו֩
אֶל־טַבְּעֹ֨ת הָאֵפֹ֜ד בִּפְתִ֣יל תְּכֵ֗לֶת לִֽהְיֹת֙ עַל־חֵ֣שֶׁב הָאֵפֹ֔ד וְלֹֽא־
יִזַּ֣ח הַחֹ֔שֶׁן מֵעַ֖ל הָאֵפֹ֑ד כַּאֲשֶׁ֛ר צִוָּ֥ה יְהוָ֖ה אֶת־מֹשֶֽׁה:

שלישי
/ששי/

וַיַּ֛עַשׂ אֶת־מְעִ֥יל הָאֵפֹ֖ד מַעֲשֵׂ֣ה אֹרֵ֑ג כְּלִ֖יל תְּכֵֽלֶת: וּפִֽי־הַמְּעִ֥יל
בְּתוֹכ֖וֹ כְּפִ֣י תַחְרָ֑א שָׂפָ֥ה לְפִ֛יו סָבִ֖יב לֹ֥א יִקָּרֵֽעַ: וַיַּעֲשׂוּ֙ עַל־שׁוּלֵ֣י
הַמְּעִ֔יל רִמּוֹנֵ֕י תְּכֵ֥לֶת וְאַרְגָּמָ֖ן וְתוֹלַ֣עַת שָׁנִ֑י מָשְׁזָֽר: וַיַּעֲשׂ֥וּ פַעֲמֹנֵ֖י
זָהָ֣ב טָה֑וֹר וַיִּתְּנ֨וּ אֶת־הַפַּֽעֲמֹנִ֜ים בְּת֣וֹךְ הָרִמֹּנִ֗ים עַל־שׁוּלֵ֤י הַמְּעִיל֙
סָבִ֔יב בְּת֖וֹךְ הָרִמֹּנִֽים: פַּעֲמֹ֤ן וְרִמֹּן֙ פַּעֲמֹ֣ן וְרִמֹּ֔ן עַל־שׁוּלֵ֥י הַמְּעִ֖יל
סָבִ֑יב לְשָׁרֵ֕ת כַּאֲשֶׁ֛ר צִוָּ֥ה יְהוָ֖ה אֶת־מֹשֶֽׁה: וַֽיַּעֲשׂ֞וּ
אֶת־הַכָּתְנֹ֥ת שֵׁ֛שׁ מַעֲשֵׂ֥ה אֹרֵ֖ג לְאַהֲרֹ֥ן וּלְבָנָֽיו: וְאֵת֙ הַמִּצְנֶ֣פֶת
שֵׁ֔שׁ וְאֶת־פַּאֲרֵ֥י הַמִּגְבָּעֹ֖ת שֵׁ֑שׁ וְאֶת־מִכְנְסֵ֥י הַבָּ֖ד שֵׁ֥שׁ מָשְׁזָֽר:
וְאֶת־הָֽאַבְנֵ֞ט שֵׁ֣שׁ מָשְׁזָ֗ר וּתְכֵ֧לֶת וְאַרְגָּמָ֛ן וְתוֹלַ֥עַת שָׁנִ֖י מַעֲשֵׂ֣ה
רֹקֵ֑ם כַּאֲשֶׁ֛ר צִוָּ֥ה יְהוָ֖ה אֶת־מֹשֶֽׁה: וַֽיַּעֲשׂ֛וּ אֶת־צִ֥יץ
נֵֽזֶר־הַקֹּ֖דֶשׁ זָהָ֣ב טָה֑וֹר וַיִּכְתְּב֣וּ עָלָ֗יו מִכְתַּב֙ פִּתּוּחֵ֣י חוֹתָ֔ם קֹ֖דֶשׁ
לַיהוָֽה: וַיִּתְּנ֤וּ עָלָיו֙ פְּתִ֣יל תְּכֵ֔לֶת לָתֵ֥ת עַל־הַמִּצְנֶ֖פֶת מִלְמָ֑עְלָה
כַּאֲשֶׁ֛ר צִוָּ֥ה יְהוָ֖ה אֶת־מֹשֶֽׁה: וַתֵּ֕כֶל כָּל־עֲבֹדַ֕ת מִשְׁכַּ֖ן
אֹ֣הֶל מוֹעֵ֑ד וַֽיַּעֲשׂוּ֙ בְּנֵ֣י יִשְׂרָאֵ֔ל כְּ֠כֹל אֲשֶׁ֨ר צִוָּ֧ה יְהוָ֛ה אֶת־מֹשֶׁ֖ה
כֵּ֥ן עָשֽׂוּ:

Shemot | Chapter 39

33 They brought the Tabernacle to Moshe: the tent and all its furnishings, its clasps, frames,
34 crossbars, posts and sockets; the covering of reddened rams' hides and the covering
35 of fine leather and the curtain that covered the screen; the Ark of the Testimony and
36/37 its carrying staves; the Ark cover; the table with all its utensils; the showbread; the pure gold candelabrum with its row of lamps and all its accessories, together with the
38 oil for lighting; the gold altar, the anointing oil, the fragrant incense, and the curtain
39 for the entrance to the tent; the bronze altar with its bronze mesh, its staves and all its
40 utensils; the laver with its base; the hangings for the courtyard, its posts and sockets, and the screen for the courtyard gate; the ropes and tent pegs for the courtyard; all
41 the furnishings for the service of the Tabernacle, the Tent of Meeting; and the woven garments for ministering in the sanctuary, both the sacred vestments for Aharon the
42 priest and the vestments for his sons to wear when serving as priests. The Israelites had
43 completed all the work exactly as the Lord commanded Moshe. Moshe saw that all the work had been done just as the Lord had commanded – and Moshe blessed them.

RABBI AVRAHAM BEN HARAMBAM

According to our Sages, of blessed memory, Moshe told the people: May it be God's will to rest His Divine Presence upon your labors. It seems to me however, that such a prayer is superfluous, considering that the entire purpose of the Tabernacle was to draw the Divine Presence into the community of Israel! Thus does the verse state early on, "They shall make Me a sanctuary and I will dwell in their midst" (25:8). Therefore, I surmise that Moshe's blessing was of a different nature, expressing a message unique to the moment, such as: May the Lord grant you success in your Torah studies and bestow His great beneficence upon you.

ר׳ אברהם בן הרמב״ם

אמרו הראשונים ז״ל שאמר להם יהי רצון שתשרה שכינה במעשה ידיכם.
וזו ברכה שאילו החריש ממנה היה די ממנה שהרי המשכן מתחילתו נעשה רק כדי שתשרה בו השכינה כמאמרו "ועשו לי מקדש ושכנתי בתוכם" ולכן אין דעתי אלא שהיא ברכה מיוחדת להם דוגמת יתן לך ה׳ הצלחה בתורה ושפע ברכות.

QUESTIONS FOR THOUGHT

- Rashi suggests that the blessing was expressed by a verse in Psalms, with an introduction. What motivated Rashi to explain it this way?
- Rabbi Avraham ben HaRambam explicitly rejects Rashi's explanation. Why? What does he offer as an alternative?
- There is a similar scene in Leviticus 9:23. How do you think the above commentaries would explain that blessing?

TEXTUAL SKILLS

1. Notice that the *menora* is identified here (39:37) as the "pure" *menora*. Suggest a reason for that.

2. Notice that the oil for the *menora* is included in the list of the vessels. Where did you see this idea earlier

שמות | פרק לט

לג וַיָּבִיאוּ אֶת־הַמִּשְׁכָּן אֶל־מֹשֶׁה אֶת־הָאֹהֶל וְאֶת־כָּל־כֵּלָיו קְרָסָיו רביעי
לד קְרָשָׁיו בְּרִיחָו וְעַמֻּדָיו וַאֲדָנָיו: וְאֶת־מִכְסֵה עוֹרֹת הָאֵילִם
הַמְאָדָּמִים וְאֶת־מִכְסֵה עֹרֹת הַתְּחָשִׁים וְאֵת פָּרֹכֶת הַמָּסָךְ:
לה אֶת־אֲרוֹן הָעֵדֻת וְאֶת־בַּדָּיו וְאֵת הַכַּפֹּרֶת: אֶת־הַשֻּׁלְחָן אֶת־
לו כָּל־כֵּלָיו וְאֵת לֶחֶם הַפָּנִים: אֶת־הַמְּנֹרָה הַטְּהֹרָה אֶת־נֵרֹתֶיהָ
לז נֵרֹת הַמַּעֲרָכָה וְאֶת־כָּל־כֵּלֶיהָ וְאֵת שֶׁמֶן הַמָּאוֹר: וְאֵת מִזְבַּח
לח הַזָּהָב וְאֵת שֶׁמֶן הַמִּשְׁחָה וְאֵת קְטֹרֶת הַסַּמִּים וְאֵת מָסַךְ פֶּתַח
לט הָאֹהֶל: אֵת ׀ מִזְבַּח הַנְּחֹשֶׁת וְאֶת־מִכְבַּר הַנְּחֹשֶׁת אֲשֶׁר־לוֹ אֶת־
מ בַּדָּיו וְאֶת־כָּל־כֵּלָיו אֶת־הַכִּיֹּר וְאֶת־כַּנּוֹ: אֵת קַלְעֵי הֶחָצֵר אֶת־
עַמֻּדֶיהָ וְאֶת־אֲדָנֶיהָ וְאֶת־הַמָּסָךְ לְשַׁעַר הֶחָצֵר אֶת־מֵיתָרָיו
מא וִיתֵדֹתֶיהָ וְאֵת כָּל־כְּלֵי עֲבֹדַת הַמִּשְׁכָּן לְאֹהֶל מוֹעֵד: אֶת־בִּגְדֵי
הַשְּׂרָד לְשָׁרֵת בַּקֹּדֶשׁ אֶת־בִּגְדֵי הַקֹּדֶשׁ לְאַהֲרֹן הַכֹּהֵן וְאֶת־
מב בִּגְדֵי בָנָיו לְכַהֵן: כְּכֹל אֲשֶׁר־צִוָּה יְהוָה אֶת־מֹשֶׁה כֵּן עָשׂוּ בְּנֵי
מג יִשְׂרָאֵל אֵת כָּל־הָעֲבֹדָה: וַיַּרְא מֹשֶׁה אֶת־כָּל־הַמְּלָאכָה וְהִנֵּה
עָשׂוּ אֹתָהּ כַּאֲשֶׁר צִוָּה יְהוָה כֵּן עָשׂוּ וַיְבָרֶךְ אֹתָם מֹשֶׁה:

CLASSIC COMMENTATORS

After inspecting what the artisans had done, Moshe blesses the people. What is the content of that blessing?

RASHI

This is how Moshe blessed the nation: May it be God's will to rest His Divine Presence within the fruits of your labor. Thus the verse states, "May the Lord our God's sweetness be upon us. Grant us success through our efforts, and may our efforts succeed!" (Ps. 90:17).

רש״י

אמר להם: יהי רצון שתשרה שכינה במעשה ידיכם, "ויהי נועם י״י וגו׳".

SHEMOT | CHAPTER 40

God instructs Moshe on the assembly of the Mishkan and its internal order.

40 ¹ Then the LORD spoke to Moshe, saying, "On the first day of the first month you shall ² set up the Tabernacle of the Tent of Meeting. Put in it the Ark of the Testimony, and ³ screen the Ark with the curtain. Bring in the table and set it. Bring in the candelabrum ⁴ and light its lamps. Put the golden incense altar in front of the Ark of the Testimony, ⁵ and hang the screen for the Tabernacle's entrance. Put the sacrificial altar in front of the ⁶ entrance of the Tabernacle of the Tent of Meeting. Place the laver between the Tent ⁷ of Meeting and the altar, and put water in it. Arrange the courtyard all around, and ⁸ put in place the screen for the courtyard gate. Take the anointing oil and anoint the ⁹ Tabernacle and everything in it. Consecrate it and all its furnishings so that it becomes ¹⁰ holy. Anoint the sacrificial altar and all its utensils, consecrating it so that it becomes ¹¹ holy of holies. Anoint the laver with its base, making it holy. Then bring Aharon and ¹² his sons to the entrance of the Tent of Meeting, and cleanse them with water. Robe

TUR

טור

Each morning during the seven days of the Tabernacle's inauguration, Moshe would assemble the structure. The Tabernacle stood throughout that entire day and night, and at dawn of the following morning, Moshe would take the Tabernacle apart and immediately rebuild it.

כל ז' ימי המלואים היה מעמידו בבקר ועומד
כל היום וכל הלילה ובעלות השחר היה
משה מפרקו וחוזר ומעמידו מיד.

QUESTIONS FOR THOUGHT

- When *Benei Yisrael* were traveling there was an entire team of Levites in charge of erecting and disassembling the *Mishkan*. How is it possible that Moshe could do that all by himself in a single day?
- At the end of his explanation, Ibn Ezra adds a fascinating comment regarding the building of the *Beit HaMikdash* nearly 500 years later. What idea do you think that comment is trying to convey?

TEXTUAL SKILLS

1. In God's instructions, some verses discuss the placement of two items, as if they are a pair. Find them.
2. Notice who is anointed in addition to the vessels. What do you think this means?
3. Which items are called קדש and where are called קדש קדשים? Why?

שמות | פרק מ

מ א וַיְדַבֵּ֥ר יְהֹוָ֖ה אֶל־מֹשֶׁ֥ה לֵּאמֹֽר: ב בְּיוֹם־הַחֹ֥דֶשׁ הָרִאשׁ֖וֹן בְּאֶחָ֣ד חמישי /שביעי/
לַחֹ֑דֶשׁ תָּקִ֕ים אֶת־מִשְׁכַּ֖ן אֹ֥הֶל מוֹעֵֽד: ג וְשַׂמְתָּ֣ שָׁ֔ם אֵ֖ת אֲר֣וֹן
הָעֵד֑וּת וְסַכֹּתָ֥ עַל־הָאָרֹ֖ן אֶת־הַפָּרֹֽכֶת: ד וְהֵֽבֵאתָ֙ אֶת־הַשֻּׁלְחָ֔ן
וְעָֽרַכְתָּ֖ אֶת־עֶרְכּ֑וֹ וְהֵֽבֵאתָ֙ אֶת־הַמְּנֹרָ֔ה וְהַֽעֲלֵיתָ֖ אֶת־נֵֽרֹתֶֽיהָ:
ה וְנָֽתַתָּ֞ה אֶת־מִזְבַּ֤ח הַזָּהָב֙ לִקְטֹ֔רֶת לִפְנֵ֖י אֲר֣וֹן הָֽעֵדֻ֑ת וְשַׂמְתָּ֛
אֶת־מָסַ֥ךְ הַפֶּ֖תַח לַמִּשְׁכָּֽן: ו וְנָ֣תַתָּ֔ה אֵ֖ת מִזְבַּ֣ח הָֽעֹלָ֑ה לִפְנֵ֕י
פֶּ֖תַח מִשְׁכַּ֥ן אֹֽהֶל־מוֹעֵֽד: ז וְנָֽתַתָּ֙ אֶת־הַכִּיֹּ֔ר בֵּֽין־אֹ֥הֶל מוֹעֵ֖ד
וּבֵ֣ין הַמִּזְבֵּ֑חַ וְנָֽתַתָּ֥ שָׁ֖ם מָֽיִם: ח וְשַׂמְתָּ֥ אֶת־הֶֽחָצֵ֖ר סָבִ֑יב וְנָ֣תַתָּ֔
אֶת־מָסַ֖ךְ שַׁ֥עַר הֶֽחָצֵֽר: ט וְלָֽקַחְתָּ֙ אֶת־שֶׁ֣מֶן הַמִּשְׁחָ֔ה וּמָֽשַׁחְתָּ֥
אֶת־הַמִּשְׁכָּ֖ן וְאֶת־כָּל־אֲשֶׁר־בּ֑וֹ וְקִדַּשְׁתָּ֥ אֹת֖וֹ וְאֶת־כָּל־כֵּלָ֖יו
וְהָ֥יָה קֹֽדֶשׁ: י וּמָֽשַׁחְתָּ֛ אֶת־מִזְבַּ֥ח הָֽעֹלָ֖ה וְאֶת־כָּל־כֵּלָ֑יו וְקִדַּשְׁתָּ֙
אֶת־הַמִּזְבֵּ֔חַ וְהָיָ֥ה הַמִּזְבֵּ֖חַ קֹ֣דֶשׁ קָֽדָשִׁ֑ים: יא וּמָֽשַׁחְתָּ֥ אֶת־הַכִּיֹּ֖ר
וְאֶת־כַּנּ֑וֹ וְקִדַּשְׁתָּ֖ אֹתֽוֹ: יב וְהִקְרַבְתָּ֤ אֶת־אַֽהֲרֹן֙ וְאֶת־בָּנָ֔יו אֶל־
פֶּ֖תַח אֹ֣הֶל מוֹעֵ֑ד וְרָֽחַצְתָּ֥ אֹתָ֖ם בַּמָּֽיִם: יג וְהִלְבַּשְׁתָּ֙ אֶת־אַֽהֲרֹ֔ן אֶת

CLASSIC COMMENTATORS

In verse 2 God tells Moshe to put everything together on the first day of the first month (of the second year after leaving Egypt). How long did it actually take to set up the *Mishkan*?

IBN EZRA — **אבן עזרא**

Based on the straightforward meaning of the text, the Tabernacle was first erected on the first day of the first month [Nisan]. Now, this was Israel's first Tabernacle, and it was put up on the first day of the first calendar month. Centuries later the construction of the First Temple – which was the nation's second Tabernacle – began on the second day of the second month (which is Iyar) as the verse states, "He [Shlomo] began construction on the second day of the second month in the fourth year of his reign" (II Chron. 3:2).

והנה על דרך הפשט: ביום החדש הראשון היתה תחלת הקמת המשכן. והנה זה המשכן הראשון, הקימוהו ביום אחד לחדש הראשון. והחלו לבנות הבית הראשון, שהוא המשכן השני, בחדש השני שהוא אייר, בשני לחדש, כי כן כתוב: בחדש השני בשני (דברי הימים ב ג׳:ב׳).

Shemot | Chapter 40 — Pekudei

יד בִּגְדֵי הַקֹּדֶשׁ וּמָשַׁחְתָּ אֹתוֹ וְקִדַּשְׁתָּ אֹתוֹ וְכִהֵן לִי: וְאֶת־בָּנָיו תַּקְרִיב
טו וְהִלְבַּשְׁתָּ אֹתָם כֻּתֳּנֹת: וּמָשַׁחְתָּ אֹתָם כַּאֲשֶׁר מָשַׁחְתָּ אֶת־אֲבִיהֶם
טז וְכִהֲנוּ לִי וְהָיְתָה לִהְיֹת לָהֶם מָשְׁחָתָם לִכְהֻנַּת עוֹלָם לְדֹרֹתָם: וַיַּעַשׂ

14 Aharon with the sacred vestments and anoint him, that he may serve Me as priest. Then
15 bring his sons forward, robe them with tunics, and anoint them as you anointed their father, that they may serve Me as priests. Through this anointing, theirs will become an
16 everlasting priesthood throughout the generations." Moshe did exactly as the Lord had
17 commanded him. On the first day of the first month of the second year the Tabernacle
18 was set up. Moshe set up the Tabernacle, placed its sockets, erected its frames, inserted
19 its bars, and put up its posts. He spread the Tent over the Tabernacle and placed the
20 covering over the Tent, as the Lord had commanded him. He took the covenant and put it in the Ark. He inserted the carrying staves into the Ark and placed the cover on
21 top of it. He brought the Ark into the Tabernacle and hung the cloth curtain, screening
22 off the Ark of the Testimony, as the Lord had commanded him. He put the table in the
23 Tent of Meeting, outside the curtain on the north side of the Tabernacle, and arranged
24 the bread on it before the Lord, as the Lord had commanded him. He placed the candelabrum in the Tent of Meeting, opposite the table, on the Tabernacle's south side,
25
26 and lit the lamps before the Lord, as the Lord had commanded him. He placed the
27 golden altar in the Tent of Meeting, in front of the curtain, and on it he burned fragrant

---

RAMBAN

רמב״ן

משה הקטיר עליו כל שבעת ימי המלואים ... והנה משה רבינו בכל העבודות הכהן הראשון, ולפיכך הקטיר גם הקטרת.

Throughout the seven days of the Tabernacle's dedication, Moshe himself burned the incense on the altar…. For during that short period Moshe our teacher served as Israel's first priest regarding all of the required services. And hence he was also the one to burn the incense.

QUESTIONS FOR THOUGHT

- Rashi quotes a verse to back up his claim. Why does Ramban disagree with him?
- According to Ramban, many of the procedures to start the *Mishkan* and inaugurate the priests required a High Priest, and Moshe served that role temporarily until Aharon could be inaugurated into the position. How was Moshe inaugurated as temporary High Priest?
- Think about the implications of Moshe being the High Priest and then handing this position off to his brother.

שמות | פרק מ | פקודי

יז מֹשֶׁה כְּכֹל אֲשֶׁר צִוָּה יְהֹוָה אֹתוֹ כֵּן עָשָׂה: וַיְהִי ששי
בַּחֹדֶשׁ הָרִאשׁוֹן בַּשָּׁנָה הַשֵּׁנִית בְּאֶחָד לַחֹדֶשׁ הוּקַם הַמִּשְׁכָּן:
יח וַיָּקֶם מֹשֶׁה אֶת־הַמִּשְׁכָּן וַיִּתֵּן אֶת־אֲדָנָיו וַיָּשֶׂם אֶת־קְרָשָׁיו וַיִּתֵּן
אֶת־בְּרִיחָיו וַיָּקֶם אֶת־עַמּוּדָיו: יט וַיִּפְרֹשׂ אֶת־הָאֹהֶל עַל־הַמִּשְׁכָּן
וַיָּשֶׂם אֶת־מִכְסֵה הָאֹהֶל עָלָיו מִלְמָעְלָה כַּאֲשֶׁר צִוָּה יְהֹוָה
אֶת־מֹשֶׁה: כ וַיִּקַּח וַיִּתֵּן אֶת־הָעֵדֻת אֶל־הָאָרֹן וַיָּשֶׂם
אֶת־הַבַּדִּים עַל־הָאָרֹן וַיִּתֵּן אֶת־הַכַּפֹּרֶת עַל־הָאָרֹן מִלְמָעְלָה:
כא וַיָּבֵא אֶת־הָאָרֹן אֶל־הַמִּשְׁכָּן וַיָּשֶׂם אֵת פָּרֹכֶת הַמָּסָךְ וַיָּסֶךְ עַל
אֲרוֹן הָעֵדוּת כַּאֲשֶׁר צִוָּה יְהֹוָה אֶת־מֹשֶׁה: כב וַיִּתֵּן אֶת־
הַשֻּׁלְחָן בְּאֹהֶל מוֹעֵד עַל יֶרֶךְ הַמִּשְׁכָּן צָפֹנָה מִחוּץ לַפָּרֹכֶת:
כג וַיַּעֲרֹךְ עָלָיו עֵרֶךְ לֶחֶם לִפְנֵי יְהֹוָה כַּאֲשֶׁר צִוָּה יְהֹוָה אֶת־
מֹשֶׁה: כד וַיָּשֶׂם אֶת־הַמְּנֹרָה בְּאֹהֶל מוֹעֵד נֹכַח הַשֻּׁלְחָן
עַל יֶרֶךְ הַמִּשְׁכָּן נֶגְבָּה: כה וַיַּעַל הַנֵּרֹת לִפְנֵי יְהֹוָה כַּאֲשֶׁר צִוָּה יְהֹוָה
אֶת־מֹשֶׁה: כו וַיָּשֶׂם אֶת־מִזְבַּח הַזָּהָב בְּאֹהֶל מוֹעֵד
לִפְנֵי הַפָּרֹכֶת: כז וַיַּקְטֵר עָלָיו קְטֹרֶת סַמִּים כַּאֲשֶׁר צִוָּה יְהֹוָה אֶת־

CLASSIC COMMENTATORS

Who did the service of the *ketoret* on the golden altar?

RASHI — רש״י

Aharon burned the incense once in the morning and once in the evening, as the verses state, "Aharon should burn incense on it every morning when he tends the lamps, and before evening when he lights the lamps" (30:7–8).

ויקטר עליו – אהרן, קטרת – שחרית וערבית, כמו שנאמר: "בבקר בבקר בהיטיבו וגומ׳, ובהעלות אהרן" (שמות ל׳:ז׳-ח׳).

28 incense, as the Lord had commanded him. He hung the curtain at the entrance of the
29 Tabernacle. He put the sacrificial altar at the entrance of the Tabernacle of the Tent of Meeting, and on it sacrificed a burnt offering and a grain offering, as the Lord had
30 commanded him. He placed the laver between the Tent of Meeting and the altar, and
31 in it he put water for washing. Moshe, Aharon and his sons would wash their hands and
32 feet there, for they washed themselves whenever they went into the Tent of Meeting or
33 approached the altar, as the Lord had commanded Moshe. Then he set up the courtyard around the Tabernacle and the altar, and hung the curtain for the courtyard gate. And so Moshe completed the work.
34 Then the cloud covered the Tent of Meeting, and the glory of the Lord filled the
35 Tabernacle. Moshe could not now enter the Tent of Meeting, because the cloud had
36 settled on it, and the glory of the Lord filled the Tabernacle. In all the journeys of the

---

RABBI SAMSON RAPHAEL HIRSCH

The Torah describes an earlier scene when it states, "The glory of the Lord rested on Mount Sinai, and the cloud covered it for six days. On the seventh, He called to Moshe from within the cloud" (24:16). Similarly now, after the Torah had been given a home among human beings, the Tabernacle became the location for God's revelation on earth. This explains the Psalm that talks about God's revelation, stating, "the Lord is among them as at Sinai in holiness" (Ps. 68:18). For God entered the community of Israel at Sinai, but later could be found in the Tabernacle. And just as regarding Sinai the verse states, "The glory of the Lord rested on Mount Sinai... On the seventh, He called to Moshe", here too the text first declares that "Moshe could not now enter the Tent of Meeting", and only subsequently does the Torah relate that, "The Lord called to Moshe. From the Tent of Meeting He spoke to him" (Lev. 1:1).

ר' שמשון רפאל הירש

כשם שנאמר בסיני: "וישכן כבוד ה' על הר סיני ויכסהו הענן" וגו' (לעיל כד, טז), כן עתה - לאחר שהתורה מצאה בית דירה עלי אדמות בין בני האדם - נעשה המשכן למקום גילוי כבוד ה' בארץ.

לקיים מה שנאמר במזמור המדבר על התגלות ה' (תהילים סח, יח): "ה' בם סיני בקדש", הווי אומר: "ה' נכנס לקרבם, ומכאן ואילך סיני יימצא במקדש".

וכשם שנאמר בסיני: "ויכסהו הענן ששת ימים ויקרא אל משה ביום השביעי מתוך הענן" (לעיל כד, טז), כן גם כאן נאמר תחילה (פסוק לה): "ולא יכל משה לבוא" וגו', ורק לאחר מכן (ויקרא א, א): "ויקרא אל משה וידבר אליו מאהל מועד".

QUESTIONS FOR THOUGHT

- Rashi does not answer the question. In fact, he seems to reinforce it. Based on what we know about Rashi's understanding that the *Mishkan* was a response to the golden calf, how do you think he might answer the question?
- How does Ibn Ezra resolve the problem? How do you think Ibn Ezra and Rashi would each understand God's accessibility to Moshe following the incident of the golden calf?
- Rav Hirsch expands on Ibn Ezra's approach and may go even further by demonstrating some amazing parallels. What are they and what message is embedded in those parallels?

שמות | פרק מ

כט מֹשֶׁה: וַיָּשֶׂם אֶת־מָסַךְ הַפֶּתַח לַמִּשְׁכָּן: וְאֵת מִזְבַּח שביעי
הָעֹלָה שָׂם פֶּתַח מִשְׁכַּן אֹהֶל־מוֹעֵד וַיַּעַל עָלָיו אֶת־הָעֹלָה וְאֶת־
ל הַמִּנְחָה כַּאֲשֶׁר צִוָּה יְהֹוָה אֶת־מֹשֶׁה: וַיָּשֶׂם אֶת־
הַכִּיֹּר בֵּין־אֹהֶל מוֹעֵד וּבֵין הַמִּזְבֵּחַ וַיִּתֵּן שָׁמָּה מַיִם לְרָחְצָה:
לא וְרָחֲצוּ מִמֶּנּוּ מֹשֶׁה וְאַהֲרֹן וּבָנָיו אֶת־יְדֵיהֶם וְאֶת־רַגְלֵיהֶם: בְּבֹאָם
לב אֶל־אֹהֶל מוֹעֵד וּבְקָרְבָתָם אֶל־הַמִּזְבֵּחַ יִרְחָצוּ כַּאֲשֶׁר צִוָּה יְהֹוָה
לג אֶת־מֹשֶׁה: וַיָּקֶם אֶת־הֶחָצֵר סָבִיב לַמִּשְׁכָּן וְלַמִּזְבֵּחַ
וַיִּתֵּן אֶת־מָסַךְ שַׁעַר הֶחָצֵר וַיְכַל מֹשֶׁה אֶת־הַמְּלָאכָה:
לד וַיְכַס הֶעָנָן אֶת־אֹהֶל מוֹעֵד וּכְבוֹד יְהֹוָה מָלֵא אֶת־הַמִּשְׁכָּן: מפטיר
לה וְלֹא־יָכֹל מֹשֶׁה לָבוֹא אֶל־אֹהֶל מוֹעֵד כִּי־שָׁכַן עָלָיו הֶעָנָן וּכְבוֹד
לו יְהֹוָה מָלֵא אֶת־הַמִּשְׁכָּן: וּבְהֵעָלוֹת הֶעָנָן מֵעַל הַמִּשְׁכָּן יִסְעוּ

CLASSIC COMMENTATORS

How could it be that Moshe was able to go up on Mount Sinai and speak with God "face to face" but unable to stay in the *Mishkan* when God's presence filled it?

רש"י

כל זמן שהיה הענן עליו – לא היה יכול משה לבוא, נסתלק הענן – נכנס משה ומדבר עמו.

RASHI

Whenever the cloud had settled on the Tent of Meeting, Moshe was unable to enter the space, but when the cloud departed, he went in and God communicated with him.

אבן עזרא

ולא יכול משה לבוא – באותה שעה, עד שקרא אליו השם מאהל מועד, כי כן כתוב (ויקרא א':א').

IBN EZRA

Moshe could not enter the Tent of Meeting at that moment until the Lord called to him from within, as the verse describes in Leviticus 1:1.

37 Israelites, when the cloud rose from the Tabernacle, they would set out. But if the cloud
38 did not lift, they did not move on; they waited until it had lifted. The Lord's cloud was over the Tabernacle by day, and fire was in it at night, in view of all the house of Israel through all their journeys.

WISDOM OF THE HEART

The cloud on the *Mishkan* represents a continuation of Mount Sinai. The Sinai experience wasn't a one time experience; the cloud will always be there. Throughout our people's journey, the "cloud" representing the Divine Presence was, and always will be there. God's watchful guidance will be a constant part of our history. Look carefully and you will always notice His footprints in the sand.

לז בְּנֵי יִשְׂרָאֵל בְּכֹל מַסְעֵיהֶֽם׃ וְאִם־לֹא יֵעָלֶה הֶעָנָן וְלֹא יִסְעוּ

לח עַד־יוֹם הֵעָלֹתֽוֹ׃ כִּי עֲנַן יְהֹוָה עַל־הַמִּשְׁכָּן יוֹמָם וְאֵשׁ תִּהְיֶה לַיְלָה בּוֹ לְעֵינֵי כָל־בֵּית־יִשְׂרָאֵל בְּכָל־מַסְעֵיהֶֽם׃   חזק

TEXTUAL SKILLS

1. Where did you see the cloud and the fire earlier in Exodus? Do you think that they are connected to Genesis chapter 15?

2. Notice that the Torah switches back and forth between the terms אוהל מועד and משכן. Are they the same thing, or two different things?

ספר שמות עם רש"י
SEFER SHEMOT WITH RASHI

שמות

פרק א

א וְאֵ֗לֶּה שְׁמוֹת֙ בְּנֵ֣י יִשְׂרָאֵ֔ל הַבָּאִ֖ים מִצְרָ֑יְמָה אֵ֣ת יַעֲקֹ֔ב אִ֥ישׁ וּבֵית֖וֹ בָּֽאוּ: ב רְאוּבֵ֣ן שִׁמְע֔וֹן לֵוִ֖י וִֽיהוּדָֽה: ג יִשָּׂשכָ֥ר זְבוּלֻ֖ן וּבִנְיָמִֽן: ד דָּ֥ן וְנַפְתָּלִ֖י גָּ֥ד וְאָשֵֽׁר: ה וַֽיְהִ֗י כָּל־נֶ֛פֶשׁ יֹצְאֵ֥י יֶֽרֶךְ־יַעֲקֹ֖ב שִׁבְעִ֣ים נָ֑פֶשׁ וְיוֹסֵ֖ף הָיָ֥ה בְמִצְרָֽיִם: ו וַיָּ֤מָת יוֹסֵף֙ וְכָל־אֶחָ֔יו וְכֹ֖ל הַדּ֥וֹר הַהֽוּא: ז וּבְנֵ֣י יִשְׂרָאֵ֗ל פָּר֧וּ וַֽיִּשְׁרְצ֛וּ וַיִּרְבּ֥וּ וַיַּֽעַצְמ֖וּ בִּמְאֹ֣ד מְאֹ֑ד וַתִּמָּלֵ֥א הָאָ֖רֶץ אֹתָֽם:

ח וַיָּ֥קָם מֶֽלֶךְ־חָדָ֖שׁ עַל־מִצְרָ֑יִם אֲשֶׁ֥ר לֹֽא־יָדַ֖ע אֶת־יוֹסֵֽף: ט וַיֹּ֖אמֶר אֶל־עַמּ֑וֹ הִנֵּ֗ה עַ֚ם בְּנֵ֣י יִשְׂרָאֵ֔ל רַ֥ב וְעָצ֖וּם מִמֶּֽנּוּ: י הָ֥בָה נִֽתְחַכְּמָ֖ה ל֑וֹ פֶּן־יִרְבֶּ֗ה וְהָיָ֞ה כִּֽי־תִקְרֶ֤אנָה מִלְחָמָה֙ וְנוֹסַ֤ף גַּם־הוּא֙ עַל־שֹׂ֣נְאֵ֔ינוּ וְנִלְחַם־בָּ֖נוּ וְעָלָ֥ה מִן־הָאָֽרֶץ: יא וַיָּשִׂ֤ימוּ עָלָיו֙ שָׂרֵ֣י מִסִּ֔ים לְמַ֥עַן עַנֹּת֖וֹ בְּסִבְלֹתָ֑ם וַיִּ֜בֶן עָרֵ֤י מִסְכְּנוֹת֙ לְפַרְעֹ֔ה אֶת־פִּתֹ֖ם וְאֶת־רַעַמְסֵֽס: יב וְכַאֲשֶׁר֙ יְעַנּ֣וּ אֹת֔וֹ כֵּ֥ן יִרְבֶּ֖ה וְכֵ֣ן יִפְרֹ֑ץ וַיָּקֻ֕צוּ מִפְּנֵ֖י

פרק א

א) **ואלה שמות בני ישראל.** אַף עַל פִּי שֶׁמְּנָאָן בְּחַיֵּיהֶם בִּשְׁמוֹתָם, חָזַר וּמְנָאָם בְּמִיתָתָם, לְהוֹדִיעַ חִבָּתָם שֶׁנִּמְשְׁלוּ לַכּוֹכָבִים, שֶׁמּוֹצִיאָם וּמַכְנִיסָם בְּמִסְפָּר וּבִשְׁמוֹתָם, שֶׁנֶּאֱמַר: "הַמּוֹצִיא בְמִסְפָּר צְבָאָם לְכֻלָּם בְּשֵׁם יִקְרָא" (ישעיה מ, כו):

ה) **ויוסף היה במצרים.** וַהֲלֹא הוּא וּבָנָיו הָיוּ בִּכְלַל שִׁבְעִים, וּמַה בָּא לְלַמְּדֵנוּ? וְכִי לֹא הָיִינוּ יוֹדְעִים שֶׁהוּא הָיָה בְּמִצְרַיִם? אֶלָּא לְהוֹדִיעֲךָ צִדְקָתוֹ שֶׁל יוֹסֵף, הוּא יוֹסֵף הָרוֹעֶה אֶת צֹאן אָבִיו, הוּא יוֹסֵף שֶׁהָיָה בְּמִצְרַיִם וְנַעֲשָׂה מֶלֶךְ, וְעוֹמֵד בְּצִדְקוֹ:

ז) **וישרצו.** שֶׁהָיוּ יוֹלְדוֹת שִׁשָּׁה בְּכֶרֶס אֶחָד:

ח) **ויקם מלך חדש.** רַב וּשְׁמוּאֵל. חַד אָמַר חָדָשׁ מַמָּשׁ, וְחַד אָמַר שֶׁנִּתְחַדְּשׁוּ גְּזֵרוֹתָיו: **אשר לא ידע.** עָשָׂה עַצְמוֹ כְּאִלּוּ לֹא יָדַע:

י) **הבה נתחכמה לו.** כָּל 'הָבָה' לְשׁוֹן הֲכָנָה וְהַזְמָנָה לְדָבָר הוּא, הָכִינוּ עַצְמְכֶם לְכָךְ: **נתחכמה לו.** לָעָם, נִתְחַכֵּם מַה לַּעֲשׂוֹת לוֹ. וְרַבּוֹתֵינוּ דָּרְשׁוּ, נִתְחַכֵּם לְמוֹשִׁיעָן שֶׁל יִשְׂרָאֵל, בְּדוּנֵם בַּמַּיִם, שֶׁכְּבָר נִשְׁבַּע שֶׁלֹּא יָבִיא מַבּוּל לָעוֹלָם: **ועלה מן הארץ.** עַל כָּרְחֵנוּ. וְרַבּוֹתֵינוּ דָּרְשׁוּ, כְּאָדָם שֶׁמְּקַלֵּל עַצְמוֹ וְתוֹלֶה קִלְלָתוֹ בַּחֲבֵרוֹ, וַהֲרֵי הוּא כְּאִלּוּ כָּתַב: 'וְעָלִינוּ מִן הָאָרֶץ' וְהֵם יִירָשׁוּהָ:

יא) **עליו. על העם: מסים.** לְשׁוֹן מַס, שָׂרִים שֶׁגּוֹבִין מֵהֶם הַמַּס. וּמַהוּ הַמַּס? שֶׁיִּבְנוּ עָרֵי מִסְכְּנוֹת לְפַרְעֹה: **למען ענתו בסבלתם.** שֶׁל מִצְרַיִם: **ערי מסכנות.** כְּתַרְגּוּמוֹ. וְכֵן: "לֶךְ בֹּא אֶל הַסֹּכֵן הַזֶּה" (ישעיה כב, טו) — גִּזְבָּר הַמְמֻנֶּה עַל הָאוֹצָרוֹת: **את פתם ואת רעמסס.** שֶׁלֹּא הָיוּ רְאוּיוֹת מִתְּחִלָּה לְכָךְ, וַעֲשָׂאוּם חֲזָקוֹת וּבְצוּרוֹת לְאוֹצָר:

יב) **וכאשר יענו אתו.** בְּכָל מַה שֶּׁהֵם נוֹתְנִין לֵב

שמות | פרק א

יד בְּנֵי יִשְׂרָאֵל: וַיַּעֲבִדוּ מִצְרַיִם אֶת־בְּנֵי יִשְׂרָאֵל בְּפָרֶךְ: וַיְמָרְרוּ אֶת־חַיֵּיהֶם בַּעֲבֹדָה קָשָׁה בְּחֹמֶר וּבִלְבֵנִים וּבְכָל־עֲבֹדָה בַּשָּׂדֶה אֵת כָּל־עֲבֹדָתָם אֲשֶׁר־עָבְדוּ בָהֶם בְּפָרֶךְ:
טו וַיֹּאמֶר מֶלֶךְ מִצְרַיִם לַמְיַלְּדֹת הָעִבְרִיֹּת אֲשֶׁר שֵׁם הָאַחַת שִׁפְרָה וְשֵׁם הַשֵּׁנִית פּוּעָה:
טז וַיֹּאמֶר בְּיַלֶּדְכֶן אֶת־הָעִבְרִיּוֹת וּרְאִיתֶן עַל־הָאָבְנָיִם אִם־בֵּן הוּא וַהֲמִתֶּן אֹתוֹ וְאִם־בַּת הִוא וָחָיָה:
יז וַתִּירֶאןָ הַמְיַלְּדֹת אֶת־הָאֱלֹהִים וְלֹא עָשׂוּ כַּאֲשֶׁר דִּבֶּר אֲלֵיהֶן מֶלֶךְ מִצְרָיִם וַתְּחַיֶּיןָ אֶת־הַיְלָדִים:
יח שני וַיִּקְרָא מֶלֶךְ־מִצְרַיִם לַמְיַלְּדֹת וַיֹּאמֶר לָהֶן מַדּוּעַ עֲשִׂיתֶן הַדָּבָר הַזֶּה וַתְּחַיֶּיןָ אֶת־הַיְלָדִים:
יט וַתֹּאמַרְןָ הַמְיַלְּדֹת אֶל־פַּרְעֹה כִּי לֹא כַנָּשִׁים הַמִּצְרִיֹּת הָעִבְרִיֹּת כִּי־חָיוֹת הֵנָּה

לְעַנּוֹת כֵּן לֵב הַקָּדוֹשׁ בָּרוּךְ הוּא לְהַרְבּוֹת וּלְהַפְרוֹת: **כֵּן יִרְבֶּה**. כֵּן רָבָה, וְכֵן פּוֹרֵץ. וּמִדְרָשׁוֹ, רוּחַ הַקֹּדֶשׁ אוֹמֶרֶת כֵּן: אַתֶּם אוֹמְרִים "פֶּן יִרְבֶּה" וַאֲנִי אוֹמֵר "כֵּן יִרְבֶּה". וַרַבּוֹתֵינוּ דָּרְשׁוּ, פְּקוּעִים הָיוּ בְּעֵינֵיהֶם.

יג **בְּפָרֶךְ**. בַּעֲבוֹדָה קָשָׁה הַמְפָרֶכֶת וּמְשַׁבֶּרֶת אֶת הַגּוּף.

טו **לַמְיַלְּדֹת**. הוּא לְשׁוֹן מוֹלִידוֹת, אֶלָּא שֶׁיֵּשׁ לְשׁוֹן קַל וְיֵשׁ לְשׁוֹן כָּבֵד, כְּמוֹ: שׁוֹבֵר וּמְשַׁבֵּר, דּוֹבֵר וּמְדַבֵּר, כָּךְ מוֹלִיד וּמְיַלֵּד: **שִׁפְרָה**. יוֹכֶבֶד, עַל שֵׁם שֶׁמְשַׁפֶּרֶת אֶת הַוָּלָד. **פּוּעָה**. מִרְיָם, שֶׁפּוֹעָה וּמְדַבֶּרֶת וְהוֹגָה לַוָּלָד כְּדֶרֶךְ הַנָּשִׁים הַמְפַיְּסוֹת תִּינוֹק הַבּוֹכֶה. "פּוּעָה" – לְשׁוֹן צְעָקָה, כְּמוֹ: "כַּיּוֹלֵדָה אֶפְעֶה" (ישעיה מב, יד):

טז **בְּיַלֶּדְכֶן**. כְּמוֹ בְּהוֹלִידְכֶן. **עַל הָאָבְנָיִם**. מוֹשַׁב הָאִשָּׁה הַיּוֹלֶדֶת, וּבְמָקוֹם אַחֵר קוֹרְאוֹ 'מַשְׁבֵּר' (ישעיה לז, ג), וְכָמוֹהוּ: "עֹשֶׂה מְלָאכָה עַל הָאָבְנָיִם" (ירמיה יח, ג) – מוֹשַׁב כְּלֵי אֻמָּנוּת יוֹצֵר חֶרֶשׂ: **אִם בֵּן הוּא וְגוֹ'**. לֹא

הָיָה מַקְפִּיד אֶלָּא עַל הַזְּכָרִים, שֶׁאָמְרוּ לוֹ אִצְטַגְנִינָיו שֶׁעֲתִידָה לֵילֵד בֵּן הַמּוֹשִׁיעַ אוֹתָם: **וָחָיָה. וְתִחְיֶה**:

יז **וַתְּחַיֶּיןָ אֶת הַיְלָדִים**. מְסַפְּקוֹת לָהֶם מָזוֹן. תַּרְגּוּם הָרִאשׁוֹן "וְקַיֵּמָא" וְהַשֵּׁנִי (בפסוק הבא) "וְקַיֵּמְתֵּן", לְפִי שֶׁלְּשׁוֹן עָבָר לִנְקֵבוֹת רַבּוֹת, תֵּבָה זוֹ וְכַיּוֹצֵא בָּהּ מְשַׁמֶּשֶׁת לְשׁוֹן פָּעֲלוּ וּלְשׁוֹן פְּעַלְתֶּן, כְּגוֹן: "וַתֹּאמַרְןָ אִישׁ מִצְרִי" (להלן ב, יט) לְשׁוֹן עָבָר, כְּמוֹ "וַיֹּאמְרוּ" לַזְּכָרִים. "וַתְּדַבֵּרְנָה בְּפִיכֶם" (ירמיה מד, כה) לְשׁוֹן דִּבַּרְתֶּם כְּמוֹ 'וַתְּדַבְּרוּ' לַזְּכָרִים. וְכֵן: "וַתְּחַלֶּלְנָה אֹתִי אֶל עַמִּי" (יחזקאל יג, יט) לְשׁוֹן עָבָר, חִלַּלְתֶּן, כְּמוֹ "וַתְּחַלְּלוּ" לַזְּכָרִים:

יט **כִּי חָיוֹת הֵנָּה**. בְּקִיאוֹת כַּמְיַלְּדוֹת, תַּרְגּוּם מְיַלְּדוֹת "חָיָתָא". וְרַבּוֹתֵינוּ דָּרְשׁוּ, הֲרֵי הֵן מְשׁוּלוֹת כְּחַיּוֹת הַשָּׂדֶה שֶׁאֵינָן צְרִיכוֹת מְיַלְּדוֹת: "גּוּר אַרְיֵה" (בראשית מט, ט), "זְאֵב יִטְרָף" (שם פסוק כז), "בְּכוֹר שׁוֹרוֹ" (דברים לג, יז), "אַיָּלָה שְׁלֻחָה" (בראשית מט, כא), וּמִי שֶׁלֹּא נִכְתַּב בּוֹ, הֲרֵי הַכָּתוּב כְּלָלָן: "מָה אִמְּךָ לְבִיָּא" (יחזקאל יט, ב):

פרק א | שמות

כ בְּטֶ֛רֶם תָּב֥וֹא אֲלֵהֶ֖ן הַמְיַלֶּ֑דֶת וְיָלָֽדוּ: וַיֵּ֥יטֶב אֱלֹהִ֖ים לַֽמְיַלְּדֹ֑ת
כא וַיִּ֧רֶב הָעָ֛ם וַיַּֽעַצְמ֖וּ מְאֹֽד: וַיְהִ֕י כִּֽי־יָרְא֥וּ הַֽמְיַלְּדֹ֖ת אֶת־הָאֱלֹהִ֑ים
כב וַיַּ֥עַשׂ לָהֶ֖ם בָּתִּֽים: וַיְצַ֣ו פַּרְעֹ֔ה לְכָל־עַמּ֖וֹ לֵאמֹ֑ר כָּל־הַבֵּ֣ן הַיִּלּ֗וֹד
הַיְאֹ֨רָה֙ תַּשְׁלִיכֻ֔הוּ וְכָל־הַבַּ֖ת תְּחַיּֽוּן:

פרק ב

א וַיֵּ֥לֶךְ אִ֖ישׁ מִבֵּ֣ית לֵוִ֑י וַיִּקַּ֖ח אֶת־בַּת־לֵוִֽי: וַתַּ֥הַר הָאִשָּׁ֖ה וַתֵּ֣לֶד בֵּ֑ן
ב וַתֵּ֤רֶא אֹתוֹ֙ כִּי־ט֣וֹב ה֔וּא וַֽתִּצְפְּנֵ֖הוּ שְׁלֹשָׁ֥ה יְרָחִֽים: וְלֹא־יָכְלָ֣ה
ג ע֘וֹד֘ הַצְּפִינוֹ֒ וַתִּֽקַּֽח־לוֹ֙ תֵּ֣בַת גֹּ֔מֶא וַתַּחְמְרָ֥ה בַחֵמָ֖ר וּבַזָּ֑פֶת וַתָּ֤שֶׂם
בָּהּ֙ אֶת־הַיֶּ֔לֶד וַתָּ֥שֶׂם בַּסּ֖וּף עַל־שְׂפַ֥ת הַיְאֹֽר: וַתֵּתַצַּ֥ב אֲחֹת֖וֹ
ד

כ-כא **וַיֵּיטֶב.** הֵיטִיב לָהֶן. וְזֶה חִלּוּק בְּתֵבָה שֶׁיְּסוֹדָהּ שְׁתֵּי אוֹתִיּוֹת וְנָתַן לָהּ וָי"ו יוֹ"ד בְּרֹאשָׁהּ, כְּשֶׁהִיא בָּאָה לְדַבֵּר בִּלְשׁוֹן וַיַּפְעִיל הוּא נוֹקֵד הַיּוֹ"ד בְּצֵירֵי שֶׁהוּא קָמָץ קָטָן, כְּגוֹן: "וַיֵּיטֶב אֱלֹהִים לַמְיַלְּדֹת", "וַיֶּרֶב בְּבַת יְהוּדָה" (איכה ב, ה), הִרְבָּה תַּאֲנִיָּה, וְכֵן "וַיֹּגֶל הַשֹּׁמְרֹנִית" (דברי הימים ב׳ לו, כ) דִּנְבוּזַרְאֲדָן, הִגְלָה אֶת הַשְּׁאֵרִית; "וַיִּפֶן זָנָב אֶל זָנָב" (שופטים טו, ד) – הִפְנָה הַזְּנָבוֹת זוֹ לָזוֹ. כָּל אֵלּוּ לְשׁוֹן הִפְעִיל אֶת אֲחֵרִים. וּכְשֶׁהוּא מְדַבֵּר בִּלְשׁוֹן וַיִּפְעַל הוּא נוֹקֵד הַיּוֹ"ד בַּחִירִיק, כְּגוֹן: "וַיִּיטַב בְּעֵינָיו" (ויקרא י, כ) – לְשׁוֹן הוּטַב; וְכֵן "וַיִּרֶב הָעָם" (להלן פסוק כ) – לְשׁוֹן רָבָה הָעָם, "וַיִּגֶל יְהוּדָה" (מלכים ב׳ כה, כא), "וַיִּפֶן כֹּה וָכֹה" (להלן ב, יב) – פָּנָה לְכָאן וּלְכָאן. וְאַל תְּשִׁיבֵנִי: וַיֵּלֶךְ, וַיֵּשֶׁב, וַיֵּרֶד, וַיֵּצֵא, לְפִי שֶׁאֵינָן מִגִּזְרָתָן שֶׁל אֵלּוּ, שֶׁהֲרֵי הַיּוֹ"ד יְסוֹד בָּהֶן: יָרַד, יָצָא, יָלַךְ, יָשַׁב, הַיּוֹ"ד אוֹת שְׁלִישִׁית בּוֹ: **וַיֵּיטֶב אֱלֹהִים לַמְיַלְּדֹת.** מַהוּ הַטּוֹבָה? **וַיַּעַשׂ לָהֶם בָּתִּים** – בָּתֵּי כְהֻנָּה וּלְוִיָּה וּמַלְכוּת, שֶׁקְּרוּיִין בָּתִּים: "לִבְנוֹת אֶת בֵּית ה׳ וְאֶת בֵּית הַמֶּלֶךְ" (מלכים א׳ ט, י), כְּהֻנָּה וּלְוִיָּה מִיּוֹכֶבֶד, וּמַלְכוּת מִמִּרְיָם, כִּדְאִיתָא בְּמַסֶּכֶת סוֹטָה (דף יא ע"ב):

כב **לְכָל עַמּוֹ.** אַף עֲלֵיהֶם גָּזַר. יוֹם שֶׁנּוֹלַד מֹשֶׁה אָמְרוּ לוֹ אִצְטַגְנִינָיו: הַיּוֹם נוֹלַד מוֹשִׁיעָן וְאֵין אָנוּ יוֹדְעִים אִם מִמִּצְרַיִם אִם מִיִּשְׂרָאֵל, וְרוֹאִים אָנוּ שֶׁסּוֹפוֹ לִלְקוֹת בַּמַּיִם, לְפִיכָךְ גָּזַר אוֹתוֹ הַיּוֹם אַף עַל הַמִּצְרִים, שֶׁנֶּאֱמַר: "כָּל הַבֵּן הַיִּלּוֹד" וְלֹא נֶאֱמַר 'הַיִּלּוֹד לָעִבְרִים'. וְהֵם לֹא הָיוּ יוֹדְעִים שֶׁסּוֹפוֹ לִלְקוֹת עַל מֵי מְרִיבָה:

פרק ב

א **וַיִּקַּח אֶת בַּת לֵוִי.** פָּרוּשׁ הָיָה מִמֶּנָּה מִפְּנֵי גְּזֵרַת פַּרְעֹה וְהֶחֱזִירָהּ וְעָשָׂה בָהּ לִקּוּחִין שְׁנִיִּים. וְאַף הִיא נֶהֶפְכָה לִהְיוֹת נַעֲרָה. וּבַת מֵאָה וּשְׁלֹשִׁים שָׁנָה הָיְתָה; שֶׁנּוֹלְדָה בְּבוֹאָהּ לְמִצְרַיִם בֵּין הַחוֹמוֹת, וּמָאתַיִם וָעֶשֶׂר נִשְׁתַּהוּ שָׁם, וּכְשֶׁיָּצְאוּ הָיָה מֹשֶׁה בֶּן שְׁמוֹנִים שָׁנָה – כְּשֶׁנִּתְעַבְּרָה מִמֶּנּוּ הָיְתָה בַּת מֵאָה וּשְׁלֹשִׁים, וְקוֹרֵא אוֹתָהּ "בַּת לֵוִי":

ב **כִּי טוֹב הוּא.** כְּשֶׁנּוֹלַד נִתְמַלֵּא הַבַּיִת כֻּלּוֹ אוֹרָה:

ג **וְלֹא יָכְלָה עוֹד הַצְּפִינוֹ.** שֶׁמָּנוּ לָהּ הַמִּצְרִים מִיּוֹם שֶׁהֶחֱזִירָהּ, וְהִיא יָלְדָה לְשִׁשָּׁה חֳדָשִׁים וְיוֹם אֶחָד, שֶׁהַיּוֹלֶדֶת לְשִׁבְעָה יוֹלֶדֶת לִמְקֻטָּעִין, וְהֵם בָּדְקוּ אַחֲרֶיהָ לִסוֹף תִּשְׁעָה: **גֹּמֶא.** גְּמִי בִּלְשׁוֹן מִשְׁנָה, וּבְלַעַז יוּנְ"ק, וְדָבָר רַךְ הוּא וְעוֹמֵד בִּפְנֵי רַךְ וּבִפְנֵי קָשֶׁה: **בַחֵמָר וּבַזָּפֶת.** זֶפֶת מִבַּחוּץ וְטִיט מִבִּפְנִים, כְּדֵי שֶׁלֹּא יָרִיחַ אוֹתוֹ צַדִּיק רֵיחַ רַע שֶׁל זֶפֶת: **וַתָּשֶׂם בַּסּוּף.** הוּא לְשׁוֹן אֲגַם, רושיי"ל בְּלַעַז, וְדוֹמֶה לוֹ: "קָנֶה וָסוּף קָמֵלוּ" (ישעיה יט, ו):

מֵרָחֹ֖ק לְדֵעָ֕ה מַה־יֵּעָשֶׂ֖ה לֽוֹ׃ וַתֵּ֤רֶד בַּת־פַּרְעֹה֙ לִרְחֹ֣ץ עַל־הַיְאֹ֔ר ה
וְנַעֲרֹתֶ֥יהָ הֹלְכֹ֖ת עַל־יַ֣ד הַיְאֹ֑ר וַתֵּ֤רֶא אֶת־הַתֵּבָה֙ בְּת֣וֹךְ הַסּ֔וּף
וַתִּשְׁלַ֥ח אֶת־אֲמָתָ֖הּ וַתִּקָּחֶֽהָ׃ וַתִּפְתַּח֙ וַתִּרְאֵ֣הוּ אֶת־הַיֶּ֔לֶד ו
וְהִנֵּה־נַ֖עַר בֹּכֶ֑ה וַתַּחְמֹ֣ל עָלָ֔יו וַתֹּ֕אמֶר מִיַּלְדֵ֥י הָֽעִבְרִ֖ים זֶֽה׃
וַתֹּ֣אמֶר אֲחֹתוֹ֮ אֶל־בַּת־פַּרְעֹה֒ הַאֵלֵ֗ךְ וְקָרָ֤אתִי לָךְ֙ אִשָּׁ֣ה מֵינֶ֔קֶת ז
מִ֖ן הָעִבְרִיֹּ֑ת וְתֵינִ֥ק לָ֖ךְ אֶת־הַיָּֽלֶד׃ וַתֹּֽאמֶר־לָ֥הּ בַּת־פַּרְעֹ֖ה ח
לֵ֑כִי וַתֵּ֨לֶךְ֙ הָֽעַלְמָ֔ה וַתִּקְרָ֖א אֶת־אֵ֥ם הַיָּֽלֶד׃ וַתֹּ֧אמֶר לָ֣הּ בַּת־ ט
פַּרְעֹ֗ה הֵילִ֜יכִי אֶת־הַיֶּ֤לֶד הַזֶּה֙ וְהֵֽינִקִ֣הוּ לִ֔י וַאֲנִ֖י אֶתֵּ֣ן אֶת־שְׂכָרֵ֑ךְ
וַתִּקַּ֧ח הָאִשָּׁ֛ה הַיֶּ֖לֶד וַתְּנִיקֵֽהוּ׃ וַיִּגְדַּ֣ל הַיֶּ֗לֶד וַתְּבִאֵ֙הוּ֙ לְבַת־ י
פַּרְעֹ֔ה וַֽיְהִי־לָ֖הּ לְבֵ֑ן וַתִּקְרָ֤א שְׁמוֹ֙ מֹשֶׁ֔ה וַתֹּ֕אמֶר כִּ֥י מִן־הַמַּ֖יִם
מְשִׁיתִֽהוּ׃ וַיְהִ֣י ׀ בַּיָּמִ֣ים הָהֵ֗ם וַיִּגְדַּ֤ל מֹשֶׁה֙ וַיֵּצֵ֣א אֶל־אֶחָ֔יו וַיַּ֖רְא יא שלישי

ה **לִרְחֹץ עַל הַיְאֹר.** סָרֵס הַמִּקְרָא וּפָרְשֵׁהוּ, וַתֵּרֶד בַּת פַּרְעֹה עַל הַיְאוֹר לִרְחֹץ בּוֹ: **עַל יַד הַיְאֹר.** אֵצֶל הַיְאוֹר, כְּמוֹ: "רְאוּ חֶלְקַת יוֹאָב אֶל יָדִי" (שמואל ב' יד, ל), וְהוּא לְשׁוֹן יָד מַמָּשׁ, שֶׁיַּד הָאָדָם סְמוּכָה לוֹ. וְרַבּוֹתֵינוּ אָמְרוּ, "הֹלְכֹת", לְשׁוֹן מִיתָה, הוֹלְכוֹת לָמוּת, לְפִי שֶׁמִּחוּ בָהּ. וְהַכָּתוּב מְסַיְּעָן, כִּי לָמָּה לָנוּ לִכְתֹּב: "וְנַעֲרֹתֶיהָ הֹלְכֹת"? **אֶת אֲמָתָהּ.** אֶת שִׁפְחָתָהּ. וְרַבּוֹתֵינוּ דָּרְשׁוּ לְשׁוֹן יָד, אֲבָל לְפִי דִּקְדּוּק לְשׁוֹן הַקֹּדֶשׁ הָיָה לוֹ לְהִנָּקֵד 'אַמָּתָהּ' מ"ם דְּגוּשָׁה, וְהֵם דָּרְשׁוּ "אֶת אֲמָתָהּ" – אֶת יָדָהּ, וְנִשְׁתַּרְבְּבָה אֲמָתָהּ אַמּוֹת הַרְבֵּה:

ו **וַתִּפְתַּח וַתִּרְאֵהוּ.** אֶת מִי רָאֲתָה? "אֶת הַיֶּלֶד", זֶהוּ פְּשׁוּטוֹ. וּמִדְרָשׁוֹ, שֶׁרָאֲתָה עִמּוֹ שְׁכִינָה: **וְהִנֵּה נַעַר בֹּכֶה.** קוֹלוֹ כְנַעַר:

ז **מִן הָעִבְרִיֹּת.** שֶׁהֶחֱזִירַתּוּ עַל מִצְרִיּוֹת הַרְבֵּה לִינֹק וְלֹא יָנַק, לְפִי שֶׁהָיָה עָתִיד לְדַבֵּר עִם הַשְּׁכִינָה:

ח **וַתֵּלֶךְ הָעַלְמָה.** הָלְכָה בְּזְרִיזוּת וְעַלְמוּת כְּעֶלֶם:

ט **הֵילִיכִי.** נִתְנַבְּאָה וְלֹא יָדְעָה מַה נִּתְנַבְּאָה, הֵי שֶׁלִּיכִי:

י **מְשִׁיתִהוּ.** "שְׁחַלְתֵּיהּ", הוּא לְשׁוֹן הוֹצָאָה בִּלְשׁוֹן אֲרַמִּי: "כְּמִשְׁחַל בִּנִיתָא מֵחֲלָבָא" (ברכות ח ע"א). וּבִלְשׁוֹן עִבְרִי "מְשִׁיתִהוּ" לְשׁוֹן הֲסִירוֹתִיו, כְּמוֹ: "לֹא יָמוּשׁ" (יהושע א, ח), "לֹא מָשׁוּ" (במדבר יד, מד), כָּךְ חִבְּרוֹ מְנַחֵם. וַאֲנִי אוֹמֵר שֶׁאֵינוֹ מִמַּחְבֶּרֶת מָשׁ וַיָּמוּשׁ, אֶלָּא מִגִּזְרַת מָשָׁה, וּלְשׁוֹן הוֹצָאָה הוּא, וְכֵן: "יַמְשֵׁנִי מִמַּיִם רַבִּים" (שמואל ב' כב, יז). שֶׁאִלּוּ הָיָה מִמַּחְבֶּרֶת מָשׁ, לֹא יִתָּכֵן לוֹמַר "מְשִׁיתִהוּ", אֶלָּא "הֲמִישׁוֹתִיהוּ", כַּאֲשֶׁר יֵאָמֵר מִן קָם "הֲקִימֹתִי", וּמִן שָׁב "הֲשִׁיבוֹתִי", וּמִן בָּא "הֲבִיאוֹתִי", אוֹ "מַשְׁתִּיהוּ", כְּמוֹ: "וּמַשְׁתִּי אֶת עֲוֹן הָאָרֶץ" (זכריה ג, ט). אֲבָל "מָשִׁיתִי" אֵינוֹ אֶלָּא מִגִּזְרַת תֵּבָה שֶׁפֹּעַל שֶׁלָּהּ מְיֻסָּד בְּה"א בְּסוֹף הַתֵּבָה, כְּגוֹן: מָשָׁה, בָּנָה, עָשָׂה, צִוָּה, פָּנָה, כְּשֶׁיָּבוֹא לוֹמַר בָּהֶם פָּעַלְתִּי תָבֹא הַיּוֹ"ד בִּמְקוֹם ה"א, כְּמוֹ: עָשִׂיתִי, בָּנִיתִי, פָּנִיתִי, צִוִּיתִי:

יא **וַיִּגְדַּל מֹשֶׁה.** וַהֲלֹא כְּבָר כָּתַב (לעיל פסוק י) "וַיִּגְדַּל הַיֶּלֶד"? אָמַר רַבִּי יְהוּדָה בְּרַבִּי אִלְּעַאי, הָרִאשׁוֹן לְקוֹמָה וְהַשֵּׁנִי לִגְדֻלָּה, שֶׁמִּנָּהוּ פַּרְעֹה עַל בֵּיתוֹ:

פרק ב | שמות

יב בְּסִבְלֹתָם וַיַּרְא אִישׁ מִצְרִי מַכֶּה אִישׁ־עִבְרִי מֵאֶחָיו: וַיִּפֶן כֹּה
וָכֹה וַיַּרְא כִּי אֵין אִישׁ וַיַּךְ אֶת־הַמִּצְרִי וַיִּטְמְנֵהוּ בַּחוֹל: וַיֵּצֵא
יג בַּיּוֹם הַשֵּׁנִי וְהִנֵּה שְׁנֵי־אֲנָשִׁים עִבְרִים נִצִּים וַיֹּאמֶר לָרָשָׁע לָמָּה
תַכֶּה רֵעֶךָ: וַיֹּאמֶר מִי שָׂמְךָ לְאִישׁ שַׂר וְשֹׁפֵט עָלֵינוּ הַלְהָרְגֵנִי
יד אַתָּה אֹמֵר כַּאֲשֶׁר הָרַגְתָּ אֶת־הַמִּצְרִי וַיִּירָא מֹשֶׁה וַיֹּאמַר אָכֵן
נוֹדַע הַדָּבָר: וַיִּשְׁמַע פַּרְעֹה אֶת־הַדָּבָר הַזֶּה וַיְבַקֵּשׁ לַהֲרֹג אֶת־
טו מֹשֶׁה וַיִּבְרַח מֹשֶׁה מִפְּנֵי פַרְעֹה וַיֵּשֶׁב בְּאֶרֶץ־מִדְיָן וַיֵּשֶׁב עַל־
הַבְּאֵר: וּלְכֹהֵן מִדְיָן שֶׁבַע בָּנוֹת וַתָּבֹאנָה וַתִּדְלֶנָה וַתְּמַלֶּאנָה
טז אֶת־הָרְהָטִים לְהַשְׁקוֹת צֹאן אֲבִיהֶן: וַיָּבֹאוּ הָרֹעִים וַיְגָרְשׁוּם
יז וַיָּקָם מֹשֶׁה וַיּוֹשִׁעָן וַיַּשְׁקְ אֶת־צֹאנָם: וַתָּבֹאנָה אֶל־רְעוּאֵל
יח אֲבִיהֶן וַיֹּאמֶר מַדּוּעַ מִהַרְתֶּן בֹּא הַיּוֹם: וַתֹּאמַרְןָ אִישׁ מִצְרִי
יט הִצִּילָנוּ מִיַּד הָרֹעִים וְגַם־דָּלֹה דָלָה לָנוּ וַיַּשְׁקְ אֶת־הַצֹּאן:

וַיַּרְא בְּסִבְלֹתָם. נָתַן עֵינָיו וְלִבּוֹ לִהְיוֹת מֵצֵר עֲלֵיהֶם: **אִישׁ מִצְרִי.** נוֹגֵשׂ הָיָה, מְמֻנֶּה עַל שׁוֹטְרֵי יִשְׂרָאֵל, וְהָיָה מַעֲמִידָם מִקְּרוֹת הַגֶּבֶר לִמְלַאכְתָּם: **מַכֶּה אִישׁ עִבְרִי.** מַלְקֵהוּ וְרוֹדֵהוּ, וּבַעְלָהּ שֶׁל שְׁלוֹמִית בַּת דִּבְרִי הָיָה, וְנָתַן עֵינָיו בָּהּ, וּבַלַּיְלָה הֶעֱמִידוֹ וְהוֹצִיאוֹ מִבֵּיתוֹ וְהוּא חָזַר וְנִכְנַס לַבַּיִת וּבָא עַל אִשְׁתּוֹ, כְּסָבוּרָה שֶׁהוּא בַּעְלָהּ. וְחָזַר הָאִישׁ לְבֵיתוֹ וְהִרְגִּישׁ בַּדָּבָר, וּכְשֶׁרָאָה אוֹתוֹ מִצְרִי שֶׁהִרְגִּישׁ בַּדָּבָר הָיָה מַכֵּהוּ וְרוֹדֵהוּ כָּל הַיּוֹם:

וַיִּפֶן כֹּה וָכֹה. רָאָה מֶה עָשָׂה לוֹ בַּבַּיִת וּמֶה עָשָׂה לוֹ בַּשָּׂדֶה. וּלְפִי פְשׁוּטוֹ כְּמַשְׁמָעוֹ: **וַיַּרְא כִּי אֵין אִישׁ.** עָתִיד לָצֵאת מִמֶּנּוּ שֶׁיִּתְגַּיֵּר:

שְׁנֵי אֲנָשִׁים עִבְרִים. דָּתָן וַאֲבִירָם, הֵם שֶׁהוֹתִירוּ מִן הַמָּן: **נִצִּים.** מְרִיבִים: **לָמָּה תַכֶּה.** אַף עַל פִּי שֶׁלֹּא הִכָּהוּ נִקְרָא רָשָׁע בַּהֲרָמַת יָד: **רֵעֶךָ.** רָשָׁע כְּמוֹתְךָ:

מִי שָׂמְךָ לְאִישׁ. וַהֲרֵי עוֹדְךָ נַעַר: **הַלְהָרְגֵנִי אַתָּה אֹמֵר.** מִכָּאן אָנוּ לְמֵדִים שֶׁהֲרָגוֹ בְּשֵׁם הַמְפֹרָשׁ: **וַיִּירָא מֹשֶׁה.** כִּפְשׁוּטוֹ. וּמִדְרָשׁוֹ, דָּאַג לוֹ עַל שֶׁרָאָה בְּיִשְׂרָאֵל רְשָׁעִים דֵּלָטוֹרִין, אָמַר: מֵעַתָּה שֶׁמָּא אֵינָם רְאוּיִין לְהִגָּאֵל: **אָכֵן נוֹדַע הַדָּבָר.** כְּמַשְׁמָעוֹ. וּמִדְרָשׁוֹ, נוֹדַע לִי הַדָּבָר שֶׁהָיִיתִי תָּמֵהַּ עָלָיו, מֶה חָטְאוּ יִשְׂרָאֵל מִכָּל שִׁבְעִים אֻמּוֹת לִהְיוֹת נִרְדִּים בַּעֲבוֹדַת פָּרֶךְ, אֲבָל רוֹאֶה אֲנִי שֶׁהֵם רְאוּיִים לְכָךְ:

וַיִּשְׁמַע פַּרְעֹה. הֵם הִלְשִׁינוּ עָלָיו: **וַיְבַקֵּשׁ לַהֲרֹג אֶת מֹשֶׁה.** מְסָרוֹ לְקוֹסְטִינָר לְהָרְגוֹ, וְלֹא שָׁלְטָה בּוֹ הַחֶרֶב, הוּא שֶׁאָמַר מֹשֶׁה: "וַיַּצִּלֵנִי מֵחֶרֶב פַּרְעֹה" (להלן יח, ד): **וַיֵּשֶׁב עַל הַבְּאֵר.** לָמַד מִיַּעֲקֹב שֶׁנִּזְדַּוֵּג לוֹ זִוּוּגוֹ מִן הַבְּאֵר:

וּלְכֹהֵן מִדְיָן. רַב שֶׁבָּהֶן, וּפֵרַשׁ לוֹ מֵעֲבוֹדָה זָרָה וְנִדּוּהוּ מֵאֶצְלָם: **אֶת הָרְהָטִים.** אֶת בְּרֵכוֹת מְרוּצוֹת הַמַּיִם הָעֲשׂוּיוֹת בָּאָרֶץ:

וַיְגָרְשׁוּם. מִפְּנֵי הַנִּדּוּי:

כ וַיֹּאמֶר אֶל־בְּנֹתָיו וְאַיּוֹ לָמָּה זֶּה עֲזַבְתֶּן אֶת־הָאִישׁ קִרְאֶן לוֹ
כא וְיֹאכַל לָחֶם: וַיּוֹאֶל מֹשֶׁה לָשֶׁבֶת אֶת־הָאִישׁ וַיִּתֵּן אֶת־צִפֹּרָה
כב בִתּוֹ לְמֹשֶׁה: וַתֵּלֶד בֵּן וַיִּקְרָא אֶת־שְׁמוֹ גֵּרְשֹׁם כִּי אָמַר גֵּר הָיִיתִי בְּאֶרֶץ נָכְרִיָּה:
כג וַיְהִי בַיָּמִים הָרַבִּים הָהֵם וַיָּמָת מֶלֶךְ מִצְרַיִם וַיֵּאָנְחוּ בְנֵי־יִשְׂרָאֵל מִן־הָעֲבֹדָה וַיִּזְעָקוּ וַתַּעַל שַׁוְעָתָם אֶל־הָאֱלֹהִים מִן־הָעֲבֹדָה:
כד וַיִּשְׁמַע אֱלֹהִים אֶת־נַאֲקָתָם וַיִּזְכֹּר אֱלֹהִים אֶת־בְּרִיתוֹ אֶת־
כה אַבְרָהָם אֶת־יִצְחָק וְאֶת־יַעֲקֹב: וַיַּרְא אֱלֹהִים אֶת־בְּנֵי יִשְׂרָאֵל וַיֵּדַע אֱלֹהִים:

ג א וּמֹשֶׁה הָיָה רֹעֶה אֶת־צֹאן יִתְרוֹ חֹתְנוֹ כֹּהֵן מִדְיָן וַיִּנְהַג אֶת־הַצֹּאן אַחַר הַמִּדְבָּר וַיָּבֹא אֶל־הַר הָאֱלֹהִים
ב חֹרֵבָה: וַיֵּרָא מַלְאַךְ יְהוָה אֵלָיו בְּלַבַּת־אֵשׁ מִתּוֹךְ הַסְּנֶה וַיַּרְא
ג וְהִנֵּה הַסְּנֶה בֹּעֵר בָּאֵשׁ וְהַסְּנֶה אֵינֶנּוּ אֻכָּל: וַיֹּאמֶר מֹשֶׁה אָסֻרָה־נָּא וְאֶרְאֶה אֶת־הַמַּרְאֶה הַגָּדֹל הַזֶּה מַדּוּעַ לֹא־יִבְעַר
ד הַסְּנֶה: וַיַּרְא יְהוָה כִּי סָר לִרְאוֹת וַיִּקְרָא אֵלָיו אֱלֹהִים מִתּוֹךְ

כב) **לָמָּה זֶּה עֲזַבְתֶּן.** הִכִּיר בּוֹ שֶׁהוּא מִזַּרְעוֹ שֶׁל יַעֲקֹב, שֶׁהַמַּיִם עוֹלִים לִקְרָאתוֹ: **וְיֹאכַל לָחֶם.** שֶׁמָּא יִשָּׂא אַחַת מִכֶּם, כְּמָה דְאַתְּ אָמַר: "כִּי אִם־הַלֶּחֶם אֲשֶׁר־הוּא אוֹכֵל" (בראשית לט, ו):

כא) **וַיּוֹאֶל.** כְּתַרְגּוּמוֹ. וְדוֹמֶה לוֹ: "הוֹאֶל נָא וְלִין" (שופטים יט, ו), "וְלוּ הוֹאַלְנוּ" (יהושע ז, ז), "הוֹאַלְתִּי לְדַבֵּר" (בראשית יח, כז). וּמִדְרָשׁוֹ, לְשׁוֹן אָלָה, נִשְׁבַּע לוֹ שֶׁלֹּא יָזוּז מִמִּדְיָן כִּי אִם בִּרְשׁוּתוֹ:

כג) **וַיָּמָת מֶלֶךְ מִצְרַיִם.** נִצְטָרַע, וְהָיָה שׁוֹחֵט תִּינוֹקוֹת יִשְׂרָאֵל וְרוֹחֵץ בְּדָמָם:

כד) **נַאֲקָתָם.** צַעֲקָתָם, וְכֵן: "מֵעִיר מְתִים יִנְאָקוּ" (איוב כד, יב): **אֶת־בְּרִיתוֹ אֶת־אַבְרָהָם.** עִם אַבְרָהָם:

כה) **וַיֵּדַע אֱלֹהִים.** נָתַן עֲלֵיהֶם לֵב וְלֹא הֶעְלִים עֵינָיו:

פרק ג

א) **אַחַר הַמִּדְבָּר.** לְהִתְרַחֵק מִן הַגֶּזֶל שֶׁלֹּא יִרְעוּ בִּשְׂדוֹת אֲחֵרִים: **אֶל־הַר הָאֱלֹהִים.** עַל שֵׁם הֶעָתִיד:

ב) **בְּלַבַּת אֵשׁ.** בְּשַׁלְהֶבֶת אֵשׁ, לִבּוֹ שֶׁל אֵשׁ, כְּמוֹ: "לֵב הַשָּׁמַיִם" (דברים ד, יא), "בְּלֵב הָאֵלָה" (שמואל ב' יח, יד), וְאַל תִּתְמַהּ עַל הַתָּי"ו, יֵשׁ לָנוּ כַּיּוֹצֵא בּוֹ: "מָה אֲמֻלָה לִבָּתֵךְ" (יחזקאל טז, ל): **מִתּוֹךְ הַסְּנֶה.** וְלֹא אִילָן אַחֵר, מִשּׁוּם "עִמּוֹ אָנֹכִי בְצָרָה" (תהלים צא, טו): **אֻכָּל.** נֶאֱכָל, כְּמוֹ: "לֹא עֻבַּד בָּהּ" (דברים כא, ג), "אֲשֶׁר לֻקַּח מִשָּׁם" (בראשית ג, כג):

ג) **אָסֻרָה.** מִכָּאן לְהִתְקָרֵב שָׁם:

פרק ג | שמות

הַסְּנֶה וַיֹּאמֶר מֹשֶׁה מֹשֶׁה וַיֹּאמֶר הִנֵּנִי: וַיֹּאמֶר אַל־תִּקְרַב
הֲלֹם שַׁל־נְעָלֶיךָ מֵעַל רַגְלֶיךָ כִּי הַמָּקוֹם אֲשֶׁר אַתָּה עוֹמֵד עָלָיו
אַדְמַת־קֹדֶשׁ הוּא: וַיֹּאמֶר אָנֹכִי אֱלֹהֵי אָבִיךָ אֱלֹהֵי אַבְרָהָם
אֱלֹהֵי יִצְחָק וֵאלֹהֵי יַעֲקֹב וַיַּסְתֵּר מֹשֶׁה פָּנָיו כִּי יָרֵא מֵהַבִּיט
אֶל־הָאֱלֹהִים: וַיֹּאמֶר יְהוָֹה רָאֹה רָאִיתִי אֶת־עֳנִי עַמִּי אֲשֶׁר
בְּמִצְרָיִם וְאֶת־צַעֲקָתָם שָׁמַעְתִּי מִפְּנֵי נֹגְשָׂיו כִּי יָדַעְתִּי אֶת־
מַכְאֹבָיו: וָאֵרֵד לְהַצִּילוֹ ׀ מִיַּד מִצְרַיִם וּלְהַעֲלֹתוֹ מִן־הָאָרֶץ
הַהִוא אֶל־אֶרֶץ טוֹבָה וּרְחָבָה אֶל־אֶרֶץ זָבַת חָלָב וּדְבָשׁ
אֶל־מְקוֹם הַכְּנַעֲנִי וְהַחִתִּי וְהָאֱמֹרִי וְהַפְּרִזִּי וְהַחִוִּי וְהַיְבוּסִי:
וְעַתָּה הִנֵּה צַעֲקַת בְּנֵי־יִשְׂרָאֵל בָּאָה אֵלָי וְגַם־רָאִיתִי אֶת־
הַלַּחַץ אֲשֶׁר מִצְרַיִם לֹחֲצִים אֹתָם: וְעַתָּה לְכָה וְאֶשְׁלָחֲךָ אֶל־
פַּרְעֹה וְהוֹצֵא אֶת־עַמִּי בְנֵי־יִשְׂרָאֵל מִמִּצְרָיִם: וַיֹּאמֶר מֹשֶׁה
אֶל־הָאֱלֹהִים מִי אָנֹכִי כִּי אֵלֵךְ אֶל־פַּרְעֹה וְכִי אוֹצִיא אֶת־בְּנֵי
יִשְׂרָאֵל מִמִּצְרָיִם: וַיֹּאמֶר כִּי־אֶהְיֶה עִמָּךְ וְזֶה־לְּךָ הָאוֹת כִּי אָנֹכִי

ה. שַׁל. שְׁלֹף וְהוֹצֵא, כְּמוֹ: "וְנָשַׁל הַבַּרְזֶל" (דברים יט),
"כִּי יִשַּׁל זֵיתֶךָ" (דברים כח, מ): אַדְמַת קֹדֶשׁ הוּא.
הַמָּקוֹם:

י. וְעַתָּה לְכָה וְאֶשְׁלָחֲךָ אֶל פַּרְעֹה. וְאִם תֹּאמַר, מַה
תּוֹעִיל? "וְהוֹצֵא אֶת עַמִּי", יוֹעִילוּ דְּבָרֶיךָ וְתוֹצִיאֵם:

יא. מִי אָנֹכִי. מָה אֲנִי חָשׁוּב לְדַבֵּר עִם הַמְּלָכִים?
וְכִי אוֹצִיא אֶת בְּנֵי יִשְׂרָאֵל. וְאַף אִם חָשׁוּב אֲנִי, מַה
זָּכוּ יִשְׂרָאֵל שֶׁיֵּעָשֶׂה לָהֶם נֵס וְאוֹצִיאֵם מִמִּצְרַיִם?

יב. וַיֹּאמֶר כִּי אֶהְיֶה עִמָּךְ. הֲשִׁיבוֹ עַל רִאשׁוֹן רִאשׁוֹן
וְעַל אַחֲרוֹן אַחֲרוֹן. שֶׁאָמַרְתָּ "מִי אָנֹכִי כִּי אֵלֵךְ
אֶל פַּרְעֹה" - לֹא שֶׁלְּךָ הִיא כִּי אִם מִשֶּׁלִּי, "כִּי

אֶהְיֶה עִמָּךְ", "וְזֶה" הַמַּרְאֶה אֲשֶׁר רָאִיתָ בַּסְּנֶה,
"לְּךָ הָאוֹת כִּי אָנֹכִי שְׁלַחְתִּיךָ" וּכְדַאי אֲנִי לְהַצִּיל, כַּאֲשֶׁר רָאִיתָ הַסְּנֶה עוֹשֶׂה שְׁלִיחוּתִי וְאֵינֶנּוּ אֻכָּל, כָּךְ תֵּלֵךְ בִּשְׁלִיחוּתִי וְאֵינְךָ נִזּוֹק. וְשֶׁשָּׁאַלְתָּ: מַה זְּכוּת יֵשׁ לְיִשְׂרָאֵל שֶׁיֵּצְאוּ מִמִּצְרָיִם? דָּבָר גָּדוֹל יֵשׁ לִי עַל הוֹצָאָה זוֹ, שֶׁהֲרֵי עֲתִידִים לְקַבֵּל הַתּוֹרָה עַל הָהָר הַזֶּה לְסוֹף שְׁלֹשָׁה חֳדָשִׁים. דָּבָר אַחֵר, "כִּי אֶהְיֶה עִמָּךְ", "וְזֶה" שֶׁתַּצְלִיחַ בִּשְׁלִיחוּתְךָ, "לְּךָ הָאוֹת" עַל הַבְטָחָה אַחֶרֶת שֶׁאֲנִי מַבְטִיחֲךָ, שֶׁכְּשֶׁתּוֹצִיאֵם מִמִּצְרַיִם תַּעַבְדוּן אוֹתִי עַל הָהָר הַזֶּה, שֶׁתְּקַבְּלוּ הַתּוֹרָה עָלָיו, וְהִיא הַזְּכוּת הָעוֹמֶדֶת לְיִשְׂרָאֵל. וְדֻגְמַת לָשׁוֹן זֶה מָצִינוּ בִּישַׁעְיָה (לז, ל): "וְזֶה לְּךָ הָאוֹת

שמות | פרק ג

שְׁלַחְתִּ֔יךָ בְּהוֹצִֽיאֲךָ֤ אֶת־הָעָם֙ מִמִּצְרַ֔יִם תַּֽעַבְדוּן֙ אֶת־הָ֣אֱלֹהִ֔ים
עַ֖ל הָהָ֥ר הַזֶּֽה׃ יג וַיֹּ֨אמֶר מֹשֶׁ֜ה אֶל־הָֽאֱלֹהִ֗ים הִנֵּ֨ה אָֽנֹכִ֣י בָא֮ אֶל־
בְּנֵ֣י יִשְׂרָאֵל֒ וְאָֽמַרְתִּ֣י לָהֶ֔ם אֱלֹהֵ֥י אֲבֽוֹתֵיכֶ֖ם שְׁלָחַ֣נִי אֲלֵיכֶ֑ם
וְאָֽמְרוּ־לִ֣י מַה־שְּׁמ֔וֹ מָ֥ה אֹמַ֖ר אֲלֵהֶֽם׃ יד וַיֹּ֤אמֶר אֱלֹהִים֙ אֶל־מֹשֶׁ֔ה
אֶֽהְיֶ֖ה אֲשֶׁ֣ר אֶֽהְיֶ֑ה וַיֹּ֗אמֶר כֹּ֤ה תֹאמַר֙ לִבְנֵ֣י יִשְׂרָאֵ֔ל אֶֽהְיֶ֖ה שְׁלָחַ֥נִי
אֲלֵיכֶֽם׃ טו וַיֹּאמֶר֩ ע֨וֹד אֱלֹהִ֜ים אֶל־מֹשֶׁ֗ה כֹּֽה־תֹאמַר֮ אֶל־בְּנֵ֣י
יִשְׂרָאֵל֒ יְהֹוָ֞ה אֱלֹהֵ֣י אֲבֹֽתֵיכֶ֗ם אֱלֹהֵ֨י אַבְרָהָ֜ם אֱלֹהֵ֥י יִצְחָ֛ק וֵֽאלֹהֵ֥י

חמישי

יַֽעֲקֹ֖ב שְׁלָחַ֣נִי אֲלֵיכֶ֑ם זֶה־שְּׁמִ֣י לְעֹלָ֔ם וְזֶ֥ה זִכְרִ֖י לְדֹ֥ר דֹּֽר׃ טז לֵ֣ךְ
וְאָֽסַפְתָּ֞ אֶת־זִקְנֵ֣י יִשְׂרָאֵ֗ל וְאָֽמַרְתָּ֤ אֲלֵהֶם֙ יְהֹוָ֞ה אֱלֹהֵ֤י אֲבֹֽתֵיכֶם֙
נִרְאָ֣ה אֵלַ֔י אֱלֹהֵ֧י אַבְרָהָ֛ם יִצְחָ֥ק וְיַֽעֲקֹ֖ב לֵאמֹ֑ר פָּקֹ֤ד פָּקַ֨דְתִּי֙
אֶתְכֶ֔ם וְאֶת־הֶֽעָשׂ֥וּי לָכֶ֖ם בְּמִצְרָֽיִם׃ יז וָֽאֹמַ֗ר אַֽעֲלֶ֣ה אֶתְכֶם֮ מֵֽעֳנִ֣י
מִצְרַ֒יִם֒ אֶל־אֶ֤רֶץ הַֽכְּנַֽעֲנִי֙ וְהַ֣חִתִּ֔י וְהָֽאֱמֹרִי֙ וְהַפְּרִזִּ֔י וְהַֽחִוִּ֖י וְהַיְבוּסִ֑י
אֶל־אֶ֛רֶץ זָבַ֥ת חָלָ֖ב וּדְבָֽשׁ׃ יח וְשָֽׁמְע֖וּ לְקֹלֶ֑ךָ וּבָאתָ֡ אַתָּה֩ וְזִקְנֵ֨י
יִשְׂרָאֵ֜ל אֶל־מֶ֣לֶךְ מִצְרַ֗יִם וַֽאֲמַרְתֶּ֤ם אֵלָיו֙ יְהֹוָ֞ה אֱלֹהֵ֤י הָֽעִבְרִיִּים֙
נִקְרָ֣ה עָלֵ֔ינוּ וְעַתָּ֗ה נֵֽלְכָה־נָּ֞א דֶּ֣רֶךְ שְׁלֹ֤שֶׁת יָמִים֙ בַּמִּדְבָּ֔ר וְנִזְבְּחָה֙

אֲכוֹל הַשָּׁנָה סָפִיחַ" וְגוֹ', "מַפֶּלֶת סַנְחֵרִיב תִּהְיֶה לְךָ אוֹת עַל הַבְטָחָה אַחֶרֶת, שֶׁאַרְצְכֶם חֲרֵבָה מִפֵּרוֹת וַאֲנִי אֲבָרֵךְ הַסְּפִיחִים:

יד-טו **אֶֽהְיֶה אֲשֶׁר אֶֽהְיֶה.** "אֶֽהְיֶה" עִמָּם בַּצָּרָה זוֹ, "אֲשֶׁר אֶֽהְיֶה" עִמָּם בְּשִׁעְבּוּד שְׁאָר מַלְכֻיּוֹת. אָמַר לְפָנָיו: רִבּוֹנוֹ שֶׁל עוֹלָם, מָה אֲנִי מַזְכִּיר לָהֶם צָרָה אַחֶרֶת? דַּיָּם בְּצָרָה זוֹ! אָמַר לוֹ: יָפֶה אָמַרְתָּ, "כֹּה תֹאמַר" וְגוֹ': **זֶה שְּׁמִי לְעֹלָם.** חָסֵר וָי"ו, לוֹמַר הַעֲלִימֵהוּ שֶׁלֹּא יִקָּרֵא כִּכְתָבוֹ: **וְזֶה זִכְרִי.** לִמְּדוֹ הֵיאַךְ נִקְרָא, וְכֵן דָּוִד הוּא אוֹמֵר: "ה' שִׁמְךָ לְעוֹלָם ה' זִכְרְךָ לְדֹר וָדֹר" (תהלים קלה, יג):

טז] **אֶת זִקְנֵי יִשְׂרָאֵל.** מְיֻחָדִים לִישִׁיבָה. וְאִם תֹּאמַר זְקֵנִים סְתָם, הֵיאַךְ אֶפְשָׁר לוֹ לֶאֱסֹף זְקֵנִים שֶׁל שִׁשִּׁים רִבּוֹא?

יח] **וְשָֽׁמְעוּ לְקֹלֶךָ.** מִכֵּיוָן שֶׁתֹּאמַר לָהֶם לָשׁוֹן זֶה יִשְׁמְעוּ לְקוֹלֶךָ, שֶׁכְּבָר סִימָן זֶה מָסוּר בְּיָדָם מִיַּעֲקֹב וּמִיּוֹסֵף שֶׁבַּלָּשׁוֹן זֶה הֵם נִגְאָלִים. יַעֲקֹב אָמַר לָהֶם: "וֵֽאלֹהִים פָּקֹד יִפְקֹד אֶתְכֶם" (בראשית נ, כד), יוֹסֵף אָמַר לָהֶם: "פָּקֹד יִפְקֹד אֱלֹהִים אֶתְכֶם" (שם פסוק כה): **נִקְרָה עָלֵינוּ.** לְשׁוֹן מִקְרֶה, וְכֵן: "וַיִּקָּר אֱלֹהִים" (במדבר כג, ד), "וְאָנֹכִי אִקָּרֶה כֹּה" (שם פסוק טו) – אֱהֵא נִקְרֶה מֵאִתּוֹ הֲלֹם:

פרק ג | שמות

לַֽיהוָ֖ה אֱלֹהֵֽינוּ: וַאֲנִ֣י יָדַ֔עְתִּי כִּ֠י לֹֽא־יִתֵּ֥ן אֶתְכֶ֛ם מֶ֥לֶךְ מִצְרַ֖יִם יט
לַהֲלֹ֑ךְ וְלֹ֖א בְּיָ֥ד חֲזָקָֽה: וְשָׁלַחְתִּ֤י אֶת־יָדִי֙ וְהִכֵּיתִ֣י אֶת־מִצְרַ֔יִם כ
בְּכֹל֙ נִפְלְאֹתַ֔י אֲשֶׁ֥ר אֶֽעֱשֶׂ֖ה בְּקִרְבּ֑וֹ וְאַחֲרֵי־כֵ֖ן יְשַׁלַּ֥ח אֶתְכֶֽם:
וְנָתַתִּ֛י אֶת־חֵ֥ן הָֽעָם־הַזֶּ֖ה בְּעֵינֵ֣י מִצְרָ֑יִם וְהָיָה֙ כִּ֣י תֵֽלֵכ֔וּן לֹ֥א כא
תֵלְכ֖וּ רֵיקָֽם: וְשָׁאֲלָ֨ה אִשָּׁ֤ה מִשְּׁכֶנְתָּהּ֙ וּמִגָּרַ֣ת בֵּיתָ֔הּ כְּלֵי־כֶ֛סֶף כב
וּכְלֵ֥י זָהָ֖ב וּשְׂמָלֹ֑ת וְשַׂמְתֶּ֗ם עַל־בְּנֵיכֶם֙ וְעַל־בְּנֹ֣תֵיכֶ֔ם וְנִצַּלְתֶּ֖ם
אֶת־מִצְרָֽיִם: וַיַּ֤עַן מֹשֶׁה֙ וַיֹּ֔אמֶר וְהֵן֙ לֹֽא־יַֽאֲמִ֣ינוּ לִ֔י וְלֹ֥א יִשְׁמְע֖וּ א ד
בְּקֹלִ֑י כִּ֣י יֹֽאמְר֔וּ לֹֽא־נִרְאָ֥ה אֵלֶ֖יךָ יְהוָֽה: וַיֹּ֧אמֶר אֵלָ֛יו יְהוָ֖ה מַזֶּ֣ה ב
בְיָדֶ֑ךָ וַיֹּ֖אמֶר מַטֶּֽה: וַיֹּ֨אמֶר֙ הַשְׁלִיכֵ֣הוּ אַ֔רְצָה וַיַּשְׁלִכֵ֥הוּ אַ֖רְצָה ג
וַיְהִ֣י לְנָחָ֑שׁ וַיָּ֥נָס מֹשֶׁ֖ה מִפָּנָֽיו: וַיֹּ֤אמֶר יְהוָה֙ אֶל־מֹשֶׁ֔ה שְׁלַח֙ ד

מַה־זֶּה

יט **לֹא יִתֵּן אֶתְכֶם מֶלֶךְ מִצְרַיִם לַהֲלֹךְ.** חָס חֵין חֲנִי מַרְאֶה לוֹ יְדֵי הַחֲזָקָה, כְּלוֹמַר, כָּל עוֹד שֶׁאֵין חֲנִי מוֹדִיעוֹ יְדֵי הַחֲזָקָה לֹא יִתֵּן אֶתְכֶם לַהֲלֹךְ: **לֹא יִתֵּן.** לֹא יַשְׁבּוֹק, כְּמוֹ: "עַל כֵּן לֹא נְתַתִּיךָ" (בראשית כ, ו), "וְלֹא נְתָנוֹ אֱלֹהִים לְהָרַע עִמָּדִי" (סם לא, ז). וְכֻלָּן לְשׁוֹן נְתִינָה הֵם. וְיֵשׁ מְפָרְשִׁים, "וְלֹא בְּיָד חֲזָקָה", וְלֹא בִּשְׁבִיל שֶׁיָּדוֹ חֲזָקָה, כִּי מֵאָז אֶשְׁלַח אֶת יָדִי "וְהִכֵּיתִי אֶת מִצְרַיִם" (פסוק כ), וְגוֹ'. וּמְתַרְגְּמִין אוֹתוֹ: "וְלָא מִן קֳדָם דְּחֵילֵיהּ תַּקִּיף". מִשְּׁמוֹ שֶׁל רַבִּי יַעֲקֹב בְּרַבִּי מְנַחֵם נֶאֱמַר לִי:

כב **וּמִגָּרַת בֵּיתָהּ.** מֵאוֹתָהּ שֶׁהִיא גָּרָה אִתָּהּ בַּבַּיִת: **וְנִצַּלְתֶּם.** כְּתַרְגּוּמוֹ: "וּתְרוֹקְנוּן", וְכֵן: "וַיְנַצְּלוּ אֶת מִצְרַיִם" (להלן יב, לו), "וַיִּתְנַצְּלוּ בְנֵי יִשְׂרָאֵל אֶת עֶדְיָם" (להלן לג, ו), וְהַנּוּ״ן בּוֹ יְסוֹד. וּמְנַחֵם חִבְּרוֹ בְּמַחְבֶּרֶת עִם "עַם" (בראשית לא, ט), "אֲשֶׁר הִצִּיל אֱלֹהִים מֵאָבִינוּ" (סם טז), וְלֹא יַאֲמִינוּ דְּבָרָיו, כִּי אִם לֹא הָיְתָה הַנּוּ״ן יְסוֹד וְהִיא נְקוּדָה בְּחִירִיק, לֹא תְּהֵא מְשַׁמֶּשֶׁת בִּלְשׁוֹן וּפְעַלְתֶּם אֶלָּא בִּלְשׁוֹן וְנִפְעַלְתֶּם, כְּמוֹ: "וְנִסַּחְתֶּם מֵעַל הָאֲדָמָה" (דברים כח, סג), "וְנִתַּתֶּם בְּיַד אוֹיֵב" (ויקרא כו, כה), "וְנִגַּפְתֶּם לִפְנֵי אוֹיְבֵיכֶם" (סם פסוק יז), "וְנִתַּתֶּם בְּתוֹכָהּ" (יחזקאל

כב, כח), "וַחֲמַרְתֶּם עֲגָלָנוּ" (ירמיה ז, י), לְשׁוֹן נִתְפַּעֵלְנוּ. וְכָל נוּ"ן שֶׁהִיא בָּאָה בַּתֵּבָה לִפְרָקִים וְנוֹפֶלֶת מִמֶּנָּה, כְּנוּ"ן שֶׁל נוֹגֵף, נוֹשֵׂא, נוֹתֵן, נוֹשֵׁךְ, כְּשֶׁהִיא מְדַבֶּרֶת לְשׁוֹן וּפְעַלְתֶּם תִּנָּקֵד בְּשָׁבָא בַּחֲטָף, כְּגוֹן: "וּנְשָׂאתֶם אֶת אֲבִיכֶם" (בראשית מה, יט), "וּנְתַתֶּם לָהֶם אֶת אֶרֶץ הַגִּלְעָד" (במדבר לב, כט), "וּנְמַלְתֶּם אֵת בְּשַׂר עָרְלַתְכֶם" (בראשית יז, יא). לְכָךְ חֲנִי אוֹמֵר שֶׁזֹּאת הַנְּקוּדָה בְּחִירִיק, מִן הַיְסוֹד הִיא, וִיסוֹד שֵׁם דָּבָר "נִצּוּל", וְהוּא מִן הַלְּשׁוֹנוֹת הַכְּבֵדִים, כְּמוֹ דִּבּוּר, כִּפּוּר, לִמּוּד, כְּשֶׁיְּדַבֵּר בִּלְשׁוֹן וּפְעַלְתֶּם יִנָּקֵד בְּחִירִיק, כְּמוֹ: "וְדִבַּרְתֶּם אֶל הַסֶּלַע" (במדבר כ, ח), "וְכִפַּרְתֶּם אֶת הַבַּיִת" (יחזקאל מה, כ), "וְלִמַּדְתֶּם אֹתָם אֶת בְּנֵיכֶם" (דברים יא, יט):

פרק ד

ב **מַזֶּה בְיָדֶךָ.** לְכָךְ נִכְתַּב תֵּבָה אַחַת, לִדְרֹשׁ: מִזֶּה שֶׁבְּיָדְךָ אַתָּה חַיָּב לִלְקוֹת, שֶׁחֲשַׁדְתָּ בִּכְשֵׁרִים. וּפְשׁוּטוֹ, כְּאָדָם שֶׁאוֹמֵר לַחֲבֵרוֹ: מוֹדֶה אַתָּה שֶׁזּוֹ שֶׁלְּפָנֶיךָ אֶבֶן הִיא? אָמַר לוֹ: הֵן. אָמַר לוֹ: הֲרֵינִי עוֹשֶׂה אוֹתָהּ עֵץ:

ג **וַיְהִי לְנָחָשׁ.** רָמַז לוֹ שֶׁסִּפֵּר לָשׁוֹן הָרַע עַל יִשְׂרָאֵל וְתָפַשׂ אֻמָּנוּתוֹ שֶׁל נָחָשׁ:

שמות | פרק ד

ה יָדְךָ֥ וֶֽאֱחֹ֖ז בִּזְנָב֑וֹ וַיִּשְׁלַ֤ח יָדוֹ֙ וַיַּ֣חֲזֶק־בּ֔וֹ וַיְהִ֥י לְמַטֶּ֖ה בְּכַפּֽוֹ: לְמַ֣עַן יַאֲמִ֔ינוּ כִּֽי־נִרְאָ֥ה אֵלֶ֛יךָ יְהֹוָ֖ה אֱלֹהֵ֣י אֲבֹתָ֑ם אֱלֹהֵ֧י אַבְרָהָ֛ם
ו אֱלֹהֵ֥י יִצְחָ֖ק וֵאלֹהֵ֥י יַעֲקֹֽב: וַיֹּאמֶר֩ יְהֹוָ֨ה ל֜וֹ ע֗וֹד הָֽבֵא־נָ֤א יָֽדְךָ֙ בְּחֵיקֶ֔ךָ וַיָּבֵ֥א יָד֖וֹ בְּחֵיק֑וֹ וַיּ֣וֹצִאָ֔הּ וְהִנֵּ֥ה יָד֖וֹ מְצֹרַ֥עַת כַּשָּֽׁלֶג:
ז וַיֹּ֗אמֶר הָשֵׁ֤ב יָֽדְךָ֙ אֶל־חֵיקֶ֔ךָ וַיָּ֥שֶׁב יָד֖וֹ אֶל־חֵיק֑וֹ וַיּֽוֹצִאָהּ֙ מֵֽחֵיק֔וֹ
ח וְהִנֵּה־שָׁ֖בָה כִּבְשָׂרֽוֹ: וְהָיָה֙ אִם־לֹ֣א יַאֲמִ֣ינוּ לָ֔ךְ וְלֹ֣א יִשְׁמְע֔וּ לְקֹ֖ל
ט הָאֹ֣ת הָרִאשׁ֑וֹן וְהֶֽאֱמִ֔ינוּ לְקֹ֖ל הָאֹ֥ת הָאַחֲרֽוֹן: וְהָיָ֡ה אִם־לֹ֣א יַאֲמִ֡ינוּ גַּם֩ לִשְׁנֵ֨י הָאֹת֜וֹת הָאֵ֗לֶּה וְלֹ֤א יִשְׁמְעוּן֙ לְקֹלֶ֔ךָ וְלָקַחְתָּ֙ מִמֵּימֵ֣י הַיְאֹ֔ר וְשָׁפַכְתָּ֖ הַיַּבָּשָׁ֑ה וְהָי֤וּ הַמַּ֨יִם֙ אֲשֶׁ֣ר תִּקַּ֣ח מִן־הַיְאֹ֔ר
י וְהָי֥וּ לְדָ֖ם בַּיַּבָּֽשֶׁת: וַיֹּ֨אמֶר מֹשֶׁ֣ה אֶל־יְהֹוָה֮ בִּ֣י אֲדֹנָי֒ לֹא֩ אִ֨ישׁ דְּבָרִ֜ים אָנֹ֗כִי גַּ֤ם מִתְּמוֹל֙ גַּ֣ם מִשִּׁלְשֹׁ֔ם גַּ֛ם מֵאָ֥ז דַּבֶּרְךָ֖ אֶל־עַבְדֶּ֑ךָ

ד | וַיַּחֲזֶק בּוֹ. לְשׁוֹן אֲחִיזָה הוּא, וְהַרְבֵּה יֵשׁ בַּמִּקְרָא: "וַיַּחֲזִיקוּ הָאֲנָשִׁים בְּיָדוֹ" (בראשית יט, טז), "וְהֶחֱזִיקָה בִּמְבֻשָׁיו" (דברים כה, יא), "וְהֶחֱזַקְתִּי בִּזְקָנוֹ" (שמואל א' יז, לה), כָּל לְשׁוֹן חִזּוּק הַדָּבוּק לְבֵי"ת לְשׁוֹן אֲחִיזָה הוּא:

ו | מְצֹרַעַת כַּשָּׁלֶג. דֶּרֶךְ צָרַעַת לִהְיוֹת לְבָנָה, "אִם בַּהֶרֶת לְבָנָה הִוא" (ויקרא יג, ד). אַף בְּאוֹת זֶה רָמַז לוֹ שֶׁלָּשׁוֹן הָרַע סִפֵּר בְּאָמְרוֹ: "לֹא יַאֲמִינוּ לִי" (לעיל פסוק א), לְפִיכָךְ הִלְקָהוּ בְּצָרַעַת, כְּמוֹ שֶׁלָּקְתָה מִרְיָם עַל לָשׁוֹן הָרַע:

ז | וַיּוֹצִאָהּ מֵחֵיקוֹ וְהִנֵּה שָׁבָה כִּבְשָׂרוֹ. מִכָּאן שֶׁמִּדָּה טוֹבָה מְמַהֶרֶת לָבוֹא מִמִּדַּת פֻּרְעָנוּת, שֶׁהֲרֵי בָּרִאשׁוֹנָה לֹא נֶאֱמַר 'מֵחֵיקוֹ':

ח | וְהֶאֱמִינוּ לְקֹל הָאֹת הָאַחֲרוֹן. מִשֶּׁתֹּאמַר לָהֶם: בִּשְׁבִילְכֶם לָקִיתִי עַל שֶׁסִּפַּרְתִּי עֲלֵיכֶם לָשׁוֹן הָרַע, יַאֲמִינוּ לָךְ, שֶׁכְּבָר לָמְדוּ בְכָךְ שֶׁהַמְזַוּוֹגִים לָהֶם לוֹקִים בִּנְגָעִים, כְּגוֹן פַּרְעֹה וַאֲבִימֶלֶךְ בִּשְׁבִיל שָׂרָה:

ט | וְהָיוּ הַמַּיִם וְגוֹ׳. וְהָיוּ וְהָיוּ, שְׁתֵּי פְעָמִים. נִרְאֶה בְעֵינַי, אִלּוּ נֶאֱמַר: 'וְהָיוּ הַמַּיִם אֲשֶׁר תִּקַּח מִן הַיְאֹר לְדָם בַּיַּבָּשֶׁת' שׁוֹמֵעַ אֲנִי שֶׁבְּיָדוֹ הֵם נֶהְפָּכִים לְדָם, וְאַף כְּשֶׁיַּגִּיעוּ לָאָרֶץ יִהְיוּ בַּהֲוָיָתָן, אֲבָל עַכְשָׁיו מְלַמְּדֵנוּ שֶׁלֹּא יִהְיוּ דָם עַד שֶׁיִּהְיוּ בַּיַּבָּשֶׁת:

י | גַּם מִתְּמוֹל וְגוֹ׳. לָמַדְנוּ שֶׁשִּׁבְעַת יָמִים הָיָה הַקָּדוֹשׁ בָּרוּךְ הוּא מְפַתֶּה אֶת מֹשֶׁה בַּסְּנֶה לֵילֵךְ בִּשְׁלִיחוּתוֹ: מִתְּמוֹל, שִׁלְשׁוֹם, גַּם שִׁלְשׁוֹם – הֲרֵי שְׁלֹשָׁה, וּגְשָׁם גְּמִין רִבּוּיִין הֵם הֲרֵי שִׁשָּׁה, וְהוּא הָיָה עוֹמֵד בַּיּוֹם הַשְּׁבִיעִי כְּשֶׁאָמַר לוֹ זֹאת, עַד "שְׁלַח נָא בְּיַד תִּשְׁלָח" (להלן פסוק יג), עַד שֶׁחָרָה בּוֹ וְקִבֵּל עָלָיו. וְכָל זֶה, שֶׁלֹּא הָיָה רוֹצֶה לִטֹּל גְּדֻלָּה עַל אַהֲרֹן אָחִיו שֶׁהָיָה גָּדוֹל הֵימֶנּוּ, וְנָבִיא הָיָה, שֶׁנֶּאֱמַר: "הֲנִגְלֹה נִגְלֵיתִי אֶל בֵּית אָבִיךָ בִּהְיוֹתָם בְּמִצְרַיִם" (שמואל א' ב, כז), הוּא אַהֲרֹן. וְכֵן בִּיחֶזְקֵאל: "וָאִוָּדַע לָהֶם בְּאֶרֶץ מִצְרַיִם וְגוֹ׳ וָאֹמַר אֲלֵהֶם אִישׁ שִׁקּוּצֵי עֵינָיו הַשְׁלִיכוּ" (יחזקאל כ, ה־ז), וְאוֹתָהּ

שמות | פרק ד

יא כִּי כְבַד־פֶּה וּכְבַד לָשׁוֹן אָנֹכִי: וַיֹּאמֶר יהוה אֵלָיו מִי שָׂם פֶּה לָאָדָם אוֹ מִי־יָשׂוּם אִלֵּם אוֹ חֵרֵשׁ אוֹ פִקֵּחַ אוֹ עִוֵּר הֲלֹא אָנֹכִי יהוה: וְעַתָּה לֵךְ וְאָנֹכִי אֶהְיֶה עִם־פִּיךָ וְהוֹרֵיתִיךָ אֲשֶׁר תְּדַבֵּר:
יג וַיֹּאמֶר בִּי אֲדֹנָי שְׁלַח־נָא בְּיַד־תִּשְׁלָח: וַיִּחַר־אַף יהוה בְּמֹשֶׁה וַיֹּאמֶר הֲלֹא אַהֲרֹן אָחִיךָ הַלֵּוִי יָדַעְתִּי כִּי־דַבֵּר יְדַבֵּר הוּא וְגַם הִנֵּה־הוּא יֹצֵא לִקְרָאתֶךָ וְרָאֲךָ וְשָׂמַח בְּלִבּוֹ: וְדִבַּרְתָּ אֵלָיו וְשַׂמְתָּ אֶת־הַדְּבָרִים בְּפִיו וְאָנֹכִי אֶהְיֶה עִם־פִּיךָ וְעִם־פִּיהוּ וְהוֹרֵיתִי אֶתְכֶם אֵת אֲשֶׁר תַּעֲשׂוּן: וְדִבֶּר־הוּא לְךָ אֶל־הָעָם וְהָיָה הוּא יִהְיֶה־לְּךָ לְפֶה וְאַתָּה תִּהְיֶה־לּוֹ לֵאלֹהִים: וְאֶת־הַמַּטֶּה הַזֶּה תִּקַּח בְּיָדֶךָ אֲשֶׁר תַּעֲשֶׂה־בּוֹ אֶת־הָאֹתֹת:

ששי יח וַיֵּלֶךְ מֹשֶׁה וַיָּשָׁב ׀ אֶל־יֶתֶר חֹתְנוֹ וַיֹּאמֶר לוֹ אֵלְכָה נָּא וְאָשׁוּבָה אֶל־אַחַי אֲשֶׁר־בְּמִצְרַיִם וְאֶרְאֶה הַעוֹדָם חַיִּים וַיֹּאמֶר

נְבוּאָה לְאַהֲרֹן נֶאֶמְרָה: **כְּבַד פֶּה.** בִּכְבֵדוּת אֲנִי מְדַבֵּר, וּבִלְשׁוֹן לַעַז בלב״ש:

יא **מִי שָׂם פֶּה וְגוֹ׳.** מִי לִמֶּדְךָ לְדַבֵּר כְּשֶׁהָיִיתָ נִדּוֹן לִפְנֵי פַרְעֹה עַל הַמִּצְרִי?: **אוֹ מִי יָשׂוּם אִלֵּם.** מִי עָשָׂה פַּרְעֹה אִלֵּם שֶׁלֹּא נִתְאַמֵּץ בְּמִצְוַת הֲרִיגָתֶךָ, וְאֶת מְשָׁרְתָיו חֵרְשִׁים שֶׁלֹּא שָׁמְעוּ בְּצַוּוֹתוֹ עָלֶיךָ, וְלָאִסְפַּקְלָטוֹרִין הַהוֹרְגִים מִי עֲשָׂאָם עִוְרִים שֶׁלֹּא רָאוּ כְּשֶׁבָּרַחְתָּ מִן הַבִּימָה וְנִמְלַטְתָּ?: **הֲלֹא אָנֹכִי.** שֶׁשְּׁמִי ה׳, עָשִׂיתִי כָּל זֹאת:

יג **בְּיַד תִּשְׁלָח.** בְּיַד מִי שֶׁאַתָּה רָגִיל לִשְׁלֹחַ, וְהוּא אַהֲרֹן. דָּבָר אַחֵר, בְּיַד אַחֵר שֶׁתִּרְצֶה לִשְׁלֹחַ, שֶׁאֵין סוֹפִי לְהַכְנִיסָם לָאָרֶץ וְלִהְיוֹת גּוֹאֲלָם לֶעָתִיד, יֵשׁ לְךָ שְׁלוּחִים הַרְבֵּה:

יד **וַיִּחַר אַף.** רַבִּי יְהוֹשֻׁעַ בֶּן קָרְחָה אוֹמֵר: כָּל חָרוֹן אַף שֶׁבַּתּוֹרָה עוֹשֶׂה רשֶׁם, וְזֶה לֹא נֶאֱמַר בּוֹ רשֶׁם, וְלֹא מָצִינוּ שֶׁבָּא עֹנֶשׁ עַל יְדֵי אוֹתוֹ חָרוֹן. אָמַר לוֹ

רַבִּי יוֹסֵי: אַף בָּזוֹ נֶאֱמַר בּוֹ רשֶׁם: ״הֲלֹא אַהֲרֹן אָחִיךָ הַלֵּוִי״, שֶׁהָיָה עָתִיד לִהְיוֹת לֵוִי וְלֹא כֹהֵן, וְהַכְּהֻנָּה הָיִיתִי אוֹמֵר לָצֵאת מִמְּךָ, מֵעַתָּה לֹא יִהְיֶה כֵן, אֶלָּא הוּא יִהְיֶה כֹהֵן וְאַתָּה לֵוִי, שֶׁנֶּאֱמַר: ״וּמֹשֶׁה אִישׁ הָאֱלֹהִים בָּנָיו יִקָּרְאוּ עַל שֵׁבֶט הַלֵּוִי״ (דברי הימים א׳ כ״ג, י״ד): **הִנֵּה הוּא יֹצֵא לִקְרָאתֶךָ.** כְּשֶׁתֵּלֵךְ לְמִצְרַיִם: **וְרָאֲךָ וְשָׂמַח בְּלִבּוֹ.** לֹא כְּשֶׁאַתָּה סָבוּר שֶׁיְּהֵא מַקְפִּיד עָלֶיךָ שֶׁאַתָּה עוֹלֶה לִגְדֻלָּה. וּמִשָּׁם זָכָה אַהֲרֹן לַעֲדִי הַחֹשֶׁן הַנָּתוּן עַל הַלֵּב:

טו **וְדִבֶּר הוּא לְךָ.** בִּשְׁבִילְךָ יְדַבֵּר אֶל הָעָם. וְזֶה יוֹכִיחַ עַל כָּל לְךָ וְלִי וְלוֹ וְלָכֶם וְלָהֶם הַסְּמוּכִים לְדִבּוּר, שֶׁכֻּלָּם לְשׁוֹן עַל הֵם: **יִהְיֶה לְךָ לְפֶה.** לְמֵלִיץ, לְפִי שֶׁאַתָּה כְּבַד פֶּה: **לֵאלֹהִים.** לְרַב וּלְשַׂר:

יח **וַיָּשָׁב אֶל יֶתֶר חֹתְנוֹ.** לִטֹּל רְשׁוּת, שֶׁהֲרֵי נִשְׁבַּע לוֹ. וְשִׁבְעָה שֵׁמוֹת הָיוּ לוֹ: רְעוּאֵל, יֶתֶר, יִתְרוֹ, קֵינִי, חוֹבָב, חֶבֶר, פּוּטִיאֵל:

שמות | פרק ד

יט יִתְרוֹ לְמֹשֶׁה לֵךְ לְשָׁלוֹם: וַיֹּאמֶר יְהוָה אֶל־מֹשֶׁה בְּמִדְיָן לֵךְ
שֻׁב מִצְרָיִם כִּי־מֵתוּ כָּל־הָאֲנָשִׁים הַמְבַקְשִׁים אֶת־נַפְשֶׁךָ:
כ וַיִּקַּח מֹשֶׁה אֶת־אִשְׁתּוֹ וְאֶת־בָּנָיו וַיַּרְכִּבֵם עַל־הַחֲמֹר וַיָּשָׁב
כא אַרְצָה מִצְרָיִם וַיִּקַּח מֹשֶׁה אֶת־מַטֵּה הָאֱלֹהִים בְּיָדוֹ: וַיֹּאמֶר
יְהוָה אֶל־מֹשֶׁה בְּלֶכְתְּךָ לָשׁוּב מִצְרַיְמָה רְאֵה כָּל־הַמֹּפְתִים
אֲשֶׁר־שַׂמְתִּי בְיָדֶךָ וַעֲשִׂיתָם לִפְנֵי פַרְעֹה וַאֲנִי אֲחַזֵּק אֶת־לִבּוֹ
כב וְלֹא יְשַׁלַּח אֶת־הָעָם: וְאָמַרְתָּ אֶל־פַּרְעֹה כֹּה אָמַר יְהוָה בְּנִי
כג בְכֹרִי יִשְׂרָאֵל: וָאֹמַר אֵלֶיךָ שַׁלַּח אֶת־בְּנִי וְיַעַבְדֵנִי וַתְּמָאֵן
כד לְשַׁלְּחוֹ הִנֵּה אָנֹכִי הֹרֵג אֶת־בִּנְךָ בְּכֹרֶךָ: וַיְהִי בַדֶּרֶךְ בַּמָּלוֹן
כה וַיִּפְגְּשֵׁהוּ יְהוָה וַיְבַקֵּשׁ הֲמִיתוֹ: וַתִּקַּח צִפֹּרָה צֹר וַתִּכְרֹת אֶת־

יט **כִּי מֵתוּ כָּל הָאֲנָשִׁים**. מִי הֵם? דָּתָן וַאֲבִירָם;
חַיִּים הָיוּ, אֶלָּא שֶׁיָּרְדוּ מִנִּכְסֵיהֶם, וְהֶעָנִי חָשׁוּב כְּמֵת:

כ **עַל הַחֲמֹר**. חֲמוֹר הַמְיֻחָד. הוּא הַחֲמוֹר שֶׁחָבַשׁ
אַבְרָהָם לַעֲקֵדַת יִצְחָק, וְהוּא שֶׁעָתִיד מֶלֶךְ הַמָּשִׁיחַ
לְהִגָּלוֹת עָלָיו, שֶׁנֶּאֱמַר: "עָנִי וְרֹכֵב עַל חֲמוֹר" (זכריה
ט, ט): **וַיָּשָׁב אַרְצָה מִצְרַיִם וַיִּקַּח מֹשֶׁה אֶת מַטֵּה**. אֵין
מֻקְדָּם וּמְאֻחָר מְדֻקְדָּקִים בַּמִּקְרָא:

כא **בְּלֶכְתְּךָ לָשׁוּב מִצְרַיְמָה וְגוֹ'**. דַּע שֶׁעַל מְנָת כֵּן
תֵּלֵךְ, שֶׁתְּהֵא גִּבּוֹר בִּשְׁלִיחוּתִי לַעֲשׂוֹת כָּל מוֹפְתַי
לִפְנֵי פַרְעֹה וְלֹא תִירָא מִמֶּנּוּ: **אֲשֶׁר שַׂמְתִּי בְיָדֶךָ**. לֹא
עַל שְׁלֹשׁ אוֹתוֹת הָאֲמוּרוֹת לְמַעְלָה, שֶׁהֲרֵי לֹא לִפְנֵי
פַרְעֹה צִוָּה לַעֲשׂוֹתָם אֶלָּא לִפְנֵי יִשְׂרָאֵל שֶׁיַּאֲמִינוּ
לוֹ, וְלֹא מָצִינוּ שֶׁעֲשָׂאָם לְפָנָיו, אֶלָּא מוֹפְתִים שֶׁאֲנִי
עָתִיד לָשׂוּם בְּיָדְךָ בְּמִצְרַיִם, כְּמוֹ: "כִּי יְדַבֵּר אֲלֵכֶם
פַּרְעֹה וְגוֹ'" (להלן ז, ט), **וְאַל תִּתְמַהּ עַל אֲשֶׁר כָּתַב**:
"אֲשֶׁר שַׂמְתִּי", שֶׁכֵּן מַשְׁמָעוֹ: כְּשֶׁתְּדַבֵּר עִמּוֹ כְּבָר
שַׂמְתִּים בְּיָדֶךָ:

כב **וְאָמַרְתָּ אֶל פַּרְעֹה**. כְּשֶׁתִּשְׁמַע שֶׁלִּבּוֹ חָזָק וִימָאֵן
לְשַׁלֵּחַ אֱמֹר לוֹ כֵּן: **בְּנִי בְכֹרִי**. לְשׁוֹן גְּדֻלָּה, כְּמוֹ: "אַף

אָנִי בְּכוֹר אֶתְּנֵהוּ" (תהלים פט, כח) זֶהוּ פְּשׁוּטוֹ. וּמִדְרָשׁוֹ,
כָּאן חָתַם הַקָּדוֹשׁ בָּרוּךְ הוּא עַל מְכִירַת הַבְּכוֹרָה
שֶׁלָּקַח יַעֲקֹב מֵעֵשָׂו:

כג **וָאֹמַר אֵלֶיךָ**. בִּשְׁלִיחוּתוֹ שֶׁל מָקוֹם: "שַׁלַּח אֶת
בְּנִי": **הִנֵּה אָנֹכִי הֹרֵג וְגוֹ'**. הִיא מַכָּה אַחֲרוֹנָה, וּבָהּ
הִתְרָהוּ תְּחִלָּה מִפְּנֵי שֶׁהִיא קָשָׁה. וְזֶה הוּא שֶׁאָמַר
אִיּוֹב: "הֶן אֵל יַשְׂגִּיב בְּכֹחוֹ" (איוב לו, כב), לְפִיכָךְ "מִי
כָמוֹהוּ מוֹרֶה" – בָּשָׂר וָדָם הַמְבַקֵּשׁ לְהִנָּקֵם מֵחֲבֵרוֹ
מַעֲלִים אֶת דְּבָרָיו, שֶׁלֹּא יְבַקֵּשׁ הַצָּלָה. אֲבָל הַקָּדוֹשׁ
בָּרוּךְ הוּא יַשְׂגִּיב בְּכֹחוֹ וְאֵין יְכוֹלֶת לְהִמָּלֵט מִיָּדוֹ
כִּי אִם בְּשׁוּבוֹ אֵלָיו, לְפִיכָךְ הוּא מוֹרֵהוּ וּמַתְרֶה
בּוֹ לָשׁוּב:

כד **וַיְהִי** מֹשֶׁה **בַדֶּרֶךְ בַּמָּלוֹן**: **וַיְבַקֵּשׁ הֲמִיתוֹ**. לְפִי
שֶׁלֹּא מָל אֶת אֱלִיעֶזֶר בְּנוֹ, וְעַל שֶׁנִּתְרַשֵּׁל נֶעֱנַשׁ
מִיתָה. תַּנְיָא, אָמַר רַבִּי יוֹסֵי: חַס וְשָׁלוֹם, לֹא נִתְרַשֵּׁל,
אֶלָּא אָמַר: אָמוּל וְאֵצֵא לַדֶּרֶךְ – סַכָּנָה הִיא לַתִּינוֹק
עַד שְׁלֹשָׁה יָמִים! אָמוּל וְאֶשְׁהֶה שְׁלֹשָׁה יָמִים –
הַקָּדוֹשׁ בָּרוּךְ הוּא צִוַּנִי: "לֵךְ שֻׁב מִצְרָיִם"! וּמִפְּנֵי
מָה נֶעֱנַשׁ? לְפִי שֶׁנִּתְעַסֵּק בַּמָּלוֹן תְּחִלָּה. בְּמַסֶּכֶת
נְדָרִים (דף לא ע״ב). **וַתְּהִי הַמַּלְאָךְ נַעֲשָׂה כְּמִין נָחָשׁ**

עָרְלַת בְּנָהּ וַתַּגַּע לְרַגְלָיו וַתֹּאמֶר כִּי חֲתַן־דָּמִים אַתָּה לִי: וַיִּרֶף
מִמֶּנּוּ אָז אָמְרָה חֲתַן דָּמִים לַמּוּלֹת:
וַיֹּאמֶר יְהוָה אֶל־אַהֲרֹן לֵךְ לִקְרַאת מֹשֶׁה הַמִּדְבָּרָה וַיֵּלֶךְ
וַיִּפְגְּשֵׁהוּ בְּהַר הָאֱלֹהִים וַיִּשַּׁק־לוֹ: וַיַּגֵּד מֹשֶׁה לְאַהֲרֹן אֵת
כָּל־דִּבְרֵי יְהוָה אֲשֶׁר שְׁלָחוֹ וְאֵת כָּל־הָאֹתֹת אֲשֶׁר צִוָּהוּ: וַיֵּלֶךְ
מֹשֶׁה וְאַהֲרֹן וַיַּאַסְפוּ אֶת־כָּל־זִקְנֵי בְּנֵי יִשְׂרָאֵל: וַיְדַבֵּר אַהֲרֹן
אֵת כָּל־הַדְּבָרִים אֲשֶׁר־דִּבֶּר יְהוָה אֶל־מֹשֶׁה וַיַּעַשׂ הָאֹתֹת
לְעֵינֵי הָעָם: וַיַּאֲמֵן הָעָם וַיִּשְׁמְעוּ כִּי־פָקַד יְהוָה אֶת־בְּנֵי יִשְׂרָאֵל
וְכִי רָאָה אֶת־עָנְיָם וַיִּקְּדוּ וַיִּשְׁתַּחֲוּוּ: וְאַחַר בָּאוּ מֹשֶׁה וְאַהֲרֹן
וַיֹּאמְרוּ אֶל־פַּרְעֹה כֹּה־אָמַר יְהוָה אֱלֹהֵי יִשְׂרָאֵל שַׁלַּח אֶת־עַמִּי
וְיָחֹגּוּ לִי בַּמִּדְבָּר: וַיֹּאמֶר פַּרְעֹה מִי יְהוָה אֲשֶׁר אֶשְׁמַע בְּקֹלוֹ
לְשַׁלַּח אֶת־יִשְׂרָאֵל לֹא יָדַעְתִּי אֶת־יְהוָה וְגַם אֶת־יִשְׂרָאֵל
לֹא אֲשַׁלֵּחַ: וַיֹּאמְרוּ אֱלֹהֵי הָעִבְרִים נִקְרָא עָלֵינוּ נֵלֲכָה־נָּא
דֶּרֶךְ שְׁלֹשֶׁת יָמִים בַּמִּדְבָּר וְנִזְבְּחָה לַיהוָה אֱלֹהֵינוּ פֶּן־יִפְגָּעֵנוּ
בַּדֶּבֶר אוֹ בֶחָרֶב: וַיֹּאמֶר אֲלֵהֶם מֶלֶךְ מִצְרַיִם לָמָּה מֹשֶׁה וְאַהֲרֹן

וּבוּלְעוֹ מֵרֹאשׁוֹ וְעַד יְרֵכָיו וְחוֹזֵר וּבוּלְעוֹ מֵרַגְלָיו וְעַד
אוֹתוֹ מָקוֹם, הַבִּינָה עֲפוּרָה שֶׁבִּשְׁבִיל הַמִּילָה הוּא:

כה | וַתַּגַּע לְרַגְלָיו. הִשְׁלִיכַתּוּ לִפְנֵי רַגְלָיו שֶׁל מֹשֶׁה.
וַתֹּאמֶר. עַל בְּנָהּ: "כִּי חֲתַן דָּמִים אַתָּה לִי" – אַתָּה
הָיִיתָ גּוֹרֵם לִהְיוֹת הֶחָתָן שֶׁלִּי נִרְצָח עָלַי, הוֹרֵג
אִישִׁי אַתָּה לִי:

כו | וַיִּרֶף. הַמַּלְאָךְ "מִמֶּנּוּ", "אָז" הֵבִינָה שֶׁעַל הַמִּילָה
בָּא לְהָרְגוֹ, "אָמְרָה", חֲתַן דָּמִים לַמּוּלֹת" – חֲתָנִי
הָיָה נִרְצָח עַל דְּבַר הַמִּילָה: לַמּוּלֹת. עַל דְּבַר
הַמּוּלוֹת, שֵׁם דָּבָר הוּא, וְהַלָּמֶ"ד מְשַׁמֶּשֶׁת בִּלְשׁוֹן

'עַל', כְּמוֹ: "וַיֹּאמֶר פַּרְעֹה לִבְנֵי יִשְׂרָאֵל" (להלן יד, ג).
וְאוּנְקְלוֹס תִּרְגֵּם "דָּמִים", עַל דַּם הַמִּילָה:

פרק ה
א | וְאַחַר בָּאוּ מֹשֶׁה וְאַהֲרֹן וְגוֹ'. אֲבָל הַזְּקֵנִים נִשְׁמְטוּ
אֶחָד אֶחָד מֵאַחַר מֹשֶׁה וְאַהֲרֹן עַד שֶׁנִּשְׁמְטוּ כֻּלָּם
קֹדֶם שֶׁהִגִּיעוּ לַפַּלְטִין, לְפִי שֶׁיָּרְאוּ לָלֶכֶת. וּבְסִינַי
נִפְרַע לָהֶם: "וְנִגַּשׁ מֹשֶׁה לְבַדּוֹ וְהֵם לֹא יִגָּשׁוּ" (להלן
כד, ב), הֶחֱזִירָם לַאֲחוֹרֵיהֶם:

ג | פֶּן יִפְגָּעֵנוּ. פֶּן יִפְגָּעֲךָ הָיָה לָהֶם לוֹמַר, אֶלָּא
שֶׁחָלְקוּ כָּבוֹד לַמַּלְכוּת. פְּגִיעָה זוֹ לְשׁוֹן מִקְרֵה מָוֶת
הוּא:

שמות | פרק ה

ה תַּפְרִיעוּ אֶת־הָעָם מִמַּעֲשָׂיו לְכוּ לְסִבְלֹתֵיכֶם: וַיֹּאמֶר פַּרְעֹה
ו הֵן־רַבִּים עַתָּה עַם הָאָרֶץ וְהִשְׁבַּתֶּם אֹתָם מִסִּבְלֹתָם: וַיְצַו
פַּרְעֹה בַּיּוֹם הַהוּא אֶת־הַנֹּגְשִׂים בָּעָם וְאֶת־שֹׁטְרָיו לֵאמֹר:
ז לֹא תֹאסִפוּן לָתֵת תֶּבֶן לָעָם לִלְבֹּן הַלְּבֵנִים כִּתְמוֹל שִׁלְשֹׁם
ח הֵם יֵלְכוּ וְקֹשְׁשׁוּ לָהֶם תֶּבֶן: וְאֶת־מַתְכֹּנֶת הַלְּבֵנִים אֲשֶׁר הֵם
עֹשִׂים תְּמוֹל שִׁלְשֹׁם תָּשִׂימוּ עֲלֵיהֶם לֹא תִגְרְעוּ מִמֶּנּוּ כִּי־נִרְפִּים
ט הֵם עַל־כֵּן הֵם צֹעֲקִים לֵאמֹר נֵלְכָה נִזְבְּחָה לֵאלֹהֵינוּ: תִּכְבַּד
הָעֲבֹדָה עַל־הָאֲנָשִׁים וְיַעֲשׂוּ־בָהּ וְאַל־יִשְׁעוּ בְּדִבְרֵי־שָׁקֶר:

ד | **תַּפְרִיעוּ אֶת הָעָם מִמַּעֲשָׂיו.** תַּבְדִּילוּ וְתַרְחִיקוּ אוֹתָם מִמְּלַאכְתָּם, שֶׁשּׁוֹמְעִין לָכֶם וּסְבוּרִים לָנוּחַ מִן הַמְּלָאכָה. וְכֵן: "פְּרָעֵהוּ אַל תַּעֲבָר בּוֹ" (משלי ד, טו) — הַרְחִיקֵהוּ. וְכֵן: "וַתִּפְרְעוּ כָל עֲצָתִי" (שם ח, כה), "כִּי פָרֻעַ הוּא" (להלן לב, כה) — נִרְחָק וְנִתְעָב: **לְכוּ לְסִבְלֹתֵיכֶם.** לְכוּ לִמְלַאכְתְּכֶם שֶׁיֵּשׁ לָכֶם לַעֲשׂוֹת בְּבָתֵּיכֶם, אֲבָל מְלֶאכֶת שִׁעְבּוּד מִצְרַיִם לֹא הָיְתָה עַל שִׁבְטוֹ שֶׁל לֵוִי, וְתֵדַע לְךָ, שֶׁהֲרֵי מֹשֶׁה וְאַהֲרֹן יוֹצְאִים וּבָאִים:

ה | **הֵן רַבִּים עַתָּה עַם הָאָרֶץ.** שֶׁהָעֲבוֹדָה מֻטֶּלֶת עֲלֵיהֶם, וְאַתֶּם מַשְׁבִּיתִים אוֹתָם מִסִּבְלוֹתָם, הֶפְסֵד גָּדוֹל הוּא זֶה:

ו | **הַנֹּגְשִׂים.** מִצְרִיִּים הָיוּ וְהַשּׁוֹטְרִים הָיוּ יִשְׂרְאֵל, הַנּוֹגֵשׂ מְמֻנֶּה עַל כַּמָּה שׁוֹטְרִים, וְהַשּׁוֹטֵר מְמֻנֶּה לִרְדּוֹת בְּעוֹשֵׂי הַמְּלָאכָה:

ז | **תֶּבֶן.** אשטובל"א, הָיוּ גוֹבְלִין אוֹתוֹ עִם הַטִּיט: **לְבֵנִים.** טיוול"ש, שֶׁעוֹשִׂים מַטִּיט וּמְיַבְּשִׁין אוֹתָן בַּחַמָּה, וְיֵשׁ שֶׁשּׂוֹרְפִין אוֹתָן בַּכִּבְשָׁן: **כִּתְמוֹל שִׁלְשֹׁם.** כַּאֲשֶׁר הֱיִיתֶם עוֹשִׂים עַד הֵנָּה: **וְקֹשְׁשׁוּ.** וְלִקְטוּ:

ח | **וְאֶת מַתְכֹּנֶת הַלְּבֵנִים.** סְכוּם חֶשְׁבּוֹן הַלְּבֵנִים שֶׁהָיָה כָּל אֶחָד עוֹשֶׂה לַיּוֹם כְּשֶׁהָיָה הַתֶּבֶן נִתָּן לָהֶם, אוֹתוֹ סְכוּם "תָּשִׂימוּ עֲלֵיהֶם" גַּם עַתָּה, לְמַעַן תִּכְבַּד הָעֲבוֹדָה עֲלֵיהֶם: **כִּי נִרְפִּים הֵם.** מִן הָעֲבוֹדָה הֵם, לְכָךְ

לִבָּם פּוֹנֶה אֶל הַבַּטָּלָה וְצוֹעֲקִים לֵאמֹר "נֵלְכָה" וְגוֹ': **מַתְכֹּנֶת.** "וְתֹכֶן לְבֵנִים" (להלן פסוק יח), "וְלֹא נִתְכְּנוּ עֲלִלוֹת" (שמואל א' ב, ג), "וְאֵת הַכֶּסֶף הַמְתֻכָּן" (מלכים ב' יב, יב), כֻּלָּם לְשׁוֹן חֶשְׁבּוֹן הֵם: **נִרְפִּים.** הַמְּלָאכָה רְפוּיָה בְּיָדָם וַעֲזוּבָה מֵהֶם וְהֵם נִרְפִּים מִמֶּנָּה, רטריי"ש בְּלַעַז:

ט | **וְאַל יִשְׁעוּ בְּדִבְרֵי שָׁקֶר.** וְאַל יֶהְגּוּ וִידַבְּרוּ תָּמִיד בְּדִבְרֵי רוּחַ לֵאמֹר: "נֵלְכָה נִזְבְּחָה". וְדוֹמֶה לוֹ: "וְאֶשְׁעָה בְחֻקֶּיךָ תָמִיד" (תהלים קיט, קיז), "לְמָשָׁל וְלִשְׁנִינָה" (דברים כח, לז), "וּלְשׁוֹנֵעַ", "וַיְסַפֵּר" (להלן יח, ח) — "וָאֶשְׁתָּעֵי". וְאִי אֶפְשָׁר לוֹמַר "וַיִּשַׁע" — "וַיִּשַׁע ה' אֶל הֶבֶל... וְאֶל קַיִן וְאֶל מִנְחָתוֹ לֹא שָׁעָה" (בראשית ד, ד-ה), "וּלְאַדְמָה 'אַל יִשְׁעוּ'" — אַל יִפְנוּ, שֶׁאִם כֵּן כֵּן הָיָה לוֹ לִכְתֹּב: "וְאַל יִשְׁעוּ אֶל דִּבְרֵי שֶׁקֶר" אוֹ "לְדִבְרֵי שֶׁקֶר", כִּי כֵן גִּזְרַת כֻּלָּם: "יִשְׁעֶה הָאָדָם עַל עוֹשֵׂהוּ" (ישעיה יז, ז), "וְלֹא שָׁעוּ עַל קְדוֹשׁ יִשְׂרָאֵל" (שם לא, א), "וְלֹא יִשְׁעֶה אֶל הַמִּזְבְּחוֹת" (שם יז, ח), "וְלֹא מְצָאתִי שָׁמוּשׁ שֶׁל בֵּי"ת סְמוּכָה לַאֲחַרֵיהֶם. אֲבָל אַחַר לְשׁוֹן דִּבּוּר כְּמִתְעַסֵּק לְדַבֵּר בַּדָּבָר נוֹפֵל לְשׁוֹן שִׁמּוּשׁ בֵּי"ת, כְּגוֹן: "הַנִּדְבָּרִים בְּךָ" (יחזקאל לג, ל), "וַתְּדַבֵּר מִרְיָם וְאַהֲרֹן בְּמֹשֶׁה" (במדבר יב, א), "הַמַּלְאָךְ הַדֹּבֵר בִּי" (זכריה ד, א), "לְדַבֵּר בָּךְ" (דברים ו, ז), "וַאֲדַבְּרָה בְעֵדֹתֶיךָ" (תהלים קיט, מו). אַף כָּאן, "אַל יִשְׁעוּ בְּדִבְרֵי שָׁקֶר" — אַל יִהְיוּ נִדְבָּרִים בְּדִבְרֵי שָׁוְא וַהֲבַאי:

פרק ה

י וַיֵּצְאוּ נֹגְשֵׂי הָעָם וְשֹׁטְרָיו וַיֹּאמְרוּ אֶל־הָעָם לֵאמֹר כֹּה אָמַר
פַּרְעֹה אֵינֶנִּי נֹתֵן לָכֶם תֶּבֶן: יא אַתֶּם לְכוּ קְחוּ לָכֶם תֶּבֶן מֵאֲשֶׁר
תִּמְצָאוּ כִּי אֵין נִגְרָע מֵעֲבֹדַתְכֶם דָּבָר: יב וַיָּפֶץ הָעָם בְּכָל־אֶרֶץ
מִצְרָיִם לְקֹשֵׁשׁ קַשׁ לַתֶּבֶן: יג וְהַנֹּגְשִׂים אָצִים לֵאמֹר כַּלּוּ מַעֲשֵׂיכֶם
דְּבַר־יוֹם בְּיוֹמוֹ כַּאֲשֶׁר בִּהְיוֹת הַתֶּבֶן: יד וַיֻּכּוּ שֹׁטְרֵי בְּנֵי יִשְׂרָאֵל
אֲשֶׁר־שָׂמוּ עֲלֵהֶם נֹגְשֵׂי פַרְעֹה לֵאמֹר מַדּוּעַ לֹא כִלִּיתֶם חָקְכֶם
לִלְבֹּן כִּתְמוֹל שִׁלְשֹׁם גַּם־תְּמוֹל גַּם־הַיּוֹם: טו וַיָּבֹאוּ שֹׁטְרֵי בְּנֵי
יִשְׂרָאֵל וַיִּצְעֲקוּ אֶל־פַּרְעֹה לֵאמֹר לָמָּה תַעֲשֶׂה כֹה לַעֲבָדֶיךָ:
טז תֶּבֶן אֵין נִתָּן לַעֲבָדֶיךָ וּלְבֵנִים אֹמְרִים לָנוּ עֲשׂוּ וְהִנֵּה עֲבָדֶיךָ
מֻכִּים וְחָטָאת עַמֶּךָ: יז וַיֹּאמֶר נִרְפִּים אַתֶּם נִרְפִּים עַל־כֵּן אַתֶּם

יא **אַתֶּם לְכוּ קְחוּ לָכֶם תֶּבֶן.** וּצְרִיכִים אַתֶּם לֵילֵךְ
בִּזְרִיזוּת, "כִּי אֵין נִגְרָע" דָּבָר מִכָּל סְכוּם הַלְּבֵנִים
שֶׁהֱיִיתֶם עוֹשִׂים לְיוֹם בִּהְיוֹת הַתֶּבֶן נִתָּן לָכֶם מִזֻּמָּן
מִבֵּית הַמֶּלֶךְ:

יב **לְקֹשֵׁשׁ קַשׁ לַתֶּבֶן.** לֶאֱסֹף אֲסִיפָה, לִלְקֹט לֶקֶט
לְצֹרֶךְ תֶּבֶן הַטִּיט. **קַשׁ.** לְשׁוֹן לִקּוּט, עַל שֵׁם שֶׁדָּבָר
הַמִּתְפַּזֵּר הוּא וְצָרִיךְ לְקוֹשְׁשׁוֹ הוּא קָרוּי 'קַשׁ' בִּשְׁאָר
מְקוֹמוֹת:

יג **אָצִים.** דּוֹחֲקִים: **דְּבַר יוֹם בְּיוֹמוֹ.** חֶשְׁבּוֹן שֶׁל כָּל
יוֹם כַּלּוּ בְּיוֹמוֹ, כַּאֲשֶׁר עֲשִׂיתֶם בִּהְיוֹת הַתֶּבֶן מוּכָן:

יד **וַיֻּכּוּ שֹׁטְרֵי בְּנֵי יִשְׂרָאֵל.** הַשּׁוֹטְרִים יִשְׂרְאֵלִים הָיוּ
וְחָסִים עַל חַבְרֵיהֶם מִלְּדָחֳקָם, וּכְשֶׁהָיוּ מַשְׁלִימִים
הַלְּבֵנִים לַנּוֹגְשִׂים שֶׁהֵם מִצְרִיִּים וְהָיָה חָסֵר מִן
הַסְּכוּם, הָיוּ מַלְקִין אוֹתָם עַל שֶׁלֹּא דָחֲקוּ אֶת
עוֹשֵׂי הַמְּלָאכָה. לְפִיכָךְ זָכוּ אוֹתָם שׁוֹטְרִים לִהְיוֹת
סַנְהֶדְרִין וְנֶאֱצַל מִן הָרוּחַ אֲשֶׁר עַל מֹשֶׁה וְהוּשַׂם

עֲלֵיהֶם, שֶׁנֶּאֱמַר "אֶסְפָה לִּי שִׁבְעִים אִישׁ מִזִּקְנֵי
יִשְׂרָאֵל", מֵאוֹתָן שֶׁיָּדַעְתָּ הַטּוֹבָה שֶׁעָשׂוּ בְּמִצְרַיִם "כִּי
הֵם זִקְנֵי הָעָם וְשֹׁטְרָיו" (במדבר יא, טז): **וַיֻּכּוּ שֹׁטְרֵי בְּנֵי
יִשְׂרָאֵל.** אֲשֶׁר שָׂמוּ גֹּשֵׂי פַרְעֹה אוֹתָם לְשׁוֹטְרִים
עֲלֵיהֶם: **לֵאמֹר מַדּוּעַ וְגוֹ'.** לָמָּה "וַיֻּכּוּ"? שֶׁהָיוּ אוֹמְרִים
לָהֶם: מַדּוּעַ לֹא כִלִּיתֶם גַּם תְּמוֹל גַּם הַיּוֹם חֹק
הַקָּצוּב עֲלֵיכֶם לִלְבֹּן כִּתְמוֹל הַשְּׁלִישִׁי, שֶׁהוּא יוֹם
שִׁלְשׁוֹם אֶתְמוֹל, וְהוּא הָיָה בִּהְיוֹת הַתֶּבֶן נִתָּן לָהֶם:
וַיֻּכּוּ. לְשׁוֹן וַיִּפְעֲלוּ, הֻכּוּ מִיַּד אֲחֵרִים, הַנּוֹגְשִׂים הִכּוּם:

טז **וּלְבֵנִים אֹמְרִים לָנוּ.** הַנּוֹגְשִׂים, "עֲשׂוּ" כַּמִּנְיָן
הָרִאשׁוֹן: **וְחָטָאת עַמֶּךָ.** אִלּוּ הָיָה נָקוּד פַּתָּח הָיִיתִי
אוֹמֵר שֶׁהוּא דָבוּק - וְדָבָר זֶה חַטָּאת עַמְּךָ הוּא.
עַכְשָׁו שֶׁהוּא קָמָץ, שֵׁם דָּבָר הוּא, וְכָךְ פֵּרוּשׁוֹ, וְדָבָר
זֶה מֵבִיא חַטָּאת עַל עַמֶּךָ, כְּאִלּוּ כָתוּב: 'וְחַטָּאת
לְעַמֶּךָ', כְּמוֹ: "כְּבוֹאֲנָה בֵּית לָחֶם" (רות א, יט) שֶׁהוּא
כְּמוֹ לְבֵית לֶחֶם, וְכֵן הַרְבֵּה:

שמות | פרק ה

יח אֹמְרִ֔ים נֵלְכָ֖ה נִזְבְּחָ֣ה לַֽיהוָ֑ה: וְעַתָּה֙ לְכ֣וּ עִבְד֔וּ וְתֶ֖בֶן לֹא־יִנָּתֵ֣ן
לָכֶ֑ם וְתֹ֥כֶן לְבֵנִ֖ים תִּתֵּֽנוּ: יט וַיִּרְא֞וּ שֹׁטְרֵ֧י בְנֵֽי־יִשְׂרָאֵ֛ל אֹתָ֖ם בְּרָ֣ע
לֵאמֹ֑ר לֹא־תִגְרְע֥וּ מִלִּבְנֵיכֶ֖ם דְּבַר־י֥וֹם בְּיוֹמֽוֹ: כ וַֽיִּפְגְּעוּ֙ אֶת־מֹשֶׁ֣ה
וְאֶֽת־אַהֲרֹ֔ן נִצָּבִ֖ים לִקְרָאתָ֑ם בְּצֵאתָ֖ם מֵאֵ֥ת פַּרְעֹֽה: כא וַיֹּאמְר֣וּ
אֲלֵהֶ֔ם יֵ֧רֶא יְהוָ֛ה עֲלֵיכֶ֖ם וְיִשְׁפֹּ֑ט אֲשֶׁ֨ר הִבְאַשְׁתֶּ֜ם אֶת־רֵיחֵ֗נוּ
בְּעֵינֵ֤י פַרְעֹה֙ וּבְעֵינֵ֣י עֲבָדָ֔יו לָֽתֶת־חֶ֥רֶב בְּיָדָ֖ם לְהָרְגֵֽנוּ: כב וַיָּ֧שָׁב מפטיר
מֹשֶׁ֛ה אֶל־יְהוָ֖ה וַיֹּאמַ֑ר אֲדֹנָ֗י לָמָ֤ה הֲרֵעֹ֙תָה֙ לָעָ֣ם הַזֶּ֔ה לָ֥מָּה זֶּ֖ה
שְׁלַחְתָּֽנִי: כג וּמֵאָ֞ז בָּ֤אתִי אֶל־פַּרְעֹה֙ לְדַבֵּ֣ר בִּשְׁמֶ֔ךָ הֵרַ֖ע לָעָ֣ם
הַזֶּ֑ה וְהַצֵּ֥ל לֹא־הִצַּ֖לְתָּ אֶת־עַמֶּֽךָ: ו א וַיֹּ֤אמֶר יְהוָה֙ אֶל־מֹשֶׁ֔ה עַתָּ֣ה
תִרְאֶ֔ה אֲשֶׁ֥ר אֶֽעֱשֶׂ֖ה לְפַרְעֹ֑ה כִּ֣י בְיָ֤ד חֲזָקָה֙ יְשַׁלְּחֵ֔ם וּבְיָ֣ד חֲזָקָ֔ה
יְגָרְשֵׁ֖ם מֵאַרְצֽוֹ:

יח | **וְתֹכֶן לְבֵנִים.** חֶשְׁבּוֹן הַלְּבֵנִים, וְכֵן: "אֶת הַכֶּסֶף הַמְתֻכָּן" (מלכים ב' י״ב, י״ב) הַמָּנוּי, כְּמוֹ שֶׁאָמוּר בָּעִנְיָן: "וַיָּצֻרוּ וַיִּמְנוּ אֶת הַכָּסֶף" (שם פסוק י״א):

יט | **וַיִּרְאוּ שֹׁטְרֵי בְנֵי יִשְׂרָאֵל.** אֶת חַבְרֵיהֶם הַנִּרְדִּים עַל יָדָם, **בְּרָע** – רָאוּ אוֹתָם בְּרָעָה וְצָרָה הַמּוֹצֵאת אוֹתָם בְּהַכְבִּידָם הָעֲבוֹדָה עֲלֵיהֶם "לֵאמֹר לֹא תִגְרְעוּ וְגוֹ':

כ | **וַיִּפְגְּעוּ.** אֲנָשִׁים מִיִּשְׂרָאֵל, "אֶת מֹשֶׁה וְאֶת אַהֲרֹן" וְגוֹ'. וְרַבּוֹתֵינוּ אָמְרוּ, כָּל 'נִצִּים' וְ'נִצָּבִים' דָּתָן וַאֲבִירָם הָיוּ, שֶׁנֶּאֱמַר בָּהֶם: "יָצְאוּ נִצָּבִים" (במדבר ט״ז, כ״ז):

כב | **לָמָה הֲרֵעֹתָה לָעָם הַזֶּה.** וְאִם תֹּאמַר, מַה אִכְפַּת לָךְ? קוֹבֵל אֲנִי עַל שֶׁשְּׁלַחְתָּנִי:

כג | **הֵרַע.** לְשׁוֹן הִפְעִיל הוּא, הִרְבָּה רָעָה עֲלֵיהֶם. וְתַרְגּוּמוֹ "אַבְאֵישׁ":

פרק ו

א | **עַתָּה תִרְאֶה וְגוֹ'.** הִרְהַרְתָּ עַל מִדּוֹתַי, לֹא כְּאַבְרָהָם שֶׁאָמַרְתִּי לוֹ: "כִּי בְיִצְחָק יִקָּרֵא לְךָ זָרַע" (בראשית כ״א, י״ב) וְאַחַר כָּךְ אָמַרְתִּי לוֹ: "הַעֲלֵהוּ... לְעֹלָה" (שם כ״ב, ב׳) וְלֹא הִרְהֵר אַחֲרַי. לְפִיכָךְ – "עַתָּה תִרְאֶה", הָעָשׂוּי לְפַרְעֹה תִרְאֶה, וְלֹא הֶעָשׂוּי לְמַלְכֵי שִׁבְעָה אֻמּוֹת כְּשֶׁאֲבִיאֵם לָאָרֶץ. **כִּי בְיָד חֲזָקָה יְשַׁלְּחֵם.** מִפְּנֵי יָדִי שֶׁתֶּחֱזַק עָלָיו יְשַׁלְּחֵם. **וּבְיָד חֲזָקָה יְגָרְשֵׁם מֵאַרְצוֹ.** עַל כָּרְחָם שֶׁל יִשְׂרָאֵל יְגָרְשֵׁם, וְלֹא יַסְפִּיקוּ לַעֲשׂוֹת לָהֶם צֵדָה, וְכֵן הוּא אוֹמֵר: "וַתֶּחֱזַק מִצְרַיִם עַל הָעָם" וְגוֹ' (להלן י״ב, ל״ג):

וארא

ד וַיְדַבֵּ֥ר אֱלֹהִ֖ים אֶל־מֹשֶׁ֑ה וַיֹּ֥אמֶר אֵלָ֖יו אֲנִ֥י יְהוָֽה׃ וָאֵרָ֗א אֶל־
אַבְרָהָ֛ם אֶל־יִצְחָ֥ק וְאֶֽל־יַעֲקֹ֖ב בְּאֵ֣ל שַׁדָּ֑י וּשְׁמִ֣י יְהוָ֔ה לֹ֥א
נוֹדַ֖עְתִּי לָהֶֽם׃ וְגַ֨ם הֲקִמֹ֤תִי אֶת־בְּרִיתִי֙ אִתָּ֔ם לָתֵ֥ת לָהֶ֖ם אֶת־
אֶ֣רֶץ כְּנָ֑עַן אֵ֛ת אֶ֥רֶץ מְגֻרֵיהֶ֖ם אֲשֶׁר־גָּ֥רוּ בָֽהּ׃ וְגַ֣ם ׀ אֲנִ֣י שָׁמַ֗עְתִּי
אֶֽת־נַאֲקַת֙ בְּנֵ֣י יִשְׂרָאֵ֔ל אֲשֶׁ֥ר מִצְרַ֖יִם מַעֲבִדִ֣ים אֹתָ֑ם וָאֶזְכֹּ֖ר אֶת־
בְּרִיתִֽי׃ לָכֵ֞ן אֱמֹ֥ר לִבְנֵֽי־יִשְׂרָאֵל֮ אֲנִ֣י יְהוָה֒ וְהוֹצֵאתִ֣י אֶתְכֶ֗ם
מִתַּ֨חַת֙ סִבְלֹ֣ת מִצְרַ֔יִם וְהִצַּלְתִּ֥י אֶתְכֶ֖ם מֵעֲבֹדָתָ֑ם וְגָאַלְתִּ֤י אֶתְכֶם֙
בִּזְר֣וֹעַ נְטוּיָ֔ה וּבִשְׁפָטִ֖ים גְּדֹלִֽים׃ וְלָקַחְתִּ֨י אֶתְכֶ֥ם לִי֙ לְעָ֔ם וְהָיִ֥יתִי
לָכֶ֖ם לֵֽאלֹהִ֑ים וִֽידַעְתֶּ֗ם כִּ֣י אֲנִ֤י יְהוָה֙ אֱלֹ֣הֵיכֶ֔ם הַמּוֹצִ֣יא אֶתְכֶ֔ם
מִתַּ֖חַת סִבְל֥וֹת מִצְרָֽיִם׃ וְהֵבֵאתִ֤י אֶתְכֶם֙ אֶל־הָאָ֔רֶץ אֲשֶׁ֤ר
נָשָׂ֙אתִי֙ אֶת־יָדִ֔י לָתֵ֣ת אֹתָ֔הּ לְאַבְרָהָ֥ם לְיִצְחָ֖ק וּֽלְיַעֲקֹ֑ב וְנָתַתִּ֨י

ב) **וידבר אלהים אל משה.** דִּבֶּר אִתּוֹ מִשְׁפָּט עַל שֶׁהִקְשָׁה לְדַבֵּר וְלוֹמַר: "לָמָה הֲרֵעֹתָה לָעָם הַזֶּה" (לעיל ה, כב). **ויאמר אליו אני ה'.** נֶאֱמָן לְשַׁלֵּם שָׂכָר טוֹב לַמִּתְהַלְּכִים לְפָנַי. וְלֹא לְחִנָּם שְׁלַחְתִּיךָ כִּי אִם לְקַיֵּם דְּבָרַי לָאָבוֹת הָרִאשׁוֹנִים. וּבַלָּשׁוֹן הַזֶּה מָצִינוּ שֶׁהוּא נִדְרָשׁ בְּכַמָּה מְקוֹמוֹת: "אֲנִי ה'" נֶאֱמָן לִפָּרַע, כְּשֶׁהוּא אָמוּר אֵצֶל עֹנֶשׁ כְּגוֹן: "וְחִלַּלְתָּ אֶת שֵׁם אֱלֹהֶיךָ אֲנִי ה'" (ויקרא יט, יב), וּכְשֶׁהוּא אָמוּר אֵצֶל קִיּוּם מִצְוֹת כְּגוֹן: "וּשְׁמַרְתֶּם מִצְוֹתַי וַעֲשִׂיתֶם אֹתָם אֲנִי ה'" (שם כב, לא) נֶאֱמָן לִתֵּן שָׂכָר:

ג) **וארא. אל האבות. באל שדי.** הִבְטַחְתִּים הַבְטָחוֹת וּבְכֻלָּן אָמַרְתִּי לָהֶם: "אֲנִי אֵל שַׁדַּי". **ושמי ה' לא נודעתי להם.** לֹא הוֹדַעְתִּי אֵין כְּתִיב כָּאן אֶלָּא "לֹא נוֹדַעְתִּי", לֹא נִכַּרְתִּי לָהֶם בְּמִדַּת אֲמִתּוּת שֶׁלִּי שֶׁעָלֶיהָ נִקְרָא שְׁמִי ה', נֶאֱמָן לְאַמֵּת דְּבָרַי, שֶׁהֲרֵי הִבְטַחְתִּים וְלֹא קִיַּמְתִּי:

ד) **וגם הקמתי את בריתי וגו'.** וְגַם כְּשֶׁנִּרְאֵיתִי לָהֶם בְּאֵל שַׁדַּי הִצַּבְתִּי וְהֶעֱמַדְתִּי בְּרִיתִי בֵּינִי וּבֵינֵיהֶם.

"לתת להם את ארץ כנען" — לאברהם בְּפָרָשַׁת מִילָה נֶאֱמַר: "אֲנִי אֵל שַׁדַּי וְגוֹ' וְנָתַתִּי לְךָ וּלְזַרְעֲךָ אַחֲרֶיךָ אֵת אֶרֶץ מְגֻרֶיךָ" (בראשית יז, א-ח). לְיִצְחָק: "כִּי לְךָ וּלְזַרְעֲךָ אֶתֵּן אֶת כָּל הָאֲרָצֹת הָאֵל וַהֲקִמֹתִי אֶת הַשְּׁבוּעָה אֲשֶׁר נִשְׁבַּעְתִּי לְאַבְרָהָם" (שם כו, ג). וְאוֹתָהּ שְׁבוּעָה שֶׁנִּשְׁבַּעְתִּי לְאַבְרָהָם בְּאֵל שַׁדַּי אָמַרְתִּי לְיַעֲקֹב: "אֲנִי אֵל שַׁדַּי פְּרֵה וּרְבֵה וְגוֹ' וְאֶת הָאָרֶץ אֲשֶׁר וְגוֹ'" (שם לה, יא-יב). הֲרֵי שֶׁנָּדַרְתִּי לָהֶם וְלֹא קִיַּמְתִּי:

ה) **וגם אני.** כְּמוֹ שֶׁהִצַּבְתִּי וְהֶעֱמַדְתִּי הַבְּרִית יֵשׁ עָלַי לְקַיֵּם, לְפִיכָךְ "שָׁמַעְתִּי אֶת נַאֲקַת בְּנֵי יִשְׂרָאֵל" הַנּוֹאֲקִים, "אֲשֶׁר מִצְרַיִם מַעֲבִדִים אֹתָם" "וָאֶזְכֹּר" אוֹתָהּ הַבְּרִית, כִּי בִּבְרִית בֵּין הַבְּתָרִים אָמַרְתִּי לוֹ: "וְגַם אֶת הַגּוֹי אֲשֶׁר יַעֲבֹדוּ דָּן אָנֹכִי" (שם טו, יד):

ו) **לכן.** עַל פִּי אוֹתָהּ הַשְּׁבוּעָה. **אמר לבני ישראל אני ה'.** הַנֶּאֱמָן בְּהַבְטָחָתִי. **והוצאתי אתכם.** כִּי כֵן הִבְטַחְתִּיו: "וְאַחֲרֵי כֵן יֵצְאוּ בִּרְכֻשׁ גָּדוֹל" (שם). **סבלת.** טֹרַח מַשָּׂא מִצְרַיִם:

ח) **נשאתי את ידי.** הֲרִימוֹתִיהָ לְהִשָּׁבַע בְּכִסְאִי:

שמות | פרק ו   ואראה | 367

ט אֹתָהּ לָכֶם מוֹרָשָׁה אֲנִי יְהוָה: וַיְדַבֵּר מֹשֶׁה כֵּן אֶל־בְּנֵי יִשְׂרָאֵל
   וְלֹא שָׁמְעוּ אֶל־מֹשֶׁה מִקֹּצֶר רוּחַ וּמֵעֲבֹדָה קָשָׁה:
יא וַיְדַבֵּר יְהוָה אֶל־מֹשֶׁה לֵּאמֹר: בֹּא דַבֵּר אֶל־פַּרְעֹה מֶלֶךְ
   מִצְרָיִם וִישַׁלַּח אֶת־בְּנֵי־יִשְׂרָאֵל מֵאַרְצוֹ: וַיְדַבֵּר מֹשֶׁה לִפְנֵי
   יְהוָה לֵאמֹר הֵן בְּנֵי־יִשְׂרָאֵל לֹא־שָׁמְעוּ אֵלַי וְאֵיךְ יִשְׁמָעֵנִי
   פַרְעֹה וַאֲנִי עֲרַל שְׂפָתָיִם:
יג וַיְדַבֵּר יְהוָה אֶל־מֹשֶׁה וְאֶל־אַהֲרֹן וַיְצַוֵּם אֶל־בְּנֵי יִשְׂרָאֵל
   וְאֶל־פַּרְעֹה מֶלֶךְ מִצְרָיִם לְהוֹצִיא אֶת־בְּנֵי־יִשְׂרָאֵל מֵאֶרֶץ

ט) **ולא שמעו אל משה.** לא קבלו תנחומין. **מקצר**
רוח. כל מי שהוא מצר, רוחו ונשימתו קצרה ואינו
יכול להאריך בנשימתו.

קרוב לענין זה שמעתי בפרשה זו מרבי ברוך ברבי
אליעזר, והביא לי ראיה ממקרא זה: "בַּפַּעַם הַזֹּאת
חוֹדִיעָם אֶת יָדִי וְאֶת גְּבוּרָתִי וְיָדְעוּ כִּי שְׁמִי ה'"
(ירמיה טז, כא), למדנו כשהקדוש ברוך הוא מאמן את
דבריו, אפילו לפורענות, מודיע שֶׁשְּׁמוֹ ה', וכל שכן
האמנה לטובה. ורבותינו דרשוהו לענין של מעלה
שאמר משה: "לָמָה הֲרֵעֹתָה" (לעיל ה, כב), אמר לו
הקדוש ברוך הוא: חבל על דאבדין ולא משתכחין!
יש לי להתאונן על מיתת האבות, הרבה פעמים
נגליתי עליהם בְּאֵל שַׁדַּי ולא אמרו לי מה שמך,
ואתה אמרת: "מַה שְּׁמוֹ, מָה אֹמַר אֲלֵהֶם" (לעיל
ג, יג). **וְגַם הֲקִמֹתִי וגו'.** וּכְשֶׁבִּקֵּשׁ אַבְרָהָם לִקְבֹּר אֶת
שָׂרָה לֹא מָצָא קֶבֶר עַד שֶׁקָּנָה בְּדָמִים מְרֻבִּים;
וְכֵן יִצְחָק - עוֹרְרוּ עָלָיו עַל הַבְּאֵרוֹת אֲשֶׁר חָפָר;
וְכֵן יַעֲקֹב - "וַיִּקֶן אֶת חֶלְקַת הַשָּׂדֶה" (בראשית לג,
יט) לִנְטוֹת אָהֳלוֹ; וְלֹא הִרְהֲרוּ אַחַר מִדּוֹתַי, וְאַתָּה
אָמַרְתָּ: "לָמָה הֲרֵעֹתָה". וְאֵין הַמִּדְרָשׁ מִתְיַשֵּׁב
אַחַר הַמִּקְרָא מִפְּנֵי כַּמָּה דְּבָרִים: אַחַת, שֶׁלֹּא
נֶאֱמַר: "וּשְׁמִי ה' לֹא שָׁאֲלוּ לִי'. וְאִם תֹּאמַר, לֹא
הוֹדִיעָם שֶׁכָּךְ שְׁמוֹ, הֲרֵי תְּחִלָּה כְּשֶׁנִּגְלָה לְאַבְרָהָם
בֵּין הַבְּתָרִים נֶאֱמַר: "אֲנִי ה' אֲשֶׁר הוֹצֵאתִיךָ מֵאוּר

כַּשְׂדִּים" (שם טו, ז)! וְעוֹד, הֵיאַךְ הַסְּמִיכָה נִמְשֶׁכֶת
בִּדְבָרִים שֶׁהוּא סוֹמֵךְ לְכָאן: "וְגַם אֲנִי שָׁמַעְתִּי וְגוֹ',
לָכֵן אֱמֹר לִבְנֵי יִשְׂרָאֵל"? לְכָךְ אֲנִי אוֹמֵר יִתְיַשֵּׁב
הַמִּקְרָא עַל פְּשׁוּטוֹ דָּבוּר עַל אָפְנָיו וְהַדְּרָשָׁה תִּדָּרֵשׁ,
שֶׁנֶּאֱמַר: "הֲלוֹא כֹה דְבָרַי כָּאֵשׁ נְאֻם ה', וּכְפַטִּישׁ יְפֹצֵץ
סָלַע" (ירמיה כג, כט), מִתְחַלֵּק לְכַמָּה נִיצוֹצוֹת.

יב) **ערל שפתים.** אֲטוּם שְׂפָתַיִם. וְכֵן כָּל לְשׁוֹן
עָרְלָה אֲנִי אוֹמֵר שֶׁהוּא אֹטֶם: "עֲרֵלָה אָזְנָם" (שם ו,
י) - אֲטוּמָה מִשְּׁמֹעַ; "עַרְלֵי לֵב" (שם ט, כה) - אֲטוּמִים
מֵהָבִין; "שְׁתֵה גַם אַתָּה וְהֵעָרֵל" (חבקוק ב, טז) - וְהֵאָטֵם
מִשָּׁכְרוּת כּוֹס הַקְּלָלָה; "עָרְלַת בָּשָׂר", שֶׁהַגִּיד אָטוּם
וּמְכֻסֶּה בָהּ; "וַעֲרַלְתֶּם עָרְלָתוֹ" (ויקרא יט, כג) - עֲשׂוּ
לוֹ אֹטֶם וּכְסוּי אִסּוּר שֶׁיַּבְדִּיל בִּפְנֵי אֲכִילָתוֹ; "שָׁלֹשׁ
שָׁנִים יִהְיֶה לָכֶם עֲרֵלִים" (שם) - אָטוּם וּמְכֻסֶּה
וּמֻבְדָּל מִלְּאָכְלוֹ: **ואיך ישמעני פרעה.** זֶה אֶחָד
מֵעֲשָׂרָה קַל וָחֹמֶר שֶׁבַּתּוֹרָה.

יג) **וידבר ה' אל משה ואל אהרן.** לְפִי שֶׁאָמַר
מֹשֶׁה: "וַאֲנִי עֲרַל שְׂפָתָיִם", צֵרַף הַקָּדוֹשׁ בָּרוּךְ הוּא
אֶת אַהֲרֹן עִמּוֹ לִהְיוֹת לוֹ לְמֵלִיץ: **ויצום אל בני**
ישראל. צִוָּם עֲלֵיהֶם לְהַנְהִיגָם בְּנַחַת וְלִסְבֹּל אוֹתָם:
ואל פרעה מלך מצרים. צִוָּם עָלָיו לַחֲלֹק לוֹ כָּבוֹד
בְּדִבְרֵיהֶם, זֶה מִדְרָשׁוֹ. וּפְשׁוּטוֹ, צִוָּם עַל דְּבַר יִשְׂרָאֵל
וְעַל שְׁלִיחוּתוֹ אֶל פַּרְעֹה. וּדְבַר הַצִּוּוּי מַהוּ, מְפֹרָשׁ
בְּפָרָשָׁה שְׁנִיָּה לְאַחַר סֵדֶר הַיַּחַס (להלן פסוק כט), חָלָק

וארא | פרק ו

שני מִצְרָיִם: ס אֵ֣לֶּה רָאשֵׁ֣י בֵית־אֲבֹתָ֑ם בְּנֵ֨י רְאוּבֵ֜ן בְּכֹ֣ר יד
יִשְׂרָאֵ֗ל חֲנ֤וֹךְ וּפַלּוּא֙ חֶצְר֣וֹן וְכַרְמִ֔י אֵ֖לֶּה מִשְׁפְּחֹ֥ת רְאוּבֵֽן: וּבְנֵ֣י טו
שִׁמְע֗וֹן יְמוּאֵ֨ל וְיָמִ֤ין וְאֹ֨הַד֙ וְיָכִ֣ין וְצֹ֔חַר וְשָׁא֖וּל בֶּן־הַכְּנַעֲנִ֑ית
אֵ֖לֶּה מִשְׁפְּחֹ֥ת שִׁמְעֽוֹן: וְאֵ֨לֶּה שְׁמ֤וֹת בְּנֵֽי־לֵוִי֙ לְתֹ֣לְדֹתָ֔ם טז
גֵּרְשׁ֕וֹן וּקְהָ֖ת וּמְרָרִ֑י וּשְׁנֵי֙ חַיֵּ֣י לֵוִ֔י שֶׁ֧בַע וּשְׁלֹשִׁ֛ים וּמְאַ֖ת שָׁנָֽה:
בְּנֵ֥י גֵרְשׁ֛וֹן לִבְנִ֥י וְשִׁמְעִ֖י לְמִשְׁפְּחֹתָֽם: וּבְנֵ֣י קְהָ֔ת עַמְרָ֣ם וְיִצְהָ֔ר יז יח
וְחֶבְר֖וֹן וְעֻזִּיאֵ֑ל וּשְׁנֵי֙ חַיֵּ֣י קְהָ֔ת שָׁלֹ֧שׁ וּשְׁלֹשִׁ֛ים וּמְאַ֖ת שָׁנָֽה:
וּבְנֵ֥י מְרָרִ֖י מַחְלִ֣י וּמוּשִׁ֑י אֵ֛לֶּה מִשְׁפְּחֹ֥ת הַלֵּוִ֖י לְתֹלְדֹתָֽם: וַיִּקַּ֨ח יט כ
עַמְרָ֜ם אֶת־יוֹכֶ֤בֶד דֹּֽדָתוֹ֙ ל֣וֹ לְאִשָּׁ֔ה וַתֵּ֣לֶד ל֔וֹ אֶֽת־אַהֲרֹ֖ן וְאֶת־
מֹשֶׁ֑ה וּשְׁנֵי֙ חַיֵּ֣י עַמְרָ֔ם שֶׁ֧בַע וּשְׁלֹשִׁ֛ים וּמְאַ֖ת שָׁנָֽה: וּבְנֵ֖י יִצְהָ֑ר כא
קֹ֥רַח וָנֶ֖פֶג וְזִכְרִֽי: וּבְנֵ֖י עֻזִּיאֵ֑ל מִֽישָׁאֵ֥ל וְאֶלְצָפָ֖ן וְסִתְרִֽי: וַיִּקַּ֨ח כב כג
אַהֲרֹ֜ן אֶת־אֱלִישֶׁ֧בַע בַּת־עַמִּינָדָ֛ב אֲח֥וֹת נַחְשׁ֖וֹן ל֣וֹ לְאִשָּׁ֑ה
וַתֵּ֣לֶד ל֗וֹ אֶת־נָדָב֙ וְאֶת־אֲבִיה֔וּא אֶת־אֶלְעָזָ֖ר וְאֶת־אִֽיתָמָֽר:
וּבְנֵ֣י קֹ֔רַח אַסִּ֥יר וְאֶלְקָנָ֖ה וַאֲבִיאָסָ֑ף אֵ֖לֶּה מִשְׁפְּחֹ֥ת הַקָּרְחִֽי: כד

מִתּוֹךְ שֶׁהִזְכִּיר מֹשֶׁה וְאַהֲרֹן, הִפְסִיק הָעִנְיָן בְּ"אֵלֶּה רָאשֵׁי בֵית אֲבוֹתָם" לְלַמְּדֵנוּ הֵיאַךְ נוֹלְדוּ מֹשֶׁה וְאַהֲרֹן וּבְמִי נִתְיַחֲסוּ:

יד אֵלֶּה רָאשֵׁי בֵית אֲבֹתָם. מִתּוֹךְ שֶׁהֻזְקַק לְיַחֵס שִׁבְטוֹ שֶׁל לֵוִי עַד מֹשֶׁה וְאַהֲרֹן בִּשְׁבִיל מֹשֶׁה וְאַהֲרֹן, הִתְחִיל לְיַחֲסָם דֶּרֶךְ תּוֹלְדוֹתָם מֵרְאוּבֵן. וּבַפְּסִיקְתָּא הַגְּדוֹלָה (פסיקתא ז) רָאִיתִי, לְפִי שֶׁקִּנְתְּרָם יַעֲקֹב אֲבִיהֶם לִשְׁלֹשָׁה שְׁבָטִים הַלָּלוּ בִּשְׁעַת מוֹתוֹ, חָזַר הַכָּתוּב לְיַחֲסָם כָּאן לְבַדָּם, לוֹמַר שֶׁחֲשׁוּבִים הֵם:

טז וּשְׁנֵי חַיֵּי לֵוִי וְגוֹ'. לָמָּה נִמְנוּ שְׁנוֹתָיו שֶׁל לֵוִי? לְהוֹדִיעַ כַּמָּה יְמֵי הַשִּׁעְבּוּד, שֶׁכָּל זְמַן שֶׁאֶחָד מִן הַשְּׁבָטִים קַיָּם לֹא הָיָה שִׁעְבּוּד, שֶׁנֶּאֱמַר: "וַיָּמָת יוֹסֵף

וְכָל אֶחָיו" (לעיל א, ו) וְאַחַר כָּךְ: "וַיָּקָם מֶלֶךְ חָדָשׁ" (פסוק ח) וְלֵוִי הֶאֱרִיךְ יָמִים עַל כֻּלָּם:

יח וּשְׁנֵי חַיֵּי קְהָת... וּשְׁנֵי חַיֵּי עַמְרָם וְגוֹ'. מֵחֶשְׁבּוֹן זֶה אָנוּ לְמֵדִים עַל מוֹשַׁב בְּנֵי יִשְׂרָאֵל אַרְבַּע מֵאוֹת שָׁנָה שֶׁאָמַר הַכָּתוּב (בראשית טו, יג ועיין להלן יב, מ), שֶׁלֹּא בְּאֶרֶץ מִצְרַיִם לְבַדָּהּ הָיוּ, אֶלָּא מִיּוֹם שֶׁנּוֹלַד יִצְחָק, שֶׁהֲרֵי קְהָת מִיּוֹרְדֵי מִצְרַיִם הָיָה, חֲשׁוֹב כָּל שְׁנוֹתָיו וּשְׁנוֹת עַמְרָם וּשְׁמוֹנִים שֶׁל מֹשֶׁה, לֹא תִמְצָאֵם אַרְבַּע מֵאוֹת שָׁנָה, וְהַרְבֵּה שָׁנִים נִבְלָעִים לַבָּנִים בִּשְׁנֵי הָאָבוֹת:

כ יוֹכֶבֶד דֹּדָתוֹ. "אֲחַת אֲבוּהִי", בַּת לֵוִי, אֲחוֹת קְהָת:

שמות | וארא | פרק ו

כה וְאֶלְעָזָ֨ר בֶּֽן־אַהֲרֹ֜ן לָקַֽח־ל֨וֹ מִבְּנ֤וֹת פּֽוּטִיאֵל֙ ל֣וֹ לְאִשָּׁ֔ה וַתֵּ֣לֶד ל֔וֹ
כו אֶת־פִּֽינְחָ֑ס אֵ֗לֶּה רָאשֵׁ֛י אֲב֥וֹת הַלְוִיִּ֖ם לְמִשְׁפְּחֹתָֽם: ה֥וּא אַהֲרֹ֖ן
וּמֹשֶׁ֑ה אֲשֶׁ֨ר אָמַ֤ר יְהוָה֙ לָהֶ֔ם הוֹצִ֜יאוּ אֶת־בְּנֵ֧י יִשְׂרָאֵ֛ל מֵאֶ֥רֶץ
מִצְרַ֖יִם עַל־צִבְאֹתָֽם:
כז הֵ֗ם הַֽמְדַבְּרִים֙ אֶל־פַּרְעֹ֣ה מֶֽלֶךְ־מִצְרַ֔יִם
לְהוֹצִ֥יא אֶת־בְּנֵֽי־יִשְׂרָאֵ֖ל מִמִּצְרָ֑יִם ה֥וּא מֹשֶׁ֖ה וְאַהֲרֹֽן:
כח וַיְהִ֗י
בְּי֨וֹם דִּבֶּ֧ר יְהוָ֛ה אֶל־מֹשֶׁ֖ה בְּאֶ֥רֶץ מִצְרָֽיִם: **שלישי** וַיְדַבֵּ֣ר
כט יְהוָ֤ה אֶל־מֹשֶׁה֙ לֵּאמֹ֔ר אֲנִ֖י יְהוָ֑ה דַּבֵּ֗ר אֶל־פַּרְעֹה֙ מֶ֣לֶךְ מִצְרַ֔יִם
ל אֵ֛ת כָּל־אֲשֶׁ֥ר אֲנִ֖י דֹּבֵ֥ר אֵלֶֽיךָ: וַיֹּ֥אמֶר מֹשֶׁ֖ה לִפְנֵ֣י יְהוָ֑ה הֵ֤ן אֲנִי֙
עֲרַ֣ל שְׂפָתַ֔יִם וְאֵ֕יךְ יִשְׁמַ֥ע אֵלַ֖י פַּרְעֹֽה:

א וַיֹּ֤אמֶר יְהוָה֙ אֶל־מֹשֶׁ֔ה רְאֵ֛ה נְתַתִּ֥יךָ אֱלֹהִ֖ים לְפַרְעֹ֑ה וְאַהֲרֹ֥ן
ב אָחִ֖יךָ יִהְיֶ֥ה נְבִיאֶֽךָ: אַתָּ֣ה תְדַבֵּ֔ר אֵ֖ת כָּל־אֲשֶׁ֣ר אֲצַוֶּ֑ךָּ וְאַהֲרֹ֤ן
ג אָחִ֨יךָ֙ יְדַבֵּ֣ר אֶל־פַּרְעֹ֔ה וְשִׁלַּ֥ח אֶת־בְּנֵֽי־יִשְׂרָאֵ֖ל מֵאַרְצֽוֹ: וַאֲנִ֥י

כה **מִבְּנוֹת פּוּטִיאֵל.** מִזֶּרַע יִתְרוֹ שֶׁפִּטֵּם עֲגָלִים לַעֲבוֹדָה זָרָה, וּמִזֶּרַע יוֹסֵף שֶׁפִּטְפֵּט בְּיִצְרוֹ:

כו **הוּא אַהֲרֹן וּמֹשֶׁה.** אֵלּוּ שֶׁהֻזְכְּרוּ לְמַעְלָה שֶׁיְּלָדָה יוֹכֶבֶד לְעַמְרָם, "הוּא אַהֲרֹן וּמֹשֶׁה אֲשֶׁר אָמַר ה'" וְגוֹ'. יֵשׁ מְקוֹמוֹת שֶׁמַּקְדִּים אַהֲרֹן לְמֹשֶׁה וְיֵשׁ מְקוֹמוֹת שֶׁמַּקְדִּים מֹשֶׁה לְאַהֲרֹן, לוֹמַר שֶׁשְּׁקוּלִים שְׁנֵיהֶם כְּאֶחָד: **עַל צִבְאֹתָם. בְּצִבְאֹתָם,** כָּל צְבָאָם לְשִׁבְטֵיהֶם. יֵשׁ עַל שֶׁאֵינוֹ אֶלָּא בִּמְקוֹם אוֹת אַחַת: "וְעַל חַרְבְּךָ תִחְיֶה" (בראשית כז, מ), כְּמוֹ בְּחַרְבְּךָ; "עֲמַדְתֶּם עַל חַרְבְּכֶם" (יחזקאל לג, כו) בְּחַרְבְּכֶם:

כז **הֵם הַמְדַבְּרִים וְגוֹ'. הֵם שֶׁנִּצְטַוּוּ הֵם שֶׁקִּיְּמוּ:** **הוּא מֹשֶׁה וְאַהֲרֹן.** הֵם בִּשְׁלִיחוּתָם וּבְצִדְקָתָם מִתְּחִלָּה וְעַד סוֹף:

כח **וַיְהִי בְּיוֹם דִּבֶּר וְגוֹ'.** מְחֻבָּר לַמִּקְרָא שֶׁל אַחֲרָיו:

כט **וַיְדַבֵּר ה'.** הוּא הַדִּבּוּר עַצְמוֹ הָאָמוּר לְמַעְלָה, "בֹּא דַבֵּר אֶל פַּרְעֹה מֶלֶךְ מִצְרַיִם", אֶלָּא מִתּוֹךְ שֶׁהִפְסִיק הָעִנְיָן בִּשְׁבִיל לְיַחֲסוֹ, חָזַר עָלָיו לְהַתְחִיל בּוֹ: **אֲנִי ה'.** כְּדַאי אֲנִי לְשָׁלְחֲךָ וּלְקַיֵּם דִּבְרֵי שְׁלִיחוּתִי:

פרק ז

א **נְתַתִּיךָ אֱלֹהִים לְפַרְעֹה.** שׁוֹפֵט וְרוֹדֶה, לִרְדּוֹתוֹ בְּמַכּוֹת וְיִסּוּרִין: **יִהְיֶה נְבִיאֶךָ.** כְּתַרְגּוּמוֹ: "מְתֻרְגְּמָנָךְ". וְכֵן כָּל לְשׁוֹן נְבוּאָה, אָדָם הַמַּכְרִיז וּמַשְׁמִיעַ לָעָם דִּבְרֵי תוֹכָחוֹת, וְהוּא מִגִּזְרַת "נִיב שְׂפָתָיִם" (ישעיה נז, יט), "נוֹב חָכְמָה" (משלי י, לא), "וַיְכַל מֵהִתְנַבּוֹת" (שמואל א' י, יג), וּבְלַעַז קוֹרְאִין לוֹ פרידיצ״ר:

ב **אַתָּה תְדַבֵּר.** פַּעַם אַחַת כָּל שְׁלִיחוּת וּשְׁלִיחוּת לְפִי שֶׁשְּׁמַעְתָּהּ מִפִּי, וְאַהֲרֹן אָחִיךָ יַמְלִיצֶנּוּ וְיַטְעִימֶנּוּ בְּאָזְנֵי פַרְעֹה:

אַקְשֶׁה אֶת־לֵב פַּרְעֹה וְהִרְבֵּיתִי אֶת־אֹתֹתַי וְאֶת־מוֹפְתַי בְּאֶרֶץ מִצְרָיִם: וְלֹא־יִשְׁמַע אֲלֵכֶם פַּרְעֹה וְנָתַתִּי אֶת־יָדִי בְּמִצְרָיִם וְהוֹצֵאתִי אֶת־צִבְאֹתַי אֶת־עַמִּי בְנֵי־יִשְׂרָאֵל מֵאֶרֶץ מִצְרַיִם בִּשְׁפָטִים גְּדֹלִים: וְיָדְעוּ מִצְרַיִם כִּי־אֲנִי יְהוָה בִּנְטֹתִי אֶת־יָדִי עַל־מִצְרָיִם וְהוֹצֵאתִי אֶת־בְּנֵי־יִשְׂרָאֵל מִתּוֹכָם: וַיַּעַשׂ מֹשֶׁה וְאַהֲרֹן כַּאֲשֶׁר צִוָּה יְהוָה אֹתָם כֵּן עָשׂוּ: וּמֹשֶׁה בֶּן־שְׁמֹנִים שָׁנָה וְאַהֲרֹן בֶּן־שָׁלֹשׁ וּשְׁמֹנִים שָׁנָה בְּדַבְּרָם אֶל־פַּרְעֹה:

רביעי

וַיֹּאמֶר יְהוָה אֶל־מֹשֶׁה וְאֶל־אַהֲרֹן לֵאמֹר: כִּי יְדַבֵּר אֲלֵכֶם פַּרְעֹה לֵאמֹר תְּנוּ לָכֶם מוֹפֵת וְאָמַרְתָּ אֶל־אַהֲרֹן קַח אֶת־מַטְּךָ וְהַשְׁלֵךְ לִפְנֵי־פַרְעֹה יְהִי לְתַנִּין: וַיָּבֹא מֹשֶׁה וְאַהֲרֹן אֶל־פַּרְעֹה וַיַּעֲשׂוּ כֵן כַּאֲשֶׁר צִוָּה יְהוָה וַיַּשְׁלֵךְ אַהֲרֹן אֶת־מַטֵּהוּ לִפְנֵי פַרְעֹה וְלִפְנֵי עֲבָדָיו וַיְהִי לְתַנִּין: וַיִּקְרָא גַּם־פַּרְעֹה לַחֲכָמִים וְלַמְכַשְּׁפִים וַיַּעֲשׂוּ גַם־הֵם חַרְטֻמֵּי מִצְרַיִם בְּלַהֲטֵיהֶם כֵּן: וַיַּשְׁלִיכוּ אִישׁ מַטֵּהוּ וַיִּהְיוּ לְתַנִּינִם וַיִּבְלַע מַטֵּה־אַהֲרֹן אֶת־מַטֹּתָם: וַיֶּחֱזַק לֵב פַּרְעֹה וְלֹא שָׁמַע אֲלֵהֶם כַּאֲשֶׁר דִּבֶּר יְהוָה:

וַיֹּאמֶר יְהוָה אֶל־מֹשֶׁה כָּבֵד לֵב פַּרְעֹה

ג׳ וַאֲנִי אַקְשֶׁה. מֵאַחַר שֶׁהִרְשִׁיעַ וְהִתְרִיס כְּנֶגְדִּי, וְגָלוּי לְפָנַי שֶׁאֵין נַחַת רוּחַ בָּאֻמּוֹת לָתֵת לֵב שָׁלֵם לָשׁוּב, טוֹב לִי שֶׁיִּתְקַשֶׁה לִבּוֹ לְמַעַן הַרְבּוֹת בּוֹ אוֹתוֹתַי וְתַכִּירוּ אַתֶּם גְּבוּרוֹתַי. וְכֵן מִדָּתוֹ שֶׁל הַקָּדוֹשׁ בָּרוּךְ הוּא, מֵבִיא פֻּרְעָנוּת עַל הָאֻמּוֹת כְּדֵי שֶׁיִּשְׁמְעוּ יִשְׂרָאֵל וְיִירְאוּ, שֶׁנֶּאֱמַר: "הִכְרַתִּי גוֹיִם נָשַׁמּוּ פִּנּוֹתָם... אָמַרְתִּי אַךְ תִּירְאִי אוֹתִי תִּקְחִי מוּסָר" (צפניה ג, ו-ז). וְאַף עַל פִּי כֵן, בְּחָמֵשׁ מַכּוֹת הָרִאשׁוֹנוֹת לֹא נֶאֱמַר: "וַיְחַזֵּק ה׳ אֶת לֵב פַּרְעֹה", אֶלָּא: "וַיֶּחֱזַק לֵב פַּרְעֹה":

ד׳ אֶת יָדִי. יָד מַמָּשׁ, לְהַכּוֹת בָּהֶם:

ט׳ מוֹפֵת. אוֹת, לְהוֹדִיעַ שֶׁיֵּשׁ עֹרֶךְ בְּמִי שֶׁשּׁוֹלֵחַ אֶתְכֶם: לְתַנִּין. נָחָשׁ:

י"א בְּלַהֲטֵיהֶם. "בְּלַחֲשֵׁיהוֹן", וְאֵין לוֹ דִּמְיוֹן בַּמִּקְרָא. וְיֵשׁ לְדַמּוֹת לוֹ: "לַהַט הַחֶרֶב הַמִּתְהַפֶּכֶת" (בראשית ג, כד), דּוֹמֶה שֶׁהִיא מִתְהַפֶּכֶת עַל יְדֵי לַחַשׁ:

י"ב וַיִּבְלַע מַטֵּה אַהֲרֹן. מֵאַחַר שֶׁחָזַר וְנַעֲשָׂה מַטֶּה בָּלַע אֶת כֻּלָּן:

י"ד כָּבֵד. תַּרְגּוּמוֹ "יַקִּיר", וְלֹא "אִתְיַקַּר", מִפְּנֵי שֶׁהוּא שֵׁם דָּבָר, כְּמוֹ: "כִּי כָבֵד מִמְּךָ הַדָּבָר" (להלן יח, יח):

טו מֵאֵ֖ן לְשַׁלַּ֣ח הָעָֽם: לֵ֣ךְ אֶל־פַּרְעֹ֞ה בַּבֹּ֗קֶר הִנֵּה֙ יֹצֵ֣א הַמַּ֔יְמָה וְנִצַּבְתָּ֥ לִקְרָאת֖וֹ עַל־שְׂפַ֣ת הַיְאֹ֑ר וְהַמַּטֶּ֛ה אֲשֶׁר־נֶהְפַּ֥ךְ לְנָחָ֖שׁ

טז תִּקַּ֥ח בְּיָדֶֽךָ: וְאָמַרְתָּ֣ אֵלָ֗יו יְהֹוָ֞ה אֱלֹהֵ֤י הָֽעִבְרִים֙ שְׁלָחַ֤נִי אֵלֶ֨יךָ֙ לֵאמֹ֔ר שַׁלַּח֙ אֶת־עַמִּ֔י וְיַֽעַבְדֻ֖נִי בַּמִּדְבָּ֑ר וְהִנֵּ֥ה לֹא־שָׁמַ֖עְתָּ עַד־

יז כֹּֽה: כֹּ֚ה אָמַ֣ר יְהֹוָ֔ה בְּזֹ֣את תֵּדַ֔ע כִּ֖י אֲנִ֣י יְהֹוָ֑ה הִנֵּ֨ה אָנֹכִ֜י מַכֶּ֣ה ׀

יח בַּמַּטֶּ֣ה אֲשֶׁר־בְּיָדִ֗י עַל־הַמַּ֛יִם אֲשֶׁ֥ר בַּיְאֹ֖ר וְנֶהֶפְכ֥וּ לְדָֽם: וְהַדָּגָ֧ה אֲשֶׁר־בַּיְאֹ֛ר תָּמ֖וּת וּבָאַ֣שׁ הַיְאֹ֑ר וְנִלְא֣וּ מִצְרַ֔יִם לִשְׁתּ֥וֹת מַ֖יִם

יט מִן־הַיְאֹֽר: וַיֹּ֨אמֶר יְהֹוָ֜ה אֶל־מֹשֶׁ֗ה אֱמֹ֣ר אֶֽל־אַהֲרֹ֡ן קַ֣ח מַטְּךָ֣ וּנְטֵֽה־יָדְךָ֩ עַל־מֵימֵ֨י מִצְרַ֜יִם עַֽל־נַהֲרֹתָ֣ם ׀ עַל־יְאֹרֵיהֶ֣ם וְעַל־אַגְמֵיהֶ֗ם וְעַ֛ל כָּל־מִקְוֵ֥ה מֵימֵיהֶ֖ם וְיִהְיוּ־דָ֑ם וְהָ֤יָה דָם֙ בְּכָל־אֶ֣רֶץ מִצְרַ֔יִם וּבָעֵצִ֖ים וּבָאֲבָנִֽים:

כ וַיַּֽעֲשׂוּ־כֵן֩ מֹשֶׁ֨ה וְאַהֲרֹ֜ן כַּֽאֲשֶׁ֣ר ׀ צִוָּ֣ה יְהֹוָ֗ה וַיָּ֤רֶם בַּמַּטֶּה֙ וַיַּ֤ךְ אֶת־הַמַּ֨יִם֙ אֲשֶׁ֣ר בַּיְאֹ֔ר לְעֵינֵ֣י פַרְעֹ֔ה וּלְעֵינֵ֖י עֲבָדָ֑יו וַיֵּהָֽפְכ֛וּ כָּל־הַמַּ֥יִם אֲשֶׁר־בַּיְאֹ֖ר

כא לְדָֽם: וְהַדָּגָ֨ה אֲשֶׁר־בַּיְאֹ֥ר מֵ֨תָה֙ וַיִּבְאַ֣שׁ הַיְאֹ֔ר וְלֹא־יָכְל֣וּ מִצְרַ֔יִם לִשְׁתּ֥וֹת מַ֖יִם מִן־הַיְאֹ֑ר וַיְהִ֥י הַדָּ֖ם בְּכָל־אֶ֥רֶץ מִצְרָֽיִם:

טו) **הִנֵּה יֹצֵא הַמַּיְמָה.** לִנְקָבָיו, שֶׁהָיָה עוֹשֶׂה עַצְמוֹ אֱלוֹהַּ וְאוֹמֵר שֶׁאֵינוֹ צָרִיךְ לִנְקָבָיו, וּמַשְׁכִּים וְיוֹצֵא לַנִּילוּס וְעוֹשֶׂה שָׁם צְרָכָיו:

טז) **עַד כֹּה. עַד הֵנָּה.** וּמִדְרָשׁוֹ, עַד שֶׁתִּשְׁמַע מִמֶּנִּי מַכַּת בְּכוֹרוֹת שֶׁאֶפְתַּח בָּהּ בְּ"כֹה אָמַר ה' כַּחֲצוֹת הַלָּיְלָה" (להלן יא, ד) וְגוֹ':

יז) **וְנֶהֶפְכוּ לְדָם.** לְפִי שֶׁאֵין גְּשָׁמִים יוֹרְדִים בְּמִצְרַיִם וְנִילוּס עוֹלֶה וּמַשְׁקֶה אֶת הָאָרֶץ וּמִצְרַיִם עוֹבְדִים לַנִּילוּס, לְפִיכָךְ הִלְקָה אֶת יִרְאָתָם וְאַחַר כָּךְ הִלְקָה אוֹתָם:

יח) **וְנִלְאוּ מִצְרַיִם.** לְבַקֵּשׁ רְפוּאָה לְמֵי הַיְאוֹר שֶׁיִּהְיוּ רְאוּיִין לִשְׁתּוֹת:

יט) **אֱמֹר אֶל אַהֲרֹן.** לְפִי שֶׁהֵגֵן הַיְאוֹר עַל מֹשֶׁה כְּשֶׁנִּשְׁלַךְ לְתוֹכוֹ, לְפִיכָךְ לֹא לָקָה עַל יָדוֹ לֹא בַדָּם וְלֹא בַצְפַרְדְּעִים, וְלָקָה עַל יְדֵי אַהֲרֹן: **נַהֲרֹתָם.** הֵם נְהָרוֹת הַמּוֹשְׁכִים כְּעֵין נְהָרוֹת שֶׁלָּנוּ: **יְאֹרֵיהֶם.** הֵם נְהָרִים הָעֲשׂוּיִים בִּידֵי אָדָם מִשְּׂפַת הַנָּהָר לַשָּׂדוֹת, וְנִילוּס מֵימָיו מִתְבָּרְכִים וְעוֹלֶה דֶּרֶךְ הַיְאוֹרִים וּמַשְׁקֶה הַשָּׂדוֹת: **אַגְמֵיהֶם.** קְבוּצַת מַיִם שֶׁאֵינָן נוֹבְעִין וְאֵינָן מוֹשְׁכִין אֶלָּא עוֹמְדִין בְּמָקוֹם אֶחָד, וְקוֹרִין לוֹ אשטנ"ק: **בְּכָל אֶרֶץ מִצְרָיִם.**

פרק ז

כב וַיַּעֲשׂוּ־כֵן חַרְטֻמֵּי מִצְרַיִם בְּלָטֵיהֶם וַיֶּחֱזַק לֵב־פַּרְעֹה וְלֹא־שָׁמַע אֲלֵהֶם כַּאֲשֶׁר דִּבֶּר יְהוָה: כג וַיִּפֶן פַּרְעֹה וַיָּבֹא אֶל־בֵּיתוֹ וְלֹא־שָׁת לִבּוֹ גַּם־לָזֹאת: כד וַיַּחְפְּרוּ כָל־מִצְרַיִם סְבִיבֹת הַיְאֹר מַיִם לִשְׁתּוֹת כִּי לֹא יָכְלוּ לִשְׁתֹּת מִמֵּימֵי הַיְאֹר: כה וַיִּמָּלֵא שִׁבְעַת יָמִים אַחֲרֵי הַכּוֹת־יְהוָה אֶת־הַיְאֹר:

כו וַיֹּאמֶר יְהוָה אֶל־מֹשֶׁה בֹּא אֶל־פַּרְעֹה וְאָמַרְתָּ אֵלָיו כֹּה אָמַר יְהוָה שַׁלַּח אֶת־עַמִּי וְיַעַבְדֻנִי: כז וְאִם־מָאֵן אַתָּה לְשַׁלֵּחַ הִנֵּה אָנֹכִי נֹגֵף אֶת־כָּל־גְּבוּלְךָ בַּצְפַרְדְּעִים: כח וְשָׁרַץ הַיְאֹר צְפַרְדְּעִים וְעָלוּ וּבָאוּ בְּבֵיתֶךָ וּבַחֲדַר מִשְׁכָּבְךָ וְעַל־מִטָּתֶךָ וּבְבֵית עֲבָדֶיךָ וּבְעַמֶּךָ וּבְתַנּוּרֶיךָ וּבְמִשְׁאֲרוֹתֶיךָ: כט וּבְכָה וּבְעַמְּךָ וּבְכָל־עֲבָדֶיךָ יַעֲלוּ הַצְפַרְדְּעִים:

פרק ח

א וַיֹּאמֶר יְהוָה אֶל־מֹשֶׁה אֱמֹר אֶל־אַהֲרֹן נְטֵה אֶת־יָדְךָ בְּמַטֶּךָ עַל־הַנְּהָרֹת עַל־הַיְאֹרִים וְעַל־הָאֲגַמִּים וְהַעַל

אַף בַּמַּרְחֲצָאוֹת וּבָאַמְבְּטָאוֹת שֶׁבַּבָּתִּים: **וּבְעֵצִים וּבָאֲבָנִים.** מַיִם שֶׁבִּכְלֵי עֵץ וּבִכְלֵי אֶבֶן.

כב] **בְּלָטֵיהֶם.** לַחַשׁ שֶׁאוֹמְרִים אוֹתוֹ בַּלָּט וּבַחֲשַׁאי. רַבּוֹתֵינוּ אָמְרוּ: 'בְּלָטֵיהֶם' – מַעֲשֵׂה שֵׁדִים, 'בְּלַהֲטֵיהֶם' – מַעֲשֵׂה כְשָׁפִים: **וַיֶּחֱזַק לֵב פַּרְעֹה.** לוֹמַר עַל יְדֵי מְכַשְּׁפוּת אַתֶּם עוֹשִׂים כֵּן, תֶּבֶן אַתֶּם מַכְנִיסִים לְעַפְרַיִם, עִיר שֶׁכֻּלָּהּ תֶּבֶן?! אַף אַתֶּם מְבִיאִין מְכַשְּׁפוּת לְמִצְרַיִם שֶׁכֻּלָּהּ כְּשָׁפִים?!

כג] **גַּם לָזֹאת.** לְמוֹפֵת הַמַּטֶּה שֶׁנֶּהְפַּךְ לְתַנִּין, וְלֹא לָזֶה שֶׁל דָּם:

כה] **וַיִּמָּלֵא.** מִנְיַן שִׁבְעַת יָמִים שֶׁלֹּא שָׁב הַיְאוֹר לְקַדְמוּתוֹ, שֶׁהָיְתָה הַמַּכָּה מְשַׁמֶּשֶׁת רְבִיעַ חֹדֶשׁ, וּשְׁלֹשָׁה חֲלָקִים הָיָה מֵעִיד וּמַתְרֶה בָּהֶם:

כז] **וְאִם מָאֵן אַתָּה.** וְאִם סָרְבָן אַתָּה. 'מָאֵן' כְּמוֹ 'מְמָאֵן', מְסָרֵב, אֶלָּא כִּנּוּי הָאָדָם עַל שֵׁם הַמִּפְעָל, כְּמוֹ: "שָׁלֵו" (איוב ט"ז, י"ב), "וְשׁוֹקֵט" (ירמיה מ"ח, י"א), "סַר וְזָעֵף" (מלכים א' כ', מ"ג): **נֹגֵף אֶת כָּל גְּבוּלְךָ.** מַכֶּה. וְכֵן כָּל לְשׁוֹן מַגֵּפָה אֵינוֹ לְשׁוֹן מִיתָה אֶלָּא לְשׁוֹן מַכָּה, וְכֵן: "וְנָגְפוּ אִשָּׁה הָרָה" (להלן כ"א, כ"ב) אֵינוֹ לְשׁוֹן מִיתָה, וְכֵן: "וּבְטֶרֶם יִתְנַגְּפוּ רַגְלֵיכֶם" (ירמיה י"ג, ט"ז), "פֶּן תִּגֹּף בָּאֶבֶן רַגְלֶךָ" (תהלים צ"א, י"ב), "וּלְאֶבֶן נֶגֶף" (ישעיה ח', י"ד):

כח] **וְעָלוּ.** מִן הַיְאוֹר: **בְּבֵיתֶךָ.** וְאַחַר כָּךְ "בְּבֵית עֲבָדֶיךָ", הוּא הִתְחִיל בָּעֵצָה תְּחִלָּה – "וַיֹּאמֶר אֶל עַמּוֹ" (לעיל א', ט') וּמִמֶּנּוּ הִתְחִילָה הַפֻּרְעָנוּת:

כט] **וּבְכָה וּבְעַמְּךָ.** בְּתוֹךְ מֵעֵיהֶם נִכְנָסִין וּמְקַרְקְרִין:

שמות | פרק ח

ב אֶת־הַֽצְפַרְדְּעִ֔ים עַל־אֶ֖רֶץ מִצְרָֽיִם: וַיֵּ֤ט אַהֲרֹן֙ אֶת־יָד֔וֹ עַ֖ל מֵימֵ֣י
ג מִצְרָ֑יִם וַתַּ֙עַל֙ הַצְּפַרְדֵּ֔עַ וַתְּכַ֖ס אֶת־אֶ֥רֶץ מִצְרָֽיִם: וַיַּֽעֲשׂוּ־כֵ֥ן
הַֽחַרְטֻמִּ֖ים בְּלָטֵיהֶ֑ם וַיַּעֲל֥וּ אֶת־הַֽצְפַרְדְּעִ֖ים עַל־אֶ֥רֶץ מִצְרָֽיִם:
ד וַיִּקְרָ֨א פַרְעֹ֜ה לְמֹשֶׁ֣ה וּֽלְאַהֲרֹ֗ן וַיֹּ֨אמֶר֙ הַעְתִּ֣ירוּ אֶל־יְהוָ֔ה וְיָסֵר֙
הַֽצְפַרְדְּעִ֔ים מִמֶּ֖נִּי וּמֵֽעַמִּ֑י וַאֲשַׁלְּחָה֙ אֶת־הָעָ֔ם וְיִזְבְּח֖וּ לַיהוָֽה:
ה וַיֹּ֣אמֶר מֹשֶׁ֣ה לְפַרְעֹה֮ הִתְפָּאֵ֣ר עָלַי֒ לְמָתַ֣י ׀ אַעְתִּ֣יר לְךָ֗ וְלַעֲבָדֶ֙יךָ֙
וּֽלְעַמְּךָ֔ לְהַכְרִית֙ הַֽצְפַרְדְּעִ֔ים מִמְּךָ֖ וּמִבָּתֶּ֑יךָ רַ֥ק בַּיְאֹ֖ר תִּשָּׁאַֽרְנָה:
ו וַיֹּ֖אמֶר לְמָחָ֑ר וַיֹּ֙אמֶר֙ כִּדְבָ֣רְךָ֔ לְמַ֣עַן תֵּדַ֔ע כִּי־אֵ֖ין כַּיהוָ֥ה אֱלֹהֵֽינוּ:
ז וְסָר֣וּ הַֽצְפַרְדְּעִ֗ים מִמְּךָ֙ וּמִבָּ֣תֶּ֔יךָ וּמֵעֲבָדֶ֖יךָ וּמֵעַמֶּ֑ךָ רַ֥ק בַּיְאֹ֖ר
ח תִּשָּׁאַֽרְנָה: וַיֵּצֵ֥א מֹשֶׁ֛ה וְאַהֲרֹ֖ן מֵעִ֣ם פַּרְעֹ֑ה וַיִּצְעַ֤ק מֹשֶׁה֙ אֶל־
ט יְהוָ֔ה עַל־דְּבַ֥ר הַֽצְפַרְדְּעִ֖ים אֲשֶׁר־שָׂ֥ם לְפַרְעֹֽה: וַיַּ֥עַשׂ יְהוָ֖ה
כִּדְבַ֣ר מֹשֶׁ֑ה וַיָּמֻ֙תוּ֙ הַֽצְפַרְדְּעִ֔ים מִן־הַבָּתִּ֥ים מִן־הַחֲצֵרֹ֖ת
י וּמִן־הַשָּׂדֹֽת: וַיִּצְבְּר֥וּ אֹתָ֖ם חֳמָרִ֣ם חֳמָרִ֑ם וַתִּבְאַ֖שׁ הָאָֽרֶץ:

חמישי (before ז)

פרק ח

ב **וַתַּעַל הַצְּפַרְדֵּעַ.** צְפַרְדֵּעַ אַחַת הָיְתָה וְהָיוּ מַכִּין אוֹתָהּ וְהִיא מַתֶּזֶת נְחִילִים נְחִילִים, זֶהוּ מִדְרָשׁוֹ. וּפְשׁוּטוֹ יֵשׁ לוֹמַר, שְׁרוֹן הַצְפַרְדְּעִים קוֹרֵא לְשׁוֹן יְחִידוּת. וְכֵן: "וַתְּהִי הַכִּנָּם" (להלן פסוק יד) הָרְחִישָׁה, פדולי"רא בְּלַעַז, וְאַף "וַתַּעַל הַצְפַרְדֵּעַ" גרינולי"רא בְּלַעַז:

ה **הִתְפָּאֵר עָלַי.** כְּמוֹ: "הֲיִתְפָּאֵר הַגַּרְזֶן עַל הַחֹצֵב בּוֹ" (ישעיה י, טו), מִשְׁתַּבֵּחַ לוֹמַר: אֲנִי גָדוֹל מִמְּךָ. וְנוטי"ר בְּלַעַז. וְכֵן: "הִתְפָּאֵר עָלַי", הִשְׁתַּבַּח לְהִתְחַכֵּם וְלִשְׁאוֹל דָּבָר גָּדוֹל וְלוֹמַר שֶׁלֹּא אוּכַל לַעֲשׂוֹתוֹ: **לְמָתַי אַעְתִּיר לְךָ.** אֵת אֲשֶׁר אַעְתִּיר לְךָ הַיּוֹם עַל הַכְרָתַת הַצְפַרְדְּעִים, לְמָתַי תִּרְצֶה שֶׁיִּכָּרְתוּ, וְתִרְאֶה אִם אַשְׁלִים דְּבָרַי לַמּוֹעֵד שֶׁאֶקְבַּע לִי. אִלּוּ נֶאֱמַר "מָתַי אַעְתִּיר", הָיָה מַשְׁמָע: מָתַי אֶתְפַּלֵּל? עַכְשָׁיו שֶׁנֶּאֱמַר "לְמָתַי", אֲנִי הַיּוֹם מִתְפַּלֵּל עָלֶיךָ שֶׁיִּכָּרְתוּ הַצְפַרְדְּעִים לִזְמַן שֶׁתִּקְבַּע לִי, אֱמֹר לְאֵיזֶה יוֹם תִּרְצֶה שֶׁיִּכָּרְתוּ: "אַעְתִּיר", "הַעְתִּירוּ", "וְהַעְתַּרְתִּי", וְלֹא נֶאֱמַר: "אֶעְתַּר", "עִתְרוּ", "וְעָתַרְתִּי", מִפְּנֵי שֶׁכָּל לְשׁוֹן "עֶתֶר" הַרְבּוֹת פַּלֵּל הוּא, וְכַאֲשֶׁר יֹאמַר: הַרְבּוּ, וְהִרְבֵּיתִי, לְשׁוֹן מַתְעִיל, כֵּן יֹאמַר: הַעְתִּירוּ, אַעְתִּיר, הַעְתִּיר דְּבָרִים, וְדֹב לְכֻלָּם: "וְהַעְתַּרְתֶּם עָלַי דִּבְרֵיכֶם" (יחזקאל לה, יג), הִרְבֵּיתֶם:

ו **וַיֹּאמֶר לְמָחָר.** הִתְפַּלֵּל הַיּוֹם שֶׁיִּכָּרְתוּ לְמָחָר:

ח **וַיֵּצֵא...וַיִּצְעַק.** מִיָּד, שֶׁיִּכָּרְתוּ לְמָחָר:

י **חֳמָרִם חֳמָרִם.** צִבּוּרִים צִבּוּרִים, כְּתַרְגּוּמוֹ "דְּגוֹרִין", גַּלִּין:

יא וַיַּ֣רְא פַּרְעֹ֗ה כִּ֤י הָֽיְתָה֙ הָֽרְוָחָ֔ה וְהַכְבֵּד֙ אֶת־לִבּ֔וֹ וְלֹ֥א שָׁמַ֖ע
אֲלֵהֶ֑ם כַּאֲשֶׁ֖ר דִּבֶּ֥ר יְהוָֽה׃   יב וַיֹּ֨אמֶר יְהוָ֜ה אֶל־מֹשֶׁ֗ה
אֱמֹר֙ אֶֽל־אַהֲרֹ֔ן נְטֵ֣ה אֶֽת־מַטְּךָ֔ וְהַ֖ךְ אֶת־עֲפַ֣ר הָאָ֑רֶץ וְהָיָ֥ה לְכִנִּ֖ם
בְּכָל־אֶ֥רֶץ מִצְרָֽיִם׃   יג וַיַּעֲשׂוּ־כֵ֗ן וַיֵּט֩ אַהֲרֹ֨ן אֶת־יָד֤וֹ בְמַטֵּ֨הוּ֙ וַיַּךְ֙
אֶת־עֲפַ֣ר הָאָ֔רֶץ וַתְּהִי֙ הַכִּנָּ֔ם בָּאָדָ֖ם וּבַבְּהֵמָ֑ה כָּל־עֲפַ֥ר הָאָ֛רֶץ
הָיָ֥ה כִנִּ֖ים בְּכָל־אֶ֥רֶץ מִצְרָֽיִם׃   יד וַיַּעֲשׂוּ־כֵ֨ן הַחַרְטֻמִּ֧ים בְּלָטֵיהֶ֛ם
לְהוֹצִ֥יא אֶת־הַכִּנִּ֖ים וְלֹ֣א יָכֹ֑לוּ וַתְּהִי֙ הַכִּנָּ֔ם בָּאָדָ֖ם וּבַבְּהֵמָֽה׃
טו וַיֹּאמְר֤וּ הַֽחַרְטֻמִּם֙ אֶל־פַּרְעֹ֔ה אֶצְבַּ֥ע אֱלֹהִ֖ים הִ֑וא וַיֶּחֱזַ֣ק לֵב־
פַּרְעֹ֗ה וְלֹֽא־שָׁמַ֣ע אֲלֵהֶ֔ם כַּאֲשֶׁ֖ר דִּבֶּ֥ר יְהוָֽה׃   טז וַיֹּ֨אמֶר
יְהוָ֜ה אֶל־מֹשֶׁ֗ה הַשְׁכֵּ֤ם בַּבֹּ֨קֶר֙ וְהִתְיַצֵּב֙ לִפְנֵ֣י פַרְעֹ֔ה הִנֵּ֖ה יוֹצֵ֣א
הַמָּ֑יְמָה וְאָמַרְתָּ֣ אֵלָ֗יו כֹּ֚ה אָמַ֣ר יְהוָ֔ה שַׁלַּ֥ח עַמִּ֖י וְיַעַבְדֻֽנִי׃   יז כִּ֣י
אִם־אֵינְךָ֮ מְשַׁלֵּ֣חַ אֶת־עַמִּי֒ הִנְנִי֩ מַשְׁלִ֨יחַ בְּךָ֜ וּבַעֲבָדֶ֤יךָ וּֽבְעַמְּךָ֙
וּבְבָתֶּ֔יךָ אֶת־הֶעָרֹ֑ב וּמָ֨לְא֜וּ בָּתֵּ֤י מִצְרַ֨יִם֙ אֶת־הֶ֣עָרֹ֔ב וְגַ֥ם הָאֲדָמָ֖ה

יא] וְהַכְבֵּד אֶת לִבּוֹ. לְשׁוֹן פָּעוֹל הוּא, "הָלוֹךְ וְכָלוֹ"
(ירמיה מא, ו), וְכֵן: "וְהַכּוֹת אֶת מוֹאָב" (מלכים ב' ג, כד),
"וְשָׁאוֹל לוֹ בֵאלֹהִים" (שמואל א' כב, יג), "הַכֵּה וּפָצֹעַ" (מלכים
א' כ, לז). כַּאֲשֶׁר דִּבֶּר ה'. וְהֵיכָן דִּבֵּר? "וְלֹא יִשְׁמַע
אֲלֵכֶם פַּרְעֹה" (לעיל ז, ד):

יב] אֱמֹר אֶל אַהֲרֹן. לֹא הֶעָפָר כְּדַאי לִלְקוֹת עַל יְדֵי
מֹשֶׁה, לְפִי שֶׁהֵגֵן עָלָיו כְּשֶׁהָרַג אֶת הַמִּצְרִי וַיִּטְמְנֵהוּ
בַּחוֹל, וְלָקָה עַל יְדֵי אַהֲרֹן:

יג] וַתְּהִי הַכִּנָּם. הָרְחִישָׁה, פדולי"ר בְּלַעַ"ז:

יד] לְהוֹצִיא אֶת הַכִּנִּים. לִבְרֹאתָם מִמָּקוֹם אַחֵר: וְלֹא
יָכֹלוּ. שֶׁאֵין הַשֵּׁד שׁוֹלֵט עַל בְּרִיָּה פְּחוּתָה מִכִּשְׂעוֹרָה:

טו] אֶצְבַּע אֱלֹהִים הִוא. מַכָּה זוֹ אֵינָהּ עַל יְדֵי
כְשָׁפִים, מֵאֵת הַמָּקוֹם הִיא: כַּאֲשֶׁר דִּבֶּר ה'. "וְלֹא
יִשְׁמַע אֲלֵכֶם פַּרְעֹה" (לעיל ז, ד):

יז] מַשְׁלִיחַ בְּךָ. מְגָרֶה בָּךְ, וְכֵן: "וְשֶׁן בְּהֵמוֹת אֲשַׁלַּח
בָּם" (דברים לב, כד) לְשׁוֹן שִׁסּוּי, אינציטיי"ר בְּלַעַ"ז: אֶת
הֶעָרֹב. כָּל מִינֵי חַיּוֹת רָעוֹת וּנְחָשִׁים וְעַקְרַבִּים
בְּעִרְבּוּבְיָא, וְהָיוּ מַשְׁחִיתִים בָּהֶם. וְיֵשׁ טַעַם בַּדָּבָר
בָּאַגָּדָה בְּכָל מַכָּה וּמַכָּה לָמָּה זוֹ וְלָמָּה זוֹ. בְּטַכְסִיסֵי
מִלְחֲמוֹת מְלָכִים בָּא עֲלֵיהֶם, כְּסֵדֶר מַלְכוּת כְּשֶׁצָּרָה
עַל עִיר, בַּתְּחִלָּה מְקַלְקֵל מַעְיְנוֹתֶיהָ, וְאַחַר כָּךְ
תּוֹקֵעַ עֲלֵיהֶם וּמְרִיעִים בַּשּׁוֹפָרוֹת לְיָרְדָם וּלְבַהֲלָם,
וְכֵן הַצְפַרְדְּעִים מְקַרְקְרִים וְהוֹמִים וְכוּ', כִּדְאִיתָא
בְּמִדְרַשׁ רַבִּי תַּנְחוּמָא (פ"ח ד):

שמות | פרק ח

יח אֲשֶׁר־הֵם עָלֶיהָ: וְהִפְלֵיתִי בַיּוֹם הַהוּא אֶת־אֶרֶץ גֹּשֶׁן אֲשֶׁר עַמִּי עֹמֵד עָלֶיהָ לְבִלְתִּי הֱיוֹת־שָׁם עָרֹב לְמַעַן תֵּדַע כִּי אֲנִי
יט יְהוָֹה בְּקֶרֶב הָאָרֶץ: וְשַׂמְתִּי פְדֻת בֵּין עַמִּי וּבֵין עַמֶּךָ לְמָחָר יִהְיֶה הָאֹת הַזֶּה: וַיַּעַשׂ יְהוָֹה כֵּן וַיָּבֹא עָרֹב כָּבֵד בֵּיתָה פַרְעֹה
כ וּבֵית עֲבָדָיו וּבְכָל־אֶרֶץ מִצְרַיִם תִּשָּׁחֵת הָאָרֶץ מִפְּנֵי הֶעָרֹב:
כא וַיִּקְרָא פַרְעֹה אֶל־מֹשֶׁה וּלְאַהֲרֹן וַיֹּאמֶר לְכוּ זִבְחוּ לֵאלֹהֵיכֶם
כב בָּאָרֶץ: וַיֹּאמֶר מֹשֶׁה לֹא נָכוֹן לַעֲשׂוֹת כֵּן כִּי תּוֹעֲבַת מִצְרַיִם נִזְבַּח לַיהוָֹה אֱלֹהֵינוּ הֵן נִזְבַּח אֶת־תּוֹעֲבַת מִצְרַיִם לְעֵינֵיהֶם
כג וְלֹא יִסְקְלֻנוּ: דֶּרֶךְ שְׁלֹשֶׁת יָמִים נֵלֵךְ בַּמִּדְבָּר וְזָבַחְנוּ לַיהוָֹה
כד אֱלֹהֵינוּ כַּאֲשֶׁר יֹאמַר אֵלֵינוּ: וַיֹּאמֶר פַּרְעֹה אָנֹכִי אֲשַׁלַּח אֶתְכֶם וּזְבַחְתֶּם לַיהוָֹה אֱלֹהֵיכֶם בַּמִּדְבָּר רַק הַרְחֵק לֹא־תַרְחִיקוּ לָלֶכֶת
כה הַעְתִּירוּ בַּעֲדִי: וַיֹּאמֶר מֹשֶׁה הִנֵּה אָנֹכִי יוֹצֵא מֵעִמָּךְ וְהַעְתַּרְתִּי אֶל־יְהוָֹה וְסָר הֶעָרֹב מִפַּרְעֹה מֵעֲבָדָיו וּמֵעַמּוֹ מָחָר רַק אַל־
כו יֹסֵף פַּרְעֹה הָתֵל לְבִלְתִּי שַׁלַּח אֶת־הָעָם לִזְבֹּחַ לַיהוָֹה: וַיֵּצֵא
כז מֹשֶׁה מֵעִם פַּרְעֹה וַיֶּעְתַּר אֶל־יְהוָֹה: וַיַּעַשׂ יְהוָֹה כִּדְבַר מֹשֶׁה

ששי

יח| וְהִפְלֵיתִי. וְהִפְרַשְׁתִּי, וְכֵן: "וְהִפְלָה ה'" (להלן ט, ד), וְכֵן: "לֹא נִפְלֵאת הִוא מִמְּךָ" (דברים ל, יא), לֹא מֻבְדֶּלֶת וּמְפֹרֶשֶׁת הִיא מִמְּךָ: לְמַעַן תֵּדַע כִּי אֲנִי ה' בְּקֶרֶב הָאָרֶץ. אַף עַל פִּי שֶׁשְּׁכִינָתִי בַּשָּׁמַיִם גְּזֵרָתִי מִתְקַיֶּמֶת בַּתַּחְתּוֹנִים:

יט| וְשַׂמְתִּי פְדֻת. שֶׁיַּבְדִּיל "בֵּין עַמִּי וּבֵין עַמֶּךָ":

כ| תִּשָּׁחֵת הָאָרֶץ. נִשְׁחֶתֶת הָאָרֶץ, "אִתְחַבַּלַת אַרְעָא":

כא| זִבְחוּ לֵאלֹהֵיכֶם בָּאָרֶץ. בִּמְקוֹמְכֶם, וְלֹא תֵלְכוּ בַּמִּדְבָּר:

כב| תּוֹעֲבַת מִצְרַיִם. יִרְאַת מִצְרַיִם, כְּמוֹ: "וּלְמִלְכֹּם תּוֹעֲבַת בְּנֵי עַמּוֹן" (מלכים ב' כג, יג), וְאֵצֶל יִשְׂרָאֵל קוֹרֵא אוֹתָהּ תּוֹעֵבָה. וְעוֹד יֵשׁ לוֹמַר בְּלָשׁוֹן אַחֵר, "תּוֹעֲבַת מִצְרַיִם", דָּבָר שָׂנוּי הוּא לְמִצְרַיִם זְבִיחָה שֶׁאָנוּ זוֹבְחִים, שֶׁהֲרֵי יִרְאָתָם אָנוּ זוֹבְחִים: וְלֹא יִסְקְלֻנוּ. בִּתְמִיהָ.

כה| הָתֵל. כְּמוֹ לְהָתֵל:

כו-כז| וְסָר הֶעָרֹב. וְלֹא מֵתוּ כְּמוֹ שֶׁמֵּתוּ הַצְפַרְדְּעִים, שֶׁאִם מֵתוּ הָיָה לָהֶם הֲנָאָה בָּעוֹרוֹת: וַיֶּעְתַּר אֶל ה'. נִתְאַמֵּץ בִּתְפִלָּה. וְכֵן אִם בָּא לוֹמַר 'וַיַּעְתִּיר' הָיָה

וַיָּ֣סַר הֶעָרֹ֗ב מִפַּרְעֹ֛ה מֵעֲבָדָ֥יו וּמֵעַמּ֖וֹ לֹ֥א נִשְׁאַ֥ר אֶחָֽד: וַיַּכְבֵּ֨ד פַּרְעֹ֤ה אֶת־לִבּ֔וֹ גַּ֖ם בַּפַּ֣עַם הַזֹּ֑את וְלֹ֥א שִׁלַּ֖ח אֶת־הָעָֽם:

וַיֹּ֤אמֶר יְהֹוָה֙ אֶל־מֹשֶׁ֔ה בֹּ֖א אֶל־פַּרְעֹ֑ה וְדִבַּרְתָּ֣ אֵלָ֗יו כֹּֽה־אָמַ֤ר יְהֹוָה֙ אֱלֹהֵ֣י הָֽעִבְרִ֔ים שַׁלַּ֥ח אֶת־עַמִּ֖י וְיַֽעַבְדֻֽנִי: כִּ֛י אִם־מָאֵ֥ן אַתָּ֖ה לְשַׁלֵּ֑חַ וְעֽוֹדְךָ֖ מַחֲזִ֥יק בָּֽם: הִנֵּ֨ה יַד־יְהֹוָ֜ה הוֹיָ֗ה בְּמִקְנְךָ֙ אֲשֶׁ֣ר בַּשָּׂדֶ֔ה בַּסּוּסִ֤ים בַּֽחֲמֹרִים֙ בַּגְּמַלִּ֔ים בַּבָּקָ֖ר וּבַצֹּ֑אן דֶּ֖בֶר כָּבֵ֥ד מְאֹֽד: וְהִפְלָ֣ה יְהֹוָ֔ה בֵּ֚ין מִקְנֵ֣ה יִשְׂרָאֵ֔ל וּבֵ֖ין מִקְנֵ֣ה מִצְרָ֑יִם וְלֹ֥א יָמ֛וּת מִכָּל־לִבְנֵ֥י יִשְׂרָאֵ֖ל דָּבָֽר: וַיָּ֥שֶׂם יְהֹוָ֖ה מוֹעֵ֣ד לֵאמֹ֑ר מָחָ֗ר יַֽעֲשֶׂ֧ה יְהֹוָ֛ה הַדָּבָ֥ר הַזֶּ֖ה בָּאָֽרֶץ: וַיַּ֨עַשׂ יְהֹוָ֜ה אֶת־הַדָּבָ֤ר הַזֶּה֙ מִֽמָּחֳרָ֔ת וַיָּ֕מָת כֹּ֖ל מִקְנֵ֣ה מִצְרָ֑יִם וּמִמִּקְנֵ֥ה בְנֵֽי־יִשְׂרָאֵ֖ל לֹא־מֵ֥ת אֶחָֽד: וַיִּשְׁלַ֣ח פַּרְעֹ֔ה וְהִנֵּ֗ה לֹא־מֵ֛ת מִמִּקְנֵ֥ה יִשְׂרָאֵ֖ל עַד־אֶחָ֑ד וַיִּכְבַּד֙ לֵ֣ב פַּרְעֹ֔ה וְלֹ֥א שִׁלַּ֖ח אֶת־הָעָֽם:

וַיֹּ֤אמֶר יְהֹוָה֙ אֶל־מֹשֶׁ֣ה וְאֶֽל־אַהֲרֹ֔ן קְח֤וּ לָכֶם֙ מְלֹ֣א חָפְנֵיכֶ֔ם פִּ֖יחַ כִּבְשָׁ֑ן וּזְרָק֥וֹ מֹשֶׁ֛ה הַשָּׁמַ֖יְמָה לְעֵינֵ֥י פַרְעֹֽה: וְהָיָ֣ה לְאָבָ֔ק עַ֖ל כָּל־אֶ֣רֶץ מִצְרָ֑יִם וְהָיָ֨ה עַל־הָֽאָדָ֜ם וְעַל־הַבְּהֵמָ֗ה לִשְׁחִ֥ין פֹּרֵ֛חַ

יָכוֹל לוֹמַר, וּמַשְׁמַע וַיִּרְבֶּה תִּפְלָה. וּכְשֶׁהוּא חוֹמֵר בִּלְשׁוֹן וַיִּפְעַל, מַשְׁמַע וַיִּרְבָּה לְהִתְפַּלֵּל:

כח] גַּם בַּפַּעַם הַזֹּאת. אַף עַל פִּי שֶׁאָמַר "חֲנֹכִי אֲשַׁלַּח אֶתְכֶם" (לעיל פסוק כד) לֹא קִיֵּם הַבְטָחָתוֹ:

פרק ט

ב] מַחֲזִיק בָּם. אוֹחֵז בָּם, כְּמוֹ: "וְהֶחֱזִיקָה בִּמְבֻשָׁיו" (דברים כה, יא):

ג] הִנֵּה יַד ה' הוֹיָה. לְשׁוֹן הֹוֶה, כִּי כֵן יֵאָמֵר בִּלְשׁוֹן נְקֵבָה עַל שֶׁעָבַר "הָיְתָה" וְעַל הֶעָתִיד "תִּהְיֶה" וְעַל הָעוֹמֵד "הֹוָה", כְּמוֹ: עוֹשָׂה, רוֹצָה, רוֹעָה:

ד] וְהִפְלָה. וְהִבְדִּיל:

ח] מְלֹא חָפְנֵיכֶם. יולויני"ש בְּלַעַ"ז. **פִּיחַ כִּבְשָׁן.** דָּבָר הַנִּפָּח מִן הַגֶּחָלִים עֲמוּמִים הַנִּשְׂרָפִים בַּכִּבְשָׁן, וּבְלַעַ"ז אולב"ש. 'פִּיחַ' לְשׁוֹן הֲפָחָה, שֶׁהָרוּחַ מְפִיחָן וּמַפְרִיחָן: **וּזְרָקוֹ מֹשֶׁה.** וְכָל דָּבָר הַנִּזְרָק בְּכֹחַ אֵינוֹ נִזְרָק אֶלָּא בְּיָד אַחַת, הֲרֵי נִסִּים הַרְבֵּה: אֶחָד, שֶׁהֶחֱזִיק קֻמְצוֹ שֶׁל מֹשֶׁה מְלֹא חָפְנַיִם שֶׁלּוֹ וְשֶׁל אַהֲרֹן. וְאֶחָד, שֶׁהָלַךְ הָאָבָק עַל כָּל אֶרֶץ מִצְרָיִם:

ט] פֹּרֵחַ אֲבַעְבֻּעֹת. כְּתַרְגּוּמוֹ: "לִשְׁחִין סָגֵי אֲבַעְבּוּעָן", שֶׁעַל יָדוֹ צוֹמְחִין בָּהֶן בּוּעוֹת: **שְׁחִין.** לְשׁוֹן חֲמִימוּת, וְהַרְבֵּה יֵשׁ בִּלְשׁוֹן מִשְׁנָה: "שָׁנָה שְׁחוּנָה" (יומא נג ע"ב):

שמות | פרק ט

אֲבַעְבֻּעֹת בְּכָל־אֶרֶץ מִצְרָיִם: וַיִּקְחוּ אֶת־פִּיחַ הַכִּבְשָׁן וַיַּעַמְדוּ לִפְנֵי פַרְעֹה וַיִּזְרֹק אֹתוֹ מֹשֶׁה הַשָּׁמָיְמָה וַיְהִי שְׁחִין אֲבַעְבֻּעֹת

יא פֹּרֵחַ בָּאָדָם וּבַבְּהֵמָה: וְלֹא־יָכְלוּ הַחַרְטֻמִּים לַעֲמֹד לִפְנֵי מֹשֶׁה

יב מִפְּנֵי הַשְּׁחִין כִּי־הָיָה הַשְּׁחִין בַּחַרְטֻמִּם וּבְכָל־מִצְרָיִם: וַיְחַזֵּק יְהוָה אֶת־לֵב פַּרְעֹה וְלֹא שָׁמַע אֲלֵהֶם כַּאֲשֶׁר דִּבֶּר יְהוָה אֶל־

יג מֹשֶׁה: וַיֹּאמֶר יְהוָה אֶל־מֹשֶׁה הַשְׁכֵּם בַּבֹּקֶר וְהִתְיַצֵּב לִפְנֵי פַרְעֹה וְאָמַרְתָּ אֵלָיו כֹּה־אָמַר יְהוָה אֱלֹהֵי הָעִבְרִים שַׁלַּח

יד אֶת־עַמִּי וְיַעַבְדֻנִי: כִּי ׀ בַּפַּעַם הַזֹּאת אֲנִי שֹׁלֵחַ אֶת־כָּל־מַגֵּפֹתַי אֶל־לִבְּךָ וּבַעֲבָדֶיךָ וּבְעַמֶּךָ בַּעֲבוּר תֵּדַע כִּי אֵין כָּמֹנִי בְּכָל־

טו הָאָרֶץ: כִּי עַתָּה שָׁלַחְתִּי אֶת־יָדִי וָאַךְ אוֹתְךָ וְאֶת־עַמְּךָ בַּדָּבֶר

טז וַתִּכָּחֵד מִן־הָאָרֶץ: וְאוּלָם בַּעֲבוּר זֹאת הֶעֱמַדְתִּיךָ בַּעֲבוּר

יז הַרְאֹתְךָ אֶת־כֹּחִי וּלְמַעַן סַפֵּר שְׁמִי בְּכָל־הָאָרֶץ: עוֹדְךָ מִסְתּוֹלֵל שביעי

יח בְּעַמִּי לְבִלְתִּי שַׁלְּחָם: הִנְנִי מַמְטִיר כָּעֵת מָחָר בָּרָד כָּבֵד מְאֹד אֲשֶׁר לֹא־הָיָה כָמֹהוּ בְּמִצְרַיִם לְמִן־הַיּוֹם הִוָּסְדָה וְעַד־עָתָּה:

י' בָּאָדָם וּבַבְּהֵמָה. וְאִם תֹּאמַר, מֵאַיִן הָיוּ לָהֶם הַבְּהֵמוֹת, וַהֲלֹא כְּבָר נֶאֱמַר: "וַיָּמָת כֹּל מִקְנֵה מִצְרַיִם" (לעיל פסוק ו)? לֹא נִגְזְרָה גְזֵרָה אֶלָּא עַל אוֹתָן שֶׁבַּשָּׂדוֹת בִּלְבַד, שֶׁנֶּאֱמַר: "בְּמִקְנְךָ אֲשֶׁר בַּשָּׂדֶה" (לעיל פסוק ג). וְהַיָּרֵא אֶת דְּבַר ה' הִכְנִיס אֶת מִקְנֵהוּ אֶל הַבָּתִּים. וְכֵן שְׁנוּיָה בַּמְּכִילְתָּא אֵצֶל "וַיִּקַּח שֵׁשׁ מֵאוֹת רֶכֶב בָּחוּר" (להלן יד, ז):

יד' אֶת כָּל מַגֵּפֹתַי. לָמַדְנוּ מִכָּאן שֶׁמַּכַּת בְּכוֹרוֹת שְׁקוּלָה כְּנֶגֶד כָּל הַמַּכּוֹת:

טו' כִּי עַתָּה שָׁלַחְתִּי אֶת יָדִי וְגוֹ'. כִּי אִלּוּ רָצִיתִי כְּשֶׁהָיְתָה יָדִי בְּמִקְנְךָ שֶׁהִכֵּיתִים בַּדֶּבֶר, שְׁלַחְתִּיהָ וְהִכֵּיתִי אוֹתְךָ וְאֶת עַמְּךָ עִם הַבְּהֵמוֹת וְנִכְחַדְתֶּם מִן הָאָרֶץ, אֲבָל "בַּעֲבוּר זֹאת הֶעֱמַדְתִּיךָ" וְגוֹ':

יז' עוֹדְךָ מִסְתּוֹלֵל בְּעַמִּי. כְּתַרְגּוּמוֹ: "כְּבִישַׁת בֵּיהּ בְּעַמִּי", וְהוּא מִגִּזְרַת "מְסִלָּה" (במדבר כ, יט) דִּמְתַרְגְּמִינַן: "אֹרַח כְּבִישָׁא", וּבִלְעַז קלקי"ר. וּכְבָר פֵּרַשְׁתִּי בְּסוֹף "וַיְהִי מִקֵּץ" (בראשית מה, טז), כָּל תֵּבָה שֶׁתְּחִלַּת יְסוֹדָהּ סמ"ך וְהִיא בָאָה לְדַבֵּר בְּלָשׁוֹן מִתְפַּעֵל נוֹתֵן הַתי"ו שֶׁל שִׁמּוּשׁ בְּאֶמְצַע אוֹתִיּוֹת שֶׁל עִקָּר, כְּגוֹן זוֹ, וּכְגוֹן: "וַיִּתְגַּלְגַּל הֶחָגָב" (קהלת יב, ה), מִגִּזְרַת "סַבָּל", "כִּי תִשְׂתָּרֵר עָלֵינוּ" (במדבר טז, יג) מִגִּזְרַת "שַׂר וְעָיַד" (דברי הימים ב לב, כח), "מִשְׂתַּכֵּל הֲוֵית" (דניאל ז, ח):

יח' כָּעֵת מָחָר. כָּעֵת הַזֹּאת לְמָחָר. שָׂרַט לוֹ שְׂרִיטָה בַּכֹּתֶל, לְמָחָר כְּשֶׁתַּגִּיעַ חַמָּה לְכָאן יֵרֵד הַבָּרָד: הִוָּסְדָה. שֶׁנִּתְיַסְּדָה. וְכָל תֵּבָה שֶׁתְּחִלַּת יְסוֹדָהּ יו"ד כְּגוֹן: יָסַד, יָלַד, יָדַע, יָסַר, כְּשֶׁהִיא מִתְפַּעֶלֶת תָּבֹא

פרק ט | שמות | וארא

יט וְעַתָּה שְׁלַח הָעֵז אֶת־מִקְנְךָ וְאֵת כָּל־אֲשֶׁר לְךָ בַּשָּׂדֶה כָּל־הָאָדָם וְהַבְּהֵמָה אֲשֶׁר־יִמָּצֵא בַשָּׂדֶה וְלֹא יֵאָסֵף הַבַּיְתָה וְיָרַד עֲלֵהֶם הַבָּרָד וָמֵתוּ:
כ הַיָּרֵא אֶת־דְּבַר יְהוָֹה מֵעַבְדֵי פַּרְעֹה הֵנִיס אֶת־עֲבָדָיו וְאֶת־מִקְנֵהוּ אֶל־הַבָּתִּים:
כא וַאֲשֶׁר לֹא־שָׂם לִבּוֹ אֶל־דְּבַר יְהוָֹה וַיַּעֲזֹב אֶת־עֲבָדָיו וְאֶת־מִקְנֵהוּ בַּשָּׂדֶה:
כב וַיֹּאמֶר יְהוָֹה אֶל־מֹשֶׁה נְטֵה אֶת־יָדְךָ עַל־הַשָּׁמַיִם וִיהִי בָרָד בְּכָל־אֶרֶץ מִצְרָיִם עַל־הָאָדָם וְעַל־הַבְּהֵמָה וְעַל כָּל־עֵשֶׂב הַשָּׂדֶה בְּאֶרֶץ מִצְרָיִם:
כג וַיֵּט מֹשֶׁה אֶת־מַטֵּהוּ עַל־הַשָּׁמַיִם וַיהוָֹה נָתַן קֹלֹת וּבָרָד וַתִּהֲלַךְ־אֵשׁ אָרְצָה וַיַּמְטֵר יְהוָֹה בָּרָד עַל־אֶרֶץ מִצְרָיִם:
כד וַיְהִי בָרָד וְאֵשׁ מִתְלַקַּחַת בְּתוֹךְ הַבָּרָד כָּבֵד מְאֹד אֲשֶׁר לֹא־הָיָה כָמֹהוּ בְּכָל־אֶרֶץ מִצְרַיִם מֵאָז הָיְתָה לְגוֹי:
כה וַיַּךְ הַבָּרָד בְּכָל־אֶרֶץ מִצְרַיִם אֵת כָּל־אֲשֶׁר בַּשָּׂדֶה מֵאָדָם וְעַד־בְּהֵמָה וְאֵת כָּל־עֵשֶׂב הַשָּׂדֶה הִכָּה הַבָּרָד וְאֶת־כָּל־עֵץ הַשָּׂדֶה שִׁבֵּר:
כו רַק בְּאֶרֶץ גֹּשֶׁן אֲשֶׁר־שָׁם בְּנֵי יִשְׂרָאֵל לֹא הָיָה בָּרָד:
כז וַיִּשְׁלַח פַּרְעֹה וַיִּקְרָא לְמֹשֶׁה וּלְאַהֲרֹן וַיֹּאמֶר אֲלֵהֶם חָטָאתִי הַפָּעַם יְהוָֹה הַצַּדִּיק וַאֲנִי וְעַמִּי הָרְשָׁעִים:
כח הַעְתִּירוּ אֶל־יְהוָֹה וְרַב מִהְיֹת קֹלֹת אֱלֹהִים וּבָרָד וַאֲשַׁלְּחָה אֶתְכֶם וְלֹא תֹסִפוּן

הֵנִ"יס בְּמָקוֹם הֵבִי"א כְּמוֹ: "הוֹסַדָה", "הוֹלָדָה" (הושע ב, ה), "וַיִּוָּדַע" (אסתר ב, כב), "וַיּוּלַד לְיוֹסֵף" (בראשית מו, כ), "בִּדְבָרִים לֹא יִוָּסֶר עָבֶד" (משלי כט, יט):

יט שְׁלַח הָעֵז. כְּתַרְגּוּמוֹ: "שְׁלַח כְּנוֹשׁ". וְכֵן: "יֹשְׁבֵי הַגֵּבִים הָעִיזוּ" (ישעיה י, לא), "הָעִזוּ בְּנֵי בִנְיָמִן" (ירמיה ו, א):

וְלֹא יֵאָסֵף הַבַּיְתָה. לְשׁוֹן הַכְנָסָה הוּא:

כ הֵנִיס. הִבְרִיחַ:

כב עַל הַשָּׁמַיִם. לְצַד הַשָּׁמַיִם. וּמִדְרַשׁ אַגָּדָה, הִגְבִּיהוֹ הַקָּדוֹשׁ בָּרוּךְ הוּא לְמֹשֶׁה לְמַעְלָה מִן הַשָּׁמַיִם:

כד מִתְלַקַּחַת בְּתוֹךְ הַבָּרָד. נֵס בְּתוֹךְ נֵס, הָאֵשׁ וְהַבָּרָד מְעֹרָבִין, וְהַבָּרָד מַיִם הוּא, וְלַעֲשׂוֹת רְצוֹן קוֹנָם עָשׂוּ שָׁלוֹם בֵּינֵיהֶם:

כח וְרַב. דַּי לוֹ בְּמַה שֶּׁהוֹרִיד כְּבָר:

שמות | פרק ט

כט וַיֹּאמֶר אֵלָיו מֹשֶׁה כְּצֵאתִי אֶת־הָעִיר אֶפְרֹשׂ אֶת־כַּפַּי אֶל־יְהֹוָה הַקֹּלוֹת יֶחְדָּלוּן וְהַבָּרָד לֹא יִהְיֶה־עוֹד לְמַעַן תֵּדַע כִּי לַיהוָֹה הָאָרֶץ: ל וְאַתָּה וַעֲבָדֶיךָ יָדַעְתִּי כִּי טֶרֶם תִּירְאוּן מִפְּנֵי יְהֹוָה אֱלֹהִים: לא וְהַפִּשְׁתָּה וְהַשְּׂעֹרָה נֻכָּתָה כִּי הַשְּׂעֹרָה אָבִיב וְהַפִּשְׁתָּה גִּבְעֹל: לב וְהַחִטָּה וְהַכֻּסֶּמֶת לֹא נֻכּוּ כִּי אֲפִילֹת הֵנָּה:

מפטיר

לג וַיֵּצֵא מֹשֶׁה מֵעִם פַּרְעֹה אֶת־הָעִיר וַיִּפְרֹשׂ כַּפָּיו אֶל־יְהֹוָה וַיַּחְדְּלוּ הַקֹּלוֹת וְהַבָּרָד וּמָטָר לֹא־נִתַּךְ אָרְצָה: לד וַיַּרְא פַּרְעֹה כִּי־חָדַל הַמָּטָר וְהַבָּרָד וְהַקֹּלֹת וַיֹּסֶף לַחֲטֹא וַיַּכְבֵּד לִבּוֹ הוּא וַעֲבָדָיו: לה וַיֶּחֱזַק לֵב פַּרְעֹה וְלֹא שִׁלַּח אֶת־בְּנֵי יִשְׂרָאֵל כַּאֲשֶׁר דִּבֶּר יְהֹוָה בְּיַד־מֹשֶׁה:

כט **כְּצֵאתִי אֶת הָעִיר.** מִן הָעִיר. אֲבָל בְּתוֹךְ הָעִיר לֹא הִתְפַּלֵּל לְפִי שֶׁהָיְתָה מְלֵאָה גִּלּוּלִים:

ל **טֶרֶם תִּירְאוּן.** עֲדַיִן לֹא תִּירְאוּן, וְכֵן כָּל טֶרֶם שֶׁבַּמִּקְרָא "עֲדַיִן לֹא" הוּא וְאֵינוֹ לְשׁוֹן קֹדֶם. "טֶרֶם יִשְׁכָּבוּ" (בראשית יט, ד) – "עַד לֹא שָׁכְבוּ", "טֶרֶם יַעֲנֶה" (ישעיה סה, כד) – "עַד לֹא עָנָה". אַף זֶה כֵּן הוּא, יָדַעְתִּי כִּי עֲדַיִן אֵינְכֶם יְרֵאִים, וּמִשֶּׁתִּהְיֶה הָרְוָחָה תַּעַמְדוּ בְּקִלְקוּלְכֶם:

לא **וְהַפִּשְׁתָּה וְהַשְּׂעֹרָה נֻכָּתָה.** נִשְׁבְּרָה, לְשׁוֹן "פַּרְעֹה נְכֹה" (מלכים ב' כג, כט), "נְכָאִים" (ישעיה טז, ז), וְכֵן "לֹא נֻכּוּ" (להלן פסוק לב). וְלֹא יִתָּכֵן לְפָרְשָׁם לְשׁוֹן הַכָּאָה, שֶׁאֵין נו"ן בִּמְקוֹם ה"א לְפָרֵשׁ 'נֻכָּתָה' כְּמוֹ 'הֻכָּתָה', 'נֻכּוּ' כְּמוֹ 'הֻכּוּ', אֶלָּא הַנּוּ"ן שֹׁרֶשׁ בַּתֵּבָה, וַהֲרֵי הוּא מִגִּזְרַת "וְנִסְּפוּ עֲמָמָיו" (איוב לג, כח):

כִּי הַשְּׂעֹרָה אָבִיב. כְּבָר בִּכְּרָה וְעוֹמֶדֶת בְּקָשֶׁיהָ וְנִשְׁתַּבְּרוּ וְנָפְלוּ. וְכֵן הַפִּשְׁתָּה גָּדְלָה כְּבָר וְהֻקְשָׁה לַעֲמֹד בְּגִבְעוֹלֶיהָ. **הַשְּׂעֹרָה אָבִיב.** עָמְדָה בְּאִבֶּיהָ, לְשׁוֹן "בְּאִבֵּי הַנָּחַל" (שיר השירים ו, יא):

לב **כִּי אֲפִילֹת הֵנָּה.** מְאֻחָרוֹת, וַעֲדַיִן הָיוּ רַכּוֹת וִיכוֹלוֹת לַעֲמֹד בִּפְנֵי קָשֶׁה. וְאַף עַל פִּי שֶׁנֶּאֱמַר: "וְאֵת כָּל עֵשֶׂב הַשָּׂדֶה הִכָּה הַבָּרָד" (לעיל פסוק כה), יֵשׁ לְיַשֵּׁב פְּשׁוּטוֹ שֶׁל מִקְרָא בָּעֲשָׂבִים הָעוֹמְדִים בְּקִלְחָם הָרְאוּיִים לִלְקוֹת בַּבָּרָד. וּבְמִדְרַשׁ רַבִּי תַּנְחוּמָא (י) יֵשׁ מֵרַבּוֹתֵינוּ שֶׁנֶּחְלְקוּ עַל זֹאת, וְדָרְשׁוּ "כִּי אֲפִילֹת" פִּלְאֵי פְלָאוֹת נַעֲשׂוּ לָהֶם שֶׁלֹּא לָקוּ:

לג **לֹא נִתַּךְ.** לֹא הִגִּיעַ, וְאַף אוֹתָן שֶׁהָיוּ בָּאֲוִיר לֹא הִגִּיעוּ לָאָרֶץ. וְדוֹמֶה לוֹ: "וַתִּתַּךְ עָלֵינוּ הָאָלָה וְהַשְּׁבֻעָה" (דניאל ט, יא), "וַתִּגַּע עָלֵינוּ". וּמְנַחֵם בֶּן סָרוּק חִבְּרוֹ בְּחֵלֶק "כְּהִתּוּךְ כֶּסֶף" (יחזקאל כב, כב), לְשׁוֹן יְצִיקַת מַתֶּכֶת, וְרוֹחַ אֱוִי אֵת דְּבָרָיו, כְּתַרְגּוּמוֹ "וַיִּצֹק" – "וְאַתִּיךְ" (להלן לח, ה), "לָצֶקֶת" (שם פסוק כז) – "לְאַתָּכָא". אַף זֶה "לֹא נִתַּךְ", לֹא הוּצַק לָאָרֶץ:

בא

א וַיֹּ֤אמֶר יְהֹוָה֙ אֶל־מֹשֶׁ֔ה בֹּ֖א אֶל־פַּרְעֹ֑ה כִּֽי־אֲנִ֞י הִכְבַּ֤דְתִּי אֶת־לִבּוֹ֙ וְאֶת־לֵ֣ב עֲבָדָ֔יו לְמַ֗עַן שִׁתִ֛י אֹתֹתַ֥י אֵ֖לֶּה בְּקִרְבּֽוֹ: ב וּלְמַ֡עַן תְּסַפֵּר֩ בְּאׇזְנֵ֨י בִנְךָ֜ וּבֶן־בִּנְךָ֗ אֵ֣ת אֲשֶׁ֤ר הִתְעַלַּ֙לְתִּי֙ בְּמִצְרַ֔יִם וְאֶת־אֹתֹתַ֖י אֲשֶׁר־שַׂ֣מְתִּי בָ֑ם וִידַעְתֶּ֖ם כִּי־אֲנִ֥י יְהֹוָֽה: ג וַיָּבֹ֨א מֹשֶׁ֤ה וְאַהֲרֹן֙ אֶל־פַּרְעֹ֔ה וַיֹּאמְר֣וּ אֵלָ֗יו כֹּֽה־אָמַ֤ר יְהֹוָה֙ אֱלֹהֵ֣י הָֽעִבְרִ֔ים עַד־מָתַ֣י מֵאַ֔נְתָּ לֵעָנֹ֖ת מִפָּנָ֑י שַׁלַּ֥ח עַמִּ֖י וְיַֽעַבְדֻֽנִי: ד כִּ֛י אִם־מָאֵ֥ן אַתָּ֖ה לְשַׁלֵּ֣חַ אֶת־עַמִּ֑י הִנְנִ֨י מֵבִ֥יא מָחָ֛ר אַרְבֶּ֖ה בִּגְבֻלֶֽךָ: ה וְכִסָּה֙ אֶת־עֵ֣ין הָאָ֔רֶץ וְלֹ֥א יוּכַ֖ל לִרְאֹ֣ת אֶת־הָאָ֑רֶץ וְאָכַ֣ל ׀ אֶת־יֶ֣תֶר הַפְּלֵטָ֗ה הַנִּשְׁאֶ֤רֶת לָכֶם֙ מִן־הַבָּרָ֔ד וְאָכַל֙ אֶת־כׇּל־הָעֵ֔ץ הַצֹּמֵ֥חַ לָכֶ֖ם מִן־הַשָּׂדֶֽה: ו וּמָלְא֨וּ בָתֶּ֜יךָ וּבָתֵּ֣י כׇל־עֲבָדֶ֘יךָ֘ וּבָתֵּ֣י כׇל־מִצְרַ֒יִם֒ אֲשֶׁ֨ר לֹֽא־רָא֤וּ אֲבֹתֶ֙יךָ֙ וַאֲב֣וֹת אֲבֹתֶ֔יךָ מִיּ֗וֹם הֱיוֹתָם֙ עַל־הָ֣אֲדָמָ֔ה עַ֖ד הַיּ֣וֹם הַזֶּ֑ה וַיִּ֥פֶן וַיֵּצֵ֖א מֵעִ֥ם פַּרְעֹֽה: ז וַיֹּאמְרוּ֩ עַבְדֵ֨י פַרְעֹ֜ה אֵלָ֗יו עַד־מָתַי֙ יִהְיֶ֨ה זֶ֥ה לָ֙נוּ֙ לְמוֹקֵ֔שׁ שַׁלַּח֙ אֶת־הָ֣אֲנָשִׁ֔ים וְיַֽעַבְד֖וּ אֶת־יְהֹוָ֣ה אֱלֹהֵיהֶ֑ם הֲטֶ֣רֶם תֵּדַ֔ע כִּ֥י אָבְדָ֖ה מִצְרָֽיִם: ח וַיּוּשַׁ֞ב אֶת־מֹשֶׁ֤ה וְאֶֽת־אַהֲרֹן֙ אֶל־פַּרְעֹ֔ה וַיֹּ֣אמֶר אֲלֵהֶ֔ם לְכ֥וּ עִבְד֖וּ אֶת־יְהֹוָ֣ה אֱלֹהֵיכֶ֑ם מִ֥י וָמִ֖י הַהֹלְכִֽים: ט וַיֹּ֤אמֶר מֹשֶׁה֙ בִּנְעָרֵ֣ינוּ

פרק י

א) **וַיֹּאמֶר ה' אֶל מֹשֶׁה בֹּא אֶל פַּרְעֹה.** וְהַתְרֵה בּוֹ: **שִׁתִי.** שׂוּמִי, שֶׁאָשִׁית אֲנִי:

ב) **הִתְעַלַּלְתִּי.** שָׂחַקְתִּי, כְּמוֹ: "כִּי הִתְעַלַּלְתְּ בִּי" (במדבר כב, כט), "הֲלוֹא כַּאֲשֶׁר הִתְעוֹלֵל בָּהֶם" (שמואל א' ו, ו) הָאָמוּר בְּמִצְרַיִם. וְאֵינוֹ לְשׁוֹן פּוֹעֵל וּמַעֲלָלִים, שֶׁאִם כֵּן הָיָה לוֹ לִכְתֹּב "עוֹלַלְתִּי", כְּמוֹ: "וְעוֹלֵל לָמוֹ כַּאֲשֶׁר עוֹלַלְתָּ לִי" (איכה א, כב), "אֲשֶׁר עוֹלַל לִי" (שם פסוק יב):

ג) **לֵעָנֹת.** כְּתַרְגּוּמוֹ: "לְאִתְכְּנָעָא", וְהוּא מִגִּזְרַת עָנִי, מֵאַנְתָּ לִהְיוֹת עָנִי וְשָׁפָל מִפָּנַי:

ה) **אֶת עֵין הָאָרֶץ.** אֶת מַרְאֵה הָאָרֶץ: **וְלֹא יוּכַל הָרֹאֶה.** "לִרְאוֹת אֶת הָאָרֶץ", וְלָשׁוֹן קְצָרָה דִּבֵּר:

ז) **הֲטֶרֶם תֵּדַע.** הַעוֹד לֹא יָדַעְתָּ "כִּי אָבְדָה מִצְרָיִם":

ח) **וַיּוּשַׁב.** הוּשְׁבוּ עַל יְדֵי שָׁלִיחַ, שֶׁשְּׁלָחוּ אַחֲרֵיהֶם וֶהֱשִׁיבוּם אֶל פַּרְעֹה:

שמות | פרק י

וּבִזְקֵנֵינוּ נֵלֵךְ בְּבָנֵינוּ וּבִבְנוֹתֵנוּ בְּצֹאנֵנוּ וּבִבְקָרֵנוּ נֵלֵךְ כִּי חַג־
יהוה לָנוּ: וַיֹּאמֶר אֲלֵהֶם יְהִי כֵן יהוה עִמָּכֶם כַּאֲשֶׁר אֲשַׁלַּח
אֶתְכֶם וְאֶת־טַפְּכֶם רְאוּ כִּי רָעָה נֶגֶד פְּנֵיכֶם: לֹא כֵן לְכוּ־נָא
הַגְּבָרִים וְעִבְדוּ אֶת־יהוה כִּי אֹתָהּ אַתֶּם מְבַקְשִׁים וַיְגָרֶשׁ אֹתָם
מֵאֵת פְּנֵי פַרְעֹה: ◂ שני ◂ וַיֹּאמֶר יהוה אֶל־מֹשֶׁה נְטֵה
יָדְךָ עַל־אֶרֶץ מִצְרַיִם בָּאַרְבֶּה וְיַעַל עַל־אֶרֶץ מִצְרָיִם וְיֹאכַל
אֶת־כָּל־עֵשֶׂב הָאָרֶץ אֵת כָּל־אֲשֶׁר הִשְׁאִיר הַבָּרָד: וַיֵּט מֹשֶׁה
אֶת־מַטֵּהוּ עַל־אֶרֶץ מִצְרַיִם וַיהוה נִהַג רוּחַ־קָדִים בָּאָרֶץ
כָּל־הַיּוֹם הַהוּא וְכָל־הַלָּיְלָה הַבֹּקֶר הָיָה וְרוּחַ הַקָּדִים נָשָׂא
אֶת־הָאַרְבֶּה: וַיַּעַל הָאַרְבֶּה עַל כָּל־אֶרֶץ מִצְרַיִם וַיָּנַח בְּכֹל
גְּבוּל מִצְרָיִם כָּבֵד מְאֹד לְפָנָיו לֹא־הָיָה כֵן אַרְבֶּה כָּמֹהוּ וְאַחֲרָיו
לֹא יִהְיֶה־כֵּן: וַיְכַס אֶת־עֵין כָּל־הָאָרֶץ וַתֶּחְשַׁךְ הָאָרֶץ וַיֹּאכַל
אֶת־כָּל־עֵשֶׂב הָאָרֶץ וְאֵת כָּל־פְּרִי הָעֵץ אֲשֶׁר הוֹתִיר הַבָּרָד
וְלֹא־נוֹתַר כָּל־יֶרֶק בָּעֵץ וּבְעֵשֶׂב הַשָּׂדֶה בְּכָל־אֶרֶץ מִצְרָיִם:

י כַּאֲשֶׁר אֲשַׁלַּח אֶתְכֶם וְאֶת טַפְּכֶם. אַךְ כִּי אֲשַׁלֵּחַ גַּם אֶת הַצֹּאן וְאֶת הַבָּקָר כַּאֲשֶׁר אֲמַרְתֶּם: רְאוּ כִּי רָעָה נֶגֶד פְּנֵיכֶם. כְּתַרְגּוּמוֹ. וּמִדְרַשׁ אַגָּדָה שָׁמַעְתִּי, כּוֹכָב אֶחָד יֵשׁ שֶׁשְּׁמוֹ רָעָה, אָמַר לָהֶם פַּרְעֹה: רוֹאֶה אֲנִי בְּאִצְטַגְנִינוּת שֶׁלִּי אוֹתוֹ כּוֹכָב עוֹלֶה לִקְרַאתְכֶם בַּמִּדְבָּר וְהוּא סִימָן דָּם וַהֲרִיגָה. וּכְשֶׁחָטְאוּ יִשְׂרָאֵל בָּעֵגֶל וּבִקֵּשׁ הַקָּדוֹשׁ בָּרוּךְ הוּא לְהָרְגָם, אָמַר מֹשֶׁה בִּתְפִלָּתוֹ: "לָמָּה יֹאמְרוּ מִצְרַיִם לֵאמֹר בְּרָעָה הוֹצִיאָם" (להלן לב, יב), זוֹ הִיא שֶׁאָמַר לָהֶם: "רְאוּ כִּי רָעָה נֶגֶד פְּנֵיכֶם". מִיָּד — "וַיִּנָּחֶם ה' עַל הָרָעָה" (שם פסוק יד) וְהָפַךְ אֶת הַדָּם לְדָם מִילָה שֶׁמָּל יְהוֹשֻׁעַ אוֹתָם. וְזֶהוּ שֶׁנֶּאֱמַר: "הַיּוֹם גַּלּוֹתִי אֶת חֶרְפַּת מִצְרַיִם מֵעֲלֵיכֶם" (יהושע ה, ט) שֶׁהָיוּ אוֹמְרִים לָכֶם: דָּם אָנוּ רוֹאִין עֲלֵיכֶם בַּמִּדְבָּר:

יא לֹא כֵן. כַּאֲשֶׁר אֲמַרְתֶּם לְהוֹלִיךְ הַטַּף עִמָּכֶם, אֶלָּא לְכוּ הַגְּבָרִים וְעִבְדוּ אֶת ה' כִּי אוֹתָהּ בִּקַּשְׁתֶּם עַד הֵנָּה, "נִזְבְּחָה לֵאלֹהֵינוּ" (לעיל ה, ח), וְאֵין דֶּרֶךְ הַטַּף לִזְבּוֹחַ: וַיְגָרֶשׁ אֹתָם. הֲרֵי זֶה לְשׁוֹן קָצָר וְלֹא פֵּרֵשׁ מִי הַמְגָרֵשׁ:

יב בָּאַרְבֶּה. בִּשְׁבִיל מַכַּת הָאַרְבֶּה:

יד וְאַחֲרָיו לֹא יִהְיֶה־כֵּן. וְאוֹתוֹ שֶׁהָיָה בִּימֵי יוֹאֵל שֶׁנֶּאֱמַר: "כָּמֹהוּ לֹא נִהְיָה מִן הָעוֹלָם" (יואל ב, ב) לָמַדְנוּ שֶׁהָיָה כָּבֵד מִשֶּׁל מֹשֶׁה — עַל יְדֵי מִינֵי הָאַרְבֶּה שֶׁהָיוּ יַחַד: אַרְבֶּה, יֶלֶק, חָסִיל, גָּזָם, אֲבָל שֶׁל מֹשֶׁה מִין אֶחָד, וְכָמוֹהוּ לֹא הָיָה וְלֹא יִהְיֶה:

טו כָּל יֶרֶק. עָלֶה יָרוֹק, וירדו"ר בְּלַעַ"ז:

פרק י | שמות

טז וַיְמַהֵר פַּרְעֹה לִקְרֹא לְמֹשֶׁה וּלְאַהֲרֹן וַיֹּאמֶר חָטָאתִי לַיהוה אֱלֹהֵיכֶם וְלָכֶם:
יז וְעַתָּה שָׂא נָא חַטָּאתִי אַךְ הַפַּעַם וְהַעְתִּירוּ לַיהוה אֱלֹהֵיכֶם וְיָסֵר מֵעָלַי רַק אֶת־הַמָּוֶת הַזֶּה:
יח וַיֵּצֵא מֵעִם פַּרְעֹה וַיֶּעְתַּר אֶל־יהוה:
יט וַיַּהֲפֹךְ יהוה רוּחַ־יָם חָזָק מְאֹד וַיִּשָּׂא אֶת־הָאַרְבֶּה וַיִּתְקָעֵהוּ יָמָּה סּוּף לֹא נִשְׁאַר אַרְבֶּה אֶחָד בְּכֹל גְּבוּל מִצְרָיִם:
כ וַיְחַזֵּק יהוה אֶת־לֵב פַּרְעֹה וְלֹא שִׁלַּח אֶת־בְּנֵי יִשְׂרָאֵל:

כא וַיֹּאמֶר יהוה אֶל־מֹשֶׁה נְטֵה יָדְךָ עַל־הַשָּׁמַיִם וִיהִי חֹשֶׁךְ עַל־אֶרֶץ מִצְרָיִם וְיָמֵשׁ חֹשֶׁךְ:
כב וַיֵּט מֹשֶׁה אֶת־יָדוֹ עַל־הַשָּׁמָיִם וַיְהִי חֹשֶׁךְ־אֲפֵלָה בְּכָל־אֶרֶץ מִצְרַיִם שְׁלֹשֶׁת יָמִים:
כג לֹא־רָאוּ אִישׁ אֶת־אָחִיו וְלֹא־קָמוּ אִישׁ מִתַּחְתָּיו שְׁלֹשֶׁת יָמִים וּלְכָל־בְּנֵי יִשְׂרָאֵל הָיָה אוֹר בְּמוֹשְׁבֹתָם:
שלישי כד וַיִּקְרָא פַרְעֹה אֶל־מֹשֶׁה וַיֹּאמֶר לְכוּ עִבְדוּ אֶת־יהוה רַק צֹאנְכֶם וּבְקַרְכֶם יֻצָּג גַּם־טַפְּכֶם יֵלֵךְ

יט) לֹא נִשְׁאַר אַרְבֶּה אֶחָד. אַף הַמְּלוּחִים שֶׁמָּלְחוּ מֵהֶן:

כא) וְיָמֵשׁ חֹשֶׁךְ. וְיַחֲשִׁיךְ עֲלֵיהֶם חֹשֶׁךְ יוֹתֵר מֵחֶשְׁכּוֹ שֶׁל לַיְלָה, וְחֹשֶׁךְ שֶׁל לַיְלָה יַחֲמִישׁ וְיַחְשִׁיךְ עוֹד. וְיָמֵשׁ. כְּמוֹ 'וְיַאֲמֵשׁ'. יֵשׁ לָנוּ תֵּבוֹת הַרְבֵּה חֲסֵרוֹת אָלֶ"ף, לְפִי שֶׁאֵין הֲבָרַת הָאָלֶ"ף נִכֶּרֶת כָּל כָּךְ, אֵין הַכָּתוּב מַקְפִּיד עַל חֶסְרוֹנָהּ, כְּגוֹן: "וְלֹא יָהֵל שָׁם עַרְבִי" (ישעיה יג, כ) כְּמוֹ 'לֹא יַאֲהֵל', לֹא יִטֶּה אָהֳלוֹ. וְכֵן: "וַתַּזְרֵנִי חַיִל" (שמואל ב' כב, מ) כְּמוֹ 'וַתְּאַזְּרֵנִי'. וְאוּנְקְלוֹס תִּרְגֵּם לְשׁוֹן הֲסָרָה, כְּמוֹ: "לֹא יָמִישׁ" (להלן יג, כב) – "בָּתַר דְּיֶעְדֵּי קְבֵל לֵילְיָא", כְּשֶׁיַּגִּיעַ סָמוּךְ לְאוֹר הַיּוֹם. אֲבָל אֵין הַדִּבּוּר מְיֻשָּׁב עַל הַיּ"וֹד שֶׁל 'וְיָמֵשׁ', לְפִי שֶׁהוּא כָּתוּב אַחַר "וִיהִי חֹשֶׁךְ". וּמִדְרַשׁ אַגָּדָה פּוֹתְרוֹ לְשׁוֹן "מְמַשֵּׁשׁ בַּצָּהֳרַיִם" (דברים כח, כט), שֶׁהָיָה כָפוּל וּמְכֻפָּל וְעָב עַד שֶׁהָיָה בּוֹ מַמָּשׁ:

כב) שְׁלֹשֶׁת יָמִים. שִׁלּוּם שֶׁל יָמִים, טרציינ"א בְּלַעַז. וְכֵן 'שִׁבְעַת יָמִים' בְּכָל מָקוֹם, שטיינ"א שֶׁל יָמִים: וַיְהִי חֹשֶׁךְ אֲפֵלָה. שְׁלֹשֶׁת יָמִים. חֹשֶׁךְ שֶׁל אֹפֶל שֶׁלֹּא רָאוּ אִישׁ אֶת אָחִיו אוֹתָן שְׁלֹשֶׁת יָמִים, וְעוֹד שְׁלֹשֶׁת יָמִים אֲחֵרִים חֹשֶׁךְ מֻכְפָּל עַל זֶה שֶׁלֹּא קָמוּ אִישׁ מִתַּחְתָּיו, יוֹשֵׁב אֵין יָכוֹל לַעֲמֹד וְעוֹמֵד אֵין יָכוֹל לֵישֵׁב. וְלָמָּה הֵבִיא עֲלֵיהֶם חֹשֶׁךְ? שֶׁהָיוּ בְּיִשְׂרָאֵל בְּאוֹתוֹ הַדּוֹר רְשָׁעִים וְלֹא הָיוּ רוֹצִים לָצֵאת, וּמֵתוּ בִּשְׁלֹשֶׁת יְמֵי אֲפֵלָה, כְּדֵי שֶׁלֹּא יִרְאוּ מִצְרִים בְּמַפַּלְתָּם וְיֹאמְרוּ: אַף הֵם לוֹקִים כָּמוֹנוּ. וְעוֹד, שֶׁחִפְּשׂוּ יִשְׂרָאֵל וְרָאוּ אֶת כְּלֵיהֶם, וּכְשֶׁיָּצְאוּ וְהָיוּ שׁוֹאֲלִים מֵהֶן וְהָיוּ אוֹמְרִים: אֵין בְּיָדֵינוּ כְּלוּם, אוֹמֵר לוֹ: אֲנִי רְאִיתִיו בְּבֵיתְךָ וּבְמָקוֹם פְּלוֹנִי הוּא:

כד) יֻצָּג. יְהֵא מֻצָּג בִּמְקוֹמוֹ:

שמות | פרק י

כה וַיֹּ֣אמֶר מֹשֶׁ֔ה גַּם־אַתָּ֛ה תִּתֵּ֥ן בְּיָדֵ֖נוּ זְבָחִ֣ים וְעֹלֹ֑ת וְעָשִׂ֕ינוּ עִמָּ֖כֶם:
לַיהוָ֥ה אֱלֹהֵֽינוּ:
כו וְגַם־מִקְנֵ֜נוּ יֵלֵ֣ךְ עִמָּ֗נוּ לֹ֤א תִשָּׁאֵר֙ פַּרְסָ֔ה כִּ֚י מִמֶּ֣נּוּ נִקַּ֔ח לַעֲבֹ֖ד אֶת־יְהוָ֣ה אֱלֹהֵ֑ינוּ וַאֲנַ֣חְנוּ לֹֽא־נֵדַ֗ע מַֽה־
נַּעֲבֹד֙ אֶת־יְהוָ֔ה עַד־בֹּאֵ֖נוּ שָֽׁמָּה:
כז וַיְחַזֵּ֥ק יְהוָ֖ה אֶת־לֵ֣ב פַּרְעֹ֑ה
וְלֹ֥א אָבָ֖ה לְשַׁלְּחָֽם:
כח וַיֹּֽאמֶר־ל֥וֹ פַרְעֹ֖ה לֵ֣ךְ מֵעָלָ֑י הִשָּׁ֣מֶר לְךָ֗
אַל־תֹּ֙סֶף֙ רְא֣וֹת פָּנַ֔י כִּ֗י בְּי֛וֹם רְאֹתְךָ֥ פָנַ֖י תָּמֽוּת:
כט וַיֹּ֥אמֶר מֹשֶׁ֖ה
כֵּ֣ן דִּבַּ֑רְתָּ לֹא־אֹסִ֥ף ע֖וֹד רְא֥וֹת פָּנֶֽיךָ:

יא א וַיֹּ֨אמֶר יְהוָ֜ה אֶל־מֹשֶׁ֗ה ע֣וֹד נֶ֤גַע אֶחָד֙ אָבִ֤יא עַל־פַּרְעֹה֙ וְעַל־ ח
מִצְרַ֔יִם אַֽחֲרֵי־כֵ֕ן יְשַׁלַּ֥ח אֶתְכֶ֖ם מִזֶּ֑ה כְּשַׁ֨לְּח֔וֹ כָּלָ֕ה גָּרֵ֛שׁ יְגָרֵ֥שׁ
אֶתְכֶ֖ם מִזֶּֽה:
ב דַּבֶּר־נָ֖א בְּאָזְנֵ֣י הָעָ֑ם וְיִשְׁאֲל֞וּ אִ֣ישׁ ׀ מֵאֵ֣ת רֵעֵ֗הוּ
וְאִשָּׁה֙ מֵאֵ֣ת רְעוּתָ֔הּ כְּלֵי־כֶ֖סֶף וּכְלֵ֥י זָהָֽב:
ג וַיִּתֵּ֧ן יְהוָ֛ה אֶת־
חֵ֥ן הָעָ֖ם בְּעֵינֵ֣י מִצְרָ֑יִם גַּ֣ם ׀ הָאִ֣ישׁ מֹשֶׁ֗ה גָּד֤וֹל מְאֹד֙ בָּאֶ֣רֶץ
מִצְרַ֔יִם בְּעֵינֵ֥י עַבְדֵֽי־פַרְעֹ֖ה וּבְעֵינֵ֥י הָעָֽם:
ד וַיֹּ֣אמֶר רביעי
מֹשֶׁ֔ה כֹּ֖ה אָמַ֣ר יְהוָ֑ה כַּחֲצֹ֣ת הַלַּ֔יְלָה אֲנִ֥י יוֹצֵ֖א בְּת֥וֹךְ מִצְרָֽיִם:

כה] **גַּם אַתָּה תִּתֵּן.** לֹא דַּיְךָ שֶׁמִּקְנֵנוּ יֵלֵךְ עִמָּנוּ, אֶלָּא אַף מִשֶּׁלְּךָ תִּתֵּן:

כו] **פַּרְסָה.** פַּרְסַת רֶגֶל, פלנט"א בְּלַעַז: **לֹא נֵדַע מַה נַּעֲבֹד.** כַּמָּה תִכְבַּד הָעֲבוֹדָה, שֶׁמָּא יִשְׁאַל יוֹתֵר מִמָּה שֶׁיֵּשׁ בְּיָדֵינוּ:

כט] **כֵּן דִּבַּרְתָּ.** יָפֶה דִּבַּרְתָּ וּבִזְמַנּוֹ דִּבַּרְתָּ, אֱמֶת שֶׁ"לֹא אֹסִף עוֹד רְאוֹת פָּנֶיךָ":

פרק יא
א] **כָּלָה.** "גְּמִירָא", כָּלִיל, כֻּלְּכֶם יְשַׁלַּח:

ב] **דַּבֶּר נָא.** אֵין "נָא" אֶלָּא לְשׁוֹן בַּקָּשָׁה, בְּבַקָּשָׁה מִמְּךָ הַזְהִירֵם עַל כָּךְ, שֶׁלֹּא יֹאמַר אוֹתוֹ צַדִּיק אַבְרָהָם,

---

ד] **וַיֹּאמֶר מֹשֶׁה כֹּה אָמַר ה'.** בְּעָמְדוֹ לִפְנֵי פַרְעֹה נֶאֶמְרָה לוֹ, שֶׁהֲרֵי מִשֶּׁיָּצָא מִלְּפָנָיו לֹא הוֹסִיף רְאוֹת פָּנָיו: **כַּחֲצֹת הַלַּיְלָה.** כְּהֵחָלֵק הַלַּיְלָה, "כַּחֲצֹת" כְּמוֹ "כַּעֲלוֹת" (יהושע ו, יח, ועוד), "כַּכְּלוֹת" (דברים כ, ט, ועוד), "בַּחֲרוֹת אַפָּם בָּנוּ" (תהלים קכד, ג). זֶהוּ פְשׁוּטוֹ לְיַשְּׁבוֹ עַל אָפְנָיו, שֶׁאֵין "חֲצוֹת" שֵׁם דָּבָר שֶׁל חֲצִי. וְרַבּוֹתֵינוּ דְּרָשׁוּהוּ כְּמוֹ "כַּחֲצִי הַלַּיְלָה", וְאָמְרוּ שֶׁאָמַר מֹשֶׁה "כַּחֲצֹת" דְּמַשְׁמַע סָמוּךְ לוֹ אוֹ לְפָנָיו אוֹ לְאַחֲרָיו, וְלֹא אָמַר "בַּחֲצוֹת", שֶׁמָּא יִטְעוּ אִצְטַגְנִינֵי פַרְעֹה וְיֹאמְרוּ מֹשֶׁה בַּדַּאי הוּא:

פרק יא | שמות

ה וּמֵת כָּל־בְּכוֹר֮ בְּאֶ֣רֶץ מִצְרַ֒יִם֒ מִבְּכ֤וֹר פַּרְעֹה֙ הַיֹּשֵׁ֣ב עַל־כִּסְא֔וֹ עַ֚ד בְּכ֣וֹר הַשִּׁפְחָ֔ה אֲשֶׁ֖ר אַחַ֣ר הָרֵחָ֑יִם וְכֹ֖ל בְּכ֥וֹר בְּהֵמָֽה:

ו וְהָ֨יְתָ֜ה צְעָקָ֤ה גְדֹלָה֙ בְּכָל־אֶ֣רֶץ מִצְרָ֔יִם אֲשֶׁ֥ר כָּמֹ֖הוּ לֹ֣א נִהְיָ֑תָה וְכָמֹ֖הוּ לֹ֥א תֹסִֽף:

ז וּלְכֹ֣ל ׀ בְּנֵ֣י יִשְׂרָאֵ֗ל לֹ֤א יֶֽחֱרַץ־כֶּ֨לֶב֙ לְשֹׁנ֔וֹ לְמֵאִ֖ישׁ וְעַד־בְּהֵמָ֑ה לְמַ֨עַן֙ תֵּֽדְע֔וּן אֲשֶׁר֙ יַפְלֶ֣ה יְהוָ֔ה בֵּ֥ין מִצְרַ֖יִם וּבֵ֥ין יִשְׂרָאֵֽל:

ח וְיָרְד֣וּ כָל־עֲבָדֶיךָ֩ אֵ֨לֶּה אֵלַ֜י וְהִשְׁתַּֽחֲווּ־לִ֣י לֵאמֹ֗ר צֵ֤א אַתָּה֙ וְכָל־הָעָ֣ם אֲשֶׁר־בְּרַגְלֶ֔יךָ וְאַחֲרֵי־כֵ֖ן אֵצֵ֑א וַיֵּצֵ֥א מֵֽעִם־פַּרְעֹ֖ה בָּחֳרִי־אָֽף:

ט וַיֹּ֤אמֶר יְהוָה֙ אֶל־מֹשֶׁ֔ה לֹֽא־יִשְׁמַ֥ע אֲלֵיכֶ֖ם פַּרְעֹ֑ה לְמַ֛עַן רְב֥וֹת מֽוֹפְתַ֖י בְּאֶ֥רֶץ מִצְרָֽיִם:

י וּמֹשֶׁ֣ה וְאַהֲרֹ֗ן עָשׂ֛וּ אֶת־כָּל־הַמֹּפְתִ֥ים הָאֵ֖לֶּה לִפְנֵ֣י פַרְעֹ֑ה וַיְחַזֵּ֤ק יְהוָה֙ אֶת־לֵ֣ב פַּרְעֹ֔ה וְלֹֽא־שִׁלַּ֥ח אֶת־בְּנֵֽי־יִשְׂרָאֵ֖ל

ה **עַד בְּכוֹר הַשְּׁבִי** (להלן יב, כט). לָמָּה לָקוּ הַשְּׁבוּיִים? כְּדֵי שֶׁלֹּא יֹאמְרוּ, יִרְאָתָם תָּבְעָה עֶלְבּוֹנָם וְהֵבִיאָה פֻּרְעָנוּת עַל מִצְרַיִם: **מִבְּכוֹר פַּרְעֹה... עַד בְּכוֹר הַשִּׁפְחָה.** כָּל הַפְּחוּתִים מִבְּכוֹר פַּרְעֹה וַחֲשׁוּבִים מִבְּכוֹר הַשִּׁפְחָה הָיוּ בַּכְּלָל. וְלָמָּה לָקוּ בְּנֵי הַשְּׁפָחוֹת? שֶׁאַף הֵם הָיוּ מִשְׁתַּעְבְּדִים בָּהֶם וּשְׂמֵחִים בְּצָרָתָם: **וְכֹל בְּכוֹר בְּהֵמָה.** לְפִי שֶׁהָיוּ עוֹבְדִין לָהּ — כְּשֶׁהַקָּדוֹשׁ בָּרוּךְ הוּא נִפְרָע מִן הָאֻמָּה נִפְרָע מֵאֱלֹהֶיהָ:

ז **לֹא יֶחֱרַץ כֶּלֶב לְשֹׁנוֹ.** אוֹמֵר אֲנִי שֶׁהוּא לְשׁוֹן שִׁנּוּן, לֹא יָשֵׁן. וְכֵן: "לֹא חָרַץ לִבְנֵי יִשְׂרָאֵל לְאִישׁ אֶת לְשֹׁנוֹ" (יהושע י, כא) — לֹא שִׁנֵּן. "אָז תֶּחֱרָץ" (שמואל ב' ה, כד) — תִּשְׁתַּנֵּן. "לַמּוֹרַג חָרוּץ" (ישעיה מא, טו) — שָׁנוּן. "מַחְשְׁבוֹת חָרוּץ" (משלי כא, ה) — "אָדָם חָרִיף וְשָׁנוּן". "וְיַד חָרוּצִים תַּעֲשִׁיר" (שם י, ד) — חֲרִיפִים, סוֹחֲרִים שֶׁעוֹסְקִים: **אֲשֶׁר יַפְלֶה.** יַבְדִּיל:

ח **וְיָרְדוּ כָל עֲבָדֶיךָ.** חָלַק כָּבוֹד לַמַּלְכוּת, שֶׁהֲרֵי סוֹף

שֶׁיָּרַד פַּרְעֹה בְּעַצְמוֹ אֵלָיו בַּלַּיְלָה, "וַיֹּאמֶר ק֥וּמוּ צְּאוּ מִתּוֹךְ עַמִּי" (להלן יב, לא), וְלֹא אָמַר לוֹ מֹשֶׁה מִתְּחִלָּה: "וְיָרַדְתָּ אֵלַי וְהִשְׁתַּחֲוִיתָ לִי": **אֲשֶׁר בְּרַגְלֶיךָ.** הַהוֹלְכִים אַחַר עֲצָתְךָ וְהִלּוּכְךָ: **וְאַחֲרֵי כֵן אֵצֵא.** עִם כָּל הָעָם מֵאַרְצְךָ: **וַיֵּצֵא מֵעִם פַּרְעֹה.** כְּשֶׁגָּמַר דְּבָרָיו יָצָא מִלְּפָנָיו: **בָּחֳרִי אָף.** עַל שֶׁאָמַר לוֹ: "אַל תֹּסֶף רְאוֹת פָּנַי" (לעיל י, כח):

ט **לְמַעַן רְבוֹת מוֹפְתַי.** מַכַּת בְּכוֹרוֹת וּקְרִיעַת יַם סוּף וּלְנַעֵר אֶת מִצְרַיִם:

י **וּמֹשֶׁה וְאַהֲרֹן עָשׂוּ וְגוֹ'.** כְּבָר כָּתַב לָנוּ זֹאת בְּכָל הַמּוֹפְתִים, וְלֹא שְׁנָאָהּ כָּאן אֶלָּא בִּשְׁבִיל לְסָמְכָהּ לַפָּרָשָׁה שֶׁל אַחֲרֶיהָ: **וַיֹּאמֶר ה' אֶל מֹשֶׁה** וְאֶל אַהֲרֹן, שֶׁבִּשְׁבִיל שֶׁאַהֲרֹן עָשָׂה וְטָרַח בַּמּוֹפְתִים כְּמֹשֶׁה, חָלַק לוֹ כָּבוֹד זֶה בְּמִצְוָה רִאשׁוֹנָה שֶׁכְּלָלוֹ עִם מֹשֶׁה בַּדִּבּוּר:

שמות | פרק יב

יב א וַיֹּאמֶר יְהוָה אֶל־מֹשֶׁה וְאֶל־אַהֲרֹן בְּאֶרֶץ מִצְרַיִם לֵאמֹר: ב הַחֹדֶשׁ הַזֶּה לָכֶם רֹאשׁ חֳדָשִׁים רִאשׁוֹן הוּא לָכֶם לְחָדְשֵׁי הַשָּׁנָה: ג דַּבְּרוּ אֶל־כָּל־עֲדַת יִשְׂרָאֵל לֵאמֹר בֶּעָשֹׂר לַחֹדֶשׁ הַזֶּה וְיִקְחוּ לָהֶם אִישׁ שֶׂה לְבֵית־אָבֹת שֶׂה לַבָּיִת: ד וְאִם־יִמְעַט הַבַּיִת מִהְיֹת מִשֶּׂה וְלָקַח הוּא וּשְׁכֵנוֹ הַקָּרֹב אֶל־בֵּיתוֹ בְּמִכְסַת נְפָשֹׁת אִישׁ לְפִי אָכְלוֹ תָּכֹסּוּ עַל־הַשֶּׂה: ה שֶׂה תָמִים זָכָר בֶּן־שָׁנָה יִהְיֶה לָכֶם מִן־הַכְּבָשִׂים וּמִן־הָעִזִּים תִּקָּחוּ: ו וְהָיָה לָכֶם לְמִשְׁמֶרֶת עַד אַרְבָּעָה עָשָׂר יוֹם לַחֹדֶשׁ הַזֶּה וְשָׁחֲטוּ

פרק יב

א בְּאֶרֶץ מִצְרַיִם. חוּץ לַכְּרַךְ. אוֹ אֵינוֹ אֶלָּא בְּתוֹךְ הַכְּרַךְ? תַּלְמוּד לוֹמַר: "כְּצֵאתִי אֶת הָעִיר" וְגוֹ' (לעיל ט, כט). וּמַה תְּפִלָּה קַלָּה לֹא הִתְפַּלֵּל בְּתוֹךְ הַכְּרַךְ, דִּבּוּר חָמוּר לֹא כָּל שֶׁכֵּן? וּמִפְּנֵי מָה לֹא נִדְבַּר עִמּוֹ בְּתוֹךְ הַכְּרַךְ? לְפִי שֶׁהָיְתָה מְלֵאָה גִלּוּלִים:

ב הַחֹדֶשׁ הַזֶּה. הֶרְאָהוּ לְבָנָה בְּחִדּוּשָׁהּ וְאָמַר לוֹ: כְּשֶׁהַיָּרֵחַ מִתְחַדֵּשׁ יִהְיֶה לְךָ רֹאשׁ חֹדֶשׁ. וְאֵין מִקְרָא יוֹצֵא מִידֵי פְשׁוּטוֹ, עַל חֹדֶשׁ נִיסָן אָמַר לוֹ, זֶה יִהְיֶה רֹאשׁ לְסֵדֶר מִנְיַן הֶחֳדָשִׁים, שֶׁיְּהֵא אִיָּר קָרוּי שֵׁנִי, סִיוָן שְׁלִישִׁי: **הַזֶּה.** נִתְקַשָּׁה מֹשֶׁה עַל מוֹלַד הַלְּבָנָה בְּאֵיזוֹ שִׁעוּר תֵּרָאֶה וְתִהְיֶה רְאוּיָה לְקַדֵּשׁ, וְהֶרְאָה לוֹ בְּאֶצְבַּע אֶת הַלְּבָנָה בָּרָקִיעַ וְאָמַר לוֹ: כָּזֶה רְאֵה וְקַדֵּשׁ. וְכֵיצַד הֶרְאָהוּ? וַהֲלֹא לֹא הָיָה נִדְבָּר עִמּוֹ אֶלָּא בַּיּוֹם, שֶׁנֶּאֱמַר: "וַיְהִי בְּיוֹם דִּבֶּר ה'" (לעיל ו, כח), "בְּיוֹם צַוֹּתוֹ" (ויקרא ז, לח), "מִן הַיּוֹם אֲשֶׁר צִוָּה ה' וָהָלְאָה" (במדבר טו, כג)? אֶלָּא סָמוּךְ לִשְׁקִיעַת הַחַמָּה נֶאֶמְרָה לוֹ פָּרָשָׁה זוֹ וְהֶרְאָהוּ עִם חֲשֵׁכָה:

ג דַּבְּרוּ אֶל כָּל עֲדַת. וְכִי אַהֲרֹן מְדַבֵּר? וַהֲלֹא כְּבָר נֶאֱמַר: "אַתָּה תְדַבֵּר" (לעיל ז, ב)! אֶלָּא חוֹלְקִין כָּבוֹד זֶה לָזֶה וְאוֹמְרִים זֶה לָזֶה: לַמְּדֵנִי, וְהַדִּבּוּר יוֹצֵא מִבֵּין שְׁנֵיהֶם כְּאִלּוּ שְׁנֵיהֶם מְדַבְּרִים: **דַּבְּרוּ אֶל כָּל עֲדַת יִשְׂרָאֵל לֵאמֹר בֶּעָשֹׂר לַחֹדֶשׁ.** דַּבְּרוּ הַיּוֹם בְּרֹאשׁ חֹדֶשׁ שֶׁיִּקָּחוּהוּ בֶּעָשׂוֹר לַחֹדֶשׁ: **הַזֶּה.** פֶּסַח מִצְרַיִם מִקָּחוֹ בֶּעָשׂוֹר וְלֹא פֶּסַח דּוֹרוֹת: **שֶׂה לְבֵית אָבֹת.** לְמִשְׁפָּחָה אֶחָת, הֲרֵי שֶׁהָיוּ מְרֻבִּין יָכוֹל שֶׂה אֶחָד לְכֻלָּן? תַּלְמוּד לוֹמַר: "שֶׂה לַבָּיִת":

ד וְאִם יִמְעַט הַבַּיִת מִהְיוֹת מִשֶּׂה. וְאִם יִהְיוּ מוּעָטִין מִהְיוֹת מִשֶּׂה אֶחָד, שֶׁאֵין יְכוֹלִין לְאָכְלוֹ וְיָבֹא לִידֵי נוֹתָר - "וְלָקַח הוּא וּשְׁכֵנוֹ" וְגוֹ', זֶהוּ מַשְׁמָעוֹ לְפִי פְשׁוּטוֹ. וְעוֹד יֵשׁ בּוֹ מִדְרָשׁ, לְלַמֵּד שֶׁאַחַר שֶׁנִּמְנוּ עָלָיו יְכוֹלִין לְהִתְמַעֵט וְלִמְשֹׁךְ יְדֵיהֶם הֵימֶנּוּ וּלְהִמָּנוֹת עַל שֶׂה אַחֵר, אַךְ אִם בָּאוּ לִמְשֹׁךְ יְדֵיהֶם וּלְהִתְמַעֵט - "מִהְיוֹת מִשֶּׂה" יִתְמַעֲטוּ, בְּעוֹד הַשֶּׂה קַיָּם, בִּהְיוֹתוֹ בַּחַיִּים, וְלֹא מִשֶּׁנִּשְׁחַט: **בְּמִכְסַת.** חֶשְׁבּוֹן, וְכֵן: "מִכְסַת הָעֶרְכְּךָ" (ויקרא כז, כג). **לְפִי אָכְלוֹ.** הָרָאוּי לַאֲכִילָה, פְּרָט לְחוֹלֶה וְלִזָקֵן שֶׁאֵינָן יְכוֹלִין לֶאֱכֹל כַּזַּיִת: **תָּכֹסּוּ.** "תִּתְמַנּוּן":

ה תָּמִים. בְּלֹא מוּם: **בֶּן שָׁנָה.** כָּל שְׁנָתוֹ קָרוּי בֶּן שָׁנָה, כְּלוֹמַר שֶׁנּוֹלַד בְּשָׁנָה זוֹ: **מִן הַכְּבָשִׂים וּמִן הָעִזִּים.** אוֹ מִזֶּה אוֹ מִזֶּה, שֶׁאַף עֵז קָרוּי 'שֶׂה', שֶׁנֶּאֱמַר: "וְשֵׂה עִזִּים" (דברים יד, ד):

ו וְהָיָה לָכֶם לְמִשְׁמֶרֶת. זֶהוּ לְשׁוֹן בִּקּוּר, שֶׁטָּעוּן בִּקּוּר מִמּוּם אַרְבָּעָה יָמִים קֹדֶם שְׁחִיטָה. וּמִפְּנֵי מָה הִקְדִּים לְקִיחָתוֹ לִשְׁחִיטָתוֹ אַרְבָּעָה יָמִים, מַה שֶּׁלֹּא צִוָּה כֵן בְּפֶסַח דּוֹרוֹת? הָיָה רַבִּי מַתְיָא בֶן

פרק יב | שמות

אֹתוֹ כֹּל קְהַל עֲדַת־יִשְׂרָאֵל בֵּין הָעַרְבָּיִם: וְלָקְחוּ מִן־הַדָּם וְנָתְנוּ עַל־שְׁתֵּי הַמְּזוּזֹת וְעַל־הַמַּשְׁקוֹף עַל הַבָּתִּים אֲשֶׁר־יֹאכְלוּ אֹתוֹ בָּהֶם: וְאָכְלוּ אֶת־הַבָּשָׂר בַּלַּיְלָה הַזֶּה צְלִי־אֵשׁ וּמַצּוֹת עַל־מְרֹרִים יֹאכְלֻהוּ: אַל־תֹּאכְלוּ מִמֶּנּוּ נָא וּבָשֵׁל מְבֻשָּׁל בַּמָּיִם כִּי אִם־צְלִי־אֵשׁ רֹאשׁוֹ עַל־כְּרָעָיו וְעַל־קִרְבּוֹ: וְלֹא־תוֹתִירוּ מִמֶּנּוּ עַד־בֹּקֶר וְהַנֹּתָר מִמֶּנּוּ עַד־בֹּקֶר בָּאֵשׁ תִּשְׂרֹפוּ:

חֶרֶשׁ חוֹמֶר: הֲרֵי הוּא חוֹמֶר: "וַתַּעֲבֹד עָלֶיךָ וַתַּחֲרֹשׁ וְהִנֵּה עַתָּךְ עֵת דֹּדִים" (יחזקאל טז, ח), הִגִּיעָה שְׁבוּעָה שֶׁנִּשְׁבַּעְתִּי לְאַבְרָהָם שֶׁאֶגְאַל אֶת בָּנָיו, וְלֹא הָיוּ בְּיָדָם מִצְוֹת לְהִתְעַסֵּק בָּהֶם כְּדֵי שֶׁיִּגָּאֲלוּ, שֶׁנֶּאֱמַר, "וְאַתְּ עֵרֹם וְעֶרְיָה" (שם פסוק ז), וְנָתַן לָהֶם שְׁתֵּי מִצְוֹת, דַּם פֶּסַח וְדַם מִילָה, שֶׁמָּלוּ בְּאוֹתוֹ הַלַּיְלָה, שֶׁנֶּאֱמַר, "מִתְבּוֹסֶסֶת בְּדָמָיִךְ" (שם פסוק ו) בִּשְׁנֵי דָמִים. וְאוֹמֵר, "גַּם אַתְּ בְּדַם בְּרִיתֵךְ שִׁלַּחְתִּי אֲסִירַיִךְ מִבּוֹר אֵין מַיִם בּוֹ" (זכריה ט, יא): וּלְפִי שֶׁהָיוּ שְׁטוּפִים בַּעֲבוֹדָה זָרָה, אָמַר לָהֶם: "מִשְׁכוּ וּקְחוּ לָכֶם" (להלן פסוק כא), מִשְׁכוּ יְדֵיכֶם מֵעֲבוֹדָה זָרָה וּקְחוּ לָכֶם צֹאן שֶׁל מִצְוָה: וְשָׁחֲטוּ אֹתוֹ וְגוֹ'. וְכִי כֻּלָּן שׁוֹחֲטִין? אֶלָּא מִכָּאן שֶׁשְּׁלוּחוֹ שֶׁל אָדָם כְּמוֹתוֹ: קְהַל עֲדַת יִשְׂרָאֵל. קָהָל וְעֵדָה וְיִשְׂרָאֵל. מִכָּאן אָמְרוּ: פִּסְחֵי צִבּוּר נִשְׁחָטִים בְּשָׁלֹשׁ כִּתּוֹת זוֹ אַחַר זוֹ. נִכְנְסָה כַּת הָרִאשׁוֹנָה נִנְעֲלוּ דַּלְתוֹת הָעֲזָרָה וְכוּ', כִּדְאִיתָא בִּפְסָחִים (דף סד ע"א): בֵּין הָעַרְבָּיִם. מִשֵּׁשׁ שָׁעוֹת וּלְמַעְלָה קָרוּי 'בֵּין הָעַרְבַּיִם', שֶׁהַשֶּׁמֶשׁ נוֹטֶה לְבֵית מְבוֹאוֹ לַעֲרֹב. וּלְשׁוֹן 'בֵּין הָעַרְבַּיִם' נִרְאֶה בְּעֵינַי, אוֹתָן שָׁעוֹת שֶׁבֵּין עֲרִיבַת הַיּוֹם לַעֲרִיבַת הַלַּיְלָה, עֲרִיבַת הַיּוֹם בִּתְחִלַּת שֶׁבַע שָׁעוֹת מִכִּי יִנָּטוּ צִלְלֵי עֶרֶב, וַעֲרִיבַת הַלַּיְלָה בִּתְחִלַּת הַלַּיְלָה. 'עֶרֶב' לְשׁוֹן נֶשֶׁף וְחֹשֶׁךְ, כְּמוֹ, "עָרְבָה כָּל שִׂמְחָה" (ישעיה כד, יא):

וְלָקְחוּ מִן הַדָּם. זוֹ קַבָּלַת הַדָּם. יָכוֹל בַּיָּד? תַּלְמוּד לוֹמַר: "אֲשֶׁר בַּסַּף" (להלן פסוק כב): **הַמְּזוּזֹת.** הֵם הַזְּקוּפוֹת, אַחַת מִכָּאן וְאַחַת מִכָּאן לַפֶּתַח: **הַמַּשְׁקוֹף.** הוּא הָעֶלְיוֹן, שֶׁהַדֶּלֶת שׁוֹקֵף עָלָיו

כְּשֶׁסּוֹגְרִין אוֹתוֹ, לינט"ל בְּלַעַ"ז. וּלְשׁוֹן 'שְׁקִיפָה' – חֲבָטָה, כְּמוֹ: "קוֹל עָלֶה נִדָּף" (ויקרא כו, לו) – "דְּשָׁקִיף", "חַבּוּרָה" (להלן כא, כה) – "מַשְׁקוֹפֵי": **עַל הַבָּתִּים אֲשֶׁר יֹאכְלוּ אֹתוֹ בָּהֶם.** וְלֹא עַל מַשְׁקוֹף וּמְזוּזוֹת שֶׁבְּבֵית הַתֶּבֶן וּבֵית הַבָּקָר, שֶׁאֵין דָּרִין בְּתוֹכוֹ:

אֶת הַבָּשָׂר. וְלֹא גִידִים וַעֲצָמוֹת: **עַל מְרֹרִים.** כָּל עֵשֶׂב מַר נִקְרָא 'מָרוֹר'. וְצִוָּם לֶאֱכֹל מַר זֵכֶר לְ"וַיְמָרְרוּ אֶת חַיֵּיהֶם" (לעיל א, יד):

אַל תֹּאכְלוּ מִמֶּנּוּ נָא. שֶׁאֵינוֹ צָלוּי כָּל צָרְכּוֹ קוֹרְהוּ 'נָא' בְּלָשׁוֹן עֲרָבִי: **וּבָשֵׁל מְבֻשָּׁל.** כָּל זֶה בְּאַזְהָרַת "אַל תֹּאכְלוּ": **בַּמָּיִם.** מִנַּיִן לִשְׁאָר מַשְׁקִין? תַּלְמוּד לוֹמַר: "וּבָשֵׁל מְבֻשָּׁל" מִכָּל מָקוֹם: **כִּי אִם צְלִי אֵשׁ.** לְמַעְלָה גָּזַר עָלָיו בְּמִצְוַת עֲשֵׂה, וְכָאן הוֹסִיף עָלָיו לֹא תַעֲשֶׂה: "אַל תֹּאכְלוּ מִמֶּנּוּ... כִּי אִם צְלִי אֵשׁ": **רֹאשׁוֹ עַל כְּרָעָיו.** צוֹלֵהוּ כֻּלּוֹ כְּאֶחָד עִם רֹאשׁוֹ וְעִם כְּרָעָיו וְעִם קִרְבּוֹ, וּבְנֵי מֵעָיו נוֹתֵן לְתוֹכוֹ לְאַחַר הֲדָחָתָן. וּלְשׁוֹן: "עַל כְּרָעָיו וְעַל קִרְבּוֹ" כִּלְשׁוֹן "עַל צִבְאֹתָם" (לעיל ו, כו) כְּמוֹ בְּצִבְאוֹתָם, כְּמוֹת שֶׁהֵן, אַף זֶה כְּמוֹת שֶׁהוּא, כָּל בְּשָׂרוֹ מְשֻׁלָּם:

וְהַנֹּתָר מִמֶּנּוּ עַד בֹּקֶר. מַה תַּלְמוּד לוֹמַר "עַד בֹּקֶר" פַּעַם שְׁנִיָּה? לִתֵּן בֹּקֶר עַל בֹּקֶר, שֶׁהַבֹּקֶר מַשְׁמָעוֹ מִשֶּׁיָּנֵץ הַחַמָּה, וּבָא הַכָּתוּב לְהַקְדִּים שֶׁאָסוּר בַּאֲכִילָה מֵעֲלוֹת הַשַּׁחַר; זֶהוּ לְפִי מַשְׁמָעוֹ. וְעוֹד מִדְרָשׁ אַחֵר, לִמֵּד שֶׁאֵינוֹ נִשְׂרָף בְּיוֹם טוֹב אֶלָּא מִמָּחֳרָת, וְכָךְ תִּדְרְשֶׁנּוּ: "וְהַנֹּתָר מִמֶּנּוּ" בְּבֹקֶר רִאשׁוֹן "עַד בֹּקֶר" שֵׁנִי תַּעֲמֹד וְתִשְׂרְפֶנּוּ:

שמות | פרק יב

יא וְכָכָה֮ תֹּאכְל֣וּ אֹתוֹ֒ מָתְנֵיכֶ֣ם חֲגֻרִ֔ים נַעֲלֵיכֶם֙ בְּרַגְלֵיכֶ֔ם וּמַקֶּלְכֶ֖ם בְּיֶדְכֶ֑ם וַאֲכַלְתֶּ֤ם אֹתוֹ֙ בְּחִפָּז֔וֹן פֶּ֥סַח ה֖וּא לַיהוָֽה:
יב וְעָבַרְתִּ֣י בְאֶֽרֶץ־מִצְרַ֘יִם֮ בַּלַּ֣יְלָה הַזֶּה֒ וְהִכֵּיתִ֤י כָל־בְּכוֹר֙ בְּאֶ֣רֶץ מִצְרַ֔יִם מֵאָדָ֖ם וְעַד־בְּהֵמָ֑ה וּבְכָל־אֱלֹהֵ֥י מִצְרַ֛יִם אֶֽעֱשֶׂ֥ה שְׁפָטִ֖ים אֲנִ֥י יְהוָֽה:
יג וְהָיָה֩ הַדָּ֨ם לָכֶ֜ם לְאֹ֗ת עַ֤ל הַבָּתִּים֙ אֲשֶׁ֣ר אַתֶּ֣ם שָׁ֔ם וְרָאִ֙יתִי֙ אֶת־הַדָּ֔ם וּפָסַחְתִּ֖י עֲלֵכֶ֑ם וְלֹֽא־יִהְיֶ֨ה בָכֶ֥ם נֶ֙גֶף֙ לְמַשְׁחִ֔ית בְּהַכֹּתִ֖י בְּאֶ֥רֶץ מִצְרָֽיִם:
יד וְהָיָה֩ הַיּ֨וֹם הַזֶּ֤ה לָכֶם֙ לְזִכָּר֔וֹן וְחַגֹּתֶ֥ם אֹת֖וֹ חַ֣ג לַֽיהוָ֑ה לְדֹרֹ֣תֵיכֶ֔ם חֻקַּ֥ת עוֹלָ֖ם תְּחָגֻּֽהוּ:
טו שִׁבְעַ֤ת יָמִים֙ מַצּ֣וֹת תֹּאכֵ֔לוּ

יא | **מָתְנֵיכֶם חֲגֻרִים.** מְזֻמָּנִים לַדֶּרֶךְ: **בְּחִפָּזוֹן.** לְשׁוֹן בֶּהָלָה וּמְהִירוּת, כְּמוֹ: "וַיְהִי דָוִד נֶחְפָּז לָלֶכֶת" (שמואל א' כג, כו), "אֲשֶׁר הִשְׁלִיכוּ אֲרָם בְּחָפְזָם" (מלכים ב' ז, טו): **פֶּסַח הוּא לַה'.** הַקָּרְבָּן קָרוּי 'פֶּסַח' עַל שֵׁם הַפְּסִיחָה, וְחִתֵּם עָשׂוּ כָּל עֲבוֹדוֹתָיו לְשֵׁם שָׁמַיִם:

יב | **וְעָבַרְתִּי.** כְּמֶלֶךְ הָעוֹבֵר מִמָּקוֹם לְמָקוֹם, וּבְהַעֲבָרָה אַחַת וּבְרֶגַע אֶחָד כֻּלָּן לוֹקִין. **כָּל בְּכוֹר בְּאֶרֶץ מִצְרַיִם.** אַף בְּכוֹרוֹת אֲחֵרִים וְהֵם בְּמִצְרַיִם. וּמִנַּיִן אַף בְּכוֹרֵי מִצְרַיִם שֶׁבִּמְקוֹמוֹת אֲחֵרִים? תַּלְמוּד לוֹמַר: "לְמַכֵּה מִצְרַיִם בִּבְכוֹרֵיהֶם" (תהלים קלו, י): **מֵאָדָם וְעַד בְּהֵמָה.** מִי שֶׁהִתְחִיל בָּעֲבֵרָה תְּחִלָּה מִמֶּנּוּ מַתְחֶלֶת הַפֻּרְעָנוּת: **וּבְכָל אֱלֹהֵי מִצְרַיִם.** שֶׁל עֵץ נִרְקֶבֶת וְשֶׁל מַתֶּכֶת נִמֶּסֶת וְנִתֶּכֶת לָאָרֶץ: **אֶעֱשֶׂה שְׁפָטִים אֲנִי ה'.** אֲנִי בְּעַצְמִי וְלֹא עַל יְדֵי שָׁלִיחַ:

יג | **וְהָיָה הַדָּם לָכֶם לְאֹת.** לָכֶם לְאוֹת וְלֹא לַאֲחֵרִים לְאוֹת. מִכָּאן שֶׁלֹּא נָתְנוּ הַדָּם אֶלָּא מִבִּפְנִים: **וְרָאִיתִי אֶת הַדָּם.** הַכֹּל גָּלוּי לְפָנָיו, אֶלָּא אָמַר הַקָּדוֹשׁ בָּרוּךְ הוּא: נוֹתֵן אֲנִי אֶת עֵינִי לִרְאוֹת שֶׁאַתֶּם עֲסוּקִים בְּמִצְוֹתַי וּפוֹסֵחַ אֲנִי עֲלֵיכֶם: **וּפָסַחְתִּי.** וְחָמַלְתִּי, וְדוֹמֶה לוֹ: "פָּסוֹחַ וְהִמְלִיט" (ישעיה לא, ה). וַאֲנִי אוֹמֵר כָּל פְּסִיחָה לְשׁוֹן דִּלּוּג וּקְפִיצָה, "וּפָסַחְתִּי" – מְדַלֵּג הָיָה מִבָּתֵּי יִשְׂרָאֵל לְבָתֵּי מִצְרַיִם, שֶׁהָיוּ שְׁרוּיִים זֶה בְּתוֹךְ זֶה. וְכֵן: "פֹּסְחִים עַל שְׁתֵּי הַסְּעִפִּים" (מלכים א' יח, כא). וְכֵן כָּל הַפִּסְחִים הוֹלְכִים כְּקוֹפְצִים. וְכֵן: "פָּסוֹחַ

והמליט", מְדַלְּגוֹ וּמַמְלִיטוֹ מִבֵּין הַמּוּמָתִים: **וְלֹא יִהְיֶה בָכֶם נֶגֶף.** הָא אִם הָיָה בְּבָתֵּי שֶׁל יִשְׂרָאֵל מִצְרִי, יָכוֹל יִמָּלֵט? תַּלְמוּד לוֹמַר: "וְלֹא יִהְיֶה בָכֶם נֶגֶף", אֲבָל הָיָה בְּמִצְרִים שֶׁבְּבָתֵּיכֶם. הֲרֵי שֶׁהָיָה יִשְׂרָאֵל בְּבֵיתוֹ שֶׁל מִצְרִי, שׁוֹמֵעַ אֲנִי יִלְקֶה כְּמוֹתוֹ? תַּלְמוּד לוֹמַר: "וְלֹא יִהְיֶה בָכֶם נֶגֶף":

יד | **לְזִכָּרוֹן.** לְדוֹרוֹת: **וְחַגֹּתֶם אֹתוֹ.** יוֹם שֶׁהוּא לְךָ לְזִכָּרוֹן אַתָּה חוֹגְגוֹ. וַעֲדַיִן לֹא שָׁמַעְנוּ אֵי זֶהוּ יוֹם הַזִּכָּרוֹן, תַּלְמוּד לוֹמַר: "זָכוֹר אֶת הַיּוֹם הַזֶּה אֲשֶׁר יְצָאתֶם" (להלן יג, ג), לָמַדְנוּ שֶׁיּוֹם הַיְצִיאָה הוּא יוֹם שֶׁל זִכָּרוֹן. וְאֵי זֶה יוֹם יָצְאוּ? תַּלְמוּד לוֹמַר: "מִמָּחֳרַת הַפֶּסַח יָצְאוּ" (במדבר לג, ג), הֱוֵי אוֹמֵר יוֹם חֲמִשָּׁה עָשָׂר בְּנִיסָן הוּא שֶׁל יוֹם טוֹב, שֶׁהֲרֵי לֵיל חֲמִשָּׁה עָשָׂר אָכְלוּ אֶת הַפֶּסַח וְלַבֹּקֶר יָצְאוּ: **לְדֹרֹתֵיכֶם.** שׁוֹמֵעַ אֲנִי מִעוּט דּוֹרוֹת שְׁנַיִם, תַּלְמוּד לוֹמַר: "חֻקַּת עוֹלָם תְּחָגֻּהוּ":

טו | **שִׁבְעַת יָמִים.** סטיי"נא שֶׁל יָמִים: **שִׁבְעַת יָמִים מַצּוֹת תֹּאכֵלוּ.** וּבְמָקוֹם אַחֵר הוּא אוֹמֵר: "שֵׁשֶׁת יָמִים תֹּאכַל מַצּוֹת" (דברים טז, ח), לִמְּדָנוּ עַל שְׁבִיעִי שֶׁאֵינוֹ חוֹבָה לֶאֱכֹל מַצָּה, וּבִלְבַד שֶׁלֹּא יֹאכַל חָמֵץ. מִנַּיִן אַף שֵׁשׁ שָׁעוֹת רְשׁוּת? דָּבָר שֶׁהָיָה בַּכְּלָל וְיָצָא מִן הַכְּלָל לְלַמֵּד, לֹא לְלַמֵּד עַל עַצְמוֹ בִּלְבַד יָצָא אֶלָּא לְלַמֵּד עַל הַכְּלָל כֻּלּוֹ יָצָא, מַה שְּׁבִיעִי רְשׁוּת אַף שֵׁשׁ שָׁעוֹת רְשׁוּת. יָכוֹל אַף לַיְלָה

אַךְ בַּיּ֣וֹם הָרִאשׁ֔וֹן תַּשְׁבִּ֥יתוּ שְּׂאֹ֖ר מִבָּתֵּיכֶ֑ם כִּ֣י ׀ כָּל־אֹכֵ֣ל חָמֵ֗ץ וְנִכְרְתָ֞ה הַנֶּ֤פֶשׁ הַהִוא֙ מִיִּשְׂרָאֵ֔ל מִיּ֥וֹם הָרִאשֹׁ֖ן עַד־י֥וֹם הַשְּׁבִעִֽי: וּבַיּ֤וֹם הָרִאשׁוֹן֙ מִקְרָא־קֹ֔דֶשׁ וּבַיּוֹם֙ הַשְּׁבִיעִ֔י מִקְרָא־קֹ֖דֶשׁ יִהְיֶ֣ה לָכֶ֑ם כָּל־מְלָאכָה֙ לֹא־יֵעָשֶׂ֣ה בָהֶ֔ם אַ֚ךְ אֲשֶׁ֣ר יֵאָכֵ֣ל לְכָל־נֶ֔פֶשׁ ה֥וּא לְבַדּ֖וֹ יֵעָשֶׂ֥ה לָכֶֽם: וּשְׁמַרְתֶּם֮ אֶת־הַמַּצּוֹת֒ כִּ֗י בְּעֶ֨צֶם֙ הַיּ֣וֹם הַזֶּ֔ה הוֹצֵ֥אתִי אֶת־צִבְאוֹתֵיכֶ֖ם מֵאֶ֣רֶץ מִצְרָ֑יִם וּשְׁמַרְתֶּ֞ם אֶת־הַיּ֥וֹם הַזֶּ֛ה לְדֹרֹתֵיכֶ֖ם חֻקַּ֥ת עוֹלָֽם: בָּרִאשֹׁ֡ן בְּאַרְבָּעָה֩ עָשָׂ֨ר י֤וֹם לַחֹ֨דֶשׁ֙ בָּעֶ֔רֶב תֹּאכְל֖וּ מַצֹּ֑ת עַ֠ד י֣וֹם הָאֶחָ֧ד וְעֶשְׂרִ֛ים לַחֹ֖דֶשׁ בָּעָֽרֶב: שִׁבְעַ֣ת יָמִ֔ים שְׂאֹ֕ר לֹ֥א יִמָּצֵ֖א בְּבָתֵּיכֶ֑ם כִּ֣י ׀ כָּל־אֹכֵ֣ל מַחְמֶ֗צֶת וְנִכְרְתָ֞ה הַנֶּ֤פֶשׁ הַהִוא֙ מֵעֲדַ֣ת יִשְׂרָאֵ֔ל בַּגֵּ֖ר וּבְאֶזְרַ֥ח

הָרִאשׁוֹן לְשִׁשִּׁית? תַּלְמוּד לוֹמַר: "בָּעֶרֶב תֹּאכְלוּ מַצֹּת" (להלן פסוק יח), הַכָּתוּב קְבָעוֹ חוֹבָה. **אַךְ בַּיּוֹם הָרִאשׁוֹן תַּשְׁבִּיתוּ שְּׂאֹר.** מֵעֶרֶב יוֹם טוֹב, וְקָרוּי רִאשׁוֹן שֶׁהוּא לִפְנֵי הַשִּׁבְעָה, וּמָצִינוּ מְקֻדָּם קָרוּי רִאשׁוֹן, "הֲרִאשׁוֹן אָדָם תִּוָּלֵד" (איוב טו, ז), הֲלִפְנֵי אָדָם נוֹלַדְתָּ. אוֹ אֵינוֹ אֶלָּא רִאשׁוֹן שֶׁל שִׁבְעָה? תַּלְמוּד לוֹמַר: "לֹא תִשְׁחַט עַל חָמֵץ" (להלן לד, כה), לֹא תִשְׁחַט הַפֶּסַח וַעֲדַיִן חָמֵץ קַיָּם: **הַנֶּפֶשׁ הַהִוא.** כְּשֶׁהִיא בְּנַפְשָׁהּ וּבְדַעְתָּהּ, פְּרָט לְאָנוּס: **מִיִּשְׂרָאֵל.** שׁוֹמֵעַ אֲנִי תִּכָּרֵת מִיִּשְׂרָאֵל וְתֵלֵךְ לָהּ לְעַם אַחֵר? תַּלְמוּד לוֹמַר בְּמָקוֹם אַחֵר: "מִלְּפָנַי" (ויקרא כב, ג), בְּכָל מָקוֹם שֶׁהוּא רְשׁוּתִי:

טז) **מִקְרָא קֹדֶשׁ.** "מִקְרָא" שֵׁם דָּבָר, קְרָא אוֹתוֹ קֹדֶשׁ לַאֲכִילָה וְשְׁתִיָּה וּכְסוּת: **לֹא יֵעָשֶׂה בָהֶם.** אֲפִלּוּ עַל יְדֵי אֲחֵרִים. הוּא וְלֹא מַכְשִׁירָיו שֶׁאֶפְשָׁר לַעֲשׂוֹתָן מֵעֶרֶב יוֹם טוֹב: **לְכָל נֶפֶשׁ.** אַף לִבְהֵמָה. יָכוֹל אַף לַגּוֹיִם? תַּלְמוּד לוֹמַר: "לָכֶם":

יז) **וּשְׁמַרְתֶּם אֶת הַמַּצּוֹת.** שֶׁלֹּא יָבוֹאוּ לִידֵי חִמּוּץ. מִכָּאן אָמְרוּ: תָּפַח, תִּלְטֹשׁ בְּצוֹנֵן. רַבִּי יֹאשִׁיָּה אוֹמֵר: אַל תְּהִי קוֹרֵא "אֶת הַמַּצּוֹת" אֶלָּא "אֶת הַמִּצְוֹת", כְּדֶרֶךְ שֶׁאֵין מַחְמִיצִין אֶת הַמַּצָּה כָּךְ אֵין מַחְמִיצִין אֶת הַמִּצְוָה, אֶלָּא אִם בָּאָה לְיָדְךָ עֲשֵׂה אוֹתָהּ מִיָּד: **וּשְׁמַרְתֶּם אֶת הַיּוֹם הַזֶּה.** מִמְּלָאכָה: **לְדֹרֹתֵיכֶם חֻקַּת עוֹלָם.** לְפִי שֶׁלֹּא נֶאֱמַר "דּוֹרוֹת" וְ"חֻקַּת עוֹלָם" עַל הַמְּלָאכָה אֶלָּא עַל הַחֲגִיגָה (לעיל פסוק יד), לְכָךְ חָזַר וּשְׁנָאוֹ כָּאן, שֶׁלֹּא תֹאמַר: "כָּל מְלָאכָה לֹא יֵעָשֶׂה" (לעיל פסוק טז) לֹא לְדוֹרוֹת נֶאֶמְרָה אֶלָּא לְאוֹתוֹ הַדּוֹר:

יח) **עַד יוֹם הָאֶחָד וְעֶשְׂרִים.** לָמָּה נֶאֱמַר. וַהֲלֹא כְּבָר נֶאֱמַר: "שִׁבְעַת יָמִים" (לעיל פסוק טו)? לְפִי שֶׁנֶּאֱמַר "יָמִים", לֵילוֹת מִנַּיִן? תַּלְמוּד לוֹמַר: "עַד יוֹם הָאֶחָד וְעֶשְׂרִים" וְגוֹ':

יט) **לֹא יִמָּצֵא בְּבָתֵּיכֶם.** מִנַּיִן לַגְּבוּלִין? תַּלְמוּד לוֹמַר: "בְּכָל גְּבֻלֶךָ" (להלן יג, ז). מַה תַּלְמוּד לוֹמַר "בְּבָתֵּיכֶם"? מַה בֵּיתְךָ בִּרְשׁוּתְךָ אַף גְּבוּלְךָ שֶׁבִּרְשׁוּתְךָ, יָצָא חֲמֵצוֹ שֶׁל נָכְרִי שֶׁהוּא אֵצֶל יִשְׂרָאֵל וְלֹא קִבֵּל עָלָיו אַחֲרָיוּת: **כִּי כָּל אֹכֵל מַחְמֶצֶת.** לַעֲנֹשׁ כָּרֵת עַל הַשְּׂאוֹר.

שמות | פרק יב

כ הָאָרֶץ: כָּל־מַחְמֶצֶת לֹא תֹאכֵלוּ בְּכֹל מוֹשְׁבֹתֵיכֶם תֹּאכְלוּ
מַצּוֹת:
כא וַיִּקְרָא מֹשֶׁה לְכָל־זִקְנֵי יִשְׂרָאֵל וַיֹּאמֶר אֲלֵהֶם מִשְׁכוּ וּקְחוּ חמישי
כב לָכֶם צֹאן לְמִשְׁפְּחֹתֵיכֶם וְשַׁחֲטוּ הַפָּסַח: וּלְקַחְתֶּם אֲגֻדַּת אֵזוֹב
וּטְבַלְתֶּם בַּדָּם אֲשֶׁר־בַּסַּף וְהִגַּעְתֶּם אֶל־הַמַּשְׁקוֹף וְאֶל־שְׁתֵּי
הַמְּזוּזֹת מִן־הַדָּם אֲשֶׁר בַּסָּף וְאַתֶּם לֹא תֵצְאוּ אִישׁ מִפֶּתַח־
כג בֵּיתוֹ עַד־בֹּקֶר: וְעָבַר יהוה לִנְגֹּף אֶת־מִצְרַיִם וְרָאָה אֶת־הַדָּם
עַל־הַמַּשְׁקוֹף וְעַל שְׁתֵּי הַמְּזוּזֹת וּפָסַח יהוה עַל־הַפֶּתַח וְלֹא
כד יִתֵּן הַמַּשְׁחִית לָבֹא אֶל־בָּתֵּיכֶם לִנְגֹּף: וּשְׁמַרְתֶּם אֶת־הַדָּבָר
כה הַזֶּה לְחָק־לְךָ וּלְבָנֶיךָ עַד־עוֹלָם: וְהָיָה כִּי־תָבֹאוּ אֶל־הָאָרֶץ
אֲשֶׁר יִתֵּן יהוה לָכֶם כַּאֲשֶׁר דִּבֵּר וּשְׁמַרְתֶּם אֶת־הָעֲבֹדָה
כו הַזֹּאת: וְהָיָה כִּי־יֹאמְרוּ אֲלֵיכֶם בְּנֵיכֶם מָה הָעֲבֹדָה הַזֹּאת

וַהֲלֹא כְּבָר עָנוּשׁ עַל הֶחָמֵץ? אֶלָּא שֶׁלֹּא תֹאמַר: חָמֵץ שֶׁרָאוּי לַאֲכִילָה עָנַשׁ עָלָיו, שְׂאוֹר שֶׁאֵינוֹ רָאוּי לַאֲכִילָה לֹא יֵעָנֵשׁ עָלָיו; וְחָמֵץ עַל הַשְּׂאוֹר וְלֹא עָנַשׁ עַל הֶחָמֵץ, הָיִיתִי אוֹמֵר: שְׂאוֹר שֶׁהוּא מְחַמֵּץ אֲחֵרִים עָנַשׁ עָלָיו, חָמֵץ שֶׁאֵינוֹ מְחַמֵּץ אֲחֵרִים לֹא יֵעָנֵשׁ עָלָיו - לְכָךְ נֶאֶמְרוּ שְׁנֵיהֶם: בַּגֵּר וּבָאֶזְרָח הָאָרֶץ. לְפִי שֶׁהַנֵּס נַעֲשָׂה לְיִשְׂרָאֵל לְרַבּוֹת אֶת הַגֵּרִים:

כ] מַחְמֶצֶת לֹא תֹאכֵלוּ. אַזְהָרָה עַל אֲכִילַת שְׂאוֹר. כָּל מַחְמֶצֶת. לְהָבִיא אֶת תַּעֲרָבְתּוֹ: בְּכֹל מוֹשְׁבֹתֵיכֶם תֹּאכְלוּ מַצּוֹת. זֶה בָּא לְלַמֵּד שֶׁתְּהֵא רְאוּיָה לְהֵאָכֵל בְּכֹל מוֹשְׁבוֹתֵיכֶם, פְּרָט לְמַעֲשֵׂר שֵׁנִי וְחַלּוֹת תּוֹדָה:

כא] מִשְׁכוּ. מִי שֶׁיֵּשׁ לוֹ צֹאן יִמְשֹׁךְ מִשֶּׁלּוֹ: וּקְחוּ. מִי שֶׁאֵין לוֹ יִקַּח מִן הַשּׁוּק: לְמִשְׁפְּחֹתֵיכֶם. "שֶׂה לְבֵית אָבֹת" (לעיל פסוק ג):

כב] אֵזוֹב. מִין יָרָק שֶׁיֵּשׁ לוֹ גִּבְעוֹלִין: אֲגֻדַּת אֵזוֹב. שְׁלֹשָׁה קְלָחִין קְרוּיִין אֲגֻדָּה: אֲשֶׁר בַּסַּף. בַּכְּלִי, כְּמוֹ "סִפּוֹת כָּסֶף" (מלכים ב יב, יד): מִן הַדָּם אֲשֶׁר בַּסָּף. לָמָּה חָזַר וּשְׁנָאוֹ? שֶׁלֹּא תֹאמַר טְבִילָה אַחַת לִשְׁלֹשׁ הַמַּתָּנוֹת, לְכָךְ נֶאֱמַר עוֹד: "אֲשֶׁר בַּסָּף", שֶׁתְּהֵא כָּל נְתִינָה וּנְתִינָה "מִן הַדָּם אֲשֶׁר בַּסָּף", עַל כָּל הַגָּעָה טְבִילָה: וְאַתֶּם לֹא תֵצְאוּ וְגוֹ'. מַגִּיד שֶׁמֵּאַחַר שֶׁנִּתְּנָה רְשׁוּת לַמַּשְׁחִית לְחַבֵּל אֵינוֹ מַבְחִין בֵּין צַדִּיק לְרָשָׁע. וְלַיְלָה רְשׁוּת לַמְחַבְּלִים הוּא, שֶׁנֶּאֱמַר: "בּוֹ תִרְמֹשׂ כָּל חַיְתוֹ יָעַר" (תהלים קד, כ):

כג] וּפָסַח. וְחָמַל, וְיֵשׁ לוֹמַר: וְדִלֵּג: וְלֹא יִתֵּן הַמַּשְׁחִית. וְלֹא יִתֵּן לוֹ יְכֹלֶת לָבוֹא, כְּמוֹ: "וְלֹא נְתָנוֹ אֱלֹהִים לְהָרַע עִמָּדִי" (בראשית לא, ז):

כה] כַּאֲשֶׁר דִּבֵּר. וְהֵיכָן דִּבֵּר? "וְהֵבֵאתִי אֶתְכֶם אֶל הָאָרֶץ" וְגוֹ' (לעיל ו, ח):

כז לָכֶֽם: וַאֲמַרְתֶּ֡ם זֶֽבַח־פֶּ֨סַח ה֜וּא לַֽיהֹוָ֗ה אֲשֶׁ֣ר פָּ֠סַ֠ח עַל־בָּתֵּ֨י בְנֵֽי־יִשְׂרָאֵ֤ל בְּמִצְרַ֙יִם֙ בְּנׇגְפּ֣וֹ אֶת־מִצְרַ֔יִם וְאֶת־בָּתֵּ֖ינוּ הִצִּ֑יל וַיִּקֹּ֥ד הָעָ֖ם וַיִּֽשְׁתַּחֲוֽוּ: כח וַיֵּלְכ֥וּ וַיַּעֲשׂ֖וּ בְּנֵ֣י יִשְׂרָאֵ֑ל כַּאֲשֶׁ֨ר צִוָּ֧ה יְהֹוָ֛ה אֶת־מֹשֶׁ֥ה וְאַהֲרֹ֖ן כֵּ֥ן עָשֽׂוּ:

ששי ט כט וַיְהִ֣י ׀ בַּחֲצִ֣י הַלַּ֗יְלָה וַֽיהֹוָה֮ הִכָּ֣ה כׇל־בְּכוֹר֮ בְּאֶ֣רֶץ מִצְרַ֒יִם֒ מִבְּכֹ֤ר פַּרְעֹה֙ הַיֹּשֵׁ֣ב עַל־כִּסְא֔וֹ עַ֚ד בְּכ֣וֹר הַשְּׁבִ֔י אֲשֶׁ֖ר בְּבֵ֣ית הַבּ֑וֹר וְכֹ֖ל בְּכ֥וֹר בְּהֵמָֽה: ל וַיָּ֨קׇם פַּרְעֹ֜ה לַ֗יְלָה ה֤וּא וְכׇל־עֲבָדָיו֙ וְכׇל־מִצְרַ֔יִם וַתְּהִ֛י צְעָקָ֥ה גְדֹלָ֖ה בְּמִצְרָ֑יִם כִּֽי־אֵ֣ין בַּ֔יִת אֲשֶׁ֥ר אֵֽין־שָׁ֖ם מֵֽת: לא וַיִּקְרָא֩ לְמֹשֶׁ֨ה וּֽלְאַהֲרֹ֜ן לַ֗יְלָה וַיֹּ֙אמֶר֙ ק֤וּמוּ צְּאוּ֙ מִתּ֣וֹךְ עַמִּ֔י גַּם־אַתֶּ֖ם גַּם־בְּנֵ֣י יִשְׂרָאֵ֑ל וּלְכ֛וּ עִבְד֥וּ אֶת־יְהֹוָ֖ה כְּדַבֶּרְכֶֽם: לב גַּם־צֹאנְכֶ֨ם גַּם־בְּקַרְכֶ֥ם קְח֛וּ

כז וַיִּקֹּד הָעָם. עַל בְּשׂוֹרַת הַגְּאֻלָּה וּבִיאַת הָאָרֶץ וּבְשׂוֹרַת הַבָּנִים שֶׁיִּהְיוּ לָהֶם וְשֶׁיִּשְׁתַּחֲווּ:

כח וַיֵּלְכוּ וַיַּעֲשׂוּ בְּנֵי יִשְׂרָאֵל. וְכִי כְבָר עָשׂוּ? וַהֲלֹא מֵרֹאשׁ חֹדֶשׁ נֶאֱמַר לָהֶם! אֶלָּא מִכֵּיוָן שֶׁקִּבְּלוּ עֲלֵיהֶם מַעֲלֶה עֲלֵיהֶם הַכָּתוּב כְּאִלּוּ עָשׂוּ: וַיֵּלְכוּ וַיַּעֲשׂוּ. אַף הַהֲלִיכָה מָנָה הַכָּתוּב, לִתֵּן שָׂכָר לַהֲלִיכָה וְשָׂכָר לַעֲשִׂיָּה: כַּאֲשֶׁר צִוָּה ה' אֶת מֹשֶׁה וְאַהֲרֹן. לְהַגִּיד שִׁבְחָן שֶׁל יִשְׂרָאֵל שֶׁלֹּא הִפִּילוּ דָּבָר מִכָּל מִצְוַת מֹשֶׁה וְאַהֲרֹן. וּמַהוּ "כֵּן עָשׂוּ"? אַף מֹשֶׁה וְאַהֲרֹן כֵּן עָשׂוּ:

כט וַה'. כָּל מָקוֹם שֶׁנֶּאֱמַר "וַה'" – ה֨וּא וּבֵית דִּינוֹ, שֶׁהַוָּי"ו לְשׁוֹן תּוֹסֶפֶת הוּא, כְּמוֹ: פְּלוֹנִי וּפְלוֹנִי: הִכָּה כָל בְּכוֹר. אַף שֶׁל אֻמָּה אַחֶרֶת וְהוּא בְּמִצְרַיִם: מִבְּכֹר פַּרְעֹה. אַף פַּרְעֹה בְּכוֹר הָיָה וְנִשְׁתַּיֵּר מִן הַבְּכוֹרוֹת, וְעָלָיו הוּא אוֹמֵר: "בַּעֲבוּר הַרְאֹתְךָ אֶת כֹּחִי" (לעיל ט, טו) – בְּיַם סוּף: עַד בְּכוֹר הַשְּׁבִי. שֶׁהָיוּ שְׂמֵחִין לְאֵידָם שֶׁל יִשְׂרָאֵל. וְעוֹד, שֶׁלֹּא יֹאמְרוּ: יִרְאָתֵנוּ הֵבִיאָה הַפֻּרְעָנוּת. וּבְכוֹר הַשִּׁפְחָה בַּכְּלָל הָיָה, שֶׁהֲרֵי מָנָה מִן הֶחָשׁוּב שֶׁבְּכֻלָּן עַד הַפָּחוּת, וּבְכוֹר הַשִּׁפְחָה חָשׁוּב מִבְּכוֹר הַשְּׁבִי:

ל וַיָּקׇם פַּרְעֹה. מִמִּטָּתוֹ: לַיְלָה. וְלֹא כְּדֶרֶךְ הַמְּלָכִים בְּשָׁלֹשׁ שָׁעוֹת בַּיּוֹם: הוּא. תְּחִלָּה וְאַחַר כָּךְ "עֲבָדָיו", מְלַמֵּד שֶׁהָיָה הוּא מְחַזֵּר עַל בָּתֵּי עֲבָדָיו וּמַעֲמִידָם: כִּי אֵין בַּיִת אֲשֶׁר אֵין שָׁם מֵת. יֵשׁ שָׁם בְּכוֹר – מֵת, אֵין שָׁם בְּכוֹר – גָּדוֹל שֶׁבַּבַּיִת קָרוּי בְּכוֹר, שֶׁנֶּאֱמַר: "אַף אָנִי בְּכוֹר אֶתְּנֵהוּ" (תהלים פט, כח). דָּבָר אַחֵר, מִצְרִיּוֹת מְזַנּוֹת תַּחַת בַּעֲלֵיהֶן וְיוֹלְדוֹת מֵרַוָּקִים פְּנוּיִים וְהָיוּ לָהֶם בְּכוֹרוֹת הַרְבֵּה, פְּעָמִים הֵם חֲמִשָּׁה לְאִשָּׁה אַחַת, כָּל אֶחָד בְּכוֹר לְאָבִיו:

לא-לב וַיִּקְרָא לְמֹשֶׁה וּלְאַהֲרֹן לַיְלָה. מַגִּיד שֶׁהָיָה מְחַזֵּר עַל פִּתְחֵי הָעִיר וְצוֹעֵק: הֵיכָן מֹשֶׁה שָׁרוּי? הֵיכָן אַהֲרֹן שָׁרוּי?: גַּם אַתֶּם. הַגְּבָרִים: גַּם בְּנֵי יִשְׂרָאֵל. הַטַּף: וּלְכוּ עִבְדוּ אֶת ה' כְּדַבֶּרְכֶם. הַכֹּל כְּמוֹ שֶׁאֲמַרְתֶּם וְלֹא כְּמוֹ שֶׁאָמַרְתִּי אֲנִי, בָּטֵל "לֹא אֲשַׁלֵּחַ" (לעיל ה, ב), בָּטֵל "מִי וָמִי הַהֹלְכִים" (לעיל י, ח), בָּטֵל "רַק צֹאנְכֶם וּבְקַרְכֶם יֻצָּג" (לעיל י, כד) – "גַּם צֹאנְכֶם גַּם בְּקַרְכֶם קְחוּ"; וּמַהוּ "כַּאֲשֶׁר דִּבַּרְתֶּם"? "גַּם אַתָּה תִּתֵּן בְּיָדֵנוּ זְבָחִים וְעֹלֹת" (לעיל י, כה) – "קְחוּ

שמות | פרק יב

לג כַּאֲשֶׁ֣ר דִּבַּרְתֶּ֑ם וּלְכ֥וּ וּבֵרַכְתֶּ֖ם גַּם־אֹתִֽי: וַתֶּחֱזַ֤ק מִצְרַ֙יִם֙ עַל־הָעָ֔ם
לד לְמַהֵ֖ר לְשַׁלְּחָ֣ם מִן־הָאָ֑רֶץ כִּ֥י אָמְר֖וּ כֻּלָּ֥נוּ מֵתִֽים: וַיִּשָּׂ֨א הָעָ֤ם
אֶת־בְּצֵקוֹ֙ טֶ֣רֶם יֶחְמָ֔ץ מִשְׁאֲרֹתָ֛ם צְרֻרֹ֥ת בְּשִׂמְלֹתָ֖ם עַל־שִׁכְמָֽם:
לה וּבְנֵי־יִשְׂרָאֵ֥ל עָשׂ֖וּ כִּדְבַ֣ר מֹשֶׁ֑ה וַֽיִּשְׁאֲלוּ֙ מִמִּצְרַ֔יִם כְּלֵי־כֶ֛סֶף וּכְלֵ֥י
לו זָהָ֖ב וּשְׂמָלֹֽת: וַֽיהוָ֞ה נָתַ֨ן אֶת־חֵ֥ן הָעָ֛ם בְּעֵינֵ֥י מִצְרַ֖יִם וַיַּשְׁאִל֑וּם
וַֽיְנַצְּל֖וּ אֶת־מִצְרָֽיִם:
לז וַיִּסְע֧וּ בְנֵֽי־יִשְׂרָאֵ֛ל מֵרַעְמְסֵ֖ס סֻכֹּ֑תָה כְּשֵׁשׁ־מֵא֨וֹת אֶ֧לֶף רַגְלִ֛י
לח הַגְּבָרִ֖ים לְבַ֥ד מִטָּֽף: וְגַם־עֵ֥רֶב רַ֖ב עָלָ֣ה אִתָּ֑ם וְצֹ֣אן וּבָקָ֔ר מִקְנֶ֖ה
לט כָּבֵ֥ד מְאֹֽד: וַיֹּאפ֨וּ אֶת־הַבָּצֵ֜ק אֲשֶׁ֨ר הוֹצִ֧יאוּ מִמִּצְרַ֛יִם עֻגֹ֥ת מַצּ֖וֹת
כִּ֣י לֹ֣א חָמֵ֑ץ כִּֽי־גֹרְשׁ֣וּ מִמִּצְרַ֗יִם וְלֹ֤א יָֽכְלוּ֙ לְהִתְמַהְמֵ֔הַּ וְגַם־צֵדָ֖ה
מ לֹא־עָשׂ֥וּ לָהֶֽם: וּמוֹשַׁב֙ בְּנֵ֣י יִשְׂרָאֵ֔ל אֲשֶׁ֥ר יָשְׁב֖וּ בְּמִצְרָ֑יִם שְׁלֹשִׁ֣ים

כַּאֲשֶׁר דִּבַּרְתֶּם. וּבֵרַכְתֶּם גַּם אֹתִי. הִתְפַּלְלוּ עָלַי שֶׁלֹּא אָמוּת, שֶׁאֲנִי בְּכוֹר:

לג **כֻּלָּנוּ מֵתִים.** אָמְרוּ: לֹא כִּגְזֵרַת מֹשֶׁה הוּא, שֶׁהֲרֵי אָמַר: "וּמֵת כָּל בְּכוֹר" (לעיל יא, ה), וְכָאן אַף הַפְּשׁוּטִים מֵתִים, חֲמִשָּׁה אוֹ עֲשָׂרָה בְּבַיִת אֶחָד:

לד **טֶרֶם יֶחְמָץ.** הַמִּצְרִים לֹא הִנִּיחוּם לִשְׁהוֹת כְּדֵי חִמּוּץ: **מִשְׁאֲרֹתָם.** שְׁיָרֵי מַצָּה וּמָרוֹר: **עַל שִׁכְמָם.** אַף עַל פִּי שֶׁבְּהֵמוֹת הַרְבֵּה הוֹלִיכוּ עִמָּהֶם, מְחַבְּבִים הָיוּ אֶת הַמִּצְוָה:

לה **כִּדְבַר מֹשֶׁה.** שֶׁאָמַר לָהֶם בְּמִצְרַיִם: "וְיִשְׁאֲלוּ אִישׁ מֵאֵת רֵעֵהוּ" (לעיל יא, ב): **וּשְׂמָלֹת.** אַף הֵן הָיוּ חֲשׁוּבוֹת לָהֶם מִן הַכֶּסֶף וּמִן הַזָּהָב, וְהַמְאֻחָר בַּפָּסוּק חָשׁוּב:

לו **וַיַּשְׁאִלוּם.** אַף מַה שֶּׁלֹּא הָיוּ שׁוֹאֲלִים מֵהֶם הָיוּ נוֹתְנִים לָהֶם, אַתָּה אוֹמֵר אֶחָד, טֹל שְׁנַיִם וָלֵךְ: **וַיְנַצְּלוּ.** וְרוֹקְנוּ:

לז **מֵרַעְמְסֵס סֻכֹּתָה.** מֵאָה וְעֶשְׂרִים מִיל הָיוּ, וּבָאוּ

שָׁם לְפִי שָׁעָה, שֶׁנֶּאֱמַר: "וָאֶשָּׂא אֶתְכֶם עַל כַּנְפֵי נְשָׁרִים" (להלן יט, ד): **הַגְּבָרִים.** מִבֶּן עֶשְׂרִים וָמַעְלָה:

לח **עֵרֶב רַב.** תַּעֲרֹבֶת אֻמּוֹת שֶׁל גֵּרִים:

לט **עֻגֹת מַצּוֹת.** חֲרָרָה שֶׁל מַצָּה. בָּצֵק שֶׁלֹּא הֶחְמִיץ קָרוּי מַצָּה: **וְגַם צֵדָה לֹא עָשׂוּ לָהֶם.** לַדֶּרֶךְ. מַגִּיד שִׁבְחָן שֶׁל יִשְׂרָאֵל, שֶׁלֹּא אָמְרוּ: הֵיאַךְ נֵצֵא לַמִּדְבָּר בְּלֹא צֵדָה? אֶלָּא הֶאֱמִינוּ וְהָלְכוּ. הוּא שֶׁמְּפֹרָשׁ בַּקַּבָּלָה: "זָכַרְתִּי לָךְ חֶסֶד נְעוּרַיִךְ אַהֲבַת כְּלוּלֹתָיִךְ לֶכְתֵּךְ אַחֲרַי בַּמִּדְבָּר בְּאֶרֶץ לֹא זְרוּעָה" (ירמיה ב, ב), מַה שָּׂכָר מְפֹרָשׁ אַחֲרָיו? "קֹדֶשׁ יִשְׂרָאֵל לַה'" וְגו' (שם פסוק ג):

מ **אֲשֶׁר יָשְׁבוּ בְּמִצְרָיִם.** אַחַר שְׁאָר הַיְּשִׁיבוֹת שֶׁיָּשְׁבוּ גֵּרִים בְּאֶרֶץ לֹא לָהֶם: **שְׁלֹשִׁים שָׁנָה וְאַרְבַּע מֵאוֹת שָׁנָה.** בֵּין הַכֹּל, מִשֶּׁנּוֹלַד יִצְחָק עַד עַכְשָׁיו הָיוּ אַרְבַּע מֵאוֹת שָׁנָה. מִשֶּׁהָיָה לוֹ זֶרַע לְאַבְרָהָם נִתְקַיֵּם: "כִּי גֵר יִהְיֶה זַרְעֲךָ" (בראשית טו, יג), וּשְׁלֹשִׁים שָׁנָה הָיוּ מִשֶּׁנִּגְזְרָה גְּזֵרָה בֵּין הַבְּתָרִים עַד שֶׁנּוֹלַד יִצְחָק. וְאִי

פרק יב | שמות | בא

שָׁנָה וְאַרְבַּע מֵאוֹת שָׁנָֽה: וַיְהִי מִקֵּץ שְׁלֹשִׁים שָׁנָה וְאַרְבַּע מֵאוֹת שָׁנָה וַיְהִי בְּעֶ֨צֶם֙ הַיּ֣וֹם הַזֶּ֔ה יָ֥צְא֛וּ כָּל־צִבְא֥וֹת יהוה מֵאֶ֥רֶץ מִצְרָֽיִם: לֵ֣יל שִׁמֻּרִ֥ים הוּא֙ לַֽיהוה לְהוֹצִיאָ֖ם מֵאֶ֣רֶץ מִצְרָ֑יִם הֽוּא־הַלַּ֤יְלָה הַזֶּה֙ לַֽיהוה שִׁמֻּרִ֛ים לְכָל־בְּנֵ֥י יִשְׂרָאֵ֖ל לְדֹרֹתָֽם: וַיֹּ֤אמֶר יהוה אֶל־מֹשֶׁ֣ה וְאַהֲרֹ֔ן זֹ֖את חֻקַּ֣ת הַפָּ֑סַח כָּל־בֶּן־נֵכָ֖ר לֹא־יֹ֥אכַל בּֽוֹ: וְכָל־עֶ֥בֶד אִ֖ישׁ מִקְנַת־כָּ֑סֶף וּמַלְתָּ֣ה אֹת֔וֹ אָ֖ז יֹ֥אכַל בּֽוֹ: תּוֹשָׁ֥ב וְשָׂכִ֖יר לֹא־יֹ֥אכַל בּֽוֹ: בְּבַ֤יִת אֶחָד֙ יֵֽאָכֵ֔ל לֹא־תוֹצִ֧יא מִן־הַבַּ֛יִת מִן־הַבָּשָׂ֖ר ח֑וּצָה וְעֶ֖צֶם לֹ֥א תִשְׁבְּרוּ־בֽוֹ:

מא

מב

מג

מד

מה
מו

אֶפְשָׁר לוֹמַר בְּאֶרֶץ מִצְרַיִם לְבַדָּהּ, שֶׁהֲרֵי קְהָת מִן הַבָּאִים עִם יַעֲקֹב הָיָה, צֵא וַחֲשֹׁב כָּל שְׁנוֹתָיו וְכָל שְׁנוֹת עַמְרָם בְּנוֹ וּשְׁמוֹנִים שֶׁל מֹשֶׁה, לֹא תִּמְצָאֵם כָּל כָּךְ. וְעַל כָּרְחֲךָ הַרְבֵּה שָׁנִים הָיוּ לִקְהָת עַד שֶׁלֹּא יָרַד לְמִצְרַיִם, וְהַרְבֵּה מִשְּׁנוֹת עַמְרָם נִבְלָעִים בִּשְׁנוֹת קְהָת, וְהַרְבֵּה מִשְּׁמוֹנִים שֶׁל מֹשֶׁה נִבְלָעִים בִּשְׁנוֹת עַמְרָם, הֲרֵי שֶׁלֹּא תִּמְצָא אַרְבַּע מֵאוֹת לְבִיאַת מִצְרַיִם. וְהֻזְקַקְתָּ לוֹמַר עַל כָּרְחֲךָ שֶׁאַף שְׁאָר הַיְשִׁיבוֹת נִקְרְאוּ גֵרוּת, וַאֲפִלּוּ בְּחֶבְרוֹן, שֶׁנֶּאֱמַר: "אֲשֶׁר גָּר שָׁם אַבְרָהָם וְיִצְחָק" (בראשית לה, כז), וְאוֹמֵר: "אֶת אֶרֶץ מְגֻרֵיהֶם אֲשֶׁר גָּרוּ בָהּ" (לעיל ו, ד). לְפִיכָךְ אַתָּה צָרִיךְ לוֹמַר "כִּי גֵר יִהְיֶה זַרְעֲךָ" - מִשֶּׁהָיָה לוֹ זֶרַע. וּכְשֶׁתִּמְנֶה אַרְבַּע מֵאוֹת שָׁנָה מִשֶּׁנּוֹלַד יִצְחָק, תִּמְצָא מִבִּיאָתָן לְמִצְרַיִם עַד יְצִיאָתָן מָאתַיִם וְעֶשֶׂר שָׁנִים. וְזֶה אֶחָד מִן הַדְּבָרִים שֶׁשִּׁנּוּ לְתַלְמַי הַמֶּלֶךְ:

מא וַיְהִי מִקֵּץ שְׁלֹשִׁים שָׁנָה... וַיְהִי בְּעֶצֶם הַיּוֹם הַזֶּה. מַגִּיד שֶׁכֵּיוָן שֶׁהִגִּיעַ הַקֵּץ לֹא עִכְּבָן הַמָּקוֹם כְּהֶרֶף עַיִן. בַּחֲמִשָּׁה עָשָׂר בְּנִיסָן בָּאוּ מַלְאֲכֵי הַשָּׁרֵת אֵצֶל אַבְרָהָם לְבַשְּׂרוֹ, בַּחֲמִשָּׁה עָשָׂר בְּנִיסָן נוֹלַד יִצְחָק, בַּחֲמִשָּׁה עָשָׂר בְּנִיסָן נִגְזְרָה גְּזֵרָה בֵּין הַבְּתָרִים:

מב לֵיל שִׁמֻּרִים. שֶׁהָיָה הַקָּדוֹשׁ בָּרוּךְ הוּא שׁוֹמֵר וּמְצַפֶּה לוֹ לְקַיֵּם הַבְטָחָתוֹ "לְהוֹצִיאָם מֵאֶרֶץ מִצְרָיִם". הוּא הַלַּיְלָה הַזֶּה לַה'. הוּא הַלַּיְלָה שֶׁאָמַר לְאַבְרָהָם: בַּלַּיְלָה הַזֶּה אֲנִי גּוֹאֵל אֶת בָּנֶיךָ: שִׁמֻּרִים לְכָל בְּנֵי

יִשְׂרָאֵל לְדֹרֹתָם. מְשֻׁמָּר וּבָא מִן הַמַּזִּיקִין, כָּעִנְיָן שֶׁנֶּאֱמַר: "וְלֹא יִתֵּן הַמַּשְׁחִית וְגוֹ'" (לעיל פסוק כג):

מג זֹאת חֻקַּת הַפָּסַח. בְּאַרְבָּעָה עָשָׂר בְּנִיסָן נֶאֶמְרָה לָהֶם פָּרָשָׁה זוֹ: כָּל בֶּן נֵכָר. שֶׁנִּתְנַכְּרוּ מַעֲשָׂיו לְאָבִיו שֶׁבַּשָּׁמַיִם, וְאֶחָד הַגּוֹי וְאֶחָד יִשְׂרָאֵל מְשֻׁמָּד בְּמַשְׁמָע:

מד וּמַלְתָּה אֹתוֹ אָז יֹאכַל בּוֹ. רַבּוֹ: מַגִּיד שֶׁמִּילַת עֲבָדָיו מְעַכַּבְתּוֹ מִלֶּאֱכֹל בַּפֶּסַח, דִּבְרֵי רַבִּי יְהוֹשֻׁעַ. רַבִּי אֱלִיעֶזֶר אוֹמֵר: אֵין מִילַת עֲבָדָיו מְעַכַּבְתּוֹ מִלֶּאֱכֹל בַּפֶּסַח, אִם כֵּן מַה תַּלְמוּד לוֹמַר: "אָז יֹאכַל בּוֹ"? הָעֶבֶד:

מה תּוֹשָׁב. זֶה גֵּר תּוֹשָׁב: וְשָׂכִיר. זֶה הַגּוֹי. וּמַה תַּלְמוּד לוֹמַר? וַהֲלֹא עֲרֵלִים הֵם, וְנֶאֱמַר: "וְכָל עָרֵל לֹא יֹאכַל בּוֹ" (להלן פסוק מח)! אֶלָּא כְּגוֹן עַרְבִי מָהוּל וְגִבְעוֹנִי מָהוּל וְהוּא תּוֹשָׁב אוֹ שָׂכִיר:

מו בְּבַיִת אֶחָד יֵאָכֵל. בַּחֲבוּרָה אַחַת, שֶׁלֹּא יֵעָשׂוּ הַנִּמְנִין עָלָיו שְׁתֵּי חֲבוּרוֹת וִיחַלְּקוּהוּ. אַתָּה אוֹמֵר בַּחֲבוּרָה אַחַת, אוֹ אֵינוֹ אֶלָּא "בְּבַיִת אֶחָד" כְּמַשְׁמָעוֹ, וּלְלַמֵּד שֶׁאִם הִתְחִילוּ וְהָיוּ אוֹכְלִים בֶּחָצֵר וְיָרְדוּ גְשָׁמִים שֶׁלֹּא יִכָּנְסוּ לַבַּיִת? תַּלְמוּד לוֹמַר: "עַל הַבָּתִּים אֲשֶׁר יֹאכְלוּ אֹתוֹ בָּהֶם" (לעיל פסוק ז), מִכָּאן שֶׁהָאוֹכֵל אוֹכֵל בִּשְׁנֵי מְקוֹמוֹת: לֹא תוֹצִיא מִן הַבַּיִת. מִן הַחֲבוּרָה: וְעֶצֶם לֹא תִשְׁבְּרוּ בוֹ. הָרָאוּי לַאֲכִילָה,

שמות | פרק יב

מח כָּל־עֲדַת יִשְׂרָאֵל יַעֲשׂוּ אֹתוֹ: וְכִי־יָגוּר אִתְּךָ גֵּר וְעָשָׂה פֶסַח לַיהוה הִמּוֹל לוֹ כָל־זָכָר וְאָז יִקְרַב לַעֲשֹׂתוֹ וְהָיָה כְּאֶזְרַח הָאָרֶץ
מט וְכָל־עָרֵל לֹא־יֹאכַל בּוֹ: תּוֹרָה אַחַת יִהְיֶה לָאֶזְרָח וְלַגֵּר הַגָּר בְּתוֹכְכֶם: וַיַּעֲשׂוּ כָּל־בְּנֵי יִשְׂרָאֵל כַּאֲשֶׁר צִוָּה יהוה אֶת־מֹשֶׁה
נא וְאֶת־אַהֲרֹן כֵּן עָשׂוּ: וַיְהִי בְּעֶצֶם הַיּוֹם הַזֶּה הוֹצִיא יהוה אֶת־בְּנֵי יִשְׂרָאֵל מֵאֶרֶץ מִצְרַיִם עַל־צִבְאֹתָם:

יג א וַיְדַבֵּר יהוה אֶל־מֹשֶׁה לֵּאמֹר: קַדֶּשׁ־לִי כָל־בְּכוֹר פֶּטֶר כָּל־רֶחֶם שביעי
ב בִּבְנֵי יִשְׂרָאֵל בָּאָדָם וּבַבְּהֵמָה לִי הוּא: וַיֹּאמֶר מֹשֶׁה אֶל־הָעָם
ג זָכוֹר אֶת־הַיּוֹם הַזֶּה אֲשֶׁר יְצָאתֶם מִמִּצְרַיִם מִבֵּית עֲבָדִים כִּי בְּחֹזֶק יָד הוֹצִיא יהוה אֶתְכֶם מִזֶּה וְלֹא יֵאָכֵל חָמֵץ: הַיּוֹם אַתֶּם
ד יֹצְאִים בְּחֹדֶשׁ הָאָבִיב: וְהָיָה כִי־יְבִיאֲךָ יהוה אֶל־אֶרֶץ הַכְּנַעֲנִי
ה וְהַחִתִּי וְהָאֱמֹרִי וְהַחִוִּי וְהַיְבוּסִי אֲשֶׁר נִשְׁבַּע לַאֲבֹתֶיךָ לָתֶת לָךְ

כְּגוֹן שֵׁיֵּשׁ עָלָיו כַּזַּיִת בָּשָׂר, יֵשׁ בּוֹ מִשּׁוּם שְׁבִירַת עֶצֶם, אֵין עָלָיו כַּזַּיִת בָּשָׂר אֵין בּוֹ מִשּׁוּם שְׁבִירַת עֶצֶם:

מז **כָּל עֲדַת יִשְׂרָאֵל יַעֲשׂוּ אֹתוֹ.** לָמָּה נֶאֱמַר? לְפִי שֶׁהוּא אוֹמֵר בְּפֶסַח מִצְרַיִם: "שֶׂה לְבֵית אָבֹת" (לעיל פסוק ג), שֶׁנִּמְנוּ עָלָיו לְמִשְׁפָּחוֹת, יָכוֹל אַף פֶּסַח דּוֹרוֹת כֵּן? תַּלְמוּד לוֹמַר: "כָּל עֲדַת יִשְׂרָאֵל יַעֲשׂוּ אֹתוֹ":

מח **וְעָשָׂה פֶסַח.** יָכוֹל כָּל הַמִּתְגַּיֵּר יַעֲשֶׂה פֶסַח מִיָּד? תַּלְמוּד לוֹמַר: "וְהָיָה כְּאֶזְרַח הָאָרֶץ", מָה אֶזְרָח בְּאַרְבָּעָה עָשָׂר, אַף גֵּר בְּאַרְבָּעָה עָשָׂר: **וְכָל עָרֵל לֹא יֹאכַל בּוֹ.** לְהָבִיא אֶת שֶׁמֵּתוּ אֶחָיו מֵחֲמַת מִילָה, שֶׁאֵינוֹ מֻפְקָד לַעֲרֵלוּת וְאֵינוֹ לָמֵד מִ"כֵּן נֵכָר לֹא יֹאכַל בּוֹ" (לעיל פסוק מג):

מט **תּוֹרָה אַחַת וְגוֹ'.** לְהַשְׁווֹת גֵּר לָאֶזְרָח אַף לִשְׁאָר מִצְווֹת שֶׁבַּתּוֹרָה:

פרק יג

ב **פֶּטֶר כָּל רֶחֶם.** שֶׁפָּתַח אֶת הָרֶחֶם תְּחִלָּה, כְּמוֹ:

"פּוֹטֵר מַיִם רֵאשִׁית מָדוֹן" (משלי יז, יד), וְכֵן: "יַפְטִירוּ בְשָׂפָה" (תהלים כב, ח) – יִפְתְּחוּ שְׂפָתַיִם: לִי הוּא. לְעַצְמִי קְנִיתִים עַל יְדֵי שֶׁהִכֵּיתִי בְכוֹרֵי מִצְרַיִם:

ג **זָכוֹר אֶת הַיּוֹם הַזֶּה.** לִמֵּד שֶׁמַּזְכִּירִין יְצִיאַת מִצְרַיִם בְּכָל יוֹם:

ד **בְּחֹדֶשׁ הָאָבִיב.** וְכִי לֹא הָיוּ יוֹדְעִין בְּאֵיזֶה חֹדֶשׁ? אֶלָּא כָּךְ אָמַר לָהֶם: רְאוּ חֶסֶד שֶׁגְּמַלְכֶם, שֶׁמּוֹצִיא אֶתְכֶם בְּחֹדֶשׁ שֶׁהוּא כָשֵׁר לָצֵאת, לֹא חַמָּה וְלֹא צִנָּה וְלֹא גְשָׁמִים. וְכֵן הוּא אוֹמֵר: "מוֹצִיא אֲסִירִים בַּכּוֹשָׁרוֹת" (תהלים סח, ז), חֹדֶשׁ שֶׁהוּא כָשֵׁר לָצֵאת:

ה **אֶל אֶרֶץ הַכְּנַעֲנִי וְגוֹ'.** אַף עַל פִּי שֶׁלֹּא מָנָה אֶלָּא חֲמִשָּׁה עַמָּמִים, כָּל שִׁבְעָה גּוֹיִם בְּמַשְׁמָע, שֶׁכֻּלָּן בִּכְלַל כְּנַעֲנִי הֵם, וְאַחַת מִמִּשְׁפְּחוֹת כְּנַעַן הָיְתָה שֶׁלֹּא נִקְרָא לָהּ שֵׁם אֶלָּא "כְּנַעֲנִי": נִשְׁבַּע לַאֲבֹתֶיךָ. בְּאַבְרָהָם הוּא אוֹמֵר: "בַּיּוֹם הַהוּא כָּרַת ה' אֶת

אֶרֶץ זָבַת חָלָב וּדְבָשׁ וְעָבַדְתָּ אֶת־הָעֲבֹדָה הַזֹּאת בַּחֹדֶשׁ הַזֶּה:
ז שִׁבְעַת יָמִים תֹּאכַל מַצֹּת וּבַיּוֹם הַשְּׁבִיעִי חַג לַיהוָה: מַצּוֹת
יֵאָכֵל אֵת שִׁבְעַת הַיָּמִים וְלֹא־יֵרָאֶה לְךָ חָמֵץ וְלֹא־יֵרָאֶה לְךָ
ח שְׂאֹר בְּכָל־גְּבֻלֶךָ: וְהִגַּדְתָּ לְבִנְךָ בַּיּוֹם הַהוּא לֵאמֹר בַּעֲבוּר
ט זֶה עָשָׂה יְהוָה לִי בְּצֵאתִי מִמִּצְרָיִם: וְהָיָה לְךָ לְאוֹת עַל־יָדְךָ
וּלְזִכָּרוֹן בֵּין עֵינֶיךָ לְמַעַן תִּהְיֶה תּוֹרַת יְהוָה בְּפִיךָ כִּי בְּיָד חֲזָקָה
י הוֹצִאֲךָ יְהוָה מִמִּצְרָיִם: וְשָׁמַרְתָּ אֶת־הַחֻקָּה הַזֹּאת לְמוֹעֲדָהּ
מִיָּמִים יָמִימָה:

יא וְהָיָה כִּי־יְבִאֲךָ יְהוָה אֶל־אֶרֶץ הַכְּנַעֲנִי כַּאֲשֶׁר נִשְׁבַּע לְךָ
יב וְלַאֲבֹתֶיךָ וּנְתָנָהּ לָךְ: וְהַעֲבַרְתָּ כָל־פֶּטֶר־רֶחֶם לַיהוָה וְכָל־
יג פֶּטֶר ׀ שֶׁגֶר בְּהֵמָה אֲשֶׁר יִהְיֶה לְךָ הַזְּכָרִים לַיהוָה: וְכָל־פֶּטֶר

אֲכַרְסֵי וְגוֹ'" (בראשית טו, יח), וּבְיִצְחָק הוּא אוֹמֵר: "גּוּר
בָּאָרֶץ הַזֹּאת וְגוֹ'" (שם כו, ג), וּבְיַעֲקֹב הוּא אוֹמֵר: "הָאָרֶץ
אֲשֶׁר אַתָּה שֹׁכֵב עָלֶיהָ" וְגוֹ' (שם כח, יג): זָבַת חָלָב
וּדְבָשׁ. חָלָב זָב מִן הָעִזִּים, וְהַדְּבַשׁ זָב מִן הַתְּמָרִים
וּמִן הַתְּאֵנִים: אֶת הָעֲבֹדָה הַזֹּאת. שֶׁל פֶּסַח. וַהֲלֹא
כְּבָר נֶאֱמַר לְמַעְלָה: "וְהָיָה כִּי־תָבֹאוּ אֶל־הָאָרֶץ" וְגוֹ'
(לעיל יב, כה), וְלָמָּה חָזַר וּשְׁנָאָהּ? בִּשְׁבִיל דָּבָר שֶׁנִּתְחַדֵּשׁ
בָּהּ. בְּפָרָשָׁה הָרִאשׁוֹנָה נֶאֱמַר: "וְהָיָה כִּי־יֹאמְרוּ אֲלֵיכֶם
בְּנֵיכֶם מָה הָעֲבֹדָה הַזֹּאת לָכֶם" (שם פסוק כו), בְּבֵן
רָשָׁע הַכָּתוּב מְדַבֵּר שֶׁהוֹצִיא עַצְמוֹ מִן הַכְּלָל, וְכָאן:
"וְהִגַּדְתָּ לְבִנְךָ" (להלן פסוק ח), בְּבֵן שֶׁאֵינוֹ יוֹדֵעַ לִשְׁאֹל,
וְהַכָּתוּב מְלַמֶּדְךָ שֶׁתִּפְתַּח לוֹ אַתָּה בְּדִבְרֵי אַגָּדָה
הַמּוֹשְׁכִין אֶת הַלֵּב:

ח בַּעֲבוּר זֶה. בַּעֲבוּר שֶׁאֲקַיֵּם מִצְוֹתָיו כְּגוֹן פֶּסַח
מַצָּה וּמָרוֹר הַלָּלוּ: עָשָׂה ה' לִי. רָמַז תְּשׁוּבָה לְבֵן
רָשָׁע, לוֹמַר: "עָשָׂה ה' לִי", וְלֹא לְךָ, שֶׁאִלּוּ הָיִיתָ שָׁם
לֹא הָיִיתָ כְּדַאי לִגָּאֵל:

ט וְהָיָה לְךָ לְאוֹת. יְצִיאַת מִצְרַיִם תִּהְיֶה לְךָ לְאוֹת
עַל יָדְךָ וּבֵין עֵינֶיךָ, שֶׁתִּכְתֹּב פָּרָשִׁיּוֹת הַלָּלוּ וְתִקְשְׁרֵם
בָּרֹאשׁ וּבַזְּרוֹעַ: עַל יָדְךָ. עַל יָד שְׂמֹאל, לְפִיכָךְ "יָדְכָה" מָלֵא
בְּפָרָשָׁה שְׁנִיָּה (להלן פסוק טז), לִדְרֹשׁ בּוֹ, יָד שֶׁהִיא כֵּהָה:

י מִיָּמִים יָמִימָה. מִשָּׁנָה לְשָׁנָה:

יא נִשְׁבַּע לְךָ. וְהֵיכָן נִשְׁבַּע לְךָ? "וְהֵבֵאתִי אֶתְכֶם אֶל
הָאָרֶץ אֲשֶׁר נָשָׂאתִי" וְגוֹ' (לעיל ו, ח): וּנְתָנָהּ לָךְ. תְּהִי
בְּעֵינֶיךָ כְּאִלּוּ נְתָנָהּ לְךָ בּוֹ בַּיּוֹם וְאַל תְּהִי בְּעֵינֶיךָ
כִּירֻשַּׁת אָבוֹת:

יב וְהַעֲבַרְתָּ. אֵין "וְהַעֲבַרְתָּ" אֶלָּא לְשׁוֹן הַפְרָשָׁה,
וְכֵן הוּא אוֹמֵר: "וְהַעֲבַרְתֶּם אֶת נַחֲלָתוֹ לְבִתּוֹ" (במדבר
כז, ח): שֶׁגֶר בְּהֵמָה. נֵפֶל שֶׁשִּׁגְּרַתּוּ אִמּוֹ וְשִׁלְּחַתּוּ בְּלֹא
עִתּוֹ. וְלִמֶּדְךָ הַכָּתוּב שֶׁהוּא קָדוֹשׁ בִּבְכוֹרָה לִפְטֹר
אֶת הַבָּא אַחֲרָיו. וְאַף שֶׁאֵינוֹ נֵפֶל קָרוּי 'שֶׁגֶר', כְּמוֹ:
"שְׁגַר אֲלָפֶיךָ" (דברים ז, יג), אֲבָל זֶה לֹא בָא פָּה לְלַמֵּד
עַל הַנֵּפֶל, שֶׁהֲרֵי כְּבָר כָּתַב "כָּל פֶּטֶר רֶחֶם". וְחֹס
תֹּאמַר, אַף בְּכוֹר בְּהֵמָה טְמֵאָה בַּמַּשְׁמָע, בָּא וּפֵרֵשׁ
בְּמָקוֹם אַחֵר: "בִּבְקָרְךָ וּבְצֹאנֶךָ" (שם טו, יט). לָשׁוֹן אַחֵר
יֵשׁ לְפָרֵשׁ, "וְהַעֲבַרְתָּ כָל פֶּטֶר רֶחֶם" – בִּבְכוֹר אָדָם
הַכָּתוּב מְדַבֵּר:

שמות | פרק יג | בשלח

חֲמוֹר תִּפְדֶּה בְשֶׂה וְאִם־לֹא תִפְדֶּה וַעֲרַפְתּוֹ וְכֹל בְּכוֹר אָדָם
בְּבָנֶיךָ תִּפְדֶּה: וְהָיָה כִּי־יִשְׁאָלְךָ בִנְךָ מָחָר לֵאמֹר מַה־זֹּאת
וְאָמַרְתָּ אֵלָיו בְּחֹזֶק יָד הוֹצִיאָנוּ יהוה מִמִּצְרַיִם מִבֵּית עֲבָדִים:
וַיְהִי כִּי־הִקְשָׁה פַרְעֹה לְשַׁלְּחֵנוּ וַיַּהֲרֹג יהוה כָּל־בְּכוֹר בְּאֶרֶץ
מִצְרַיִם מִבְּכֹר אָדָם וְעַד־בְּכוֹר בְּהֵמָה עַל־כֵּן אֲנִי זֹבֵחַ לַיהוה
כָּל־פֶּטֶר רֶחֶם הַזְּכָרִים וְכָל־בְּכוֹר בָּנַי אֶפְדֶּה: וְהָיָה לְאוֹת
עַל־יָדְכָה וּלְטוֹטָפֹת בֵּין עֵינֶיךָ כִּי בְּחֹזֶק יָד הוֹצִיאָנוּ יהוה
מִמִּצְרָיִם:

מפטיר

יד

טו

טז

בשלח

וַיְהִי בְּשַׁלַּח פַּרְעֹה אֶת־הָעָם וְלֹא־נָחָם אֱלֹהִים דֶּרֶךְ אֶרֶץ
פְּלִשְׁתִּים כִּי קָרוֹב הוּא כִּי ׀ אָמַר אֱלֹהִים פֶּן־יִנָּחֵם הָעָם בִּרְאֹתָם

יז

יג) **פֶּטֶר חֲמוֹר.** ולא פֶּטֶר שְׁאָר בְּהֵמָה טְמֵאָה, וּגְזֵרַת
הַכָּתוּב הִיא, לְפִי שֶׁנִּמְשְׁלוּ בְּכוֹרֵי מִצְרַיִם לַחֲמוֹרִים.
וְעוֹד, שֶׁסִּיְּעוּ אֶת יִשְׂרָאֵל בִּיצִיאָתָן מִמִּצְרַיִם, שֶׁאֵין
לְךָ אֶחָד מִיִּשְׂרָאֵל שֶׁלֹּא נָטַל עִמּוֹ הַרְבֵּה חֲמוֹרִים
טְעוּנִים מִכַּסְפָּה וּמִזְּהָבָה שֶׁל מִצְרַיִם: **תִּפְדֶּה בְשֶׂה.**
נוֹתֵן שֶׂה לַכֹּהֵן וּפֶטֶר חֲמוֹר מֻתָּר בַּהֲנָאָה, וְהַשֶּׂה
חֻלִּין בְּיַד כֹּהֵן: **וַעֲרַפְתּוֹ.** עוֹרְפוֹ בְּקוֹפִיץ מֵאֲחוֹרָיו
וְהוֹרְגוֹ. הוּא הִפְסִיד מָמוֹנוֹ שֶׁל כֹּהֵן לְפִיכָךְ יֻפְסַד
מָמוֹנוֹ: **וְכֹל בְּכוֹר אָדָם בְּבָנֶיךָ תִּפְדֶּה.** חָמֵשׁ סְלָעִים
פִּדְיוֹנוֹ קָצוּב בְּמָקוֹם אַחֵר (במדבר יח, טז):

יד) **כִּי־יִשְׁאָלְךָ בִנְךָ מָחָר.** יֵשׁ 'מָחָר' שֶׁהוּא עַכְשָׁו וְיֵשׁ
'מָחָר' שֶׁהוּא לְאַחַר זְמַן, כְּגוֹן זֶה וּכְגוֹן: "מָחָר יֹאמְרוּ
בְנֵיכֶם לְבָנֵינוּ" (יהושע כב, כד) דִּבְנֵי גָד וּדְבְנֵי רְאוּבֵן:
מַה־זֹּאת. זֶה תִּינוֹק טִפֵּשׁ שֶׁאֵינוֹ יוֹדֵעַ לְהַעֲמִיק
שְׁאֵלָתוֹ וְסוֹתֵם וְשׁוֹאֵל "מַה זֹּאת". וּבְמָקוֹם אַחֵר הוּא
אוֹמֵר: "מָה הָעֵדֹת וְהַחֻקִּים וְהַמִּשְׁפָּטִים וְגוֹ'" (דברים
ו, כ). הֲרֵי זֹאת שְׁאֵלַת בֵּן חָכָם. דִּבְּרָה תוֹרָה כְּנֶגֶד

אַרְבָּעָה בָנִים: רָשָׁע, וְשֶׁאֵינוֹ יוֹדֵעַ לִשְׁאֹל, וְהַשּׁוֹאֵל
דֶּרֶךְ סְתוּמָה, וְהַשּׁוֹאֵל דֶּרֶךְ חָכְמָה:

טז) **וּלְטוֹטָפֹת.** תְּפִלִּין, וְעַל שֵׁם שֶׁהֵם אַרְבָּעָה בָתִּים
קְרוּיִין 'טוֹטָפֹת', 'טָט' בְּכַתְפִּי שְׁתַּיִם, 'פַּת' בְּאַפְרִיקִי
שְׁתַּיִם. וּמְנַחֵם חִבְּרוֹ עִם "וְהַטֵּף אֶל דָּרוֹם" (יחזקאל כא,
ב), "אַל תַּטִּפוּ" (מיכה ב, ו), לְשׁוֹן דִּבּוּר, כְּמוֹ: "וּלְזִכָּרוֹן
בֵּין עֵינֶיךָ" (לעיל פסוק ט), שֶׁהָרוֹאֶה אוֹתָם קְשׁוּרִים בֵּין
הָעֵינַיִם יִזְכֹּר הַנֵּס וִידַבֵּר בּוֹ:

יז) **וַיְהִי בְּשַׁלַּח פַּרְעֹה.** **וְלֹא־נָחָם.** נְהָגָם, כְּמוֹ: "לֵךְ נְחֵה
אֶת הָעָם" (להלן לב, לד), "בְּהִתְהַלֶּכְךָ תַּנְחֶה אֹתָךְ" (משלי
ו, כב): **כִּי קָרוֹב הוּא.** וְנוֹחַ לָשׁוּב בְּאוֹתוֹ הַדֶּרֶךְ לְמִצְרַיִם.
וּמִדְרְשֵׁי אַגָּדָה יֵשׁ הַרְבֵּה: **בִּרְאֹתָם מִלְחָמָה.** כְּגוֹן
מִלְחֶמֶת "וַיֵּרֶד הָעֲמָלֵקִי וְהַכְּנַעֲנִי וְגוֹ'" (במדבר יד, מה).
אִם הָלְכוּ דֶּרֶךְ יָשָׁר הָיוּ חוֹזְרִים. מָה אִם כְּשֶׁהִקִּיפָם
דֶּרֶךְ מְעֻקָּם אָמְרוּ: "נִתְּנָה רֹאשׁ וְנָשׁוּבָה מִצְרָיְמָה"
(שם פסוק ד), אִם הוֹלִיכָם בִּפְשׁוּטָה עַל אַחַת כַּמָּה
וְכַמָּה: **פֶּן יִנָּחֵם.** יַחְשְׁבוּ מַחֲשָׁבָה עַל שֶׁיָּצְאוּ וְיִתְּנוּ
לֵב לָשׁוּב:

פרק יג

מִלְחָמָה וְשָׁבוּ מִצְרָיְמָה: וַיַּסֵּב אֱלֹהִים ׀ אֶת־הָעָם דֶּרֶךְ הַמִּדְבָּר יח
יַם־סוּף וַחֲמֻשִׁים עָלוּ בְנֵי־יִשְׂרָאֵל מֵאֶרֶץ מִצְרָיִם: וַיִּקַּח מֹשֶׁה יט
אֶת־עַצְמוֹת יוֹסֵף עִמּוֹ כִּי הַשְׁבֵּעַ הִשְׁבִּיעַ אֶת־בְּנֵי יִשְׂרָאֵל
לֵאמֹר פָּקֹד יִפְקֹד אֱלֹהִים אֶתְכֶם וְהַעֲלִיתֶם אֶת־עַצְמֹתַי מִזֶּה
אִתְּכֶם: וַיִּסְעוּ מִסֻּכֹּת וַיַּחֲנוּ בְאֵתָם בִּקְצֵה הַמִּדְבָּר: וַיהוָה הֹלֵךְ כא
לִפְנֵיהֶם יוֹמָם בְּעַמּוּד עָנָן לַנְחֹתָם הַדֶּרֶךְ וְלַיְלָה בְּעַמּוּד אֵשׁ
לְהָאִיר לָהֶם לָלֶכֶת יוֹמָם וָלָיְלָה: לֹא־יָמִישׁ עַמּוּד הֶעָנָן יוֹמָם כב
וְעַמּוּד הָאֵשׁ לָיְלָה לִפְנֵי הָעָם:

וַיְדַבֵּר יְהוָה אֶל־מֹשֶׁה לֵּאמֹר: דַּבֵּר אֶל־בְּנֵי יִשְׂרָאֵל וְיָשֻׁבוּ יד
וְיַחֲנוּ לִפְנֵי פִּי הַחִירֹת בֵּין מִגְדֹּל וּבֵין הַיָּם לִפְנֵי בַּעַל צְפֹן נִכְחוֹ

יח. **וַיַּסֵּב.** הֱסִבָּם מִן הַדֶּרֶךְ הַפְּשׁוּטָה לַדֶּרֶךְ הָעֲקֻמָּה.
יַם סוּף. כְּמוֹ לְיַם סוּף. וְ"סוּף" הוּא לְשׁוֹן אֲגַם שֶׁגְּדֵלִים
בּוֹ קָנִים, וְכֵן: "וַתָּשֶׂם בַּסּוּף" (לעיל ב, ג), "קָנֶה וָסוּף
קָמֵלוּ" (ישעיה יט, ו): **וַחֲמֻשִׁים.** אֵין "חֲמֻשִׁים" אֶלָּא
מְזֻיָּנִים, וְכֵן הוּא אוֹמֵר: "וְאַתֶּם תַּעַבְרוּ חֲמֻשִׁים" (יהושע
א, יד). וְכֵן תִּרְגֵּם אוּנְקְלוֹס "מְזָרְזִין", כְּמוֹ: "וַיָּרֶק אֶת
חֲנִיכָיו" (בראשית יד, יד), "וְזָרִיז". דָּבָר אַחֵר, "חֲמֻשִׁים",
מְחֻמָּשִׁים, אֶחָד מֵחֲמִשָּׁה יָצְאוּ וְאַרְבָּעָה חֲלָקִים מֵתוּ
בִּשְׁלֹשֶׁת יְמֵי אֲפֵלָה:

יט. **הַשְׁבֵּעַ הִשְׁבִּיעַ.** הִשְׁבִּיעָם שֶׁיַּשְׁבִּיעוּ לִבְנֵיהֶם.
וְלָמָּה לֹא הִשְׁבִּיעַ לְבָנָיו שֶׁיִּשָּׂאוּהוּ לְאֶרֶץ כְּנַעַן מִיָּד
כְּמוֹ שֶׁהִשְׁבִּיעַ יַעֲקֹב? אָמַר יוֹסֵף: אֲנִי שַׁלִּיט הָיִיתִי
בְּמִצְרַיִם וְהָיָה סֵפֶק בְּיָדִי לַעֲשׂוֹת, אֲבָל בָּנַי לֹא יַנִּיחוּ
מִצְרַיִם לַעֲשׂוֹת, לְכָךְ הִשְׁבִּיעָם לִכְשֶׁיִּגָּאֲלוּ וְיֵצְאוּ מִשָּׁם
שֶׁיִּשָּׂאוּהוּ: **וְהַעֲלִיתֶם אֶת עַצְמֹתַי מִזֶּה אִתְּכֶם.** לְאֶחָיו
הִשְׁבִּיעַ כֵּן, לִמְּדָנוּ שֶׁאַף עַצְמוֹת כָּל הַשְּׁבָטִים הֶעֱלוּ
עִמָּהֶם, שֶׁנֶּאֱמַר "אִתְּכֶם":

כ. **וַיִּסְעוּ מִסֻּכֹּת.** בַּיּוֹם הַשֵּׁנִי, שֶׁהֲרֵי בָּרִאשׁוֹן בָּאוּ
מֵרַעְמְסֵס לְסֻכּוֹת (לעיל יב, לו).

כא. **לַנְחֹתָם הַדֶּרֶךְ.** נָקוּד פַּתָּח, שֶׁהוּא כְּמוֹ לְהַנְחֹתָם,

כְּמוֹ: "לַרְאֹתְכֶם בַּדֶּרֶךְ אֲשֶׁר תֵּלְכוּ בָהּ" (דברים א, לג)
שֶׁהוּא כְּמוֹ לְהַרְאוֹתְכֶם, אַף כָּאן לְהַנְחֹתָם עַל יְדֵי
שָׁלִיחַ. וּמִי הוּא הַשָּׁלִיחַ? עַמּוּד הֶעָנָן, וְהַקָּדוֹשׁ בָּרוּךְ
הוּא בִּכְבוֹדוֹ מוֹלִיכוֹ לִפְנֵיהֶם, וּמִכָּל מָקוֹם אֶת עַמּוּד
הֶעָנָן הֵכִין לְהַנְחוֹתָם עַל יָדוֹ, שֶׁהֲרֵי עַל יְדֵי עַמּוּד
הֶעָנָן הֵם הוֹלְכִים. עַמּוּד הֶעָנָן אֵינוֹ לְאוֹרָה אֶלָּא
לְהוֹרוֹתָם הַדֶּרֶךְ:

כב. **לֹא יָמִישׁ.** הַקָּדוֹשׁ בָּרוּךְ הוּא אֶת "עַמּוּד הֶעָנָן
יוֹמָם וְעַמּוּד הָאֵשׁ לָיְלָה", מַגִּיד שֶׁעַמּוּד הֶעָנָן
מַשְׁלִים לְעַמּוּד הָאֵשׁ וְעַמּוּד הָאֵשׁ מַשְׁלִים לְעַמּוּד
הֶעָנָן, שֶׁעַד שֶׁלֹּא יִשְׁקַע זֶה עוֹלֶה זֶה:

פרק יד

ב. **וְיָשֻׁבוּ.** לַאֲחוֹרֵיהֶם, לְצַד מִצְרַיִם הָיוּ מְקָרְבִין
כָּל יוֹם הַשְּׁלִישִׁי, כְּדֵי לְהַטְעוֹת אֶת פַּרְעֹה שֶׁיֹּאמַר
תּוֹעִים הֵם בַּדֶּרֶךְ, כְּמוֹ שֶׁנֶּאֱמַר: "וְאָמַר פַּרְעֹה לִבְנֵי
יִשְׂרָאֵל" וְגוֹ' (להלן פסוק ג): **וְיַחֲנוּ לִפְנֵי פִּי הַחִירֹת.** הִיא
פִּיתוֹם, וְעַכְשָׁו נִקְרֵאת "פִּי הַחִירֹת" עַל שֵׁם שֶׁנַּעֲשׂוּ
שָׁם בְּנֵי חוֹרִין. וְהֵם שְׁנֵי סְלָעִים גְּבוֹהִים זְקוּפִים,
וְהַגַּיְא שֶׁבֵּינֵיהֶם קָרוּי פִּי הַסְּלָעִים: **לִפְנֵי בַּעַל צְפֹן.**
הוּא נִשְׁאַר מִכָּל אֱלֹהֵי מִצְרַיִם כְּדֵי לְהַטְעוֹתָן

שמות | פרק יד

ג תַחֲנוּ עַל־הַיָּם: וְאָמַר פַּרְעֹה לִבְנֵי יִשְׂרָאֵל נְבֻכִים הֵם בָּאָרֶץ
ד סָגַר עֲלֵיהֶם הַמִּדְבָּר: וְחִזַּקְתִּי אֶת־לֵב־פַּרְעֹה וְרָדַף אַחֲרֵיהֶם וְאִכָּבְדָה בְּפַרְעֹה וּבְכָל־חֵילוֹ וְיָדְעוּ מִצְרַיִם כִּי־אֲנִי יְהוָה
ה וַיַּעֲשׂוּ־כֵן: וַיֻּגַּד לְמֶלֶךְ מִצְרַיִם כִּי בָרַח הָעָם וַיֵּהָפֵךְ לְבַב פַּרְעֹה וַעֲבָדָיו אֶל־הָעָם וַיֹּאמְרוּ מַה־זֹּאת עָשִׂינוּ כִּי־שִׁלַּחְנוּ אֶת־יִשְׂרָאֵל מֵעָבְדֵנוּ: וַיֶּאְסֹר אֶת־רִכְבּוֹ וְאֶת־עַמּוֹ לָקַח עִמּוֹ:
ז וַיִּקַּח שֵׁשׁ־מֵאוֹת רֶכֶב בָּחוּר וְכֹל רֶכֶב מִצְרָיִם וְשָׁלִשִׁם עַל־

שֶׁיֹּאמְרוּ: קָשָׁה יִרְדְּתָן. וְעָלָיו פֵּרֵשׁ אִיּוֹב: "מַשְׂגִּיא לַגּוֹיִם וַיְאַבְּדֵם" (איוב יב, כג):

ג) וְאָמַר פַּרְעֹה. כְּשֶׁיִּשְׁמַע שֶׁהֵם שָׁבִים לַאֲחוֹרֵיהֶם: לִבְנֵי יִשְׂרָאֵל. עַל בְּנֵי יִשְׂרָאֵל. וְכֵן: "ה' יִלָּחֵם לָכֶם" (להלן פסוק יד) – עֲלֵיכֶם; "אִמְרִי לִי אָחִי הוּא" (בראשית כ, יג) – אִמְרִי עָלָי: נְבֻכִים הֵם. כְּלוּאִים וּמְשֻׁקָּעִים, וּבְלַעַז שיר״ר. כְּמוֹ: "בְּעִמְקֵי יָם" (איוב לח, טז), "בְּעֵמֶק הַבָּכָא" (תהלים פד, ז), "מִבְּכִי נְהָרוֹת" (איוב כח, יא). נְבֻכִים הֵם – כְּלוּאִים הֵם בַּמִּדְבָּר, שֶׁאֵינָן יוֹדְעִין לָצֵאת מִמֶּנּוּ וּלְהֵיכָן יֵלְכוּ:

ד) וְאִכָּבְדָה בְּפַרְעֹה. כְּשֶׁהַקָּדוֹשׁ בָּרוּךְ הוּא מִתְנַקֵּם בָּרְשָׁעִים שְׁמוֹ מִתְגַּדֵּל וּמִתְכַּבֵּד. וְכֵן הוּא אוֹמֵר: "וְנִשְׁפַּטְתִּי אִתּוֹ" וְגוֹ' וְאַחַר כָּךְ: "וְהִתְגַּדִּלְתִּי וְהִתְקַדִּשְׁתִּי וְנוֹדַעְתִּי" וְגוֹ' (יחזקאל לח, כב-כג), וְאוֹמֵר: "שָׁמָּה שִׁבַּר רִשְׁפֵי קָשֶׁת" וְאַחַר כָּךְ: "נוֹדָע בִּיהוּדָה אֱלֹהִים" (תהלים עו, ב-ד), וְאוֹמֵר: "נוֹדַע ה' מִשְׁפָּט עָשָׂה" (שם ט, יז): בְּפַרְעֹה וּבְכָל־חֵילוֹ. הוּא הִתְחִיל בַּעֲבֵרָה וּמִמֶּנּוּ הִתְחִיל הַפֻּרְעָנוּת: וַיַּעֲשׂוּ־כֵן. לְהַגִּיד שִׁבְחָן שֶׁשָּׁמְעוּ לְקוֹל מֹשֶׁה, וְלֹא אָמְרוּ: הֵיאַךְ נִתְקָרֵב אֶל רוֹדְפֵינוּ? אָנוּ צְרִיכִים לִבְרֹחַ! אֶלָּא אָמְרוּ: אֵין לָנוּ אֶלָּא דִבְרֵי בֶן עַמְרָם:

ה) וַיֻּגַּד לְמֶלֶךְ מִצְרָיִם. אִיקְטוֹרִין שָׁלַח עִמָּהֶם, וְכֵיוָן שֶׁהִגִּיעוּ לִשְׁלֹשֶׁת יָמִים שֶׁקָּבְעוּ לֵילֵךְ וְלָשׁוּב וְרָאוּ שֶׁאֵינָן חוֹזְרִין לְמִצְרַיִם, בָּאוּ וְהִגִּידוּ לְפַרְעֹה בַּיּוֹם הָרְבִיעִי. וּבַחֲמִישִׁי וּבַשִּׁשִּׁי רָדְפוּ אַחֲרֵיהֶם, לֵיל שְׁבִיעִי

יָרְדוּ לַיָּם, בְּשַׁחֲרִית אָמְרוּ שִׁירָה, וְהוּא יוֹם שְׁבִיעִי שֶׁל פֶּסַח. לְכָךְ אָנוּ קוֹרִין הַשִּׁירָה בַּיּוֹם הַשְּׁבִיעִי: וַיֵּהָפֵךְ. נֶהְפַּךְ מִמַּה שֶּׁהָיָה, שֶׁהֲרֵי אָמַר לָהֶם: "קוּמוּ צְּאוּ מִתּוֹךְ עַמִּי" (לעיל יב, לא), וְנֶהְפַּךְ לֵב עֲבָדָיו, שֶׁהֲרֵי לְשֶׁעָבַר הָיוּ אוֹמְרִים לוֹ: "עַד מָתַי יִהְיֶה זֶה לָנוּ לְמוֹקֵשׁ" (לעיל י, ז) וְעַכְשָׁיו נֶהֶפְכוּ לִרְדֹּף אַחֲרֵיהֶם בִּשְׁבִיל מָמוֹנָם שֶׁשִּׁלְּחוּם: מֵעָבְדֵנוּ. מֵעֲבֹד אוֹתָנוּ:

ו) וַיֶּאְסֹר אֶת־רִכְבּוֹ. וְאֶת־עַמּוֹ. הוּא בְּעַצְמוֹ: לָקַח עִמּוֹ. מְשָׁכָם בִּדְבָרִים: לָקִינוּ וְנָטְלוּ מָמוֹנֵנוּ וְשִׁלַּחְנוּם! בּוֹאוּ עִמִּי וַאֲנִי לֹא אֶתְנַהֵג עִמָּכֶם כִּשְׁאָר מְלָכִים, דֶּרֶךְ שְׁאָר מְלָכִים עֲבָדָיו קוֹדְמִין לוֹ בַּמִּלְחָמָה, וַאֲנִי אַקְדִּים לִפְנֵיכֶם, שֶׁנֶּאֱמַר: "וּפַרְעֹה הִקְרִיב" (להלן פסוק י) – הִקְרִיב עַצְמוֹ וּמִהֵר לִפְנֵי חֲיָלוֹתָיו, דֶּרֶךְ שְׁאָר מְלָכִים לִטֹּל בִּזָּה בָּרֹאשׁ כְּמוֹ שֶׁיִּבְחָר, אֲנִי אֲשַׁוֶּה עִמָּכֶם חֵלֶק, שֶׁנֶּאֱמַר: "אֲחַלֵּק שָׁלָל" (להלן טו, ט):

ז) בָּחוּר. נְבְחָרִים. 'בָּחוּר' לְשׁוֹן יָחִיד, כָּל רֶכֶב וָרֶכֶב שֶׁבַּמִּנְיָן זֶה הָיָה בָּחוּר: וְכֹל רֶכֶב מִצְרָיִם. וְעִמָּהֶם כָּל שְׁאָר הָרָכֶב. וּמֵהֵיכָן הָיוּ הַבְּהֵמוֹת הַלָּלוּ? אִם תֹּאמַר מִשֶּׁל מִצְרַיִם, הֲרֵי נֶאֱמַר: "וַיָּמָת כֹּל מִקְנֵה מִצְרָיִם" (לעיל ט, ו)! וְאִם מִשֶּׁל יִשְׂרָאֵל, וַהֲלֹא נֶאֱמַר: "וְגַם מִקְנֵנוּ יֵלֵךְ עִמָּנוּ" (לעיל י, כו)! מִשֶּׁל מִי הָיוּ? מִ"הַיָּרֵא אֶת דְּבַר ה'" (לעיל ט, כ). מִכָּאן הָיָה רַבִּי שִׁמְעוֹן אוֹמֵר: כָּשֵׁר שֶׁבַּגּוֹיִם הֲרֹג, טוֹב שֶׁבַּנְּחָשִׁים רְצֹץ אֶת מֹחוֹ: וְשָׁלִשִׁם עַל כֻּלּוֹ. שָׂרֵי צְבָאוֹת כְּתַרְגּוּמוֹ:

פרק יד | שמות | בשלח

ח וַיְחַזֵּק יְהוָה אֶת־לֵב פַּרְעֹה מֶלֶךְ מִצְרַיִם וַיִּרְדֹּף אַחֲרֵי בְּנֵי יִשְׂרָאֵל וּבְנֵי יִשְׂרָאֵל יֹצְאִים בְּיָד רָמָה: ט וַיִּרְדְּפוּ מִצְרַיִם אַחֲרֵיהֶם וַיַּשִּׂיגוּ אוֹתָם חֹנִים עַל־הַיָּם כָּל־סוּס רֶכֶב פַּרְעֹה וּפָרָשָׁיו וְחֵילוֹ עַל־פִּי הַחִירֹת לִפְנֵי בַּעַל צְפֹן: י וּפַרְעֹה הִקְרִיב וַיִּשְׂאוּ בְנֵי־יִשְׂרָאֵל אֶת־עֵינֵיהֶם וְהִנֵּה מִצְרַיִם ׀ נֹסֵעַ אַחֲרֵיהֶם וַיִּירְאוּ מְאֹד וַיִּצְעֲקוּ בְנֵי־יִשְׂרָאֵל אֶל־יְהוָה: יא וַיֹּאמְרוּ אֶל־מֹשֶׁה הֲמִבְּלִי אֵין־קְבָרִים בְּמִצְרַיִם לְקַחְתָּנוּ לָמוּת בַּמִּדְבָּר מַה־זֹּאת עָשִׂיתָ לָּנוּ לְהוֹצִיאָנוּ מִמִּצְרָיִם: יב הֲלֹא־זֶה הַדָּבָר אֲשֶׁר דִּבַּרְנוּ אֵלֶיךָ בְמִצְרַיִם לֵאמֹר חֲדַל מִמֶּנּוּ וְנַעַבְדָה אֶת־מִצְרָיִם כִּי טוֹב לָנוּ עֲבֹד אֶת־מִצְרַיִם מִמֻּתֵנוּ בַּמִּדְבָּר: יג וַיֹּאמֶר מֹשֶׁה אֶל־הָעָם אַל־תִּירָאוּ הִתְיַצְּבוּ וּרְאוּ אֶת־יְשׁוּעַת יְהוָה אֲשֶׁר־יַעֲשֶׂה לָכֶם הַיּוֹם כִּי אֲשֶׁר רְאִיתֶם אֶת־מִצְרַיִם הַיּוֹם לֹא תֹסִפוּ לִרְאֹתָם עוֹד עַד־עוֹלָם: יד יְהוָה יִלָּחֵם לָכֶם וְאַתֶּם תַּחֲרִשׁוּן:

ח] וַיְחַזֵּק ה' אֶת לֵב פַּרְעֹה. שֶׁהָיָה תוֹלֶה אִם לִרְדֹּף אִם לָאו, וְחִזֵּק אֶת לִבּוֹ לִרְדֹּף: **בְּיָד רָמָה.** בִּגְבוּרָה גְבוֹהָה וּמְפֻרְסֶמֶת:

י] וּפַרְעֹה הִקְרִיב. הָיָה לוֹ לִכְתֹּב: "וּפַרְעֹה קָרַב", מַהוּ "הִקְרִיב"? הִקְרִיב עַצְמוֹ וְנִתְאַמֵּץ לְקַדֵּם לִפְנֵיהֶם כְּמוֹ שֶׁהִתְנָה עִמָּהֶם: **נֹסֵעַ אַחֲרֵיהֶם.** בְּלֵב אֶחָד כְּאִישׁ אֶחָד. דָּבָר אַחֵר, "וְהִנֵּה מִצְרַיִם נֹסֵעַ אַחֲרֵיהֶם", רָאוּ שַׂר שֶׁל מִצְרַיִם נוֹסֵעַ מִן הַשָּׁמַיִם לַעֲזֹר לְמִצְרַיִם. תַּנְחוּמָא: **וַיִּצְעֲקוּ.** תָּפְשׂוּ אֻמָּנוּת אֲבוֹתָם, בְּאַבְרָהָם הוּא אוֹמֵר: "אֶל הַמָּקוֹם אֲשֶׁר עָמַד שָׁם" (בראשית יט), בְּיִצְחָק: "לָשׂוּחַ בַּשָּׂדֶה" (שם כד, סג), בְּיַעֲקֹב: "וַיִּפְגַּע בַּמָּקוֹם" (שם כח, יא):

יא] הֲמִבְּלִי אֵין קְבָרִים. וְכִי מֵחֲמַת חֶסְרוֹן קְבָרִים, שֶׁאֵין קְבָרִים בְּמִצְרַיִם לִקְבֹּר שָׁם, לְקַחְתָּנוּ מִשָּׁם? שִׂיפוֹ"ר פלענ"ש דינ"ו פוסי"ש בלע"ז:

יב] אֲשֶׁר דִּבַּרְנוּ אֵלֶיךָ בְּמִצְרָיִם. וְהֵיכָן דִּבְּרוּ? "יֵרֶא ה' עֲלֵיכֶם וְיִשְׁפֹּט" (לעיל ה, כא): **מִמֻּתֵנוּ.** מֵאֲשֶׁר נָמוּת. וְאִם הָיָה נָקוּד מְלָאפוּם הָיָה נִבְאָר 'מִמִּיתָתֵנוּ', עַכְשָׁיו שֶׁנָּקוּד בְּשׁוּרוּק נִבְאָר 'מֵאֲשֶׁר נָמוּת'. וְכֵן: "מִי יִתֵּן מוּתֵנוּ" (להלן טז, ג), שֶׁנָּמוּת, וְכֵן: "מִי יִתֵּן מוּתִי" דְּאַבְשָׁלוֹם (שמואל ב' יט, א), שֶׁאָמוּת, כְּמוֹ: "לְיוֹם קוּמִי לְעַד" (צפניה ג, ח), "עַד שׁוּבִי בְשָׁלוֹם" (דברי הימים ב' יח, כו), שֶׁאָקוּם, שֶׁאָשׁוּב:

יג] כִּי אֲשֶׁר רְאִיתֶם אֶת מִצְרַיִם וְגוֹ'. מַה שֶּׁרְאִיתֶם אוֹתָם אֵינוֹ אֶלָּא הַיּוֹם, הַיּוֹם הוּא שֶׁרְאִיתֶם אוֹתָם וְלֹא תוֹסִיפוּ עוֹד:

יד] יִלָּחֵם לָכֶם. בִּשְׁבִילְכֶם. וְכֵן: "כִּי ה' נִלְחָם לָהֶם" (להלן פסוק כה), וְכֵן: "אִם לָאֵל תְּרִיבוּן" (איוב יג, ח), וְכֵן:

שמות | פרק יד

יא שלישי

טו וַיֹּאמֶר יהוה אֶל־מֹשֶׁה מַה־תִּצְעַק אֵלָי דַּבֵּר אֶל־בְּנֵי־יִשְׂרָאֵל
טז וְיִסָּעוּ: וְאַתָּה הָרֵם אֶת־מַטְּךָ וּנְטֵה אֶת־יָדְךָ עַל־הַיָּם וּבְקָעֵהוּ
יז וְיָבֹאוּ בְנֵי־יִשְׂרָאֵל בְּתוֹךְ הַיָּם בַּיַּבָּשָׁה: וַאֲנִי הִנְנִי מְחַזֵּק אֶת־לֵב
מִצְרַיִם וְיָבֹאוּ אַחֲרֵיהֶם וְאִכָּבְדָה בְּפַרְעֹה וּבְכָל־חֵילוֹ בְּרִכְבּוֹ
יח וּבְפָרָשָׁיו: וְיָדְעוּ מִצְרַיִם כִּי־אֲנִי יהוה בְּהִכָּבְדִי בְּפַרְעֹה בְּרִכְבּוֹ
יט וּבְפָרָשָׁיו: וַיִּסַּע מַלְאַךְ הָאֱלֹהִים הַהֹלֵךְ לִפְנֵי מַחֲנֵה יִשְׂרָאֵל וַיֵּלֶךְ
מֵאַחֲרֵיהֶם וַיִּסַּע עַמּוּד הֶעָנָן מִפְּנֵיהֶם וַיַּעֲמֹד מֵאַחֲרֵיהֶם: וַיָּבֹא
כ בֵּין ׀ מַחֲנֵה מִצְרַיִם וּבֵין מַחֲנֵה יִשְׂרָאֵל וַיְהִי הֶעָנָן וְהַחֹשֶׁךְ וַיָּאֶר
כא אֶת־הַלָּיְלָה וְלֹא־קָרַב זֶה אֶל־זֶה כָּל־הַלָּיְלָה: וַיֵּט מֹשֶׁה אֶת־יָדוֹ
עַל־הַיָּם וַיּוֹלֶךְ יהוה ׀ אֶת־הַיָּם בְּרוּחַ קָדִים עַזָּה כָּל־הַלַּיְלָה
כב וַיָּשֶׂם אֶת־הַיָּם לֶחָרָבָה וַיִּבָּקְעוּ הַמָּיִם: וַיָּבֹאוּ בְנֵי־יִשְׂרָאֵל

"וַאֲשֶׁר דִּבֶּר לִי" (בראשית כד, ז). וְכֵן: "הַחַתֵּם תְּרִיבוּן
לַבָּעַל" (שופטים ו, לא).

טו) מַה תִּצְעַק אֵלָי. לָמַדְנוּ שֶׁהָיָה מֹשֶׁה עוֹמֵד
וּמִתְפַּלֵּל, אָמַר לוֹ הַקָּדוֹשׁ בָּרוּךְ הוּא: לֹא עֵת עַתָּה
לְהַאֲרִיךְ שֶׁיִּשְׂרָאֵל נְתוּנִין בְּצָרָה. דָּבָר אַחֵר, "מַה
תִּצְעַק אֵלָי", עָלַי הַדָּבָר וְלֹא עָלֶיךָ, כְּמוֹ שֶׁנֶּאֱמַר
לְהַלָּן: "עַל בָּנַי וְעַל פֹּעַל יָדַי תְּצַוֻּנִי" (ישעיה מה, יא): **דַּבֵּר
אֶל בְּנֵי יִשְׂרָאֵל וְיִסָּעוּ.** אֵין לָהֶם אֶלָּא לִסַּע, שֶׁאֵין
הַיָּם עוֹמֵד בִּפְנֵיהֶם, כְּדַאי זְכוּת אֲבוֹתֵיהֶם וְהֵמָּה
שֶׁהֶאֱמִינוּ בִּי וְיָצְאוּ, לִקְרֹעַ לָהֶם אֶת הַיָּם:

יט-כ) וַיֵּלֶךְ מֵאַחֲרֵיהֶם. לְהַבְדִּיל בֵּין מַחֲנֵה מִצְרַיִם
וּבֵין מַחֲנֵה יִשְׂרָאֵל וּלְקַבֵּל חִצִּים וּבַלִּיסְטְרָאוֹת שֶׁל
מִצְרַיִם. בְּכָל מָקוֹם הוּא אוֹמֵר: "מַלְאַךְ ה'", וְכָאן
"מַלְאַךְ הָאֱלֹהִים", אֵין "אֱלֹהִים" בְּכָל מָקוֹם אֶלָּא
דִּין, מְלַמֵּד שֶׁהָיוּ יִשְׂרָאֵל נְתוּנִין בַּדִּין בְּאוֹתָהּ שָׁעָה
אִם לְהִנָּצֵל אִם לְהֵאָבֵד עִם מִצְרַיִם: **וַיָּבֹא בֵּין מַחֲנֵה
מִצְרַיִם.** מָשָׁל לִמְהַלֵּךְ בַּדֶּרֶךְ וּבְנוֹ מְהַלֵּךְ לְפָנָיו,
בָּאוּ לִסְטִים לִשְׁבּוֹתוֹ, נְטָלוֹ מִלְּפָנָיו וּנְתָנוֹ לְאַחֲרָיו,

בָּא זְאֵב מֵאַחֲרָיו, נְתָנוֹ לְפָנָיו. בָּאוּ לִסְטִים לְפָנָיו
וְזְאֵבִים מֵאַחֲרָיו, נְתָנוֹ עַל זְרוֹעוֹ וְנִלְחַם בָּהֶם. כָּךְ:
"וְאָנֹכִי תִרְגַּלְתִּי לְאֶפְרַיִם קָחָם עַל זְרוֹעֹתָיו" (הושע יא,
ג): **וַיִּסַּע עַמּוּד הֶעָנָן.** כְּשֶׁחָשְׁכָה וְהִשְׁלִים עַמּוּד הֶעָנָן
אֶת הַמַּחֲנֶה לְעַמּוּד הָאֵשׁ, לֹא נִסְתַּלֵּק הֶעָנָן כְּמוֹ
שֶׁהָיָה רָגִיל לְהִסְתַּלֵּק עַרְבִית לְגַמְרֵי, אֶלָּא נָסַע
וְהָלַךְ לוֹ מֵאַחֲרֵיהֶם לְהַחֲשִׁיךְ לְמִצְרַיִם: **וַיְהִי הֶעָנָן
וְהַחֹשֶׁךְ.** לְמִצְרַיִם: **וַיָּאֶר.** עַמּוּד הָאֵשׁ "אֶת הַלַּיְלָה"
לְיִשְׂרָאֵל, וְהוֹלֵךְ לִפְנֵיהֶם כְּדַרְכּוֹ לָלֶכֶת כָּל הַלַּיְלָה,
וְהַחֹשֶׁךְ שֶׁל עֲרָפֶל לְצַד מִצְרַיִם: **וְלֹא קָרַב זֶה אֶל זֶה.**
מַחֲנֶה אֶל מַחֲנֶה:

כא) בְּרוּחַ קָדִים עַזָּה. בְּרוּחַ קָדִים שֶׁהִיא עַזָּה
שֶׁבָּרוּחוֹת, הִיא הָרוּחַ שֶׁהַקָּדוֹשׁ בָּרוּךְ הוּא נִפְרָע
בָּהּ מִן הָרְשָׁעִים, שֶׁנֶּאֱמַר: "כְּרוּחַ קָדִים אֲפִיצֵם"
(ירמיה יח, יז), "יָבוֹא קָדִים רוּחַ ה'" (הושע יג, טו), "רוּחַ
הַקָּדִים שְׁבָרֵךְ בְּלֵב יַמִּים" (יחזקאל כז, כו), "הָגָה בְּרוּחוֹ
הַקָּשָׁה בְּיוֹם קָדִים" (ישעיה כז, ח): **וַיִּבָּקְעוּ הַמָּיִם.** כָּל
מַיִם שֶׁבָּעוֹלָם:

בְּתוֹךְ הַיָּם בַּיַּבָּשָׁה וְהַמַּיִם לָהֶם חוֹמָה מִימִינָם וּמִשְּׂמֹאלָם:
כג וַיִּרְדְּפוּ מִצְרַיִם וַיָּבֹאוּ אַחֲרֵיהֶם כֹּל סוּס פַּרְעֹה רִכְבּוֹ וּפָרָשָׁיו אֶל־תּוֹךְ הַיָּם: כד וַיְהִי בְּאַשְׁמֹרֶת הַבֹּקֶר וַיַּשְׁקֵף יְהֹוָה אֶל־מַחֲנֵה מִצְרַיִם בְּעַמּוּד אֵשׁ וְעָנָן וַיָּהָם אֵת מַחֲנֵה מִצְרָיִם: כה וַיָּסַר אֵת אֹפַן מַרְכְּבֹתָיו וַיְנַהֲגֵהוּ בִּכְבֵדֻת וַיֹּאמֶר מִצְרַיִם אָנוּסָה מִפְּנֵי יִשְׂרָאֵל כִּי יְהֹוָה נִלְחָם לָהֶם בְּמִצְרָיִם:

רביעי כו וַיֹּאמֶר יְהֹוָה אֶל־מֹשֶׁה נְטֵה אֶת־יָדְךָ עַל־הַיָּם וְיָשֻׁבוּ הַמַּיִם עַל־מִצְרַיִם עַל־רִכְבּוֹ וְעַל־פָּרָשָׁיו: כז וַיֵּט מֹשֶׁה אֶת־יָדוֹ עַל־הַיָּם וַיָּשָׁב הַיָּם לִפְנוֹת בֹּקֶר לְאֵיתָנוֹ וּמִצְרַיִם נָסִים לִקְרָאתוֹ וַיְנַעֵר יְהֹוָה אֶת־מִצְרַיִם בְּתוֹךְ הַיָּם: כח וַיָּשֻׁבוּ הַמַּיִם וַיְכַסּוּ אֶת־הָרֶכֶב וְאֶת־הַפָּרָשִׁים לְכֹל חֵיל פַּרְעֹה הַבָּאִים אַחֲרֵיהֶם בַּיָּם לֹא־נִשְׁאַר

כג **כֹּל סוּס פַּרְעֹה.** וְכִי סוּס אֶחָד הָיָה?! מַגִּיד שֶׁאֵין כֻּלָּם חֲשׁוּבִין לִפְנֵי הַמָּקוֹם אֶלָּא כְּסוּס אֶחָד:

כד **בְּאַשְׁמֹרֶת הַבֹּקֶר.** שְׁלֹשֶׁת חֶלְקֵי הַלַּיְלָה קְרוּיִין אַשְׁמֹרֶת, וְאוֹתָהּ שֶׁלִּפְנֵי הַיּוֹם קוֹרֵא "אַשְׁמֹרֶת הַבֹּקֶר". וְאוֹמֵר אֲנִי, שֶׁהִוא חֲלוּק לְמִשְׁמְרוֹת שִׁיר מַלְאֲכֵי הַשָּׁרֵת כַּת אַחַר כַּת לִשְׁלֹשָׁה חֲלָקִים, לְכָךְ קָרוּי אַשְׁמֹרֶת, וְזֶהוּ שֶׁתִּרְגֵּם אֻנְקְלוֹס: "מַטְּרַת": **וַיַּשְׁקֵף.** וַיַּבֵּט, כְּלוֹמַר פָּנָה אֲלֵיהֶם לְהַשְׁחִיתָם. וְתַרְגּוּמוֹ: "וְאִסְתְּכִי" אַף הוּא לְשׁוֹן הַבָּטָה, כְּמוֹ "שְׂדֵה צֹפִים" (במדבר כג, יד), "חֲקַל סָכוּתָא": **בְּעַמּוּד אֵשׁ וְעָנָן.** עַמּוּד עָנָן יוֹרֵד וְעוֹשֶׂה אוֹתוֹ פָטִיט, וְעַמּוּד אֵשׁ מַרְתִּיחוֹ, וְטַלְפֵי סוּסֵיהֶם מִשְׁתַּמְּטוֹת: **וַיָּהָם.** לְשׁוֹן מְהוּמָה, אשטורדי"שון בְּלַעַז. עִרְבְּבָם, נָטַל סִגְנִיּוֹת שֶׁלָּהֶם. וְשָׁנִינוּ בְּפִרְקֵי רַבִּי אֱלִיעֶזֶר בְּנוֹ שֶׁל רַבִּי יוֹסֵי הַגְּלִילִי, כָּל מָקוֹם שֶׁנֶּאֱמַר 'מְהוּמָה' הַרְעָשַׁת קוֹל הוּא, וְזֶה אָב לְכֻלָּן: "וַיַּרְעֵם ה' בְּקוֹל גָּדוֹל... עַל פְּלִשְׁתִּים וַיְהֻמֵּם" (שמואל א' ז, י):

כה **וַיָּסַר אֵת אֹפַן מַרְכְּבֹתָיו.** מִכֹּחַ הָאֵשׁ נִשְׂרְפוּ הַגַּלְגַּלִּים, וְהַמֶּרְכָּבוֹת נִגְרָרוֹת, וְהַיּוֹשְׁבִים בָּהֶם נָעִים

וְאֵיבְרֵיהֶן מִתְפָּרְקִים: **וַיְנַהֲגֵהוּ בִּכְבֵדֻת.** בְּהַנְהָגָה כְּבֵדָה וְקָשָׁה לָהֶם, בְּמִדָּה שֶׁמָּדְדוּ, "וַיִּכְבַּד לִבּוֹ הוּא וַעֲבָדָיו" (לעיל ט, לד), אַף כָּאן, "וַיְנַהֲגֵהוּ בִּכְבֵדֻת": **נִלְחָם לָהֶם בְּמִצְרָיִם.** בְּמִצְרַיִם. דָּבָר אַחֵר "בְּמִצְרַיִם", בְּאֶרֶץ מִצְרַיִם, שֶׁכְּשֵׁם שֶׁאֵלּוּ לוֹקִים עַל הַיָּם כָּךְ לוֹקִים אוֹתָם שֶׁנִּשְׁאֲרוּ בְּמִצְרַיִם:

כו **וְיָשֻׁבוּ הַמָּיִם.** שֶׁזְּקוּפִים וְעוֹמְדִים כְּחוֹמָה, יָשׁוּבוּ לִמְקוֹמָם וִיכַסּוּ "עַל מִצְרָיִם":

כז **לִפְנוֹת בֹּקֶר.** לְעֵת שֶׁהַבֹּקֶר פּוֹנֶה לָבֹא: **לְאֵיתָנוֹ.** לְתָקְפּוֹ הָרִאשׁוֹן: **נָסִים לִקְרָאתוֹ.** שֶׁהָיוּ מְהֻמָּמִים וּמְטֹרָפִים וְרָצִין לִקְרַאת הַמַּיִם: **וַיְנַעֵר ה'.** כְּאָדָם שֶׁמְּנַעֵר אֶת הַקְּדֵרָה וְהוֹפֵךְ הָעֶלְיוֹן לְמַטָּה וְהַתַּחְתּוֹן לְמַעְלָה, כָּךְ הָיוּ עוֹלִין וְיוֹרְדִין וּמִשְׁתַּבְּרִין בַּיָּם. וְנָתַן הַקָּדוֹשׁ בָּרוּךְ הוּא בָּהֶם חַיּוּת לְקַבֵּל הַיִּסּוּרִין: "וַיְנַעֵר", הוּא לְשׁוֹן טֵרוּף בְּלָשׁוֹן אֲרַמִּי, וְהַרְבֵּה יֵשׁ בְּמִדְרְשֵׁי אַגָּדָה:

כח **וַיְכַסּוּ אֶת הָרֶכֶב... לְכֹל חֵיל פַּרְעֹה.** כֵּן דֶּרֶךְ הַמִּקְרָאוֹת לִכְתֹּב לָמֶ"ד יְתֵרָה, כְּמוֹ: "לְכָל כֵּלָיו

שמות | פרק יד

כט בָּהֶ֖ם עַד־אֶחָֽד׃ וּבְנֵ֧י יִשְׂרָאֵ֛ל הָלְכ֥וּ בַיַּבָּשָׁ֖ה בְּת֣וֹךְ הַיָּ֑ם וְהַמַּ֤יִם
ל לָהֶם֙ חֹמָ֔ה מִֽימִינָ֖ם וּמִשְּׂמֹאלָֽם׃ וַיּ֨וֹשַׁע יְהֹוָ֜ה בַּיּ֥וֹם הַה֛וּא אֶת־
יִשְׂרָאֵ֖ל מִיַּ֣ד מִצְרָ֑יִם וַיַּ֤רְא יִשְׂרָאֵל֙ אֶת־מִצְרַ֔יִם מֵ֖ת עַל־שְׂפַ֥ת
לא הַיָּֽם׃ וַיַּ֨רְא יִשְׂרָאֵ֜ל אֶת־הַיָּ֣ד הַגְּדֹלָ֗ה אֲשֶׁ֨ר עָשָׂ֤ה יְהֹוָה֙ בְּמִצְרַ֔יִם
וַיִּֽירְא֥וּ הָעָ֖ם אֶת־יְהֹוָ֑ה וַיַּֽאֲמִ֨ינוּ֙ בַּֽיהֹוָ֔ה וּבְמֹשֶׁ֖ה עַבְדּֽוֹ׃

טו א אָ֣ז יָשִֽׁיר־מֹשֶׁה֩ וּבְנֵ֨י יִשְׂרָאֵ֜ל אֶת־הַשִּׁירָ֤ה הַזֹּאת֙ לַֽיהֹוָ֔ה וַיֹּאמְר֖וּ
לֵאמֹ֑ר   אָשִׁ֤ירָה לַֽיהֹוָה֙ כִּֽי־גָאֹ֣ה גָּאָ֔ה   ס֥וּס
ב וְרֹכְב֖וֹ רָמָ֥ה בַיָּֽם׃   עָזִּ֤י וְזִמְרָת֙ יָ֔הּ וַֽיְהִי־לִ֖י

תַּעֲשֶׂה נָחֹשֶׁת" (להלן כז, ג), וְכֵן: "לְכָל כְּלֵי הַמִּשְׁכָּן בְּכֹל עֲבֹדָתוֹ" (שם פסוק יט), "וִיתֵדֹתָם וּמֵיתְרֵיהֶם לְכָל כְּלֵיהֶם" (במדבר ד, לב), וַחֲנִינָה חַלָּף תִּקּוּן לָשׁוֹן:

וַיַּרְא יִשְׂרָאֵל אֶת מִצְרַיִם מֵת. שֶׁפְּלָטָן הַיָּם עַל שְׂפָתוֹ, כְּדֵי שֶׁלֹּא יֹאמְרוּ יִשְׂרָאֵל: כְּשֵׁם שֶׁאָנוּ עוֹלִים מֵעַד זֶה כָּךְ הֵם עוֹלִין מֵעַד אַחֵר רָחוֹק מִמֶּנּוּ וְיִרְדְּפוּ אַחֲרֵינוּ:

לא **אֶת הַיָּד הַגְּדֹלָה.** אֶת הַגְּבוּרָה הַגְּדוֹלָה שֶׁעָשְׂתָה יָדוֹ שֶׁל הַקָּדוֹשׁ בָּרוּךְ הוּא. וְהַרְבֵּה לְשׁוֹנוֹת נוֹפְלִין עַל לְשׁוֹן "יָד", וְכֻלָּן לְשׁוֹן יָד מַמָּשׁ הֵן, וְהַמְפָרֵשׁ יְתַקֵּן הַלָּשׁוֹן אַחַר עִנְיַן הַדִּבּוּר:

פרק טו

א **אָז יָשִׁיר מֹשֶׁה.** אָז כְּשֶׁרָאָה הַנֵּס עָלָה בְלִבּוֹ שֶׁיָּשִׁיר שִׁירָה. וְכֵן: "אָז יְדַבֵּר יְהוֹשֻׁעַ" (יהושע י, יב), וְכֵן: "וּבַיִת יַעֲשֶׂה לְבַת פַּרְעֹה" (מלכים א׳ ז, ח), חָשַׁב בְּלִבּוֹ שֶׁיַּעֲשֶׂה לָהּ. אַף כָּאן, "יָשִׁיר", אָמַר לוֹ לִבּוֹ שֶׁיָּשִׁיר, וְכֵן עָשָׂה: "וַיֹּאמְרוּ לֵאמֹר אָשִׁירָה לַה'". וְכֵן בִּיהוֹשֻׁעַ, כְּשֶׁרָאָה הַנֵּס אָמַר לוֹ לִבּוֹ שֶׁיְּדַבֵּר, וְכֵן עָשָׂה: "וַיֹּאמֶר לְעֵינֵי יִשְׂרָאֵל" (יהושע שם). וְכֵן שִׁירַת הַבְּאֵר שֶׁפָּתַח בָּהּ: "אָז יָשִׁיר יִשְׂרָאֵל" (במדבר כא, יז), פֵּרַשׁ אַחֲרָיו: "עֲלִי בְאֵר עֱנוּ לָהּ". "אָז יִבְנֶה שְׁלֹמֹה בָּמָה" (מלכים א׳ יא, ז), פֵּרְשׁוּ בוֹ חַכְמֵי יִשְׂרָאֵל שֶׁבִּקֵּשׁ לִבְנוֹת וְלֹא בָנָה. לָמַדְנוּ שֶׁהַיּוּ"ד עַל שֵׁם הַמַּחֲשָׁבָה נֶאֶמְרָה. זֶהוּ לְיַשֵּׁב

פְּשׁוּטוֹ. אֲבָל מִדְרָשׁוֹ אָמְרוּ רַבּוֹתֵינוּ זִכְרוֹנָם לִבְרָכָה, מִכָּאן רֶמֶז לִתְחִיַּת הַמֵּתִים מִן הַתּוֹרָה, וְכֵן בְּכֻלָּן, חוּץ מִשֶּׁל שְׁלֹמֹה שֶׁפֵּרְשׁוּהוּ בִּקֵּשׁ לִבְנוֹת וְלֹא בָנָה. וְאֵין לוֹמַר וּלְיַשֵּׁב לָשׁוֹן הַזֶּה כִּשְׁאָר דְּבָרִים הַנִּכְתָּבִים בִּלְשׁוֹן עָתִיד וְהֵן מִיָּד, כְּגוֹן: "כָּכָה יַעֲשֶׂה אִיּוֹב" (איוב א, ה), "עַל פִּי ה' יַחֲנוּ" (במדבר ט, כ), "וְיֵשׁ אֲשֶׁר יִהְיֶה הֶעָנָן" (שם), לְפִי שֶׁהֵן דְּבַר הֹוֶה תָּמִיד וְנוֹפֵל בּוֹ בֵּין לְשׁוֹן עָתִיד בֵּין לְשׁוֹן עָבָר, אֲבָל זֶה שֶׁלֹּא הָיָה אֶלָּא לְשָׁעָה אֵינִי יָכוֹל לְיַשְּׁבוֹ בַּלָּשׁוֹן הַזֶּה. **כִּי גָאֹה גָּאָה.** כְּתַרְגּוּמוֹ. דָּבָר אַחֵר, "כִּי גָאֹה גָּאָה", עַל כָּל הַשִּׁירוֹת. וְכָל מַה שֶּׁאֲקַלֵּס בּוֹ עוֹד יֵשׁ תּוֹסֶפֶת, וְלֹא כְמִדַּת מֶלֶךְ בָּשָׂר וָדָם שֶׁמְּקַלְּסִין אוֹתוֹ וְאֵין בּוֹ: **סוּס וְרֹכְבוֹ.** שְׁנֵיהֶם קְשׁוּרִים זֶה בָזֶה, וְהַמַּיִם מַעֲלִין אוֹתָן לָרוּם וּמוֹרִידִין לָעֹמֶק וַעֲדַיִן נִפְרָדִין. **רָמָה.** הִשְׁלִיךְ, וְכֵן: "וְרָמוּ לְגוֹא אַתּוּן נוּרָא" (דניאל ג, כא). וּמִדְרַשׁ אַגָּדָה, כָּתוּב אֶחָד אוֹמֵר "רָמָה" וְכָתוּב אֶחָד אוֹמֵר "יָרָה", מְלַמֵּד שֶׁהָיוּ עוֹלִין לָרוּם וְיוֹרְדִין לַתְּהוֹם, כְּמוֹ: "מִי יָרָה אֶבֶן פִּנָּתָהּ" (איוב לח, ו) מִלְמַעְלָה לְמַטָּה:

ב **עָזִּי וְזִמְרָת יָהּ.** אוּנְקְלוֹס תִּרְגֵּם "עָזִּי" כְּמוֹ 'עֻזִּי', "וְזִמְרָת" כְּמוֹ 'וְזִמְרָתִי'. וַאֲנִי תָּמֵהַּ עַל הַמִּקְרָא, שֶׁאֵין לְךָ כָּמוֹהוּ בְנִקּוּדָתוֹ בַּמִּקְרָא חַלָּף בִּשְׁלֹשָׁה מְקוֹמוֹת שֶׁהוּא סָמוּךְ אֵצֶל "וְזִמְרָת", וְכָל שְׁאָר מְקוֹמוֹת נָקוּד שׁוּרֵק, "ה' עָזִּי וּמָעֻזִּי" (ירמיה טז, יט), "עָזְךָ אֵלֶךָ אֶשְׁמֹרָה" (תהלים נט, י). וְכֵן כָּל תֵּבָה בַּת

פרק טו | שמות | בשלח | 402

לִישׁוּעָ֑ה זֶ֤ה אֵלִי֙ וְאַנְוֵ֔הוּ אֱלֹהֵ֥י
אָבִ֖י וַאֲרֹמְמֶֽנְהוּ: יְהוָ֖ה אִ֣ישׁ מִלְחָמָ֑ה יְהוָ֖ה ג
שְׁמֽוֹ: מַרְכְּבֹ֥ת פַּרְעֹ֛ה וְחֵיל֖וֹ יָרָ֣ה בַיָּ֑ם וּמִבְחַ֥ר ד
שָׁלִשָׁ֖יו טֻבְּע֥וּ בְיַם־סֽוּף: תְּהֹמֹ֖ת יְכַסְיֻ֑מוּ יָרְד֥וּ בִמְצוֹלֹ֖ת ה

שְׁתֵּי אוֹתִיּוֹת הַנְּקוּדָה מִלְּחַפּוֹס, כְּשֶׁהִיא מְחֻלֶּקֶת בְּחָלוּק שְׁלִישִׁית וְחֵין הַשְּׁנִית בְּשָׁבָח חֲטוּף, הָרִאשׁוֹנָה נְקוּדָה בְּשׁוּרֻק, כְּגוֹן: עַז עָזִי, לֹק רְקִי, חֹק חִקְקִי, עַל עֹלוּ, "יְסוֹד... עֹלוּ" (ישעיה יד, כה), כֹּל כֻּלוֹ, "וְשִׁלֵּשׁ עַל כֻּלוֹ" (לעיל יד, ז). וְאֵלּוּ שְׁלֹשָׁה "עָזִּי וְזִמְרָת" שֶׁל כָּאן וְשֶׁל יְשַׁעְיָה (יב, ב) וְשֶׁל תְּהִלִּים (קיח, יד) נְקוּדִים בַּחֲטוּף קָמַץ, וְעוֹד, אֵין בְּאֶחָד מֵהֶם כָּתוּב "וְזִמְרָתִי" אֶלָּא "וְזִמְרָת", וְכֻלָּם סְמוּכִים לָהֶם: "וַיְהִי לִי לִישׁוּעָה". לְכָךְ אֲנִי אוֹמֵר לְיַשֵּׁב לְשׁוֹן הַמִּקְרָא, שֶׁאֵין "עָזִּי" כְּמוֹ "עָזִּי", וְלֹא "וְזִמְרָת" כְּמוֹ "וְזִמְרָתִי", אֶלָּא "עָזִּי" שֵׁם דָּבָר הוּא, כְּמוֹ: "הַיֹּשְׁבִי בַּשָּׁמַיִם" (שם קכג, א), "שֹׁכְנִי בְּחַגְוֵי סֶלַע" (עובדיה א, ג), "שֹׁכְנִי סְנֶה" (דברים לג, טז). וְזֶהוּ הַשֶּׁבַח: עָזִּי וְזִמְרָת יָהּ הוּא הָיָה לִי לִישׁוּעָה. וְ"זִמְרָת" דָּבוּק הוּא לְתֵבַת ה', כְּמוֹ "לְעֶזְרַת ה'" (שופטים ה, כג), "בְּעֶבְרַת ה'" (ישעיה ט, יח), "עַל דִּבְרַת בְּנֵי הָאָדָם" (קהלת ג, יח). וּלְשׁוֹן "וְזִמְרָת" לְשׁוֹן "לֹא תִזְמֹר" (ויקרא כה, ד), "זְמִיר עָרִיצִים" (ישעיה כה, ה), כְּסוּחִים וּכְרִיתָה, עֻזּוֹ וְנִקְמָתוֹ שֶׁל אֱלֹהֵינוּ הָיָה לָנוּ לִישׁוּעָה. וְאַל תִּתְמַהּ עַל לְשׁוֹן "וַיְהִי" שֶׁלֹּא נֶאֱמַר "הָיָה", שֶׁיֵּשׁ לָנוּ מִקְרָאוֹת מְדַבְּרִים בַּלָּשׁוֹן זֶה, וְזֶה דֻגְמָתוֹ: "אֶת קִירוֹת הַבַּיִת סָבִיב לַהֵיכָל וְלַדְּבִיר וַיַּעַשׂ צְלָעוֹת סָבִיב" (מלכים א ו, ה), הָיָה לוֹ לוֹמַר: עָשָׂה צְלָעוֹת סָבִיב; וְכֵן בְּדִבְרֵי הַיָּמִים (ב י, יח): "וּבְנֵי יִשְׂרָאֵל הַיֹּשְׁבִים בְּעָרֵי יְהוּדָה וַיִּמְלֹךְ עֲלֵיהֶם רְחַבְעָם", הָיָה לוֹ לוֹמַר: מָלַךְ עֲלֵיהֶם רְחַבְעָם; "מִבַּלְתִּי יְכֹלֶת ה' וְגוֹ' וַיִּשְׁחָטֵם" (במדבר יד, טז), הָיָה לוֹ לוֹמַר: שְׁחָטָם; "וְהָאֲנָשִׁים אֲשֶׁר שָׁלַח מֹשֶׁה... וַיָּמֻתוּ" (שם פסוקים לו-לז), "מֵתוּ" הָיָה לוֹ לוֹמַר; "וַאֲשֶׁר לֹא שָׂם לִבּוֹ אֶל דְּבַר ה' וַיַּעֲזֹב" (לעיל ט, כא), הָיָה לוֹ לוֹמַר: עָזַב. זֶה אֵלִי. בִּכְבוֹדוֹ עָלָה עֲלֵיהֶם וְהָיוּ מַרְאִין אוֹתוֹ בָּאֶצְבַּע, רָאֲתָה שִׁפְחָה עַל הַיָּם מַה שֶּׁלֹּא רָאוּ נְבִיאִים. וְאַנְוֵהוּ. אוּנְקְלוֹס תִּרְגֵּם לְשׁוֹן נָוֶה, "נָוֶה שַׁאֲנָן" (ישעיה לג, כ), "לִנְוֵה צֹאן" (שם

סה, י). דָּבָר אַחֵר, "וְאַנְוֵהוּ", לְשׁוֹן נוֹי, אֲסַפֵּר נוֹיוֹ וְשִׁבְחוֹ לְבָאֵי עוֹלָם, כְּגוֹן: "מַה דּוֹדֵךְ מִדּוֹד" (שיר השירים ה, ט), "דּוֹדִי צַח וְאָדוֹם" (שם פסוק י) וְכָל הָעִנְיָן: אֱלֹהֵי אָבִי. הוּא זֶה, וַאֲרוֹמְמֶנְהוּ: אֱלֹהֵי אָבִי. לֹא אֲנִי תְּחִלַּת הַקְּדֻשָּׁה, מֻחְזֶקֶת וְעוֹמֶדֶת לִי הַקְּדֻשָּׁה וֶאֱלֹהוּתוֹ עָלַי מִימֵי אֲבוֹתַי:

ג. ה' אִישׁ מִלְחָמָה. בַּעַל מִלְחָמוֹת, כְּמוֹ: "אִישׁ נָעֳמִי" (רות א, ג), וְכָל "אִישׁ" וְ"חֹשֶׁךְ" מִתַּרְגְּמִין בַּעַל. וְכֵן: "וְחָזַקְתָּ וְהָיִיתָ לְאִישׁ" (מלכים א ב, ב), לְגִבּוֹר: ה' שְׁמוֹ. מִלְחֲמוֹתָיו לֹא בִּכְלֵי זַיִן אֶלָּא בִּשְׁמוֹ הוּא נִלְחָם, "וַאֲנֹכִי בָא אֵלֶיךָ בְּשֵׁם ה' צְבָאוֹת" (שמואל א יז, מה). דָּבָר אַחֵר, "ה' שְׁמוֹ", אַף בְּשָׁעָה שֶׁהוּא נִלְחָם וְנוֹקֵם מֵאוֹיְבָיו, אוֹחֵז הוּא בְּמִדָּתוֹ לָרַחֵם עַל קְלָחָיו וְלָזוּן אֶת כָּל בָּאֵי עוֹלָם, וְלֹא כְּמִדַּת מַלְכֵי אֲדָמָה כְּשֶׁהוּא עוֹסֵק בְּמִלְחָמָה פּוֹנֶה עַצְמוֹ מִכָּל עֲסָקִים וְאֵין בּוֹ כֹּחַ לַעֲשׂוֹת זוֹ וָזוֹ:

ד. יָרָה בַיָּם. "שָׁדֵי בְיַמָּא", "שָׁדֵי" לְשׁוֹן יְרִיָּה, וְכֵן הוּא אוֹמֵר: "אוֹ יָרֹה יִיָּרֶה" (להלן יט, יג), "אוֹ חֲשָׁתְדָּאָה אִשְׁתְּדִי", וְהִתְפַּעֵל מְשַׁמֵּשׁ בְּחָלוּק בִּמְקוֹם יִתְפָּעֵל. וּמִבְחַר. שֵׁם דָּבָר, כְּמוֹ: "מִרְכָּב" (ויקרא טו, ט), "מִשְׁכָּב" (שם פסוק ד), "מִקְרָא קֹדֶשׁ" (לעיל יב, טז): טֻבְּעוּ. אֵין טְבִיעָה אֶלָּא בִּמְקוֹם טִיט, כְּמוֹ: "טָבַעְתִּי בִּיוֵן מְצוּלָה" (תהלים סט, ג), "וַיִּטְבַּע יִרְמְיָהוּ בַּטִּיט" (ירמיה לח, ו), מְלַמֵּד שֶׁנַּעֲשָׂה הַיָּם טִיט, לִגְמֹל לָהֶם כְּמִדָּתָם שֶׁשִּׁעְבְּדוּ אֶת יִשְׂרָאֵל בְּחֹמֶר וּבִלְבֵנִים:

ה. יְכַסְיֻמוּ. כְּמוֹ "יְכַסּוּם". הַיּוּ"ד הָאֶמְצָעִית יְתֵרָה בּוֹ וְדֶרֶךְ מִקְרָאוֹת בְּכָךְ, כְּמוֹ: "וּבְקִרְךָ וְצֹאנְךָ יִרְבְּיֻן" (דברים ח, יג), "יִרְוְיֻן מִדֶּשֶׁן בֵּיתֶךָ" (תהלים לו, ט), וְהַיּוּ"ד הָרִאשׁוֹנָה שֶׁמַּשְׁמָעָהּ לְשׁוֹן עָתִיד, כָּךְ פֵּרוּשָׁהּ: טֻבְּעוּ בְּיַם סוּף כְּדֵי שֶׁיַּחְזְרוּ הַמַּיִם וִיכַסּוּ אוֹתָן. "יְכַסְיֻמוּ" אֵין דּוֹמֶה לוֹ בַּמִּקְרָא בִּנְקֻדָּתוֹ, וְדַרְכּוֹ לִהְיוֹת נָקוּד

שמות | פרק טו   בשלח | 403

ו   יְמִינְךָ֣ יְהוָ֔ה נֶאְדָּרִ֖י בַּכֹּ֑חַ   יְמִֽינְךָ֥   כְּמוֹ־אָֽבֶן:
ז   יְהוָ֖ה תִּרְעַ֥ץ אוֹיֵֽב: וּבְרֹ֥ב גְּאוֹנְךָ֖ תַּהֲרֹ֣ס
ח   קָמֶ֑יךָ   תְּשַׁלַּח֙ חֲרֹ֣נְךָ֔ יֹאכְלֵ֖מוֹ כַּקַּֽשׁ:   וּבְר֤וּחַ
    אַפֶּ֙יךָ֙ נֶ֣עֶרְמוּ מַ֔יִם   נִצְּב֥וּ
ט   כְמוֹ־נֵ֖ד נֹזְלִ֑ים   קָֽפְא֥וּ תְהֹמֹ֖ת בְּלֶב־יָֽם: אָמַ֥ר
    אוֹיֵ֛ב אֶרְדֹּ֥ף אַשִּׂ֖יג   אֲחַלֵּ֣ק שָׁלָ֑ל תִּמְלָאֵ֣מוֹ

"יְכַסְיֻ֖מוֹ" מִלְחַפּוּשׂ. וּבְמָקוֹם אַחֵר "צָלֲלוּ כַּעוֹפֶרֶת" (להלן פסוק י), וּבְמָקוֹם אַחֵר "יֹאכְלֵמוֹ כַּקַּשׁ" (להלן פסוק ז). הָרְשָׁעִים כַּקַּשׁ הַהוֹלְכִים וּמְטוֹרָפִין עוֹלִין וְיוֹרְדִין, בֵּינוֹנִים כָּאֶבֶן, וְהַכְּשֵׁרִים כַּעוֹפֶרֶת שֶׁנָּחוּ מִיָּד:

ו יְמִינְךָ יְמִינְךָ. שְׁתֵּי פְעָמִים. כְּשֶׁיִּשְׂרָאֵל עוֹשִׂין רְצוֹנוֹ שֶׁל מָקוֹם הַשְּׂמֹאל נַעֲשֵׂית יָמִין: יְמִינְךָ ה' נֶאְדָּרִי בַּכֹּחַ. לְהַצִּיל אֶת יִשְׂרָאֵל, וִימִינְךָ הַשֵּׁנִית "תִּרְעַץ אוֹיֵב". נֶאְדָּרִי. כְּמוֹ: "רַבָּתִי עָם" (איכה א, א), "שָׂרָתִי בַּמְּדִינוֹת" (שם), "גְּנֻבְתִי יוֹם" (בראשית לא, לט): תִּרְעַץ אוֹיֵב. תָּמִיד הִיא רוֹעֶצֶת וּמְשַׁבֶּרֶת הָאוֹיֵב, וְדוֹמֶה לוֹ: "וַיִּרְעֲצוּ וַיְרֹצְצוּ אֶת בְּנֵי יִשְׂרָאֵל" בְּשׁוֹפְטִים (י, ח):

ז תַּהֲרֹס קָמֶיךָ. תָּמִיד אַתָּה הוֹרֵס קָמֶיךָ הַקָּמִים נֶגְדֶּךָ. וּמִי הֵם הַקָּמִים כְּנֶגְדּוֹ? אֵלּוּ הַקָּמִים עַל יִשְׂרָאֵל. וְכֵן הוּא אוֹמֵר: "כִּי הִנֵּה אוֹיְבֶיךָ יֶהֱמָיוּן" (תהלים פג, ג). וּמָה הִיא הַהֲמָיָה? "עַל עַמְּךָ יַעֲרִימוּ סוֹד" (שם פסוק ד), וְעַל זֶה קוֹרֵא אוֹתָם אוֹיְבָיו:

ח וּבְרוּחַ אַפֶּיךָ. הַיּוֹצֵא מִשְּׁנֵי נְחִירִים שֶׁל אַף. דִּבֶּר הַכָּתוּב כִּבְיָכוֹל בַּשְּׁכִינָה דֻּגְמַת מֶלֶךְ בָּשָׂר וָדָם, כְּדֵי לְהַשְׁמִיעַ אֹזֶן הַבְּרִיּוֹת כְּפִי הַהֹוֶה שֶׁיּוּכְלוּ לְהָבִין דָּבָר. כְּשֶׁאָדָם כּוֹעֵס יוֹצֵא רוּחַ מִנְּחִירָיו, וְכֵן: "עָלָה עָשָׁן בְּאַפּוֹ" (שם יח, ט), וְכֵן: "וּמֵרוּחַ אַפּוֹ יִכְלוּ" (איוב ד, ט). וְזֶהוּ שֶׁנֶּאֱמַר: "לְמַעַן שְׁמִי אַאֲרִיךְ אַפִּי" (ישעיה מח, ט). כְּשֶׁזַּעְפּוֹ נָח נְשִׁימָתוֹ אֲרֻכָּה וּכְשֶׁהוּא כּוֹעֵס נְשִׁימָתוֹ קְצָרָה, "וּתְהִלָּתִי אֶחֱטָם לָךְ" (שם), וּלְמַעַן תְּהִלָּתִי חָשַׂם חוֹטֶם שֶׁלִּי בְּאַפִּי לִסְתֹּם נְחִירַי בִּפְנֵי הָאַף וְהָרוּחַ שֶׁלֹּא יֵצְאוּ "לָךְ", בִּשְׁבִילְךָ. "אֶחֱטָם" כְּמוֹ 'נָאקָה בַּחֲטָם' בְּמַסֶּכֶת שַׁבָּת (דף נד עב), כָּךְ נִרְאָה בְעֵינַי. וְכָל לְשׁוֹן חָרוֹן שֶׁבַּמִּקְרָא אֲנִי אוֹמֵר כֵּן: "חָרָה

אַף" (ישעיה ה, כה) כְּמוֹ: "וְעַצְמִי חָרָה מִנִּי חֹרֶב" (איוב ל, ל) לְשׁוֹן שְׂרֵפָה וּמוֹקֵד, שֶׁהַנְּחִירַיִם מִתְחַמְּמִים וְנֶחֱרִים בְּעֵת הַקֶּצֶף, וְחָרוֹן מִגִּזְרַת חָרָה כְּמוֹ מִגִּזְרַת דָּעָה, וְכֵן חֵמָה לְשׁוֹן חֲמִימוּת, עַל כֵּן הוּא אוֹמֵר: "וַחֲמָתוֹ בָּעֲרָה בוֹ" (אסתר א, יב), וּבְנוּחַ הַחֵמָה אוֹמֵר: "נִתְקָרְרָה דַעְתּוֹ" (יבמות סג עא): נֶעֶרְמוּ מַיִם. אֻנְקְלוֹס תִּרְגֵּם לְשׁוֹן עַרְמִימוּת, וּלְשׁוֹן צַחוּת הַמִּקְרָא כְּמוֹ: "עֲרֵמַת חִטִּים" (שיר השירים ז, ג), "וְנִצְּבוּ כְמוֹ נֵד" יוֹכִיחַ: נֶעֶרְמוּ. מִמֹּקֶד רוּחַ שֶׁיָּצָא מֵאַפְּךָ יָבְשׁוּ הַמַּיִם וְהֵם נַעֲשׂוּ כְמִינֵי גַּלִּים וּכְרִיּוֹת שֶׁל עֲרֵמָה שֶׁהֵם גְּבוֹהִים: כְּמוֹ נֵד. כְּתַרְגּוּמוֹ "כְּשׁוּר", כַּחוֹמָה. לְשׁוֹן עִבּוּר וְכִנּוּס, כְּמוֹ: "נֵד קָצִיר בְּיוֹם נַחֲלָה" (ישעיה יז, יא), לֹא כָּתַב 'כִּנּוּס קָצִיר' אֶלָּא "נֵד קָצִיר". "כֹּנֵס כַּנֵּד" (תהלים לג, ז), אִלּוּ הָיָה "כְּנֵד" כְּמוֹ 'כַּנֹּאד' לְשׁוֹן הַכְנָסָה, הָיָה לוֹ לִכְתֹּב 'מַכְנִיס כַּנֹּאד מֵי הַיָּם'. אֶלָּא 'כֹּנֵס' לְשׁוֹן אוֹסֵף וְעוֹדֵר הוּא, וְכֵן: "קָמוּ נֵד אֶחָד" (יהושע ג, טז), "וַיַּעַמְדוּ נֵד אֶחָד" (שם פסוק יג), וְאֵין לְשׁוֹן קִימָה וַעֲמִידָה בִּגְדוּדֵי חֵלֶף בְּחוֹמוֹת וְעִבּוּרִים, וְלֹא מָצִינוּ 'נֹאד' נָקוּד חֵלֶף בְּמִלְחַפּוּשׂ, כְּמוֹ: "שִׂימָה דִמְעָתִי בְנֹאדֶךָ" (תהלים נו, ט), "אֶת נֹאוד הֶחָלָב" (שופטים ד, יט): קָפְאוּ. כְּמוֹ: "וְכַגְּבִינָה תַּקְפִּיאֵנִי" (איוב י, י), שֶׁהֻקְשׁוּ וְנַעֲשׂוּ כַּאֲבָנִים, וְהַמַּיִם זוֹרְקִים אֶת הַמִּצְרִים עַל הָאֶבֶן בְּכֹחַ וְנִלְחָמִים בָּם בְּכָל מִינֵי קֹשִׁי: בְּלֶב יָם. בְּחֹזֶק הַיָּם. וְדֶרֶךְ הַמִּקְרָאוֹת לְדַבֵּר כֵּן: "עַד לֵב הַשָּׁמַיִם" (דברים ד, יא), "בְּלֵב הָאֵלָה" (שמואל ב יח, יד), לְשׁוֹן עִקְּרוֹ וְתָקְפּוֹ שֶׁל דָּבָר:

ט אָמַר אוֹיֵב. לְעַמּוֹ כְּשֶׁפִּתָּם בִּדְבָרִים, אֶרְדֹּף וְאַשִּׂיגֵם וַאֲחַלֵּק שָׁלָל עִם שָׂרַי וַעֲבָדַי: תִּמְלָאֵמוֹ.

נָשַׁפְתָּ	אָרִיק חַרְבִּי תּוֹרִישֵׁמוֹ יָדִי׃	נַפְשִׁי
צָלֲלוּ כַּעוֹפֶרֶת בְּמַיִם	בְּרוּחֲךָ כִּסָּמוֹ יָם	
מִי	מִי־כָמֹכָה בָּאֵלִם יְהוה	אַדִּירִים׃
נוֹרָא תְהִלֹּת עֹשֵׂה	כָּמֹכָה נֶאְדָּר בַּקֹּדֶשׁ	
נָחִיתָ	נָטִיתָ יְמִינְךָ תִּבְלָעֵמוֹ אָרֶץ׃	פֶלֶא׃
נֵהַלְתָּ בְעָזְּךָ אֶל־נְוֵה	בְחַסְדְּךָ עַם־זוּ גָּאָלְתָּ	
חִיל	שָׁמְעוּ עַמִּים יִרְגָּזוּן	קָדְשֶׁךָ׃
אָז נִבְהֲלוּ אַלּוּפֵי	אָחַז יֹשְׁבֵי פְּלָשֶׁת׃	
נָמֹגוּ	אֵילֵי מוֹאָב יֹאחֲזֵמוֹ רָעַד	אֱדוֹם

תִּמָּלֵא מֵהֶם: **נַפְשִׁי.** רוּחִי וְרְצוֹנִי. וְאַל תִּתְמַהּ עַל תֵּבָה הַמְדַבֶּרֶת בִּשְׁתַּיִם, "תִּמְלָאֵמוֹ" תִּמָּלֵא מֵהֶם, יֵשׁ הַרְבֵּה בַּלָּשׁוֹן הַזֶּה: "כִּי אֶרֶץ הַנֶּגֶב נְתַתָּנִי" (שופטים א, טו), כְּמוֹ נָתַתָּ לִי; "וְלֹא יָכְלוּ דַבְּרוֹ לְשָׁלֹם" (בראשית לז, ד), כְּמוֹ דַּבֵּר עִמּוֹ; "בְּנֵי יְצָאֻנִי" (ירמיה י, כ), כְּמוֹ יָצְאוּ מִמֶּנִּי; "מִסְפַּר צְעָדַי אַגִּידֶנּוּ" (איוב לא, לז), כְּמוֹ אַגִּיד לוֹ; אַף כָּאן "תִּמְלָאֵמוֹ" תִּמָּלֵא נַפְשִׁי מֵהֶם: **אָרִיק חַרְבִּי.** אֶשְׁלֹף. וְעַל שֵׁם שֶׁהוּא מֵרִיק אֶת הַתַּעַר בִּשְׁלִיפָתָהּ וְנִשְׁאַר רֵיק, נוֹפֵל בּוֹ לְשׁוֹן הֲרָקָה, כְּמוֹ: "מְרִיקִים שַׂקֵּיהֶם" (בראשית מב, לה), "וְכֵלָיו יָרִיקוּ" (ירמיה מח, יב). וְאַל תֹּאמַר, אֵין לְשׁוֹן רֵיקוּת נוֹפֵל עַל הַיּוֹצֵא אֶלָּא עַל הַתִּיק וְעַל הַשַּׂק וְעַל הַכְּלִי שֶׁיָּצָא מִמֶּנּוּ, אֲבָל לֹא עַל הַחֶרֶב וְעַל הַיַּיִן, וְלִדְחֹק וּלְפָרֵשׁ "אָרִיק חַרְבִּי" כִּלְשׁוֹן "וַיָּרֶק אֶת חֲנִיכָיו" (בראשית יד, יד), חֲזֹן בַּחַרְבִּי - מָעֲנוּ הַלָּשׁוֹן מוּסָב אַף עַל הַיּוֹצֵא, "שֶׁמֶן תּוּרַק" (שיר השירים א, ג), "וְלֹא הוּרַק מִכְּלִי אֶל כֶּלִי" (ירמיה מח, יא), "לֹא הוּרַק הַכְּלִי" אֵין כָּתוּב כָּאן, אֶלָּא "לֹא הוּרַק הַיַּיִן מִכְּלִי אֶל כֶּלִי", מָעֲנוּ הַלָּשׁוֹן מוּסָב עַל הַיַּיִן. וְכֵן: "וְהֵרִיקוּ חַרְבוֹתָם עַל יְפִי חָכְמָתֶךָ" (יחזקאל כח, ז) דְחִירָם: **תּוֹרִישֵׁמוֹ.** לְשׁוֹן רִישׁוּת וְדַלּוּת, כְּמוֹ: "מוֹרִישׁ וּמַעֲשִׁיר" (שמואל א ב, ז):

י) **נָשַׁפְתָּ.** לְשׁוֹן הֲפָחָה, וְכֵן "וְגַם נָשַׁף בָּהֶם" (ישעיה מ,

צָלֲלוּ. שָׁקְעוּ, עָמְקוּ, לְשׁוֹן "מְצוּלָה". **כַּעוֹפֶרֶת.** אֲבָךְ, פלו"ם בְּלַעַ"ז:

יא) **בָּאֵלִם.** בַּחֲזָקִים, כְּמוֹ: "וְאֶת אֵילֵי הָאָרֶץ לָקָח" (יחזקאל יז, יג), "אֵילוּתִי לְעֶזְרָתִי חוּשָׁה" (תהלים כב, כ): **נוֹרָא תְהִלֹּת.** יְרֵאוּי מִלְּהַגִּיד תְּהִלּוֹתֶיךָ פֶּן יִמְעֲטוּ, עַל כֵּן: "לְךָ דֻמִיָּה תְהִלָּה" (תהלים סה, ב):

יב) **נָטִיתָ יְמִינְךָ.** כְּשֶׁהַקָּדוֹשׁ בָּרוּךְ הוּא נוֹטֶה יָדוֹ הָרְשָׁעִים כָּלִים וְנוֹפְלִים, לְפִי שֶׁהַכֹּל נָתוּן בְּיָדוֹ וְנוֹפְלִים בְּהַטָּיָתָהּ, וְכֵן הוּא אוֹמֵר: "זֶה יִטֶּה יָדוֹ וְכָשַׁל עוֹזֵר וְנָפַל עָזֻר" (ישעיה לא, ג). מָשָׁל לִכְלִי זְכוּכִית הַנְּתוּנִין בְּיַד אָדָם, מַטֶּה יָדוֹ מְעַט וְהֵם נוֹפְלִים וּמִשְׁתַּבְּרִים: **תִּבְלָעֵמוֹ אָרֶץ.** מִכָּאן שֶׁזָּכוּ לִקְבוּרָה, בִּשְׂכַר שֶׁאָמְרוּ: "ה' הַצַּדִּיק" (לעיל ט, כז):

יג) **נֵהַלְתָּ.** לְשׁוֹן מְנַהֵל. וְאוּנְקְלוּס תִּרְגֵּם לְשׁוֹן נוֹשֵׂא וְסוֹבֵל, וְלֹא דִקְדֵּק לְפָרֵשׁ אַחַר לְשׁוֹן הָעִבְרִית:

יד) **יִרְגָּזוּן.** מִתְרַגְּזִין: **יֹשְׁבֵי פְּלָשֶׁת.** מִפְּנֵי שֶׁהָרְגוּ אֶת בְּנֵי אֶפְרַיִם שֶׁמִהֲרוּ אֶת הַקֵּץ וְיָצְאוּ בְּחָזְקָה, כַּמְפֹרָשׁ בְּדִבְרֵי הַיָּמִים (א ז, כא), "וַהֲרָגוּם אַנְשֵׁי גַת":

טו) **אַלּוּפֵי אֱדוֹם אֵילֵי מוֹאָב.** וַהֲלֹא לֹא הָיָה לָהֶם לִירֹא כְּלוּם, שֶׁהֲרֵי לֹא עֲלֵיהֶם הוֹלְכִים? אֶלָּא מִפְּנֵי

שמות | פרק טו

טז כֹּל יֹשְׁבֵי כְנָעַן׃ תִּפֹּל עֲלֵיהֶם אֵימָתָה
וָפַחַד בִּגְדֹל זְרוֹעֲךָ יִדְּמוּ כָּאָבֶן עַד־
יַעֲבֹר עַמְּךָ יְהֹוָה עַד־יַעֲבֹר עַם־זוּ
יז קָנִיתָ׃ תְּבִאֵמוֹ וְתִטָּעֵמוֹ בְּהַר נַחֲלָתְךָ מָכוֹן
לְשִׁבְתְּךָ פָּעַלְתָּ יְהֹוָה מִקְּדָשׁ אֲדֹנָי כּוֹנְנוּ
יח יָדֶיךָ׃ יְהֹוָה ׀ יִמְלֹךְ לְעֹלָם וָעֶד׃ כִּי
בָא סוּס פַּרְעֹה בְּרִכְבּוֹ וּבְפָרָשָׁיו בַּיָּם וַיָּשֶׁב יְהֹוָה עֲלֵהֶם אֶת־מֵי
הַיָּם וּבְנֵי יִשְׂרָאֵל הָלְכוּ בַיַּבָּשָׁה בְּתוֹךְ הַיָּם׃

כ וַתִּקַּח מִרְיָם הַנְּבִיאָה אֲחוֹת אַהֲרֹן אֶת־הַתֹּף בְּיָדָהּ וַתֵּצֶאןָ
כא כָל־הַנָּשִׁים אַחֲרֶיהָ בְּתֻפִּים וּבִמְחֹלֹת׃ וַתַּעַן לָהֶם מִרְיָם שִׁירוּ

חֲנִיתוֹת שֶׁהָיוּ מִתְחוֹנְנִים וּמִתְעָרְעִים עַל כְּבוֹדָם שֶׁל יִשְׂרָאֵל. נָמֹגוּ. נָמַסּוּ, כְּמוֹ: "בִּרְבִיבִים תְּמֹגְגֶנָּה" (תהלים סה, יא), אָמְרוּ: עָלֵינוּ הֵם בָּאִים לְכַלּוֹתֵנוּ וְלִירַשׁ אֶת אַרְצֵנוּ:

טז. **תִּפֹּל עֲלֵיהֶם אֵימָתָה.** עַל הָרְחוֹקִים: **וָפַחַד.** עַל הַקְּרוֹבִים, כָּעִנְיָן שֶׁנֶּאֱמַר: "כִּי שָׁמַעְנוּ אֵת אֲשֶׁר הוֹבִישׁ" וְגוֹ' (יהושע ב, י): **עַד יַעֲבֹר... עַד יַעֲבֹר.** כְּתַרְגּוּמוֹ: **קָנִיתָ.** חִבַּבְתָּ מִשְּׁאָר אֻמּוֹת, כְּחֵפֶץ הַקָּנוּי בְּדָמִים יְקָרִים שֶׁחָבִיב עַל הָאָדָם:

יז-יח. **תְּבִאֵמוֹ.** נִתְנַבֵּא מֹשֶׁה שֶׁלֹּא יִכָּנֵס לָאָרֶץ, לְכָךְ לֹא נֶאֱמַר 'תְּבִיאֵנוּ': **מָכוֹן לְשִׁבְתְּךָ.** מִקְדָּשׁ שֶׁל מַטָּה מְכֻוָּן כְּנֶגֶד כִּסֵּא שֶׁל מַעְלָה אֲשֶׁר "פָּעַלְתָּ" מִקְדָּשׁ. הַטַּעַם עָלָיו זָקֵף גָּדוֹל לְהַפְרִידוֹ מִתֵּבַת הַשֵּׁם שֶׁלְּאַחֲרָיו, הַמִּקְדָּשׁ אֲשֶׁר כּוֹנְנוּ יָדֶיךָ ה'. חָבִיב בֵּית הַמִּקְדָּשׁ, שֶׁהָעוֹלָם נִבְרָא בְּיַד אַחַת, שֶׁנֶּאֱמַר "אַף יָדִי יָסְדָה אֶרֶץ" (ישעיה מח, יג), וּמִקְדָּשׁ בִּשְׁתֵּי יָדַיִם. וְאֵימָתַי יִבָּנֶה בִּשְׁתֵּי יָדַיִם? בִּזְמַן שֶׁה' יִמְלֹךְ לְעֹלָם

וָעֶד", לֶעָתִיד לָבֹא שֶׁכָּל הַמְּלוּכָה שֶׁלּוֹ. וּ"לְעֹלָם וָעֶד" לְשׁוֹן עוֹלָמִית הוּא, וְהַוָּי"ו בּוֹ יְסוֹד, לְפִיכָךְ הִיא פְּתוּחָה, אֲבָל "וְחַנָּנִי הַיּוֹדֵעַ וָעֵד" (ירמיה כט, כג) שֶׁהַוָּי"ו בּוֹ שִׁמּוּשׁ, קְמוּצָה הִיא:

יט. **כִּי בָא סוּס פַּרְעֹה** וְגוֹ'. כַּאֲשֶׁר בָּא סוּס פַּרְעֹה וְגוֹ':

כ. **וַתִּקַּח מִרְיָם הַנְּבִיאָה.** הֵיכָן נִתְנַבְּאָה? כְּשֶׁהָיְתָה "אֲחוֹת אַהֲרֹן" קֹדֶם שֶׁנּוֹלַד מֹשֶׁה, אָמְרָה: עֲתִידָה אִמִּי שֶׁתֵּלֵד בֵּן וְכוּ' כִּדְאִיתָא בְּסוֹטָה (דף יב ע"ב). דָּבָר אַחֵר, "אֲחוֹת אַהֲרֹן," לְפִי שֶׁמָּסַר נַפְשׁוֹ עָלֶיהָ כְּשֶׁנִּצְטָרְעָה נִקְרֵאת עַל שְׁמוֹ: **אֶת הַתֹּף.** כְּלִי שֶׁל מִינֵי זֶמֶר: **בְּתֻפִּים וּבִמְחֹלֹת.** מֻבְטָחוֹת הָיוּ צִדְקָנִיּוֹת שֶׁבַּדּוֹר שֶׁהַקָּדוֹשׁ בָּרוּךְ הוּא עוֹשֶׂה לָהֶם נִסִּים, וְהוֹצִיאוּ תֻפִּים מִמִּצְרָיִם:

כא. **וַתַּעַן לָהֶם מִרְיָם.** מֹשֶׁה אָמַר שִׁירָה לָאֲנָשִׁים, הוּא אוֹמֵר וְהֵם עוֹנִין אַחֲרָיו, וּמִרְיָם אָמְרָה שִׁירָה לַנָּשִׁים:

פרק טו | שמות | בשלח

לַֽיהוָ֖ה כִּֽי־גָאֹ֣ה גָּאָ֑ה ס֥וּס וְרֹכְב֖וֹ רָמָ֥ה בַיָּֽם׃ **וַיַּסַּ֨ע** כב
מֹשֶׁ֤ה אֶת־יִשְׂרָאֵל֙ מִיַּם־ס֔וּף וַיֵּצְא֖וּ אֶל־מִדְבַּר־שׁ֑וּר וַיֵּלְכ֧וּ
שְׁלֹֽשֶׁת־יָמִ֛ים בַּמִּדְבָּ֖ר וְלֹא־מָ֥צְאוּ מָֽיִם׃ וַיָּבֹ֣אוּ מָרָ֔תָה וְלֹ֣א כג
יָֽכְל֗וּ לִשְׁתֹּ֥ת מַ֙יִם֙ מִמָּרָ֔ה כִּ֥י מָרִ֖ים הֵ֑ם עַל־כֵּ֥ן קָרָֽא־שְׁמָ֖הּ
מָרָֽה׃ וַיִּלֹּ֧נוּ הָעָ֛ם עַל־מֹשֶׁ֥ה לֵּאמֹ֖ר מַה־נִּשְׁתֶּֽה׃ וַיִּצְעַ֣ק אֶל־ כד כה
יְהוָ֗ה וַיּוֹרֵ֤הוּ יְהוָה֙ עֵ֔ץ וַיַּשְׁלֵךְ֙ אֶל־הַמַּ֔יִם וַֽיִּמְתְּק֖וּ הַמָּ֑יִם שָׁ֣ם
שָׂ֥ם ל֛וֹ חֹ֥ק וּמִשְׁפָּ֖ט וְשָׁ֥ם נִסָּֽהוּ׃ וַיֹּאמֶר֩ אִם־שָׁמ֨וֹעַ תִּשְׁמַ֜ע כו
לְק֣וֹל ׀ יְהוָ֣ה אֱלֹהֶ֗יךָ וְהַיָּשָׁ֤ר בְּעֵינָיו֙ תַּעֲשֶׂ֔ה וְהַֽאֲזַנְתָּ֙ לְמִצְוֹתָ֔יו
וְשָׁמַרְתָּ֖ כָּל־חֻקָּ֑יו כָּֽל־הַמַּֽחֲלָ֞ה אֲשֶׁר־שַׂ֤מְתִּי בְמִצְרַ֙יִם֙ לֹא־
אָשִׂ֣ים עָלֶ֔יךָ כִּ֛י אֲנִ֥י יְהוָ֖ה רֹפְאֶֽךָ׃ וַיָּבֹ֣אוּ אֵילִ֔מָה כז

חמישי

כב **וַיַּסַּע משֶׁה.** הִסִּיעָן בְּעַל כָּרְחָם, שֶׁעִטְּרוּ מִצְרַיִם אֶת סוּסֵיהֶם בְּתַכְשִׁיטֵי זָהָב וָכֶסֶף וַאֲבָנִים טוֹבוֹת, וְהָיוּ יִשְׂרָאֵל מוֹצְאִין אוֹתָן בַּיָּם. וּגְדוֹלָה הָיְתָה בִּזַּת הַיָּם מִבִּזַּת מִצְרַיִם, שֶׁנֶּאֱמַר: ״תּוֹרֵי זָהָב נַעֲשֶׂה לָּךְ עִם נְקֻדּוֹת הַכָּסֶף״ (שיר השירים א, יא), לְפִיכָךְ הִצְרַךְ לְהַסִּיעָן בְּעַל כָּרְחָם:

כג **וַיָּבֹאוּ מָרָתָה.** כְּמוֹ ׳לְמָרָה׳, ה״א בְּסוֹף תֵּבָה בִּמְקוֹם לָמֶ״ד בִּתְחִלָּתָהּ, וְהַתָּי״ו הִיא בִּמְקוֹם הַנִּשְׁרֶשֶׁת בְּתֵבַת ׳מָרָה׳, וּבִסְמִיכָתָהּ, כְּשֶׁהִיא מִדֻּבֶּקֶת לְה״א שֶׁהִיא מוֹסִיף בְּמָקוֹם הַלָּמֶ״ד, תֵּהָפֵךְ הָה״א שֶׁל עִקַּר לְתָי״ו. וְכֵן כָּל ה״א שֶׁהִיא שֹׁרֶשׁ בַּתֵּיבָה, תֵּהָפֵךְ לְתָי״ו בִּסְמִיכָתָהּ, כְּמוֹ: ״חֵמָה אֵין לִי״ (ישעיה כז, ד), ״וַחֲמָתוֹ בָּעֲרָה בוֹ״ (אסתר ז, יב), הֲרֵי ה״א שֶׁל שֹׁרֶשׁ נֶהְפָּכָה לְתָי״ו מִפְּנֵי שֶׁנִּסְמְכָה עַל הַוָּי״ו הַנּוֹסֶפֶת. וְכֵן: ״עֶבֶד וְחָמָה״ (ויקרא כה, מד), ״הִנֵּה חֲמָתִי כַּלְיָה״ (בראשית ל, ג), ״לְנֶפֶשׁ חַיָּה״ (בראשית ב, ז), ״בֵּין הָרָמָה״ (שופטים ד, ה), ״וַתִּשְׁתַּבַּח עַל הָרָמָתָה״ (שמואל א׳ א, יט):

כד **וַיִּלֹּנוּ.** לְשׁוֹן נִפְעָלוּ הוּא. וְכֵן הַתַּרְגּוּם לְשׁוֹן נִפְעָלוּ הוּא, ״וְאִתְרַעֲמוּ״. וְכֵן דֶּרֶךְ לְשׁוֹן תְּלוּנָה לְהָסֵב הַדִּבּוּר

אֶל הָאָדָם: מִתְלוֹנֵן, מִתְרוֹעֵם, וְלֹא יֹאמַר: לוֹנֵן, רוֹעֵם. וְכֵן יֹאמַר הַלּוֹעֵז דְקוֹמְפְּלַיְנְש״ט ש״יי, מֵסֵב הַדִּבּוּר אֶצְלוֹ בְּאָמְרוֹ ש״יי:

כה **שָׂם שָׂם לוֹ.** בְּמָרָה נָתַן לָהֶם מִקְצָת פָּרָשִׁיּוֹת שֶׁל תּוֹרָה שֶׁיִּתְעַסְּקוּ בָהֶם: שַׁבָּת וּפָרָה אֲדֻמָּה וְדִינִין: **וְשָׁם נִסָּהוּ.** לָעָם, וְרָאָה קְשִׁי עָרְפּוֹ שֶׁלֹּא נִמְלְכוּ בְּמֹשֶׁה בְּלָשׁוֹן יָפָה: ״בַּקֵּשׁ עָלֵינוּ שֶׁיִּהְיוּ לָנוּ מַיִם לִשְׁתּוֹת״, אֶלָּא נִתְלוֹנְנוּ:

כו **אִם שָׁמוֹעַ תִּשְׁמַע.** זוֹ קַבָּלָה שֶׁיְּקַבְּלוּ עֲלֵיהֶם: **תַּעֲשֶׂה.** הִיא עֲשִׂיָּה: **וְהַאֲזַנְתָּ.** תַּטֶּה אָזְנֶיךָ לְדַקְדֵּק בָּהֶם: **כָּל חֻקָּיו.** דְּבָרִים שֶׁאֵינָן אֶלָּא גְּזֵרַת מֶלֶךְ בְּלֹא שׁוּם טַעַם, וְיֵצֶר הָרַע מְקַנְטֵר עֲלֵיהֶם, מַה אִסּוּר בְּאֵלּוּ? לָמָּה נֶאֶסְרוּ? כְּגוֹן לְבִישַׁת כִּלְאַיִם וַאֲכִילַת חֲזִיר וּפָרָה אֲדֻמָּה וְכַיּוֹצֵא בָּהֶם: **לֹא אָשִׂים עָלֶיךָ.** וְאִם אָשִׂים הֲרֵי הִיא כְּלֹא הוּשְׂמָה, ״כִּי אֲנִי ה׳ רֹפְאֶךָ״. וּלְפִי פְּשׁוּטוֹ, ״כִּי אֲנִי ה׳״ הַמְלַמֶּדְךָ תּוֹרָה וּמִצְוֹת לְמַעַן תִּנָּצֵל מֵהֶם, כָּרוֹפֵא הַזֶּה הָאוֹמֵר לָאָדָם: אַל תֹּאכַל דָּבָר זֶה פֶּן יְבִיאֲךָ לִידֵי חֹלִי זֶה. וְכֵן הוּא אוֹמֵר: ״רִפְאוּת תְּהִי לְשָׁרֶּךָ״ (משלי ג, ח):

שמות | פרק טז | בשלח

וְשָׁ֗ם שְׁתֵּ֥ים עֶשְׂרֵ֛ה עֵינֹ֥ת מַ֖יִם וְשִׁבְעִ֣ים תְּמָרִ֑ים וַיַּחֲנוּ־שָׁ֖ם עַל־הַמָּֽיִם: וַיִּסְעוּ֙ מֵֽאֵילִ֔ם וַיָּבֹ֜אוּ כָּל־עֲדַ֤ת בְּנֵֽי־יִשְׂרָאֵל֙ אֶל־מִדְבַּר־סִ֔ין אֲשֶׁ֥ר בֵּין־אֵילִ֖ם וּבֵ֣ין סִינָ֑י בַּחֲמִשָּׁ֨ה עָשָׂ֥ר יוֹם֙ לַחֹ֣דֶשׁ הַשֵּׁנִ֔י לְצֵאתָ֖ם מֵאֶ֥רֶץ מִצְרָֽיִם: וַיִּלּ֜וֹנוּ כָּל־עֲדַ֧ת בְּנֵי־יִשְׂרָאֵ֛ל עַל־מֹשֶׁ֥ה וְעַֽל־אַהֲרֹ֖ן בַּמִּדְבָּֽר: וַיֹּאמְר֨וּ אֲלֵהֶ֜ם בְּנֵ֣י יִשְׂרָאֵ֗ל מִֽי־יִתֵּ֨ן מוּתֵ֤נוּ בְיַד־יְהוָה֙ בְּאֶ֣רֶץ מִצְרַ֔יִם בְּשִׁבְתֵּ֨נוּ֙ עַל־סִ֣יר הַבָּשָׂ֔ר בְּאָכְלֵ֥נוּ לֶ֖חֶם לָשֹׂ֑בַע כִּֽי־הוֹצֵאתֶ֤ם אֹתָ֨נוּ֙ אֶל־הַמִּדְבָּ֣ר הַזֶּ֔ה לְהָמִ֛ית אֶת־כָּל־הַקָּהָ֥ל הַזֶּ֖ה בָּרָעָֽב: וַיֹּ֤אמֶר יְהוָה֙ אֶל־מֹשֶׁ֔ה הִנְנִ֨י מַמְטִ֥יר לָכֶ֛ם לֶ֖חֶם מִן־הַשָּׁמָ֑יִם וְיָצָ֨א הָעָ֤ם וְלָֽקְטוּ֙ דְּבַר־י֣וֹם בְּיוֹמ֔וֹ לְמַ֧עַן אֲנַסֶּ֛נּוּ הֲיֵלֵ֥ךְ בְּתוֹרָתִ֖י אִם־לֹֽא: וְהָיָה֙ בַּיּ֣וֹם הַשִּׁשִּׁ֔י וְהֵכִ֖ינוּ אֵ֣ת אֲשֶׁר־יָבִ֑יאוּ וְהָיָ֣ה מִשְׁנֶ֔ה עַ֥ל אֲשֶֽׁר־יִלְקְט֖וּ י֥וֹם ׀ יֽוֹם: וַיֹּ֤אמֶר מֹשֶׁה֙ וְאַהֲרֹ֔ן אֶֽל־כָּל־בְּנֵ֖י יִשְׂרָאֵ֑ל עֶ֕רֶב וִֽידַעְתֶּ֕ם כִּ֧י יְהוָ֛ה הוֹצִ֥יא אֶתְכֶ֖ם מֵאֶ֥רֶץ מִצְרָֽיִם: וּבֹ֗קֶר וּרְאִיתֶם֙

כג שְׁתֵּים עֶשְׂרֵה עֵינֹת מָיִם. כְּנֶגֶד שְׁנֵים עָשָׂר שְׁבָטִים נִזְדַּמְּנוּ לָהֶם: וְשִׁבְעִים תְּמָרִים. כְּנֶגֶד שִׁבְעִים זְקֵנִים:

פרק טז

א בַּחֲמִשָּׁה עָשָׂר יוֹם. נִתְפָּרֵשׁ הַיּוֹם שֶׁל חֲנָיָה זוֹ לְפִי שֶׁבּוֹ בַּיּוֹם כָּלְתָה הַחֲרָרָה שֶׁהוֹצִיאוּ מִמִּצְרַיִם וְהֻצְרְכוּ לַמָּן, לְלַמְּדֵנוּ שֶׁאָכְלוּ מִשְּׁיָרֵי הַבָּצֵק שִׁשִּׁים וְאַחַת סְעֻדּוֹת, וְיָרַד לָהֶם הַמָּן בְּשִׁשָּׁה עָשָׂר בְּאִיָּר, וְיוֹם אֶחָד בְּשַׁבָּת הָיָה, כִּדְאִיתָא בְּמַסֶּכֶת שַׁבָּת (דף פז ע"ב):

ב וַיִּלּוֹנוּ. לְפִי שֶׁכָּלָה הַלֶּחֶם:

ג מִי יִתֵּן מוּתֵנוּ. שֶׁנָּמוּת. וְאֵינוֹ שֵׁם דָּבָר כְּמוֹ 'מוֹתֵנוּ', אֶלָּא כְּמוֹ: עֲשׂוֹתֵנוּ, חֲנוֹתֵנוּ, שׁוּבֵנוּ – לַעֲשׂוֹת חֲנַיְתֵנוּ, לַחֲנוֹת חֲנוֹתֵנוּ, לָמוּת חֲנוֹתֵנוּ. "לְוַי דְּמִיתְנָא" – לוּ מֵיתְנוּ, הַלְוַאי וְהָיִינוּ מֵתִים:

ד דְּבַר יוֹם בְּיוֹמוֹ. צֹרֶךְ אֲכִילַת יוֹם יִלְקְטוּ בְּיוֹמוֹ, וְלֹא יִלְקְטוּ הַיּוֹם לְצֹרֶךְ מָחָר: לְמַעַן אֲנַסֶּנּוּ. כִּי חֲמָצֵנוּ "הֲיֵלֵךְ בְּתוֹרָתִי", אִם יִשְׁמְרוּ מִצְווֹת הַתְּלוּיוֹת בּוֹ, שֶׁלֹּא יוֹתִירוּ מִמֶּנּוּ וְלֹא יֵצְאוּ בְשַׁבָּת לִלְקֹט:

ה וְהָיָה מִשְׁנֶה. לַיּוֹם וְלַמָּחֳרָת: מִשְׁנֶה. עַל שֶׁהָיוּ רְגִילִים לִלְקֹט יוֹם יוֹם שֶׁל שְׁאָר יְמוֹת הַשָּׁבוּעַ:

ו עֶרֶב. כְּמוֹ לָעֶרֶב: וִידַעְתֶּם כִּי ה' הוֹצִיא אֶתְכֶם מֵאֶרֶץ מִצְרָיִם. לְפִי שֶׁאֲמַרְתֶּם לָנוּ: "כִּי הוֹצֵאתֶם אֹתָנוּ" (לעיל פסוק ג), תֵּדְעוּ כִּי לֹא אֲנַחְנוּ הַמּוֹצִיאִים אֶלָּא ה' הוֹצִיא אֶתְכֶם, שֶׁיָּזִיז לָכֶם אֶת הַשְּׂלָו:

ז וּבֹקֶר וּרְאִיתֶם. לֹא עַל הַכָּבוֹד שֶׁנֶּאֱמַר: "וְהִנֵּה כְּבוֹד ה' נִרְאָה בֶּעָנָן" (להלן פסוק י) נֶאֱמַר, אֶלָּא כָּךְ אָמַר לָהֶם: עֶרֶב וִידַעְתֶּם כִּי הַיְּכֹלֶת בְּיָדוֹ לִתֵּן תַּאֲוַתְכֶם, וּבָשָׂר יִתֵּן, אַךְ לֹא בְּפָנִים מְאִירוֹת יִתְּנֶנָּה לָכֶם, כִּי

אֶת־כְּבוֹד יְהוָה בְּשָׁמְעוֹ אֶת־תְּלֻנֹּתֵיכֶם עַל־יְהוָה וְנַחְנוּ מָה
כִּי תַלִּינוּ עָלֵינוּ: וַיֹּאמֶר מֹשֶׁה בְּתֵת יְהוָה לָכֶם בָּעֶרֶב בָּשָׂר ח
לֶאֱכֹל וְלֶחֶם בַּבֹּקֶר לִשְׂבֹּעַ בִּשְׁמֹעַ יְהוָה אֶת־תְּלֻנֹּתֵיכֶם אֲשֶׁר־
אַתֶּם מַלִּינִם עָלָיו וְנַחְנוּ מָה לֹא־עָלֵינוּ תְלֻנֹּתֵיכֶם כִּי עַל־יְהוָה:
וַיֹּאמֶר מֹשֶׁה אֶל־אַהֲרֹן אֱמֹר אֶל־כָּל־עֲדַת בְּנֵי יִשְׂרָאֵל קִרְבוּ ט
לִפְנֵי יְהוָה כִּי שָׁמַע אֵת תְּלֻנֹּתֵיכֶם: וַיְהִי כְּדַבֵּר אַהֲרֹן אֶל־כָּל־ י
עֲדַת בְּנֵי־יִשְׂרָאֵל וַיִּפְנוּ אֶל־הַמִּדְבָּר וְהִנֵּה כְּבוֹד יְהוָה נִרְאָה
בֶּעָנָן:

וַיְדַבֵּר יְהוָה אֶל־מֹשֶׁה לֵּאמֹר: שָׁמַעְתִּי אֶת־תְּלוּנֹּת בְּנֵי יִשְׂרָאֵל יא יב
דַּבֵּר אֲלֵהֶם לֵאמֹר בֵּין הָעַרְבַּיִם תֹּאכְלוּ בָשָׂר וּבַבֹּקֶר תִּשְׂבְּעוּ־
לָחֶם וִידַעְתֶּם כִּי אֲנִי יְהוָה אֱלֹהֵיכֶם: וַיְהִי בָעֶרֶב וַתַּעַל הַשְּׂלָו יג
וַתְּכַס אֶת־הַמַּחֲנֶה וּבַבֹּקֶר הָיְתָה שִׁכְבַת הַטַּל סָבִיב לַמַּחֲנֶה:
וַתַּעַל שִׁכְבַת הַטָּל וְהִנֵּה עַל־פְּנֵי הַמִּדְבָּר דַּק מְחֻסְפָּס דַּק יד

שֶׁלֹּא כַהוֹגֶן, שֶׁחֲלָטָהּ אוֹתוֹ, וּמְכָרֵס מְלֵאָה. וְהַלֶּחֶם שֶׁשְּׁאֵלְתֶּם לְצֹרֶךְ, בִּירִידָתוֹ לַבֹּקֶר תִּרְאוּ אֶת כְּבוֹד אוֹר פָּנָיו, שֶׁיּוֹרִידֵהוּ לָכֶם דֶּרֶךְ חִבָּה בַּבֹּקֶר שֵׁם שָׁהוּת לַהֲכִינוֹ, וְטַל מִלְמַעְלָה וְטַל מִלְמַטָּה כִּמְנֻחָּה בְּקֻפְסָא: אֶת תְּלֻנֹּתֵיכֶם עַל ה'. כְּמוֹ אֲשֶׁר עַל ה': וְנַחְנוּ מָה. מָה אֲנַחְנוּ חֲשׁוּבִין: כִּי תַלִּינוּ עָלֵינוּ. שֶׁתַּרְעִימוּ עָלֵינוּ אֶת הַכֹּל, אֶת בְּנֵיכֶם וּנְשֵׁיכֶם וּבְנוֹתֵיכֶם וְעֵרֶב רַב. וְעַל כָּרְחִי אֲנִי זָקוּק לְפָרֵשׁ "תַּלִּינוּ" בִּלְשׁוֹן תַּפְעִילוּ, מִפְּנֵי דָּגְשׁוּתוֹ וּקְרִיָּתוֹ. שֶׁאִלּוּ הָיָה רָפֶה הָיִיתִי מְפָרְשׁוֹ בִּלְשׁוֹן תִּפְעֲלוּ, כְּמוֹ: "וַיָּלֶן הָעָם עַל מֹשֶׁה" (להלן יז, ג), אוֹ אִם הָיָה דָּגוּשׁ וְאֵין בּוֹ יוּ"ד וְנִקְרָא "תָּלֹנּוּ" הָיִיתִי מְפָרְשׁוֹ לְשׁוֹן תִּפְעֹלוּנָה. עַכְשָׁיו הוּא מַשְׁמַע תַּלִּינוּ אֶת אֲחֵרִים, כְּמוֹ בַּמְרַגְּלִים: "וַיַּלִּינוּ עָלָיו אֶת כָּל הָעֵדָה" (במדבר יד, לו):

ח בָּשָׂר לֶאֱכֹל. וְלֹא לִשְׂבֹּעַ, לִמְּדָה תּוֹרָה דֶּרֶךְ אֶרֶץ שֶׁאֵין אוֹכְלִין בָּשָׂר לָשֹׂבַע. וּמָה רָאָה לְהוֹרִיד לֶחֶם בַּבֹּקֶר וּבָשָׂר בָּעֶרֶב? לְפִי שֶׁהַלֶּחֶם שָׁאֲלוּ כַּהוֹגֶן, שֶׁאִי אֶפְשָׁר לוֹ לָאָדָם בְּלֹא לֶחֶם, אֲבָל בָּשָׂר שָׁאֲלוּ שֶׁלֹּא כַהוֹגֶן, שֶׁהַרְבֵּה בְּהֵמוֹת הָיוּ לָהֶם, וְעוֹד שֶׁהָיָה אֶפְשָׁר לָהֶם בְּלֹא בָּשָׂר, לְפִיכָךְ נָתַן לָהֶם בְּשָׁעַת טֹרַח שֶׁלֹּא כַהוֹגֶן: אֲשֶׁר אַתֶּם מַלִּינִם עָלָיו. אֶת הָאֲחֵרִים הַשּׁוֹמְעִים אֶתְכֶם מִתְלוֹנְנִים:

ט קִרְבוּ. לַמָּקוֹם שֶׁהֶעָנָן יֵרֵד:

יג הַשְּׂלָו. מִין עוֹף, וְשָׁמֵן מְאֹד: הָיְתָה שִׁכְבַת הַטָּל. הַטַּל שׁוֹכֵב עַל הַמָּן, וּבְמָקוֹם אַחֵר הוּא אוֹמֵר: "וּבְרֶדֶת הַטַּל וְגוֹ'" (במדבר יא, ט), הַטַּל יוֹרֵד עַל הָאָרֶץ וְהַמָּן יוֹרֵד עָלָיו וְחוֹזֵר וְיוֹרֵד טַל עָלָיו, וַהֲרֵי הוּא כִּמְנֻחָּה בְּקֻפְסָא:

יד וַתַּעַל שִׁכְבַת הַטָּל. כְּשֶׁהַחַמָּה זוֹרַחַת עוֹלֶה הַטַּל

שמות | פרק טז

טו כַּכְּפֹ֖ר עַל־הָאָֽרֶץ: וַיִּרְא֣וּ בְנֵֽי־יִשְׂרָאֵ֗ל וַיֹּ֨אמְר֜וּ אִ֤ישׁ אֶל־אָחִיו֙ מָ֣ן ה֔וּא כִּ֛י לֹ֥א יָדְע֖וּ מַה־ה֑וּא וַיֹּ֤אמֶר מֹשֶׁה֙ אֲלֵהֶ֔ם ה֣וּא הַלֶּ֔חֶם

טז אֲשֶׁ֨ר נָתַ֧ן יְהוָ֛ה לָכֶ֖ם לְאָכְלָֽה: זֶ֤ה הַדָּבָר֙ אֲשֶׁ֣ר צִוָּ֣ה יְהוָ֔ה לִקְט֣וּ מִמֶּ֔נּוּ אִ֖ישׁ לְפִ֣י אָכְל֑וֹ עֹ֣מֶר לַגֻּלְגֹּ֗לֶת מִסְפַּר֙ נַפְשֹׁ֣תֵיכֶ֔ם אִ֛ישׁ

יז לַאֲשֶׁ֥ר בְּאָהֳל֖וֹ תִּקָּֽחוּ: וַיַּעֲשׂוּ־כֵ֖ן בְּנֵ֣י יִשְׂרָאֵ֑ל וַֽיִּלְקְט֔וּ הַמַּרְבֶּ֖ה

יח וְהַמַּמְעִֽיט: וַיָּמֹ֣דּוּ בָעֹ֔מֶר וְלֹ֤א הֶעְדִּיף֙ הַמַּרְבֶּ֔ה וְהַמַּמְעִ֖יט לֹ֣א

יט הֶחְסִ֑יר אִ֥ישׁ לְפִֽי־אָכְל֖וֹ לָקָֽטוּ: וַיֹּ֥אמֶר מֹשֶׁ֖ה אֲלֵהֶ֑ם אִ֕ישׁ אַל־

כ יוֹתֵ֥ר מִמֶּ֖נּוּ עַד־בֹּֽקֶר: וְלֹא־שָׁמְע֣וּ אֶל־מֹשֶׁ֗ה וַיּוֹתִ֨רוּ אֲנָשִׁ֤ים מִמֶּ֨נּוּ֙ עַד־בֹּ֔קֶר וַיָּ֥רֻם תּוֹלָעִ֖ים וַיִּבְאַ֑שׁ וַיִּקְצֹ֥ף עֲלֵהֶ֖ם מֹשֶֽׁה:

כא וַיִּלְקְט֤וּ אֹתוֹ֙ בַּבֹּ֣קֶר בַּבֹּ֔קֶר אִ֖ישׁ כְּפִ֣י אָכְל֑וֹ וְחַ֥ם הַשֶּׁ֖מֶשׁ וְנָמָֽס:

שֶׁעַל הַמָּן לִקְרַאת הַחַמָּה כְּדֶרֶךְ טַל עוֹלֶה לִקְרַאת חַמָּה, אַף חַם תְּמַלֵּא שְׁפוֹפֶרֶת שֶׁל בֵּיצָה טַל וְתִסְתֹּם אֶת פִּיהָ וּתְנִיחֶנָּה בַּחַמָּה, הִיא עוֹלָה מֵאֵלֶיהָ בָּאֲוִיר. וְרַבּוֹתֵינוּ דָּרְשׁוּ שֶׁהַטַּל עוֹלֶה מִן הָאָרֶץ, וְכַעֲלוֹת שִׁכְבַת הַטַּל נִתְגַּלָּה הַמָּן, וְרָאוּ וְהִנֵּה עַל פְּנֵי הַמִּדְבָּר דָּבָר דַּק מְחֻסְפָּס – מְגֻלֶּה, וְאֵין דֻּמֶּה לוֹ בַּמִּקְרָא. וְיֵשׁ לוֹמַר "מְחֻסְפָּס" לְשׁוֹן "חֲפִיסָה וּדְלוּסְקְמָא" שֶׁבִּלְשׁוֹן מִשְׁנָה, כְּשֶׁנִּתְגַּלָּה מִשִּׁכְבַת הַטַּל רָאוּ שֶׁהָיָה דָּבָר דַּק מְחֻסְפָּס בְּתוֹכוֹ בֵּין שְׁתֵּי שִׁכְבוֹת הַטַּל. וְאוּנְקְלוֹס תִּרְגֵּם: "מְקֻלָּף", לְשׁוֹן "מַחְשׂוֹף הַלָּבָן" (בראשית ל, לז). **כַּכְּפֹר**. כְּפוֹר – גליד"א בְּלַעַז. "דַּעְדַּק כְּגִיר", "כְּאַבְנֵי גִר" (ישעיה כז, ט), וְהוּא מִין צֶבַע שָׁחוֹר כְּדְאָמְרִינַן גַּבֵּי כִּסּוּי הַדָּם: "הַגִּיר וְהַזַּרְנִיךְ" (חולין פח ע״ב). "דַּעְדַּק כְּגִיר כְּגְלִידָא עַל אַרְעָא", דַּק הָיָה כְּגִיר וְשׁוֹכֵב מְגֻלָּד כִּכְפוֹר עַל הָאָרֶץ. וְכֵן פֵּרוּשׁוֹ, "דַּק כַּכְּפֹר", שָׁטוּחַ קָלוּשׁ וּמְחֻבָּר כִּגְלִיד. "דַּק" טינב״ש בְּלַעַז, שֶׁהָיָה מַגְלִיד גֶּלֶד דַּק מִלְמַעְלָה. וּ"כְגִיר" שֶׁתִּרְגֵּם אוּנְקְלוֹס, תּוֹסֶפֶת הוּא עַל לְשׁוֹן הָעִבְרִית וְאֵין לוֹ תֵּבָה בַּפָּסוּק.

טו **מָן הוּא**. הֲכָנַת מָזוֹן הוּא, כְּמוֹ: "וַיְמַן לָהֶם הַמֶּלֶךְ" (דניאל א, ה). **כִּי לֹא יָדְעוּ מַה הוּא**. שֶׁיִּקְרָאוּהוּ בִּשְׁמוֹ.

טז **עֹמֶר**. שֵׁם מִדָּה: **מִסְפַּר נַפְשֹׁתֵיכֶם**. כְּפִי מִנְיַן נְפָשׁוֹת שֶׁיֵּשׁ לְאִישׁ בְּאָהֳלוֹ תִּקָּחוּ, עֹמֶר לְכָל גֻּלְגֹּלֶת:

יז **הַמַּרְבֶּה וְהַמַּמְעִיט**. יֵשׁ שֶׁלָּקְטוּ הַרְבֵּה וְיֵשׁ שֶׁלָּקְטוּ מְעַט, וּכְשֶׁבָּאוּ לְבֵיתָם מָדְדוּ בָּעֹמֶר אִישׁ אִישׁ מַה שֶּׁלָּקְטוּ, וּמָצְאוּ שֶׁהַמַּרְבֶּה לִלְקֹט לֹא הֶעְדִּיף עַל עֹמֶר לַגֻּלְגֹּלֶת אֲשֶׁר בְּאָהֳלוֹ, וְהַמַּמְעִיט לִלְקֹט לֹא מָצָא חָסֵר מֵעֹמֶר לַגֻּלְגֹּלֶת, וְזֶהוּ נֵס גָּדוֹל שֶׁנַּעֲשָׂה בּוֹ:

כ **וַיּוֹתִרוּ אֲנָשִׁים**. דָּתָן וַאֲבִירָם: **וַיָּרֻם תּוֹלָעִים**. לְשׁוֹן רִמָּה: **וַיִּבְאַשׁ**. הֲרֵי זֶה מִקְרָא הָפוּךְ, שֶׁבַּתְּחִלָּה הִבְאִישׁ וּלְבַסּוֹף הִתְלִיעַ, כָּעִנְיָן שֶׁנֶּאֱמַר: "וְלֹא הִבְאִישׁ וְרִמָּה לֹא הָיְתָה בּוֹ" (להלן פסוק כד), וְכֵן דֶּרֶךְ כָּל הַמַּתְלִיעִים:

כא **וְחַם הַשֶּׁמֶשׁ וְנָמָס**. הַנִּשְׁאָר בַּשָּׂדֶה נַעֲשֶׂה נְחָלִים וְשׁוֹתִין מִמֶּנּוּ אַיָּלִים וּצְבָאִים, וְאֻמּוֹת הָעוֹלָם צָדִין מֵהֶם וְטוֹעֲמִים בָּהֶם טַעַם מָן וְיוֹדְעִים מַה שִׁבְחָן שֶׁל יִשְׂרָאֵל. "פָּשַׁר" (אונקלוס), לְשׁוֹן פּוֹשְׁרִין, עַל יְדֵי הַשֶּׁמֶשׁ מִתְחַמֵּם וּמַפְשִׁיר: **וְנָמָס**. דישטנפרי"ר. וְאַגָּדָתוֹ בְּסַנְהֶדְרִין בְּסוֹף 'אַרְבַּע מִיתוֹת' (דף סז ע״ב):

פרק טז

כב וַיְהִ֣י ׀ בַּיּ֣וֹם הַשִּׁשִּׁ֗י לָֽקְט֥וּ לֶ֙חֶם֙ מִשְׁנֶ֔ה שְׁנֵ֥י הָעֹ֖מֶר לָאֶחָ֑ד וַיָּבֹ֙אוּ֙ כָּל־נְשִׂיאֵ֣י הָֽעֵדָ֔ה וַיַּגִּ֖ידוּ לְמֹשֶֽׁה:
כג וַיֹּ֣אמֶר אֲלֵהֶ֗ם ה֚וּא אֲשֶׁ֣ר דִּבֶּ֣ר יְהוָ֔ה שַׁבָּת֧וֹן שַׁבַּת־קֹ֛דֶשׁ לַיהוָ֖ה מָחָ֑ר אֵ֣ת אֲשֶׁר־תֹּאפ֞וּ אֵפ֗וּ וְאֵ֤ת אֲשֶׁר־תְּבַשְּׁלוּ֙ בַּשֵּׁ֔לוּ וְאֵת֙ כָּל־הָ֣עֹדֵ֔ף הַנִּ֧יחוּ לָכֶ֛ם לְמִשְׁמֶ֖רֶת עַד־הַבֹּֽקֶר:
כד וַיַּנִּ֤יחוּ אֹתוֹ֙ עַד־הַבֹּ֔קֶר כַּאֲשֶׁ֖ר צִוָּ֣ה מֹשֶׁ֑ה וְלֹ֣א הִבְאִ֔ישׁ וְרִמָּ֖ה לֹא־הָ֥יְתָה בּֽוֹ:
כה וַיֹּ֤אמֶר מֹשֶׁה֙ אִכְלֻ֣הוּ הַיּ֔וֹם כִּֽי־שַׁבָּ֥ת הַיּ֖וֹם לַיהוָ֑ה הַיּ֕וֹם לֹ֥א תִמְצָאֻ֖הוּ בַּשָּׂדֶֽה:
כו שֵׁ֥שֶׁת יָמִ֖ים תִּלְקְטֻ֑הוּ וּבַיּ֧וֹם הַשְּׁבִיעִ֛י שַׁבָּ֖ת לֹ֥א יִֽהְיֶה־בּֽוֹ:
כז וַֽיְהִי֙ בַּיּ֣וֹם הַשְּׁבִיעִ֔י יָצְא֥וּ מִן־הָעָ֖ם לִלְקֹ֑ט וְלֹ֖א מָצָֽאוּ:
כח וַיֹּ֥אמֶר יְהוָ֖ה אֶל־מֹשֶׁ֑ה עַד־אָ֙נָה֙ מֵֽאַנְתֶּ֔ם לִשְׁמֹ֥ר מִצְוֺתַ֖י וְתוֹרֹתָֽי:
כט רְא֗וּ כִּֽי־יְהוָה֮ נָתַ֣ן לָכֶ֣ם הַשַּׁבָּת֒ עַל־כֵּ֠ן ה֣וּא נֹתֵ֥ן לָכֶ֛ם בַּיּ֥וֹם הַשִּׁשִּׁ֖י לֶ֣חֶם יוֹמָ֑יִם שְׁב֣וּ ׀ אִ֣ישׁ תַּחְתָּ֗יו אַל־יֵ֥צֵא אִ֛ישׁ מִמְּקֹמ֖וֹ בַּיּ֥וֹם

כב] לָקְטוּ לֶחֶם מִשְׁנֶה. כְּשֶׁמָּדְדוּ אֶת לְקִיטָתָם בְּאָהֳלֵיהֶם מָצְאוּ כִּפְלַיִם, "שְׁנֵי הָעֹמֶר לָאֶחָד". וּמִדְרַשׁ אַגָּדָה, "לֶחֶם מִשְׁנֶה" מְשֻׁנֶּה, אוֹתוֹ הַיּוֹם נִשְׁתַּנָּה לְשֶׁבַח בְּרֵיחוֹ וּבְטַעֲמוֹ: **וַיַּגִּידוּ לְמֹשֶׁה.** שְׁאָלוּהוּ מַה יּוֹם מִיּוֹמַיִם? וּמִכָּאן יֵשׁ לִלְמֹד שֶׁעֲדַיִן לֹא הִגִּיד לָהֶם מֹשֶׁה פָּרָשַׁת שַׁבָּת שֶׁנִּצְטַוָּה לוֹמַר לָהֶם: "וְהָיָה בַּיּוֹם הַשִּׁשִּׁי וְהֵכִינוּ" וְגוֹ' (לעיל פסוק ה), עַד שֶׁשָּׁאֲלוּ אֶת זֹאת, אָמַר לָהֶם: "הוּא אֲשֶׁר דִּבֶּר ה'" (בפסוק הבא), שֶׁנִּצְטַוֵּיתִי לוֹמַר לָכֶם. וּלְכָךְ עֲנָשׁוֹ הַכָּתוּב, שֶׁאָמַר לוֹ: "עַד אָנָה מֵאַנְתֶּם" (להלן פסוק כח) וְלֹא הוֹצִיאוֹ מִן הַכְּלָל:

כג] אֵת אֲשֶׁר תֹּאפוּ אֵפוּ. מַה שֶּׁאַתֶּם רוֹצִים לֶאֱפוֹת בַּתַּנּוּר, "אֵפוּ" הַיּוֹם הַכֹּל לִשְׁנֵי יָמִים. וּמַה שֶּׁאַתֶּם צְרִיכִים לְבַשֵּׁל מִמֶּנּוּ בַּמַּיִם, "בַּשְּׁלוּ" הַיּוֹם. לְשׁוֹן אֲפִיָּה נוֹפֵל בְּלֶחֶם וּלְשׁוֹן בִּשּׁוּל בְּתַבְשִׁיל: **לְמִשְׁמֶרֶת.** לִגְנִיזָה:

כה] וַיֹּאמֶר מֹשֶׁה אִכְלֻהוּ הַיּוֹם. שַׁחֲרִית, שֶׁהָיוּ רְגִילִים

כו] וּבַיּוֹם הַשְּׁבִיעִי שַׁבָּת. "שַׁבָּת" הוּא, הַמָּן, "לֹא יִהְיֶה בּוֹ". וְלֹא בָא הַכָּתוּב אֶלָּא לְרַבּוֹת יוֹם הַכִּפּוּרִים וְיָמִים טוֹבִים:

כח] עַד אָנָה מֵאַנְתֶּם. מָשָׁל הֶדְיוֹט הוּא, בַּהֲדֵי הוּצָא לָקֵי כָּרְבָא, עַל יְדֵי הָרְשָׁעִים מִתְגַּנִּין הַכְּשֵׁרִים:

כט] רְאוּ. בְּעֵינֵיכֶם כִּי ה' בִּכְבוֹדוֹ מַזְהִיר אֶתְכֶם עַל הַשַּׁבָּת, שֶׁהֲרֵי נֵס נַעֲשֶׂה בְּכָל עֶרֶב שַׁבָּת לָתֵת לָכֶם לֶחֶם יוֹמָיִם: **שְׁבוּ אִישׁ תַּחְתָּיו.** מִכָּאן סָמְכוּ חֲכָמִים אַרְבַּע אַמּוֹת לַיּוֹצֵא חוּץ לַתְּחוּם: **אַל יֵצֵא אִישׁ מִמְּקֹמוֹ.** אֵלּוּ אַלְפַּיִם אַמָּה, וְלֹא בְּמִפֹרָשׁ, שֶׁאֵין

שמות | פרק טז

לא הַשְּׁבִיעִֽי: וַיִּשְׁבְּת֖וּ הָעָ֑ם בַּיּ֥וֹם הַשְּׁבִעִֽי: וַיִּקְרְא֧וּ בֵֽית־יִשְׂרָאֵ֛ל אֶת־שְׁמ֖וֹ מָ֑ן וְה֗וּא כְּזֶ֤רַע גַּד֙ לָבָ֔ן וְטַעְמ֖וֹ כְּצַפִּיחִ֥ת בִּדְבָֽשׁ:
לב וַיֹּ֣אמֶר מֹשֶׁ֗ה זֶ֤ה הַדָּבָר֙ אֲשֶׁ֣ר צִוָּ֣ה יְהֹוָ֔ה מְלֹ֤א הָעֹ֨מֶר֙ מִמֶּ֔נּוּ לְמִשְׁמֶ֖רֶת לְדֹרֹֽתֵיכֶ֑ם לְמַ֣עַן ׀ יִרְא֣וּ אֶת־הַלֶּ֗חֶם אֲשֶׁ֨ר הֶאֱכַ֤לְתִּי אֶתְכֶם֙ בַּמִּדְבָּ֔ר בְּהוֹצִיאִ֥י אֶתְכֶ֖ם מֵאֶ֥רֶץ מִצְרָֽיִם:
לג וַיֹּ֨אמֶר מֹשֶׁ֜ה אֶֽל־אַהֲרֹ֗ן קַ֚ח צִנְצֶ֣נֶת אַחַ֔ת וְתֶן־שָׁ֥מָּה מְלֹֽא־הָעֹ֖מֶר מָ֑ן וְהַנַּ֤ח אֹתוֹ֙ לִפְנֵ֣י יְהֹוָ֔ה לְמִשְׁמֶ֖רֶת לְדֹרֹֽתֵיכֶֽם:
לד כַּאֲשֶׁ֛ר צִוָּ֥ה יְהֹוָ֖ה אֶל־מֹשֶׁ֑ה וַיַּנִּיחֵ֧הוּ אַהֲרֹ֛ן לִפְנֵ֥י הָעֵדֻ֖ת לְמִשְׁמָֽרֶת:
לה וּבְנֵ֣י יִשְׂרָאֵ֗ל אָֽכְל֤וּ אֶת־הַמָּן֙ אַרְבָּעִ֣ים שָׁנָ֔ה עַד־בֹּאָ֖ם אֶל־אֶ֣רֶץ נוֹשָׁ֑בֶת אֶת־הַמָּן֙ אָֽכְל֔וּ עַד־בֹּאָ֕ם אֶל־קְצֵ֖ה אֶ֥רֶץ כְּנָֽעַן:
לו וְהָעֹ֕מֶר עֲשִׂרִ֥ית הָאֵיפָ֖ה הֽוּא:

תְּחוּמִין חֶלֶּק מִדִּבְרֵי סוֹפְרִים, וְעִקְּרוּ שֶׁל מִקְרָא עַל לוֹקְטֵי הַמָּן נֶאֱמָר:

לא) וְהוּא כְּזֶרַע גַּד. עֵשֶׂב שֶׁשְּׁמוֹ חֶלִידְ"א, וְזֶרַע שֶׁלּוֹ עָגֹל וְאֵינוֹ לָבָן, וְהַמָּן הָיָה לָבָן, וְאֵינוֹ נִמְשָׁל לְזֶרַע גַּד אֶלָּא לָעִנְיָן הָעִגּוּל, "כְּזֶרַע גַּד" הָיָה וְהוּא "לָבָן": **כְּצַפִּיחִת.** בָּצֵק שֶׁמְּטַגְּנִין אוֹתוֹ בִּדְבַשׁ, וְקוֹרִין לוֹ 'אִסְקְרִיטִין' בִּלְשׁוֹן מִשְׁנָה (חלה א, ד; פסחים לז ע"א), וְהוּא תַּרְגּוּם שֶׁל אוּנְקְלוֹס:

לב) לְמִשְׁמֶרֶת. לִגְנִיזָה: **לְדֹרֹתֵיכֶם.** בִּימֵי יִרְמְיָהוּ, כְּשֶׁהָיָה יִרְמְיָהוּ מוֹכִיחָם: לָמָּה אֵין אַתֶּם עוֹסְקִים בַּתּוֹרָה? וְהֵם אוֹמְרִים: נַנִּיחַ מְלַאכְתֵּנוּ וְנַעֲסֹק בַּתּוֹרָה, מֵהֵיכָן נִתְפַּרְנֵס? הוֹצִיא לָהֶם צִנְצֶנֶת הַמָּן, אָמַר לָהֶם: "הַדּ֔וֹר אַתֶּ֖ם רְא֣וּ דְבַר־יְהֹוָ֑ה" (ירמיה ב, לא), 'שִׁמְעוּ' לֹא נֶאֱמַר אֶלָּא 'רְאוּ', בָּזֶה נִתְפַּרְנְסוּ אֲבוֹתֵיכֶם, הַרְבֵּה שְׁלוּחִין יֵשׁ לוֹ לַמָּקוֹם לְהָכִין מָזוֹן לִירֵאָיו:

לג) צִנְצֶנֶת. צְלוֹחִית שֶׁל חֶרֶס, כְּתַרְגּוּמוֹ: **וְהַנַּח אוֹתוֹ לִפְנֵי ה'.** לִפְנֵי הָאָרוֹן. וְלֹא נֶאֱמַר מִקְרָא זֶה עַד שֶׁנִּבְנָה אֹהֶל מוֹעֵד, אֶלָּא שֶׁנִּכְתַּב כָּאן בְּפָרָשַׁת הַמָּן:

לה) אַרְבָּעִים שָׁנָה. וַהֲלֹא חָסֵר שְׁלֹשִׁים יוֹם, שֶׁהֲרֵי בַּחֲמִשָּׁה עָשָׂר בְּאִיָּר יָרַד לָהֶם הַמָּן תְּחִלָּה, וּבַחֲמִשָּׁה עָשָׂר בְּנִיסָן פָּסַק, שֶׁנֶּאֱמַר: "וַיִּשְׁבֹּ֤ת הַמָּן֙ מִמָּ֣חֳרָ֔ת" (יהושע ה, יב)? אֶלָּא מַגִּיד שֶׁהָעוּגוֹת שֶׁהוֹצִיאוּ יִשְׂרָאֵל מִמִּצְרַיִם טָעֲמוּ בָּהֶם טַעַם מָן: **אֶל אֶרֶץ נוֹשָׁבֶת.** לְאַחַר שֶׁעָבְרוּ אֶת הַיַּרְדֵּן: **אֶל קְצֵה אֶרֶץ כְּנָעַן.** בִּתְחִלַּת הַגְּבוּל קֹדֶם שֶׁעָבְרוּ אֶת הַיַּרְדֵּן, וְהֵם עַרְבוֹת מוֹאָב. נִמְצְאוּ מַכְחִישִׁין זֶה אֶת זֶה! אֶלָּא בְּעַרְבוֹת מוֹאָב כְּשֶׁמֵּת מֹשֶׁה בְּשִׁבְעָה בַּאֲדָר פָּסַק הַמָּן מִלֵּירֵד, וְנִסְתַּפְּקוּ מִמָּן שֶׁלִּקְּטוּ בּוֹ בַּיּוֹם עַד שֶׁהִקְרִיבוּ הָעֹמֶר בְּשִׁשָּׁה עָשָׂר בְּנִיסָן, שֶׁנֶּאֱמַר: "וַיֹּ֨אכְל֜וּ מֵעֲב֥וּר הָאָ֛רֶץ מִמָּחֳרַ֥ת הַפֶּ֖סַח" (יהושע ה, יא):

לו) עֲשִׂרִית הָאֵיפָה. הָאֵיפָה שָׁלֹשׁ סְאִין, וְהַסְּאָה שֵׁשֶׁת קַבִּין, וְהַקַּב אַרְבָּעָה לֻגִּין, וְהַלֹּג שֵׁשׁ בֵּיצִים; נִמְצָא עֲשִׂירִית הָאֵיפָה אַרְבָּעִים וְשָׁלֹשׁ בֵּיצִים וְחֹמֶשׁ בֵּיצָה, וְהוּא שִׁעוּר לַחַלָּה וְלַמְּנָחוֹת:

בשלח | פרק יז | שמות

שביעי
א וַיִּסְעוּ כָּל־עֲדַת בְּנֵי־יִשְׂרָאֵל מִמִּדְבַּר־סִין לְמַסְעֵיהֶם עַל־פִּי יְהוָה וַיַּחֲנוּ בִּרְפִידִים וְאֵין מַיִם לִשְׁתֹּת הָעָם: ב וַיָּרֶב הָעָם עִם־מֹשֶׁה וַיֹּאמְרוּ תְּנוּ־לָנוּ מַיִם וְנִשְׁתֶּה וַיֹּאמֶר לָהֶם מֹשֶׁה מַה־תְּרִיבוּן עִמָּדִי מַה־תְּנַסּוּן אֶת־יְהוָה: ג וַיִּצְמָא שָׁם הָעָם לַמַּיִם וַיָּלֶן הָעָם עַל־מֹשֶׁה וַיֹּאמֶר לָמָּה זֶּה הֶעֱלִיתָנוּ מִמִּצְרַיִם לְהָמִית אֹתִי וְאֶת־בָּנַי וְאֶת־מִקְנַי בַּצָּמָא: ד וַיִּצְעַק מֹשֶׁה אֶל־יְהוָה לֵאמֹר מָה אֶעֱשֶׂה לָעָם הַזֶּה עוֹד מְעַט וּסְקָלֻנִי: ה וַיֹּאמֶר יְהוָה אֶל־מֹשֶׁה עֲבֹר לִפְנֵי הָעָם וְקַח אִתְּךָ מִזִּקְנֵי יִשְׂרָאֵל וּמַטְּךָ אֲשֶׁר הִכִּיתָ בּוֹ אֶת־הַיְאֹר קַח בְּיָדְךָ וְהָלָכְתָּ: ו הִנְנִי עֹמֵד לְפָנֶיךָ שָּׁם ׀ עַל־הַצּוּר בְּחֹרֵב וְהִכִּיתָ בַצּוּר וְיָצְאוּ מִמֶּנּוּ מַיִם וְשָׁתָה הָעָם וַיַּעַשׂ כֵּן מֹשֶׁה לְעֵינֵי זִקְנֵי יִשְׂרָאֵל: ז וַיִּקְרָא שֵׁם הַמָּקוֹם מַסָּה וּמְרִיבָה עַל־רִיב ׀ בְּנֵי יִשְׂרָאֵל וְעַל נַסֹּתָם אֶת־יְהוָה לֵאמֹר הֲיֵשׁ יְהוָה בְּקִרְבֵּנוּ אִם־אָיִן:

ח וַיָּבֹא עֲמָלֵק וַיִּלָּחֶם עִם־יִשְׂרָאֵל בִּרְפִידִם: ט וַיֹּאמֶר מֹשֶׁה אֶל־

פרק יז
ב | **מַה תְּנַסּוּן.** לוֹמַר, הֲיוּכַל לָתֵת מַיִם בְּאֶרֶץ צִיָּה:

ד | **עוֹד מְעַט.** אִם אַמְתִּין "עוֹד מְעַט, וּסְקָלֻנִי":

ה | **עֲבֹר לִפְנֵי הָעָם.** וּרְאֵה אִם יִסְקְלוּךָ, לָמָּה הוֹצֵאתָ לַעַז עַל בָּנַי? **וְקַח אִתְּךָ מִזִּקְנֵי יִשְׂרָאֵל.** לְעֵדוּת, שֶׁיִּרְאוּ שֶׁעַל יָדְךָ הַמַּיִם יוֹצְאִים מִן הַצּוּר, וְלֹא יֹאמְרוּ: מַעְיָנוֹת הָיוּ שָׁם מִימֵי קֶדֶם: **וּמַטְּךָ אֲשֶׁר הִכִּיתָ בּוֹ אֶת הַיְאֹר.** מַה תַּלְמוּד לוֹמַר: "אֲשֶׁר הִכִּיתָ בּוֹ אֶת הַיְאֹר"? אֶלָּא שֶׁהָיוּ יִשְׂרָאֵל אוֹמְרִים עַל הַמַּטֶּה שֶׁאֵינוֹ מוּכָן אֶלָּא לְפוּרְעָנוּת, בּוֹ לָקָה פַרְעֹה וּמִצְרַיִם כַּמָּה מַכּוֹת בְּמִצְרַיִם וְעַל הַיָּם, לְכָךְ נֶאֱמַר: "אֲשֶׁר הִכִּיתָ בּוֹ אֶת הַיְאֹר", וְהֵם אוֹמְרִים עָלָיו שֶׁאֵינוֹ אֶלָּא לְפוּרְעָנוּת, יִרְאוּ עַתָּה שֶׁאַף לְטוֹבָה הוּא מוּכָן:

ו | **וְהִכִּיתָ בַצּוּר.** 'עַל הַצּוּר' לֹא נֶאֱמַר אֶלָּא "בַצּוּר", מִכָּאן שֶׁהַמַּטֶּה הָיָה שֶׁל מִין דָּבָר חָזָק וּשְׁמוֹ סַנְפִּירִינוֹן, וְהַצּוּר נִבְקַע מִפָּנָיו:

ח | **וַיָּבֹא עֲמָלֵק.** סָמַךְ פָּרָשָׁה זוֹ לְמִקְרָא זֶה, לוֹמַר, תָּמִיד אֲנִי בֵּינֵיכֶם וּמְזֻמָּן לְכָל צָרְכֵיכֶם, וְאַתֶּם אוֹמְרִים: "הֲיֵשׁ ה' בְּקִרְבֵּנוּ אִם אָיִן" (לעיל פסוק ז)?! חַיֵּיכֶם שֶׁהַכֶּלֶב בָּא וְנוֹשֵׁךְ אֶתְכֶם וְאַתֶּם צוֹעֲקִים לִי וְתֵדְעוּ הֵיכָן אֲנִי. מָשָׁל לְאֶחָד שֶׁהִרְכִּיב בְּנוֹ עַל כְּתֵפוֹ וְיָצָא לַדֶּרֶךְ, הָיָה אוֹתוֹ הַבֵּן רוֹאֶה חֵפֶץ וְאוֹמֵר: אַבָּא, טֹל חֵפֶץ זֶה וְתֶן לִי, וְהוּא נוֹתֵן לוֹ, וְכֵן שְׁנִיָּה וְכֵן שְׁלִישִׁית. פָּגְעוּ בְּאָדָם אֶחָד, אָמַר לוֹ אוֹתוֹ הַבֵּן: רָאִיתָ אֶת אַבָּא? אָמַר לוֹ אָבִיו: אֵינְךָ יוֹדֵעַ הֵיכָן אֲנִי?! הִשְׁלִיכוֹ מֵעָלָיו, וּבָא הַכֶּלֶב וּנְשָׁכוֹ.

יְהוֹשֻׁעַ בְּחַר־לָנוּ אֲנָשִׁים וְצֵא הִלָּחֵם בַּעֲמָלֵק מָחָר אָנֹכִי נִצָּב עַל־רֹאשׁ הַגִּבְעָה וּמַטֵּה הָאֱלֹהִים בְּיָדִי: וַיַּעַשׂ יְהוֹשֻׁעַ כַּאֲשֶׁר אָמַר־לוֹ מֹשֶׁה לְהִלָּחֵם בַּעֲמָלֵק וּמֹשֶׁה אַהֲרֹן וְחוּר עָלוּ רֹאשׁ הַגִּבְעָה: וְהָיָה כַּאֲשֶׁר יָרִים מֹשֶׁה יָדוֹ וְגָבַר יִשְׂרָאֵל וְכַאֲשֶׁר יָנִיחַ יָדוֹ וְגָבַר עֲמָלֵק: וִידֵי מֹשֶׁה כְּבֵדִים וַיִּקְחוּ־אֶבֶן וַיָּשִׂימוּ תַחְתָּיו וַיֵּשֶׁב עָלֶיהָ וְאַהֲרֹן וְחוּר תָּמְכוּ בְיָדָיו מִזֶּה אֶחָד וּמִזֶּה אֶחָד וַיְהִי יָדָיו אֱמוּנָה עַד־בֹּא הַשָּׁמֶשׁ: וַיַּחֲלֹשׁ יְהוֹשֻׁעַ אֶת־עֲמָלֵק וְאֶת־עַמּוֹ לְפִי־חָרֶב:

יא

יב

יג

וַיֹּאמֶר יְהֹוָה אֶל־מֹשֶׁה כְּתֹב זֹאת זִכָּרוֹן בַּסֵּפֶר וְשִׂים בְּאָזְנֵי יְהוֹשֻׁעַ כִּי־מָחֹה אֶמְחֶה אֶת־זֵכֶר עֲמָלֵק מִתַּחַת הַשָּׁמָיִם:

יד   מפטיר

ט| בְּחַר לָנוּ. לִי וּלְךָ, הִשְׁוָהוּ לוֹ. מִכָּאן אָמְרוּ: "יְהִי כְבוֹד תַּלְמִידְךָ חָבִיב עָלֶיךָ כְּשֶׁלָּךְ" (אבות ד, טו). כְּבוֹד חֲבֵרְךָ כְּמוֹרָא רַבָּךְ, מִנַּיִן? "וַיֹּאמֶר אַהֲרֹן אֶל מֹשֶׁה בִּי אֲדֹנִי" (במדבר יב, יא), וַהֲלֹא גְדוֹל הָאַחִין הָיָה, וְעוֹשֶׂה אֶת חֲבֵרוֹ כְּרַבּוֹ. וּמוֹרָא רַבָּךְ כְּמוֹרָא שָׁמַיִם, שֶׁנֶּאֱמַר: "אֲדֹנִי מֹשֶׁה כְּלָאֵם" (שם יא, כח), כַּלֵּם מִן הָעוֹלָם, חַיָּבִין הֵם כְּלָיָה הַמּוֹרְדִים בְּךָ כְּאִלּוּ פָּשְׁעוּ בְּהַקָּדוֹשׁ בָּרוּךְ הוּא: וְצֵא הִלָּחֵם. צֵא מִן הֶעָנָן וְהִלָּחֵם בּוֹ: מָחָר. בְּעֵת הַמִּלְחָמָה "אָנֹכִי נִצָּב": בְּחַר לָנוּ אֲנָשִׁים. גִּבּוֹרִים וְיִרְאֵי חֵטְא, שֶׁתְּהֵא זְכוּתָן מְסַיַּעְתָּן. דָּבָר אַחֵר, בְּחַר לָנוּ אֲנָשִׁים שֶׁיּוֹדְעִין לְבַטֵּל כְּשָׁפִים, לְפִי שֶׁבְּנֵי עֲמָלֵק מְכַשְּׁפִים הָיוּ:

י| וּמֹשֶׁה אַהֲרֹן וְחוּר. מִכָּאן לְתַעֲנִית שֶׁמַּעֲרִיכִין שְׁלֹשָׁה לַעֲבֹר לִפְנֵי הַתֵּבָה, שֶׁבְּתַעֲנִית הָיוּ שְׁרוּיִים: חוּר. בְּנָהּ שֶׁל מִרְיָם הָיָה:

יא| כַּאֲשֶׁר יָרִים מֹשֶׁה יָדוֹ. וְכִי יָדָיו שֶׁל מֹשֶׁה נוֹצְחוֹת הָיוּ הַמִּלְחָמָה? וְכוּ', כִּדְאִיתָא בְּרֹאשׁ הַשָּׁנָה (דף כט ע"א):

יב| וִידֵי מֹשֶׁה כְּבֵדִים. בִּשְׁבִיל שֶׁנִּתְעַצֵּל בַּמִּצְוָה וּמִנָּה אַחֵר תַּחְתָּיו, נִתְיַקְּרוּ יָדָיו: וַיִּקְחוּ. אַהֲרֹן וְחוּר: וַיָּשִׂימוּ תַחְתָּיו. וְלֹא יָשַׁב לוֹ עַל כַּר וָכֶסֶת, אָמַר, יִשְׂרָאֵל שְׁרוּיִין בְּצַעַר, אַף אֲנִי אֶהְיֶה עִמָּהֶם בְּצַעַר: וַיְהִי יָדָיו אֱמוּנָה. וַיְהִי מֹשֶׁה יָדָיו בֶּאֱמוּנָה פְּרוּשׂוֹת הַשָּׁמַיִם בִּתְפִלָּה נֶאֱמָנָה וּנְכוֹנָה: עַד בֹּא הַשָּׁמֶשׁ. שֶׁהָיוּ עֲמָלֵקִים מְחַשְּׁבִין אֶת הַשָּׁעוֹת בְּאִצְטְרוֹלוֹגְיָאָה בְּאֵיזוֹ שָׁעָה הֵם נוֹצְחִים, וְהֶעֱמִיד לָהֶם מֹשֶׁה חַמָּה וְעִרְבֵּב אֶת הַשָּׁעוֹת:

יג| וַיַּחֲלֹשׁ יְהוֹשֻׁעַ. חָתַךְ רָאשֵׁי גִבּוֹרָיו וְלֹא הִשְׁאִיר אֶלָּא חַלָּשִׁים שֶׁבָּהֶם, וְלֹא הֲרָגָם כֻּלָּם. מִכָּאן אָנוּ לְמֵדִים שֶׁעָשׂוּ עַל פִּי הַדִּבּוּר שֶׁל שְׁכִינָה:

יד| כְּתֹב זֹאת זִכָּרוֹן. שֶׁבָּא עֲמָלֵק לְהִזְדַּוֵּג לְיִשְׂרָאֵל קֹדֶם לְכָל הָאֻמּוֹת: וְשִׂים בְּאָזְנֵי יְהוֹשֻׁעַ. הַמַּכְנִיס אֶת יִשְׂרָאֵל לָאָרֶץ, שֶׁיְּצַוֶּה אֶת יִשְׂרָאֵל לְשַׁלֵּם לוֹ אֶת גְּמוּלוֹ. כָּאן נִרְמַז לוֹ לְמֹשֶׁה שֶׁיְּהוֹשֻׁעַ מַכְנִיס אֶת יִשְׂרָאֵל לָאָרֶץ: כִּי מָחֹה אֶמְחֶה. לְכָךְ אֲנִי מַזְהִירְךָ כֵּן, כִּי חָפֵץ אֲנִי לִמְחוֹתוֹ:

פרק יז

טו וַיִּבֶן מֹשֶׁה מִזְבֵּחַ וַיִּקְרָא שְׁמוֹ יְהוָה׀ נִסִּי: וַיֹּאמֶר כִּי־יָד עַל־כֵּס יָהּ מִלְחָמָה לַיהוָה בַּעֲמָלֵק מִדֹּר דֹּר:

פרק יח

א וַיִּשְׁמַע יִתְרוֹ כֹהֵן מִדְיָן חֹתֵן מֹשֶׁה אֵת כָּל־אֲשֶׁר עָשָׂה אֱלֹהִים לְמֹשֶׁה וּלְיִשְׂרָאֵל עַמּוֹ כִּי־הוֹצִיא יְהוָה אֶת־יִשְׂרָאֵל מִמִּצְרָיִם: ב וַיִּקַּח יִתְרוֹ חֹתֵן מֹשֶׁה אֶת־צִפֹּרָה אֵשֶׁת מֹשֶׁה אַחַר שִׁלּוּחֶיהָ: ג וְאֵת שְׁנֵי בָנֶיהָ אֲשֶׁר שֵׁם הָאֶחָד גֵּרְשֹׁם כִּי אָמַר גֵּר הָיִיתִי בְּאֶרֶץ נָכְרִיָּה: ד וְשֵׁם הָאֶחָד אֱלִיעֶזֶר כִּי־אֱלֹהֵי אָבִי בְּעֶזְרִי וַיַּצִּלֵנִי מֵחֶרֶב פַּרְעֹה: ה וַיָּבֹא יִתְרוֹ חֹתֵן מֹשֶׁה וּבָנָיו וְאִשְׁתּוֹ אֶל־מֹשֶׁה אֶל־הַמִּדְבָּר אֲשֶׁר־הוּא חֹנֶה שָׁם הַר הָאֱלֹהִים: ו וַיֹּאמֶר אֶל־

טו וַיִּקְרָא שְׁמוֹ. שֶׁל מִזְבֵּחַ "ה' נִסִּי" – הַקָּדוֹשׁ בָּרוּךְ הוּא עָשָׂה לָנוּ כָּאן נֵס. לֹא שֶׁהַמִּזְבֵּחַ קָרוּי ה', אֶלָּא הַמַּזְכִּיר שְׁמוֹ שֶׁל מִזְבֵּחַ זוֹכֵר אֶת הַנֵּס שֶׁעָשָׂה הַמָּקוֹם, ה' הוּא נֵס שֶׁלָּנוּ:

טז וַיֹּאמֶר. מֹשֶׁה "כִּי יָד עַל כֵּס יָהּ" – יָדוֹ שֶׁל הַקָּדוֹשׁ בָּרוּךְ הוּא הוּרְמָה לִשָּׁבַע בְּכִסְאוֹ לִהְיוֹת לוֹ מִלְחָמָה וְאֵיבָה בַּעֲמָלֵק עוֹלָמִית. וּמַהוּ "כֵּס" וְלֹא נֶאֱמַר "כִּסֵּא", וְאַף הַשֵּׁם נֶחֱלַק לְחֶצְיוֹ? נִשְׁבַּע הַקָּדוֹשׁ בָּרוּךְ הוּא שֶׁאֵין שְׁמוֹ שָׁלֵם וְאֵין כִּסְאוֹ שָׁלֵם עַד שֶׁיִּמָּחֶה שְׁמוֹ שֶׁל עֲמָלֵק כֻּלּוֹ, וּכְשֶׁיִּמָּחֶה שְׁמוֹ יִהְיֶה הַשֵּׁם שָׁלֵם וְהַכִּסֵּא שָׁלֵם, שֶׁנֶּאֱמַר: "הָאוֹיֵב תַּמּוּ חֳרָבוֹת לָנֶצַח" (תהלים ט, ז) – זֶהוּ עֵשָׂו שֶׁכָּתוּב בּוֹ: "וְעֶבְרָתוֹ שְׁמָרָה נֶצַח" (עמוס א, יא), "וְעָרִים נָתַשְׁתָּ אָבַד זִכְרָם הֵמָּה" (תהלים שם), מַהוּ אוֹמֵר אַחֲרָיו? "וַה' לְעוֹלָם יֵשֵׁב" (שם פסוק ח), הֲרֵי הַשֵּׁם שָׁלֵם. "כּוֹנֵן לַמִּשְׁפָּט כִּסְאוֹ" (שם), הֲרֵי הַכִּסֵּא שָׁלֵם:

פרק יח

א וַיִּשְׁמַע יִתְרוֹ. מַה שְּׁמוּעָה שָׁמַע? קְרִיעַת יַם סוּף וּמִלְחֶמֶת עֲמָלֵק: **יִתְרוֹ.** שִׁבְעָה שֵׁמוֹת נִקְרְאוּ לוֹ: רְעוּאֵל, יֶתֶר, יִתְרוֹ, חוֹבָב, חֶבֶר, קֵינִי, פּוּטִיאֵל. יֶתֶר, עַל שֵׁם שֶׁיִּתֵּר פָּרָשָׁה אַחַת בַּתּוֹרָה: "וְאַתָּה תֶחֱזֶה" (להלן פסוק כא). יִתְרוֹ, לִכְשֶׁנִּתְגַּיֵּר וְקִיֵּם הַמִּצְווֹת הוֹסִיפוּ לוֹ אוֹת. חוֹבָב, שֶׁחִבֵּב אֶת הַתּוֹרָה. חוֹבָב הוּא יִתְרוֹ, שֶׁנֶּאֱמַר: "מִבְּנֵי חֹבָב חֹתֵן מֹשֶׁה" (שופטים ד, יא). וְיֵשׁ אוֹמְרִים: רְעוּאֵל אֲבִיו שֶׁל יִתְרוֹ הָיָה, וּמַהוּ אוֹמֵר: "וַתָּבֹאנָה אֶל רְעוּאֵל אֲבִיהֶן" (לעיל ב, יח)? שֶׁהַתִּינוֹקוֹת קוֹרִין לַאֲבִי אֲבִיהֶן אַבָּא. בְּסִפְרֵי (בהעלותך עח): **חֹתֵן מֹשֶׁה.** כָּאן הָיָה יִתְרוֹ מִתְכַּבֵּד בְּמֹשֶׁה: אֲנִי חֹתֵן הַמֶּלֶךְ, וּלְשֶׁעָבַר הָיָה מֹשֶׁה תוֹלֶה הַגְּדֻלָּה בְּחָמִיו, שֶׁנֶּאֱמַר: "וַיָּשָׁב אֶל יֶתֶר חֹתְנוֹ" (לעיל ד, יח): **לְמֹשֶׁה וּלְיִשְׂרָאֵל.** שָׁקוּל מֹשֶׁה כְּנֶגֶד כָּל יִשְׂרָאֵל: **אֵת כָּל אֲשֶׁר עָשָׂה.** לָהֶם בִּירִידַת הַמָּן וּבַבְּאֵר וּבַעֲמָלֵק: **כִּי הוֹצִיא ה' וְגוֹ'.** זוֹ גְדוֹלָה עַל כֻּלָּם:

ב אַחַר שִׁלּוּחֶיהָ. כְּשֶׁאָמַר לוֹ הַקָּדוֹשׁ בָּרוּךְ הוּא בְּמִדְיָן: "לֵךְ שֻׁב מִצְרָיִם", "וַיִּקַּח מֹשֶׁה אֶת אִשְׁתּוֹ וְאֶת בָּנָיו וְגוֹ'" (לעיל ד, יט-כ), וְיָצָא אַהֲרֹן לִקְרָאתוֹ "וַיִּפְגְּשֵׁהוּ בְּהַר הָאֱלֹהִים" (שם פסוק כז), אָמַר לוֹ: מִי הֵם הַלָּלוּ? אָמַר לוֹ: זוֹ הִיא אִשְׁתִּי שֶׁנָּשָׂאתִי בְּמִדְיָן וְאֵלּוּ בָּנַי. אָמַר לוֹ: וְהֵיכָן אַתָּה מוֹלִיכָן? אָמַר לוֹ: לְמִצְרָיִם. אָמַר לוֹ: עַל הָרִאשׁוֹנִים אָנוּ מִצְטַעֲרִים וְאַתָּה בָּא לְהוֹסִיף עֲלֵיהֶם? אָמַר לָהּ: לְכִי לְבֵית אָבִיךְ. נָטְלָה שְׁנֵי בָנֶיהָ וְהָלְכָה לָהּ:

ד וַיַּצִּלֵנִי מֵחֶרֶב פַּרְעֹה. כְּשֶׁגִּלּוּ דָּתָן וַאֲבִירָם עַל דְּבַר הַמִּצְרִי וּבִקֵּשׁ לַהֲרֹג אֶת מֹשֶׁה, נַעֲשָׂה צַוָּארוֹ כְּעַמּוּד שֶׁל שַׁיִשׁ:

ה אֶל הַמִּדְבָּר. אַף אָנוּ יוֹדְעִים שֶׁבַּמִּדְבָּר הָיוּ, אֶלָּא

ז מֹשֶׁה אֲנִי חֹתֶנְךָ יִתְרוֹ בָּא אֵלֶיךָ וְאִשְׁתְּךָ וּשְׁנֵי בָנֶיהָ עִמָּהּ: וַיֵּצֵא מֹשֶׁה לִקְרַאת חֹתְנוֹ וַיִּשְׁתַּחוּ וַיִּשַּׁק־לוֹ וַיִּשְׁאֲלוּ אִישׁ־לְרֵעֵהוּ לְשָׁלוֹם וַיָּבֹאוּ הָאֹהֱלָה:
ח וַיְסַפֵּר מֹשֶׁה לְחֹתְנוֹ אֵת כָּל־אֲשֶׁר עָשָׂה יְהוָה לְפַרְעֹה וּלְמִצְרַיִם עַל אוֹדֹת יִשְׂרָאֵל אֵת כָּל־הַתְּלָאָה אֲשֶׁר מְצָאָתַם בַּדֶּרֶךְ וַיַּצִּלֵם יְהוָה:
ט וַיִּחַדְּ יִתְרוֹ עַל כָּל־הַטּוֹבָה אֲשֶׁר־עָשָׂה יְהוָה לְיִשְׂרָאֵל אֲשֶׁר הִצִּילוֹ מִיַּד מִצְרָיִם:
י וַיֹּאמֶר יִתְרוֹ בָּרוּךְ יְהוָה אֲשֶׁר הִצִּיל אֶתְכֶם מִיַּד מִצְרַיִם וּמִיַּד פַּרְעֹה אֲשֶׁר הִצִּיל אֶת־הָעָם מִתַּחַת יַד־מִצְרָיִם:
יא עַתָּה יָדַעְתִּי כִּי־גָדוֹל יְהוָה מִכָּל־הָאֱלֹהִים כִּי בַדָּבָר אֲשֶׁר זָדוּ עֲלֵיהֶם:
יב וַיִּקַּח יִתְרוֹ חֹתֵן מֹשֶׁה עֹלָה וּזְבָחִים לֵאלֹהִים וַיָּבֹא אַהֲרֹן וְכֹל ׀ זִקְנֵי

בְּשִׁבְחוֹ שֶׁל יִתְרוֹ דִּבֶּר הַכָּתוּב, שֶׁהָיָה יוֹשֵׁב בִּכְבוֹדוֹ שֶׁל עוֹלָם, וְנָדְבוּ לִבּוֹ לָצֵאת אֶל הַמִּדְבָּר מְקוֹם תֹּהוּ לִשְׁמוֹעַ דִּבְרֵי תוֹרָה:

ו וַיֹּאמֶר אֶל מֹשֶׁה. עַל יְדֵי שָׁלִיחַ: **אֲנִי חֹתֶנְךָ יִתְרוֹ וְגוֹ׳.** אִם אֵין אַתָּה יוֹצֵא בְּגִין חָמִיךָ, צֵא בְּגִין אִשְׁתְּךָ, וְאִם אֵין אַתָּה יוֹצֵא בְּגִין אִשְׁתְּךָ, צֵא בְּגִין שְׁנֵי בָנֶיהָ:

ז וַיֵּצֵא מֹשֶׁה. כָּבוֹד גָּדוֹל נִתְכַּבֵּד יִתְרוֹ בְּאוֹתָהּ שָׁעָה; כֵּיוָן שֶׁיָּצָא מֹשֶׁה יָצָא אַהֲרֹן נָדָב וַאֲבִיהוּא, וּמִי הוּא שֶׁרָאָה אֶת אֵלּוּ יוֹצְאִין וְלֹא יָצָא? **וַיִּשְׁתַּחוּ וַיִּשַּׁק לוֹ.** אֵינִי יוֹדֵעַ מִי הִשְׁתַּחֲוָה לְמִי, כְּשֶׁהוּא אוֹמֵר "אִישׁ לְרֵעֵהוּ", מִי הַקָּרוּי "אִישׁ"? זֶה מֹשֶׁה (במדבר יב, ג):

ח וַיְסַפֵּר מֹשֶׁה לְחֹתְנוֹ. לִמְשֹׁךְ אֶת לִבּוֹ לְקָרְבוֹ לַתּוֹרָה: **אֵת כָּל הַתְּלָאָה.** שֶׁעַל הַיָּם וְשֶׁל עֲמָלֵק: **הַתְּלָאָה.** לָמֶ״ד מִן הַיְסוֹד שֶׁל תֵּבָה, וְהַתָּי״ו הוּא תִּקּוּן וִיסוֹד הַנּוֹפֵל מִמֶּנּוּ לִפְרָקִים, וְכֵן: תְּרוּמָה, תְּנוּפָה, תְּקוּמָה, תְּנוּחָה:

ט וַיִּחַדְּ יִתְרוֹ. וַיִּשְׂמַח יִתְרוֹ, זֶהוּ פְּשׁוּטוֹ. וּמִדְרָשׁוֹ, נַעֲשָׂה בְּשָׂרוֹ חִדּוּדִין חִדּוּדִין, מֵצַר עַל אִבּוּד מִצְרַיִם.

"הַיְנוּ דְּאַמְרֵי אֱנָשֵׁי: גִּיּוֹרָא, עַד עַשְׂרָה דָּרֵי לָא תְּבַזֵּי אֲרַמָּאָה בְּאַפֵּיהּ" (סנהדרין צד ע״א): **עַל כָּל הַטּוֹבָה.** טוֹבַת הַמָּן וְהַבְּאֵר וְהַתּוֹרָה. וְעַל כֻּלָּן "אֲשֶׁר הִצִּילוֹ מִיַּד מִצְרָיִם", עַד עַכְשָׁיו לֹא הָיָה עֶבֶד יָכוֹל לִבְרוֹחַ מִמִּצְרַיִם, שֶׁהָיְתָה הָאָרֶץ מְסֻגֶּרֶת, וְאֵלּוּ יָצְאוּ שִׁשִּׁים רִבּוֹא:

י אֲשֶׁר הִצִּיל אֶתְכֶם מִיַּד מִצְרַיִם. אֻמָּה קָשָׁה: **וּמִיַּד פַּרְעֹה.** מֶלֶךְ קָשֶׁה: **מִתַּחַת יַד מִצְרָיִם.** כְּתַרְגּוּמוֹ, לְשׁוֹן רִדּוּי וּמָרוּת הַיָּד שֶׁהָיוּ מַכְבִּידִים עֲלֵיהֶם, הִיא הָעֲבוֹדָה:

יא עַתָּה יָדַעְתִּי. מַכִּירוֹ הָיִיתִי לְשֶׁעָבַר, וְעַכְשָׁיו בְּיוֹתֵר: **מִכָּל הָאֱלֹהִים.** מְלַמֵּד שֶׁהָיָה מַכִּיר בְּכָל עֲבוֹדָה זָרָה שֶׁבָּעוֹלָם, שֶׁלֹּא הִנִּיחַ עֲבוֹדָה זָרָה שֶׁלֹּא עֲבָדָהּ: **כִּי בַדָּבָר אֲשֶׁר זָדוּ עֲלֵיהֶם.** כְּתַרְגּוּמוֹ, בַּמַּיִם דִּמּוּ לְאַבְּדָם וְהֵם נֶאֶבְדוּ בַּמַּיִם: **אֲשֶׁר זָדוּ.** אֲשֶׁר הִרְשִׁיעוּ. וְרַבּוֹתֵינוּ דְּרָשׁוּהוּ לְשׁוֹן: "וַיָּזֶד יַעֲקֹב נָזִיד" (בראשית כה, כט), בַּקְּדֵרָה שֶׁבִּשְּׁלוּ בָּהּ נִתְבַּשְּׁלוּ:

יב עֹלָה. כְּמַשְׁמָעָהּ, שֶׁהִיא כָּלָהּ כָּלִיל: **וּזְבָחִים.** שְׁלָמִים: **וַיָּבֹא אַהֲרֹן וְגוֹ׳.** וּמֹשֶׁה הֵיכָן הָלַךְ? וַהֲלֹא

שני יִשְׂרָאֵ֛ל לֶאֱכָל־לֶ֥חֶם עִם־חֹתֵ֥ן מֹשֶׁ֖ה לִפְנֵ֥י הָאֱלֹהִֽים׃ יג וַיְהִי֙ מִֽמָּחֳרָ֔ת וַיֵּ֥שֶׁב מֹשֶׁ֖ה לִשְׁפֹּ֣ט אֶת־הָעָ֑ם וַיַּעֲמֹ֤ד הָעָם֙ עַל־מֹשֶׁ֔ה מִן־הַבֹּ֖קֶר עַד־הָעָֽרֶב׃ יד וַיַּרְא֙ חֹתֵ֣ן מֹשֶׁ֔ה אֵ֛ת כָּל־אֲשֶׁר־ה֥וּא עֹשֶׂ֖ה לָעָ֑ם וַיֹּ֗אמֶר מָֽה־הַדָּבָ֤ר הַזֶּה֙ אֲשֶׁ֨ר אַתָּ֤ה עֹשֶׂה֙ לָעָ֔ם מַדּ֗וּעַ אַתָּ֤ה יוֹשֵׁב֙ לְבַדֶּ֔ךָ וְכָל־הָעָ֛ם נִצָּ֥ב עָלֶ֖יךָ מִן־בֹּ֥קֶר עַד־עָֽרֶב׃ טו וַיֹּ֥אמֶר מֹשֶׁ֖ה לְחֹתְנ֑וֹ כִּֽי־יָבֹ֥א אֵלַ֛י הָעָ֖ם לִדְרֹ֥שׁ אֱלֹהִֽים׃ טז כִּֽי־יִהְיֶ֨ה לָהֶ֤ם דָּבָר֙ בָּ֣א אֵלַ֔י וְשָׁ֣פַטְתִּ֔י בֵּ֥ין אִ֖ישׁ וּבֵ֣ין רֵעֵ֑הוּ וְהוֹדַעְתִּ֛י אֶת־חֻקֵּ֥י הָאֱלֹהִ֖ים וְאֶת־תּוֹרֹתָֽיו׃ יז וַיֹּ֛אמֶר חֹתֵ֥ן מֹשֶׁ֖ה אֵלָ֑יו לֹא־טוֹב֙ הַדָּבָ֔ר אֲשֶׁ֥ר אַתָּ֖ה עֹשֶֽׂה׃ יח נָבֹ֣ל תִּבֹּ֔ל גַּם־אַתָּ֕ה גַּם־הָעָ֥ם הַזֶּ֖ה אֲשֶׁ֣ר עִמָּ֑ךְ כִּֽי־כָבֵ֤ד מִמְּךָ֙ הַדָּבָ֔ר לֹא־תוּכַ֥ל עֲשֹׂ֖הוּ לְבַדֶּֽךָ׃ יט עַתָּ֞ה שְׁמַ֤ע

הוּא שֶׁיָּצָא לִקְרָאתוֹ וְגֵרַס לוֹ אֵת כָּל הַכָּבוֹד? אֶלָּא שֶׁהָיָה עוֹמֵד וּמְשַׁמֵּשׁ לִפְנֵיהֶם: **לִפְנֵי הָאֱלֹהִים.** מִכָּאן שֶׁהַנֶּהֱנֶה מִסְּעוּדָה שֶׁתַּלְמִידֵי חֲכָמִים מְסֻבִּין בָּהּ כְּאִלּוּ נֶהֱנֶה מִזִּיו הַשְּׁכִינָה:

יג **וַיְהִי מִמָּחֳרָת.** מוֹצָאֵי יוֹם הַכִּפּוּרִים הָיָה, כָּךְ שָׁנִינוּ בְּסִפְרֵי (ראה מכילתא יתרו, עמלק ח). וּמַהוּ "מִמָּחֳרָת"? לְמָחֳרַת רִדְתּוֹ מִן הָהָר. וְעַל כָּרְחֲךָ אִי אֶפְשָׁר לוֹמַר אֶלָּא מִמָּחֳרַת יוֹם הַכִּפּוּרִים, שֶׁהֲרֵי קֹדֶם מַתַּן תּוֹרָה אִי אֶפְשָׁר לוֹמַר "וְהוֹדַעְתִּי אֶת חֻקֵּי" וְגוֹ׳ (להלן פסוק טז), וּמִשֶּׁנִּתְּנָה תּוֹרָה עַד יוֹם הַכִּפּוּרִים לֹא יָשַׁב מֹשֶׁה לִשְׁפֹּט אֶת הָעָם, שֶׁהֲרֵי בְּשִׁבְעָה עָשָׂר בְּתַמּוּז יָרַד וְשִׁבֵּר אֶת הַלּוּחוֹת, וּלְמָחֳרָת עָלָה בְּהַשְׁכָּמָה וְשָׁהָה שְׁמוֹנִים יוֹם וְיָרַד בְּיוֹם הַכִּפּוּרִים. וְאֵין פָּרָשָׁה זוֹ כְּתוּבָה כְּסֵדֶר, שֶׁלֹּא נֶאֱמַר "וַיְהִי מִמָּחֳרָת" עַד שָׁנָה שְׁנִיָּה. אַף לְדִבְרֵי הָאוֹמֵר יִתְרוֹ קֹדֶם מַתַּן תּוֹרָה בָּא, שִׁלּוּחוֹ אֶל אַרְצוֹ לֹא הָיָה אֶלָּא עַד שָׁנָה שְׁנִיָּה, שֶׁהֲרֵי נֶאֱמַר כָּאן: "וַיְשַׁלַּח מֹשֶׁה אֶת חֹתְנוֹ" (להלן פסוק כז), וּמָצִינוּ בְּמַסַּע הַדְּגָלִים שֶׁאָמַר לוֹ מֹשֶׁה: "נֹסְעִים אֲנַחְנוּ אֶל הַמָּקוֹם וְגוֹ׳ אַל נָא תַּעֲזֹב אֹתָנוּ" (במדבר י, כט-לא), וְאִם זֶה קֹדֶם מַתַּן תּוֹרָה מִשֶּׁשִּׁלְּחוֹ, הֵיכָן מָצִינוּ שֶׁחָזַר? וְאִם תֹּאמַר, שָׁם לֹא נֶאֱמַר יִתְרוֹ אֶלָּא חוֹבָב, וּבְנוֹ שֶׁל יִתְרוֹ הָיָה – הוּא חוֹבָב

הוּא יִתְרוֹ, שֶׁהֲרֵי כָּתוּב: "מִבְּנֵי חֹבָב חֹתֵן מֹשֶׁה" (שופטים ד, יא): **וַיֵּשֶׁב מֹשֶׁה... וַיַּעֲמֹד הָעָם.** יוֹשֵׁב כְּמֶלֶךְ וְכֻלָּן עוֹמְדִים, וְהֻקְשָׁה הַדָּבָר לְיִתְרוֹ שֶׁהָיָה מְזַלְזֵל בִּכְבוֹדָן שֶׁל יִשְׂרָאֵל וְהוֹכִיחוֹ עַל כָּךְ, שֶׁנֶּאֱמַר: "מַדּוּעַ אַתָּה יוֹשֵׁב לְבַדֶּךָ" וְכֻלָּם נִצָּבִים: **מִן הַבֹּקֶר עַד הָעָרֶב.** אֶפְשָׁר לוֹמַר כֵּן?! אֶלָּא כָּל דַּיָּן שֶׁדָּן דִּין אֱמֶת לַאֲמִתּוֹ אֲפִלּוּ שָׁעָה אַחַת מַעֲלֶה עָלָיו הַכָּתוּב כְּאִלּוּ עוֹסֵק בַּתּוֹרָה כָּל הַיּוֹם, וּכְאִלּוּ נַעֲשָׂה שֻׁתָּף לְהַקָּדוֹשׁ בָּרוּךְ הוּא בְּמַעֲשֵׂה בְרֵאשִׁית שֶׁנֶּאֱמַר בּוֹ: "וַיְהִי עֶרֶב וַיְהִי בֹקֶר יוֹם אֶחָד" (בראשית א, ה):

טו **כִּי יָבֹא.** כִּי בָא, לְשׁוֹן הֹוֶה, "לְמִתְבַּע אוּלְפָן", לִשְׁאֹל תַּלְמוּד מִפִּי הַגְּבוּרָה:

טז **כִּי יִהְיֶה לָהֶם דָּבָר.** מִי שֶׁיִּהְיֶה לוֹ דָּבָר בָּא אֵלַי:

יז **וַיֹּאמֶר חֹתֵן מֹשֶׁה.** דֶּרֶךְ כָּבוֹד קוֹרְאֵהוּ הַכָּתוּב, חוֹתְנוֹ שֶׁל מֶלֶךְ:

יח **נָבֹל תִּבֹּל.** כְּתַרְגּוּמוֹ. וּלְשׁוֹנוֹ לְשׁוֹן כְּמִישָׁה, פלישטר"א בְּלַעַז, כְּמוֹ: "וְהֶעָלֶה נָבֵל" (ירמיה ח, יג), "כִּנְבֹל עָלֶה מִגֶּפֶן" (ישעיה לד, ד), שֶׁהוּא כָּמוּשׁ עַל יְדֵי חַמָּה וְעַל יְדֵי קֶרַח וְכֹחוֹ תָּשׁ וְנִלְאֶה: **גַּם אַתָּה.** לְרַבּוֹת אַהֲרֹן וְחוּר וְשִׁבְעִים זְקֵנִים: **כִּי כָבֵד מִמְּךָ.** כָּבְדּוֹ רַב יוֹתֵר מִכֹּחֲךָ:

יט **אִיעָצְךָ וִיהִי אֱלֹהִים עִמָּךְ.** בָּעֵצָה, אָמַר לוֹ: צֵא

בְּקֹלִי אִיעָצְךָ וִיהִי אֱלֹהִים עִמָּךְ הֱיֵה אַתָּה לָעָם מוּל הָאֱלֹהִים
ב וְהֵבֵאתָ אַתָּה אֶת־הַדְּבָרִים אֶל־הָאֱלֹהִים: וְהִזְהַרְתָּה אֶתְהֶם
אֶת־הַחֻקִּים וְאֶת־הַתּוֹרֹת וְהוֹדַעְתָּ לָהֶם אֶת־הַדֶּרֶךְ יֵלְכוּ בָהּ
כא וְאֶת־הַמַּעֲשֶׂה אֲשֶׁר יַעֲשׂוּן: וְאַתָּה תֶחֱזֶה מִכָּל־הָעָם אַנְשֵׁי־
חַיִל יִרְאֵי אֱלֹהִים אַנְשֵׁי אֱמֶת שֹׂנְאֵי בָצַע וְשַׂמְתָּ עֲלֵהֶם שָׂרֵי
כב אֲלָפִים שָׂרֵי מֵאוֹת שָׂרֵי חֲמִשִּׁים וְשָׂרֵי עֲשָׂרֹת: וְשָׁפְטוּ אֶת־
הָעָם בְּכָל־עֵת וְהָיָה כָּל־הַדָּבָר הַגָּדֹל יָבִיאוּ אֵלֶיךָ וְכָל־הַדָּבָר
הַקָּטֹן יִשְׁפְּטוּ־הֵם וְהָקֵל מֵעָלֶיךָ וְנָשְׂאוּ אִתָּךְ: אִם אֶת־הַדָּבָר
כג הַזֶּה תַּעֲשֶׂה וְצִוְּךָ אֱלֹהִים וְיָכָלְתָּ עֲמֹד וְגַם כָּל־הָעָם הַזֶּה עַל־
כד מְקֹמוֹ יָבֹא בְשָׁלוֹם: וַיִּשְׁמַע מֹשֶׁה לְקוֹל חֹתְנוֹ וַיַּעַשׂ כֹּל אֲשֶׁר שלישי
כה אָמָר: וַיִּבְחַר מֹשֶׁה אַנְשֵׁי־חַיִל מִכָּל־יִשְׂרָאֵל וַיִּתֵּן אֹתָם רָאשִׁים
עַל־הָעָם שָׂרֵי אֲלָפִים שָׂרֵי מֵאוֹת שָׂרֵי חֲמִשִּׁים וְשָׂרֵי עֲשָׂרֹת:
כו וְשָׁפְטוּ אֶת־הָעָם בְּכָל־עֵת אֶת־הַדָּבָר הַקָּשֶׁה יְבִיאוּן אֶל־מֹשֶׁה
כז וְכָל־הַדָּבָר הַקָּטֹן יִשְׁפּוּטוּ הֵם: וַיְשַׁלַּח מֹשֶׁה אֶת־חֹתְנוֹ וַיֵּלֶךְ
לוֹ אֶל־אַרְצוֹ:

הַמֶּלֶךְ בַּגְּבוּרָה. הֱיֵה אַתָּה לָעָם מוּל הָאֱלֹהִים. שָׁלִיחַ
וּמֵלִיץ בֵּינוֹתָם לַמָּקוֹם וְשׁוֹאֵל מִשְׁפָּטִים מֵאִתּוֹ: אֶת
הַדְּבָרִים. דִּבְרֵי רִיבוֹתָם:
כא | וְאַתָּה תֶחֱזֶה. בְּרוּחַ הַקֹּדֶשׁ שֶׁעָלֶיךָ: אַנְשֵׁי חַיִל.
עֲשִׁירִים, שֶׁאֵין צְרִיכִין לְהַחֲנִיף וּלְהַכִּיר פָּנִים: אַנְשֵׁי
אֱמֶת. אֵלּוּ בַּעֲלֵי הַבְטָחָה שֶׁהֵם כְּדַאי לִסְמֹךְ עַל
דִּבְרֵיהֶם, שֶׁעַל יְדֵי כָּךְ יִהְיוּ דִּבְרֵיהֶם נִשְׁמָעִין: שֹׂנְאֵי
בָצַע. שֶׁשּׂוֹנְאִים אֶת מָמוֹנָם בַּדִּין, כְּהַהִיא דְּאָמְרִינַן:
כָּל דַּיָּן דְּמַפְּקִין מָמוֹנָא מִנֵּהּ בְּדִינָא לָאו דַּיָּנָא
הוּא: שָׂרֵי אֲלָפִים. הֵם הָיוּ שֵׁם מֵאוֹת שָׂרִים לְשֵׁשׁ
מֵאוֹת אֶלֶף: שָׂרֵי מֵאוֹת. שֵׁשֶׁת אֲלָפִים הָיוּ: שָׂרֵי
חֲמִשִּׁים. שְׁנֵים עָשָׂר אֶלֶף: וְשָׂרֵי עֲשָׂרֹת. שִׁשִּׁים אֶלֶף:
כב | וְשָׁפְטוּ. "וִידוּנוּן", לְשׁוֹן צִוּוּי: וְהָקֵל מֵעָלֶיךָ. דָּבָר

זֶה לְהָקֵל מֵעָלֶיךָ. "וְהָקֵל" כְּמוֹ: "וְהַכְבֵּד אֶת לִבּוֹ"
(לעיל ח, יח), "וְהַכּוֹת אֶת מוֹאָב" (מלכים ב' ג, כד), לְשׁוֹן הוֹוֶה:
כג | וְצִוְּךָ אֱלֹהִים וְיָכָלְתָּ עֲמֹד. הַמֶּלֶךְ בַּגְּבוּרָה, אִם
יְצַוְּךָ מִצְוָה חוֹתָם לַעֲשׂוֹת כֵּן - תּוּכַל לַעֲמֹד, וְאִם יְעַכֵּב
עַל יָדְךָ - לֹא תּוּכַל לַעֲמֹד: וְגַם כָּל הָעָם הַזֶּה. אַהֲרֹן
נָדָב וַאֲבִיהוּא וְשִׁבְעִים זְקֵנִים הַנִּלְוִים עַתָּה עִמָּךְ:
כו | וְשָׁפְטוּ. "וְדָיְנִין יָת עַמָּא": יְבִיאוּן. "מַיְתָן":
יִשְׁפּוּטוּ הֵם. כְּמוֹ יִשְׁפְּטוּ. וְכֵן: "לֹא תַעֲבוּרִי" (רות ב, ח)
כְּמוֹ לֹא תַעֲבֹרִי. וְתַרְגּוּמוֹ: "דָּיְנִין אִנּוּן". מִקְרָאוֹת
הָעֶלְיוֹנִים (לעיל פסוק כב) הָיוּ לְשׁוֹן צִוּוּי, לְכָךְ מְתַרְגְּמִין:
וִידוּנוּן, יַיְתוּן, יְדוּעוֹן, וּמִקְרָאוֹת הַלָּלוּ לְשׁוֹן עֲשִׂיָּה:
כז | וַיֵּלֶךְ לוֹ אֶל אַרְצוֹ. לְגַיֵּר בְּנֵי מִשְׁפַּחְתּוֹ:

פרק יט

רביעי א בַּחֹדֶשׁ הַשְּׁלִישִׁי לְצֵאת בְּנֵי־יִשְׂרָאֵל מֵאֶרֶץ מִצְרָיִם בַּיּוֹם הַזֶּה בָּאוּ מִדְבַּר סִינָי: ב וַיִּסְעוּ מֵרְפִידִים וַיָּבֹאוּ מִדְבַּר סִינַי וַיַּחֲנוּ בַּמִּדְבָּר וַיִּחַן־שָׁם יִשְׂרָאֵל נֶגֶד הָהָר: ג וּמֹשֶׁה עָלָה אֶל־הָאֱלֹהִים וַיִּקְרָא אֵלָיו יְהֹוָה מִן־הָהָר לֵאמֹר כֹּה תֹאמַר לְבֵית יַעֲקֹב וְתַגֵּיד לִבְנֵי יִשְׂרָאֵל: ד אַתֶּם רְאִיתֶם אֲשֶׁר עָשִׂיתִי לְמִצְרָיִם וָאֶשָּׂא אֶתְכֶם עַל־כַּנְפֵי נְשָׁרִים וָאָבִא אֶתְכֶם אֵלָי: ה וְעַתָּה אִם־שָׁמוֹעַ תִּשְׁמְעוּ בְּקֹלִי וּשְׁמַרְתֶּם אֶת־בְּרִיתִי וִהְיִיתֶם לִי סְגֻלָּה מִכָּל־הָעַמִּים כִּי־לִי כָּל־הָאָרֶץ: ו וְאַתֶּם תִּהְיוּ־לִי מַמְלֶכֶת כֹּהֲנִים וְגוֹי קָדוֹשׁ אֵלֶּה הַדְּבָרִים אֲשֶׁר תְּדַבֵּר אֶל־בְּנֵי יִשְׂרָאֵל:

פרק יט

א בַּיּוֹם הַזֶּה. בְּרֹאשׁ חֹדֶשׁ. לֹא הָיָה צָרִיךְ לִכְתֹּב אֶלָּא 'בַּיּוֹם הַהוּא', מַהוּ 'בַּיּוֹם הַזֶּה'? שֶׁיִּהְיוּ דִּבְרֵי תוֹרָה חֲדָשִׁים עָלֶיךָ כְּאִלּוּ הַיּוֹם נִתְּנוּ:

ב וַיִּסְעוּ מֵרְפִידִים. מַה תַּלְמוּד לוֹמַר לַחֲזֹר וּלְפָרֵשׁ מֵהֵיכָן נָסְעוּ? וַהֲלֹא כְּבָר כָּתַב שֶׁבִּרְפִידִים הָיוּ חוֹנִים (לעיל יז, א), בְּיָדוּעַ שֶׁמִּשָּׁם נָסְעוּ! אֶלָּא לְהַקִּישׁ נְסִיעָתָן מֵרְפִידִים לְבִיאָתָן לְמִדְבַּר סִינַי, מַה בִּיאָתָן לְמִדְבַּר סִינַי בִּתְשׁוּבָה, אַף נְסִיעָתָן מֵרְפִידִים בִּתְשׁוּבָה: **וַיִּחַן שָׁם יִשְׂרָאֵל.** כְּאִישׁ אֶחָד בְּלֵב אֶחָד, אֲבָל שְׁאָר כָּל הַחֲנִיּוֹת בְּתַרְעֹמֶת וּבְמַחֲלֹקֶת: **נֶגֶד הָהָר.** לְמִזְרָחוֹ, וְכָל מָקוֹם שֶׁאַתָּה מוֹצֵא 'נֶגֶד' – פָּנִים לַמִּזְרָח:

ג וּמֹשֶׁה עָלָה. בַּיּוֹם הַשֵּׁנִי, וְכָל עֲלִיּוֹתָיו בְּהַשְׁכָּמָה הָיוּ, שֶׁנֶּאֱמַר: "וַיַּשְׁכֵּם מֹשֶׁה בַבֹּקֶר" (להלן לד, ד): **כֹּה תֹאמַר.** בַּלָּשׁוֹן הַזֶּה וְכַסֵּדֶר הַזֶּה: **לְבֵית יַעֲקֹב.** אֵלּוּ הַנָּשִׁים, תֹּאמַר לָהֶן בְּלָשׁוֹן רַכָּה: **וְתַגֵּיד לִבְנֵי יִשְׂרָאֵל.** עֳנָשִׁין וְדִקְדּוּקִין פָּרֵשׁ לַזְּכָרִים, דְּבָרִים הַקָּשִׁין כְּגִידִין:

ד אַתֶּם רְאִיתֶם. וְלֹא מָסֹרֶת הִיא בְּיֶדְכֶם בִּדְבָרִים אֲשֶׁר עָשִׂיתִי בְּמִצְרַיִם, עַל כַּמָּה עֲבֵרוֹת הָיוּ חַיָּבִין לִי קֹדֶם שֶׁנִּזְדַּוְּגוּ לָכֶם, וְלֹא נִפְרַעְתִּי מֵהֶם אֶלָּא עַל יֶדְכֶם: **וָאֶשָּׂא אֶתְכֶם.** זֶה יוֹם שֶׁבָּאוּ יִשְׂרָאֵל לְרַעְמְסֵס, שֶׁהָיוּ יִשְׂרָאֵל מְפֻזָּרִין בְּכָל אֶרֶץ גֹּשֶׁן, וּלְשָׁעָה קַלָּה כְּשֶׁבָּאוּ לִסַּע וְלָצֵאת נִקְבְּצוּ כֻלָּם לְרַעְמְסֵס. וְאוּנְקְלוֹס תִּרְגֵּם "וַאֲסָּח" כְּמוֹ וָאַסִּיעַ אֶתְכֶם: "וְאַטֵּלִית יָתְכוֹן", תִּקֵּן אֶת הַדִּבּוּר דֶּרֶךְ כָּבוֹד לְמַעְלָה: **עַל כַּנְפֵי נְשָׁרִים.** כַּנֶּשֶׁר הַנּוֹשֵׂא גּוֹזָלָיו עַל כְּנָפָיו, שֶׁכָּל שְׁאָר הָעוֹפוֹת נוֹתְנִים אֶת בְּנֵיהֶם בֵּין רַגְלֵיהֶם, לְפִי שֶׁמִּתְיָרְאִין מֵעוֹף אַחֵר שֶׁפּוֹרֵחַ עַל גַּבֵּיהֶם, אֲבָל הַנֶּשֶׁר הַזֶּה אֵינוֹ מִתְיָרֵא אֶלָּא מִן הָאָדָם שֶׁמָּא יִזְרֹק בּוֹ חֵץ, לְפִי שֶׁאֵין עוֹף פּוֹרֵחַ עַל גַּבָּיו, לְכָךְ נוֹתְנוֹ עַל כְּנָפָיו, אוֹמֵר: מוּטָב יִכָּנֵס הַחֵץ בִּי וְלֹא בִבְנִי. אַף אֲנִי עָשִׂיתִי כֵן: "וַיִּסַּע מַלְאַךְ הָאֱלֹהִים וְגוֹ' וַיָּבֹא בֵּין מַחֲנֵה מִצְרַיִם וְגוֹ'" (לעיל יד, יט-כ), וְהָיוּ מִצְרִיִּים זוֹרְקִים חִצִּים וְאַבְנֵי בַּלִּסְטְרָאוֹת וְהֶעָנָן מְקַבְּלָם: **וָאָבִא אֶתְכֶם אֵלָי.** כְּתַרְגּוּמוֹ:

ה וְעַתָּה. אִם עַתָּה תְּקַבְּלוּ עֲלֵיכֶם יֶעֱרַב לָכֶם מִכָּאן וְאֵילָךְ, שֶׁכָּל הַתְחָלוֹת קָשׁוֹת: **וּשְׁמַרְתֶּם אֶת בְּרִיתִי.** שֶׁאֶכְרֹת עִמָּכֶם עַל שְׁמִירַת הַתּוֹרָה: **סְגֻלָּה.** אוֹצָר חָבִיב, כְּמוֹ: "וּסְגֻלַּת מְלָכִים" (קהלת ב, ח), כְּלֵי יְקָר וַאֲבָנִים טוֹבוֹת שֶׁהַמְּלָכִים גּוֹנְזִים אוֹתָם, כָּךְ אַתֶּם תִּהְיוּ לִי סְגֻלָּה מִשְּׁאָר אֻמּוֹת, וְלֹא תֹאמְרוּ, אַתֶּם לְבַדְּכֶם שֶׁלִּי וְאֵין לִי אֲחֵרִים עִמָּכֶם, וּמַה יֵּשׁ לִי עוֹד שֶׁתְּהֵא חִבַּתְכֶם נִכֶּרֶת? – "כִּי לִי כָּל הָאָרֶץ", וְהֵם בְּעֵינַי וּלְפָנַי לִכְלוּם:

ו וְאַתֶּם תִּהְיוּ לִי מַמְלֶכֶת כֹּהֲנִים. שָׂרִים, כְּמָה דְאַתְּ

שמות | פרק יט

חמישי

ז וַיָּבֹא מֹשֶׁה וַיִּקְרָא לְזִקְנֵי הָעָם וַיָּשֶׂם לִפְנֵיהֶם אֵת כָּל־הַדְּבָרִים
הָאֵלֶּה אֲשֶׁר צִוָּהוּ יהוה: ח וַיַּעֲנוּ כָל־הָעָם יַחְדָּו וַיֹּאמְרוּ כֹּל
אֲשֶׁר־דִּבֶּר יהוה נַעֲשֶׂה וַיָּשֶׁב מֹשֶׁה אֶת־דִּבְרֵי הָעָם אֶל־יהוה:
ט וַיֹּאמֶר יהוה אֶל־מֹשֶׁה הִנֵּה אָנֹכִי בָּא אֵלֶיךָ בְּעַב הֶעָנָן בַּעֲבוּר
יִשְׁמַע הָעָם בְּדַבְּרִי עִמָּךְ וְגַם־בְּךָ יַאֲמִינוּ לְעוֹלָם וַיַּגֵּד מֹשֶׁה
אֶת־דִּבְרֵי הָעָם אֶל־יהוה: י וַיֹּאמֶר יהוה אֶל־מֹשֶׁה לֵךְ אֶל־
הָעָם וְקִדַּשְׁתָּם הַיּוֹם וּמָחָר וְכִבְּסוּ שִׂמְלֹתָם: יא וְהָיוּ נְכֹנִים לַיּוֹם
הַשְּׁלִישִׁי כִּי ׀ בַּיּוֹם הַשְּׁלִשִׁי יֵרֵד יהוה לְעֵינֵי כָל־הָעָם עַל־הַר
סִינָי: יב וְהִגְבַּלְתָּ אֶת־הָעָם סָבִיב לֵאמֹר הִשָּׁמְרוּ לָכֶם עֲלוֹת
בָּהָר וּנְגֹעַ בְּקָצֵהוּ כָּל־הַנֹּגֵעַ בָּהָר מוֹת יוּמָת: יג לֹא־תִגַּע בּוֹ יָד
כִּי־סָקוֹל יִסָּקֵל אוֹ־יָרֹה יִיָּרֶה אִם־בְּהֵמָה אִם־אִישׁ לֹא יִחְיֶה
בִּמְשֹׁךְ הַיֹּבֵל הֵמָּה יַעֲלוּ בָהָר: יד וַיֵּרֶד מֹשֶׁה מִן־הָהָר אֶל־הָעָם

אָמַר: "וּבְנֵי דָוִד כֹּהֲנִים הָיוּ" (שמואל ב׳ ח, יח): **אֵלֶּה הַדְּבָרִים.** לֹא פָּחוֹת וְלֹא יוֹתֵר:

ח] **וַיָּשֶׁב מֹשֶׁה אֶת דִּבְרֵי הָעָם וְגוֹ׳.** בְּיוֹם הַמָּחֳרָת שֶׁהוּא שְׁלִישִׁי, שֶׁהֲרֵי בְּהַשְׁכָּמָה עָלָה. וְכִי צָרִיךְ הָיָה מֹשֶׁה לְהָשִׁיב? אֶלָּא בָּא הַכָּתוּב לְלַמֶּדְךָ דֶּרֶךְ אֶרֶץ מִמֹּשֶׁה, שֶׁלֹּא אָמַר: הוֹאִיל וְיוֹדֵעַ מִי שֶׁשְּׁלָחַנִי, אֵינִי צָרִיךְ לְהָשִׁיב:

ט] **בְּעַב הֶעָנָן.** בְּמַעֲבֵה הֶעָנָן, וְזֶהוּ עֲרָפֶל. **וְגַם בְּךָ.** גַּם בַּנְּבִיאִים הַבָּאִים אַחֲרֶיךָ: **וַיַּגֵּד מֹשֶׁה אֶת דִּבְרֵי וְגוֹ׳.** בַּיּוֹם הַמָּחֳרָת שֶׁהוּא רְבִיעִי לַחֹדֶשׁ: **אֶת דִּבְרֵי הָעָם וְגוֹ׳.** תְּשׁוּבָה עַל דָּבָר זֶה שָׁמַעְתִּי מֵהֶם, שֶׁרְצוֹנָם לִשְׁמֹעַ מִמְּךָ, אֵינוֹ דּוֹמֶה הַשּׁוֹמֵעַ מִפִּי שָׁלִיחַ לַשּׁוֹמֵעַ מִפִּי הַמֶּלֶךְ, רְצוֹנֵנוּ לִרְאוֹת אֶת מַלְכֵּנוּ:

י] **וְקִדַּשְׁתָּם.** וְזִמַּנְתָּם. וְזִמַּנְתָּם, שֶׁיִּהְיוּ נְכוֹנִים "הַיּוֹם וּמָחָר":

יא] **וְהָיוּ נְכֹנִים: לַיּוֹם הַשְּׁלִישִׁי.** שֶׁהוּא שִׁשָּׁה בַחֹדֶשׁ, וּבַחֲמִישִׁי בָּנָה מֹשֶׁה אֶת הַמִּזְבֵּחַ תַּחַת הָהָר

וּשְׁתֵּים עֶשְׂרֵה מַצֵּבָה, כָּל הָעִנְיָן הָאָמוּר בְּפָרָשַׁת וְאֵלֶּה הַמִּשְׁפָּטִים (להלן פרק כד), וְאֵין מֻקְדָּם וּמְאֻחָר בַּתּוֹרָה: **לְעֵינֵי כָל הָעָם.** מְלַמֵּד שֶׁלֹּא הָיָה בָּהֶם סוּמָא, שֶׁנִּתְרַפְּאוּ כֻּלָּם:

יב] **וְהִגְבַּלְתָּ.** קְבַע לָהֶם תְּחוּמִין לְסִימָן, שֶׁלֹּא יִקְרְבוּ מִן הַגְּבוּל וָהָלְאָה: **לֵאמֹר.** הַגְּבוּל אוֹמֵר לָהֶם: הִשָּׁמְרוּ מֵעֲלוֹת מִכָּאן וָהָלְאָן, וְאַתָּה הַזְהִירֵם עַל כָּךְ: **וּנְגֹעַ בְּקָצֵהוּ.** אֲפִלּוּ בְּקָצֵהוּ:

יג] **יָרֹה יִיָּרֶה.** מִכָּאן לַנִּסְקָלִין שֶׁהֵם נִדְחִין לְמַטָּה מִבֵּית הַסְּקִילָה, שֶׁהָיְתָה גְבוֹהָה שְׁתֵּי קוֹמוֹת: **יִיָּרֶה.** יֻשְׁלַךְ לְמַטָּה לָאָרֶץ, כְּמוֹ: "יָרָה בַיָּם" (לעיל טו, ד): **בִּמְשֹׁךְ הַיֹּבֵל.** כְּשֶׁיִּמְשֹׁךְ הַיּוֹבֵל קוֹל אָרֹךְ, הוּא סִימָן סִלּוּק שְׁכִינָה וְהַפְסָקַת הַקּוֹל, וְכֵיוָן שֶׁאֶסְתַּלֵּק הֵם רַשָּׁאִין לַעֲלוֹת: **הַיֹּבֵל.** הוּא שׁוֹפָר שֶׁל אַיִל, שֶׁכֵּן בַּעֲרַבְיָא קוֹרִין לְדִכְרָא יוֹבְלָא. וְשׁוֹפָר שֶׁל אֵילוֹ שֶׁל יִצְחָק הָיָה:

יד] **מִן הָהָר אֶל הָעָם.** מְלַמֵּד שֶׁלֹּא הָיָה מֹשֶׁה פוֹנֶה לַעֲסָקָיו, אֶלָּא מִן הָהָר אֶל הָעָם:

וַיְקַדֵּשׁ אֶת־הָעָם וַיְכַבְּסוּ שִׂמְלֹתָם: וַיֹּאמֶר אֶל־הָעָם הֱיוּ נְכֹנִים טו
לִשְׁלֹשֶׁת יָמִים אַל־תִּגְּשׁוּ אֶל־אִשָּׁה: וַיְהִי בַיּוֹם הַשְּׁלִישִׁי בִּהְיֹת טז
הַבֹּקֶר וַיְהִי קֹלֹת וּבְרָקִים וְעָנָן כָּבֵד עַל־הָהָר וְקֹל שֹׁפָר חָזָק
מְאֹד וַיֶּחֱרַד כָּל־הָעָם אֲשֶׁר בַּמַּחֲנֶה: וַיּוֹצֵא מֹשֶׁה אֶת־הָעָם יז
לִקְרַאת הָאֱלֹהִים מִן־הַמַּחֲנֶה וַיִּתְיַצְּבוּ בְּתַחְתִּית הָהָר: וְהַר יח
סִינַי עָשַׁן כֻּלּוֹ מִפְּנֵי אֲשֶׁר יָרַד עָלָיו יְהוָה בָּאֵשׁ וַיַּעַל עֲשָׁנוֹ כְּעֶשֶׁן
הַכִּבְשָׁן וַיֶּחֱרַד כָּל־הָהָר מְאֹד: וַיְהִי קוֹל הַשּׁוֹפָר הוֹלֵךְ וְחָזֵק יט
מְאֹד מֹשֶׁה יְדַבֵּר וְהָאֱלֹהִים יַעֲנֶנּוּ בְקוֹל: וַיֵּרֶד יְהוָה עַל־הַר סִינַי כ
אֶל־רֹאשׁ הָהָר וַיִּקְרָא יְהוָה לְמֹשֶׁה אֶל־רֹאשׁ הָהָר וַיַּעַל מֹשֶׁה:

ששי

טו הֱיוּ נְכֹנִים לִשְׁלֹשֶׁת יָמִים. לְסוֹף שְׁלֹשֶׁת יָמִים, הוּא יוֹם רְבִיעִי, שֶׁהוֹסִיף מֹשֶׁה יוֹם אֶחָד מִדַּעְתּוֹ, כְּדִבְרֵי רַבִּי יוֹסֵי. וּלְדִבְרֵי הָאוֹמֵר בְּשִׁשָּׁה בַחֹדֶשׁ נִתְּנוּ עֲשֶׂרֶת הַדִּבְּרוֹת, לֹא הוֹסִיף מֹשֶׁה כְּלוּם, וְ"לִשְׁלֹשֶׁת יָמִים" כְּמוֹ "לַיּוֹם הַשְּׁלִישִׁי": אַל תִּגְּשׁוּ אֶל אִשָּׁה. כָּל שְׁלֹשֶׁת יָמִים הַלָּלוּ, כְּדֵי שֶׁיִּהְיוּ הַנָּשִׁים טוֹבְלוֹת לַיּוֹם הַשְּׁלִישִׁי וְיִהְיוּ טְהוֹרוֹת לְקַבֵּל תּוֹרָה, שֶׁאִם יְשַׁמְּשׁוּ תּוֹךְ שְׁלֹשָׁה שֶׁמָּא תִּפְלֹט הָאִשָּׁה שִׁכְבַת זֶרַע לְאַחַר טְבִילָתָהּ וְתַחֲזוֹר וְתִטַּמֵּא, אֲבָל מִשֶּׁשָּׁהֲתָה שְׁלֹשָׁה יָמִים כְּבָר הַזֶּרַע מַסְרִיחַ וְאֵינוֹ רָאוּי לְהַזְרִיעַ, וְטָהוֹר מִלְּטַמֵּא אֶת הַפּוֹלֶטֶת:

טז בִּהְיֹת הַבֹּקֶר. מְלַמֵּד שֶׁהִקְדִּים עַל יָדָם, מַה שֶּׁאֵין דֶּרֶךְ בָּשָׂר וָדָם לַעֲשׂוֹת כֵּן שֶׁיְּהֵא הָרַב מַמְתִּין לַתַּלְמִיד. וְכֵן מָצִינוּ בִּיחֶזְקֵאל: "קוּם צֵא אֶל הַבִּקְעָה... וָאָקוּם וָאֵצֵא אֶל הַבִּקְעָה וְהִנֵּה שָׁם כְּבוֹד ה' עֹמֵד" (יחזקאל ג, כב-כג):

יז לִקְרַאת הָאֱלֹהִים. מַגִּיד שֶׁהַשְּׁכִינָה יָצְתָה לִקְרָאתָם כְּחָתָן הַיּוֹצֵא לִקְרַאת כַּלָּה, וְזֶהוּ שֶׁנֶּאֱמַר: "ה' מִסִּינַי בָּא" (דברים לג, ב), וְלֹא נֶאֱמַר: "לְסִינַי בָּא": בְּתַחְתִּית הָהָר. לְפִי פְשׁוּטוֹ בְּרַגְלֵי הָהָר. וּמִדְרָשׁוֹ, שֶׁנִּתְלַשׁ הָהָר מִמְּקוֹמוֹ וְנִכְפָּה עֲלֵיהֶם כְּגִיגִית:

יח עָשַׁן כֻּלּוֹ. אֵין "עָשַׁן" זֶה שֵׁם דָּבָר, שֶׁהֲרֵי נָקוּד הַשִּׁי"ן פַּתָּח, אֶלָּא לְשׁוֹן פָּעַל, כְּמוֹ אָמַר, שָׁמַר, שָׁמַע, לְכָךְ תַּרְגּוּמוֹ: "תָּנַן כֻּלֵּיהּ" וְלֹא תִרְגֵּם "תְּנָנָא". וְכָל עָשָׁן שֶׁבַּמִּקְרָא נְקוּדִים קָמַ"ץ, מִפְּנֵי שֶׁהֵם שֵׁם דָּבָר: הַכִּבְשָׁן. שֶׁל סִיד. יָכוֹל כְּכִבְשָׁן זֶה וְלֹא יוֹתֵר? תַּלְמוּד לוֹמַר: "בֹּעֵר בָּאֵשׁ עַד לֵב הַשָּׁמַיִם" (דברים ד, יא). וּמַה תַּלְמוּד לוֹמַר: "כִּבְשָׁן"? לְשַׂבֵּר אֶת הָאֹזֶן מַה שֶּׁיְּכוֹלָה לִשְׁמֹעַ, נוֹתֵן לַבְּרִיּוֹת סִימָן הַנִּכָּר לָהֶם. כַּיּוֹצֵא בוֹ: "כְּאַרְיֵה יִשְׁאָג" (הושע יא, י), וְכִי מִי נָתַן כֹּחַ בָּאֲרִי אֶלָּא הוּא, וְהַכָּתוּב מוֹשְׁלוֹ כָּאֲרִי? אֶלָּא אָנוּ מְכַנִּין וּמְדַמִּין אוֹתוֹ לִבְרִיּוֹתָיו כְּדֵי לְשַׂבֵּר אֶת הָאֹזֶן מַה שֶּׁיְּכוֹלָה לִשְׁמֹעַ. כַּיּוֹצֵא בוֹ: "וְקוֹלוֹ כְּקוֹל מַיִם רַבִּים" (יחזקאל מג, ב), וְכִי מִי נָתַן קוֹל לַמַּיִם אֶלָּא הוּא, וְאַתָּה מְכַנֶּה אוֹתוֹ לְדַמּוֹתוֹ לִבְרִיּוֹתָיו, כְּדֵי לְשַׂבֵּר אֶת הָאֹזֶן:

יט הוֹלֵךְ וְחָזֵק מְאֹד. מִנְהַג הֶדְיוֹט, כָּל זְמַן שֶׁהוּא מַאֲרִיךְ לִתְקֹעַ קוֹלוֹ מַחֲלִישׁ וְכוֹשֵׁל, אֲבָל כָּאן "הוֹלֵךְ וְחָזֵק מְאֹד". וְלָמָּה כָּךְ מִתְּחִלָּה? לְשַׂבֵּר אָזְנֵיהֶם מַה שֶּׁיְּכוֹלִין לִשְׁמֹעַ: מֹשֶׁה יְדַבֵּר. כְּשֶׁהָיָה מֹשֶׁה מְדַבֵּר וּמַשְׁמִיעַ הַדִּבְּרוֹת לְיִשְׂרָאֵל, שֶׁהֲרֵי לֹא שָׁמְעוּ מִפִּי הַגְּבוּרָה אֶלָּא "אָנֹכִי" וְ"לֹא יִהְיֶה לְךָ", וְהַקָּדוֹשׁ בָּרוּךְ הוּא מַסִּיעוֹ לָתֵת בּוֹ כֹּחַ לִהְיוֹת קוֹלוֹ מַגְבִּיר וְנִשְׁמָע: יַעֲנֶנּוּ בְקוֹל. עַל דְּבַר הַקּוֹל, כְּמוֹ: "אֲשֶׁר יַעֲנֶה בָאֵשׁ" (מלכים א יח, כד), עַל דְּבַר הָאֵשׁ לְהוֹרִידוֹ:

כ וַיֵּרֶד ה' עַל הַר סִינַי. יָכוֹל יָרַד עָלָיו מַמָּשׁ?

שמות | פרק יט

כא וַיֹּאמֶר יְהוָה אֶל־מֹשֶׁה רֵד הָעֵד בָּעָם פֶּן־יֶהֶרְסוּ אֶל־יְהוָה
כב לִרְאוֹת וְנָפַל מִמֶּנּוּ רָב: וְגַם הַכֹּהֲנִים הַנִּגָּשִׁים אֶל־יְהוָה יִתְקַדָּשׁוּ
כג פֶּן־יִפְרֹץ בָּהֶם יְהוָה: וַיֹּאמֶר מֹשֶׁה אֶל־יְהוָה לֹא־יוּכַל הָעָם
לַעֲלֹת אֶל־הַר סִינָי כִּי־אַתָּה הַעֵדֹתָה בָּנוּ לֵאמֹר הַגְבֵּל אֶת־
כד הָהָר וְקִדַּשְׁתּוֹ: וַיֹּאמֶר אֵלָיו יְהוָה לֶךְ־רֵד וְעָלִיתָ אַתָּה וְאַהֲרֹן
עִמָּךְ וְהַכֹּהֲנִים וְהָעָם אַל־יֶהֶרְסוּ לַעֲלֹת אֶל־יְהוָה פֶּן־יִפְרָץ־
כה בָּם: וַיֵּרֶד מֹשֶׁה אֶל־הָעָם וַיֹּאמֶר אֲלֵהֶם: וַיְדַבֵּר
ב אֱלֹהִים אֵת כָּל־הַדְּבָרִים הָאֵלֶּה לֵאמֹר: אָנֹכִי
יְהוָה אֱלֹהֶיךָ אֲשֶׁר הוֹצֵאתִיךָ מֵאֶרֶץ מִצְרַיִם מִבֵּית עֲבָדִים:

תַּלְמוּד לוֹמַר: "כִּי מִן הַשָּׁמַיִם דִּבַּרְתִּי עִמָּכֶם" (להלן כ, יט)! מְלַמֵּד שֶׁהִרְכִּין שָׁמַיִם הַתַּחְתּוֹנִים וְהָעֶלְיוֹנִים וְהִצִּיעָן עַל גַּבֵּי הָהָר כְּמַצָּע עַל הַמִּטָּה, וַיֵּרֶד כִּסֵּא הַכָּבוֹד עֲלֵיהֶם.

כא | הָעֵד בָּעָם. הַתְרֵה בָּהֶם שֶׁלֹּא לַעֲלוֹת בָּהָר. **פֶּן יֶהֶרְסוּ וְגוֹ׳.** שֶׁלֹּא יֶהֶרְסוּ אֶת מַצָּבָם עַל יְדֵי שֶׁתַּאֲוָתָם "אֶל ה׳ לִרְאוֹת" וְיִקְרְבוּ לְצַד הָהָר: **וְנָפַל מִמֶּנּוּ רָב.** כָּל מַה שֶּׁיִּפֹּל מֵהֶם, וַאֲפִלּוּ הוּא יְחִידִי, חָשׁוּב לְפָנַי רָב: **פֶּן יֶהֶרְסוּ.** כָּל הֲרִיסָה מַפְרֶדֶת אֲסֵפַת הַבִּנְיָן, אַף הַנִּפְרָדִין מִמַּצַּב אֲנָשִׁים הוֹרְסִים אֶת הַמַּצָּב:

כב | וְגַם הַכֹּהֲנִים. אַף הַבְּכוֹרוֹת שֶׁהָעֲבוֹדָה בָּהֶם: **הַנִּגָּשִׁים אֶל ה׳.** לְהַקְרִיב קָרְבָּנוֹת, אַף הֵם אַל יִסְמְכוּ עַל חֲשִׁיבוּתָם לַעֲלוֹת: **יִתְקַדָּשׁוּ.** יְהִיוּ מְזֻמָּנִים לְהִתְיַצֵּב עַל עָמְדָן: **פֶּן יִפְרֹץ.** לְשׁוֹן פִּרְצָה, יַהֲרֹג בָּהֶם וְיַעֲשֶׂה בָהֶם פְּרָצוֹת:

כג | לֹא יוּכַל הָעָם. אֵינִי צָרִיךְ לְהָעִיד בָּהֶם, שֶׁהֲרֵי מֻתְרִים וְעוֹמְדִים הֵם הַיּוֹם שְׁלֹשֶׁת יָמִים, וְלֹא יוּכְלוּ לַעֲלוֹת, שֶׁאֵין לָהֶם רְשׁוּת:

כד | לֶךְ רֵד. וְהָעֵד בָּהֶם שֵׁנִית, שֶׁמְּזָרְזִין אֶת הָאָדָם קֹדֶם מַעֲשֶׂה וְחוֹזְרִין וּמְזָרְזִין אוֹתוֹ בִּשְׁעַת מַעֲשֶׂה: **וְעָלִיתָ אַתָּה וְאַהֲרֹן עִמָּךְ וְהַכֹּהֲנִים.** יָכוֹל אַף הֵם עִמְּךָ? תַּלְמוּד לוֹמַר: "וְעָלִיתָ אַתָּה". אֱמֹר מֵעַתָּה:

אַתָּה מְחִצָּה לְעַצְמְךָ, וְאַהֲרֹן מְחִצָּה לְעַצְמוֹ, וְהַכֹּהֲנִים מְחִצָּה לְעַצְמָם, מֹשֶׁה נִגַּשׁ יוֹתֵר מֵאַהֲרֹן וְאַהֲרֹן יוֹתֵר מִן הַכֹּהֲנִים, וְהָעָם כָּל עִקָּר "אַל יֶהֶרְסוּ" אֶת מַצָּבָם "לַעֲלֹת אֶל ה׳": **פֶּן יִפְרָץ בָּם.** אַף עַל פִּי שֶׁהוּא נָקוּד חֲטַף קָמָץ אֵינוֹ זָז מִגְּזֵרָתוֹ, כָּךְ דֶּרֶךְ כָּל תֵּבָה שֶׁנְּקֻדָּתָהּ מְלָאֻפוּם, כְּשֶׁהִיא סְמוּכָה בְּמַקָּף מִשְׁתַּנֶּה הַנִּקּוּד לַחֲטַף קָמָץ:

כה | וַיֹּאמֶר אֲלֵהֶם. הַתְרָאָה זוֹ:

פרק כ

א | וַיְדַבֵּר אֱלֹהִים. אֵין "אֱלֹהִים" אֶלָּא דַּיָּן, לְפִי שֶׁיֵּשׁ פָּרָשִׁיּוֹת בַּתּוֹרָה שֶׁאִם עֲשָׂאָן אָדָם מְקַבֵּל שָׂכָר וְאִם לָאו אֵינוֹ מְקַבֵּל עֲלֵיהֶם פֻּרְעָנוּת, יָכוֹל אַף עֲשֶׂרֶת הַדִּבְּרוֹת כֵּן? תַּלְמוּד לוֹמַר: "וַיְדַבֵּר אֱלֹהִים", דַּיָּן לִפָּרַע: **אֵת כָּל הַדְּבָרִים הָאֵלֶּה.** מְלַמֵּד שֶׁאָמַר הַקָּדוֹשׁ בָּרוּךְ הוּא עֲשֶׂרֶת הַדִּבְּרוֹת בְּדִבּוּר אֶחָד, מַה שֶּׁאִי אֶפְשָׁר לְאָדָם לוֹמַר כֵּן. אִם כֵּן מַה תַּלְמוּד לוֹמַר עוֹד "אָנֹכִי" וְ"לֹא יִהְיֶה לְךָ"? שֶׁחָזַר וּפֵרַשׁ עַל כָּל דִּבּוּר וְדִבּוּר בִּפְנֵי עַצְמוֹ: **לֵאמֹר.** מְלַמֵּד שֶׁהָיוּ עוֹנִין עַל הֵן – הֵן, וְעַל לָאו – לָאו:

ב | אֲשֶׁר הוֹצֵאתִיךָ מֵאֶרֶץ מִצְרַיִם. כְּדַאי הִיא הַהוֹצָאָה שֶׁתִּהְיוּ מְשֻׁעְבָּדִים לִי. דָּבָר אַחֵר, לְפִי שֶׁנִּגְלָה בַּיָּם כִּגְבּוֹר מִלְחָמָה וְנִגְלָה כָּאן כְּזָקֵן מָלֵא רַחֲמִים, שֶׁנֶּאֱמַר: "וְתַחַת רַגְלָיו כְּמַעֲשֵׂה לִבְנַת הַסַּפִּיר" (להלן כד,

פרק כ | שמות | יתרו

ג לֹא־יִהְיֶה לְךָ אֱלֹהִים אֲחֵרִים עַל־פָּנָי: לֹא־תַעֲשֶׂה לְךָ פֶסֶל ד
וְכָל־תְּמוּנָה אֲשֶׁר בַּשָּׁמַיִם מִמַּעַל וַאֲשֶׁר בָּאָרֶץ מִתַּחַת וַאֲשֶׁר
בַּמַּיִם מִתַּחַת לָאָרֶץ: לֹא־תִשְׁתַּחֲוֶה לָהֶם וְלֹא תָעָבְדֵם כִּי אָנֹכִי ה
יהוה אֱלֹהֶיךָ אֵל קַנָּא פֹּקֵד עֲוֹן אָבֹת עַל־בָּנִים עַל־שִׁלֵּשִׁים
וְעַל־רִבֵּעִים לְשֹׂנְאָי: וְעֹשֶׂה חֶסֶד לַאֲלָפִים לְאֹהֲבַי וּלְשֹׁמְרֵי ו
מִצְוֹתָי: לֹא תִשָּׂא אֶת־שֵׁם־יהוה אֱלֹהֶיךָ לַשָּׁוְא כִּי ז
לֹא יְנַקֶּה יהוה אֵת אֲשֶׁר־יִשָּׂא אֶת־שְׁמוֹ לַשָּׁוְא:
זָכוֹר אֶת־יוֹם הַשַּׁבָּת לְקַדְּשׁוֹ: שֵׁשֶׁת יָמִים תַּעֲבֹד וְעָשִׂיתָ כָּל־ ח

ג זוֹ הָיְתָה לְפָנַי בִּשְׁעַת הַשִּׁעְבּוּד, "וּכְעַנֶּנֶךְ הַשָּׁמַיִם" (שם) מִשֶּׁנְּגָאֲלוּ, הוֹחִיל וְאָנוּ מִשְׁתַּנָּה בְּמֶרְחָוֹת, אַל תֹּאמְרוּ שְׁתֵּי רָשׁוּיוֹת הֵן, חָלִילָה הוּא אֲשֶׁר הוֹצִיאֲתִיךָ מִמִּצְרַיִם וְעַל הַיָּם. דָּבָר אַחֵר, לְפִי שֶׁהָיוּ שׁוֹמְעִין קוֹלוֹת הַרְבֵּה, שֶׁנֶּאֱמַר "אֶת הַקּוֹלֹת" (להלן פסוק טו), קוֹלוֹת בָּאִין מֵאַרְבַּע רוּחוֹת וּמִן הַשָּׁמַיִם וּמִן הָאָרֶץ, אַל תֹּאמְרוּ רָשׁוּיוֹת הַרְבֵּה הֵן: וְלָמָּה אָמַר לְשׁוֹן יָחִיד, "אֱלֹהֶיךָ"? לִתֵּן פִּתְחוֹן פֶּה לְמֹשֶׁה לְלַמֵּד סָנֵגוֹרְיָה בְּמַעֲשֵׂה הָעֵגֶל, וְזֶה הוּא שֶׁאָמַר: "לָמָה ה' יֶחֱרֶה אַפְּךָ בְּעַמֶּךָ" (להלן לב, יא), לֹא לָהֶם צִוִּיתָ "לֹא יִהְיֶה לָכֶם אֱלֹהִים אֲחֵרִים", אֶלָּא לִי לְבַדִּי: מִבֵּית עֲבָדִים. מִבֵּית פַּרְעֹה שֶׁהֱיִיתֶם עֲבָדִים לוֹ. אוֹ אֵינוֹ אוֹמֵר אֶלָּא "מִבֵּית עֲבָדִים" שֶׁהָיוּ עֲבָדִים לַעֲבָדִים? תַּלְמוּד לוֹמַר: "וַיִּפְדְּךָ מִבֵּית עֲבָדִים מִיַּד פַּרְעֹה מֶלֶךְ מִצְרָיִם" (דברים ז, ח), אֱמוֹר מֵעַתָּה, עֲבָדִים לַמֶּלֶךְ הָיוּ וְלֹא עֲבָדִים לַעֲבָדִים:

ג לֹא יִהְיֶה לְךָ. לָמָּה נֶאֱמַר? לְפִי שֶׁנֶּאֱמַר: "לֹא תַעֲשֶׂה לְךָ", אֵין לִי אֶלָּא שֶׁלֹּא יַעֲשֶׂה, הֶעָשׂוּי כְּבָר מִנַּיִן שֶׁלֹּא יְקַיֵּם? תַּלְמוּד לוֹמַר: "לֹא יִהְיֶה לְךָ": אֱלֹהִים אֲחֵרִים. שֶׁאֵינָן אֱלֹהוּת, אֶלָּא אֲחֵרִים עֲשָׂאוּם אֱלֹהִים עֲלֵיהֶם. וְלֹא יִתָּכֵן לְפָרֵשׁ "אֱלֹהִים אֲחֵרִים" זוּלָתִי, שֶׁגְּנַאי הוּא כְּלַפֵּי מַעֲלָה לִקְרוֹתָם אֱלֹהוּת אֶצְלוֹ. דָּבָר אַחֵר, "אֱלֹהִים אֲחֵרִים", שֶׁהֵם אֲחֵרִים לְעוֹבְדֵיהֶם, צוֹעֲקִים אֲלֵיהֶם וְאֵינָן עוֹנִין

אוֹתָם, וְדוֹמֶה כְּאִלּוּ הוּא אַחֵר שֶׁאֵינוֹ מַכִּירוֹ מֵעוֹלָם: עַל פָּנָי. כָּל זְמַן שֶׁאֲנִי קַיָּם, שֶׁלֹּא תֹאמַר, לֹא נִצְטַוּוּ עַל עֲבוֹדָה זָרָה אֶלָּא אוֹתוֹ הַדּוֹר:

ד פֶּסֶל. עַל שֵׁם שֶׁנִּפְסָל כָּל תְּמוּנַת דָּבָר "אֲשֶׁר בַּשָּׁמַיִם" וְגוֹ':

ה-ו אֵל קַנָּא. מְקַנֵּא לִפָּרַע וְאֵינוֹ עוֹבֵר עַל מִדָּתוֹ לִמְחֹל עַל עֲבוֹדָה זָרָה. כָּל לְשׁוֹן "קַנָּא" אונפרי"מנט בְּלַעַז, נוֹתֵן לֵב לִפָּרַע: לְשֹׂנְאָי. כְּתַרְגּוּמוֹ, כְּשֶׁאוֹחֲזִין מַעֲשֵׂה אֲבוֹתֵיהֶם בִּידֵיהֶם. וְנֹצֵר חֶסֶד שֶׁאָדָם עוֹשֶׂה, לְשַׁלֵּם שָׂכָר עַד לַאֲלָפִים דּוֹר. נִמְצֵאת מִדָּה טוֹבָה יְתֵרָה עַל מִדַּת פֻּרְעָנוּת אַחַת עַל חֲמֵשׁ מֵאוֹת, שֶׁזּוֹ לְאַרְבָּעָה דוֹרוֹת וְזוֹ לַאֲלָפִים:

ז לַשָּׁוְא. חִנָּם, לַהֶבֶל. וְאֵי זֶהוּ שְׁבוּעַת שָׁוְא? נִשְׁבַּע לְשַׁנּוֹת אֶת הַיָּדוּעַ, עַל עַמּוּד שֶׁל אֶבֶן שֶׁהוּא שֶׁל זָהָב:

ח "זָכוֹר" וְ"שָׁמוֹר" בְּדִבּוּר אֶחָד נֶאֶמְרוּ. וְכֵן: "מְחַלְלֶיהָ מוֹת יוּמָת" (להלן לא, יד), "וּבְיוֹם הַשַּׁבָּת שְׁנֵי כְבָשִׂים" (במדבר כח, ט), וְכֵן: "לֹא תִלְבַּשׁ שַׁעַטְנֵז", "גְּדִלִים תַּעֲשֶׂה לָּךְ" (דברים כב, יא-יב), וְכֵן: "עֶרְוַת אֵשֶׁת אָחִיךָ" (ויקרא יח, טז), "יְבָמָהּ יָבֹא עָלֶיהָ" (דברים כה, ה), הוּא שֶׁנֶּאֱמַר: "אַחַת דִּבֶּר אֱלֹהִים שְׁתַּיִם זוּ שָׁמָעְתִּי" (תהלים סב, יב).

שמות | פרק כ | יתרו

^י מְלַאכְתֶּךָ: וְיוֹם הַשְּׁבִיעִי שַׁבָּת לַיהוה אֱלֹהֶיךָ לֹא־תַעֲשֶׂה כָל־מְלָאכָה אַתָּה ׀ וּבִנְךָ וּבִתֶּךָ עַבְדְּךָ וַאֲמָתְךָ וּבְהֶמְתֶּךָ וְגֵרְךָ אֲשֶׁר

^{יא} בִּשְׁעָרֶיךָ: כִּי שֵׁשֶׁת־יָמִים עָשָׂה יהוה אֶת־הַשָּׁמַיִם וְאֶת־הָאָרֶץ אֶת־הַיָּם וְאֶת־כָּל־אֲשֶׁר־בָּם וַיָּנַח בַּיּוֹם הַשְּׁבִיעִי עַל־כֵּן בֵּרַךְ יהוה אֶת־יוֹם הַשַּׁבָּת וַיְקַדְּשֵׁהוּ:

^{יב} כַּבֵּד אֶת־אָבִיךָ וְאֶת־אִמֶּךָ לְמַעַן יַאֲרִכוּן יָמֶיךָ עַל הָאֲדָמָה אֲשֶׁר־יהוה אֱלֹהֶיךָ נֹתֵן לָךְ:

^{יג} לֹא תִרְצָח: לֹא תִנְאָף: לֹא תִגְנֹב: לֹא־

^{יד} תַעֲנֶה בְרֵעֲךָ עֵד שָׁקֶר: לֹא תַחְמֹד בֵּית רֵעֶךָ לֹא־תַחְמֹד אֵשֶׁת רֵעֶךָ וְעַבְדּוֹ וַאֲמָתוֹ וְשׁוֹרוֹ וַחֲמֹרוֹ וְכֹל אֲשֶׁר לְרֵעֶךָ:

"זָכוֹר" לְשׁוֹן פָּעוֹל הוּא, כְּמוֹ: "אָכוֹל וְשָׁתוֹ" (ישעיה כב, יג), "הָלוֹךְ וּבָכֹה" (שמואל ב' ג, טז), וְכֵן פִּתְרוֹנוֹ: תְּנוּ לֵב לִזְכֹּר תָּמִיד אֶת יוֹם הַשַּׁבָּת, שֶׁאִם נִזְדַּמֵּן לְךָ חֵפֶץ יָפֶה תְּהֵא מַזְמִינוֹ לַשַּׁבָּת:

^ט **וְעָשִׂיתָ כָּל מְלַאכְתֶּךָ.** כְּשֶׁתָּבוֹא שַׁבָּת יְהֵא בְּעֵינֶיךָ כְּאִלּוּ כָּל מְלַאכְתְּךָ עֲשׂוּיָה, שֶׁלֹּא תְהַרְהֵר אַחַר מְלָאכָה:

^י **אַתָּה וּבִנְךָ וּבִתֶּךָ.** אֵלּוּ קְטַנִּים. אוֹ אֵינוֹ אֶלָּא גְּדוֹלִים? אָמַרְתָּ, הֲרֵי כְּבָר מֻזְהָרִין הֵם, אֶלָּא לֹא בָא אֶלָּא לְהַזְהִיר הַגְּדוֹלִים עַל שְׁבִיתַת הַקְּטַנִּים, וְזֶהוּ שֶׁשָּׁנִינוּ: קָטָן שֶׁבָּא לְכַבּוֹת אֵין שׁוֹמְעִין לוֹ, מִפְּנֵי שֶׁשְּׁבִיתָתוֹ עָלֶיךָ:

^{יא} **וַיָּנַח בַּיּוֹם הַשְּׁבִיעִי.** כִּבְיָכוֹל הִכְתִּיב בְּעַצְמוֹ מְנוּחָה, לְלַמֵּד הֵימֶנּוּ קַל וָחֹמֶר לָאָדָם שֶׁמְּלַאכְתּוֹ

בְּעָמָל וּבִיגִיעָה שֶׁיְּהֵא נָח בַּשַּׁבָּת: **בֵּרַךְ... וַיְקַדְּשֵׁהוּ.** בֵּרְכוֹ בַּמָּן, לְכָפְלוֹ בַּשִּׁשִּׁי לֶחֶם מִשְׁנֶה, וְקִדְּשׁוֹ בַּמָּן, שֶׁלֹּא הָיָה יוֹרֵד בּוֹ:

^{יב} **לְמַעַן יַאֲרִכוּן יָמֶיךָ.** אִם תְּכַבֵּד - יַאֲרִיכוּן, וְאִם לָאו - יִקְצְרוּן, שֶׁדִּבְרֵי תּוֹרָה נוֹטָרִיקוֹן הֵם, נִדְרָשִׁים מִכְּלָל הֵן לָאו וּמִכְּלָל לָאו הֵן:

^{יג} **לֹא תִנְאָף.** אֵין נִאוּף אֶלָּא בְּאֵשֶׁת אִישׁ, שֶׁנֶּאֱמַר: "מוֹת יוּמַת הַנֹּאֵף וְהַנֹּאָפֶת" (ויקרא כ, י), וְאוֹמֵר: "הָאִשָּׁה הַמְּנָאֶפֶת תַּחַת אִישָׁהּ תִּקַּח אֶת זָרִים" (יחזקאל טז, לב): **לֹא תִגְנֹב.** בְּגוֹנֵב נְפָשׁוֹת הַכָּתוּב מְדַבֵּר, "לֹא תִגְנֹבוּ" (ויקרא יט, יא) בְּגוֹנֵב מָמוֹן. אוֹ אֵינוֹ אֶלָּא זֶה בְּגוֹנֵב מָמוֹן וּלְהַלָּן בְּגוֹנֵב נְפָשׁוֹת? אָמַרְתָּ, דָּבָר לָמֵד מֵעִנְיָנוֹ, "לֹא תִרְצָח", "לֹא תִנְאָף", מִיתַת בֵּית דִּין, אַף "לֹא תִגְנֹב" דָּבָר שֶׁחַיָּבִין עָלָיו מִיתַת בֵּית דִּין:

שביעי
טו וְכָל־הָעָם רֹאִים אֶת־הַקּוֹלֹת וְאֶת־הַלַּפִּידִם וְאֵת קוֹל הַשֹּׁפָר
טז וְאֶת־הָהָר עָשֵׁן וַיַּרְא הָעָם וַיָּנֻעוּ וַיַּעַמְדוּ מֵרָחֹק: וַיֹּאמְרוּ אֶל־
מֹשֶׁה דַּבֵּר־אַתָּה עִמָּנוּ וְנִשְׁמָעָה וְאַל־יְדַבֵּר עִמָּנוּ אֱלֹהִים
יז פֶּן־נָמוּת: וַיֹּאמֶר מֹשֶׁה אֶל־הָעָם אַל־תִּירָאוּ כִּי לְבַעֲבוּר
נַסּוֹת אֶתְכֶם בָּא הָאֱלֹהִים וּבַעֲבוּר תִּהְיֶה יִרְאָתוֹ עַל־פְּנֵיכֶם
יח לְבִלְתִּי תֶחֱטָאוּ: וַיַּעֲמֹד הָעָם מֵרָחֹק וּמֹשֶׁה נִגַּשׁ אֶל־הָעֲרָפֶל
מפטיר
אֲשֶׁר־שָׁם הָאֱלֹהִים: וַיֹּאמֶר יְהוָֹה אֶל־מֹשֶׁה כֹּה
יט תֹאמַר אֶל־בְּנֵי יִשְׂרָאֵל אַתֶּם רְאִיתֶם כִּי מִן־הַשָּׁמַיִם דִּבַּרְתִּי
כ עִמָּכֶם: לֹא תַעֲשׂוּן אִתִּי אֱלֹהֵי כֶסֶף וֵאלֹהֵי זָהָב לֹא תַעֲשׂוּ לָכֶם:

טו **וְכָל הָעָם רֹאִים.** מְלַמֵּד שֶׁלֹּא הָיָה בָּהֶם אֶחָד סוּמָא. וּמִנַּיִן שֶׁלֹּא הָיָה בָּהֶם חֵלֵשׁ? תַּלְמוּד לוֹמַר: "וַיַּעֲנוּ כָל הָעָם" (לעיל יט, ח). וּמִנַּיִן שֶׁלֹּא הָיָה בָּהֶם חֵרֵשׁ? תַּלְמוּד לוֹמַר: "נַעֲשֶׂה וְנִשְׁמָע" (להלן כד, ז): **רֹאִים אֶת הַקּוֹלֹת.** רוֹאִין אֶת הַנִּשְׁמָע, שֶׁאִי אֶפְשָׁר לִרְאוֹת בְּמָקוֹם אַחֵר: **אֶת הַקּוֹלֹת.** הַיּוֹצְאִין מִפִּי הַגְּבוּרָה: **וַיָּנֻעוּ.** אֵין "נוֹעַ" אֶלָּא זִיעַ: **וַיַּעַמְדוּ מֵרָחֹק.** הָיוּ נִרְתָּעִין לַאֲחוֹרֵיהֶם שְׁנֵים עָשָׂר מִיל כְּאֹרֶךְ מַחֲנֵיהֶם, וּמַלְאֲכֵי הַשָּׁרֵת בָּאִין וּמְסַיְּעִין אוֹתָן לְהַחֲזִירָם, שֶׁנֶּאֱמַר: "מַלְאֲכֵי צְבָאוֹת יִדֹּדוּן יִדֹּדוּן" (תהלים סח, יג):

יז **לְבַעֲבוּר נַסּוֹת אֶתְכֶם.** לְגַדֵּל אֶתְכֶם בָּעוֹלָם, שֶׁיֵּצֵא לָכֶם שֵׁם בָּאֻמּוֹת שֶׁהוּא בִּכְבוֹדוֹ נִגְלָה עֲלֵיכֶם: **נַסּוֹת.** לְשׁוֹן הֲרָמָה וְגַדְלָה, כְּמוֹ: "הָרִימוּ נֵס" (ישעיה סב, י), "אָרִים נִסִּי" (שם מט, כב), "וְכַנֵּס עַל הַגִּבְעָה" (שם ל, יז), שֶׁהוּא זָקוּף: **וּבַעֲבוּר תִּהְיֶה יִרְאָתוֹ.** עַל יְדֵי שֶׁרְאִיתֶם אוֹתוֹ יָרֹא וְאָיֹם, תֵּדְעוּ כִּי אֵין זוּלָתוֹ וְתִירְאוּ מִפָּנָיו:

יח **נִגַּשׁ אֶל הָעֲרָפֶל.** לִפְנִים מִשְּׁלֹשׁ מְחִצּוֹת: חֹשֶׁךְ, עָנָן וַעֲרָפֶל, שֶׁנֶּאֱמַר: "וְהָהָר בֹּעֵר בָּאֵשׁ עַד לֵב הַשָּׁמַיִם חֹשֶׁךְ עָנָן וַעֲרָפֶל" (דברים ד, יא). **עֲרָפֶל** הוּא עַב הֶעָנָן, שֶׁאָמַר לוֹ: "הִנֵּה אָנֹכִי בָּא אֵלֶיךָ בְּעַב הֶעָנָן" (לעיל יט, ט):

יט **כֹּה תֹאמַר.** בַּלָּשׁוֹן הַזֶּה: **אַתֶּם רְאִיתֶם.** יֵשׁ הֶפְרֵשׁ בֵּין מַה שֶּׁאָדָם רוֹאֶה לְמַה שֶּׁאֲחֵרִים מְשִׂיחִין לוֹ, שֶׁמַּה שֶּׁאֲחֵרִים מְשִׂיחִין לוֹ פְּעָמִים שֶׁלִּבּוֹ חָלוּק מִלְּהַאֲמִין: **כִּי מִן הַשָּׁמַיִם דִּבַּרְתִּי.** וְכָתוּב אַחֵר אוֹמֵר: "וַיֵּרֶד ה' עַל הַר סִינַי" (לעיל יט, כ)! בָּא הַכָּתוּב הַשְּׁלִישִׁי וְהִכְרִיעַ בֵּינֵיהֶם: "מִן הַשָּׁמַיִם הִשְׁמִיעֲךָ אֶת קֹלוֹ לְיַסְּרֶךָּ וְעַל הָאָרֶץ הֶרְאֲךָ אֶת אִשּׁוֹ הַגְּדוֹלָה" (דברים ד, לו), כְּבוֹדוֹ בַּשָּׁמַיִם וְאִשּׁוֹ וּגְבוּרָתוֹ עַל הָאָרֶץ. דָּבָר אַחֵר, הִרְכִּין שָׁמַיִם וּשְׁמֵי שָׁמַיִם וְהִצִּיעָן עַל הָהָר, וְכֵן הוּא אוֹמֵר: "וַיֵּט שָׁמַיִם וַיֵּרַד" (שמואל ב' כב, י):

כ **לֹא תַעֲשׂוּן אִתִּי.** לֹא תַעֲשׂוּן דְּמוּת שַׁמָּשַׁי הַמְשַׁמְּשִׁים לְפָנַי בַּמָּרוֹם: **אֱלֹהֵי כֶסֶף.** בָּא לְהַזְהִיר עַל הַכְּרוּבִים, שֶׁאַתָּה עוֹשֶׂה לַעֲמֹד אִתִּי, שֶׁלֹּא יִהְיוּ שֶׁל כֶּסֶף, שֶׁאִם שִׁנִּיתָם לַעֲשׂוֹתָם שֶׁל כֶּסֶף הֲרֵי הֵן לְפָנַי כֶּאֱלֹהוּת: **וֵאלֹהֵי זָהָב.** בָּא לְהַזְהִיר שֶׁלֹּא יוֹסִיף עַל שְׁנַיִם, שֶׁאִם עָשִׂיתָ אַרְבָּעָה הֲרֵי הֵן לְפָנַי כֶּאֱלֹהֵי זָהָב: **לֹא תַעֲשׂוּ לָכֶם.** שֶׁלֹּא תֹאמַר, הֲרֵינִי עוֹשֶׂה

שמות | פרק כ

כא מִזְבַּ֣ח אֲדָמָה֮ תַּעֲשֶׂה־לִּי֒ וְזָבַחְתָּ֣ עָלָ֗יו אֶת־עֹלֹתֶ֙יךָ֙ וְאֶת־שְׁלָמֶ֔יךָ אֶת־צֹֽאנְךָ֖ וְאֶת־בְּקָרֶ֑ךָ בְּכָל־הַמָּקוֹם֙ אֲשֶׁ֣ר אַזְכִּ֣יר אֶת־שְׁמִ֔י
כב אָב֥וֹא אֵלֶ֖יךָ וּבֵרַכְתִּֽיךָ: וְאִם־מִזְבַּ֤ח אֲבָנִים֙ תַּֽעֲשֶׂה־לִּ֔י לֹֽא־
כג תִבְנֶ֥ה אֶתְהֶ֖ן גָּזִ֑ית כִּ֣י חַרְבְּךָ֤ הֵנַ֙פְתָּ֙ עָלֶ֔יהָ וַתְּחַֽלְלֶֽהָ: וְלֹֽא־תַעֲלֶ֥ה בְמַעֲלֹ֖ת עַֽל־מִזְבְּחִ֑י אֲשֶׁ֛ר לֹֽא־תִגָּלֶ֥ה עֶרְוָתְךָ֖ עָלָֽיו:

כרובים בבתי כנסיות ובבתי מדרשות כדרך שאני עושה בבית עולמים, לכך נאמר: "לא תעשו לכם":

כא | מזבח אדמה. מחובר באדמה, שלא יבננו על גבי עמודים או על גבי כפים. דבר אחר, שהיה ממלא את חלל מזבח הנחשת אדמה בשעת חנייתן: **תעשה לי.** שתהא תחלת עשייתו לשמי: **וזבחת עליו.** אצלו, כמו: "ועליו מטה מנשה" (במדבר ב, כ). או אינו אלא עליו ממש? תלמוד לומר: "הבשר והדם על מזבח ה' אלהיך" (דברים יב, כז), ואין שחיטה בראש המזבח: **את עלתיך ואת שלמיך.** אשר מצאנך ומבקרך. "את צאנך ואת בקרך" פרוש ל"את עלתיך ואת שלמיך": **בכל המקום אשר אזכיר את שמי.** אשר אתן לך רשות להזכיר שם המפרש שלי, שם "אבוא אליך", אשרה את שכינתי, "וברכתיך". מכאן אתה למד שלא נתן רשות להזכיר שם המפרש אלא במקום שהשכינה באה שם, וזהו בית הבחירה, שם נתן רשות לכהנים להזכיר שם המפרש בנשיאות כפים ולברך את העם:

כב | ואם מזבח אבנים. רבי ישמעאל אומר: כל "אם" ו"אם" שבתורה רשות חוץ משלשה: "ואם מזבח אבנים תעשה לי", הרי "אם" זה משמש בלשון "כאשר", וכאשר תעשה לי מזבח אבנים "לא תבנה אתהן גזית", שהרי חובה עליך לבנות מזבח אבנים, שנאמר: "אבנים שלמות תבנה" (דברים כז, ו). וכן: "אם כסף תלוה" (שמות כב, כד) חובה הוא, שנאמר: "והעבט תעביטנו" (דברים טו, ח), ואף זה משמש בלשון "כאשר". וכן: "ואם תקריב מנחת בכורים" (ויקרא ב, יד), זו מנחת

העומר שהיא חובה. ועל כרחך אין "אם" הללו תלויין אלא ודאין, ובלשון "כאשר" הם משמשים: **גזית.** לשון גזיזה, שפוסלן ומכתתן בברזל: **כי חרבך הנפת עליה.** הרי "כי" זה משמש בלשון "פן", שהוא כמו "דלמא", פן תניף חרבך עליה: **ותחללה.** הא למדת שאם הנפת עליה ברזל – חללת, שהמזבח נברא להאריך ימיו של אדם, והברזל נברא לקצר ימיו של אדם, אין זה בדין שיונף המקצר על המאריך. ועוד, שהמזבח מטיל שלום בין ישראל לאביהם שבשמים, לפיכך לא יבא עליו כורת ומחבל. והרי דברים קל וחמר: ומה אבנים שאינן רואות ולא שומעות ולא מדברות, על ידי שמטילות שלום אמרה תורה: "לא תניף עליהם ברזל" (דברים כז, ה), המטיל שלום בין איש לאשתו, בין משפחה למשפחה, בין אדם לחברו, על אחת כמה וכמה שלא תבואהו פרענות:

כג | ולא תעלה במעלת. כשאתה בונה כבש למזבח לא תעשהו מעלות מעלות, אשקלונ"ש בלעז, אלא חלק יהא ומשפע: **אשר לא תגלה ערותך.** שעל ידי המעלות אתה צריך להרחיב פסיעותיך. ואף על פי שאינן גלוי ערוה ממש, שהרי כתיב: "ועשה להם מכנסי בד" (שמות כח, מב), מכל מקום הרחבת הפסיעות קרוב לגלוי ערוה הוא, ואתה נוהג בהם מנהג בזיון. והרי דברים קל וחומר: ומה אבנים הללו שאין בהם דעת להקפיד על בזיונן, אמרה תורה: הואיל ויש בהם צורך לא תנהג בהם מנהג בזיון, חברך שהוא בדמות יוצרך ומקפיד על בזיונו, על אחת כמה וכמה:

משפטים

פרק כא

וְאֵ֣לֶּה הַמִּשְׁפָּטִ֔ים אֲשֶׁ֥ר תָּשִׂ֖ים לִפְנֵיהֶֽם: כִּ֤י תִקְנֶה֙ עֶ֣בֶד עִבְרִ֔י שֵׁ֥שׁ שָׁנִ֖ים יַעֲבֹ֑ד וּבַ֨שְּׁבִעִ֔ת יֵצֵ֥א לַֽחָפְשִׁ֖י חִנָּֽם: אִם־בְּגַפּ֣וֹ יָבֹ֔א בְּגַפּ֖וֹ יֵצֵ֑א אִם־בַּ֤עַל אִשָּׁה֙ ה֔וּא וְיָצְאָ֥ה אִשְׁתּ֖וֹ עִמּֽוֹ: אִם־אֲדֹנָיו֙ יִתֶּן־ל֣וֹ אִשָּׁ֔ה וְיָלְדָה־ל֥וֹ בָנִ֖ים א֣וֹ בָנ֑וֹת הָאִשָּׁ֣ה וִֽילָדֶ֗יהָ תִּהְיֶה֙ לַֽאדֹנֶ֔יהָ וְה֖וּא יֵצֵ֥א בְגַפּֽוֹ: וְאִם־אָמֹ֤ר יֹאמַר֙ הָעֶ֔בֶד אָהַ֙בְתִּי֙ אֶת־אֲדֹנִ֔י אֶת־אִשְׁתִּ֖י וְאֶת־בָּנָ֑י לֹ֥א אֵצֵ֖א חָפְשִֽׁי: וְהִגִּישׁ֤וֹ אֲדֹנָיו֙ אֶל־הָ֣אֱלֹהִ֔ים וְהִגִּישׁוֹ֙ אֶל־הַדֶּ֔לֶת א֖וֹ אֶל־הַמְּזוּזָ֑ה

פרק כא

א וְאֵלֶּה הַמִּשְׁפָּטִים. כָּל מָקוֹם שֶׁנֶּאֱמַר 'אֵלֶּה' – פָּסַל אֶת הָרִאשׁוֹנִים, 'וְאֵלֶּה' – מוֹסִיף עַל הָרִאשׁוֹנִים, מָה הָרִאשׁוֹנִים מִסִּינַי, אַף אֵלּוּ מִסִּינָי. וְלָמָּה נִסְמְכָה פָּרָשַׁת דִּינִין לְפָרָשַׁת מִזְבֵּחַ? לוֹמַר לְךָ שֶׁתָּשִׂים סַנְהֶדְרִין אֵצֶל הַמִּקְדָּשׁ: אֲשֶׁר תָּשִׂים לִפְנֵיהֶם. אָמַר לוֹ הַקָּדוֹשׁ בָּרוּךְ הוּא לְמֹשֶׁה: לֹא תַעֲלֶה עַל דַּעְתְּךָ לוֹמַר אֶשְׁנֶה לָהֶם הַפֶּרֶק וְהַהֲלָכָה שְׁנַיִם אוֹ שְׁלֹשָׁה פְּעָמִים עַד שֶׁתְּהֵא סְדוּרָה בְּפִיהֶם כְּמִשְׁנָתָהּ, וְאֵינִי מַטְרִיחַ עַצְמִי לַהֲבִינָם טַעֲמֵי הַדָּבָר וּפֵרוּשׁוֹ, לְכָךְ נֶאֱמַר: "אֲשֶׁר תָּשִׂים לִפְנֵיהֶם", כְּשֻׁלְחָן הֶעָרוּךְ וּמוּכָן לֶאֱכוֹל לִפְנֵי הָאָדָם: לִפְנֵיהֶם. וְלֹא לִפְנֵי גוֹיִם, וַאֲפִלּוּ יָדַעְתָּ בְּדִין אֶחָד שֶׁהַגּוֹיִם דָּנִין אוֹתוֹ כְּדִינֵי יִשְׂרָאֵל אַל תְּבִיאֵהוּ בְּעַרְכָּאוֹת שֶׁלָּהֶם, שֶׁהַמֵּבִיא דִּינֵי יִשְׂרָאֵל לִפְנֵי גוֹיִם מְחַלֵּל אֶת הַשֵּׁם וּמְיַקֵּר שֵׁם עֲבוֹדָה זָרָה לְהַחֲשִׁיבָהּ, שֶׁנֶּאֱמַר: "כִּי לֹא כְצוּרֵנוּ צוּרָם וְאֹיְבֵינוּ פְּלִילִים" (דברים לב, לא), כְּשֶׁאוֹיְבֵינוּ פְּלִילִים זֶהוּ עֵדוּת לְעִלּוּי יִרְאָתָם:

ב כִּי תִקְנֶה עֶבֶד עִבְרִי. עֶבֶד שֶׁהוּא עִבְרִי, אוֹ אֵינוֹ אֶלָּא עַבְדּוֹ שֶׁל עִבְרִי, עֶבֶד כְּנַעֲנִי שֶׁלְּקָחוֹ מִיִּשְׂרָאֵל, וְעָלָיו הוּא אוֹמֵר: "שֵׁשׁ שָׁנִים יַעֲבֹד", וּמָה אֲנִי מְקַיֵּם "וְהִתְנַחַלְתֶּם אֹתָם" (ויקרא כה, מו) – בִּלְקוּחַ מִן הַגּוֹי, אֲבָל בִּלְקוּחַ מִיִּשְׂרָאֵל יֵצֵא בְּשֵׁשׁ? תַּלְמוּד לוֹמַר: "כִּי יִמָּכֵר לְךָ אָחִיךָ הָעִבְרִי" (דברים טו, יב), לֹא אָמַרְתִּי אֶלָּא בְּאָחִיךָ: כִּי תִקְנֶה. מִיַּד בֵּית דִּין שֶׁמְּכָרוּהוּ בִּגְנֵבָתוֹ, כְּמוֹ שֶׁנֶּאֱמַר: "אִם אֵין לוֹ וְנִמְכַּר בִּגְנֵבָתוֹ"

(להלן כב, ב). אוֹ אֵינוֹ אֶלָּא בְּמוֹכֵר עַצְמוֹ מִפְּנֵי דָּחֳקוֹ, אֲבָל מְכָרוּהוּ בֵּית דִּין לֹא יֵצֵא בְּשֵׁשׁ? כְּשֶׁהוּא אוֹמֵר: "וְכִי יָמוּךְ אָחִיךָ עִמָּךְ וְנִמְכַּר לָךְ" (ויקרא כה, לט) הֲרֵי מוֹכֵר עַצְמוֹ מִפְּנֵי דָּחֳקוֹ אָמוּר, וּמָה אֲנִי מְקַיֵּם "כִּי תִקְנֶה"? בְּנִמְכָּר בְּבֵית דִּין: לַחָפְשִׁי. לְחֵרוּת:

ג אִם בְּגַפּוֹ יָבֹא. שֶׁלֹּא הָיָה נָשׂוּי אִשָּׁה, כְּתַרְגּוּמוֹ: "אִם בִּלְחוֹדוֹהִי". וּלְשׁוֹן 'בְּגַפּוֹ', בִּכְנָפוֹ, שֶׁלֹּא בָּא אֶלָּא כְּמוֹת שֶׁהוּא יְחִידִי בְּתוֹךְ לְבוּשׁוֹ, בִּכְנַף בִּגְדוֹ: בְּגַפּוֹ יֵצֵא. מַגִּיד שֶׁאִם לֹא הָיָה נָשׂוּי מִתְּחִלָּה, אֵין רַבּוֹ מוֹסֵר לוֹ שִׁפְחָה כְּנַעֲנִית לְהוֹלִיד מִמֶּנָּה עֲבָדִים: אִם בַּעַל אִשָּׁה הוּא. יִשְׂרְאֵלִית: וְיָצְאָה אִשְׁתּוֹ עִמּוֹ. וְכִי מִי הִכְנִיסָהּ שֶׁתֵּצֵא? אֶלָּא מַגִּיד הַכָּתוּב שֶׁהַקּוֹנֶה עֶבֶד עִבְרִי חַיָּב בִּמְזוֹנוֹת אִשְׁתּוֹ וּבָנָיו:

ד אִם אֲדֹנָיו יִתֶּן לוֹ אִשָּׁה. מִכָּאן שֶׁהָרְשׁוּת בְּיַד רַבּוֹ לִמְסוֹר לוֹ שִׁפְחָה כְּנַעֲנִית לְהוֹלִיד מִמֶּנָּה עֲבָדִים. אוֹ אֵינוֹ אֶלָּא בְּיִשְׂרְאֵלִית? תַּלְמוּד לוֹמַר: "הָאִשָּׁה וִילָדֶיהָ תִּהְיֶה לַאדֹנֶיהָ", הָא אֵינוֹ מְדַבֵּר אֶלָּא בִּכְנַעֲנִית, שֶׁהֲרֵי הָעִבְרִיָּה אַף הִיא יוֹצְאָה בְּשֵׁשׁ, וַאֲפִלּוּ לִפְנֵי שֵׁשׁ אִם הֵבִיאָה סִימָנִין יוֹצְאָה, שֶׁנֶּאֱמַר: "אָחִיךָ הָעִבְרִי אוֹ הָעִבְרִיָּה" (דברים טו, יב), מְלַמֵּד שֶׁאַף הָעִבְרִיָּה יוֹצְאָה בְּשֵׁשׁ:

ה אֶת אִשְׁתִּי. הַשִּׁפְחָה:

ו אֶל הָאֱלֹהִים. לְבֵית דִּין, צָרִיךְ שֶׁיִּמָּלֵךְ בְּמוֹכְרָיו שֶׁמְּכָרוּהוּ לוֹ: אֶל הַדֶּלֶת אוֹ אֶל הַמְּזוּזָה. יָכוֹל שֶׁתְּהֵא הַמְּזוּזָה כְּשֵׁרָה לִרְצוֹעַ עָלֶיהָ? תַּלְמוּד לוֹמַר: "וְנָתַתָּה

שמות | פרק כא | משפטים

ז וְרָצַע אֲדֹנָיו אֶת־אָזְנוֹ בַּמַּרְצֵעַ וַעֲבָדוֹ לְעֹלָם: ח וְכִי־יִמְכֹּר אִישׁ אֶת־בִּתּוֹ לְאָמָה לֹא תֵצֵא כְּצֵאת הָעֲבָדִים: ח אִם־רָעָה בְּעֵינֵי אֲדֹנֶיהָ אֲשֶׁר־לא יְעָדָהּ וְהֶפְדָּהּ לְעַם נָכְרִי לֹא־יִמְשֹׁל לְמָכְרָהּ בְּבִגְדוֹ־בָהּ: ט וְאִם־לִבְנוֹ יִיעָדֶנָּה כְּמִשְׁפַּט

בְּחֶזְקוֹ וּבַדֶּלֶת (דברים טו, יז), בַּדֶּלֶת וְלֹא בַּמְּזוּזָה, הָא מַה תַּלְמוּד לוֹמַר: "אוֹ אֶל הַמְּזוּזָה"? הִקִּישׁ דֶּלֶת לַמְּזוּזָה, מַה מְּזוּזָה מֵעוֹמֵד אַף דֶּלֶת מֵעוֹמֵד. רַבִּי שִׁמְעוֹן הָיָה דּוֹרֵשׁ מִקְרָא זֶה כְּמִין חֹמֶר: מַה נִּשְׁתַּנּוּ דֶלֶת וּמְזוּזָה מִכָּל כֵּלִים שֶׁבַּבַּיִת? אָמַר הַקָּדוֹשׁ בָּרוּךְ הוּא: דֶּלֶת וּמְזוּזָה שֶׁהָיוּ עֵדַי בְּמִצְרַיִם כְּשֶׁפָּסַחְתִּי עַל הַמַּשְׁקוֹף וְעַל שְׁתֵּי הַמְּזוּזוֹת, וְאָמַרְתִּי: "כִּי לִי בְנֵי יִשְׂרָאֵל עֲבָדִים" (ויקרא כה, נה), וְלֹא עֲבָדִים לַעֲבָדִים, וְהָלַךְ זֶה וְקָנָה אָדוֹן לְעַצְמוֹ, יֵרָצַע בִּפְנֵיהֶם: וְרָצַע אֲדֹנָיו אֶת אָזְנוֹ. הַיְמָנִית, אוֹ אֵינוֹ אֶלָּא שֶׁל שְׂמֹאל? תַּלְמוּד לוֹמַר: "אֹזֶן" "אֹזֶן" לִגְזֵרָה שָׁוָה, נֶאֱמַר בַּמְּצֹרָע: "תְּנוּךְ אֹזֶן הַמְּטֹהָר הַיְמָנִית" (ויקרא יד, יד), וּמָה רָאָה אֹזֶן לֵרָצַע מִכָּל הָאֵיבָרִים? אָמַר רַבָּן יוֹחָנָן בֶּן זַכַּאי: אֹזֶן שֶׁשָּׁמְעָה בְּסִינַי: "לֹא תִגְנֹב" (לעיל כ, יג), וְהָלַךְ וְגָנַב, תֵּרָצַע. וְאִם מוֹכֵר עַצְמוֹ הוּא, אֹזֶן שֶׁשָּׁמְעָה "כִּי לִי בְנֵי יִשְׂרָאֵל עֲבָדִים" (ויקרא כה, נה), וְהָלַךְ וְקָנָה אָדוֹן לְעַצְמוֹ, תִּלָּקֶה. וַעֲבָדוֹ לְעֹלָם. עַד הַיּוֹבֵל, אוֹ אֵינוֹ אֶלָּא כְּמַשְׁמָעוֹ? תַּלְמוּד לוֹמַר: "וְאִישׁ אֶל מִשְׁפַּחְתּוֹ תָּשֻׁבוּ" (ויקרא כה, י), מַגִּיד שֶׁחֲמִשִּׁים שָׁנָה קְרוּיִים 'עוֹלָם'. וְלֹא שֶׁיְּהֵא עוֹבְדוֹ כָּל חֲמִשִּׁים שָׁנָה, אֶלָּא עוֹבְדוֹ עַד הַיּוֹבֵל, בֵּין סָמוּךְ בֵּין מֻפְלָג:

ז וְכִי יִמְכֹּר אִישׁ אֶת בִּתּוֹ לְאָמָה. בִּקְטַנָּה הַכָּתוּב מְדַבֵּר. יָכוֹל אֲפִלּוּ הֵבִיאָה סִימָנִים? אָמַרְתָּ, קַל וָחֹמֶר: וּמָה מְכוּרָה קֹדֶם לָכֵן יוֹצְאָה בְּסִימָנִין, כְּמוֹ שֶׁכָּתוּב: "וְיָצְאָה חִנָּם אֵין כָּסֶף" (להלן פסוק יא), שֶׁאָנוּ דּוֹרְשִׁים אוֹתוֹ לְסִימָנֵי נַעֲרוּת, שֶׁאֵינָהּ מְכוּרָה אֵינוֹ דִּין שֶׁלֹּא תִּמָּכֵר?: לֹא תֵצֵא כְּצֵאת הָעֲבָדִים. כִּיצִיאַת עֲבָדִים כְּנַעֲנִים שֶׁיּוֹצְאִים בְּשֵׁן וָעַיִן, אֲבָל זוֹ לֹא תֵצֵא בְּשֵׁן וָעַיִן, אֶלָּא עוֹבֶדֶת שֵׁשׁ, אוֹ עַד הַיּוֹבֵל, אוֹ עַד שֶׁתָּבִיא סִימָנִין, וְכָל הַקּוֹדֵם לַחֲרוּתָהּ, וְנוֹתֵן לָהּ דְּמֵי עֵינָהּ אוֹ דְמֵי שִׁנָּהּ. אוֹ אֵינוֹ אֶלָּא "לֹא תֵצֵא

כְּצֵאת הָעֲבָדִים" בְּשֵׁשׁ וּבַיּוֹבֵל? תַּלְמוּד לוֹמַר: "כִּי יִמָּכֵר לְךָ אָחִיךָ הָעִבְרִי אוֹ הָעִבְרִיָּה" (דברים טו, יב), מַקִּישׁ עִבְרִיָּה לְעִבְרִי לְכָל יְצִיאוֹתָיו: מָה עִבְרִי יוֹצֵא בְּשֵׁשׁ וּבַיּוֹבֵל, אַף עִבְרִיָּה יוֹצְאָה בְּשֵׁשׁ וּבַיּוֹבֵל. וּמַהוּ "לֹא תֵצֵא כְּצֵאת הָעֲבָדִים"? לֹא תֵצֵא בְּרָאשֵׁי אֵיבָרִים כַּעֲבָדִים כְּנַעֲנִים. יָכוֹל הָעִבְרִי יוֹצֵא בְּרָאשֵׁי אֵיבָרִים? תַּלְמוּד לוֹמַר: "הָעִבְרִי אוֹ הָעִבְרִיָּה", מַקִּישׁ עִבְרִי לְעִבְרִיָּה, מָה הָעִבְרִיָּה אֵינָהּ יוֹצְאָה בְּרָאשֵׁי אֵיבָרִים, אַף הוּא אֵינוֹ יוֹצֵא בְּרָאשֵׁי אֵיבָרִים:

ח אִם רָעָה בְּעֵינֵי אֲדֹנֶיהָ. שֶׁלֹּא נָשְׂאָה חֵן בְּעֵינָיו לְכָנְסָהּ: אֲשֶׁר לֹא יְעָדָהּ. שֶׁהָיָה לוֹ לְיַעֲדָהּ וּלְהַכְנִיסָהּ לוֹ לְאִשָּׁה, וְכֶסֶף קְנִיָּתָהּ הוּא כֶּסֶף קִדּוּשֶׁיהָ. וְכָאן רָמַז לְךָ הַכָּתוּב שֶׁמִּצְוָה בְּיִעוּד, וְרָמַז לְךָ שֶׁאֵינָהּ צְרִיכָה קִדּוּשִׁין אֲחֵרִים: וְהֶפְדָּהּ. יִתֵּן לָהּ מָקוֹם לְהִפָּדוֹת וְלָצֵאת, שֶׁאַף הוּא מְסַיֵּעַ בְּפִדְיוֹנָהּ. וּמַה הוּא מָקוֹם שֶׁנּוֹתֵן לָהּ? שֶׁמְּגָרֵעַ מִפִּדְיוֹנָהּ כְּמִסְפַּר הַשָּׁנִים שֶׁעָשְׂתָה אֶצְלוֹ, כְּאִלּוּ הִיא שְׂכוּרָה אֶצְלוֹ. כֵּיצַד? הֲרֵי שֶׁקְּנָאָהּ בְּמָנֶה וְעָשְׂתָה אֶצְלוֹ שְׁתֵּי שָׁנִים, אוֹמְרִים לוֹ, יוֹדֵעַ הָיִיתָ שֶׁעֲתִידָה לָצֵאת לְסוֹף שֵׁשׁ, נִמְצֵאתָ קוֹנֶה עֲבוֹדַת כָּל שָׁנָה וְשָׁנָה בִּשְׁתוּת הַמָּנֶה, וְעָשְׂתָה אֶצְלְךָ שְׁתֵּי שָׁנִים, הֲרֵי שְׁלִישִׁית הַמָּנֶה, טֹל שְׁנֵי שְׁלִישֵׁי מָנֶה וְתֵצֵא מֵאֶצְלְךָ: לְעַם נָכְרִי לֹא יִמְשֹׁל לְמָכְרָהּ. אֵינוֹ רַשַּׁאי לְמָכְרָהּ לְאַחֵר, לֹא הָאָדוֹן וְלֹא הָאָב: בְּבִגְדוֹ בָהּ. אִם בָּא לִבְגֹּד בָּהּ שֶׁלֹּא לְקַיֵּם בָּהּ מִצְוַת יִעוּד, וְכֵן אָבִיהָ, מֵאַחַר שֶׁבָּגַד בָּהּ וּמְכָרָהּ לָזֶה:

ט וְאִם לִבְנוֹ יִיעָדֶנָּה. הָאָדוֹן, מְלַמֵּד שֶׁאַף בְּנוֹ קָם תַּחְתָּיו לְיַעֲדָהּ אִם יִרְצֶה אָבִיו, וְאֵינוֹ צָרִיךְ לְקַדְּשָׁהּ קִדּוּשִׁין אֲחֵרִים, אֶלָּא אוֹמֵר לָהּ: הֲרֵי אַתְּ מְיֹעֶדֶת לִי בַּכֶּסֶף שֶׁקִּבֵּל אָבִיךְ בִּדְמַיִךְ: כְּמִשְׁפַּט הַבָּנוֹת. שְׁאֵר כְּסוּת וְעוֹנָה.

פרק כא | שמות

הַבָּנוֹת יַעֲשֶׂה־לָּהּ: אִם־אַחֶרֶת יִקַּח־לוֹ שְׁאֵרָהּ כְּסוּתָהּ
וְעֹנָתָהּ לֹא יִגְרָע: וְאִם־שְׁלָשׁ־אֵלֶּה לֹא יַעֲשֶׂה לָהּ וְיָצְאָה חִנָּם
אֵין כָּסֶף: מַכֵּה אִישׁ וָמֵת מוֹת יוּמָת: וַאֲשֶׁר
לֹא צָדָה וְהָאֱלֹהִים אִנָּה לְיָדוֹ וְשַׂמְתִּי לְךָ מָקוֹם אֲשֶׁר יָנוּס

י **אִם אַחֶרֶת יִקַּח לוֹ.** עָלֶיהָ: **שְׁאֵרָהּ כְּסוּתָהּ וְעֹנָתָהּ לֹא יִגְרָע.** מִן הָאָמָה שֶׁיִּעֵד לוֹ כְּבָר: **שְׁאֵרָהּ.** מְזוֹנוֹת: **כְּסוּתָהּ.** כְּמַשְׁמָעוֹ: **עֹנָתָהּ.** תַּשְׁמִישׁ:

יא **וְאִם שְׁלָשׁ אֵלֶּה לֹא יַעֲשֶׂה לָהּ.** אִם אַחַת מִשָּׁלֹשׁ אֵלֶּה לֹא יַעֲשֶׂה לָהּ. וּמָה הֵן הַשָּׁלֹשׁ? יִיעָדֶנָּה לוֹ, אוֹ לִבְנוֹ, אוֹ יִגְרַע מִפִּדְיוֹנָהּ וְתֵצֵא, וְזֶה לֹא יְעָדָהּ לוֹ וְלֹא לִבְנוֹ, וְהִיא לֹא הָיָה בְיָדָהּ לִפְדּוֹת אֶת עַצְמָהּ: **וְיָצְאָה חִנָּם.** רִבָּה לָהּ יְצִיאָה לָזוֹ יוֹתֵר מִמַּה שֶּׁרִבָּה לַעֲבָדִים. וּמַה הָיָה יְצִיאָתָהּ? לִמֶּדְךָ שֶׁתֵּצֵא בְסִימָנִים. וְהִם תִּשְׁהֶא עִמּוֹ עַד שֶׁתֵּצֵא בְסִימָנִים, אִם הִגִּיעוּ שֵׁשׁ שָׁנִים קוֹדֶם סִימָנִים, כְּבָר לָמַדְנוּ שֶׁתֵּצֵא, שֶׁנֶּאֱמַר: "הָעִבְרִי אוֹ הָעִבְרִיָּה וַעֲבָדְךָ שֵׁשׁ שָׁנִים" (דברים טו, יב), וּמָה הָאָמוּר כָּאן? "וְיָצְאָה חִנָּם", שֶׁאִם קָדְמוּ סִימָנִים לְשֵׁשׁ שָׁנִים תֵּצֵא בָהֶן, אוֹ אֵינוֹ אוֹמֵר שֶׁתֵּצֵא בְּבַגְרוּת? תַּלְמוּד לוֹמַר: "אֵין כָּסֶף" לְרַבּוֹת יְצִיאַת בַּגְרוּת. וְאִם לֹא נֶאֶמְרוּ שְׁנֵיהֶם, הָיִיתִי אוֹמֵר: "וְיָצְאָה חִנָּם" זוֹ בַגְרוּת, לְכָךְ נֶאֶמְרוּ שְׁנֵיהֶם, שֶׁלֹּא לִתֵּן פִּתְחוֹן פֶּה לְבַעַל הַדִּין לַחֲלֹק:

יב **מַכֵּה אִישׁ וָמֵת.** כַּמָּה כְּתוּבִים נֶאֶמְרוּ בְפָרָשַׁת רוֹצְחִין, וּמַה שֶּׁבְּיָדִי לְפָרֵשׁ לָמָּה בָאוּ כֻּלָּם אֲפָרֵשׁ: **מַכֵּה אִישׁ וָמֵת.** לָמָּה נֶאֱמַר? לְפִי שֶׁנֶּאֱמַר: "וְאִישׁ כִּי יַכֶּה כָּל נֶפֶשׁ אָדָם מוֹת יוּמָת" (ויקרא כד, יז), שׁוֹמֵעַ אֲנִי הַכָּאָה בְּלֹא מִיתָה? תַּלְמוּד לוֹמַר: "מַכֵּה אִישׁ וָמֵת", אֵינוֹ חַיָּב אֶלָּא בְהַכָּאָה שֶׁל מִיתָה. וְאִם נֶאֱמַר "מַכֵּה אִישׁ" וְלֹא נֶאֱמַר "וְיָךְ כִּי יַכֶּה", הָיִיתִי אוֹמֵר אֵינוֹ חַיָּב עַד שֶׁיַּכֶּה אִישׁ, הִכָּה אֶת הָאִשָּׁה וְאֶת הַקָּטָן מִנַּיִן? תַּלְמוּד לוֹמַר: "כִּי יַכֶּה כָּל נֶפֶשׁ אָדָם", אֲפִלּוּ קָטָן וַאֲפִלּוּ אִשָּׁה. וְעוֹד, אִלּוּ נֶאֱמַר "מַכֵּה אִישׁ" שׁוֹמֵעַ אֲנִי אֲפִלּוּ קָטָן שֶׁהִכָּה וְהָרַג יְהֵא חַיָּב? תַּלְמוּד לוֹמַר: "וְכִי יַכֶּה כָּל נֶפֶשׁ אָדָם", וְלֹא קָטָן שֶׁהִכָּה. וְעוֹד, "כִּי יַכֶּה כָּל נֶפֶשׁ אָדָם" אֲפִלּוּ נְפָלִים בְּמַשְׁמָע.

תַּלְמוּד לוֹמַר: "מַכֵּה אִישׁ", עַד שֶׁיִּהְיֶה בֶן קְיָמָא הָרָאוּי לִהְיוֹת אִישׁ:

יג **וַאֲשֶׁר לֹא צָדָה.** לֹא אָרַב לוֹ וְלֹא נִתְכַּוֵּן. 'צָדָה' לְשׁוֹן מַאֲרָב, וְכֵן הוּא אוֹמֵר: "וְאַתָּה צֹדֶה אֶת נַפְשִׁי לְקַחְתָּהּ" (שמואל א' כד, יא). וְלֹא יִתָּכֵן לוֹמַר 'צָדָה' לְשׁוֹן "הַצָּד צָיִד" (בראשית כה, כח), שֶׁצֵּידַת חַיּוֹת אֵין נוֹפֵל ה"א בַּפֹּעַל שֶׁלָּהּ, וְשֵׁם דָּבָר בָּהּ 'צַיִד', וְזֶה שֵׁם דָּבָר בּוֹ 'צְדִיָּה', וּפֹעַל שֶׁלּוֹ 'צוֹדֶה', וְזֶה פֹּעַל שֶׁלּוֹ 'צָד'. וְאוֹמֵר אֲנִי, פִּתְרוֹנוֹ כְּתַרְגּוּמוֹ: "וּדְלָא כְמַן לֵיהּ". וּמְנַחֵם חִבְּרוֹ בְּחֵלֶק 'צָד עַד', וְאֵין אֲנִי מוֹדֶה לוֹ. וְאִם יֵשׁ לְחַבְּרוֹ בְּאַחַת מִמַּחְלְקוֹת שֶׁל 'צָד', נְחַבְּרֶנּוּ בְּחֵלֶק "עַד תְּנַאֲשׁוּ" (ישעיה סו, יב), "עָדָה חֻלְיָהּ" (שמואל ב' א, כד), "וּמִלִּין לְצַד עִלָּאָה יְמַלֵּל" (דניאל ז, כה). אַף כָּאן "אֲשֶׁר לֹא צָדָה" לֹא צִדֵּד לְמַעְלָה לוֹ שׁוּם עַד מִיתָה. וְאַף זֶה יֵשׁ לְהַרְהֵר עָלָיו, מִכָּל מָקוֹם לְשׁוֹן אוֹרֵב הוּא: **וְהָאֱלֹהִים אִנָּה לְיָדוֹ.** זִמֵּן לְיָדוֹ, לְשׁוֹן: "לֹא תְאֻנֶּה אֵלֶיךָ רָעָה" (תהלים צא, י), "לֹא יְאֻנֶּה לַצַּדִּיק כָּל אָוֶן" (משלי יב, כא), "מִתְאַנֶּה הוּא לִי" (מלכים ב' ה, ז) – מִזְדַּמֵּן לִמְצֹא לִי עִלָּה: **וְהָאֱלֹהִים אִנָּה לְיָדוֹ.** וְלָמָּה תֵצֵא זֹאת מִלְּפָנָיו? הוּא שֶׁאָמַר דָּוִד: "כַּאֲשֶׁר יֹאמַר מְשַׁל הַקַּדְמֹנִי מֵרְשָׁעִים יֵצֵא רֶשַׁע" (שמואל א' כד, יג). וּמְשַׁל הַקַּדְמֹנִי הִיא הַתּוֹרָה שֶׁהִיא מְשַׁל הַקָּדוֹשׁ בָּרוּךְ הוּא שֶׁהוּא קַדְמוֹנוֹ שֶׁל עוֹלָם. וְהֵיכָן אָמְרָה תוֹרָה: "מֵרְשָׁעִים יֵצֵא רֶשַׁע"? – "וְהָאֱלֹהִים אִנָּה לְיָדוֹ". בַּמֶּה הַכָּתוּב מְדַבֵּר? בִּשְׁנֵי בְנֵי אָדָם, אֶחָד הָרַג שׁוֹגֵג וְאֶחָד הָרַג מֵזִיד, וְלֹא הָיוּ עֵדִים בַּדָּבָר שֶׁיָּעִידוּ, זֶה לֹא נֶהֱרָג וְזֶה לֹא גָלָה. הַקָּדוֹשׁ בָּרוּךְ הוּא מְזַמְּנָן לְפֻנְדָּק אֶחָד, זֶה שֶׁהָרַג מֵזִיד יוֹשֵׁב תַּחַת הַסֻּלָּם וְזֶה שֶׁהָרַג שׁוֹגֵג עוֹלֶה בַסֻּלָּם וְנוֹפֵל עַל זֶה שֶׁהָרַג מֵזִיד וְהוֹרְגוֹ, וְעֵדִים מְעִידִים עָלָיו וּמְחַיְּבִים אוֹתוֹ לִגְלוֹת. נִמְצָא זֶה שֶׁהָרַג שׁוֹגֵג גּוֹלֶה וְזֶה שֶׁהָרַג מֵזִיד נֶהֱרָג: **וְשַׂמְתִּי לְךָ מָקוֹם.** אַף בַּמִּדְבָּר, שֶׁיָּנוּס שָׁמָּה. וְאֵי זֶה מָקוֹם קוֹלְטוֹ? זֶה מַחֲנֵה לְוִיָּה:

שמות | פרק כא — משפטים

יד שָׁמָּה: וְכִי־יָזִד אִישׁ עַל־רֵעֵהוּ לְהָרְגוֹ בְעָרְמָה
טו מֵעִם מִזְבְּחִי תִּקָּחֶנּוּ לָמוּת: וּמַכֵּה אָבִיו וְאִמּוֹ
טז מוֹת יוּמָת: וְגֹנֵב אִישׁ וּמְכָרוֹ וְנִמְצָא בְיָדוֹ מוֹת
יז יוּמָת: וּמְקַלֵּל אָבִיו וְאִמּוֹ מוֹת יוּמָת: וְכִי־
יח יְרִיבֻן אֲנָשִׁים וְהִכָּה־אִישׁ אֶת־רֵעֵהוּ בְּאֶבֶן אוֹ בְאֶגְרֹף וְלֹא יָמוּת
יט וְנָפַל לְמִשְׁכָּב: אִם־יָקוּם וְהִתְהַלֵּךְ בַּחוּץ עַל־מִשְׁעַנְתּוֹ וְנִקָּה
כ הַמַּכֶּה רַק שִׁבְתּוֹ יִתֵּן וְרַפֹּא יְרַפֵּא: וְכִי־יַכֶּה אִישׁ שני

יד) **וְכִי יָזִד.** לָמָּה נֶאֱמַר? לְפִי שֶׁנֶּאֱמַר: "מַכֵּה אִישׁ" וְגוֹ' (לעיל פסוק יב), שׁוֹמֵעַ אֲנִי חַבְלוּ גּוֹי, וְהָרוֹפֵא שֶׁהֵמִית, וּשְׁלִיחַ בֵּית דִּין שֶׁהֵמִית בְּמַלְקוּת אַרְבָּעִים, וְהָאָב הַמַּכֶּה אֶת בְּנוֹ, וְהָרַב הָרוֹדֶה אֶת תַּלְמִידוֹ, וְהַשּׁוֹגֵג? תַּלְמוּד לוֹמַר: "וְכִי יָזִד" וְלֹא שׁוֹגֵג, "עַל רֵעֵהוּ" וְלֹא עַל גּוֹי, "לְהָרְגוֹ בְעָרְמָה" וְלֹא שְׁלִיחַ בֵּית דִּין וְהָרוֹפֵא וְהָרוֹדֶה בְּנוֹ וְתַלְמִידוֹ, שֶׁאַף עַל פִּי שֶׁהֵם מְזִידִין אֵין מַעֲרִימִין: **מֵעִם מִזְבְּחִי.** אִם הָיָה כֹהֵן וְרוֹצֶה לַעֲבוֹד עֲבוֹדָה, "תִּקָּחֶנּוּ לָמוּת":

טו) **וּמַכֵּה אָבִיו וְאִמּוֹ.** לְפִי שֶׁלָּמַדְנוּ עַל הַחוֹבֵל בַּחֲבֵרוֹ שֶׁהוּא בְּתַשְׁלוּמִין וְלֹא בְּמִיתָה, הֻצְרַךְ לוֹמַר עַל הַחוֹבֵל בְּאָבִיו שֶׁהוּא בְּמִיתָה. וְאֵינוֹ חַיָּב אֶלָּא בְּהַכָּאָה שֶׁיֵּשׁ בָּהּ חַבּוּרָה: **אָבִיו וְאִמּוֹ.** אוֹ זֶה אוֹ זֶה: **מוֹת יוּמָת.** בְּחֶנֶק:

טז) **וְגֹנֵב אִישׁ וּמְכָרוֹ.** לָמָּה נֶאֱמַר? לְפִי שֶׁנֶּאֱמַר: "כִּי יִמָּצֵא אִישׁ גֹּנֵב נֶפֶשׁ מֵאֶחָיו" (דברים כד, ז), אֵין לִי אֶלָּא אִישׁ שֶׁגָּנַב נֶפֶשׁ, אִשָּׁה אוֹ טֻמְטוּם אוֹ אַנְדְּרוֹגִינוֹס שֶׁגָּנְבוּ מִנַּיִן? תַּלְמוּד לוֹמַר: "וְגֹנֵב אִישׁ וּמְכָרוֹ". וּלְפִי שֶׁנֶּאֱמַר כָּאן: "וְגֹנֵב אִישׁ", אֵין לִי אֶלָּא גּוֹנֵב אִישׁ, גּוֹנֵב אִשָּׁה מִנַּיִן? תַּלְמוּד לוֹמַר: "גֹּנֵב נֶפֶשׁ". לְכָךְ הֶעֱרִיךְ שְׁנֵיהֶם, מַה שֶּׁחָסֵר זֶה גִּלָּה זֶה: **וְנִמְצָא בְיָדוֹ.** שֶׁרָאוּהוּ עֵדִים שֶׁגְּנָבוֹ וּמְכָרוֹ, "וְנִמְצָא" כְּבָר קֹדֶם הַמְּכִירָה: **מוֹת יוּמָת.** בְּחֶנֶק. כָּל מִיתָה הָאֲמוּרָה בַּתּוֹרָה סְתָם חֶנֶק הִיא:

יז) **וּמְקַלֵּל אָבִיו וְאִמּוֹ.** לָמָּה נֶאֱמַר? לְפִי שֶׁהוּא אוֹמֵר: "אִישׁ אִישׁ אֲשֶׁר יְקַלֵּל אֶת אָבִיו" (ויקרא כ, ט), אֵין לִי אֶלָּא אִישׁ שֶׁקִּלֵּל אֶת אָבִיו, אִשָּׁה שֶׁקִּלְּלָה אֶת אָבִיהָ מִנַּיִן? תַּלְמוּד לוֹמַר: "וּמְקַלֵּל אָבִיו וְאִמּוֹ", סְתָם, בֵּין אִישׁ וּבֵין אִשָּׁה. אִם כֵּן לָמָּה נֶאֱמַר: "אִישׁ אֲשֶׁר יְקַלֵּל"? לְהוֹצִיא אֶת הַקָּטָן. **מוֹת יוּמָת.** בִּסְקִילָה, וְכָל מָקוֹם שֶׁנֶּאֱמַר "דָּמָיו בּוֹ", בִּסְקִילָה, וּבִנְיַן אָב לְכֻלָּם: "בָּאֶבֶן יִרְגְּמוּ אֹתָם דְּמֵיהֶם בָּם" (ויקרא כ, כז), וּבִמְקַלֵּל אָבִיו נֶאֱמַר: "דָּמָיו בּוֹ" (שם פסוק ט):

יח) **וְכִי יְרִיבֻן אֲנָשִׁים.** לָמָּה נֶאֱמַר? לְפִי שֶׁנֶּאֱמַר: "עַיִן תַּחַת עַיִן" (להלן פסוק כד), לֹא לָמַדְנוּ אֶלָּא דְּמֵי אֵבָרָיו, אֲבָל שֶׁבֶת וְרִפּוּי לֹא לָמַדְנוּ, לְכָךְ נֶאֶמְרָה פָּרָשָׁה זוֹ: **וְנָפַל לְמִשְׁכָּב.** כְּתַרְגּוּמוֹ: "וְיִפּוֹל לְבוּטְלָן", לְחֹלִי שֶׁמְּבַטְּלוֹ מִמְּלַאכְתּוֹ:

יט) **עַל מִשְׁעַנְתּוֹ.** עַל בֻּרְיוֹ וְכֹחוֹ: **וְנִקָּה הַמַּכֶּה.** וְכִי תַעֲלֶה עַל דַּעְתְּךָ שֶׁיֵּהָרֵג זֶה שֶׁלֹּא הָרַג?! אֶלָּא לִמֶּדְךָ כָּאן שֶׁחוֹבְשִׁים אוֹתוֹ עַד שֶׁנִּרְאֶה אִם יִתְרַפֵּא זֶה, וְכֵן מַשְׁמָעוֹ: כְּשֶׁקָּם זֶה וְהוֹלֵךְ עַל מִשְׁעַנְתּוֹ אָז נִקָּה הַמַּכֶּה, אֲבָל עַד שֶׁלֹּא יָקוּם זֶה לֹא נִקָּה הַמַּכֶּה: **רַק שִׁבְתּוֹ.** בִּטּוּל מְלַאכְתּוֹ מֵחֲמַת הַחֹלִי. אִם קָטַע יָדוֹ אוֹ רַגְלוֹ רוֹאִין בִּטּוּל מְלֶאכֶת הַחֹלִי כְּאִלּוּ הוּא שׁוֹמֵר קִשּׁוּאִין, שֶׁהֲרֵי אַף לְאַחַר הַחֹלִי אֵינוֹ רָאוּי לִמְלֶאכֶת יָד וְרֶגֶל, וְהוּא כְבָר נָתַן לוֹ מֵחֲמַת נִזְקוֹ דְּמֵי יָדוֹ וְרַגְלוֹ, שֶׁנֶּאֱמַר: "יָד תַּחַת יָד, רֶגֶל תַּחַת רָגֶל" (להלן פסוק כד): **וְרַפֹּא יְרַפֵּא.** כְּתַרְגּוּמוֹ, יְשַׁלֵּם שְׂכַר הָרוֹפֵא:

כ) **וְכִי יַכֶּה אִישׁ אֶת עַבְדּוֹ אוֹ אֶת אֲמָתוֹ.** בְּעֶבֶד כְּנַעֲנִי הַכָּתוּב מְדַבֵּר, אוֹ אֵינוֹ אֶלָּא בְּעִבְרִי? תַּלְמוּד

משפטים | פרק כא

אֶת־עַבְדּ֛וֹ א֥וֹ אֶת־אֲמָת֖וֹ בַּשֵּׁ֑בֶט וּמֵ֖ת תַּ֣חַת יָד֑וֹ נָקֹ֖ם יִנָּקֵֽם: אַ֥ךְ כא
אִם־י֛וֹם א֥וֹ יוֹמַ֖יִם יַעֲמֹ֑ד לֹ֣א יֻקַּ֔ם כִּ֥י כַסְפּ֖וֹ הֽוּא: וְכִֽי־ כב
יִנָּצ֣וּ אֲנָשִׁ֗ים וְנָ֨גְפ֜וּ אִשָּׁ֤ה הָרָה֙ וְיָצְא֣וּ יְלָדֶ֔יהָ וְלֹ֥א יִהְיֶ֖ה אָס֑וֹן
עָנ֣וֹשׁ יֵעָנֵ֗שׁ כַּֽאֲשֶׁ֨ר יָשִׁ֤ית עָלָיו֙ בַּ֣עַל הָֽאִשָּׁ֔ה וְנָתַ֖ן בִּפְלִלִֽים:
וְאִם־אָס֖וֹן יִֽהְיֶ֑ה וְנָֽתַתָּ֥ה נֶ֖פֶשׁ תַּ֥חַת נָֽפֶשׁ: עַ֚יִן תַּ֣חַת עַ֔יִן שֵׁ֖ן כג
תַּ֣חַת שֵׁ֑ן יָ֚ד תַּ֣חַת יָ֔ד רֶ֖גֶל תַּ֥חַת רָֽגֶל: כְּוִיָּה֙ תַּ֣חַת כְּוִיָּ֔ה פֶּ֖צַע כה
תַּ֣חַת פָּ֑צַע חַבּוּרָ֖ה תַּ֥חַת חַבּוּרָֽה: וְכִֽי־יַכֶּ֥ה אִ֛ישׁ אֶת־ כו

לוֹמַר: "כִּי כַסְפּוֹ הוּא", מָה כַּסְפּוֹ קָנוּי לוֹ עוֹלָמִית, אַף עֶבֶד הַקָּנוּי לוֹ עוֹלָמִית. וַהֲרֵי הָיָה בִּכְלָל "מַכֵּה אִישׁ וָמֵת" (לעיל פסוק יב), חֻלַּק בָּהּ הַכָּתוּב וְהוֹצִיאוֹ מִן הַכְּלָל לִהְיוֹת נָדוֹן בְּדִין יוֹם אוֹ יוֹמַיִם, שֶׁאִם לֹא מֵת תַּחַת יָדוֹ וְשָׁהָה מֵעֵת לְעֵת – פָּטוּר: בַּשֵּׁבֶט. כְּשֶׁיֵּשׁ בּוֹ כְּדֵי לְהָמִית הַכָּתוּב מְדַבֵּר. אוֹ אֵפִלּוּ אֵין בּוֹ כְּדֵי לְהָמִית? תַּלְמוּד לוֹמַר בְּיִשְׂרָאֵל: "וְאִם בְּאֶבֶן יָד אֲשֶׁר יָמוּת בָּהּ הִכָּהוּ" (במדבר לה, יז), וַהֲלֹא דְּבָרִים קַל וָחֹמֶר. וּמַה יִּשְׂרָאֵל חָמוּר, אֵין חַיָּב עָלָיו חֶלָּא אִם כֵּן הִכָּהוּ בְּדָבָר שֶׁיֵּשׁ בּוֹ כְּדֵי לְהָמִית וְעַל אֵבֶר שֶׁהוּא כְּדֵי לָמוּת בְּהַכָּאָה זוֹ, עֶבֶד הַקַּל לֹא כָּל שֶׁכֵּן?: נָקֹם יִנָּקֵם. מִיתַת סַיִף, וְכֵן הוּא אוֹמֵר: "חֶרֶב נֹקֶמֶת נְקַם בְּרִית" (ויקרא כו, כה):

כא) אַךְ אִם יוֹם אוֹ יוֹמַיִם יַעֲמֹד לֹא יֻקַּם. אִם עַל יוֹם אֶחָד הוּא פָּטוּר עַל יוֹמַיִם לֹא כָּל שֶׁכֵּן?! אֶלָּא יוֹם שֶׁהוּא כְּיוֹמַיִם, וְאֵי זֶה זֶה? זֶה מֵעֵת לְעֵת: לֹא יֻקַּם כִּי כַסְפּוֹ הוּא. הָא אַחֵר שֶׁהִכָּהוּ, אַף עַל פִּי שֶׁשָּׁהָה מֵעֵת לְעֵת קֹדֶם שֶׁמֵּת, חַיָּב:

כב) וְכִי יִנָּצוּ אֲנָשִׁים. זֶה עִם זֶה, וְנִתְכַּוְּנוּ לְהַכּוֹת אֶת חֲבֵרוֹ וְהִכָּה אֶת הָאִשָּׁה: וְנָגְפוּ. אֵין נְגִיפָה אֶלָּא לְשׁוֹן דְּחִיפָה וְהַכָּאָה, כְּמוֹ: "פֶּן תִּגֹּף בָּאֶבֶן רַגְלֶךָ" (תהלים צא, יב), "וּבְטֶרֶם יִתְנַגְּפוּ רַגְלֵיכֶם" (ירמיה יג, טז), "וּלְאֶבֶן נֶגֶף" (ישעיה ח, יד): וְלֹא יִהְיֶה אָסוֹן. בָּאִשָּׁה: עָנוֹשׁ יֵעָנֵשׁ. לְשַׁלֵּם דְּמֵי וְלָדוֹת לַבַּעַל, שָׁמִין אוֹתָהּ כַּמָּה הָיְתָה רְאוּיָה לִמָּכֵר בַּשּׁוּק לְהַעֲלוֹת בִּדְמֶיהָ בִּשְׁבִיל הֵרָיוֹנָהּ: עָנוֹשׁ יֵעָנֵשׁ. יִגְבּוּ מָמוֹן מִמֶּנּוּ, כְּמוֹ "וְעָנְשׁוּ

אוֹתוֹ מֵאָה כֶסֶף" (דברים כב, יט): כַּאֲשֶׁר יָשִׁית עָלָיו וְגוֹ׳. כְּשֶׁיִּתְבָּעֶנּוּ הַבַּעַל בְּבֵית דִּין לְהָשִׁית עָלָיו עֹנֶשׁ עַל כָּךְ: וְנָתַן. הַמַּכֶּה דְּמֵי וְלָדוֹת: בִּפְלִלִים. עַל פִּי הַדַּיָּנִים:

כג) וְאִם אָסוֹן יִהְיֶה. בָּאִשָּׁה: וְנָתַתָּה נֶפֶשׁ תַּחַת נָפֶשׁ. רַבּוֹתֵינוּ חוֹלְקִים בַּדָּבָר: יֵשׁ אוֹמְרִים נֶפֶשׁ מַמָּשׁ, וְיֵשׁ אוֹמְרִים מָמוֹן, אֲבָל לֹא נֶפֶשׁ מַמָּשׁ, שֶׁהַמִּתְכַּוֵּן לַהֲרֹג אֶת זֶה וְהָרַג אֶת זֶה פָּטוּר מִמִּיתָה, וּמְשַׁלֵּם לְיוֹרְשָׁיו דָּמָיו כְּמוֹ שֶׁהָיָה נִמְכָּר בַּשּׁוּק:

כד) עַיִן תַּחַת עַיִן. סִמֵּא עֵין חֲבֵרוֹ נוֹתֵן לוֹ דְּמֵי עֵינוֹ כַּמָּה שֶׁפָּחֲתוּ דָּמָיו לִמְכֹּר בַּשּׁוּק, וְכֵן כֻּלָּם, וְלֹא נְטִילַת אֵבֶר מַמָּשׁ, כְּמוֹ שֶׁדָּרְשׁוּ רַבּוֹתֵינוּ בְּפֶרֶק הַחוֹבֵל (בבא קמא פג ע"ב - פד ע"א):

כה) כְּוִיָּה תַּחַת כְּוִיָּה. מִכְוַת אֵשׁ. וְעַד עַכְשָׁו לֹא דִּבֵּר בַּחֲבָלָה שֶׁיֵּשׁ בָּהּ פְּחַת דָּמִים, וְעַכְשָׁו בְּשֶׁאֵין בָּהּ פְּחַת דָּמִים, כְּגוֹן כְּוָאוֹ בְּשַׁפּוּד עַל צִפָּרְנוֹ, אוֹמְדִים כַּמָּה אָדָם כַּיּוֹצֵא בָּזֶה רוֹצֶה לִטֹּל לִהְיוֹת מִצְטַעֵר כָּךְ: פֶּצַע. הִיא מַכָּה הַמּוֹצִיאָה דָּם, שֶׁפָּצַע אֶת בְּשָׂרוֹ, נברדו"רא בְּלַעַ"ז. הַכֹּל לְפִי מַה שֶּׁהוּא, אִם יֵשׁ בּוֹ פְּחַת דָּמִים נוֹתֵן נֶזֶק, וְאִם נָפַל לְמִשְׁכָּב נוֹתֵן שֶׁבֶת וְרִפּוּי וּבֹשֶׁת וָצַעַר. וּמִקְרָא זֶה יָתֵר הוּא, וּבְ"הַחוֹבֵל" דְּרָשׁוּהוּ רַבּוֹתֵינוּ לְחַיֵּב עַל הַצַּעַר אֲפִלּוּ בִּמְקוֹם נֶזֶק, שֶׁאַף עַל פִּי שֶׁנּוֹתֵן לוֹ דְּמֵי יָדוֹ אֵין פּוֹטְרִין אוֹתוֹ מִן הַצַּעַר, לוֹמַר הוֹאִיל וְקָנָה יָדוֹ יֵשׁ עָלָיו לְחָתְכָהּ בְּכָל מַה שֶּׁיִּרְצֶה, אֶלָּא אוֹמְרִים יֵשׁ לוֹ לְחָתְכָהּ בְּסַם שֶׁאֵינוֹ מִצְטַעֵר כָּל כָּךְ, וְזֶה חֲתָכָהּ בְּבַרְזֶל וְצִעֲרוֹ: חַבּוּרָה. הִיא מַכָּה שֶׁהַדָּם נֶאֱצָר בָּהּ

שמות | פרק כא

עֵין עַבְדּ֛וֹ אוֹ־אֶת־עֵ֥ין אֲמָת֖וֹ וְשִׁחֵתָ֑הּ לַֽחָפְשִׁ֥י יְשַׁלְּחֶ֖נּוּ תַּ֥חַת
עֵינֽוֹ: וְאִם־שֵׁ֥ן עַבְדּ֛וֹ אֽוֹ־שֵׁ֥ן אֲמָת֖וֹ יַפִּ֑יל לַֽחָפְשִׁ֥י יְשַׁלְּחֶ֖נּוּ תַּ֥חַת כז
שִׁנּֽוֹ:

וְכִֽי־יִגַּ֨ח שׁ֥וֹר אֶת־אִ֛ישׁ א֥וֹ אֶת־אִשָּׁ֖ה וָמֵ֑ת סָק֤וֹל יִסָּקֵל֙ הַשּׁ֔וֹר כח
וְלֹ֥א יֵֽאָכֵ֖ל אֶת־בְּשָׂר֑וֹ וּבַ֥עַל הַשּׁ֖וֹר נָקִֽי: וְאִ֡ם שׁוֹר֩ נַגָּ֨ח ה֜וּא כט
מִתְּמֹ֣ל שִׁלְשֹׁ֗ם וְהוּעַ֤ד בִּבְעָלָיו֙ וְלֹ֣א יִשְׁמְרֶ֔נּוּ וְהֵמִ֥ית אִ֖ישׁ א֣וֹ
אִשָּׁ֑ה הַשּׁוֹר֙ יִסָּקֵ֔ל וְגַם־בְּעָלָ֖יו יוּמָֽת: אִם־כֹּ֖פֶר יוּשַׁ֣ת עָלָ֑יו ל
וְנָתַ֛ן פִּדְיֹ֥ן נַפְשׁ֖וֹ כְּכֹ֥ל אֲשֶׁר־יוּשַׁ֥ת עָלָֽיו: אוֹ־בֵ֥ן יִגָּ֖ח אוֹ־בַ֥ת לא

וְהִנּוֹ יוֹצֵא חָלָק שֶׁמְּאַחֲדִים הַבָּשָׂר כְּנֶגְדּוֹ. וּלְשׁוֹן חַבּוּרָה טיק״א בלעז, כְּמוֹ: "וַנָּמֵר חֲבַרְבֻּרֹתָיו" (ירמיה יג, כג), וְתַרְגּוּמוֹ "מַשְׁקוֹפֵי", לְשׁוֹן חֲבָטָה, בטדו״ר בלעז, וְכֵן: "שִׁדְפוֹת קָדִים" (בראשית מא, כג), "שְׁקִיפָן קִדּוּם", חֲבוּטוֹת בָּרוּחַ. וְכֵן: "עַל הַמַּשְׁקוֹף" (לעיל יב, ז), עַל שֵׁם שֶׁהַדֶּלֶת נוֹקֵשׁ עָלָיו:

כו אֶת עֵין עַבְדּוֹ. כְּנַעֲנִי, אֲבָל עִבְרִי אֵינוֹ יוֹצֵא בְּשֵׁן וָעַיִן, כְּמוֹ שֶׁנֶּאֱמַר אֵצֶל "לֹא תֵצֵא כְּצֵאת הָעֲבָדִים" (לעיל פסוק ז): תַּחַת עֵינוֹ. וְכֵן בְּעֶשְׂרִים וְאַרְבָּעָה רָאשֵׁי אֵבָרִים: אֶצְבְּעוֹת הַיָּדַיִם וְהָרַגְלַיִם וּשְׁתֵּי אָזְנַיִם וְהַחֹטֶם וְרֹאשׁ הַגְּוִיָּה שֶׁהוּא גִּיד הַחַמָּה. וְלָמָּה נֶאֶמְרוּ שֵׁן וָעַיִן? שֶׁאִם נֶאֱמַר עַיִן וְלֹא נֶאֱמַר שֵׁן, הָיִיתִי אוֹמֵר, מָה עַיִן שֶׁנִּבְרְאָה עִמּוֹ אַף כָּל שֶׁנִּבְרָא עִמּוֹ, וַהֲרֵי שֵׁן לֹא נִבְרְאָה עִמּוֹ. וְאִם נֶאֱמַר שֵׁן וְלֹא נֶאֱמַר עַיִן, הָיִיתִי אוֹמֵר, אֲפִלּוּ שֵׁן תִּינוֹק שֶׁיֵּשׁ לָהּ חֲלִיפִין, לְכָךְ נֶאֱמַר עַיִן:

כח וְכִי יִגַּח שׁוֹר. אֶחָד שׁוֹר וְאֶחָד כָּל בְּהֵמָה וְחַיָּה וָעוֹף, אֶלָּא שֶׁדִּבֵּר הַכָּתוּב בַּהֹוֶה: וְלֹא יֵאָכֵל אֶת בְּשָׂרוֹ. מִמַּשְׁמָע שֶׁנֶּאֱמַר: "סָקוֹל יִסָּקֵל הַשּׁוֹר" אֵינִי יוֹדֵעַ שֶׁהוּא נְבֵלָה וּנְבֵלָה אֲסוּרָה בַּאֲכִילָה? אֶלָּא מַה תַּלְמוּד לוֹמַר: "וְלֹא יֵאָכֵל אֶת בְּשָׂרוֹ"? שֶׁאֲפִלּוּ שְׁחָטוֹ לְאַחַר שֶׁנִּגְמַר דִּינוֹ אָסוּר בַּאֲכִילָה. בַּהֲנָאָה מִנַּיִן? תַּלְמוּד לוֹמַר: "וּבַעַל הַשּׁוֹר נָקִי", כְּאָדָם

הָאוֹמֵר לַחֲבֵרוֹ: יָצָא פְּלוֹנִי נָקִי מִנְּכָסָיו וְאֵין לוֹ בָּהֶם הֲנָאָה שֶׁל כְּלוּם. זֶהוּ מִדְרָשׁוֹ. וּפְשׁוּטוֹ כְּמַשְׁמָעוֹ, לְפִי שֶׁנֶּאֱמַר: "וְגַם בְּעָלָיו יוּמָת", הָצְרַךְ לוֹמַר פָּתַח: "וּבַעַל הַשּׁוֹר נָקִי":

כט מִתְּמֹל שִׁלְשֹׁם. הֲרֵי שָׁלֹשׁ נְגִיחוֹת: וְהוּעַד בִּבְעָלָיו. לְשׁוֹן הַתְרָאָה בְּעֵדִים, כְּמוֹ: "הָעֵד הֵעִד בָּנוּ הָאִישׁ" (בראשית מג, ג): וְהֵמִית אִישׁ וְגוֹ'. לְפִי שֶׁנֶּאֱמַר: "וְכִי יִגַּח" (לעיל פסוק כח), אֵין לִי אֶלָּא שֶׁהֵמִית בִּנְגִיחָה, הֵמִית בִּנְשִׁיכָה דְּחִיפָה בְּעִיטָה מִנַּיִן? תַּלְמוּד לוֹמַר: "וְהֵמִית": וְגַם בְּעָלָיו יוּמָת. בִּידֵי שָׁמַיִם. יָכוֹל בִּידֵי אָדָם? תַּלְמוּד לוֹמַר: "מוֹת יוּמַת הַמַּכֶּה רֹצֵחַ הוּא" (במדבר לה, כא), עַל רְצִיחָתוֹ אַתָּה הוֹרְגוֹ וְאִי אַתָּה הוֹרְגוֹ עַל רְצִיחַת שׁוֹרוֹ:

ל אִם כֹּפֶר יוּשַׁת עָלָיו. 'אִם' זֶה אֵינוֹ תָּלוּי, וַהֲרֵי הוּא כְּמוֹ: "אִם כֶּסֶף תַּלְוֶה" (להלן כב, כד), לְשׁוֹן 'אֲשֶׁר', זֶה מִשְׁפָּטוֹ שֶׁיָּשִׁיתוּ עָלָיו בֵּית דִּין כֹּפֶר: וְנָתַן פִּדְיֹן נַפְשׁוֹ. דְּמֵי נִזָּק, דִּבְרֵי רַבִּי יִשְׁמָעֵאל. רַבִּי עֲקִיבָא אוֹמֵר: דְּמֵי מַזִּיק:

לא אוֹ בֵן יִגָּח. בֵּן שֶׁהוּא קָטָן: אוֹ בַת. שֶׁהִיא קְטַנָּה. לְפִי שֶׁנֶּאֱמַר: "וְהֵמִית אִישׁ אוֹ אִשָּׁה" (לעיל פסוק כט), יָכוֹל אֵינוֹ חַיָּב אֶלָּא עַל הַגְּדוֹלִים? תַּלְמוּד לוֹמַר: "אוֹ בֵן יִגַּח וְגוֹ'", לְחַיֵּב עַל הַקְּטַנִּים כַּגְּדוֹלִים:

פרק כא

לב יִגָּח כַּמִּשְׁפָּט הַזֶּה יֵעָשֶׂה לּוֹ: אִם־עֶבֶד יִגַּח הַשּׁוֹר אוֹ אָמָה כֶּסֶף שְׁלֹשִׁים שְׁקָלִים יִתֵּן לַאדֹנָיו וְהַשּׁוֹר יִסָּקֵל: לג וְכִי־יִפְתַּח אִישׁ בּוֹר אוֹ כִּי־יִכְרֶה אִישׁ בֹּר וְלֹא יְכַסֶּנּוּ וְנָפַל־שָׁמָּה שּׁוֹר אוֹ חֲמוֹר: לד בַּעַל הַבּוֹר יְשַׁלֵּם כֶּסֶף יָשִׁיב לִבְעָלָיו וְהַמֵּת יִהְיֶה־לּוֹ: לה וְכִי־יִגֹּף שׁוֹר־אִישׁ אֶת־שׁוֹר רֵעֵהוּ וָמֵת וּמָכְרוּ אֶת־הַשּׁוֹר הַחַי וְחָצוּ אֶת־כַּסְפּוֹ וְגַם אֶת־הַמֵּת יֶחֱצוּן:

לב **אִם עֶבֶד אוֹ אָמָה.** כְּנַעֲנִים: **שְׁלֹשִׁים שְׁקָלִים יִתֵּן.** גְּזֵרַת הַכָּתוּב הוּא, בֵּין שֶׁהוּא שָׁוֶה אֶלֶף זוּז בֵּין שֶׁאֵינוֹ שָׁוֶה אֶלָּא דִּינָר. וְהַשֶּׁקֶל מִשְׁקָלוֹ אַרְבָּעָה זְהוּבִים שֶׁהֵם חֲצִי אוּנְקִיָּא לְמִשְׁקַל הַיָּשָׁר שֶׁל קוֹלוֹנְיָא:

לג **וְכִי יִפְתַּח אִישׁ בּוֹר.** שֶׁהָיָה מְכֻסֶּה וְגִלָּהוּ: **אוֹ כִּי יִכְרֶה.** לָמָּה נֶאֱמַר? אִם עַל הַפְּתִיחָה חַיָּב עַל הַכְּרִיָּה לֹא כָּל שֶׁכֵּן?! אֶלָּא לְהָבִיא כּוֹרֶה אַחַר כּוֹרֶה שֶׁהוּא חַיָּב: **וְלֹא יְכַסֶּנּוּ.** הָא אִם כִּסָּהוּ פָּטוּר, וּבְחוֹפֵר בִּרְשׁוּת הָרַבִּים דִּבֶּר הַכָּתוּב: **שׁוֹר אוֹ חֲמוֹר.** הוּא הַדִּין לְכָל בְּהֵמָה וְחַיָּה, שֶׁבְּכָל מָקוֹם שֶׁנֶּאֱמַר שׁוֹר וַחֲמוֹר אָנוּ לְמֵדִין אוֹתוֹ 'שׁוֹר' מִשַּׁבָּת, שֶׁנֶּאֱמַר: "לְמַעַן יָנוּחַ שׁוֹרְךָ וַחֲמֹרֶךָ" (להלן כג, יב), מָה לְהַלָּן כָּל בְּהֵמָה וְחַיָּה כַּשּׁוֹר, שֶׁהֲרֵי נֶאֱמַר בְּמָקוֹם אַחֵר: "וְכָל בְּהֶמְתֶּךָ" (דברים ה, יד), אַף כָּאן כָּל בְּהֵמָה וְחַיָּה כַּשּׁוֹר, וְלֹא נֶאֱמַר שׁוֹר וַחֲמוֹר אֶלָּא 'שׁוֹר' וְלֹא אָדָם, 'חֲמוֹר' וְלֹא כֵּלִים:

לד **בַּעַל הַבּוֹר.** בַּעַל הַתַּקָּלָה, אַף עַל פִּי שֶׁאֵין הַבּוֹר שֶׁלּוֹ, שֶׁעֲשָׂאוֹ בִּרְשׁוּת הָרַבִּים, עֲשָׂאוֹ הַכָּתוּב בְּעָלָיו לְהִתְחַיֵּב בִּנְזָקָיו: **כֶּסֶף יָשִׁיב לִבְעָלָיו.** "יָשִׁיב" לְרַבּוֹת שָׁוֶה כֶסֶף וַאֲפִלּוּ סֻבִּין: **וְהַמֵּת יִהְיֶה לּוֹ.** לַנִּזָּק, שָׁמִין אֶת הַנְּבֵלָה וְנוֹטְלָהּ בַּדָּמִים, וּמְשַׁלֵּם לוֹ הַמַּזִּיק עָלֶיהָ תַּשְׁלוּמֵי נִזְקוֹ:

לה **וְכִי יִגֹּף.** יִדְחֹף, בֵּין בְּקַרְנָיו בֵּין בְּגוּפוֹ בֵּין בְּרַגְלָיו בֵּין שֶׁנְּשָׁכוֹ בְּשִׁנָּיו כֻּלָּן בִּכְלָל נְגִיפָה הֵם, שֶׁאֵין נְגִיפָה

אֶלָּא לְשׁוֹן מַכָּה: **שׁוֹר אִישׁ.** שׁוֹר שֶׁל אִישׁ: **וּמָכְרוּ אֶת הַשּׁוֹר וְגוֹ'.** בְּשָׁוִים הַכָּתוּב מְדַבֵּר, שׁוֹר שָׁוֶה מָאתַיִם שֶׁהֵמִית שׁוֹר שָׁוֶה מָאתַיִם, בֵּין שֶׁהַנְּבֵלָה שָׁוָה הַרְבֵּה בֵּין שֶׁהִיא שָׁוָה מְעַט, כְּשֶׁנּוֹטֵל זֶה חֲצִי הַחַי וַחֲצִי הַמֵּת וְזֶה חֲצִי הַחַי וַחֲצִי הַמֵּת נִמְצָא כָּל אֶחָד מַפְסִיד חֲצִי נֶזֶק שֶׁהִזִּיקָה הַמִּיתָה. לִמְּדֵנוּ שֶׁהַתָּם מְשַׁלֵּם חֲצִי נֶזֶק, שֶׁמִּן הַשָּׁוִין אַתָּה לָמֵד לַשֶּׁאֵינָן שָׁוִין כִּי דִין הַתָּם לְשַׁלֵּם חֲצִי נֶזֶק, לֹא פָּחוֹת וְלֹא יוֹתֵר. אוֹ יָכוֹל אַף בְּשֶׁאֵינָן שָׁוִין בִּדְמֵיהֶן כְּשֶׁהֵן חַיִּים אָמַר הַכָּתוּב: וְחָצוּ אֶת שְׁנֵיהֶם? אִם אָמַרְתָּ כֵּן, פְּעָמִים שֶׁהַמַּזִּיק מִשְׂתַּכֵּר הַרְבֵּה, כְּשֶׁהַנְּבֵלָה שָׁוָה לִמָּכֵר לְגוֹיִם הַרְבֵּה יוֹתֵר מִדְּמֵי שׁוֹר הַמַּזִּיק, וְאִי אֶפְשָׁר שֶׁיֹּאמַר הַכָּתוּב שֶׁיְּהֵא הַמַּזִּיק נִשְׂכָּר. אוֹ פְּעָמִים שֶׁהַנִּזָּק נוֹטֵל הַרְבֵּה יוֹתֵר מִדְּמֵי נֵזֶק שָׁלֵם, שֶׁאֲנִי דְּמֵי שׁוֹר הַמַּזִּיק שָׁוִין יוֹתֵר מִכָּל דְּמֵי שׁוֹר הַנִּזָּק, וְאִם אָמַרְתָּ כֵּן, הֲרֵי תָּם מְשַׁלֵּם מוּעָד. עַל כָּרְחֲךָ לֹא דִבֶּר הַכָּתוּב אֶלָּא בְּשָׁוִין בְּשָׁוֶה, וְלִמֶּדְךָ שֶׁהַתָּם מְשַׁלֵּם חֲצִי נֶזֶק, וּמִן הַשָּׁוִין תִּלְמֹד לְשֶׁאֵינָן שָׁוִין, שֶׁהַמִּשְׁתַּלֵּם חֲצִי נִזְקוֹ שָׁמִין לוֹ אֶת הַנְּבֵלָה, וּמַה שֶּׁפָּחֲתָה מִדָּמֶיהָ בִּשְׁבִיל הַמִּיתָה נוֹטֵל חֲצִי פַחַת וְהוֹלֵךְ. וְלָמָּה אָמַר הַכָּתוּב בִּלְשׁוֹן הַזֶּה, וְלֹא אָמַר: יְשַׁלֵּם חֶצְיוֹ? לְלַמֵּד שֶׁאֵין הַתָּם מְשַׁלֵּם אֶלָּא מִגּוּפוֹ, וְאִם נָגַח וָמֵת אֵין הַנִּזָּק נוֹטֵל אֶלָּא הַנְּבֵלָה, וְאִם אֵינָהּ מַגַּעַת לַחֲצִי נִזְקוֹ יַפְסִיד. אוֹ שׁוֹר שָׁוֶה מָנֶה שֶׁנָּגַח שׁוֹר שָׁוֶה חָמֵשׁ מֵאוֹת זוּז אֵינוֹ נוֹטֵל אֶלָּא אֶת הַשּׁוֹר, שֶׁלֹּא נִתְחַיֵּב הַתָּם לְשַׁלֵּם אֶת בְּעָלָיו מִן הָעֲלִיָּה:

שמות | פרק כא | משפטים

לו אוֹ נוֹדַע כִּי שׁוֹר נַגָּח הוּא מִתְּמוֹל שִׁלְשֹׁם וְלֹא יִשְׁמְרֶנּוּ בְּעָלָיו
שַׁלֵּם יְשַׁלֵּם שׁוֹר תַּחַת הַשּׁוֹר וְהַמֵּת יִהְיֶה־לּוֹ:
לז כִּי יִגְנֹב־אִישׁ שׁוֹר אוֹ־שֶׂה וּטְבָחוֹ אוֹ מְכָרוֹ חֲמִשָּׁה בָקָר יְשַׁלֵּם
תַּחַת הַשּׁוֹר וְאַרְבַּע־צֹאן תַּחַת הַשֶּׂה:
כב א אִם־בַּמַּחְתֶּרֶת יִמָּצֵא הַגַּנָּב וְהֻכָּה וָמֵת אֵין לוֹ דָּמִים:
ב אִם־זָרְחָה הַשֶּׁמֶשׁ עָלָיו דָּמִים לוֹ
שַׁלֵּם יְשַׁלֵּם אִם־אֵין לוֹ וְנִמְכַּר בִּגְנֵבָתוֹ:
ג אִם־הִמָּצֵא תִמָּצֵא בְיָדוֹ הַגְּנֵבָה מִשּׁוֹר עַד־חֲמוֹר עַד־שֶׂה חַיִּים שְׁנַיִם יְשַׁלֵּם: שלישי
ד כִּי יַבְעֶר־אִישׁ שָׂדֶה אוֹ־כֶרֶם וְשִׁלַּח אֶת־בְּעִירוֹ וּבִעֵר בִּשְׂדֵה

לו) או נודע. אוֹ לֹא הָיָה תָם, אֶלָּא "נוֹדַע כִּי שׁוֹר נַגָּח הוּא" הַיּוֹם וּמִתְּמוֹל שִׁלְשֹׁם, הֲרֵי שָׁלֹשׁ נְגִיחוֹת: **שַׁלֵּם יְשַׁלֵּם שׁוֹר.** נֶזֶק שָׁלֵם: **וְהַמֵּת יִהְיֶה־לּוֹ.** לַנִּזָּק, וְעָלָיו יַשְׁלִים הַמַּזִּיק עַד שֶׁיִּשְׁתַּלֵּם נֶזֶק כָּל מָקוֹם:

לז) חֲמִשָּׁה בָקָר וְגוֹ'. אָמַר רַבִּי יוֹחָנָן בֶּן זַכַּאי: חָס הַמָּקוֹם עַל כְּבוֹדָן שֶׁל בְּרִיּוֹת, שׁוֹר שֶׁהוֹלֵךְ בְּרַגְלָיו וְלֹא נִתְבַּזָּה בּוֹ הַגַּנָּב לְנָשְׂאוֹ עַל כְּתֵפוֹ – מְשַׁלֵּם חֲמִשָּׁה, שֶׂה שֶׁנּוֹשְׂאוֹ עַל כְּתֵפוֹ – מְשַׁלֵּם אַרְבָּעָה הוֹאִיל וְנִתְבַּזָּה בּוֹ. אָמַר רַבִּי מֵאִיר: בֹּא וּרְאֵה כַּמָּה גְדוֹלָה כֹּחָהּ שֶׁל מְלָאכָה, שׁוֹר שֶׁבִּטְּלוֹ מִמְּלַאכְתּוֹ – חֲמִשָּׁה, שֶׂה שֶׁלֹּא בִטְּלוֹ מִמְּלַאכְתּוֹ – אַרְבָּעָה: **תַּחַת הַשּׁוֹר... תַּחַת הַשֶּׂה.** שְׁנָאָן הַכָּתוּב, לוֹמַר שֶׁאֵין מִדַּת תַּשְׁלוּמֵי אַרְבָּעָה וַחֲמִשָּׁה נוֹהֶגֶת אֶלָּא בְּשׁוֹר וָשֶׂה בִּלְבָד:

פרק כב

א) אִם־בַּמַּחְתֶּרֶת. כְּשֶׁהָיָה חוֹתֵר אֶת הַבַּיִת: **אֵין לוֹ דָּמִים.** אֵין זוֹ רְצִיחָה, הֲרֵי הוּא כְּמֵת מֵעִקָּרוֹ. כָּאן לִמֶּדְתְךָ תּוֹרָה: אִם בָּא לַהָרְגְּךָ הַשְׁכֵּם לְהָרְגוֹ, וְזֶה לַהָרְגְּךָ בָּא, שֶׁהֲרֵי יוֹדֵעַ הוּא שֶׁאֵין אָדָם מַעֲמִיד עַצְמוֹ וְרוֹאֶה שֶׁנּוֹטְלִין מָמוֹנוֹ בְּפָנָיו וְשׁוֹתֵק, לְפִיכָךְ עַל מְנָת כֵּן בָּא שֶׁאִם יַעֲמֹד בַּעַל הַמָּמוֹן כְּנֶגְדּוֹ יַהַרְגֶנּוּ:

ב) אִם־זָרְחָה הַשֶּׁמֶשׁ עָלָיו. אֵין זֶה אֶלָּא כְּמִין מָשָׁל,

---

אִם בָּרוּר לְךָ הַדָּבָר שֶׁיֵּשׁ לוֹ שָׁלוֹם עִמְּךָ, כַּשֶּׁמֶשׁ הַזֶּה שֶׁהוּא שָׁלוֹם בָּעוֹלָם כָּךְ פָּשׁוּט לְךָ שֶׁאֵינוֹ בָא לַהֲרֹג אֲפִלּוּ יַעֲמֹד בַּעַל הַמָּמוֹן כְּנֶגְדּוֹ, כְּגוֹן אָב הַחוֹתֵר לִגְנֹב מָמוֹן הַבֵּן, בְּיָדוּעַ שֶׁרַחֲמֵי הָאָב עַל הַבֵּן וְאֵינוֹ בָא עַל עִסְקֵי נְפָשׁוֹת: **דָּמִים לוֹ.** כְּחַי הוּא חָשׁוּב, וּרְצִיחָה הִיא אִם יַהַרְגֶנּוּ בַּעַל הַבַּיִת: **שַׁלֵּם יְשַׁלֵּם.** הַגַּנָּב מָמוֹן שֶׁגָּנַב וְאֵינוֹ חַיָּב מִיתָה. וְאוּנְקְלוּס שֶׁתִּרְגֵּם: "אִם עֵינָא דְסָהֲדַיָּא נְפַלַת עֲלוֹהִי" לָקַח לוֹ שִׁטָּה אַחֶרֶת, לוֹמַר שֶׁאִם מְצָאוּהוּ עֵדִים קֹדֶם שֶׁבָּא בַּעַל הַבַּיִת וּכְשֶׁבָּא בַּעַל הַבַּיִת לְנֶגְדּוֹ הִתְרוּ בוֹ שֶׁלֹּא יַהַרְגֵהוּ, "דָּמִים לוֹ", חַיָּב עָלָיו אִם הֲרָגוֹ, שֶׁמֵּאַחַר שֶׁיֵּשׁ רוֹאִים לָהֶם אֵין הַגַּנָּב זֶה בָא עַל עִסְקֵי נְפָשׁוֹת, וְלֹא יַהֲרֹג אֶת בַּעַל הַמָּמוֹן:

ג) אִם־הִמָּצֵא תִמָּצֵא בְיָדוֹ. בִּרְשׁוּתוֹ, שֶׁלֹּא טָבַח וְלֹא מָכַר: **מִשּׁוֹר עַד חֲמוֹר.** כָּל דָּבָר בִּכְלַל תַּשְׁלוּמֵי כֶפֶל, בֵּין שֶׁיֵּשׁ בּוֹ רוּחַ חַיִּים בֵּין שֶׁאֵין בּוֹ רוּחַ חַיִּים, שֶׁהֲרֵי נֶאֱמַר מִקְרָא אַחֵר: "עַל שֶׂה עַל שַׂלְמָה עַל כָּל אֲבֵדָה וְגוֹ' יְשַׁלֵּם שְׁנַיִם לְרֵעֵהוּ" (להלן פסוק ח): **חַיִּים שְׁנַיִם יְשַׁלֵּם.** וְלֹא יְשַׁלֵּם לוֹ מֵתִים, אֶלָּא חַיִּים אוֹ דְּמֵי חַיִּים:

ד) כִּי יַבְעֶר... אֶת בְּעִירֹה וּבִעֵר. כֻּלָּם לְשׁוֹן בְּהֵמָה, כְּמוֹ: "אֲנַחְנוּ וּבְעִירֵנוּ" (במדבר כ, ד): **כִּי יַבְעֶר.** יוֹלִיךְ בְּהֶמְתּוֹ בְּשָׂדֶה וְכֶרֶם שֶׁל חֲבֵרוֹ וְיַזִּיק אוֹתָהּ בְּאַחַת מִשְּׁתֵּי אֵלּוּ: אוֹ בְּשִׁלּוּחַ בְּעִירָהּ אוֹ בְּבִעוּר. וּפֵרְשׁוּ

אַחַר מֵיטַב שָׂדֵהוּ וּמֵיטַב כַּרְמוֹ יְשַׁלֵּם: כִּי־תֵצֵא ה
אֵשׁ וּמָצְאָה קֹצִים וְנֶאֱכַל גָּדִישׁ אוֹ הַקָּמָה אוֹ הַשָּׂדֶה שַׁלֵּם
יְשַׁלֵּם הַמַּבְעִר אֶת־הַבְּעֵרָה: כִּי־יִתֵּן אִישׁ אֶל־רֵעֵהוּ ו
כֶּסֶף אוֹ־כֵלִים לִשְׁמֹר וְגֻנַּב מִבֵּית הָאִישׁ אִם־יִמָּצֵא הַגַּנָּב
יְשַׁלֵּם שְׁנָיִם: אִם־לֹא יִמָּצֵא הַגַּנָּב וְנִקְרַב בַּעַל־הַבַּיִת אֶל־ ז
הָאֱלֹהִים אִם־לֹא שָׁלַח יָדוֹ בִּמְלֶאכֶת רֵעֵהוּ: עַל־כָּל־דְּבַר־ ח
פֶּשַׁע עַל־שׁוֹר עַל־חֲמוֹר עַל־שֶׂה עַל־שַׂלְמָה עַל־כָּל־אֲבֵדָה
אֲשֶׁר יֹאמַר כִּי־הוּא זֶה עַד הָאֱלֹהִים יָבֹא דְּבַר־שְׁנֵיהֶם אֲשֶׁר
יַרְשִׁיעֻן אֱלֹהִים יְשַׁלֵּם שְׁנַיִם לְרֵעֵהוּ: כִּי־יִתֵּן אִישׁ ט
אֶל־רֵעֵהוּ חֲמוֹר אוֹ־שׁוֹר אוֹ־שֶׂה וְכָל־בְּהֵמָה לִשְׁמֹר וּמֵת

רַבּוֹתֵינוּ: ׳שָׁלּוּחַ׳ הוּא מִקְצֵי מִדְרָךְ כַּף רֶגֶל, ״וּבְעֵר״
הוּא מִקְצֵי הַשֵּׁן הַחוֹכֶלֶת וּמְבַעֶרֶת. בִּשְׂדֵה אַחֵר.
בִּשְׂדֵה שֶׁל אִישׁ אַחֵר: מֵיטַב שָׂדֵהוּ... יְשַׁלֵּם.
אֶת הַנִּזָּק, וְאִם בָּא לְשַׁלֵּם לוֹ קַרְקַע דְּמֵי נִזְקוֹ יְשַׁלֵּם
לוֹ מִמֵּיטַב שְׂדוֹתָיו, אִם הָיָה נִזְקוֹ סֶלַע יִתֵּן לוֹ שָׁוֶה
סֶלַע מֵעִדִּית שֶׁיֵּשׁ לוֹ. לִמֶּדְךָ הַכָּתוּב שֶׁהַנִּזּוֹקִין שָׁמִין
לָהֶם בָּעִידִית:

ה כִּי תֵצֵא אֵשׁ. אֲפִלּוּ מֵעַצְמָהּ: וּמָצְאָה קֹצִים.
קרדו״נש בְּלַעַז: וְנֶאֱכַל גָּדִישׁ. שֶׁלִּחֲכָה בַּקּוֹצִים עַד
שֶׁהִגִּיעָה לַגָּדִישׁ אוֹ לַקָּמָה הַמְחֻבֶּרֶת לַקַּרְקַע: אוֹ
הַשָּׂדֶה. שֶׁלִּחֲכָה אֶת נִירוֹ וְצָרִיךְ לָנִיר אוֹתָהּ פַּעַם
שְׁנִיָּה: שַׁלֵּם יְשַׁלֵּם הַמַּבְעִר. אַף עַל פִּי שֶׁהִדְלִיק
בְּתוֹךְ שֶׁלּוֹ וְהִיא יָצְאָה מֵעַצְמָהּ עַל יְדֵי קוֹצִים
שֶׁמָּצְאָה, חַיָּב לְשַׁלֵּם, לְפִי שֶׁלֹּא שָׁמַר אֶת גַּחַלְתּוֹ
שֶׁלֹּא תֵצֵא וְתַזִּיק:

ו וְגֻנַּב מִבֵּית הָאִישׁ. לְפִי דְּבָרָיו: אִם־יִמָּצֵא הַגַּנָּב.
יְשַׁלֵּם הַגַּנָּב שְׁנַיִם לַבְּעָלִים:

ז אִם לֹא יִמָּצֵא הַגַּנָּב. וּבָא הַשּׁוֹמֵר הַזֶּה שֶׁהוּא בַּעַל
הַבַּיִת: וְנִקְרַב. אֶל הַדַּיָּנִין לָדוּן עִם זֶה וְלִשָּׁבַע לוֹ
שֶׁלֹּא שָׁלַח יָדוֹ בְּשֶׁלּוֹ:

ח עַל כָּל דְּבַר פֶּשַׁע. שֶׁיִּמָּצֵא שַׁקְרָן בִּשְׁבוּעָתוֹ,

שֶׁיָּעִידוּ עֵדִים שֶׁהוּא עַצְמוֹ גְּנָבוֹ, וְיַרְשִׁיעֻהוּ אֱלֹהִים
עַל פִּי הָעֵדִים: יְשַׁלֵּם שְׁנַיִם לְרֵעֵהוּ. לִמֶּדְךָ הַכָּתוּב
שֶׁהַטּוֹעֵן בְּפִקָּדוֹן לוֹמַר נִגְנַב הֵימֶנּוּ, וְנִמְצָא שֶׁהוּא
עַצְמוֹ גְּנָבוֹ, מְשַׁלֵּם תַּשְׁלוּמֵי כֶפֶל. בִּזְמַן
שֶׁנִּשְׁבַּע וְאַחַר כָּךְ בָּאוּ עֵדִים, שֶׁכָּךְ דָּרְשׁוּ רַבּוֹתֵינוּ:
״וְנִקְרַב בַּעַל הַבַּיִת אֶל הָאֱלֹהִים״, קְרִיבָה זוֹ שְׁבוּעָה
הִיא. אַתָּה אוֹמֵר לִשְׁבוּעָה אוֹ אֵינוֹ אֶלָּא לָדִין, שֶׁכֵּיוָן
שֶׁבָּא לַדִּין וְכָפַר לוֹמַר נִגְנְבָה, מִיָּד יִתְחַיֵּב כֶּפֶל
אִם בָּאוּ עֵדִים שֶׁהוּא בְּיָדוֹ? נֶאֱמַר כָּאן שְׁלִיחוּת
יָד וְנֶאֱמַר לְמַטָּה שְׁלִיחוּת יָד: ״שְׁבֻעַת ה׳ תִּהְיֶה
בֵּין שְׁנֵיהֶם אִם לֹא שָׁלַח יָדוֹ״ (להלן פסוק י), מַה לְּהַלָּן
שְׁבוּעָה אַף כָּאן שְׁבוּעָה: אֲשֶׁר יֹאמַר כִּי הוּא זֶה. לְפִי
פְּשׁוּטוֹ, אֲשֶׁר יֹאמַר הָעֵד: ״כִּי הוּא זֶה״ שֶׁנִּשְׁבַּעְתָּ
עָלָיו הֲרֵי הוּא אֶצְלְךָ, עַד הַדַּיָּנִין ״יָבֹא דְּבַר שְׁנֵיהֶם״
וְיַחְקְרוּ אֶת הָעֵדִים, וְאִם כְּשֵׁרִים הֵם וְיַרְשִׁיעוּהוּ
לַשּׁוֹמֵר זֶה – ״יְשַׁלֵּם שְׁנַיִם״, וְאִם יַרְשִׁיעוּ אֶת הָעֵדִים
שֶׁנִּמְצְאוּ זוֹמְמִין, יְשַׁלְּמוּ הֵם שְׁנַיִם לַשּׁוֹמֵר. וְרַבּוֹתֵינוּ
זִכְרוֹנָם לִבְרָכָה דָּרְשׁוּ: ״כִּי הוּא זֶה״ לְלַמֵּד שֶׁאֵין
מְחַיְּבִין אוֹתוֹ שְׁבוּעָה אֶלָּא אִם כֵּן הוֹדָה בְּמִקְצָת
לוֹמַר: כָּךְ וְכָךְ אֲנִי חַיָּב לְךָ וְהַמּוֹתָר נִגְנַב מִמֶּנִּי:

ט-י כִּי יִתֵּן אִישׁ אֶל רֵעֵהוּ חֲמוֹר אוֹ שׁוֹר. פָּרָשָׁה
רִאשׁוֹנָה נֶאֶמְרָה בְּשׁוֹמֵר חִנָּם, לְפִיכָךְ פָּטַר בּוֹ

שמות | פרק כב | משפטים

י אוֹ־נִשְׁבַּ֥ר אוֹ־נִשְׁבָּ֖ה אֵ֣ין רֹאֶֽה: שְׁבֻעַ֣ת יְהֹוָ֗ה תִּֽהְיֶה֙ בֵּ֣ין שְׁנֵיהֶ֔ם אִם־לֹ֥א שָׁלַ֛ח יָד֖וֹ בִּמְלֶ֣אכֶת רֵעֵ֑הוּ וְלָקַ֥ח בְּעָלָ֖יו וְלֹ֥א יְשַׁלֵּֽם:

יא וְאִם־גָּנֹ֥ב יִגָּנֵ֖ב מֵֽעִמּ֑וֹ יְשַׁלֵּ֖ם לִבְעָלָֽיו: אִם־טָרֹ֣ף יִטָּרֵ֔ף יְבִאֵ֖הוּ עֵ֑ד הַטְּרֵפָ֖ה לֹ֥א יְשַׁלֵּֽם:

יב וְכִֽי־יִשְׁאַ֥ל אִ֛ישׁ מֵעִ֥ם רֵעֵ֖הוּ וְנִשְׁבַּ֣ר אוֹ־מֵ֑ת בְּעָלָ֥יו אֵין־עִמּ֖וֹ שַׁלֵּ֥ם יְשַׁלֵּֽם:

יג אִם־בְּעָלָ֥יו עִמּ֖וֹ לֹ֣א יְשַׁלֵּ֑ם אִם־שָׂכִ֣יר ה֔וּא בָּ֖א בִּשְׂכָרֽוֹ:

יד וְכִֽי־יְפַתֶּ֣ה אִ֗ישׁ בְּתוּלָ֛ה אֲשֶׁ֥ר לֹא־אֹרָ֖שָׂה וְשָׁכַ֣ב עִמָּ֑הּ מָהֹ֛ר יִמְהָרֶ֥נָּה לּ֖וֹ לְאִשָּֽׁה:

טו אִם־מָאֵ֧ן יְמָאֵ֛ן אָבִ֖יהָ לְתִתָּ֣הּ ל֑וֹ כֶּ֣סֶף יִשְׁקֹ֔ל כְּמֹ֖הַר הַבְּתוּלֹֽת:

טז מְכַשֵּׁפָ֖ה

אֶת הַגְּנֵבָה, כְּמוֹ שֶׁכָּתוּב: "וְגֻנַּב מִבֵּית הָאִישׁ... אִם לֹא יִמָּצֵא הַגַּנָּב וְנִקְרַב בַּעַל הַבַּיִת" (לעיל פסוקים ו-ז) לִשְׁבוּעָה, לָמַדְתָּ שֶׁפּוֹטֵר עַצְמוֹ בִּשְׁבוּעָה זוֹ, וְכָל שֶׁכֵּן שׁוֹמֵר שָׂכָר, לְפִיכָךְ אִם אָמַר חִנָּם פָּטוּר אִם גְּנֵבָה, כְּמוֹ שֶׁכָּתוּב: "אִם גֻּנֹּב יִגָּנֵב מֵעִמּוֹ יְשַׁלֵּם" (להלן פסוק יח). חוֹבֵל עַל הֶחָכָם, כְּמוֹ "מֵת" מֵעַצְמוֹ אוֹ נִשְׁבַּר אוֹ נִשְׁבָּה בְּחָזְקָה עַל יְדֵי לִסְטִים, וְ"אֵין רֹאֶה" שֶׁיָּעִיד בַּדָּבָר – "שְׁבֻעַת ה' תִּהְיֶה", יִשָּׁבַע שֶׁכֵּן הוּא כִּדְבָרָיו, וְהוּא לֹא שָׁלַח בָּהּ יָד לְהִשְׁתַּמֵּשׁ בָּהּ לְעַצְמוֹ, שֶׁאִם שָׁלַח בָּהּ יָד וְאַחַר כָּךְ נֶאֶנְסָה חַיָּב בָּאֳנָסֶיהָ: וְלָקַח בְּעָלָיו. הַשְּׁבוּעָה. וְלֹא יְשַׁלֵּם. לוֹ הַשּׁוֹמֵר כְּלוּם:

יא] אִם טָרֹף יִטָּרֵף. עַל יְדֵי חַיָּה רָעָה: יְבִאֵהוּ עֵד. יָבִיא עֵדִים שֶׁנִּטְרְפָה בְּאֹנֶס וּפָטוּר: הַטְּרֵפָה לֹא יְשַׁלֵּם. אֵינוֹ אוֹמֵר 'טְרֵפָה לֹא יְשַׁלֵּם' אֶלָּא "הַטְּרֵפָה", יֵשׁ טְרֵפָה שֶׁהוּא מְשַׁלֵּם וְיֵשׁ טְרֵפָה שֶׁאֵינוֹ מְשַׁלֵּם: טְרֵפַת חָתוּל וְשׁוּעָל וּנְמִיָּה מְשַׁלֵּם, טְרֵפַת זְאֵב אֲרִי וְדֹב וְנָחָשׁ אֵינוֹ מְשַׁלֵּם. וּמִי לְחָשְׁךָ לָדוּן כֵּן? שֶׁהֲרֵי כָּתוּב: "וּמֵת אוֹ נִשְׁבַּר אוֹ נִשְׁבָּה", מַה מִּיתָה שֶׁאֵין יָכוֹל לְהַצִּיל, אַף שֶׁבֶר וּשְׁבִיָּה שֶׁאֵין יָכוֹל לְהַצִּיל:

יג] וְכִי יִשְׁאַל. בָּא לְלַמֵּד עַל הַשּׁוֹאֵל שֶׁחַיָּב בָּאֳנָסִין:

בְּעָלָיו אֵין עִמּוֹ. אִם בְּעָלָיו שֶׁל שׁוֹר אֵינוֹ עִם הַשּׁוֹאֵל בִּמְלַאכְתּוֹ:

יד] אִם בְּעָלָיו עִמּוֹ. בֵּין שֶׁהוּא בְּאוֹתָהּ מְלָאכָה בֵּין שֶׁהוּא בִּמְלָאכָה אַחֶרֶת, הָיָה עִמּוֹ בִּשְׁעַת שְׁאֵלָה אֵינוֹ צָרִיךְ לִהְיוֹת עִמּוֹ בִּשְׁעַת שְׁבִירָה וּמִיתָה: אִם שָׂכִיר הוּא. אִם הַשּׁוֹר אֵינוֹ שָׁאוּל אֶלָּא שָׂכוּר, "בָּא בִּשְׂכָרוֹ" לְיַד הַשּׂוֹכֵר הַזֶּה וְלֹא בִּשְׁאֵלָה, וְאֵין כָּל הֲנָאָה שֶׁלּוֹ שֶׁהֲרֵי עַל יְדֵי שְׂכָרוֹ נִשְׁתַּמֵּשׁ, וְאֵין לוֹ מִשְׁפָּט שׁוֹאֵל לְהִתְחַיֵּב בָּאֳנָסִין. וְלֹא פֵּרַשׁ מַה דִּינוֹ כְּשׁוֹמֵר חִנָּם אוֹ כְּשׁוֹמֵר שָׂכָר, לְפִיכָךְ נֶחְלְקוּ בּוֹ חַכְמֵי יִשְׂרָאֵל שׂוֹכֵר כֵּיצַד מְשַׁלֵּם? רַבִּי מֵאִיר אוֹמֵר: כְּשׁוֹמֵר חִנָּם, רַבִּי יְהוּדָה אוֹמֵר: כְּשׁוֹמֵר שָׂכָר:

טו] וְכִי יְפַתֶּה. מְדַבֵּר עַל לִבָּהּ עַד שֶׁשּׁוֹמַעַת לוֹ, וְכֵן תַּרְגּוּמוֹ: "וַאֲרֵי יְשַׁדֵּל". שִׁדּוּל בִּלְשׁוֹן חֲכָמִים כְּפִתּוּי בִּלְשׁוֹן עִבְרִי: מָהֹר יִמְהָרֶנָּה. יִפְסֹק לָהּ מֹהַר כְּמִשְׁפַּט אִישׁ לְאִשְׁתּוֹ, שֶׁכּוֹתֵב לָהּ כְּתֻבָּה וְיִשָּׂאֶנָּה:

טז] כְּמֹהַר הַבְּתוּלֹת. שֶׁהוּא קָצוּב חֲמִשִּׁים כֶּסֶף אֵצֶל הַתּוֹפֵס אֶת הַבְּתוּלָה וְשׁוֹכֵב עִמָּהּ בְּאֹנֶס, שֶׁנֶּאֱמַר: "וְנָתַן הָאִישׁ הַשֹּׁכֵב עִמָּהּ לַאֲבִי הַנַּעֲרָ חֲמִשִּׁים כָּסֶף" (דברים כב, כט):

יז] מְכַשֵּׁפָה לֹא תִחְיֶה. אֶלָּא תּוּמַת בְּבֵית דִּין. וְאֶחָד

משפטים | פרק כב

יח לֹא תְחַיֶּה: כָּל־שֹׁכֵב עִם־בְּהֵמָה מוֹת יוּמָת: יט זֹבֵחַ לָאֱלֹהִים יָחֳרָם בִּלְתִּי לַיהוָה לְבַדּוֹ: כ וְגֵר לֹא־תוֹנֶה וְלֹא תִלְחָצֶנּוּ כִּי־גֵרִים הֱיִיתֶם בְּאֶרֶץ מִצְרָיִם: כא כָּל־אַלְמָנָה וְיָתוֹם לֹא תְעַנּוּן: כב אִם־עַנֵּה תְעַנֶּה אֹתוֹ כִּי אִם־צָעֹק יִצְעַק אֵלַי שָׁמֹעַ אֶשְׁמַע צַעֲקָתוֹ: כג וְחָרָה אַפִּי וְהָרַגְתִּי אֶתְכֶם בֶּחָרֶב וְהָיוּ נְשֵׁיכֶם אַלְמָנוֹת וּבְנֵיכֶם יְתֹמִים:

זְכָרִים וְאֶחָד נְקֵבוֹת, חֶלָּא שֶׁדִּבֶּר הַכָּתוּב בַּהֹוֶה, שֶׁהֵם מְצוּיוֹת בִּכְשָׁפִים:

יח) כָּל שׁוֹכֵב עִם בְּהֵמָה מוֹת יוּמָת. בִּסְקִילָה, רוֹבֵעַ כְּנִרְבַּעַת, שֶׁכָּתוּב בָּהֶם: "דְּמֵיהֶם בָּם" (ויקרא כ, טז):

יט) לָאֱלֹהִים. לַעֲבוֹדָה זָרָה. אִלּוּ הָיָה נָקוּד 'לֵאלֹהִים', הָיָה צָרִיךְ לְפָרֵשׁ וְלִכְתֹּב 'אֲחֵרִים', עַכְשָׁיו שֶׁאָמַר "לָאֱלֹהִים" אֵין צָרִיךְ לְפָרֵשׁ 'אֲחֵרִים', שֶׁכָּל לָמֶ"ד וּבֵי"ת הַמְשַׁמֶּשֶׁת בְּרֹאשׁ הַתֵּבָה, אִם נְקוּדָה בַּחֲטָף, כְּגוֹן: לְמֶלֶךְ, לְמִדְבָּר, לְעִיר, צָרִיךְ לְפָרֵשׁ לְאֵיזֶה מֶלֶךְ, לְאֵיזֶה מִדְבָּר, לְאֵיזֶה עִיר. וְכֵן. לִמְלָכִים, לִרְגָלִים, צָרִיךְ לְפָרֵשׁ לְאֵיזֶה, וְאִם אֵינוֹ מְפָרֵשׁ, כָּל מְלָכִים בַּמַּשְׁמָע. וְכֵן "לָאֱלֹהִים" כָּל אֱלֹהִים בַּמַּשְׁמָע, אֲפִלּוּ קֹדֶשׁ. אֲבָל כְּשֶׁהִיא נְקוּדָה פַּתָּח, כְּמוֹ: לַמֶּלֶךְ, לַמִּדְבָּר, לָעִיר, יוֹדֵעַ בְּאֵיזֶה מֶלֶךְ מְדַבֵּר, וְכֵן 'לָעִיר' יוֹדֵעַ בְּאֵיזֶה עִיר מְדַבֵּר, וְכֵן "לָאֱלֹהִים", לְאוֹתָן שֶׁהֻזְהַרְתֶּם עֲלֵיהֶם בְּמָקוֹם אַחֵר. כַּיּוֹצֵא בּוֹ: "אֵין כָּמוֹךָ בָאֱלֹהִים" (תהלים פו, ח), לְפִי שֶׁלֹּא פֵּרֵשׁ הֻצְרַךְ לִנְקֹד פַּתָּח. יָחֳרָם. יוּמָת. וְלָמָּה נֶאֱמַר "יָחֳרָם"? וַהֲלֹא כְּבָר נֶאֶמְרָה בּוֹ מִיתָה בְּמָקוֹם אַחֵר: "הוֹצֵאתָ אֶת הָאִישׁ הַהוּא אוֹ אֶת הָאִשָּׁה הַהִיא" וְגוֹ' (דברים יז, ה), אֶלָּא לְפִי שֶׁלֹּא פֵּרֵשׁ עַל אֵיזוֹ עֲבוֹדָה חַיָּב מִיתָה, שֶׁלֹּא תֹאמַר כָּל עֲבוֹדוֹת בְּמִיתָה, בָּא וּפֵרֵשׁ לְךָ כָּאן: "זֹבֵחַ לָאֱלֹהִים", מַה זְּבִיחָה עֲבוֹדָה הַנַּעֲשֵׂית בִּפְנִים לַשָּׁמַיִם, אַף אֲנִי מְרַבֶּה הַמַּקְטִיר וְהַמְנַסֵּךְ שֶׁהֵן עֲבוֹדָה בִּפְנִים, וְחַיָּבִים עֲלֵיהֶם לְכָל עֲבוֹדָה זָרָה, בֵּין

שֶׁדַּרְכָּהּ לְעָבְדָהּ בְּכָךְ בֵּין שֶׁאֵין דַּרְכָּהּ לְעָבְדָהּ בְּכָךְ. אֲבָל שְׁאָר עֲבוֹדוֹת, כְּגוֹן: הַמְכַבֵּד וְהַמְרַבֵּץ וְהַמְגַפֵּף וְהַמְנַשֵּׁק, אֵינוֹ בְּמִיתָה:

כ) וְגֵר לֹא תוֹנֶה. אוֹנָאַת דְּבָרִים, קונטרליי"ר בְּלַעַז, כְּמוֹ: "וְהַאֲכַלְתִּי אֶת מוֹנַיִךְ אֶת בְּשָׂרָם" (ישעיה מט, כו): וְלֹא תִלְחָצֶנּוּ. בִּגְזֵלַת מָמוֹן. כִּי גֵרִים הֱיִיתֶם. אִם הוֹנֵיתוֹ אַף הוּא יָכוֹל לְהוֹנוֹתְךָ וְלוֹמַר לְךָ: אַף אַתָּה מִגֵּרִים בָּאתָ. מוּם שֶׁבְּךָ אַל תֹּאמַר לַחֲבֵרְךָ. כָּל לְשׁוֹן 'גֵּר', אָדָם שֶׁלֹּא נוֹלַד בְּאוֹתָהּ מְדִינָה, אֶלָּא בָּא מִמְּדִינָה אַחֶרֶת לָגוּר שָׁם:

כא) כָּל אַלְמָנָה וְיָתוֹם לֹא תְעַנּוּן. הוּא הַדִּין לְכָל אָדָם, אֶלָּא שֶׁדִּבֶּר הַכָּתוּב בַּהֹוֶה, לְפִי שֶׁהֵם תְּשׁוּשֵׁי כֹחַ וְדָבָר מָצוּי לְעַנּוֹתָם:

כב) אִם עַנֵּה תְעַנֶּה אֹתוֹ. הֲרֵי זֶה מִקְרָא קָצָר. גָּזַם וְלֹא פֵּרֵשׁ עָנְשׁוֹ, כְּמוֹ: "לָכֵן כָּל הֹרֵג קַיִן" (בראשית ד, טו), וְלֹא פֵּרֵשׁ עָנְשׁוֹ. אַף כָּאן: "אִם עַנֵּה תְעַנֶּה אֹתוֹ" לְשׁוֹן גָּזַם, כְּלוֹמַר, סוֹפְךָ לִטֹּל אֶת שֶׁלְּךָ, לָמָּה? "כִּי אִם צָעֹק יִצְעַק אֵלַי" וְגוֹ':

כג) וְהָיוּ נְשֵׁיכֶם אַלְמָנוֹת. מִמַּשְׁמָע שֶׁנֶּאֱמַר: "וְהָרַגְתִּי אֶתְכֶם" אֵינִי יוֹדֵעַ שֶׁנְּשֵׁיכֶם אַלְמָנוֹת וּבְנֵיכֶם יְתוֹמִים? אֶלָּא הֲרֵי זוֹ קְלָלָה אַחֶרֶת, שֶׁיִּהְיוּ הַנָּשִׁים עֲגוּנוֹת כְּאַלְמָנוֹת חַיּוֹת, שֶׁלֹּא יִהְיוּ עֵדִים לְמִיתַת בַּעֲלֵיהֶן וְתִהְיֶינָה אֲסוּרוֹת לְהִנָּשֵׂא, וְהַבָּנִים יִהְיוּ יְתוֹמִים, שֶׁלֹּא יַנִּיחוּם בֵּית דִּין לֵירֵד לְנִכְסֵי אֲבִיהֶם, לְפִי שֶׁאֵין יוֹדְעִים אִם מֵת אִם נִשְׁבָּה:

שמות | פרק כב | משפטים

כד אִם־כֶּ֣סֶף ׀ תַּלְוֶ֣ה אֶת־עַמִּ֗י אֶת־הֶֽעָנִי֙ עִמָּ֔ךְ לֹא־תִהְיֶ֥ה ל֖וֹ

כה כְּנֹשֶׁ֑ה לֹֽא־תְשִׂימ֥וּן עָלָ֖יו נֶֽשֶׁךְ: אִם־חָבֹ֥ל תַּחְבֹּ֖ל שַׂלְמַ֣ת רֵעֶ֑ךָ

כו עַד־בֹּ֥א הַשֶּׁ֖מֶשׁ תְּשִׁיבֶ֥נּוּ לֽוֹ: כִּ֣י הִ֤וא כְסוּתֹה֙ לְבַדָּ֔הּ הִ֥וא שִׂמְלָת֖וֹ לְעֹר֑וֹ בַּמֶּ֣ה יִשְׁכָּ֔ב וְהָיָה֙ כִּֽי־יִצְעַ֣ק אֵלַ֔י וְשָׁמַעְתִּ֖י כִּֽי־

כז חַנּ֥וּן אָֽנִי: אֱלֹהִ֖ים לֹ֣א תְקַלֵּ֑ל וְנָשִׂ֥יא בְעַמְּךָ֖

כח לֹ֥א תָאֹֽר: מְלֵאָתְךָ֥ וְדִמְעֲךָ֖ לֹ֣א תְאַחֵ֑ר בְּכ֥וֹר בָּנֶ֖יךָ תִּתֶּן־לִֽי:

כט כֵּֽן־תַּעֲשֶׂ֥ה לְשֹׁרְךָ֖ לְצֹאנֶ֑ךָ שִׁבְעַ֤ת יָמִים֙ יִהְיֶ֣ה עִם־אִמּ֔וֹ בַּיּ֥וֹם

רביעי

כד) **אם כסף תלוה את עמי.** רַבִּי יִשְׁמָעֵאל אוֹמֵר: כָּל אִם וְאִם שֶׁבַּתּוֹרָה רְשׁוּת מִשְּׁלֹשָׁה, וְזֶה אֶחָד מֵהֶן: **את עמי.** עַמִּי וְגוֹי, עַמִּי קוֹדֵם. עָנִי וְעָשִׁיר, עָנִי קוֹדֵם. עֲנִיֵּי עִירְךָ וַעֲנִיֵּי עִיר אַחֶרֶת, עֲנִיֵּי עִירְךָ קוֹדְמִין. וְזֶה מַשְׁמָעוֹ: "אִם כֶּסֶף תַּלְוֶה, אֶת עַמִּי" תַּלְוֵהוּ, וְלֹא לְגוֹי. וּלְאֵיזֶה מֵעַמִּי? "אֶת הֶעָנִי". וּלְאֵיזֶה עָנִי? לְאוֹתוֹ שֶׁ"עִמָּךְ". דָּבָר אַחֵר "אֶת עַמִּי", שֶׁלֹּא תִנְהַג בּוֹ מִנְהַג בִּזָּיוֹן בְּהַלְוָאָה, שֶׁהוּא עַמִּי: **את העני עמך.** הֱוֵי מִסְתַּכֵּל בְּעַצְמְךָ כְּאִלּוּ אַתָּה עָנִי: **לא תהיה לו כנשה.** לֹא תִתְבָּעֶנּוּ בְּחָזְקָה. אִם אַתָּה יוֹדֵעַ שֶׁאֵין לוֹ, אַל תְּהִי דוֹמֶה עָלָיו כְּאִלּוּ הִלְוִיתוֹ, אֶלָּא כְּאִלּוּ לֹא הִלְוִיתוֹ, כְּלוֹמַר לֹא תַכְלִימֵהוּ: **נשך.** רִבִּית, שֶׁהוּא כִּנְשִׁיכַת נָחָשׁ, שֶׁנּוֹשֵׁךְ חַבּוּרָה קְטַנָּה בְּרַגְלוֹ וְאֵינוֹ מַרְגִּישׁ, וּפִתְאֹם הוּא מְבַצְבֵּץ וְנוֹפֵחַ עַד קָדְקֳדוֹ, כָּךְ רִבִּית אֵינוֹ מַרְגִּישׁ וְאֵינוֹ נִכָּר, עַד שֶׁהָרִבִּית עוֹלָה וּמְחַסְּרוֹ מָמוֹן הַרְבֵּה:

כה) **אם חבל תחבל.** כָּל לְשׁוֹן חֲבָלָה אֵינוֹ מַשְׁכּוֹן בִּשְׁעַת הַלְוָאָה, אֶלָּא שֶׁמְּמַשְׁכְּנִין אֶת הַלֹּוֶה כְּשֶׁמַּגִּיעַ הַזְּמָן וְאֵינוֹ פּוֹרֵעַ: **חבל תחבל.** כָּפַל לְךָ בַּחֲבָלָה עַד כַּמָּה פְעָמִים, אָמַר הַקָּדוֹשׁ בָּרוּךְ הוּא, כַּמָּה אַתָּה חַיָּב לִי, וַהֲרֵי נַפְשְׁךָ עוֹלָה אֶצְלִי בְּכָל לַיְלָה וְלַיְלָה וְנוֹתֶנֶת דִּין וְחֶשְׁבּוֹן וּמִתְחַיֶּבֶת לְפָנַי וַאֲנִי מַחֲזִירָהּ לָךְ, אַף אַתָּה טֹל וְהָשֵׁב: **עד בא השמש תשיבנו לו.** כָּל הַיּוֹם תְּשִׁיבֶנּוּ לוֹ עַד בֹּא הַשֶּׁמֶשׁ, וּכְבוֹא הַשֶּׁמֶשׁ תַּחֲזֹר וְתִטְּלֶנּוּ עַד שֶׁיָּבוֹא

בֹּקֶר שֶׁל מָחָר. וּבִכְסוּת יוֹם הַכָּתוּב מְדַבֵּר, שֶׁאֵין צָרִיךְ לָהּ בַּלַּיְלָה:

כו) **כי הוא כסותה.** זוֹ טַלִּית: **שמלתו.** זוֹ חָלוּק: **במה ישכב.** לְרַבּוֹת אֶת הַמַּצָּע:

כז) **אלהים לא תקלל.** הֲרֵי זוֹ אַזְהָרָה לְבִרְכַּת הַשֵּׁם, וְאַזְהָרָה לְקִלְלַת דַּיָּן:

כח) **מלאתך.** חוֹבָה הַמֻּטֶּלֶת עָלֶיךָ כְּשֶׁתִּתְמַלֵּא תְּבוּאָתְךָ לְהִתְבַּשֵּׁל, וְהֵם בִּכּוּרִים: **ודמעך.** הִיא תְּרוּמָה, וְאֵינִי יוֹדֵעַ מַהוּ לְשׁוֹן דֶּמַע: **לא תאחר.** לֹא תְשַׁנֶּה סֵדֶר הַפְרָשָׁתָן לְאַחֵר אֶת הַמֻּקְדָּם וּלְהַקְדִּים אֶת הַמְאֻחָר, שֶׁלֹּא יַקְדִּים תְּרוּמָה לְבִכּוּרִים וּמַעֲשֵׂר לִתְרוּמָה: **בכור בניך תתן לי.** לִפְדּוֹתוֹ חָמֵשׁ סְלָעִים מִן הַכֹּהֵן. וַהֲלֹא כְבָר צִוָּה עָלָיו בְּמָקוֹם אַחֵר (במדבר יח, טו)? אֶלָּא כְּדֵי לִסְמֹךְ לוֹ: "כֵּן תַּעֲשֶׂה לְשֹׁרְךָ", מַה בְּכוֹר אָדָם לְאַחַר שְׁלֹשִׁים יוֹם פּוֹדֵהוּ, שֶׁנֶּאֱמַר: "וּפְדוּיָו מִבֶּן חֹדֶשׁ תִּפְדֶּה" (שם), אַף בְּכוֹר בְּהֵמָה גַּסָּה מְטַפֵּל בּוֹ שְׁלֹשִׁים יוֹם וְאַחַר כָּךְ נוֹתְנוֹ לַכֹּהֵן:

כט) **שבעת ימים יהיה עם אמו.** זוֹ אַזְהָרָה לַכֹּהֵן, שֶׁאִם בָּא לְמַהֵר הַקְרָבָתוֹ לֹא יְמַהֵר קֹדֶם שְׁמוֹנָה, לְפִי שֶׁהוּא מְחֻסַּר זְמָן: **ביום השמיני תתנו לי.** יָכוֹל יְהֵא חוֹבָה לְכוֹ בַיּוֹם? נֶאֱמַר כָּאן: "שְׁמִינִי" וְנֶאֱמַר לְהַלָּן: "וּמִיּוֹם הַשְּׁמִינִי וָהָלְאָה יֵרָצֶה" (ויקרא כב, כז), מַה שְּׁמִינִי הָאָמוּר לְהַלָּן לְהַכְשִׁיר מִשְּׁמִינִי וָהָלְאָה, אַף שְׁמִינִי הָאָמוּר כָּאן לְהַכְשִׁיר מִשְּׁמִינִי וָהָלְאָה, וְכֵן מַשְׁמָעוֹ: וּבַיּוֹם הַשְּׁמִינִי אַתָּה רַשַּׁאי לִתְּנוֹ לִי:

הַשְּׁמִינִי תִּתְּנוֹ־לִי: וְאַנְשֵׁי־קֹדֶשׁ תִּהְיוּן לִי וּבָשָׂר בַּשָּׂדֶה טְרֵפָה לֹא תֹאכֵלוּ לַכֶּלֶב תַּשְׁלִכוּן אֹתוֹ: לֹא תִשָּׂא שֵׁמַע שָׁוְא אַל־תָּשֶׁת יָדְךָ עִם־רָשָׁע לִהְיֹת עֵד חָמָס: לֹא־תִהְיֶה אַחֲרֵי־רַבִּים לְרָעֹת וְלֹא־תַעֲנֶה עַל־רִב לִנְטֹת אַחֲרֵי רַבִּים לְהַטֹּת: וְדָל לֹא תֶהְדַּר בְּרִיבוֹ: כִּי תִפְגַּע שׁוֹר

ל וְאַנְשֵׁי קֹדֶשׁ תִּהְיוּן לִי. הֱוּוּ אַתֶּם קְדוֹשִׁים וּפְרוּשִׁים מִשִּׁקּוּצֵי נְבֵלוֹת וּטְרֵפוֹת, הֲרֵי אַתֶּם שֶׁלִּי, וְאִם לָאו אֵינְכֶם שֶׁלִּי. וּבָשָׂר בַּשָּׂדֶה טְרֵפָה. אַף הַבַּיִת כֵּן, אֶלָּא שֶׁדִּבֵּר הַכָּתוּב בַּהוֹוֶה, מְקוֹם שֶׁדֶּרֶךְ בְּהֵמוֹת לִטָּרֵף. וְכֵן: "כִּי בַשָּׂדֶה מְצָאָהּ" (דברים כב, כז). וְכֵן: "אֲשֶׁר לֹא יִהְיֶה טָהוֹר מִקְרֵה לָיְלָה" (שם כג, יא), הוּא הַדִּין לְמִקְרֵה יוֹם, אֶלָּא שֶׁדִּבֵּר הַכָּתוּב בַּהוֹוֶה. "וּבָשָׂר תָּלוּשׁ מִן חַיָּיא חַיָּא", בָּשָׂר שֶׁנִּתְלַשׁ עַל יְדֵי טְרֵפַת זְאֵב אוֹ אֲרִי מִן חַיָּה כְּשֵׁרָה אוֹ בְהֵמָה כְּשֵׁרָה בְּחַיֶּיהָ: לַכֶּלֶב תַּשְׁלִכוּן אֹתוֹ. אַף הַגּוֹי כַּכֶּלֶב, אוֹ אֵינוֹ אֶלָּא כֶּלֶב כְּמַשְׁמָעוֹ, תַּלְמוּד לוֹמַר בִּנְבֵלָה: "אוֹ מָכֹר לְנָכְרִי" (שם יד, כא), קַל וָחֹמֶר לִטְרֵפָה שֶׁמֻּתֶּרֶת בְּכָל הֲנָאוֹת. אִם כֵּן מַה תַּלְמוּד לוֹמַר: "לַכֶּלֶב"? לְלַמֶּדְךָ שֶׁהַכֶּלֶב מְכֻבָּד מִן הַגּוֹי שֶׁהַנְּבֵלָה לַגּוֹי וְהַטְּרֵפָה לַכֶּלֶב. וּלְלַמֶּדְךָ שֶׁאֵין הַקָּדוֹשׁ בָּרוּךְ הוּא מְקַפֵּחַ שְׂכַר כָּל בְּרִיָּה, שֶׁנֶּאֱמַר: "וּלְכֹל בְּנֵי יִשְׂרָאֵל לֹא יֶחֱרַץ כֶּלֶב לְשֹׁנוֹ" (לעיל יא, ז), אָמַר הַקָּדוֹשׁ בָּרוּךְ הוּא, תְּנוּ לוֹ שְׂכָרוֹ:

פרק כג
א לֹא תִשָּׂא שֵׁמַע שָׁוְא. כְּתַרְגּוּמוֹ, "לָא תְקַבֵּל שְׁמַע דִּשְׁקַר", אַזְהָרָה לִמְקַבֵּל לָשׁוֹן הָרָע וְלַדַּיָּן שֶׁלֹּא יִשְׁמַע דִּבְרֵי בַּעַל דִּין עַד שֶׁיָּבֹא בַּעַל דִּין חֲבֵרוֹ: אַל תָּשֶׁת יָדְךָ עִם רָשָׁע. הַטּוֹעֵן אֶת חֲבֵרוֹ תְּבִיעַת שֶׁקֶר, שֶׁהִבְטִיחֵהוּ לִהְיוֹת לוֹ עֵד חָמָס:

ב לֹא תִהְיֶה אַחֲרֵי רַבִּים לְרָעֹת. יֵשׁ בְּמִקְרָא זֶה מִדְרְשֵׁי חַכְמֵי יִשְׂרָאֵל, אֲבָל אֵין לְשׁוֹן הַמִּקְרָא מְיֻשָּׁב בָּהֶן עַל אָפְנָיו. מִכָּאן דָּרְשׁוּ שֶׁאֵין מַטִּין לְחוֹבָה בְּהַכְרָעַת דַּיָּן אֶחָד. וְסוֹף הַמִּקְרָא דָּרְשׁוּ: "אַחֲרֵי רַבִּים לְהַטֹּת", שֶׁאִם יֵשׁ שְׁנַיִם בַּמְחַיְּבִין יוֹתֵר עַל

הַמְזַכִּין, הַטֵּה הַדִּין עַל פִּיהֶם לְחוֹבָה, וּבְדִינֵי נְפָשׁוֹת הַכָּתוּב מְדַבֵּר. וְאֶמְצַע הַמִּקְרָא דָּרְשׁוּ: "וְלֹא תַעֲנֶה עַל רִב", עַל רַב, שֶׁאֵין חוֹלְקִין עַל מֻפְלָא שֶׁבְּבֵית דִּין, לְפִיכָךְ מַתְחִילִין בְּדִינֵי נְפָשׁוֹת מִן הַצַּד, לַקְּטַנִּים שֶׁבָּהֶם שׁוֹאֲלִין תְּחִלָּה שֶׁיֹּאמְרוּ אֶת דַּעְתָּם. וּלְפִי דִּבְרֵי רַבּוֹתֵינוּ כָּךְ פִּתְרוֹן הַמִּקְרָא: "לֹא תִהְיֶה אַחֲרֵי רַבִּים לְרָעֹת", לְחַיֵּב מִיתָה בִּשְׁבִיל דַּיָּן אֶחָד שֶׁיִּרְבּוּ מְחַיְּבִין עַל הַמְזַכִּין, "וְלֹא תַעֲנֶה עַל הָרַב לִנְטוֹת" מִדְּבָרָיו, וּלְפִי שֶׁהוּא חָסֵר יוֹ"ד דָּרְשׁוּ בוֹ כֵּן, "אַחֲרֵי רַבִּים לְהַטֹּת", וְיֵשׁ רַבִּים שֶׁאַתָּה נוֹטֶה אַחֲרֵיהֶם, וְאֵימָתַי? בִּזְמַן שֶׁהֵן שְׁנַיִם הַמַּכְרִיעִין בַּמְחַיְּבִין יוֹתֵר מִן הַמְזַכִּין, וּמִמַּשְׁמַע שֶׁנֶּאֱמַר: "לֹא תִהְיֶה אַחֲרֵי רַבִּים לְרָעֹת", שׁוֹמֵעַ אֲנִי אֲבָל הֱיֵה עִמָּהֶם לְטוֹבָה, מִכָּאן אָמְרוּ: דִּינֵי נְפָשׁוֹת מַטִּין עַל פִּי אֶחָד לִזְכוּת וְעַל פִּי שְׁנַיִם לְחוֹבָה. וְאוּנְקְלוֹס תִּרְגֵּם: "לָא תִתְמְנַע מִלְּאַלָּפָא מָא דִּבְעֵינָךְ עַל דִּינָא", וּלְשׁוֹן הָעִבְרִי לְפִי הַתַּרְגּוּם כָּךְ הוּא נִדְרָשׁ: "לֹא תַעֲנֶה עַל רַב לִנְטוֹת", אִם יִשְׁאָלְךָ דָּבָר לְמִשְׁפָּט לֹא תַעֲנֶה לִנְטוֹת לְצַד אֶחָד וּלְסַלֵּק עַצְמְךָ מִן הָרִיב, אֶלָּא הֱוֵי דָּן דִּין לַאֲמִתּוֹ. וַאֲנִי אוֹמֵר לְיַשְּׁבוֹ עַל אָפְנָיו כִּפְשׁוּטוֹ כָּךְ פִּתְרוֹנוֹ: "לֹא תִהְיֶה אַחֲרֵי רַבִּים לְרָעֹת" – אִם רָאִיתָ רְשָׁעִים מַטִּין מִשְׁפָּט, לֹא תֹאמַר: הוֹאִיל וְרַבִּים הֵם הִנְנִי נוֹטֶה אַחֲרֵיהֶם. "וְלֹא תַעֲנֶה עַל רִב וְגוֹ'" – וְאִם יִשְׁאָלְךָ הַנִּדּוֹן עַל אוֹתוֹ הַמִּשְׁפָּט, אַל תַּעֲנֶנּוּ עַל הָרִיב דָּבָר הַנּוֹטֶה אַחֲרֵי אוֹתָן רַבִּים לְהַטּוֹת אֶת הַמִּשְׁפָּט מֵאֲמִתּוֹ, אֶלָּא אֱמֹר אֶת הַמִּשְׁפָּט כַּאֲשֶׁר הוּא, וְקוֹלָר יְהֵא תָּלוּי בְּצַוַּאר הָרַבִּים:

ג וְדָל לֹא תֶהְדַּר. לֹא תַחֲלֹק לוֹ כָּבוֹד לְזַכּוֹתוֹ בַּדִּין, וְלוֹמַר: דַּל הוּא, אֲזַכֶּנּוּ וַאֲכַבְּדֶנּוּ:

שמות | פרק כג — משפטים | 439

ה אֹיִבְךָ֔ אוֹ חֲמֹר֖וֹ תֹּעֶ֑ה הָשֵׁ֥ב תְּשִׁיבֶ֖נּוּ לֽוֹ: כִּֽי־תִרְאֶ֞ה
חֲמ֣וֹר שֹׂנַאֲךָ֗ רֹבֵץ֙ תַּ֣חַת מַשָּׂא֔וֹ וְחָדַלְתָּ֖ מֵעֲזֹ֣ב ל֑וֹ עָזֹ֥ב תַּעֲזֹ֖ב
עִמּֽוֹ:
ו לֹ֥א תַטֶּ֛ה מִשְׁפַּ֥ט אֶבְיֹנְךָ֖ בְּרִיבֽוֹ: מִדְּבַר־שֶׁ֖קֶר חמישי
ז תִּרְחָ֑ק וְנָקִ֤י וְצַדִּיק֙ אַֽל־תַּהֲרֹ֔ג כִּ֥י לֹא־אַצְדִּ֖יק רָשָֽׁע: וְשֹׁ֖חַד
ח לֹ֣א תִקָּ֑ח כִּ֤י הַשֹּׁ֙חַד֙ יְעַוֵּ֣ר פִּקְחִ֔ים וִֽיסַלֵּ֖ף דִּבְרֵ֥י צַדִּיקִֽים:
ט וְגֵ֖ר לֹ֣א תִלְחָ֑ץ וְאַתֶּ֗ם יְדַעְתֶּם֙ אֶת־נֶ֣פֶשׁ הַגֵּ֔ר כִּֽי־גֵרִ֥ים הֱיִיתֶ֖ם
י בְּאֶ֥רֶץ מִצְרָֽיִם: וְשֵׁ֥שׁ שָׁנִ֖ים תִּזְרַ֣ע אֶת־אַרְצֶ֑ךָ וְאָסַפְתָּ֖ אֶת־
יא תְּבוּאָתָֽהּ: וְהַשְּׁבִיעִ֞ת תִּשְׁמְטֶ֣נָּה וּנְטַשְׁתָּ֗הּ וְאָֽכְלוּ֙ אֶבְיֹנֵ֣י עַמֶּ֔ךָ

ה כי תראה חמור שנאך וגו'. הרי "כי" משמש
לשון "דלמא", שהוא מארבע לשונות של שמושי "כי".
וכה פתרונו: שמא תראה חמורו "רבץ תחת משאו",
"וחדלת מעזב לו", בתמיה; "עזב תעזב עמו" —
עזיבה זו לשון עזרה, וכן: "עצור ועזוב" (דברים לב, לו),
וכן: "ויעזבו ירושלם עד החומה" (נחמיה ג, ח), מלחומה
עפר לעצור ולהשביע את חזק החומה. כיוצא בו: "כי
תאמר בלבבך רבים הגוים האלה ממני" וגו' (דברים
ז, יז), שמא תאמר כן, בתמיה — "לא תירא מהם"
(שם פסוק יח). ומדרשו, כך דרשו רבותינו: "כי תראה
וחדלת", פעמים שאתה חודל ופעמים שאתה עוזב.
הא כיצד? זקן ואינה לפי כבודו — "וחדלת", או
בהמת גוי ומשאו של ישראל — "עזב תעזב": עזב
תעזב עמו. לפרק המשא. "מלמשקל ליה", מלטול
משאו ממנו:

ו אביונך. לשון חובה, שהוא מדלדל ותאב לכל
טובה:

ז ונקי וצדיק אל תהרג. מנין ליוצא מבית דין חייב,
ואמר אחד: יש לי ללמד עליו זכות, שמחזירין
אותו? תלמוד לומר: "ונקי אל תהרג", ואף על פי
שאינו "צדיק", שלא נצטדק בבית דין, מכל מקום
"נקי" הוא מדין מיתה, שהרי יש לך לזכותו. ומנין

ליוצא מבית דין זכאי, ואמר אחד: יש לי ללמד
עליו חובה, שאין מחזירין אותו לבית דין? תלמוד
לומר: "וצדיק אל תהרג", וזה צדיק הוא שנצטדק
בבית דין. כי לא אצדיק רשע. אין עליך להחזירו,
כי אני לא אצדיקנו בדיני, אם יצא מידך זכאי יש
לי שלוחים הרבה להמיתו במיתה שנתחייב בה:

ח ושחד לא תקח. אפלו לשפט אמת, וכל שכן
כדי להטות הדין, שהרי כדי להטות את הדין כבר
נאמר: "לא תטה משפט" (לעיל פסוק ו). יעור פקחים.
אפלו חכם בתורה ונוטל שחד, סוף שתטרף
דעתו עליו, וישתכח תלמודו ויכהה מאור עיניו:
ויסלף. כתרגומו: "ומקלקל". דברי צדיקים. דברים
המצדקים, משפטי אמת. וכן תרגומו: "פתגמין
תריצין", ישרים:

ט וגר לא תלחץ. בהרבה מקומות הזהירה תורה
על הגר, מפני שסורו רע. את נפש הגר. כמה קשה
לו כשלוחצין אותו:

י ואספת את תבואתה. לשון הכנסה לבית, כמו:
"ואספתו אל תוך ביתך" (דברים כב, ב):

יא תשמטנה. מעבודה. ונטשתה. מאכילה
אחר זמן הבעור. דבר אחר: "תשמטנה" מעבודה
גמורה, כגון חרישה וזריעה. "ונטשתה" מלזבל

פרק כג | שמות | משפטים

יב וְיִתְרָ֕ם תֹּאכַ֖ל חַיַּ֣ת הַשָּׂדֶ֑ה כֵּֽן־תַּעֲשֶׂ֥ה לְכַרְמְךָ֖ לְזֵיתֶֽךָ׃ שֵׁ֤שֶׁת יָמִים֙ תַּעֲשֶׂ֣ה מַעֲשֶׂ֔יךָ וּבַיּ֥וֹם הַשְּׁבִיעִ֖י תִּשְׁבֹּ֑ת לְמַ֣עַן יָנ֗וּחַ שֽׁוֹרְךָ֙ וַחֲמֹרֶ֔ךָ וְיִנָּפֵ֥שׁ בֶּן־אֲמָתְךָ֖ וְהַגֵּֽר׃ יג וּבְכֹ֛ל אֲשֶׁר־אָמַ֥רְתִּי אֲלֵיכֶ֖ם תִּשָּׁמֵ֑רוּ וְשֵׁ֨ם אֱלֹהִ֤ים אֲחֵרִים֙ לֹ֣א תַזְכִּ֔ירוּ לֹ֥א יִשָּׁמַ֖ע עַל־פִּֽיךָ׃ יד שָׁלֹ֥שׁ רְגָלִ֖ים תָּחֹ֥ג לִ֖י בַּשָּׁנָֽה׃ טו אֶת־חַ֣ג הַמַּצּוֹת֮ תִּשְׁמֹר֒ שִׁבְעַ֣ת יָמִים֩ תֹּאכַ֨ל מַצּ֜וֹת כַּאֲשֶׁ֣ר צִוִּיתִ֗ךָ לְמוֹעֵד֙ חֹ֣דֶשׁ הָֽאָבִ֔יב כִּי־ב֖וֹ יָצָ֣אתָ מִמִּצְרָ֑יִם וְלֹא־יֵרָא֥וּ פָנַ֖י רֵיקָֽם׃ טז וְחַ֤ג הַקָּצִיר֙ בִּכּוּרֵ֣י מַעֲשֶׂ֔יךָ אֲשֶׁ֥ר תִּזְרַ֖ע בַּשָּׂדֶ֑ה וְחַ֤ג הָֽאָסִף֙ בְּצֵ֣את הַשָּׁנָ֔ה בְּאָסְפְּךָ֥ אֶֽת־מַעֲשֶׂ֖יךָ מִן־הַשָּׂדֶֽה׃ יז שָׁלֹ֥שׁ פְּעָמִ֖ים בַּשָּׁנָ֑ה יֵרָאֶה֙ כָּל־זְכ֣וּרְךָ֔

וְיִתְרָם תֹּאכַל חַיַּת הַשָּׂדֶה. לְהָקִישׁ מַאֲכַל אֶבְיוֹן לְמַאֲכַל חַיָּה, מַה חַיָּה אוֹכֶלֶת בְּלֹא מַעֲשֵׂר אַף אֶבְיוֹנִים אוֹכְלִים בְּלֹא מַעֲשֵׂר, מִכָּאן אָמְרוּ: אֵין מַעֲשֵׂר בַּשְּׁבִיעִית: **כֵּן תַּעֲשֶׂה לְכַרְמֶךָ.** וּתְחִלַּת הַמִּקְרָא מְדַבֵּר בִּשְׂדֵה הַלָּבָן, כְּמוֹ שֶׁאָמוּר לְמַעְלָה הֵימֶנּוּ: "תִּזְרַע אֶת אַרְצֶךָ" (בפסוק הקודם):

יב) וּבַיּוֹם הַשְּׁבִיעִי תִּשְׁבֹּת. אַף בַּשָּׁנָה הַשְּׁבִיעִית לֹא תֵעָקֵר שַׁבַּת בְּרֵאשִׁית מִמְּקוֹמָהּ, שֶׁלֹּא תֹאמַר: הוֹאִיל וְכָל הַשָּׁנָה קְרוּיָה שַׁבָּת לֹא תִנְהַג בָּהּ שַׁבַּת בְּרֵאשִׁית: **לְמַעַן יָנוּחַ שׁוֹרְךָ וַחֲמֹרֶךָ.** תֵּן לוֹ נְיַח, לְהַתִּיר שֶׁיְּהֵא תוֹלֵשׁ וְאוֹכֵל עֲשָׂבִים מִן הַקַּרְקַע. אוֹ אֵינוֹ אֶלָּא יַחְבְּשֶׁנּוּ בְּתוֹךְ הַבַּיִת? אָמַרְתָּ, אֵין זֶה נְיַח אֶלָּא צַעַר: **בֶּן אֲמָתֶךָ.** בְּעֶבֶד עָרֵל הַכָּתוּב מְדַבֵּר: **וְהַגֵּר.** זֶה גֵּר תּוֹשָׁב:

יג) וּבְכֹל אֲשֶׁר אָמַרְתִּי אֲלֵיכֶם תִּשָּׁמֵרוּ. לַעֲשׂוֹת כָּל מִצְוֹת עֲשֵׂה בְּאַזְהָרָה, שֶׁכָּל שְׁמִירָה שֶׁבַּתּוֹרָה אַזְהָרָה הִיא בִּמְקוֹם לָאו: **לֹא תַזְכִּירוּ.** שֶׁלֹּא יֹאמַר לוֹ: שְׁמֹר לִי בְּצַד עֲבוֹדָה זָרָה פְּלוֹנִית, אוֹ תַּעֲמֹד עִמִּי בְּיוֹם עֲבוֹדָה זָרָה פְּלוֹנִית. דָּבָר אַחֵר, "וּבְכֹל אֲשֶׁר אָמַרְתִּי אֲלֵיכֶם תִּשָּׁמֵרוּ וְשֵׁם אֱלֹהִים אֲחֵרִים לֹא תַזְכִּירוּ",

לְלַמֶּדְךָ שֶׁשְּׁקוּלָה עֲבוֹדָה זָרָה כְּנֶגֶד כָּל הַמִּצְוֹת כֻּלָּן, וְהַנִּזְהָר בָּהּ כְּשׁוֹמֵר אֶת כֻּלָּן: **לֹא יִשָּׁמַע.** מִן הַגּוֹי: **עַל פִּיךָ** - שֶׁלֹּא תַּעֲשֶׂה שֻׁתָּפוּת עִם הַגּוֹי וְיִשָּׁבַע לְךָ בַּעֲבוֹדָה זָרָה שֶׁלּוֹ, נִמְצֵאתָ שֶׁאַתָּה גּוֹרֵם שֶׁיִּזָּכֵר עַל יָדְךָ:

יד) רְגָלִים. פְּעָמִים, וְכֵן: "כִּי הִכִּיתַנִי זֶה שָׁלֹשׁ רְגָלִים" (במדבר כב, כח):

טו) חֹדֶשׁ הָאָבִיב. שֶׁהַתְּבוּאָה מִתְמַלֵּאת בּוֹ בְּאִבֶּיהָ, לְשׁוֹן אַחֵר, "אָבִיב", לְשׁוֹן אָב, בְּכוֹר וְרִאשׁוֹן לְבַשֵּׁל פֵּרוֹת: **וְלֹא יֵרָאוּ פָנַי רֵיקָם.** כְּשֶׁתָּבוֹאוּ לֵרָאוֹת פָּנַי בָּרְגָלִים, הָבִיאוּ לִי עוֹלוֹת:

טז) וְחַג הַקָּצִיר. הוּא חַג שָׁבוּעוֹת: **בִּכּוּרֵי מַעֲשֶׂיךָ.** שֶׁהוּא זְמַן הֲבָאַת בִּכּוּרִים, שֶׁשְּׁתֵּי הַלֶּחֶם הַבָּאִין בַּעֲצֶרֶת הָיוּ מַתִּירִין הֶחָדָשׁ לַמְּנָחוֹת וּלְהָבִיא בִּכּוּרִים לַמִּקְדָּשׁ, שֶׁנֶּאֱמַר: "וּבְיוֹם הַבִּכּוּרִים" וְגוֹ' (שם כח, כו): **וְחַג הָאָסִף.** הוּא חַג הַסֻּכּוֹת: **בְּאָסְפְּךָ אֶת מַעֲשֶׂיךָ.** שֶׁכָּל יְמוֹת הַחַמָּה הַתְּבוּאָה מִתְיַבֶּשֶׁת בַּשָּׂדוֹת, וּבֶחָג אוֹסְפִים אוֹתָהּ אֶל הַבַּיִת מִפְּנֵי הַגְּשָׁמִים:

יז) שָׁלֹשׁ פְּעָמִים וְגוֹ'. לְפִי שֶׁהָעִנְיָן מְדַבֵּר בַּשְּׁבִיעִית, הֻצְרַךְ לוֹמַר שֶׁלֹּא יִסְתָּרְסוּ רְגָלִים מִמְּקוֹמָן: **כָּל זְכוּרְךָ.** הַזְּכָרִים שֶׁבְּךָ:

שמות | פרק כג

יח אֶל־פְּנֵ֖י הָאָדֹ֥ן ׀ יְהוָֽה: לֹֽא־תִזְבַּ֥ח עַל־חָמֵ֖ץ דַּם־זִבְחִ֑י וְלֹֽא־יָלִ֥ין
חֵֽלֶב־חַגִּ֖י עַד־בֹּֽקֶר: יט רֵאשִׁ֗ית בִּכּוּרֵי֙ אַדְמָ֣תְךָ֔ תָּבִ֕יא בֵּ֖ית יְהוָ֣ה
אֱלֹהֶ֑יךָ לֹֽא־תְבַשֵּׁ֥ל גְּדִ֖י בַּחֲלֵ֥ב אִמּֽוֹ:

ששי

כ הִנֵּ֨ה אָנֹכִ֜י שֹׁלֵ֤חַ מַלְאָךְ֙ לְפָנֶ֔יךָ לִשְׁמָרְךָ֖ בַּדָּ֑רֶךְ וְלַהֲבִ֣יאֲךָ֔ אֶל־
כא הַמָּק֖וֹם אֲשֶׁ֥ר הֲכִנֹֽתִי: הִשָּׁ֧מֶר מִפָּנָ֛יו וּשְׁמַ֥ע בְּקֹל֖וֹ אַל־תַּמֵּ֣ר בּ֑וֹ כִּ֣י
כב לֹ֤א יִשָּׂא֙ לְפִשְׁעֲכֶ֔ם כִּ֥י שְׁמִ֖י בְּקִרְבּֽוֹ: כִּ֣י אִם־שָׁמ֤וֹעַ תִּשְׁמַע֙ בְּקֹל֔וֹ
וְעָשִׂ֕יתָ כֹּ֖ל אֲשֶׁ֣ר אֲדַבֵּ֑ר וְאָֽיַבְתִּי֙ אֶת־אֹ֣יְבֶ֔יךָ וְצַרְתִּ֖י אֶת־צֹרְרֶֽיךָ:
כג כִּֽי־יֵלֵ֣ךְ מַלְאָכִי֮ לְפָנֶיךָ֒ וֶהֱבִֽיאֲךָ֗ אֶל־הָֽאֱמֹרִי֙ וְהַ֣חִתִּ֔י וְהַפְּרִזִּי֙
כד וְהַֽכְּנַעֲנִ֔י הַחִוִּ֖י וְהַיְבוּסִ֑י וְהִכְחַדְתִּֽיו: לֹֽא־תִשְׁתַּחֲוֶ֤ה לֵאלֹֽהֵיהֶם֙
וְלֹ֣א תָֽעָבְדֵ֔ם וְלֹ֥א תַעֲשֶׂ֖ה כְּמַעֲשֵׂיהֶ֑ם כִּ֤י הָרֵס֙ תְּהָ֣רְסֵ֔ם וְשַׁבֵּ֥ר

יח | **לֹא תִזְבַּח עַל חָמֵץ וְגוֹ׳.** לֹא תִשְׁחַט אֶת הַפֶּסַח
בְּאַרְבָּעָה עָשָׂר בְּנִיסָן עַד שֶׁתְּבַעֵר הֶחָמֵץ: **וְלֹא יָלִין
חֵלֶב חַגִּי וְגוֹ׳.** חוּץ לַמִּזְבֵּחַ: **עַד בֹּקֶר.** יָכוֹל אַף עַל
הַמַּעֲרָכָה יִפָּסֵל בְּלִינָה? תַּלְמוּד לוֹמַר: "עַל מוֹקְדָה
עַל הַמִּזְבֵּחַ כָּל הַלַּיְלָה" (ויקרא ו, ב): **וְלֹא יָלִין.** אֵין לִינָה
אֶלָּא בְּעַמּוּד הַשַּׁחַר, שֶׁנֶּאֱמַר: "עַד בֹּקֶר", אֲבָל כָּל
הַלַּיְלָה יָכוֹל לְהַעֲלוֹתוֹ מִן הָרִצְפָּה לַמִּזְבֵּחַ:

יט | **רֵאשִׁית בִּכּוּרֵי אַדְמָתְךָ.** אַף הַשְּׁבִיעִית חַיֶּבֶת
בַּבִּכּוּרִים, לְכָךְ נֶאֱמְרָה אַף כָּאן: **בִּכּוּרֵי אַדְמָתְךָ.**
כֵּיצַד? אָדָם נִכְנָס לְתוֹךְ שָׂדֵהוּ, רוֹאֶה תְּאֵנָה שֶׁבִּכְּרָה,
כּוֹרֵךְ עָלֶיהָ גֶּמִי לְסִימָן וּמַקְדִּישָׁהּ (ביכורים ג, א). וְאֵין
בִּכּוּרִים אֶלָּא מִשִּׁבְעַת הַמִּינִין הָאֲמוּרִים בַּמִּקְרָא:
"אֶרֶץ חִטָּה וּשְׂעֹרָה וְגוֹ׳" (דברים ח, ח): **לֹא תְבַשֵּׁל גְּדִי.**
אַף עֵגֶל וָכֶבֶשׂ בִּכְלַל 'גְּדִי', שֶׁאֵין גְּדִי אֶלָּא לְשׁוֹן
וָלָד רַךְ, מִמַּה שֶּׁאַתָּה מוֹצֵא בְּכַמָּה מְקוֹמוֹת בַּתּוֹרָה
שֶׁכָּתוּב 'גְּדִי' וְהֻצְרַךְ לְפָרֵשׁ אַחֲרָיו 'עִזִּים', כְּגוֹן: "חֲלִי
אֲשַׁלַּח גְּדִי עִזִּים" (בראשית לח, יז), "אֶת גְּדִי הָעִזִּים"
(שם פסוק כ; שופטים יג, יט), "שְׁנֵי גְּדָיֵי עִזִּים" (בראשית כז, ט),
לְלַמֶּדְךָ שֶׁכָּל מָקוֹם שֶׁנֶּאֱמַר 'גְּדִי' סְתָם אַף עֵגֶל
וָכֶבֶשׁ בַּמַּשְׁמָע. וּבִשְׁלֹשָׁה מְקוֹמוֹת נִכְתַּב בַּתּוֹרָה,

אֶחָד לְאִסּוּר אֲכִילָה וְאֶחָד לְאִסּוּר הֲנָאָה וְאֶחָד
לְאִסּוּר בִּשּׁוּל:

כ | **הִנֵּה אָנֹכִי שֹׁלֵחַ מַלְאָךְ.** כָּאן נִתְבַּשְּׂרוּ שֶׁעֲתִידִין
לַחֲטוֹא וּשְׁכִינָה אוֹמֶרֶת לָהֶם: "כִּי לֹא אֶעֱלֶה בְּקִרְבְּךָ"
(להלן לג, ג): **אֲשֶׁר הֲכִנֹתִי.** אֲשֶׁר זִמַּנְתִּי לָתֵת לָכֶם,
זֶהוּ פְּשׁוּטוֹ. וּמִדְרָשׁוֹ, "אֶל הַמָּקוֹם אֲשֶׁר הֲכִנֹתִי",
כְּבָר מְקוֹמִי נִכָּר כְּנֶגְדּוֹ, וְזֶה אֶחָד מִן הַמִּקְרָאוֹת
שֶׁאוֹמְרִים שֶׁבֵּית הַמִּקְדָּשׁ שֶׁל מַעְלָה מְכֻוָּן כְּנֶגֶד בֵּית
הַמִּקְדָּשׁ שֶׁל מַטָּה:

כא | **אַל תַּמֵּר בּוֹ.** לְשׁוֹן הַמְרָאָה, "אֲשֶׁר יַמְרֶה
אֶת פִּיךָ" (יהושע א, יח), "וַיַּמְרוּ בִי" (יחזקאל כ, ח): **כִּי לֹא
יִשָּׂא לְפִשְׁעֲכֶם.** אֵינוֹ מְלֻמָּד בְּכָךְ, שֶׁהוּא מִן הַכַּת
שֶׁאֵין חוֹטְאִין. וְעוֹד, שֶׁהוּא שָׁלִיחַ וְאֵינוֹ עוֹשֶׂה אֶלָּא
שְׁלִיחוּתוֹ: **כִּי שְׁמִי בְּקִרְבּוֹ.** מְחֻבָּר לְרֹאשׁ הַמִּקְרָא,
"הִשָּׁמֶר מִפָּנָיו" כִּי שְׁמִי מְשֻׁתָּף בּוֹ, וְרַבּוֹתֵינוּ אָמְרוּ,
זֶה מְטַטְרוֹן שֶׁשְּׁמוֹ כְּשֵׁם רַבּוֹ. מְטַטְרוֹן בְּגִמַטְרִיָּא
שַׁדַּי:

כב | **וְצַרְתִּי.** כְּתַרְגּוּמוֹ: "וַאֲעִיק":

כד | **הָרֵס תְּהָרְסֵם.** לְאוֹתָם אֱלֹהוֹת: **מַצֵּבֹתֵיהֶם.**
אֲבָנִים שֶׁהֵם מַצִּיבִין לְהִשְׁתַּחֲווֹת לָהֶם:

משפטים | פרק כג

תְּשַׁבֵּ֖ר מַצֵּבֹתֵיהֶֽם: וַעֲבַדְתֶּ֗ם אֵ֚ת יְהֹוָ֣ה אֱלֹֽהֵיכֶ֔ם וּבֵרַ֥ךְ אֶת־ כה
לַֽחְמְךָ֖ וְאֶת־מֵימֶ֑יךָ וַהֲסִרֹתִ֥י מַחֲלָ֖ה מִקִּרְבֶּֽךָ: לֹ֥א שביעי
תִהְיֶ֛ה מְשַׁכֵּלָ֥ה וַעֲקָרָ֖ה בְּאַרְצֶ֑ךָ אֶת־מִסְפַּ֥ר יָמֶ֖יךָ אֲמַלֵּֽא: כו
אֶת־אֵֽימָתִי֙ אֲשַׁלַּ֣ח לְפָנֶ֔יךָ וְהַמֹּתִי֙ אֶת־כָּל־הָעָ֔ם אֲשֶׁ֥ר תָּבֹ֖א כז
בָּהֶ֑ם וְנָתַתִּ֧י אֶת־כָּל־אֹיְבֶ֛יךָ אֵלֶ֖יךָ עֹֽרֶף: וְשָׁלַחְתִּ֥י אֶת־הַצִּרְעָ֖ה כח
לְפָנֶ֑יךָ וְגֵרְשָׁ֗ה אֶת־הַחִוִּ֧י אֶת־הַֽכְּנַעֲנִ֛י וְאֶת־הַחִתִּ֖י מִלְּפָנֶֽיךָ:
לֹ֧א אֲגָרְשֶׁ֛נּוּ מִפָּנֶ֖יךָ בְּשָׁנָ֣ה אֶחָ֑ת פֶּן־תִּהְיֶ֤ה הָאָ֨רֶץ֙ שְׁמָמָ֔ה כט
וְרַבָּ֥ה עָלֶ֖יךָ חַיַּ֥ת הַשָּׂדֶֽה: מְעַ֥ט מְעַ֛ט אֲגָרְשֶׁ֖נּוּ מִפָּנֶ֑יךָ עַ֚ד אֲשֶׁ֣ר ל
תִּפְרֶ֔ה וְנָחַלְתָּ֖ אֶת־הָאָֽרֶץ: וְשַׁתִּ֣י אֶת־גְּבֻלְךָ֗ מִיַּם־סוּף֙ וְעַד־ לא
יָ֣ם פְּלִשְׁתִּ֔ים וּמִמִּדְבָּ֖ר עַד־הַנָּהָ֑ר כִּ֣י ׀ אֶתֵּ֣ן בְּיֶדְכֶ֗ם אֵ֚ת יֹשְׁבֵ֣י
הָאָ֔רֶץ וְגֵרַשְׁתָּ֖מוֹ מִפָּנֶֽיךָ: לֹֽא־תִכְרֹ֥ת לָהֶ֛ם וְלֵאלֹֽהֵיהֶ֖ם בְּרִֽית: לב

כו) **לֹא תִהְיֶה מְשַׁכֵּלָה.** אִם תַּעֲשֶׂה רְצוֹנִי: **מְשַׁכֵּלָה.** מַפֶּלֶת נְפָלִים אוֹ קוֹבֶרֶת אֶת בָּנֶיהָ קְרוּיָה מְשַׁכֵּלָה:

כז) **וְהַמֹּתִי.** כְּמוֹ וְהֵמַמְתִּי, וְתַרְגּוּמוֹ: "וֶאֱשַׁגֵּשׁ". וְכֵן כָּל תֵּבָה שֶׁפֹּעַל שֶׁלָּהּ בְּכֶפֶל אוֹת אַחֲרוֹנָה, כְּשֶׁתְּהַפְּכֶנּוּ לְדַבֵּר בִּלְשׁוֹן פָּעַלְתִּי יֵשׁ מְקוֹמוֹת שֶׁנּוֹטֵל אוֹת הַכְּפוּלָה וּמַדְגֵּשׁ אֶת הָאוֹת וְנוֹקְדוֹ בִּמְלָאפוּם, כְּגוֹן: "וְהַמֹּתִי" מִגִּזְרַת "וְהָמַם גַּלְגַּל עֶגְלָתוֹ" (ישעיה כח, כח), "וְסַבּוֹתִי" מִגִּזְרַת "וְסָבַב בֵּית אֵל" (שמואל א׳ ז, טז), "דַּלּוֹתִי" (תהלים קטז, ו) מִגִּזְרַת "דְּלָלוּ וְחָרְבוּ" (ישעיה יט, ו), "עַל כַּפַּיִם חַקֹּתִיךְ" (שם מט, טז) מִגִּזְרַת "חִקְקֵי לֵב" (שופטים ה, טו), "אֶת מִי רַצּוֹתִי" (שמואל א׳ יב, ג) מִגִּזְרַת "רֶצַץ עָבַד דַּלִּים" (איוב כ, יט). וְהַמְתַרְגֵּם "וְהַמֹּתִי" - "וַאֲקַטֵּיל" טוֹעֶה הוּא, שֶׁאִלּוּ מִגִּזְרַת מִיתָה הָיָה, אֵין ה"א שֶׁלָּהּ בְּפַתָּח וְלֹא מ"ם שֶׁלָּהּ מֻדְגֶּשֶׁת וְלֹא נְקוּדָה מְלָאפוּם, אֶלָּא "וְהֵמַתִּי", כְּגוֹן: "וְהֵמַתָּה אֶת הָעָם הַזֶּה" (במדבר יד, טו), וְהַתָּי"ו מֻדְגֶּשֶׁת לְפִי שֶׁתָּבוֹא בִּמְקוֹם שְׁתֵּי תָוִי"ן, הָאַחַת נִשְׁרֶשֶׁת, לְפִי שֶׁאֵין מִיתָה בְּלֹא תָי"ו, וְהָאַחֶרֶת מְשַׁמֶּשֶׁת, כְּמוֹ: אָמַרְתִּי, חָטָאתִי, עָשִׂיתִי, וְכֵן "וְנָתַתִּי" הַתָּי"ו מֻדְגֶּשֶׁת, שֶׁהִיא בָאָה בִּמְקוֹם שְׁתֵּי תָוִי"ן, לְפִי שֶׁהָיָה

עָרִיךְ שָׁלֹשׁ תָוִי"ן, שְׁתַּיִם לַיְסוֹד כְּמוֹ: "בְּיוֹם תֵּת ה'" (יהושע י, יב), "מַתַּת אֱלֹהִים הִיא" (קהלת ג, יג), וְהַשְּׁלִישִׁית לְשִׁמּוּשׁ: **עֹרֶף.** שֶׁיָּנוּסוּ לְפָנֶיךָ וְיַהַפְכוּ לְךָ עָרְפָּם:

כח) **הַצִּרְעָה.** מִין שֶׁרֶץ הָעוֹף, וְהָיְתָה מַכָּה אוֹתָם בְּעֵינֵיהֶם וּמְטִילָה בָּם אֶרֶס וְהֵם מֵתִים. וְהַצִּרְעָה לֹא עָבְרָה אֶת הַיַּרְדֵּן. וְחִוִּי וּכְנַעֲנִי הֵם אֶרֶץ סִיחוֹן וְעוֹג, לְפִיכָךְ מִכָּל שֶׁבַע אֻמּוֹת לֹא מָנָה כָּאן אֶלָּא אֵלּוּ. וְחִוִּי, אַף עַל פִּי שֶׁהוּא מֵעֵבֶר הַיַּרְדֵּן וָהָלְאָה, שָׁנוּ רַבּוֹתֵינוּ בְּמַסֶּכֶת סוֹטָה (דף לו ע"א): עַל שְׂפַת הַיַּרְדֵּן עָמְדָה וְזָרְקָה בָּהֶם מָרָה:

כט) **שְׁמָמָה.** רֵיקָנִית מִבְּנֵי אָדָם, לְפִי שֶׁאַתֶּם מְעַט וְאֵין בָּכֶם כְּדֵי לְמַלֹּאות אוֹתָהּ: **וְרַבָּה עָלֶיךָ.** וְתִרְבֶּה עָלֶיךָ:

ל) **עַד אֲשֶׁר תִּפְרֶה.** תִּרְבֶּה, לְשׁוֹן פְּרִי, כְּמוֹ: "פְּרוּ וּרְבוּ" (בראשית ח, כב):

לא) **וְשַׁתִּי.** לְשׁוֹן הֲשָׁתָה, וְהַתָּי"ו מֻדְגֶּשֶׁת מִפְּנֵי שֶׁבָּאָה תַּחַת שְׁתַּיִם, שֶׁאֵין שִׁיתָה בְּלֹא תָי"ו, וְהָאַחַת לְשִׁמּוּשׁ: **עַד הַנָּהָר.** פְּרָת: **וְגֵרַשְׁתָּמוֹ.** וּתְגָרְשֵׁם:

שמות | פרק כג — משפטים | 443

לג לֹא יֵשְׁבוּ בְּאַרְצְךָ פֶּן־יַחֲטִיאוּ אֹתְךָ לִי כִּי תַעֲבֹד אֶת־אֱלֹהֵיהֶם כִּי־יִהְיֶה לְךָ לְמוֹקֵשׁ:

כד א וְאֶל־מֹשֶׁה אָמַר עֲלֵה אֶל־יְהוָה אַתָּה וְאַהֲרֹן נָדָב וַאֲבִיהוּא
ב וְשִׁבְעִים מִזִּקְנֵי יִשְׂרָאֵל וְהִשְׁתַּחֲוִיתֶם מֵרָחֹק: וְנִגַּשׁ מֹשֶׁה
לְבַדּוֹ אֶל־יְהוָה וְהֵם לֹא יִגָּשׁוּ וְהָעָם לֹא יַעֲלוּ עִמּוֹ: וַיָּבֹא מֹשֶׁה
ג וַיְסַפֵּר לָעָם אֵת כָּל־דִּבְרֵי יְהוָה וְאֵת כָּל־הַמִּשְׁפָּטִים וַיַּעַן
כָּל־הָעָם קוֹל אֶחָד וַיֹּאמְרוּ כָּל־הַדְּבָרִים אֲשֶׁר־דִּבֶּר יְהוָה
ד נַעֲשֶׂה: וַיִּכְתֹּב מֹשֶׁה אֵת כָּל־דִּבְרֵי יְהוָה וַיַּשְׁכֵּם בַּבֹּקֶר וַיִּבֶן
מִזְבֵּחַ תַּחַת הָהָר וּשְׁתֵּים עֶשְׂרֵה מַצֵּבָה לִשְׁנֵים עָשָׂר שִׁבְטֵי
ה יִשְׂרָאֵל: וַיִּשְׁלַח אֶת־נַעֲרֵי בְּנֵי יִשְׂרָאֵל וַיַּעֲלוּ עֹלֹת וַיִּזְבְּחוּ
ו זְבָחִים שְׁלָמִים לַיהוָה פָּרִים: וַיִּקַּח מֹשֶׁה חֲצִי הַדָּם וַיָּשֶׂם
ז בָּאַגָּנֹת וַחֲצִי הַדָּם זָרַק עַל־הַמִּזְבֵּחַ: וַיִּקַּח סֵפֶר הַבְּרִית וַיִּקְרָא
בְּאָזְנֵי הָעָם וַיֹּאמְרוּ כֹּל אֲשֶׁר־דִּבֶּר יְהוָה נַעֲשֶׂה וְנִשְׁמָע:

לג| כִּי תַעֲבֹד וְגוֹ'. הֲרֵי אֵלּוּ "כִּי" מְשַׁמְּשִׁין בִּמְקוֹם 'אֲשֶׁר', וְכֵן בְּכַמָּה מְקוֹמוֹת. וְזֶהוּ לְשׁוֹן 'אִי', שֶׁהוּא אֶחָד מֵאַרְבָּעָה לְשׁוֹנוֹת שֶׁהַ"כִּי" מְשַׁמֵּשׁ. וְגַם מָצִינוּ בְּהַרְבֵּה מְקוֹמוֹת 'אִם' מְשַׁמֵּשׁ בִּלְשׁוֹן 'אֲשֶׁר', כְּמוֹ: "וְאִם תַּקְרִיב מִנְחַת בִּכּוּרִים" (ויקרא ב, יד) שֶׁהוּא חוֹבָה:

פרק כד
א| וְאֶל מֹשֶׁה אָמַר. פָּרָשָׁה זוֹ נֶאֶמְרָה קֹדֶם עֲשֶׂרֶת הַדִּבְּרוֹת, בְּאַרְבָּעָה בְּסִיוָן נֶאֱמַר לוֹ: "עֲלֵה":

ב| וְנִגַּשׁ מֹשֶׁה לְבַדּוֹ. אֶל הָעֲרָפֶל:

ג| וַיָּבֹא מֹשֶׁה וַיְסַפֵּר לָעָם. בּוֹ בַּיּוֹם: אֵת כָּל דִּבְרֵי ה'. מִצְוַת פְּרִישָׁה וְהַגְבָּלָה: וְאֵת כָּל הַמִּשְׁפָּטִים. שֶׁבַע

מִצְוֹת שֶׁנִּצְטַוּוּ בְּנֵי נֹחַ, וְשַׁבָּת וְכִבּוּד אָב וָאֵם וּפָרָה אֲדֻמָּה וְדִינִין שֶׁנִּתְּנוּ לָהֶם בְּמָרָה:

ד| וַיִּכְתֹּב מֹשֶׁה. מִבְּרֵאשִׁית וְעַד מַתַּן תּוֹרָה, וְכָתַב מִצְוֹת שֶׁנִּצְטַוּוּ בְּמָרָה: וַיַּשְׁכֵּם בַּבֹּקֶר. בַּחֲמִשָּׁה בְּסִיוָן:

ה| אֶת נַעֲרֵי. הַבְּכוֹרוֹת:

ו| וַיִּקַּח מֹשֶׁה חֲצִי הַדָּם. מִי חִלְּקוֹ? מַלְאָךְ בָּא וְחִלְּקוֹ: בָּאַגָּנֹת. שְׁתֵּי אַגָּנוֹת, אֶחָד לַחֲצִי דַּם עוֹלָה וְאֶחָד לַחֲצִי דַּם שְׁלָמִים לְהַזּוֹת אוֹתָם עַל הָעָם. וּמִכָּאן לָמְדוּ רַבּוֹתֵינוּ שֶׁנִּכְנְסוּ אֲבוֹתֵינוּ לַבְּרִית בְּמִילָה וּטְבִילָה וְהַרְצָאַת דָּמִים, שֶׁאֵין הַזָּאָה בְּלֹא טְבִילָה:

ז| סֵפֶר הַבְּרִית. מִבְּרֵאשִׁית וְעַד מַתַּן תּוֹרָה, וּמִצְוֹת שֶׁנִּצְטַוּוּ בְּמָרָה:

פרק כד | שמות

ח וַיִּקַּ֤ח מֹשֶׁה֙ אֶת־הַדָּ֔ם וַיִּזְרֹ֖ק עַל־הָעָ֑ם וַיֹּ֗אמֶר הִנֵּ֤ה דַֽם־הַבְּרִית֙
ט אֲשֶׁ֨ר כָּרַ֤ת יְהוָֹה֙ עִמָּכֶ֔ם עַ֥ל כָּל־הַדְּבָרִ֖ים הָאֵֽלֶּה: וַיַּ֥עַל מֹשֶׁ֖ה
י וְאַהֲרֹ֑ן נָדָב֙ וַאֲבִיה֔וּא וְשִׁבְעִ֖ים מִזִּקְנֵ֥י יִשְׂרָאֵֽל: וַֽיִּרְא֕וּ אֵ֖ת
אֱלֹהֵ֣י יִשְׂרָאֵ֑ל וְתַ֣חַת רַגְלָ֗יו כְּמַעֲשֵׂה֙ לִבְנַ֣ת הַסַּפִּ֔יר וּכְעֶ֥צֶם
יא הַשָּׁמַ֖יִם לָטֹֽהַר: וְאֶל־אֲצִילֵי֙ בְּנֵ֣י יִשְׂרָאֵ֔ל לֹ֥א שָׁלַ֖ח יָד֑וֹ וַֽיֶּחֱזוּ֙
יב אֶת־הָ֣אֱלֹהִ֔ים וַיֹּאכְל֖וּ וַיִּשְׁתּֽוּ: וַיֹּ֨אמֶר יְהוָֹ֜ה אֶל־
מֹשֶׁ֗ה עֲלֵ֥ה אֵלַ֛י הָהָ֖רָה וֶהְיֵה־שָׁ֑ם וְאֶתְּנָ֨ה לְךָ֜ אֶת־לֻחֹ֣ת הָאֶ֗בֶן
וְהַתּוֹרָה֙ וְהַמִּצְוָ֔ה אֲשֶׁ֥ר כָּתַ֖בְתִּי לְהֽוֹרֹתָֽם: וַיָּ֣קָם מֹשֶׁ֔ה וִיהוֹשֻׁ֖עַ
יג מְשָׁרְת֑וֹ וַיַּ֥עַל מֹשֶׁ֖ה אֶל־הַ֥ר הָאֱלֹהִֽים: וְאֶל־הַזְּקֵנִ֤ים אָמַר֙
יד שְׁבוּ־לָ֣נוּ בָזֶ֔ה עַ֥ד אֲשֶׁר־נָשׁ֖וּב אֲלֵיכֶ֑ם וְהִנֵּ֨ה אַהֲרֹ֤ן וְחוּר֙ עִמָּכֶ֔ם

ח וַיִּזְרֹק. עִנְיַן הַזָּאָה, וְתַרְגּוּמוֹ: "וּזְרַק עַל מַדְבְּחָא לְכַפָּרָא עַל עַמָּא":

י וַיִּרְאוּ אֵת אֱלֹהֵי יִשְׂרָאֵל. נִסְתַּכְּלוּ וְהֵצִיצוּ וְנִתְחַיְּבוּ מִיתָה, אֶלָּא שֶׁלֹּא רָצָה הַקָּדוֹשׁ בָּרוּךְ הוּא לְעַרְבֵּב שִׂמְחַת הַתּוֹרָה, וְהִמְתִּין לְנָדָב וַאֲבִיהוּא עַד יוֹם חֲנֻכַּת הַמִּשְׁכָּן, וְלַזְּקֵנִים עַד "וַיְהִי הָעָם כְּמִתְאֹנְנִים... וַתִּבְעַר בָּם אֵשׁ ה' וַתֹּאכַל בִּקְצֵה הַמַּחֲנֶה" (במדבר יא, א), בִּקְצִינִים שֶׁבַּמַּחֲנֶה: כְּמַעֲשֵׂה לִבְנַת הַסַּפִּיר. הִיא הָיְתָה לְפָנָיו בִּשְׁעַת הַשִּׁעְבּוּד, לִזְכֹּר צָרָתָן שֶׁל יִשְׂרָאֵל שֶׁהָיוּ מְשֻׁעְבָּדִים בְּמַעֲשֵׂה לְבֵנִים: וּכְעֶצֶם הַשָּׁמַיִם לָטֹהַר. מִשֶּׁנִּגְאֲלוּ הָיָה אוֹר וְחֶדְוָה לְפָנָיו: וּכְעֶצֶם. כְּתַרְגּוּמוֹ, לְשׁוֹן מַרְאֶה: לָטֹהַר. לְשׁוֹן בָּרוּר וְצָלוּל:

יא וְאֶל אֲצִילֵי. הֵם נָדָב וַאֲבִיהוּא וְהַזְּקֵנִים: לֹא שָׁלַח יָדוֹ. מִכְּלָל שֶׁהָיוּ רְאוּיִים לְהִשְׁתַּלֵּחַ בָּם יָד: וַיֶּחֱזוּ אֶת הָאֱלֹהִים. הָיוּ מִסְתַּכְּלִין בּוֹ בְּלֵב גַּס מִתּוֹךְ אֲכִילָה וּשְׁתִיָּה, כָּךְ מִדְרַשׁ תַּנְחוּמָא, וְאֻנְקְלוֹס לֹא תִּרְגֵּם כֵּן, "אֲצִילֵי" לְשׁוֹן גְּדוֹלִים, כְּמוֹ: "וּמֵאֲצִילֶיהָ קְרָאתִיךָ" (ישעיה מא, ט), "וַיֶּאצֶל מִן הָרוּחַ" (במדבר יא, כה), "שֵׁשׁ אַמּוֹת אַצִּילָה" (יחזקאל מא, ח):

יב וַיֹּאמֶר ה' אֶל מֹשֶׁה. לְאַחַר מַתַּן תּוֹרָה: עֲלֵה אֵלַי הָהָרָה וֶהְיֵה שָׁם. אַרְבָּעִים יוֹם: אֶת לֻחֹת הָאֶבֶן וְהַתּוֹרָה וְהַמִּצְוָה אֲשֶׁר כָּתַבְתִּי לְהוֹרֹתָם. כָּל שֵׁשׁ מֵאוֹת וּשְׁלֹשׁ עֶשְׂרֵה מִצְוֹת בִּכְלַל עֲשֶׂרֶת הַדִּבְּרוֹת הֵן, וְרַבֵּנוּ סְעַדְיָה פֵּרַשׁ בָּאַזְהָרוֹת שֶׁיָּסַד לְכָל דִּבּוּר וְדִבּוּר מִצְוֹת הַתְּלוּיוֹת בּוֹ:

יג וַיָּקָם מֹשֶׁה וִיהוֹשֻׁעַ מְשָׁרְתוֹ. לֹא יָדַעְתִּי מַה טִּיבוֹ שֶׁל יְהוֹשֻׁעַ כָּאן, וְאוֹמֵר אֲנִי, שֶׁהָיָה הַתַּלְמִיד מְלַוֶּה לָרַב עַד מְקוֹם הַגְבָּלַת תְּחוּמֵי הָהָר, שֶׁאֵינוֹ רַשַּׁאי לֵילֵךְ מִשָּׁם וָהָלְאָה, וּמִשָּׁם "וַיַּעַל מֹשֶׁה" לְבַדּוֹ "אֶל הַר הָאֱלֹהִים", וִיהוֹשֻׁעַ נָטָה שָׁם אָהֳלוֹ וְנִתְעַכֵּב שָׁם כָּל אַרְבָּעִים יוֹם, שֶׁכֵּן מָצִינוּ כְּשֶׁיָּרַד מֹשֶׁה: "וַיִּשְׁמַע יְהוֹשֻׁעַ אֶת קוֹל הָעָם בְּרֵעֹה" (להלן לב, יז), לָמַדְנוּ שֶׁלֹּא הָיָה יְהוֹשֻׁעַ עִמָּהֶם:

יד וְאֶל הַזְּקֵנִים אָמַר. בְּצֵאתוֹ מִן הַמַּחֲנֶה: שְׁבוּ לָנוּ בָזֶה. וְהִתְעַכְּבוּ כָּאן עִם שְׁאָר הָעָם בַּמַּחֲנֶה לִהְיוֹת נְכוֹנִים לִשְׁפֹּט לְכָל אִישׁ רִיבוֹ: חוּר. בְּנָהּ שֶׁל מִרְיָם הָיָה, וְאָבִיו כָּלֵב בֶּן יְפֻנֶּה, שֶׁנֶּאֱמַר: "וַיִּקַּח לוֹ כָּלֵב אֶת אֶפְרָת וַתֵּלֶד לוֹ אֶת חוּר" (דברי הימים א' ב, יט), אֶפְרָת זוֹ מִרְיָם, כִּדְאִיתָא בְסוֹטָה (דף יא ע״ב): מִי בַעַל דְּבָרִים. מִי שֶׁיֵּשׁ לוֹ דִין:

שמות | פרק כד   תרומה | 445

מפטיר
טו מִֽי־בַ֥עַל דְּבָרִ֖ים יִגַּ֥שׁ אֲלֵהֶֽם: וַיַּ֥עַל מֹשֶׁ֖ה אֶל־הָהָ֑ר וַיְכַ֥ס הֶעָנָ֖ן
טז אֶת־הָהָֽר: וַיִּשְׁכֹּ֤ן כְּבוֹד־יְהֹוָה֙ עַל־הַ֣ר סִינַ֔י וַיְכַסֵּ֥הוּ הֶעָנָ֖ן שֵׁ֣שֶׁת
יז יָמִ֑ים וַיִּקְרָ֧א אֶל־מֹשֶׁ֛ה בַּיּ֥וֹם הַשְּׁבִיעִ֖י מִתּ֥וֹךְ הֶעָנָֽן: וּמַרְאֵה֙
יח כְּב֣וֹד יְהֹוָ֔ה כְּאֵ֥שׁ אֹכֶ֖לֶת בְּרֹ֣אשׁ הָהָ֑ר לְעֵינֵ֖י בְּנֵ֥י יִשְׂרָאֵֽל: וַיָּבֹ֥א
מֹשֶׁ֛ה בְּת֥וֹךְ הֶעָנָ֖ן וַיַּ֣עַל אֶל־הָהָ֑ר וַיְהִ֤י מֹשֶׁה֙ בָּהָ֔ר אַרְבָּעִ֣ים י֔וֹם
וְאַרְבָּעִ֖ים לָֽיְלָה׃

כה א וַיְדַבֵּ֥ר יְהֹוָ֖ה אֶל־מֹשֶׁ֥ה לֵּאמֹֽר: דַּבֵּר֙ אֶל־בְּנֵ֣י יִשְׂרָאֵ֔ל וְיִקְחוּ־לִ֖י   יח תרומה
תְּרוּמָ֑ה מֵאֵ֤ת כָּל־אִישׁ֙ אֲשֶׁ֣ר יִדְּבֶ֣נּוּ לִבּ֔וֹ תִּקְח֖וּ אֶת־תְּרוּמָתִֽי:
ג וְזֹאת֙ הַתְּרוּמָ֔ה אֲשֶׁ֥ר תִּקְח֖וּ מֵֽאִתָּ֑ם זָהָ֥ב וָכֶ֖סֶף וּנְחֹֽשֶׁת: וּתְכֵ֧לֶת
ד וְאַרְגָּמָ֛ן וְתוֹלַ֥עַת שָׁנִ֖י וְשֵׁ֥שׁ וְעִזִּֽים: וְעֹרֹ֨ת אֵילִ֧ם מְאָדָּמִ֛ים

טו) וַיְכַסֵּהוּ הֶעָנָן. רַבּוֹתֵינוּ חוֹלְקִים בַּדָּבָר: יֵשׁ מֵהֶם   לִקְעוֹת מֵהֶן קָרְבָּנוֹת צִבּוּר; וְאַחַת תְּרוּמַת הַמִּשְׁכָּן
אוֹמְרִים, אֵלּוּ שִׁשָּׁה יָמִים שֶׁמֵּרֹאשׁ חֹדֶשׁ; "וַיְכַסֵּהוּ   נִדְבַת כָּל אֶחָד וְאֶחָד שֶׁהִתְנַדְּבוּ שָׁלֹשׁ עֲשָׂרֵה דְּבָרִים
הֶעָנָן" לָהָר, "וַיִּקְרָא אֶל מֹשֶׁה בַּיּוֹם הַשְּׁבִיעִי" לוֹמַר   הָאֲמוּרִים בָּעִנְיָן כֻּלָּם הֻצְרְכוּ לִמְלֶאכֶת הַמִּשְׁכָּן אוֹ
עֲשֶׂרֶת הַדִּבְּרוֹת, וּמֹשֶׁה וְכָל בְּנֵי יִשְׂרָאֵל עוֹמְדִים   לְבִגְדֵי כְהֻנָּה כְּשֶׁתְּדַקְדֵּק בָּהֶם:
אֶלָּא שֶׁחָלַק הַכָּתוּב כָּבוֹד לְמֹשֶׁה. וְיֵשׁ אוֹמְרִים,
"וַיְכַסֵּהוּ הֶעָנָן" לְמֹשֶׁה "שֵׁשֶׁת יָמִים" לְאַחַר עֲשֶׂרֶת   ג) זָהָב וָכֶסֶף וּנְחֹשֶׁת וְגוֹ'. כֻּלָּם בָּאוּ בִּנְדָבָה אִישׁ אִישׁ
הַדִּבְּרוֹת, וְהֵם הָיוּ בִּתְחִלַּת אַרְבָּעִים יוֹם שֶׁעָלָה מֹשֶׁה   מַה שֶּׁנְּדָבוֹ לִבּוֹ, חוּץ מִן הַכֶּסֶף שֶׁבָּא בְשָׁוֶה, מַחֲצִית
לְקַבֵּל הַלּוּחוֹת, וּלְלַמֶּדְךָ שֶׁכָּל הַנִּכְנָס לַמַּחֲנֵה שְׁכִינָה   הַשֶּׁקֶל לְכָל אֶחָד. וְלֹא מָצִינוּ בְּכָל מְלֶאכֶת הַמִּשְׁכָּן
טָעוּן פְּרִישָׁה שִׁשָּׁה יָמִים: שֶׁהֻצְרַךְ שָׁם כֶּסֶף יוֹתֵר, שֶׁנֶּאֱמַר: "וְכֶסֶף פְּקוּדֵי הָעֵדָה
                                                                       וְגוֹ' בֶּקַע לַגֻּלְגֹּלֶת וְגוֹ'" (להלן לח, כה-כו). וּשְׁאָר הַכֶּסֶף
יח) בְּתוֹךְ הֶעָנָן. עָנָן זֶה כְּמִין עָשָׁן הוּא, וְעָשָׂה לוֹ   הַבָּא שָׁם בִּנְדָבָה (להלן לח, כד) עֲשָׂאוּהוּ לִכְלֵי שָׁרֵת:
הַקָּדוֹשׁ בָּרוּךְ הוּא לְמֹשֶׁה שְׁבִיל בְּתוֹכוֹ:
                                                                       ד) וּתְכֵלֶת. צֶמֶר צָבוּעַ בְּדַם חִלָּזוֹן, וְצִבְעוֹ יָרֹק:
פרק כה
                                                                       וְאַרְגָּמָן. צֶמֶר צָבוּעַ מִמִּין צֶבַע שֶׁשְּׁמוֹ אַרְגָּמָן: וְשֵׁשׁ.
ב) וְיִקְחוּ לִי תְּרוּמָה. "לִי" – לִשְׁמִי: תְּרוּמָה.   הוּא פִּשְׁתָּן: וְעִזִּים. נוֹצָה שֶׁל עִזִּים, לְכָךְ תִּרְגֵּם
הַפְרָשָׁה, יַפְרִישׁוּ לִי מִמָּמוֹנָם נְדָבָה: יִדְּבֶנּוּ לִבּוֹ:   אֻנְקְלוֹס: "וּמַעֲזֵי", דָּבָר הַבָּא מִן הָעִזִּים וְלֹא עִזִּים
לְשׁוֹן נְדָבָה, וְהוּא לְשׁוֹן רָצוֹן טוֹב, פייש"נט בְּלַעַז: עַצְמָן, שֶׁתַּרְגּוּם שֶׁל עִזִּים "עִזַּיָּא":
תִּקְחוּ אֶת תְּרוּמָתִי. אָמְרוּ רַבּוֹתֵינוּ, שָׁלֹשׁ תְּרוּמוֹת
אֲמוּרוֹת כָּאן: אַחַת תְּרוּמַת בֶּקַע לַגֻּלְגֹּלֶת שֶׁנַּעֲשׂוּ   ה) מְאָדָּמִים. צְבוּעוֹת הָיוּ אָדֹם לְאַחַר עִבּוּדָן:
מֵהֶם הָאֲדָנִים, כְּמוֹ שֶׁמְּפֹרָשׁ בְּ"אֵלֶּה פְקוּדֵי" (להלן לח,   תְּחָשִׁים. מִין חַיָּה, וְלֹא הָיְתָה אֶלָּא לְשָׁעָה, וְהַרְבֵּה
כה-כח). וְאַחַת תְּרוּמַת הַמִּזְבֵּחַ בֶּקַע לַגֻּלְגֹּלֶת, לִקְעוֹת   גְּוָנִים הָיוּ לָהּ, לְכָךְ מְתַרְגֵּם "סַסְגּוֹנָא", שֶׁשָּׂשׂ

תרומה | פרק כה | שמות

ו וְעֹרֹת תְּחָשִׁים וַעֲצֵי שִׁטִּים: ס שֶׁמֶן לַמָּאֹר בְּשָׂמִים לְשֶׁמֶן הַמִּשְׁחָה וְלִקְטֹרֶת הַסַּמִּים: ז אַבְנֵי־שֹׁהַם וְאַבְנֵי מִלֻּאִים לָאֵפֹד וְלַחֹשֶׁן: ח וְעָשׂוּ לִי מִקְדָּשׁ וְשָׁכַנְתִּי בְּתוֹכָם: ט כְּכֹל אֲשֶׁר אֲנִי מַרְאֶה אוֹתְךָ אֵת תַּבְנִית הַמִּשְׁכָּן וְאֵת תַּבְנִית כָּל־כֵּלָיו וְכֵן תַּעֲשׂוּ: ס י וְעָשׂוּ אֲרוֹן עֲצֵי שִׁטִּים אַמָּתַיִם וָחֵצִי אָרְכּוֹ וְאַמָּה וָחֵצִי רָחְבּוֹ וְאַמָּה וָחֵצִי קֹמָתוֹ: יא וְצִפִּיתָ אֹתוֹ זָהָב טָהוֹר מִבַּיִת וּמִחוּץ תְּצַפֶּנּוּ וְעָשִׂיתָ עָלָיו זֵר זָהָב סָבִיב: יב וְיָצַקְתָּ לּוֹ אַרְבַּע טַבְּעֹת זָהָב וְנָתַתָּה עַל אַרְבַּע פַּעֲמֹתָיו וּשְׁתֵּי

וּמִתְפָּאֵר בְּגִוְנִין שֶׁלוֹ. **וַעֲצֵי שִׁטִּים.** וּמֵאַיִן הָיוּ לָהֶם בַּמִּדְבָּר? פֵּרֵשׁ רַבִּי תַּנְחוּמָא, יַעֲקֹב אָבִינוּ צָפָה בְּרוּחַ הַקֹּדֶשׁ שֶׁעֲתִידִין יִשְׂרָאֵל לִבְנוֹת מִשְׁכָּן בַּמִּדְבָּר, וְהֵבִיא אֲרָזִים לְמִצְרַיִם וּנְטָעָם, וְצִוָּה לְבָנָיו לִטְּלָם עִמָּהֶם כְּשֶׁיֵּצְאוּ מִמִּצְרַיִם:

ו **שֶׁמֶן לַמָּאֹר.** שֶׁמֶן זַיִת זָךְ לְהַעֲלוֹת נֵר תָּמִיד: **בְּשָׂמִים לְשֶׁמֶן הַמִּשְׁחָה.** שֶׁנַּעֲשָׂה לִמְשֹׁחַ כְּלֵי הַמִּשְׁכָּן וְהַמִּשְׁכָּן לְקַדְּשׁוֹ, וְהֻצְרְכוּ לוֹ בְּשָׂמִים, כְּמוֹ שֶׁמְּפֹרָשׁ בְּ"כִי תִשָּׂא" (להלן ל, כג-כה): **וְלִקְטֹרֶת הַסַּמִּים.** שֶׁהָיוּ מַקְטִירִין בְּכָל בֹּקֶר וָעֶרֶב, כְּמוֹ שֶׁמְּפֹרָשׁ בְּ"וְאַתָּה תְּצַוֶּה" (להלן ל, ז-ח). וּלְשׁוֹן קְטֹרֶת, הַעֲלָאַת קִיטוֹר וְתִמְרוֹת עָשָׁן:

ז **אַבְנֵי שֹׁהַם.** שְׁתַּיִם הֻצְרְכוּ שָׁם לְצֹרֶךְ הָאֵפוֹד הָאָמוּר בְּ"וְאַתָּה תְּצַוֶּה" (שם כח, ט-יב): **מִלֻּאִים.** עַל שֵׁם שֶׁעוֹשִׂין לָהֶם בַּזָּהָב מוֹשָׁב כְּמִין גֻּמָּא וְנוֹתְנִין הָאֶבֶן שָׁם לְמַלֹּאות הַגֻּמָּא, קְרוּיִים "אַבְנֵי מִלֻּאִים", וּמְקוֹם הַמּוֹשָׁב קָרוּי מִשְׁבֶּצֶת: **לָאֵפוֹד וְלַחֹשֶׁן.** הַשֹּׁהַם לָאֵפוֹד וְאַבְנֵי הַמִּלֻּאִים לַחֹשֶׁן. וְחֹשֶׁן וְאֵפוֹד מְפֹרָשִׁים בְּ"וְאַתָּה תְּצַוֶּה" (שם כח, ו-ל), וְהֵם מִינֵי תַכְשִׁיט:

ח **וְעָשׂוּ לִי מִקְדָּשׁ.** וְעָשׂוּ לִשְׁמִי בֵּית קְדֻשָּׁה:

ט **כְּכֹל אֲשֶׁר אֲנִי מַרְאֶה אוֹתְךָ.** כָּאן "אֵת תַּבְנִית הַמִּשְׁכָּן". הַמִּקְרָא הַזֶּה מְחֻבָּר לַמִּקְרָא שֶׁלְּמַעְלָה הֵימֶנּוּ: "וְעָשׂוּ לִי מִקְדָּשׁ... כְּכֹל אֲשֶׁר אֲנִי מַרְאֶה

אוֹתְךָ... וְכֵן תַּעֲשׂוּ לַדּוֹרוֹת, אִם יֹאבַד אֶחָד מִן הַכֵּלִים, אוֹ כְּשֶׁתַּעֲשׂוּ לִי כְּלֵי בֵּית עוֹלָמִים כְּגוֹן שֻׁלְחָנוֹת וּמְנוֹרוֹת וְכִיּוֹרוֹת וּמְכוֹנוֹת שֶׁעָשָׂה שְׁלֹמֹה, כְּתַבְנִית אֵלּוּ תַּעֲשׂוּ אוֹתָם. וְאִם לֹא הָיָה הַמִּקְרָא מְחֻבָּר לְמַעְלָה הֵימֶנּוּ, לֹא הָיָה לוֹ לִכְתֹּב: "וְכֵן תַּעֲשׂוּ" אֶלָּא "כֵּן תַּעֲשׂוּ", וְהָיָה מְדַבֵּר עַל עֲשִׂיַּת אֹהֶל מוֹעֵד וְכֵלָיו:

י **וְעָשׂוּ אֲרוֹן.** כְּמִין אֲרוֹנוֹת שֶׁעוֹשִׂים בְּלֹא רַגְלַיִם עֲשׂוּיִם כְּמִין אַרְגָּז שֶׁקּוֹרִין אשקרי"ן, יוֹשֵׁב עַל שׁוּלָיו:

יא **מִבַּיִת וּמִחוּץ תְּצַפֶּנּוּ.** שְׁלֹשָׁה אֲרוֹנוֹת עָשָׂה בְּצַלְאֵל, שְׁנַיִם שֶׁל זָהָב וְאֶחָד שֶׁל עֵץ, אַרְבָּעָה כְּתָלִים וְשׁוּלַיִם לְכָל אֶחָד, וּפְתוּחִים מִלְמַעְלָה. נָתַן שֶׁל עֵץ בְּתוֹךְ שֶׁל זָהָב, וְשֶׁל זָהָב בְּתוֹךְ שֶׁל עֵץ, וְחִפָּה שְׂפָתוֹ הָעֶלְיוֹנָה בְּזָהָב, נִמְצָא מְצֻפֶּה מִבַּיִת וּמִחוּץ: **זֵר זָהָב.** כְּמִין כֶּתֶר מַקִּיף לוֹ סָבִיב לְמַעְלָה מִשְּׂפָתוֹ, שֶׁעָשָׂה הָאָרוֹן הַחִיצוֹן גָּבוֹהַּ מִן הַפְּנִימִי עַד שֶׁעָלָה לְמוּל עֳבִי הַכַּפֹּרֶת וּלְמַעְלָה הֵימֶנּוּ מַשֶּׁהוּ, וּכְשֶׁהַכַּפֹּרֶת שׁוֹכֵב עַל עֳבִי הַכְּתָלִים עוֹלֶה הַזֵּר לְמַעְלָה מִכָּל עֳבִי הַכַּפֹּרֶת כָּל שֶׁהוּא, וְהוּא סִימָן לְכֶתֶר תּוֹרָה:

יב **וְיָצַקְתָּ.** לְשׁוֹן הַתָּכָה, כְּתַרְגּוּמוֹ. **פַּעֲמֹתָיו.** כְּתַרְגּוּמוֹ: "זִוְיָתֵיהּ". וּבְזָוִיּוֹת הָעֶלְיוֹנוֹת סָמוּךְ לַכַּפֹּרֶת הָיוּ נְתוּנוֹת, שְׁתַּיִם מִכָּאן וּשְׁתַּיִם מִכָּאן לְרָחְבּוֹ שֶׁל אָרוֹן, וְהַבַּדִּים נְתוּנִים בָּהֶם, וְאָרְכּוֹ שֶׁל אָרוֹן מַפְסִיק

שמות | פרק כה   תרומה | 447

טַבָּעֹ֖ת עַל־צַלְע֣וֹ הָאֶחָ֑ת וּשְׁתֵי֙ טַבָּעֹ֔ת עַל־צַלְע֖וֹ הַשֵּׁנִֽית:
יג וְעָשִׂ֥יתָ בַדֵּ֖י עֲצֵ֣י שִׁטִּ֑ים וְצִפִּיתָ֥ אֹתָ֖ם זָהָֽב: וְהֵבֵאתָ֤ אֶת־הַבַּדִּים֙
יד בַּטַּבָּעֹ֔ת עַ֖ל צַלְעֹ֣ת הָאָרֹ֑ן לָשֵׂ֥את אֶת־הָאָרֹ֖ן בָּהֶֽם: בְּטַבְּעֹת֙
טו הָאָרֹ֔ן יִהְי֖וּ הַבַּדִּ֑ים לֹ֥א יָסֻ֖רוּ מִמֶּֽנּוּ: וְנָתַתָּ֖ אֶל־הָאָרֹ֑ן אֵ֚ת
טז הָעֵדֻ֔ת אֲשֶׁ֥ר אֶתֵּ֖ן אֵלֶֽיךָ: ◆ וְעָשִׂ֥יתָ כַפֹּ֖רֶת זָהָ֣ב טָה֑וֹר אַמָּתַ֤יִם   שני
יז וָחֵ֨צִי֙ אָרְכָּ֔הּ וְאַמָּ֥ה וָחֵ֖צִי רָחְבָּֽהּ: וְעָשִׂ֥יתָ שְׁנַ֖יִם כְּרֻבִ֣ים זָהָ֑ב
יח מִקְשָׁה֙ תַּעֲשֶׂ֣ה אֹתָ֔ם מִשְּׁנֵ֖י קְצ֥וֹת הַכַּפֹּֽרֶת: וַ֠עֲשֵׂ֠ה כְּר֨וּב אֶחָ֤ד
יט מִקָּצָה֙ מִזֶּ֔ה וּכְרוּב־אֶחָ֥ד מִקָּצָ֖ה מִזֶּ֑ה מִן־הַכַּפֹּ֛רֶת תַּעֲשׂ֥וּ אֶת־
הַכְּרֻבִ֖ים עַל־שְׁנֵ֥י קְצוֹתָֽיו: וְהָי֣וּ הַכְּרֻבִים֩ פֹּרְשֵׂ֨י כְנָפַ֜יִם לְמַ֗עְלָה
כ סֹכְכִ֤ים בְּכַנְפֵיהֶם֙ עַל־הַכַּפֹּ֔רֶת וּפְנֵיהֶ֖ם אִ֣ישׁ אֶל־אָחִ֑יו אֶל־

בֵּין הַבַּדִּים אַמָּתַיִם וָחֵצִי בֵּין בַּד לְבַד, שֶׁיִּהְיוּ שְׁנֵי בְנֵי אָדָם הַנּוֹשְׂאִים אֶת הֶחָרוֹן מְהַלְּכִין בֵּינֵיהֶם, וְכֵן מְפֹרָשׁ בִּמְנָחוֹת בְּפֶרֶק 'שְׁתֵּי הַלֶּחֶם' (דף צח ע״ב):
וּשְׁתֵּי טַבָּעוֹת עַל צַלְעוֹ הָאֶחָת. הֵן הֵן אַרְבַּע טַבָּעוֹת שֶׁבִּתְחִלַּת הַמִּקְרָא, וּפֵרֵשׁ לְךָ הֵיכָן הָיוּ. וְהַוָּי״ו זוֹ יְתֵרָה הִיא, וּפִתְרוֹנוֹ כְּמוֹ שְׁתֵּי טַבָּעוֹת. וְיֵשׁ לְךָ לְיַשְּׁבָהּ כֵּן: וּשְׁתַּיִם מִן הַטַּבָּעוֹת הַלָּלוּ עַל צַלְעוֹ הָאֶחָת:
צַלְעוֹ. צִדּוֹ:

יג **בַּדֵּי.** מוֹטוֹת:

טו **לֹא יָסֻרוּ מִמֶּנּוּ.** לְעוֹלָם:

טז **וְנָתַתָּ אֶל הָאָרֹן.** כְּמוֹ בָּאָרוֹן: **הָעֵדֻת.** הַתּוֹרָה שֶׁהִיא לְעֵדוּת בֵּינִי וּבֵינֵיכֶם שֶׁצִּוִּיתִי אֶתְכֶם מִצְוֹת הַכְּתוּבוֹת בָּהּ:

יז **כַּפֹּרֶת.** כִּסּוּי עַל הָאָרוֹן, שֶׁהָיָה פָּתוּחַ מִלְמַעְלָה וּמַנִּיחוֹ עָלָיו כְּמִין דַּף: **אַמָּתַיִם וָחֵצִי אָרְכָּהּ.** כְּאָרְכּוֹ שֶׁל אָרוֹן, וְרָחְבָּהּ כְּרָחְבּוֹ שֶׁל אָרוֹן, וּמֻנַּחַת עַל עֳבִי הַכְּתָלִים אַרְבַּעְתָּם. וְאַף עַל פִּי שֶׁלֹּא

נָתַן שִׁעוּר לְעָבְיָהּ, פֵּרְשׁוּ רַבּוֹתֵינוּ שֶׁהָיָה עָבְיָהּ טֶפַח:

יח **כְּרֻבִים.** דְּמוּת פַּרְצוּף תִּינוֹק לָהֶם: **מִקְשָׁה תַּעֲשֶׂה אֹתָם.** שֶׁלֹּא תַעֲשֵׂם בִּפְנֵי עַצְמָם וּתְחַבְּרֵם בְּרָאשֵׁי הַכַּפֹּרֶת לְאַחַר עֲשִׂיָּתָם כְּמַעֲשֵׂה צוֹרְפִים שֶׁקּוֹרִין שולדרי״ץ, אֶלָּא הַטֵּל זָהָב הַרְבֵּה בִּתְחִלַּת עֲשִׂיַּת הַכַּפֹּרֶת, וְהַכֵּה בְּפַטִּישׁ וּבְקֻרְנָס בָּאֶמְצַע וְרָאשִׁין בּוֹלְטִין לְמַעְלָה, וְצַיֵּר הַכְּרוּבִים בִּבְלִיטַת קְצוֹתָיו: **מִקְשָׁה.** בטדי״ץ בְּלַעַ״ז, כְּמוֹ: ״דָּא לְדָא נָקְשָׁן״ (דניאל ה, ו): **קְצוֹת הַכַּפֹּרֶת.** רָאשֵׁי הַכַּפֹּרֶת:

יט **וַעֲשֵׂה כְּרוּב אֶחָד מִקָּצָה.** שֶׁלֹּא תֹאמַר, שְׁנַיִם כְּרוּבִים לְכָל קָצֶה וְקָצֶה, לְכָךְ הֻצְרַךְ לְפָרֵשׁ: ״כְּרוּב אֶחָד מִקָּצָה מִזֶּה״: **מִן הַכַּפֹּרֶת.** עַצְמָהּ ״תַּעֲשׂוּ אֶת הַכְּרֻבִים״. זֶהוּ פֵּרוּשׁוֹ שֶׁל ״מִקְשָׁה תַּעֲשֶׂה אֹתָם״, שֶׁלֹּא תַעֲשֵׂם בִּפְנֵי עַצְמָם וּתְחַבְּרֵם לַכַּפֹּרֶת:

כ **פֹּרְשֵׂי כְנָפַיִם.** שֶׁלֹּא תַעֲשֶׂה כַנְפֵיהֶם שׁוֹכְבִים, אֶלָּא פְּרוּשִׂים וּגְבוֹהִים לְמַעְלָה אֵצֶל רָאשֵׁיהֶם, שֶׁיְּהֵא עֲשָׂרָה טְפָחִים בַּחֲלַל שֶׁבֵּין הַכְּנָפַיִם לַכַּפֹּרֶת, כִּדְאִיתָא בְּסֻכָּה (דף ה ע״ב):

פרק כה | שמות | תרומה | 448

הַכַּפֹּ֛רֶת יִהְי֖וּ פְּנֵ֥י הַכְּרֻבִֽים: וְנָתַתָּ֧ אֶת־הַכַּפֹּ֛רֶת עַל־הָאָרֹ֖ן כא
מִלְמָ֑עְלָה וְאֶל־הָ֣אָרֹ֔ן תִּתֵּן֙ אֶת־הָ֣עֵדֻ֔ת אֲשֶׁ֥ר אֶתֵּ֖ן אֵלֶֽיךָ:
וְנוֹעַדְתִּ֣י לְךָ֮ שָׁם֒ וְדִבַּרְתִּ֨י אִתְּךָ֜ מֵעַ֣ל הַכַּפֹּ֗רֶת מִבֵּין֙ שְׁנֵ֣י הַכְּרֻבִ֔ים כב
אֲשֶׁ֖ר עַל־אֲר֣וֹן הָעֵדֻ֑ת אֵ֣ת כָּל־אֲשֶׁ֧ר אֲצַוֶּ֛ה אֽוֹתְךָ֖ אֶל־בְּנֵ֥י
יִשְׂרָאֵֽל:
וְעָשִׂ֥יתָ שֻׁלְחָ֖ן עֲצֵ֣י שִׁטִּ֑ים אַמָּתַ֤יִם אָרְכּוֹ֙ וְאַמָּ֣ה רָחְבּ֔וֹ וְאַמָּ֥ה כג
וָחֵ֖צִי קֹמָתֽוֹ: וְצִפִּיתָ֥ אֹת֖וֹ זָהָ֣ב טָה֑וֹר וְעָשִׂ֥יתָ לּ֛וֹ זֵ֥ר זָהָ֖ב סָבִֽיב: כד
וְעָשִׂ֨יתָ לּ֥וֹ מִסְגֶּ֛רֶת טֹ֖פַח סָבִ֑יב וְעָשִׂ֧יתָ זֵר־זָהָ֛ב לְמִסְגַּרְתּ֖וֹ כה
סָבִֽיב: וְעָשִׂ֣יתָ לּ֔וֹ אַרְבַּ֖ע טַבְּעֹ֣ת זָהָ֑ב וְנָֽתַתָּ֙ אֶת־הַטַּבָּעֹ֔ת עַ֚ל כו
אַרְבַּ֣ע הַפֵּאֹ֔ת אֲשֶׁ֖ר לְאַרְבַּ֥ע רַגְלָֽיו: לְעֻמַּת֙ הַמִּסְגֶּ֔רֶת תִּהְיֶ֖יןָ כז
הַטַּבָּעֹ֑ת לְבָתִּ֣ים לְבַדִּ֔ים לָשֵׂ֖את אֶת־הַשֻּׁלְחָֽן: וְעָשִׂ֤יתָ אֶת־ כח

כא] וְאֶל הָאָרֹן תִּתֵּן אֶת הָעֵדֻת. לֹא יָדַעְתִּי לָמָה נֶכְפַּל, שֶׁהֲרֵי כְּבָר נֶאֱמַר: "וְנָתַתָּ אֶל הָאָרֹן אֵת הָעֵדֻת" (לעיל פסוק טז)! וְיֵשׁ לוֹמַר, שֶׁבָּא לְלַמֵּד שֶׁבְּעוֹדוֹ אָרוֹן לְבַדּוֹ בְּלֹא כַּפֹּרֶת יִתֵּן תְּחִלָּה הָעֵדוּת לְתוֹכוֹ, וְאַחַר כָּךְ יִתֵּן אֶת הַכַּפֹּרֶת עָלָיו, וְכֵן מָצִינוּ כְּשֶׁהֵקִים אֶת הַמִּשְׁכָּן, נֶאֱמַר: "וַיִּתֵּן אֶת הָעֵדֻת אֶל הָאָרֹן" וְאַחַר כָּךְ: "וַיִּתֵּן אֶת הַכַּפֹּרֶת עַל הָאָרֹן מִלְמָעְלָה" (להלן מ, כ):

כב] וְנוֹעַדְתִּי. כְּשֶׁאֶקְבַּע מוֹעֵד לְךָ לְדַבֵּר עִמְּךָ, אוֹתוֹ מָקוֹם אֶקְבַּע לַמּוֹעֵד, שֶׁאָבוֹא שָׁם לְדַבֵּר אֵלֶיךָ: וְדִבַּרְתִּי אִתְּךָ מֵעַל הַכַּפֹּרֶת. וּבְמָקוֹם אַחֵר הוּא אוֹמֵר: "וַיְדַבֵּר ה' אֵלָיו מֵאֹהֶל מוֹעֵד לֵאמֹר" (ויקרא א, א), זֶה הַמִּשְׁכָּן מִחוּץ לַפָּרֹכֶת, נִמְצְאוּ שְׁנֵי כְתוּבִים מַכְחִישִׁים זֶה אֶת זֶה! בָּא הַכָּתוּב הַשְּׁלִישִׁי וְהִכְרִיעַ בֵּינֵיהֶם: "וּבְבֹא מֹשֶׁה אֶל אֹהֶל מוֹעֵד וַיִּשְׁמַע אֶת הַקּוֹל מִדַּבֵּר אֵלָיו מֵעַל הַכַּפֹּרֶת וְגוֹ'" (במדבר ז, פט), מֹשֶׁה הָיָה נִכְנָס לַמִּשְׁכָּן, וְכֵיוָן שֶׁבָּא בְּתוֹךְ הַפֶּתַח קוֹל יוֹרֵד מִן הַשָּׁמַיִם לְבֵין הַכְּרוּבִים, וּמִשָּׁם יוֹצֵא וְנִשְׁמָע לְמֹשֶׁה בְּאֹהֶל מוֹעֵד:

וְאֵת כָּל אֲשֶׁר אֲצַוֶּה אוֹתְךָ אֶל בְּנֵי יִשְׂרָאֵל. הֲרֵי וָי"ו זוֹ יְתֵרָה וּטְפֵלָה, וְכָמוֹהָ הַרְבֵּה בַּמִּקְרָא, וְכֹה תִּפְתָּרֶהוּ: וְאֵת אֲשֶׁר אֲדַבֵּר עִמְּךָ שָׁם "אֵת כָּל אֲשֶׁר אֲצַוֶּה אוֹתְךָ אֶל בְּנֵי יִשְׂרָאֵל" הוּא:

כג] קֹמָתוֹ. גָּבְהוֹ רַגְלָיו עִם עֳבִי הַשֻּׁלְחָן:

כד] זֵר זָהָב. סִימָן לְכֶתֶר מַלְכוּת, שֶׁהַשֻּׁלְחָן שֵׁם עֹשֶׁר וּגְדֻלָּה, כְּמוֹ שֶׁאוֹמְרִים: שֻׁלְחַן מְלָכִים:

כה] מִסְגֶּרֶת. כְּתַרְגּוּמוֹ: "גְּדַנְפָא". וְנֶחְלְקוּ חַכְמֵי יִשְׂרָאֵל בַּדָּבָר: יֵשׁ אוֹמְרִים לְמַעְלָה הָיְתָה סָבִיב לַשֻּׁלְחָן, כְּמוֹ לִבְזִבִּין שֶׁבִּשְׂפַת שֻׁלְחַן שָׂרִים, וְיֵשׁ אוֹמְרִים לְמַטָּה הָיְתָה תְּקוּעָה מֵרֶגֶל לְרֶגֶל בְּאַרְבַּע רוּחוֹת הַשֻּׁלְחָן, וְדַף הַשֻּׁלְחָן שׁוֹכֵב עַל אוֹתָהּ מִסְגֶּרֶת: וְעָשִׂיתָ זֵר זָהָב לְמִסְגַּרְתּוֹ. הוּא זֵר הָאָמוּר לְמַעְלָה, וּפֵרַשׁ לְךָ כָּאן שֶׁעַל שְׂפַת הַמִּסְגֶּרֶת הָיָה:

כו] לְעֻמַּת הַמִּסְגֶּרֶת תִּהְיֶיןָ הַטַּבָּעוֹת. בְּרַגְלַיִם תְּקוּעוֹת כְּנֶגֶד רָאשֵׁי הַמִּסְגֶּרֶת: לְבָתִּים לְבַדִּים. אוֹתָן הַטַּבָּעוֹת יִהְיוּ בָּתִּים לְהַכְנִיס בָּהֶן הַבַּדִּים: לְבָתִּים. לְצֹרֶךְ בָּתִּים: לְבַדִּים. כְּתַרְגּוּמוֹ: "לְאַתְרָא לַאֲרִיחַיָּא":

שמות | פרק כה | תרומה

הַבַּדִּים עֲצֵי שִׁטִּים וְצִפִּיתָ אֹתָם זָהָב וְנִשָּׂא־בָם אֶת־הַשֻּׁלְחָן: כט וְעָשִׂיתָ קְּעָרֹתָיו וְכַפֹּתָיו וּקְשׂוֹתָיו וּמְנַקִּיֹּתָיו אֲשֶׁר יֻסַּךְ בָּהֵן זָהָב טָהוֹר תַּעֲשֶׂה אֹתָם: ל וְנָתַתָּ עַל־הַשֻּׁלְחָן לֶחֶם פָּנִים לְפָנַי תָּמִיד: לא וְעָשִׂיתָ מְנֹרַת זָהָב טָהוֹר מִקְשָׁה תֵּיעָשֶׂה הַמְּנוֹרָה יְרֵכָהּ וְקָנָהּ

כח) וְנִשָּׂא בָם. לְשׁוֹן נִפְעַל. יִהְיֶה נִשָּׂא בָּם אֶת הַשֻּׁלְחָן:

כט) וְעָשִׂיתָ קְּעָרֹתָיו וְכַפֹּתָיו. קְעָרֹתָיו זֶה דְּפוּס, שֶׁהָיָה עָשׂוּי כִּדְפוּס הַלֶּחֶם. וְהַלֶּחֶם הָיָה עָשׂוּי כְּמִין תֵּבָה פְּרוּצָה, מִשְּׁתֵּי רוּחוֹתֶיהָ, שׁוּלַיִם לוֹ לְמַטָּה, וְקוֹפֵל מִכָּאן וּמִכָּאן כְּלַפֵּי מַעְלָה כְּמִין כְּתָלִים, וּלְכָךְ קָרוּי לֶחֶם הַפָּנִים, שֶׁיֵּשׁ לוֹ פָּנִים רוֹאִים לְכָאן וּלְכָאן לְצִדֵּי הַבַּיִת מִזֶּה וּמִזֶּה. וְנוֹתֵן אָרְכּוֹ לְרָחְבּוֹ שֶׁל שֻׁלְחָן, וְכָתְלָיו זְקוּפִים כְּנֶגֶד שְׂפַת הַשֻּׁלְחָן. וְהָיָה עָשׂוּי לוֹ דְּפוּס וּדְפוּס בַּרְזֶל, בְּשֶׁל בַּרְזֶל הוּא נֶאֱפֶה, וּכְשֶׁמּוֹצִיאוֹ מִן הַתַּנּוּר נוֹתְנוֹ בְּשֶׁל זָהָב עַד לְמָחָר, בְּשַׁבָּת, שֶׁמְּסַדְּרוֹ עַל הַשֻּׁלְחָן, וְאוֹתוֹ דְּפוּס קָרוּי קְעָרָה: **וְכַפֹּתָיו.** בָּזִיכִין שֶׁנּוֹתְנִין בָּהֶם לְבוֹנָה, וּשְׁתַּיִם הָיוּ לִשְׁנֵי קֹמְצֵי לְבוֹנָה שֶׁנּוֹתְנִין עַל שְׁתֵּי הַמַּעֲרָכוֹת, שֶׁנֶּאֱמַר: "וְנָתַתָּ עַל הַמַּעֲרֶכֶת לְבֹנָה זַכָּה" (ויקרא כד, ז): **וּקְשׂוֹתָיו.** הֵן כְּמִין חֲצָאֵי קָנִים חֲלוּלִים הַנִּסְדָּקִין לְאָרְכָּן, דֻּגְמָתָן עָשׂוּי שֶׁל זָהָב, וּמְסַדֵּר שְׁלֹשָׁה עַל רֹאשׁ כָּל לֶחֶם, שֶׁיֵּשֵׁב לֶחֶם הָאֶחָד עַל גַּבֵּי אוֹתָן הַקָּנִים, וּמַבְדִּילִין בֵּין לֶחֶם לְלֶחֶם כְּדֵי שֶׁתִּכָּנֵס הָרוּחַ בֵּינֵיהֶם וְלֹא יִתְעַפְּשׁוּ. וּבִלְשׁוֹן עֲרָבִי כָּל דָּבָר חָלוּל קָרוּי קְסוּ"ח: **וּמְנַקִּיֹּתָיו.** תַּרְגּוּמוֹ "וּמְכִילָתֵיהּ", הֵן סְנִיפִין כְּמִין יְתֵדוֹת זָהָב עוֹמְדִין בָּאָרֶץ וּגְבוֹהִין עַד לְמַעְלָה מִן הַשֻּׁלְחָן הַרְבֵּה כְּנֶגֶד גֹּבַהּ מַעֲרֶכֶת הַלֶּחֶם, וּמְפֻצָּלִים שִׁשָּׁה פִּצּוּלִים, זֶה לְמַעְלָה מִזֶּה, וְקִצְווֹת הַקָּנִים שֶׁבֵּין לֶחֶם לְלֶחֶם סְמוּכִין עַל אוֹתָן פִּצּוּלִין, כְּדֵי שֶׁלֹּא יִכְבַּד מַשָּׂא הַלֶּחֶם הָעֶלְיוֹנִים עַל הַתַּחְתּוֹנִים וְיִשָּׁבְרוּ. וּלְשׁוֹן "מְכִילָתֵיהּ" סוֹבְלוֹתָיו, כְּמוֹ: "נִלְאֵיתִי הָכִיל" (ירמיה ו, יא). אֲבָל לְשׁוֹן "מְנַקִּיֹּת" אֵינִי יוֹדֵעַ אֵיךְ נוֹפֵל עַל סְנִיפִין. וְיֵשׁ מֵחַכְמֵי יִשְׂרָאֵל אוֹמְרִים, "קְשׂוֹתָיו" אֵלּוּ סְנִיפִין, שֶׁמַּקְשִׁין אוֹתוֹ וּמַחֲזִיקִים אוֹתוֹ שֶׁלֹּא יִשָּׁבֵר, "וּמְנַקִּיֹּתָיו" אֵלּוּ

הַקָּנִים, שֶׁמְּנַקִּין אוֹתוֹ שֶׁלֹּא יִתְעַפֵּשׁ. אֲבָל אוּנְקְלוּס שֶׁתִּרְגֵּם: "וּמְכִילָתֵיהּ" הָיָה שׁוֹנֶה כְּדִבְרֵי הָאוֹמֵר מְנַקִּיּוֹת הֵן סְנִיפִין: **אֲשֶׁר יֻסַּךְ בָּהֵן.** אֲשֶׁר יְכֻסֶּה בָּהֵן. וְעַל קְשׂוֹתָיו הוּא אוֹמֵר: "אֲשֶׁר יֻסַּךְ", שֶׁהָיוּ עָלָיו כְּמִין סְכָךְ וְכִסּוּי, וְכֵן בְּמָקוֹם אַחֵר הוּא אוֹמֵר: "וְאֶת קְשׂוֹת הַנָּסֶךְ" (במדבר ד, ז). וְזֶה וָזֶה, "יֻסַּךְ" וְ"הַנָּסֶךְ", לְשׁוֹן סְכָךְ וְכִסּוּי הֵם:

ל) לֶחֶם פָּנִים. שֶׁהָיוּ לוֹ פָּנִים כְּמוֹ שֶׁפֵּרַשְׁתִּי. וּמִנְיַן הַלֶּחֶם וְסֵדֶר מַעַרְכוֹתָיו מְפֹרָשִׁים בְּ"אֱמֹר אֶל הַכֹּהֲנִים" (ויקרא כד, ה-ט):

לא) מִקְשָׁה תֵּיעָשֶׂה הַמְּנוֹרָה. שֶׁלֹּא יַעֲשֶׂנָּה חֻלְיוֹת, וְלֹא יַעֲשֶׂה קָנֶיהָ וְנֵרוֹתֶיהָ אֵבָרִים אֵבָרִים וְאַחַר כָּךְ יְדַבְּקֵם כְּדֶרֶךְ הַצּוֹרְפִים שֶׁקּוֹרִין שולדיר"ן, אֶלָּא כֻּלָּהּ בָּאָה מֵחֲתִיכָה אַחַת, וּמַקִּישׁ בַּקֻּרְנָס וְחוֹתֵךְ בִּכְלֵי הָאֻמָּנוּת וּמַפְרִיד הַקָּנִים אֵילָךְ וְאֵילָךְ. תַּרְגּוּמוֹ שֶׁל "מִקְשָׁה": "נְגִיד", לְשׁוֹן הַמְשָׁכָה, שֶׁמַּמְשִׁיךְ הָאֵבָרִים מִן הָעֶשֶׁת לְכָאן וּלְכָאן בְּהַקָּשַׁת הַקֻּרְנָס. וּלְשׁוֹן "מִקְשָׁה" מַכַּת קֻרְנָס, בטדי"ץ בְּלַעַז. **תֵּיעָשֶׂה הַמְּנוֹרָה.** מֵאֵלֶיהָ, לְפִי שֶׁהָיָה מֹשֶׁה מִתְקַשֶּׁה בָּהּ, אָמַר לוֹ הַקָּדוֹשׁ בָּרוּךְ הוּא: הַשְׁלֵךְ אֶת הַכִּכָּר לָאוּר וְהִיא נַעֲשֵׂית מֵאֵלֶיהָ, לְכָךְ לֹא נִכְתַּב "תַּעֲשֶׂה": **יְרֵכָהּ.** הוּא הָרֶגֶל שֶׁלְּמַטָּה הֶעָשׂוּי כְּמִין תֵּבָה, וּשְׁלֹשֶׁת הָרַגְלַיִם יוֹצְאִין הֵימֶנָּה מַטָּה: **וְקָנָהּ.** הַקָּנֶה הָאֶמְצָעִי שֶׁלָּהּ הָעוֹלֶה בְּאֶמְצַע הַיָּרֵךְ זָקוּף כְּלַפֵּי מַעְלָה, וְעָלָיו נֵר הָאֶמְצָעִי עָשׂוּי כְּמִין בַּזָּךְ לָצוּק הַשֶּׁמֶן לְתוֹכוֹ וְלָתֵת הַפְּתִילָה: **גְּבִיעֶיהָ.** הֵן כְּמִין כּוֹסוֹת שֶׁעוֹשִׂין מִזְכוּכִית אֲרֻכִּים וּקְצָרִים, וְקוֹרִין לָהֶם מדרי"נש, וְאֵלּוּ עֲשׂוּיִין שֶׁל זָהָב וּבוֹלְטִין וְיוֹצְאִין מִכָּל קָנֶה וְקָנֶה כְּמִנְיָן שֶׁנָּתַן בָּהֶם הַכָּתוּב, וְלֹא הָיוּ בָּהֶם אֶלָּא לְנוֹי: **כַּפְתֹּרֶיהָ.** כְּמִין תַּפּוּחִים הָיוּ עֲגֻלִּין סָבִיב, בּוֹלְטִין

פרק כה

לב גְּבִיעֶיהָ כַּפְתֹּרֶיהָ וּפְרָחֶיהָ מִמֶּנָּה יִהְיוּ: וְשִׁשָּׁה קָנִים יֹצְאִים מִצִּדֶּיהָ שְׁלֹשָׁה ׀ קְנֵי מְנֹרָה מִצִּדָּהּ הָאֶחָד וּשְׁלֹשָׁה קְנֵי מְנֹרָה

לג מִצִּדָּהּ הַשֵּׁנִי: שְׁלֹשָׁה גְבִעִים מְשֻׁקָּדִים בַּקָּנֶה הָאֶחָד כַּפְתֹּר וָפֶרַח וּשְׁלֹשָׁה גְבִעִים מְשֻׁקָּדִים בַּקָּנֶה הָאֶחָד כַּפְתֹּר וָפָרַח

לד כֵּן לְשֵׁשֶׁת הַקָּנִים הַיֹּצְאִים מִן־הַמְּנֹרָה: וּבַמְּנֹרָה אַרְבָּעָה

לה גְבִעִים מְשֻׁקָּדִים כַּפְתֹּרֶיהָ וּפְרָחֶיהָ: וְכַפְתֹּר תַּחַת שְׁנֵי הַקָּנִים מִמֶּנָּה וְכַפְתֹּר תַּחַת שְׁנֵי הַקָּנִים מִמֶּנָּה וְכַפְתֹּר תַּחַת־שְׁנֵי

לו הַקָּנִים מִמֶּנָּה לְשֵׁשֶׁת הַקָּנִים הַיֹּצְאִים מִן־הַמְּנֹרָה: כַּפְתֹּרֵיהֶם

סְבִיבוֹת הַקָּנֶה הַחָמְצָעִי, כְּדֶרֶךְ שֶׁעוֹשִׂין לַמְּנוֹרוֹת שֶׁלִּפְנֵי הַשָּׂרִים וְקוֹרִין לָהֶם פומיל"ש, וּמִנְיַן שֶׁלָּהֶם כָּתוּב בַּפָּרָשָׁה, כַּמָּה כַּפְתּוֹרִים בּוֹלְטִין מִמֶּנָּה וְכַמָּה חֵלֶק בֵּין כַּפְתּוֹר לְכַפְתּוֹר: וּפְרָחֶיהָ. עִיּוּרִין עֲשׂוּיִין בָּהּ כְּמִין פְּרָחִים: מִמֶּנָּה יִהְיוּ. הַכֹּל מִקְשָׁה יוֹצֵא מִתּוֹךְ חֲתִיכַת הָעֶשֶׁת, וְלֹא יַעֲשֶׂה לְבַדָּם וְיַדְבִּיקֵם:

לב יֹצְאִים מִצִּדֶּיהָ. לְכָאן וּלְכָאן בַּאֲלַכְסוֹן, נִמְשָׁכִים וְעוֹלִין עַד כְּנֶגֶד גָּבְהָהּ שֶׁל מְנוֹרָה שֶׁהוּא הַקָּנֶה הָאֶמְצָעִי, וְיוֹצְאִים מִתּוֹךְ קְנֵה הָאֶמְצָעִי זֶה לְמַעְלָה מִזֶּה, הַתַּחְתּוֹן אָרֹךְ וְשֶׁל מַעְלָה קָצָר הֵימֶנּוּ וְהָעֶלְיוֹן קָצָר הֵימֶנּוּ, לְפִי שֶׁהָיָה גֹּבַהּ רָאשֵׁיהֶן שָׁוֶה לְגָבְהוֹ שֶׁל קָנֶה הָאֶמְצָעִי הַשְּׁבִיעִי שֶׁמִּמֶּנּוּ יוֹצְאִים הַשִּׁשָּׁה:

לג מְשֻׁקָּדִים. כְּתַרְגּוּמוֹ, מְצַיָּרִים הָיוּ כְּדֶרֶךְ שֶׁעוֹשִׂין לְכֵלֵי כֶסֶף וְזָהָב שֶׁקּוֹרִין ניילי"ר: שְׁלֹשָׁה גְבִעִים. בּוֹלְטִין מִכָּל קָנֶה וְקָנֶה: כַּפְתֹּר וָפֶרַח. הָיָה לְכָל קָנֶה וְקָנֶה:

לד וּבַמְּנֹרָה אַרְבָּעָה גְבִעִים. בְּגוּפָהּ שֶׁל מְנוֹרָה הָיוּ אַרְבָּעָה גְבִעִים, אֶחָד בּוֹלֵט בָּהּ לְמַטָּה מִן הַקָּנִים, וְהַשְּׁלֹשָׁה לְמַעְלָה מִן יְצִיאַת הַקָּנִים הַיּוֹצְאִים מִצִּדֶּיהָ: מְשֻׁקָּדִים כַּפְתֹּרֶיהָ וּפְרָחֶיהָ. זֶה אֶחָד מֵחֲמִשָּׁה מִקְרָאוֹת שֶׁאֵין לָהֶם הֶכְרֵעַ, אֵין יָדוּעַ אִם "גְּבִעִים מְשֻׁקָּדִים" אוֹ "מְשֻׁקָּדִים כַּפְתֹּרֶיהָ וּפְרָחֶיהָ":

לה וְכַפְתֹּר תַּחַת שְׁנֵי הַקָּנִים. מִתּוֹךְ הַכַּפְתּוֹר הָיוּ הַקָּנִים נִמְשָׁכִים מִשְּׁנֵי צִדָּיו אֵילָךְ וָאֵילָךְ. כָּךְ

שָׁנִינוּ בִּמְלֶאכֶת הַמִּשְׁכָּן: גָּבְהָהּ שֶׁל מְנוֹרָה שְׁמוֹנָה עָשָׂר טְפָחִים. הָרַגְלַיִם וְהַפֶּרַח שְׁלֹשָׁה טְפָחִים, הוּא הַפֶּרַח הָאָמוּר בַּיְרֵךְ שֶׁנֶּאֱמַר: "עַד יְרֵכָהּ עַד פִּרְחָהּ" (במדבר ח, ד), וּטְפָחַיִם חָלָק, וְטֶפַח שֶׁבּוֹ גָבִיעַ מֵאַרְבָּעָה גְבִיעִים וְכַפְתּוֹר וָפֶרַח מִשְּׁנֵי כַפְתּוֹרִים וּשְׁנֵי פְרָחִים הָאֲמוּרִים בַּמְּנוֹרָה עַצְמָהּ, שֶׁנֶּאֱמַר: "מְשֻׁקָּדִים כַּפְתֹּרֶיהָ וּפְרָחֶיהָ" (בפסוק הקודם), לָמַדְנוּ שֶׁהָיוּ בַּקָּנֶה שְׁנֵי כַפְתּוֹרִים וּשְׁנֵי פְרָחִים לְבַד מִן הַשְּׁלֹשָׁה כַּפְתּוֹרִים שֶׁהַקָּנִים נִמְשָׁכִין מִתּוֹכָן, שֶׁנֶּאֱמַר: "וְכַפְתֹּר תַּחַת שְׁנֵי הַקָּנִים וְגוֹ'", וּטְפָחַיִם חָלָק, וְטֶפַח כַּפְתּוֹר, וּשְׁנֵי קָנִים יוֹצְאִים מִמֶּנּוּ אֵילָךְ וָאֵילָךְ נִמְשָׁכִים וְעוֹלִים כְּנֶגֶד גָּבְהָהּ שֶׁל מְנוֹרָה, וְטֶפַח חָלָק, וְטֶפַח כַּפְתּוֹר, וּשְׁנֵי קָנִים יוֹצְאִים מִמֶּנּוּ, וְטֶפַח חָלָק, וְטֶפַח כַּפְתּוֹר, וּשְׁנֵי קָנִים יוֹצְאִים מִמֶּנּוּ, וְטֶפָחַיִם חָלָק, נִשְׁתַּיְּרוּ שָׁם שְׁלֹשָׁה טְפָחִים, שֶׁבָּהֶם שְׁלֹשָׁה גְבִיעִים וְכַפְתּוֹר וָפֶרַח. נִמְצְאוּ גְבִיעִים שְׁנֵים וְעֶשְׂרִים, שְׁמוֹנָה עָשָׂר לְשִׁשָּׁה קָנִים שְׁלֹשָׁה לְכָל אֶחָד וְאֶחָד, וְאַרְבָּעָה בְגוּפָהּ שֶׁל מְנוֹרָה; וְאַחַד עָשָׂר כַּפְתּוֹרִים, שִׁשָּׁה בְּשֵׁשֶׁת הַקָּנִים, וּשְׁלֹשָׁה בְגוּפָהּ שֶׁל מְנוֹרָה שֶׁהַקָּנִים יוֹצְאִים מֵהֶם, וּשְׁנַיִם עוֹד בַּמְּנוֹרָה שֶׁנֶּאֱמַר: "מְשֻׁקָּדִים כַּפְתֹּרֶיהָ" וּמִעוּט כַּפְתּוֹרִים שְׁנַיִם, הָאֶחָד לְמַטָּה אֵצֶל הַיָּרֵךְ וְהָאֶחָד בִּשְׁלֹשָׁה טְפָחִים הָעֶלְיוֹנִים עִם הַשְּׁלֹשָׁה גְבִיעִים. וְתִשְׁעָה פְרָחִים הָיוּ לָהּ, שִׁשָּׁה לְשֵׁשֶׁת הַקָּנִים, שֶׁנֶּאֱמַר: "בַּקָּנֶה הָאֶחָד כַּפְתֹּר וָפָרַח" (לעיל פסוק לג), וּשְׁלֹשָׁה

שמות | פרק כה · תרומה

לו וּמִקְשָׁה מִמֶּנָּה יִהְיוּ כֻּלָּהּ מִקְשָׁה אַחַת זָהָב טָהוֹר: וְעָשִׂיתָ
אֶת־נֵרֹתֶיהָ שִׁבְעָה וְהֶעֱלָה אֶת־נֵרֹתֶיהָ וְהֵאִיר עַל־עֵבֶר פָּנֶיהָ:
לח וּמַלְקָחֶיהָ וּמַחְתֹּתֶיהָ זָהָב טָהוֹר: כִּכָּר זָהָב טָהוֹר יַעֲשֶׂה אֹתָהּ
מ אֵת כָּל־הַכֵּלִים הָאֵלֶּה: וּרְאֵה וַעֲשֵׂה בְּתַבְנִיתָם אֲשֶׁר־אַתָּה
מָרְאֶה בָּהָר:

פרק כו שלישי
א וְאֶת־הַמִּשְׁכָּן תַּעֲשֶׂה עֶשֶׂר יְרִיעֹת שֵׁשׁ
מָשְׁזָר וּתְכֵלֶת וְאַרְגָּמָן וְתוֹלַעַת שָׁנִי כְּרֻבִים מַעֲשֵׂה חֹשֵׁב
ב תַּעֲשֶׂה אֹתָם: הַיְרִיעָה הָאַחַת שְׁמֹנֶה וְעֶשְׂרִים בָּאַמָּה
וְרֹחַב אַרְבַּע בָּאַמָּה הַיְרִיעָה הָאֶחָת מִדָּה אַחַת לְכָל־הַיְרִיעֹת:

לַמְּנוֹרָה, שֶׁנֶּאֱמַר: "מְשֻׁקָּדִים כַּפְתֹּרֶיהָ וּפְרָחֶיהָ" (בפסוק הקודם) וּמִעוּט פְּרָחִים שְׁנַיִם, וְאֶחָד הָאָמוּר בְּפָרָשַׁת 'בְּהַעֲלֹתְךָ' (במדבר ח, ד) "עַד יְרֵכָהּ עַד פִּרְחָהּ". וְחֵס תְּדַקְדֵּק בְּמִשְׁנָה זוֹ הַכְּתוּבָה לְמַעְלָה תִּמְצָאֵם כְּמִנְיָנָם אִישׁ אִישׁ בִּמְקוֹמוֹ:

אֶת נֵרֹתֶיהָ. כְּמִין בָּזִיכִין שֶׁנּוֹתְנִין בְּתוֹכָם הַשֶּׁמֶן וְהַפְּתִילוֹת: **וְהֵאִיר עַל עֵבֶר פָּנֶיהָ.** עֲשֵׂה פִּי שֵׁשֶׁת הַנֵּרוֹת שֶׁבְּרָאשֵׁי הַקָּנִים הַיּוֹצְאִים מִצִּדֶּיהָ מֻסְבִּים כְּלַפֵּי הָאֶמְצָעִי, כְּדֵי שֶׁיִּהְיוּ הַנֵּרוֹת כְּשֶׁתַּדְלִיקֵם מְאִירִים "אֶל עֵבֶר פָּנֶיהָ", מוּסָב חוּדָּם שֶׁל אוֹר הַנֵּרוֹת אֶל עֵבֶר פָּנֶיהָ שֶׁל הַקָּנֶה הָאֶמְצָעִי שֶׁהוּא גּוּף הַמְּנוֹרָה:

וּמַלְקָחֶיהָ. הֵם הַצְּבָתִים הָעֲשׂוּיִין לִקַּח בָּהֶם הַפְּתִילוֹת מִתּוֹךְ הַשֶּׁמֶן לְיַשְּׁבָן וּלְמָשְׁכָן בְּפִי הַנֵּרוֹת, וְעַל שֵׁם שֶׁלּוֹקְחִים בָּהֶם קְרוּיִים מֶלְקָחַיִם, וְ"צִבְתָהָא" שֶׁתִּרְגֵּם אוּנְקְלוֹס, לְשׁוֹן צְבָת, טנליי"ש בְּלַעַז: **וּמַחְתֹּתֶיהָ.** כְּמִין בָּזִיכִין קְטַנִּים שֶׁחוֹתֶה בָהֶן אֶת הָאֵפֶר שֶׁבַּנֵּר בַּבֹּקֶר כְּשֶׁהוּא מֵטִיב אֶת הַנֵּרוֹת מֵאֵפֶר הַפְּתִילוֹת שֶׁדָּלְקוּ הַלַּיְלָה וְכָבוּ, וּלְשׁוֹן מַחְתָּה פוּשידוי"א בְּלַעַז, כְּמוֹ: "לַחְתּוֹת אֵשׁ מִיָּקוּד" (ישעיה ל, יד):

לח כִּכָּר זָהָב טָהוֹר. שֶׁלֹּא יִהְיֶה מִשְׁקָלָהּ עִם כָּל כֵּלֶיהָ אֶלָּא כִּכָּר, לֹא פָחוֹת וְלֹא יוֹתֵר. וְהַכִּכָּר שֶׁל חֹל שִׁשִּׁים מָנֶה, וְשֶׁל קֹדֶשׁ הָיָה כָּפוּל, מֵאָה וְעֶשְׂרִים

מָנֶה, וְהַמָּנֶה הוּא לִיטְרָא שֶׁשּׁוֹקְלִין בָּהּ כֶּסֶף לְמִשְׁקַל קוֹלוֹנְיָא, וְהֵם מֵאָה זְהוּבִים, עֶשְׂרִים וַחֲמִשָּׁה סְלָעִים, וְהַסֶּלַע אַרְבָּעָה זְהוּבִים:

מ **וּרְאֵה וַעֲשֵׂה.** רְאֵה כָּאן בָּהָר תַּבְנִית שֶׁאֲנִי מַרְאֶה אוֹתְךָ, מַגִּיד שֶׁנִּתְקַשָּׁה מֹשֶׁה בְּמַעֲשֵׂה הַמְּנוֹרָה עַד שֶׁהֶרְאָה לוֹ הַקָּדוֹשׁ בָּרוּךְ הוּא מְנוֹרָה שֶׁל אֵשׁ: **אֲשֶׁר אַתָּה מָרְאֶה.** כְּתַרְגּוּמוֹ: "דְּאַתְּ מִתְחֲזֵי בְּטוּרָא". אִלּוּ הָיָה נָקוּד 'מַרְאֶה' בְּפַתָּח, הָיָה פִּתְרוֹנוֹ, אַתָּה מַרְאֶה לַאֲחֵרִים, עַכְשָׁיו שֶׁנָּקוּד חֲטַף קָמָץ, פִּתְרוֹנוֹ 'דְּאַתְּ מִתְחֲזֵי', שֶׁאֲחֵרִים מַרְאִים לָךְ:

פרק כו

א **וְאֶת הַמִּשְׁכָּן תַּעֲשֶׂה עֶשֶׂר יְרִיעֹת.** לִהְיוֹת לוֹ לְגַג וְלִמְחִצוֹת מִחוּץ לַקְּרָשִׁים, שֶׁהַיְרִיעוֹת תְּלוּיוֹת מֵאֲחוֹרֵיהֶן לְכַסּוֹתָן: **שֵׁשׁ מָשְׁזָר וּתְכֵלֶת וְאַרְגָּמָן וְתוֹלַעַת שָׁנִי.** הֲרֵי אַרְבָּעָה מִינִין בְּכָל חוּט וָחוּט, אֶחָד שֶׁל פִּשְׁתִּים וּשְׁלֹשָׁה שֶׁל צֶמֶר, וְכָל מִין וָמִין חוּטוֹ כָּפוּל שִׁשָּׁה, הֲרֵי אַרְבָּעָה מִינִין כְּשֶׁהֵן שְׁזוּרִין יַחַד עֶשְׂרִים וְאַרְבָּעָה כְּפָלִים לַחוּט: **כְּרֻבִים מַעֲשֵׂה חֹשֵׁב.** כְּרוּבִים הָיוּ מְצוּיָרִין בָּהֶם בַּאֲרִיגָתָן, וְלֹא בִּרְקִימָה שֶׁהוּא מַעֲשֵׂה מַחַט, אֶלָּא בָּאֲרִיגָה בִּשְׁנֵי כְתָלִים, פַּרְצוּף אֶחָד מִכָּאן וּפַרְצוּף אֶחָד מִכָּאן, אֲרִי מִצַּד זֶה וְנֶשֶׁר מִצַּד זֶה, כְּמוֹ שֶׁאוֹרְגִין חֲגוֹרוֹת שֶׁל מֶשִׁי שֶׁקּוֹרִין בְּלַעַז פיישי"ש:

חֲמֵשׁ הַיְרִיעֹת תִּֽהְיֶ֙יןָ֙ חֹֽבְרֹ֔ת אִשָּׁ֖ה אֶל־אֲחֹתָ֑הּ וְחָמֵ֤שׁ יְרִיעֹת֙ ג
חֹֽבְרֹ֔ת אִשָּׁ֖ה אֶל־אֲחֹתָֽהּ: וְעָשִׂ֜יתָ לֻֽלְאֹ֣ת תְּכֵ֗לֶת עַ֣ל שְׂפַ֤ת ד
הַיְרִיעָה֙ הָֽאֶחָ֔ת מִקָּצָ֖ה בַּחֹבָ֑רֶת וְכֵ֤ן תַּֽעֲשֶׂה֙ בִּשְׂפַ֣ת הַיְרִיעָ֔ה
הַקִּ֣יצוֹנָ֔ה בַּמַּחְבֶּ֖רֶת הַשֵּׁנִֽית: חֲמִשִּׁ֣ים לֻֽלָאֹ֗ת תַּֽעֲשֶׂה֮ בַּיְרִיעָ֣ה ה
הָֽאֶחָת֒ וַֽחֲמִשִּׁ֣ים לֻֽלָאֹ֗ת תַּֽעֲשֶׂה֙ בִּקְצֵ֣ה הַיְרִיעָ֔ה אֲשֶׁ֖ר בַּמַּחְבֶּ֣רֶת
הַשֵּׁנִ֑ית מַקְבִּילֹת֙ הַלֻּ֣לָאֹ֔ת אִשָּׁ֖ה אֶל־אֲחֹתָֽהּ: וְעָשִׂ֕יתָ חֲמִשִּׁ֖ים ו
קַרְסֵ֣י זָהָ֑ב וְחִבַּרְתָּ֙ אֶת־הַיְרִיעֹ֜ת אִשָּׁ֤ה אֶל־אֲחֹתָהּ֙ בַּקְּרָסִ֔ים
וְהָיָ֥ה הַמִּשְׁכָּ֖ן אֶחָֽד: וְעָשִׂ֨יתָ֙ יְרִיעֹ֣ת עִזִּ֔ים לְאֹ֖הֶל עַל־הַמִּשְׁכָּ֑ן ז

ג׀ תִּהְיֶיןָ חֹבְרֹת. תּוֹפְרָן בַּמַּחַט זוֹ בְּצַד זוֹ, חָמֵשׁ לְבַד
וְחָמֵשׁ לְבַד: אִשָּׁה אֶל אֲחֹתָהּ. כָּךְ דֶּרֶךְ הַמִּקְרָא
לְדַבֵּר בְּדָבָר שֶׁהוּא לְשׁוֹן נְקֵבָה; וּבְדָבָר שֶׁהוּא לְשׁוֹן
זָכָר חוֹמֵר: ׳אִישׁ אֶל אָחִיו׳, כְּמוֹ שֶׁנֶּאֱמַר בַּכְּרוּבִים:
"וּפְנֵיהֶם אִישׁ אֶל אָחִיו" (לעיל כה, כ):

ד׀ לֻלָאֹת. לעוּל״ש בְּלַעַז, וְכֵן תִּרְגֵּם אוּנְקְלוֹס: "עֲנוּבִין",
לְשׁוֹן עֲנִיבָה: מִקָּצָה בַּחֹבָרֶת. בְּאוֹתָהּ יְרִיעָה שֶׁבְּסוֹף
הַחִבּוּר, קְבוּצַת חֲמֵשֶׁת הַיְרִיעוֹת קְרוּיָה חוֹבֶרֶת: וְכֵן
תַּעֲשֶׂה בִּשְׂפַת הַיְרִיעָה הַקִּיצוֹנָה בַּמַּחְבֶּרֶת הַשֵּׁנִית.
בְּאוֹתָהּ יְרִיעָה שֶׁהִיא קִיצוֹנָה, לְשׁוֹן קָצֶה, כְּלוֹמַר לְסוֹף
הַחוֹבֶרֶת:

ה׀ מַקְבִּילֹת הַלֻּלָאֹת אִשָּׁה אֶל אֲחֹתָהּ. שְׁמוֹר
שֶׁתַּעֲשֶׂה הַלּוּלָאוֹת מְכֻוָּנוֹת בְּמִדָּה אַחַת הַבְדָּלָתָן זוֹ
מִזּוֹ, וּכְמִדָּתָן בִּירִיעָה זוֹ כֵּן יְהֵא בַּחֲבֶרְתָּהּ, כְּשֶׁתִּפְרֹשׂ
חוֹבֶרֶת אֵצֶל חוֹבֶרֶת יִהְיוּ הַלּוּלָאוֹת שֶׁל יְרִיעָה זוֹ
מְכֻוָּנוֹת כְּנֶגֶד לוּלָאוֹת שֶׁל זוֹ. וְזֶהוּ לְשׁוֹן ׳מַקְבִּילֹת׳, זוֹ
כְּנֶגֶד זוֹ, תַּרְגּוּמוֹ שֶׁל ׳נֶגֶד׳ (לעיל י) – ׳לָקֳבֵל׳. הַיְרִיעוֹת
אָרְכָּן עֶשְׂרִים וּשְׁמוֹנֶה וְרָחְבָּן אַרְבַּע, וּכְשֶׁחִבֵּר חָמֵשׁ
יְרִיעוֹת יַחַד נִמְצָא רָחְבָּן עֶשְׂרִים, וְכֵן הַחוֹבֶרֶת
הַשֵּׁנִית. וְהַמִּשְׁכָּן אָרְכּוֹ שְׁלֹשִׁים מִן הַמִּזְרָח לַמַּעֲרָב,
שֶׁנֶּאֱמַר: "עֶשְׂרִים קְרָשִׁים לִפְאַת נֶגֶב תֵּימָנָה" (להלן
לו, כג), וְכֵן לַצָּפוֹן (להלן פסוק יח), וְכָל
קֶרֶשׁ אַמָּה וַחֲצִי הָאַמָּה (להלן פסוק טז), הֲרֵי שְׁלֹשִׁים
מִן הַמִּזְרָח לַמַּעֲרָב, רֹחַב הַמִּשְׁכָּן מִן הַצָּפוֹן לַדָּרוֹם

עֶשֶׂר אַמּוֹת, שֶׁנֶּאֱמַר: "וּלְיַרְכְּתֵי הַמִּשְׁכָּן יָמָּה וְגוֹ׳
וּשְׁנֵי קְרָשִׁים... לַמְּקֻצָעֹת" (להלן פסוקים כב-כג) הֲרֵי עֶשֶׂר,
וּבִמְקוֹמָם אֲפָרְשֵׁם לַמִּקְרָאוֹת הַלָּלוּ. נוֹתֵן הַיְרִיעוֹת
אָרְכָּן לְרָחְבּוֹ שֶׁל מִשְׁכָּן, עֶשֶׂר אַמּוֹת אֶמְצָעִיּוֹת
לְגַג חֲלַל הַמִּשְׁכָּן, וְאַמָּה מִכָּאן וְאַמָּה מִכָּאן
לַעֲבִי רָאשֵׁי הַקְּרָשִׁים, שֶׁעָבְיָן אַמָּה, נִשְׁתַּיְּרוּ שָׁם
עֶשְׂרֵה אַמָּה, שְׁמוֹנֶה לַצָּפוֹן וּשְׁמוֹנֶה לַדָּרוֹם, מְכַסּוֹת
קוֹמַת הַקְּרָשִׁים שֶׁגָּבְהָן עֶשֶׂר, נִמְצְאוּ שְׁתֵּי אַמּוֹת
הַתַּחְתּוֹנוֹת מְגֻלּוֹת. רָחְבָּן שֶׁל יְרִיעוֹת אַרְבָּעִים אַמָּה
כְּשֶׁהֵן מְחֻבָּרוֹת, עֶשְׂרִים אַמָּה לַחוֹבֶרֶת. שְׁלֹשִׁים מֵהֶן
לְגַג חֲלַל הַמִּשְׁכָּן לְאָרְכּוֹ, וְאַמָּה כְּנֶגֶד עֳבִי רָאשֵׁי
הַקְּרָשִׁים שֶׁבַּמַּעֲרָב, וְאַמָּה לְכַסּוֹת עֳבִי הָעַמּוּדִים
שֶׁבַּמִּזְרָח, שֶׁלֹּא הָיוּ קְרָשִׁים בַּמִּזְרָח אֶלָּא אַרְבָּעָה
עַמּוּדִים שֶׁהַמָּסָךְ פָּרוּשׂ וְתָלוּי בַּוָּוִין שֶׁבָּהֶן כְּמִין וִילוֹן,
נִשְׁתַּיְּרוּ שְׁמוֹנֶה אַמּוֹת הַתְּלוּיִין עַל אֲחוֹרֵי הַמִּשְׁכָּן
שֶׁבַּמַּעֲרָב, וּשְׁתֵּי אַמּוֹת הַתַּחְתּוֹנוֹת מְגֻלּוֹת. זוֹ מָצָאתִי
בְּבָרַיְתָא דְּאַרְבָּעִים וְתֵשַׁע מִדּוֹת. אֲבָל בְּמַסֶּכֶת שַׁבָּת
(דף צח ע"ב) אֵין יְרִיעוֹת הַתַּחְתּוֹנוֹת מְכַסּוֹת אֶת עַמּוּדֵי הַמִּזְרָח,
וּתְשַׁע אַמּוֹת תְּלוּיוֹת אֲחוֹרֵי הַמִּשְׁכָּן, וְהַכָּתוּב
מְסַיְּעֵנוּ: "וְנָתַתָּה אֶת הַפָּרֹכֶת תַּחַת הַקְּרָסִים" (להלן
פסוק לג) וְאִם כְּדִבְרֵי הַבָּרַיְתָא הַזֹּאת, נִמְצֵאת פָּרֹכֶת
מְשׁוּכָה מִן הַקְּרָסִים וְלַמַּעֲרָב אַמָּה:

ו׀ קַרְסֵי זָהָב. פירמיל״ש בְּלַעַז, וּמַכְנִיסִין לְחֹשֶׁן

ח עַשְׁתֵּי־עֶשְׂרֵה יְרִיעֹת תַּעֲשֶׂה אֹתָם: הַיְרִיעָה הָאַחַת שְׁלֹשִׁים בָּאַמָּה וְרֹחַב אַרְבַּע בָּאַמָּה הַיְרִיעָה הָאֶחָת מִדָּה אַחַת לְעַשְׁתֵּי עֶשְׂרֵה יְרִיעֹת:
ט וְחִבַּרְתָּ אֶת־חֲמֵשׁ הַיְרִיעֹת לְבָד וְאֶת־שֵׁשׁ הַיְרִיעֹת לְבָד וְכָפַלְתָּ אֶת־הַיְרִיעָה הַשִּׁשִּׁית אֶל־מוּל פְּנֵי הָאֹהֶל:
י וְעָשִׂיתָ חֲמִשִּׁים לֻלָאֹת עַל שְׂפַת הַיְרִיעָה הָאֶחָת הַקִּיצֹנָה בַּחֹבָרֶת וַחֲמִשִּׁים לֻלָאֹת עַל שְׂפַת הַיְרִיעָה הַחֹבֶרֶת הַשֵּׁנִית:
יא וְעָשִׂיתָ קַרְסֵי נְחֹשֶׁת חֲמִשִּׁים וְהֵבֵאתָ אֶת־הַקְּרָסִים בַּלֻּלָאֹת וְחִבַּרְתָּ אֶת־הָאֹהֶל וְהָיָה אֶחָד:
יב וְסֶרַח הָעֹדֵף בִּירִיעֹת הָאֹהֶל חֲצִי הַיְרִיעָה הָעֹדֶפֶת תִּסְרַח עַל אֲחֹרֵי הַמִּשְׁכָּן:
יג וְהָאַמָּה מִזֶּה וְהָאַמָּה מִזֶּה בָּעֹדֵף בְּאֹרֶךְ יְרִיעֹת הָאֹהֶל יִהְיֶה סָרוּחַ עַל־צִדֵּי הַמִּשְׁכָּן מִזֶּה וּמִזֶּה לְכַסֹּתוֹ:
יד וְעָשִׂיתָ מִכְסֶה לָאֹהֶל עֹרֹת אֵילִם מְאָדָּמִים וּמִכְסֵה עֹרֹת תְּחָשִׁים מִלְמָעְלָה:

אֶחָד בַּלּוּלָאוֹת שֶׁבַּחוֹבֶרֶת זוֹ וְרֹאשָׁן אֶחָד בַּלּוּלָאוֹת שֶׁבַּחוֹבֶרֶת זוֹ וּמְחַבְּרָן בָּהֶן:

זּ יְרִיעֹת עִזִּים. מִנּוֹצָה שֶׁל עִזִּים: לְאֹהֶל עַל הַמִּשְׁכָּן. לִפְרֹשׂ אוֹתָן עַל הַיְרִיעוֹת הַתַּחְתּוֹנוֹת:

חַ שְׁלֹשִׁים בָּאַמָּה. שֶׁכְּשֶׁנּוֹתֵן אָרְכָּן לְרֹחַב הַמִּשְׁכָּן כְּמוֹ שֶׁנָּתַן אֶת הָרִאשׁוֹנוֹת, נִמְצְאוּ אֵלּוּ עוֹדְפוֹת אַמָּה מִכָּאן וְאַמָּה מִכָּאן, לְכַסּוֹת אַחַת מֵהַשְּׁתֵּי אַמּוֹת שֶׁנִּשְׁאֲרוּ מְגֻלּוֹת בַּקְּרָשִׁים. וְהָאַמָּה הַתַּחְתּוֹנָה שֶׁל קֶרֶשׁ שֶׁאֵין הַיְרִיעָה מְכַסָּה אוֹתוֹ, הִיא הָאַמָּה הַתְּחוּבָה בְּנֶקֶב הָאֶדֶן, שֶׁהָאֲדָנִים גְּבָהָן אַמָּה:

ט וְכָפַלְתָּ אֶת הַיְרִיעָה הַשִּׁשִּׁית. שֶׁעוֹדֶפֶת בָּאֵלּוּ הָעֶלְיוֹנוֹת יוֹתֵר מִן הַתַּחְתּוֹנוֹת: אֶל מוּל פְּנֵי הָאֹהֶל. חֲצִי רָחְבָּהּ הָיָה תָּלוּי וְכָפוּל עַל הַמָּסָךְ שֶׁבַּמִּזְרָח כְּנֶגֶד הַפֶּתַח, דּוֹמֶה לְכַלָּה צְנוּעָה הַמְכֻסָּה בִּצְעִיף עַל פָּנֶיהָ:

יב־יג וְסֶרַח הָעֹדֵף בִּירִיעֹת הָאֹהֶל. עַל יְרִיעֹת הַמִּשְׁכָּן. יְרִיעֹת הָאֹהֶל הֵן הָעֶלְיוֹנוֹת שֶׁל עִזִּים שֶׁקְּרוּיִים אֹהֶל, כְּמוֹ שֶׁאָמוּר בָּהֶן: "לָאֹהֶל עַל הַמִּשְׁכָּן" (לעיל פסוק ז), וְכָל אֹהֶל הָאָמוּר בָּהֶן אֵינוֹ אֶלָּא לְשׁוֹן גַּג, שֶׁמַּאֲהִילוֹת וּמְסַכְּכוֹת עַל הַתַּחְתּוֹנוֹת. וְהֵן הָיוּ עוֹדְפוֹת עַל הַתַּחְתּוֹנוֹת חֲצִי הַיְרִיעָה לַמַּעֲרָב, שֶׁהַחֲצִי שֶׁל יְרִיעָה אַחַת עֲשִׂירִית הַיְתֵרָה הָיָה נִכְפָּל אֶל מוּל פְּנֵי הָאֹהֶל, נִשְׁאֲרוּ שְׁתֵּי אַמּוֹת רֹחַב חֶצְיָהּ עוֹדֵף עַל רֹחַב הַתַּחְתּוֹנוֹת: תִּסְרַח עַל אֲחֹרֵי הַמִּשְׁכָּן. לְכַסּוֹת שְׁתֵּי אַמּוֹת שֶׁהָיוּ מְגֻלּוֹת בַּקְּרָשִׁים: וְהָאַמָּה מִזֶּה וְהָאַמָּה מִזֶּה. לַצָּפוֹן וְלַדָּרוֹם: בָּעֹדֵף בְּאֹרֶךְ יְרִיעֹת הָאֹהֶל. שֶׁהֵן עוֹדְפוֹת עַל אֹרֶךְ יְרִיעוֹת הַמִּשְׁכָּן שְׁתֵּי אַמּוֹת: יִהְיֶה סָרוּחַ עַל צִדֵּי הַמִּשְׁכָּן. לַצָּפוֹן וְלַדָּרוֹם, כְּמוֹ שֶׁפֵּרַשְׁתִּי לְמַעְלָה. לִמְּדָה תּוֹרָה דֶּרֶךְ אֶרֶץ, שֶׁיְּהֵא אָדָם חָס עַל הַיָּפֶה: אַחֲרֵי הַמִּשְׁכָּן. הוּא צַד מַעֲרָב, לְפִי שֶׁהַפֶּתַח בַּמִּזְרָח שֶׁהֵן פָּנָיו, וְצָפוֹן וְדָרוֹם קְרוּיִין צְדָדִין לַיָּמִין וְלַשְּׂמֹאל:

יד מִכְסֶה לָאֹהֶל. לְאוֹתוֹ גַּג שֶׁל יְרִיעוֹת עִזִּים, עֲשֵׂה עוֹד מִכְסֶה אֶחָד שֶׁל "עֹרֹת אֵילִם מְאָדָּמִים",

| תרומה | 454   פרק כו | שמות

רביעי

טו וְעָשִׂ֥יתָ אֶת־הַקְּרָשִׁ֖ים לַמִּשְׁכָּ֑ן עֲצֵ֥י שִׁטִּ֖ים עֹמְדִֽים: עֶ֣שֶׂר אַמּ֔וֹת
טז אֹ֖רֶךְ הַקָּ֑רֶשׁ וְאַמָּה֙ וַחֲצִ֣י הָֽאַמָּ֔ה רֹ֖חַב הַקֶּ֥רֶשׁ הָאֶחָֽד: שְׁתֵּ֣י
יז יָד֗וֹת לַקֶּ֙רֶשׁ֙ הָאֶחָ֔ד מְשֻׁ֨לָּבֹ֔ת אִשָּׁ֖ה אֶל־אֲחֹתָ֑הּ כֵּ֣ן תַּעֲשֶׂ֔ה
לְכֹ֖ל קַרְשֵׁ֥י הַמִּשְׁכָּֽן: וְעָשִׂ֥יתָ אֶת־הַקְּרָשִׁ֖ים לַמִּשְׁכָּ֑ן עֶשְׂרִ֣ים
יח קֶ֔רֶשׁ לִפְאַ֖ת נֶ֥גְבָּה תֵימָֽנָה: וְאַרְבָּעִים֙ אַדְנֵי־כֶ֔סֶף תַּעֲשֶׂ֕ה תַּ֖חַת
יט עֶשְׂרִ֣ים הַקָּ֑רֶשׁ שְׁנֵ֣י אֲדָנִ֡ים תַּֽחַת־הַקֶּ֤רֶשׁ הָאֶחָד֙ לִשְׁתֵּ֣י יְדֹתָ֔יו
וּשְׁנֵ֧י אֲדָנִ֛ים תַּֽחַת־הַקֶּ֥רֶשׁ הָאֶחָ֖ד לִשְׁתֵּ֥י יְדֹתָֽיו: וּלְצֶ֧לַע הַמִּשְׁכָּ֛ן
כ הַשֵּׁנִ֖ית לִפְאַ֣ת צָפ֑וֹן עֶשְׂרִ֖ים קָֽרֶשׁ: וְאַרְבָּעִ֥ים אַדְנֵיהֶ֖ם כָּ֑סֶף שְׁנֵ֣י
כא אֲדָנִ֗ים תַּ֚חַת הַקֶּ֣רֶשׁ הָאֶחָ֔ד וּשְׁנֵ֣י אֲדָנִ֔ים תַּ֖חַת הַקֶּ֥רֶשׁ הָאֶחָֽד:

ועוד למעלה ממנו "מכסה עורות תחשים", ואותן מכסאות לא היו מכסין אלא את הגג, ארכן שלשים ורחבן עשר, אלו דברי רבי נחמיה. ולדברי רבי יהודה מכסה אחד היה, חציו של עורות אילים מאדמים וחציו של עורות תחשים:

טו וְעָשִׂיתָ אֶת הַקְּרָשִׁים. היה לו לומר: ׳ועשית קרשים׳, כמו שנאמר בכל דבר ודבר. ומהו "הקרשים"? מאותן העומדין ומיחדין לכך, יעקב אבינו נטע ארזים במצרים, וכשמת צוה לבניו להעלותם עמהם כשיצאו ממצרים, ואמר להם שעתיד הקדוש ברוך הוא לצוות אותן לעשות משכן במדבר מעצי שטים, ראו שיהיו מזמנים בידכם. הוא שיסד הבבלי בפיוטו שלו: "טס מטע מזורזים, קורות בתינו ארזים" (יוצר ליום ראשון של פסח), שנזדרזו להיות מוכנים בידם מקדם לכך: עֲצֵי שִׁטִּים עֹמְדִים. אישטנטיב"ש בלעז, שיהא ארך הקרשים זקוף למעלה בקירות המשכן, ולא תעשה הכתלים בקרשים שוכבים להיות רחב הקרשים לגובה הכתלים קרש על קרש:

טו עֶשֶׂר אַמּוֹת אֹרֶךְ הַקָּרֶשׁ. למדנו גבהו של משכן עשר אמות: וְאַמָּה וַחֲצִי הָאַמָּה רֹחַב. למדנו ארכו של משכן לעשרים הקרשים שהיו בצפון ובדרום מן המזרח למערב, שלשים אמה:

יז שְׁתֵּי יָדוֹת לַקֶּרֶשׁ הָאֶחָד. היה חורץ את הקרש מלמטה באמצעו בגבהו אמה, מניח רביע לרחבו מכאן ורביע לרחבו מכאן והן הן הידות, והחריץ חצי לרחב הקרש באמצע. ואותן הידות מכניס באדנים שהיו חלולים, והאדנים גבהן אמה ויושבים רצופים ארבעים זה אצל זה. וידות הקרש הנכנסות בחלל האדנים חרוצות משלשת עדיין, לרחב החריץ כעבי שפת האדן, שיכסה הקרש את כל ראש האדן, שאם לא כן נמצא רוח בין קרש לקרש כעבי שפת שני האדנים שיפסיקו ביניהם, וזהו שנאמר "וְיִהְיוּ תֹאֲמִים מִלְּמַטָּה" (להלן פסוק כד), שיחלץ את עבי הידות כדי שיתחברו הקרשים זה אצל זה: מְשֻׁלָּבֹת. עשויות כמין שליבות סלם מבדלות זו מזו, ומשפין ראשיהם לכנס בתוך חלל האדן כשליבה הנכנסת בנקב עמודי הסלם: אִשָּׁה אֶל אֲחֹתָהּ. מכוונות זו כנגד זו, שיהיו חריציהם שוים זו כמדת זו, כדי שלא יהיו שתי ידות זו משוכה לצד פנים וזו משוכה לצד חוץ בעבי הקרש שהוא אמה. ותרגום של "ידות" - "צירין", לפי שדומות לצירי הדלת הנכנסים בחורי המפתן:

יח לִפְאַת נֶגְבָּה תֵימָנָה. אין "פאה" זו לשון מקצוע, אלא כל הרוח קרויה פאה. כתרגומו: "לרוח עבר דרומא":

שמות | פרק כו   455 | תרומה

כב וּלְיַרְכְּתֵ֥י הַמִּשְׁכָּ֖ן יָ֑מָּה תַּעֲשֶׂ֖ה שִׁשָּׁ֥ה קְרָשִֽׁים: כג וּשְׁנֵ֤י קְרָשִׁים֙
תַּעֲשֶׂ֔ה לִמְקֻצְעֹ֖ת הַמִּשְׁכָּ֑ן בַּיַּרְכָתָֽיִם: כד וְיִֽהְי֣וּ תֹֽאֲמִם֘ מִלְּמַ֒טָּה֒
וְיַחְדָּ֗ו יִהְי֤וּ תַמִּים֙ עַל־רֹאשׁ֔וֹ אֶל־הַטַּבַּ֖עַת הָאֶחָ֑ת כֵּ֚ן יִהְיֶ֣ה
לִשְׁנֵיהֶ֔ם לִשְׁנֵ֥י הַמִּקְצֹעֹ֖ת יִהְיֽוּ: כה וְהָיוּ֙ שְׁמֹנָ֣ה קְרָשִׁ֔ים וְאַדְנֵיהֶ֣ם
כֶּ֔סֶף שִׁשָּׁ֥ה עָשָׂ֖ר אֲדָנִ֑ים שְׁנֵ֣י אֲדָנִ֗ים תַּ֚חַת הַקֶּ֣רֶשׁ הָאֶחָ֔ד וּשְׁנֵ֣י
אֲדָנִ֔ים תַּ֖חַת הַקֶּ֥רֶשׁ הָאֶחָֽד: כו וְעָשִׂ֥יתָ בְרִיחִ֖ם עֲצֵ֣י שִׁטִּ֑ים חֲמִשָּׁ֕ה

כב) וּלְיַרְכְּתֵי. לְשׁוֹן סוֹף, כְּתַרְגּוּמוֹ: "וְלִסְיָפֵי". וּלְפִי שֶׁהַפֶּתַח בַּמִּזְרָח, קְרוּי מִזְרָח פָּנִים וְהַמַּעֲרָב אֲחוֹרַיִם, וְזֶהוּ סוֹף, שֶׁהַפָּנִים הֵן הָרֹאשׁ: תַּעֲשֶׂה שִׁשָּׁה קְרָשִׁים. הֲרֵי תֵּשַׁע אַמּוֹת לְרֹחַב:

כג) וּשְׁנֵי קְרָשִׁים תַּעֲשֶׂה לִמְקֻצְעֹת. אֶחָד לְמִקְצוֹעַ צְפוֹנִית מַעֲרָבִית וְאֶחָד לְמַעֲרָבִית דְּרוֹמִית. כָּל שְׁמוֹנָה קְרָשִׁים בְּסֵדֶר אֶחָד הֵן, אֶלָּא שֶׁאֵלּוּ הַשְּׁתַּיִם אֵינָן בַּחֲלַל הַמִּשְׁכָּן, אֶלָּא חֲצִי אַמָּה מִזּוֹ וַחֲצִי אַמָּה מִזּוֹ נִרְאוֹת בֶּחָלָל, לְהַשְׁלִים רָחְבּוֹ לְעֶשֶׂר, וְהָאַמָּה מִזֶּה וְהָאַמָּה מִזֶּה בָּאוֹת כְּנֶגֶד אַמַּת עֳבִי קַרְשֵׁי הַמִּשְׁכָּן הַצָּפוֹן וְהַדָּרוֹם, כְּדֵי שֶׁיְּהֵא הַמִּקְצוֹעַ מִבַּחוּץ שָׁוֶה:

כד) וְיִֽהְי֣וּ תֹֽאֲמִם. כָּל הַקְּרָשִׁים "תּוֹאֲמִים" זֶה לָזֶה "מִלְּמַטָּה", שֶׁלֹּא יַפְסִיק עֳבִי שְׂפַת שְׁנֵי הָאֲדָנִים בֵּינֵיהֶם לְהַרְחִיקָם זֶה מִזֶּה. זֶהוּ שֶׁפֵּרַשְׁתִּי שֶׁיִּהְיוּ עִצְרֵי הַיָּדוֹת חֲרוּצִים מֵעֶצְיָן, שֶׁיְּהֵא לַחַב הַקֶּרֶשׁ בּוֹלֵט לְעֶבְרָיו חוּץ לְיַד הַקֶּרֶשׁ לְכַסּוֹת אֶת שְׂפַת הָאֶדֶן, וְכֵן הַקֶּרֶשׁ שֶׁאֶצְלוֹ, וְנִמְצְאוּ תוֹאֲמִים זֶה לָזֶה. וְהַקֶּרֶשׁ הַמִּקְצוֹעַ שֶׁבְּסֵדֶר הַמַּעֲרָב חָרוּץ לְרָחְבּוֹ בְּעָבְיוֹ, כְּנֶגֶד חָרִיץ שֶׁל עֳבִי קֶרֶשׁ הַצָּפוֹנִי וְהַדְּרוֹמִי, כְּדֵי שֶׁלֹּא יַפְרִידוּ הָאֲדָנִים בֵּינֵיהֶם. וְיַחְדָּו יִהְיוּ תַמִּים. כְּמוֹ "תְּאוֹמִים": עַל רֹאשׁוֹ. שֶׁל קֶרֶשׁ: אֶל הַטַּבַּעַת הָאֶחָת. כָּל קֶרֶשׁ וָקֶרֶשׁ הָיָה חָרוּץ לְמַעְלָה בְּרָחְבּוֹ שְׁנֵי חֲרִיצִין בִּשְׁנֵי עֶדְיָו, כְּדֵי עֳבִי שְׂפַת טַבַּעַת, וּמַכְנִיסוֹ בְּטַבַּעַת אַחַת, נִמְצָא מַתְאִים לַקֶּרֶשׁ שֶׁאֶצְלוֹ. אֲבָל אוֹתָן טַבָּעוֹת לֹא יָדַעְתִּי אִם קְבוּעוֹת הֵן אִם מִטַּלְטְלוֹת. וּבַקֶּרֶשׁ שֶׁבַּמִּקְצוֹעַ הָיְתָה טַבַּעַת בְּעֶבְרֵי הַקֶּרֶשׁ הַדְּרוֹמִי וְהַצְּפוֹנִי, וְרֹאשׁ קֶרֶשׁ הַמִּקְצוֹעַ שֶׁבְּסֵדֶר מַעֲרָב נִכְנָס לְתוֹכוֹ, נִמְצְאוּ

שְׁנֵי הַכְּתָלִים מְחֻבָּרִים: כֵּן יִהְיֶה לִשְׁנֵיהֶם. הַקְּרָשִׁים שֶׁבַּמִּקְצוֹעַ, לַקֶּרֶשׁ שֶׁבְּסוֹף צָפוֹן וְלַקֶּרֶשׁ הַמַּעֲרָבִי, וְכֵן "לִשְׁנֵי הַמִּקְצֹעֹת":

כה) וְהָיוּ שְׁמֹנָה קְרָשִׁים. הֵן הָאֲמוּרוֹת לְמַעְלָה: "תַּעֲשֶׂה שִׁשָּׁה קְרָשִׁים וּשְׁנֵי קְרָשִׁים תַּעֲשֶׂה לִמְקֻצְעֹת" (לעיל פסוקים כב-כג), נִמְצְאוּ שְׁמוֹנָה קְרָשִׁים בְּסֵדֶר מַעֲרָבִי. כָּךְ שְׁנוּיָה בִּמְלֶאכֶת מַעֲשֵׂה סֵדֶר הַקְּרָשִׁים בִּמְלֶאכֶת הַמִּשְׁכָּן (ברייתא דמלאכת המשכן, פרק ח): הָיָה עוֹשֶׂה אֶת הָאֲדָנִים חֲלוּלִים, וְחוֹרֵץ אֶת הַקֶּרֶשׁ מִלְּמַטָּה רְבִיעַ מִכָּאן וּרְבִיעַ מִכָּאן וְהֶחָרִיץ חֶצְיוֹ בָּאֶמְצַע, וְעָשָׂה לוֹ שְׁתֵּי יָדוֹת כְּמִין שְׁנֵי חִמּוּקִין, וְלֹא נִרְאֶה שֶׁהַגִּרְסָא כְּמִין שְׁנֵי חִוָּקִין, כְּמִין שְׁתֵּי שְׁלִיבוֹת סֻלָּם הַמֻּבְדָּלוֹת זוֹ מִזּוֹ, וּמְשֻׁפּוֹת לִכָּנֵס בַּחֲלַל הָאֶדֶן כִּשְׁלִיבָה הַנִּכְנֶסֶת בְּנֶקֶב עַמּוּד הַסֻּלָּם, וְהוּא לְשׁוֹן "מְשֻׁלָּבוֹת", עֲשׂוּיוֹת כְּמִין שְׁלִיבָה. וּמַכְנִיסָן לְתוֹךְ שְׁנֵי אֲדָנִים, שֶׁנֶּאֱמַר: "שְׁנֵי אֲדָנִים... וּשְׁנֵי אֲדָנִים" (לעיל פסוק יט). וְחוֹרֵץ אֶת הַקֶּרֶשׁ מִלְמַעְלָה אֶצְבַּע מִכָּאן וְאֶצְבַּע מִכָּאן וְנוֹתֵן לְתוֹךְ טַבַּעַת אַחַת שֶׁל זָהָב, כְּדֵי שֶׁלֹּא יִהְיוּ נִפְרָדִים זֶה מִזֶּה, שֶׁנֶּאֱמַר: "וְיִהְיוּ תֹאֲמִם מִלְּמַטָּה" וְגוֹ' (לעיל פסוק כד). כָּךְ הִיא הַמִּשְׁנָה, וּפֵרוּשׁ שֶׁלָּהּ הַצַּעְתִּי לְמַעְלָה בְּסֵדֶר הַמִּקְרָאוֹת:

כו) בְרִיחִם. כְּתַרְגּוּמוֹ: "עַבְרִין", וּבְלַעַז אשפרי"ש: חֲמִשָּׁה לְקַרְשֵׁי צֶלַע הַמִּשְׁכָּן. אֵלּוּ חֲמִשָּׁה שְׁלוֹשָׁה הֵן, אֶלָּא שֶׁהַבְּרִיחַ הָעֶלְיוֹן וְהַתַּחְתּוֹן עֲשׂוּי מִשְּׁתֵּי חֲתִיכוֹת, זֶה מַבְרִיחַ עַד חֲצִי הַכֹּתֶל וְזֶה מַבְרִיחַ עַד חֲצִי הַכֹּתֶל, זֶה נִכְנָס בַּטַּבַּעַת מִצַּד זֶה וְזֶה נִכְנָס בַּטַּבַּעַת מִצַּד זֶה עַד שֶׁמַּגִּיעִין זֶה לָזֶה, נִמְצְאוּ שֶׁהָעֶלְיוֹן וְהַתַּחְתּוֹן שְׁנַיִם שֶׁהֵן אַרְבָּעָה. אֲבָל הָאֶמְצָעִי אָרְכּוֹ

תרומה | פרק כו

כו לְקַרְשֵׁי צֶלַע־הַמִּשְׁכָּן הָאֶחָד: וַחֲמִשָּׁה בְרִיחִם לְקַרְשֵׁי צֶלַע־
הַמִּשְׁכָּן הַשֵּׁנִית וַחֲמִשָּׁה בְרִיחִם לְקַרְשֵׁי צֶלַע הַמִּשְׁכָּן לַיַּרְכָתַיִם
יָמָּה: וְהַבְּרִיחַ הַתִּיכֹן בְּתוֹךְ הַקְּרָשִׁים מַבְרִחַ מִן־הַקָּצֶה אֶל־
כח הַקָּצֶה: וְאֶת־הַקְּרָשִׁים תְּצַפֶּה זָהָב וְאֶת־טַבְּעֹתֵיהֶם תַּעֲשֶׂה
כט זָהָב בָּתִּים לַבְּרִיחִם וְצִפִּיתָ אֶת־הַבְּרִיחִם זָהָב: וַהֲקֵמֹתָ אֶת־
ל הַמִּשְׁכָּן כְּמִשְׁפָּטוֹ אֲשֶׁר הָרְאֵיתָ בָּהָר: חמישי וְעָשִׂיתָ פָרֹכֶת
לא תְּכֵלֶת וְאַרְגָּמָן וְתוֹלַעַת שָׁנִי וְשֵׁשׁ מָשְׁזָר מַעֲשֵׂה חֹשֵׁב יַעֲשֶׂה
לב אֹתָהּ כְּרֻבִים: וְנָתַתָּה אֹתָהּ עַל־אַרְבָּעָה עַמּוּדֵי שִׁטִּים מְצֻפִּים

כְּנֶגֶד כָּל הַכֹּתֶל, וּמַבְרִיחַ מִקְצֵה הַכֹּתֶל וְעַד קָצֵהוּ, שֶׁנֶּאֱמַר: "וְהַבְּרִיחַ הַתִּיכֹן וְגוֹ׳ מַבְרִחַ מִן־הַקָּצֶה אֶל־הַקָּצֶה" (להלן פסוק כח). שֶׁהָעֶלְיוֹנִים וְהַתַּחְתּוֹנִים הָיוּ לָהֶן טַבָּעוֹת בַּקְּרָשִׁים לִכָּנֵס לְתוֹכָן, שְׁתֵּי טַבָּעוֹת לְכָל קֶרֶשׁ, מְשֻׁלָּשִׁים בְּתוֹךְ עֶשֶׂר אַמּוֹת שֶׁל גֹּבַהּ הַקֶּרֶשׁ, חֵלֶק אֶחָד מִן הַטַּבַּעַת הָעֶלְיוֹנָה וּלְמַעְלָה וְחֵלֶק אֶחָד מִן הַתַּחְתּוֹנָה וּלְמַטָּה, וְכָל חֵלֶק הוּא רְבִיעַ אֹרֶךְ הַקֶּרֶשׁ, וּשְׁנֵי חֲלָקִים בֵּין טַבַּעַת לְטַבַּעַת, כְּדֵי שֶׁיִּהְיוּ כָּל הַטַּבָּעוֹת מְכֻוָּנוֹת זוֹ כְּנֶגֶד זוֹ. אֲבָל לַבְּרִיחַ הַתִּיכוֹן אֵין טַבָּעוֹת, אֶלָּא הַקְּרָשִׁים נְקוּבִין בְּעָבְיָן, וְהוּא נִכְנָס בָּהֶם דֶּרֶךְ הַנְּקָבִים שֶׁהֵם מְכֻוָּנִין זֶה מוּל זֶה, וְזֶהוּ שֶׁנֶּאֱמַר: "בְּתוֹךְ הַקְּרָשִׁים" (שם). הַבְּרִיחִים הָעֶלְיוֹנִים וְהַתַּחְתּוֹנִים שֶׁבַּצְּדָדִים וְשֶׁבַּדָּרוֹם אֹרֶךְ כָּל אֶחָד חֲמֵשׁ עֶשְׂרֵה אַמָּה, וְהַתִּיכוֹן אָרְכּוֹ שְׁלֹשִׁים אַמָּה, וְזֶהוּ "מִן הַקָּצֶה אֶל הַקָּצֶה" (שם), מִן הַמִּזְרָח וְעַד הַמַּעֲרָב. וַחֲמִשָּׁה בְרִיחִים שֶׁבַּמַּעֲרָב אֹרֶךְ הָעֶלְיוֹנִים וְהַתַּחְתּוֹנִים שֵׁשׁ אַמּוֹת, וְהַתִּיכוֹן אָרְכּוֹ שְׁתֵּים עֶשְׂרֵה, כְּנֶגֶד רֹחַב שְׁמוֹנֶה קְרָשִׁים. כָּךְ הִיא מְפֹרֶשֶׁת בִּמְלֶאכֶת הַמִּשְׁכָּן:

כט **בָּתִּים לַבְּרִיחִם.** הַטַּבָּעוֹת שֶׁתַּעֲשֶׂה בָהֶן יִהְיוּ בָּתִּים לִכָּנֵס בָּהֶן הַבְּרִיחִים: **וְצִפִּיתָ אֶת הַבְּרִיחִים זָהָב.** לֹא שֶׁהָיָה הַזָּהָב מְדֻבָּק עַל הַבְּרִיחִים, שֶׁאֵין עֲלֵיהֶם שׁוּם צִפּוּי, אֶלָּא בַּקֶּרֶשׁ הָיָה קוֹבֵעַ כְּמִין שְׁנֵי פִיפִיּוֹת שֶׁל זָהָב כְּמִין שְׁנֵי סִדְקֵי קָנֶה חָלוּק

וְקוֹבְעָן אֵצֶל הַטַּבָּעוֹת לְכָאן וּלְכָאן, אָרְכָּן מְמַלֵּא אֶת רֹחַב הַקֶּרֶשׁ מִן הַטַּבַּעַת לְכָאן וּמִמֶּנָּה לְכָאן, וְהַבְּרִיחַ נִכְנָס לְתוֹכוֹ וּמִן הַטַּבַּעַת לַפֶּה הַשֵּׁנִי, נִמְצְאוּ הַבְּרִיחִים מְצֻפִּים זָהָב כְּשֶׁהֵן תְּחוּבִין בַּקְּרָשִׁים. וְהַבְּרִיחִים הַלָּלוּ מִבַּחוּץ הָיוּ; בְּלִיטַת הַטַּבָּעוֹת וְהַפִּיפִיּוֹת לֹא הָיְתָה נִרְאֵית בְּתוֹךְ הַמִּשְׁכָּן, אֶלָּא כָּל הַכֹּתֶל חָלָק מִבִּפְנִים:

ל **וַהֲקֵמֹתָ אֶת הַמִּשְׁכָּן.** לְאַחַר שֶׁיִּגָּמֵר הֲקִימֵהוּ: **הָרְאֵיתָ בָּהָר.** קֹדֶם לָכֵן, שֶׁאֲנִי עָתִיד לְלַמֶּדְךָ וּלְהַרְאוֹתְךָ סֵדֶר הֲקָמָתוֹ:

לא **פָּרֹכֶת.** לְשׁוֹן מְחִצָּה הוּא, וּבִלְשׁוֹן חֲכָמִים: פַּרְגּוֹד, דָּבָר הַמַּבְדִּיל בֵּין הַמֶּלֶךְ וּבֵין הָעָם: **תְּכֵלֶת וְאַרְגָּמָן.** כָּל מִין וָמִין הָיָה כָּפוּל, בְּכָל חוּט וָחוּט שִׁשָּׁה חוּטִין: **מַעֲשֵׂה חֹשֵׁב.** כְּבָר פֵּרַשְׁתִּי שֶׁזּוֹ הִיא אֲרִיגָה שֶׁל שְׁתֵּי קִירוֹת, שֶׁהַצּוּרִין שֶׁמִּשְּׁנֵי עֲבָרֶיהָ אֵינָן דּוֹמִין זֶה לָזֶה: **כְּרֻבִים.** צוּרִין שֶׁל בְּרִיּוֹת יַעֲשֶׂה בָהּ:

לב **אַרְבָּעָה עַמּוּדִים.** תְּקוּעִים בְּתוֹךְ אַרְבָּעָה אֲדָנִים, וְאֻנְקְלָיוֹת קְבוּעִין בָּהֶן עֲקוּמִין לְמַעְלָה, לְהוֹשִׁיב עֲלֵיהֶם כְּלוּנָס שֶׁל הַפָּרֹכֶת שְׁלוּחָה בָרֹאשׁ בָּהּ, וְהָאֻנְקְלָיוֹת הֵן הַוָּוִין, שֶׁהֲרֵי כְּמִין וָוִין הֵן עֲשׂוּיִים. וְהַפָּרֹכֶת אָרְכָּהּ עֶשֶׂר אַמּוֹת לְרָחְבּוֹ שֶׁל מִשְׁכָּן, וְרָחְבָּהּ עֶשֶׂר אַמּוֹת כְּגָבְהָן שֶׁל קְרָשִׁים, פְּרוּסָה בִּשְׁלִישׁוֹ שֶׁל מִשְׁכָּן, שֶׁיְּהֵא הֵימֶנָּה וּלְפָנִים עֶשֶׂר אַמּוֹת וְהֵימֶנָּה וְלַחוּץ עֶשְׂרִים אַמָּה. נִמְצָא בֵּית קָדְשֵׁי הַקֳּדָשִׁים עֶשֶׂר עַל

שמות | פרק כו

לג זָהָב וָוֵיהֶם זָהָב עַל־אַרְבָּעָה אַדְנֵי־כָסֶף: וְנָתַתָּה אֶת־הַפָּרֹכֶת תַּחַת הַקְּרָסִים וְהֵבֵאתָ שָׁמָּה מִבֵּית לַפָּרֹכֶת אֵת אֲרוֹן הָעֵדוּת

לד וְהִבְדִּילָה הַפָּרֹכֶת לָכֶם בֵּין הַקֹּדֶשׁ וּבֵין קֹדֶשׁ הַקֳּדָשִׁים: וְנָתַתָּ

לה אֶת־הַכַּפֹּרֶת עַל אֲרוֹן הָעֵדֻת בְּקֹדֶשׁ הַקֳּדָשִׁים: וְשַׂמְתָּ אֶת־הַשֻּׁלְחָן מִחוּץ לַפָּרֹכֶת וְאֶת־הַמְּנֹרָה נֹכַח הַשֻּׁלְחָן עַל צֶלַע

לו הַמִּשְׁכָּן תֵּימָנָה וְהַשֻּׁלְחָן תִּתֵּן עַל־צֶלַע צָפוֹן: וְעָשִׂיתָ מָסָךְ לְפֶתַח הָאֹהֶל תְּכֵלֶת וְאַרְגָּמָן וְתוֹלַעַת שָׁנִי וְשֵׁשׁ מָשְׁזָר מַעֲשֵׂה רֹקֵם:

לז וְעָשִׂיתָ לַמָּסָךְ חֲמִשָּׁה עַמּוּדֵי שִׁטִּים וְצִפִּיתָ אֹתָם זָהָב וָוֵיהֶם

כז א זָהָב וְיָצַקְתָּ לָהֶם חֲמִשָּׁה אַדְנֵי נְחֹשֶׁת: ששי וְעָשִׂיתָ אֶת־הַמִּזְבֵּחַ עֲצֵי שִׁטִּים חָמֵשׁ אַמּוֹת אֹרֶךְ וְחָמֵשׁ אַמּוֹת רֹחַב

ב רָבוּעַ יִהְיֶה הַמִּזְבֵּחַ וְשָׁלֹשׁ אַמּוֹת קֹמָתוֹ: וְעָשִׂיתָ קַרְנֹתָיו עַל אַרְבַּע פִּנֹּתָיו מִמֶּנּוּ תִּהְיֶיןָ קַרְנֹתָיו וְצִפִּיתָ אֹתוֹ נְחֹשֶׁת:

עָשָׂר, שֶׁנֶּאֱמַר: "וְנָתַתָּה אֶת הַפָּרֹכֶת תַּחַת הַקְּרָסִים" (להלן פסוק לג) הַמְחַבְּרִים אֶת שְׁתֵּי חוֹבְרוֹת שֶׁל יְרִיעוֹת הַמִּשְׁכָּן; רֹחַב הַחוֹבֶרֶת עֶשְׂרִים אַמָּה, וּכְשֶׁפּוֹרְשָׂהּ עַל גַּג הַמִּשְׁכָּן מִן הַפֶּתַח לַמַּעֲרָב, כָּלְתָה בִּשְׁנֵי שְׁלִישֵׁי הַמִּשְׁכָּן, וְהַחוֹבֶרֶת הַשֵּׁנִית כִּסְּתָה שְׁלִישׁוֹ שֶׁל מִשְׁכָּן, וְהַמּוֹתָר תָּלוּי לַאֲחוֹרָיו לְכַסּוֹת אֶת הַקְּרָשִׁים:

לה] וְשַׂמְתָּ אֶת הַשֻּׁלְחָן. שֻׁלְחָן בַּצָּפוֹן מָשׁוּךְ מִן הַכֹּתֶל הַצְּפוֹנִי שְׁתֵּי אַמּוֹת וּמֶחֱצָה, וּמְנוֹרָה בַּדָּרוֹם מְשׁוּכָה מִן הַכֹּתֶל הַדְּרוֹמִי שְׁתֵּי אַמּוֹת וּמֶחֱצָה, וּמִזְבַּח הַזָּהָב נָתוּן כְּנֶגֶד אֲוִיר שֶׁבֵּין שֻׁלְחָן לַמְּנוֹרָה מָשׁוּךְ קִמְעָא כְּלַפֵּי הַמִּזְרָח, וְכֻלָּם נְתוּנִים מִן חֲצִי הַמִּשְׁכָּן וְלִפְנִים. כֵּיצַד? אֹרֶךְ הַמִּשְׁכָּן מִן הַפֶּתַח לַפָּרֹכֶת עֶשְׂרִים אַמָּה, הַמִּזְבֵּחַ וְהַשֻּׁלְחָן וְהַמְּנוֹרָה מְשׁוּכִים מִן הַפֶּתַח לְצַד מַעֲרָב עֶשֶׂר אַמּוֹת:

לו] וְעָשִׂיתָ מָסָךְ. וִילוֹן שֶׁהוּא מָסָךְ כְּנֶגֶד הַפֶּתַח,

כְּמוֹ: "שַׂכְתָּ בַעֲדוֹ" (איוב א, י), לְשׁוֹן מָגֵן: מַעֲשֵׂה רֹקֵם. הַצּוּרוֹת עֲשׂוּיוֹת בּוֹ מַעֲשֵׂה מַחַט, כְּפַרְצוּף שֶׁל עֵבֶר זֶה כָּךְ פַּרְצוּף שֶׁל עֵבֶר זֶה: רֹקֵם. שֵׁם הָאֻמָּן וְלֹא שֵׁם הָאֻמָּנוּת, וְתַרְגּוּמוֹ: "עוֹבַד צַיָּר" וְלֹא "עוֹבֵד צִיּוּר": מִדַּת הַמָּסָךְ כְּמִדַּת הַפָּרֹכֶת, עֶשֶׂר אַמּוֹת עַל עֶשֶׂר אַמּוֹת:

פרק כז

א] וְעָשִׂיתָ אֶת הַמִּזְבֵּחַ וְגוֹ' וְשָׁלֹשׁ אַמּוֹת קֹמָתוֹ. דְּבָרִים כִּכְתָבָן, דִּבְרֵי רַבִּי יְהוּדָה. רַבִּי יוֹסֵי אוֹמֵר: נֶאֱמַר כָּאן "רָבוּעַ" וְנֶאֱמַר בַּפְּנִימִי "רָבוּעַ" (להלן ל, ח), מַה לְּהַלָּן גָּבְהוֹ פִּי שְׁנַיִם כְּאָרְכּוֹ, אַף כָּאן גָּבְהוֹ פִּי שְׁנַיִם כְּאָרְכּוֹ, וּמָה אֲנִי מְקַיֵּם "וְשָׁלֹשׁ אַמּוֹת קֹמָתוֹ"? מִשְּׂפַת סוֹבֵב וּלְמָעְלָה:

ב] מִמֶּנּוּ תִּהְיֶיןָ קַרְנֹתָיו. שֶׁלֹּא יַעֲשֵׂם לְבַדָּם וִיחַבְּרֵם בּוֹ: וְצִפִּיתָ אֹתוֹ נְחֹשֶׁת. לְכַפֵּר עַל עַזּוּת מֵצַח, שֶׁנֶּאֱמַר: "וּמִצְחֲךָ נְחוּשָׁה" (ישעיה מח, ד):

וְעָשִׂיתָ סִּירֹתָיו לְדַשְּׁנוֹ וְיָעָיו וּמִזְרְקֹתָיו וּמִזְלְגֹתָיו וּמַחְתֹּתָיו ג
לְכָל־כֵּלָיו תַּעֲשֶׂה נְחֹשֶׁת: וְעָשִׂיתָ לּוֹ מִכְבָּר מַעֲשֵׂה רֶשֶׁת נְחֹשֶׁת ד
וְעָשִׂיתָ עַל־הָרֶשֶׁת אַרְבַּע טַבְּעֹת נְחֹשֶׁת עַל אַרְבַּע קְצוֹתָיו:
וְנָתַתָּה אֹתָהּ תַּחַת כַּרְכֹּב הַמִּזְבֵּחַ מִלְּמָטָּה וְהָיְתָה הָרֶשֶׁת עַד ה

ג סִירֹתָיו. כְּמִין יוֹרוֹת: לְדַשְּׁנוֹ. לְהָסִיר דִּשְׁנוֹ לְתוֹכָם; וְהוּא שֶׁתִּרְגֵּם אוּנְקְלוֹס: "לְמִסְפֵּי קִטְמֵיהּ", לִסְפּוֹת הַדֶּשֶׁן לְתוֹכָם. כִּי יֵשׁ מִלּוֹת בִּלְשׁוֹן עִבְרִית מִלָּה אַחַת מִתְחַלֶּפֶת בַּפִּתְרוֹן לְשַׁמֵּשׁ בִּנְיָן וּסְתִירָה, כְּמוֹ "וַתַּשְׁרֵשׁ שָׁרָשֶׁיהָ" (תהלים פ, י), "חֲצִיר מַצְמִיחַ" (חיוב ה, ג), וְחִלּוּפוֹ: "וּבְכָל תְּבוּאָתִי תְשָׁרֵשׁ" (איוב לא, יב), וְכָמוֹהוּ: "בִּסְעִפֶיהָ פֹּרִיָּה" (ישעיה יז, ו), וְחִלּוּפוֹ: "מְסָעֵף פֻּארָה" (ישעיה י, לג), מְפַשֵּׁחַ סְעִיפֶיהָ. וְכָמוֹהוּ: "זֶה הָאַחֲרוֹן עִצְּמוֹ" (ירמיה נ, יז), שָׁבַר עַצְמוֹתָיו, וְכָמוֹהוּ: "וַיִּסְקְלֻהוּ בָאֲבָנִים" (מלכים א כא, יג), וְחִלּוּפוֹ: "סַקְּלוּ מֵאֶבֶן" (ישעיה סב, י), הָסִירוּ אֲבָנֶיהָ, וְכֵן: "וַיְעַזְּקֵהוּ וַיְסַקְּלֵהוּ" (ישעיה ה, ב). אַף כָּאן "לְדַשְּׁנוֹ" לְהָסִיר דִּשְׁנוֹ, וּבְלַעַז אדשצנד"ר: וְיָעָיו. כְּתַרְגּוּמוֹ, מַגְרֵפוֹת שֶׁנּוֹטֵל בָּהֶן הַדֶּשֶׁן, וְהֵן כְּמִין כִּסּוּי הַקְּדֵרָה, וְהוּא שֶׁל מַתֶּכֶת דַּק וְלוֹ בֵּית יָד, וּבְלַעַז וודי"ל: וּמִזְרְקֹתָיו. לְקַבֵּל בָּהֶם דַּם הַזְּבָחִים: וּמִזְלְגֹתָיו. כְּמִין אֻנְקְלִיּוֹת כְּפוּפִין, וּמַכֶּה בָּהֶן בַּבָּשָׂר וְנִתְקָעִין בּוֹ, וּמְהַפֵּךְ בָּהֶן עַל גַּחֲלֵי הַמַּעֲרָכָה שֶׁיְּהֵא מְמַהֵר שְׂרֵפָתָן, וּבְלַעַז קרוצינ"ש, וּבִלְשׁוֹן חֲכָמִים: צִנּוֹרִיּוֹת: וּמַחְתֹּתָיו. בֵּית קִבּוּל יֵשׁ לָהֶם לִטֹּל בָּהֶן גֶּחָלִים מִן הַמִּזְבֵּחַ לְשֵׂאתָן עַל מִזְבַּח הַפְּנִימִי לַקְּטֹרֶת, וְעַל שֵׁם חֲתִיָּתָן קְרוּיִים מַחְתּוֹת, כְּמוֹ: "לַחְתּוֹת אֵשׁ מִיָּקוּד" (ישעיה ל, יד), לְשׁוֹן שְׁאִיבַת אֵשׁ מִמְּקוֹמָהּ, וְכֵן: "הֲיַחְתֶּה אִישׁ אֵשׁ בְּחֵיקוֹ" (משלי ו, כז). כְּמוֹ כָּל כֵּלָיו:

ד מִכְבָּר. לְשׁוֹן כְּבָרָה שֶׁקּוֹרִין קריב"ל, כְּמִין לְבוּשׁ עָשׂוּי לוֹ לַמִּזְבֵּחַ, עָשׂוּי חוֹרִין חוֹרִין כְּמִין רֶשֶׁת. וּמִקְרָא זֶה מְסֹרָס, וְכֹה פִּתְרוֹנוֹ: וְעָשִׂיתָ לּוֹ מִכְבָּר נְחֹשֶׁת מַעֲשֵׂה רֶשֶׁת:

ה כַּרְכֹּב הַמִּזְבֵּחַ. סוֹבֵב. כָּל דָּבָר הַמַּקִּיף סָבִיב בְּעִגּוּל קָרוּי כַּרְכֹּב, כְּמוֹ שֶׁשָּׁנִינוּ בְּ"הַכֹּל שׁוֹחֲטִין": "אֵלּוּ הֵן גְּלָמֵי כְלֵי עֵץ, כָּל שֶׁעָתִיד לָשׁוּף וּלְכַרְכֵּב" (חולין כה ע"א), וְהוּא שֶׁעוֹשִׂין חֲרִיצִין עֲגֻלִּין בְּקַרְשֵׁי הַתֵּבוֹת וְסַפְסְלֵי הָעֵץ. אַף לַמִּזְבֵּחַ עָשָׂה חָרִיץ סְבִיבוֹ בְּדָפְנוֹ לְנוֹי, וְהוּא לְסוֹף שֵׁשׁ אַמּוֹת שֶׁל גָּבְהוֹ כְּדִבְרֵי הָאוֹמֵר (זבחים נט ע"ב – ס ע"א): "וְשָׁלֹשׁ אַמּוֹת קוֹמָתוֹ" מָה אֲנִי מְקַיֵּם? מִשְּׂפַת סוֹבֵב וּלְמַעְלָה. אֲבָל סוֹבֵב לַהֲלוֹךְ הַכֹּהֲנִים לֹא הָיָה לְמִזְבַּח הַנְּחֹשֶׁת, אֶלָּא עַל רֹאשׁוֹ לִפְנִים מִקַּרְנוֹתָיו. וְכֵן שָׁנִינוּ בִּזְבָחִים (דף סב ע"א): אֵיזֶהוּ כַרְכֹּב? בֵּין קֶרֶן לְקֶרֶן, וְלִפְנִים מֵהֶן אַמָּה שֶׁל הִלּוּךְ רַגְלֵי הַכֹּהֲנִים, שְׁתֵּי אַמּוֹת הַלָּלוּ קְרוּיִים כַּרְכֹּב. וְדִקְדַּקְנוּ שָׁם: וְהָכְתִיב: "תַּחַת כַּרְכֻּבּוֹ מִלְּמָטָּה" (להלן לח, ד), לָמַדְנוּ שֶׁהַכַּרְכֹּב בְּדָפְנוֹ הוּא וּלְבוּשׁ הַמִּכְבָּר תַּחְתָּיו! וְתֵרֵץ הַמְתָרֵץ: תְּרֵי הֲווֹ, חַד לְנוֹי וְחַד לַכֹּהֲנִים דְּלֹא נִשְׁתַּרְקוּ, זֶה שֶׁבְּדָפְנוֹ לְנוֹי הָיָה, וּמִתַּחְתָּיו הִלְבִּישׁוֹ הַמִּכְבָּר, וְהִגִּיעַ רָחְבּוֹ עַד חֲצִי הַמִּזְבֵּחַ, וְהוּא הָיָה סִימָן לַחֲצִי גָּבְהוֹ לְהַבְדִּיל בֵּין דָּמִים הָעֶלְיוֹנִים לְדָמִים הַתַּחְתּוֹנִים, וּכְנֶגְדּוֹ עָשׂוּ לְמִזְבֵּחַ בֵּית עוֹלָמִים חֲגוֹרַת חוּט הַסִּקְרָא בְּאֶמְצָעוֹ (מדות ג, א). וְכֶבֶשׁ שֶׁהָיוּ עוֹלִין בּוֹ, אַף עַל פִּי שֶׁלֹּא פֵּרְשׁוֹ בְּעִנְיָן זֶה, כְּבָר שְׁמָעֲנוּ בְּפָרָשַׁת "מִזְבַּח אֲדָמָה תַּעֲשֶׂה לִּי": "וְלֹא תַעֲלֶה בְמַעֲלֹת" (לעיל כ, כב), לֹא תַּעֲשֶׂה לוֹ מַעֲלוֹת בְּכִבְשׁוֹ שֶׁלּוֹ, אֶלָּא כֶּבֶשׁ חָלָק, לָמַדְנוּ שֶׁהָיָה לוֹ כֶּבֶשׁ. כָּךְ שָׁנִינוּ בִּמְכִילְתָּא (בחדש פרשה יא): וּ'מִזְבַּח אֲדָמָה' הוּא מִזְבַּח הַנְּחֹשֶׁת, שֶׁהָיוּ מְמַלְּאִין חֲלָלוֹ אֲדָמָה בִּמְקוֹם חֲנִיָּתָן. וְהַכֶּבֶשׁ הָיָה בִּדְרוֹם הַמִּזְבֵּחַ מֻבְדָּל מִן הַמִּזְבֵּחַ מְלֹא חוּט הַשַּׂעֲרָה, וְרַגְלָיו מַגִּיעִין עַד אַמָּה סָמוּךְ לְקַלְעֵי הֶחָצֵר שֶׁבַּדָּרוֹם, כְּדִבְרֵי הָאוֹמֵר עֶשֶׂר אַמּוֹת קוֹמָתוֹ, וּלְדִבְרֵי הָאוֹמֵר דְּבָרִים כִּכְתָבָן "שָׁלֹשׁ אַמּוֹת קוֹמָתוֹ" (זבחים נט ע"ב), לֹא הָיָה אֹרֶךְ הַכֶּבֶשׁ אֶלָּא עֶשֶׂר אַמּוֹת. כָּךְ מָצָאתִי בְּמִשְׁנַת אַרְבָּעִים וְתֵשַׁע מִדּוֹת. וְזֶה שֶׁהוּא מֻבְדָּל מִן הַמִּזְבֵּחַ מְלֹא הַחוּט, בְּמַסֶּכֶת זְבָחִים (דף סב ע"ב) לְמֵדוּהוּ מִן הַמִּקְרָא:

שמות | פרק כז | תרומה

ו חֲצִי הַמִּזְבֵּחַ: וְעָשִׂיתָ בַדִּים לַמִּזְבֵּחַ בַּדֵּי עֲצֵי שִׁטִּים וְצִפִּיתָ אֹתָם
ז נְחֹשֶׁת: וְהוּבָא אֶת־בַּדָּיו בַּטַּבָּעֹת וְהָיוּ הַבַּדִּים עַל־שְׁתֵּי צַלְעֹת
ח הַמִּזְבֵּחַ בִּשְׂאֵת אֹתוֹ: נְבוּב לֻחֹת תַּעֲשֶׂה אֹתוֹ כַּאֲשֶׁר הֶרְאָה
ט אֹתְךָ בָּהָר כֵּן יַעֲשׂוּ: וְעָשִׂיתָ אֵת חֲצַר הַמִּשְׁכָּן לִפְאַת שביעי
נֶגֶב־תֵּימָנָה קְלָעִים לֶחָצֵר שֵׁשׁ מָשְׁזָר מֵאָה בָאַמָּה אֹרֶךְ לַפֵּאָה
י הָאֶחָת: וְעַמֻּדָיו עֶשְׂרִים וְאַדְנֵיהֶם עֶשְׂרִים נְחֹשֶׁת וָוֵי הָעַמֻּדִים
יא וַחֲשֻׁקֵיהֶם כָּסֶף: וְכֵן לִפְאַת צָפוֹן בָּאֹרֶךְ קְלָעִים מֵאָה אֹרֶךְ
וְעַמֻּדָו עֶשְׂרִים וְאַדְנֵיהֶם עֶשְׂרִים נְחֹשֶׁת וָוֵי הָעַמֻּדִים וַחֲשֻׁקֵיהֶם
יב כָּסֶף: וְרֹחַב הֶחָצֵר לִפְאַת־יָם קְלָעִים חֲמִשִּׁים אַמָּה עַמֻּדֵיהֶם
יג עֲשָׂרָה וְאַדְנֵיהֶם עֲשָׂרָה: וְרֹחַב הֶחָצֵר לִפְאַת קֵדְמָה מִזְרָחָה

ז **בַּטַּבָּעֹת.** בְּאַרְבַּע טַבָּעוֹת שֶׁנַּעֲשׂוּ לַמִּכְבָּר:

ח **נְבוּב לֻחֹת.** כְּתַרְגּוּמוֹ: "חֲלִיל לוּחִין", לוּחוֹת עֲצֵי שִׁטִּים מִכָּל צַד וְהֶחָלָל בָּאֶמְצַע, וְלֹא יְהֵא כֻלּוֹ עֵץ אֶחָד שֶׁיְּהֵא עָבְיוֹ חָמֵשׁ אַמּוֹת עַל חָמֵשׁ אַמּוֹת כְּמִין סַדָּן:

ט **קְלָעִים.** עֲשׂוּיִין כְּמִין קַלְעֵי סְפִינָה נְקָבִים נְקָבִים, מַעֲשֵׂה קְלִיעָה וְלֹא מַעֲשֵׂה אוֹרֵג. וְתַרְגּוּמוֹ: "סְרָדִין", כְּתַרְגּוּמוֹ שֶׁל "מִכְבָּר" (לעיל פסוק ד) הַמְּתֻרְגָּם: "סְרָדָא", לְפִי שֶׁהֵן מְנֻקָּבִין כִּכְבָרָה: **לַפֵּאָה הָאֶחָת.** כָּל הָרוּחַ קָרוּי פֵּאָה:

י **וְעַמֻּדָיו עֶשְׂרִים.** חָמֵשׁ אַמּוֹת בֵּין עַמּוּד לְעַמּוּד: **וְאַדְנֵיהֶם נְחֹשֶׁת.** שֶׁל הָעַמּוּדִים. הָאֲדָנִים יוֹשְׁבִין עַל הָאָרֶץ וְהָעַמּוּדִים תְּקוּעִים לְתוֹכָן. וְהָיָה עוֹשֶׂה כְּמִין קֻנְדָּסִין שֶׁקּוֹרִין פלא"ש [בְּלַעַז] שָׁשׁ טְפָחִים וְרָחְבָּן שְׁלֹשָׁה, וְטַבַּעַת נְחֹשֶׁת קְבוּעָה בּוֹ בָּאֶמְצַע, וְכוֹרֵךְ שְׂפַת הַקֶּלַע סְבִיבָיו בְּמֵיתָרִים כְּנֶגֶד כָּל עַמּוּד, וְתוֹלֶה הַקֻּנְדָּס דֶּרֶךְ טַבַּעְתּוֹ בְּאֻנְקְלִי שֶׁבָּעַמּוּד הֶעָשׂוּי כְּמִין וָי"ו, רֹאשׁוֹ זָקוּף לְמַעְלָה

וְלֹאשׁוֹ אֶחָד תָּקוּעַ בָּעַמּוּד, כְּחוֹטָן שֶׁעוֹשִׂין לְהַצִּיב דְּלָתוֹת שֶׁקּוֹרִין גוני"ש, וְרֹחַב הַקֶּלַע תָּלוּי מִלְמַטָּה וְהִיא קוֹמַת מְחִצּוֹת הֶחָצֵר: **וָוֵי הָעַמֻּדִים.** הֵם הָאֻנְקְלָיוֹת: **וַחֲשֻׁקֵיהֶם.** מֻקָּפִין הָיוּ הָעַמּוּדִים בְּחוּטֵי כֶסֶף סָבִיב. וְאֵינִי יוֹדֵעַ אִם עַל פְּנֵי כֻלָּם אִם בְּרֹאשָׁם אִם בְּאֶמְצָעָם, אַךְ יוֹדֵעַ אֲנִי שֶׁ"חִשּׁוּק" לְשׁוֹן חֲגוֹרָה, שֶׁכָּךְ מָצִינוּ בִּפְלַגּוֹת רְאוּבֵן "גְּדוֹלִים חִקְקֵי לֵב" (שופטים ה, טו) תִּרְגּוּמוֹ: 'חֲשִׁיקִין':

יג **לִפְאַת קֵדְמָה מִזְרָחָה.** פְּנֵי הַמִּזְרָח קָרוּי 'קֶדֶם', לְשׁוֹן פָּנִים, 'אָחוֹר' לְשׁוֹן אֲחוֹרַיִם, לְפִיכָךְ מִזְרָח קָרוּי קֶדֶם שֶׁהוּא פָנִים, וּמַעֲרָב קָרוּי אָחוֹר, כְּמָה דְאַתְּ אָמַר: "הַיָּם הָאַחֲרוֹן" (דברים יא, כד) – "יַמָּא מַעַרְבָאָה" (אונקלוס שם): **חֲמִשִּׁים אַמָּה.** אוֹתָן חֲמִשִּׁים אַמָּה לֹא הָיוּ סְתוּמִים כֻּלָּם בִּקְלָעִים, לְפִי שֶׁשָּׁם הַפֶּתַח, אֶלָּא חָמֵשׁ עֶשְׂרֵה אַמָּה קְלָעִים לְכֶתֶף הַפֶּתַח מִכָּאן וְכֵן לַכָּתֵף הַשֵּׁנִית, נִשְׁאַר רֹחַב חֲלַל הַפֶּתַח בֵּינְתַיִם עֶשְׂרִים אַמָּה, וְזֶהוּ שֶׁנֶּאֱמַר: "וּלְשַׁעַר הֶחָצֵר מָסָךְ עֶשְׂרִים אַמָּה" (להלן פסוק טז), וִילוֹן לְהֶסֶךְ כְּנֶגֶד הַפֶּתַח עֶשְׂרִים אַמָּה אֹרֶךְ, כְּרֹחַב הַפֶּתַח:

יד חֲמִשִּׁים אַמָּה: וַחֲמֵשׁ עֶשְׂרֵה אַמָּה קְלָעִים לַכָּתֵף עַמֻּדֵיהֶם
טו שְׁלֹשָׁה וְאַדְנֵיהֶם שְׁלֹשָׁה: וְלַכָּתֵף הַשֵּׁנִית חֲמֵשׁ עֶשְׂרֵה קְלָעִים
טז עַמֻּדֵיהֶם שְׁלֹשָׁה וְאַדְנֵיהֶם שְׁלֹשָׁה: וּלְשַׁעַר הֶחָצֵר מָסָךְ
עֶשְׂרִים אַמָּה תְּכֵלֶת וְאַרְגָּמָן וְתוֹלַעַת שָׁנִי וְשֵׁשׁ מָשְׁזָר מַעֲשֵׂה

מפטיר
יז רֹקֵם עַמֻּדֵיהֶם אַרְבָּעָה וְאַדְנֵיהֶם אַרְבָּעָה: כָּל־עַמּוּדֵי הֶחָצֵר
יח סָבִיב מְחֻשָּׁקִים כֶּסֶף וָוֵיהֶם כָּסֶף וְאַדְנֵיהֶם נְחֹשֶׁת: אֹרֶךְ הֶחָצֵר
מֵאָה בָאַמָּה וְרֹחַב חֲמִשִּׁים בַּחֲמִשִּׁים וְקֹמָה חָמֵשׁ אַמּוֹת שֵׁשׁ
יט מָשְׁזָר וְאַדְנֵיהֶם נְחֹשֶׁת: לְכֹל כְּלֵי הַמִּשְׁכָּן בְּכֹל עֲבֹדָתוֹ וְכָל־
יְתֵדֹתָיו וְכָל־יִתְדֹת הֶחָצֵר נְחֹשֶׁת:

יד. **עַמֻּדֵיהֶם שְׁלֹשָׁה.** חָמֵשׁ אַמּוֹת בֵּין עַמּוּד לְעַמּוּד, בֵּין עַמּוּד שֶׁבְּרֹאשׁ הַדָּרוֹם הָעוֹמֵד בְּמִקְצוֹעַ דְּרוֹמִית מִזְרָחִית עַד עַמּוּד שֶׁהוּא מִן הַשְּׁלֹשָׁה שֶׁבַּמִּזְרָח חָמֵשׁ אַמּוֹת, וּמִמֶּנּוּ לַשֵּׁנִי חָמֵשׁ אַמּוֹת, וּמִן הַשֵּׁנִי לַשְּׁלִישִׁי חָמֵשׁ אַמּוֹת, וְכֵן לַכָּתֵף הַשֵּׁנִית, וְאַרְבָּעָה עַמּוּדִים לַמָּסָךְ. הֲרֵי עֲשָׂרָה עַמּוּדִים לַמִּזְרָח כְּנֶגֶד עֲשָׂרָה לַמַּעֲרָב:

יז. **כָּל עַמּוּדֵי הֶחָצֵר סָבִיב וְגוֹ'.** לְפִי שֶׁלֹּא פֵּרֵשׁ וָוִין וַחֲשׁוּקִים וְאַדְנֵי נְחֹשֶׁת אֶלָּא לַעַמּוּד וְלַדָּרוֹם, אֲבָל לַמִּזְרָח וְלַמַּעֲרָב לֹא נֶאֱמַר וָוִין וַחֲשׁוּקִים וְאַדְנֵי נְחֹשֶׁת, לְכָךְ בָּא וְלִמֵּד כָּאן:

יח. **אֹרֶךְ הֶחָצֵר.** הַצָּפוֹן וְהַדָּרוֹם שֶׁמִּן הַמִּזְרָח לַמַּעֲרָב ״מֵאָה בָאַמָּה״: **וְרֹחַב חֲמִשִּׁים בַּחֲמִשִּׁים.** חָצֵר שֶׁבַּמִּזְרָח הָיְתָה מְרֻבַּעַת חֲמִשִּׁים עַל חֲמִשִּׁים, שֶׁהַמִּשְׁכָּן אָרְכּוֹ שְׁלֹשִׁים וְרָחְבּוֹ עֶשֶׂר, הֶעֱמִיד מִזְרַח פִּתְחוֹ בִּשְׂפַת חֲמִשִּׁים הַחִיצוֹנִים שֶׁל אֹרֶךְ הֶחָצֵר, נִמְצָא כֻלּוֹ בַּחֲמִשִּׁים הַפְּנִימִיִּים, וְכָלֶה אָרְכּוֹ לְסוֹף שְׁלֹשִׁים, נִמְצְאוּ עֶשְׂרִים אַמָּה רֶוַח לַאֲחוֹרָיו בֵּין הַקְּלָעִים שֶׁבַּמַּעֲרָב לִירִיעוֹת שֶׁל אֲחוֹרֵי הַמִּשְׁכָּן.

וְרֹחַב הַמִּשְׁכָּן עֶשֶׂר אַמּוֹת בְּאֶמְצַע רֹחַב הֶחָצֵר, נִמְצְאוּ לוֹ עֶשְׂרִים אַמָּה רֶוַח לַצָּפוֹן וְלַדָּרוֹם מִן קַלְעֵי הֶחָצֵר לִירִיעוֹת הַמִּשְׁכָּן, וְכֵן לַמַּעֲרָב, וַחֲמִשִּׁים עַל חֲמִשִּׁים חָצֵר לְפָנָיו: **וְקֹמָה חָמֵשׁ אַמּוֹת.** גֹּבַהּ מְחִצּוֹת הֶחָצֵר, וְהוּא רֹחַב הַקְּלָעִים: **וְאַדְנֵיהֶם נְחֹשֶׁת.** לְהָבִיא אַדְנֵי הַמָּסָךְ, שֶׁלֹּא תֹאמַר לֹא נֶאֶמְרוּ אַדְנֵי נְחֹשֶׁת אֶלָּא לְעַמּוּדֵי הַקְּלָעִים, אֲבָל אַדְנֵי הַמָּסָךְ שֶׁל מִין אַחֵר. כָּךְ נִרְאֶה בְעֵינַי שֶׁלְּכָךְ חָזַר וּשְׁנָאָן:

יט. **לְכֹל כְּלֵי הַמִּשְׁכָּן.** שֶׁהָיוּ צְרִיכִין לַהֲקָמָתוֹ וּלְהוֹרָדָתוֹ, כְּגוֹן מַקָּבוֹת לִתְקֹעַ יְתֵדוֹת וְעַמּוּדִים: **יְתֵדֹת.** כְּמִין נַגְרֵי נְחֹשֶׁת עֲשׂוּיִין לִירִיעוֹת הָאֹהֶל וּלְקַלְעֵי הֶחָצֵר קְשׁוּרִים בְּמֵיתָרִים סָבִיב סָבִיב בְּשִׁפּוּלֵיהֶן, כְּדֵי שֶׁלֹּא תָּהֵא הָרוּחַ מַגְבִּיהָתָן, וְאֵינִי יוֹדֵעַ אִם תְּחוּבִין בָּאָרֶץ, אוֹ קְשׁוּרִין וּתְלוּיִין וְכָבְדָּן מַכְבִּיד שִׁפּוּלֵי הַיְרִיעוֹת שֶׁלֹּא יָנוּעוּ בָרוּחַ. וְאוֹמֵר אֲנִי שֶׁשְּׁמָן מוֹכִיחַ עֲלֵיהֶם שֶׁהֵם תְּקוּעִים בָּאָרֶץ, לְכָךְ נִקְרְאוּ ״יְתֵדֹת״, וּמִקְרָא זֶה מְסַיְּעֵנִי: ״אֹהֶל בַּל יִצְעָן בַּל יִסַּע יְתֵדֹתָיו לָנֶצַח״ (ישעיה לג, כ):

שמות | פרק כח

כא תצוה

כא וְאַתָּה תְּצַוֶּה ׀ אֶת־בְּנֵי יִשְׂרָאֵל וְיִקְחוּ אֵלֶיךָ שֶׁמֶן זַיִת זָךְ כָּתִית לַמָּאוֹר לְהַעֲלֹת נֵר תָּמִיד: בְּאֹהֶל מוֹעֵד מִחוּץ לַפָּרֹכֶת אֲשֶׁר עַל־הָעֵדֻת יַעֲרֹךְ אֹתוֹ אַהֲרֹן וּבָנָיו מֵעֶרֶב עַד־בֹּקֶר לִפְנֵי יְהֹוָה חֻקַּת עוֹלָם לְדֹרֹתָם מֵאֵת בְּנֵי יִשְׂרָאֵל:

כח א וְאַתָּה הַקְרֵב אֵלֶיךָ אֶת־אַהֲרֹן אָחִיךָ וְאֶת־בָּנָיו אִתּוֹ מִתּוֹךְ בְּנֵי יִשְׂרָאֵל לְכַהֲנוֹ־לִי אַהֲרֹן נָדָב וַאֲבִיהוּא אֶלְעָזָר וְאִיתָמָר בְּנֵי אַהֲרֹן: ב וְעָשִׂיתָ בִגְדֵי־קֹדֶשׁ לְאַהֲרֹן אָחִיךָ לְכָבוֹד וּלְתִפְאָרֶת: ג וְאַתָּה תְּדַבֵּר אֶל־כָּל־חַכְמֵי־לֵב אֲשֶׁר מִלֵּאתִיו רוּחַ חָכְמָה וְעָשׂוּ אֶת־בִּגְדֵי אַהֲרֹן לְקַדְּשׁוֹ לְכַהֲנוֹ־לִי: ד וְאֵלֶּה הַבְּגָדִים אֲשֶׁר יַעֲשׂוּ חֹשֶׁן וְאֵפוֹד

כ וְאַתָּה תְּצַוֶּה. זָךְ. בְּלִי שְׁמָרִים, כְּמוֹ שֶׁשָּׁנִינוּ בִּמְנָחוֹת (דף פ ע"ח), מְגַרְגְּרוֹ בְּרֹאשׁ הַזַּיִת וְכוּ': כָּתִית: הַזֵּיתִים, כּוֹתֵשׁ בְּמַכְתֶּשֶׁת וְאֵינוֹ טוֹחֲנָן בָּרֵחַיִם, כְּדֵי שֶׁלֹּא יְהוּ בּוֹ שְׁמָרִים, וְאַחַר שֶׁהוֹצִיא טִפָּה רִאשׁוֹנָה מַכְנִיסָן לָרֵחַיִם וְטוֹחֲנָן. וְהַשֶּׁמֶן הַשֵּׁנִי פָּסוּל לַמְּנוֹרָה וְכָשֵׁר לַמְּנָחוֹת, שֶׁנֶּאֱמַר: "כָּתִית לַמָּאוֹר", וְלֹא כָתִית לַמְּנָחוֹת (סם): לְהַעֲלֹת נֵר תָּמִיד. מַדְלִיק עַד שֶׁתְּהֵא שַׁלְהֶבֶת עוֹלָה מֵאֵלֶיהָ: תָּמִיד. כָּל לַיְלָה וָלַיְלָה קָרוּי 'תָּמִיד', כְּמוֹ שֶׁאַתָּה אוֹמֵר: "עֹלַת תָּמִיד" (להלן כט, מב; במדבר כח, ו) וְאֵינָהּ אֶלָּא מִיּוֹם לְיוֹם, וְכֵן בְּמִנְחַת חֲבִתִּין: "תָּמִיד" (ויקרא ו, ג) וְאֵינָהּ אֶלָּא מַחֲצִיתָהּ בַּבֹּקֶר וּמַחֲצִיתָהּ בָּעֶרֶב. אֲבָל "תָּמִיד" הָאָמוּר בְּלֶחֶם הַפָּנִים (לעיל כה, ל) מִשַּׁבָּת לְשַׁבָּת הוּא:

כא] מֵעֶרֶב עַד בֹּקֶר. תֵּן לָהּ מִדָּתָהּ שֶׁתְּהֵא דוֹלֶקֶת מֵעֶרֶב וְעַד בֹּקֶר. וְשִׁעֲרוּ חֲכָמִים חֲצִי לֹג לְלֵילֵי טֵבֵת הָאֲרֻכִּין, וְכֵן לְכָל הַלֵּילוֹת, וְאִם יִוָּתֵר אֵין בְּכָךְ כְּלוּם:

פרק כח

א] וְאַתָּה הַקְרֵב אֵלֶיךָ. לְאַחַר שֶׁתִּגָּמֵר מְלֶאכֶת הַמִּשְׁכָּן:

ג] לְקַדְּשׁוֹ לְכַהֲנוֹ־לִי. לְקַדְּשׁוֹ לְהַכְנִיסוֹ בִּכְהֻנָּה עַל יְדֵי הַבְּגָדִים, שֶׁיְּהֵא כֹהֵן לִי. וּלְשׁוֹן 'כְּהֻנָּה' שֵׁרוּת הוּא, שירייטרי"א בְּלַעַז:

ד] חֹשֶׁן. תַּכְשִׁיט כְּנֶגֶד הַלֵּב: וְאֵפוֹד. לֹא שָׁמַעְתִּי וְלֹא מָצָאתִי בַּבָּרַיְתָא פֵּרוּשׁ תַּבְנִיתוֹ, וְלִבִּי אוֹמֵר לִי שֶׁהוּא חָגוּר לוֹ מֵאֲחוֹרָיו, רָחָב כְּרֹחַב גַּב אִישׁ כְּמִין סִינָר שֶׁקּוֹרִין רענ"ט שֶׁחוֹגְרוֹת הַשָּׂרוֹת כְּשֶׁרוֹכְבוֹת עַל הַסּוּסִים, כָּךְ מַעֲשֵׂהוּ מִלְּמַטָּה, שֶׁנֶּאֱמַר: "וְדָוִד חָגוּר אֵפוֹד בָּד" (שמואל ב' ו, יד), לָמַדְנוּ שֶׁהָאֵפוֹד חֲגוֹרָה הִיא. וְאִי אֶפְשָׁר לוֹמַר שֶׁאֵין בּוֹ אֶלָּא הַחֲגוֹרָה לְבַדָּהּ, שֶׁהֲרֵי נֶאֱמַר: "וַיִּתֵּן עָלָיו אֶת הָאֵפֹד" (ויקרא ח, ז), וְאַחַר כָּךְ: "וַיַּחְגֹּר אֹתוֹ בְּחֵשֶׁב הָאֵפֹד" וְתִרְגֵּם אוּנְקְלוּס: "בְּהֶמְיַן אֵפוֹדָא", לָמַדְנוּ שֶׁהַחֵשֶׁב הוּא הַחֲגוֹר, וְהָאֵפוֹד שֵׁם תַּכְשִׁיט לְבַדּוֹ. וְאִי אֶפְשָׁר לוֹמַר שֶׁעַל שֵׁם שְׁתֵּי הַכְּתֵפוֹת שֶׁבּוֹ הוּא קָרוּי אֵפוֹד, שֶׁהֲרֵי נֶאֱמַר: "שְׁתֵּי כִתְפוֹת הָאֵפוֹד" (להלן פסוק כו), לָמַדְנוּ שֶׁהָאֵפוֹד שֵׁם לְבַד, וְהַכְּתֵפוֹת שֵׁם לְבַד, וְהַחֵשֶׁב שֵׁם לְבַד. לְכָךְ אֲנִי אוֹמֵר שֶׁעַל שֵׁם הַסִּינָר שֶׁל מַטָּה קָרוּי אֵפוֹד, עַל שֵׁם שֶׁאוֹפְדוֹ וּמְקַשְּׁטוֹ בּוֹ, כְּמוֹ שֶׁנֶּאֱמַר: "וַיֶּאְפֹּד לוֹ בּוֹ" (ויקרא ח, ז), וְהַחֵשֶׁב הוּא חֲגוֹר שֶׁלְּמַעְלָה הֵימֶנּוּ, וְהַכְּתֵפוֹת קְבוּעוֹת בּוֹ. וְעוֹד אוֹמֵר לִי לִבִּי שֶׁיֵּשׁ רְאָיָה שֶׁהוּא מִין לְבוּשׁ, שֶׁתִּרְגֵּם יוֹנָתָן: "וְדָוִד חָגוּר אֵפוֹד בָּד" (שמואל ב' ו, יד) – "כַּרְדּוּט דְּבוּץ",

פרק כח | שמות

וּמְעִיל וּכְתֹנֶת תַּשְׁבֵּץ מִצְנֶפֶת וְאַבְנֵט וְעָשׂוּ בִגְדֵי־קֹדֶשׁ לְאַהֲרֹן אָחִיךָ וּלְבָנָיו לְכַהֲנוֹ־לִי: וְהֵם יִקְחוּ אֶת־הַזָּהָב וְאֶת־הַתְּכֵלֶת וְאֶת־הָאַרְגָּמָן וְאֶת־תּוֹלַעַת הַשָּׁנִי וְאֶת־הַשֵּׁשׁ: וְעָשׂוּ אֶת־הָאֵפֹד זָהָב תְּכֵלֶת וְאַרְגָּמָן תּוֹלַעַת שָׁנִי וְשֵׁשׁ מָשְׁזָר

ה

ו

וְתִרְגֵּם כְּמוֹ כֵן "מְעִילִים" – "כַּרְדּוּטִין" בְּמַעֲשֵׂה תָּמָר אֲחוֹת אַבְשָׁלוֹם, "כִּי כֵן תִּלְבַּשְׁןָ בְנוֹת הַמֶּלֶךְ הַבְּתוּלוֹת מְעִילִים" (שמואל ב׳ יג, יח). וּמְעִיל. הוּא כְּמִין חָלוּק, וְכֵן הַכְּתֹנֶת, אֶלָּא שֶׁהַכְּתֹנֶת סָמוּךְ לִבְשָׂרוֹ, וּמְעִיל קָרוּי חָלוּק הָעֶלְיוֹן: תַּשְׁבֵּץ. עֲשׂוּיִין מִשְׁבְּצוֹת לְנוֹי. וְהַמִּשְׁבְּצוֹת הֵם כְּמִין גּוּמּוֹת הָעֲשׂוּיוֹת בְּתַכְשִׁיטֵי זָהָב לְמוֹשַׁב קְבִיעַת אֲבָנִים טוֹבוֹת וּמַרְגָּלִיּוֹת, כְּמוֹ שֶׁנֶּאֱמַר בְּאַבְנֵי הָאֵפוֹד: "מֻסַבֹּת מִשְׁבְּצוֹת זָהָב" (להלן פסוק יא), וּבִלְעַז קוֹרְחִין אוֹתוֹ קשטונ"ש: מִצְנֶפֶת. כְּמִין כִּפַּת כּוֹבַע שֶׁקּוֹרִין קוֹפיי"א, שֶׁהֲרֵי בְּמָקוֹם אַחֵר קוֹרֵא לָהֶם "מִגְבָּעוֹת" (להלן כט, ט) וּמְתַרְגְּמִינַן "כּוֹבָעִין": וְאַבְנֵט. הִיא חֲגוֹרָה עַל הַכְּתֹנֶת, וְהָאֵפוֹד חֲגוֹרָה עַל הַמְּעִיל, כְּמוֹ שֶׁמָּצִינוּ בְּסֵדֶר לְבִישָׁתָן: "וַיִּתֵּן עָלָיו אֶת הַכֻּתֹּנֶת וַיַּחְגֹּר אֹתוֹ בָּאַבְנֵט, וַיַּלְבֵּשׁ אֹתוֹ אֶת הַמְּעִיל וַיִּתֵּן עָלָיו אֶת הָאֵפֹד" (ויקרא ח): בִּגְדֵי קֹדֶשׁ. מִתְּרוּמָה הַמֻּקְדֶּשֶׁת לִשְׁמִי יַעֲשׂוּ אוֹתָם:

ה. וְהֵם יִקְחוּ. חוֹתָם חַכְמֵי לֵב שֶׁיַּעֲשׂוּ הַבְּגָדִים יְקַבְּלוּ מִן הַמִּתְנַדְּבִים "אֶת הַזָּהָב וְאֶת הַתְּכֵלֶת" לַעֲשׂוֹת מֵהֶן אֶת הַבְּגָדִים:

ו. וְעָשׂוּ אֶת הָאֵפֹד. אִם בָּאתִי לְפָרֵשׁ מַעֲשֵׂה הָאֵפוֹד וְהַחֹשֶׁן עַל סֵדֶר הַמִּקְרָאוֹת, הֲרֵי פֵּרוּשָׁן פְּרָקִים, וְיִשְׁגֶּה הַקּוֹרֵא בְּצֵרוּפָן. לְכָךְ אֲנִי כּוֹתֵב מַעֲשֵׂיהֶם כְּמוֹת שֶׁהוּא לְמַעַן יָרוּץ קוֹרֵא בוֹ, וְאַחַר כָּךְ אֲפָרֵשׁ עַל סֵדֶר הַמִּקְרָאוֹת. הָאֵפוֹד עָשׂוּי כְּמִין סִינָר שֶׁל נָשִׁים רוֹכְבוֹת סוּסִים, וְחוֹגֵר אוֹתוֹ מֵאֲחוֹרָיו כְּנֶגֶד לִבּוֹ לְמַטָּה מֵאֲצִילָיו, רָחְבּוֹ כְּמִדַּת רֹחַב גַּבּוֹ שֶׁל אָדָם וְיוֹתֵר, וּמַגִּיעַ עַד עֲקֵבָיו. וְהַחֵשֶׁב מְחֻבָּר בְּרֹאשׁוֹ עַל פְּנֵי רָחְבּוֹ מַעֲשֵׂה אוֹרֵג, וּמַאֲרִיךְ לְכָאן וּלְכָאן כְּדֵי לְהַקִּיף וְלֶאֱגֹד בּוֹ. וְהַכְּתֵפוֹת מְחֻבָּרוֹת בַּחֵשֶׁב, אַחַת לְיָמִין וְאַחַת לִשְׂמֹאל, מֵאֲחוֹרֵי הַכֹּהֵן לִשְׁנֵי קְצוֹת רָחְבּוֹ שֶׁל סִינָר, וּכְשֶׁזּוֹקְפָן עוֹמְדוֹת לוֹ עַל שְׁנֵי כְּתֵפָיו. וְהֵן כְּמִין שְׁתֵּי רְצוּעוֹת עֲשׂוּיוֹת מִמִּין הָאֵפוֹד, אֲרֻכּוֹת כְּדֵי שִׁעוּר לְזָקְפָן אֵצֶל צַוָּארוֹ מִכָּאן וּמִכָּאן, וְנִכְפָּלוֹת לִפְנֵי לְמַטָּה מִכְּתֵפָיו מְעַט. וְאַבְנֵי הַשֹּׁהַם קְבוּעוֹת בָּהֶם, אַחַת עַל כֶּתֵף יָמִין וְאַחַת עַל כֶּתֵף שְׂמֹאל, וְהַמִּשְׁבְּצוֹת נְתוּנוֹת בְּרָאשֵׁיהֶם לִפְנֵי כְּתֵפָיו, וּשְׁתֵּי עֲבוֹתוֹת הַזָּהָב תְּחוּבוֹת בִּשְׁתֵּי טַבָּעוֹת שֶׁבַּחֹשֶׁן בִּשְׁנֵי קְצוֹת רָחְבּוֹ הָעֶלְיוֹן, אַחַת לְיָמִין וְאַחַת לִשְׂמֹאל, וּשְׁנֵי רָאשֵׁי הַשַּׁרְשֶׁרֶת תְּקוּעִין בַּמִּשְׁבֶּצֶת לְיָמִין, וְכֵן שְׁנֵי רָאשֵׁי הַשַּׁרְשֶׁרֶת הַשְּׂמָאלִית תְּקוּעִין בַּמִּשְׁבֶּצֶת שֶׁבַּכָּתֵף שְׂמֹאל, נִמְצָא הַחֹשֶׁן תָּלוּי בַּמִּשְׁבְּצוֹת הָאֵפוֹד עַל לִבּוֹ מִלְּפָנָיו. וְעוֹד שְׁתֵּי טַבָּעוֹת בִּשְׁנֵי קְצוֹת הַחֹשֶׁן בְּתַחְתִּיתוֹ, וּכְנֶגְדָּם שְׁתֵּי טַבָּעוֹת בִּשְׁתֵּי כִתְפוֹת הָאֵפוֹד מִלְּמַטָּה בְּרֹאשׁוֹ הַתַּחְתּוֹן הַמְחֻבָּר בַּחֵשֶׁב, טַבְּעוֹת הַחֹשֶׁן אֶל מוּל טַבְּעוֹת הָאֵפוֹד שׁוֹכְבִים זֶה עַל זֶה, וּמְרַכְּסָן בִּפְתִיל תְּכֵלֶת תָּחוּב בַּטַּבָּעוֹת שֶׁל אֵפוֹד וְחֹשֶׁן, שֶׁיְּהֵא תַחְתִּית הַחֹשֶׁן דָּבוּק לַחֵשֶׁב הָאֵפוֹד, וְלֹא יְהֵא נָד וְנִבְדָּל הוֹלֵךְ וָחוֹזֵר: זָהָב תְּכֵלֶת וְאַרְגָּמָן תּוֹלַעַת שָׁנִי וְשֵׁשׁ מָשְׁזָר. חֲמֵשֶׁת מִינִים הַלָּלוּ שְׁזוּרִין בְּכָל חוּט וָחוּט. הָיוּ מְרַדְּדִין אֶת הַזָּהָב כְּמִין טַסִּים דַּקִּים וְקוֹצְצִין פְּתִילִים מֵהֶם, וְטוֹוִין אוֹתָן חוּט שֶׁל זָהָב עִם שִׁשָּׁה חוּטִין שֶׁל תְּכֵלֶת, וְחוּט שֶׁל זָהָב עִם שִׁשָּׁה חוּטִין שֶׁל אַרְגָּמָן, וְכֵן בְּתוֹלַעַת שָׁנִי וְכֵן בַּשֵּׁשׁ, שֶׁכָּל הַמִּינִין חוּטָן כָּפוּל שִׁשָּׁה, וְחוּט שֶׁל זָהָב עִם כָּל אֶחָד וְאֶחָד. וְאַחַר כָּךְ שׁוֹזֵר אֶת כֻּלָּם כְּאֶחָד, נִמְצָא חוּטָן כָּפוּל עֶשְׂרִים וּשְׁמוֹנָה. וְכֵן מְפֹרָשׁ בְּמַסֶּכֶת יוֹמָא (דף עב ע"א), וְלָמֵד מִן הַמִּקְרָא הַזֶּה: "וַיְרַקְּעוּ אֶת פַּחֵי הַזָּהָב וְקִצֵּץ פְּתִילִם לַעֲשׂוֹת בְּתוֹךְ הַתְּכֵלֶת וּבְתוֹךְ הָאַרְגָּמָן" וְגוֹ' (להלן לט, ג), לְמַדְנוּ שֶׁחוּט שֶׁל זָהָב שָׁזוּר עִם כָּל מִין וָמִין: מַעֲשֵׂה חֹשֵׁב. כְּבָר פֵּרַשְׁתִּי (רש"י לעיל כו, א) שֶׁהִיא אֲרִיגַת שְׁתֵּי קִירוֹת, שֶׁאֵין צוּרַת שְׁנֵי עֲבָרֶיהָ דּוֹמוֹת זוֹ לָזוֹ:

ז מַעֲשֵׂה חֹשֵׁב: שְׁתֵּי כְתֵפֹת חֹבְרֹת יִהְיֶה־לּוֹ אֶל־שְׁנֵי קְצוֹתָיו
ח וְחֻבָּר: וְחֵשֶׁב אֲפֻדָּתוֹ אֲשֶׁר עָלָיו כְּמַעֲשֵׂהוּ מִמֶּנּוּ יִהְיֶה זָהָב
ט תְּכֵלֶת וְאַרְגָּמָן וְתוֹלַעַת שָׁנִי וְשֵׁשׁ מָשְׁזָר: וְלָקַחְתָּ אֶת־שְׁתֵּי
י אַבְנֵי־שֹׁהַם וּפִתַּחְתָּ עֲלֵיהֶם שְׁמוֹת בְּנֵי יִשְׂרָאֵל: שִׁשָּׁה
מִשְּׁמֹתָם עַל הָאֶבֶן הָאֶחָת וְאֶת־שְׁמוֹת הַשִּׁשָּׁה הַנּוֹתָרִים עַל־
יא הָאֶבֶן הַשֵּׁנִית כְּתוֹלְדֹתָם: מַעֲשֵׂה חָרַשׁ אֶבֶן פִּתּוּחֵי חֹתָם
תְּפַתַּח אֶת־שְׁתֵּי הָאֲבָנִים עַל־שְׁמֹת בְּנֵי יִשְׂרָאֵל מֻסַבֹּת
יב מִשְׁבְּצוֹת זָהָב תַּעֲשֶׂה אֹתָם: וְשַׂמְתָּ אֶת־שְׁתֵּי הָאֲבָנִים עַל
כִּתְפֹת הָאֵפֹד אַבְנֵי זִכָּרֹן לִבְנֵי יִשְׂרָאֵל וְנָשָׂא אַהֲרֹן אֶת־שְׁמוֹתָם

ז **שְׁתֵּי כְתֵפֹת וְגוֹ׳.** הַסִּינָר מִלְּמַטָּה, וְהַחֵשֶׁב הָאָחוּד הִיא הַחֲגוֹרָה, וְעוֹמְדָה לוֹ מִלְּמַעְלָה כְּנֶגֶד סִינָר הַנָּשִׁים. וּמִגַּבּוֹ שֶׁל כֹּהֵן הָיוּ מְחֻבָּרוֹת בַּחֵשֶׁב שְׁתֵּי חֲתִיכוֹת כְּמִין שְׁתֵּי רְצוּעוֹת רְחָבוֹת, אַחַת כְּנֶגֶד כָּל כָּתֵף וְכָתֵף, וְזוֹקְפָן עַל שְׁתֵּי כְתֵפוֹתָיו עַד שֶׁנִּכְפָּלוֹת לְפָנָיו כְּנֶגֶד הֶחָזֶה, וְעַל יְדֵי חִבּוּרָן לְטַבְּעוֹת הַחֹשֶׁן נֶאֱחָזִין מִלְּפָנָיו כְּנֶגֶד לִבּוֹ שֶׁאֵין נוֹפְלוֹת, כְּמוֹ שֶׁמְּפֹרָשׁ בָּעִנְיָן; וְהָיוּ זְקוּפוֹת וְהוֹלְכוֹת כְּנֶגֶד כְּתֵפָיו, וּשְׁתֵּי אַבְנֵי הַשֹּׁהַם קְבוּעוֹת בָּהֶן, אַחַת בְּכָל אַחַת: **אֶל שְׁנֵי קְצוֹתָיו.** אֶל רֹחְבּוֹ שֶׁל אֵפוֹד, שֶׁלֹּא הָיָה רָחְבּוֹ מָלֵא כְּנֶגֶד גַּבּוֹ שֶׁל כֹּהֵן, וְגָבְהוֹ עַד כְּנֶגֶד הָאֲצִילִים שֶׁקּוֹרִין קוּדי״ש, שֶׁנֶּאֱמַר: "לֹא יַחְגְּרוּ בַּיָּזַע" (יחזקאל מד, יח), אֵין חוֹגְרִין בִּמְקוֹם זֵעָה, לֹא לְמַעְלָה מֵאַצִּילֵיהֶם וְלֹא לְמַטָּה מִמָּתְנֵיהֶם, אֶלָּא כְּנֶגֶד אַצִּילֵיהֶם: **וְחֻבָּר.** הָאֵפוֹד עִם אוֹתָן שְׁתֵּי כְּתֵפוֹת הָאֵפוֹד, יְחַבֵּר אוֹתָם בִּמְחַט לְמַטָּה בַּחֵשֶׁב, וְלֹא יְאַרְגֵם עִמּוֹ, אֶלָּא אוֹרְגָם לְבַד וְאַחַר כָּךְ מְחַבְּרָם:

ח **וְחֵשֶׁב אֲפֻדָּתוֹ.** חֲגוֹר שֶׁעַל יָדוֹ הוּא מְאַפְּדוֹ וּמְתַקְּנוֹ לַכֹּהֵן וּמְקַשְּׁטוֹ: **אֲשֶׁר עָלָיו.** לְמַעְלָה בִּשְׂפַת הַסִּינָר, וְהִיא הַחֲגוֹרָה: **כְּמַעֲשֵׂהוּ.** כַּאֲרִיגַת הַסִּינָר מַעֲשֵׂה חוֹשֵׁב וּמֵחֲמֵשֶׁת מִינִים, כָּךְ אֲרִיגַת הַחֵשֶׁב

מַעֲשֵׂה חוֹשֵׁב וּמֵחֲמֵשֶׁת מִינִים: **מִמֶּנּוּ יִהְיֶה.** עִמּוֹ הָיָה אָרוּג, וְלֹא יַאַרְגֶנּוּ לְבַד וִיחַבְּרֶנּוּ:

י **כְּתוֹלְדֹתָם.** כַּסֵּדֶר שֶׁנּוֹלְדוּ: רְאוּבֵן, שִׁמְעוֹן, לֵוִי, יְהוּדָה, דָּן, נַפְתָּלִי עַל הָאַחַת; וְעַל הַשֵּׁנִית; גָּד, אָשֵׁר, יִשָּׂשכָר, זְבוּלֻן, יוֹסֵף, בִּנְיָמִין מָלֵא, שֶׁכֵּן הוּא כָתוּב בִּמְקוֹם תּוֹלַדְתּוֹ (בראשית לה, יח), עֶשְׂרִים וְחָמֵשׁ אוֹתִיּוֹת בְּכָל אַחַת וְאַחַת:

יא **מַעֲשֵׂה חָרַשׁ אֶבֶן.** מַעֲשֵׂה אֻמָּן שֶׁל אֲבָנִים. "חָרָשׁ" זֶה, דָּבוּק הוּא לַתֵּבָה שֶׁלְּאַחֲרָיו וּלְפִיכָךְ הוּא נָקוּד פַּתָּח בְּסוֹפוֹ, וְכֵן: "חָרַשׁ עֵצִים נָטָה קָו" (ישעיה מד, יג), חָרָשׁ שֶׁל עֵצִים, וְכֵן: "חָרַשׁ בַּרְזֶל מַעֲצָד" (שם פסוק יב), כָּל אֵלֶּה דְּבוּקִים וּפְתוּחִים: **פִּתּוּחֵי חֹתָם.** כְּתַרְגוּמוֹ: "כְּתָב מְפֹרָשׁ כִּגְלָף דְּעִזְקָא", חֲרוּצוֹת הָאוֹתִיּוֹת בְּתוֹכָן כְּמוֹ שֶׁחוֹרְצִין חוֹתְמֵי טַבָּעוֹת שֶׁהֵם לַחְתּוֹם אִגְּרוֹת, כְּתָב נִכָּר וּמְפֹרָשׁ: **עַל שְׁמֹת.** כְּמוֹ בִּשְׁמוֹת: **מֻסַבֹּת מִשְׁבְּצוֹת.** מֻקָּפוֹת הָאֲבָנִים בְּמִשְׁבְּצוֹת זָהָב, שֶׁעוֹשֶׂה מוֹשַׁב הָאֶבֶן בְּזָהָב כְּמִין גּוּמָא לְמִדַּת הָאֶבֶן וּמַשְׁקִיעָהּ בַּמִּשְׁבֶּצֶת, נִמְצֵאת הַמִּשְׁבֶּצֶת סוֹבֶבֶת אֶת הָאֶבֶן סָבִיב, וּמְחַבֵּר הַמִּשְׁבָּצוֹת בְּכִתְפוֹת הָאֵפוֹד:

יב **לְזִכָּרֹן.** שֶׁיִּרְאֶה הַקָּדוֹשׁ בָּרוּךְ הוּא הַשְּׁבָטִים כְּתוּבִים לְפָנָיו וְיִזְכֹּר צִדְקָתָם:

תצוה | 464   פרק כח | שמות

שני לִפְנֵ֥י יְהוָ֖ה עַל־שְׁתֵ֣י כְתֵפָ֑יו לְזִכָּרֹֽן׃ וְעָשִׂ֥יתָ יג
מִשְׁבְּצֹ֖ת זָהָֽב׃ וּשְׁתֵּ֤י שַׁרְשְׁרֹת֙ זָהָ֣ב טָה֔וֹר מִגְבָּלֹ֖ת תַּעֲשֶׂ֣ה יד
אֹתָ֑ם מַעֲשֵׂ֣ה עֲבֹ֑ת וְנָתַתָּ֛ה אֶת־שַׁרְשְׁרֹ֥ת הָעֲבֹתֹ֖ת עַל־
הַֽמִּשְׁבְּצֹֽת׃ וְעָשִׂ֜יתָ חֹ֣שֶׁן מִשְׁפָּט֮ מַעֲשֵׂ֣ה חֹשֵׁב֒ טו
כְּמַעֲשֵׂ֣ה אֵפֹ֖ד תַּעֲשֶׂ֑נּוּ זָ֠הָב תְּכֵ֨לֶת וְאַרְגָּמָ֜ן וְתוֹלַ֧עַת שָׁנִ֛י וְשֵׁ֥שׁ
מָשְׁזָ֖ר תַּעֲשֶׂ֥ה אֹתֽוֹ׃ רָב֥וּעַ יִֽהְיֶ֖ה כָּפ֑וּל זֶ֥רֶת אָרְכּ֖וֹ וְזֶ֥רֶת רָחְבּֽוֹ׃ טז
וּמִלֵּאתָ֥ בוֹ֙ מִלֻּ֣אַת אֶ֔בֶן אַרְבָּעָ֖ה טוּרִ֣ים אָ֑בֶן ט֗וּר אֹ֤דֶם פִּטְדָה֙ יז
וּבָרֶ֔קֶת הַטּ֖וּר הָאֶחָֽד׃ וְהַטּ֖וּר הַשֵּׁנִ֑י נֹ֥פֶךְ סַפִּ֖יר וְיָהֲלֹֽם׃ וְהַטּ֖וּר יח
הַשְּׁלִישִׁ֑י לֶ֥שֶׁם שְׁב֖וֹ וְאַחְלָֽמָה׃ וְהַטּוּר֙ הָרְבִיעִ֔י תַּרְשִׁ֥ישׁ וְשֹׁ֖הַם יט
וְיָשְׁפֵ֑ה מְשֻׁבָּצִ֥ים זָהָ֛ב יִהְי֖וּ בְּמִלּוּאֹתָֽם׃ וְהָאֲבָנִ֗ים תִּֽהְיֶ֨יןָ֙ עַל־ כ
כא

יג **וְעָשִׂיתָ מִשְׁבְּצֹת.** מְעוּט "מִשְׁבְּצֹת" שְׁתַּיִם, וְלֹא פֵּרַשׁ לְךָ עַתָּה בְּפָרָשָׁה זוֹ אֶלָּא מִקְצָת צָרְכָּן, וּבְפָרָשַׁת הַחֹשֶׁן גּוֹמֵר לְךָ פֵּרוּשָׁן:

יד **שַׁרְשְׁרֹת זָהָב.** שַׁלְשְׁלָאוֹת: **מִגְבָּלֹת.** לְסוֹף גְּבוּל הַחֹשֶׁן תַּעֲשֶׂה: **מַעֲשֵׂה עֲבֹת.** מַעֲשֵׂה קְלִיעַת חוּטִין, וְלֹא מַעֲשֵׂה נְקָבִים וּכְפָלִים כְּאוֹתָן שֶׁעוֹשִׂין לַבּוֹרוֹת, אֶלָּא כְּאוֹתָן שֶׁעוֹשִׂין לַעֲרַדְסְקָאוֹת שֶׁקּוֹרִין אנצינשייר"ש: **וְנָתַתָּה אֶת שַׁרְשְׁרֹת.** שֶׁל עֲבוֹתוֹת הָעֲשׂוּיוֹת מַעֲשֵׂה עֲבֹת, עַל מִשְׁבְּצוֹת הַלָּלוּ. וְלֹא זֶה הוּא מְקוֹם צַוָּאַת עֲשִׂיָּתָן שֶׁל שַׁרְשְׁרוֹת וְלֹא צַוָּאַת קְבִיעָתָן, וְאֵין "תַּעֲשֶׂה" הָאָמוּר כָּאן לְשׁוֹן צִוּוּי, וְאֵין "וְנָתַתָּה" הָאָמוּר כָּאן לְשׁוֹן צִוּוּי, אֶלָּא לְשׁוֹן עָתִיד, כִּי בְּפָרָשַׁת הַחֹשֶׁן חוֹזֵר וּמְצַוֶּה עַל עֲשִׂיָּתָן וְעַל קְבִיעָתָן, וְלֹא נִכְתַּב כָּאן אֶלָּא לְהוֹדִיעַ מִקְצָת צֹרֶךְ הַמִּשְׁבְּצוֹת שֶׁצִּוָּה לַעֲשׂוֹתָן עִם הָאֵפוֹד, וְכָתַב לְךָ זֹאת לוֹמַר לְךָ, הַמִּשְׁבְּצוֹת הַלָּלוּ יִזָּקְקוּ לְךָ, לִכְשֶׁתַּעֲשֶׂה שַׁרְשְׁרוֹת מִגְבָּלוֹת עַל הַחֹשֶׁן, תִּתְּנֵם עַל הַמִּשְׁבְּצוֹת הַלָּלוּ:

טו **חֹשֶׁן מִשְׁפָּט.** שֶׁמְּכַפֵּר עַל קִלְקוּל הַדִּין. דָּבָר אַחֵר, "מִשְׁפָּט", שֶׁמְּבָרֵר דְּבָרָיו וְהַבְטָחָתוֹ אֱמֶת

דְּרִישֵׁנמֵנ"ט בְּלַעַ"ז. שֶׁהַמִּשְׁפָּט מְשַׁמֵּשׁ שָׁלֹשׁ לְשׁוֹנוֹת: דִּבְרֵי בַּעֲלֵי הַדִּין, וּגְמַר הַדִּין, וְעֹנֶשׁ הַדִּין, חִם עֹנֶשׁ מִיתָה חִם עֹנֶשׁ מַכּוֹת חִם עֹנֶשׁ מָמוֹן. וְזֶה מְשַׁמֵּשׁ לְשׁוֹן בֵּרוּר דְּבָרִים, שֶׁמְּפָרֵשׁ וּמְבָרֵר דְּבָרָיו: **כְּמַעֲשֵׂה אֵפֹד.** מַעֲשֵׂה חוֹשֵׁב וּמֵחֲמֵשֶׁת מִינִין:

טז **זֶרֶת אָרְכּוֹ וְזֶרֶת רָחְבּוֹ.** כָּפוּל וּמֻטָּל לוֹ לְפָנָיו כְּנֶגֶד לִבּוֹ, שֶׁנֶּאֱמַר: "וְהָיוּ עַל לֵב אַהֲרֹן" (להלן פסוק ל), תָּלוּי בִּכְתֵפוֹת הָאֵפוֹד הַבָּאוֹת מֵאֲחוֹרָיו עַל כְּתֵפָיו וְנִכְפָּלוֹת וְיוֹרְדוֹת לְפָנָיו מְעַט, וְהַחֹשֶׁן תָּלוּי בָּהֶן בְּשַׁרְשְׁרוֹת וְטַבָּעוֹת, כְּמוֹ שֶׁמְּפֹרָשׁ בָּעִנְיָן:

יז **וּמִלֵּאתָ בוֹ.** עַל שֵׁם שֶׁהָאֲבָנִים מְמַלְּאוֹת גֻּמּוֹת הַמִּשְׁבְּצוֹת הַמְּתֻקָּנוֹת לָהֶן, קוֹרֵא אוֹתָן בִּלְשׁוֹן מִלּוּאִים:

כ **מְשֻׁבָּצִים זָהָב יִהְיוּ.** הַטּוּרִים "בְּמִלּוּאֹתָם", מְקוֹמוֹת מִשְׁבְּצוֹת זָהָב יִהְיוּ בְּעֹמֶק שֶׁיִּתְמַלֵּא בְּעֹבִי הָאֶבֶן. זֶהוּ לְשׁוֹן "בְּמִלּוּאֹתָם", כְּשִׁעוּר מִלּוּי עָבְיָן שֶׁל אֲבָנִים יִהְיֶה עֹמֶק הַמִּשְׁבְּצוֹת, לֹא פָּחוֹת וְלֹא יָתֵר:

שמות | פרק כח

כב שְׁמֹת בְּנֵי־יִשְׂרָאֵל שְׁתֵּים עֶשְׂרֵה עַל־שְׁמֹתָם פִּתּוּחֵי חוֹתָם אִישׁ עַל־שְׁמוֹ תִּהְיֶיןָ לִשְׁנֵי עָשָׂר שָׁבֶט: וְעָשִׂיתָ עַל־הַחֹשֶׁן
כג שַׁרְשֹׁת גַּבְלֻת מַעֲשֵׂה עֲבֹת זָהָב טָהוֹר: וְעָשִׂיתָ עַל־הַחֹשֶׁן שְׁתֵּי טַבְּעוֹת זָהָב וְנָתַתָּ אֶת־שְׁתֵּי הַטַּבָּעוֹת עַל־שְׁנֵי קְצוֹת
כד הַחֹשֶׁן: וְנָתַתָּה אֶת־שְׁתֵּי עֲבֹתֹת הַזָּהָב עַל־שְׁתֵּי הַטַּבָּעֹת אֶל־
כה קְצוֹת הַחֹשֶׁן: וְאֵת שְׁתֵּי קְצוֹת שְׁתֵּי הָעֲבֹתֹת תִּתֵּן עַל־שְׁתֵּי
כו הַמִּשְׁבְּצוֹת וְנָתַתָּה עַל־כִּתְפוֹת הָאֵפֹד אֶל־מוּל פָּנָיו: וְעָשִׂיתָ שְׁתֵּי טַבְּעוֹת זָהָב וְשַׂמְתָּ אֹתָם עַל־שְׁנֵי קְצוֹת הַחֹשֶׁן עַל־שְׂפָתוֹ

כא) **אִישׁ עַל שְׁמוֹ.** כְּסֵדֶר תּוֹלְדוֹתָם סֵדֶר הָאֲבָנִים: אֹדֶם לִרְאוּבֵן, פִּטְדָה לְשִׁמְעוֹן, וְכֵן כֻּלָּם:

כב) **עַל הַחֹשֶׁן.** בִּשְׁבִיל הַחֹשֶׁן, לְהִקָּבֵעַ בְּטַבְּעוֹתָיו, כְּמוֹ שֶׁמְּפֹרָשׁ לְמַטָּה בָּעִנְיָן: **שַׁרְשֹׁת.** לְשׁוֹן שָׁרְשֵׁי אִילָן שֶׁהֵן מְחֻזָּקִין לָאִילָן לְהַאֲחִיז וּלְהִתָּקַע בָּאָרֶץ, אַף אֵלּוּ יִהְיוּ מְחֻזָּקִין לַחֹשֶׁן, שֶׁבָּהֶם יִהְיֶה תָּלוּי בָּאֵפוֹד, וְהֵן שְׁתֵּי שַׁרְשְׁרוֹת הָאֲמוּרוֹת לְמַעְלָה בָּעִנְיָן הַמִּשְׁבְּצוֹת (לעיל פסוק יד). וְאַף 'שַׁרְשְׁרוֹת' פָּתַר מְנַחֵם בֶּן סָרוּק לְשׁוֹן שָׁרָשִׁים, וְאָמַר שֶׁהָרֵי"שׁ יְתֵרָה כְּמוֹ מֵ"ם שֶׁבְּ"שַׁלְשֹׁם" (בראשית לא, ב) וּמֵ"ם שֶׁבְּ"רֵיקָם" (שם פסוק מב). וְאֵינִי רוֹאֶה אֶת דְּבָרָיו, אֶלָּא 'שַׁרְשֶׁרֶת' בִּלְשׁוֹן עִבְרִית כְּ"שַׁלְשֶׁלֶת" בִּלְשׁוֹן מִשְׁנָה (כלים יד, ג): **גַּבְלֻת.** הוּא "מִגְבָּלֹת" הָאָמוּר לְמַעְלָה (לעיל פסוק יד), שֶׁתִּתְקָעֵם בַּטַּבָּעוֹת שֶׁיִּהְיוּ בִּגְבוּל הַחֹשֶׁן. וְכָל 'גְּבוּל' לְשׁוֹן קָצֶה, אשוֹמי"ל בְּלַעַ"ז: **מַעֲשֵׂה עֲבֹת.** מַעֲשֵׂה קְלִיעָה:

כג) **עַל הַחֹשֶׁן.** לְצָרְכּוֹ שֶׁל חֹשֶׁן, כְּדֵי לְקָבְעָם בּוֹ. וְלֹא יִתָּכֵן לוֹמַר שֶׁתְּהֵא תְּחִלַּת עֲשִׂיָּתָן עָלָיו, שֶׁאִם כֵּן מַה הוּא שֶׁחוֹזֵר וְאוֹמֵר: "וְנָתַתָּ אֶת שְׁתֵּי הַטַּבָּעוֹת", וַהֲלֹא כְּבָר נְתוּנוֹת בּוֹ! הָיָה לוֹ לִכְתֹּב בִּתְחִלַּת הַמִּקְרָא: "וְעָשִׂיתָ עַל קְצוֹת הַחֹשֶׁן שְׁתֵּי טַבְּעוֹת זָהָב! וְאַף בַּשַּׁרְשְׁרוֹת צָרִיךְ אַתָּה לִפְתֹּר כֵּן: **עַל שְׁנֵי קְצוֹת הַחֹשֶׁן.** לִשְׁתֵּי פֵּאוֹת שֶׁכְּנֶגֶד הַצַּוָּאר, לַיְמָנִית וְלַשְּׂמָאלִית, הַבָּאִים מוּל כִּתְפוֹת הָאֵפוֹד:

כד) **וְנָתַתָּה אֶת שְׁתֵּי עֲבֹתֹת הַזָּהָב.** הֵן הֵן "שַׁרְשֹׁת גַּבְלֻת" הַכְּתוּבוֹת לְמַעְלָה (לעיל פסוק כב), וְלֹא פֵּרַשׁ מְקוֹם קְבִיעָתָן בַּחֹשֶׁן, עַכְשָׁיו מְפָרֵשׁ לְךָ שֶׁיִּהְיֶה תּוֹחֵב אוֹתָן בַּטַּבָּעוֹת. וְתֵדַע לְךָ שֶׁהֵן הֵן הָרִאשׁוֹנוֹת, שֶׁהֲרֵי בְּפָרָשַׁת 'אֵלֶּה פְקוּדֵי' לֹא הֻכְפְּלוּ:

כה) **וְאֵת שְׁתֵּי קְצוֹת.** שֶׁל "שְׁתֵּי הָעֲבֹתֹת", שְׁנֵי רָאשֵׁיהֶן שֶׁל כָּל אַחַת וְאַחַת: **תִּתֵּן עַל שְׁתֵּי הַמִּשְׁבְּצוֹת.** הֵן הֵן הַכְּתוּבוֹת לְמַעְלָה בֵּין פָּרָשַׁת הַחֹשֶׁן וּפָרָשַׁת הָאֵפוֹד, וְלֹא פֵּרַשׁ אֶת עָרְכָּן וְאֶת מְקוֹמָן, עַכְשָׁיו מְפָרֵשׁ לְךָ שֶׁיִּתְקַע בָּהֶן רָאשֵׁי הָעֲבוֹתוֹת הַתְּחוּבוֹת בְּטַבְּעוֹת הַחֹשֶׁן לַיָּמִין וְלַשְּׂמֹאל אֵצֶל הַצַּוָּאר, שְׁנֵי רָאשֵׁי שַׁרְשֶׁרֶת הַיְמָנִית תּוֹקֵעַ בַּמִּשְׁבֶּצֶת שֶׁל יָמִין, וְכֵן בְּשֶׁל שְׂמֹאל שְׁנֵי רָאשֵׁי שַׁרְשֶׁרֶת הַשְּׂמָאלִית: **וְנָתַתָּה.** הַמִּשְׁבְּצוֹת **עַל כִּתְפוֹת הָאֵפוֹד.** אַחַת בְּזוֹ וְאַחַת בְּזוֹ, נִמְצְאוּ כִּתְפוֹת הָאֵפוֹד מַחֲזִיקִין אֶת הַחֹשֶׁן שֶׁלֹּא יִפֹּל, וּבָהֶן הוּא תָּלוּי. וַעֲדַיִן שְׂפַת הַחֹשֶׁן הַתַּחְתּוֹנָה הוֹלֶכֶת וּבָאָה וְנוֹקֶשֶׁת עַל כְּרֵסוֹ וְאֵינָהּ דְּבוּקָה לוֹ יָפֶה, לְכָךְ הֻצְרַךְ עוֹד שְׁתֵּי טַבָּעוֹת לְתַחְתִּיתוֹ כְּמוֹ שֶׁמְּפָרֵשׁ וְהוֹלֵךְ: **אֶל מוּל פָּנָיו.** שֶׁל אֵפוֹד, שֶׁלֹּא יִתֵּן הַמִּשְׁבְּצוֹת בְּעֵבֶר הַכְּתֵפוֹת שֶׁכְּלַפֵּי הַמְּעִיל, אֶלָּא בָּעֵבֶר הָעֶלְיוֹן שֶׁכְּלַפֵּי הַחוּץ, וְהוּא קָרוּי 'מוּל פָּנָיו' שֶׁל אֵפוֹד, כִּי אוֹתוֹ עֵבֶר שֶׁאֵינוֹ נִרְאֶה אֵינוֹ קָרוּי פָּנִים:

כו) **עַל שְׁנֵי קְצוֹת הַחֹשֶׁן.** הֵן שְׁתֵּי פִּאוֹתָיו הַתַּחְתּוֹנוֹת לַיְמִין וְלַשְּׂמֹאל: **עַל שְׂפָתוֹ אֲשֶׁר אֶל עֵבֶר הָאֵפוֹד**

אֲשֶׁר אֶל־עֵבֶר הָאֵפֹד בָּיְתָה: וְעָשִׂיתָ שְׁתֵּי טַבְּעוֹת זָהָב וְנָתַתָּה כז
אֹתָם עַל־שְׁתֵּי כִתְפוֹת הָאֵפוֹד מִלְּמַטָּה מִמּוּל פָּנָיו לְעֻמַּת
מֶחְבַּרְתּוֹ מִמַּעַל לְחֵשֶׁב הָאֵפוֹד: וְיִרְכְּסוּ אֶת־הַחֹשֶׁן מִטַּבְּעֹתָו כח
אֶל־טַבְּעֹת הָאֵפוֹד בִּפְתִיל תְּכֵלֶת לִהְיוֹת עַל־חֵשֶׁב הָאֵפוֹד
וְלֹא־יִזַּח הַחֹשֶׁן מֵעַל הָאֵפוֹד: וְנָשָׂא אַהֲרֹן אֶת־שְׁמוֹת כט
בְּנֵי־יִשְׂרָאֵל בְּחֹשֶׁן הַמִּשְׁפָּט עַל־לִבּוֹ בְּבֹאוֹ אֶל־הַקֹּדֶשׁ
לְזִכָּרֹן לִפְנֵי־יהוה תָּמִיד: וְנָתַתָּ אֶל־חֹשֶׁן הַמִּשְׁפָּט אֶת־ ל
הָאוּרִים וְאֶת־הַתֻּמִּים וְהָיוּ עַל־לֵב אַהֲרֹן בְּבֹאוֹ לִפְנֵי יהוה
וְנָשָׂא אַהֲרֹן אֶת־מִשְׁפַּט בְּנֵי־יִשְׂרָאֵל עַל־לִבּוֹ לִפְנֵי יהוה

בָּיְתָה. הֲרֵי לְךָ שְׁנֵי סִימָנִין: הָאֶחָד שְׁתֵּיהֶן בִּשְׁנֵי קְצוֹת שֶׁל תַּחְתִּיתוֹ שֶׁהוּא כְּנֶגֶד הָאֵפוֹד, שֶׁעֶלְיוֹנוֹ אֵינוֹ כְּנֶגֶד הָאֵפוֹד, שֶׁהֲרֵי סָמוּךְ לַצַּוָּאר הוּא וְהָאֵפוֹד נָתוּן עַל מָתְנָיו. וְעוֹד נָתַן סִימָן, שֶׁלֹּא יִקָּבְעֵם בָּעֵבֶר הַחֹשֶׁן שֶׁכְּלַפֵּי הַחוּץ אֶלָּא בָּעֵבֶר שֶׁכְּלַפֵּי פְנִים, שֶׁנֶּאֱמַר "בָּיְתָה", וְאוֹתוֹ הָעֵבֶר הוּא לְצַד הָאֵפוֹד, שֶׁחֵשֶׁב הָאֵפוֹד חוֹגְרוֹ לַכֹּהֵן וְנִקְפָּל הַסִּינָר לִפְנֵי הַכֹּהֵן עַל מָתְנָיו וּקְצָת כְּרֵסוֹ מִכָּאן וּמִכָּאן עַד כְּנֶגֶד קְצוֹת הַחֹשֶׁן, וּקְצוֹתָיו שׁוֹכְבִין עָלָיו:

כז עַל שְׁתֵּי כִתְפוֹת הָאֵפוֹד מִלְּמַטָּה. שֶׁהַמִּשְׁבְּצוֹת נְתָנוֹ בְּרָאשֵׁי כִתְפֵי הָאֵפוֹד הָעֶלְיוֹנִים הַבָּאִים עַל כְּתֵפָיו כְּנֶגֶד גְּרוֹנוֹ וְנִקְפָּלוֹת וְיוֹרְדוֹת לְפָנָיו, וְהַטַּבָּעוֹת עָשָׂה לָתֵת בְּרֹאשָׁן הַשֵּׁנִי שֶׁהוּא מְחֻבָּר לָאֵפוֹד, וְהוּא שֶׁנֶּאֱמַר: "לְעֻמַּת מֶחְבַּרְתּוֹ", סָמוּךְ לִמְקוֹם חִבּוּרָן בָּאֵפוֹד לְמַעְלָה מִן הַחֲגוֹרָה מְעַט, שֶׁהַמַּחְבֶּרֶת לְעֻמַּת הַחֲגוֹרָה, וְאֵלּוּ נְתוּנִים מְעַט בְּגֹבַהּ זְקִיפַת הַכְּתֵפוֹת, הוּא שֶׁנֶּאֱמַר: "מִמַּעַל לְחֵשֶׁב הָאֵפוֹד", וְהֵן כְּנֶגֶד סוֹף הַחֹשֶׁן. וְנוֹתֵן פְּתִיל תְּכֵלֶת בְּאוֹתָן הַטַּבָּעוֹת וּבְטַבְּעוֹת הַחֹשֶׁן, וְרוֹכְסָן בְּאוֹתָן פְּתִיל לְיָמִין וְלִשְׂמֹאל, שֶׁלֹּא יְהֵא תַּחְתִּית הַחֹשֶׁן הוֹלֵךְ

לְפָנִים וְחוֹזֵר לְאָחוֹר וְנוֹקֵשׁ עַל כְּרֵסוֹ, וְנִמְצָא מְיֻשָּׁב עַל הַמְּעִיל יָפֶה. מִמּוּל פָּנָיו. בָּעֵבֶר הַחִיצוֹן:

כח וְיִרְכְּסוּ. לְשׁוֹן חִבּוּר, וְכֵן: "מֵרֻכְסֵי אִישׁ" (תהלים לא,
כא), חִבּוּרֵי חֶבְלֵי רְשָׁעִים, וְכֵן: "וְהָרְכָסִים לְבִקְעָה"
(ישעיה מ, ד), הֶהָרִים הַסְּמוּכִים זֶה לָזֶה שֶׁאִי אֶפְשָׁר לֵירֵד
לַגַּיְא שֶׁבֵּינֵיהֶם אֶלָּא בְּקֹשִׁי גָדוֹל, שֶׁמִּתּוֹךְ סְמִיכָתָן
הַגַּיְא זְקוּפָה וַעֲמֻקָּה, יִהְיוּ לְבִקְעַת מִישׁוֹר וְנוֹחָה
לֵילֵךְ: לִהְיוֹת עַל חֵשֶׁב הָאֵפוֹד. לִהְיוֹת הַחֹשֶׁן דָּבוּק
אֶל חֵשֶׁב הָאֵפוֹד: וְלֹא יִזַּח. לְשׁוֹן נִתּוּק, וּלְשׁוֹן עֲרָבִי
הוּא, כְּדִבְרֵי דּוּנָשׁ בֶּן לַבְרָט:

ל אֶת הָאוּרִים וְאֶת הַתֻּמִּים. הוּא כְּתָב שֵׁם הַמְפֹרָשׁ שֶׁהָיָה נוֹתְנוֹ בְּתוֹךְ כִּפְלֵי הַחֹשֶׁן, שֶׁעַל יָדוֹ הוּא מֵאִיר דְּבָרָיו וּמְתַמֵּם אֶת דְּבָרָיו. וּבְמִקְדָּשׁ שֵׁנִי הָיָה הַחֹשֶׁן, שֶׁאִי אֶפְשָׁר לְכֹהֵן גָּדוֹל לִהְיוֹת מְחֻסָּר בְּגָדִים, אֲבָל אוֹתוֹ הַשֵּׁם לֹא הָיָה בְתוֹכוֹ. וְעַל שֵׁם אוֹתוֹ הַכְּתָב הוּא קָרוּי 'מִשְׁפָּט', שֶׁנֶּאֱמַר: "וְשָׁאַל לוֹ בְּמִשְׁפַּט הָאוּרִים" (במדבר כז, כא): אֶת מִשְׁפַּט בְּנֵי יִשְׂרָאֵל. דָּבָר שֶׁהֵם נִשְׁפָּטִים וְנוֹכָחִים עַל יָדוֹ אִם לַעֲשׂוֹת דָּבָר אוֹ לֹא לַעֲשׂוֹת. וּלְפִי מִדְרַשׁ אַגָּדָה שֶׁהַחֹשֶׁן מְכַפֵּר עַל מְעַוְּתֵי הַדִּין, נִקְרָא "מִשְׁפָּט" עַל שֵׁם סְלִיחַת הַמִּשְׁפָּט:

שמות | פרק כח

לא וְעָשִׂיתָ אֶת־מְעִיל הָאֵפוֹד כְּלִיל תְּכֵלֶת: תָּמִיד: שלישי

לב וְהָיָה פִי־רֹאשׁוֹ בְּתוֹכוֹ שָׂפָה יִהְיֶה לְפִיו סָבִיב מַעֲשֵׂה אֹרֵג כְּפִי תַחְרָא יִהְיֶה־לּוֹ לֹא יִקָּרֵעַ:

לג וְעָשִׂיתָ עַל־שׁוּלָיו רִמֹּנֵי תְּכֵלֶת וְאַרְגָּמָן וְתוֹלַעַת שָׁנִי עַל־שׁוּלָיו סָבִיב וּפַעֲמֹנֵי זָהָב בְּתוֹכָם סָבִיב:

לד פַּעֲמֹן זָהָב וְרִמּוֹן פַּעֲמֹן זָהָב וְרִמּוֹן עַל־שׁוּלֵי הַמְּעִיל סָבִיב:

לה וְהָיָה עַל־אַהֲרֹן לְשָׁרֵת וְנִשְׁמַע קוֹלוֹ בְּבֹאוֹ אֶל־הַקֹּדֶשׁ לִפְנֵי יְהוָה וּבְצֵאתוֹ וְלֹא יָמוּת:

לו וְעָשִׂיתָ צִּיץ זָהָב טָהוֹר וּפִתַּחְתָּ עָלָיו פִּתּוּחֵי חֹתָם קֹדֶשׁ לַיהוָה:

לז וְשַׂמְתָּ אֹתוֹ עַל־פְּתִיל תְּכֵלֶת וְהָיָה עַל־הַמִּצְנָפֶת אֶל־מוּל פְּנֵי־הַמִּצְנֶפֶת

לא| **אֶת מְעִיל הָאֵפוֹד**. שֶׁהָאֵפוֹד נָתוּן עָלָיו לַחֲגוֹרָה: **כְּלִיל תְּכֵלֶת**. כֻּלּוֹ תְּכֵלֶת, שֶׁאֵין מִין אַחֵר מְעֹרָב בּוֹ:

לב| **וְהָיָה פִי רֹאשׁוֹ**. פִּי הַמְּעִיל שֶׁבְּגָבְהוֹ, הוּא פְּתִיחַת בֵּית הַצַּוָּאר: **בְּתוֹכוֹ**. כְּתַרְגּוּמוֹ: "כָּפִיל לְגַוֵּהּ", כָּפוּל לְתוֹכוֹ לִהְיוֹת לוֹ לְשָׂפָה כְּפִילָתוֹ. וְהָיָה מַעֲשֵׂה אוֹרֵג וְלֹא בְּמַחַט: **כְּפִי תַחְרָא**. לָמַדְנוּ שֶׁהַשִּׁרְיוֹנִים שֶׁלָּהֶם פִּיהֶם כָּפוּל: **לֹא יִקָּרֵעַ**. כְּדֵי שֶׁלֹּא יִקָּרֵעַ, וְהַקּוֹרְעוֹ עוֹבֵר בְּלָאו, שֶׁזֶּה מִמִּנְיַן לָאוִין שֶׁבַּתּוֹרָה. וְכֵן: "לֹא יִזַּח הַחֹשֶׁן", וְכֵן: "לֹא יָסֻרוּ מִמֶּנּוּ" (לעיל כה, טו) הַנֶּאֱמַר בְּבַדֵּי הָאָרוֹן: (לעיל פסוק כח)

לג| **רִמֹּנֵי**. עֲגֻלִּים וַחֲלוּלִים הָיוּ, כְּמִין רִמּוֹנִים הָעֲשׂוּיִים כְּבֵיצַת תַּרְנְגֹלֶת: **וּפַעֲמֹנֵי זָהָב**. זַגִּים עִם עִנְבָּלִים שֶׁבְּתוֹכָם: **בְּתוֹכָם סָבִיב**. בֵּינֵיהֶם סָבִיב, בֵּין שְׁנֵי רִמּוֹנִים פַּעֲמֹן אֶחָד דָּבוּק וְתָלוּי בְּשׁוּלֵי הַמְּעִיל:

לד| **פַּעֲמֹן זָהָב וְרִמּוֹן**. אֶצְלוֹ. פַּעֲמֹן זָהָב וְרִמּוֹן. אֶצְלוֹ:

לה| **וְלֹא יָמוּת**. מִכְּלַל לָאו אַתָּה שׁוֹמֵעַ הֵן יִהְיֶה לוֹ לֹא יִתְחַיֵּב מִיתָה, הָא אִם נִכְנַס מְחֻסָּר אֶחָד מִן הַבְּגָדִים הַלָּלוּ חַיָּב מִיתָה בִּידֵי שָׁמַיִם:

לו| **צִיץ**. כְּמִין טַס שֶׁל זָהָב הָיָה, רֹחַב שְׁתֵּי אֶצְבָּעוֹת, מַקִּיף עַל הַמֵּצַח מֵאֹזֶן לְאֹזֶן:

לז| **עַל פְּתִיל תְּכֵלֶת**. וּבְמָקוֹם אַחֵר הוּא אוֹמֵר: "וַיִּתְּנוּ עָלָיו פְּתִיל תְּכֵלֶת" (להלן לט, לא), וְעוֹד, כְּתִיב כָּאן: "וְהָיָה עַל הַמִּצְנָפֶת", וּלְמַטָּה הוּא אוֹמֵר: "וְהָיָה עַל מֵצַח אַהֲרֹן" (בפסוק הבא), וּבִשְׁחִיטַת קָדָשִׁים שָׁנִינוּ: "שְׂעָרוֹ הָיָה נִרְאֶה בֵּין צִיץ לַמִּצְנֶפֶת שֶׁשָּׁם מַנִּיחַ תְּפִלִּין" (זבחים יט ע״א), לָמַדְנוּ שֶׁהַמִּצְנֶפֶת לְמַעְלָה בְּגֹבַהּ הָרֹאשׁ וְחֵיתָהּ עֲמֻקָּה לִכְנֹס בָּהּ כָּל הָרֹאשׁ עַד הַמֵּצַח, וְהַצִּיץ מִלְּמַטָּה, וְהַפְּתִילִים הָיוּ עֲוֹקִין וּתְלוּיִין בּוֹ בִּשְׁנֵי רָאשִׁים וּבְאֶמְצָעִיתוֹ, שָׁשָׁה בִּשְׁלֹשָׁה מְקוֹמוֹת הַלָּלוּ, פְּתִיל מִלְמַעְלָה – אֶחָד מִבַּחוּץ וְאֶחָד מִבִּפְנִים כְּנֶגְדּוֹ, וְקוֹשֵׁר רָאשֵׁי הַפְּתִילִים מֵאֲחוֹרֵי הָעֹרֶף שְׁלָשְׁתָּן, וְנִמְצְאוּ בֵּין אֹרֶךְ הַטַּס וּפְתִילֵי רָאשָׁיו מַקִּיפִין אֶת הַקָּדְקֹד, וְהַפְּתִיל הָאֶמְצָעִי, שֶׁבְּרֹאשׁוֹ קָשׁוּר עִם רָאשֵׁי הַשְּׁנַיִם, הוֹלֵךְ עַל פְּנֵי רֹחַב הָרֹאשׁ מִלְּמַעְלָה, וְנִמְצָא עָשׂוּי כְּמִין כּוֹבַע, וְעַל פְּתִיל הָאֶמְצָעִי הוּא אוֹמֵר: "וְהָיָה עַל הַמִּצְנָפֶת", וְהָיָה נוֹתֵן הַצִּיץ עַל רֹאשׁוֹ כְּמִין כּוֹבַע עַל הַמִּצְנֶפֶת, וְהַפְּתִיל הָאֶמְצָעִי מַחֲזִיקוֹ שֶׁאֵינוֹ נוֹפֵל, וְהַטַּס תָּלוּי כְּנֶגֶד מִצְחוֹ. וְנִתְקַיְּמוּ כָּל הַמִּקְרָאוֹת: פְּתִיל עַל הַצִּיץ, וְצִיץ עַל הַפְּתִיל, וּפְתִיל עַל הַמִּצְנֶפֶת מִלְמַעְלָה:

פרק כח | שמות

לח וְהָיָה עַל־מֵצַח אַהֲרֹן וְנָשָׂא אַהֲרֹן אֶת־עֲוֹן הַקֳּדָשִׁים אֲשֶׁר יַקְדִּישׁוּ בְּנֵי יִשְׂרָאֵל לְכָל־מַתְּנֹת קָדְשֵׁיהֶם וְהָיָה עַל־מִצְחוֹ תָּמִיד לְרָצוֹן לָהֶם לִפְנֵי יהוה: לט וְשִׁבַּצְתָּ הַכְּתֹנֶת שֵׁשׁ וְעָשִׂיתָ מִצְנֶפֶת שֵׁשׁ וְאַבְנֵט תַּעֲשֶׂה מַעֲשֵׂה רֹקֵם: מ וְלִבְנֵי אַהֲרֹן תַּעֲשֶׂה כֻתֳּנֹת וְעָשִׂיתָ לָהֶם אַבְנֵטִים וּמִגְבָּעוֹת תַּעֲשֶׂה לָהֶם לְכָבוֹד וּלְתִפְאָרֶת: מא וְהִלְבַּשְׁתָּ אֹתָם אֶת־אַהֲרֹן אָחִיךָ וְאֶת־בָּנָיו אִתּוֹ וּמָשַׁחְתָּ אֹתָם וּמִלֵּאתָ אֶת־יָדָם וְקִדַּשְׁתָּ אֹתָם וְכִהֲנוּ־לִי: מב וַעֲשֵׂה לָהֶם מִכְנְסֵי־בָד לְכַסּוֹת בְּשַׂר עֶרְוָה מִמָּתְנַיִם וְעַד־יְרֵכַיִם יִהְיוּ: מג וְהָיוּ עַל־אַהֲרֹן וְעַל־בָּנָיו בְּבֹאָם ׀ אֶל־אֹהֶל מוֹעֵד אוֹ בְגִשְׁתָּם אֶל־הַמִּזְבֵּחַ לְשָׁרֵת בַּקֹּדֶשׁ וְלֹא־יִשְׂאוּ עָוֹן וָמֵתוּ חֻקַּת

לח | **וְנָשָׂא אַהֲרֹן.** לְשׁוֹן סְלִיחָה, וְאַף עַל פִּי כֵן אֵינוֹ זָז מִמַּשְׁמָעוֹ, שֶׁאַהֲרֹן נוֹשֵׂא אֶת הַמַּשָּׂא שֶׁל עָוֹן, נִמְצָא מְסֻלָּק הֶעָוֹן מִן הַקֳּדָשִׁים: **אֶת עֲוֹן הַקֳּדָשִׁים.** לְרַצּוֹת עַל הַדָּם וְעַל הַחֵלֶב שֶׁקְּרֵבוּ בְטֻמְאָה, כְּמוֹ שֶׁשָּׁנִינוּ: חֵי זֶה עָוֹן הוּא נוֹשֵׂא? אִם עֲוֹן פִּגּוּל, הֲרֵי כְּבָר נֶאֱמַר וְכוּ'. וְאֵין לוֹמַר שֶׁיְּכַפֵּר עַל הַכֹּהֲנִים שֶׁהִקְרִיבוּם טְמֵאִים, שֶׁהֲרֵי "עֲוֹן הַקֳּדָשִׁים" נֶאֱמַר וְלֹא עֲוֹן הַמַּקְרִיבִין! אֵינוֹ מְרַצֶּה אֶלָּא לְהַכְשִׁיר הַקָּרְבָּן: **וְהָיָה עַל מִצְחוֹ תָּמִיד.** אִי אֶפְשָׁר לוֹמַר שֶׁיְּהֵא עַל מִצְחוֹ תָּמִיד, שֶׁהֲרֵי אֵינוֹ עָלָיו אֶלָּא בִשְׁעַת הָעֲבוֹדָה! אֶלָּא "תָּמִיד לְרָצוֹן לָהֶם", אֵינוֹ עַל מִצְחוֹ, שֶׁלֹּא הָיָה כֹהֵן גָּדוֹל עוֹבֵד בְּאוֹתָהּ שָׁעָה. וּלְדִבְרֵי הָאוֹמֵר עוֹדֵהוּ עַל מִצְחוֹ מְכַפֵּר וּמְרַצֶּה וְאִם לָאו אֵינוֹ מְרַצֶּה, נִדְרָשׁ "עַל מִצְחוֹ תָּמִיד" לְלַמֵּד שֶׁיְּמַשְׁמֵשׁ בּוֹ בְּעוֹדוֹ עַל מִצְחוֹ, שֶׁלֹּא יַסִּיחַ דַּעְתּוֹ מִמֶּנּוּ:

לט | **וְשִׁבַּצְתָּ.** עֲשֵׂה אוֹתָהּ מִשְׁבְּצוֹת מִשְׁבְּצוֹת, וְכֻלָּהּ שֶׁל שֵׁשׁ:

מ | **וְלִבְנֵי אַהֲרֹן תַּעֲשֶׂה.** אַרְבָּעָה בְגָדִים הַלָּלוּ וְלֹא יוֹתֵר: כֻּתֹּנֶת, וְאַבְנֵט, וּמִגְבָּעוֹת הִיא מִצְנֶפֶת, וּמִכְנָסַיִם כְּתוּבִים לְמַטָּה בַּפָּרָשָׁה (להלן פסוק מב):

מא | **וְהִלְבַּשְׁתָּ אֹתָם אֶת אַהֲרֹן.** אוֹתָם הָאֲמוּרִים בְּאַהֲרֹן: חֹשֶׁן, וְאֵפוֹד, וּמְעִיל, וּכְתֹנֶת תַּשְׁבֵּץ מִצְנֶפֶת וְאַבְנֵט, "(לעיל פסוק ד) וְצִיץ, וּמִכְנָסַיִם כְּתוּבִים לְמַטָּה בְּכֻלָּם: **וְאֶת בָּנָיו אִתּוֹ.** אוֹתָם הַכְּתוּבִים בָּהֶם: **וּמָשַׁחְתָּ אֹתָם.** אֶת אַהֲרֹן וְאֶת בָּנָיו בְּשֶׁמֶן הַמִּשְׁחָה: **וּמִלֵּאתָ אֶת יָדָם.** כָּל מִלּוּי יָדַיִם לְשׁוֹן חִנּוּךְ, כְּשֶׁהוּא נִכְנָס לַדָּבָר לִהְיוֹת מֻחְזָק בּוֹ מֵאוֹתוֹ יוֹם וָהָלְאָה הוּא, וּבִלְשׁוֹן לַעַז כְּשֶׁמְּמַנִּין אָדָם עַל פְּקִידַת דָּבָר, נוֹתֵן הַשַּׁלִּיט בְּיָדוֹ בֵּית יָד שֶׁל עוֹר שֶׁקּוֹרִין גוואנ"ט, וְעַל יָדוֹ הוּא מַחֲזִיקוֹ בַּדָּבָר, וְקוֹרִין לְאוֹתָהּ מְסִירָה רווישטי"ר, וְהוּא מִלּוּי יָדַיִם:

מב | **וַעֲשֵׂה לָהֶם.** לְאַהֲרֹן וּלְבָנָיו: **מִכְנְסֵי בָד.** הֲרֵי שְׁמוֹנָה בְגָדִים לְכֹהֵן גָּדוֹל וְאַרְבָּעָה לְכֹהֵן הֶדְיוֹט:

מג | **וְהָיוּ.** כָּל הַבְּגָדִים הָאֵלֶּה, "עַל אַהֲרֹן" הָרְאוּיִין לוֹ, "וְעַל בָּנָיו" הָאֲמוּרִים בָּהֶם: **בְּבֹאָם אֶל אֹהֶל מוֹעֵד.** לַהֵיכָל, וְכֵן לַמִּשְׁכָּן: **וָמֵתוּ.** הָא לָמַדְתָּ שֶׁהַמְשַׁמֵּשׁ מְחֻסַּר בְּגָדִים – בְּמִיתָה: **חֻקַּת עוֹלָם לוֹ.** כָּל מָקוֹם שֶׁנֶּאֱמַר 'חֻקַּת' לְעַכֵּב:

שמות | פרק כט

א וְזֶה הַדָּבָר אֲשֶׁר תַּעֲשֶׂה עוֹלָם לוֹ וּלְזַרְעוֹ אַחֲרָיו: כב רביעי
לָהֶם לְקַדֵּשׁ אֹתָם לְכַהֵן לִי לְקַח פַּר אֶחָד בֶּן־בָּקָר וְאֵילִם שְׁנַיִם
ב תְּמִימִם: וְלֶחֶם מַצּוֹת וְחַלֹּת מַצֹּת בְּלוּלֹת בַּשֶּׁמֶן וּרְקִיקֵי מַצּוֹת
ג מְשֻׁחִים בַּשָּׁמֶן סֹלֶת חִטִּים תַּעֲשֶׂה אֹתָם: וְנָתַתָּ אוֹתָם עַל־סַל
אֶחָד וְהִקְרַבְתָּ אֹתָם בַּסָּל וְאֶת־הַפָּר וְאֵת שְׁנֵי הָאֵילִם: וְאֶת־
ד אַהֲרֹן וְאֶת־בָּנָיו תַּקְרִיב אֶל־פֶּתַח אֹהֶל מוֹעֵד וְרָחַצְתָּ אֹתָם
ה בַּמָּיִם: וְלָקַחְתָּ אֶת־הַבְּגָדִים וְהִלְבַּשְׁתָּ אֶת־אַהֲרֹן אֶת־הַכֻּתֹּנֶת
וְאֵת מְעִיל הָאֵפֹד וְאֶת־הָאֵפֹד וְאֶת־הַחֹשֶׁן וְאָפַדְתָּ לוֹ בְּחֵשֶׁב
ו הָאֵפֹד: וְשַׂמְתָּ הַמִּצְנֶפֶת עַל־רֹאשׁוֹ וְנָתַתָּ אֶת־נֵזֶר הַקֹּדֶשׁ עַל־
ז הַמִּצְנָפֶת: וְלָקַחְתָּ אֶת־שֶׁמֶן הַמִּשְׁחָה וְיָצַקְתָּ עַל־רֹאשׁוֹ
ח וּמָשַׁחְתָּ אֹתוֹ: וְאֶת־בָּנָיו תַּקְרִיב וְהִלְבַּשְׁתָּם כֻּתֳּנֹת: וְחָגַרְתָּ
אֹתָם אַבְנֵט אַהֲרֹן וּבָנָיו וְחָבַשְׁתָּ לָהֶם מִגְבָּעֹת וְהָיְתָה לָהֶם
י כְּהֻנָּה לְחֻקַּת עוֹלָם וּמִלֵּאתָ יַד־אַהֲרֹן וְיַד־בָּנָיו: וְהִקְרַבְתָּ אֶת־
הַפָּר לִפְנֵי אֹהֶל מוֹעֵד וְסָמַךְ אַהֲרֹן וּבָנָיו אֶת־יְדֵיהֶם עַל־רֹאשׁ

פרק כט
א| לָקַח. כְּמוֹ קַח. וּשְׁתֵּי גְזֵרוֹת הֵן, אַחַת שֶׁל קִיחָה וְאַחַת שֶׁל לְקִיחָה, וְלָהֶן פִּתְרוֹן אֶחָד: פַּר אֶחָד. לְכַפֵּר עַל מַעֲשֵׂה הָעֵגֶל שֶׁהוּא פָר:

ב| וְלֶחֶם מַצּוֹת וְחַלֹּת מַצֹּת... וּרְקִיקֵי מַצּוֹת. הֲרֵי אֵלּוּ שְׁלֹשָׁה מִינִין: רְבוּכָה וְחַלּוֹת וּרְקִיקִין. "לֶחֶם מַצּוֹת" הִיא הַקְּרוּיָה לְמַטָּה בָעִנְיָן: "חַלַּת לֶחֶם שֶׁמֶן" (להלן פסוק כג), עַל שֵׁם שֶׁנּוֹתֵן שֶׁמֶן בָּרְבוּכָה כְּנֶגֶד הַחַלּוֹת וְהָרְקִיקִין. וְכָל הַמִּינִין בָּאִים עֶשֶׂר עֶשֶׂר חַלּוֹת. בְּלוּלֹת בַּשֶּׁמֶן. כְּשֶׁהֵן קֶמַח יוֹצֵק בָּהֶן שֶׁמֶן וּבוֹלְלָן: מְשֻׁחִים בַּשָּׁמֶן. אַחַר אֲפִיָּתָן מוֹשְׁחָן כְּמִין כָ"ף, כָּךְ יְוָנִית, שֶׁהִיא עֲשׂוּיָה כְנוּ"ן שֶׁלָּנוּ:

ג| וְהִקְרַבְתָּ אֹתָם. אֶל חֲצַר הַמִּשְׁכָּן בְּיוֹם הֲקָמָתוֹ:

ד| וְרָחַצְתָּ. טְבִילַת כָּל הַגּוּף:

ה| וְאָפַדְתָּ. קַשֵּׁט וְתַקֵּן הַחֲגוֹרָה וְהַסִּינָר סְבִיבוֹתָיו:

ו| נֵזֶר הַקֹּדֶשׁ. זֶה הַצִּיץ: עַל הַמִּצְנָפֶת. כְּמוֹ שֶׁפֵּרַשְׁתִּי לְמַעְלָה (לעיל כח, לו), עַל יְדֵי הַפְּתִיל הַחֶמְצָעִי וּשְׁנֵי פְתִילִין שֶׁבְּרֹאשׁוֹ הַקְּשׁוּרִין שְׁלָשְׁתָּן מֵאֲחוֹרֵי הָעֹרֶף הוּא נָתוּן עַל הַמִּצְנֶפֶת כְּמִין כּוֹבַע:

ז| וּמָשַׁחְתָּ אֹתוֹ. אַף מְשִׁיחָה זוֹ כְּמִין כָ"י, נוֹתֵן שֶׁמֶן עַל רֹאשׁוֹ וּבֵין רִיסֵי עֵינָיו וּמְחַבְּרָן בְּאֶצְבָּעוֹ:

ט| וְהָיְתָה לָהֶם. מִלּוּי יָדַיִם זֶה לִכְהֻנַּת עוֹלָם: וּמִלֵּאתָ. עַל יְדֵי הַדְּבָרִים הָאֵלֶּה: יַד אַהֲרֹן וְיַד בָּנָיו. בְּמִלּוּי וּפְקֻדַּת הַכְּהֻנָּה:

הַפָּר: וְשָׁחַטְתָּ אֶת־הַפָּר לִפְנֵי יְהוה פֶּתַח אֹהֶל מוֹעֵד: וְלָקַחְתָּ יב
מִדַּם הַפָּר וְנָתַתָּה עַל־קַרְנֹת הַמִּזְבֵּחַ בְּאֶצְבָּעֶךָ וְאֶת־כָּל־הַדָּם
תִּשְׁפֹּךְ אֶל־יְסוֹד הַמִּזְבֵּחַ: וְלָקַחְתָּ אֶת־כָּל־הַחֵלֶב הַמְכַסֶּה יג
אֶת־הַקֶּרֶב וְאֵת הַיֹּתֶרֶת עַל־הַכָּבֵד וְאֵת שְׁתֵּי הַכְּלָיֹת וְאֶת־
הַחֵלֶב אֲשֶׁר עֲלֵיהֶן וְהִקְטַרְתָּ הַמִּזְבֵּחָה: וְאֶת־בְּשַׂר הַפָּר וְאֶת־ יד
עֹרוֹ וְאֶת־פִּרְשׁוֹ תִּשְׂרֹף בָּאֵשׁ מִחוּץ לַמַּחֲנֶה חַטָּאת הוּא:
וְאֶת־הָאַיִל הָאֶחָד תִּקָּח וְסָמְכוּ אַהֲרֹן וּבָנָיו אֶת־יְדֵיהֶם עַל־ טו
רֹאשׁ הָאָיִל: וְשָׁחַטְתָּ אֶת־הָאָיִל וְלָקַחְתָּ אֶת־דָּמוֹ וְזָרַקְתָּ עַל־ טז
הַמִּזְבֵּחַ סָבִיב: וְאֶת־הָאַיִל תְּנַתֵּחַ לִנְתָחָיו וְרָחַצְתָּ קִרְבּוֹ וּכְרָעָיו יז
וְנָתַתָּ עַל־נְתָחָיו וְעַל־רֹאשׁוֹ: וְהִקְטַרְתָּ אֶת־כָּל־הָאַיִל הַמִּזְבֵּחָה יח
עֹלָה הוּא לַיהוה רֵיחַ נִיחוֹחַ אִשֶּׁה לַיהוה הוּא: וְלָקַחְתָּ אֵת יט
הָאַיִל הַשֵּׁנִי וְסָמַךְ אַהֲרֹן וּבָנָיו אֶת־יְדֵיהֶם עַל־רֹאשׁ הָאָיִל:
וְשָׁחַטְתָּ אֶת־הָאַיִל וְלָקַחְתָּ מִדָּמוֹ וְנָתַתָּה עַל־תְּנוּךְ אֹזֶן אַהֲרֹן כ

חמישי

יא) **פֶּתַח אֹהֶל מוֹעֵד.** בַּחֲצַר הַמִּשְׁכָּן שֶׁלִּפְנֵי הַפֶּתַח:

יב) **עַל קַרְנֹת.** לְמַעְלָה בַּקְּרָנוֹת מַמָּשׁ: **וְאֶת כָּל הַדָּם.** שְׁיָרֵי הַדָּם: **אֶל יְסוֹד הַמִּזְבֵּחַ.** כְּמִין בְּלִיטַת בֵּית קִבּוּל עָשׂוּי לוֹ סָבִיב סָבִיב לְאַחַר שֶׁעָלָה אַמָּה מִן הָאָרֶץ:

יג) **הַחֵלֶב הַמְכַסֶּה אֶת הַקֶּרֶב.** הוּא הַקְּרוּם שֶׁעַל הַכֶּרֶס שֶׁקּוֹרִין טיל"א: **וְאֵת הַיֹּתֶרֶת.** הוּא טַרְפְּשָׁא דְּכַבְדָא שֶׁקּוֹרִין אייב"לש: **עַל הַכָּבֵד.** אַף מִן הַכָּבֵד יִטֹּל עִמָּהּ:

יד) **תִּשְׂרֹף בָּאֵשׁ.** לֹא מָצִינוּ חַטָּאת חִיצוֹנָה נִשְׂרֶפֶת אֶלָּא זוֹ:

טו) **וְזָרַקְתָּ.** בַּכְּלִי, אוֹחֵז בַּמִּזְרָק וְזוֹרֵק כְּנֶגֶד הַקֶּרֶן, כְּדֵי שֵׁיֵּרָאֶה לְכָאן וּלְכָאן. וְאֵין קָרְבָּן טָעוּן מַתָּנָה

בְּאֶצְבַּע חוּץ מֵחַטָּאת בִּלְבַד. אֲבָל שְׁאָר זְבָחִים אֵינָן טְעוּנִין קֶרֶן וְלֹא אֶצְבַּע, שֶׁמַּתַּן דָּמָם מֵחֲצִי הַמִּזְבֵּחַ וּלְמַטָּה, וְאֵינוֹ עוֹלֶה בְּכֶבֶשׁ אֶלָּא עוֹמֵד בָּאָרֶץ וְזוֹרֵק. כָּךְ מְפֹרָשׁ בִּשְׁחִיטַת קָדָשִׁים (זבחים נ"ג ע"ב), שֶׁאֵין "סָבִיב" אֶלָּא שְׁתֵּי מַתָּנוֹת שֶׁהֵן אַרְבַּע, הָאַחַת בְּפִקְרָן זָוִית זוֹ וְהָאַחַת בִּכְנֶגְדָּה בַּאֲלַכְסוֹן, וְכָל מַתָּנָה נִרְאֵית בִּשְׁנֵי צִדֵּי הַקֶּרֶן אֵילָךְ וָאֵילָךְ, נִמְצָא הַדָּם נָתוּן בְּאַרְבַּע רוּחוֹת סָבִיב, לְכָךְ קָרוּי סָבִיב:

יז) **עַל נְתָחָיו.** עִם נְתָחָיו, מוּסָף עַל שְׁאָר הַנְּתָחִים:

יח) **רֵיחַ נִיחוֹחַ.** נַחַת רוּחַ לְפָנַי שֶׁאָמַרְתִּי וְנַעֲשָׂה רְצוֹנִי: **אִשֶּׁה.** לְשׁוֹן אֵשׁ, וְהִיא הַקְטָרַת אֵבָרִים שֶׁעַל הָאֵשׁ:

כ) **תְּנוּךְ.** הוּא הַסְּחוּס הָאֶמְצָעִי שֶׁבְּתוֹךְ הָאֹזֶן שֶׁקּוֹרִין טנדרו"ם: **בֹּהֶן יָדָם.** הַגּוּדָל, וּבַפֶּרֶק הָאֶמְצָעִי:

וְעַל־תְּנוּךְ אֹזֶן בָּנָיו הַיְמָנִית וְעַל־בֹּהֶן יָדָם הַיְמָנִית וְעַל־בֹּהֶן
כא רַגְלָם הַיְמָנִית וְזָרַקְתָּ אֶת־הַדָּם עַל־הַמִּזְבֵּחַ סָבִיב: וְלָקַחְתָּ
מִן־הַדָּם אֲשֶׁר עַל־הַמִּזְבֵּחַ וּמִשֶּׁמֶן הַמִּשְׁחָה וְהִזֵּיתָ עַל־אַהֲרֹן
וְעַל־בְּגָדָיו וְעַל־בָּנָיו וְעַל־בִּגְדֵי בָנָיו אִתּוֹ וְקָדַשׁ הוּא וּבְגָדָיו
כב וּבָנָיו וּבִגְדֵי בָנָיו אִתּוֹ: וְלָקַחְתָּ מִן־הָאַיִל הַחֵלֶב וְהָאַלְיָה וְאֶת־
הַחֵלֶב ׀ הַמְכַסֶּה אֶת־הַקֶּרֶב וְאֵת יֹתֶרֶת הַכָּבֵד וְאֵת ׀ שְׁתֵּי
הַכְּלָיֹת וְאֶת־הַחֵלֶב אֲשֶׁר עֲלֵהֶן וְאֵת שׁוֹק הַיָּמִין כִּי אֵיל
כג מִלֻּאִים הוּא: וְכִכַּר לֶחֶם אַחַת וְחַלַּת לֶחֶם שֶׁמֶן אַחַת וְרָקִיק
כד אֶחָד מִסַּל הַמַּצּוֹת אֲשֶׁר לִפְנֵי יהוה: וְשַׂמְתָּ הַכֹּל עַל כַּפֵּי אַהֲרֹן
וְעַל כַּפֵּי בָנָיו וְהֵנַפְתָּ אֹתָם תְּנוּפָה לִפְנֵי יהוה: וְלָקַחְתָּ אֹתָם
כה מִיָּדָם וְהִקְטַרְתָּ הַמִּזְבֵּחָה עַל־הָעֹלָה לְרֵיחַ נִיחוֹחַ לִפְנֵי יהוה
כו אִשֶּׁה הוּא לַיהוה: וְלָקַחְתָּ אֶת־הֶחָזֶה מֵאֵיל הַמִּלֻּאִים אֲשֶׁר
לְאַהֲרֹן וְהֵנַפְתָּ אֹתוֹ תְּנוּפָה לִפְנֵי יהוה וְהָיָה לְךָ לְמָנָה:

כב] הַחֵלֶב. זֶה חֵלֶב הַדַּקִּין אוֹ הַקֵּבָה: וְהָאַלְיָה. מִן הַכְּלָיוֹת וּלְמַטָּה, כְּמוֹ שֶׁמְּפֹרָשׁ בְּ"וַיִּקְרָא" (ג, ט), שֶׁנֶּאֱמַר: "לְעֻמַּת הֶעָצֶה יְסִירֶנָּה", מָקוֹם שֶׁהַכְּלָיוֹת יוֹעֲצוֹת. וּבְאֵמוּרֵי הַפָּר לֹא נֶאֱמַר חֶלְיָה, שֶׁאֵין אַלְיָה קְרֵבָה אֶלָּא בְּכֶבֶשׂ וְכִבְשָׂה וְאַיִל, אֲבָל שׁוֹר וָעֵז אֵין טְעוּנִים אַלְיָה: וְאֵת שׁוֹק הַיָּמִין. לֹא מָצִינוּ הַקְטָרָה בְּשׁוֹק הַיָּמִין עִם הָאֵמוּרִים אֶלָּא זוֹ בִּלְבַד: כִּי אֵיל מִלֻּאִים הוּא. שְׁלָמִים, לְשׁוֹן שְׁלֵמוּת, שֶׁמַּשְׁלִים בַּכֹּל. מַגִּיד הַכָּתוּב שֶׁהַמִּלּוּאִים שְׁלָמִים, שֶׁמְּשִׂימִים שָׁלוֹם לַמִּזְבֵּחַ וְלָעוֹבֵד הָעֲבוֹדָה וְלַבְּעָלִים, לְכָךְ אֲנִי מַעֲרִיכוֹ הֶחָזֶה לִהְיוֹת לָעוֹבֵד הָעֲבוֹדָה לְמָנָה, וְזֶהוּ מֹשֶׁה שֶׁשִּׁמֵּשׁ בַּמִּלּוּאִים, וְהַשְּׁאָר אָכְלוּ אַהֲרֹן וּבָנָיו שֶׁהֵם בְּעָלִים כִּמְפֹרָשׁ בְּעִנְיָן:

כג] וְכִכַּר לֶחֶם. מִן הַחַלּוֹת: וְחַלַּת לֶחֶם שֶׁמֶן. מִמִּין הָרְבוּכָה: וְרָקִיק. מִן הָרְקִיקִין, אֶחָד מֵעֲשָׂרָה שֶׁבְּכָל

מִין וָמִין. וְלֹא מָצִינוּ תְּרוּמַת לֶחֶם עִם זֶבַח נִקְטֶרֶת חֵלֶב זוֹ בִּלְבַד, שֶׁתְּרוּמַת לַחְמֵי תּוֹדָה וְאֵיל נָזִיר נְתוּנָה לַכֹּהֲנִים עִם חָזֶה וָשׁוֹק, וּמִזֶּה לֹא הָיָה לְמֹשֶׁה לְמָנָה אֶלָּא חָזֶה בִּלְבַד:

כד] עַל כַּפֵּי אַהֲרֹן... וְהֵנַפְתָּ. שְׁנֵיהֶם עֲסוּקִין בַּתְּנוּפָה, הַבְּעָלִים וְהַכֹּהֵן. הָא כֵּיצַד? כֹּהֵן מַנִּיחַ יָדוֹ תַּחַת יַד הַבְּעָלִים וּמֵנִיף, וּבָזֶה הָיוּ אַהֲרֹן וּבָנָיו בְּעָלִים וּמֹשֶׁה כֹהֵן: תְּנוּפָה. מוֹלִיךְ וּמֵבִיא, לְמִי שֶׁאַרְבַּע רוּחוֹת הָעוֹלָם שֶׁלּוֹ, וּתְנוּפָה מְעַכֶּבֶת וּמְבַטֶּלֶת פֻּרְעָנוּיּוֹת רוּחוֹת רָעוֹת. מַעֲלֶה וּמוֹרִיד, לְמִי שֶׁהַשָּׁמַיִם וְהָאָרֶץ שֶׁלּוֹ, וּמְעַכֶּבֶת טְלָלִים רָעִים:

כה] עַל הָעֹלָה. עַל הָאַיִל הָרִאשׁוֹן שֶׁהֶעֱלֵיתָ עוֹלָה: לְרֵיחַ נִיחוֹחַ. לְנַחַת רוּחַ לְמִי שֶׁאָמַר וְנַעֲשָׂה רְצוֹנוֹ: אִשֶּׁה. לָאֵשׁ נִתַּן: לַה'. לִשְׁמוֹ שֶׁל מָקוֹם:

פרק כט | שמות | תצוה

כז וְקִדַּשְׁתָּ אֵת ׀ חֲזֵה הַתְּנוּפָה וְאֵת שׁוֹק הַתְּרוּמָה אֲשֶׁר הוּנַף וַאֲשֶׁר הוּרָם מֵאֵיל הַמִּלֻּאִים מֵאֲשֶׁר לְאַהֲרֹן וּמֵאֲשֶׁר לְבָנָיו:
כח וְהָיָה לְאַהֲרֹן וּלְבָנָיו לְחָק־עוֹלָם מֵאֵת בְּנֵי יִשְׂרָאֵל כִּי תְרוּמָה הוּא וּתְרוּמָה יִהְיֶה מֵאֵת בְּנֵי־יִשְׂרָאֵל מִזִּבְחֵי שַׁלְמֵיהֶם תְּרוּמָתָם לַיהוה:
כט וּבִגְדֵי הַקֹּדֶשׁ אֲשֶׁר לְאַהֲרֹן יִהְיוּ לְבָנָיו אַחֲרָיו לְמָשְׁחָה בָהֶם וּלְמַלֵּא־בָם אֶת־יָדָם:
ל שִׁבְעַת יָמִים יִלְבָּשָׁם הַכֹּהֵן תַּחְתָּיו מִבָּנָיו אֲשֶׁר יָבֹא אֶל־אֹהֶל מוֹעֵד לְשָׁרֵת בַּקֹּדֶשׁ:
לא וְאֵת אֵיל הַמִּלֻּאִים תִּקָּח וּבִשַּׁלְתָּ אֶת־בְּשָׂרוֹ בְּמָקֹם קָדֹשׁ:
לב וְאָכַל אַהֲרֹן וּבָנָיו אֶת־בְּשַׂר הָאַיִל וְאֶת־הַלֶּחֶם אֲשֶׁר בַּסָּל פֶּתַח אֹהֶל מוֹעֵד:
לג וְאָכְלוּ אֹתָם אֲשֶׁר כֻּפַּר בָּהֶם לְמַלֵּא אֶת־יָדָם לְקַדֵּשׁ אֹתָם וְזָר לֹא־יֹאכַל כִּי־קֹדֶשׁ הֵם:
לד וְאִם־יִוָּתֵר מִבְּשַׂר הַמִּלֻּאִים וּמִן־הַלֶּחֶם עַד־הַבֹּקֶר וְשָׂרַפְתָּ אֶת־הַנּוֹתָר בָּאֵשׁ לֹא יֵאָכֵל כִּי־קֹדֶשׁ הוּא:

כז-כח | וְקִדַּשְׁתָּ אֵת חֲזֵה הַתְּנוּפָה וְאֵת שׁוֹק הַתְּרוּמָה וְגוֹ'. קַדֵּשׁ לְדוֹרוֹת לִהְיוֹת נוֹהֶגֶת תְּרוּמָתָם וַהֲנָפָתָם בֶּחָזֶה וָשׁוֹק שֶׁל שְׁלָמִים, אֲבָל לֹא לְהַקְטָרָה, אֶלָּא "וְהָיָה לְאַהֲרֹן וּלְבָנָיו" לֶאֱכֹל. לְחָק עוֹלָם מֵאֵת בְּנֵי יִשְׂרָאֵל. שֶׁהַשְּׁלָמִים לַבְּעָלִים, וְאֶת הֶחָזֶה וְהַשּׁוֹק יִתְּנוּ לַכֹּהֵן. תְּנוּפָה. לְשׁוֹן הוֹלָכָה וַהֲבָאָה, ונטיל"ד בְּלַעַ"ז. הוּרַם. לְשׁוֹן מַעֲלֶה וּמוֹרִיד: כִּי תְרוּמָה הוּא. הֶחָזֶה וְהַשּׁוֹק הַזֶּה:

כט | יִהְיוּ לְבָנָיו אַחֲרָיו. לְמִי שֶׁבָּא בִגְדֻלָּה אַחֲרָיו. לְמָשְׁחָה. לְהִתְגַּדֵּל בָּהֶם, שֶׁיֵּשׁ מְשִׁיחָה שֶׁהִיא לְשׁוֹן שְׂרָרָה, כְּמוֹ: "לְךָ נְתַתִּים לְמָשְׁחָה" (במדבר יח, ח), "אַל תִּגְּעוּ בִמְשִׁיחָי" (תהלים קה, טו): וּלְמַלֵּא בָם אֶת יָדָם. עַל יְדֵי הַבְּגָדִים הוּא מִתְלַבֵּשׁ בִּכְהֻנָּה גְדוֹלָה:

ל | שִׁבְעַת יָמִים. רְצוּפִין: יִלְבָּשָׁם הַכֹּהֵן. אֲשֶׁר יָקוּם מִבָּנָיו תַּחְתָּיו לִכְהֻנָּה גְדוֹלָה, כְּשֶׁיְּמַנּוּהוּ לִהְיוֹת כֹּהֵן גָּדוֹל: אֲשֶׁר יָבֹא אֶל אֹהֶל מוֹעֵד. אוֹתוֹ כֹּהֵן הַמּוּכָן לִכָּנֵס לִפְנַי וְלִפְנִים בְּיוֹם הַכִּפּוּרִים, וְזֶהוּ כֹּהֵן גָּדוֹל, שֶׁאֵין עֲבוֹדַת יוֹם הַכִּפּוּרִים כְּשֵׁרָה אֶלָּא בּוֹ. מִבָּנָיו. מְלַמֵּד שֶׁאִם יֵשׁ לוֹ לַכֹּהֵן גָּדוֹל בֵּן מְמַלֵּא אֶת מְקוֹמוֹ, יְמַנּוּהוּ כֹהֵן גָּדוֹל תַּחְתָּיו:

לא | בְּמָקֹם קָדֹשׁ. בַּחֲצַר אֹהֶל מוֹעֵד, שֶׁהַשְּׁלָמִים הַלָּלוּ קָדְשֵׁי קָדָשִׁים הָיוּ:

לב | פֶּתַח אֹהֶל מוֹעֵד. כָּל הֶחָצֵר קָרוּי כֵּן:

לג | וְאָכְלוּ אֹתָם. אַהֲרֹן וּבָנָיו, לְפִי שֶׁהֵם בַּעֲלֵיהֶם: אֲשֶׁר כֻּפַּר בָּהֶם. כָּל זָרוּת וְתִעוּב: לְמַלֵּא אֶת יָדָם. בָּאַיִל וּבַלֶּחֶם הַלָּלוּ: לְקַדֵּשׁ אֹתָם. שֶׁעַל יְדֵי הַמִּלּוּאִים הַלָּלוּ נִתְמַלְּאוּ יְדֵיהֶם וְנִתְקַדְּשׁוּ לִכְהֻנָּה: כִּי קֹדֶשׁ הֵם. קָדְשֵׁי קָדָשִׁים. וּמִכָּאן לָמַדְנוּ אַזְהָרָה לְזָר הָאוֹכֵל קָדְשֵׁי קָדָשִׁים (מכילתא עח,א), שֶׁנָּתַן הַמִּקְרָא טַעַם לַדָּבָר מִשּׁוּם דְּ"קֹדֶשׁ הֵם":

שמות | פרק כט

לה וְעָשִׂ֜יתָ לְאַהֲרֹ֤ן וּלְבָנָיו֙ כָּ֔כָה כְּכֹ֥ל אֲשֶׁר־צִוִּ֖יתִי אֹתָ֑כָה שִׁבְעַ֥ת
לו יָמִ֖ים תְּמַלֵּ֥א יָדָֽם: וּפַ֨ר חַטָּ֜את תַּעֲשֶׂ֤ה לַיּוֹם֙ עַל־הַכִּפֻּרִ֔ים
וְחִטֵּאתָ֙ עַל־הַמִּזְבֵּ֔חַ בְּכַפֶּרְךָ֖ עָלָ֑יו וּמָשַׁחְתָּ֥ אֹת֖וֹ לְקַדְּשֽׁוֹ:
לז שִׁבְעַ֣ת יָמִ֗ים תְּכַפֵּר֙ עַל־הַמִּזְבֵּ֔חַ וְקִדַּשְׁתָּ֖ אֹת֑וֹ וְהָיָ֤ה הַמִּזְבֵּ֙חַ֙
לח קֹ֣דֶשׁ קָֽדָשִׁ֔ים כָּל־הַנֹּגֵ֥עַ בַּמִּזְבֵּ֖חַ יִקְדָּֽשׁ: וְזֶ֕ה אֲשֶׁ֥ר ‏<small>ששי</small>
לט תַּעֲשֶׂ֖ה עַל־הַמִּזְבֵּ֑חַ כְּבָשִׂ֧ים בְּנֵֽי־שָׁנָ֛ה שְׁנַ֥יִם לַיּ֖וֹם תָּמִֽיד: אֶת־
הַכֶּ֥בֶשׂ הָאֶחָ֖ד תַּעֲשֶׂ֣ה בַבֹּ֑קֶר וְאֵת֙ הַכֶּ֣בֶשׂ הַשֵּׁנִ֔י תַּעֲשֶׂ֖ה בֵּ֥ין
מ הָעַרְבָּֽיִם: וְעִשָּׂרֹ֨ן סֹ֜לֶת בָּל֨וּל בְּשֶׁ֤מֶן כָּתִית֙ רֶ֣בַע הַהִ֔ין וְנֵ֕סֶךְ
מא רְבִיעִ֥ת הַהִ֖ין יָ֣יִן לַכֶּ֣בֶשׂ הָאֶחָֽד: וְאֵת֙ הַכֶּ֣בֶשׂ הַשֵּׁנִ֔י תַּעֲשֶׂ֖ה בֵּ֥ין

לה) וְעָשִׂיתָ לְאַהֲרֹן וּלְבָנָיו כָּכָה. שָׁנָה הַכָּתוּב וְכָפַל לְעַכֵּב, שֶׁאִם חָסֵר דָּבָר אֶחָד מִכָּל הָאָמוּר בָּעִנְיָן, לֹא נִתְמַלְּאוּ יְדֵיהֶם לִהְיוֹת כֹּהֲנִים וַעֲבוֹדָתָם פְּסוּלָה: **אֹתָכָה.** כְּמוֹ אוֹתָךְ: **שִׁבְעַת יָמִים תְּמַלֵּא.** בָּעִנְיָן הַזֶּה וּבַקָּרְבָּנוֹת הַלָּלוּ בְּכָל יוֹם:

לו) עַל הַכִּפֻּרִים. בִּשְׁבִיל הַכִּפּוּרִים, לְכַפֵּר עַל הַמִּזְבֵּחַ מִכָּל זָרוּת וְתִעוּב. וּלְפִי שֶׁנֶּאֱמַר: "שִׁבְעַת יָמִים תְּמַלֵּא יָדָם" (בפסוק הקודם), אֵין לִי אֶלָּא דָבָר הַבָּא בִּשְׁבִילָם, כְּגוֹן הַחֲלִיטִים וְהַלֶּחֶם, אֲבָל הַבָּא בִּשְׁבִיל הַמִּזְבֵּחַ, כְּגוֹן פַּר שֶׁהוּא לְחִטּוּי הַמִּזְבֵּחַ, לֹא שָׁמַעְנוּ, לְכָךְ הֻצְרַךְ מִקְרָא זֶה. וּמִדְרַשׁ תּוֹרַת כֹּהֲנִים (ויקרא ח, יד מלואים טו) אוֹמֵר: כַּפָּרַת הַמִּזְבֵּחַ הַעֲרָכָה שֶׁמָּא הִתְנַדֵּב אִישׁ מִיִּשְׂרָאֵל דָּבָר גָּזֵל בִּמְלֶאכֶת הַמִּשְׁכָּן: **וְחִטֵּאתָ.** "וְתִדַּכֵּי", לְשׁוֹן מַתְּנַת דָּמִים הַנִּתָּנִים בָּאֶצְבַּע קָרוּי חִטּוּי: **וּמָשַׁחְתָּ אֹתוֹ.** בְּשֶׁמֶן הַמִּשְׁחָה. וְכָל הַמְּשִׁיחוֹת כְּמִין כ״ף:

לז) וְהָיָה הַמִּזְבֵּחַ קֹדֶשׁ. וּמַה הִיא קְדֻשָּׁתוֹ? **כָּל הַנֹּגֵעַ בַּמִּזְבֵּחַ יִקְדָּשׁ.** אֲפִלּוּ קָרְבָּן פָּסוּל שֶׁעָלָה עָלָיו, קִדְּשׁוֹ הַמִּזְבֵּחַ לְהַכְשִׁירוֹ שֶׁלֹּא יֵרֵד. מִתּוֹךְ שֶׁנֶּאֱמַר: "כָּל הַנֹּגֵעַ... יִקְדָּשׁ", שׁוֹמֵעַ אֲנִי בֵּין רָאוּי בֵּין שֶׁאֵינוֹ רָאוּי, כְּגוֹן דָּבָר שֶׁלֹּא הָיָה פְּסוּלוֹ בַקֹּדֶשׁ, כְּגוֹן הָרוֹבֵעַ וְהַנִּרְבָּע וּמֻקְצֶה וְנֶעֱבַד וְהָאֶתְנָן וְהַמְּחִיר וְכַיּוֹצֵא בָהֶן, תַּלְמוּד לוֹמַר: "וְזֶה אֲשֶׁר תַּעֲשֶׂה" הַסָּמוּךְ אַחֲרָיו, מָה עוֹלָה רְאוּיָה אַף כָּל רָאוּי, שֶׁנִּרְאָה לוֹ כְּבָר וְנִפְסַל מִשֶּׁבָּא לָעֲזָרָה, כְּגוֹן הַלָּן וְהַיּוֹצֵא וְהַטָּמֵא וְשֶׁנִּשְׁחַט בְּמַחֲשֶׁבֶת חוּץ לִזְמַנּוֹ וְחוּץ לִמְקוֹמוֹ וְכַיּוֹצֵא בָהֶן:

מ) וְעִשָּׂרֹן סֹלֶת. עֲשִׂירִית הָאֵיפָה, אַרְבָּעִים וְשָׁלֹשׁ בֵּיצִים וְחֹמֶשׁ בֵּיצָה: **בְּשֶׁמֶן כָּתִית.** לֹא לְחוֹבָה נֶאֱמַר "כָּתִית", אֶלָּא לְהַכְשִׁיר, לְפִי שֶׁנֶּאֱמַר: "כָּתִית לַמָּאוֹר" (לעיל כז, כ), וּמַשְׁמָע לַמָּאוֹר וְלֹא לַמְּנָחוֹת, יָכוֹל לְפָסְלוֹ לַמְּנָחוֹת? תַּלְמוּד לוֹמַר כָּאן: "כָּתִית", וְלֹא נֶאֱמַר "כָּתִית לַמָּאוֹר" אֶלָּא לְמַעֵט מְנָחוֹת שֶׁאֵין צָרִיךְ כָּתִית, שֶׁאַף הַטָּחוּן בָּרֵחַיִם כָּשֵׁר בָּהֶן: **רֶבַע הַהִין.** שְׁלֹשֶׁת לוֹגִין: **וָנֶסֶךְ.** לַסְּפָלִים, כְּמוֹ שֶׁשָּׁנִינוּ בְּמַסֶּכֶת סֻכָּה (דף מח ע״ב): שְׁנֵי סְפָלִים שֶׁל כֶּסֶף הָיוּ בְּרֹאשׁ הַמִּזְבֵּחַ וּמְנֻקָּבִים כְּמִין שְׁנֵי חֳטָמִין דַּקִּים, נוֹתֵן הַיַּיִן לְתוֹכוֹ וְהוּא מְקַלֵּחַ וְיוֹצֵא דֶּרֶךְ הַחֹטֶם וְנוֹפֵל עַל גַּג הַמִּזְבֵּחַ, וּמִשָּׁם יוֹרֵד לַשִּׁיתִין בְּמִזְבַּח בֵּית עוֹלָמִים, וּבַמִּזְבֵּחַ הַנְּחֹשֶׁת יוֹרֵד מִן הַמִּזְבֵּחַ לָאָרֶץ:

הָעַרְבָּיִם כְּמִנְחַת הַבֹּקֶר וּכְנִסְכָּהּ תַּעֲשֶׂה־לָּהּ לְרֵיחַ נִיחֹחַ אִשֶּׁה לַיהוה: עֹלַת תָּמִיד לְדֹרֹתֵיכֶם פֶּתַח אֹהֶל־מוֹעֵד לִפְנֵי יהוה אֲשֶׁר אִוָּעֵד לָכֶם שָׁמָּה לְדַבֵּר אֵלֶיךָ שָׁם: וְנֹעַדְתִּי שָׁמָּה לִבְנֵי יִשְׂרָאֵל וְנִקְדַּשׁ בִּכְבֹדִי: וְקִדַּשְׁתִּי אֶת־אֹהֶל מוֹעֵד וְאֶת־הַמִּזְבֵּחַ וְאֶת־אַהֲרֹן וְאֶת־בָּנָיו אֲקַדֵּשׁ לְכַהֵן לִי: וְשָׁכַנְתִּי בְּתוֹךְ בְּנֵי יִשְׂרָאֵל וְהָיִיתִי לָהֶם לֵאלֹהִים: וְיָדְעוּ כִּי אֲנִי יהוה אֱלֹהֵיהֶם אֲשֶׁר הוֹצֵאתִי אֹתָם מֵאֶרֶץ מִצְרַיִם לְשָׁכְנִי בְתוֹכָם אֲנִי יהוה אֱלֹהֵיהֶם:

שביעי וְעָשִׂיתָ מִזְבֵּחַ מִקְטַר קְטֹרֶת עֲצֵי שִׁטִּים תַּעֲשֶׂה אֹתוֹ: אַמָּה אָרְכּוֹ וְאַמָּה רָחְבּוֹ רָבוּעַ יִהְיֶה וְאַמָּתַיִם קֹמָתוֹ מִמֶּנּוּ קַרְנֹתָיו: וְצִפִּיתָ אֹתוֹ זָהָב טָהוֹר אֶת־גַּגּוֹ וְאֶת־קִירֹתָיו סָבִיב וְאֶת־קַרְנֹתָיו וְעָשִׂיתָ לּוֹ זֵר זָהָב סָבִיב: וּשְׁתֵּי טַבְּעֹת זָהָב תַּעֲשֶׂה־לּוֹ ׀ מִתַּחַת לְזֵרוֹ עַל שְׁתֵּי צַלְעֹתָיו תַּעֲשֶׂה עַל־שְׁנֵי צִדָּיו וְהָיָה לְבָתִּים לְבַדִּים

מא] לְרֵיחַ נִיחֹחַ. עַל הַמִּנְחָה נֶאֱמַר, שֶׁמִּנְחַת נְסָכִים כֻּלָּהּ כָּלִיל. וְסֵדֶר הַקְרָבָתָם, הָאֵבָרִים בַּתְּחִלָּה וְאַחַר כָּךְ הַמִּנְחָה, שֶׁנֶּאֱמַר: "עֹלָה וּמִנְחָה" (ויקרא כג, לז):

מב] תָּמִיד. מִיּוֹם אֶל יוֹם, לֹא יַפְסִיק יוֹם בֵּינְתַיִם: **אֲשֶׁר אִוָּעֵד לָכֶם.** כְּשֶׁאֶקְבַּע מוֹעֵד לְדַבֵּר אֵלֶיךָ, שָׁם אֶקְבָּעֶנּוּ לָבֹא. וְיֵשׁ מֵרַבּוֹתֵינוּ לְמֵדִים מִכָּאן שֶׁמֵּעַל מִזְבַּח הַנְּחֹשֶׁת הָיָה הַקָּדוֹשׁ בָּרוּךְ הוּא מְדַבֵּר עִם מֹשֶׁה מִשֶּׁהוּקַם הַמִּשְׁכָּן. וְיֵשׁ אוֹמְרִים מֵעַל הַכַּפֹּרֶת, כְּמוֹ שֶׁנֶּאֱמַר: "וְדִבַּרְתִּי אִתְּךָ מֵעַל הַכַּפֹּרֶת" (לעיל כה, כב), וַ"אֲשֶׁר אִוָּעֵד לָכֶם" הָאָמוּר כָּאן אֵינוֹ אָמוּר עַל הַמִּזְבֵּחַ, אֶלָּא עַל "אֹהֶל מוֹעֵד" הַנִּזְכָּר בַּמִּקְרָא:

מג] וְנֹעַדְתִּי שָׁמָּה. אֶתְוַעֵד עִמָּם בְּדִבּוּר, כְּמֶלֶךְ הַקּוֹבֵעַ מְקוֹם מוֹעֵד לְדַבֵּר עִם עֲבָדָיו שָׁם: **וְנִקְדַּשׁ** בִּ"כְבֹדִי", שֶׁתִּשְׁרֶה שְׁכִינָתִי בּוֹ. וּמִדְרַשׁ אַגָּדָה, אַל תִּקְרֵי "בִּכְבֹדִי" אֶלָּא 'בִּכְבוּדַי', בַּמְכֻבָּדִים שֶׁלִּי, כָּאן רָמַז לוֹ מִיתַת בְּנֵי אַהֲרֹן בְּיוֹם הֲקָמָתוֹ, וְזֶהוּ שֶׁאָמַר מֹשֶׁה: "הוּא אֲשֶׁר דִּבֶּר ה' לֵאמֹר בִּקְרֹבַי אֶקָּדֵשׁ" (ויקרא י, ג), וְהֵיכָן דִּבֶּר? "וְנִקְדַּשׁ בִּכְבֹדִי":

מו] לְשָׁכְנִי בְתוֹכָם. עַל מְנָת לִשְׁכֹּן אֲנִי בְּתוֹכָם:

פרק ל

א] מִקְטַר קְטֹרֶת. לְהַעֲלוֹת עָלָיו קִטּוֹר עֲשַׁן סַמִּים:

ג] אֶת גַּגּוֹ. זֶה הָיָה לוֹ גַג, אֲבָל מִזְבַּח הָעוֹלָה לֹא הָיָה לוֹ גַג, אֶלָּא מְמַלְּאִים חֲלָלוֹ אֲדָמָה בְּכָל חֲנִיָּתָן: **זֵר זָהָב.** סִימָן לְכֶתֶר כְּהֻנָּה:

ד] צַלְעֹתָיו. כָּאן הוּא לְשׁוֹן זָוִיּוֹת, כְּתַרְגּוּמוֹ, לְפִי שֶׁנֶּאֱמַר: "עַל שְׁנֵי צִדָּיו", שְׁתֵּי זָוִיּוֹתָיו שֶׁבִּשְׁנֵי צְדָדָיו: **וְהָיָה.** מַעֲשֵׂה הַטַּבָּעוֹת הָאֵלֶּה "לְבָתִּים לְבַדִּים", בֵּית תִּהְיֶה הַטַּבַּעַת לַבָּד:

שמות | פרק ל | כי תשא

ה לָשֵׂאת אֹתוֹ בָּהֵֽמָּה: וְעָשִׂיתָ אֶת־הַבַּדִּים עֲצֵי שִׁטִּים וְצִפִּיתָ
ו אֹתָם זָהָֽב: וְנָתַתָּה אֹתוֹ לִפְנֵי הַפָּרֹכֶת אֲשֶׁר עַל־אֲרֹן הָעֵדֻת
ז לִפְנֵי הַכַּפֹּרֶת אֲשֶׁר עַל־הָעֵדֻת אֲשֶׁר אִוָּעֵד לְךָ שָֽׁמָּה: וְהִקְטִיר
עָלָיו אַהֲרֹן קְטֹרֶת סַמִּים בַּבֹּקֶר בַּבֹּקֶר בְּהֵיטִיבוֹ אֶת־הַנֵּרֹת
ח יַקְטִירֶֽנָּה: וּבְהַעֲלֹת אַהֲרֹן אֶת־הַנֵּרֹת בֵּין הָעַרְבַּיִם יַקְטִירֶנָּה [מפטיר]
ט קְטֹרֶת תָּמִיד לִפְנֵי יְהֹוָה לְדֹרֹתֵיכֶֽם: לֹא־תַעֲלוּ עָלָיו קְטֹרֶת זָרָה
י וְעֹלָה וּמִנְחָה וְנֵסֶךְ לֹא תִסְּכוּ עָלָֽיו: וְכִפֶּר אַהֲרֹן עַל־קַרְנֹתָיו
אַחַת בַּשָּׁנָה מִדַּם חַטַּאת הַכִּפֻּרִים אַחַת בַּשָּׁנָה יְכַפֵּר עָלָיו
לְדֹרֹתֵיכֶם קֹֽדֶשׁ־קָֽדָשִׁים הוּא לַיהֹוָֽה:

יב וַיְדַבֵּר יְהֹוָה אֶל־מֹשֶׁה לֵּאמֹֽר: כִּי תִשָּׂא אֶת־רֹאשׁ בְּנֵי־יִשְׂרָאֵל [כי תשא]
לִפְקֻדֵיהֶם וְנָתְנוּ אִישׁ כֹּפֶר נַפְשׁוֹ לַיהֹוָה בִּפְקֹד אֹתָם וְלֹא־
יג יִהְיֶה בָהֶם נֶגֶף בִּפְקֹד אֹתָֽם: זֶה ׀ יִתְּנוּ כָּל־הָעֹבֵר עַל־הַפְּקֻדִים

ו) **לִפְנֵי הַפָּרֹכֶת.** שֶׁמָּא תֹּאמַר מָשׁוּךְ מִכְּנֶגֶד הָאָרוֹן לַצָּפוֹן אוֹ לַדָּרוֹם? תַּלְמוּד לוֹמַר: "לִפְנֵי הַכַּפֹּרֶת", מְכֻוָּן כְּנֶגֶד הָאָרוֹן מִבַּחוּץ:

ז-ח) **בְּהֵיטִיבוֹ.** לְשׁוֹן נִקּוּי הַבָּזִיכִין שֶׁל הַמְּנוֹרָה מִדֶּשֶׁן הַפְּתִילוֹת שֶׁנִּשְׂרְפוּ בַּלַּיְלָה, וְהָיָה מְטִיבָן בְּכָל בֹּקֶר וָבֹקֶר: **הַנֵּרֹת.** לוֹעַ"ז בְּלַעַ"ז, וְכֵן כָּל נֵרוֹת הָאֲמוּרוֹת בַּמְּנוֹרָה, חוּץ מִמָּקוֹם שֶׁנֶּאֱמַר שָׁם הַעֲלָאָה, שֶׁהוּא לְשׁוֹן הַדְלָקָה: **וּבְהַעֲלֹת.** כְּשֶׁיַּדְלִיקֵם לְהַעֲלוֹת לַהַבְתָּן "יַקְטִירֶנָּה". בְּכָל יוֹם מַקְטִיר פֶּרֶס שַׁחֲרִית וּפֶרֶס בֵּין הָעַרְבַּיִם:

ט) **לֹא תַעֲלוּ עָלָיו.** עַל מִזְבֵּחַ זֶה: **קְטֹרֶת זָרָה.** שׁוּם קְטֹרֶת שֶׁל נְדָבָה, כֻּלָּן זָרוֹת לוֹ חוּץ מִזּוֹ: **וְעֹלָה וּמִנְחָה.** וְלֹא עוֹלָה וּמִנְחָה. עוֹלָה שֶׁל בְּהֵמָה וָעוֹף, וּמִנְחָה הִיא שֶׁל מִין לֶחֶם:

י) **וְכִפֶּר אַהֲרֹן.** מַתַּן דָּמִים: **עַל קַרְנֹתָיו.** אַחַת בַּשָּׁנָה. בְּיוֹם הַכִּפּוּרִים, הוּא שֶׁנֶּאֱמַר בְּ"אַחֲרֵי מוֹת":

"וַיִּצַע אֶל הַמִּזְבֵּחַ אֲשֶׁר לִפְנֵי ה' וְכִפֶּר עָלָיו" (ויקרא טז, יח): **חַטַּאת הַכִּפֻּרִים.** הֵם פַּר וְשָׂעִיר שֶׁל יוֹם הַכִּפּוּרִים הַמְּכַפְּרִים עַל טֻמְאַת מִקְדָּשׁ וְקָדָשָׁיו: **קֹדֶשׁ קָדָשִׁים הוּא.** הַמִּזְבֵּחַ מְקֻדָּשׁ לַדְּבָרִים הַלָּלוּ בִּלְבַד וְלֹא לַעֲבוֹדָה אַחֶרֶת:

יב) **כִּי תִשָּׂא.** לְשׁוֹן קַבָּלָה, כְּתַרְגּוּמוֹ. כְּשֶׁתַּחְפֹּץ לְקַבֵּל סְכוּם מִנְיָנָם לָדַעַת כַּמָּה הֵם, אַל תִּמְנֵם לַגֻּלְגֹּלֶת, אֶלָּא יִתְּנוּ כָּל אֶחָד מַחֲצִית הַשֶּׁקֶל, וְתִמְנֶה אֶת הַשְּׁקָלִים וְתֵדַע מִנְיָנָם: **וְלֹא יִהְיֶה בָהֶם נֶגֶף.** שֶׁהַמִּנְיָן שׁוֹלֵט בּוֹ עַיִן הָרָע וְהַדֶּבֶר בָּא עֲלֵיהֶם, כְּמוֹ שֶׁמָּצִינוּ בִּימֵי דָּוִד (שמואל ב' כד, א-י):

יג) **זֶה יִתְּנוּ.** הֶרְאָה לוֹ כְּמִין מַטְבֵּעַ שֶׁל אֵשׁ וּמִשְׁקָלָהּ מַחֲצִית הַשֶּׁקֶל, וְאָמַר לוֹ: כָּזֶה יִתְּנוּ: **הָעֹבֵר עַל הַפְּקֻדִים.** דֶּרֶךְ הַמּוֹנִין מַעֲבִירִין אֶת הַנִּמְנִין זֶה אַחַר זֶה, וְכֵן: "כֹּל אֲשֶׁר יַעֲבֹר תַּחַת הַשָּׁבֶט" (ויקרא כז, לב), וְכֵן: "תַּעֲבֹרְנָה הַצֹּאן עַל יְדֵי מוֹנֶה" (ירמיה לג, יג):

מַחֲצִית הַשֶּׁקֶל בְּשֶׁקֶל הַקֹּדֶשׁ עֶשְׂרִים גֵּרָה הַשֶּׁקֶל מַחֲצִית הַשֶּׁקֶל תְּרוּמָה לַיהוה: יד כֹּל הָעֹבֵר עַל־הַפְּקֻדִים מִבֶּן עֶשְׂרִים שָׁנָה וָמָעְלָה יִתֵּן תְּרוּמַת יהוה: טו הֶעָשִׁיר לֹא־יַרְבֶּה וְהַדַּל לֹא יַמְעִיט מִמַּחֲצִית הַשָּׁקֶל לָתֵת אֶת־תְּרוּמַת יהוה לְכַפֵּר עַל־נַפְשֹׁתֵיכֶם: טז וְלָקַחְתָּ אֶת־כֶּסֶף הַכִּפֻּרִים מֵאֵת בְּנֵי יִשְׂרָאֵל וְנָתַתָּ אֹתוֹ עַל־עֲבֹדַת אֹהֶל מוֹעֵד וְהָיָה לִבְנֵי יִשְׂרָאֵל לְזִכָּרוֹן לִפְנֵי יהוה לְכַפֵּר עַל־נַפְשֹׁתֵיכֶם:

מַחֲצִית הַשֶּׁקֶל בְּשֶׁקֶל הַקֹּדֶשׁ. בְּמִשְׁקַל הַשֶּׁקֶל שֶׁקָּצַבְתִּי לְךָ לִשְׁקֹל בּוֹ שִׁקְלֵי הַקֹּדֶשׁ, כְּגוֹן שְׁקָלִים הָאֲמוּרִין בְּפָרָשַׁת עֲרָכִין (ויקרא כז, ג-ח) וּשְׂדֵה אֲחֻזָּה (שם פסוק טז-יט): **עֶשְׂרִים גֵּרָה הַשָּׁקֶל.** עַכְשָׁו פֵּרֵשׁ לְךָ כַּמָּה הוּא: **גֵּרָה.** לְשׁוֹן מָעָה, וְכֵן בִּשְׁמוּאֵל: "יָבוֹא לְהִשְׁתַּחֲוֹת לוֹ לַאֲגוֹרַת כֶּסֶף וְכִכַּר לָחֶם" (שמואל א' ב, לו): **עֶשְׂרִים גֵּרָה הַשָּׁקֶל.** הַשָּׁלֵם, שֶׁהַשֶּׁקֶל אַרְבָּעָה זוּזִים, וְהַזּוּז מִתְּחִלָּתוֹ חֲמֵשׁ מָעוֹת, אֶלָּא בָּא וְהוֹסִיפוּ עָלָיו שְׁתוּת וְהֶעֱלוּהוּ לְשֵׁשׁ מָעָה כֶּסֶף, וּמַחֲצִית הַשֶּׁקֶל הַזֶּה שֶׁאָמַרְתִּי לְךָ יִתְּנוּ תְּרוּמָה לַה':

יד **מִבֶּן עֶשְׂרִים שָׁנָה וָמָעְלָה.** לִמֶּדְךָ כָּאן שֶׁאֵין פָּחוֹת מִבֶּן עֶשְׂרִים יוֹצֵא לַצָּבָא וְנִמְנֶה בִּכְלַל אֲנָשִׁים:

טו **לְכַפֵּר עַל נַפְשֹׁתֵיכֶם.** שֶׁלֹּא תִנָּגְפוּ עַל יְדֵי מִנְיָן, דָּבָר אַחֵר, "לְכַפֵּר עַל נַפְשֹׁתֵיכֶם", לְפִי שֶׁרָמַז לָהֶם כָּאן שָׁלֹשׁ תְּרוּמוֹת, שֶׁנִּכְתַּב כָּאן "תְּרוּמַת ה'" שָׁלֹשׁ פְּעָמִים: אַחַת תְּרוּמַת אֲדָנִים, שֶׁמְּנָאָן כְּשֶׁהִתְחִילוּ בְּנִדְבַת הַמִּשְׁכָּן, שֶׁנָּתְנוּ כָּל אֶחָד וְאֶחָד מַחֲצִית הַשֶּׁקֶל וְעָלָה לִמְחַת הַכִּכָּר, שֶׁנֶּאֱמַר: "וְכֶסֶף פְּקוּדֵי הָעֵדָה מְאַת כִּכָּר" (להלן לח, כה), וּמֵהֶם נַעֲשׂוּ הָאֲדָנִים, שֶׁנֶּאֱמַר: "וַיְהִי מְאַת כִּכַּר הַכֶּסֶף" וְגוֹ' (שם פסוק כז). וְהַשֵּׁנִית אַף הִיא עַל יְדֵי מִנְיָן שֶׁמְּנָאָן מִשֶּׁהוּקַם הַמִּשְׁכָּן, הוּא הַמִּנְיָן הָאָמוּר בִּתְחִלַּת חוּמָשׁ הַפְּקוּדִים "בְּאֶחָד לַחֹדֶשׁ הַשֵּׁנִי בַּשָּׁנָה הַשֵּׁנִית" (במדבר א, א), וְנָתְנוּ כָל אֶחָד מַחֲצִית הַשֶּׁקֶל, וְהֵן לִקְנוֹת מֵהֶן קָרְבְּנוֹת צִבּוּר שֶׁל כָּל שָׁנָה וְשָׁנָה, וְהֻשְׁווּ בָהֶם עֲנִיִּים וַעֲשִׁירִים, וְעַל אוֹתָהּ תְּרוּמָה נֶאֱמַר: "לְכַפֵּר עַל נַפְשֹׁתֵיכֶם",

שֶׁהַקָּרְבָּנוֹת לְכַפָּרָה הֵם בָּאִים; וְהַשְּׁלִישִׁית הִיא תְּרוּמַת הַמִּשְׁכָּן, כְּמוֹ שֶׁנֶּאֱמַר: "כָּל מֵרִים תְּרוּמַת כֶּסֶף וּנְחֹשֶׁת" (להלן לה, כד), וְלֹא הָיְתָה יַד כֻּלָּם שָׁוָה בָהּ, אֶלָּא אִישׁ אִישׁ מַה שֶּׁנְּדָבוֹ לִבּוֹ:

טז **וְנָתַתָּ אֹתוֹ עַל עֲבֹדַת אֹהֶל מוֹעֵד.** לָמַדְתָּ שֶׁנִּצְטַוָּה לִמְנוֹתָם בִּתְחִלַּת נִדְבַת הַמִּשְׁכָּן אַחַר מַעֲשֵׂה הָעֵגֶל, מִפְּנֵי שֶׁנִּתְנָה בָּהֶם מַגֵּפָה, כְּמוֹ שֶׁנֶּאֱמַר: "וַיִּגֹּף ה' אֶת הָעָם" (להלן לב, לה). מָשָׁל לְצֹאן הַחֲבִיבָה עַל בְּעָלֶיהָ שֶׁנָּפַל בָּהּ דֶּבֶר, וּמִשֶּׁפָּסַק אָמַר לוֹ לָרוֹעֶה: בְּבַקָּשָׁה מִמְּךָ, מְנֵה אֶת צֹאנִי וְדַע כַּמָּה נוֹתְרוּ בָהּ, לְהוֹדִיעוֹ שֶׁהִיא חֲבִיבָה עָלָיו. וְאִי אֶפְשָׁר לוֹמַר שֶׁהַמִּנְיָן הַזֶּה הוּא הָאָמוּר בְּחוּמַשׁ הַפְּקוּדִים, שֶׁהֲרֵי נֶאֱמַר בּוֹ: "בְּאֶחָד לַחֹדֶשׁ הַשֵּׁנִי" (במדבר א, א), וְהַמִּשְׁכָּן הוּקַם בְּאֶחָד לַחֹדֶשׁ הָרִאשׁוֹן, שֶׁנֶּאֱמַר: "בְּיוֹם הַחֹדֶשׁ הָרִאשׁוֹן בְּאֶחָד לַחֹדֶשׁ תָּקִים" וְגוֹ' (להלן מ, ב), וּמֵהַמִּנְיָן הַזֶּה נַעֲשׂוּ הָאֲדָנִים מִשְּׁקָלִים שֶׁלּוֹ, שֶׁנֶּאֱמַר: "וַיְהִי מְאַת כִּכַּר הַכֶּסֶף לָצֶקֶת" וְגוֹ' (להלן לח, כז), הָא לָמַדְתָּ שְׁנַיִם הָיוּ: אֶחָד בִּתְחִלַּת נִדְבָתָן אַחַר יוֹם הַכִּפּוּרִים בַּשָּׁנָה הָרִאשׁוֹנָה, וְאֶחָד בַּשָּׁנָה הַשֵּׁנִית בְּאִיָּר מִשֶּׁהוּקַם הַמִּשְׁכָּן. וְאִם תֹּאמַר, וְכִי אֶפְשָׁר שֶׁבִּשְׁנֵיהֶם הָיוּ יִשְׂרָאֵל שָׁוִים שֵׁשׁ מֵאוֹת אֶלֶף וּשְׁלֹשֶׁת אֲלָפִים וַחֲמֵשׁ מֵאוֹת וַחֲמִשִּׁים? שֶׁהֲרֵי בְּכֶסֶף פְּקוּדֵי הָעֵדָה נֶאֱמַר כֵּן (להלן לח, כו), וּבְחוּמַשׁ הַפְּקוּדִים אַף בּוֹ נֶאֱמַר כֵּן: "וַיִּהְיוּ כָּל הַפְּקֻדִים שֵׁשׁ מֵאוֹת אֶלֶף וּשְׁלֹשֶׁת אֲלָפִים וַחֲמֵשׁ מֵאוֹת וַחֲמִשִּׁים" (במדבר א, מו), וַהֲלֹא בִּשְׁתֵּי שָׁנִים הָיוּ, וְאִי אֶפְשָׁר שֶׁלֹּא הָיוּ בְּשָׁעַת מִנְיָן

שמות | פרק ל | כי תשא | 477

יח וַיְדַבֵּר יְהוָה אֶל־מֹשֶׁה לֵּאמֹר: וְעָשִׂיתָ כִּיּוֹר נְחֹשֶׁת וְכַנּוֹ נְחֹשֶׁת
לְרָחְצָה וְנָתַתָּ אֹתוֹ בֵּין־אֹהֶל מוֹעֵד וּבֵין הַמִּזְבֵּחַ וְנָתַתָּ שָׁמָּה
יט מָיִם: וְרָחֲצוּ אַהֲרֹן וּבָנָיו מִמֶּנּוּ אֶת־יְדֵיהֶם וְאֶת־רַגְלֵיהֶם: בְּבֹאָם
אֶל־אֹהֶל מוֹעֵד יִרְחֲצוּ־מַיִם וְלֹא יָמֻתוּ אוֹ בְגִשְׁתָּם אֶל־הַמִּזְבֵּחַ
כא לְשָׁרֵת לְהַקְטִיר אִשֶּׁה לַיהוָה: וְרָחֲצוּ יְדֵיהֶם וְרַגְלֵיהֶם וְלֹא
יָמֻתוּ וְהָיְתָה לָהֶם חָק־עוֹלָם לוֹ וּלְזַרְעוֹ לְדֹרֹתָם: ־
כב וַיְדַבֵּר יְהוָה אֶל־מֹשֶׁה לֵּאמֹר: וְאַתָּה קַח־לְךָ בְּשָׂמִים רֹאשׁ
מָר־דְּרוֹר חֲמֵשׁ מֵאוֹת וְקִנְּמָן־בֶּשֶׂם מַחֲצִיתוֹ חֲמִשִּׁים וּמָאתָיִם

הָרִאשׁוֹן בְּנֵי תֵּשַׁע עֶשְׂרֵה שָׁנָה שֶׁלֹּא נִמְנוּ וּבַשְּׁנִיָּה נַעֲשׂוּ בְּנֵי עֶשְׂרִים? תְּשׁוּבָה לַדָּבָר, חֲצִי שְׁנוֹת הַחֲנָנִים בְּשָׁנָה אַחַת נִמְנוּ, לְמַעַן יְצִיאַת מִצְרַיִם הָיוּ שְׁתֵּי שָׁנִים, לְפִי שֶׁלִּיצִיאַת מִצְרַיִם מוֹנִין מִנִּיסָן, כְּמוֹ שֶׁשָּׁנִינוּ בְּמַסֶּכֶת רֹאשׁ הַשָּׁנָה (דף ב ע"ב), וְנִבְנָה הַמִּשְׁכָּן בָּרִאשׁוֹנָה וְהוּקַם בַּשְּׁנִיָּה, שֶׁנִּתְחַדְּשָׁה שָׁנָה בְּאֶחָד בְּנִיסָן, חֲצִי שְׁנוֹת הַחֲנָנִים מְנוּיִין לְמִנְיַן שְׁנוֹת עוֹלָם הַמַּתְחִילִין מִתִּשְׁרֵי, נִמְצְאוּ שְׁנַיִם הַמְּנוּיִים בְּשָׁנָה אַחַת, הַמִּנְיָן הָאֶחָד הָיָה בְּתִשְׁרֵי לְאַחַר יוֹם הַכִּפּוּרִים, שֶׁנִּתְרַצָּה הַמָּקוֹם לְיִשְׂרָאֵל לִסְלוֹחַ לָהֶם וְנִצְטַוּוּ עַל הַמִּשְׁכָּן, וְהַשֵּׁנִי בְּאֶחָד בְּאִיָּר: **עַל עֲבֹדַת אֹהֶל מוֹעֵד.** הֵן הָאֲדָנִים שֶׁנַּעֲשׂוּ בוֹ:

יח) **כִּיּוֹר.** כְּמִין דּוּד גָּדוֹל וְלוֹ דַּדִּים הַמְּרִיקִים בְּפִיהֶם מַיִם: **וְכַנּוֹ.** כְּתַרְגּוּמוֹ: "בְּסִיסֵיהּ", מוֹשָׁב מְתֻקָּן לַכִּיּוֹר: **לְרָחְצָה.** מוּסָב עַל הַכִּיּוֹר: **וּבֵין הַמִּזְבֵּחַ.** מִזְבַּח הָעוֹלָה, שֶׁכָּתוּב בּוֹ שֶׁהוּא לִפְנֵי פֶּתַח מִשְׁכַּן אֹהֶל מוֹעֵד (להלן מ, כט), וְהָיָה הַכִּיּוֹר מָשׁוּךְ קִמְעָא וְעוֹמֵד כְּנֶגֶד אֲוִיר שֶׁבֵּין הַמִּזְבֵּחַ וְהַמִּשְׁכָּן וְאֵינוֹ מַפְסִיק כְּלָל בֵּינְתַיִם, מִשּׁוּם שֶׁנֶּאֱמַר: "וְאֶת מִזְבַּח הָעוֹלָה שָׂם פֶּתַח מִשְׁכַּן אֹהֶל מוֹעֵד" (שם), כְּלוֹמַר, מִזְבֵּחַ לִפְנֵי אֹהֶל מוֹעֵד וְאֵין כִּיּוֹר לִפְנֵי אֹהֶל מוֹעֵד, הָא כֵּיצַד? מָשׁוּךְ קִמְעָא כְּלַפֵּי הַדָּרוֹם. כָּךְ שְׁנוּיָה בִּזְבָחִים (דף נט ע"א):

יט) **אֶת יְדֵיהֶם וְאֶת רַגְלֵיהֶם.** בְּבַת אַחַת הָיָה

מְקַדֵּשׁ יָדָיו וְרַגְלָיו. וְכָךְ שָׁנִינוּ בִּזְבָחִים (דף יט ע"ב): כֵּיצַד קִדּוּשׁ יָדַיִם וְרַגְלַיִם? מַנִּיחַ יָדוֹ עַל גַּבֵּי רַגְלוֹ הַיְמָנִית, וְיָדוֹ הַשְּׂמָאלִית עַל גַּבֵּי רַגְלוֹ הַשְּׂמָאלִית, וּמְקַדֵּשׁ:

כ) **בְּבֹאָם אֶל אֹהֶל מוֹעֵד.** לְהַקְטִיר שַׁחֲרִית וּבֵין הָעַרְבַּיִם קְטֹרֶת, אוֹ לְהַזּוֹת מִדַּם פַּר כֹּהֵן הַמָּשִׁיחַ וּשְׂעִירֵי עֲבוֹדָה זָרָה: **וְלֹא יָמֻתוּ.** הָא אִם לֹא יִרְחֲצוּ – יָמוּתוּ, שֶׁבַּתּוֹרָה נֶאֶמְרוּ כְלָלוֹת, וּמִכְּלַל לָאו אַתָּה שׁוֹמֵעַ הֵן: **אֶל הַמִּזְבֵּחַ.** הַחִיצוֹן, שֶׁאֵין כָּאן בְּיאַת אֹהֶל מוֹעֵד אֶלָּא בֶּחָצֵר:

כא) **וְלֹא יָמֻתוּ.** לְחַיֵּב מִיתָה עַל הַמְּשַׁמֵּשׁ בַּמִּזְבֵּחַ וְאֵינוֹ רְחוּץ יָדַיִם וְרַגְלַיִם, שֶׁהַמִּיתָה הָרִאשׁוֹנָה לֹא שְׁמַעֲנוּ אֶלָּא עַל הַנִּכְנָס לַהֵיכָל:

כג) **בְּשָׂמִים רֹאשׁ.** חֲשׁוּבִים: **וְקִנְּמָן בֶּשֶׂם.** לְפִי שֶׁהַקִּנָּמוֹן קְלִפַּת עֵץ הוּא, יֵשׁ שֶׁהוּא טוֹב וְיֵשׁ בּוֹ רֵיחַ טוֹב וָטַעַם, וְיֵשׁ שֶׁאֵינוֹ אֶלָּא כְּעֵץ, לְכָךְ הֻצְרַךְ לוֹמַר "קִנְּמָן בֶּשֶׂם", מִן הַטּוֹב: **מַחֲצִיתוֹ חֲמִשִּׁים וּמָאתָיִם.** מַחֲצִית הֲבָאָתוֹ תְּהֵא "חֲמִשִּׁים וּמָאתָיִם", נִמְצָא כֻּלּוֹ חֲמֵשׁ מֵאוֹת, כְּמוֹ שִׁעוּר מָר דְּרוֹר. אִם כֵּן לָמָּה נֶאֱמַר בּוֹ חֲצָאִין? גְּזֵרַת הַכָּתוּב הִיא לַהֲבִיאוֹ לַחֲצָאִין, לְהַרְבּוֹת בּוֹ שְׁנֵי הַכְרָעוֹת, שֶׁאֵין שׁוֹקְלִין עַיִן בְּעַיִן. וְכָךְ שְׁנוּיָה בִּכְרֵתוֹת (דף ה ע"א): **וּקְנֵה בֶשֶׂם.** קְנֵה שֶׁל בֹּשֶׂם, לְפִי שֶׁיֵּשׁ קָנִים שֶׁאֵינָן שֶׁל בֹּשֶׂם, הֻצְרַךְ לוֹמַר: "בֶּשֶׂם": **חֲמִשִּׁים וּמָאתָיִם.** סַךְ מִשְׁקָלוֹ כֻּלּוֹ:

וְקִנְּמָן־בֶּשֶׂם חֲמִשִּׁים וּמָאתָיִם: וְקִדָּה חֲמֵשׁ מֵאוֹת בְּשֶׁקֶל כד
הַקֹּדֶשׁ וְשֶׁמֶן זַיִת הִין: וְעָשִׂיתָ אֹתוֹ שֶׁמֶן מִשְׁחַת־קֹדֶשׁ רֹקַח כה
מִרְקַחַת מַעֲשֵׂה רֹקֵחַ שֶׁמֶן מִשְׁחַת־קֹדֶשׁ יִהְיֶה: וּמָשַׁחְתָּ בוֹ כו
אֶת־אֹהֶל מוֹעֵד וְאֵת אֲרוֹן הָעֵדֻת: וְאֶת־הַשֻּׁלְחָן וְאֶת־כָּל־כֵּלָיו כז
וְאֶת־הַמְּנֹרָה וְאֶת־כֵּלֶיהָ וְאֵת מִזְבַּח הַקְּטֹרֶת: וְאֶת־מִזְבַּח כח
הָעֹלָה וְאֶת־כָּל־כֵּלָיו וְאֶת־הַכִּיֹּר וְאֶת־כַּנּוֹ: וְקִדַּשְׁתָּ אֹתָם וְהָיוּ כט
קֹדֶשׁ קָדָשִׁים כָּל־הַנֹּגֵעַ בָּהֶם יִקְדָּשׁ: וְאֶת־אַהֲרֹן וְאֶת־בָּנָיו ל
תִּמְשָׁח וְקִדַּשְׁתָּ אֹתָם לְכַהֵן לִי: וְאֶל־בְּנֵי יִשְׂרָאֵל תְּדַבֵּר לֵאמֹר לא
שֶׁמֶן מִשְׁחַת־קֹדֶשׁ יִהְיֶה זֶה לִי לְדֹרֹתֵיכֶם: עַל־בְּשַׂר אָדָם לב
לֹא יִיסָךְ וּבְמַתְכֻּנְתּוֹ לֹא תַעֲשׂוּ כָּמֹהוּ קֹדֶשׁ הוּא קֹדֶשׁ יִהְיֶה

כד **וְקִדָּה.** שֵׁם עֵשֶׂב, וּבִלְשׁוֹן חֲכָמִים 'קְצִיעָה': **הִין.** שְׁנֵים עָשָׂר לֻגִּין. וְנֶחְלְקוּ בּוֹ חַכְמֵי יִשְׂרָאֵל. רַבִּי מֵאִיר אוֹמֵר: בּוֹ שָׁלְקוּ אֶת הָעִקָּרִין. אָמַר לוֹ רַבִּי יְהוּדָה: וַהֲלֹא לָסוּךְ אֶת הָעִקָּרִין אֵינוֹ סִפֵּק, אֶלָּא שֶׁרִחֲצוּם בְּמַיִם שֶׁלֹּא יִבְלְעוּ אֶת הַשֶּׁמֶן, וְאַחַר כָּךְ הֵצִיף עֲלֵיהֶם הַשֶּׁמֶן עַד שֶׁקָּלַט הָרֵיחַ, וְקִפְּחוֹ לַשֶּׁמֶן מֵעַל הָעִקָּרִין:

כה **רֹקַח מִרְקַחַת.** 'רֹקַח' שֵׁם דָּבָר הוּא, וְהַטַּעַם מוֹכִיחַ, שֶׁהוּא לְמַעְלָה. וַהֲרֵי הוּא כְּמוֹ 'רֶקַח' (שיר השירים ח, ב), 'רֶגַע' (להלן לג, ה), וְחִנּוּ כְּמוֹ 'רֹגַע הַיָּם' (ישעיה נא, טו) וּכְמוֹ "רֹקַע הָאָרֶץ" (תהלים קלו, ו) שֶׁהַטַּעַם לְמַטָּה. וְכָל דָּבָר הַמְעֹרָב בַּחֲבֵרוֹ עַד שֶׁזֶּה קוֹפֵחַ מִזֶּה אוֹ רֵיחַ אוֹ טַעַם, קָרוּי 'מִרְקַחַת': רֹקַח מִרְקַחַת. רֹקַח הֶעָשׂוּי עַל יְדֵי אֻמָּנוּת וְתַעֲרֹבֶת: מַעֲשֵׂה רֹקֵחַ. שֵׁם הָאֻמָּן בַּדָּבָר:

כו **וּמָשַׁחְתָּ בּוֹ.** כָּל הַמְּשִׁיחוֹת כְּמִין כַ"ף, חוּץ מִשֶּׁל מְלָכִים שֶׁהֵן כְּמִין נֵזֶר:

כט **וְקִדַּשְׁתָּ אֹתָם.** מְשִׁיחָה זוֹ מְקַדַּשְׁתָּם לִהְיוֹת קֹדֶשׁ קָדָשִׁים. וּמַה הִיא קְדֻשָּׁתָם? "כָּל הַנֹּגֵעַ וְגוֹ'" – כָּל הָרָאוּי לִכְלִי שָׁרֵת מִשֶּׁנִּכְנַס לְתוֹכוֹ, קָדוֹשׁ קְדֻשַּׁת

הַגּוּף לִפָּסֵל בְּיוֹצֵא וְלִינָה וּטְבוּל יוֹם, וְאֵינוֹ נִפְדֶּה לָצֵאת לְחֻלִּין, אֲבָל דָּבָר שֶׁאֵינוֹ רָאוּי לָהֶם אֵין הֵן מְקַדְּשִׁין. וּשְׁנוּיָה הִיא מִשְׁנָה שְׁלֵמָה אֵצֶל מִזְבֵּחַ מִתּוֹךְ שֶׁנֶּאֱמַר: "כָּל הַנֹּגֵעַ בַּמִּזְבֵּחַ יִקְדָּשׁ" (לעיל כט, לז), שׁוֹמֵעַ אֲנִי בֵּין רָאוּי בֵּין שֶׁאֵינוֹ רָאוּי, תַּלְמוּד לוֹמַר: "כְּבָשִׂים", מַה כְּבָשִׂים רְאוּיִים אַף כָּל רָאוּי (זבחים פג ע"ב). כָּל מְשִׁיחַת מִשְׁכָּן וְכֹהֲנִים וּמְלָכִים מְתֻרְגָּם לְשׁוֹן 'רִבּוּי', לְפִי שֶׁאֵין עֶרֶךְ מְשִׁיחָתָן אֶלָּא לִגְדֻלָּה, כִּי כֵן יָסַד הַמֶּלֶךְ שֶׁזֶּה חֹזֶק גִּדּוּלָתָן. וּשְׁאָר מְשִׁיחוֹת, כְּגוֹן 'רְקִיקִין מְשׁוּחִין', "וְרֵאשִׁית שְׁמָנִים יִמְשָׁחוּ" (עמוס ו, ו) לְשׁוֹן אֲרַמִּית בָּהֶן כִּלְשׁוֹן עִבְרִית:

לא **לְדֹרֹתֵיכֶם.** מִכָּאן לָמְדוּ רַבּוֹתֵינוּ לוֹמַר שֶׁכֻּלּוֹ קַיָּם לֶעָתִיד לָבוֹא, "זֶה" בְּגִימַטְרִיָּא תְּרֵיסַר לֻגִּין הֲוָה:

לב **לֹא יִיסָךְ.** בִּשְׁנֵי יוּדִי"ן, לְשׁוֹן לֹא יִפְעַל, כְּמוֹ: "לְמַעַן יִיטַב לָךְ" (דברים ה, טו): **עַל בְּשַׂר אָדָם לֹא יִיסָךְ.** מִן הַשֶּׁמֶן הַזֶּה עַצְמוֹ: **וּבְמַתְכֻּנְתּוֹ לֹא תַעֲשׂוּ כָּמֹהוּ.** בְּסְכוּם סַמָּנָיו לֹא תַעֲשׂוּ אַחֵר כָּמוֹהוּ בְּמִשְׁקַל סַמָּנִין הַלָּלוּ לְפִי מִדַּת הִין שֶׁמֶן, אֲבָל אִם פִּחֵת אוֹ רִבָּה סַמָּנִין לְפִי מִדַּת הִין שֶׁמֶן – מֻתָּר. וְאַף הֶעָשׂוּי בְּמַתְכֻּנְתּוֹ שֶׁל זֶה, אֵין הַסָּךְ מִמֶּנּוּ חַיָּב, אֶלָּא

שמות | פרק ל   כי תשא | 479

לג אִישׁ אֲשֶׁר יִרְקַח כָּמֹהוּ וַאֲשֶׁר יִתֵּן מִמֶּנּוּ עַל־זָר וְנִכְרַת
מֵעַמָּיו׃   לד וַיֹּאמֶר יְהֹוָה אֶל־מֹשֶׁה קַח־לְךָ סַמִּים נָטָף ׀
לה וּשְׁחֵלֶת וְחֶלְבְּנָה סַמִּים וּלְבֹנָה זַכָּה בַּד בְּבַד יִהְיֶה׃ וְעָשִׂיתָ אֹתָהּ
קְטֹרֶת רֹקַח מַעֲשֵׂה רוֹקֵחַ מְמֻלָּח טָהוֹר קֹדֶשׁ׃ וְשָׁחַקְתָּ מִמֶּנָּה
הָדֵק וְנָתַתָּה מִמֶּנָּה לִפְנֵי הָעֵדֻת בְּאֹהֶל מוֹעֵד אֲשֶׁר אִוָּעֵד
לו לְךָ שָׁמָּה קֹדֶשׁ קָדָשִׁים תִּהְיֶה לָכֶם׃ וְהַקְּטֹרֶת אֲשֶׁר תַּעֲשֶׂה
לז בְּמַתְכֻּנְתָּהּ לֹא תַעֲשׂוּ לָכֶם קֹדֶשׁ תִּהְיֶה לְךָ לַיהוָה׃ אִישׁ אֲשֶׁר
לח יַעֲשֶׂה כָמוֹהָ לְהָרִיחַ בָּהּ וְנִכְרַת מֵעַמָּיו׃   לא א וַיְדַבֵּר יְהוָה

הָרוֹקְחוֹ. וּבְמַתְכֻּנְתָּהּ. לְשׁוֹן חֶשְׁבּוֹן, כְּמוֹ "מַתְכֹּנֶת
הַלְּבֵנִים" (לעיל ה, ח), וְכֵן "בְּמַתְכֻּנְתָּהּ" (הֲרֵי פָּסוּק לוֹ)
שֶׁל קְטֹרֶת:

לג וַאֲשֶׁר יִתֵּן מִמֶּנּוּ. מִשְּׁחִיתוֹ שֶׁל מֹשֶׁה. עַל זָר. שֶׁאֵינוֹ
צֹרֶךְ כְּהֻנָּה וּמַלְכוּת:

לד נָטָף. הוּא צֳרִי. וְעַל שֶׁאֵינוֹ אֶלָּא שְׂרָף הַנּוֹטֵף
מֵעֲצֵי הַקְּטָף קָרוּי 'נָטָף', וּבְלַעַז גומ"א, וְהַצֳּרִי
קוֹרִין לוֹ טריא"ק. וּשְׁחֵלֶת. שֹׁרֶשׁ בֹּשֶׂם חָלָק
וּמַזְהִיר כַּצִּפֹּרֶן, וּבִלְשׁוֹן הַמִּשְׁנָה קָרוּי צִפֹּרֶן, וְזֶהוּ
שֶׁתִּרְגֵּם אוּנְקְלוֹס: "וְטוּפְרָא". וְחֶלְבְּנָה. בֹּשֶׂם שֶׁרֵיחוֹ
רַע וְקוֹרִין לוֹ גַלְבְּנָא. וּמָנָה הַכָּתוּב בֵּין סַמָּנֵי
הַקְּטֹרֶת, לְלַמְּדֵנוּ שֶׁלֹּא יֵקַל בְּעֵינֵינוּ לְצָרֵף עִמָּנוּ
בַּאֲגֻדַּת תַּעֲנִיּוֹתֵינוּ וּתְפִלּוֹתֵינוּ אֶת פּוֹשְׁעֵי יִשְׂרָאֵל
שֶׁיִּהְיוּ נִמְנִין עִמָּנוּ. סַמִּים. אֲחֵרִים. וּלְבֹנָה זַכָּה. מִכָּאן
לָמְדוּ רַבּוֹתֵינוּ אַחַד עָשָׂר סַמָּנִין נֶאֶמְרוּ לוֹ לְמֹשֶׁה
בְּסִינַי: מִעוּט "סַמִּים" שְׁנַיִם, "נָטָף וּשְׁחֵלֶת וְחֶלְבְּנָה"
שְׁלֹשָׁה, הֲרֵי חֲמִשָּׁה. "סַמִּים", לִרְבּוֹת עוֹד כְּמוֹ אֵלּוּ,
הֲרֵי עֲשָׂרָה. "וּלְבוֹנָה", הֲרֵי אַחַד עָשָׂר. וְאֵלּוּ הֵן: הַצֳּרִי
וְהַצִּפֹּרֶן, הַחֶלְבְּנָה וְהַלְּבוֹנָה, מוֹר וּקְצִיעָה, שִׁבֹּלֶת נֵרְדְּ
וְכַרְכֹּם, הֲרֵי שְׁמוֹנָה, שֶׁהַשִּׁבֹּלֶת וְנֵרְדְּ אֶחָד, שֶׁהַנֵּרְדְּ
דּוֹמֶה לְשִׁבֹּלֶת, הַקֹּשְׁטְ וְהַקִּלּוּפָה וְהַקִּנָּמוֹן, הֲרֵי אַחַד
עָשָׂר. בּוֹרִית כַּרְשִׁינָה אֵינוֹ נִקְטָר, אֶלָּא בּוֹ שָׁפִין אֶת
הַצִּפֹּרֶן לְלַבְּנָהּ שֶׁתְּהֵא נָאָה. בַּד בְּבַד יִהְיֶה. אֵלּוּ

הָאַרְבָּעָה הַנִּזְכָּרִים כָּאן יִהְיוּ שָׁוִין מִשְׁקָל בְּמִשְׁקָל,
כְּמִשְׁקָלוֹ שֶׁל זֶה כָּךְ מִשְׁקָלוֹ שֶׁל זֶה, וְכֵן שָׁנִינוּ:
"הַצֳּרִי וְהַצִּפֹּרֶן הַחֶלְבְּנָה וְהַלְּבוֹנָה מִשְׁקַל שִׁבְעִים
שִׁבְעִים מָנֶה" (כריתות ו ע"א), וּלְשׁוֹן "בַּד" נִרְאֶה בְּעֵינַי
שֶׁהוּא לְשׁוֹן יָחִיד, אֶחָד בְּאֶחָד יִהְיֶה, זֶה כְּמוֹת זֶה:

לה מְמֻלָּח. כְּתַרְגּוּמוֹ, "מְעָרַב", שֶׁיְּעָרֵב שְׁחִיקָתָן
יָפֶה יָפֶה זֶה עִם זֶה. וְאוֹמֵר אֲנִי שֶׁדּוֹמֶה לוֹ: "וַיִּירְאוּ
הַמַּלָּחִים" (יונה א, ה), "מַלָּחַיִךְ וְחוֹבְלָיִךְ" (יחזקאל כז, כז),
עַל שֵׁם שֶׁמְּהַפְּכִין אֶת הַמַּיִם בְּמִשּׁוֹטוֹת כְּשֶׁמַּנְהִיגִים
אֶת הַסְּפִינָה, כְּאָדָם הַמְהַפֵּךְ בְּכַף בֵּיצִים טְרוּפוֹת
לְעָרְבָן עִם הַמַּיִם, וְכָל דָּבָר שֶׁאָדָם רוֹצֶה לְעָרֵב יָפֶה
יָפֶה מְהַפְּכוֹ בְּאֶצְבַּע אוֹ בְּכַף: מְמֻלָּח טָהוֹר קֹדֶשׁ.
מְמֻלָּח יִהְיֶה, וְטָהוֹר יִהְיֶה, וְקֹדֶשׁ יִהְיֶה:

לו וְנָתַתָּה מִמֶּנָּה וְגוֹ'. הִיא קְטֹרֶת שֶׁבְּכָל יוֹם וָיוֹם
שֶׁעַל מִזְבֵּחַ הַפְּנִימִי, שֶׁהוּא "בְּאֹהֶל מוֹעֵד": אֲשֶׁר
אִוָּעֵד לְךָ שָׁמָּה. כָּל מוֹעֲדֵי דִּבּוּר שֶׁאֶקְבַּע לְךָ, אֲנִי
קוֹבְעָם לְאוֹתוֹ מָקוֹם:

לז בְּמַתְכֻּנְתָּהּ. בְּמִנְיַן סַמָּנֶיהָ: קֹדֶשׁ תִּהְיֶה לְךָ לַה'.
שֶׁלֹּא תַעֲשֶׂנָּה אֶלָּא לִשְׁמִי:

לח לְהָרִיחַ בָּהּ. אֲבָל עוֹשֶׂה אַתָּה בְּמַתְכֻּנְתָּהּ מִשֶּׁלְּךָ
כְּדֵי לְמָסְרָהּ לַצִּבּוּר:

אֶל־מֹשֶׁה לֵּאמֹֽר: רְאֵה קָרָאתִי בְשֵׁם בְּצַלְאֵל בֶּן־אוּרִי בֶן־חוּר לְמַטֵּה יְהוּדָֽה: וָאֲמַלֵּא אֹתוֹ רוּחַ אֱלֹהִים בְּחָכְמָה וּבִתְבוּנָה וּבְדַעַת וּבְכָל־מְלָאכָֽה: לַחְשֹׁב מַחֲשָׁבֹת לַעֲשׂוֹת בַּזָּהָב וּבַכֶּסֶף וּבַנְּחֹֽשֶׁת: וּבַחֲרֹשֶׁת אֶבֶן לְמַלֹּאת וּבַחֲרֹשֶׁת עֵץ לַעֲשׂוֹת בְּכָל־מְלָאכָֽה: וַאֲנִי הִנֵּה נָתַתִּי אִתּוֹ אֵת אָהֳלִיאָב בֶּן־אֲחִֽיסָמָךְ לְמַטֵּה־דָן וּבְלֵב כָּל־חֲכַם־לֵב נָתַתִּי חָכְמָה וְעָשׂוּ אֵת כָּל־אֲשֶׁר צִוִּיתִֽךָ: אֵת ׀ אֹהֶל מוֹעֵד וְאֶת־הָאָרֹן לָעֵדֻת וְאֶת־הַכַּפֹּרֶת אֲשֶׁר עָלָיו וְאֵת כָּל־כְּלֵי הָאֹֽהֶל: וְאֶת־הַשֻּׁלְחָן וְאֶת־כֵּלָיו וְאֶת־הַמְּנֹרָה הַטְּהֹרָה וְאֶת־כָּל־כֵּלֶיהָ וְאֵת מִזְבַּח הַקְּטֹֽרֶת: וְאֶת־מִזְבַּח הָעֹלָה וְאֶת־כָּל־כֵּלָיו וְאֶת־הַכִּיּוֹר וְאֶת־כַּנּֽוֹ: וְאֵת בִּגְדֵי הַשְּׂרָד וְאֶת־בִּגְדֵי הַקֹּדֶשׁ לְאַהֲרֹן הַכֹּהֵן וְאֶת־בִּגְדֵי בָנָיו לְכַהֵֽן:

ב

ג

ד

ה

ו

ז

ח

ט

י

פרק לא

ב) קָרָאתִי בְשֵׁם. לַעֲשׂוֹת מְלַאכְתִּי, אֶת בְּצַלְאֵל.

ג) בְּחָכְמָה. מַה שֶּׁאָדָם שׁוֹמֵעַ מֵאֲחֵרִים וְלָמֵד. וּבִתְבוּנָה. מֵבִין דָּבָר מִלִּבּוֹ מִתּוֹךְ דְּבָרִים שֶׁלָּמַד. וּבְדַעַת. רוּחַ הַקֹּדֶשׁ:

ד) לַחְשֹׁב מַחֲשָׁבֹת. אֲרִיגַת מַעֲשֵׂה חוֹשֵׁב:

ה) וּבַחֲרֹשֶׁת. לְשׁוֹן אֻמָּנוּת, כְּמוֹ: "חָרַשׁ חָכָם" (ישעיה מ, כ). וְאוּנְקְלוֹס פֵּרַשׁ וְשִׁנָּה בְּפֵרוּשָׁן, שֶׁאֻמָּן אֲבָנִים קָרוּי 'אֻמָּן', וְחָרָשׁ עֵץ קָרוּי 'נַגָּר': לְמַלֹּאת. לְהוֹשִׁיבָהּ בַּמִּשְׁבֶּצֶת שֶׁלָּהּ בְּמִלּוּאָהּ, לַעֲשׂוֹת הַמִּשְׁבֶּצֶת לְמִדַּת מוֹשַׁב הָאֶבֶן וְעָבְיָהּ:

ו) וּבְלֵב כָּל חֲכַם לֵב וְגוֹ'. וְעוֹד שְׁאָר חַכְמֵי לֵב יֵשׁ בָּכֶם, וְכֹל אֲשֶׁר נָתַתִּי בּוֹ חָכְמָה, "וְעָשׂוּ אֵת כָּל אֲשֶׁר צִוִּיתִֽךָ":

ז) וְאֵת הָאָרֹן לָעֵדֻת. לְצֹרֶךְ לוּחוֹת הָעֵדוּת:

ח) הַטְּהֹרָה. עַל שֵׁם זָהָב טָהוֹר:

י) וְאֶת בִּגְדֵי הַשְּׂרָד. אוֹמֵר אֲנִי לְפִי פְּשׁוּטוֹ שֶׁל מִקְרָא שֶׁאִי אֶפְשָׁר לוֹמַר שֶׁבְּבִגְדֵי כְהֻנָּה מְדַבֵּר, לְפִי שֶׁנֶּאֱמַר אֶצְלָם: "וְאֶת בִּגְדֵי הַקֹּדֶשׁ לְאַהֲרֹן הַכֹּהֵן וְאֶת בִּגְדֵי בָנָיו לְכַהֵן", אֶלָּא אֵלּוּ בִּגְדֵי הַשְּׂרָד הֵם בִּגְדֵי הַתְּכֵלֶת וְהָאַרְגָּמָן וְתוֹלַעַת שָׁנִי הָאֲמוּרִים בְּפָרָשַׁת מַסְעוֹת: וְנָתְנוּ עָלָיו בֶּגֶד תְּכֵלֶת (עיין במדבר ד, ז), וְנָתְנוּ עָלָיו בֶּגֶד אַרְגָּמָן (שם פסוק יג-יד), וְנָתְנוּ עֲלֵיהֶם בֶּגֶד תּוֹלַעַת שָׁנִי (שם פסוק ח). וְנִרְאִין דְּבָרַי, שֶׁנֶּאֱמַר: "וּמִן הַתְּכֵלֶת וְהָאַרְגָּמָן וְתוֹלַעַת הַשָּׁנִי עָשׂוּ בִגְדֵי שְׂרָד לְשָׁרֵת בַּקֹּדֶשׁ" (להלן לט, א), וְלֹא הֻזְכַּר שֵׁשׁ עִמָּהֶם, וְאִם בְּבִגְדֵי כְהֻנָּה מְדַבֵּר, לֹא מָצִינוּ בְּאֶחָד מֵהֶם אַרְגָּמָן אוֹ תּוֹלַעַת שָׁנִי בְּלֹא שֵׁשׁ: בִּגְדֵי הַשְּׂרָד. יֵשׁ מְפָרְשִׁים לְשׁוֹן עֲבוֹדָה וּשְׁרָרוּת, כְּתַרְגּוּמוֹ: "לְבוּשֵׁי שִׁמּוּשָׁא", וְאֵין לוֹ דִּמְיוֹן בַּמִּקְרָא. וַאֲנִי אוֹמֵר שֶׁהוּא לְשׁוֹן אֲרַמִּי כְּתַרְגּוּמוֹ שֶׁל "קְלָעִים" (לעיל כז, ט) וְתַרְגּוּם שֶׁל "מִכְבָּר" (שם פסוק ד), שֶׁהָיוּ מְאֻרָגִים בְּמַחַט, עֲשׂוּיִים נְקָבִים נְקָבִים, לעיי"ץ בְּלַעַ"ז:

שמות | פרק לא

יא וְאֵת שֶׁמֶן הַמִּשְׁחָה וְאֶת־קְטֹרֶת הַסַּמִּים לַקֹּדֶשׁ כְּכֹל אֲשֶׁר־צִוִּיתִךָ יַעֲשׂוּ׃

יב וַיֹּאמֶר יְהוָה אֶל־מֹשֶׁה לֵּאמֹר׃ יג וְאַתָּה דַּבֵּר אֶל־בְּנֵי יִשְׂרָאֵל לֵאמֹר אַךְ אֶת־שַׁבְּתֹתַי תִּשְׁמֹרוּ כִּי אוֹת הִוא בֵּינִי וּבֵינֵיכֶם לְדֹרֹתֵיכֶם לָדַעַת כִּי אֲנִי יְהוָה מְקַדִּשְׁכֶם׃ יד וּשְׁמַרְתֶּם אֶת־הַשַּׁבָּת כִּי קֹדֶשׁ הִוא לָכֶם מְחַלְלֶיהָ מוֹת יוּמָת כִּי כָּל־הָעֹשֶׂה בָהּ מְלָאכָה וְנִכְרְתָה הַנֶּפֶשׁ הַהִוא מִקֶּרֶב עַמֶּיהָ׃ טו שֵׁשֶׁת יָמִים יֵעָשֶׂה מְלָאכָה וּבַיּוֹם הַשְּׁבִיעִי שַׁבַּת שַׁבָּתוֹן קֹדֶשׁ לַיהוָה כָּל־הָעֹשֶׂה מְלָאכָה בְּיוֹם הַשַּׁבָּת מוֹת יוּמָת׃ טז וְשָׁמְרוּ בְנֵי־יִשְׂרָאֵל אֶת־הַשַּׁבָּת לַעֲשׂוֹת אֶת־הַשַּׁבָּת לְדֹרֹתָם בְּרִית עוֹלָם׃ יז בֵּינִי וּבֵין בְּנֵי יִשְׂרָאֵל אוֹת הִוא לְעֹלָם כִּי־שֵׁשֶׁת יָמִים עָשָׂה יְהוָה אֶת־הַשָּׁמַיִם וְאֶת־הָאָרֶץ וּבַיּוֹם הַשְּׁבִיעִי שָׁבַת וַיִּנָּפַשׁ׃ יח וַיִּתֵּן אֶל־ שני מֹשֶׁה כְּכַלֹּתוֹ לְדַבֵּר אִתּוֹ בְּהַר סִינַי שְׁנֵי לֻחֹת הָעֵדֻת לֻחֹת אֶבֶן

יא **וְאֶת קְטֹרֶת הַסַּמִּים לַקֹּדֶשׁ.** לְצֹרֶךְ הַקְּטָרַת הֵיכָל שֶׁהוּא קֹדֶשׁ:

יג **וְאַתָּה דַּבֵּר אֶל בְּנֵי יִשְׂרָאֵל. וְאַתָּה.** אַף עַל פִּי שֶׁהִפְקַדְתִּיךָ לְצַוּוֹתָם עַל מְלֶאכֶת הַמִּשְׁכָּן, אַל יֵקַל בְּעֵינֶיךָ לִדְחוֹת אֶת הַשַּׁבָּת מִפְּנֵי אוֹתָהּ מְלָאכָה: **אַךְ אֶת שַׁבְּתֹתַי תִּשְׁמֹרוּ.** אַף עַל פִּי שֶׁתִּהְיוּ רְדוּפִין וּזְרִיזִין בִּזְרִיזוּת הַמְּלָאכָה, שַׁבָּת אַל תִּדָּחֶה מִפָּנֶיהָ. כָּל אַכִּין וְרַקִּין מִעוּטִין, לְמַעֵט שַׁבָּת מִמְּלֶאכֶת הַמִּשְׁכָּן: **כִּי אוֹת הִוא בֵּינִי וּבֵינֵיכֶם.** אוֹת גְּדֻלָּה הִיא בֵּינֵינוּ שֶׁבָּחַרְתִּי בָכֶם, בְּהַנְחִילִי לָכֶם אֶת יוֹם מְנוּחָתִי לִמְנוּחָה: **לָדַעַת.** הָאֻמּוֹת בָּהּ "כִּי אֲנִי ה' מְקַדִּשְׁכֶם":

יד **מוֹת יוּמָת.** אִם יֵשׁ עֵדִים וְהַתְרָאָה: **וְנִכְרְתָה.** בְּלֹא הַתְרָאָה: **מְחַלְלֶיהָ.** הַנּוֹהֵג בָּהּ חֹל בִּקְדֻשָּׁתָהּ:

טו **שַׁבַּת שַׁבָּתוֹן.** מְנוּחַת מַרְגּוֹעַ וְלֹא מְנוּחַת עֲרַאי: **קֹדֶשׁ לַה'.** שְׁמִירַת קְדֻשָּׁתָהּ לִשְׁמִי וּבְמִצְוָתִי:

יז **וַיִּנָּפַשׁ.** כְּתַרְגּוּמוֹ "וְנָח". וְכָל לְשׁוֹן "נֹפֶשׁ" הוּא לְשׁוֹן נֶפֶשׁ, שֶׁמֵּשִׁיב נַפְשׁוֹ וּנְשִׁימָתוֹ בְּהַרְגִּיעוֹ מִטֹּרַח הַמְּלָאכָה. וּמִי שֶׁכָּתוּב בּוֹ: "לֹא יִיעַף וְלֹא יִיגַע" (ישעיה מ, כח), וְכָל פָּעֳלוֹ בְּמַאֲמָר, הִכְתִּיב מְנוּחָה בְּעַצְמוֹ, לְשַׂבֵּר הָאֹזֶן מַה שֶּׁהִיא יְכוֹלָה לִשְׁמֹעַ:

יח **וַיִּתֵּן אֶל מֹשֶׁה וְגוֹ'.** אֵין מֻקְדָּם וּמְאֻחָר בַּתּוֹרָה. מַעֲשֵׂה הָעֵגֶל קֹדֶם לְצִוּוּי מְלֶאכֶת הַמִּשְׁכָּן יָמִים רַבִּים הָיָה, שֶׁהֲרֵי בְּשִׁבְעָה עָשָׂר בְּתַמּוּז נִשְׁתַּבְּרוּ הַלּוּחוֹת, וּבְיוֹם הַכִּפּוּרִים נִתְרַצָּה הַקָּדוֹשׁ בָּרוּךְ הוּא לְיִשְׂרָאֵל, וּלְמָחֳרָת הִתְחִילוּ בְּנִדְבַת הַמִּשְׁכָּן וְהוּקַם בְּאֶחָד בְּנִיסָן: **כְּכַלֹּתוֹ.** "כְּכַלֹּתוֹ" כְּתִיב חָסֵר, שֶׁנִּמְסְרָה לוֹ תוֹרָה בְּמַתָּנָה כְּכַלָּה לֶחָתָן, שֶׁלֹּא הָיָה יָכוֹל

פרק לב | שמות | כי תשא

כְּתֻבִים בְּאֶצְבַּע אֱלֹהִים: וַיַּרְא הָעָם כִּי־בֹשֵׁשׁ מֹשֶׁה לָרֶדֶת א לב
מִן־הָהָר וַיִּקָּהֵל הָעָם עַל־אַהֲרֹן וַיֹּאמְרוּ אֵלָיו קוּם עֲשֵׂה־לָנוּ
אֱלֹהִים אֲשֶׁר יֵלְכוּ לְפָנֵינוּ כִּי־זֶה ׀ מֹשֶׁה הָאִישׁ אֲשֶׁר הֶעֱלָנוּ
מֵאֶרֶץ מִצְרַיִם לֹא יָדַעְנוּ מֶה־הָיָה לוֹ: וַיֹּאמֶר אֲלֵהֶם אַהֲרֹן ב
פָּרְקוּ נִזְמֵי הַזָּהָב אֲשֶׁר בְּאָזְנֵי נְשֵׁיכֶם בְּנֵיכֶם וּבְנֹתֵיכֶם וְהָבִיאוּ
אֵלָי: וַיִּתְפָּרְקוּ כָּל־הָעָם אֶת־נִזְמֵי הַזָּהָב אֲשֶׁר בְּאָזְנֵיהֶם וַיָּבִיאוּ ג
אֶל־אַהֲרֹן: וַיִּקַּח מִיָּדָם וַיָּצַר אֹתוֹ בַּחֶרֶט וַיַּעֲשֵׂהוּ עֵגֶל מַסֵּכָה ד
וַיֹּאמְרוּ אֵלֶּה אֱלֹהֶיךָ יִשְׂרָאֵל אֲשֶׁר הֶעֱלוּךָ מֵאֶרֶץ מִצְרָיִם:

לְלַמֵּד כַּלָּה בִּזְמַן מוּעָט כָּזֶה. דָּבָר אַחֵר, מַה כַּלָּה
מִתְקַשֶּׁטֶת בְּעֶשְׂרִים וְאַרְבָּעָה קִשּׁוּטִין, הֵן הָאֲמוּרִים
בְּסֵפֶר יְשַׁעְיָה (ג, יח-כד), אַף תַּלְמִיד חָכָם צָרִיךְ לִהְיוֹת
בָּקִי בְּעֶשְׂרִים וְאַרְבָּעָה סְפָרִים: לְדַבֵּר אִתּוֹ. הַחֻקִּים
וְהַמִּשְׁפָּטִים שֶׁבְּוָאֵלֶּה הַמִּשְׁפָּטִים: לְדַבֵּר אִתּוֹ.
מְלַמֵּד שֶׁהָיָה מֹשֶׁה שׁוֹמֵעַ מִפִּי הַגְּבוּרָה וְחוֹזְרִין
וְשׁוֹנִין אֶת הַהֲלָכָה שְׁנֵיהֶם יַחַד. לֻחֹת. "לֻחֹת" כְּתִיב,
שֶׁהָיוּ שְׁתֵּיהֶן שָׁווֹת:

פרק לב

א] **כִּי בֹשֵׁשׁ מֹשֶׁה.** כְּתַרְגּוּמוֹ לְשׁוֹן אִחוּר, וְכֵן "בֹּשֵׁשׁ
רִכְבּוֹ" (שופטים ה, כח), "וַיָּחִילוּ עַד בּוֹשׁ" (שם ג, כה). כִּי
כְּשֶׁעָלָה מֹשֶׁה לָהָר אָמַר לָהֶם: לְסוֹף אַרְבָּעִים יוֹם
אֲנִי בָּא בְּתוֹךְ שֵׁשׁ שָׁעוֹת. כְּסְבוּרִים הֵם שֶׁאוֹתוֹ יוֹם
שֶׁעָלָה מִן הַמִּנְיָן הוּא, וְהוּא אָמַר לָהֶם שְׁלֵמִים,
אַרְבָּעִים יוֹם וְלֵילוֹ עִמּוֹ, וְיוֹם עֲלִיָּתוֹ אֵין לֵילוֹ עִמּוֹ.
בְּשִׁבְעָה בְּסִיוָן עָלָה, נִמְצָא יוֹם אַרְבָּעִים בְּשִׁבְעָה עָשָׂר
בְּתַמּוּז. בְּשִׁשָּׁה עָשָׂר בָּא שָׂטָן וְעִרְבֵּב אֶת הָעוֹלָם
וְהֶרְאָה דְּמוּת חֹשֶׁךְ וַאֲפֵלָה וַעֲרַבּוּבְיָא, לוֹמַר וַדַּאי
מֵת מֹשֶׁה לְכָךְ בָּא עִרְבּוּבְיָא לָעוֹלָם. אָמַר לָהֶם:
מֵת מֹשֶׁה, שֶׁכְּבָר בָּאוּ שֵׁשׁ שָׁעוֹת וְלֹא בָּא וְכוּ׳,
כִּדְאִיתָא בְּמַסֶּכֶת שַׁבָּת (דף פט ע"א). וְאִי אֶפְשָׁר לוֹמַר
שֶׁלֹּא טָעוּ אֶלָּא בְּיוֹם הַמְעֻנָּן בֵּין קֹדֶם חֲצוֹת בֵּין
לְאַחַר חֲצוֹת, שֶׁהֲרֵי לֹא יָרַד מֹשֶׁה עַד יוֹם הַמָּחֳרָת,
שֶׁנֶּאֱמַר: "וַיַּשְׁכִּימוּ מִמָּחֳרָת וַיַּעֲלוּ עֹלֹת" (להלן פסוק

ה] **אֲשֶׁר יֵלְכוּ לְפָנֵינוּ.** אֱלֹהוֹת הַרְבֵּה אִוּוּ לָהֶם: **כִּי
זֶה מֹשֶׁה הָאִישׁ.** כְּמִין דְּמוּת מֹשֶׁה הֶרְאָה לָהֶם
הַשָּׂטָן שֶׁנּוֹשְׂאִים אוֹתוֹ בַּאֲוִיר רְקִיעַ הַשָּׁמַיִם: **אֲשֶׁר
הֶעֱלָנוּ מֵאֶרֶץ מִצְרַיִם.** וְהָיָה מוֹרֶה לָנוּ דֶּרֶךְ אֲשֶׁר
נַעֲלֶה בָּהּ, עַתָּה צְרִיכִין אָנוּ לֶאֱלֹהוֹת "אֲשֶׁר יֵלְכוּ
לְפָנֵינוּ":

ב] **בְּאָזְנֵי נְשֵׁיכֶם.** אָמַר אַהֲרֹן בְּלִבּוֹ: הַנָּשִׁים וְהַיְלָדִים
חָסִים עַל תַּכְשִׁיטֵיהֶן, שֶׁמָּא יִתְעַכֵּב הַדָּבָר וּבְתוֹךְ
כָּךְ יָבֹא מֹשֶׁה. וְהֵם לֹא הִמְתִּינוּ וּפָרְקוּ מֵעַל עַצְמָן:
פָּרְקוּ. לְשׁוֹן צִוּוּי מִגִּזְרַת "פְּרֹק" לְיָחִיד, כְּמוֹ "בָּרְכוּ"
מִגִּזְרַת "בָּרֵךְ":

ג] **וַיִּתְפָּרְקוּ.** לְשׁוֹן פְּרִיקַת מַשָּׂא, כְּשֶׁנְּטָלוּם מֵאָזְנֵיהֶם
נִמְצְאוּ הֵם מְפֹרָקִים מִנִּזְמֵיהֶם, דיסקרייד"ר בְּלַעַ"ז:
אֶת נִזְמֵי. כְּמוֹ מִנִּזְמֵי, כְּמוֹ "כְּצֵאתִי אֶת הָעִיר" (לעיל
ט, כט) - מִן הָעִיר:

ד] **וַיָּצַר אֹתוֹ בַּחֶרֶט.** יֵשׁ לְתַרְגְּמוֹ בִּשְׁנֵי פָּנִים:
הָאֶחָד - "וַיָּצַר" לְשׁוֹן קְשִׁירָה, "בַּחֶרֶט" לְשׁוֹן סוּדָר,
כְּמוֹ "וְהַמִּטְפָּחוֹת וְהָחֲרִיטִים" (ישעיה ג, כב) "וַיָּצַר
כִּכְּרַיִם כֶּסֶף בִּשְׁנֵי חֲרִטִים" (מלכים ב' ה, כג). וְהַשֵּׁנִי -
"וַיָּצַר" לְשׁוֹן צוּרָה, "בַּחֶרֶט" כְּלִי אֻמָּנוּת הַצּוֹרְפִין
שֶׁחוֹרְצִין וְחוֹתְכִין בּוֹ צוּרוֹת בַּזָּהָב כְּעֵט סוֹפֵר
הַחוֹרֵץ אוֹתִיּוֹת בְּלוּחוֹת וּפִנְקָסִין, כְּמוֹ "וּכְתֹב עָלָיו
בְּחֶרֶט אֱנוֹשׁ" (ישעיה ח, א), וְזֶהוּ שֶׁתִּרְגֵּם אוּנְקְלוֹס: "וְצָר

שמות | פרק לב

ה וַיַּרְא אַהֲרֹן וַיִּבֶן מִזְבֵּחַ לְפָנָיו וַיִּקְרָא אַהֲרֹן וַיֹּאמַר חַג לַיהוה
ו מָחָר: וַיַּשְׁכִּימוּ מִמָּחֳרָת וַיַּעֲלוּ עֹלֹת וַיַּגִּשׁוּ שְׁלָמִים וַיֵּשֶׁב הָעָם
לֶאֱכֹל וְשָׁתוֹ וַיָּקֻמוּ לְצַחֵק:
ז וַיְדַבֵּר יהוה אֶל־מֹשֶׁה לֶךְ־רֵד כִּי שִׁחֵת עַמְּךָ אֲשֶׁר הֶעֱלֵיתָ
מֵאֶרֶץ מִצְרָיִם: סָרוּ מַהֵר מִן־הַדֶּרֶךְ אֲשֶׁר צִוִּיתִם עָשׂוּ לָהֶם עֵגֶל
ח מַסֵּכָה וַיִּשְׁתַּחֲווּ־לוֹ וַיִּזְבְּחוּ־לוֹ וַיֹּאמְרוּ אֵלֶּה אֱלֹהֶיךָ יִשְׂרָאֵל
ט אֲשֶׁר הֶעֱלוּךָ מֵאֶרֶץ מִצְרָיִם: וַיֹּאמֶר יהוה אֶל־מֹשֶׁה רָאִיתִי
י אֶת־הָעָם הַזֶּה וְהִנֵּה עַם־קְשֵׁה־עֹרֶף הוּא: וְעַתָּה הַנִּיחָה לִּי

יָתֵיהּ בְּזוּזָא". לְשׁוֹן זִיּוּף, הוּא כְּלִי אֻמָּנוּת שֶׁחוֹרְצִין בּוֹ בַּזָּהָב אוֹתִיּוֹת וּנְקֻדּוֹת שֶׁקּוֹרִין בְּלַעַ"ז נייל"ר, וּמַזִּיפִין עַל יָדוֹ חוֹתָמוֹת. **עֵגֶל מַסֵּכָה.** כֵּיוָן שֶׁהִשְׁלִיכוֹ לָאוּר בַּכּוּר, בָּאוּ מְכַשְּׁפֵי עֵרֶב רַב שֶׁעָלוּ עִמָּהֶם מִמִּצְרַיִם וַעֲשָׂאוּהוּ בִּכְשָׁפִים. וְיֵשׁ אוֹמְרִים: מִיכָה הָיָה שָׁם, שֶׁיָּצָא מִתּוֹךְ דִּמּוּסֵי בִּנְיָן שֶׁנִּתְמַעֵךְ בּוֹ בְּמִצְרַיִם, וְהָיָה בְּיָדוֹ שֵׁם וְטַס שֶׁכָּתַב בּוֹ מֹשֶׁה: "עֲלֵה שׁוֹר עֲלֵה שׁוֹר" לְהַעֲלוֹת אֲרוֹנוֹ שֶׁל יוֹסֵף מִתּוֹךְ נִילוּס, וְהִשְׁלִיכוֹ לְתוֹךְ הַכּוּר וְיָצָא הָעֵגֶל. **מַסֵּכָה.** לְשׁוֹן מַתֶּכֶת. דָּבָר אַחֵר, מֵאָה וְעֶשְׂרִים וַחֲמִשָּׁה קַנְטְרִין זָהָב הָיוּ בּוֹ כְּגִימַטְרִיָּא שֶׁל מַסֵּכָה. **אֵלֶּה אֱלֹהֶיךָ.** וְלֹא נֶאֱמַר 'אֵלֶּה אֱלֹהֵינוּ', מִכָּאן שֶׁעֵרֶב רַב שֶׁעָלוּ מִמִּצְרַיִם הֵם שֶׁנִּקְהֲלוּ עַל אַהֲרֹן וְהֵם שֶׁעֲשָׂאוּהוּ, וְאַחַר כָּךְ הִטְעוּ אֶת יִשְׂרָאֵל אַחֲרָיו:

ה **וַיַּרְא אַהֲרֹן.** שֶׁהָיָה בּוֹ רוּחַ חַיִּים, שֶׁנֶּאֱמַר: "בְּתַבְנִית שׁוֹר אֹכֵל עֵשֶׂב" (תהלים קו, כ), וְרָאָה שֶׁהִצְלִיחַ מַעֲשֵׂה שָׂטָן, וְלֹא הָיָה לוֹ פֶה לִדְחוֹתָם לְגַמְרֵי: **וַיִּבֶן מִזְבֵּחַ.** לִדְחוֹתָם: **וַיִּקְרָא... חַג לַה' מָחָר.** וְלֹא הַיּוֹם, שֶׁמָּא יָבֹא מֹשֶׁה קֹדֶם שֶׁיַּעַבְדוּהוּ, זֶהוּ פְּשׁוּטוֹ. וּמִדְרָשׁוֹ בְּוַיִּקְרָא רַבָּה (י, ג): דְּבָרִים הַרְבֵּה רָאָה אַהֲרֹן; רָאָה חוּר בֶּן אֲחוֹתוֹ שֶׁהָיָה מוֹכִיחָם וַהֲרָגוּהוּ, וְזֶהוּ "וַיִּבֶן מִזְבֵּחַ לְפָנָיו", וַיָּבֶן מִזָּבוּחַ לְפָנָיו, וְעוֹד רָאָה וְאָמַר, מוּטָב שֶׁיִּתָּלֶה בִּי הַסֵּרָחוֹן וְלֹא בָהֶם, וְעוֹד רָאָה וְאָמַר, אִם הֵם בּוֹנִים אוֹתוֹ הַמִּזְבֵּחַ, זֶה מֵבִיא צְרוֹר

וְזֶה מֵבִיא אֶבֶן וְנִמְצֵאת מְלַאכְתָּן בְּבַת אַחַת, מִתּוֹךְ שֶׁאֲנִי בּוֹנֶה אוֹתוֹ וַאֲנִי מִתְעַצֵּל בִּמְלַאכְתִּי, בֵּין כָּךְ וּבֵין כָּךְ מֹשֶׁה בָּא. **חַג לַה'.** בְּלִבּוֹ הָיָה לַשָּׁמַיִם, בָּטוּחַ הָיָה שֶׁיָּבֹא מֹשֶׁה וְיַעַבְדוּ אֶת הַמָּקוֹם:

ו **וַיַּשְׁכִּימוּ.** הַשָּׂטָן זֵרְזָם כְּדֵי שֶׁיֶּחֶטְאוּ: **לְצַחֵק.** יֵשׁ בְּמַשְׁמָע הַזֶּה גִּלּוּי עֲרָיוֹת, כְּמוֹ שֶׁנֶּאֱמַר: "לְצַחֶק בִּי" (בראשית לט, יז), וּשְׁפִיכוּת דָּמִים, כְּמוֹ שֶׁנֶּאֱמַר: "יָקוּמוּ נָא הַנְּעָרִים וִישַׂחֲקוּ לְפָנֵינוּ" (שמואל ב' ב, יד), אַף כָּאן נֶהֱרַג חוּר:

ז **וַיְדַבֵּר.** לְשׁוֹן קֹשִׁי הוּא, כְּמוֹ: "וַיְדַבֵּר אִתָּם קָשׁוֹת" (בראשית מב, ז): **לֶךְ־רֵד.** מִגְּדֻלָּתְךָ, לֹא נָתַתִּי לְךָ גְּדֻלָּה אֶלָּא בִּשְׁבִילָם. בְּאוֹתָהּ שָׁעָה נִתְנַדָּה מֹשֶׁה מִפִּי בֵּית דִּין שֶׁלְּמַעְלָה: **שִׁחֵת עַמְּךָ.** שִׁחֵת הָעָם לֹא נֶאֱמַר, אֶלָּא "עַמְּךָ", עֵרֶב רַב שֶׁקִּבַּלְתָּ מֵעַצְמְךָ וְגִיַּרְתָּם וְלֹא נִמְלַכְתָּ בִּי, וְאָמַרְתָּ: טוֹב שֶׁיִּדְבְּקוּ גֵּרִים בַּשְּׁכִינָה - הֵם שִׁחֲתוּ וְהִשְׁחִיתוּ:

ט **קְשֵׁה־עֹרֶף.** מַחֲזִירִין קְשִׁי עָרְפָּם לְנֶגֶד מוֹכִיחֵיהֶם וּמְמָאֲנִים לִשְׁמֹעַ:

י **הַנִּיחָה לִּי.** עֲדַיִן לֹא שָׁמַעְנוּ שֶׁהִתְפַּלֵּל מֹשֶׁה עֲלֵיהֶם, וְהוּא אוֹמֵר "הַנִּיחָה לִּי"? אֶלָּא כָּאן פָּתַח לוֹ פֶתַח וְהוֹדִיעוֹ שֶׁהַדָּבָר תָּלוּי בּוֹ, שֶׁאִם יִתְפַּלֵּל עֲלֵיהֶם לֹא יְכַלֶּה:

פרק לב | שמות

יא וַיִּחַר־אַפִּי בָהֶם וַאֲכַלֵּם וְאֶעֱשֶׂה אוֹתְךָ לְגוֹי גָּדוֹל: וַיְחַל מֹשֶׁה אֶת־פְּנֵי יְהוָה אֱלֹהָיו וַיֹּאמֶר לָמָה יְהוָה יֶחֱרֶה אַפְּךָ בְּעַמֶּךָ
יב אֲשֶׁר הוֹצֵאתָ מֵאֶרֶץ מִצְרַיִם בְּכֹחַ גָּדוֹל וּבְיָד חֲזָקָה: לָמָּה יֹאמְרוּ מִצְרַיִם לֵאמֹר בְּרָעָה הוֹצִיאָם לַהֲרֹג אֹתָם בֶּהָרִים וּלְכַלֹּתָם מֵעַל פְּנֵי הָאֲדָמָה שׁוּב מֵחֲרוֹן אַפֶּךָ וְהִנָּחֵם עַל־
יג הָרָעָה לְעַמֶּךָ: זְכֹר לְאַבְרָהָם לְיִצְחָק וּלְיִשְׂרָאֵל עֲבָדֶיךָ אֲשֶׁר נִשְׁבַּעְתָּ לָהֶם בָּךְ וַתְּדַבֵּר אֲלֵהֶם אַרְבֶּה אֶת־זַרְעֲכֶם כְּכוֹכְבֵי הַשָּׁמָיִם וְכָל־הָאָרֶץ הַזֹּאת אֲשֶׁר אָמַרְתִּי אֶתֵּן לְזַרְעֲכֶם
יד וְנָחֲלוּ לְעֹלָם: וַיִּנָּחֶם יְהוָה עַל־הָרָעָה אֲשֶׁר דִּבֶּר לַעֲשׂוֹת לְעַמּוֹ:

כה
טו וַיִּפֶן וַיֵּרֶד מֹשֶׁה מִן־הָהָר וּשְׁנֵי לֻחֹת הָעֵדֻת בְּיָדוֹ לֻחֹת כְּתֻבִים
טז מִשְּׁנֵי עֶבְרֵיהֶם מִזֶּה וּמִזֶּה הֵם כְּתֻבִים: וְהַלֻּחֹת מַעֲשֵׂה אֱלֹהִים הֵמָּה וְהַמִּכְתָּב מִכְתַּב אֱלֹהִים הוּא חָרוּת עַל־הַלֻּחֹת:

יא] **לָמָה ה' יֶחֱרֶה אַפְּךָ.** כְּלוּם מִתְקַנֵּא אֶלָּא חָכָם בְּחָכָם גִּבּוֹר בְּגִבּוֹר:

יב] **וְהִנָּחֵם.** הִתְעַשֵּׁת לָהֶם מַחֲשָׁבָה אַחֶרֶת לְהֵיטִיב **עַל הָרָעָה.** אֲשֶׁר חָשַׁבְתָּ לָהֶם:

יג] **זְכֹר לְאַבְרָהָם.** אִם עָבְרוּ עַל עֲשֶׂרֶת הַדִּבְּרוֹת, אַבְרָהָם אֲבִיהֶם נִתְנַסָּה בַּעֲשָׂרָה נִסְיוֹנוֹת וַעֲדַיִן לֹא קִבֵּל שְׂכָרוֹ, תְּנֵהוּ לוֹ, וְיֵצְאוּ עֲשָׂרָה בַּעֲשָׂרָה: **לְאַבְרָהָם לְיִצְחָק וּלְיִשְׂרָאֵל.** אִם שְׂרוּפִין הֵן, זְכֹר לְאַבְרָהָם שֶׁמָּסַר עַצְמוֹ לִשָּׂרֵף עָלֶיךָ בְּאוּר כַּשְׂדִּים. אִם הֲרוּגִים, זְכֹר לְיִצְחָק שֶׁפָּשַׁט צַוָּארוֹ לָעֲקֵדָה. אִם גּוֹלִים, זְכֹר לְיַעֲקֹב שֶׁגָּלָה לְחָרָן. וְאִם אֵינָן נִצּוֹלִין בִּזְכוּתָן, מָה אַתָּה אוֹמֵר לִי: "וְאֶעֱשֶׂה אוֹתְךָ לְגוֹי גָּדוֹל"? אִם כִּסֵּא שֶׁל שָׁלֹשׁ רַגְלַיִם אֵינוֹ עוֹמֵד לְפָנֶיךָ, קַל וָחֹמֶר לְכִסֵּא שֶׁל רֶגֶל אֶחָד: **אֲשֶׁר נִשְׁבַּעְתָּ לָהֶם בָּךְ.** לֹא נִשְׁבַּעְתָּ לָהֶם בְּדָבָר שֶׁהוּא כָּלֶה, לֹא בַשָּׁמַיִם וְלֹא בָאָרֶץ, לֹא בֶהָרִים וְלֹא בַגְּבָעוֹת, אֶלָּא בְּךָ שֶׁאַתָּה

קַיָּם וְכֵן שְׁבוּעָתְךָ תִּתְקַיֵּם, שֶׁנֶּאֱמַר: "בִּי נִשְׁבַּעְתִּי נְאֻם ה'" (בראשית כב, טז), וּלְיִצְחָק נֶאֱמַר: "וַהֲקִמֹתִי אֶת הַשְּׁבוּעָה אֲשֶׁר נִשְׁבַּעְתִּי לְאַבְרָהָם אָבִיךָ" (שם כו, ג), וּלְיַעֲקֹב נֶאֱמַר: "אֲנִי אֵל שַׁדַּי פְּרֵה וּרְבֵה" (שם לה, יא), נִשְׁבַּע לוֹ בְּאֵל שַׁדָּי:

טו] **מִשְּׁנֵי עֶבְרֵיהֶם.** הָיוּ הָאוֹתִיּוֹת נִקְרָאוֹת, וּמַעֲשֵׂה נִסִּים הוּא:

טז] **מַעֲשֵׂה אֱלֹהִים הֵמָּה.** כְּמַשְׁמָעוֹ, הוּא בִּכְבוֹדוֹ עֲשָׂאָן. דָּבָר אַחֵר, כְּאָדָם הָאוֹמֵר לַחֲבֵרוֹ: כָּל עֲסָקָיו שֶׁל פְּלוֹנִי בִּמְלָאכָה פְּלוֹנִית, כָּךְ כָּל שַׁעֲשׁוּעָיו שֶׁל הַקָּדוֹשׁ בָּרוּךְ הוּא בַּתּוֹרָה: **חָרוּת.** לְשׁוֹן 'חֶרֶט' וְ"חָרוּת" אֶחָד הוּא, שְׁנֵיהֶם לְשׁוֹן חִקּוּק, אנטלי"ר בְּלַעַז:

שמות | פרק לב

יז וַיִּשְׁמַע יְהוֹשֻׁעַ אֶת־קוֹל הָעָם בְּרֵעֹה וַיֹּאמֶר אֶל־מֹשֶׁה קוֹל
יח מִלְחָמָה בַּמַּחֲנֶה: וַיֹּאמֶר אֵין קוֹל עֲנוֹת גְּבוּרָה וְאֵין קוֹל עֲנוֹת
יט חֲלוּשָׁה קוֹל עַנּוֹת אָנֹכִי שֹׁמֵעַ: וַיְהִי כַּאֲשֶׁר קָרַב אֶל־הַמַּחֲנֶה
וַיַּרְא אֶת־הָעֵגֶל וּמְחֹלֹת וַיִּחַר־אַף מֹשֶׁה וַיַּשְׁלֵךְ מִיָּדָו אֶת־
כ הַלֻּחֹת וַיְשַׁבֵּר אֹתָם תַּחַת הָהָר: וַיִּקַּח אֶת־הָעֵגֶל אֲשֶׁר עָשׂוּ
וַיִּשְׂרֹף בָּאֵשׁ וַיִּטְחַן עַד אֲשֶׁר־דָּק וַיִּזֶר עַל־פְּנֵי הַמַּיִם וַיַּשְׁקְ אֶת־
כא בְּנֵי יִשְׂרָאֵל: וַיֹּאמֶר מֹשֶׁה אֶל־אַהֲרֹן מֶה־עָשָׂה לְךָ הָעָם הַזֶּה
כב כִּי־הֵבֵאתָ עָלָיו חֲטָאָה גְדֹלָה: וַיֹּאמֶר אַהֲרֹן אַל־יִחַר אַף אֲדֹנִי
כג אַתָּה יָדַעְתָּ אֶת־הָעָם כִּי בְרָע הוּא: וַיֹּאמְרוּ לִי עֲשֵׂה־לָנוּ אֱלֹהִים
אֲשֶׁר יֵלְכוּ לְפָנֵינוּ כִּי־זֶה ׀ מֹשֶׁה הָאִישׁ אֲשֶׁר הֶעֱלָנוּ מֵאֶרֶץ
כד מִצְרַיִם לֹא יָדַעְנוּ מֶה־הָיָה לוֹ: וָאֹמַר לָהֶם לְמִי זָהָב הִתְפָּרָקוּ
כה וַיִּתְּנוּ־לִי וָאַשְׁלִכֵהוּ בָאֵשׁ וַיֵּצֵא הָעֵגֶל הַזֶּה: וַיַּרְא מֹשֶׁה אֶת־הָעָם
כו כִּי פָרֻעַ הוּא כִּי־פְרָעֹה אַהֲרֹן לְשִׁמְצָה בְּקָמֵיהֶם: וַיַּעֲמֹד מֹשֶׁה

יז| בְּרֵעֹה. בַּהֲרִיעוֹ, שֶׁהָיוּ מְרִיעִים וּשְׂמֵחִים וְצוֹחֲקִים:

יח| אֵין קוֹל עֲנוֹת גְּבוּרָה. אֵין קוֹל הַזֶּה נִרְאֶה קוֹל עֲנִיַּת גִּבּוֹרִים הַצּוֹעֲקִים 'נַצָּחוֹן', וְלֹא קוֹל חַלָּשִׁים הַצּוֹעֲקִים 'וַי' אוֹ 'נִסָה': קוֹל עַנּוֹת. קוֹל חֵרוּפִין וְגִדּוּפִין הַמְעַנִּין אֶת נֶפֶשׁ שׁוֹמְעָן כְּשֶׁנֶּאֱמָרִין לוֹ:

יט| וַיַּשְׁלֵךְ מִיָּדָו וְגו'. אָמַר: מַה פֶּסַח שֶׁהוּא אַחַת מִן הַמִּצְוֹת, אָמְרָה תּוֹרָה: "כָּל בֶּן נֵכָר לֹא יֹאכַל בּוֹ" (לעיל יב, מג), הַתּוֹרָה כֻּלָּהּ כָּאן וְכָל יִשְׂרָאֵל מְשֻׁמָּדִים, וְאֶתְּנֶנָּה לָהֶם?!: תַּחַת הָהָר. לְרַגְלֵי הָהָר:

כ| וַיִּזֶר. לְשׁוֹן נִפּוּץ, וְכֵן: "יְזֹרֶה עַל נָוֵהוּ גָפְרִית" (איוב יח, טו), וְכֵן: "כִּי חִנָּם מְזֹרָה הָרָשֶׁת" (משלי א, יז), שֶׁזּוֹרִין בָּהּ דָּגָן וְקִטְנִיּוֹת: וַיַּשְׁקְ אֶת בְּנֵי יִשְׂרָאֵל. נִתְכַּוֵּן לְבָדְקָן כְּסוֹטוֹת. שָׁלֹשׁ מִיתוֹת נִדּוֹנוּ שָׁם: אִם יֵשׁ עֵדִים וְהַתְרָאָה, בְּסַיִף, כְּמִשְׁפַּט אַנְשֵׁי עִיר הַנִּדַּחַת שֶׁהֵן מְרֻבִּין; עֵדִים בְּלֹא הַתְרָאָה, בְּמַגֵּפָה, שֶׁנֶּאֱמַר: "וַיִּגֹּף ה' אֶת הָעָם" (להלן פסוק לה), לֹא עֵדִים וְלֹא הַתְרָאָה, בְּהִדְרוֹקָן, שֶׁבְּדָקוּם הַמַּיִם וְצָבוּ בִטְנֵיהֶם:

כא| מֶה עָשָׂה לְךָ הָעָם הַזֶּה. כַּמָּה יִסּוּרִים סָבַלְתָּ שֶׁיִּסְּרוּךָ עַד שֶׁלֹּא תָּבִיא עֲלֵיהֶם חֵטְא זֶה:

כב| כִּי בְרָע הוּא. בְּדֶרֶךְ רַע הֵם הוֹלְכִין תָּמִיד וּבְנִסְיוֹנוֹת לִפְנֵי הַמָּקוֹם:

כד| וָאֹמַר לָהֶם. דָּבָר אֶחָד, וְהֵם מִהֲרוּ וְ"הִתְפָּרָקוּ" וַיִּתְּנוּ לִי: וָאַשְׁלִכֵהוּ בָאֵשׁ. וְלֹא יָדַעְתִּי שֶׁיֵּצֵא הָעֵגֶל הַזֶּה, "וַיֵּצֵא":

כה| פָרֻעַ. מְגֻלֶּה, נִתְגַּלָּה שִׁמְצוֹ וּקְלוֹנוֹ, כְּמוֹ: "וּפָרַע אֶת רֹאשׁ הָאִשָּׁה" (במדבר ה, יח): לְשִׁמְצָה בְּקָמֵיהֶם. לִהְיוֹת לָהֶם הַדָּבָר הַזֶּה לִגְנוּת בְּפִי כָּל הַקָּמִים עֲלֵיהֶם:

בְּשַׁעַר הַמַּחֲנֶה וַיֹּאמֶר מִי לַיהוה אֵלָי וַיֵּאָסְפוּ אֵלָיו כָּל־בְּנֵי לֵוִי:
וַיֹּאמֶר לָהֶם כֹּה־אָמַר יהוה אֱלֹהֵי יִשְׂרָאֵל שִׂימוּ אִישׁ־חַרְבּוֹ
עַל־יְרֵכוֹ עִבְרוּ וָשׁוּבוּ מִשַּׁעַר לָשַׁעַר בַּמַּחֲנֶה וְהִרְגוּ אִישׁ־אֶת־
אָחִיו וְאִישׁ אֶת־רֵעֵהוּ וְאִישׁ אֶת־קְרֹבוֹ: וַיַּעֲשׂוּ בְנֵי־לֵוִי כִּדְבַר
מֹשֶׁה וַיִּפֹּל מִן־הָעָם בַּיּוֹם הַהוּא כִּשְׁלֹשֶׁת אַלְפֵי אִישׁ: וַיֹּאמֶר
מֹשֶׁה מִלְאוּ יֶדְכֶם הַיּוֹם לַיהוה כִּי אִישׁ בִּבְנוֹ וּבְאָחִיו וְלָתֵת
עֲלֵיכֶם הַיּוֹם בְּרָכָה: וַיְהִי מִמָּחֳרָת וַיֹּאמֶר מֹשֶׁה אֶל־הָעָם אַתֶּם
חֲטָאתֶם חֲטָאָה גְדֹלָה וְעַתָּה אֶעֱלֶה אֶל־יהוה אוּלַי אֲכַפְּרָה
בְּעַד חַטַּאתְכֶם: וַיָּשָׁב מֹשֶׁה אֶל־יהוה וַיֹּאמַר אָנָּא חָטָא הָעָם
הַזֶּה חֲטָאָה גְדֹלָה וַיַּעֲשׂוּ לָהֶם אֱלֹהֵי זָהָב: וְעַתָּה אִם־תִּשָּׂא
חַטָּאתָם וְאִם־אַיִן מְחֵנִי נָא מִסִּפְרְךָ אֲשֶׁר כָּתָבְתָּ: וַיֹּאמֶר יהוה
אֶל־מֹשֶׁה מִי אֲשֶׁר חָטָא־לִי אֶמְחֶנּוּ מִסִּפְרִי: וְעַתָּה לֵךְ ׀ נְחֵה
אֶת־הָעָם אֶל אֲשֶׁר־דִּבַּרְתִּי לָךְ הִנֵּה מַלְאָכִי יֵלֵךְ לְפָנֶיךָ וּבְיוֹם

כו | **מִי לַהֹ׳ אֵלָי.** יָבֹא אֵלָי: **כָּל בְּנֵי לֵוִי.** מִכָּאן שֶׁכָּל הַשֵּׁבֶט כָּשֵׁר:

כז | **כֹּה אָמַר וְגוֹ׳.** וְהֵיכָן אָמַר? "זֹבֵחַ לָאֱלֹהִים יָחֳרָם" (לעיל כב, יט), כָּךְ שְׁנוּיָה בַּמְּכִילְתָּא: **אָחִיו.** מֵאִמּוֹ, וְהוּא יִשְׂרָאֵל:

כט | **מִלְאוּ יֶדְכֶם.** אַתֶּם הַהוֹרְגִים אוֹתָם, בַּדָּבָר זֶה תִּתְחַנְּכוּ לִהְיוֹת כֹּהֲנִים לַמָּקוֹם: **כִּי אִישׁ.** מִכֶּם, יְמַלֵּא יָדוֹ "בִּבְנוֹ וּבְאָחִיו":

ל | **אֲכַפְּרָה בְּעַד חַטַּאתְכֶם.** אָשִׂים כֹּפֶר וְקִנּוּחַ וּסְתִימָה לְנֶגֶד חַטַּאתְכֶם, לְהַבְדִּיל בֵּינֵיכֶם וּבֵין הַחֵטְא:

לא | **אֱלֹהֵי זָהָב.** אַתָּה הוּא שֶׁגָּרַמְתָּ לָהֶם, שֶׁהִשְׁפַּעְתָּ לָהֶם זָהָב וְכָל חֶפְצָם, מַה יַּעֲשׂוּ שֶׁלֹּא יֶחֶטְאוּ? מָשָׁל

לְמֶלֶךְ שֶׁהָיָה מַאֲכִיל וּמַשְׁקֶה וּמְקַשְּׁטוֹ וְתוֹלֶה לוֹ כִּיס בְּצַוָּארוֹ, וּמַעֲמִידוֹ בְּפֶתַח בֵּית זוֹנוֹת, מַה יַּעֲשֶׂה הַבֵּן שֶׁלֹּא יֶחֱטָא?

לב | **וְעַתָּה אִם תִּשָּׂא חַטָּאתָם.** הֲרֵי טוֹב, אֵינִי אוֹמֵר לְךָ "מְחֵנִי", וְאִם אַיִן – "מְחֵנִי", וְזֶה מִקְרָא קָצָר, וְכֵן הַרְבֵּה: **מִסִּפְרְךָ.** מִכָּל הַתּוֹרָה כֻּלָּהּ, שֶׁלֹּא יֹאמְרוּ עָלַי שֶׁלֹּא הָיִיתִי כְּדַאי לְבַקֵּשׁ עֲלֵיהֶם רַחֲמִים:

לד | **אֶל אֲשֶׁר דִּבַּרְתִּי לָךְ.** יֵשׁ כָּאן "לָךְ" אֵצֶל דִּבּוּר בִּמְקוֹם "אֵלֶיךָ", וְכֵן: "לְדַבֶּר לוֹ עַל אֲדֹנִיָּהוּ" (מלכים א ב, יט): **הִנֵּה מַלְאָכִי.** וְלֹא אֲנִי: **וּבְיוֹם פָּקְדִי וְגוֹ׳.** עַתָּה שָׁמַעְתִּי אֵלֶיךָ מִלְּכַלּוֹתָם יַחַד, וְתָמִיד תָּמִיד כְּשֶׁאֶפְקֹד עֲלֵיהֶם עֲוֹנוֹתֵיהֶם, "וּפָקַדְתִּי עֲלֵיהֶם" מְעַט מִן הֶעָוֹן הַזֶּה עִם שְׁאָר הָעֲוֹנוֹת, וְאֵין פֻּרְעָנוּת בָּאָה עַל יִשְׂרָאֵל שֶׁאֵין בָּהּ קְצָת מִפִּרְעוֹן עֲוֹן הָעֵגֶל:

שמות | פרק לב

לה פְּקֻדִּי וּפָקַדְתִּי עֲלֵהֶם חַטָּאתָם: וַיִּגֹּף יהוה אֶת־הָעָם עַל אֲשֶׁר
לג א עָשׂוּ אֶת־הָעֵגֶל אֲשֶׁר עָשָׂה אַהֲרֹן: וַיְדַבֵּר יהוה אֶל־
מֹשֶׁה לֵךְ עֲלֵה מִזֶּה אַתָּה וְהָעָם אֲשֶׁר הֶעֱלִיתָ מֵאֶרֶץ מִצְרָיִם
אֶל־הָאָרֶץ אֲשֶׁר נִשְׁבַּעְתִּי לְאַבְרָהָם לְיִצְחָק וּלְיַעֲקֹב לֵאמֹר
ב לְזַרְעֲךָ אֶתְּנֶנָּה: וְשָׁלַחְתִּי לְפָנֶיךָ מַלְאָךְ וְגֵרַשְׁתִּי אֶת־הַכְּנַעֲנִי
ג הָאֱמֹרִי וְהַחִתִּי וְהַפְּרִזִּי הַחִוִּי וְהַיְבוּסִי: אֶל־אֶרֶץ זָבַת חָלָב
וּדְבָשׁ כִּי לֹא אֶעֱלֶה בְּקִרְבְּךָ כִּי עַם־קְשֵׁה־עֹרֶף אַתָּה פֶּן־
ד אֲכֶלְךָ בַּדָּרֶךְ: וַיִּשְׁמַע הָעָם אֶת־הַדָּבָר הָרָע הַזֶּה וַיִּתְאַבָּלוּ
ה וְלֹא־שָׁתוּ אִישׁ עֶדְיוֹ עָלָיו: וַיֹּאמֶר יהוה אֶל־מֹשֶׁה אֱמֹר אֶל־
בְּנֵי־יִשְׂרָאֵל אַתֶּם עַם־קְשֵׁה־עֹרֶף רֶגַע אֶחָד אֶעֱלֶה בְקִרְבְּךָ
וְכִלִּיתִיךָ וְעַתָּה הוֹרֵד עֶדְיְךָ מֵעָלֶיךָ וְאֵדְעָה מָה אֶעֱשֶׂה־לָּךְ:
ו וַיִּתְנַצְּלוּ בְנֵי־יִשְׂרָאֵל אֶת־עֶדְיָם מֵהַר חוֹרֵב: וּמֹשֶׁה יִקַּח אֶת־

לה] וַיִּגֹּף ה' אֶת הָעָם. מִיתָה בִּידֵי שָׁמַיִם לָעֵדִים
בְּלֹא הַתְרָאָה:

פרק לג

א] לֵךְ עֲלֵה מִזֶּה. אֶרֶץ יִשְׂרָאֵל גְּבוֹהָה מִכָּל הָאֲרָצוֹת,
לְכָךְ נֶאֱמַר "עֲלֵה". דָּבָר אַחֵר, כְּלַפֵּי שֶׁאָמַר לוֹ
בִּשְׁעַת הַכַּעַס: "לֶךְ רֵד" (לעיל לב, ז), אָמַר לוֹ בִּשְׁעַת
רָצוֹן: "לֵךְ עֲלֵה": אַתָּה וְהָעָם. כָּאן לֹא נֶאֱמַר "וְעַמְּךָ":

ב] וְגֵרַשְׁתִּי אֶת הַכְּנַעֲנִי וְגוֹ'. שֵׁשׁ אֻמּוֹת הֵן, וְהַגִּרְגָּשִׁי
עָמַד וּפִנָּה מִפְּנֵיהֶם מֵאֵלָיו:

ג] אֶל אֶרֶץ זָבַת חָלָב וּדְבָשׁ. אֲנִי אוֹמֵר לְךָ
לְהַעֲלוֹתָם: כִּי לֹא אֶעֱלֶה בְּקִרְבְּךָ. לְכָךְ אֲנִי אוֹמֵר
לְךָ: "וְשָׁלַחְתִּי לְפָנֶיךָ מַלְאָךְ": כִּי עַם קְשֵׁה עֹרֶף אָתָּה.
וּכְשֶׁשְּׁכִינָתִי בְּקִרְבְּכֶם וְאַתֶּם מַמְרִים בִּי מַרְבֶּה אֲנִי
עֲלֵיכֶם זַעַם: אֲכֶלְךָ. לְשׁוֹן כִּלָּיוֹן:

ד] הַדָּבָר הָרָע. שֶׁאֵין הַשְּׁכִינָה שׁוֹרָה וּמְהַלֶּכֶת עִמָּם:
אִישׁ עֶדְיוֹ. כְּתָרִים שֶׁנִּתְּנוּ לָהֶם בְּחוֹרֵב כְּשֶׁאָמְרוּ:
"נַעֲשֶׂה וְנִשְׁמָע" (לעיל כד, ז):

ה] רֶגַע אֶחָד אֶעֱלֶה בְקִרְבְּךָ וְכִלִּיתִיךָ. אִם מַעֲלֶה
בְּקִרְבְּךָ וְאַתֶּם מַמְרִים בִּי בְּקַשְׁיוּת עָרְפְּכֶם, אֶזְעַם
עֲלֵיכֶם רֶגַע אֶחָד – שֶׁהוּא שִׁעוּר זַעְמוֹ, שֶׁנֶּאֱמַר:
"חֲבִי כִּמְעַט רֶגַע עַד יַעֲבָר זָעַם" (ישעיה כו, כ) – וַאֲכַלֶּה
אֶתְכֶם, לְפִיכָךְ טוֹב לָכֶם שֶׁאֶשְׁלַח מַלְאָךְ: וְעַתָּה.
פֻּרְעָנוּת זוֹ תִּלְקוּ מִיָּד, שֶׁתּוֹרִידוּ עֶדְיְכֶם מֵעֲלֵיכֶם:
וְאֵדְעָה מָה אֶעֱשֶׂה לָּךְ. בִּפְקֻדַּת שְׁאָר הֶעָווֹן אֲנִי יוֹדֵעַ
מַה בְּלִבִּי לַעֲשׂוֹת:

ו] אֶת עֶדְיָם מֵהַר חוֹרֵב. אֶת הָעֲדִי שֶׁהָיָה בְּיָדָם
מֵהַר חוֹרֵב:

ו] וּמֹשֶׁה. מֵחַטֹּאתוֹ עָוֹן וְהָלְאָה "יִקַּח אֶת הָאֹהֶל",
לְשׁוֹן הֹוֶה הוּא, לוֹקֵחַ אָהֳלוֹ וְנוֹטֵהוּ מִחוּץ לַמַּחֲנֶה.

הָאֹהֶל וְנָטָה־לוֹ ׀ מִחוּץ לַמַּחֲנֶה הַרְחֵק מִן־הַמַּחֲנֶה וְקָרָא לוֹ אֹהֶל מוֹעֵד וְהָיָה כָּל־מְבַקֵּשׁ יְהוָה יֵצֵא אֶל־אֹהֶל מוֹעֵד אֲשֶׁר מִחוּץ לַמַּחֲנֶה: וְהָיָה כְּצֵאת מֹשֶׁה אֶל־הָאֹהֶל יָקוּמוּ כָּל־הָעָם וְנִצְּבוּ אִישׁ פֶּתַח אָהֳלוֹ וְהִבִּיטוּ אַחֲרֵי מֹשֶׁה עַד־בֹּאוֹ הָאֹהֱלָה: וְהָיָה כְּבֹא מֹשֶׁה הָאֹהֱלָה יֵרֵד עַמּוּד הֶעָנָן וְעָמַד פֶּתַח הָאֹהֶל וְדִבֶּר עִם־מֹשֶׁה: וְרָאָה כָל־הָעָם אֶת־עַמּוּד הֶעָנָן עֹמֵד פֶּתַח הָאֹהֶל וְקָם כָּל־הָעָם וְהִשְׁתַּחֲווּ אִישׁ פֶּתַח אָהֳלוֹ: וְדִבֶּר יְהוָה אֶל־מֹשֶׁה פָּנִים אֶל־פָּנִים כַּאֲשֶׁר יְדַבֵּר אִישׁ אֶל־רֵעֵהוּ וְשָׁב אֶל־הַמַּחֲנֶה וּמְשָׁרְתוֹ יְהוֹשֻׁעַ בִּן־נוּן נַעַר לֹא יָמִישׁ מִתּוֹךְ הָאֹהֶל:

ח

ט

י

יא

חָמַר. מְנָדֶּה לָרַב מְנָדֶּה לַתַּלְמִיד: **הַרְחֵק.** אַלְפַּיִם אַמָּה, כְּעִנְיָן שֶׁנֶּאֱמַר: "אַךְ רָחוֹק יִהְיֶה בֵּינֵיכֶם וּבֵינָיו כְּאַלְפַּיִם אַמָּה בַּמִּדָּה" (יהושע ג, ד): **וְקָרָא לוֹ.** וְהָיָה קוֹרֵא לוֹ "אֹהֶל מוֹעֵד", הוּא בֵּית וַעַד לַמְבַקְּשֵׁי תוֹרָה: **כָּל מְבַקֵּשׁ ה'.** מִכָּאן לַמְבַקֵּשׁ פְּנֵי זָקֵן כִּמְקַבֵּל פְּנֵי שְׁכִינָה: **יֵצֵא אֶל אֹהֶל מוֹעֵד.** כְּמוֹ 'יוֹצֵא'. דָּבָר אַחֵר, "וְהָיָה כָּל מְבַקֵּשׁ ה'", אֲפִלּוּ מַלְאֲכֵי הַשָּׁרֵת כְּשֶׁהָיוּ שׁוֹאֲלִים מְקוֹם שְׁכִינָה, חַבְרֵיהֶם אוֹמְרִים לָהֶם הֲרֵי הוּא בְּאָהֳלוֹ שֶׁל מֹשֶׁה:

ח וְהָיָה. לְשׁוֹן הוֶֹה: **כְּצֵאת מֹשֶׁה מִן הַמַּחֲנֶה.** לָלֶכֶת אֶל הָאֹהֶל: **יָקוּמוּ כָּל הָעָם.** עוֹמְדִים מִפָּנָיו, וְאֵין יוֹשְׁבִין עַד שֶׁנִּתְכַּסֶּה מֵהֶם: **וְהִבִּיטוּ אַחֲרֵי מֹשֶׁה.** לְשֶׁבַח: אַשְׁרֵי יְלוּד אִשָּׁה שֶׁכָּךְ מֻבְטָח שֶׁהַשְּׁכִינָה תִּכָּנֵס אַחֲרָיו לְפֶתַח אָהֳלוֹ:

ט וְדִבֶּר עִם מֹשֶׁה. כְּמוֹ וּמְדַבֵּר עִם מֹשֶׁה, וְתַרְגּוּמוֹ: "וּמִתְמַלֵּל עִם מֹשֶׁה" שֶׁהוּא כְּבוֹד שְׁכִינָה, כְּמוֹ: "וַיִּשְׁמַע אֶת הַקּוֹל מִדַּבֵּר אֵלָיו" (במדבר ז, פט), וְאֵינוֹ קוֹרֵא 'מְדַבֵּר' אֵלָיו, כְּשֶׁהוּא קוֹרֵא 'מְדַבֵּר' פִּתְרוֹנוֹ, הַקּוֹל מְדַבֵּר בֵּינוֹ לְבֵין עַצְמוֹ וְהַהֶדְיוֹט שׁוֹמֵעַ מֵאֵלָיו, וּכְשֶׁהוּא קוֹרֵא 'מְדַבֵּר' מַשְׁמַע שֶׁהַמֶּלֶךְ מְדַבֵּר עִם הַהֶדְיוֹט:

י וְהִשְׁתַּחֲווּ. לַשְּׁכִינָה:

יא וְדִבֶּר ה' אֶל מֹשֶׁה פָּנִים אֶל פָּנִים. וּמִתְמַלֵּל עִם מֹשֶׁה. וְשָׁב אֶל הַמַּחֲנֶה. לְאַחַר שֶׁנִּדְבַּר עִמּוֹ הָיָה מֹשֶׁה שָׁב אֶל הַמַּחֲנֶה וּמְלַמֵּד לַזְּקֵנִים מַה שֶּׁלָּמַד. וְהַדָּבָר הַזֶּה נָהַג מֹשֶׁה מִיּוֹם הַכִּפּוּרִים עַד שֶׁהוּקַם הַמִּשְׁכָּן וְלֹא יוֹתֵר, שֶׁהֲרֵי בְּשִׁבְעָה עָשָׂר בְּתַמּוּז נִשְׁתַּבְּרוּ הַלּוּחוֹת, וּבְשִׁמוֹנָה עָשָׂר שָׂרַף אֶת הָעֵגֶל וְדָן אֶת הַחוֹטְאִים, וּבְתִשְׁעָה עָשָׂר עָלָה, שֶׁנֶּאֱמַר: "וַיְהִי מִמָּחֳרָת וַיֹּאמֶר מֹשֶׁה אֶל הָעָם" וְגוֹ' (לעיל לב, ל), עָשָׂה שָׁם אַרְבָּעִים יוֹם וּבִקֵּשׁ רַחֲמִים, שֶׁנֶּאֱמַר: "וָאֶתְנַפַּל לִפְנֵי ה'" וְגוֹ' (דברים ט, יח), וּבְרֹאשׁ חֹדֶשׁ אֱלוּל נֶאֱמַר לוֹ: "וְעָלִיתָ בַבֹּקֶר אֶל הַר סִינַי" (לעיל לד, ב) לְקַבֵּל לוּחוֹת הָאַחֲרוֹנוֹת, וְעָשָׂה שָׁם אַרְבָּעִים יוֹם, שֶׁנֶּאֱמַר בָּהֶם: "וְאָנֹכִי עָמַדְתִּי בָהָר כַּיָּמִים הָרִאשֹׁנִים" וְגוֹ' (דברים י, י), מָה הָרִאשׁוֹנִים בְּרָצוֹן אַף הָאַחֲרוֹנִים בְּרָצוֹן, אֱמוֹר מֵעַתָּה אֶמְצָעִיִּים הָיוּ בְכַעַס. בַּעֲשָׂרָה בְּתִשְׁרֵי נִתְרַצָּה הַקָּדוֹשׁ בָּרוּךְ הוּא לְיִשְׂרָאֵל בְּשִׂמְחָה וּבְלֵב שָׁלֵם, וְאָמַר לוֹ לְמֹשֶׁה: סָלַחְתִּי כִּדְבָרֶךָ, וּמָסַר לוֹ לוּחוֹת אַחֲרוֹנוֹת, וְיָרַד, וְהִתְחִיל לְצַוֹּתָם עַל מְלֶאכֶת הַמִּשְׁכָּן, וַעֲשָׂאוּהוּ עַד אֶחָד בְּנִיסָן, וּמִשֶּׁהוּקַם לֹא נִדְבַּר עִמּוֹ עוֹד אֶלָּא מֵאֹהֶל מוֹעֵד:

שמות | פרק לג | כי תשא

יב וַיֹּאמֶר מֹשֶׁה אֶל־יְהֹוָה רְאֵה אַתָּה אֹמֵר אֵלַי הַעַל אֶת־הָעָם הַזֶּה וְאַתָּה לֹא הוֹדַעְתַּנִי אֵת אֲשֶׁר־תִּשְׁלַח עִמִּי וְאַתָּה אָמַרְתָּ
יג יְדַעְתִּיךָ בְשֵׁם וְגַם־מָצָאתָ חֵן בְּעֵינָי: וְעַתָּה אִם־נָא מָצָאתִי חֵן בְּעֵינֶיךָ הוֹדִעֵנִי נָא אֶת־דְּרָכֶךָ וְאֵדָעֲךָ לְמַעַן אֶמְצָא־חֵן בְּעֵינֶיךָ
יד וּרְאֵה כִּי עַמְּךָ הַגּוֹי הַזֶּה: וַיֹּאמַר פָּנַי יֵלֵכוּ וַהֲנִחֹתִי לָךְ: וַיֹּאמֶר
טו אֵלָיו אִם־אֵין פָּנֶיךָ הֹלְכִים אַל־תַּעֲלֵנוּ מִזֶּה: וּבַמֶּה ׀ יִוָּדַע אֵפוֹא
טז כִּי־מָצָאתִי חֵן בְּעֵינֶיךָ אֲנִי וְעַמֶּךָ הֲלוֹא בְּלֶכְתְּךָ עִמָּנוּ וְנִפְלֵינוּ אֲנִי וְעַמְּךָ מִכָּל־הָעָם אֲשֶׁר עַל־פְּנֵי הָאֲדָמָה:
יז וַיֹּאמֶר יְהֹוָה אֶל־מֹשֶׁה גַּם אֶת־הַדָּבָר הַזֶּה אֲשֶׁר דִּבַּרְתָּ אֶעֱשֶׂה

שלישי

רביעי

וַיָּשָׁב אֶל הַמַּחֲנֶה. תַּרְגּוּמוֹ: "וְתָאֵיב לְמַשְׁרִיתָא", לְפִי שֶׁהוּא לְשׁוֹן הֹוֶה, וְכֵן כָּל הָעִנְיָן: "וְרָחָה כָל הָעָם" (לעיל פסוק י), "וְנִצְּבוּ", (לעיל פסוק ח) "וְקָמִין", "וְהִבִּיטוּ" (שם), "וּמִסְתַּכְּלִין", "וְהִשְׁתַּחֲווּ" (לעיל פסוק י) – "וְסָגְדִין". וּמִדְרָשׁוֹ: "וְדִבֶּר ה' אֶל מֹשֶׁה" שֶׁיָּשׁוּב אֶל הַמַּחֲנֶה, אָמַר לוֹ: אֲנִי בְּכַעַס וְאַתָּה בְּכַעַס, אִם כֵּן מִי יְקָרְבֵם?

יב רְאֵה אַתָּה אֹמֵר אֵלַי. רְאֵה, תֵּן עֵינֶיךָ וְלִבְּךָ עַל דְּבָרֶיךָ: אַתָּה אֹמֵר אֵלַי וְגוֹ' וְאַתָּה לֹא הוֹדַעְתַּנִי וְגוֹ'. שֶׁאָמַרְתָּ לִי: "הִנֵּה אָנֹכִי שֹׁלֵחַ מַלְאָךְ" (לעיל כג, כ), אֵין זוֹ הוֹדָעָה, שֶׁאֵינִי חָפֵץ בּוֹ: וְאַתָּה אָמַרְתָּ. הַפְרִיתִיךָ מִשְּׁאָר בְּנֵי אָדָם בְּשֵׁם חֲשִׁיבוּת, שֶׁהֲרֵי אָמַרְתָּ לִי: "הִנֵּה אָנֹכִי בָּא אֵלֶיךָ בְּעַב הֶעָנָן וְגוֹ' וְגַם בְּךָ יַאֲמִינוּ לְעוֹלָם" (לעיל יט, ט):

יג וְעַתָּה. אִם אֱמֶת שֶׁמָּצָאתִי חֵן בְּעֵינֶיךָ: הוֹדִעֵנִי נָא אֶת דְּרָכֶךָ. מַה שָּׂכָר אַתָּה נוֹתֵן לְמוֹצְאֵי חֵן בְּעֵינֶיךָ: וְאֵדָעֲךָ לְמַעַן אֶמְצָא חֵן בְּעֵינֶיךָ. וְאֵדַע בְּזוֹ מִדַּת תַּגְמוּלֶךָ, מַה הִיא מְצִיאַת חֵן שֶׁמָּצָאתִי בְּעֵינֶיךָ. וּפִתְרוֹן "לְמַעַן אֶמְצָא חֵן" – לְמַעַן אַכִּיר כַּמָּה שְׂכַר מְצִיאַת הַחֵן: וּרְאֵה כִּי עַמְּךָ הַגּוֹי הַזֶּה. שֶׁלֹּא תֹּאמַר: "וְאֶעֱשֶׂה אוֹתְךָ לְגוֹי גָּדוֹל" (לעיל לב, י) וְאֵת חֶלָּה תַּעֲזֹב,

רְאֵה כִּי עַמְּךָ הֵם מִקֶּדֶם, וְאִם בָּהֶם תִּמְאַס, אֵינִי סוֹמֵךְ עַל הַיּוֹצְאִים מֵחֲלָצַי שֶׁיִּתְקַיְּמוּ, וְאֶת תַּשְׁלוּם הַשָּׂכָר שֶׁלִּי בָּעָם הַזֶּה תּוֹדִיעֵנִי. וְרַבּוֹתֵינוּ דְּרָשׁוּהוּ בְּמַסֶּכֶת בְּרָכוֹת (דף ז ע"א), וַאֲנִי לְיַשֵּׁב הַמִּקְרָאוֹת עַל אָפְנֵיהֶם וְעַל סִדְרָם בָּאתִי:

יד וַיֹּאמַר פָּנַי יֵלֵכוּ. כְּתַרְגּוּמוֹ: לֹא אֶשְׁלַח עוֹד מַלְאָךְ, אֲנִי בְּעַצְמִי אֵלֵךְ, כְּמוֹ: "וּפָנֶיךָ הֹלְכִים בַּקְּרָב" (שמואל ב' יז, יא):

טו וַיֹּאמֶר אֵלָיו. בְּזוֹ אֲנִי חָפֵץ, כִּי עַל יְדֵי מַלְאָךְ "אַל תַּעֲלֵנוּ מִזֶּה":

טז וּבַמֶּה יִוָּדַע אֵפוֹא. יִוָּדַע מְצִיאַת הַחֵן, "הֲלוֹא בְּלֶכְתְּךָ עִמָּנוּ". וְעוֹד דָּבָר אַחֵר אֲנִי שׁוֹאֵל מִמְּךָ, שֶׁלֹּא תַּשְׁרֶה שְׁכִינָתְךָ עוֹד עַל אֻמּוֹת הָעוֹלָם: וְנִפְלֵינוּ אֲנִי וְעַמְּךָ. וְנִהְיֶה מֻבְדָּלִים בַּדָּבָר הַזֶּה "מִכָּל הָעָם", כְּמוֹ: "וְהִפְלָה ה' בֵּין מִקְנֵה יִשְׂרָאֵל וְגוֹ'" (לעיל ט, ד):

יז גַּם אֶת הַדָּבָר הַזֶּה. שֶׁלֹּא תִּשְׁרֶה שְׁכִינָתִי עוֹד עַל אֻמּוֹת הָעוֹלָם, "אֶעֱשֶׂה". וְאֵין דְּבָרָיו שֶׁל בִּלְעָם עַל יְדֵי שְׁרִיַּת שְׁכִינָה, אֶלָּא "נֹפֵל וּגְלוּי עֵינָיִם" (במדבר כד, ד), כְּגוֹן: "וְאֵלַי דָּבָר יְגֻנָּב" (איוב ד, יב), שׁוֹמְעִין עַל יְדֵי שָׁלִיחַ:

כי תשא

יח כִּֽי־מָצָ֤אתָ חֵן֙ בְּעֵינַ֔י וָאֵדָעֲךָ֖ בְּשֵׁ֑ם: וַיֹּאמַ֑ר הַרְאֵ֥נִי נָ֖א אֶת־כְּבֹדֶֽךָ:
יט וַיֹּ֗אמֶר אֲנִ֨י אַעֲבִ֤יר כׇּל־טוּבִי֙ עַל־פָּנֶ֔יךָ וְקָרָ֧אתִֽי בְשֵׁ֛ם יְהֹוָ֖ה לְפָנֶ֑יךָ
וְחַנֹּתִי֙ אֶת־אֲשֶׁ֣ר אָחֹ֔ן וְרִחַמְתִּ֖י אֶת־אֲשֶׁ֥ר אֲרַחֵֽם: וַיֹּ֕אמֶר לֹ֥א
כ תוּכַ֖ל לִרְאֹ֣ת אֶת־פָּנָ֑י כִּ֛י לֹֽא־יִרְאַ֥נִי הָאָדָ֖ם וָחָֽי: וַיֹּ֣אמֶר יְהֹוָ֔ה
כא הִנֵּ֥ה מָק֖וֹם אִתִּ֑י וְנִצַּבְתָּ֖ עַל־הַצּֽוּר: וְהָיָה֙ בַּעֲבֹ֣ר כְּבֹדִ֔י וְשַׂמְתִּ֖יךָ
כב בְּנִקְרַ֣ת הַצּ֑וּר וְשַׂכֹּתִ֥י כַפִּ֛י עָלֶ֖יךָ עַד־עׇבְרִֽי: וַהֲסִרֹתִי֙ אֶת־כַּפִּ֔י
כג וְרָאִ֖יתָ אֶת־אֲחֹרָ֑י וּפָנַ֖י לֹ֥א יֵרָאֽוּ:

חמישי לד א וַיֹּ֤אמֶר יְהֹוָה֙ אֶל־מֹשֶׁ֔ה פְּסׇל־לְךָ֛ שְׁנֵֽי־לֻחֹ֥ת אֲבָנִ֖ים כָּרִאשֹׁנִ֑ים

יח וַיֹּאמֶר הַרְאֵנִי נָא אֶת כְּבֹדֶךָ. רָאָה מֹשֶׁה שֶׁהָיָה עֵת רָצוֹן וּדְבָרָיו מְקֻבָּלִים, וְהוֹסִיף לִשְׁאֹל לְהַרְאוֹתוֹ מַרְאִית כְּבוֹדוֹ:

יט וַיֹּאמֶר אֲנִי אַעֲבִיר וְגוֹ׳. הִגִּיעָה שָׁעָה שֶׁתִּרְאֶה בִּכְבוֹדִי מַה שֶּׁאַרְשֶׁה אוֹתְךָ לִרְאוֹת, לְפִי שֶׁאֲנִי רוֹצֶה וְצָרִיךְ לְלַמֶּדְךָ סֵדֶר תְּפִלָּה, שֶׁכְּשֶׁנִּצְרַכְתָּ לְבַקֵּשׁ רַחֲמִים עַל יִשְׂרָאֵל הִזְכַּרְתָּ לִי זְכוּת אָבוֹת, כִּסְבוּר אַתָּה שֶׁאִם תַּמָּה זְכוּת אָבוֹת אֵין עוֹד תִּקְוָה, אֲנִי אַעֲבִיר כׇּל מִדַּת טוּבִי לְפָנֶיךָ עַל הַצּוּר וְאַתָּה נָתוּן בַּמְּעָרָה: וְקָרָאתִי בְשֵׁם ה׳ לְפָנֶיךָ. לְלַמֶּדְךָ סֵדֶר בַּקָּשַׁת רַחֲמִים אַף אִם תִּכְלֶה זְכוּת אָבוֹת, וּכַסֵּדֶר שֶׁאַתָּה רוֹאֶה אוֹתִי מְעֻטָּף וּקְרָא שְׁלשׁ עֶשְׂרֵה מִדּוֹת הֱוֵי מְלַמֵּד אֶת יִשְׂרָאֵל לַעֲשׂוֹת כֵּן, וְעַל יְדֵי שֶׁיַּזְכִּירוּ לְפָנַי "רַחוּם וְחַנּוּן", כִּי רַחֲמַי לֹא כָלִים: וְחַנֹּתִי אֶת אֲשֶׁר אָחֹן. וְרִחַמְתִּי לָחֹן. עֵת שֶׁאֶחְפֹּץ לָחֹן. עַד כָּאן לֹא הִבְטִיחוֹ אֶלָּא עִתִּים אֶעֱנֶה וְעִתִּים לֹא אֶעֱנֶה, אֲבָל בִּשְׁעַת מַעֲשֶׂה אָמַר לוֹ: "הִנֵּה אָנֹכִי כֹּרֵת בְּרִית" (להלן לד, י), הִבְטִיחוֹ שֶׁאֵינָן חוֹזְרוֹת רֵיקָם:

כ וַיֹּאמֶר לֹא תוּכַל וְגוֹ׳. אַף כְּשֶׁאַעֲבִיר כׇּל טוּבִי עַל פָּנֶיךָ, אֵינִי נוֹתֵן לְךָ רְשׁוּת לִרְאוֹת אֶת פָּנָי:

כא הִנֵּה מָקוֹם אִתִּי. בָּהָר אֲשֶׁר אֲנִי מְדַבֵּר עִמְּךָ תָּמִיד, יֵשׁ מָקוֹם מוּכָן לִי לְצָרְכְּךָ שֶׁאַטְמִינְךָ שָׁם שֶׁלֹּא תִזֹּק, וּמִשָּׁם תִּרְאֶה מַה שֶּׁתִּרְאֶה, זֶהוּ פְּשׁוּטוֹ. וּמִדְרָשׁוֹ, עַל מָקוֹם שֶׁהַשְּׁכִינָה שָׁם מְדַבֵּר, וְאוֹמֵר "הַמָּקוֹם אִתִּי" וְאֵינוֹ אוֹמֵר 'אֲנִי בַּמָּקוֹם', שֶׁהַקָּדוֹשׁ בָּרוּךְ הוּא מְקוֹמוֹ שֶׁל עוֹלָם וְאֵין עוֹלָמוֹ מְקוֹמוֹ:

כב בַּעֲבֹר כְּבֹדִי. כְּשֶׁאֶעֱבֹר לְפָנֶיךָ: בְּנִקְרַת הַצּוּר. כְּמוֹ: "הַעֵינֵי הָאֲנָשִׁים הָהֵם תְּנַקֵּר" (במדבר טז, יד), "יִקְּרוּהָ עֹרְבֵי נַחַל" (משלי ל, יז), "אֲנִי קַרְתִּי וְשָׁתִיתִי מָיִם" (ישעיה לז, כה), גִּזְרָה אַחַת לָהֶם: נִקְרַת הַצּוּר. כְּרִית הַצּוּר: וְשַׂכֹּתִי כַפִּי. מִכָּאן שֶׁנִּתְּנָה רְשׁוּת לַמְחַבְּלִים לְחַבֵּל, וְתַרְגּוּמוֹ: "וְאַגֵּין בְּמֵימְרִי", כִּנּוּי הוּא לְדֶרֶךְ כָּבוֹד שֶׁל מַעְלָה, שֶׁאֵינוֹ צָרִיךְ לְסוֹכֵךְ עָלָיו בְּכַף מַמָּשׁ:

כג וַהֲסִרֹתִי אֶת כַּפִּי. "וְאַעֲדֵי יָת דִּבְרַת יְקָרִי", כְּשֶׁאֲסַלֵּק הַנְהָגַת כְּבוֹדִי מִכְּנֶגֶד פָּנֶיךָ לָלֶכֶת מִשָּׁם וּלְהַלָּן: וְרָאִיתָ אֶת אֲחֹרָי. הֶרְאָהוּ קֶשֶׁר שֶׁל תְּפִלִּין:

פרק לד

א פְּסָל לְךָ. הֶרְאָהוּ מַחְצָב סַנְפִּירִינוֹן מִתּוֹךְ אָהֳלוֹ, וְאָמַר לוֹ: הַפְּסֹלֶת יִהְיֶה שֶׁלָּךְ, וּמִשָּׁם נִתְעַשֵּׁר מֹשֶׁה הַרְבֵּה: פְּסָל לְךָ. אַתָּה שִׁבַּרְתָּ הָרִאשׁוֹנוֹת, אַתָּה פְּסָל לְךָ אֲחֵרוֹת. מָשָׁל לְמֶלֶךְ שֶׁהָלַךְ לִמְדִינַת הַיָּם וְהִנִּיחַ אֲרוּסָתוֹ עִם הַשְּׁפָחוֹת. מִתּוֹךְ קִלְקוּל הַשְּׁפָחוֹת יָצָא עָלֶיהָ שֵׁם רָע. עָמַד שׁוֹשְׁבִינָהּ וְקָרַע כְּתֻבָּתָהּ, אָמַר: אִם יֹאמַר הַמֶּלֶךְ לְהׇרְגָהּ, אֹמַר לוֹ: עֲדַיִן אֵינָהּ אִשְׁתְּךָ. בָּדַק הַמֶּלֶךְ וּמָצָא שֶׁלֹּא הָיָה

שמות | פרק לד | כי תשא

וְכָתַבְתִּי עַל־הַלֻּחֹת אֶת־הַדְּבָרִים אֲשֶׁר הָיוּ עַל־הַלֻּחֹת
ב הָרִאשֹׁנִים אֲשֶׁר שִׁבַּרְתָּ: וֶהְיֵה נָכוֹן לַבֹּקֶר וְעָלִיתָ בַבֹּקֶר אֶל־
הַר סִינַי וְנִצַּבְתָּ לִי שָׁם עַל־רֹאשׁ הָהָר: וְאִישׁ לֹא־יַעֲלֶה עִמָּךְ
ג וְגַם־אִישׁ אַל־יֵרָא בְּכָל־הָהָר גַּם־הַצֹּאן וְהַבָּקָר אַל־יִרְעוּ אֶל־
מוּל הָהָר הַהוּא: וַיִּפְסֹל שְׁנֵי־לֻחֹת אֲבָנִים כָּרִאשֹׁנִים וַיַּשְׁכֵּם
ד מֹשֶׁה בַבֹּקֶר וַיַּעַל אֶל־הַר סִינַי כַּאֲשֶׁר צִוָּה יהוה אֹתוֹ וַיִּקַּח
בְּיָדוֹ שְׁנֵי לֻחֹת אֲבָנִים: וַיֵּרֶד יהוה בֶּעָנָן וַיִּתְיַצֵּב עִמּוֹ שָׁם וַיִּקְרָא
ה בְשֵׁם יהוה: וַיַּעֲבֹר יהוה ׀ עַל־פָּנָיו וַיִּקְרָא יהוה ׀ יהוה אֵל
ו רַחוּם וְחַנּוּן אֶרֶךְ אַפַּיִם וְרַב־חֶסֶד וֶאֱמֶת: נֹצֵר חֶסֶד לָאֲלָפִים
ז נֹשֵׂא עָוֹן וָפֶשַׁע וְחַטָּאָה וְנַקֵּה לֹא יְנַקֶּה פֹּקֵד ׀ עֲוֹן אָבוֹת עַל־
בָּנִים וְעַל־בְּנֵי בָנִים עַל־שִׁלֵּשִׁים וְעַל־רִבֵּעִים: וַיְמַהֵר מֹשֶׁה
ח

הַקִּלְקוּל אֶלָּא מִן הַשְּׁפָתַיִם, נִתְרַצָּה לָהּ. אָמַר
לוֹ שׁוֹשְׁבִינָהּ: כְּתֹב לָהּ כְּתֻבָּה אַחֶרֶת, שֶׁנִּקְרְעָה
הָרִאשׁוֹנָה. אָמַר לוֹ הַמֶּלֶךְ: אַתָּה קְרַעְתָּהּ אוֹתָהּ,
אַתָּה קְנֵה לָךְ נְיָר אַחֵר וַאֲנִי אֶכְתֹּב לָךְ בִּכְתָב יָדִי.
כָּךְ הַמֶּלֶךְ זֶה הַקָּדוֹשׁ בָּרוּךְ הוּא, הַשְּׁפָתַיִם אֵלּוּ
עֶרֶב רַב, וְהַשּׁוֹשְׁבִין זֶה מֹשֶׁה. לְכָךְ נֶאֱמַר: "פְּסָל לָךְ":

ב) **נָכוֹן.** מְזֻמָּן:

ג) **וְאִישׁ לֹא יַעֲלֶה עִמָּךְ.** הָרִאשׁוֹנוֹת עַל יְדֵי שֶׁהָיוּ
בִּתְשׁוּאוֹת וְקוֹלוֹת וּקְהִלָּה, שָׁלְטָה בָּהֶן עַיִן רָעָה, אֵין
לְךָ יָפֶה מִן הַצְּנִיעוּת:

ה) **וַיִּקְרָא בְשֵׁם ה'.** מְתַרְגְּמִינָן: "וּקְרָא בִשְׁמָא דַה'":

ו) **ה' ה'.** הוּא מִדַּת רַחֲמִים, אַחַת קֹדֶם שֶׁיֶּחֱטָא
וְאַחַת לְאַחַר שֶׁיֶּחֱטָא וְיָשׁוּב. **אֵל.** אַף זוֹ מִדַּת רַחֲמִים,
וְכֵן הוּא אוֹמֵר: "אֵלִי אֵלִי לָמָה עֲזַבְתָּנִי" (תהלים כב,
ב), וְאֵין לוֹמַר לְמִדַּת הַדִּין: "לָמָה עֲזַבְתָּנִי". כָּךְ
מְצָאתִי בַּמְּכִילְתָּא (שירה ג, טו, כ): **אֶרֶךְ אַפַּיִם.** מַאֲרִיךְ

אַפּוֹ וְאֵינוֹ מְמַהֵר לִפְרֹעַ, שֶׁמָּא יַעֲשֶׂה תְשׁוּבָה: **וְרַב
חֶסֶד.** לִצְרִיכֵי חֶסֶד, שֶׁאֵין לָהֶם זְכֻיּוֹת כָּל כָּךְ: **וֶאֱמֶת.**
לְשַׁלֵּם שָׂכָר טוֹב לְעוֹשֵׂי רְצוֹנוֹ:

ז) **נֹצֵר חֶסֶד.** שֶׁהָאָדָם עוֹשֶׂה לְפָנָיו: **לָאֲלָפִים.** לִשְׁנֵי
אֲלָפִים דּוֹרוֹת. **עֲוֹנוֹת** אֵלּוּ הַזְּדוֹנוֹת, **פְּשָׁעִים** אֵלּוּ
הַמְּרָדִים שֶׁאָדָם עוֹשֶׂה לְהַכְעִיס: **וְנַקֵּה לֹא יְנַקֶּה.** לְפִי
פְשׁוּטוֹ מַשְׁמַע שֶׁאֵינוֹ מְוַתֵּר עַל הֶעָוֹן לְגַמְרֵי, אֶלָּא
נִפְרָע מִמֶּנּוּ מְעַט מְעַט. וְרַבּוֹתֵינוּ דָּרְשׁוּ: "מְנַקֶּה"
הוּא לַשָּׁבִים "וְלֹא יְנַקֶּה" לְשֶׁאֵינָן שָׁבִים: **פֹּקֵד
עֲוֹן אָבוֹת עַל בָּנִים.** כְּשֶׁאוֹחֲזִים מַעֲשֵׂה אֲבוֹתֵיהֶם
בִּידֵיהֶם, שֶׁכְּבָר פֵּרַשׁ בְּמִקְרָא אַחֵר "לְשֹׂנְאָי" (לעיל
כ, ה): **וְעַל רִבֵּעִים.** דּוֹר רְבִיעִי. נִמְצֵאת מִדָּה טוֹבָה
מְרֻבָּה עַל מִדַּת פֻּרְעָנוּת אַחַת לַחֲמֵשׁ מֵאוֹת,
שֶׁבְּמִדָּה טוֹבָה הוּא אוֹמֵר: "נֹצֵר חֶסֶד לָאֲלָפִים":

ח) **וַיְמַהֵר מֹשֶׁה.** כְּשֶׁרָאָה מֹשֶׁה שְׁכִינָה עוֹבֶרֶת וְשָׁמַע
קוֹל הַקְּרִיאָה, מִיָּד "וַיִּשְׁתָּחוּ":

ט וַיִּקֹּ֥ד אַ֖רְצָה וַיִּשְׁתָּֽחוּ: וַיֹּ֡אמֶר אִם־נָא֩ מָצָ֨אתִי חֵ֤ן בְּעֵינֶ֙יךָ֙ אֲדֹנָ֔י יֵֽלֶךְ־נָ֥א אֲדֹנָ֖י בְּקִרְבֵּ֑נוּ כִּ֤י עַם־קְשֵׁה־עֹ֙רֶף֙ ה֔וּא וְסָלַחְתָּ֛ לַעֲוֺנֵ֥נוּ וּלְחַטָּאתֵ֖נוּ וּנְחַלְתָּֽנוּ:

ששי י וַיֹּ֗אמֶר הִנֵּ֣ה אָנֹכִי֮ כֹּרֵ֣ת בְּרִית֒ נֶ֤גֶד כׇּל־עַמְּךָ֙ אֶעֱשֶׂ֣ה נִפְלָאֹ֔ת אֲשֶׁ֛ר לֹֽא־נִבְרְא֥וּ בְכׇל־הָאָ֖רֶץ וּבְכׇל־הַגּוֹיִ֑ם וְרָאָ֣ה כׇל־הָ֠עָ֠ם אֲשֶׁר־אַתָּ֨ה בְקִרְבּ֜וֹ אֶת־מַעֲשֵׂ֤ה יְהֹוָה֙ כִּֽי־נוֹרָ֣א ה֔וּא אֲשֶׁ֥ר אֲנִ֖י עֹשֶׂ֥ה עִמָּֽךְ: יא שְׁמׇ֨ר־לְךָ֔ אֵ֛ת אֲשֶׁ֥ר אָנֹכִ֖י מְצַוְּךָ֣ הַיּ֑וֹם הִנְנִ֧י גֹרֵ֣שׁ מִפָּנֶ֗יךָ אֶת־הָאֱמֹרִי֙ וְהַֽכְּנַעֲנִ֔י וְהַֽחִתִּי֙ וְהַפְּרִזִּ֔י וְהַחִוִּ֖י וְהַיְבוּסִֽי: יב הִשָּׁ֣מֶר לְךָ֗ פֶּן־תִּכְרֹ֤ת בְּרִית֙ לְיוֹשֵׁ֣ב הָאָ֔רֶץ אֲשֶׁ֥ר אַתָּ֖ה בָּ֣א עָלֶ֑יהָ פֶּן־יִהְיֶ֥ה לְמוֹקֵ֖שׁ בְּקִרְבֶּֽךָ: יג כִּ֤י אֶת־מִזְבְּחֹתָם֙ תִּתֹּצ֔וּן וְאֶת־מַצֵּבֹתָ֖ם תְּשַׁבֵּר֑וּן וְאֶת־אֲשֵׁרָ֖יו תִּכְרֹתֽוּן: יד כִּ֛י לֹ֥א תִֽשְׁתַּחֲוֶ֖ה לְאֵ֣ל אַחֵ֑ר כִּ֤י יְהֹוָה֙ קַנָּ֣א שְׁמ֔וֹ אֵ֥ל קַנָּ֖א הֽוּא: טו פֶּן־תִּכְרֹ֥ת בְּרִ֖ית לְיוֹשֵׁ֣ב הָאָ֑רֶץ וְזָנ֣וּ ׀ אַחֲרֵ֣י אֱלֹֽהֵיהֶ֗ם וְזָבְחוּ֙ לֵאלֹ֣הֵיהֶ֔ם וְקָרָ֣א לְךָ֔ וְאָכַלְתָּ֖ מִזִּבְחֽוֹ: טז וְלָקַחְתָּ֥ מִבְּנֹתָ֖יו לְבָנֶ֑יךָ וְזָנ֣וּ בְנֹתָ֗יו אַחֲרֵי֙ אֱלֹ֣הֵיהֶ֔ן וְהִזְנוּ֙ אֶת־בָּנֶ֔יךָ אַחֲרֵ֖י אֱלֹהֵיהֶֽן: יז אֱלֹהֵ֥י מַסֵּכָ֖ה לֹ֣א תַעֲשֶׂה־לָּֽךְ: יח אֶת־חַ֣ג הַמַּצּוֹת֮

ט] יֵלֶךְ נָא ה' בְּקִרְבֵּנוּ. כְּמוֹ שֶׁהִבְטַחְתָּ, מֵאַחַר שֶׁאַתָּה נוֹשֵׂא עָוֺן, וְאִם "עַם קְשֵׁה עֹרֶף הוּא" וְיַמְרוּ בְךָ וְאָמַרְתָּ עַל זֹאת: "פֶּן אֲכֶלְךָ בַּדָּרֶךְ" (לעיל לג):

י] — אַתָּה תִּסְלַח "לַעֲוֺנֵנוּ" וְגוֹ'. יֵשׁ "כִּי" בִּמְקוֹם "אִם": וּנְחַלְתָּנוּ. וּתְנֵנוּ לְךָ לְנַחֲלָה מְיֻחֶדֶת, זוֹ הִיא בַּקָּשַׁת "וְנִפְלִינוּ אֲנִי וְעַמְּךָ" (עם פסוק טז), שֶׁלֹּא תִשְׁרֶה שְׁכִינָתְךָ עַל הָאֻמּוֹת:

י] כֹּרֵת בְּרִית. עַל זֹאת: אֶעֱשֶׂה נִפְלָאֹת. לְשׁוֹן "וְנִפְלִינוּ", שֶׁתִּהְיוּ מֻבְדָּלִים בָּזוֹ מִכָּל הָאֻמּוֹת, שֶׁלֹּא תִשְׁרֶה שְׁכִינָתִי עֲלֵיהֶם:

יא] אֶת הָאֱמֹרִי וְגוֹ'. שֵׁשׁ אֻמּוֹת יֵשׁ כָּאן, כִּי הַגִּרְגָּשִׁי עָמַד וּפִנָּה מִפְּנֵיהֶם:

יג] אֲשֵׁרָיו. הוּא אִילָן שֶׁעוֹבְדִים אוֹתוֹ:

יד] קַנָּא שְׁמוֹ. מְקַנֵּא לִפָּרַע וְאֵינוֹ מְוַתֵּר, וְזֶהוּ כָּל לְשׁוֹן קִנְאָה, אוֹחֵז בְּנִצְחוֹנוֹ וּפוֹרֵעַ מֵעוֹזְבָיו:

טו-טז] וְאָכַלְתָּ מִזִּבְחוֹ. כִּסְבוּר אַתָּה שֶׁאֵין עֹנֶשׁ בַּאֲכִילָתוֹ, וַאֲנִי מַעֲלֶה עָלֶיךָ כְּמוֹדֶה בַּעֲבוֹדָתָם, שֶׁמִּתּוֹךְ כָּךְ אַתָּה בָּא וְלוֹקֵחַ "מִבְּנֹתָיו לְבָנֶיךָ":

שמות | פרק לד | כי תשא

תִּשְׁמֹר שִׁבְעַת יָמִים תֹּאכַל מַצּוֹת אֲשֶׁר צִוִּיתִךָ לְמוֹעֵד חֹדֶשׁ הָאָבִיב כִּי בְּחֹדֶשׁ הָאָבִיב יָצָאתָ מִמִּצְרָיִם: כָּל־פֶּטֶר רֶחֶם לִי וְכָל־מִקְנְךָ תִּזָּכָר פֶּטֶר שׁוֹר וָשֶׂה: וּפֶטֶר חֲמוֹר תִּפְדֶּה בְשֶׂה וְאִם־לֹא תִפְדֶּה וַעֲרַפְתּוֹ כֹּל בְּכוֹר בָּנֶיךָ תִּפְדֶּה וְלֹא־יֵרָאוּ פָנַי רֵיקָם: שֵׁשֶׁת יָמִים תַּעֲבֹד וּבַיּוֹם הַשְּׁבִיעִי תִּשְׁבֹּת בֶּחָרִישׁ וּבַקָּצִיר תִּשְׁבֹּת: וְחַג שָׁבֻעֹת תַּעֲשֶׂה לְךָ בִּכּוּרֵי קְצִיר חִטִּים וְחַג הָאָסִיף תְּקוּפַת הַשָּׁנָה: שָׁלֹשׁ פְּעָמִים בַּשָּׁנָה יֵרָאֶה כָּל־זְכוּרְךָ

יט | **כֹּל פֶּטֶר רֶחֶם לִי**. בָּאָדָם. **וְכָל מִקְנְךָ תִּזָּכָר וְגוֹ׳**. וְכָל מִקְנְךָ אֲשֶׁר תִּזָּכָר בְּפֶטֶר שׁוֹר וָשֶׂה, אֲשֶׁר יִפְטֹר זָכָר אֶת רַחְמָהּ. ״פֶּטֶר״ לְשׁוֹן פְּתִיחָה, וְכֵן: ״פּוֹטֵר מַיִם רֵאשִׁית מָדוֹן״ (משלי יז, יד). תַּ״י שֶׁל ״תִּזָּכָר״ לְשׁוֹן נְקֵבָה הִיא, מוּסָב עַל הַיּוֹלֶדֶת:

יח | **חֹדֶשׁ הָאָבִיב**. חֹדֶשׁ הַבִּכּוּר, שֶׁהַתְּבוּאָה מְבֻכֶּרֶת בְּבִשּׁוּלָהּ:

כ | **וּפֶטֶר חֲמוֹר**. וְלֹא שְׁאָר בְּהֵמָה טְמֵאָה. **תִּפְדֶּה בְשֶׂה**. נוֹתֵן שֶׂה לַכֹּהֵן וְהוּא חֻלִּין בְּיַד כֹּהֵן, וּפֶטֶר חֲמוֹר מֻתָּר בַּעֲבוֹדָה לַבְּעָלִים. **וַעֲרַפְתּוֹ**. עוֹרְפוֹ בְּקוֹפִיץ. הוּא הִפְסִיד מָמוֹן כֹּהֵן, לְפִיכָךְ יִפָּסֵד מָמוֹנוֹ. **כֹּל בְּכוֹר בָּנֶיךָ תִּפְדֶּה**. חֲמִשָּׁה סְלָעִים פִּדְיוֹנוֹ קָצוּב, שֶׁנֶּאֱמַר: ״וּפְדוּיָו מִבֶּן חֹדֶשׁ תִּפְדֶּה וְגוֹ׳״ (במדבר יח, טז). **וְלֹא יֵרָאוּ פָנַי רֵיקָם**. לְפִי פְּשׁוּטוֹ שֶׁל מִקְרָא דָּבָר בִּפְנֵי עַצְמוֹ הוּא וְאֵינוֹ מוּסָב עַל הַבְּכוֹר, שֶׁאֵין בְּמִצְוַת בְּכוֹר רְאִיַּת פָּנִים, אֶלָּא אַזְהָרָה אַחֶרֶת הִיא. וּכְשֶׁתַּעֲלוּ לָרֶגֶל לֵרָאוֹת ״לֹא יֵרָאוּ פָנַי רֵיקָם״, מִצְוָה עֲלֵיכֶם לְהָבִיא עוֹלַת רְאִיַּת פָּנִים. וּלְפִי מִדְרַשׁ בָּרַיְתָא, מִקְרָא יָתֵר הוּא וּמֻפְנֶה לִגְזֵרָה שָׁוָה, לְלַמֵּד עַל הָעֲנָקָתוֹ שֶׁל עֶבֶד עִבְרִי שֶׁהוּא חֲמִשָּׁה סְלָעִים מִכָּל מִין וָמִין כְּפִדְיוֹן בְּכוֹר. בְּמַסֶּכֶת קִדּוּשִׁין (דף יז ע״א):

כא | **בֶּחָרִישׁ וּבַקָּצִיר תִּשְׁבֹּת**. לָמָּה נִזְכַּר חָרִישׁ

וְקָצִיר? יֵשׁ מֵרַבּוֹתֵינוּ אוֹמְרִים: עַל חָרִישׁ שֶׁל עֶרֶב שְׁבִיעִית הַנִּכְנָס לַשְּׁבִיעִית וְקָצִיר שֶׁל שְׁבִיעִית הַיּוֹצֵא לְמוֹצָאֵי שְׁבִיעִית, לְלַמֶּדְךָ שֶׁמּוֹסִיפִין מֵחֹל עַל הַקֹּדֶשׁ. וְכָךְ מַשְׁמָעוֹ: ״שֵׁשֶׁת יָמִים תַּעֲבֹד וּבַיּוֹם הַשְּׁבִיעִי תִּשְׁבֹּת״, וַעֲבוֹדַת שֵׁשֶׁת הַיָּמִים שֶׁהִתַּרְתִּי לְךָ, יֵשׁ שָׁנָה שֶׁהֶחָרִישׁ וְהַקָּצִיר אָסוּר. וְאֵין צָרִיךְ לוֹמַר חָרִישׁ וְקָצִיר שֶׁל שְׁבִיעִית, שֶׁהֲרֵי כְּבָר נֶאֱמַר: ״שָׂדְךָ לֹא תִזְרָע וְגוֹ׳״ (ויקרא כה, ד). וְיֵשׁ מֵהֶם אוֹמְרִים: אֵינוֹ מְדַבֵּר אֶלָּא בְּשַׁבָּת, וְחָרִישׁ וְקָצִיר שֶׁנִּזְכַּר בּוֹ לוֹמַר לְךָ, מַה חָרִישׁ רְשׁוּת אַף קָצִיר רְשׁוּת, יָצָא קְצִיר הָעֹמֶר שֶׁהוּא מִצְוָה וְדוֹחֶה אֶת הַשַּׁבָּת:

כב | **בִּכּוּרֵי קְצִיר חִטִּים**. שֶׁאַתָּה מֵבִיא בּוֹ שְׁתֵּי הַלֶּחֶם מִן הַחִטִּים בִּכּוּרִים, שֶׁהִיא מִנְחָה רִאשׁוֹנָה הַבָּאָה מִן הֶחָדָשׁ חִטִּים לַמִּקְדָּשׁ, כִּי מִנְחַת הָעֹמֶר הַבָּאָה בַּפֶּסַח, מִן הַשְּׂעוֹרִים הִיא. **וְחַג הָאָסִיף**. בִּזְמַן שֶׁאַתָּה אוֹסֵף תְּבוּאָתְךָ מִן הַשָּׂדֶה לַבַּיִת. אֲסִיפָה זוֹ לְשׁוֹן הַכְנָסָה לַבַּיִת, כְּמוֹ: ״וַאֲסַפְתּוֹ אֶל תּוֹךְ בֵּיתֶךָ״ (דברים כב, ב). **תְּקוּפַת הַשָּׁנָה**. שֶׁהִיא בַּחֲזָרַת הַשָּׁנָה, בִּתְחִלַּת הַשָּׁנָה הַבָּאָה. **תְּקוּפַת**. לְשׁוֹן מְסִבָּה וְהַקָּפָה:

כג | **כָּל זְכוּרְךָ**. כָּל הַזְּכָרִים שֶׁבָּךְ. הַרְבֵּה מִצְווֹת בַּתּוֹרָה נֶאֶמְרוּ וְנִכְפְּלוּ, וְיֵשׁ מֵהֶם שָׁלֹשׁ פְּעָמִים וְאַרְבַּע, לְחַיֵּב וְלַעֲנֹשׁ עַל מִנְיַן לָאוִין שֶׁבָּהֶם וְעַל מִנְיַן עֲשֵׂה שֶׁבָּהֶם:

אֶת־פְּנֵי הָאָדֹן ׀ יְהֹוָה אֱלֹהֵי יִשְׂרָאֵל: כִּי־אוֹרִישׁ גּוֹיִם מִפָּנֶיךָ כד
וְהִרְחַבְתִּי אֶת־גְּבֻלֶךָ וְלֹא־יַחְמֹד אִישׁ אֶת־אַרְצְךָ בַּעֲלֹתְךָ
לֵרָאוֹת אֶת־פְּנֵי יְהֹוָה אֱלֹהֶיךָ שָׁלֹשׁ פְּעָמִים בַּשָּׁנָה: לֹא־תִשְׁחַט כה
עַל־חָמֵץ דַּם־זִבְחִי וְלֹא־יָלִין לַבֹּקֶר זֶבַח חַג הַפָּסַח: רֵאשִׁית כו
בִּכּוּרֵי אַדְמָתְךָ תָּבִיא בֵּית יְהֹוָה אֱלֹהֶיךָ לֹא־תְבַשֵּׁל גְּדִי בַּחֲלֵב
אִמּוֹ:

שביעי כז וַיֹּאמֶר יְהֹוָה אֶל־מֹשֶׁה כְּתָב־לְךָ אֶת־הַדְּבָרִים הָאֵלֶּה כִּי עַל־
פִּי ׀ הַדְּבָרִים הָאֵלֶּה כָּרַתִּי אִתְּךָ בְּרִית וְאֶת־יִשְׂרָאֵל: וַיְהִי־שָׁם כח
עִם־יְהֹוָה אַרְבָּעִים יוֹם וְאַרְבָּעִים לַיְלָה לֶחֶם לֹא אָכַל וּמַיִם לֹא
שָׁתָה וַיִּכְתֹּב עַל־הַלֻּחֹת אֵת דִּבְרֵי הַבְּרִית עֲשֶׂרֶת הַדְּבָרִים:
וַיְהִי בְּרֶדֶת מֹשֶׁה מֵהַר סִינַי וּשְׁנֵי לֻחֹת הָעֵדֻת בְּיַד־מֹשֶׁה כט
בְּרִדְתּוֹ מִן־הָהָר וּמֹשֶׁה לֹא־יָדַע כִּי קָרַן עוֹר פָּנָיו בְּדַבְּרוֹ אִתּוֹ:
וַיַּרְא אַהֲרֹן וְכָל־בְּנֵי יִשְׂרָאֵל אֶת־מֹשֶׁה וְהִנֵּה קָרַן עוֹר פָּנָיו ל

כד אוֹרִישׁ. כְּתַרְגּוּמוֹ: "אֲתָרֵךְ", וְכֵן: "הָחֵל רָשׁ" (דברים ב, לא), וְכֵן: "וַיּוֹרֶשׁ אֶת הָאֱמֹרִי" (במדבר כא, לב), לְשׁוֹן גֵּרוּשִׁין: וְהִרְחַבְתִּי אֶת גְּבֻלְךָ. וְאַתָּה רָחוֹק מִבֵּית הַבְּחִירָה וְאֵינְךָ יָכוֹל לֵרָאוֹת לְפָנַי תָּמִיד, לְכָךְ אֲנִי קוֹבֵעַ לְךָ שָׁלֹשׁ רְגָלִים הַלָּלוּ:

כה לֹא תִשְׁחַט וְגוֹ'. לֹא תִשְׁחַט אֶת הַפֶּסַח וַעֲדַיִן חָמֵץ קַיָּם, אַזְהָרָה לַשּׁוֹחֵט אוֹ לַזּוֹרֵק אוֹ לְאֶחָד מִבְּנֵי חֲבוּרָה: וְלֹא יָלִין. כְּתַרְגּוּמוֹ. אֵין לִינָה מוֹעֶלֶת בְּרֹאשׁ הַמִּזְבֵּחַ, וְאֵין לִינָה אֶלָּא בְּעַמּוּד הַשָּׁחַר: זֶבַח חַג הַפָּסַח. אֵמוּרָיו, וּמִכָּאן אַתָּה לָמֵד לְכָל הֶקְטֵר חֲלָבִים וְאֵבָרִים:

כו רֵאשִׁית בִּכּוּרֵי אַדְמָתְךָ. מִשִּׁבְעַת הַמִּינִין הָאֲמוּרִים בְּשֶׁבַח אַרְצְךָ: "אֶרֶץ חִטָּה וּשְׂעֹרָה וְגֶפֶן וְגוֹ'" (דברים ח, ח) "וּדְבַשׁ" - הֵן תְּמָרִים: לֹא תְבַשֵּׁל גְּדִי. אַזְהָרָה לְבָשָׂר בְּחָלָב. וּשְׁלֹשָׁה פְּעָמִים כָּתוּב בַּתּוֹרָה: אֶחָד לַאֲכִילָה, וְאֶחָד לַהֲנָאָה, וְאֶחָד לְאִסּוּר בִּשּׁוּל: גְּדִי. כָּל וָלָד רַךְ בְּמַשְׁמָע וְאַף עֵגֶל וָכֶבֶשׂ, מִמַּה שֶׁהֻצְרַךְ לְפָרֵשׁ בְּכַמָּה מְקוֹמוֹת: "גְּדִי עִזִּים" (בראשית לח, יז, ועוד) לָמַדְתָּ שֶׁ"גְּדִי" סְתָם כָּל יוֹנְקִים בַּמַּשְׁמָע: בַּחֲלֵב אִמּוֹ. פְּרָט לְעוֹף, שֶׁאֵין לוֹ חֲלֵב אֵם, שֶׁאֵין אִסּוּרוֹ מִן הַתּוֹרָה אֶלָּא מִדִּבְרֵי סוֹפְרִים:

כז אֶת הַדְּבָרִים הָאֵלֶּה. וְלֹא אַתָּה רַשַּׁאי לִכְתֹּב תּוֹרָה שֶׁבְּעַל פֶּה:

כט וַיְהִי בְּרֶדֶת מֹשֶׁה. כְּשֶׁהֵבִיא לוּחוֹת אַחֲרוֹנוֹת בְּיוֹם הַכִּפּוּרִים: כִּי קָרַן. לְשׁוֹן קַרְנַיִם, שֶׁהָאוֹר מַבְהִיק וּבוֹלֵט כְּמִין קֶרֶן. וּמֵהֵיכָן זָכָה מֹשֶׁה לְקַרְנֵי הַהוֹד? רַבּוֹתֵינוּ אָמְרוּ: מִן הַמְּעָרָה, שֶׁנָּתַן הַקָּדוֹשׁ בָּרוּךְ הוּא יָדוֹ עַל פָּנָיו, שֶׁנֶּאֱמַר: "וְשַׂכֹּתִי כַפִּי" (לעיל לג, כב):

שמות | פרק לד

לא וַיִּרְאוּ מִגֶּשֶׁת אֵלָיו: וַיִּקְרָא אֲלֵהֶם מֹשֶׁה וַיָּשֻׁבוּ אֵלָיו אַהֲרֹן
לב וְכָל־הַנְּשִׂאִים בָּעֵדָה וַיְדַבֵּר מֹשֶׁה אֲלֵהֶם: וְאַחֲרֵי־כֵן נִגְּשׁוּ כָּל־
לג בְּנֵי יִשְׂרָאֵל וַיְצַוֵּם אֵת כָּל־אֲשֶׁר דִּבֶּר יְהֹוָה אִתּוֹ בְּהַר סִינָי: וַיְכַל
לד מֹשֶׁה מִדַּבֵּר אִתָּם וַיִּתֵּן עַל־פָּנָיו מַסְוֶה: וּבְבֹא מֹשֶׁה לִפְנֵי יְהֹוָה
לְדַבֵּר אִתּוֹ יָסִיר אֶת־הַמַּסְוֶה עַד־צֵאתוֹ וְיָצָא וְדִבֶּר אֶל־בְּנֵי
לה יִשְׂרָאֵל אֵת אֲשֶׁר יְצֻוֶּה: וְרָאוּ בְנֵי־יִשְׂרָאֵל אֶת־פְּנֵי מֹשֶׁה כִּי
קָרַן עוֹר פְּנֵי מֹשֶׁה וְהֵשִׁיב מֹשֶׁה אֶת־הַמַּסְוֶה עַל־פָּנָיו עַד־בֹּאוֹ
לְדַבֵּר אִתּוֹ:

מפטיר

ויקהל

לה א וַיַּקְהֵל מֹשֶׁה אֶת־כָּל־עֲדַת בְּנֵי יִשְׂרָאֵל וַיֹּאמֶר אֲלֵהֶם אֵלֶּה
ב הַדְּבָרִים אֲשֶׁר־צִוָּה יְהֹוָה לַעֲשֹׂת אֹתָם: שֵׁשֶׁת יָמִים תֵּעָשֶׂה

לו] **וַיִּרְאוּ מִגֶּשֶׁת אֵלָיו.** בֹּא וּרְאֵה כַּמָּה גָדוֹל כֹּחָהּ שֶׁל עֲבֵרָה, שֶׁעַד שֶׁלֹּא פָּשְׁטוּ יְדֵיהֶם בַּעֲבֵרָה מַהוּ אוֹמֵר? "וּמַרְאֵה כְּבוֹד ה' כְּאֵשׁ אֹכֶלֶת בְּרֹאשׁ הָהָר לְעֵינֵי בְּנֵי יִשְׂרָאֵל" (לעיל כד, יז), וְלֹא יְרֵאִים וְלֹא מִזְדַּעְזְעִים, וּמִשֶּׁעָשׂוּ אֶת הָעֵגֶל, אַף מִקַּרְנֵי הוֹדוֹ שֶׁל מֹשֶׁה הָיוּ מַרְתִּיעִים וּמִזְדַּעְזְעִים:

לא] **הַנְּשִׂאִים בָּעֵדָה.** כְּמוֹ נְשִׂיאֵי הָעֵדָה. **וַיְדַבֵּר מֹשֶׁה אֲלֵהֶם.** שְׁלִיחוּתוֹ שֶׁל מָקוֹם. וּלְשׁוֹן הֹוֶה הוּא כָּל הָעִנְיָן הַזֶּה:

לב] **וְאַחֲרֵי כֵן נִגְּשׁוּ.** אַחַר שֶׁלִּמַּד לַזְּקֵנִים חוֹזֵר וּמְלַמֵּד הַפָּרָשָׁה אוֹ הַהֲלָכָה לְיִשְׂרָאֵל. תָּנוּ רַבָּנָן: כֵּיצַד סֵדֶר הַמִּשְׁנָה? מֹשֶׁה הָיָה לָמֵד מִפִּי הַגְּבוּרָה. נִכְנַס אַהֲרֹן, שָׁנָה לוֹ מֹשֶׁה פִּרְקוֹ, נִסְתַּלֵּק אַהֲרֹן וְיָשַׁב לוֹ לִשְׂמֹאל מֹשֶׁה. נִכְנְסוּ בָּנָיו, שָׁנָה לָהֶם מֹשֶׁה פִּרְקָם, נִסְתַּלְּקוּ הֵם, יָשַׁב אֶלְעָזָר לִימִין מֹשֶׁה וְאִיתָמָר לִשְׂמֹאל אַהֲרֹן. נִכְנְסוּ זְקֵנִים, שָׁנָה לָהֶם מֹשֶׁה פִּרְקָם, נִסְתַּלְּקוּ זְקֵנִים, יָשְׁבוּ לַצְּדָדִין. נִכְנְסוּ כָּל הָעָם, שָׁנָה לָהֶם מֹשֶׁה פִּרְקָם. נִמְצָא בְּיַד כָּל הָעָם אֶחָד, בְּיַד הַזְּקֵנִים שְׁנַיִם, בְּיַד בְּנֵי אַהֲרֹן שְׁלֹשָׁה, בְּיַד אַהֲרֹן אַרְבָּעָה וְכוּ', כִּדְאִיתָא בְּעֵרוּבִין (דף נד ע"ב):

לג-לה] **וַיִּתֵּן עַל פָּנָיו מַסְוֶה.** כְּתַרְגּוּמוֹ: "בֵּית אַפֵּי", לְשׁוֹן אֲרַמִּי הוּא בַּתַּלְמוּד (כתובות סב ע"ב): "סְוֵי לִבַּהּ", וְעוֹד בִּכְתֻבּוֹת (דף ס ע"א): "הֲוָה קָא מַסְוֵי לְאַפֵּהּ", לְשׁוֹן הַבָּטָה, הָיָה מִסְתַּכֵּל בָּהּ. אַף כָּאן "מַסְוֶה", בֶּגֶד הַנִּתָּן כְּנֶגֶד הַפַּרְצוּף וּבֵית הָעֵינַיִם. וְלִכְבוֹד קַרְנֵי הַהוֹד שֶׁלֹּא יִזּוֹנוּ הַכֹּל מֵהֶם הָיָה נוֹתֵן הַמַּסְוֶה כְּנֶגְדָּן, וְנוֹטְלוֹ בְּשָׁעָה שֶׁהָיָה מְדַבֵּר עִם יִשְׂרָאֵל, וּבְשָׁעָה שֶׁהַמָּקוֹם נִדְבָּר עִמּוֹ "עַד צֵאתוֹ", וּבְצֵאתוֹ – "וְיָצָא" בְּלֹא מַסְוֶה "וְדִבֶּר אֶל בְּנֵי יִשְׂרָאֵל" וְרָאוּ קַרְנֵי הַהוֹד בְּפָנָיו. וּכְשֶׁהוּא מִסְתַּלֵּק מֵהֶם, "וְהֵשִׁיב... אֶת הַמַּסְוֶה עַל פָּנָיו עַד בֹּאוֹ לְדַבֵּר אִתּוֹ", וּכְשֶׁבָּא לְדַבֵּר אִתּוֹ – נוֹטְלוֹ מֵעַל פָּנָיו:

פרק לה

א] **וַיַּקְהֵל מֹשֶׁה.** לְמָחֳרַת יוֹם הַכִּפּוּרִים כְּשֶׁיָּרַד מִן הָהָר. וְהוּא לְשׁוֹן הִפְעִיל, שֶׁאֵינוֹ אוֹסֵף אֲנָשִׁים בַּיָּדַיִם, אֶלָּא הֵן נֶאֱסָפִים עַל פִּי דִבּוּרוֹ, וְתַרְגּוּמוֹ: "וְאַכְנֵשׁ":

ב] **שֵׁשֶׁת יָמִים.** הִקְדִּים לָהֶם אַזְהָרַת שַׁבָּת לְצִוּוּי מְלֶאכֶת הַמִּשְׁכָּן, לוֹמַר שֶׁאֵינוֹ דּוֹחֶה אֶת הַשַּׁבָּת:

מְלָאכָ֔ה וּבַיּ֣וֹם הַשְּׁבִיעִ֗י יִהְיֶ֨ה לָכֶ֥ם קֹ֛דֶשׁ שַׁבַּ֥ת שַׁבָּת֖וֹן לַיהֹוָ֑ה כָּל־הָעֹשֶׂ֥ה ב֛וֹ מְלָאכָ֖ה יוּמָֽת: לֹא־תְבַעֲר֣וּ אֵ֔שׁ בְּכֹ֖ל מֹשְׁבֹֽתֵיכֶ֑ם בְּי֖וֹם הַשַּׁבָּֽת:

וַיֹּ֣אמֶר מֹשֶׁ֔ה אֶל־כָּל־עֲדַ֥ת בְּנֵֽי־יִשְׂרָאֵ֖ל לֵאמֹ֑ר זֶ֣ה הַדָּבָ֔ר אֲשֶׁר־צִוָּ֥ה יְהֹוָ֖ה לֵאמֹֽר: קְח֨וּ מֵֽאִתְּכֶ֤ם תְּרוּמָה֙ לַֽיהֹוָ֔ה כֹּ֚ל נְדִ֣יב לִבּ֔וֹ יְבִיאֶ֕הָ אֵ֖ת תְּרוּמַ֣ת יְהֹוָ֑ה זָהָ֥ב וָכֶ֖סֶף וּנְחֹֽשֶׁת: וּתְכֵ֧לֶת וְאַרְגָּמָ֛ן וְתוֹלַ֥עַת שָׁנִ֖י וְשֵׁ֣שׁ וְעִזִּֽים: וְעֹרֹ֨ת אֵילִ֧ם מְאָדָּמִ֛ים וְעֹרֹ֥ת תְּחָשִׁ֖ים וַעֲצֵ֥י שִׁטִּֽים: וְשֶׁ֖מֶן לַמָּא֑וֹר וּבְשָׂמִים֙ לְשֶׁ֣מֶן הַמִּשְׁחָ֔ה וְלִקְטֹ֖רֶת הַסַּמִּֽים: וְאַ֨בְנֵי־שֹׁ֔הַם וְאַבְנֵ֖י מִלֻּאִ֑ים לָאֵפ֖וֹד וְלַחֹֽשֶׁן: וְכָל־חֲכַם־לֵ֖ב בָּכֶ֑ם יָבֹ֣אוּ וְיַעֲשׂ֔וּ אֵ֛ת כָּל־אֲשֶׁ֥ר צִוָּ֖ה יְהֹוָֽה:

אֶת־הַ֨מִּשְׁכָּ֔ן אֶת־אָהֳל֖וֹ וְאֶת־מִכְסֵ֑הוּ אֶת־קְרָסָיו֙ וְאֶת־קְרָשָׁ֔יו אֶת־בְּרִיחָ֖יו אֶת־עַמֻּדָ֥יו וְאֶת־אֲדָנָֽיו: אֶת־הָאָרֹ֥ן וְאֶת־בַּדָּ֖יו אֶת־הַכַּפֹּ֑רֶת וְאֵ֖ת פָּרֹ֥כֶת הַמָּסָֽךְ: אֶת־הַשֻּׁלְחָ֥ן וְאֶת־בַּדָּ֖יו וְאֶת־כָּל־כֵּלָ֑יו וְאֵ֖ת לֶ֥חֶם הַפָּנִֽים: וְאֶת־מְנֹרַ֧ת הַמָּא֛וֹר וְאֶת־כֵּלֶ֖יהָ וְאֶת־

ג) לֹא תְבַעֲרוּ אֵשׁ. יֵשׁ מֵרַבּוֹתֵינוּ אוֹמְרִים הַבְעָרָה לְלָאו יָצָאת, וְיֵשׁ אוֹמְרִים לְחַלֵּק יָצָאת:

ד) זֶה הַדָּבָר אֲשֶׁר צִוָּה ה'. לִי "לֵאמֹר" לָכֶם:

ה) נְדִיב לִבּוֹ. עַל שֵׁם שֶׁלִּבּוֹ נוֹדְבוֹ קָרוּי 'נְדִיב לֵב'. כְּבָר פֵּרַשְׁתִּי נִדְבַת הַמִּשְׁכָּן וּמְלַאכְתּוֹ בִּמְקוֹם עֲשִׂיָּתָם:

יא) אֶת הַמִּשְׁכָּן. יְרִיעוֹת הַתַּחְתּוֹנוֹת הַנִּרְאוֹת בְּתוֹכוֹ קָרוּי 'מִשְׁכָּן': אֶת אָהֳלוֹ. הוּא אֹהֶל יְרִיעוֹת עִזִּים הֶעָשׂוּי לְגָג: וְאֶת מִכְסֵהוּ. מִכְסֵה עוֹרוֹת אֵילִים וְהַתְּחָשִׁים:

יב) וְאֶת פָּרֹכֶת הַמָּסָךְ. פָּרֹכֶת הַמְּחִצָּה. כָּל דָּבָר הַמֵּגֵן בֵּין מִלְמַעְלָה בֵּין מִכְּנֶגֶד קָרוּי 'מָסָךְ' וּ'סְכָךְ', וְכֵן: "שַׂכְתָּ בַעֲדוֹ" (איוב א, י), "הִנְנִי שָׂךְ אֶת דַּרְכֵּךְ" (הושע ב, ח):

יג) לֶחֶם הַפָּנִים. כְּבָר פֵּרַשְׁתִּי (לעיל כה, כט) עַל שֵׁם שֶׁהָיוּ לוֹ פָנִים לְכָאן וּלְכָאן, שֶׁהָיָה עָשׂוּי כְּמִין תֵּבָה פְּרוּצָה:

יד) וְאֶת כֵּלֶיהָ. מֶלְקָחַיִם וּמַחְתּוֹת: נֵרֹתֶיהָ. לוימ"ש בְּלַעַז, בָּזִיכִים שֶׁהַשֶּׁמֶן וְהַפְּתִילוֹת נְתוּנִין בָּהֶן: וְאֶת שֶׁמֶן הַמָּאוֹר. אַף הוּא צָרִיךְ חֲכַם לֵב, שֶׁהוּא מְשֻׁנֶּה מִשְּׁאָר שְׁמָנִים, כְּמוֹ שֶׁמְּפֹרָשׁ בִּמְנָחוֹת (דף פו ע"א) מְגַרְגְּרוֹ בְּרֹאשׁ הַזַּיִת, וְהוּא כָתִית וְזַךְ:

שמות | פרק לה

טו נֵרֹתֶיהָ וְאֵת שֶׁמֶן הַמָּאוֹר: וְאֶת־מִזְבַּח הַקְּטֹרֶת וְאֶת־בַּדָּיו וְאֵת שֶׁמֶן הַמִּשְׁחָה וְאֵת קְטֹרֶת הַסַּמִּים וְאֶת־מָסַךְ הַפֶּתַח לְפֶתַח הַמִּשְׁכָּן:

טז אֵת ׀ מִזְבַּח הָעֹלָה וְאֶת־מִכְבַּר הַנְּחֹשֶׁת אֲשֶׁר־לוֹ אֶת־בַּדָּיו וְאֶת־כָּל־כֵּלָיו אֶת־הַכִּיֹּר וְאֶת־כַּנּוֹ:

יז אֵת קַלְעֵי הֶחָצֵר אֶת־עַמֻּדָיו וְאֶת־אֲדָנֶיהָ וְאֵת מָסַךְ שַׁעַר הֶחָצֵר:

יח אֶת־יִתְדֹת הַמִּשְׁכָּן וְאֶת־יִתְדֹת הֶחָצֵר וְאֶת־מֵיתְרֵיהֶם:

יט אֶת־בִּגְדֵי הַשְּׂרָד לְשָׁרֵת בַּקֹּדֶשׁ אֶת־בִּגְדֵי הַקֹּדֶשׁ לְאַהֲרֹן הַכֹּהֵן וְאֶת־בִּגְדֵי בָנָיו לְכַהֵן:

כ וַיֵּצְאוּ כָּל־עֲדַת בְּנֵי־יִשְׂרָאֵל מִלִּפְנֵי מֹשֶׁה: כא וַיָּבֹאוּ כָּל־אִישׁ אֲשֶׁר־נְשָׂאוֹ לִבּוֹ וְכֹל אֲשֶׁר נָדְבָה רוּחוֹ אֹתוֹ הֵבִיאוּ אֶת־תְּרוּמַת יהוה לִמְלֶאכֶת אֹהֶל מוֹעֵד וּלְכָל־עֲבֹדָתוֹ וּלְבִגְדֵי הַקֹּדֶשׁ:

כב וַיָּבֹאוּ הָאֲנָשִׁים עַל־הַנָּשִׁים כֹּל ׀ נְדִיב לֵב הֵבִיאוּ חָח וָנֶזֶם וְטַבַּעַת וְכוּמָז כָּל־כְּלִי זָהָב וְכָל־אִישׁ אֲשֶׁר הֵנִיף תְּנוּפַת זָהָב לַיהוה:

כג וְכָל־אִישׁ אֲשֶׁר־נִמְצָא אִתּוֹ תְּכֵלֶת וְאַרְגָּמָן וְתוֹלַעַת שָׁנִי וְשֵׁשׁ וְעִזִּים וְעֹרֹת אֵילִם מְאָדָּמִים וְעֹרֹת תְּחָשִׁים הֵבִיאוּ:

טו מָסַךְ הַפֶּתַח. וִילוֹן שֶׁלִּפְנֵי הַמִּזְרָח, שֶׁלֹּא הָיוּ שָׁם קְרָשִׁים וְלֹא יְרִיעוֹת:

טז אֶת עַמֻּדָיו וְאֶת אֲדָנֶיהָ. הֲרֵי 'חָצֵר' קָרוּי כָּאן לְשׁוֹן זָכָר וּלְשׁוֹן נְקֵבָה, וְכֵן דְּבָרִים הַרְבֵּה: וְאֵת מָסַךְ שַׁעַר הֶחָצֵר. וִילוֹן פָּרוּס לְצַד הַמִּזְרָח, עֶשְׂרִים אַמָּה אֶמְצָעִיּוֹת שֶׁל רֹחַב הֶחָצֵר, שֶׁהָיָה חֲמִשִּׁים רֹחַב, וּסְתוּמִין הֵימֶנּוּ לְצַד צָפוֹן חָמֵשׁ עֶשְׂרֵה אַמָּה וְכֵן לַדָּרוֹם, שֶׁנֶּאֱמַר: "וַחֲמֵשׁ עֶשְׂרֵה אַמָּה קְלָעִים לַכָּתֵף" (לעיל כז, יד):

יח יְתֵדֹת. לִתְקֹעַ וְלִקְשֹׁר בָּהֶם סוֹפֵי הַיְרִיעוֹת בָּאָרֶץ שֶׁלֹּא יָנוּעוּ בָּרוּחַ: מֵיתְרֵיהֶם. חֲבָלִים לִקְשֹׁר:

יט בִּגְדֵי הַשְּׂרָד. לְכַסּוֹת הָאָרוֹן וְהַשֻּׁלְחָן וְהַמְּנוֹרָה וְהַמִּזְבְּחוֹת בִּשְׁעַת סִלּוּק הַמַּסָּעוֹת:

כב עַל הַנָּשִׁים. עִם הַנָּשִׁים וּסְמוּכִין אֲלֵיהֶם: חָח. הוּא תַּכְשִׁיט שֶׁל זָהָב עָגֹל נָתוּן עַל הַזְּרוֹעַ וְהוּא הֶעָמִיד: וְכוּמָז. כְּלִי זָהָב הוּא נָתוּן כְּנֶגֶד אוֹתוֹ מָקוֹם לָאִשָּׁה. וְרַבּוֹתֵינוּ פֵּרְשׁוּ שֵׁם 'כּוּמָז': כָּאן מְקוֹם זִמָּה:

כג וְכָל אִישׁ אֲשֶׁר נִמְצָא אִתּוֹ. תְּכֵלֶת אוֹ אַרְגָּמָן אוֹ תוֹלַעַת שָׁנִי אוֹ עוֹרוֹת אֵילִים אוֹ תְּחָשִׁים, כֻּלָּם "הֵבִיאוּ":

כד כָּל־מֵרִים תְּרוּמַת כֶּסֶף וּנְחֹשֶׁת הֵבִיאוּ אֵת תְּרוּמַת יהוה וְכֹל אֲשֶׁר נִמְצָא אִתּוֹ עֲצֵי שִׁטִּים לְכָל־מְלֶאכֶת הָעֲבֹדָה הֵבִיאוּ:
כה וְכָל־אִשָּׁה חַכְמַת־לֵב בְּיָדֶיהָ טָווּ וַיָּבִיאוּ מַטְוֶה אֶת־הַתְּכֵלֶת וְאֶת־הָאַרְגָּמָן אֶת־תּוֹלַעַת הַשָּׁנִי וְאֶת־הַשֵּׁשׁ:
כו וְכָל־הַנָּשִׁים אֲשֶׁר נָשָׂא לִבָּן אֹתָנָה בְּחָכְמָה טָווּ אֶת־הָעִזִּים:
כז וְהַנְּשִׂאִם הֵבִיאוּ אֵת אַבְנֵי הַשֹּׁהַם וְאֵת אַבְנֵי הַמִּלֻּאִים לָאֵפוֹד וְלַחֹשֶׁן:
כח וְאֶת־הַבֹּשֶׂם וְאֶת־הַשָּׁמֶן לְמָאוֹר וּלְשֶׁמֶן הַמִּשְׁחָה וְלִקְטֹרֶת הַסַּמִּים:
כט כָּל־אִישׁ וְאִשָּׁה אֲשֶׁר נָדַב לִבָּם אֹתָם לְהָבִיא לְכָל־הַמְּלָאכָה אֲשֶׁר צִוָּה יהוה לַעֲשׂוֹת בְּיַד־מֹשֶׁה הֵבִיאוּ בְנֵי־יִשְׂרָאֵל נְדָבָה לַיהוה:

שלישי /שני/

ל וַיֹּאמֶר מֹשֶׁה אֶל־בְּנֵי יִשְׂרָאֵל רְאוּ קָרָא יהוה בְּשֵׁם בְּצַלְאֵל בֶּן־אוּרִי בֶן־חוּר לְמַטֵּה יְהוּדָה:
לא וַיְמַלֵּא אֹתוֹ רוּחַ אֱלֹהִים בְּחָכְמָה בִּתְבוּנָה וּבְדַעַת וּבְכָל־מְלָאכָה:
לב וְלַחְשֹׁב מַחֲשָׁבֹת לַעֲשֹׂת בַּזָּהָב וּבַכֶּסֶף וּבַנְּחֹשֶׁת:
לג וּבַחֲרֹשֶׁת אֶבֶן לְמַלֹּאת וּבַחֲרֹשֶׁת עֵץ לַעֲשׂוֹת בְּכָל־מְלֶאכֶת מַחֲשָׁבֶת:
לד וּלְהוֹרֹת נָתַן בְּלִבּוֹ הוּא וְאָהֳלִיאָב בֶּן־אֲחִיסָמָךְ לְמַטֵּה־דָן:
לה מִלֵּא אֹתָם חָכְמַת־לֵב

כו **טָווּ אֶת הָעִזִּים.** הִיא הָיְתָה אֻמָּנוּת יְתֵרָה, שֶׁמֵּעַל גַּבֵּי הָעִזִּים טוֹוִין אוֹתָם:

כז **וְהַנְּשִׂאִם הֵבִיאוּ.** אָמַר רַבִּי נָתָן: מַה רָאוּ נְשִׂיאִים לְהִתְנַדֵּב בַּחֲנֻכַּת הַמִּזְבֵּחַ בַּתְּחִלָּה, וּבִמְלֶאכֶת הַמִּשְׁכָּן לֹא הִתְנַדְּבוּ בַּתְּחִלָּה? אֶלָּא כָּךְ אָמְרוּ נְשִׂיאִים: יִתְנַדְּבוּ צִבּוּר מַה שֶּׁמִּתְנַדְּבִין, וּמַה שֶּׁמְּחַסְּרִין — אָנוּ מַשְׁלִימִין אוֹתוֹ. כֵּיוָן שֶׁהִשְׁלִימוּ צִבּוּר אֶת הַכֹּל, שֶׁנֶּאֱמַר: "וְהַמְּלָאכָה הָיְתָה דַיָּם" (להלן לו, ז), אָמְרוּ נְשִׂיאִים: מָה עָלֵינוּ לַעֲשׂוֹת? "הֵבִיאוּ אֶת אַבְנֵי הַשֹּׁהַם" וְגוֹ׳, לְכָךְ הִתְנַדְּבוּ בַּחֲנֻכַּת הַמִּזְבֵּחַ תְּחִלָּה. וּלְפִי שֶׁנִּתְעַצְּלוּ מִתְּחִלָּה נֶחְסְרָה אוֹת מִשְּׁמָם, "וְהַנְּשִׂאִם" כְּתִיב:

ל **חוּר.** בְּנָהּ שֶׁל מִרְיָם הָיָה:

לד **וְאָהֳלִיאָב.** מִשֵּׁבֶט דָּן, מִן הַיְרוּדִין שֶׁבַּשְּׁבָטִים, מִבְּנֵי הַשְּׁפָחוֹת, וְהִשְׁוָהוּ הַמָּקוֹם לִבְצַלְאֵל לִמְלֶאכֶת הַמִּשְׁכָּן, וְהוּא מִגְּדוֹלֵי הַשְּׁבָטִים, לְקַיֵּם מַה שֶּׁנֶּאֱמַר: "וְלֹא נִכַּר שׁוֹעַ לִפְנֵי דָל" (איוב לד, יט):

לַעֲשׂוֹת כָּל־מְלֶאכֶת חָרָשׁ וְחֹשֵׁב וְרֹקֵם בַּתְּכֵלֶת וּבָאַרְגָּמָן בְּתוֹלַעַת הַשָּׁנִי וּבַשֵּׁשׁ וְאֹרֵג עֹשֵׂי כָּל־מְלָאכָה וְחֹשְׁבֵי מַחֲשָׁבֹת:

לו א וְעָשָׂה בְצַלְאֵל וְאָהֳלִיאָב וְכֹל ׀ אִישׁ חֲכַם־לֵב אֲשֶׁר נָתַן יְהֹוָה חָכְמָה וּתְבוּנָה בָּהֵמָּה לָדַעַת לַעֲשֹׂת אֶת־כָּל־מְלֶאכֶת עֲבֹדַת הַקֹּדֶשׁ לְכֹל אֲשֶׁר־צִוָּה יְהֹוָה: ב וַיִּקְרָא מֹשֶׁה אֶל־בְּצַלְאֵל וְאֶל־אָהֳלִיאָב וְאֶל כָּל־אִישׁ חֲכַם־לֵב אֲשֶׁר נָתַן יְהֹוָה חָכְמָה בְּלִבּוֹ כֹּל אֲשֶׁר נְשָׂאוֹ לִבּוֹ לְקָרְבָה אֶל־הַמְּלָאכָה לַעֲשֹׂת אֹתָהּ: ג וַיִּקְחוּ מִלִּפְנֵי מֹשֶׁה אֵת כָּל־הַתְּרוּמָה אֲשֶׁר הֵבִיאוּ בְּנֵי יִשְׂרָאֵל לִמְלֶאכֶת עֲבֹדַת הַקֹּדֶשׁ לַעֲשֹׂת אֹתָהּ וְהֵם הֵבִיאוּ אֵלָיו עוֹד נְדָבָה בַּבֹּקֶר בַּבֹּקֶר: ד וַיָּבֹאוּ כָּל־הַחֲכָמִים הָעֹשִׂים אֵת כָּל־מְלֶאכֶת הַקֹּדֶשׁ אִישׁ־אִישׁ מִמְּלַאכְתּוֹ אֲשֶׁר־הֵמָּה עֹשִׂים: ה וַיֹּאמְרוּ אֶל־מֹשֶׁה לֵּאמֹר מַרְבִּים הָעָם לְהָבִיא מִדֵּי הָעֲבֹדָה לַמְּלָאכָה אֲשֶׁר־צִוָּה יְהֹוָה לַעֲשֹׂת אֹתָהּ: ו וַיְצַו מֹשֶׁה וַיַּעֲבִירוּ קוֹל בַּמַּחֲנֶה לֵאמֹר אִישׁ וְאִשָּׁה אַל־יַעֲשׂוּ־עוֹד מְלָאכָה לִתְרוּמַת הַקֹּדֶשׁ וַיִּכָּלֵא הָעָם מֵהָבִיא: ז וְהַמְּלָאכָה הָיְתָה דַיָּם לְכָל־הַמְּלָאכָה לַעֲשׂוֹת אֹתָהּ וְהוֹתֵר:

רביעי ח וַיַּעֲשׂוּ כָל־חֲכַם־לֵב בְּעֹשֵׂי הַמְּלָאכָה אֶת־הַמִּשְׁכָּן עֶשֶׂר יְרִיעֹת שֵׁשׁ מָשְׁזָר

פרק לו

ה) מִדֵּי הָעֲבֹדָה. יוֹתֵר מִכְּדֵי צֹרֶךְ הָעֲבוֹדָה:

ו) וַיִּכָּלֵא. לְשׁוֹן מְנִיעָה:

ז) וְהַמְּלָאכָה הָיְתָה דַיָּם לְכָל הַמְּלָאכָה. וּמְלֶאכֶת הַהֲבָאָה "הָיְתָה דַיָּם" שֶׁל עוֹשֵׂי הַמִּשְׁכָּן, "לְכָל הַמְּלָאכָה" שֶׁל מִשְׁכָּן "לַעֲשׂוֹת אוֹתָהּ" וּלְהוֹתֵר. וְהוֹתֵר. כְּמוֹ: "וְהַכְבֵּד אֶת לִבּוֹ" (לעיל ח, יח), "וְהַכּוֹת אֶת מוֹאָב" (מלכים ב ג, כד):

וּתְכֵ֧לֶת וְאַרְגָּמָ֛ן וְתוֹלַ֥עַת שָׁנִ֖י כְּרֻבִ֑ים מַעֲשֵׂ֥ה חֹשֵׁ֖ב עָשָׂ֥ה אֹתָֽם׃
ט אֹ֜רֶךְ הַיְרִיעָ֣ה הָֽאַחַ֗ת שְׁמֹנֶ֤ה וְעֶשְׂרִים֙ בָּֽאַמָּ֔ה וְרֹ֨חַב֙ אַרְבַּ֣ע בָּֽאַמָּ֔ה הַיְרִיעָ֖ה הָאֶחָ֑ת מִדָּ֥ה אַחַ֖ת לְכָל־הַיְרִיעֹֽת׃
י וַיְחַבֵּ֛ר אֶת־חֲמֵ֥שׁ הַיְרִיעֹ֖ת אַחַ֣ת אֶל־אֶחָ֑ת וְחָמֵ֤שׁ יְרִיעֹת֙ חִבַּ֔ר אַחַ֖ת אֶל־אֶחָֽת׃
יא וַיַּ֜עַשׂ לֻֽלְאֹ֣ת תְּכֵ֗לֶת עַ֚ל שְׂפַ֣ת הַיְרִיעָ֣ה הָֽאֶחָ֔ת מִקָּצָ֖ה בַּמַּחְבָּ֑רֶת כֵּ֣ן עָשָׂ֗ה בִּשְׂפַת֙ הַיְרִיעָ֣ה הַקִּיצוֹנָ֔ה בַּמַּחְבֶּ֖רֶת הַשֵּׁנִֽית׃
יב חֲמִשִּׁ֣ים לֻֽלָאֹ֗ת עָשָׂה֙ בַּיְרִיעָ֣ה הָֽאֶחָ֔ת וַֽחֲמִשִּׁ֣ים לֻֽלָאֹ֗ת עָשָׂה֙ בִּקְצֵ֣ה הַיְרִיעָ֔ה אֲשֶׁ֖ר בַּמַּחְבֶּ֣רֶת הַשֵּׁנִ֑ית מַקְבִּילֹת֙ הַלֻּ֣לָאֹ֔ת אַחַ֖ת אֶל־אֶחָֽת׃
יג וַיַּ֕עַשׂ חֲמִשִּׁ֖ים קַרְסֵ֣י זָהָ֑ב וַיְחַבֵּ֨ר אֶת־הַיְרִיעֹ֜ת אַחַ֤ת אֶל־אַחַת֙ בַּקְּרָסִ֔ים וַֽיְהִ֥י הַמִּשְׁכָּ֖ן אֶחָֽד׃
יד וַיַּ֨עַשׂ֙ יְרִיעֹ֣ת עִזִּ֔ים לְאֹ֖הֶל עַל־הַמִּשְׁכָּ֑ן עַשְׁתֵּֽי־עֶשְׂרֵ֥ה יְרִיעֹ֖ת עָשָׂ֥ה אֹתָֽם׃
טו אֹ֜רֶךְ הַיְרִיעָ֣ה הָֽאַחַ֗ת שְׁלֹשִׁים֙ בָּֽאַמָּ֔ה וְאַרְבַּ֣ע אַמּ֔וֹת רֹ֖חַב הַיְרִיעָ֣ה הָאֶחָ֑ת מִדָּ֣ה אַחַ֔ת לְעַשְׁתֵּ֥י עֶשְׂרֵ֖ה יְרִיעֹֽת׃
טז וַיְחַבֵּ֛ר אֶת־חֲמֵ֥שׁ הַיְרִיעֹ֖ת לְבָ֑ד וְאֶת־שֵׁ֥שׁ הַיְרִיעֹ֖ת לְבָֽד׃
יז וַיַּ֜עַשׂ לֻֽלָאֹ֣ת חֲמִשִּׁ֗ים עַ֚ל שְׂפַ֣ת הַיְרִיעָ֔ה הַקִּיצֹנָ֖ה בַּמַּחְבָּ֑רֶת וַֽחֲמִשִּׁ֣ים לֻֽלָאֹ֗ת עָשָׂה֙ עַל־שְׂפַ֣ת הַיְרִיעָ֔ה הַֽחֹבֶ֖רֶת הַשֵּׁנִֽית׃
יח וַיַּ֛עַשׂ קַרְסֵ֥י נְחֹ֖שֶׁת חֲמִשִּׁ֑ים לְחַבֵּ֥ר אֶת־הָאֹ֖הֶל לִֽהְיֹ֥ת אֶחָֽד׃
יט וַיַּ֤עַשׂ מִכְסֶה֙ לָאֹ֔הֶל עֹרֹ֥ת אֵלִ֖ים מְאָדָּמִ֑ים וּמִכְסֵ֛ה עֹרֹ֥ת תְּחָשִׁ֖ים מִלְמָֽעְלָה׃

חמישי כ וַיַּ֥עַשׂ אֶת־הַקְּרָשִׁ֖ים לַמִּשְׁכָּ֑ן עֲצֵ֥י שִׁטִּ֖ים עֹמְדִֽים׃
כא עֶ֥שֶׂר אַמֹּ֖ת אֹ֣רֶךְ הַקָּ֑רֶשׁ וְאַמָּה֙ וַֽחֲצִ֣י הָֽאַמָּ֔ה רֹ֖חַב הַקֶּ֥רֶשׁ הָאֶחָֽד׃
כב שְׁתֵּ֣י יָד֗וֹת לַקֶּ֨רֶשׁ֙ הָאֶחָ֔ד מְשֻׁלָּבֹ֔ת אַחַ֖ת אֶל־אֶחָ֑ת כֵּ֣ן עָשָׂ֔ה לְכֹ֖ל קַרְשֵׁ֥י הַמִּשְׁכָּֽן׃
כג וַיַּ֥עַשׂ אֶת־הַקְּרָשִׁ֖ים

כד לַמִּשְׁכָּן עֶשְׂרִים קְרָשִׁים לִפְאַת נֶגֶב תֵּימָנָה: וְאַרְבָּעִים אַדְנֵי־
כֶסֶף עָשָׂה תַּחַת עֶשְׂרִים הַקְּרָשִׁים שְׁנֵי אֲדָנִים תַּחַת־הַקֶּרֶשׁ
הָאֶחָד לִשְׁתֵּי יְדֹתָיו וּשְׁנֵי אֲדָנִים תַּחַת־הַקֶּרֶשׁ הָאֶחָד לִשְׁתֵּי
כה יְדֹתָיו: וּלְצֶלַע הַמִּשְׁכָּן הַשֵּׁנִית לִפְאַת צָפוֹן עָשָׂה עֶשְׂרִים
כו קְרָשִׁים: וְאַרְבָּעִים אַדְנֵיהֶם כָּסֶף שְׁנֵי אֲדָנִים תַּחַת הַקֶּרֶשׁ
כז הָאֶחָד וּשְׁנֵי אֲדָנִים תַּחַת הַקֶּרֶשׁ הָאֶחָד: וּלְיַרְכְּתֵי הַמִּשְׁכָּן יָמָּה
כח עָשָׂה שִׁשָּׁה קְרָשִׁים: וּשְׁנֵי קְרָשִׁים עָשָׂה לִמְקֻצְעֹת הַמִּשְׁכָּן
כט בַּיַּרְכָתָיִם: וְהָיוּ תוֹאֲמִם מִלְּמַטָּה וְיַחְדָּו יִהְיוּ תַמִּים אֶל־רֹאשׁוֹ
ל אֶל־הַטַּבַּעַת הָאֶחָת כֵּן עָשָׂה לִשְׁנֵיהֶם לִשְׁנֵי הַמִּקְצֹעֹת: וְהָיוּ
שְׁמֹנָה קְרָשִׁים וְאַדְנֵיהֶם כֶּסֶף שִׁשָּׁה עָשָׂר אֲדָנִים שְׁנֵי
לא אֲדָנִים תַּחַת הַקֶּרֶשׁ הָאֶחָד: וַיַּעַשׂ בְּרִיחֵי עֲצֵי שִׁטִּים חֲמִשָּׁה
לב לְקַרְשֵׁי צֶלַע־הַמִּשְׁכָּן הָאֶחָת: וַחֲמִשָּׁה בְרִיחִם לְקַרְשֵׁי צֶלַע־
הַמִּשְׁכָּן הַשֵּׁנִית וַחֲמִשָּׁה בְרִיחִם לְקַרְשֵׁי הַמִּשְׁכָּן לַיַּרְכָתַיִם
לג יָמָּה: וַיַּעַשׂ אֶת־הַבְּרִיחַ הַתִּיכֹן לִבְרֹחַ בְּתוֹךְ הַקְּרָשִׁים מִן־
לד הַקָּצֶה אֶל־הַקָּצֶה: וְאֶת־הַקְּרָשִׁים צִפָּה זָהָב וְאֶת־טַבְּעֹתָם
עָשָׂה זָהָב בָּתִּים לַבְּרִיחִם וַיְצַף אֶת־הַבְּרִיחִם זָהָב: וַיַּעַשׂ אֶת־
לה הַפָּרֹכֶת תְּכֵלֶת וְאַרְגָּמָן וְתוֹלַעַת שָׁנִי וְשֵׁשׁ מָשְׁזָר מַעֲשֵׂה
לו חֹשֵׁב עָשָׂה אֹתָהּ כְּרֻבִים: וַיַּעַשׂ לָהּ אַרְבָּעָה עַמּוּדֵי שִׁטִּים
וַיְצַפֵּם זָהָב וָוֵיהֶם זָהָב וַיִּצֹק לָהֶם אַרְבָּעָה אַדְנֵי־כָסֶף: וַיַּעַשׂ
לז מָסָךְ לְפֶתַח הָאֹהֶל תְּכֵלֶת וְאַרְגָּמָן וְתוֹלַעַת שָׁנִי וְשֵׁשׁ מָשְׁזָר
לח מַעֲשֵׂה רֹקֵם: וְאֶת־עַמּוּדָיו חֲמִשָּׁה וְאֶת־וָוֵיהֶם וְצִפָּה רָאשֵׁיהֶם
וַחֲשֻׁקֵיהֶם זָהָב וְאַדְנֵיהֶם חֲמִשָּׁה נְחֹשֶׁת:

לז א וַיַּעַשׂ בְּצַלְאֵל אֶת־הָאָרֹן עֲצֵי שִׁטִּים אַמָּתַיִם וָחֵצִי אָרְכּוֹ וְאַמָּה
ב וָחֵצִי רָחְבּוֹ וְאַמָּה וָחֵצִי קֹמָתוֹ: וַיְצַפֵּהוּ זָהָב טָהוֹר מִבַּיִת וּמִחוּץ
ג וַיַּעַשׂ לוֹ זֵר זָהָב סָבִיב: וַיִּצֹק לוֹ אַרְבַּע טַבְּעֹת זָהָב עַל אַרְבַּע
פַּעֲמֹתָיו וּשְׁתֵּי טַבָּעֹת עַל־צַלְעוֹ הָאֶחָת וּשְׁתֵּי טַבָּעֹת עַל־צַלְעוֹ
ד ה הַשֵּׁנִית: וַיַּעַשׂ בַּדֵּי עֲצֵי שִׁטִּים וַיְצַף אֹתָם זָהָב: וַיָּבֵא אֶת־
ו הַבַּדִּים בַּטַּבָּעֹת עַל צַלְעֹת הָאָרֹן לָשֵׂאת אֶת־הָאָרֹן: וַיַּעַשׂ
כַּפֹּרֶת זָהָב טָהוֹר אַמָּתַיִם וָחֵצִי אָרְכָּהּ וְאַמָּה וָחֵצִי רָחְבָּהּ:
ז וַיַּעַשׂ שְׁנֵי כְרֻבִים זָהָב מִקְשָׁה עָשָׂה אֹתָם מִשְּׁנֵי קְצוֹת הַכַּפֹּרֶת:
ח כְּרוּב־אֶחָד מִקָּצָה מִזֶּה וּכְרוּב־אֶחָד מִקָּצָה מִזֶּה מִן־הַכַּפֹּרֶת
ט עָשָׂה אֶת־הַכְּרֻבִים מִשְּׁנֵי קְצוֹתָיו: וַיִּהְיוּ הַכְּרֻבִים פֹּרְשֵׂי כְנָפַיִם
לְמַעְלָה סֹכְכִים בְּכַנְפֵיהֶם עַל־הַכַּפֹּרֶת וּפְנֵיהֶם אִישׁ אֶל־אָחִיו
אֶל־הַכַּפֹּרֶת הָיוּ פְּנֵי הַכְּרֻבִים:
י וַיַּעַשׂ אֶת־הַשֻּׁלְחָן עֲצֵי שִׁטִּים אַמָּתַיִם אָרְכּוֹ וְאַמָּה רָחְבּוֹ וְאַמָּה
יא וָחֵצִי קֹמָתוֹ: וַיְצַף אֹתוֹ זָהָב טָהוֹר וַיַּעַשׂ לוֹ זֵר זָהָב סָבִיב: וַיַּעַשׂ
יב לוֹ מִסְגֶּרֶת טֹפַח סָבִיב וַיַּעַשׂ זֵר־זָהָב לְמִסְגַּרְתּוֹ סָבִיב: וַיִּצֹק לוֹ
אַרְבַּע טַבְּעֹת זָהָב וַיִּתֵּן אֶת־הַטַּבָּעֹת עַל אַרְבַּע הַפֵּאֹת אֲשֶׁר
יד לְאַרְבַּע רַגְלָיו: לְעֻמַּת הַמִּסְגֶּרֶת הָיוּ הַטַּבָּעֹת בָּתִּים לַבַּדִּים
טו לָשֵׂאת אֶת־הַשֻּׁלְחָן: וַיַּעַשׂ אֶת־הַבַּדִּים עֲצֵי שִׁטִּים וַיְצַף אֹתָם

פרק לו

א| וַיַּעַשׂ בְּצַלְאֵל. לְפִי שֶׁנָּתַן נַפְשׁוֹ עַל הַמְּלָאכָה יוֹתֵר מִשְּׁאָר חֲכָמִים, נִקְרֵאת עַל שְׁמוֹ:

שמות | פרק לז

טז זָהָב לָשֵׂאת אֶת־הַשֻּׁלְחָן: וַיַּעַשׂ אֶת־הַכֵּלִים ׀ אֲשֶׁר עַל־הַשֻּׁלְחָן אֶת־קְעָרֹתָיו וְאֶת־כַּפֹּתָיו וְאֵת מְנַקִּיֹּתָיו וְאֶת־הַקְּשָׂוֺת אֲשֶׁר יֻסַּךְ בָּהֵן זָהָב טָהוֹר:

ששי
/שלישי/

יז וַיַּעַשׂ אֶת־הַמְּנֹרָה זָהָב טָהוֹר מִקְשָׁה עָשָׂה אֶת־הַמְּנֹרָה יְרֵכָהּ וְקָנָהּ גְּבִיעֶיהָ כַּפְתֹּרֶיהָ וּפְרָחֶיהָ מִמֶּנָּה הָיוּ: יח וְשִׁשָּׁה קָנִים יֹצְאִים מִצִּדֶּיהָ שְׁלֹשָׁה ׀ קְנֵי מְנֹרָה מִצִּדָּהּ הָאֶחָד וּשְׁלֹשָׁה קְנֵי מְנֹרָה מִצִּדָּהּ הַשֵּׁנִי: יט שְׁלֹשָׁה גְבִעִים מְשֻׁקָּדִים בַּקָּנֶה הָאֶחָד כַּפְתֹּר וָפֶרַח וּשְׁלֹשָׁה גְבִעִים מְשֻׁקָּדִים בְּקָנֶה אֶחָד כַּפְתֹּר וָפָרַח כֵּן לְשֵׁשֶׁת הַקָּנִים הַיֹּצְאִים מִן־הַמְּנֹרָה: כ וּבַמְּנֹרָה אַרְבָּעָה גְבִעִים מְשֻׁקָּדִים כַּפְתֹּרֶיהָ וּפְרָחֶיהָ: כא וְכַפְתֹּר תַּחַת שְׁנֵי הַקָּנִים מִמֶּנָּה וְכַפְתֹּר תַּחַת שְׁנֵי הַקָּנִים מִמֶּנָּה וְכַפְתֹּר תַּחַת־שְׁנֵי הַקָּנִים מִמֶּנָּה לְשֵׁשֶׁת הַקָּנִים הַיֹּצְאִים מִמֶּנָּה: כב כַּפְתֹּרֵיהֶם וּקְנֹתָם מִמֶּנָּה הָיוּ כֻּלָּהּ מִקְשָׁה אַחַת זָהָב טָהוֹר: כג וַיַּעַשׂ אֶת־נֵרֹתֶיהָ שִׁבְעָה וּמַלְקָחֶיהָ וּמַחְתֹּתֶיהָ זָהָב טָהוֹר: כד כִּכַּר זָהָב טָהוֹר עָשָׂה אֹתָהּ וְאֵת כָּל־כֵּלֶיהָ:

כה וַיַּעַשׂ אֶת־מִזְבַּח הַקְּטֹרֶת עֲצֵי שִׁטִּים אַמָּה אָרְכּוֹ וְאַמָּה רָחְבּוֹ רָבוּעַ וְאַמָּתַיִם קֹמָתוֹ מִמֶּנּוּ הָיוּ קַרְנֹתָיו: כו וַיְצַף אֹתוֹ זָהָב טָהוֹר אֶת־גַּגּוֹ וְאֶת־קִירֹתָיו סָבִיב וְאֶת־קַרְנֹתָיו וַיַּעַשׂ לוֹ זֵר זָהָב סָבִיב: כז וּשְׁתֵּי טַבְּעֹת זָהָב עָשָׂה־לוֹ ׀ מִתַּחַת לְזֵרוֹ עַל שְׁתֵּי צַלְעֹתָיו עַל שְׁנֵי צִדָּיו לְבָתִּים לְבַדִּים לָשֵׂאת אֹתוֹ בָּהֶם: כח וַיַּעַשׂ אֶת־הַבַּדִּים עֲצֵי שִׁטִּים וַיְצַף אֹתָם זָהָב: כט וַיַּעַשׂ אֶת־שֶׁמֶן הַמִּשְׁחָה קֹדֶשׁ

שביעי
/רביעי/

וְאֶת־קְטֹרֶת הַסַּמִּים טָהוֹר מַעֲשֵׂה רֹקֵחַ: וַיַּעַשׂ
אֶת־מִזְבַּח הָעֹלָה עֲצֵי שִׁטִּים חָמֵשׁ אַמּוֹת אָרְכּוֹ וְחָמֵשׁ־אַמּוֹת
רָחְבּוֹ רָבוּעַ וְשָׁלֹשׁ אַמּוֹת קֹמָתוֹ: וַיַּעַשׂ קַרְנֹתָיו עַל אַרְבַּע
פִּנֹּתָיו מִמֶּנּוּ הָיוּ קַרְנֹתָיו וַיְצַף אֹתוֹ נְחֹשֶׁת: וַיַּעַשׂ אֶת־כָּל־
כְּלֵי הַמִּזְבֵּחַ אֶת־הַסִּירֹת וְאֶת־הַיָּעִים וְאֶת־הַמִּזְרָקֹת אֶת־
הַמִּזְלָגֹת וְאֶת־הַמַּחְתֹּת כָּל־כֵּלָיו עָשָׂה נְחֹשֶׁת: וַיַּעַשׂ לַמִּזְבֵּחַ
מִכְבָּר מַעֲשֵׂה רֶשֶׁת נְחֹשֶׁת תַּחַת כַּרְכֻּבּוֹ מִלְּמַטָּה עַד־חֶצְיוֹ:
וַיִּצֹק אַרְבַּע טַבָּעֹת בְּאַרְבַּע הַקְּצָוֹת לְמִכְבַּר הַנְּחֹשֶׁת בָּתִּים
לַבַּדִּים: וַיַּעַשׂ אֶת־הַבַּדִּים עֲצֵי שִׁטִּים וַיְצַף אֹתָם נְחֹשֶׁת: וַיָּבֵא
אֶת־הַבַּדִּים בַּטַּבָּעֹת עַל צַלְעֹת הַמִּזְבֵּחַ לָשֵׂאת אֹתוֹ בָּהֶם
נְבוּב לֻחֹת עָשָׂה אֹתוֹ: וַיַּעַשׂ אֵת הַכִּיּוֹר נְחֹשֶׁת
וְאֵת כַּנּוֹ נְחֹשֶׁת בְּמַרְאֹת הַצֹּבְאֹת אֲשֶׁר צָבְאוּ פֶּתַח אֹהֶל
מוֹעֵד: וַיַּעַשׂ אֶת־הֶחָצֵר לִפְאַת ׀ נֶגֶב תֵּימָנָה קַלְעֵי
הֶחָצֵר שֵׁשׁ מָשְׁזָר מֵאָה בָּאַמָּה: עַמּוּדֵיהֶם עֶשְׂרִים וְאַדְנֵיהֶם

פרק לח

ז׀ נְבוּב לֻחֹת. "נָבוּב" הוּא חָלוּל, וְכֵן: "וְעָבְיוֹ אַרְבַּע אֶצְבָּעוֹת נָבוּב" (ירמיה נב, כא). נְבוּב לֻחֹת. הַלּוּחוֹת שֶׁל עֲצֵי שִׁטִּים לְכָל רוּחַ, וְהֶחָלָל בָּאֶמְצַע:

ח׀ בְּמַרְאֹת הַצֹּבְאֹת. בְּנוֹת יִשְׂרָאֵל הָיוּ בְּיָדָן מַרְאוֹת שֶׁרוֹאוֹת בָּהֶן כְּשֶׁהֵן מִתְקַשְּׁטוֹת, וְאַף אוֹתָן לֹא עִכְּבוּ מִלְּהָבִיא לְנִדְבַת הַמִּשְׁכָּן, וְהָיָה מוֹאֵס מֹשֶׁה בָּהֶן מִפְּנֵי שֶׁעֲשׂוּיִים לְיֵצֶר הָרָע, אָמַר לוֹ הַקָּדוֹשׁ בָּרוּךְ הוּא: קַבֵּל, כִּי אֵלּוּ חֲבִיבִין עָלַי מִן הַכֹּל, שֶׁעַל יְדֵיהֶם הֶעֱמִידוּ הַנָּשִׁים צְבָאוֹת רַבּוֹת בְּמִצְרַיִם. כְּשֶׁהָיוּ בַּעְלֵיהֶן יְגֵעִים בַּעֲבוֹדַת פֶּרֶךְ בַּשָּׂדֶה, הָיוּ הוֹלְכוֹת וּמוֹלִיכוֹת לָהֶם מַאֲכָל וּמִשְׁתֶּה וּמַאֲכִילוֹת אוֹתָם, וְנוֹטְלוֹת הַמַּרְאוֹת, וְכָל אַחַת רוֹאָה עַצְמָהּ עִם בַּעְלָהּ בַּמַּרְאָה, וּמְשַׁדַּלְתּוֹ בִדְבָרִים: 'אֲנִי נָאָה מִמְּךָ', וּמִתּוֹךְ כָּךְ מְבִיאוֹת לְבַעְלֵיהֶן לִידֵי תַאֲוָה וְנִזְקָקוֹת לָהֶם וּמִתְעַבְּרוֹת וְיוֹלְדוֹת שָׁם, שֶׁנֶּאֱמַר: "תַּחַת הַתַּפּוּחַ עוֹרַרְתִּיךָ" (שיר השירים ח, ה), וְזֶהוּ שֶׁנֶּאֱמַר: "בְּמַרְאֹת הַצֹּבְאֹת". וְנַעֲשָׂה הַכִּיּוֹר מֵהֶם שֶׁהוּא לָשׂוּם שָׁלוֹם בֵּין אִישׁ לְאִשְׁתּוֹ, לְהַשְׁקוֹת מִמַּיִם שֶׁבְּתוֹכוֹ אֶת שֶׁקִּנֵּא לָהּ בַּעְלָהּ. וְתֵדַע לְךָ שֶׁהֵן מַרְאוֹת מַמָּשׁ, שֶׁהֲרֵי נֶאֱמַר: "וּנְחֹשֶׁת הַתְּנוּפָה שִׁבְעִים כִּכָּר וְגוֹ׳ וַיַּעַשׂ בָּהּ וְגוֹ׳" (להלן פסוקים כט-ל), וְכִיּוֹר וְכַנּוֹ לֹא הֻזְכְּרוּ שָׁם, לָמַדְתָּ שֶׁלֹּא הָיְתָה נְחֹשֶׁת שֶׁל כִּיּוֹר מִנְּחֹשֶׁת הַתְּנוּפָה. כָּךְ דָּרַשׁ רַבִּי תַּנְחוּמָא (פקודי ט). וְכֵן תִּרְגֵּם אוּנְקְלוֹס: "בְּמַחְזְיָת נְשַׁיָּא", וְהוּא תַּרְגּוּמוֹ שֶׁל 'מַרְאוֹת', מִירוֹאֵ"רְשׂ בְּלַעַ"ז. וְכֵן מָצִינוּ בְּיִשַׁעְיָה: "וְהַגִּלְיֹנִים" (ג, כג) מְתַרְגְּמִינָן: "וּמַחְזְיָתָא". אֲשֶׁר צָבְאוּ. לְהָבִיא נִדְבָתָן:

שמות | פרק לח

יא עֶשְׂרִים נְחֹ֔שֶׁת וָוֵ֧י הָעַמּוּדִ֛ים וַחֲשֻׁקֵיהֶ֖ם כָּֽסֶף׃ וְלִפְאַ֣ת צָפ֗וֹן מֵאָ֣ה בָֽאַמָּ֔ה עַמּֽוּדֵיהֶ֣ם עֶשְׂרִ֔ים וְאַדְנֵיהֶ֥ם עֶשְׂרִ֖ים נְחֹ֑שֶׁת וָוֵ֧י
יב הָעַמּוּדִ֛ים וַחֲשֻׁקֵיהֶ֖ם כָּֽסֶף׃ וְלִפְאַת־יָ֗ם קְלָעִים֙ חֲמִשִּׁ֣ים בָּֽאַמָּ֔ה עַמּֽוּדֵיהֶ֥ם עֲשָׂרָ֖ה וְאַדְנֵיהֶ֣ם עֲשָׂרָ֑ה וָוֵ֧י הָעַמֻּדִ֛ים וַחֲשֽׁוּקֵיהֶ֖ם
יג כָּֽסֶף׃ וְלִפְאַ֛ת קֵ֥דְמָה מִזְרָ֖חָה חֲמִשִּׁ֥ים אַמָּֽה׃ קְלָעִ֛ים חֲמֵשׁ־
יד עֶשְׂרֵ֥ה אַמָּ֖ה אֶל־הַכָּתֵ֑ף עַמּֽוּדֵיהֶ֣ם שְׁלֹשָׁ֔ה וְאַדְנֵיהֶ֖ם שְׁלֹשָֽׁה׃
טו וְלַכָּתֵ֣ף הַשֵּׁנִ֗ית מִזֶּ֤ה וּמִזֶּה֙ לְשַׁ֣עַר הֶֽחָצֵ֔ר קְלָעִ֕ים חֲמֵ֥שׁ עֶשְׂרֵ֖ה
טז אַמָּ֑ה עַמֻּֽדֵיהֶ֣ם שְׁלֹשָׁ֔ה וְאַדְנֵיהֶ֖ם שְׁלֹשָֽׁה׃ כָּל־קַלְעֵ֧י הֶֽחָצֵ֛ר
יז סָבִ֖יב שֵׁ֥שׁ מָשְׁזָֽר׃ וְהָאֲדָנִ֣ים לָֽעַמֻּדִים֮ נְחֹשֶׁת֒ וָוֵ֨י הָֽעַמּוּדִ֜ים וַחֲשׁוּקֵיהֶם֙ כֶּ֔סֶף וְצִפּ֥וּי רָֽאשֵׁיהֶ֖ם כָּ֑סֶף וְהֵם֙ מְחֻשָּׁקִ֣ים כֶּ֔סֶף כֹּ֖ל
יח עַמֻּדֵ֥י הֶֽחָצֵֽר׃ וּמָסַ֞ךְ שַׁ֤עַר הֶֽחָצֵר֙ מַעֲשֵׂ֣ה רֹקֵ֔ם תְּכֵ֧לֶת וְאַרְגָּמָ֛ן וְתוֹלַ֥עַת שָׁנִ֖י וְשֵׁ֣שׁ מָשְׁזָ֑ר וְעֶשְׂרִ֤ים אַמָּה֙ אֹ֔רֶךְ וְקוֹמָ֤ה בְרֹ֙חַב֙
יט חָמֵ֣שׁ אַמּ֔וֹת לְעֻמַּ֖ת קַלְעֵ֥י הֶֽחָצֵֽר׃ וְעַמֻּֽדֵיהֶ֣ם אַרְבָּעָ֔ה וְאַדְנֵיהֶ֥ם אַרְבָּעָ֖ה נְחֹ֑שֶׁת וָוֵיהֶ֣ם כֶּ֔סֶף וְצִפּ֧וּי רָֽאשֵׁיהֶ֛ם וַחֲשֻׁקֵיהֶ֖ם כָּֽסֶף׃
כ וְכָל־הַיְתֵדֹ֞ת לַמִּשְׁכָּ֧ן וְלֶֽחָצֵ֛ר סָבִ֖יב נְחֹֽשֶׁת׃

מפטיר

כח פקודי

כא אֵ֣לֶּה פְקוּדֵ֤י הַמִּשְׁכָּן֙ מִשְׁכַּ֣ן הָֽעֵדֻ֔ת אֲשֶׁ֥ר פֻּקַּ֖ד עַל־פִּ֣י מֹשֶׁ֑ה
כב עֲבֹדַת֙ הַלְוִיִּ֔ם בְּיַד֙ אִֽיתָמָ֔ר בֶּֽן־אַהֲרֹ֖ן הַכֹּהֵֽן׃ וּבְצַלְאֵ֛ל בֶּן־אוּרִ֥י

יח | לְעֻמַּת קַלְעֵי הֶחָצֵר. כְּמִדַּת קַלְעֵי הֶחָצֵר:

כא | אֵלֶּה פְקוּדֵי. בְּפָרָשָׁה זוֹ נִמְנוּ כָּל מִשְׁקְלֵי נִדְבַת הַמִּשְׁכָּן לַכֶּסֶף, לַזָּהָב וְלַנְּחֹשֶׁת, וְנִמְנוּ כָּל כֵּלָיו לְכָל עֲבוֹדָתוֹ: הַמִּשְׁכָּן מִשְׁכַּן. שְׁנֵי פְעָמִים, רֶמֶז לַמִּקְדָּשׁ שֶׁנִּתְמַשְׁכֵּן בִּשְׁנֵי חֻרְבָּנִין עַל עֲוֹנוֹתֵיהֶן שֶׁל יִשְׂרָאֵל: מִשְׁכַּן הָעֵדֻת. עֵדוּת לְיִשְׂרָאֵל שֶׁוִּתֵּר לָהֶם הַקָּדוֹשׁ בָּרוּךְ הוּא עַל מַעֲשֵׂה הָעֵגֶל, שֶׁהֲרֵי הִשְׁרָה שְׁכִינָתוֹ בֵּינֵיהֶם: עֲבֹדַת הַלְוִיִּם. פְּקוּדֵי הַמִּשְׁכָּן וְכֵלָיו הִיא עֲבוֹדָה הַמְּסוּרָה לַלְוִיִּם בַּמִּדְבָּר, לָשֵׂאת וּלְהוֹרִיד וּלְהָקִים אִישׁ אִישׁ לְמַשָּׂאוֹ הַמֻּפְקָד עָלָיו, כְּמוֹ שֶׁאָמוּר בְּפָרָשַׁת נָשֹׂא (במדבר ד): בְּיַד אִיתָמָר. הוּא הָיָה פָקִיד עֲלֵיהֶם, לִמְסֹר לְכָל בֵּית אָב עֲבוֹדָה שֶׁעָלָיו:

כב | וּבְצַלְאֵל בֶּן אוּרִי... עָשָׂה. ״אֵת כָּל אֲשֶׁר צִוָּה״ אוֹתוֹ מֹשֶׁה אֵין כְּתִיב כָּאן אֶלָּא ״אֵת כָּל אֲשֶׁר צִוָּה

בֶּן־ח֔וּר לְמַטֵּ֖ה יְהוּדָ֑ה עָשָׂ֕ה אֵ֛ת כׇּל־אֲשֶׁר־צִוָּ֥ה יְהֹוָ֖ה אֶת־מֹשֶֽׁה׃

כג וְאִתּ֗וֹ אׇהֳלִיאָ֞ב בֶּן־אֲחִיסָמָ֛ךְ לְמַטֵּה־דָ֖ן חָרָ֣שׁ וְחֹשֵׁ֑ב וְרֹקֵ֗ם בַּתְּכֵ֙לֶת֙ וּבָֽאַרְגָּמָ֔ן וּבְתוֹלַ֥עַת הַשָּׁנִ֖י וּבַשֵּֽׁשׁ׃ ס

כד כׇּל־הַזָּהָ֗ב הֶֽעָשׂוּי֙ לַמְּלָאכָ֔ה בְּכֹ֖ל מְלֶ֣אכֶת הַקֹּ֑דֶשׁ וַיְהִ֣י ׀ זְהַ֣ב הַתְּנוּפָ֗ה תֵּ֤שַׁע וְעֶשְׂרִים֙ כִּכָּ֔ר וּשְׁבַ֨ע מֵא֧וֹת וּשְׁלֹשִׁ֛ים שֶׁ֖קֶל בְּשֶׁ֥קֶל הַקֹּֽדֶשׁ׃

כה וְכֶ֛סֶף פְּקוּדֵ֥י הָעֵדָ֖ה מְאַ֣ת כִּכָּ֑ר וְאֶ֩לֶף֩ וּשְׁבַ֨ע מֵא֜וֹת וַחֲמִשָּׁ֧ה וְשִׁבְעִ֛ים שֶׁ֖קֶל בְּשֶׁ֥קֶל הַקֹּֽדֶשׁ׃

כו בֶּ֚קַע לַגֻּלְגֹּ֔לֶת מַחֲצִ֥ית הַשֶּׁ֖קֶל בְּשֶׁ֣קֶל הַקֹּ֑דֶשׁ לְכֹ֨ל הָעֹבֵ֜ר עַל־הַפְּקֻדִ֗ים מִבֶּ֨ן עֶשְׂרִ֤ים שָׁנָה֙ וָמַ֔עְלָה לְשֵׁשׁ־מֵא֥וֹת אֶ֙לֶף֙ וּשְׁלֹ֣שֶׁת אֲלָפִ֔ים וַחֲמֵ֥שׁ מֵא֖וֹת וַחֲמִשִּֽׁים׃

כז וַיְהִ֗י מְאַת֙ כִּכַּ֣ר הַכֶּ֔סֶף לָצֶ֗קֶת אֵ֚ת אַדְנֵ֣י הַקֹּ֔דֶשׁ וְאֵ֖ת אַדְנֵ֣י הַפָּרֹ֑כֶת מְאַ֧ת אֲדָנִ֛ים לִמְאַ֥ת הַכִּכָּ֖ר כִּכָּ֥ר לָאָֽדֶן׃

כח וְאֶת־הָאֶ֜לֶף וּשְׁבַ֤ע הַמֵּאוֹת֙ וַחֲמִשָּׁ֣ה וְשִׁבְעִ֔ים עָשָׂ֥ה וָוִ֖ים לָעַמּוּדִ֑ים וְצִפָּ֥ה רָאשֵׁיהֶ֖ם וְחִשַּׁ֥ק אֹתָֽם׃

כט וּנְחֹ֥שֶׁת הַתְּנוּפָ֖ה שִׁבְעִ֣ים כִּכָּ֑ר וְאַלְפַּ֥יִם וְאַרְבַּע־מֵא֖וֹת שָֽׁקֶל׃

ל וַיַּ֣עַשׂ בָּ֔הּ אֶת־אַדְנֵ֕י פֶּ֖תַח אֹ֣הֶל מוֹעֵ֑ד וְאֵת֙ מִזְבַּ֣ח הַנְּחֹ֔שֶׁת וְאֶת־מִכְבַּ֥ר הַנְּחֹ֖שֶׁת אֲשֶׁר־ל֑וֹ וְאֵ֖ת כׇּל־

ה' אֶת מֹשֶׁה", חָשְׁבוּ דְבָרִים שֶׁלֹּא חָמַר לוֹ רַבּוֹ הִסְכִּימָה דַּעְתּוֹ לְמָה שֶׁנֶּאֱמַר לְמֹשֶׁה בְּסִינַי:

כד בְּכִכָּר. שִׁשִּׁים מָנֶה. וּמָנֶה שֶׁל קֹדֶשׁ כָּפוּל הָיָה, הֲרֵי הַכִּכָּר מֵאָה וְעֶשְׂרִים מָנֶה, וְהַמָּנֶה עֶשְׂרִים וַחֲמִשָּׁה סְלָעִים, הֲרֵי כִּכָּר שֶׁל קֹדֶשׁ שְׁלֹשֶׁת אֲלָפִים שְׁקָלִים, לְפִיכָךְ מָנָה בִּפְרוֹטְרוֹט כָּל הַשְּׁקָלִים שֶׁפְּחוּתִין בְּמִנְיָנָם מִשְּׁלֹשֶׁת אֲלָפִים שֶׁאֵין מַגִּיעִין לְכִכָּר:

כו בֶּקַע. הוּא שֵׁם מִשְׁקַל שֶׁל מַחֲצִית הַשֶּׁקֶל: לְשֵׁשׁ מֵאוֹת אֶלֶף וְגוֹ'. כָּךְ הָיוּ יִשְׂרָאֵל, וְכָךְ עָלָה מִנְיָנָם אַחַר שֶׁהוּקַם הַמִּשְׁכָּן בְּסֵפֶר וַיְדַבֵּר (במדבר ב, לב), וְאַף עַתָּה בִּנְדָבַת הַמִּשְׁכָּן כָּךְ הָיוּ. וּמִנְיַן חֲצָאֵי הַשְּׁקָלִים שֶׁל שֵׁשׁ מֵאוֹת אֶלֶף עוֹלֶה מְאַת כִּכָּר, כָּל אֶחָד שֶׁל שְׁלֹשֶׁת אֲלָפִים שְׁקָלִים. כֵּיצַד? שֵׁשׁ מֵאוֹת אֶלֶף חֲצָאִין, הֲרֵי הֵן שְׁלֹשׁ מֵאוֹת אֶלֶף שְׁלֵמִים, הֲרֵי מְאַת כִּכָּר, וְהַשְּׁלֹשֶׁת אֲלָפִים וַחֲמֵשׁ מֵאוֹת וַחֲמִשִּׁים חֲצָאִין, עוֹלִין אֶלֶף וּשְׁבַע מֵאוֹת וַחֲמִשָּׁה וְשִׁבְעִים שְׁקָלִים:

כז לָצֶקֶת. לְמַתָּכָא: אֶת אַדְנֵי הַקֹּדֶשׁ. שֶׁל קַרְשֵׁי הַמִּשְׁכָּן, שֶׁהֵם אַרְבָּעִים וּשְׁמוֹנָה קְרָשִׁים וְלָהֶן תִּשְׁעִים וְשִׁשָּׁה אֲדָנִים, וְאַדְנֵי הַפָּרֹכֶת אַרְבָּעָה, הֲרֵי מֵאָה. וְכָל שְׁאָר הָאֲדָנִים 'נְחֹשֶׁת' כָּתוּב בָּהֶם:

כח וְצִפָּה רָאשֵׁיהֶם. שֶׁל עַמּוּדִים מֵהֶם, שֶׁבְּכֻלָּן כָּתוּב וְצִפָּה רָאשֵׁיהֶם וַחֲשׁוּקֵיהֶם כָּסֶף (עיין לעיל לח, י-כ):

שמות | פרק לח

לא כְּלֵי הַמִּזְבֵּחַ: וְאֶת־אַדְנֵי הֶחָצֵר סָבִיב וְאֶת־אַדְנֵי שַׁעַר הֶחָצֵר
לט א וְאֵת כָּל־יִתְדֹת הַמִּשְׁכָּן וְאֶת־כָּל־יִתְדֹת הֶחָצֵר סָבִיב: וּמִן־
הַתְּכֵלֶת וְהָאַרְגָּמָן וְתוֹלַעַת הַשָּׁנִי עָשׂוּ בִגְדֵי־שְׂרָד לְשָׁרֵת
בַּקֹּדֶשׁ וַיַּעֲשׂוּ אֶת־בִּגְדֵי הַקֹּדֶשׁ אֲשֶׁר לְאַהֲרֹן כַּאֲשֶׁר צִוָּה יְהוָה
אֶת־מֹשֶׁה: ּ

ב וַיַּעַשׂ אֶת־הָאֵפֹד זָהָב תְּכֵלֶת וְאַרְגָּמָן וְתוֹלַעַת שָׁנִי וְשֵׁשׁ   שני
מָשְׁזָר: וַיְרַקְּעוּ אֶת־פַּחֵי הַזָּהָב וְקִצֵּץ פְּתִילִם לַעֲשׂוֹת בְּתוֹךְ /חמישי/
הַתְּכֵלֶת וּבְתוֹךְ הָאַרְגָּמָן וּבְתוֹךְ תּוֹלַעַת הַשָּׁנִי וּבְתוֹךְ הַשֵּׁשׁ
ד מַעֲשֵׂה חֹשֵׁב: כְּתֵפֹת עָשׂוּ־לוֹ חֹבְרֹת עַל־שְׁנֵי קצוותו חֻבָּר: קצוותיו
ה וְחֵשֶׁב אֲפֻדָּתוֹ אֲשֶׁר עָלָיו מִמֶּנּוּ הוּא כְּמַעֲשֵׂהוּ זָהָב תְּכֵלֶת
וְאַרְגָּמָן וְתוֹלַעַת שָׁנִי וְשֵׁשׁ מָשְׁזָר כַּאֲשֶׁר צִוָּה יְהוָה אֶת־
ו מֹשֶׁה: וַיַּעֲשׂוּ אֶת־אַבְנֵי הַשֹּׁהַם מֻסַבֹּת מִשְׁבְּצֹת
ז זָהָב מְפֻתָּחֹת פִּתּוּחֵי חוֹתָם עַל־שְׁמוֹת בְּנֵי יִשְׂרָאֵל: וַיָּשֶׂם
אֹתָם עַל כִּתְפֹת הָאֵפֹד אַבְנֵי זִכָּרוֹן לִבְנֵי יִשְׂרָאֵל כַּאֲשֶׁר צִוָּה
יְהוָה אֶת־מֹשֶׁה:

פרק לט
א וּמִן הַתְּכֵלֶת וְהָאַרְגָּמָן וְגוֹ׳. שֵׁם לֹא נֶאֱמַר כָּאן,
מִכָּאן אֲנִי אוֹמֵר שֶׁאֵין בִּגְדֵי שְׂרָד הַלָּלוּ בִּגְדֵי כְהֻנָּה,
שֶׁבְּבִגְדֵי כְהֻנָּה הָיָה שֵׁשׁ, אֶלָּא הֵם בְּגָדִים שֶׁמְּכַסִּים
בָּהֶם כְּלֵי הַקֹּדֶשׁ בִּשְׁעַת סִלּוּק מַסָּעוֹת, שֶׁלֹּא הָיָה
בָּהֶם שֵׁשׁ:

ג וַיְרַקְּעוּ. כְּמוֹ: "לְרוֹקַע הָאָרֶץ" (תהלים קלו, ו), כְּתַרְגּוּמוֹ
"וְרַדִּידוּ". טַסִּין הָיוּ מְרַדְּדִין מִן הַזָּהָב, אשטנדר״א

בְּלַעַז, טַסִּין דַּקּוֹת. כָּאן הוּא מְלַמֶּדְךָ הֵיאַךְ הָיוּ
טוֹוִין אֶת הַזָּהָב עִם הַחוּטִין: מְרַדְּדִין הַטַּסִּין דַּקִּין,
וְקוֹצְצִין מֵהֶן פְּתִילִים לְחֹרֶךְ הַטַּס, לַעֲשׂוֹת אוֹתָן
פְּתִילִים תַּעֲרֹבֶת עִם כָּל מִין בַּחֹשֶׁן וְאֵפוֹד,
שֶׁנֶּאֱמַר בָּהֶן "זָהָב" (לעיל כח, ו, טו), חוּט אֶחָד שֶׁל זָהָב
עִם שִׁשָּׁה חוּטִין שֶׁל תְּכֵלֶת, וְכֵן עִם כָּל מִין וָמִין,
שֶׁכָּל הַמִּינִים חוּטָן כָּפוּל שִׁשָּׁה, וְהַזָּהָב חוּט שְׁבִיעִי
עִם כָּל אֶחָד וְאֶחָד:

ח וַיַּ֧עַשׂ אֶת־הַחֹ֛שֶׁן מַעֲשֵׂ֥ה חֹשֵׁ֖ב כְּמַעֲשֵׂ֣ה אֵפֹ֑ד זָהָ֗ב תְּכֵ֧לֶת
ט וְאַרְגָּמָ֛ן וְתוֹלַ֥עַת שָׁנִ֖י וְשֵׁ֥שׁ מָשְׁזָֽר: רָב֧וּעַ הָיָ֛ה כָּפ֖וּל עָשׂ֣וּ אֶת־
הַחֹ֑שֶׁן זֶ֧רֶת אָרְכּ֛וֹ וְזֶ֥רֶת רָחְבּ֖וֹ כָּפֽוּל: וַיְמַלְאוּ־ב֔וֹ אַרְבָּעָ֖ה ט֣וּרֵי
י אָ֑בֶן ט֗וּר אֹ֤דֶם פִּטְדָה֙ וּבָרֶ֔קֶת הַטּ֖וּר הָאֶחָֽד: וְהַטּ֖וּר הַשֵּׁנִ֑י נֹ֥פֶךְ
יא סַפִּ֖יר וְיָהֲלֹֽם: וְהַטּ֖וּר הַשְּׁלִישִׁ֑י לֶ֥שֶׁם שְׁב֖וֹ וְאַחְלָֽמָה: וְהַטּוּר֙
יב/יג הָֽרְבִיעִ֔י תַּרְשִׁ֥ישׁ שֹׁ֖הַם וְיָשְׁפֵ֑ה מֽוּסַבֹּ֛ת מִשְׁבְּצֹ֥ת זָהָ֖ב בְּמִלֻּאֹתָֽם:
יד וְ֠הָאֲבָנִ֠ים עַל־שְׁמֹ֨ת בְּנֵֽי־יִשְׂרָאֵ֥ל הֵ֛נָּה שְׁתֵּ֥ים עֶשְׂרֵ֖ה עַל־שְׁמֹתָ֑ם
טו פִּתּוּחֵ֤י חֹתָם֙ אִ֣ישׁ עַל־שְׁמ֔וֹ לִשְׁנֵ֥ים עָשָׂ֖ר שָֽׁבֶט: וַיַּעֲשׂ֧וּ עַל־
הַחֹ֛שֶׁן שַׁרְשְׁרֹ֥ת גַּבְלֻ֖ת מַעֲשֵׂ֣ה עֲבֹ֑ת זָהָ֖ב טָהֽוֹר: וַֽיַּעֲשׂ֗וּ שְׁתֵּי֙
טז מִשְׁבְּצֹ֣ת זָהָ֔ב וּשְׁתֵּ֖י טַבְּעֹ֣ת זָהָ֑ב וַֽיִּתְּנ֗וּ אֶת־שְׁתֵּי֙ הַטַּבָּעֹ֔ת
יז עַל־שְׁנֵ֖י קְצ֥וֹת הַחֹֽשֶׁן: וַֽיִּתְּנ֗וּ שְׁתֵּי֙ הָעֲבֹתֹ֣ת הַזָּהָ֔ב עַל־שְׁתֵּ֖י
יח הַטַּבָּעֹ֑ת עַל־קְצ֖וֹת הַחֹֽשֶׁן: וְאֵ֨ת שְׁתֵּ֤י קְצוֹת֙ שְׁתֵּ֣י הָֽעֲבֹתֹ֔ת
נָֽתְנ֖וּ עַל־שְׁתֵּ֣י הַֽמִּשְׁבְּצֹ֑ת וַֽיִּתְּנֻ֛ם עַל־כִּתְפֹ֥ת הָאֵפֹ֖ד אֶל־מ֥וּל
יט פָּנָֽיו: וַֽיַּעֲשׂ֗וּ שְׁתֵּי֙ טַבְּעֹ֣ת זָהָ֔ב וַיָּשִׂ֕ימוּ עַל־שְׁנֵ֖י קְצ֣וֹת הַחֹ֑שֶׁן
כ עַל־שְׂפָת֕וֹ אֲשֶׁ֛ר אֶל־עֵ֥בֶר הָאֵפֹ֖ד בָּֽיְתָה: וַֽיַּעֲשׂוּ֮ שְׁתֵּ֣י טַבְּעֹ֣ת
זָהָב֒ וַֽיִּתְּנֻ֗ם עַל־שְׁתֵּ֨י כִתְפֹ֤ת הָאֵפֹד֙ מִלְּמַ֔טָּה מִמּ֖וּל פָּנָ֑יו לְעֻמַּ֣ת
כא מַחְבַּרְתּ֔וֹ מִמַּ֕עַל לְחֵ֖שֶׁב הָאֵפֹֽד: וַיִּרְכְּס֣וּ אֶת־הַחֹ֡שֶׁן מִטַּבְּעֹתָיו֩
אֶל־טַבְּעֹ֨ת הָאֵפֹ֜ד בִּפְתִ֣יל תְּכֵ֗לֶת לִֽהְיֹת֙ עַל־חֵ֣שֶׁב הָאֵפֹ֔ד וְלֹֽא־
יִזַּ֣ח הַחֹ֔שֶׁן מֵעַ֖ל הָאֵפֹ֑ד כַּאֲשֶׁ֛ר צִוָּ֥ה יְהוָ֖ה אֶת־מֹשֶֽׁה:
כב וַיַּ֛עַשׂ אֶת־מְעִ֥יל הָאֵפֹ֖ד מַעֲשֵׂ֣ה אֹרֵ֑ג כְּלִ֖יל תְּכֵֽלֶת: וּפִֽי־הַמְּעִ֥יל
כג בְּתוֹכ֖וֹ כְּפִ֣י תַחְרָ֑א שָׂפָ֥ה לְפִ֛יו סָבִ֖יב לֹ֥א יִקָּרֵֽעַ: וַֽיַּעֲשׂוּ֙ עַל־שׁוּלֵ֣י
כד הַמְּעִ֔יל רִמּוֹנֵ֕י תְּכֵ֥לֶת וְאַרְגָּמָ֖ן וְתוֹלַ֣עַת שָׁנִ֑י מָשְׁזָֽר: וַיַּעֲשׂ֥וּ פַעֲמֹנֵ֖י
כה

שלישי
/ששי/

שמות | פרק לט | פקודי

זָהָב טָהֻוֹר וַיִּתְּנוּ אֶת־הַפַּעֲמֹנִים בְּתָוֹךְ הָרִמֹּנִים עַל־שׁוּלֵי הַמְּעִיל
סָבִיב בְּתָוֹךְ הָרִמֹּנִים: פַּעֲמֹן וְרִמֹּן פַּעֲמֹן וְרִמֹּן עַל־שׁוּלֵי הַמְּעִיל כו
סָבִיב לְשָׁרֵת כַּאֲשֶׁר צִוָּה יְהוָה אֶת־מֹשֶׁה: וַיַּעֲשׂוּ כז
אֶת־הַכָּתְנֹת שֵׁשׁ מַעֲשֵׂה אֹרֵג לְאַהֲרֹן וּלְבָנָיו: וְאֵת הַמִּצְנֶפֶת כח
שֵׁשׁ וְאֶת־פַּאֲרֵי הַמִּגְבָּעֹת שֵׁשׁ וְאֶת־מִכְנְסֵי הַבָּד שֵׁשׁ מָשְׁזָר:
וְאֶת־הָאַבְנֵט שֵׁשׁ מָשְׁזָר וּתְכֵלֶת וְאַרְגָּמָן וְתוֹלַעַת שָׁנִי מַעֲשֵׂה כט
רֹקֵם כַּאֲשֶׁר צִוָּה יְהוָה אֶת־מֹשֶׁה: וַיַּעֲשׂוּ אֶת־צִיץ ל
נֵזֶר־הַקֹּדֶשׁ זָהָב טָהֻוֹר וַיִּכְתְּבוּ עָלָיו מִכְתַּב פִּתּוּחֵי חֹתָם קֹדֶשׁ
לַיהוָה: וַיִּתְּנוּ עָלָיו פְּתִיל תְּכֵלֶת לָתֵת עַל־הַמִּצְנֶפֶת מִלְמָעְלָה לא
כַּאֲשֶׁר צִוָּה יְהוָה אֶת־מֹשֶׁה: וַתֵּכֶל כָּל־עֲבֹדַת מִשְׁכַּן לב
אֹהֶל מוֹעֵד וַיַּעֲשׂוּ בְּנֵי יִשְׂרָאֵל כְּכֹל אֲשֶׁר צִוָּה יְהוָה אֶת־מֹשֶׁה
כֵּן עָשׂוּ:
וַיָּבִיאוּ אֶת־הַמִּשְׁכָּן אֶל־מֹשֶׁה אֶת־הָאֹהֶל וְאֶת־כָּל־כֵּלָיו קְרָסָיו לג רביעי כט

כח| וְאֵת פַּאֲרֵי הַמִּגְבָּעֹת. תִּפְאֶרֶת הַמִּגְבָּעוֹת, הַמִּגְבָּעוֹת הַמְפֹאָרִין:

לא| לָתֵת עַל הַמִּצְנֶפֶת מִלְמָעְלָה. שֶׁעַל יְדֵי הַפְּתִילִים הָיָה מוֹשִׁיבוֹ עַל הַמִּצְנֶפֶת כְּמִין כֶּתֶר. וְאִי אֶפְשָׁר לוֹמַר עַל הַצִּיץ עַל הַמִּצְנֶפֶת, שֶׁהֲרֵי בִּשְׁחִיטַת קָדָשִׁים שָׁנִינוּ: שְׂעָרוֹ הָיָה נִרְאֶה בֵּין צִיץ לַמִּצְנֶפֶת שֶׁשָּׁם מֵנִיחַ תְּפִלִּין (זבחים יט ע״א), וְהַצִּיץ הָיָה נָתוּן עַל הַמֵּצַח, הֲרֵי הַמִּצְנֶפֶת לְמַעְלָה וְהַצִּיץ לְמַטָּה. כָּאן הוּא אוֹמֵר: ״וַיִּתְּנוּ עָלָיו פְּתִיל תְּכֵלֶת״, וּבְעִנְיַן הַצַּוָּאָה הוּא אוֹמֵר: ״וְשַׂמְתָּ אֹתוֹ עַל פְּתִיל תְּכֵלֶת״ (לעיל כח, לו)? שְׁנֵי חוּטִין הָיוּ בְּכָל קָצֶה וְקָצֶה, אֶחָד מִמַּעַל וְאֶחָד מִתַּחַת לְצַד מִצְחוֹ, וְכֵן בָּאֶמְצַע וְקוֹשֵׁר רָאשֵׁיהֶם הַשְּׁנַיִם כֻּלָּם יַחַד מֵאֲחוֹרָיו לְמוּל עָרְפּוֹ, וּמוֹשִׁיבוֹ עַל הַמִּצְנֶפֶת. וְאַל תִּתְמַהּ שֶׁלֹּא נֶאֱמַר ״פְּתִילֵי״ תְּכֵלֶת הוֹחִיל וּמֻרְבִּין הֵן, שֶׁהֲרֵי

מָצִינוּ בַּחֹשֶׁן וְאֵפוֹד: ״וַיִּרְכְּסוּ אֶת הַחֹשֶׁן וְגוֹ׳״ (לעיל פסוק כא), וְעַל כָּרְחֲךָ פָּחוֹת מִשְּׁנַיִם לֹא הָיוּ, שֶׁהֲרֵי בִּשְׁנֵי קְצוֹת הַחֹשֶׁן הָיוּ שְׁתֵּי טַבְּעוֹת הַחֹשֶׁן וּבִשְׁתֵּי כְּתֵפוֹת הָאֵפוֹד הָיוּ טַבְּעוֹת הָאֵפוֹד שֶׁכְּנֶגְדָּן, וּלְפִי דֶּרֶךְ קְשִׁירָה אַרְבָּעָה חוּטִין הָיוּ, וּמִכָּל מָקוֹם פָּחוֹת מִשְּׁנַיִם אִי אֶפְשָׁר:

לב| וַיַּעֲשׂוּ בְּנֵי יִשְׂרָאֵל. אֶת הַמְּלָאכָה. ״כְּכֹל אֲשֶׁר צִוָּה ה׳״ וְגוֹ׳:

לג| וַיָּבִיאוּ אֶת הַמִּשְׁכָּן וְגוֹ׳. שֶׁלֹּא הָיוּ יְכוֹלִין לַהֲקִימוֹ, וּלְפִי שֶׁלֹּא עָשָׂה מֹשֶׁה שׁוּם מְלָאכָה בַּמִּשְׁכָּן הִנִּיחַ לוֹ הַקָּדוֹשׁ בָּרוּךְ הוּא הֲקָמָתוֹ, שֶׁלֹּא הָיָה יָכוֹל לַהֲקִימוֹ שׁוּם אָדָם מֵחֲמַת כֹּבֶד הַקְּרָשִׁים שֶׁאֵין כֹּחַ בָּאָדָם לְזָקְפָן, וּמֹשֶׁה הֶעֱמִידוֹ. אָמַר מֹשֶׁה לִפְנֵי הַקָּדוֹשׁ בָּרוּךְ הוּא: אֵיךְ אֶפְשָׁר הֲקָמָתוֹ עַל יְדֵי אָדָם? אָמַר לוֹ: עֲסֹק אַתָּה בְּיָדְךָ נִרְאֶה כִּמְקִימוֹ, וְהוּא נִזְקָף

פקודי | שמות · פרק לט

קְרָשָׁיו בְּרִיחָיו וְעַמֻּדָיו וַאֲדָנָיו: וְאֶת־מִכְסֵה עוֹרֹת הָאֵילִם לד
הַמְאָדָּמִים וְאֶת־מִכְסֵה עֹרֹת הַתְּחָשִׁים וְאֵת פָּרֹכֶת הַמָּסָךְ:
אֶת־אֲרוֹן הָעֵדֻת וְאֶת־בַּדָּיו וְאֵת הַכַּפֹּרֶת: אֶת־הַשֻּׁלְחָן אֶת־ לה
כָּל־כֵּלָיו וְאֵת לֶחֶם הַפָּנִים: אֶת־הַמְּנֹרָה הַטְּהֹרָה אֶת־נֵרֹתֶיהָ לו
נֵרֹת הַמַּעֲרָכָה וְאֶת־כָּל־כֵּלֶיהָ וְאֵת שֶׁמֶן הַמָּאוֹר: וְאֵת מִזְבַּח לז
הַזָּהָב וְאֵת שֶׁמֶן הַמִּשְׁחָה וְאֵת קְטֹרֶת הַסַּמִּים וְאֵת מָסַךְ פֶּתַח לח
הָאֹהֶל: אֵת ׀ מִזְבַּח הַנְּחֹשֶׁת וְאֶת־מִכְבַּר הַנְּחֹשֶׁת אֲשֶׁר־לוֹ אֶת־ לט
בַּדָּיו וְאֶת־כָּל־כֵּלָיו אֶת־הַכִּיֹּר וְאֶת־כַּנּוֹ: אֵת קַלְעֵי הֶחָצֵר אֶת־ מ
עַמֻּדֶיהָ וְאֶת־אֲדָנֶיהָ וְאֶת־הַמָּסָךְ לְשַׁעַר הֶחָצֵר אֶת־מֵיתָרָיו
וִיתֵדֹתֶיהָ וְאֵת כָּל־כְּלֵי עֲבֹדַת הַמִּשְׁכָּן לְאֹהֶל מוֹעֵד: אֶת־בִּגְדֵי מא
הַשְּׂרָד לְשָׁרֵת בַּקֹּדֶשׁ אֶת־בִּגְדֵי הַקֹּדֶשׁ לְאַהֲרֹן הַכֹּהֵן וְאֶת־
בִּגְדֵי בָנָיו לְכַהֵן: כְּכֹל אֲשֶׁר־צִוָּה יְהוָה אֶת־מֹשֶׁה כֵּן עָשׂוּ בְּנֵי מב
יִשְׂרָאֵל אֵת כָּל־הָעֲבֹדָה: וַיַּרְא מֹשֶׁה אֶת־כָּל־הַמְּלָאכָה וְהִנֵּה מג
עָשׂוּ אֹתָהּ כַּאֲשֶׁר צִוָּה יְהוָה כֵּן עָשׂוּ וַיְבָרֶךְ אֹתָם מֹשֶׁה:

חמישי /שביעי

וַיְדַבֵּר יְהוָה אֶל־מֹשֶׁה לֵּאמֹר: בְּיוֹם־הַחֹדֶשׁ הָרִאשׁוֹן בְּאֶחָד מ א-ב
לַחֹדֶשׁ תָּקִים אֶת־מִשְׁכַּן אֹהֶל מוֹעֵד: וְשַׂמְתָּ שָׁם אֵת אֲרוֹן ג
הָעֵדוּת וְסַכֹּתָ עַל־הָאָרֹן אֶת־הַפָּרֹכֶת: וְהֵבֵאתָ אֶת־הַשֻּׁלְחָן ד
וְעָרַכְתָּ אֶת־עֶרְכּוֹ וְהֵבֵאתָ אֶת־הַמְּנֹרָה וְהַעֲלֵיתָ אֶת־נֵרֹתֶיהָ:

וְקָם מֵאֵלָיו. וְזֶהוּ שֶׁנֶּאֱמַר: "הוּקַם הַמִּשְׁכָּן" (להלן מ, יז), הוּקַם מֵאֵלָיו. מִדְרַשׁ רַבִּי תַּנְחוּמָא (פקודי יא):

מג׀ וַיְבָרֶךְ אֹתָם מֹשֶׁה. אָמַר לָהֶם: יְהִי רָצוֹן שֶׁתִּשְׁרֶה שְׁכִינָה בְּמַעֲשֵׂה יְדֵיכֶם, "וִיהִי נֹעַם ה' אֱלֹהֵינוּ עָלֵינוּ וְגוֹ'" (תהלים צ, יז), וְהוּא מֵאֶחָד עָשָׂר מִזְמוֹרִים שֶׁבִּתְפִלָּה לְמֹשֶׁה (תהלים צ-ק):

פרק מ

ג׀ וְסַכֹּתָ עַל־הָאָרֹן. לְשׁוֹן הֲגָנָה, שֶׁהֲרֵי מְחִצָּה הָיְתָה:

ד׀ וְעָרַכְתָּ אֶת־עֶרְכּוֹ. שְׁתֵּי מַעֲרָכוֹת שֶׁל לֶחֶם הַפָּנִים:

ה וְנָתַתָּה אֶת־מִזְבַּח הַזָּהָב לִקְטֹרֶת לִפְנֵי אֲרוֹן הָעֵדֻת וְשַׂמְתָּ
ו אֶת־מָסַךְ הַפֶּתַח לַמִּשְׁכָּן: וְנָתַתָּה אֵת מִזְבַּח הָעֹלָה לִפְנֵי
ז פֶּתַח מִשְׁכַּן אֹהֶל־מוֹעֵד: וְנָתַתָּ אֶת־הַכִּיֹּר בֵּין־אֹהֶל מוֹעֵד
ח וּבֵין הַמִּזְבֵּחַ וְנָתַתָּ שָׁם מָיִם: וְשַׂמְתָּ אֶת־הֶחָצֵר סָבִיב וְנָתַתָּ
ט אֶת־מָסַךְ שַׁעַר הֶחָצֵר: וְלָקַחְתָּ אֶת־שֶׁמֶן הַמִּשְׁחָה וּמָשַׁחְתָּ
אֶת־הַמִּשְׁכָּן וְאֶת־כָּל־אֲשֶׁר־בּוֹ וְקִדַּשְׁתָּ אֹתוֹ וְאֶת־כָּל־כֵּלָיו
י וְהָיָה קֹדֶשׁ: וּמָשַׁחְתָּ אֶת־מִזְבַּח הָעֹלָה וְאֶת־כָּל־כֵּלָיו וְקִדַּשְׁתָּ
יא אֶת־הַמִּזְבֵּחַ וְהָיָה הַמִּזְבֵּחַ קֹדֶשׁ קָדָשִׁים: וּמָשַׁחְתָּ אֶת־הַכִּיֹּר
יב וְאֶת־כַּנּוֹ וְקִדַּשְׁתָּ אֹתוֹ: וְהִקְרַבְתָּ אֶת־אַהֲרֹן וְאֶת־בָּנָיו אֶל־
יג פֶּתַח אֹהֶל מוֹעֵד וְרָחַצְתָּ אֹתָם בַּמָּיִם: וְהִלְבַּשְׁתָּ אֶת־אַהֲרֹן
אֵת בִּגְדֵי הַקֹּדֶשׁ וּמָשַׁחְתָּ אֹתוֹ וְקִדַּשְׁתָּ אֹתוֹ וְכִהֵן לִי: וְאֶת־
יד בָּנָיו תַּקְרִיב וְהִלְבַּשְׁתָּ אֹתָם כֻּתֳּנֹת: וּמָשַׁחְתָּ אֹתָם כַּאֲשֶׁר
טו מָשַׁחְתָּ אֶת־אֲבִיהֶם וְכִהֲנוּ לִי וְהָיְתָה לִהְיֹת לָהֶם מָשְׁחָתָם
טז לִכְהֻנַּת עוֹלָם לְדֹרֹתָם: וַיַּעַשׂ מֹשֶׁה כְּכֹל אֲשֶׁר צִוָּה יהוה אֹתוֹ
יז כֵּן עָשָׂה: ששי וַיְהִי בַּחֹדֶשׁ הָרִאשׁוֹן בַּשָּׁנָה הַשֵּׁנִית בְּאֶחָד
יח לַחֹדֶשׁ הוּקַם הַמִּשְׁכָּן: וַיָּקֶם מֹשֶׁה אֶת־הַמִּשְׁכָּן וַיִּתֵּן אֶת־
אֲדָנָיו וַיָּשֶׂם אֶת־קְרָשָׁיו וַיִּתֵּן אֶת־בְּרִיחָיו וַיָּקֶם אֶת־עַמּוּדָיו:
יט וַיִּפְרֹשׂ אֶת־הָאֹהֶל עַל־הַמִּשְׁכָּן וַיָּשֶׂם אֶת־מִכְסֵה הָאֹהֶל עָלָיו
כ מִלְמָעְלָה כַּאֲשֶׁר צִוָּה יהוה אֶת־מֹשֶׁה: וַיִּקַּח וַיִּתֵּן
אֶת־הָעֵדֻת אֶל־הָאָרֹן וַיָּשֶׂם אֶת־הַבַּדִּים עַל־הָאָרֹן וַיִּתֵּן אֶת־

יט| וַיִּפְרֹשׂ אֶת הָאֹהֶל. הֵן יְרִיעוֹת הָעִזִּים: כ| אֶת הָעֵדֻת. הַלּוּחוֹת:

פקודי | פרק מ

כא הַכַּפֹּרֶת עַל־הָאָרֹן מִלְמָעְלָה: וַיָּבֵא אֶת־הָאָרֹן אֶל־הַמִּשְׁכָּן וַיָּשֶׂם אֵת פָּרֹכֶת הַמָּסָךְ וַיָּסֶךְ עַל אֲרוֹן הָעֵדוּת כַּאֲשֶׁר צִוָּה יהוה אֶת־מֹשֶׁה:
כב וַיִּתֵּן אֶת־הַשֻּׁלְחָן בְּאֹהֶל מוֹעֵד עַל יֶרֶךְ הַמִּשְׁכָּן צָפֹנָה מִחוּץ לַפָּרֹכֶת:
כג וַיַּעֲרֹךְ עָלָיו עֵרֶךְ לֶחֶם לִפְנֵי יהוה כַּאֲשֶׁר צִוָּה יהוה אֶת־מֹשֶׁה:
כד וַיָּשֶׂם אֶת־הַמְּנֹרָה בְּאֹהֶל מוֹעֵד נֹכַח הַשֻּׁלְחָן עַל יֶרֶךְ הַמִּשְׁכָּן נֶגְבָּה:
כה וַיַּעַל הַנֵּרֹת לִפְנֵי יהוה כַּאֲשֶׁר צִוָּה יהוה אֶת־מֹשֶׁה:
כו וַיָּשֶׂם אֶת־מִזְבַּח הַזָּהָב בְּאֹהֶל מוֹעֵד לִפְנֵי הַפָּרֹכֶת:
כז וַיַּקְטֵר עָלָיו קְטֹרֶת סַמִּים כַּאֲשֶׁר צִוָּה יהוה אֶת־מֹשֶׁה: *שביעי*
כח וַיָּשֶׂם אֶת־מָסַךְ הַפֶּתַח לַמִּשְׁכָּן:
כט וְאֵת מִזְבַּח הָעֹלָה שָׂם פֶּתַח מִשְׁכַּן אֹהֶל־מוֹעֵד וַיַּעַל עָלָיו אֶת־הָעֹלָה וְאֶת־הַמִּנְחָה כַּאֲשֶׁר צִוָּה יהוה אֶת־מֹשֶׁה:
ל וַיָּשֶׂם אֶת־הַכִּיֹּר בֵּין־אֹהֶל מוֹעֵד וּבֵין הַמִּזְבֵּחַ וַיִּתֵּן שָׁמָּה מַיִם לְרָחְצָה:
לא וְרָחֲצוּ מִמֶּנּוּ מֹשֶׁה וְאַהֲרֹן וּבָנָיו אֶת־יְדֵיהֶם וְאֶת־רַגְלֵיהֶם:
לב בְּבֹאָם אֶל־אֹהֶל מוֹעֵד וּבְקָרְבָתָם אֶל־הַמִּזְבֵּחַ יִרְחָצוּ כַּאֲשֶׁר צִוָּה יהוה אֶת־

כב> **עַל יֶרֶךְ הַמִּשְׁכָּן צָפֹנָה.** בַּחֲצִי הַצָּפוֹנִי שֶׁל רֹחַב הַבַּיִת. **יֶרֶךְ.** כְּתַרְגּוּמוֹ: "צִדָּא", כְּיָרֵךְ הַזֶּה שֶׁהוּא בְּצִדּוֹ שֶׁל אָדָם:

כז> **וַיַּקְטֵר עָלָיו קְטֹרֶת.** שַׁחֲרִית וְעַרְבִית, כְּמוֹ שֶׁנֶּאֱמַר: "בַּבֹּקֶר בַּבֹּקֶר בְּהֵיטִיבוֹ אֶת הַנֵּרֹת וְגוֹ' וּבְהַעֲלֹת אַהֲרֹן וְגוֹ'" (לעיל ל, ז-ח):

כט> אַף בַּיּוֹם הַשְּׁמִינִי לַמִּלּוּאִים שֶׁהוּא יוֹם הֲקָמַת הַמִּשְׁכָּן, שִׁמֵּשׁ מֹשֶׁה וְהִקְרִיב קָרְבָּנוֹת צִבּוּר, חוּץ

כב> מֵחוֹתָן שֶׁנִּצְטַוּוּ לְבוֹ בַּיּוֹם, שֶׁנֶּאֱמַר: "קְרַב אֶל הַמִּזְבֵּחַ וְגוֹ'" (ויקרא ט, ז): **אֶת הָעֹלָה.** עוֹלַת הַתָּמִיד. **וְאֶת הַמִּנְחָה.** מִנְחַת נְסָכִים שֶׁל תָּמִיד, כְּמוֹ שֶׁנֶּאֱמַר: "וְעִשָּׂרוֹן סֹלֶת בָּלוּל בְּשֶׁמֶן" וְגוֹ' (לעיל כט, מ):

לא> **וְרָחֲצוּ מִמֶּנּוּ מֹשֶׁה וְאַהֲרֹן וּבָנָיו.** יוֹם שְׁמִינִי לַמִּלּוּאִים הֻשְׁווּ כֻלָּם לְכֻהֻנָּה, וְתַרְגּוּמוֹ: "וּמְקַדְּשִׁין מִנֵּהּ", בּוֹ בַּיּוֹם קִדֵּשׁ מֹשֶׁה עִמָּהֶם:

לב> **וּבְקָרְבָתָם.** כְּמוֹ וּבְקָרְבָם, כְּפֵירוּקוֹ:

שמות | פרק מ

לג מֹשֶֽׁה: וַיָּ֣קֶם אֶת־הֶחָצֵ֗ר סָבִיב֙ לַמִּשְׁכָּ֣ן וְלַמִּזְבֵּ֔חַ וַיִּתֵּ֕ן אֶת־מָסַ֖ךְ שַׁ֣עַר הֶחָצֵ֑ר וַיְכַ֥ל מֹשֶׁ֖ה אֶת־הַמְּלָאכָֽה:

לד וַיְכַ֥ס הֶעָנָ֖ן אֶת־אֹ֣הֶל מוֹעֵ֑ד וּכְב֣וֹד יְהֹוָ֔ה מָלֵ֖א אֶת־הַמִּשְׁכָּֽן: מפטיר

לה וְלֹא־יָכֹ֣ל מֹשֶׁ֗ה לָבוֹא֙ אֶל־אֹ֣הֶל מוֹעֵ֔ד כִּֽי־שָׁכַ֥ן עָלָ֖יו הֶעָנָ֑ן וּכְב֣וֹד יְהֹוָ֔ה מָלֵ֖א אֶת־הַמִּשְׁכָּֽן:

לו וּבְהֵעָל֤וֹת הֶֽעָנָן֙ מֵעַ֣ל הַמִּשְׁכָּ֔ן יִסְע֖וּ בְּנֵ֥י יִשְׂרָאֵ֑ל בְּכֹ֖ל מַסְעֵיהֶֽם:

לז וְאִם־לֹ֥א יֵעָלֶ֖ה הֶעָנָ֑ן וְלֹ֣א יִסְע֔וּ עַד־י֖וֹם הֵעָלֹתֽוֹ:

לח כִּי֩ עֲנַ֨ן יְהֹוָ֤ה עַֽל־הַמִּשְׁכָּן֙ יוֹמָ֔ם וְאֵ֕שׁ תִּהְיֶ֥ה לַ֖יְלָה בּ֑וֹ לְעֵינֵ֥י כָל־בֵּֽית־יִשְׂרָאֵ֖ל בְּכָל־מַסְעֵיהֶֽם:

לה | וְלֹא יָכֹל מֹשֶׁה לָבוֹא אֶל אֹהֶל מוֹעֵד. וְכָתוּב אֶחָד אוֹמֵר: "וּבְבֹא מֹשֶׁה אֶל אֹהֶל מוֹעֵד" (במדבר ז, פט), בָּא הַכָּתוּב הַשְּׁלִישִׁי וְהִכְרִיעַ בֵּינֵיהֶם: "כִּי שָׁכַן עָלָיו הֶעָנָן", אֱמֹר מֵעַתָּה, כָּל זְמַן שֶׁהָיָה הֶעָנָן עָלָיו לֹא הָיָה יָכוֹל לָבֹא, נִסְתַּלֵּק הֶעָנָן, נִכְנָס וּמְדַבֵּר עִמּוֹ:

לח | לְעֵינֵי כָל בֵּית יִשְׂרָאֵל בְּכָל מַסְעֵיהֶם. בְּכָל מַסָּע שֶׁהָיוּ נוֹסְעִים, הָיָה הֶעָנָן שׁוֹכֵן בִּמְקוֹם אֲשֶׁר יַחֲנוּ שָׁם. מְקוֹם חֲנִיָּתָן אַף הוּא קָרוּי מַסָּע, וְכֵן: "וַיֵּלֶךְ לְמַסָּעָיו" (בראשית יג, ג), וְכֵן: "אֵלֶּה מַסְעֵי" (במדבר לג, א), לְפִי שֶׁמִּמְּקוֹם הַחֲנִיָּה חָזְרוּ וְנָסְעוּ, לְכָךְ נִקְרְאוּ כֻּלָּן מַסָּעוֹת:

APPENDIX

THE CLASSIC COMMENTATORS

Rabbi Yitzḥak **Abarbanel** (1437–1508) wrote an extensive commentary on most of Tanakh. His commentary does not flow verse by verse, but is divided into sections that cover several verses. He is famous for opening each section with an extensive list of questions, followed by an essay in which he answers them all. Abarbanel's commentary is based on rational analysis, and he often disagrees with many of the traditional commentators who preceded him. Abarbanel served as finance minister to King Ferdinand of Spain until the expulsion of the Jews from Spain in 1492.

Rabbi Yitzḥak Arama (1420–1494) wrote a complex commentary to the Torah known as *Akedat Yitzḥak*. He was a contemporary of Abarbanel, and upon his expulsion from Spain he moved to Italy. He was an original thinker who blended Kabbala and philosophy with deep human insights in his Torah commentary.

Rabbi Avraham ben HaRambam (1186–1237), the Rambam's son, was for many years the head of the Jewish community in Cairo, succeeding his father. He continued his father's rationalist methodology, while adding on his own mystical approach to Judaism. He too was a prominent medical doctor. His commentary on the Torah puts its primary focus on understanding the literal meaning of the words and then moves on to explore their significance.

Rabbeinu Baḥya ben Asher (1255–1340) was a Spanish commentator. He frequently cites commentators who came before him, and his original insights are mostly in the realm of mysticism, especially as he tries to explain the mystical comments of Ramban.

Rabbi David Tzvi Hoffman (1843–1921) was a rabbi in Germany who also earned a doctorate and was eventually head of the Hildesheimer Rabbinical Seminary in Berlin. He was considered a leading authority in halakha, and in addition to his halakhic writings he authored a commentary on the Torah which incorporated elements of the new academic study of Tanakh, including history, archaeology, and linguistic analysis. He believed that the modern methods of study, which many were using to challenge the authority of the Torah, could and should be used to enhance our Torah study and deepen our understanding.

Rabbi Eliyahu ben Amozegh (1822–1900) was an Italian rabbi, kabbalist, philosopher, and scholar. His commentary to the Torah draws from a wide range of disciplines, and he was known for his universalist thinking. His commentary was printed only once and is not readily available.

Haamek Davar is the name of a commentary written by Rabbi Naftali Tzvi Yehuda Berlin (aka Netziv, 1816–1893), who was head of the Volozhin Yeshiva. His commentary on the Torah crosses many boundaries – he was interested in both a *peshat* reading of the text and deeper exploration drawing on the Gemara and halakha. Surprisingly for a Lithuanian rosh yeshiva, he sometimes makes reference to scientific discoveries as they impact our understanding of the Torah.

HaKetav VehaKabbala is the name of the book written by Rabbi Yaakov Tzvi Mecklenburg (1785–1865), who was a rabbi in eastern Prussia. His commentary was intended to demonstrate the link between the Written Torah and its

◂ literal

APPENDIX – THE CLASSIC COMMENTATORS

literal meaning on the one hand, and the Oral Torah and the halakha on the other. Along with those of Malbim and Rabbi Hirsch, his commentary was an important defense against the challenges of the growing Reform movement.

Ḥizkuni is the commentary written by Rabbi Ḥizkiya ben Manoaḥ (13th century), a French rabbi. His commentary is based largely on Rashi, but he draws from others as well and adds some of his own ideas. He builds on Midrash and rabbinic commentary to try to arrive at a closer reading of the Torah text.

Ho'il Moshe is a commentary written by Rabbi Moshe Yitzḥak Ashkenazi (1821–1898), an Italian rabbi. His commentary, not very well-known, spans all the books of Tanakh. Like many of the Italian commentaries, his approach was grounded in trying to appreciate the meaning of the text as written, and diverges from both the Ashkenazi and the Sephardic traditions.

Rabbi Avraham **Ibn Ezra** (1089–1172) was a prominent commentator focusing primarily on *peshat*, the literal meaning of the text, and logic. Born in Muslim Spain, he moved extensively throughout his life, spending time in Portugal, Italy, France, and England (where he died). Ibn Ezra had extensive secular learning, having studied medicine and other sciences, and was an acclaimed Hebrew poet. He is also known for his sharp wit and his disputes with the Karaite sect. While respectful of the rabbinic tradition, he did not feel bound to accept all of rabbinic commentary, especially on the non-halakhic portions of the Torah.

Rabbi Isaac Samuel Reggio (1784–1855) was an Italian rabbi, linguist, and mathematician. His commentary aims to understand the literal reading of the Torah while being aware of and sensitive to traditional rabbinic interpretations. He has many novel and creative ideas in understanding the big picture in the Torah.

Keli Yakar is the name of the commentary written by Rabbi Shlomo Ephraim Luntschitz (1550–1619), a rabbi and rosh yeshiva in Prague. He cites frequently from Rashi, Ramban, Sforno, Abarbanel and others, and says that he is interested in trying to "get close" to the *peshat*, or plain reading of the text. In addition to his desire to figure out what the text actually means, his commentary is filled with moral teachings and ideas for deeper meaning.

Rabbi Meir Leibush ben Yeḥiel Mikhel (**Malbim**, 1809–1879) was a rabbi who taught in Romania and other European countries. In his commentary, which covers most of Tanakh, he argues that no two Hebrew words are exact synonyms, and that each has a unique meaning. Malbim draws heavily on earlier commentaries like Ramban and Abarbanel and tries to demonstrate the connection between the Oral Torah and the Written Torah. Malbim dedicated many of his efforts, including a significant part of his Torah commentary, to debate with the Reform movement.

Rabbi Meir Simḥa HaCohen (**Meshekh Ḥokhma**, 1843–1926) was a prominent rabbi in Latvia who spent his entire rabbinical career in Dvinsk. He was best known as a great talmudic scholar, but he wrote a fascinating commentary on the Torah which blends talmudic thinking, halakhic analysis, and original and creative readings of the Torah text.

Rabbi Ḥayyim Ibn Attar (1696–1743) was a Moroccan rabbi known primarily for his commentary on the Torah, **Or HaḤayyim**. His commentary focuses heavily on spiritual and mystical understandings of the Torah, and he is often referred to (especially in Ḥasidic circles) as the Or HaḤayyim Hakadosh – the Holy Or HaḤayyim.

Ralbag (Rabbi Levi ben Gershon, aka Gersonides, 1288–1344) was a French Jewish philosopher, talmudist, mathematician, physician and astronomer. His commentary on the Torah is divided into two parts – one is an explanation of the words, the other is an exploration of the big ideas and messages he derives from the Torah.

The **Rambam** (Rabbi Moshe ben Maimon, 1135–1204) was known primarily for his great works of halakha (*Mishne Torah*) and philosophy (*Moreh Nevukhim*). He did not write a commentary on the Torah, but within his two major works, especially *Moreh Nevukhim*, there are many passages in which he explains various passages

◄ from the

from the Torah. The Rambam's approach is rationalist and often has philosophical grounding.

Ramban (Rabbi Moshe ben Naḥman, aka Nahmanides, 1194–1270) was a leading Spanish rabbi, philosopher, and kabbalist. Aside from his extensive commentary on the Talmud, he wrote a very rich commentary on the Torah, which includes a literal understanding of the text, discussion of context and broad themes, analysis of Midrash (especially those cited by Rashi), and Jewish mysticism. Ramban frequently quotes both Rashi and Ibn Ezra, and often disagrees with both. He was most fierce in his disagreements with the Rambam's writings on the Torah.

Rashbam (Rabbi Shmuel ben Meir, 1085–1158) was a well-known talmudic scholar in France. He was both a student and a grandson of Rashi, and he is quoted frequently in the Tosafot on the pages of the Talmud. He also wrote his own commentary to parts of the Talmud where Rashi's commentary was missing. Rashbam's commentary on the Torah was focused almost exclusively on what the verses mean and has many original insights, including those which are dramatically different from those of the rabbis of the Talmud. Rashbam is famous for his polite but firm disagreements with his grandfather Rashi, especially about Rashi's reliance on midrash.

Rashi (Rabbi Shlomo Yitzḥaki, 1040–1105) was a French rabbi considered by many to be the father of all the commentaries. Aside from his comprehensive commentary on the Talmud, he wrote an extensive commentary on all of Tanakh. Rashi's commentary on the Torah was distributed widely during his own lifetime and was embraced by both scholars and non-scholars. His commentary focuses on his unique understanding of what *peshat*, or the simple reading of the text is, but is based mostly on midrash. Rashi's commentary also includes many educational messages, and his commentary is so popular that many people do not know whether some of the stories they have learned are in the Torah itself or in Rashi's commentary on the Torah.

Rabbi Samson Raphael Hirsch (1808–1888) was a German rabbi often credited with having saved German Orthodoxy from the challenges of the Reform movement. He believed in integrating traditional Jewish learning with modern German life, an approach which he termed Torah *Im Derekh Eretz*, and served in the Moravian parliament when he was chief rabbi. Hirsch wrote extensively, including many works of philosophy, but mostly in German. Rabbi Hirsch's commentary on the Torah, translated from German, combines a careful look at the text of the Torah, details of halakha, creative grammar, psychology, and philosophy. His commentary is considered both modern and traditional, and it was an important weapon in his battle with the Reform movement as he tried to demonstrate the unbreakable bond between the Oral Torah and the Tanakh.

The *Sefer HaḤinukh* (13th century) is not a Torah commentary but a book which follows the order of the Torah and presents a list of the 613 mitzvot with a brief explanation for each. As part of those explanations, the author occasionally discusses the Torah text. The author, who lived in Spain, chose to be anonymous, but he is thought to have been Rabbi Pinḥas HaLevi, brother of the more well-known Rabbi Aharon HaLevi, who wrote a commentary on the Talmud.

Rabbi Ovadya Sforno (1475–1550) lived in Italy, where he studied Hebrew, mathematics and medicine in addition to his primary interest, Torah. In his commentary to the Torah, he often paraphrases Rashi, Ibn Ezra, Rashbam, and Ramban, but he adds many original thoughts. His primary interest is understanding what the verses mean, but he also tries to derive meaning for contemporary life.

Rabbi Yaakov Baal HaTurim (1269–1343) is most famous for his halakhic masterpiece, the **Tur**, which eventually served as the foundation for the *Shulḥan Arukh*. He was born in Ashkenaz and moved to Spain, so that he was aware of the two main halakhic traditions. He wrote a brief Torah commentary which focuses on *gematria* and finding rare occurrences of words – this commentary is printed in many editions of the *Mikraot Gedolot*. Lesser known is a longer commentary which is largely based on Rashi, Ramban, and his father, Rabbeinu Asher (Rosh).

◂ Rabbi Yosef

APPENDIX – THE CLASSIC COMMENTATORS

Rabbi Yosef Bekhor Shor (12th century) was a French rabbi and talmudic scholar who studied with Rabbeinu Tam and is cited frequently in Tosafot as "Ri of Orleans." His commentary on the Torah relies heavily on rational thinking and focuses on understanding the literal meaning of the text. It is filled with original ideas.

Rabbi Yosef Ibn Kaspi (1280–1345) was a philosopher in Spain and Provence. His commentary on the Torah is aimed very much at a rational understanding of the *peshat*, and he was influenced by rational thinkers such as the Rambam as well as by *peshat* commentaries like those of Rashbam and Ibn Ezra. Like many in his circle, he held that the search for *peshat* should take precedence over accepting traditional rabbinic explanations to Tanakh in non-halakhic matters.

Rabbi Yosef Kara (c. 1050–1130) was a student and colleague of Rashi in northern France. He was an older colleague of Rashbam, and he is recognized as a creative and innovative commentator who was one of the champions of the approach to try to find the simple reading of the text. He dedicated many of his efforts to refuting challenges from and debating with the Christian church.

In Appreciation

We feel fortunate to be involved in a publication partnering with Rabbi Shlomo Einhorn, who embodies the impactful teachings and Torah values crucial for today's Jewish youth.

Rabbi Einhorn understood the priority our father, Jack M. Nagel z"l, placed on Torah Education and Religious Zionism. In addition to a weekly shiur that they shared, he became his cherished teacher, spiritual leader and close friend.

We gratefully acknowledge and thank Rabbi Shlomo for his insightful commentary and vision as Executive Editor of The Koren Lev Ladaat Ḥumash.

May he and his dear Rebbitzen Shira be blessed to continue to lead and inspire the greater Los Angeles community and see much happiness and nachas from their wonderful family.

THE NAGEL, LERER & PARKER FAMILIES

NOTES

NOTES

NOTES

NOTES

NOTES

NOTES

NOTES